# Shooter's Bible ®

## ABOUT OUR COVER

This year's cover features two special edition Browning Ducks Unlimited commemorative shotguns. The new 1997 (top) 60th Anniversary Model Gold self-loader was crafted in high-grade walnut with beautifully engraved and plated receiver designed by Leon Burrows. The lower classic A5 Light 12 was introduced in 1987 as the 50th Anniversary limited edition. Made of 4–5 American walnut, the engraving on the satin grey receiver was also designed by Leon Burrows.

**NO. 89**
**1998 EDITION**

**EDITOR:**
William S. Jarrett

**PRODUCTION EDITOR:**
Charlene Cruson Step

**PRODUCTION & DESIGN:**
Loretta Luongo Associates

**EDITORIAL ASSISTANTS:**
Susan Baldassano
Dasi Goldsmith

**FIREARMS CONSULTANTS:**
Bill Meade
Vincent A. Pestilli
Paul Rochelle

**COVER PHOTOGRAPHER:**
Ray Wells

**PUBLISHER:**
David C. Perkins

**PRESIDENT**
Brian T. Herrick

Shooter's Bible®

### STOEGER PUBLISHING COMPANY

Every effort has been made to record specifications and descriptions of guns, ammunition and accessories accurately, but the Publisher can take no responsibility for errors or omissions. The prices shown for guns, ammunition and accessories are manufacturers' suggested retail prices (unless otherwise noted) and are furnished for information only. These were in effect at press time and are subject to change without notice. Purchasers of this book have complete freedom of choice in pricing for resale.

Published by Stoeger Publishing Company
5 Mansard Court
Wayne, New Jersey 07470

Library of Congress Catalog Card No.: 63-6200
International Standard Book No.: 0-88317-198-8

Manufactured in the United States of America

In the United States:
Distributed to the book trade and to the sporting goods trade by
Stoeger Industries
5 Mansard Court
Wayne, New Jersey 07470
Tel: 201-872-9500  Fax: 201-872-2230

In Canada:
Distributed to the book trade and to the sporting goods trade by
Stoeger Canada Ltd.
1801 Wentworth Street, Unit 16
Whitby, Ontario, L1N 8R6, Canada

# Contents

# FOREWORD

Welcome to the 89th publication of the nation's oldest gun annual. As usual, we've worked hard to bring you the latest goings-on in the sporting world. We start, as always, with a series of articles by some of the best outdoor writers in the business, who cover everything from hunting "primitive style" to what's new in gun scopes. Among our regulars is Wayne van Zwoll, who was recently named "Outdoor Writer of the Year" by the Outdoor Writers Association. Wayne has produced another gem of an article on mountain rifles, and some of his conclusions may surprise you. Next we introduce veteran writer Bud Journey to our pages. His piece is all about hunting with a muzzleloader that "kicks like a mule" and requires shooters to stalk their prey as close as possible. And for an entertaining profile of Roy Chapman Andrews, the great adventurer and explorer, we've borrowed a chapter from Sam Fadala's popular book, *Great Shooters of the World* (Stoeger, 1990).

Looking for some real action? Take a look at Wilf Pyle's informative piece on choosing the right action for your particular needs. Ralph Quinn is sure to please his many fans with an informative look at scopes—how to find, install and use the right one for your needs. On a totally different tack, we urge you to read Howard Harlan's colorful examples of duck calls in all their guises (this article has been adapted from a new book by Dr. Stephen Irwin, entitled *Sporting Collectibles*, published in 1997 by Stoeger). Sako's new, eagerly awaited rifle—Model 75—has been analyzed thoroughly by Layne Simpson, who describes it as "the finest bolt-action centerfire rifle this world renowned Finnish company has ever built."

No stranger to these pages is our handgun expert, Gene Gangarosa Jr., who continues his series on Walther pistols—the HP, in this instance. And Don Lewis, our technical writer extraordinaire, delivers still another incisive report on the intricate subject of ballistic coefficients. Moving in a totally different direction, we highly recommend Jim Casada's entertaining piece on Corey Ford, arguably the world's best outdoor humor writer in his time. And finally, we've included another illustrative piece by Dr.

Steve Irwin of Montana, who has gathered together some beautiful sporting prints created by some of the best outdoor artists of this century.

If you're shopping for a new rifle or an accessory of some kind, be sure to check out the Manufacturers' Showcase, which follows the article section. Most of these products won't be found in the Specifications section, so we highly recommend that you take a look. From there, go directly to the extensive and invaluable Specifications segment, which covers firearms of every description. New to this section are several up-and-coming manufacturers, importers and representatives. In the handgun category, we note especially the Downsizer Corporation, FEG, Israel Arms and Jennings. For rifles, check out Beretta, Henry Repeating Arms, Prairie Gun Works and Christensen Arms models. And for shotguns, we've added Brolin and Charles Daly, plus returnees Ithaca, Savage, SIG and Rizzini. The newcomers to the blackpowder group this year are Austin & Halleck, American Frontier, Marlin and Peifer. Gone from our spec section, unfortunately, are Mitchell Arms, CZ pistols, Connecticut Valley Classics, Stone Mountain and Mountain State.

After all the firearms have been accounted for, turn next to the Sights and Scopes pages, followed by an array of ballistic tables, bullet manufacturers, and reloading equipment of all kinds, followed by a complete Directory of Manufacturers and Suppliers. And if you're searching for a particular caliber or firearm, we present once again our two popular reference guides: Caliberfinder and Gunfinder. With these guides in hand, you can easily locate what's available in your favorite caliber, then find the relevant page(s) in the Gunfinder. All this vital information crammed into 576 pages ends with another helpful guide—the Product Index—which provides an overview of the book's contents and page references.

As always, we welcome your suggestions, critiques and whatever else is required to make this country's oldest and most respected gun reference book even better the next time around. We've already begun planning for it.

William S.Jarrett
Editor

Articles

# Mountain Rifles: Comin' Full Circle, Only Better!

## by Wayne van Zwoll

Slender and shapely, the modern mountain rifle swings with grace and agility. Like a fine dancer, she is light to the hand, with more sizzle than her trim lines suggest. But it was not always so.

Fortunately, during the last 30 years American gunmakers and hunters have transformed the mountain rifle into a svelte bolt-action chambered for the .270, .280 and 7x57; or, as some might define them, sheep cartridges and mule-deer medicine. Purists might reject 30-calibers because they are too fat in the neck; some might consider the 7mm-08 too young. Nor do belted magnums have any place in this club. To enthusiasts, a rifle meant for the peaks must exude a certain cachet. As autoloading shotguns seem out of their element on driven grouse, so rifles that don't look and feel like mountain types don't belong among the crags.

Most shooters aren't all that particular, though. Those who opt for a rifle to carry into steep places may choose one that's lighter and perhaps shorter than what they've come to know as standard. At the same time, they prefer powerful cartridges. Flat-shooting bullets appeal to them, no matter the size or origin of the case. They accept synthetic stocks that don't break easily or warp. They commonly screw burly scopes on top of dainty rifles so they can see better across alpine basins in the fading light of day. The result is a hybrid rifle, one that retains some elements of the traditional mountain rifle but with less understatement, exhibiting more bulk and muscle than its forebears.

Actually, the mountain rifle is returning to its roots. The first of its kind appeared not in the Rockies, but in the southern Appalachian chain, where early 19th-century frontiersmen found the vaunted Kentucky rifle ill-suited to conditions there. These pioneers needed sturdy rifles to withstand the hard knocks of wilderness hunting. Gunsmiths in the new land were, moreover, limited as to facilities and materials. Brass patchboxes were replaced by iron furniture. To ensure one-shot kills on bears and hostile Indians, bigger bores became popular. The result was the "southern," "mountain" or "Tennessee" rifle (to distinguish it from traditional Kentucky version), whose lineage included the short "jaeger" rifles made in Germany and the fowling pieces crafted in England. Among the most highly prized mountain guns were those made by Youmans in North Carolina, which later inspired the Hawken rifles of frontier fame.

Few people know much about the *real* Hawkens, which were built in a St. Louis shop beginning in 1822. Relatively few of these rifles were made, but they did nevertheless define the Plains rifle, which represented the mountain rifle one step removed in place and time. It all began sometime before the American Revolution in Pennsylvania, where a colonial gunsmith named Henry Hawkins was living and raising a family (the proper Dutch spelling was Hawken, but the Anglicized name hewed to the custom of the day). By the late 1700s, after Hawkins moved to Schenectady, New York, Daniel Boone and other explorers began to probe the wilderness west of the Cumberlands. This frontier eventually enticed restless settlers from the already crowded towns and cities along the East Coast. Hawkins later moved to Hagerstown, Maryland, from which two of his five boys—Jacob and Samuel—headed west to seek their fortunes on the prairie. Most historians agree that by 1807 Jacob took up work in St. Louis,

building rifles for the hardy people who pushed beyond the Missouri River onto the Great Plains. A few years later in 1822, Samuel closed his gun shop in Xenia, Ohio, and joined his brother.

## ST. LOUIS—THE DEPOT FOR FRONTIER RIFLES

About this time, General William H. Ashley, head of the Rocky Mountain Fur Company, developed a rendezvous system for getting his furs to market. Pelts from the Rockies soon flooded St. Louis, fueling rapid growth in the city. Trappers were outfitted there and business prospered, especially those that supplied rifles. It was there that Jake and Sam Hawken actually got their

*Slender form, light weight and fine balance characterize the traditional bolt-action mountain rifle, developed not only for easy carrying but for quick, accurate shots on steep slopes.*

*Light rifles by Ultra Light Arms are built from the blueprint up to become the most coveted of mountain rifles by knowledgeable hunters. The sleek Model 20 is pictured above.*

start repairing rifles. One submitted by the Hawken brothers in 1826 to the U.S. Indian Department itemized charges of 50 cents for fixing a rifle, a dollar and a quarter for cutting a barrel and "britch," 18¾ cents for a pin, and 50 cents for shoeing a horse!

As the American frontier shifted from New England westward past the Cumberlands and across the Plains to the Rockies, changes in rifle design were called for. Barrels were lopped for easier carrying on horseback, while at the same time rifles were made heavier to allow for stout powder charges. Patchboxes were often omitted, and full-length stocks gave way to half-stocks, commonly keyed in two places.

According to some historians, the Plains rifle (as fashioned by the Hawkens and their contemporaries) was essentially a modified 1803 Harpers Ferry rifle. Others say the Harpers Ferry and its descendants, most notably the 1817 "common" rifle and the 1841 "Mississippi" percussion rifle, were borrowed from the frontier. Both schools of thought have merit; indeed, the slow-twist, seven-groove, 32-inch, 54-caliber barrel featured in the Harpers Ferry rifle surely resembled the barrel found on the Plains rifles. In any event, the Hawken quickly became popular and remained the first pick among many hunters and trappers between 1820 and 1865. During that period, several prominent British sportsmen visited the American West on hunting trips, bringing with them rifles that were in some ways more sophisticated than those of

their hosts. But the Englishmen's quick rifling twist and thin barrel walls were poorly suited to the huge powder charges needed for killing large game at long range or keeping Indians at a distance. As a result, most American hunters stuck with their Hawkens, which in 1850 cost $22.50.

Typically, a Hawken rifle weighed 9.5 pounds, with a plain maple stock, wide buttplate and oval cheekpiece. Double-set triggers were standard equipment. Most Hawkens had an iron buckhorn rear sight and a silver blade front sight in a copper base. Their octagon barrels, which averaged 38 inches in length and an inch across the flats, were made of soft iron, with a slow rifling pitch and most commonly a 50-caliber bore. The iron came from "skelps" measuring 12 to 18 inches in length and a quarter-inch thick. Massey's Iron Works, located about 100 miles from St. Louis, supplied many of these skelps, which were then hand-welded into barrels (the Hawken brothers also bought unrifled barrel blanks from a Pittsburgh steel works).

After Jake Hawken died of cholera in 1849, Sam continued the family business, making his first trip in 1859 to the Rocky Mountains where so many of his rifles had gone before him. The following year Sam hired J.P. Gemmer, a German immigrant, to hep him run the shop in St. Louis. Gemmer proved so capable that when Sam retired in 1862, Gemmer bought the business. He changed locations in St. Louis several times during the next five decades before shutting down the business in 1915. He died four years later at the age of 92.

Plains rifles were credited with kills at what seemed like absurd distances. Author Francis Parkman once wrote that he'd downed a pronghorn at 204 paces with one and watched another hunter drop a buffalo at nearly 300. The thick-walled barrels of these venerable rifles could safely bottle huge powder charges, but iron sights and imperfect projectiles limited their effective ranges. Hunters who used round balls carried patch material, usually cheap but tough pillow ticking. Buckskin patches served as well, but they couldn't be pared down as thin as ticking could. Patches of whatever type were greased with animal fat or, in a pinch, with saliva.    The Plains rifle remained popular well into the era of breechloaders. John Hall's breechloading rifle snared a military contract in 1817 and became standard issue for the U.S. cavalry in 1833. Christian Sharps patented an ingenious sliding-breech action in 1848, about the time Walter Hunt announced his "rocket ball" repeating rifle that later evolved into Winchester's famous 1873 lever-action "gun that won the West."

Those early breechloading mechanisms, however, were too complex and fragile for many hunters and trappers. They also leaked gas, and none of them could handle the powder charges needed for long-range shooting with heavy bullets. During and after the Civil War, tougher competition came along. Spencer carbines flooded the frontier market, and soon the Sharps mechanism was beefed up to handle more potent cartridges.

Jake and Sam Hawken were not designers like Walter Hunt or industrialists like Oliver Winchester. They built rifles of proven design, modified slightly according to their customers' desires. These modifications came to define the rifle. Frontiersmen and target shooters bought enough Hawken rifles to absorb production up to the turn of the century. Because Plains rifles got such hard use and thus led short lives, some historians speculate that many more Hawkens were built than is generally thought. After hunters all but wiped out the bison, these rifles saw more service in the mountains than they ever had on the prairies. Indeed, long before that the fabled

*Remington has combined the best of the old and the new in its bolt-action Model 700 and Model Seven "mountain" rifles. The Model 700 MTN DM (top) features a slender 22-inch barrel and trim, mountain-profile stock. Some hunters prefer a traditional magazine over the standard four-shot stainless detachable one. The Model Seven Stainless Synthetic (bottom) is available in .243 Win., 7mm-08 Rem. and .308 Win. A compact action, black synthetic stock and stainless 20-inch barrel make it a pleasure to carry and swing in difficult terrain.*

"Mountain Man" had contributed heavily to the design of the Plains rifle.

Other makers either emulated the Hawken brothers or developed their own Plains rifles, mostly in and around St. Louis. Henry Lehman, who opened shop in 1834, earned high praise for his work, as did contemporaries James Henry and George Tryon. These gunsmiths probably built as many rifles as had Jake and Sam Hawken, selling mostly to the fur companies.

## MOUNTAIN RIFLES MAKE WAY FOR "MODERN" GUNS

Beginning in the 1880s, after the bison market had hit bottom, conservation measures put the lid on market hunting. Sport hunters found depleted game reserves even in the mountains; but where pioneers had lived on venison, their offspring now raised cattle and sheep. From then on until after World War II, when lightweight sporting rifles found a commercial niche,

*This iron-sighted Springfield is too bulky and heavy to win any kudos from mountain rifle purists. Nonetheless, it's a serviceable hunting rifle, as were its forebears following World War I.*

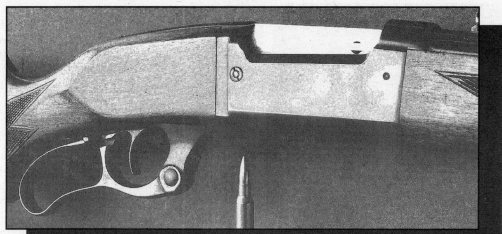

*Roy Chapman Andrews used a Savage 99 like this one in .250-3000 for much of his mountain hunting. Lever-action rifles are not popular among sheep and mule deer hunters now, but they're no less effective than bolt guns in accomplished hands.*

no such thing as an American mountain rifle existed. European hunters, meanwhile, were chasing chamois over the Alps with their lovely little Mannlicher-Schoenauer sporting rifles that handled like wands.

The German army during World War I was quick to see the merits of a compact, lightweight rifle for its elite assault units. The G33/40 Mauser, originally a Czech development, made its way into German paratroop and ski divisions. It featured a short, slim barrel, cuts in the receiver and a hollowed bolt knob to pare ounces. This "small thread, small ring" Mauser still ranks among the most sought after military weapons as raw material for custom mountain rifles.

Between the world wars, many American hunters pursued mountain game with surplus Springfields and Enfields. Well-heeled customers bought commercial Mausers, Remington Model 30s and custom rifles by Sedgley or Griffin & Howe. The Great War had shifted American tastes away from lever rifles to bolt guns. Savage, Marlin and Winchester continued to supply whitetail hunters in the East and cowboys in the West with slab-sided carbines. These quick-handling, easy-carrying guns lacked the reach needed by hunters who were now probing the high basins for bighorn sheep and mule deer.

Winchester's Model 1886 (and later 1871) offered more punch, but its tubular magazines mandated flat bullet noses. A spool magazine in the 99 Savage—the same model used by famed explorer Roy Chapman Andrews while hunting the world's great mountain ranges—allowed mountain hunters to use pointed bullets, thus extending their effective range.

In 1925 Winchester announced that its Model 54 bolt rifle was now available in the .270 cartridge. The 7x57 Mauser had been around since 1893, and the more potent .30-06 since 1906. But the .270, with a 130-grain bullet at 3,000 fps, excited hunters and placated handloaders looking for something as snappy as the wildcat .25-06. Though early .270 bullets often failed on game, a tide of good will, thanks in large part to the popular outdoor writer Jack O'Connor, carried the round until bullet design improved.

In 1937 the Winchester Model 54 was supplanted by the Model 70. Winchester immediately fashioned a carbine version of the new rifle, but it was certainly no mountain rifle. It was simply a standard 70 with a shorter barrel. Heavy and poorly balanced, it failed to catch on, so Winchester eventually dropped it. But in the early 1950s, with the introduction of its .243 and .308 cartridges, Winchester trotted out a true Featherweight, one that boasted a slim barrel

*This excellent Ruger 77 Mannlicher-style rifle is short but still heavier than the 77 Ultralight. The 2.5x scope adds only a few ounces and keeps the center of balance low. The stainless-barreled Model 77 preferred by sheep hunters tolerates mountain storms and rock slides better than do walnut-stocked, chrome-moly rifles.*

.30-06-length actions, Weatherby did not see them as fodder for lightweight rifles. Slow powders called for long barrels, and substantial recoil made weight savings a mixed blessing. When the .458 Winchester appeared in 1956—the first of several short magnums to be chambered in rifles by the major gun firms—it was properly viewed as a specialized cartridge for African hunters. The Model 70 that chambered it weighed as much as a small wrecking ball and cost a daunting $310. The .338 and .264 Winchester Magnums that followed were more in keeping with the needs of American hunters. By then Roy Weatherby and Fred Jennie had developed the Mark V rifle which, like the Winchester Model 70 in magnum chamberings, came with a long barrel. It weighed over eight pounds, slightly more than the Model 70.

By the early 1960s, after Remington had announced its new Model 700 rifle and belted 7mm cartridge, Winchester countered with its own .300 Winchester Magnum. The lightweight rifle had indeed begun to catch on. Chambered initially only for short-action rounds such as the .243 and .308, plus the perennially popular .270 and .30-06, the Model 700 Featherweight was introduced by Winchester in .264 Magnum. A poorer match is hard to imagine. Because the huge charge of slow powder had such a small tunnel in which to burn, the light 22-inch barrel acted as a flame thrower. Velocities fell off so badly in the short tube that this loud, hard-bucking rifle delivered no more zip than a standard .270. Fast throat erosion and expensive ammunition, plus a hostile gun press, helped kill the .264 Featherweight and severely cripple the cartridge.

## HUNTERS ENCOURAGE A COMEBACK

Nevertheless, during the 1960s and 1970s lightweight rifles found increasing favor with sportsmen. By the 1980s, many custom gun builders were specializing in what is now known as the "mountain rifle." Remington even brought out a Model 700 with a trim stock and slender barrel. Synthetic stocks had become a popular option, but the weight advantage many hunters expected did not always appear. Synthetics offered extra durability and stability, but some proved as heavy as wood—and some were even heavier. The lightest and most expensive models shaved only about a

and an unmodified stock (i.e., it was bulkier and heavier than barrel and action warranted). But the rifle sold well, as did its trim offspring.

During World War II, Roy Weatherby introduced his sharp-shouldered magnums. Based on the .300 H&H case, they offered greater range and striking energy (because of their higher velocity) than most other cartridges could muster. But while some were engineered to fit in quarter-pound off the rifle weight. A Sako short-action rifle tips the scale at roughly 7¼ pounds, whereas a wood stock weighs 7¾ (the difference is substantially less percentage-wise when the rifle is scoped, loaded and equipped with a sling). Most mountain rifles now wear walnut stocks. Remington's Model 700 Mountain Rifle, weighing in at 6.5 pounds, offers no synthetic option. Winchester's Model 70 Featherweight, a true mountain rifle in form and chambering, is available with synthetic or wood in .270, .280 and .30-06; but a .243, 7mm-08 or .308 comes in wood only. A Featherweight in 7mm Remington or .300 Winchester Magnum is available in synthetic only. Remington's Model Seven—a short-action rifle that replaced the 600 and 660 carbines of the 1960s—is at home in thickets as well as on alpine shale. It comes in synthetic or walnut stock; but whatever the material, a mountain rifle's stock should have a rubber or synthetic recoil pad.

Few gunmakers have followed Remington's lead in producing rifles marketed specifically to mountain hunters, which seems odd considering how easy it would be to cobble a "new" rifle from an existing workhorse action. All one has to do is change the barrel and stock contours. Some companies already manufacture lightweight rifles with trim lines, including Savage's standard Model 111, which weighs only 6½ pounds with either wood or synthetic stock. Browning short- and standard-action A-Bolts with their 22-inch barrels weigh only 6¼ and 6¾ pounds, respectively. Ruger's Ultra Light Model 77 weighs a mere 6 pounds, thanks to its thin 20-inch barrel. Ruger's Model 77 RSI weighs 7 pounds and features a full-length stock on its 18-inch barrel.

Rifles, Incorporated, a custom shop in Cedar City, Utah, offers models as light as 4¾ pounds on 700 Remington actions. And Mountain Rifles (Palmer, Alaska) manufactures one that weighs only 4¼ pounds! But perhaps the best known and most respected name in mountain rifles is Ultra Light Arms of Granville, West Virginia. Ranging in weight from 4¾ to 5¼ pounds in standard chamberings, its svelte rifles are finely sculpted with great attention to fit and finish. Rather than skeletonizing standard-weight actions from other companies, Ultra Light has designed a 700-like mechanism for mountain

*Ruger's single-shot Number One is not a lightweight rifle, but it is certainly compact.*

rifle purists that is trim and aesthetically delightful. A Timney trigger is standard, and a two-position safety allows bolt removal while the striker stays blocked. Ultra Light supplies its own scope mounts that are clean, one-piece affairs weighing about as much as a cough drop. Dakota, a name synonymous with top-grade production rifles, offers a slim, handsome 6-pound single-shot, called the Model 10. Designed almost from scratch, it's the only dropping-block model available that can qualify as a mountain rifle. Both the Ruger Number One and Browning's Model 1885 weigh considerably more and cannot equal the Dakota rifle for shape, fit and smoothness of function.

The variation in weight among mountain rifles begs the question: Is lighter always better? Not if you intend to fire the rifle as well as carry

*Long treks into Oregon's mule deer country above 8,000 feet call for not only a trim rifle, but a lightweight scope and rings, and a slender shooting sling as well.*

it. Weight not only reduces recoil, it helps hold the rifle steady in a breeze or while you're still puffing after a climb. Weight in the barrel keeps it from "crawling" as it heats up. Extra bulk is best jettisoned, but weight beyond that needed for safety and function is not all bad. The correct length of pull, for example, depends on one's build, shooting style and personal preference. Moreover, the proper distribution of weight is as important as total poundage, because it determines balance.

Custom rifles come in many chamberings. Remington's 700 Mountain Rifle is available only in .243 and 7mm-08 in the short action, and .25-06, .270, .280 and .30-06 in the standard-length version—a lineup similar to Winchester's M70 Featherweight. Remington offers its Model Seven carbine with 18 1/2- and 20-inch barrels in .243, 7mm-08 and .308, while the Ruger 77 Ultra Light comes in .243, .257 Roberts, .270, .308 and .30-06.

## MID-WEIGHT BULLETS/MID-RANGE SCOPES
Given that mountain rifles are built for sheep, goats and mule deer, the .243 is adequate; but few experienced hunters would call it a good choice. Long ranges and stiff winds dictate more potent cartridges, such as the .270, .280 and .30-06. In short rifle actions, the 7mm-08 has its fans, too, but the .270 offers a heavier bullet in the same case. Assuming equal ballistic coefficients, that extra bullet weight helps in the

wind and can also boost penetration.

For most mountain game, bullets in the middle of the weight range for the caliber serve best; i.e., 140 grains for the .270, 150 grains for the 7mms, and 165 grains for the .30s. If elk is the target, it's smart to increase bullet weight by 10 to 15 grains. All bullets, of course, must have pointed noses for efficient long-distance flight. Boattail bases, which are optional, shoot flatter than flatbase bullets, but the difference is generally not noticeable at normal hunting ranges. In any event, bullet choice depends in part on accuracy. Rifles—especially those with light barrels—can be fussy in that regard, so it's smart to test a variety of bullets and loads. For those who don't handload, many choices are still available, including Hornady's Light Magnum and Federal's High Energy super-velocity ammunition. Internal construction matters, too. Unless you're after elk, standard softpoint design is adequate; a deep-penetrating bullet for deer and bighorn sheep is not necessary. The most sudden kills come with a bullet that opens quickly.

Scopes for the high country need not be big and powerful. It makes little sense to pare all the weight and bulk possible from a rifle only to load it back on with an oversize scope. Most of the time, a 4x scope is more than adequate for big game. For variable scopes, choose a 2-7x or a 1.5-6x. Whatever the magnification, though, keep the objective lens diameter at 40mm or below. A 36mm lens will give you all the light needed at 6x, the highest power anyone is likely to need even in the dimmest conditions.

The first mountain rifles had features that increased their utility on the rough Appalachian frontier. Although many custom mountain rifles are now built more for display than for hunting, their design reveals a practical heritage. The best are trim, lightweight, accurate and finely balanced, steady to the hand, quick to aim—and always dependable. Many modern shooters seek to combine the trim lines of a traditional mountain rifle with the great reach and bone-blasting power of Herculean rounds like the .30-378 Weatherby or 7mm STW. Unfortunately, they're not likely to succeed. Odds are, they'll wind up with a modern plains rifle. The mountain rifle has made that jump before.

*WAYNE VAN ZWOLL is a writer known for his expertise on big-game hunting and the technical aspects of shooting. He has written for most of the major outdoor magazines, including Field & Stream, Sports Afield, and Rifle and Bugle, and has served as editor of Kansas Wildlife magazine. He has authored three books: MASTERING MULE DEER (1988, North American Hunting Club), ELK RIFLES, CARTRIDGES AND HUNTING TACTICS (1993) and AMERICA'S GREAT GUNMAKERS, (1992, Stoeger Publishing). Van Zwoll has been a wildlife agent with the Washington State Dept. of Game and a field director for the Rocky Mountain Elk Foundation. He recently received the 1997 Shooting Sports Writer of the Year award from the Outdoor Writer's Assn. of America.*

# The New Sako Model 75

## by Layne Simpson

Some experts have called the new Model 75 "the finest bolt-action centerfire rifle Sako has ever built." That's a powerful statement considering the thousands of hunters around the world who look upon the Sako as one of the all-time great sporting rifles—but it's true! The lines of this rifle are trimmer and more graceful, its action smoother and its styling classier. It might even be a bit more accurate.

When I first learned that Sako planned to "bring in the new and phase out the old," I visualized a firearm designed by penny- squeezers who opted for plastic parts here and pot metal ones there, all assembled by unfeeling robots— in sum, just another one of those "modern" rifles designed to cut production costs at the expense of pride in ownership. But as I discovered, nothing could be further from the truth. Everything that looks like genuine wood and steel actually *is* genuine wood and steel. And while space-age robotic equipment may have been used in the manufacturing process, human hands played an equally important role in the final product.

Sako engineers have also managed to incorporate the best ideas from the old rifle into the design of the new one. The overall classic styling is still there, and the Turkish walnut stock is hand-checkered the way it should be on a rifle of *this* quality. Both old and new versions share the spring-loaded, claw-type rotating extractor; their cocking indicators are quite similar, too, but the Model 75 has a different ejector. On the original Sako rifle, a combination bolt release and pivoting-type ejector are housed on the left side of the receiver. The bolt release on the Model 75 is in the same location but it's trimmer. It also has a fixed ejector attached to the floor of its receiver.

The fully adjustable trigger on the Model 75 is similar to that found on Sako's TRG-S rifle. The one tested for this article had no perceptible creep or overtravel, and it broke crisply at a consistent 46 ounces. Capable of adjusting to a pull weight of only a few ounces, it should prove ideal for the Model 75 heavy- barrel varmint rifle. The two-position, three-function safety on Sako's new rifle is admirable. With the serrated thumb tab pushed all the way back, the unit is on "Safe," the bolt is locked from rotation and the firing pin is blocked from forward travel. As sporting rifles go, you can't get any safer than that. A push forward moves the safety lever to its "Fire" position, then swings the combination firing-pin block and bolt lock downward to the disengaged position.

Among the impressive safety aspects of this made-in-Finland product is that the bolt can be released for rotation while the safety is engaged. All that's needed is to press downward on a small tab located just forward of the primary safety tab. The rifle chamber can then be loaded or unloaded with the safety on. And you can do

*The new bolt action Model 75 from Sako.*

all this with only one hand (even when wearing heavy gloves) merely by holding down the override tab with the thumb while lifting the bolt handle with a finger.

The Model 75 also inherited the famous Sako scope mounting system, one of the best ever designed. Since the base is actually an integral part of the receiver, it is stronger than a multiple-piece mount, not to mention the fact that the tiny and inaccessible screws that hold other types of scope-mounting bases to the rifle are totally eliminated.

Whereas the old Sako rifle had dual-opposed locking lugs, the Model 75 bolt has three lugs located at 12, 4 and 8 o'clock. Adding the third lug reduces bolt rotation to 70 degrees, allowing the bolt to operate a bit quicker. Moreover, the handle on a short-rotating bolt of this type is less likely to interfere with the extremely large ocular lens housing found on some fat- tube scopes now being built.

Turnbolt rifles with multiple locking lugs have never been universally accepted. Anyone who knows anything about bolt-action rifle design knows that a reduction in bolt rotation usually requires a drastic increase in the angle of the cocking cam surface. As a result, more muscle is required to rotate the bolt to its cocked position after the rifle has been fired. This explains why the bolts found on some multiple locking-lug rifles are extremely difficult to operate with the butt of the stock held against the shoulder. Thanks to the Sako engineers, though, the bolt of the Model 75 action actually takes less effort to operate than any two-lug bolt you

can think of. Such a smooth, effortless system is a result of several novel design and manufacturing details.

To smooth out bolt lift, the bearing surfaces of all the action parts are honed to a glass-hard smoothness. Then grooves are machined into the locking lugs of the bolt, allowing it to glide smoothly along tracks that have been machined into the guide rails. Equally important, the top cartridge in the magazine is more closely aligned with the chamber of the barrel than in other bolt-action rifles. With its shallower feed angle, the bolt is able to trip a cartridge from the magazine and push it into the chamber with less resistance.

*One of the writer's favorite features: the new two-position, three-function safety.*

*Sako's excellent scope mounting system, with its base an integral part of the receiver.*

## FIVE ACTIONS FOR FAST ACTION

Sako may well be the only manufacturer who builds rifles around five cartridge-specific actions. While it's not uncommon for rifle makers to offer both long and short actions, Sako is the only one that offers actions in five different sizes: No. 1 action is built to scale for the .222 Remington family of cartridges, including the .223 Remington and .17 Remington. No. II action is a perfect home for the .22 PPC, 6mm PPC and 7.62X39mm Russian. Action No. III is ideal in length and diameter for the .243 Winchester, 7mm-08 Remington and .308 Winchester. No. IV handles longer cartridges—the .270 Winchester, 7X64mm Brenneke, .30-06 and 9.3X62mm Mauser. And finally, No. V is designed for belted magnums ranging from the .270 Weatherby to the .458 Winchester. For still another reason why the new Model 75 action operates like grease on glass, consider this: the .223 Remington cartridge cannot feed smoothly from an action built for the .30-06, nor can an action made for the .375 H&H Magnum handle a .270 Winchester.

To discover just how smooth the Model 75 action is, I had to travel all the way to Finland for a moose hunt. But to qualify for a hunting license there, I first had to pass Finland's tough shooting proficiency test. It consisted of firing six rounds at a full-size moose target, three while the target traveled left-to- right and vice versa, and three more shots while it stood still. The target was just over 80 yards from the firing point and all shots had to be taken from the offhand

position—with no rest! As it moved swiftly across a shooting window, the target was exposed to my view for only four seconds. If I failed to place all six shots into a vital area, no hunting license would be granted.

As luck would have it, I managed to pass the shooting test on my first try, which entitled me to shoot the same course of fire several more times for fun. It might be possible, I thought, to get off three aimed shots within the time limit instead of just one. I was right. Three shots went into the vital area in just under four seconds. I mention this anecdote not to boast of my prowess with a rifle, but to make an important point: if not for the uncommonly easy bolt lift and smoothness of the Model 75 action, it would have been impossible to hit those targets.

Soon after returning home, I asked some friends to help me compare the smoothness of the Model 75 action with that of six other rifles. Some had the usual twin locking lugs, while others were of the multiple-lug design. After shooting the seven rifles, we all agreed that the Model 75's bolt was the easiest to operate. In fact, to quote one of my colleagues, the Model 75 bolt lift felt like it was already cocked.

In another experiment, I asked a friend to close his eyes, whereupon I placed an empty Model 75 rifle in his hands and asked him to operate the bolt. I then loaded a dummy car-

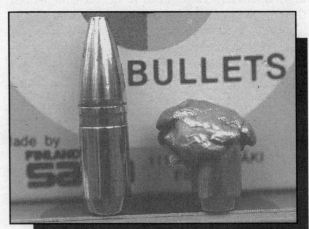

*This 30-caliber 180-grain Super Hammerhead bullet was recovered from a moose. It expanded to 55 caliber and retained over 78 percent of its original weight.*

tridge into the magazine and asked him to operate the bolt once again. This experiment was repeated several times with another shooter and, incredible as it might sound, no one could tell if the magazine was empty or loaded. That's how smooth and effortless the bolt pushed a cartridge from magazine to chamber.

### DISASSEMBLING THE BOLT

To my knowledge, the Model 75 is the only sporting rifle whose bolt can be completely disassembled to its component parts without using tools. During a cold-weather hunt, water can easily enter the bolt and freeze, thereby preventing the

*An important feature to the big-game hunter is the Model 75 bolt, which can be taken down completely for cleaning in the field and then reassembled without a tool of any type.*

rifle from firing. Having the ability to take the bolt apart quickly in the field avoids that problem. A bolt that's easily disassembled also encourages shooters to clean their rifles more thoroughly. I've had occasion to examine other hunters' rifles that wouldn't fire and have discovered that rust inside the bolts had completely tied up the works. True, the bolts on some rifles—including the old Sako and the pre-64 Winchester Model 70—can be partially disassembled. But their firing pins, springs, cocking pieces and bolt shrouds can be removed from the bolt body only as a single unit; further bolt disassembly requires tools most rifle owners don't

have at home, much less in the field.

With the Model 75, however, complete disassembly is easily accomplished. Start by holding the bolt bottomside up in one hand and rotating the bolt shroud clockwise with the other. You must twist hard enough so that the nose of the cocking piece is forced up and out of the full-cock detent at the back of the bolt body. As the shroud rotates (about one-quarter inch beyond the detent), two small lugs at the front of the collar disengage from retaining grooves located inside the bolt body. Now the compressed firing pin spring pushes the shroud to the rear, and it— along with the firing pin, spring, spring guide

*The bolt on the Model 75 has three locking lugs; but unlike other multiple locking lug systems, it is easy to operate.*

and cocking piece — are easily withdrawn from the bolt body. The bolt has now been completely disassembled into its five component parts.

When reassembling the bolt, it's a good idea to fit the shroud into the back of the bolt body before installing any other parts. Doing so enables you to note how the shroud should be positioned so that the two retaining lugs are properly aligned with their retention grooves inside the bolt body. After that, remove the shroud, drop in the firing pin, spring and spring guide, push the shroud all the way into the bolt body, and slowly rotate it counterclockwise until the nose of the cocking piece drops into the full-cock detent at the rear of the bolt body. When twisting the shroud in that direction, though, go easy. If it moves too far beyond the detent, it can drop into the full-forward slot at the root of the bolt handle, allowing the firing pin to travel all the way forward. In that case, the firing pin must be recocked. To do this, simply apply pressure on the cocking piece with your thumb while rotating the bolt shroud.

Among the early variations of the Model 75 are the Hunter and Synthetic Stainless. The latter has a stainless-steel barreled action and synthetic stock. Soft rubber inserts imbedded into the wrist and forearm of the stock make this one of the most shooter-friendly synthetic stocks available. Both versions are made with standard Mauser-style fixed magazines with hinged floorplates (or one of the new quick-detachable magazines). The release for the detachable magazine is found in a cavity slightly ahead of the magazine floorplate (which, by the way, is machined from steel barstock). The magazine can be loaded by removing it from the rifle or by pushing cartridges through the ejection port.

Depending on caliber and style of a given rifle, barrel lengths can vary. But basically those models in standard chamberings are 22 inches, while the belted magnums measure two inches longer (some heavy-barrel varmint rifles also have 26-inch tubes). The barrels on all Model 75

*Model 75 Hunter and Model 75 Stainless Synthetic*

*The detachable magazine can be loaded while still in the rifle or after it's been removed.*

rifles are completely free-floated for top accuracy and long-term maintenance of zero. These features are rarely found in wood-stocked rifles simply because the forearm has a tendency to warp against one side of the barrel, spoiling accuracy. Sako has solved this problem by allowing the walnut stock blanks to dry much longer than other manufacturers traditionally do. The blank is then rough-shaped and put through

*The writer is shown with his Model 75 Hunter in the field.*

another lengthy drying process before it's inlet-ted for the barreled action. After the stock has been finish-sanded, its moisture content is stabilized with a penetrating space-age sealant. Only then is the final satin finish applied.

All that weatherproofing pays off. While hunting moose in Finland, I zeroed my .30-06 caliber test Model 75 three inches high at 100 yards using Sako ammo loaded with the new 180-grain Super Hammerhead bullet. The damp and slightly rainy conditions encountered during the hunt played havoc with the zeros of some

other wood-stock rifles, but not so with the Model 75. Weeks later, that same rifle arrived at my home still topped by the same Zeiss scope it had worn in Finland. Using cartridges from the same box of ammo used on the moose hunt, I checked to see how well the rifle had held its zero. To my astonishment, it printed exactly three inches high at 100 yards. After being subjected to Finland's harsh hunting weather, after being hauled several hundred miles in the luggage compartment of a bus during the trip to and from the moose hunt, after making a 4,000-

# SAKO AMMO

Sako began manufacturing metallic centerfire cartridges during the early days of World War II, when the Finnish Army awarded the company a contract for several million rounds of 9X19mm Luger ammunition. But a condition came with the contract: the ammunition had to be manufactured in a bomb-proof factory. Sake met that condition by tunneling into a mountain of solid granite, carving out enough room for the necessary machinery and people. That little ammo factory still exists behind the main building of the Sako facility, but now the ammunition is manufactured on more modern machinery at another location.

Sako ammunition is imported to the U.S. by Stoeger Industries (Wayne, NJ). Made of top-quality materials, the cases are drawn to extremely close tolerances, to the point where the 6mm PPC absolutely dominates benchrest competition in the U.S., holding more accuracy records than most other cartridges combined. The main reason for this success is the uncommon uniformity of the Sako case. Sako ammunition also boasts phenomenal precision. The writer has been shooting and measuring groups for over 40 years, and during that time only two off-the-shelf, standard-production factory rifle/cartridge combinations have consistently averaged less than half an inch at 100 yards. One was the Sako Varmint in 22 PPC with a Sako 52-grain factory load. The other was a Sako Varmint in 6mm PPC firing a Sako 70-grain factory load.

All Sako ammo contains Finnish-made Vihtavuori powders, although some other components are made in the U.S. All the match ammo— 52-grain .222 Remington, 52-grain .22 PPC, 70-grain 6mm PPC, 168- and 190-grain .308 Winchester, 168-grain .300 Winchester Magnum and 168- and 180-grain .30-06—feature Sierra MatchKing bullets (Sako also uses CCI primers in some loads). In addition, Sako's 9.3X62mm Mauser, 9.3X74R and .375 H&H Magnum loads feature Powerhead bullets, which are essentially Barnes X-Bullets with a Finnish accent.

Because practically everyone in Finland hunts moose, deer and other game, Sako has naturally gained a worldwide reputation for making some of the world's finest big-game ammo. The company's latest development is the Super Hammerhead, a premium-grade, controlled-expansion bullet of spitzer, cavity-point, boattail design. The bullet is made by bonding a special lead core to a thick tapered jacket. How good is Sako's new super bullet? I tested it during my moose-hunting venture in Finland, using a new Sako Model 75 rifle in .30-06 with a Zeiss 1.5-4.5X scope. The Sako factory ammo was loaded with the 180-grain Super Hammerhead bullet at 2700 fps. On the first day of the hunt, a moose came running by broadside. Standing in a tower stand about 75 paces away, I plastered the crosshairs on the front of its chest and squeezed off a round. The Super Hammerhead smashed through the moose's shoulder, then traveled at a slight downward angle through the chest cavity, blasted through the offside shoulder and came to rest beneath the hide. Even after smashing through all that heavy bone, the recovered bullet weighed 141 grains, or more than 78 percent weight retention. It had expanded to .55 caliber frontal area, retaining 56 percent of its original length.

While in Finland, I also tried the 30-06 factory ammo in a Model 75 rifle on Sako's 110-yard underground tunnel and kept three shots consistently within an inch. Later I tried the 180-grain Super Hammerhead load in the same gun, but this time on an outdoor 100-yard range. Again, the load averaged a remarkable 1.2 inches. The Super Hammerhead is now made in 30 caliber and is available only in Sako's 308 Winchester, 30-06 and 300 Winchester ammo. One of my favorite loads is the 42-grain 22 Hornet. Using a custom heavy-barrel Ruger 77/22H, the 42-grain hollowpoint bullet tripped mychronograph at almost 2700 fps, averaging .77 inch for several five-shot groups at 100 yards.

## PERFORMANCE RESULTS — SAKO MODEL 75 HUNTER
## Caliber .30-06

| Factory Load | Bullet | Velocity fps | Accuracy (Inches) |
|---|---|---|---|
| Sako | 123-gr. PSN | 3037 | 1.34 |
| Federal Premium | 150-gr. Nosler BT | 2866 | 1.18 |
| Winchester Supreme | 165-gr. STBT | 2718 | 1.16 |
| Federal GM Match | 168-gr. Sierra MK | 2643 | 1.14 |
| Sako | 180-gr. Super Hammerhead | 2662 | 1.21 |
| SakoSuper Match | 180-gr. Sierra MK | 2556 | 0.92 |
| Federal Premium | 180-gr. Nosler Part. | 2631 | 1.32 |
| Winchester Supreme | 180-gr. STBT | 2668 | 1.03 |
| Hornady Light Magnum | 180-gr. PSN | 2704 | 1.77 |
| Norma | 180-gr. RSN | 2583 | 1.26 |
| Federal Premium | 180-gr. SBT | 2595 | 1.87 |
| Remington | 180-gr. PCL | 2689 | 1.42 |
| | Aggregate Accuracy | | 1.30 |

NOTES: Accuracy shown for each load is an average of two three- shot groups fired at 100 yards from a benchrest. Velocities are averages of six rounds clocked 12 feet from the muzzle.

mile ride from the Sako factory in Finland to Stoeger's headquarters in New Jersey in the cargo hold of a jet airliner, and after traveling by UPS from New Jersey to my home in South Carolina, that rifle with its gorgeous wood stock was still perfectly sighted in.

Sako rifles have long been known for their excellent accuracy, and the new Model 75 is carrying on that same tradition. The test rifle used for this article chalked up an overall average of 1.3 inches for three-shot groups at 100 yards using a dozen factory loads. With Sako Super Match ammo loaded with Sierra's 168-grain MatchKing, it broke minute-of-angle by averaging .92 inch. When shooting its preferred loads, the rifle averaged 1.03 inches with Winchester Supreme 180-grain Silvertip boattails. For additional test firing results, see the table above.

The craftsmen at Sako have long been noted for their ability to combine Old World quality, styling and workmanship with the latest in materials and technology, all designed to produce some of the all-time great sporting rifles. They did it back in the 1950s when they introduced their first varmint and big-game rifles, and now they've done it again with their bright new star: the Model 75.

# Roy Chapman Andrews: World Explorer

## by Sam Fadala

Adventurer. Explorer. That was Roy Chapman Andrews—and a great hunter and rifleman, too, although he was never noted as such in most circles. But what else would you call a man who collected more wild animals with rifle than most dedicated sportsman could ever come close to equaling in two lifetimes?

Although Roy gained fame as a naturalist, he spent his early life as a tenderfoot hunter and outdoorsman. His hunting interest followed precisely the path trod by those who harvest wildlife. Hunting coincided with a strong love of animals and a desire to know as much about them as possible through books. Two of his early favorites, the *Handbook of North American Birds* and *Robinson Crusoe*, blended perfectly to describe his nature. Roy quickly became a dedicated student of wildlife and an inveterate vagabond, his sparkling career as a naturalist nurtured by early hunting.

When Roy was in grade school, his father, Ezra, gave the boy a single-barreled shotgun. In his autobiography, *Under a Lucky Star*, Andrews wrote: "The greatest event of my early life was when, on my ninth birthday [January 26, 1893], Father gave me a single-barrel shotgun. Previous to this I had been allowed to shoot Grandfather's muzzle loader once or twice, but it was too much for me to negotiate with its forty-inch long barrel." Roy's mother, Cora May Chapman, was against the idea of her son having the firearm, but it was his all the same.

Roy's first success with his new shotgun was a duck, followed by some geese he bagged in the marshes of Beloit, Wisconsin—but there was a problem. The young lad made a good stalk that day, and his aim was true. But unfortunately the three geese he shot turned out to be decoys belonging to one Fred Fenton, a man intensely disliked by Roy's father, who immediately rewarded his son with a brand new double-barreled hammergun. Since he no longer needed the single-barreled shotgun, Roy sold it for three dollars

Andrews once wrote, "All my life I have been a sportsman. Beginning with whales, I have shot big game and dangerous game in most countries of the world." He went on to explain how he had pursued evidence of ancient man with similar hunting instincts. A book called *Taxidermy and Home Decoration* by William T. Hornaday taught the young man how to mount specimens that were good enough to fetch a profit. Although he was an animal-lover of the highest order, Roy never did care for reptiles, having been frightened by a snake as a youngster. His aversion to them was matched somewhat by his attitude toward school. Except for science and literature, in which he excelled, the young Andrews was never considered a star pupil.

*Roy Chapman Andrews led several Central Asiatic Expeditions for the American Museum of Natural History in the early 1900s. Carrying two rifles on most of his adventures, the 250-3000 Savage lever-action and the 6.5mm Mannlicher carbine, he found that smaller calibers minimized the damage to scientific specimens.*

A grave incident befell Roy in his youth one day. A young English instructor who was accompanying him on a duck hunting trip dropped a paddle from their boat into the icy water. As he lunged forward to retrieve it, the vessel tipped over. Roy emerged safely, but sadly his instructor was drowned. As Roy trudged toward home, drenched and freezing, a passing farmer covered the lad with blankets and gave him shelter. Andrews never forgot that terrible accident.

In 1906, the young taxidermist graduated with honors from Beloit College. His study habits had improved markedly from his earlier days, earning him a degree *cum laude*. While his intelligence and curiosity had obviously blossomed, Roy admitted that he had really not labored long and hard in securing his excellent grades. In fact, he never really felt well-educated after graduating from college. But at least he knew now what he wanted to be: a naturalist.

### THE ADVENTURE BEGINS

It was July 6, 1906, and Teddy Roosevelt was president when Roy Chapman Andrews ventured all the way from Beloit, Wisconsin, to New York City. Standing outside the American Museum of Natural History for the first time, he gazed in awe at this great structure that had occupied his thoughts for so long. When informed there was no opening for him, Roy told the man in charge that he'd gladly mop the floors in exchange for access to the museum's treasures. He was hired at 40 dollars a month, working under Jimmy Clark at the Department of Taxidermy. In keeping with his desire to be part of the museum, Andrews was entrusted with mopping the tiles of the taxidermy department each morning. "They were not ordinary floors to me and I didn't mind scrubbing them," he said. "Those floors were walked on by my scientific gods."

Andrews's first real assignment for the museum was a whale hunt in 1908 along the Pacific coast of Alaska. During the first week he killed three whales with a harpoon gun. He never became merely a hunter of museum specimens, though; in fact, it was his outdoor lore, his enthusiasm for the hunt and his marksmanship that brought many treasures to the museum for study and display. To obtain certain species for collection, Andrews turned to trapping on uninhabited islands. There he acquired boar, monkeys and giant lizards for the museum, seeking the small as well as the large. On one adventure, he even found a previously unknown species of ant, which was named in his honor.

Meanwhile, Roy continued his whaling expeditions, gathering new and important data on whales from all the oceans of the world. He also found time to hunt in several countries. In a Korean village, for example, with another hunter as his guide, Andrews set out to locate and shoot a tiger that was killing livestock and even some local villagers. Three weeks of tracking and hard labor proved fruitless; meanwhile, the beast had added several more people to its list of victims. At one point, Paik, the guide, wanted to follow the tiger into a cave. Roy, deciding that was not a bad idea, went along. Fortunately for the two men, the tiger evacuated the cave through a rear entrance and escaped. Later, a wild boar struck at Paik from the brush and Roy had to fire three shots before the boar was downed.

More adventures in Korea were in store for Roy. On one trek he ran into some Manchurian bandits, but after explaining who he was and what he was doing, they let him go. But everyone back home believed Andrews was now a corpse lying in a faraway land. As with Mark Twain before him, Roy's demise has been "greatly exaggerated." A memorial service in his honor was even held in his home town. Later, on a trip to Russia, Roy hunted for two months with a Russian prince before returning to the museum to resume his normal duties. In 1913, Roy, after completing his Ph.D. at Columbia University, gathered up another degree as well: a marriage certificate certifying his marriage to Yvette Borup. Roy's bride was an accomplished photographer whose camera skills came in handy on future expeditions with her husband. During Roy's study of whales, their efforts produced Andrews's first book, *Whale Hunting with Gun and Camera*, which was published in 1916.

His experience as an explorer and his insatiable thirst for discovery naturally led Andrews to taking charge of an expedition to central Asia on behalf of the Museum. In 1916 on the first expedition to    Tibet, Southwest China and Burma, the party of 40 men included experts in geology, paleontology, archaeology and topology, plus eight automobiles and 150 camels. All researchers combed the Gobi Desert for fossils, rare animals, birds, vegetation and whatever they could unearth. Hunting was, of course, an integral part of the exploration. Another tiger, known as the "Great Invisible" and the "Blue Tiger," eluded them all. The marauder went on to kill some 100 men, women and children. Roy did not travel alone now, and Yvette levied no complaints—at least not in those early years of nuptial bliss—about her husband's wanderlust. For a time, Andrews hunted near the Burmese border searching for camp food as well as museum specimens. Armed with a 6.5mm Mannlicher rifle and a pair of binoculars, he took thousands of specimens for science including 2,100 mammals, 800 birds and 200 reptiles. Yvette, meanwhile, documented it all with 8,000 feet of film.

As a man who loved hunting, Roy Chapman Andrews succumbed to what some call the "Old Hunter Syndrome," stating once that "I kill animals for good or science [not sport]." That bit of fluff sometimes emanated from sporting hunters who'd had a wonderful time in the field, all the while making up unwarranted excuses for hunting. In a more candid moment, Andrews confessed, "Some men tell me that they never get excited when they hunt. Thank God, I do."

He was certainly excited when he hunted rams in China and wrote this account in *Mongolian Plains*:

> Almost in a daze, I lifted my rifle, saw the little ivory bead of the front sight center on that gray neck, and touched the trigger. A thousand echoes crashed back upon us. There

*Andrews's third Asiatic Expedition in the 1920s led him again into the Gobi Desert, where camel travel was relied on. The digs uncovered the first-known dinosaur eggs as well as skeletons of the oldest and largest land mammals known at that time.*

*Andrews admired and often used the lever-action Savage in caliber 250-3000 Savage. Here Bill Fadala demonstrates the Savage Model 1899, later known as the Model 99.*

was a clatter of stones, a confused vision of a ponderous bulk heaving up and back—and all was still. But it was enough for me; there could be no mistake this time. The ram was mine. . . I yelled and pounded the old Mongol on the back until he begged for mercy; then I whirled him about in a war dance on the summit of the ridge. I wanted to leap down the rocks where the sheep had disappeared, but the hunter held my arm.

Roy became especially animated about a man-eating tiger he'd tracked down in China. His hunting partner, Caldwell, had fired several times at close range with buckshot, but none of the pellets had penetrated enough to stop the cat. "Next day," Andrews wrote, "I followed the blood trail with a lot of natives and found her dead nearly a half mile away. Her whole face and

neck were full of buckshot but most were flattened against the heavy bones and hadn't penetrated. I think she bled to death."

When the tiger was brought back to the village, a mother who'd lost a child to the cat began beating it with a stick and screaming curses at the lifeless animal. The villagers took all but the hide, sopping up the blood with rags. They sold the meat for medicinal purposes in the belief that a little bite would give them "tiger-courage." The bones, whiskers and claws were stewed into a jelly and turned into pills, which the Chinese druggists sold to ailing patients.

Afterwards, Roy and his hunter friend discussed the ballistics of the situation. Andrews, a smallbore fan (recall his 6.5mm rifle), had no faith in Caldwell's .22 Savage Hi Power for hunting tigers. "Your .22 Hi Power doesn't have enough shocking power for dangerous game," Roy told him. But Caldwell, who had taken several tigers with a 303 Savage, found the .22 Hi Power quite deadly on the big cats. "The Savage Company sent me out this rifle," he recalled, "and the first time I ever fired it was at a tiger. You ought to have seen what that tiny bullet did to him! He was a big tiger, too—a man-eater that had killed several people in this very village."

Andrews had his own theory about the .22 Hi Power's effect on the tiger, and he warned Caldwell that he must not expect the same results on the next tiger he tried to down with the little cartridge. Andrews believed that the full stomach of the cat had contributed to its demise. "I've seen the same thing happen when I've shot woodchucks with a hardnose .22 Hi Power bullet. They just blow up if I get them through the body when the stomach is packed with food; if it is empty, I lose my 'chuck."

As a collector of specimens, Andrews felt the smaller calibers made sense and caused less destruction to specimens that were to be mounted for the museum. But when hunting antelope, Roy preferred his 250 Savage. In *Across Mongolian Plains, A Naturalist's Account of China's 'Great Northwest,'* he wrote: "The one I killed was 400 yards away, and I held four feet ahead when I pulled the trigger . . . that antelope I killed was four hundred yards away. I know how far it was, for I paced it off. I may say, in passing, that I had never before killed a running animal at that range. Ninety percent of my shooting had been well within one hundred and fifty yards, but in Mongolia conditions are most extraordinary."

Andrews led two more Asiatic Expeditions, the last one taking place in the 1920s. Then his group discovered the first known dinosaur eggs as well as skeletons of the oldest and largest land mammals known at that time. He still found it impossible to settle down to a routine life; and as for city living, he felt it was far more dangerous than the perils he had faced during his life as a world explorer. Unfortunately, his wandering ways proved too much for his marriage, which ended in divorce in 1931. He and Yvette had two boys—George Borup and Roy Kevin—but once the divorce was final Roy seldom saw his family. It seemed more important for him to be known as the naturalist who first discovered dinosaur eggs, or the deliverer of the huge whale that was suspended in the museum for all to see and study. Sadly, Yvette was killed a few years later in a car accident in Spain. In 1935, Andrews married Wilhelmina Anderson Christmas, with whom he shared the remainder of his life.

In January of 1935, Roy had become director of the American Museum of Natural History, a post he kept until 1941, when he retired at age 57. His career was far from over, however. He lectured, wrote monographs and authored many books, including *Camps and Trails in China, On the Trail of Ancient Man, The New Conquest of Central Asia, This Business of Exploring, This Amazing Planet, An Explorer Comes Home, Beyond Adventure: The Lives of Three Explorers* [himself, Admiral Peary and Carl Akeley] and

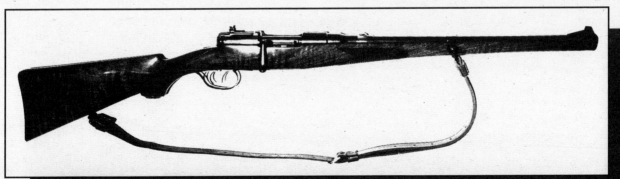

*When Andrews finally gave up hunting for good, he gave his reliable Mannlicher to his son, George. As Andrews wrote in An Explorer Comes Home, the gun had been his ". . . constant companion during more than a quarter of a century. . .and to its bullets had fallen game in almost every country of the world."*

others. One of his last books—*In the Days of the Dinosaurs*—was published a year before his death.

When Andrews finally gave up hunting for good, he left his favorite Mannlicher carbine to his son, George, with the following commentary (from *An Explorer Comes Home*):

> For his protection he had the Mannlicher rifle that was my constant companion during more than a quarter of a century. To its bullets had fallen game in almost every country of the world. Two notches on the stock were reminders of how it had saved my life from Chinese brigands. In Arctic snows or tropic jungles it never failed.

The famous naturalist and world hunter died from a heart attack at age 76 on March 11, 1960, in Carmel, California. Roy Chapman Andrews had led a full life, the kind many of us dream about. We may have adventure in our souls, but Andrews was able to live it out. And it all began with a nine-year-old boy who inherited a strong hunting instinct—and a gun.

SAM FADALA is currently Technical Editor for *Rifle Magazine* and *Handloader Magazine*, and writes regularly for *Muzzleloader Magazine* and *Guns Magazine*. A freelance writer for over 25 years, his articles have also appeared in *Gun World, Bow and Arrow Hunter, Outdoor Life* and *Sports Afield*. Fadala has authored many books, including THE BOOK OF THE 22: THE ALL-AMERICAN CALIBER (Stoeger, 1989). The excerpt above was taken from his anthology GREAT SHOOTERS OF THE WORLD (Stoeger, 1990).

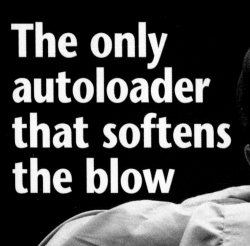

# The only autoloader that softens the blow

## here...

## and here.

### The Soft Shooting System™ that handles target loads to 3″ Mags without ever changing barrels.

Now, one autoloader can cover every shot-gunner's game. When the season changes, you only change chokes, not barrels. Mossberg's exclusive gas compensation system is the key. Its simple, yet rugged, design vents excess pressure while operating the action. The result is a substantial reduction in recoil without any reduction in reliability. You'll also like the reduction in cost compared to other autoloaders.

**A. gas from barrel
B. action movement
C. vents excess gas**

### Camo, Slugs and Combos make the Model 9200 the most versatile autoloader.

Mossy Oak® Treestand, new Realtree® All Purpose Gray and affordable OFM Woodland... turkey hunters and water-fowlers can find a Model 9200 for the cover they hunt. Slug hunters enjoy less recoil and still get all of the accuracy of a scope mounted, fully rifled barrel with the Trophy Slugster™ version. With both a 28" vent rib barrel and a 24" rifled slug barrel, the Model 9200 Combo is Mossberg's best deal.

### Even the new, more affordable Viking Grade™ Model 9200 has a Lifetime Limited Warranty.

The new Viking Grade™ Model 9200 delivers soft shooting, gas operated performance in an even more attractively priced model. Outfitted with a rugged, good looking Moss green synthetic stock and a Mil-Spec Parkerized barrel, the Viking Grade Model 9200 is loaded with Mossberg Value. Just like every other Model 9200, it's backed by Mossberg's Lifetime Limited Warranty.

## MOSSBERG

**NEW!** Viking Grade™ Model 9200 Autoloader

MOSSBERG LIFETIME LIMITED WARRANTY 9200

O.F. Mossberg & Sons, Inc. • 7 Grasso Avenue • P.O. Box 497 • North Haven, CT 06473-9844

© 1996, O.F. Mossberg & Sons, Inc.                    Safety and safe firearms handling is everyone's responsibility.

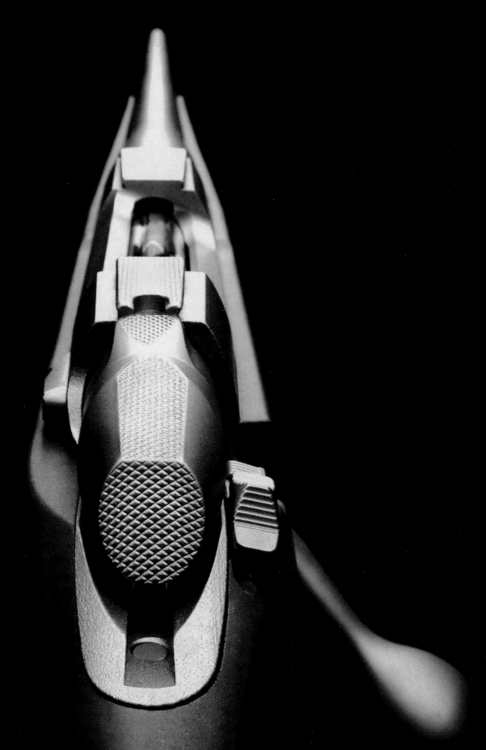

# Action Actions: There IS One For You

## by Wilf E Pyle

Let's set the record straight: Gone are the days when one type of action was considered preferable to another for a given purpose. Today, good shooting and hunting can be enjoyed with all types of actions. For years, gun experts compared the six action types, pointing out the benefits of one against the faults of another. But modern action designs are all capable of delivering cartridges of similar power and accuracy. It's easy now to find both bolt-action and lever rifles that will handle high-pressure cartridges, deliver flat-shooting bullets and provide good down-range performance. For those who've always preferred one type of action over others, there's certain to be a rifle that suits their purposes with the kind of action they prefer. In the end, personal preference dictates each shooter's choice of action, just as it does in selecting one cartridge or one stock type over another for certain types and styles of shooting. One shooter might choose a lever-action carbine, while another opts for a bolt-action sporter or Mannlicher. There's no longer any technical reason—whether reliability, accuracy or quality—to choose one action over another.

For those who want to build a personal rifle battery, one good strategy is to pick a combination of action types. This allows a shooter to meet the differing demands of hunting and shooting according to personal preference, and to cover as well most situations requiring a specific rifle

type. For example, a shooter may use a short barrel on his lever rifle for hunting in heavy cover or on horseback, while for plains hunting a long barrel on a favorite sporter is called for. Other choices include a full stock on a bolt rifle for carrying on horseback, a short barrel on a sporter for hauling on foot, a heavy-barreled bolt for varmints, or a short lightweight lever or pump for women and young shooters. Still others may require a heavy-barreled single-shot action for target and plinking work. And don't forget those warm Saturday afternoons when a fast-shooting autoloader is the hot ticket to success in the field.

True, times change. The action that interests a shooter's hunt today may not seem the right answer for tomorrow. For this writer, an old military bolt-action made up the early components of my rifle battery. At that time, cost was the driving factor in making choices, so as a result my gun rack had strong World War II overtones. Then came a love affair with lever-actions, followed by a Trapper Nelson packboard and a Model 94 Winchester .30-30. For a teenaged deer hunter, these were considered the ultimate in outdoor gear. Later as my interest in reloading grew, high—quality bolt-actions took a more dominant place in my gun rack. Over the years, this interest in collecting has translated into plenty of room for single-shots, pumps, semiautos and one or two combination guns. Nevertheless, to this day my personal preference is still a lever or bolt-action rifle for all hunting and shooting needs.

## HOW AND WHERE THE ACTIONS ORIGINATED

The first action was the single-shot that evolved from the earliest muzzleloader. But a breechloading rifle was every shooter's dream, with the first model originating in England around the time of Henry VIII during the 16th century. The advantages of having a second, third and perhaps even

*Repeating rifles were not perfected until the invention of the metallic cartridge. Then followed a series of Winchesters, including the Model '86, which identified the lever as America's most popular design.*

a fourth shot were readily apparent, thus spearheading the steady evolution of the early repeaters. Even during the muzzleloading days, a follow-up shot was considered essential, leading to the first crude attempts. In doing so, common sense was sometimes ignored. As an example, there was an early Colt revolving-cylinder rifle that came onto the market in 1858. A blast from its barrel-cylinder interface burned many a beard and singed countless sideburns. But it did provide five to six powerful shots in rapid succession, for which recruits were grateful during the Civil War. More important, this rifle affirmed the principle that repeating shots were possible, encouraging many inventors who sought lucrative contracts to design repeating rifles in remarkably short order.

Repeating rifles were not perfected, however, until the invention of the metallic cartridge. Interest among frontiersmen and military planners kept inventors around the world motivated to seek new designs. But it was an American gun designer, B. Tyler Henry, who was one of the first to marry the metallic cartridge to a repeating rifle. The Henry and Spencer rifles both saw action during the Civil War, with the Mauser bolt-action appearing in the mid-1860s as a breech-operated, single-shot rifle. Within a brief period of time, though, it evolved into a repeating bolt.

As one of the first successful repeating rifles, the Spencer held seven cartridges, which during the Civil War years was considered nothing less than an astounding feat. Among the rifle's innovations was a tubular magazine that passed through the center of the stock from butt to receiver. The rifle was loaded through a buttplate trap, and the action was operated by lowering the trigger guard. The hammer was cocked manually for each shot. By Civil War standards the rifle performed well, although the mechanism was delicate and the metal soft, making it susceptible to quick wear.

A series of Winchesters followed—notably the Models '92, and '94—all of which turned the lever into the most preferred design of its kind in America, especially among the pioneers who were busy opening the country for settlement. About the same time, Marlin produced a series of excellent lever-action rifles, including the Model '81 in the then powerful military .45-70 round. Later, the company introduced a new design— the Model '91—featuring a solid top and side ejection. Other companies, Colt and Stevens among them, began producing levers as well.

After the Civil War, civilian interest in repeating arms continued to grow, whereas the U.S. military drifted back toward single-shots in search of an improved breechloading design. This resulted in the .50-70 (and later the .45-70) Springfield rifle. The continuing use of volley shooting, during which great numbers of troops fired simultaneously at large targets, remained military doctrine. For that reason, only a single-shot equipped with crude sights was required. Besides, the single-shot was cheaper to manufacture and proved more reliable in the hands of what were then poorly trained soldiers. They were also built better than any of the repeating rifles then in use.

Meanwhile, hunters and adventurers favored lever-actions. Keep in mind that the .45-70 Springfield single-shot was still in use up to the Spanish-American War (although the .30-40 Krag Jorgenson had been adopted by the army in 1892). It was then that America's military designers learned an important lesson, one that proved a pivotal point in firearm design. By then the bolt-action Mauser had, after undergoing several refinements, evolved into a strong and reliable repeating rifle. This action type found favor everywhere with hunters; even the U.S. military came to realize that repeating Mausers in reasonably powered cartridges performed well in battle. The 1893 Mauser was obviously superior to the .30-40 Krag Jorgensen and the old .45-70.

During the Spanish-American War, some 700 Spaniards inflicted 1,400 casualties on the U.S. force of 15,000 men at the battle of San Juan Hill in 1898. This was the turning point at which the single-shot as a military action was cast aside in favor of the Mauser. The military establishment now recognized that a clip-loaded rifle with Mauser designs was needed. The result was the Model 1903 Springfield. The Krag-Jorgensen was soon relegated to the sidelines. Although a repeater in design, its cartridges had to be

*The Savage Model 99 lever-action rifle is shown with an early Model 40 bolt.*

loaded in single-shot fashion. This was thought at first to be an economical device on the theory that soldiers would drop fewer cartridges. Tests showed, however, that it was much slower to reload than the clip-fed Mauser. In military situations, this meant less firepower compared to the Mauser.

As bolt actions changed, the shooter's dream of a rifle that could eject a spent cartridge, chamber another and cock the rifle in sequence remained strong. The product was the first workable semiautomatic rifle, invented by an American living in England named Hiram

Maxim. Maxim succeeded in making a Winchester 1873 lever-action rifle that functioned in semiautomatic mode. Military establishments throughout the world were definitely interested in the firepower this type of action could deliver. Thus did European design activity remain brisk, with most major advancements being made by Germany and Belgium.

As for hunters, they have always favored the quick follow-up shots made possible by any of the semiautomatics. The first semiautomatic rifle created for their needs was the Remington Model 8. But it was not until recent times that top-quality semiautomatic rifles became available in high-powered cartridges, beginning with the Remington Model 742 "Woodmaster."

### COMBINATION RIFLES

Few hunters in North America bother with the combination or double rifle. This British invention and its action type have never proved popular with American hunters because of their weight and lack of firepower, although double rifles made by Krieghoff are available in the caliber models preferred by African hunters. These rifles are popular in Africa among well-heeled hunters who travel on safari and live in comparative luxury. Their rifles typically weigh more than 12 pounds when fully loaded and outfitted with a sling. Most safari hunters freely admit that a double rifle or drilling adds tradition to a hunting trip through Africa. The action in these rifles is short compared to the rifles's overall length, making them easy to handle. Sighting-in a double rifle is difficult, however, with both barrels typically failing to shoot to the same point of aim.

Among the last shotgun-rifle combos on the market today are those made by Tikka (imported by Stoeger Industries) and Savage. The Tikka ranks among the most popular guns of its type in the U.S., offering a choice of four calibers (222, 30-06, 308, and 9.3X74R) for the under barrel and a 12-gauge upper barrel. The Savage, by contrast, has been marketed in many different combinations of rifle cartridges and shotgun shells. In western Canada, fur trappers still use these guns to dispatch game taken in traps and for use in pest control, while others

pack the Savage as a survival rifle. In any case, the hunter must carry two kinds of ammunition, which can prove a disadvantage. Scoping the shotgun-rifle is also a problem. A scope may work well with a rim or centerfire cartridge, but its application with the shotgun frequently requires the scope to be removed and resighted. In a survival situation, this process wastes ammo and proves inconvenient in the field. Thus, few of these combination rifles carry scopes.

### SINGLE-SHOT RIFLES

During the 1880s, Winchester crafted the beautiful and functional Model 1885 single-shot rifle. Browning still makes a faithful copy of this in calibers ranging from the once-popular .22 Hornet to the 7mm Remington Magnum. Other popular rifles in their day were the Sharps, the hammerless Sharps-Borchardt, the Remington-Hepburn, the Remington-Rider rolling block and the Stevens famous 44½. All were considered more accurate than other action types, at the

*Ruger is credited with reviving single-shot rifles in the late 1960s. Their longer barrel lengths and the rigorous application of modern machining make these guns highly accurate.*

*Despite having the fastest manual action available, the pump-action rifle may go the way of the dinosaur. The Remington Model 7600 pictured above is the only high-powered pump-action rifle on the market today.*

same time firing some of the most powerful cartridges of the day.

During the late 1960s, Sturm, Ruger & Company was credited with sparking a revival in single-shot rifles. Extremely accurate due in part to the extra barrel length they carry, they were built to the rigorous standards of modern machining. Thompson/Center now offers interchangeable barrels, stainless steel components and composite stocks for its single-shots.

For hunters, a certain snobbery is associated with going afield carrying a single-shot rifle. It's the knowledge that there's only one shot, and it better count. Adding to this kind of one-upmanship, Ruger offers enough barrel lengths, calibers and stock configurations to satisfy every superior taste. Indeed, the fact that single-shot actions produce only one shot is the reason why inventors and gun cranks sought out new actions in the first place. This shortcoming of the single-shot can't be ignored when planning expensive trips or in hunting situations that demand more than one shot. Most modern big-game hunters must take this into consideration when selecting a rifle action.

## PUMP ACTIONS

The pump is in trouble. This uniquely American invention, which is more closely related to a shotgun, has failed to attract a large and enthusiastic following. That's unfortunate, because the pump is the fastest manual action available. Moreover, it can be worked from the shoulder, it can be recocked with one finger still on the trigger, and it can be fired by either left- or right-handed shooters. At one time, Savage made a

Model 170 pump in .30-30 and .35 Remington that proved excellent for short-range, quick-shooting in close cover.

Today, the Remington 7600 is the only high-powered pump-action rifle available. The modern Remington 7600 (a spinoff from the Model 760 Gamemaster) points more naturally than any rifle on the market and readily lines up on target. It's also available in 35 Whelen, making it the most powerful pump-action rifle ever. Unfortunately, few shooters are interested. The gun's predecessor—the Model 760—was available in .35 Remington, creating an almost cult following among those eastern deer hunters who like to work in thick cedar swamps flushing out game at close range.

In addition to maintaining critical case lengths with the Model 7600, reloaders must use small base dies. While the action is quite strong, it lacks the camming power found in bolt guns; the chambers are also cut slightly larger for easier extraction. Finally, the rifle's breech, multiple-rotating locking lugs and receiver recesses must be kept very clean. Don't ever use cartridges that were dropped in the snow; it takes only a thin layer of moisture or detritus to foul the action.

## AUTOLOADERS

The best action for making a second loaded round available is without a doubt an autoloader. Levers are quick and pumps are even faster, but only an autoloader can deliver a well-aimed shot quicker with a level of accuracy consistent with the rifle model used. Even a poorly trained shooter can get off a second shot

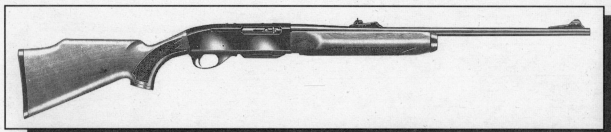

*The best action for bringing up a second loaded round is undoubtedly the autoloader. Among the current best-sellers is Remington's centerfire Model 7400, shown here with high-gloss finish.*

within five seconds of firing. All he must do is recover from the recoil, realign the sights and squeeze the trigger. All shots can be delivered on target in 10 to 12 seconds. It all adds up to power with acute accuracy that's not to be taken lightly.

Current best-selling autoloaders include the Remington 7400 and the Browning BAR. The Remington has evolved from a long line of successful autoloaders, beginning in 1955 with the gas-operated Model 740 Woodsmaster. That was followed by the Model 7400 and its offshoots, the Models 4, 742 and Sportsman 74. Having become popular with the same group of hunters that preferred the pumps, these rifles have often competed against each other. Stories abound of fathers who went hunting with their Remington pumps while their sons carried autoloaders. The Browning BAR, on the other hand, began as a

military action. It went civilian in 1955 as a gas-operated autoloading rifle with a seven-lug locking bolt and a rotary head. Today as the most powerful autoloader on the market, it's available in 7mm Magnum, .300 Winchester Magnum and the powerful .338 Winchester Magnum. A strikingly beautiful rifle, the BAR features cut-checkering, highly polished and blued steel with a near-perfect marriage of wood to metal.

An autoloader offers a lot more than quick follow-up shots, however. Its design allows the action to soak up some of the felt recoil as gas is siphoned off to drive the action. For the shooter, this translates into a gentle push rather than the sharp kick other rifles produce. Autos also feature clip loading, making them easier and quicker to reload. They're also fun to shoot at moving targets and tin cans, testing as they do the shooter's reflexes and eye-hand coordination

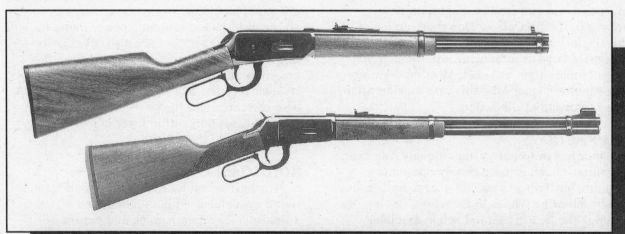

*The Winchester Model 94 Trapper (top) represents a very specialized kind of rifle, one whose short barrel meets the demands of some contemporary hunters. Winchester's big-bore .375 Model 94 (bottom) fills the need for a rifle that performs like an old .38-55 Winchester.*

as no other rifles can do.

On the negative side, autoloaders are sometimes considered inaccurate for long-range varmint shooting, although they perform well for hide hunters. They also consume ammunition in a hurry, forcing hunters to fight the urge to shoot quickly and repeatedly. In addition, the action ejects cases away from the gun, which can mean much time wasted in the field looking for spent brass. Handloaders must use small base dies exclusively with autoloaders. They must also ensure that the brass is trimmed to length correctly, otherwise a misfire or jam may result. Handloaders armed with autoloaders should always perform extensive load-testing and monitor brass conditions carefully before going afield with reloaded cartridges.

## LEVER ACTIONS

The lever-action rifle remains a perennial favorite, with Winchester and Marlin rifles leading the field because of their light weight, compact design and easy access to hunting cartridges.

Readers will recall the old western movies in which levers meant the difference between good and evil. Television audiences nowadays laugh at the simple premises behind those films; but by the same token, they're quick to replace lever- actions with phaser guns and the like.

When it comes to getting back on target and taking repeat shots, levers are faster than bolts. The comfort they provide when carried on horseback is related more to their slim profile than their short barrels; indeed, a longer-barreled rifle is actually easier to get out of a scabbard. But then old myths die hard. Still, a hunter can dismount, grab his lever-action rifle, bring it to his shoulder and place a well-aimed shot in one smooth motion. Speed is of the essence, so the second shot can be delivered from a solid stance and with good aim. This sequence of events during the lever's heyday contributed to the success and popularity of this action.

Winchester, Marlin and Savage were the first to offer levers (Browning entering the market later on). Marlin, with its solid top receiver,

*Browning dominated the market for lever-action rifles. This Lightning model is available in a long-action version offering .30-06, .270 and 7mm Remington Magnum chamberings. The inset shows a full view of the Browning Lightning BLR in short action.*

claimed an early safety advantage over the Winchester dating back to 1881. It remains the major design difference between the two competing levers. The Savage Model 99 continues to survive, although it disappeared for nearly two years. It has changed little, gaining its major reputation from the .250-3000, with more than two million sold worldwide. Today, Browning dominates the lever-action rifle market. Its Lightning model, first produced in 1981, has undergone some cosmetic changes. In addition, a long-action version now offers .30-06, .270 and 7mm Remington Magnum cartridges, bringing the lever up to modern hunting standards. In some respects, it has recaptured the firepower that was previously available only to hunters armed with such legendary levers as the Model 71 Winchester and the Model 88. Many now feel that lever shooting has caught up to where it was when Winchester's Model 1895 was available.

The Browning Lightning has eliminated most of the early concerns about the lever. Small-based reloading dies have made handloaded cartridges reliable. The two-piece stock remains a problem for rifle purists, but its accuracy and performance are indisputable. The line-up of cartridges available today means there is plenty of power for all types of game. But for the Browning Lightning to survive it must continue to evolve, both in caliber offerings and design configurations. Hunters can look forward to carbine versions with shorter barrels, other models featuring more open levers for winter shooting, and full wood models—plus, of course, a broader selection of cartridges. That's a big challenge, especially since bolt-action guns already cover most of these bases.

### BOLT ACTIONS

A large percentage of serious shooters simply dismiss all the other action types in favor of the bolt. For some, it's the only action that supports the cartridge they have in mind. Moreover, it offers more models, variations and designs than any other action type. Handloaders prefer the bolt-action, too. Mauser designed its rifles so their high camming power would extract dirty, oversized, out-of-shape cases. The powerful extractor grips each cartridge firmly and pulls it from the breech. Early Mausers featured a posi-

*Most big-game hunters prefer the bolt. More bolt models, variations and designs are available than for any other action type, making the choice simple for many shooters.*

tive feed, with the extractor picking up and holding the cartridge firmly as the bolt closed. This ensured a positive loading and extraction process. Because the bolt action closes so tightly on the cartridge, it contains the high pressures accompanying most high-intensity cartridges. A typical action has two locking lugs that mesh with cuts in the breech, sealing the chamber and cartridge head. It's important for reloaders that the cases do not stretch excessively once the bolt is locked at the head.

All other things being equal, the bolt is usually more accurate than other actions. The one-piece stock supports both barrel and action. Frequently, the barrel is free-floated, barely

*Bolt-action rifles built by Sako (left) and Ruger enjoy high preference among hunters.*

spring. It takes a deliberate effort to unload a magazine rifle; but still, a practiced hunter can fire quick repeat shots without taking the gun from his/her shoulder.

For American hunters, the big three bolt guns—the Winchester Model 70, Remington Model 700 and Ruger Model 77—have remained virtually unchanged for nearly 30 years and still account for most of the sporting rifles sold in the U.S. Dozens of other gun makers manufacture bolt guns, but none produce the array offered by the big three. The choices abound. The Remington Model 700 comes in 17 calibers and 34 different configurations. The Winchester Model 70 offers slightly more than a dozen versions, while Ruger provides eight. No other action can compare with this variety. Indeed, a hunter can, with some smart shopping, pick a bolt gun for every hunting situation he might ever encounter.

So you can see, based on an overview of all the current rifle actions that good shooting and hunting can be enjoyed with any type of action. Modern action designs are capable of delivering similar firepower and accuracy, even though they may have dissimilar features. For those sportsmen who have always favored one type of action over another, there *is* a rifle that suits your purposes with the kind of action you prefer. In the end, personal preference will dictate your choice, but keep in mind that with the newer, modern actions, there's no longer any real technical reason to choose one over another.

touching the forend and thus preserving shot-to-shot accuracy. These features enable the barrel and action to form an unencumbered sine wave during recoil. On the negative side, bolts are slower to operate and some models are difficult to reload quickly because of their staggered magazines. Some shooters complain about how slow the bolt unloads as shooters move from field to vehicle, with each round having to be jacked through the action and ejected. On models with floorplates, spent rounds are often sprung into the ground by tension in the clip

*WILF PYLE is an avid sportsman who has hunted nearly all game species with a wide variety of firearms. A well-known authority on sporting arms and reloading, he has a passion for sporting rifles, hence his ability to discuss all action types. His books include SMALL GAME AND VARMINT HUNTING and HUNTING PREDATORS FOR HIDES AND PROFIT (Stoeger Publishing). He has also co-authored THE HUNTER'S BOOK OF THE PRONGHORN ANTELOPE (New Century).*

# Scopes: Simplifying The Search

## by Ralph F. Quinn

For shooters who grew up during World War II and the two decades following, it's tough to recall a time when the telescopic sight was not a permanent part of the American hunting scene. It's been that way ever since 1933, when W.E. "Bill" Weaver, an inventor based in El Paso, Texas, introduced his now-famous models M 330 and 440 to the shooting public. True, a California instrument maker named Rudolph Noske had earlier come up with the idea of placing both windage and elevation adjustments inside a scope tube; but it was the entrepreneurial-minded Weaver who put a simple, quality optic device in the hands of the average hunter at an affordable price (a 3X scope during the post-depression days retailed for something less than $20.00). After World War II, a number of prominent manufacturers—Bausch & Lomb, Lyman, Kollmorgen Optical (Redfield) and Leupold-Stevens among others— jumped into the scope business. The rest, as they say, is history.

It's hard to believe, but 1998 marks the 65th anniversary of Weaver's excellent K series of scopes. What began as a simple, low-volume market has evolved into a high-profile, multi-million-dollar industry. With so many scope makers and importers active in the field today, and with dozens of new and improved models being offered each season, it's difficult for shooters and hunters to make wise decisions with some assurance that their money has been well-spent. Today, an average variable scope made by a reputable firm retails in the $450-$500 range, so it pays to know something about the product and one's specific needs. By dividing scopes into general categories and discussing their nomenclature along the way, readers should be in a better position to make informed decisions about the pros and cons of a particular scope.

### POWER IS ONLY ONE CONSIDERATION

For big-game hunting limited to 100 yards, a scope with a fixed power of 1X (no magnification) or 2X (twice as large as the unaided eye) makes a fine choice, but a 4X (four times magnified) or a variable of 1X-5X is much better. With scope sights, magnifying power comes with some sacrifice: the higher the power, the narrower the field of view—FOV, or the area seen through the scope and generally measured at 100 yards. All things being equal, high magnification equals a low FOV, a more critical eye relief, and a shallow depth of focus. Conversely, the lower the power, the greater the FOV. Thus, eye relief is less critical and focus depth is increased.

A large field of view may be required for quick shooting of all kinds, but for running game it is essential. For example, a 2½X scope at 100 yards has a FOV of 40 yards. A 4X scope has a FOV equal to 28–30 feet, and with a 6X it's approximately 20 feet. Going further, a 12X FOV equals 10 feet while a 3X-9X variable has a FOV of 10–35 feet. Since field of view is cone-shaped, it becomes wider as distance increases. The wider the field, the faster the scope can get on target. For jump shooting in brush or timber, a wide FOV is needed along with good light gathering, a quick-centering reticle (crosshair module) and non-critical eye relief (the clearance between the ocular lens and the shooter's eye). In addition, most rifle scopes need to adjust for recoil. When the eye gets closer than 3" or farther away than 4½"–5", the FOV blacks out—and that's where the real problems begin. Lateral eye movement can also cause a blackout of the FOV, a critical factor in the low light levels of dusk and dawn.

This raises a very important consideration. In fixed-power scopes of 8X or more, and with variables set on the top end, the usable field of view grows narrow and eye relief typically becomes critical. With a scope that has poor eye relief, the FOV grows small as the eye moves away from the optimum field; when the eye is too close or too far, the view blacks out completely. This problem occurs particularly with compact variables at dusk when the power ring is set on 9X.

For most big-game hunters in the Midwest and East, the best bet is a fixed-power scope of 3X to 4X or a variable of 1X to 5X equipped with

*This lineup of hunting and target scopes includes (top to bottom): Simmon's ATEC 2.8-10X/44mm WA; Weaver V9 3-9X/38mm; Leupold 6X/40mm; Aimpoint 5000 2X/46mm Electronic Sight. Birchwood Casey's Precision Squares make sighting-in an easy process.*

a duplex crosshair (i.e., a wide outside wire that slims down abruptly near the intersect). Actually, an increase in power is not needed for whitetail or bear hunting because these animals

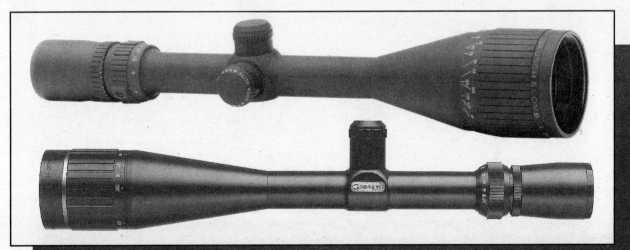

*Bausch & Lomb's Elite 4-16x50mm (top) and Simmon's Gold Metal Silhouette-Varmint (6-20X/44mm) are top-drawer adjustable objective scopes. Both require high mounts to clear the barrel and work best on custom or special-use rifles.*

are highly visible targets with conspicuous kill zones. Some of the longest shots taken on mulies, moose, elk, caribou and antelope have been with a 4X scope or a variable set on 4/5 power. A good stock fit, by the way, is essential for accuracy and proper scope use (*see also* SHOOTER'S BIBLE 1993 on this subject).

Many hunters in the western mountain and plains regions prefer 6X scopes equipped with standard crosshairs because they ensure a steadier, more exact aim. Moreover, it's often easier with a 6X to pick out an animal in a herd, or to evaluate details of horns and racks. Using this increased magnification, however, sacrifices field and focus, making eye relief more critical.

***Variable or Fixed Power?*** Ever since the technicians at Bausch & Lomb and Burris Optics figured out how to keep the relative size of a crosswire reticles constant throughout a power range, the variable scope has dominated the marketplace. Indeed variables outsell fixed-powers 4-to-1 in most regions of the U.S. and Canada. At first glance, the shooter who selects a variable for a multi-use rifle can seemingly have his cake and eat it too—but there are trade-offs.

Although some compact variables weigh as little as 9.5 ounces, the average 3-9X 40mm comes in at 13 to 17 ounces. The cause of this added weight is the optical glass and brass needed for these advanced lens and mechanical systems. With more reflective surfaces to catch light as it travels the length of the scope tube, more anti-reflective coatings must be applied to all lens surfaces. This complicated process involves molecular bombardment in a vacuum

*The author's favorite deer rifles include this custom 7mm/250 topped with a 3-9X/40mm Leupold scope (top). Low rings and a one-piece base make a solid mounting system. The bottom rifle, a Ruger M77 in .257 Roberts with a maple stock, wears Ruger integral rings and bases with Bausch & Lomb's Elite 3000 3-9X/40mm variable scope.*

chamber, which means there's no economic short-cut. This translates into more dollars for the final product (many variables cost $100 to $200 more than a fixed-power scope).

In order to "stuff" additional light into the scope tube, manufacturers have gone to an outside objective lens measuring 44-50mm. The objective lens is the large bell-shaped part of the scope that lies opposite the ocular (eye piece). Admittedly, the objective lens is closely associated with the brightness and light-gathering aspects of a scope, but these new designs require high scope mounts to clear the barrel. This puts the shooter's eye well above the bore; moreover, the cheek is in poor contact with the stock's comb. The net result is mediocre accuracy.

Those who are bent on going the variable route are urged to select a top-of-the line unit in 2X-7X or 3X-9X with a 40mm objective. Some low-cost scopes have a tendency to shift bullet impact through power change. These run-out errors occur when the internal lens mechanisms produce off-axis images to the reticle, causing accuracy to suffer. If it comes down to a choice between topping a light-to-medium bore rifle with a quality fixed-power or a middle-of-the-road variable for the same amount of cash, the fixed-power route is the way to go.

## CROSSHAIRS AND RETICLES: SIMPLE IS BETTER

Even though 90 percent of all scopes sold today are equipped with a version of the thick/thin crosshair (4-plex, quadplex, duplex, etc.), the subject of crosshairs or reticles deserves attention. Several styles of aiming modules are available, including crosshair, dot, post and rangefinder. Again, shooters need to evaluate the type of shooting or hunting they plan to pursue when making a decision. If the answer is target work, small varmint hunting or open country big game, the standard crosshair is ideal.

For close-in work, the standard 4-minute-dot (covering 4 inches at 100 yards) centers the eye quickly, a feature that serves whitetail hunters. If there's a chance of getting a long-range shot at a browsing animal, though, the dot tends to be too large for precise aiming. The same story goes for the post-and- horizontal wire combination. In

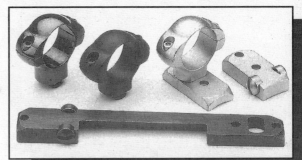

*Scope bases should be matched to each rifle model, while rings are selected to clear scope objectives. The rotary base ring is a solid connection with the base. The one-piece base makes a rigid mount system. Note the rough windage adjustment on these Redfield bases.*

bushy terrain with low light, the concept works fine; but at longer ranges it proves imprecise.

Rangefinder reticles are typically a combination of duplex crosshairs and a pair of horizontal stadia wires that are used to "bracket" the chest region of big game. Knowing the standard measurement of a mature animal enables the

*A good work and maintenance center makes scope mounting easy and accurate. Here a screwdriver tip is matched to a screw slot. Loctite is used to secure the threads against recoil.*

*Using a collimator, the shooter can quickly zero his rifle by matching the scope reticle with a boresighter crosshair. Note the one-piece base on a custom 7mm/250 rifle.*

*A rifle vise is ideal for boresighting and making initial scope adjustments. Remove the bolt and align the bore with the target center.*

*With ear plugs and shooting glasses in place, carefully squeeze off one round. Here extra support for the stock is supplied by a sandbag.*

hunter to estimate distance and collect the trophy with one shot. In theory, this concept sounds appealing, but it doesn't work that well in actuality. When hunting unsuspecting late-season trophies, such as elk, mule deer and antelope, we sometimes forget to hold precisely, particularly on uphill and downhill shots. These momentary lapses are usually caused by the confusing nature of reticle configuration. The bottom line, on reticles, therefore, is: Simple is better.

## SIGHTING IN AND INSTALLING

Once the scope is in hand, it's up to the shooter to mount it properly and "sight it in". For those who are technicians and follow directions, that may sound easy enough. But too often a hunter will purchase a top-drawer variable from a mail-order house, then take it to a local gunsmith for installation. This involves the use of an optical collimator to bore-sight the outfit. The rifle is then targeted with a handful of factory ammo and declared ready for action. Steps one and two may be acceptable, but NOBODY should sight in a rifle except its owner or whoever's going to use the firearm. Nothing takes the place of a shooter who knows his own rifle. Modern hunting scopes may be technical marvels, but they sure aren't miracle workers.

Anytime a new scope is mounted to a rifle or shotgun it becomes part of a system, not just "a scope on a gun." Even though quick-detachable ring systems are available, it's better to put a scope on a rifle and leave it there. Also, keep in mind that three different manufacturers are involved in building a mount, scope and firearm. Therefore, you can expect tolerance variations in receiver rings, holes, mount and saddle configurations. Any deviation from standard can affect how you mount and sight in a hunting scope. The following procedures for installing scopes are recommended:

*1.* Make sure the rings and bases are correct for your particular rifle or shotgun. If a rifle has integral bases, or if scope rings are furnished, proceed with the knowledge that there's one less variable to affect accuracy.

*2.* Remove all oil from the ring and action screw holes. Birchwood Casey's aerosol Gun

*Eliminating parallax is important for pinpoint accuracy. By adjusting the objective, it's possible to fine-tune an optical system to distance and make the reticle seem "pasted" on the target. Note how a rifle rest is used to enhance precision shooting.*

Scrubber is recommended for this tedious job. Simply insert the plastic tube and press the button. To simplify the entire job, work (if possible) from a gun vise or a work station like MTM's Portable Maintenance Center. Its rubber-coated supports are designed specifically for holding a forend and buttstock securely.

*3.* Install base and rings with a screwdriver blade that "fits" the slot, otherwise a sloppy job will result. If base and ring screws are Allen or socket-style heads, the job will go smoothly (a thread tightener, such as Loctite, will ensure a firm hold). To remove these parts later on, a soldering gun applied to the head will break the bond. (Tip: for rotary-type front rings, place an anti-seize grease on the aluminum dovetail to prevent galling).

*4.* With the top saddle rings removed, proceed to the next step: checking ring alignment. A piece of one-inch aluminum bar stock measuring 12 inches can serve as a gauge (a one-inch wood dowel will also work). Place the rod in the rings, check for lateral variation, then adjust. Next, lap the inside saddles (top and bottom) with a piece

of #320 wet-dry sandpaper wrapped around the rod or dowel. A few strokes should do it. This small task will eliminate ring variations and prevent damage to the scope's exterior once the ring screws have been tightened.

*5.* Place the scope in the bottom rings, mate the top saddles and re-install the screws—but don't tighten them. For rifles chambered in a magnum or medium-bore caliber, coat the bottom and top ring with rubber cement to prevent slippage during recoil.

*6.* Adjust the reticle until it is centered on its axis and eye relief is established. The horizontal wire should be dead level with the receiver. Even a slight slant can lead to misses, particularly on long-range, angular shots. Eye relief is correct when a full field of view is visible in the eye piece. Now, with one cheek flush against the stock comb, slide the scope forward until the FOV is a bright and complete circle; then tighten all screws alternately to equalize ring pressure. By taking a few extra moments now, any accuracy problem caused by scope mounting can be avoided. The goal, remember, is long-term zero, not just for the sight-in period.

## OCULAR FOCUS

Before beginning the initial sight-in session, make sure the eye piece is adjusted to the master or aiming eye. With the rifle held tightly in a shooting vise, aim toward an opaque or neutral background, such as the sky. Loosen the lock ring and adjust the ocular counter clockwise until the crosshair begins to look fuzzy. Then back-focus until the reticle is in sharp focus and tighten the lock ring. Be sure to look away several times during the process; this will allow the

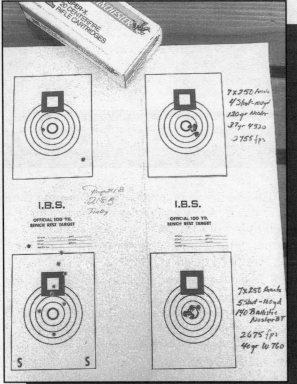

*Reading targets is part of the sighting-in process. Top left: the first round was low, right. Adjusting the click value puts the second round in the center. Bottom left: note how each bullet walked toward the center and beyond. The shooter should discount odd shots, then make an adjustment. Right top and bottom: minute groups like these are possible for shooters who work to eliminate shooting errors and who mount their scopes correctly. Note the IBS target with a one-inch aiming square above each ring target.*

eye's ciliary muscles to adjust to the final focus. Otherwise, the eye will automatically accommodate small deviations in the sharpness of the focus. Those who have an adjustable objective can focus to the range being used (calibrations are marked on the objective bell in yards and meters).

With the rifle clamped firmly in a vise, the next task is to check for parallax. Most centerfire hunting scopes—including variables and fixed powers—are factory adjusted parallax-free at 100 yards (rimfire optics are generally set at 50 yards to accommodate closer ranges). Parallax is an optical phenomenon in which images viewed through the scope and reticle are not in the same focal plane; thus, when the shooter's head moves left or right, up or down, the crosshair appears to move across the target ever so slightly. Turning the front lens with an adjustable objective is relatively easy—just keep turning until the reticle does not move. At that point, the scope is said to be parallax-free. When hunting big game at practical distances, parallax is of little consequence; but when sighting in or when hunting small varmints at long range, it's important to have this kind of pinpoint accuracy.

## TARGETS AND AIMING POINT

Most shooters give little thought to target selection during the sighting process. They simply bang away at a black dot tacked to a suitable backdrop and, once a bullet cuts the mark, they declare the scope sighted in. The best targets for sight-in consist of small squares printed on a measured background with a clearly defined aiming spot. A good example of this style is Birchwood Casey's Precision Squares. Equipped with a crosshair or duplex reticle, a shooter finds it easy to dissect the target face into quadrants before calling his shots. And with a spotting scope, bullet holes are readily located and measured for windage and elevation adjustment. The International Benchrest Society (IBS) uses an ideal target consisting of a one-inch black square with a half-inch white center aiming point printed an inch above center of a 2½-inch concentric target.

## BORE SIGHTING AND RANGE TESTING

The boresighter, or optical collimator, ranks high

among the great time-saving devices designed for rifle users. By locking the instrument in the muzzle of a rifle, it's possible to tune in the scope's zero point quickly by adjusting the reticle to intersect with the grid crosshair. This tool represents a major investment, but it will quickly pay for itself in unwasted ammo and sight-in time.

A rifle can also be boresighted by aligning the target and adjusting the reticle to intersect the target center. The rifle must be clamped firmly in a gun vise during this process; otherwise, windage and elevation become a guess-by-guess situation. Tip: if the rear base of a rifle contains a windage adjustment screw, use the gross adjustment first, then fine-tune with the reticle. Also, should the elevation screw bottom out, try "shimming" the front or rear ring or base. To move impact up, place the shim (an empty aluminum soda can is ideal) in the rear saddle. Then down, front saddle; right, right front or left rear base; left, left front or right rear base.

With the rifle clamped firmly in the vise, and with ear and eye protection in place, carefully align the crosshair and fire one round. Locate the bullet hole with the spotting scope and calculate the distance in inches to the target center. Make the necessary adjustment according to the scope's click values. Measured in 1/4 (or quarter of a minute), it means that for every click, bullet impact moves 1/4 inch at 100 yards. For example, with an impact three inches high and four inches left, move the elevation screw 12 clicks down and 16 clicks right.

With a 25 yard setup, instead of zeroing the reticle on the target center, raise the impact 1 to 2 1/2 inches high. Depending on caliber and load, the natural parabolic trajectory curve of the bullet's rising and falling will take care of the 100- and 200-yard marks. To avoid mistakes, it's always a good idea to check the rifle and project-ed load at hunting distances. So you won't forget, mark all click values and trajectory information for the hunting load used inside the scope adjustment cover.

Once several groups have been fired, average the centers and move or adjust the reticle only as required. Ignore eccentric off-the-mark shots. They may be caused by a variety of factors: poor handloads, increased internal cartridge pressures, loose action screws, poor holding, solvent in the barrel, and so on. Some rifle barrels shift their impact as the steel heats and expands, causing pressure in the inletting. This shifting, or "walking," is caused by a straightened barrel trying to regain its "memory." That explains why some barrel manufacturers refuse to straighten a tube after it's been rifled; they prefer having the bullet fly through one long curve than a lot of short ones. When a rifle exhibits this tendency, it's best to fire several rounds, then let the barrel cool. Zeroing the rifle with a cold barrel ensures you'll be on the mark.

As with all shooting sports, poor rifle accuracy can usually be traced to bad shooting habits, such as flinching, poor holding, aiming and faulty trigger squeeze. Sighting-in that expensive scope on an equally expensive rifle calls for finely honed technique and plenty of practice. Keep things simple, and let the scope's built-in technology take care of the rest.

*RALPH F. QUINN is a Senior Active Member of Outdoor Writers of America, with more than 22 years of freelance writing for gun and outdoor periodicals, including Wing and Shot, American Rifleman, Aquafield's Accuracy & Shooting, Sigarms Quarterly and Handgunning. The information in this article stems from more than 35 years of Quinn's big-game hunting experiences from Alaska to Africa. He is a regular contributor to SHOOTER'S BIBLE.*

# Duck Calls and Their Dedicated Makers

## by Howard L. Harlan

Who made the first duck call? No one really knows, but he was probably a duck hunter from the Mississippi flyway, or perhaps a Native American with one of those thin leaf affairs still used today by some duck and turkey hunters. They would place the leaves or stems in their mouths and blow over them to create sounds imitating their favorite fowl. Whoever that first creator of duck calls was, he certainly knew what ducks sounded like and what their habits were.

The duck call as we know it probably developed from the "tongue pincher" call brought into North America by hunters and trappers during the late 1600s and early 1700s. These calls were referred to as tongue pinchers simply because, if you weren't careful, the reed would pinch your tongue. All contemporary duck and goose calls began with this design. Tongue pinchers were made of two pieces of wood with a metal reed or cane strips sliced very thin. Sometimes a metal bell or turned horn bell was attached for added volume. The French, Germans, Spanish and Italians were probably the first to develop this game call, which was surely the predecessor of our American calls.

Tongue-pincher calls began as double tone boards, but later one of the tone boards was either lost or discarded because it wasn't effective. Perhaps someone conceived an idea about how to build a better duck trap. In any event,

after removing the top or bottom tone board and exposing the reed, someone decided to enclose the reed and tone board with a barrel. All that was required then was to blow a little air into the end of the tube or barrel. As a result of this device, more ducks ended up on American dinner tables than any other invention, with the exception of

The "grandfather" of American tongue pinchers was Elam Fisher, who in 1870 designed and patented a copy of a French and English design.

the shotgun itself.

The contemporary duck call came into its own around 1860, when production call makers entered the scene. The most important of these were F.A. Allen and Charles W. Grubb, who introduced contemporary duck call to the masses. A lot of speculation has circulated about who marketed the first commercial duck call. Allen claimed to be first, but most historians accept Grubb's claim that he was the first, even though Allen's first public announcements in 1863 predated Grubb's by five years. Grubb claimed that his company made the first commercial duck call in 1868. It was a wooden affair with one turned-up metal reed on a flat tone board and one straight metal reed on a curved tone board. He made several models and marketed them for many years. They were made with fine materials and still sound good, which explains why they were so popular in the early 20th century (some are still used by hunters along the Illinois River).

There's no question, though, about who produced the most calls. Allen by far boasts the greater numbers—and probably also the prize—for greater coverage across the country. He advertised in many early periodicals, including Forest and Stream (the forerunner of Field & Stream) and many of the nation's foremost sporting goods stores. Grubb ads are found in these same publications, but not as often as Allen's. Today, many of Allen's calls do not fetch the same price as Grubb's, simply because they were produced in greater numbers even as late as the 1930s. While many other makers must be given credit during this period of development, it was Allen and Grubb who furnished hunters with good, reliable calling devices at cheap prices.

Despite the fact that Allen and Grubb produced many calls on a large commercial basis, they never patented their products. The man who became known as the grandfather of the American tongue pincher was a manufacturer from Detroit named Elam Fisher, who in 1870 designed and patented a copy of a French and English design. Other makers of American tongue-pincher calls were doubtless successful, too, but Fisher was the first we know of who patented his call. Crow and hawk calls of this same design, as well as some early predator

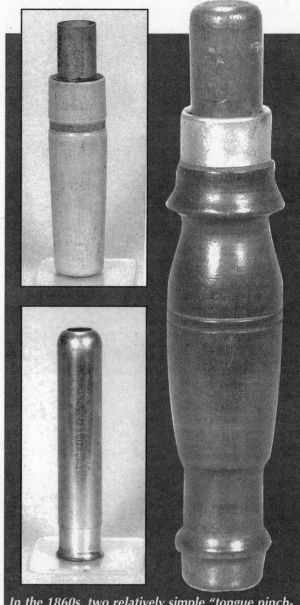

*In the 1860s, two relatively simple "tongue pinchers" by F.A. Allen (left two) and a more elaborate one by Charles Grubb (right) were popular. Allen and Grubb produced duck calls in large numbers and furnished hunters with good, reliable calling devices at cheap prices.*

calls, evolved much later.

Other early Illinois River-type call makers—chiefly Charles Ditto, P.S. Olt, Dick Burns and J.W. Reynolds—also deserve attention. Ditto used the wooden-barrel designs of Grubb and

Allen, plus the metal ball for the stopper (made famous by Allen). He combined these two previous developments, then added molded tone boards and reeds made of hard rubber to develop a wonderful combination, one that worked back in 1905 and still does today. His products were found throughout the Illinois River area and are still marketed by his son.

P.S. Olt entered the calling scene around 1904 and his company still produces his famous D2 duck call. Olt has probably made more duck calls than any other company in history. It remains a family-owned business and continues to be a leader in game-call production in this country and throughout the world. Olt's greatest contribution was the introduction of hard rubber as the chief material in duck calls. Others had used this material previously, but never on Olt's scale. Dick Burns fashioned his idea of a duck

call in hard, molded rubber. Another designer, August R. Kuhlemeier, patented his hard rubber device in 1903, then added a brass band to his barrel to keep the hard rubber from bursting. Hard rubber did indeed make a great duck call, but in cold weather it became brittle. Kuhlemeier's Mascot call was one of the first to feature a rolled radius on the tone board.

Other call makers of note were the Slinn brothers, who combined rosewood stoppers with their hard rubber barrels, which featured scenes of ducks, rabbits and other game molded on. They are very rare and highly desired by duck-call collectors today.

Around the turn of the century another duck-call artist, Charles H. Perdew, used his talents to fashioned duck calls from red cedar and walnut. These were a combination of both the Arkansas and the flat tone boards of the Illinois and

*The early Illinois River call makers included Charles Ditto, Dick Burns and J.W. Reynolds. Ditto, whose call is shown at left, began with the wooden barrel designs of Grubb and Allen, then added molded tone boards and reeds made of hard rubber. Burns' and Reynolds' popular designs are shown center*

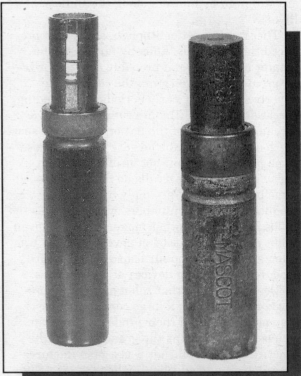

*Duck calls by P.S. Olt, another Illinois River maker (left), and August Kuhlemeier featured hard rubber extensively in their designs. Kuhlemeier's Mascot call (right) was also one of the first to feature a rolled radius on the tone board.*

*Charles Perdew and the Slinn brothers added highly prized art to their craft. Perdew fashioned duck calls from red cedar and walnut with handsomely carved barrels (right). The brothers Slinn combined rosewood stoppers with their hard rubber barrels, which featured game scenes molded on (left). Both types of calls are collectors' items today.*

*Among the rarest of the duck calls are those crafted by Victor Glodo and J.T. Beckhart. Glodo is credited as the forefather of the Reelfoot Lake style (left), while Beckhart is known for his hand-carved black walnut barrels with cut-checkering (right).*

Reelfoot styles. Some were carved with handsome checkering; others had ducks and hunting scenes on the barrels. Sometimes Perdew's wife, Edna, painted the ducks to add a wonderful folk art slant to his work. Perdew was one of the first to add art to the craft and his calls still bring very high prices at call and decoy auctions along the East Coast and throughout the Midwest.

Olt and Kuhlemeier introduced the contemporary-style tone board to the American duck hunter on a large scale, and while it remains the choice of most hunters today, the metal reeds of the Reelfoot style are still used by hunters in the Reelfoot Lake area of northwest Tennessee, northeast Arkansas and southern Illinois. This con-

struction was used for duck calls from the very beginning of their existence and was developed from the tongue-pincher design found mostly on the lakes of southern Illinois by the Glodo family. He was copied by many call makers, but never marketed his products except by word of mouth.

Tom Turpin, George Leonard Herter, J.T. Beckhart, G.D. Kinney, John Cochran and Doug and Nat Porter all had their own ideas of what a Glodo duck call should look and sound like. The most successful of these copies were by Leonard

*Tom Turpin, G.D. Kinney, Doug and Nat Porter, and John "Sundown" Cochran had their own ideas of what a Glodo duck call should look and sound like. Here left to right are their interpretations and contributions to the duck-call industry.*

Herter, who was a mass-market genius and sold many calls from coast to coast during the first half of this century. Next to Herter, there was Tom Turpin, who made an outstanding metal-reed call and sold his products all over the country by way of *Field & Stream* and other publications of his day. G.D. Kinney, Nat Porter and Earl Dennison, all call makers from western Tennessee, worked on a small scale compared to Herter.

Another important call maker was J.T. Beckhart, whose extraordinary duck calls were carved from black walnut with German silver reeds on flat tone boards. He lived on Big Lake along the Arkansas and Missouri border and, like Victor Glodo, used checkering designs probably copied from the fancy gun stocks of the sportsmen they hunted with back East. Beckhart's calls were made by hand and were not produced in large quantities. He and Glodo are, in fact, recognized as the premier call makers of the early 1900s era. Although Beckhart

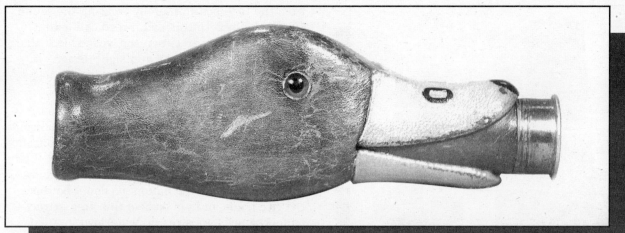

*Although the famous Kinney Harlow duck-head call shown above has brought $12,000 to $13,000 in private sales, it has never reached the prices paid for the rare Glodo calls.*

advertised his calls in some early catalogs published in New York and Chicago, they were never recognized as Beckhart calls, but were listed as St. Francis River duck calls. These calls are rare and high priced in antique shops and flea markets. Glodo calls, however, are the rarest of the metal-reed calls (only a dozen or so have been found). The famous Kinney Harlow duck head call has brought $12,000 to $13,000 in private sales but has never reached the prices paid for Glodo calls. Duck-call prices in this range are justifiable when one considers the value reached in the decoy trade. Prices ranging from $200,000 to $300,000 are not uncommon for buyers seeking the decoy of their dreams. Duck calls are, in fact, much rarer sporting collectibles than decoys or fishing lures.

Another metal-reed maker of note was Earl Dennison and family, who have made calls since the late 1920s. More Dennison calls have been produced than those of any other Tennessee maker and have been marketed all over the U.S. Earl Dennison, who advertised himself as the "Duck Call Man," often carried a mallard hen on his sales visits to sporting goods stores. If the owners didn't buy his calls, at least they remembered him for the real duck squawking from his shoulder. He sold many calls, though, and was featured on early radio shows across the nation. Each Dennison call was boiled in linseed oil to protect it from moisture, which explains why so many have survived and are still in use today.

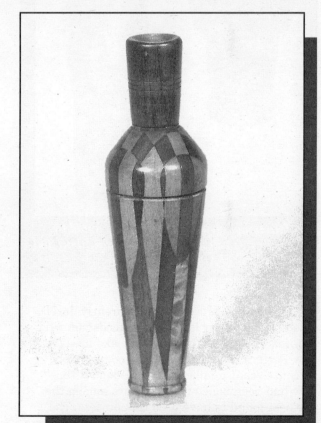

*The Earl Dennison and family duck calls that were made from the 1920s still survive in excellent condition because each one was boiled in linseed oil to protect it from moisture.*

*Two unique types of calls can be found by Tennessee call maker, John Morrow (left) and John Jolly of Arkansas (right).*

from the tone board, thereby creating the sound. One problem with this metal-reed call is that the stopper tends to loosen the wedge block that holds it in place. Porter's gun-sight design ensures that the stopper will stay inside the barrel.

Reelfoot calls will survive as long as there are ducks to shoot, but they are difficult to keep in tune. Thus, the more contemporary calls from Arkansas have become more commonplace. Arkansas has produced more duck-call makers than any other in the nation, no doubt because the rice fields and pin oaks of this area attracted more ducks. As a result, waterfowl in great numbers have wintered in Arkansas since the early part of the century. Arkansas still produces the largest wintering populations, so it figures that the state also boasts a large concentration of call makers. The early calls of Olt, Ditto and others made a great impact on the Arkansas-style call; and while Ditto's and Olt's

This boiling process was apparently developed by the Porter family, backwoodsmen who hunted and fished the Reelfoot Lake area. Very few Porter calls have been located, probably because scant numbers were made; but those few had been boiled in oil and are among the earliest found to have used this process. The Porter calls feature an unusual gun-sight design used by only one other Tennessee call maker, John Morrow. This style of tone board is like any other metal-reed call except that the end of the tone board is round, with a small hole drilled into it. This allows the air flow to lift the reed

*Chick Major's design has won more world championships than any other call maker's.*

are still used there in great numbers, these styles were expanded by such local makers as Chic Major, Jake Gartner, A.M. Bowles, John Jolly and Joe Willingham, to name a few. Indeed, no other call maker has had a greater impact on the industry than the world-famous Chic Major, who must be referred to as the grandfather of all call makers. His design has won more world championships than any other call maker. Edy Holt, Butch Richenback, Wendell Carlson and Buck Gardner have all carried on Major's tradition of call making.

Fortunately, the cottage craft of call making is alive and well. It brings to mind Bruce Leffingwell's book, *Wild-Fowl Shooting*, published in 1888, in which he wrote:

The power of mimicry in man has full-scope for vent in wild-fowl shooting. Some men are natural mimics, others are sadly deficient in such powers, and for the latter the artificial duck's quack is a blessing—that is, if properly used. But when we take into consideration the great army of duck hunters and think for a moment how little they know the art of calling, we are at a loss to know the reason why. The majority of hunters invest in a duck call. They gaze upon it with admiration, squint into its muzzle of bell-shaped horn, look cautiously around to see if they are observed, then place it in their mouth, fill their lungs with air, give a violent blow, and the air resounds with a discordant 'bla-a-a.' Not to be discouraged at the first attempt, they try again, and by thrusting the extreme end against the palate a sound is blown out in A Minor, which faintly resembles a wild duck. A little practice soon obviates this, and the aspirant soon learns to imitate a duck. Imitate how? As the bird calls in its different moods? No, he doesn't think of that, the very thing he ought to think of. The result is, he seeks at times to call them to his decoys, and tries this, when he cries to them in tones which they utter only when in

fright. The beginner should be a student of nature and birds, and watch them in their feeding grounds. Once in a while, some corpulent matron will forget herself and call out 'quack, quack, quack' in 'Won't go home till morning' strains; but the majority are quiet, feeding along with a 'sip-sip-sip,' just as you have often seen tame ducks do. Learn to imitate these; learn to imitate the whistling pintail, the widgeon, the 'meow,' the purring sound of the redheads, the tenor quack of the shoveller, the soprano of the teal. Listen to the mallard hen, as she calls her mate. Try to call like her. How your blood tingles, as his grating, vibrating call reaches you, so mellow, so tender as it travels through the woods—'M-amph, M-amph.' Practice this call, not on the wooden one, but with the one nature provided you with. The best artificial calls I have ever seen are those made by Fred A. Allen. If one is apt he can readily learn to blow them, but bear in mind, the secret of duck calling is the right call in the right place, as the birds call in their different flights and resorts.

As long as mallards fly and there are habitats for them to visit, and as long as our Creator provides water on the prairie, we will continue to call these wonderful waterfowl from Canada to Louisiana with our man-made mimics.

*HOWARD L. HARLAN is a sportsman, collector, author and internationally known champion call maker, and is ranked among the most widely acknowledged game call historians and experts of our time. Harlan is also co-founder of the Call Makers and Collectors Assn. and curator of the largest collection of American game calls and sporting memorabilia. His efforts to authenticate the game call as a unique American folk art have received worldwide recognition. This article is adapted from a chapter contributed by Harlan to the new book, SPORTING COLLECTIBLES (Stoeger, 1997), written and edited by Stephen Irwin, M.D.*

# The Walther HP Pistol: A Collector's Dream

*by Gene Gangarosa Jr.*

Beginning in the late 1920s, the Carl Walther Waffenfabrik, known to the firearms world as simply "Walther," began a series of experiments intended to create a double-action military pistol in 9mm automatic. At first, the company, located in Zella-Mehlis, an industrial city in then eastern Germany, attempted to enlarge its successful .32 ACP (7.65mm) Model PP to accept the more powerful 9mm cartridge. The result was a pistol—dubbed the *Militarisches Pistole* or Model MP—that attracted only limited interest from the German military, mostly because it had a blowback (unlocked breech) mechanism that was considered unsafe with the high-pressure 9mm cartridge.

Next came a locked-breech pistol, again named the Model MP, which was the creation of Fritz Walther, son of the late founder of the factory who became the company's pistol design genius. Another design, called the Model AP (meaning *Armee Pistole*), appeared around 1936. Similar in mechanical function and appearance to today's P.38, it received favorable notice from the German Army Weapons Office, or *Heereswaffenamt*, the agency responsible for approving new weapons for service in the armed forces. The Model AP's only shortcoming, at least from the German military's point of view, was its enclosed hammer, which made it difficult to determine the weapon's state of readiness at a glance. Its manual safety was actually too good, because when it broke the gun could not be fired at all.

Thus did the Heereswaffenamt return the Model AP to Walther with suggestions for improvements. These changes having been made, the perfected pistol, called the Model HP, was born. It featured a modified safety mechanism and a shortened slide with an opening at the rear to allow for a prominent exposed hammer. These changes were all that set the HP apart from the earlier, failed Model AP. In late 1938, this modified pistol—which eventually became the famous P.38—received a tentative German army order for 410,600 pistols. While still in the tooling stage for mass production, the pistol appeared in April 1939 for the first time in the Wehrmacht's official weapons inventory, as well as in Walther ads aimed at commercial sale of the new weapon. Nevertheless, the problems involved in producing the pistols at the enormous rate requested by the army (the monthly rate was set in November 1939 at 10,000 pistols) delayed production for well over a year. During this time, Walther continued to develop the Model HP as a commercial venture, albeit on a limited scale.

The largest single order for the HP came from Sweden, though world events prevented Walther from filling the order. In late 1939, the Swedes,

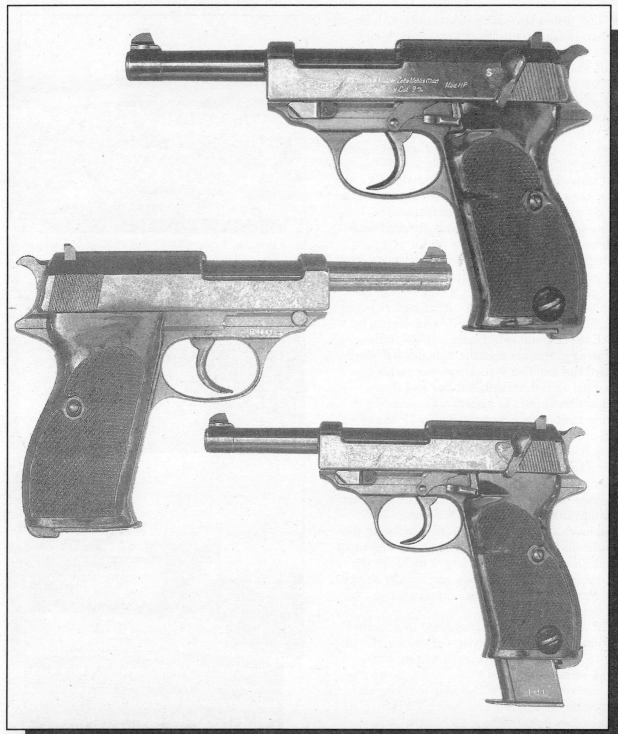

*The Model HPs that were sent to Sweden in 1940 featured distinctive black checkered plastic grips with a circular relief hole for the lanyard loop (top). To easily distinguish these guns, an "H" prefix before the serial numbers, which ran from H1001 to H2885, was stamped on the gun (center) as well as the magazine (bottom). (Tom Tozer collection)*

who had tested several foreign pistols with an eye to replacing their Husqvarna-made Model 1907s, adopted the HP as their official military pistol. The Swedish armed forces then asked Walther to supply them with 11,000 pistols. In 1940 Walther sent 1500 HPs to Sweden, each with a distinctive pattern and with serial numbers beginning at H1001 and running to H2885. These distinctive HPs had black, checkered plastic grips with a circular relief hole for the lanyard loop. The rear sights were also slightly narrower than those found in later production runs. The Swedish-contract guns also featured a squared-head firing pin that was automatically withdrawn into the slide once the shooter applied the manual safety lever. This safety system made it impossible for the hammer to strike the firing pin during the decocking stroke. To simplify manufacture, the Walther factory soon switched to a simpler rounded-head design, in which the manual safety, once applied, locked the firing pin in place as the hammer fell. Even though the hammer struck the rear end of the firing pin as it decocked, Walther and the German army felt the system was adequate. Horror stories have circulated about P.38s being fired accidentally during the decocking motion, but this was never a problem with guns made during the early war or postwar periods.

One interesting comment on Walther's attempts to market the Model HP was an advertisement that appeared in A.F. Stoeger Company's 1939 catalog. This ad testified to the high hopes Walther entertained for its well-made pistol. Despite its high price ($75 in 1939), the HP would certainly have become a major success had World War II not cut off exports before they had begun.

HP commercial sales continued in a limited fashion during the early years of the war. Until late 1940, Walther kept experimenting with slight variations on the basic design. Some pistols marked "Mod. P38" had four-inch barrels (the standard barrel length being 4.9 inches) and dual-caliber 9mm/7.65mm (.30 Luger) sets, whereby the caliber was changed simply by switching barrels. The deluxe models had beautiful carved wooden grips, yellow and red highlights on the front and rear sights, lightweight aluminum-alloy frames, and single-action target

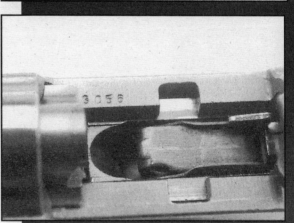

*The Model HP's slide markings, which were in use until early 1945, made clear exactly who built the pistol and where it came from (top). Most HPs built after April 1940 had the German Nazi Eagle-over-N commercial proofmark placed on the slide. Note also the serial number—13056—on the frame (center) and the inside of the slide (bottom). The "1" here is not visible unless the pistol is disassembled.*

versions. Once large-scale production of P.38s for Germany's armed forces got underway, however, such experimentation virtually ceased. The Model HP made during World War II was to all intents and purposes a P.38 with commercial markings and ribbed brown plastic grips instead of wooden or black checkered ones.

In addition to HP sales in Germany itself, Walther made modest foreign sales, including the Croatian fascist party, or Ustacha, whom Walther supplied with slightly under 200 Model HPs. These pistols were made late, around serial number 12400, each bearing a distinctive shield emblem engraved into the left side of the slide. Smaller numbers of HPs probably were sold during the war years to Portugal and various Central and South American countries. In each case, the number of pistols involved was quite small, probably no more than a few hundred in all.

*The early commercial HP (1939-1940) sometimes appeared with black checkered plastic grips and a rectangular opening for the lanyard loop, similar to the modern P.38 grip.*

*The well-made Model HP is inherently accurate. This slow-fire group shot from a rest at a distance of 50 feet placed a full magazine of 8 rounds into a hole less than an inch across.*

*The Model HP, like all other P.38-type pistols, featured the clever loaded-chamber indicator pin introduced by Walther as an optional feature in the PP/PPK series pistols. Here the pistol is shown cocked for single-action shooting.*

The Model HP served in Nazi Germany's armed forces, too, with an estimated 6,200 pistols having been acquired by the Wehrmacht. These military HPs can be easily identified by a military acceptance stamp appearing on the right side of the slide in the form of a stylized eagle over the number 359. Of these, an estimated 2,400 HPs featured a high-polish blued finish. Reported serial numbers on those specimens extended to about 16000, after which the pistols mostly bore a duller matte blued finish more suited to a military pistol (some HPs, though, did show up with the original high-polish blued finish in the 19000 serial number range). Serial numbers on this second military-blue variation reached about serial number 24000, with the German armed forces buying an estimated 2,600 of them. In the final months of the war a third variation, called the Zero Series HP, appeared. These pistols, marked "P.38" and "ac 45" on the left side of the slide, were given full military acceptance marks on the right side, continuing the HP serial number range with an 0 prefix (hence, the "Zero Series" designation). These late-war pistols are technically considered HPs, although with their crude finish they are a far cry from the beautifully made models of 1940 and 1941. Serial numbers on the Zero Series designation range from 025900 up to 027700 (estimates), with the German Wehrmacht having bought about 1,200 such pistols from Walther. With all the serial numbers reported, most of the HPs produced were intended for commercial sale and therefore lacked the military acceptance stamp.

Throughout the war years (except for the Zero Series), Walther marked the slide of all Model HPs with its company name and location. This procedure was unlike the much more common practice with the P.38s, which, having been made to military specifications, were coded. Very early in HP production—and again in late 1944 to early 1945—Walther marked a quantity of Model HPs with the designation "Mod. P.38" instead of "Mod. HP." Those pistols so marked are relatively scarce, including perhaps a few hundred early-war and slightly fewer than 1,800 late-war pistols.

The postwar Austrian armed forces, called the *Bundesheer*, also used the HP to a considerable extent. These pistols were actually donated to Austria around 1955 by the Allied forces of World War II. Several hundred of these weapons saw Austrian service until they were phased out of service between 1985 and 1987, at which time U.S. importers brought them into the United States. Regrettably for collectors, most of the Austrian Model HPs underwent extensive rebuilding programs, which in most cases involved rebluing and adding Austrian markings, thus largely destroying the collector value of these pistols. Since the end of World War II, HPs have surfaced in Austria, Australia, Canada, China, France, Germany, Russia, Sweden and the U.S.

Walther's Model HP would undoubtedly have become a major commercial success had not the war intervened. As it was, Walther built fewer than 30,000 of them, making it a rare gun indeed. Those who have an excellent-to-mint-condition Model HP in their collections are most fortunate.

## TIPS FOR COLLECTORS

Made to a higher standard than contemporary P.38s, the HP generally has a slightly better trigger pull and is equally durable, reliable and accurate. As the late firearms authority W.H.B. Smith remarked in 1961, "A Model HP is wonderful to shoot for fun or for keeps." His statement remains true today. Several cautions are in order before a collector puts one of these guns through its paces, however. First, as with any old gun that has been previously owned by several people, it should be closely examined by a qualified gunsmith with expertise in the P.38 design. Areas of special concern include the presence and proper function of the locking block located beneath the breech end of the barrel. Another concern involves integrity of the

*This Model HP, called the "Bundesheer", saw service with the postwar Austrian army. The Austrians reblued the pistol, thus obliterating the slide markings, and added two sets of serial numbers to the slide and frame (along with the "BH" property mark).*

hammer-decocking function, which is part of the safety mechanism. After all, nobody wants this powerful service pistol to be fired as an unlocked-breech blowback; nor does anyone relish the thought of firing the gun accidentally with the manual safety on.

Satisfied that the HP in question is in sound condition, the prospective owner should consider the gun's inherent value and collectibility. Collectors base such considerations on how close the gun is to its original factory condition, its scarcity (in that particular variation), and whatever historical interest is associated with it. Some HP variants are so rare today that one found to be in excellent to mint condition should never be fired at all lest its collector value be compromised. Such HPs include any pre-production prototypes with concealed or rounded hammers. Swedish contract pistols in excellent condition are also vary rare; most of those that come up for sale have seen considerable use and show extensive finish wear. And any Model HP made originally to fire the 7.65mm (.30 Luger) caliber cartridge (rather than the 9mm) is exceedingly rare. Finally, late-war Model HPs marked with 0-prefix serial numbers are not only scarce, they are so crudely made that none of them should ever be fired.

The more common, mechanically sound variations of the Model HP can be shot in moderation without undue harm to their collectible status. These include most mid-war models with ribbed P.38-style grips, particularly those in less-than-excellent condition. Any of the refinished or reworked guns modified after the war, particularly those formerly in Austrian official service, have no real collector value and are thus qualified to shoot. Model HPs that came out of Austrian surplus often appear at gun shows. Although few in number—probably only a hundred or so have been converted—these former Austrian guns lack collector status. The main reasons for this are their refinished metal surfaces, partially obliterated slide markings and heavy use of replacement parts. While these improvements have enhanced the gun's handling and shooting characteristics, they destroy their value to advanced collectors who are willing to pay top dollar for vintage guns. Such collectors, often fussy by nature, diligently look instead for

**FURTHER READING**

Buxton, Warren. *The P.38 Pistol*. Ucross Books, Los Alamos, New Mexico, 1990

Gangarosa, Gene. *P.38 Automatic Pistol—the First 50 Years*. Stoeger Publishing Company, Inc., Wayne, NJ, 1993

Smith, Walther, *H.B. Walther, Mannlicher and Mauser Pistols*. Stackpole Publishing Company, PA, 1971

Still, Jan. *Axis Pistols*. Walsworth Publishing Company, Marceline, MO, 1989

guns in mint, original-issue condition.

A final caution: any Model HP should be fired in moderation only. The 7.65 and 9mm Parabellum cartridges chambered for these pistols are high-intensity, high-pressure cartridges. The basic P.38 design may be durable enough for standard factory loadings, but it is not an inherently stronger pistol. While a P.38 of more recent vintage can still provide excellent service as a military, police or civilian self-defense sidearm, one should not put an elderly Model HP through any severe strains. Parts that are almost impossible to replace will inevitably break. For all these reasons it's wise to reserve even the functional specimens of a Model IIP for occasional shooting only.

GENE GANGAROSA JR. is a teacher and technical writer who lives in Florida. His long association with handguns began during his naval service as a helicopter aircrewman and in naval intelligence. Since 1988, Gangarosa has written more than 200 articles on firearms, his work appearing in Guns and Gun World magazines, among many others. This is Gangarosa's second appearance in SHOOT-ER'S BIBLE. His new book — COMPLETE GUIDE TO COMPACT HANDGUNS — debuted this spring (Stoeger, 1997); the companion volume, COMPLETE GUIDE TO SERVICE HANDGUNS, is in progress. These follow two earlier titles: P38 AUTOMATIC PIS-TOL — THE FIRST 50 YEARS (1993) and MODERN BERETTA FIREARMS (1994), also published by Stoeger.

# Gold Rush.

*Gold shotgun*
*$735 (suggested retail)*
*Available in 12 and 20 gauge*

The heart pounds. Adrenaline flows. Time stands still. All this while your Gold shotgun is still cradled in your arm.

Imagine what happens when its perfect balance brings it to your shoulder. When its gas-dampened recoil keeps it there for a fast follow-up on a double — maybe even a triple. With the bolt locked back, its speed loading feature automatically sends the first shell you thumb into the magazine directly to the chamber, ready to be fired. It's more excitement than most people can handle, but it's all in a day's work for the Gold.

If you're ready for the heart-pounding rush of the Gold shotgun, see your Browning dealer. If not, see your cardiologist.

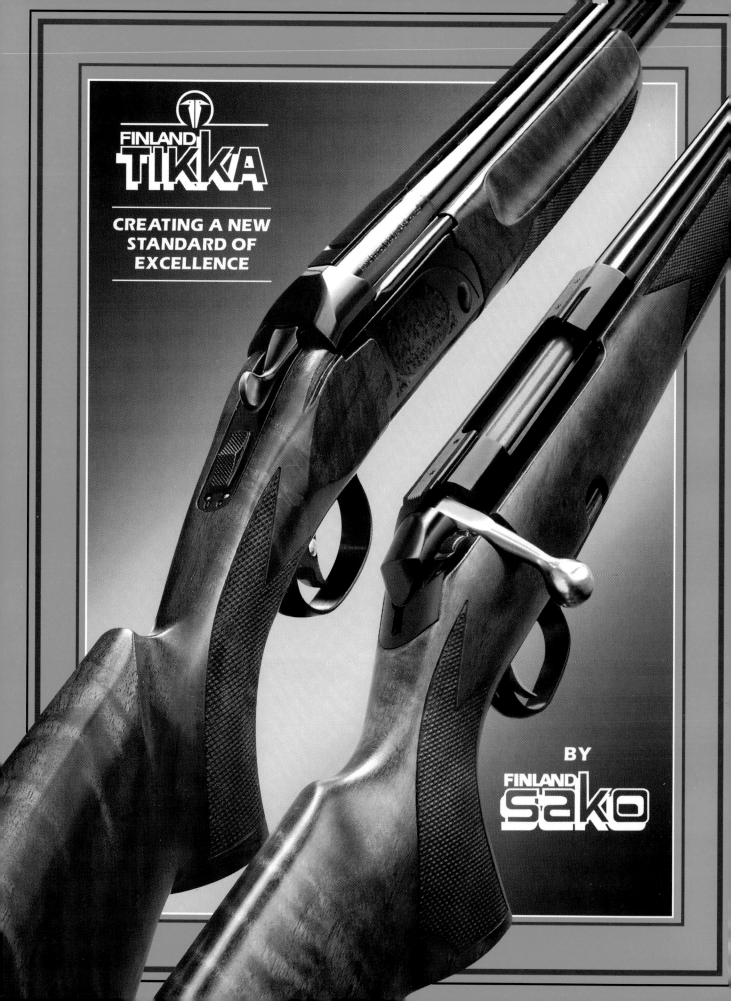

FINLAND
TIKKA

CREATING A NEW
STANDARD OF
EXCELLENCE

BY

FINLAND
sako

# Understanding Bullet Behavior

## by Don Lewis

Long before the black dust known as gunpowder was invented, the armies of the Dark Ages used various devices to hurl arrows and large stones and iron balls into enemy forts. The Old Testament (Chronicles 25–26) states that Uzziah made a vast array of weaponry for his army, "And he made in Jerusalem engines, invented by cunning men, to be on the towers and upon the bulwarks, to shoot arrows and great stones withal."

Undoubtedly, these monstrous "engines" referred to catapults, which could hurl large objects into enemy forts and lines. The only problem was, they had little or no accuracy. When the first cannon appeared, it offered more range; but, like the catapult, it couldn't be aimed properly. Large balls could batter the walls of a fort, but they had little impact on ranks of soldiers. Later on; the shoulder weapon (musket) proved effective in throwing small balls at a single enemy. Unlike the massive catapults and cumbersome cannons, the shoulder weapon could be carried by individual soldiers.

Early shoulder weapons were plagued with ignition problems, though, and were difficult to reload. A musket could be pointed at a specific target, but it didn't guarantee a hit (a problem somewhat overcome by adding sights). Accuracy was not significantly enhanced until spiral grooves (rifling) were cut into the bore, causing the ball (projectile) to spin. This helped stabilize its flight and at the same time improved accuracy. Exactly why a rotating sphere traveled straighter than one that flew without rotation was not completely understood at the time. It was known, however, that feathers set at an angle made an arrow rotate in flight, thus rendering it more stable in the air. It's quite possible that a tinkering gunsmith somewhere reasoned that the same principle ought to work with a spinning ball.

By the early 1800s, a variety of experiments had been carried out with elongated projectiles—bullets, not balls. Gunsmiths had learned by now that elongated bullets must rotate faster than balls to retain stability and improve accuracy. And yet, despite many advances in ignition and barrel design, the flight of the bullet still perplexed cartridge designers. A bullet exiting from the muzzle at a high rate of speed, they observed, struck the target almost instantly. Because it was physically impossible for early shooters to watch a bullet in flight, they naturally thought all bullets traveled in a straight line. That theory probably died when it was learned that changing the angle of the muzzle increased the distance a bullet traveled before it hit the ground. Tinkering gunsmiths eventually discovered that not all bullet shapes produced the same accuracy. It became evident that a bullet was more than just a piece of elongated lead; its shape played an important role in how it traveled through the air. That principle—how a bullet reacts as it flies through the air—became known as *external ballistics*.

Sierra's *50th Anniversary Rifle Reloading Manual* states that, "Ballistics has existed as a technical art for thousands of years. . . . Evidence of the development of throwing instruments and specialized projectiles dates back to Stone Age Man." It's impossible to determine how much was known about external ballistics in prehistoric times, but dedicated experimenters soon learned that a strong crosswind was detrimental to a bullet's flight, and that powder charges of different weights made bullets react differently. One thing became quite clear: the flight of a bullet was subject to gravity and other atmospheric conditions. Then around 1710, famed British scientist Sir Isaac Newton proved that faster moving projectiles were subject to greater air resistance, or drag. Thereafter, gunsmiths assumed that the faster a bullet exited the muzzle, the quicker it slowed down. Once it left the muzzle, the bullet was subject to the same physical laws of gravity as any falling object. Its speed could not prevent gravity from pulling it down, nor could it stop air resistance from slowing it down. Once the effects of gravity and air resistance became common knowledge among ballisticians, the path of a particular bullet in flight—i.e., ballistics—could at last be determined with accuracy.

## BALLISTICS BECOMES A REAL SCIENCE

Today three types of ballistics are studied: interior, exterior and terminal. *Interior ballistics*—the study of chamber pressure, velocity, temperature and time—starts with primer ignition and ends when the bullet exits the muzzle. At that moment, *exterior ballistics*—or the flight of the bullet—takes over until the bullet strikes the target. The third type of ballistics—*terminal*—is described in the *Speer Rifle # 12 Reloading Manual* as "the study of bullet behavior from the moment it enters that target until it stops." Thus, bullet construction and velocity play important parts in terminal ballistics, advising the hunter which bullet will take the game animal he seeks most effectively.

For the hunter, though, the most critical stage lies in exterior ballistics. Once the path of a bullet is known, a hunter can easily determine

*The author fires a 22-250 at a chuck more than 300 yards away. Bullets with high ballistic coefficients are more accurate and retain velocity at long ranges.*

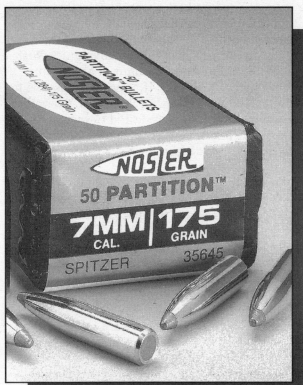

*The 175-grain Nosler Partition bullet with a high ballistic coefficient of .519 and a sectional density of .310 is an ideal game bullet, especially when used in a Remington 7mm Magnum at velocities above 2600 fps.*

where the bullet will strike at different ranges—a ballistic that's especially critical for long-range shooting. As discussed, the flight of a bullet is not a straight line. A bullet begins falling the instant it exits the muzzle, and it falls faster the farther it travels. Its speed does not prevent it from being pulled down by gravity. A 220 Swift with a 40-grain bullet producing a muzzle velocity of 4000 fps falls about one inch during the first 100 yards of flight. On the other hand, a 40-grain 22-rimfire bullet generating 1200 fps or so will fall 12 inches over the same distance. That doesn't mean the 220 Swift overcame the Law of Gravity; it simply spent less time in gravity's grasp.

That raises the important subject of gunsights. A sight that's aligned with the bore cannot intersect the bullet, which falls steadily below the bore line. An adjustable sight allows the shooter to make the line of sight intersect the bore line instead of being parallel to it. Adjusting the sights for elevation automatically raises the muzzle, causing the bullet to go through the line of sight twice — once immediately in front of the muzzle, and again at the point at which the rifle is sighted in. After the bullet has passed through the line of sight (a few yards in front of the muzzle), it flies in an arc above the line of sight, then drops back through the line of sight at a predetermined sight-in distance. The curve of the bullet above the line of sight is not a true arc, however. Some call it parabolic, or simply an elongated arc.

When looking at the arc, there is a difference between the mid-range trajectory and the highest point of the arc. The mid-range trajectory is really the halfway point between the muzzle and the sight-in distance, not the highest point of the bullet's arc as many shooters assume. The highest part of the arc is called *maximum ordinate*, or MO. There's no easy formula in fixing the MO, but in general it occurs about 60 percent or more to the sight-in point. Thus, a rifle zeroed in for 300 yards has an MO at about 185 yards, with a mid-range trajectory set at 150 yards.

As firearms became more efficient, some astute gunsmith realized that bullets had a scientific nature of sorts. Archers had long known that to add distance to the flight of an arrow, one must start it out on an arc; i.e., changing the angle of flight. For the same reason, cannoneers tilted the muzzle upward to throw the ball farther. Those familiar with mathematics began to develop formulas to prove that a moving projectile was subject to air resistance. Galileo had proven that both heavy and light objects fall at the same rate; but if that were true, why does a sheet of metal fall faster than a sheet of styrofoam? The answer: density and air resistance. Styrofoam and metal may be identical in size, but a sheet of metal has more density, while by comparison a sheet of styrofoam has little mass. Thus, the low mass of styrofoam does not overcome air resistance as efficiently as metal, which is more dense. Because lead has more mass than lighter materials, such as steel or aluminum, bullet makers have always used the heavier metal.

According to the new *Sierra 50th Reloading Manual,*

A bullet traveling through the air is acted on by two distinct kinds of forces, the force of gravity and the force due to the air flow around the body. After a bullet leaves the gun barrel, the trajectory is completely determined by these forces. In the early days of ballistic science, nothing was known about the aerodynamic force, and very little was known about gravity. It seems strange now, but for about 200 years after firearms first appeared in western Europe in the early 1300s, it was not known that the shape of a bullet's trajectory is a curve.

In 1537, an Italian scientist named Tartaglia claimed that the trajectory of a bullet was a continuous curve. Later, in 1636, Galileo published the results of his experiments, which proved that the trajectory of a bullet was a type of curve called a parabola. From this point on, external ballistics was given high priority; after all, battles in those days were won by armies with the most accurate guns. War was literally a way of life then, so governments allocated large sums of

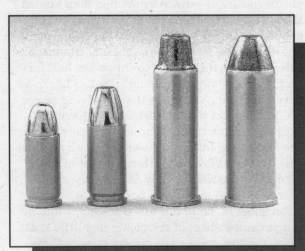

*Note the various shapes found in a random selection of handgun bullets, each with its own ballistic coefficient. The slightest change in shape adds to or decreases the BC.*

money to produce better weapons. In their quest for more sophisticated weaponry, scientists began in earnest to develop ballistics and other physical sciences, including aerodynamics. With the birth of the electromechanical analog computer during World War II, it became possible to solve calculus problems mechanically, where previously ballisticians were forced to work with slow, inefficient manual computations. "For the first time," according to the *Sierra Reloading Manual,*

"ballisticians began to see themselves emancipated from tedious manual computations, and this opened a new vista for ballistic research. The electromechanical computer helped solve the very complex trajectory computation problem for aerial bombs dropped from high-flying World War II bombers, and this was a major step forward in ballistics."

Ballisticians had known for a long time that a single standard drag function was not practical for all bullet shapes. It seemed logical, therefore, to classify bullets into families. Finally, in 1965, Winchester announced it had developed a set of ballistic tables using four families of bullets: $G_1$, $G_5$, $G_6$ and $G_L$ (drag functions for standard bullets are designated by the letter G, thanks to extensive work done in France by the Gavre Commission). The instruction manual for operating the Oehler Model 43 Personal Ballistic Laboratory has this to say about drag functions:

A few decades ago the commercial firearms and ammo people decided on a standard model to describe the exterior ballistic performance of sporting ammo. They chose a drag function named G to represent typical performance of a sporting bullet. While the G drag function sounds impressive, it's only a table showing how fast the standard projectile is losing velocity versus the momentary velocity of the projectile. If a tested bullet loses velocity twice as fast as does the standard bullet, it has a ballistic coefficient of ½

*The five 150-grain, 308 bullets shown have the same sectional density, but different ballistic coefficients. For example, the roundnose bullet (right) registers a low BC of .266 while the Spitzer on the left has a high BC of .423, making it more efficient for long-range shooting.*

or 0.500. If the tested bullet loses velocity three times as fast as does the standard bullet, it has a BC of 1/3 or 0.444. If the tested bullet loses velocity at the same rate as the standard bullet, it has a BC of 1/1 or 1.000. If the tested bullet retains its velocity better than the standard bullet, it has a BC of greater than 1.000. To measure BC, you must know both how fast your bullet is going and how fast the bullet is losing velocity. Suppose that your bullet starts at 2500 fps and loses 312 fps in 100 yards. The standard bullet loses only 84 fps starting at the same velocity under the same atmospheric conditions. The BC of your bullet is approximately 84/312 or 0.269.

A bullet's energy output and flight are also governed by such things as sectional density and ballistic coefficient. These two terms are blamed for many field-shooting problems, but it's a rare case when either of these elements is the direct cause of a miss. Still, to get a better grasp on external ballistics, it's important to understand these elements of a bullet's makeup. Sectional density (SD) is a bullet's weight in pounds divided by the square of its diameter. The formula for calculating it, therefore, is $SD = W/D^2$. All else being equal, the higher the SD reading, the better the penetration. As an example: to convert the weight of a 105-grain 6mm bullet in pounds,

divide 7000 (the number of grains in a pound) into 105, which gives 0.015. Divide that number by .243 (the bullet diameter in inches) squared, or 0.059. The sectional density (SD) of this bullet is therefore .254. Since SD is determined solely by a bullet's weight and diameter, any change in shape is irrelevant. Thus, 105-grain 6mm bullets have the same SD no matter what their shape or style.

Sectional density is not the primary reason for choosing a bullet, however. It's possible to have two bullets with nearly identical SDs, but that doesn't mean they have identical power or efficiency. For example, following our formula, the SD of a 90-grain .243 bullet is .218, while that of a 150-grain .308 bullet is .224. With a muzzle velocity of 2900 fps, the .243 bullet has a kinetic energy of 1,345 foot-pounds at 100 yards, while the 150-grain .308 at 2900 fps has far greater energy at 2,312 foot-pounds. Obviously a big-game hunter would be better off with the .308 bullet, even though the sectional density of the two bullets is nearly the same.

Next, let's consider the *ballistic coefficient* of a bullet, which is determined by its shape. William C. Davis Jr., the ballistic editor for *American Rifleman*, describes BC as: "A quantitative indicator of a bullet's ability to maintain its velocity as it flies through the air. It is defined mathematically by the expression $C = W/(1xD^2)$." That means shape is important as a bullet moves through the atmosphere. A more streamlined bullet naturally slips through the air easier than does a blunt-shaped one, hence it doesn't lose velocity as fast. It retains more kinetic energy at long range.

To show how BC is related to SD, Davis further explains:

The same equation can be rearranged to read $C=W/D^2/1$ ($W/D^2$=sectional density of the bullet), which means the ballistic coefficient can also be defined as the sectional density divided by the form factor. This is a dimensionless number expressing the aerodynamic efficiency of a bullet's shape; or more specifically, the ratio of the drag coefficient of any given bullet to the drag coefficient of a standard projectile. If all bullets were of the exact same shape as the standard projectiles to which they are compared, the form factor would always be exactly 1, and the ballistic coefficient would always be exactly equal to the sectional density.

The highly sophisticated Oehler Model 43

Personal Ballistic Laboratory (PBL) offers a maze of ballistic information, including chamber pressure readings in individual rifles, instrumental velocity, time of flight, downrange velocity and the ballistic coefficient of each bullet fired through the Acoustic Target. As the PBL's creator, Dr. Kenneth Oehler, explains:

A BC of .41 means simply that a bullet is 41% as efficient at retaining its velocity as was the 'standard' bullet for which the drag table was determined. . . . If you measure the BC at a different velocity level, you may get a different BC. Nothing about the bullet changes as velocity changes, but a different key, or BC, may be required to make the bullet's behavior fit the standard table at the new velocity.

Kevin Thomas, Chief Ballistician at Sierra Bullets, further explains: "Unlike physical dimensions of weight and diameter, the BC of a given bullet will vary tremendously depending on a range of outside factors, such as initial

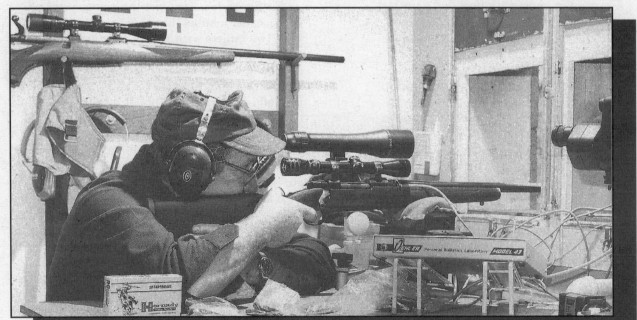

*The Oehler Model 43 Personal Ballistic Laboratory is used for velocity tests for both factory and hand-loaded .222 Swift ammunition. The M-43 also gives the ballistic coefficient of each bullet fired through the downrange Acoustic Target.*

*Helen Lewis (the author's wife) did not need to know the BC of the .25-06 hollowpoint 120-grain GS-SP Speer bullet (BC-.328) when she dropped this five-point buck at 80 yards.*

velocity, twist rate and the more commonly recognized variables of temperature, humidity and barometric pressure."

Until handloaders could purchase affordable equipment to measure both interior and exterior ballistics, the term *ballistic coefficient* was really meaningless. It was generally known that a bullet with a high BC would retain velocity longer and also have a lower trajectory arc. Few handloaders knew that the BC changed when velocities changed. *The Sierra 50th Reloading Manual* includes a table of ballistic coefficients for three velocities computed for sea-level altitude and standard atmospheric conditions. For example: a 130 Spitzer 277 (270 Winchester) has a sectional density of .242 and a BC of .370 at 2700 fps; .379 between 2700 and 2200 fps; and .383 at 2200 fps and below. The .277 Spitzer Boat Tail has the same sectional density but a BC of .436 at 2800 fps and above; .418 between 2800 and 2200 fps; .402 between 2200 and 1800 fps; and .387 at 1800 fps and below. These measurements illus-

trate how much the BC changes significantly with increases or decreases in velocity.

Many chronographs claim an accuracy rating of 0.5%. At 3000 fps, 0.5 translates into 15 fps, which is admittedly small compared to the average velocity of 3000 fps. However, the range of measurements for a good load may vary no more than 10 to 30 fps from the average velocity; moreover, a 0.5% accuracy applies only to average velocities measured under ideal conditions. Most handloaders will likely experience more than a 15 fps error on individual shots. When trying to measure uniformity, and with all readings falling within 25 fps of the average, a 15 fps error become huge. A handloader's chronograph should show a consistency of approximately 0.1%, or 3 fps out of 3000 fps on each shot, before uniformity measurements can be relied upon.

To obtain reliable velocity data, all measurements—distance to skyscreens, distance between skyscreens and range measurement—must be held to critical standards. For one recent range test with the Oehler Model 43 PBL, the range was measured electronically to within one inch from a point on the shooter's window sill to an Acoustic Target armed with three microphones to pick up the sonic boom (mach cone) of a passing bullet. No matter which chronograph is used, all measurements must be held to close tolerances.

Knowing the SD or BC of a bullet definitely can lead a hunter to success in the field or a competitor to win a match. Handloaders who have a deep understanding of internal and external ballistics will more often than not produce handloads that result in superb accuracy.

*DON LEWIS is an experienced hunter who tests and evaluates firearms and shooting equipment. A regular contributor to SHOOTER'S BIBLE, Lewis writes gun-related articles for several publications, including Handloader's Digest and Pennsylvania Game News, for which he has served as gun columnist for the past 32 years. He also contributes regularly to Varmint Hunter, Precision Shooting and, for the past 24 years, as outdoors writer for Leader Times. Helen Lewis, Don's wife and hunting companion of many years, took the photos for this article.*

# Hunting "Primitive Style"

## by Bud Journey

Trying to figure out why some modern shooters deliberately use a primitive weapon that puts them at a disadvantage is probably fruitless. Such people are undoubtedly a few grains short of a full load, as the saying goes. The purpose here is not to analyze their motives, but to explore the clever schemes they devise when dealing with their so-called "outmoded" weapons, not to mention coping with the odds that are stacked against them.

The muzzleloader whose virtues are extolled here is the old-fashioned type. It shoots a ball propelled by blackpowder that's set off by a percussion cap struck from the top of the magazine by a hand-cocked hammer. It has open sights, and its practical shooting range is 100 yards, preferably less. What's more, it kicks like a mule fighting off a pack of coyotes.

The overriding concern when hunting with this intriguing but temperamental weapon is to make the most of the first shot. That calls for such vital elements as consistent powder charges, proper sight alignment, and a steady aim (using a rest whenever possible). One should never underestimate, however, the value of being within reasonable shooting range before pulling the trigger on game. People naturally disagree on exactly what is a reasonable shooting range, but you can't go wrong by striving for a 50-yard shot. In fact, limiting all shots at game to 100 yards or less is probably a good standard to follow. Proper shot placement is another critical element in hunting with a muzzleloader. As with virtually every other type of hunting firearm, the heart/lung area remains the best target, and an animal quartering away provides the best angle.

### CHASING DEER WITH A PRIMITIVE MUZZLELOADER

Whitetails may be the easiest game to hunt with a muzzleloader, with their natural habitat often so thick with vegetation that shots frequently fall inside 100 yards. The question is: How do you see the deer to get the shot? For patient hunters, a treestand or groundstand next to an area of deer activity can often provide a close shot. Areas of activity include easy access to water, a travel corridor or a food source such as acorns, tree moss or apples. These areas can be found easiest during the season by scouting for tracks, scrapes and rubs. Why during the season? Because that's when you hunt. Deer behavior varies, depending on weather, seasons and other factors, so it doesn't necessarily make sense to conduct a fall hunt in an area that was scouted in the summer (although summer scouting is better than no scouting at all).

Impatient hunters are generally at a major disadvantage when hunting whitetails. If you're one of those who simply can't sit quietly, success can still be realized by moving through the woods a few steps at a time, stopping frequently to scan the area thoroughly. This method—which some people call "still-hunting"—makes it tougher for advocates of primitive weapons to take game simply because it's harder to get into range. On the other hand, it does keep the hyperactive types from going nuts on a stand.

During the weeks immediately prior to the rut, try rattling deer antlers during rest stops to attract aggressive bucks. When rattling, however, keep the rest stops to a minimum of 15 minutes, preferably half an hour for best results. Whether you're rattling or not, when a doe or a small buck appears, it's a good idea to wait for several minutes to see if another buck is in the vicinity. That's often the case, especially during the rut.

Mule deer require a different approach because of their dramatically different habits. For example, during the fall of 1996 I was glassing a large clearing in a remote section of north-western Montana. Suddenly, at dawn, I spotted a big five-pointer feeding on some serviceberry bushes. After admiring the buck for several minutes, I looked around for others—and a good thing, too. For within minutes a forked horn, a small 4X4, another nice 5X5, and a monstrous 5X5 all made their appearance. I was definitely looking at a record-book buck, perhaps two of them, but how could I get within my muzzle-loader's shooting range way out there in the middle of that huge opening? The answer was clear: I couldn't. I had to find a way to close the gap. Instead of trying an impossible stalk, I kept watching until the bucks had finished feeding. Then they moved up the hill and into the timber to bed down for the day. I noted precisely their exit route, then withdrew.

The next morning, an hour before daylight, I was sitting along that same exit trail with my back to a tree and my Thompson/Center Hawken Replica dry and ready. I had to wait for three hours, but finally I heard the deer moving my way. I froze and waited. The forked horn walked

*A groundstand near a travel corridor can put you within range of a whitetail.*

Having made my fateful decision, I lowered the Hawken. The buck I had passed up moved quickly up the trail and out of sight, whereupon the last and largest beauty turned and sauntered straight down the hill, keeping the bush between us before he disappeared. The other 5X5 had already left, as had the first three bucks long since. So I just sat there—empty-handed, feeling distinctly less intelligent than those five mulies.

### STALKING THE ELUSIVE PRONGHORN

An almost impossible quarry for the short-ranged muzzleloader is the pronghorn. Its habits,

*Just at dawn, a big mulie buck is spotted high on a hill in northwestern Montana.*

*Blending in with the environment can help primitive-weapons hunters stalk big game.*

cautiously by, followed by the 4X4 and the smallest of the 5X5s. All were well within my preferred range of 50 yards, but I passed them up, waiting for one of the two biggest 5X5s I had seen a day earlier. A long pause ensued, and I was about to question the wisdom of letting the first three animals walk by, when another buck walked into view. I raised the muzzleloader and set my open sights just behind the shoulder of the buck. But before I could squeeze off, a movement caught my eye. The biggest buck had now moved into view and stopped behind a bush. Should I take the sure buck or wait for the monster to move into the open?

*Hunting on a prairie with a muzzleloader requires careful planning and well-executed stalks.*

habitat and physical attributes make hunting with a muzzleloader something like trying to hit a Roger Clemens fast ball with a golf club. Pronghorns usually hang out in the middle of huge expanses of land where their phenomenal eyesight and dazzling speed seemingly create impossible targets for a cruise missile, much less a blackpowder rifle. With some astute hunting and a little luck, though, antelope can be reasonable quarries for a muzzleloader, as I once discovered during a hunt on Montana's eastern prairies.

After several days of roaming the prairie and glassing for stalkable bucks, I finally hit on the right approach. I'd been walking along a gully for several hours, emerging on occasion to glass the terrain around me. On one such occasion, I crawled on my belly to the top of a low rise and peeked over. There I spotted a lone antelope bedded down about 200 yards away. Even without

binoculars, I could tell it was a good buck. Moreover, no other antelope were in the area, which meant I had only one set of super eyes to deal with. It was the opportunity I'd been seeking for several days.

After carefully perusing the terrain, I knew that if I returned to the gully without being seen, I could then move to another location where a small hill separated me from the resting pronghorn. From there, all I had to do was crawl to the top of the hill and place myself within good shooting range. It worked. As I had expected, the buck was out of sight behind the shallow hill. I moved briskly toward the antelope, keeping the high ground between us. As I approached the top of the hill, I peeked over. The pronghorn was still there, on his feet and browsing. I continued crawling laboriously on my belly for another 15 yards, then stopped behind a clump of prairie grass. Meanwhile, the buck,

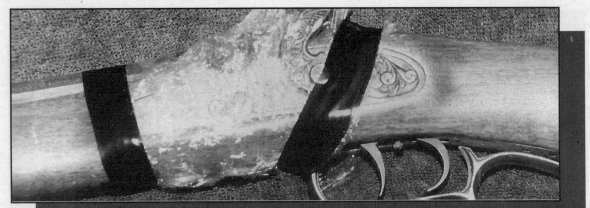

*If there is any doubt about the weather, it's a good idea to moisture-proof your muzzleloader.*

who was now about 50 yards away, kept on feeding, unaware of my presence. I couldn't get any closer without being spotted, but it didn't matter; I was close enough.

Shoving my day pack in front of me, I laid the barrel of the Hawken across the softest part, making it a perfect rest. I lined up the open sights and set them behind the buck's right shoulder. After admonishing myself to hold firm through recoil, I squeezed off. Black smoke billowed from the barrel, the butt smacking my shoulder and cheek. Then, almost in slow motion, the buck collapsed under the heavy impact of the ball. He never got up.

All hunters should know that antelope depend mainly on their eyesight and speed to

*Muzzleloading for elk in the high country is best done during the rut.*

protect themselves. As a result, they most often hang out in the middle of large flats where they can spot danger and escape the moment potential danger shows itself. However, they can't always stay in big flats. Sometimes they are forced to travel through broken terrain, which is virtually the only time a primitive-weapon hunter can stalk them effectively, taking advantage of gullies and hills to stay out of sight. Using a blind and an antelope silhouette on the horizon is another reasonably effective method for getting within range, especially when bucks are still in the rutting mode.

### LEARNING THE HARD WAY

I was hunting elk in Montana during the first week of the regular season (Montana doesn't have a blackpowder season; incidentally, many believe—quite rightly, in my opinion—that blackpowder hunting season should be limited to those who choose to hunt with primitive weapons only; modern muzzleloaders should be allowed only during the regular season, when other weapons of comparable efficiency are allowed).

It was foggy and damp, the rain having stopped the night before. Still, the dampness was pervasive, and I worried about my powder and firing mechanism. After running across some fresh elk tracks in the duff of the forest floor, I tried a few subtle cow calls. Immediately,

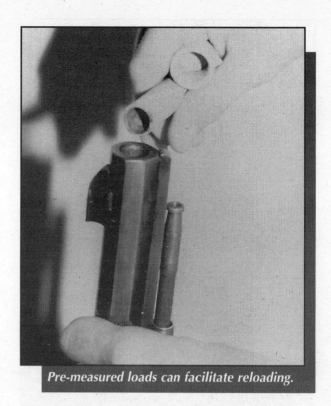

*Pre-measured loads can facilitate reloading.*

an elk answered close by. I called again and suddenly a spike walked out, haloed by fog and vegetation less than 40 yards away. I raised the Hawken, pulled back the hammer and set the sights directly behind the young bull's shoulder. I pulled the trigger and, because of the dampness,

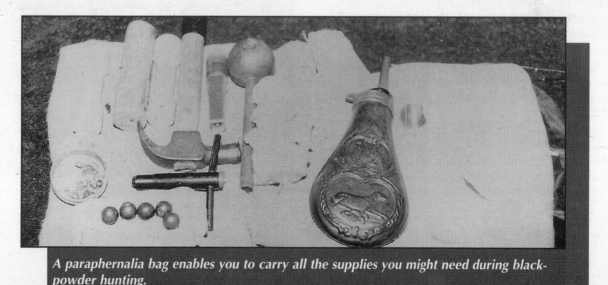

*A paraphernalia bag enables you to carry all the supplies you might need during black-powder hunting.*

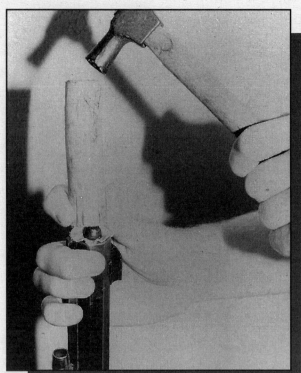

*To facilitate starting the ball, try tapping it in with a hammer and a shock absorber.*

things, though, by pre-measuring powder into individual loads kept in small plastic containers with caps (or 1/2" x 3" PVC tubing with caps). Having several of these pre-measured loads in your paraphernalia bag can speed up the reloading process and minimize the possibility of using a wrong load under duress. It also helps to keep a dry rag handy for a variety of purposes—from drying off the gun and tools to providing ball patches in an emergency. Ziplock-type plastic bags work well for keeping rags and other gear dry.

Once the dry powder charge is safely down the barrel, the next potential hang-up is getting the ball started. One way to deal with this frustrating and often aggravating problem is to carry a small mallet or hammer for tapping in the ball. But be sure to use a sturdy piece of wood or some other shock-absorbing material to prevent mutilating the ball. The most sensible paraphernalia bag, by the way, is one that is waterproof and opens and closes easily. Some diehards insist on using something totally impractical, such as rawhide or buckskin. But then, if blackpowder hunters were practical, they would hunt with modern, scoped, bolt-action rifles and forget those hard-kicking, temperamental, primitive weapons. Who's to say what motivates us old-fashioned types?

concentrated on holding on target. The hammer clicked against the cap. It popped. I jerked. The gun went off and the elk ran away, untouched. Even though I'd suspected a delayed shot or a misfire, I still hadn't been able to hold a steady bead until the gun went off. My dampness problem could have been handled effectively by covering the entire area around the powder with plastic wrap. That includes the magazine, hammer, cap nipple, and so forth. It's not necessary to remove the plastic before firing, nor can it affect accuracy.

Another characteristic of hunting with an old-fashioned muzzleloader is the single-shot aspect of the sport. The nature of the weapon precludes quick second shots. A hunter can facilitate

*BUD JOURNEY is a veteran writer/photographer who specializes in outdoor topics, including hunting and fishing. He has contributed to over 50 regional and national publications, including Outdoor Life, Field & Stream, In-Fisherman and Sports Afield. He was Montana editor for Outdoor Life from 1986 to 1993 and is a past Montana Director for Northwest Outdoor Writers Association (NOWA). He has won regional and national contests for his writing and photography. Journey has lived in Libby, Montana, for 24 years.*

# *Cory Ford,*
# *Sporting Humorist*

## *by Jim Casada*

How well I remember as a lad the joys of growing up in the simpler days of the 1950s. Among them were my regular visits to the local barber shop, a favorite gathering place where male camaraderie, gentle ribbing and plenty of talk about sports were standard fare. To a youngster for whom hunting and fishing were the central features of his life, these weekly trips to the barber also offered free access to the pages of the latest issue of *Field & Stream*. My visits were carefully timed to make sure plenty of customers were in line ahead of me, so that I had ample time to devour the rollicking humor of Corey Ford's monthly column, "The Lower Forty," along with Robert Ruark's tales of "The Old Man and The Boy." Ford truly touched my life through that column, and I suspect the same can be said for countless others who've been privileged to share his keen wit. Reading his words, you knew instinctively he was a man with whom you'd want to share a day afield. He was, as one admirer put it, "The quintessential American sportsman who loved the flex of a fine fly rod, the thrust of a 20 gauge Parker, and the flash of an English setter."

Born in New York City on April 29, 1902, Corey Ford was an only child who in all likelihood enjoyed a pampered early life. Unlike many fine outdoor writers of his generation, Ford had no exposure to sport during his adolescence. According to his biographer, Laurie Morrow, there is precious little to be learned about Ford's early years. Throughout his life, in fact, he remained a private man who chose to reveal little about his childhood. In 1907 his family moved to Mount Vernon, an affluent suburb of New York where young Ford grew up. After earning honors in poetry and drama at the local high school, he attended Columbia University. Bright and witty, Ford's literary talents led him to become editor of the *Columbia Jester*, the university's student humor magazine. There he gained early notoriety by writing a parody— "The Laughing Jackass Association"—in which he suggested that Nicholas Murray, then president of Columbia, was a "charter jackass." Finding nothing funny in this example of student iconoclasm, Murray immediately placed Ford on a lengthy probation. Disillusioned, and with only a few credit hours short of graduation, Ford promptly left the university to join the staff of *Life* magazine. He never completed work on his college degree.

At *Life*, Ford worked shoulder to shoulder with some of the greatest humorists America has produced—writers like Ogden Nash, Robert Benchley, Dorothy Parker and Frank Sullivan. In 1924 Ford moved to *Vanity Fair* and later

*Ford poses outside his home in Freedom, New Hampshire, with his favorite Parker double-barrel and Cider, his "dog of a lifetime."*

held a position at *The New Yorker*, where he shared quarters with the likes of E.B. White and James Thurber. In the fashion of the "Roaring Twenties," Ford lived a fast and hard social life.

Then suddenly, with the Depression clenching New York and the western part of the globe in its grip, Ford's world fell apart. His parents died in 1930 within a half year of one another, and then his fiance was killed in an automobile accident only weeks before their scheduled marriage. In Laurie Morrow's words, "This was the time when Corey shut the door to his personal past, never to speak about it, or even allude to it, again." There may have been a hidden blessing in all this heartbreak, however, for eventually Ford found solace in hunting, fishing and the wild outdoors that eventually became key aspects of his life.

Meanwhile, he had discovered his personal paradise in the charming hamlet of Freedom, New Hampshire, which he had first discovered in his late teens while working with the National Park Service. Ford loved the simple ways of Freedom and its people, who in time adopted him as one of their own. Freedom soon became his home, the place where he learned how to hunt and fish, where he met the local personalities who inspired his delightful stories of the "Lower Forty Shooting, Fishing and Inside Straight Club." He also bought a 100-acre tract of land in Freedom and built a hunting lodge, calling it Stoney Broke, ". . . because," as he put it, "I was stone broke by the time it was finished."

From then on, sport became an integral part of Ford's life. He yearned for the opening day of grouse season, when his hunting dogs became his constant companions. During the late 1920s and throughout the Depression era, articles continued to pour from his prolific pen, including three lighthearted spoofs: *The Gazelle's Ears, Salt Water Taffy,* and *Coconut Oil.*

By the time World War II erupted, Ford had become a well-established sportsman. Ever a fervent patriot, he pulled enough strings to win a lieutenant colonel's position in the Air Corps, leaving Freedom far behind. As an official historian of the air war, Ford traveled to Alaska, which he often revisited for sport, as well as the Aleutians, Asia and Europe. Several of his books, including *Short Cut to Tokyo, Cloak and Dagger, A Peculiar Service,* and *Where the Sea Breaks Its*

*Ford and his long-time hunting partner, Everett Wood, swap stories at the lodge overlooking the "Lower Forty" in Freedom.*

*Back*, were all inspired by his wartime travels and experiences.

At war's end, Ford's gifts as a humorist were in demand as never before. His humor appealed to readers because it reminded them of themselves and their friends. "Take, for example," he once wrote, "your real dyed-in-the-wool wing-shooter. The walls of his office are hung with pictures of himself in Carolina or Saskatchewan or Maine. His cigarette boxes are decorated with game birds, he subscribes only to outdoor magazines, and his filing cabinet is entirely filled with boxes of shells. A million-dollar contract awaits unsigned while he dreamily sits at his desk, making a slingshot out of a rubber-band and shooting paper clips at the stuffed pheasant on the bookcase."

And then there is Ford's description of a true duck hunter: "An individual whose season begins on the morning of Opening Day and ends 354 days later, the night before the beginning of next season. This give him approximately twelve hours to get acquainted with his wife, check up on any new children that may have arrived during his absence, glance over his mail, and wrap up a few sandwiches for an early start tomorrow morning. Otherwise his home is a place to clean his guns, drape his waders in the front hall, and hang his wet socks in front of the living room fireplace."

In the late 1940s and early 1950s Ford's solid reputation as a humorist was further enhanced

*Even while ice fishing, Ford makes sure Cider is at his side.*

by several books, including *How to Guess Your Age, The Office Party,* and *Never Say Diet.* He also turned his love affair with dogs to good effect with *A Man of His Own, Every Dog Should Have a Man*, and *Cold Noses and Warm Hearts.* Another, called *Just a Dog,* appeared in *Field & Stream* in 1940, long before "The Lower Forty" became a fixture in the pages of that magazine. In this heart-wrenching account of how his beloved English setter was shot by a careless hunter, Ford wrote with telling phrases, making as powerful a plea for gun safety as was ever written. As one reader urged, "A copy of it should be handed out with every hunting license issued in the country." Ford's concluding words in *Just a Dog* still bring sadness to those who share his compassion:

I know you didn't mean it, Mr. Coggins. You felt very sorry afterward. You told me that it really spoiled your deer hunting the rest of

the day. It spoiled my bird hunting the rest of a lifetime.

At least, I hope one thing, Mr. Coggins. That is why I am writing you. I hope that you will remember how she looked. I hope that the next time you raise a rifle to your shoulder you will see her over the sights, dragging herself toward you across the field, with blood running from her mouth and down her white chest. I hope you will see her eyes.

I hope you will always see her eyes, Mr. Coggins, whenever there is a flick in the bushes and you bring your rifle to your shoulder before you know what is there.

While Corey Ford's evolution as an outdoor writer was a slow and gradual one, a faithful reader suggested in February 1935 that he write a story for *Field & Stream.* That made sense to Ray Holland, the magazine's editor, and thus began Ford's association with *Field & Stream*. It was a literary marriage that lasted until the author's death. Over the years he wrote a number of features on varying subjects for the magazine, but it was his monthly column—"The Lower Forty"—that will be best remembered. It made its debut in September 1953 and was an immediate hit. In Ford's words, it described

. . . the misadventures of a group of average, everyday sportsmen who prevaricate, steal, cheat, grumble loudly and desert their wives on weekends, just

like the rest of us. I started this series because I firmly believe that sportsmen, above all others, have a sense of humor and like to laugh at themselves.

Ford hit such a responsive chord with his readers because they could identify with the quirky cast of characters who peopled his column. The foibles and peculiarities of Uncle Park, Doc Hall, Cousin Sid, Mister McNab, Judge Parker and others who regularly appeared in "The Lower Forty" shared the same characteristics most serious hunters associated with them-

*Corey (left), Everett Wood and "Cousin Sid" Hayward relax after a day of grouse hunting.*

*Corey and Cider on the alert while hunting grouse in New Hampshire sometime in the latter part of the 1960s.*

selves or someone they knew. They brought "Everyman" to life, doing so in Ford's inimitable fashion and delighting a generation of readers. Many of his finest episodes remain accessible to readers in the pages of several out-of-print books, chiefly *Uncle Perk's Jug, Minutes of the Lower Forty, The Best of Corey Ford* and *The Corey Ford Sporting Treasury.*

Eventually, Ford left Freedom, but he remained in New Hampshire, serving as writer-in-residence at Dartmouth College. He continued to write, hunt grouse and raise a whole generation of English setters. Failing health gradually diminished his hours afield—but not his literary output or his zest for life. Heart trouble, culminating in a massive stroke, finally felled this giant of American sporting humor on July 27, 1969.

For all his quick wit and love of whimsy, Corey Ford was a simple man whose humor was at its best when it related to the outdoor sports. To read his rollicking tales of "The Lower Forty" or his winsome stories of hunting dogs is to realize he was precisely the sort of man you'd want as a hunting buddy or fellow club member. Ford once wrote that all sportsmen have been bopped

# BOOKS BY COREY FORD

Corey Ford's literary legacy is an impressive one. He wrote hundreds, if not thousands of magazine and newspaper articles, using both his own name and pseudonyms (in particular, John Riddell and June Triplett). So prolific was he in this regard that volume after volume of The Reader's Guide to Periodical Literature during the 1950s and 1960s lists dozens or even scores of his articles. It is his books, however, along with "The Road to Tinkhamtown" and "Only a Dog," which constitute Ford's most enduring work. A list of his books (in chronological order of their first publication) follows. Those marked with an asterisk (*) will appeal especially to sporting or outdoor interests.

*You Can Always Tell a Fisherman—But You Can't Tell Him Much (1958)
The Day Nothing Happened (1959)
What Every Bachelor Knows (1961)
Corey Ford's Guide to Thinking (1961)
*Minutes of the Lower Forty (1962)
*Uncle Perk's Jug: The Misadventures of the Lower Forty Shooting, Angling and Inside Straight Club (1964)
A Peculiar Service (1965)
*Where the Sea Breaks Its Back (1966)
The Time of Laughter (1967)
Donovan of the O.S.S. (1970)
*The Best of Corey Ford (Edited by Jack Samson and with a Foreword by Hugh Grey, (1975)
*The Trickiest Thing in Feathers (Compiled and with a Foreword by Laurie Morrow (1996)
The Gazelle's Ears (1926)

Salt Water Taffy (1929)
Coconut Oil (1931)
Short Cut to Tokyo (1943)
Cloak and Dagger: The Secret Story of O.S.S. (1946)
*A Man of His Own, and Other Dog Stories (1949)
How to Guess Your Age (1950)
The Office Party (1951)
*Every Dog Should Have a Man (1952)
*My Dog Likes It Here (1953)
Never Say Diet: How to Live Older and Longer (1954)
*Has Anybody Seen Me Lately? (1958. An anthology containing four earlier books—How to Guess Your Age, The Office Party, Never Say Diet, and Every Dog Should Have a Man—plus other material)
*Cold Noses and Warm Hearts (1958)

*Because bird dogs were high among the great loves of Ford's life, stories about them figure prominently in his literary legacy. Readers may enjoy a good sampling of his work in The Corey Ford Treasury.*

on the head by a divine madness. Nowhere is that "divine madness" better exemplified than in his tales of the "Lower Forty Shooting, Angling and Inside Straight Club." According to Ford, the organization's constitution, as typed on a sheet of wrapping paper by erstwhile member Uncle Perk while the membership was assembled at his store, read:

### Constitution of the Lower Fourty

Artickle One: Rules
   There ain't no rules.

Artickle Two: President
   Everybody's President.

Artickle Three: Membership
   If ennybody else wants to join this club, go ahead, but don't bother us about it. We've went fishing.

Ford then observed, in words that still ring true:

   The Lower Forty will never change, because sportsmen never change. They're the same the world over, arguing and bragging and swapping tall tales around a jug and a dog and a fire.

The Lower Forty is the name of this particular club, but it could be any club and any group of sportsmen who have hunted together in the cold, and fished in the rain, and shared the same memories over the years.

It was Ford's uncanny ability to evoke such memories, and in a humorous way, that made him a sporting scribe for the ages.

*JIM CASADA is a regular contributor to SHOOTER'S BIBLE of profiles of noted sportsmen and gun scribes. A Senior Editor for Sporting Classics magazine and editor-at-large for Turkey & Turkey Hunting, he writes weekly columns for two newspapers and serves on the staffs of several other outdoor publications, including Southern Outdoors, Deer & Deer Hunting, TroutSouth, and Tennessee Valley Outdoors. His most recent book is THE LOST CLASSICS OF ROBERT RUARK, a collection of works never before published in book form. Casada is also the editor of a trilogy comprising the writings of Archibald Rutledge: HUNTING & HOME IN THE SOUTHERN HEARTLAND, TALES OF WHITETAILS, and AMERICA'S GREATEST GAME BIRD.*

# The Art of the Sporting Print

## by R. Stephen Irwin, M.D.

The following pages represent only a sampling of the best sporting prints ever created by America's graphic artists. The one who has proven the most responsible for bringing this genre to the sporting scene—and whose work earned him the title "Dean of American Sporting Art"—is Frank W. Benson (1862-1951). His ducks seemed to abound with the motion of flight. An ardent waterfowler, he was a master at blending actions into his sporting scenes.

Benson, who produced his first print in 1915, was an expert draftsman. He believed that competence in drawing was the foundation of art and that economy of line was an essential of good drawing. As important as what he included in a print was what he left out. As a result, open space contributed profoundly to his overall effect. He set the standard for his field and in so doing inspired other graphic artists to follow in his footsteps.

[Editor's Note: This article is the first in a series featuring the art of sporting prints collected and edited by Dr. Stephen Irwin, a regular contributor to these pages.]

## MG-42 STOCK KIT

GLASER's MG-42 Stock Cit transforms your Ruger 10/22 into a 2/3-scale semi-auto replica of the WWII MG-42 machine gun. The lightweight MG-42 stock fully encloses the 10/22 receiver and barrel to give the appearance and feel of the original machine gun. Ventilation slots in the barrel shroud provide barrel cooling just like the original. Front and rear sights are adjustable for windage and elevation. Fully assembled, the replica weighs no more than the original 10/22. No alterations to the 10/22 are required, and the old stock can be replaced in minutes. For a free brochure, contact:

**GLASER SAFETY SLUG, INC.**
P.O. Box 8223, Foster City, CA 94404
Tel: 800-221-3489  Fax: 510-785-6685

# MANUFACTURERS' SHOWCASE

CONTINUOUS ON / HOURS  0  1  2  3  4  5  6  7  8  9  10  11  12  13  14  15  16  17  18  19  20

**BEAMSHOT**

Their Laser Sight

## NOBODY BEATS BEAMSHOT

Only **BEAMSHOT Laser Sights** can supply continuous "on" usage for more than 20 hours—25 times the life of other laser sights. Designed and built better than other average laser sights, these sights cost less initially and less in battery usage over the long run. And what good is a laser sight if you can't mount it securely to your firearm? Other manufacturers claim their lasers will mount "any" arm. In fact, **BEAMSHOT** produces the widest variety of mounts available—and all in stock.

Is there a gun **BEAMSHOT** can't be mounted to with ease? Not likely.

**BEAMSHOT**
PROFESSIONAL LASER SIGHTING SYSTEMS™

**QUARTON USA**
7042 Alamo Downs Pkwy, Suite 370, San Antonio, TX 78238
Tel: 210-520-8430  Fax: 210-520-8433

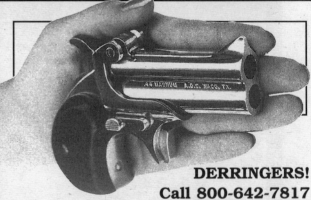

## DERRINGERS!
### Call 800-642-7817
### for our '97 Dealer Program

**NEW**

### Model 1 Black Powder PERCUSSION .45 over/under (Stainless)

Model 1 Series. Stainless Steel; from 22 LR to 45-70
Affordable. Lightweight.  Made in USA!
Lifetime Warranty Guarantee

**AMERICAN DERRINGER CORP.**
127 North Lacy Drive, Waco, Texas 76705
Fax: 817-799-7935
ladyderringer.com  amderringer.com

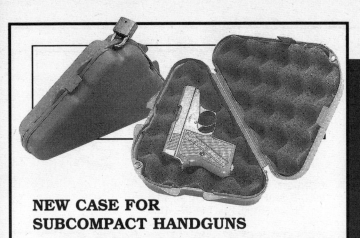
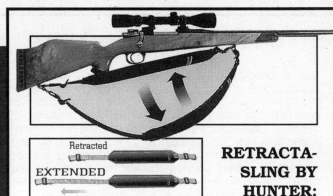

## GUNLINE CHECKERING TOOLS

Gunline Checkering Tools are precisely made and come with illustrated instructions and easy-to-follow sample checkering patterns. Easy to use, their cutting qualities and simple design make them useful for both hobbyist and professional stockmaker. The company offers a full line of medium and fine-cut replacement cutters from 16 to 32 lines/inch. They are available in 60° and 90° in short or long cutter sizes. Three types of handles are offered, one with an offset rearview feature. Tool set prices start at **$37.95**; the NEW Premier Set (8 tools) lists at **$77.95**. Mention SHOOTER's BIBLE and receive a FREE brochure.

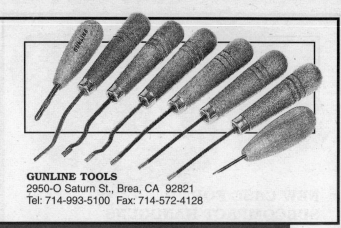

**GUNLINE TOOLS**
2950-O Saturn St., Brea, CA 92821
Tel: 714-993-5100  Fax: 714-572-4128

**KOWA OPTIMED INC.**
20001 South Vermont Ave.
Torrance, CA 90502
Tel: 310-327-1913  Fax: 310-327-4177

## NEW SPOTTING SCOPE SERIES FROM KOWA

KOWA introduces the new TSN-820 Series of waterproof spotting scopes with 82mm objective lens. With more than 30 years' experience in the manufacture of scopes and other precision optical instruments, KOWA has acquired in-depth knowledge about the requirements of field use. The TSN-820 Series offers state-of-the-art optics with unmatched quality and fast, easy use under all conditions. Full multi-coatings on the 82mm objective lens produce the ultimate in bright, clear, high-definition imagery. The superb sharpness is especially noticeable at extended distances or under low-light conditions.

# MANUFACTURERS' SHOWCASE

## FORREST INC. OFFERS RIFLE/PISTOL MAGAZINES

Whether you're looking for a few spare magazines for that obsolete 22 rifle or pistol, or wish to replace a 10-shot with the higher-capacity pre-ban original, all are available from FORREST INC. With one of the largest selections of magazines, they offer competitive pricing especially for dealers who buy in quantity.

FORREST INC. also stocks parts and accessories for the Colt 1911 45 Auto Pistol, the SKS and MAK-90 rifles, and many U.S. military rifles. One of their specialty parts is firing pins for obsolete weapons.

Call or write for more information and a **FREE** brochure. **DEALERS WELCOME!**

**FORREST INC.**
P.O. Box 326, Lakeside, CA 92040
Tel: 619-561-5800  Fax: 619-561-0227

## SAKO AMMO: ACCURATE, DEPENDABLE

SAKO cartridges deliver outstanding accuracy and uniform performance—every time. These qualities have halped SAKO capture more than 200 Bench Rest world records, more than any other maker of fine ammunition. All primers used by SAKO ignite the powder evenly and dependably. SAKO bullets are made of the finest materials, reducing barrel wear to an absolute minimum. The ballistic characteristics of each bullet are matched perfectly to the cartridge caliber for every shooting purpose. SAKO supplies the right bullet for every situation.

**STOEGER INDUSTRIES**
5 Mansard Court, Wayne, NJ 07470
Tel: 800-631-0722 (Toll Free)
Tel: 973-872-9500  Fax: 973-872-2230

# BEAMSHOT
## PROFESSIONAL LASER SIGHTING SYSTEMS™

## SIGHTS DESIGNED FOR REVOLVERS

Designed specifically for the special demands of revolver use, **BEAMSHOT Professional Laser Sighting Systems** will maintain their accuracy in extreme conditions. Constructed of high-grade, lightweight aluminum, they are available in black or silver. **BEAMSHOT's** 1000 series and 3000 series have various ranges from 670nm/300 yards to 635nm/800 yards. A special **BEAMSHOT** 780nm is visible only when viewed through night vision equipment. All **BEAMSHOTs** are quality constructed and powered by unmatched, continuous "on" operation (20+ hours). Easily mounted to virtually all revolvers. One year warranty.

**QUARTON USA**
7042 Alamo Downs Pkwy, Suite 370, San Antonio, TX 78238
Tel: 210-520-8430  Fax: 210-520-8433

## ULTRA™ LINE
## COMPENSATED MODELS
## BY HARRINGTON & RICHARDSON

The well-known producer of single-shot, break-action centerfire rifles has added two new compensated models in both 270 Win. and 30-06 Springfield. Each features an integral muzzle brake or compensator on the end of the barrel that allows escaping gas to vent radially, reducing felt recoil dramatically. The stock has a Monte Carlo configuration and the forend is of a semi-beavertail design. The high-pressure laminate wood blanks stand up under harsh weather conditions and are as tough as synthetics. A transfer-bar system virtually eliminates the possibility of accidental discharge. For further information contact:

**HARRINGTON & RICHARDSON**
Industrial Rowe, Gardner, MA 01440
Tel: 506-632-9393  Fax: 506-632-2300

# MANUFACTURERS' SHOWCASE

## NEW ENGLAND FIREARMS'
## SUPER LIGHT 223 REM RIFLE

NEW ENGLAND FIREARMS, maker of the Handi-Rifle single-shot rifle, introduces its new Super Light version. NEF engineers have reduced the weight of a 223 Rem Handi-Rifle to a mere 5.5 lbs. (without scope), making it the lightest single-shot centerfire rifle available from a U.S. manufacturer. Each rifle features a non-slip finish and includes sling swivel studs and a recoil pad. The overall matte black finish is ideal for reducing reflection. The new Super Light includes the patented NEW ENGLAND FIREARMS transfer-bar system, virtually eliminating the possibility of accidental discharge. For more information contact:

**NEW ENGLAND FIREARMS**
Industrial Rowe, Gardner, MA 01440
Tel: 508-632-9393  Fax: 508-632-2300

**NEW**

## TRIUS 1-STEP
## "Setting the Standard
## for 41 Years"

The new TRIUS 1-Step is almost effortless to use: (1) Set arm; (2) Place target on arm without tension; (3) Step on pedal to put tension on arm and release target in one motion. Adjustable without tools. Easy cocking, lay-on loading, singles, doubles, plus piggy-back doubles offer unparalleled variety. **Birdshooter**: quality at a budget price — now with high-angle retainer. **Model 92**: a best-seller with high-angle clip and can thrower. **TrapMaster**: sit-down comfort plus pivoting action.

**TRIUS PRODUCTS INC.**
P.O. Box 25, Cleves, OH 45002
Tel: 513-941-5682  Fax: 513-941-7970

Satisfying Shooters Since 1955
TRIUS TRAPS

## "ACCURATE" HANDLOADER PROPELLANTS

ACCURATE offers a full line of pistol, rifle and shotshell propellants for handloaders. Whether reloading for hunting, competition or just practice, ACCURATE propellants have been formulated to meet your needs. ACCURATE's disc, flake, ball and extruder powders offer burning speeds for all kinds of cartridges—from the most popular to the little-known. There are 4 shotshell burning-speed formulations, plus 4 for pistol and 12 for rifle-class cartridges. And rifle-cartridge reloaders have a choice of two propellants: the ball variety (including the popular ACCURATE® 2230) and X-truded™ line (from XMP-5744 to XMR-4350 powder).

**ACCURATE ARMS**
Dept. SB, 5891 Hwy. 230W, McEwen, TN 37101
Tel: 615-729-4207 Fax: 615-729-4211

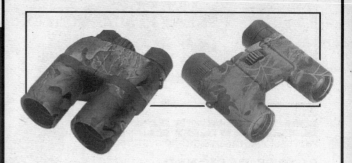

## VIVITAR® SPORTS OPTICS

VIVITAR offers a complete line of top-quality optics for shooters and outdoorsmen, including the extremely popular Hawkeye Series of binoculars and cameras finished in Advantage Camouflage. New to the Hawkeye Series for '97 are: 10X42 and 10X26 binoculars and the exciting new weatherproof A35 Camera. The newest Hawkeyes feature precision-ground BaK4 prisms and lenses for brighter colors, more brilliant resolution and superior contrast in low light situations. For a free catalog, contact:

**VIVITAR**
1280 Rancho Conejo Blvd., Newbury Park, CA 91320
Tel: 805-498-7008

# MANUFACTURERS' SHOWCASE

## BLUE BOOK OF GUN VALUES 18TH EDITION

The new 18th edition of the **Blue Book of Gun Values** by S.P. Fjestad contains 1,408 pages and includes pricing and detailed technical information on domestic, foreign and military guns (both new and discontinued), plus major trademark antiques, commemoratives, special editions, and most new models. Included in the 18th edition is a revised 40-page full-color section of high-resolution photographs showing rifles, shotgun and handguns in various percentages of condition from zero to 100 percent. The retail price is **$27.95** (add **$4.00** for domestic 4th Class S/H). To order, call or write (ISBN #1-886768-08-0):

**BLUE BOOK PUBLICATIONS, INC.**
8009 34th Avenue S., Suite #175, Minneapolis, MN 55425
Tel: 800-877-4867 or 612-854-5229 Fax: 612-853-1486
E-mail: bluebook@bluebookinc.com
Web Site: www.bluebookinc.com

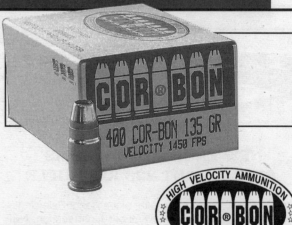

## AMMO OFFERINGS

COR-BON is a manufacturer of premium self-defense ammunition for law enforcement, special operations and personal self-defense. In addition, COR-BON Handgun Hunting ammunition is offered in various loads, from 10mm to 454 Casull. Plus, a special Single Shot Hunter line is specifically designed to give optimum ballistics in the reduced barrel length of high-performance pistols.

**COR-BON BULLET CO.**
1311 Industry Road, Sturgis, SD 57785
Tel: 800-626-7266 Fax: 800-923-2666

## NEW
## LYMAN GREAT PLAINS HUNTER

LYMAN PRODUCTS introduces a new edition of their popular Great Plains rifle—specifically for hunters. The "Great Plains Hunter," this model features a 1:32" twist and shallow rifling groove for shooting modern sabots and blackpowder hunting bullets. As Ed Schmitt, LYMAN's Product Mgr., states, "A Great Plains Hunter model with a faster twist has been one of the most requested products from consumers." This new Hunter has all the features of Lyman's Great Plains, including 32" octagonal barrel and oil-finished walnut stock. It is pre-drilled and tapped for LYMAN's 57GPR peep sight. For more information, please write to:

Ed Schmitt
**LYMAN PRODUCTS CORPORATION**
475 Smith Street, Middletown, CT 06457
Tel:1-800-22-LYMAN  Fax: 860-349-1840

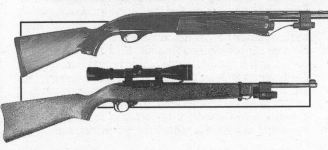

**QUARTON USA**
7042 Alamo Downs Pkwy, Suite 370, San Antonio, TX 78238
Tel: 210-520-8430  Fax: 210-520-8433

## BEAMSHOT
PROFESSIONAL LASER SIGHTING SYSTEMS™

## SIGHTS FOR RIFLES AND SHOTGUNS

BEAMSHOT **Professional Laser Sighting Systems** for use on rifles and shotguns are available in black or silver. BEAMSHOT's 1000 and 3000 series have various ranges, from 670nm/300 yards to 635nm/800 yards; the 1001U projects a precise 1.5" laser dot at 100 yards. A special BEAMSHOT 780nm is visible only when viewed through night vision equipment. All BEAMSHOTS are battery powered for continuous "on" operation (20+ hours). Easily mounted to all rifles/shotguns. One year warranty.

# MANUFACTURERS' SHOWCASE

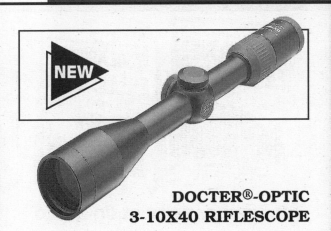

## NEW

## DOCTER®-OPTIC
## 3-10X40 RIFLESCOPE

DOCTER®-OPTIC's new 3-10X40 Riflescope features precision-crafted German optics in an American-style scope. Top-quality multi-coated optics, 40mm objective lens and one-inch tube produce unsurpassed light-gathering capabilities. Engineered to handle with ease the recoil from large-caliber rifles. Docter's 3-10X40 Riflescope is perfect for late evening and early morning hunting. 30-Year Warranty!

**DOCTER-OPTIC TECHNOLOGIES, INC.**
4685 Boulder Highway, Las Vegas, NV 89121
Tel: 800-290-3634  Fax: 702-898-3737

## WHITETAILS
## UNLIMITED 1997
## COMMEMORATIVE
## RIFLE

HARRINGTON & RICHARDSON's limited edition version of the 45-70 Govt. ULTRA rifle is designed especially to commemorate the work of Whitetails Unlimited. It is the first-ever ULTRA Rifle with hand-checkered American black walnut on its stock and forend. Included are high-polish blued actions and barrels, a classic pistol-grip stock with sling swivel studs, and a premium recoil pad. Each rifle features a laser engraving of the WTU logo, plus a pewter-finished WTU medallion inletted into the stock.

**HARRINGTON & RICHARDSON**
Industrial Rowe, Gardner, MA 01440
Tel: 506-632-9393  Fax: 506-632-2300

95

## BENCH MASTER RIFLE REST

The Bench Master Rifle Rest is a rugged, compact and highly adjustable rifle-shooting accessory— one that offers precision line-up and recoil reduction when sighting in a rifle, testing ammunition or shooting varmints. It features three course positions totaling 5½″, with 1½″ fine adjustment in each course position, plus leveling and shoulder height adjustments for maximum control and comfort. Because of its unique design, the Bench Master can easily double as a rifle vise for scope mounting, bore sighting and cleaning. It comes with a LIFETIME Warranty and a list price of only **$119.95**. For a free brochure, call or write:

**DESERT MOUNTAIN MFG.**
P.O. Box 130184, Coram, MT 59913
Tel: 800-477-0762 (Toll Free)

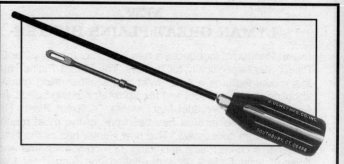

## NYLON-COATED GUN CLEANING RODS

J. Dewey cleaning rods have been used by the U.S. Olympic shooting team and the benchrest community for over 20 years. These one-piece, spring-tempered, steel-based rods will not gall delicate rifling or damage the muzzle area of front-cleaned firearms. Each nylon-coated rod comes with a non-breakable plastic handle supported by ball-bearings for ease of cleaning. The brass cleaning jags are designed to pierce the center of the cleaning patch or wrap around the knurled area to keep the patch centered in the bore. Available from 17-caliber to shotgun bore size in several lengths. For more information, contact:

**J. DEWEY MANUFACTURING CO., INC.**
P. O. Box 2014, Southbury, CT 06488
Tel: 203-264-3064   Fax: 203-262-6907

# MANUFACTURERS' SHOWCASE

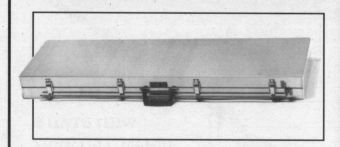

## PROTECTIVE METAL CASES

A complete line of Protective Metal Transport/Shipping Cases are available through ICC (IMPACT CASE COMPANY) and KK AIR INTERNATIONAL. Both lines are products of KNOUFF & KNOUFF, INC. In addition to the "flat case" design, three-piece and "Trunk"-style cases are part of the standard lines. KK AIR also manufactures customized cases to each owner's sizing and specifications. These case products are designed for STRENGTH, with third-party handling in mind, and are "proven." For detailed specification sheets, contact:

**KNOUFF & KNOUFF, INC.**
P.O. Box 9912, Spokane, WA 99209
Tel: 1-800-262-3322 (Toll Free)

## GLASER SAFETY SLUG AMMO

GLASER SAFETY SLUG'S state-of-the-art professional-grade personal defense ammunition is now offered in two bullet styles: BLUE uses a #12 compressed shot core for maximum ricochet protection, and SILVER uses a #6 compressed shot core for maximum penetration. The manufacturing process results in outstanding accuracy, with documented groups of less than an inch at 100 yards! That's why GLASER is the top choice among professional and private law enforcement agencies worldwide. Currently available in every caliber from 25 ACP–30-06, including 40 S&W, 10mm, 223 and 7.62 × 39. For a free brochure contact:

**GLASER SAFETY SLUG, INC.**
P.O. Box 8223, Foster City, CA 94404
Tel: 1-800-221-3489 (Toll Free)

# When you have to be quick, you need a gun that won't slow you down.

## *Beretta Field Grades: the fastest over-and-unders you can own.*

It happens in an instant: an explosion of sound and color and more speed than you're ready for. And yet, you *are* ready for it. You swing, mount and fire in one smooth, continuous motion, as though

*Silver Pigeon*

*S686 Onyx*

*NEW! Silver Essential*

the Beretta Field Grade in your hands is actually a part of you. It's a sensation Beretta shooters never tire of...the result of over a century of refining the Beretta Over-and-Unders into the world's finest – and fastest – production shotguns.

This is a gun that's built for speed. Its low profile, special steel alloy closed receiver and chrome-nickel-moly

tri-alloy steel barrels provide remarkable strength without burdensome bulk. Its compact fore-end design contributes to proper hand-eye alignment, near-perfect balance and lighter weight.

Yet, this is also a gun that's built to last. Beretta's dual conical locking lugs adjust automatically, and our bores are hard-chromed for maximum strength and corrosion-resistance. So your Beretta Field Grade will keep locking snugly and firing dependably year after year.

Beretta Field Grades: you'll never know how fast you can be until you try one. See your authorized Beretta dealer, or contact Beretta U.S.A. Corp., 17601 Beretta Dr., Accokeek, MD 20607, (301) 283-2191.

## Beretta

*A Tradition of Excellence Since 1526.*

# STOEGER IGA

## SHOTGUNS

**RUGGED. RELIABLE. PERFORMANCE AT AN AFFORDABLE PRICE!**

# Handguns

For addresses and phone/fax numbers of manufacturers and distributors included in this section, please turn to DIRECTORY OF MANUFACTURERS AND SUPPLIERS on page 554.

# AMERICAN ARMS

**ESCORT .380 ACP**
**$349.00**

## ESCORT .380 ACP

**SPECIFICATIONS**
**Caliber**: .380 ACP
**Action**: DA  **Capacity**: 7-shot magazine
**Barrel length**: 3³/₈"  **Overall length**: 6¹/₈"
**Width**: ¹³/₁₆"  **Weight**: 19 oz.
**Sights**: Fixed; low profile
**Features**: Stainless steel frame, slide & trigger; nickel-steel barrel; soft polymer grips; loaded chamber indicator

## MATEBA AUTO REVOLVER (not shown)
**$1295.00**

This newly designed firearm incorporates the quickness and handling of a semi-auto pistol with the reliability and accuracy of a revolver. May be fired as a single-action or double-action handgun. When fired, the cylinder and slide assembly move back and the recoil causes the cylinder to rotate. The speed of firing is comparable to a semi-auto pistol. The "auto pistol" aspect of this gun aligns the barrel with the bottom chamber of the cylinder. This reduces muzzle recoil allowing the shooter to stay "on target" with the least amount of movement.

**SPECIFICATIONS**
**Caliber**: 357  **Capacity**: 6 rounds
**Overall length**: 8.77"
**Barrel length**: 4"
**Weight**: 2.75 lbs.
**Features**: The Mateba has an all blue finish, solid steel alloy frame and walnut grips

## UBERTI .454 SINGLE ACTION (not shown)
$869.00

**SPECIFICATIONS**
**Caliber**: .454
**Barrel lengths**: 6", 7¹/₂"
**Features**: Top ported barrels; satin nickel finish; fully adj. sight; hammer block safety; hardwood grips; wide serrated trigger guard with off-hand finger rest for two-handed hold

**REGULATOR SINGLE ACTION REVOLVER**

## REGULATOR SINGLE ACTION

**SPECIFICATIONS**
**Calibers**: 45 Long Colt, 44-40, 357 Mag.
**Barrel length**: 4³/₄", 5¹/₂" and 7¹/₂"
**Overall length**: 8¹/₁₆"
**Weight**: 2 lb. 3 oz. (4³/₄" barrel)
**Sights**: Fixed
**Safety**: Hammer block
**Features**: Brass trigger guard and backstrap; two-cylinder combos avail. (45 L.C./45 ACP and 44-40/44 Special)
**Prices**:
**Regulator Single Action Revolver** . . . . . . . . . . . $365.00
**Two-cylinder Set** . . . . . . . . . . . . . . . . . . . . . . . . 435.00

**REGULATOR DELUXE**

## REGULATOR DELUXE

**SPECIFICATIONS**
**Features**: Blued steel backstrap and trigger guard; hammer block safety;
**Prices**:
**Bird's-head grip** . . . . . . . . . . . . . . . . . . . . . . . . . $425.00
**Two-cylinder Set** . . . . . . . . . . . . . . . . . . . . . . . . 495.00

# AMERICAN DERRINGER PISTOLS

## MODEL 1

**SPECIFICATIONS**
**Calibers:** See below
**Action:** Single action w/automatic barrel selection
**Capacity:** 2 shots
**Barrel length:** 3"  **Overall length:** 4.82"
**Weight:** 15 oz. (in 45 Auto)

| Calibers: | Prices |
|---|---|
| 22 Long Rifle w/rosewood grips | $250.00 |
| 10mm Auto, 32 Magnum/32 S&W Long | 260.00 |
| 32-20 | 250.00 |
| 357 Magnum w/rosewood grips | 262.00 |
| 357 Maximum w/rosewood grips | 270.00 |
| 9mm Luger, 38 Special w/rosewood grips | 250.00 |
| 38 Super w/rosewood grips | 258.00 |
| 38 Special +P+ (Police) | 258.00 |
| 38 Special Shot Shells | 258.00 |
| 380 Auto | 250.00 |
| 40 S&W, 45 Auto, 30 M-1 Carbine | 262.00 |
| 45/.410 | 325.00 |
|    Stainless B | 345.00 |
|    Stainless G | 365.00 |
| 45-70 (single shot) | 317.00 |
| 45 Colt, 2½" Snake (45-cal. rifled barrel), 44-40 Win., 44 Special | 325.00 |
| 45 Win. Mag., 44 Magnum, 41 Magnum | 390.00 |
| 30-30 Win., 357 Mag., 223 Rem., Comm. Ammo dual calibers | 380.00 |
| Engraved Series | 1317.00 |

**MODEL 7 Ultra Lightweight Single Action** (7½ oz.)
**(not shown)**

| | |
|---|---|
| 22 LR, 22 Mag. Rimfire, 32 Mag./32 S&W Long, 38 Special, 380 Auto | $245.00 |
| 44 Special | 505.00 |

**MODEL 10 Stainless Steel Barrel** (10 oz.)
**(not shown)**

| | |
|---|---|
| 38 Special | $245.00 |
| 45 Auto | 262.00 |
| 45 Colt | 325.00 |

**MODEL 11 Lightweight Double Derringer** (11 oz.)

| | |
|---|---|
| 22 LR, 22 Mag. Rim., 32 Mag./SW, 38 Special, 380 Auto | $230.00 |

## 38 DOUBLE ACTION DERRINGER

**SPECIFICATIONS**
**Calibers:** See below   **Capacity:** 2 shots
**Barrel length:** 3"  **Overall length:** 4.85"
**Weight:** 14.5 oz.
**Height:** 3.3"  **Width:** 1.1"
**Finish:** Stainless steel
**Safety:** Hammerblock thumb

| Calibers | Prices |
|---|---|
| 22 LR, 38 Special | $305.00 |
| 9mm Luger | 330.00 |
| 357 Magnum, 40 S&W | 355.00 |

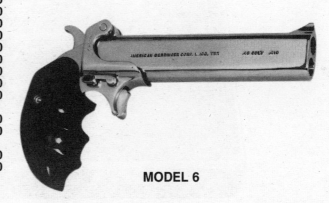

## MODEL 6

## MODEL 6
## STAINLESS STEEL DOUBLE DERRINGER

**SPECIFICATIONS**
**Calibers**: See below   **Capacity**: 2 shots
**Barrel length**: 6"  **Overall length**: 8.2"
**Weight**: 21 oz.

| Calibers: | Prices |
|---|---|
| 22 Win. Mag. | $305.00 |
| 357 Mag. | 305.00 |
| 45 Auto | 350.00 |
| 45/.410, 45 Colt | 368.00 |

# AMERICAN DERRINGER PISTOLS

**MODEL 4**

## MODEL 4
### STAINLESS STEEL DOUBLE DERRINGER

**SPECIFICATIONS**
**Calibers:** 45 Colt and 3".410
**Capacity:** 2 shots
**Barrel length:** 4.1"
**Overall length:** 6"
**Weight:** 16.5 oz.
**Finish:** Satin or high-polish stainless steel
**Price:** . . . . . . . . . . . . . . . . . . . . . . . . . . . . . . . . . . $357.00

Also available:
In 357 Mag., 357 Maximum . . . . . . . . . . . . . . . $374.00
In 45-70 w/oversized grips, both barrels . . . . . . . . 501.00
In 44 Mag. w/oversized grips. . . . . . . . . . . . . . . 427.00
**MODEL M-4 ALASKAN SURVIVAL**
   in 45-70/45-.410, 45-70/45 Colt . . . . . . . . . . . 393.00
**Engraved Series** . . . . . . . . . . . . . . . . . . . . . . . . . 1517.00

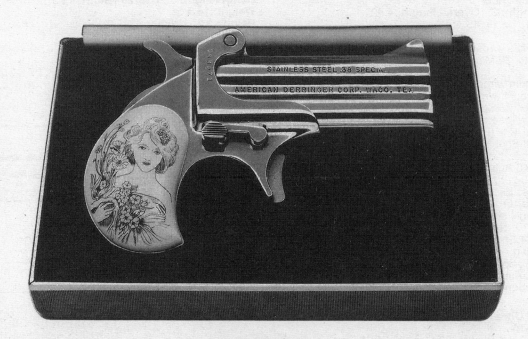

**LADY DERRINGER**
**STAINLESS STEEL DOUBLE**

**LADY DERRINGER** (Stainless Steel Double)

| Calibers: | Prices |
|---|---|
| 38 Special . . . . . . . . . . . . . . . . . . . . . . . . . . . . . | $265.00 |
| 32 Mag. . . . . . . . . . . . . . . . . . . . . . . . . . . . . . . | 285.00 |
| 357 Mag. . . . . . . . . . . . . . . . . . . . . . . . . . . . . . | 305.00 |
| 45 Colt . . . . . . . . . . . . . . . . . . . . . . . . . . . . . . | 350.00 |

**TEXAS DOUBLE DERRINGER**
**COMMEMORATIVE**
**(not shown)**

| Calibers: | Prices |
|---|---|
| 38 Special (Brass) . . . . . . . . . . . . . . . . . . . . . . . | $285.00 |
| 44-40 or 45 Colt (Brass) . . . . . . . . . . . . . . . . . . | 350.00 |
| 45 Colt Brass Frame Special SN . . . . . . . . . . . . . | 360.00 |

# AMT PISTOLS

### BACKUP

**SPECIFICATIONS**
**Calibers:** 357 SIG, 380 ACP (9mm Short), 38 Super, 40 S&W, 45 ACP
**Capacity:** 5-shot (40 S&W, 45 ACP); 6-shot (other calibers)
**Barrel length:** 3"
**Overall length:** 5 3/4"
**Weight:** 23 oz.
**Width:** 1"
**Features:** Locking-barrel action, checkered fiberglass grips, grooved slide sight
**Prices:**
In 380 ACP . . . . . . . . . . . . . . . . . . . . . . . . . . . . . $329.99
Other calibers . . . . . . . . . . . . . . . . . . . . . . . . . . . 449.99

**BACKUP**
**(380 or 9mm Short)**

### 380 BACKUP II

**SPECIFICATIONS**
**Caliber:** 380 ACP
**Capacity:** 5 shots
**Barrel length:** 2 1/2"   **Overall length:** 5"
**Weight:** 18 oz.   **Width:** 11/16"
**Sights:** Open
**Grips:** Carbon fiber
**Prices:**
Single Action only . . . . . . . . . . . . . . . . . . . . . . . $309.99

### 1911 GOVERNMENT
### 45 ACP LONGSLIDE (not shown)

**SPECIFICATIONS**
**Caliber:** 45 ACP
**Capacity:** 7 shots
**Barrel length:** 7" **Overall length:** 10 1/2"
**Weight:** 46 oz.
**Sights:** 3-dot, adjustable
**Features:** Wide adjustable trigger; Neoprene wraparound grips
**Price:** . . . . . . . . . . . . . . . . . . . . . . . . . . . . . . . . $595.99
Also available:
**Conversion Kit** (7") . . . . . . . . . . . . . . . . . . . . . . . 299.99

**380 BACKUP II**

### 1911 GOVERNMENT MODEL

**SPECIFICATIONS**
**Caliber:** 45 ACP  **Capacity:** 7 shots
**Barrel length:** 5"  **Overall length:** 8 1/2"
**Weight:** 38 oz.  **Width:** 1 1/4"
**Sights:** Fixed
**Features:** Long grip safety; rubber wraparound Neoprene grips; beveled magazine well; wide adjustable trigger
**Price:** . . . . . . . . . . . . . . . . . . . . . . . . . . . . . . . . $489.99

Also available:
**1911 HARDBALLER.** Same specifications as Standard Model, but with adjustable sights and matte rib. .$549.99
**Conversion Kit** (5") . . . . . . . . . . . . . . . . . . . . . . . 279.00

**1911 GOVERNMENT**

# AMT PISTOLS

**22 AUTOMAG II**

## 22 AUTOMAG II RIMFIRE MAGNUM

The only production semiautomatic handgun in this caliber, the Automag II is ideal for the small-game hunter or shooting enthusiast who wants more power and accuracy in a light, trim handgun. The pistol features a bold open-slide design and employs a unique gas-channeling system for smooth, trouble-free action.

### SPECIFICATIONS
**Caliber**: 22 Rimfire Magnum
**Barrel lengths**: 3³/₈", 4¹/₂" or 6"
**Magazine capacity**: 9 shots (4¹/₂" & 6"), 7 shots (3³/₈")
**Weight**: 32 oz. (6"), 30 oz. (4¹/₂"), 24 oz. (3³/₈")
**Sights**: Adjustable 3-dot
**Finish**: Stainless steel
**Features**: Squared trigger guard; grooved carbon fiber grips; gas channeling system
**Price**:. . . . . . . . . . . . . . . . . . . . . . . . . . . . . . . . . $405.95

**AUTOMAG III**

**AUTOMAG III**

### SPECIFICATIONS
**Caliber**: 30 M1 Carbine
**Capacity**: 8 shots
**Barrel length**: 6³/₈"    **Overall length**: 10¹/₂"
**Weight**: 43 oz.
**Sights**: Adjustable
**Grips**: Carbon fiber
**Finish**: Stainless steel
**Price**:. . . . . . . . . . . . . . . . . . . . . . . . . . . . . . . $469.79

**AUTOMAG IV**

**AUTOMAG IV**

### SPECIFICATIONS
**Caliber**: 45 Win. Mag.
**Capacity**: 7 shots
**Barrel length**: 6¹/₂"    **Overall length**: 10¹/₂"
**Weight**: 46 oz.
**Sights**: Adjustable
**Grips**: Carbon fiber
**Finish**: Stainless steel
**Price**:. . . . . . . . . . . . . . . . . . . . . . . . . . . . . . . $699.99

# AUTO-ORDNANCE

### MODEL 1911A1 THOMPSON

**SPECIFICATIONS**
**Caliber:** 45 ACP
**Capacity:** 9 rounds (9mm, 10mm & 38 Super); 7 rounds (45 ACP)
**Barrel length:** 5"  **Overall length:** 8 1/2"
**Weight:** 39 oz.
**Sights:** Blade front; rear adjustable for windage
**Stock:** Checkered plastic with medallion
**Prices:**
45 ACP, blued. . . . . . . . . . . . . . . . . . . . . . . . . . . **$397.50**
**PIT BULL MODEL** (45 ACP w/3 1/2" barrel). . . . . . 474.50
**WW II PARKERIZED PISTOL** (45 cal. only) . . . . . 399.95
**DELUXE MODEL** (45 cal. only) . . . . . . . . . . . . 438.00
   **CUSTOM HIGH POLISH** . . . . . . . . . . . . . . 585.00

**MODEL 1911A1
THOMPSON (9mm)**

**PITBULL
(4 3/8" barrel)**

**MODEL 1911A1
CUSTOM HIGH POLISH
(5" barrel)**

### MODEL 1911 "THE GENERAL"
(not shown)

**SPECIFICATIONS**
**Caliber:** 45 ACP
**Capacity:** 7 rounds
**Barrel length:** 4 1/2"
**Overall length:** 8"
**Weight:** 37 oz.
**Stock:** Black textured, rubber wraparound with medallion
**Sights:** White 3-dot system
**Feature:** Full-length recoil guide system
**Price:** . . . . . . . . . . . . . . . . . . . . . . . . . . . . . . **$465.00**

# BERETTA PISTOLS

## COMPACT FRAME PISTOLS

### COUGAR SERIES
### MODEL 8000 (9mm)  MODEL 8040 (40 cal.)

Beretta's 8000/8040 Cougar Series semiautomatics use a proven locked-breech system with a rotating barrel. This design makes the pistol compact and easy to conceal and operate with today's high-powered 9mm and 40-caliber ammunition. When the pistol is fired, the initial thrust of recoil energy is partially absorbed as it pushes slide and barrel back, with the barrel rotating by cam action against a tooth on the rigid central block. When the barrel has turned about 30 degrees, the locking lugs on the barrel clear the locking recesses, which free the slide to continue rearward. The recoil spring absorbs the remaining recoil energy as the slide extracts and ejects the spent shell casing, rotates the hammer, and then reverses direction to chamber the next round. By channeling part of the recoil energy into barrel rotation and by partially absorbing the barrel and slide recoil shock through the central block before it is transferred to the frame, the Cougar shows an unusually low felt recoil.

### SPECIFICATIONS
**Calibers:** 9mm and 40 semiauto
**Capacity:** 10 rounds
**Action:** Double/Single or Double Action only
**Barrel length:** 3.6"
**Overall length:** 7"
**Weight:** 33.5 oz.
**Overall height:** 5.5"
**Sight radius:** 5.2"
**Sights:** Front and rear sights dovetailed to slide
**Finish:** Bruniton/Plastic
**Features:** Firing-pin block; chrome-lined barrel; short recoil, rotating barrel; anodized aluminum alloy frame
**Prices:**
Double action only . . . . . . . . . . . . . . . . . . . . . . . $663.00
Double or Single action . . . . . . . . . . . . . . . . . . . . 699.00

**MODEL 8000/8040
COUGAR**

**MODEL 8040
MINI-COUGAR**

### MODEL 8000/8040 MINI-COUGAR

**Caliber:** 9mm and 40 S&W
**Capacity:** 10 rounds (9mm); 8 rounds (40 S&W)
**Action:** Double/Single or Double Action only
**Weight:** 27.6 oz. (9mm); 27.4 oz. (40 S&W)
**Features:** One inch shorter in the grip than the standard Cougar
**Prices:** Available on request

# BERETTA PISTOLS

## SMALL FRAME PISTOLS

**MODEL 3032 TOMCAT**

### MODEL 3032 TOMCAT

**SPECIFICATIONS**
**Caliber:** 32 Auto
**Capacity:** 7-shot magazine
**Barrel length:** 2.45"
**Overall length:** 5"
**Weight:** 15 oz.
**Sights:** Blade front, drift-adjustable rear
**Features:** Double action, thumb safety, tip-up barrel for direct loading/unloading, blued or matte finish
**Prices:**
Matte/Plastic. . . . . . . . . . . . . . . . . . . . . . . . . . . . $269.00
Blued/Plastic . . . . . . . . . . . . . . . . . . . . . . . . . . . 330.00

### MODEL 21 BOBCAT DA SEMIAUTOMATIC

A safe, dependable, accurate small-bore pistol in 22 LR or 25 Auto. Easy to load with its unique barrel tip-up system.

**SPECIFICATIONS**
**Caliber:** 22 LR or 25 ACP. **Magazine capacity:** 7 rounds 22 LR); 8 rounds (25 ACP). **Overall length:** 4.9". **Barrel length:** 2.4". **Weight:** 11.5 oz. (25 ACP); 11.8 oz. (22 LR) **Sights:** Blade front; V-notch rear. **Safety:** Thumb operated. **Grips:** Plastic or Walnut. **Frame:** Forged aluminum.
**Prices:**
Matte/Plastic. . . . . . . . . . . . . . . . . . . . . . . . . . . . $209.00
Blued/Plastic . . . . . . . . . . . . . . . . . . . . . . . . . . . 259.00
Nickel/Plastic . . . . . . . . . . . . . . . . . . . . . . . . . . . 269.00
Blued/Engraved/Wood . . . . . . . . . . . . . . . . . . . . . 309.00

**MODEL 21 BOBCAT**

**MODEL 950 JETFIRE**

### MODEL 950 JETFIRE
### SINGLE-ACTION SEMIAUTOMATIC

**SPECIFICATIONS**
**Caliber:** 25 ACP. **Barrel length:** 2.4". **Overall length:** 4.7". **Overall height:** 3.4". **Safety:** External, thumb-operated **Magazine capacity:** 8 rounds. **Sights:** Blade front; V-notch rear. **Weight:** 9.9 oz. **Frame:** Forged aluminum.
**Prices:**
Matte/Plastic. . . . . . . . . . . . . . . . . . . . . . . . . . . . $187.00
Blued/Plastic . . . . . . . . . . . . . . . . . . . . . . . . . . . 216.00
Nickel/Plastic . . . . . . . . . . . . . . . . . . . . . . . . . . . 250.00
Blued/Engraved/Wood . . . . . . . . . . . . . . . . . . . . . 296.00

# BERETTA PISTOLS

## MEDIUM-FRAME PISTOLS

### MODEL 84 CHEETAH

This pistol is pocket size with a large magazine capacity. The first shot (with hammer down, chamber loaded) can be fired by a double-action pull on the trigger without cocking the hammer manually.

The pistol also features a favorable grip angle for natural pointing, positive thumb safety (designed for both right- and left-handed operation), quick takedown (by means of special takedown button) and a conveniently located magazine release. Black plastic grips. Wood grips extra.

**SPECIFICATIONS**
**Caliber:** 380 Auto (9mm Short). **Magazine capacity:** 10 rounds. **Barrel length:** 3.8". (approx.) **Overall length:** 6.8". (approx.) **Weight:** 23.3 oz. (approx.). **Sights:** Fixed front; rear dovetailed to slide. **Height overall:** 4.85" (approx.).
**Prices:**
Bruniton/Plastic . . . . . . . . . . . . . . . . . . . . . . . **$529.00**
Bruniton/Wood . . . . . . . . . . . . . . . . . . . . . . . . . . **557.00**
Nickel/Wood . . . . . . . . . . . . . . . . . . . . . . . . . . . . **600.00**

**MODEL 84 CHEETAH**

### MODEL 85 CHEETAH (not shown)

Some basic specifications as the model 84 Cheetah, except has single line 8-round magazine, ambidextrous safety.
**Prices:**
Bruniton/Plastic . . . . . . . . . . . . . . . . . . . . . . . **$500.00**
Bruniton/Wood . . . . . . . . . . . . . . . . . . . . . . . . . . **530.00**
Nickel/Wood . . . . . . . . . . . . . . . . . . . . . . . . . . . . **559.00**
Also available:
**MODEL 87** in 22 LR. **Capacity:** 7 rounds. Straight blow-back open slide design **Width:** 1.3". **Overall height:** 4.7". **Weight:** 20.1 oz. **Finish:** Blued with wood . . . . . . **$529.00**

### MODEL 86 CHEETAH

**SPECIFICATIONS**
**Caliber:** 380 Auto. **Barrel length:** 4.4". **Overall length:** 7.3". **Capacity:** 8 rounds. **Weight:** 23.3 oz. **Sight radius:** 4.9". **Overall height:** 4.8". **Overall width:** 1.4". **Grip:** Walnut. **Features:** Same as other Medium Frame, straight blow-back models, plus safety and convenience of a tip-up barrel (rounds can be loaded directly into chamber without operating the slide).
**Price:** Bruniton/Wood Grips . . . . . . . . . . . . . . . . **$530.00**

**MODEL 86 CHEETAH**

### MODEL 89 GOLD STANDARD SA

This sophisticated single-action, target pistol features an eight-round magazine, adjustable target sights, and target-style contoured walnut grips with thumbrest.
**SPECIFICATIONS**
**Caliber:** 22 LR. **Capacity:** 8 rounds. **Barrel length:** 6". **Overall length:** 9.5". **Height:** 5.3". **Weight:** 41 oz. **Features:** Adjustable target sights, and target style contuored walnut grips with thumbrest.
**Price** . . . . . . . . . . . . . . . . . . . . . . . . . . . . . . . . . **$750.00**

**MODEL 89 GOLD STANDARD**

# BERETTA PISTOLS

## LARGE FRAME PISTOLS

### MODELS 92FS (9mm) & 96 (40 Cal.)

**SPECIFICATIONS**
**Calibers:** 9mm and 40 cal.
**Capacity:** 10 rounds
**Action:** Double/Single
**Barrel length:** 4.9" **Overall length:** 8.5"
**Weight:** 34.4 oz.
**Overall height:** 5.4" **Overall width:** 1.5"
**Sights:** Integral front; windage adjustable rear; 3-dot or tritium night sights
**Grips:** Wood or plastic
**Finish:** Bruniton (also available in blued, stainless, silver or gold)
**Features:** Chrome-lined bore; visible firing-pin block; open slide design; safety drop catch (half-cock); combat trigger guard; external hammer; reversible magazine release

Also available:
**MODELS 92D** (9mm) and 96D (40 cal.). Same specifications but in DA only and with Bruniton finish and plastic grips only. Also features chamber loaded indicator on extractor; bobbed external hammer; "slick" slide (no external levers)
**MODEL CENTURION** (9mm and 40 cal.). Same as above but more compact upper slide barrel assembly. **Barrel length:** 4.3". **Overall length:** 7.8". **Weight:** 33.2 oz.

**MODEL 92D/ 96D**

**MODEL 96**

| Models | Prices |
|---|---|
| **Model 92FS Plastic** w/3-Dot sights | $ 626.00 |
| For wood grips, **add** | 20.00 |
| For tritium sights, **add** | 90.00 |
| **Model 92F** Stainless w/3-dot sights | 757.00 |
| **Model 92FS** Plastic Centurion 9mm/40 cal. w/3-dot sights | 626.00 |
| w/tritium sights | 716.00 |
| **Model 92D** (DA only, bobbed hammer) w/3-dot sights | 586.00 |
| w/tritium sight | 676.00 |
| **Model 92F** Deluxe gold-plated engraved | 5429.00 |
| **Model 96** w/3-dot sights | 626.00 |
| w/tritium sights | 676.00 |
| **Model 96D** (DA only) | 586.00 |
| w/tritium sights | 676.00 |
| **Model 96 Centurion** | 626.00 |
| w/tritium sights | 716.00 |

### MODEL 96 COMBAT/MODEL 96 STOCK

**SPECIFICATIONS**
**Calibers:** 40 **Capacity:** 10 rounds
**Action:** Single action only (Combat); single/double (Stock)
**Barrel length:** 4.9" (Stock); 5.9" (Combat)
**Overall length:** 8.5" (Stock); 9.5" (Combat)
**Weight:** 35 oz. (Stock); 40 oz. (Combat)
**Sights:** 3 interchangable front sights (Stock)
**Features:** Rubber magazine bumpers; replaceable accurizing barrel bushings; checkered grips; machine-checkered front and backstraps; fitted ABS cases; Brigadier slide; extended frame-mounted safety; competition-tuned trigger and adjustable rear target set and tool set (Combat only)
**Prices:**
Model 96 Combat .......................... $1371.00
Model 96 Stock ........................... 1593.00

**MODEL 96 COMBAT**

# BERNARDELLI PISTOLS

## MODEL P.018 TARGET PISTOL
### $725.00 (Black Plastic)
### $780.00 (Chrome)

**SPECIFICATIONS**
**Caliber:** 9mm
**Capacity:** 16 rounds
**Barrel length:** 4.8"
**Overall length:** 8.25"
**Weight:** 34.2 oz.
**Sights:** Low micrometric sights adjustable for windage and elevation
**Sight radius:** 5.4"
**Features:** Thumb safety decocks hammer; magazine press button release reversible for right- and left-hand shooters; hardened steel barrel; can be carried cocked and locked; squared and serrated trigger guard and grip; frame and barrel forged in steel and milled with CNC machines; manual thumb, half cock, magazine and auto-locking firing-pin block safeties; low-profile 3-dot interchangeable combat sights

**MODEL P.018
TARGET PISTOL**

## MODEL P.018 COMPACT TARGET PISTOL
### $725.00 (Black Plastic)
### $780.00 (Chrome)

**SPECIFICATIONS**
**Calibers:** 380, 9mm, 40 S&W (chrome only)
**Capacity:** 14 rounds
**Barrel length:** 4"
**Overall length:** 7.44"
**Weight:** 31.7 oz.
**Sight radius:** 5.4"
**Grips:** Walnut or plastic
**Features:** Same as Model P.018

**MODEL P.018
COMPACT TARGET**

## MODEL P.010 TARGET PISTOL
### $899.00

**SPECIFICATIONS**
**Caliber:** 22 LR
**Capacity:** 5 or 10 rounds
**Barrel length:** 5.9"
**Weight:** 40 oz.
**Sights:** Interchangeable front sight; rear sight adjustable for windage and elevation
**Sight radius:** 7.5"
**Features:** All steel construction; external hammer with safety notch; external slide catch for hold-open device; inertia safe firing pin; oil-finished walnut grips for right- and left-hand shooters; matte black or chrome finish; pivoted trigger with adjustable weight and take-ups

**MODEL P.010
TARGET**

# BERSA AUTOMATIC PISTOLS

## THUNDER 9 DOUBLE ACTION
### $458.95 (Duo-Tone)  $475.00 (Satin Nickel)
### $448.95 (Matte)

**SPECIFICATIONS**
**Caliber:** 9mm  **Capacity:** 10 rounds
**Action:** Double
**Barrel length:** 4"  **Overall length:** 7 3/8"
**Weight:** 30 oz.  **Height:** 5.5"
**Sights:** Blade front (integral w/slide); fully adjustable rear
**Safety:** Manual, firing pin and decocking lever
**Grips:** Black polymer
**Finish:** Matte blue, satin nickel or duo-tone
**Features:** Reversible extended magazine release; adjustable trigger release; "Link-Free" design system (ensures positive lockup); instant disassembly; ambidextrous slide release

**THUNDER 9 DOUBLE ACTION**

**THUNDER 22**

**THUNDER 380**

**SERIES 95**

## THUNDER 22
### $249.95 (Matte)  $274.95 (Satin Nickel)

**SPECIFICATIONS**
**Caliber:** 22 LR  **Capacity:** 10 rounds
**Action:** Double
**Barrel length:** 3.5"  **Overall length:** 6 5/8"
**Weight:** 23 oz.
**Sights:** Notched-bar dovetailed rear; blade integral with slide front; 3-dot
**Safety:** Manual firing pin
**Grips:** Black polymer

## THUNDER 380
### $258.95 (Matte)  $274.95 (Satin Nickel)

**SPECIFICATIONS**
**Caliber:** 380 ACP  **Capacity:** 7 rounds
**Barrel length:** 3.5"  **Overall length:** 6 5/8"
**Weight:** 23 oz.
**Sights:** Notched-bar dovetailed rear; blade integral with slide front
**Safety:** Manual firing pin
**Grips:** Black polymer
**Finish:** Blue, satin nickel.
Also available:
**THUNDER 380 Deluxe** (29 oz.; 9 shots) **Price:** $274.95

## SERIES 95
### $231.95 (Matte)  $253.95 (Nickel)

**SPECIFICATIONS**
**Caliber:** 380 ACP  **Capacity:** 7 rounds
**Action:** Double
**Barrel length:** 3.5"  **Overall length:** 6 5/8"
**Weight:** 23 oz.
**Sights:** Notched-bar dovetailed rear; blade integral with slide front
**Safety:** Manual firing pin
**Grips:** Black polymer
**Finish:** Matte blue, satin nickel

# BROLIN ARMS

## PRO SERIES

### MODEL PRO-COMP PISTOL
### $919.00 ($929.00 Stainless or Two-Tone)

**SPECIFICATIONS**
**Caliber:** 45 ACP  **Capacity:** 8+1
**Action:** Single
**Barrel length:** 4"  **Overall length:** 8.5"
**Weight:** 37 oz.
**Finish:** Blue, Stainless or Two-Tone
**Features:** Signature wood grip; beveled magazine well;
beavertail grip safety; adj. rear sight; black ramp front
sight; recoil guide rod; adj. aluminum match trigger; slot-
ted commander hammer; dual-port compensator

Also available:
**MODEL PRO-STOCK.** Same specifications as the Pro-
Comp Pistol, except without dual-port compensator.
**Price: $779.00 ($799.00 in Stainless or Two-Tone)**

**PRO SERIES**
**PRO-COMP TWO-TONE**

## PATRIOT SERIES

### MODEL P45C COMPENSATED
### $689.00 ($709.00 Stainless or Two-Tone)
### $699.00 (Compact Comp)

**SPECIFICATIONS**
**Caliber:** 45 ACP  **Capacity:** 7+1
**Action:** Single
**Barrel length:** 3.25"  **Overall Length:** 7.5"
**Weight:** 33 oz.
**Features:** DPC Compensator w/conical lock-up match bar-
rel; orange- ramp front sight, white-outline rear sight;
slotted commander hammer; beavertail grip safety;
checkered wood grip; adj. aluminum match trigger; dual
recoil springs; Millett sights (Novak sights optional)

Also available:
**MODEL P45 COMP STANDARD.** Same specifications as
the P45C Comp Compact, except w/o DPC Compensator
and dual recoil springs. **Price: $649.00 ($669.00
Stainless or Two-Tone)**

**MODEL P45C COMP
COMPACT**

## LEGEND SERIES

### MODEL L45 STANDARD
### $459.00 ($489.00 with Compact Slide)

**SPECIFICATIONS**
**Caliber:** 45 ACP  **Capacity:** 7+1
**Action:** Single
**Barrel length:** 5"  **Overall length:** 8.5"
**Weight:** 46 oz.
**Finish:** Matte blue
**Features:** Throated match barrel; orange-ramp front sight;
white-outlined rear sight; beveled magazine well; check-
ered walnut grip; aluminum match trigger

Also available:
**MODEL L45C COMPACT.** Same specifications as the L45
Standard, except with integral conical lock-up. **Price:
$489.00**

**LEGEND SERIES L45
STANDARD**

# BROWNING AUTOMATIC PISTOLS

**9mm HI-POWER
SINGLE ACTION**

## HI-POWER SINGLE ACTION

Both the 9mm and 40 S&W models come with either a fixed-blade front sight and a windage-adjustable rear sight or a nonglare rear sight, screw adjustable for both windage and elevation. The front sight is an 1/8-inch-wide blade mounted on a ramp. The rear surface of the blade is serrated to prevent glare. All models have an ambidextrous safety. See table below for specifications and prices.

## HI-POWER SPECIFICATIONS 9mm & 40 S&W

| Model | Sights | Grips | Barrel Length | Overall Length | Overall Width | Overall Height | Weight* | Mag. Cap. | Prices |
|---|---|---|---|---|---|---|---|---|---|
| Mark III | Fixed | Molded | 4.75" | 7.75" | 1 3/8" | 5" | 32 oz. | 10 | $550.95 |
| Standard | Fixed | Walnut | 4.75" | 7.75" | 1 3/8" | 5" | 32 oz. | 10 | 584.95 |
| Standard | Adj. | Walnut | 4.75" | 7.75" | 1 3/8" | 5" | 32 oz. | 10 | 635.95 |
| HP-Practical | Fixed | Pachmayr | 4.75" | 7.75" | 1 3/8" | 5" | 36 oz. | 10 | 629.95 |
| HP-Practical | Adj. | Pachmayr | 4.75" | 7.75" | 1 3/8" | 5" | 36 oz. | 10 | 681.95 |
| Silver Chrome | Adj. | Pachmayr | 4.75" | 7.75" | 1 3/8" | 5" | 36 oz. | 10 | 650.95 |
| Capitan (9mm only) | Adj. | Walnut | 4.75" | 7.75" | 1 3/8" | 5" | 32 oz. | 10 | 692.95 |

\* 9mm weight listed. Overall weight of the 40 S&W Hi-Power is 3 oz. heavier than the 9mm.

## MODEL BDM 9mm DOUBLE ACTION

Browning's Model BDM (for Browning Double Mode) pistol provides shooters with convenience and safety by combining the best advantages of double-action pistols with those of the revolver. In just seconds, the shooter can set the BDM to conventional double-action "pistol" mode or to the all-new double-action "revolver" mode.

**SPECIFICATIONS**
**Caliber:** 9mm Luger
**Capacity:** 10 rounds
**Barrel length:** 4.73"
**Overall length:** 7.85"
**Weight:** 31 oz. (empty)
**Sight radius:** 6.26"
**Sights:** Low-profile front (removable); rear screw adjustable for windage; includes 3-dot sight system
**Finish:** Matte blue
**Features:** Dual-purpose ambidextrous decocking lever/safety designed with a short stroke for easy operation (also functions as slide release); contoured grip is checkered on all four sides
**Prices:**
Standard . . . . . . . . . . . . . . . . . . . . . . . . . . . . . $550.95

**MODEL BDM
9mm DOUBLE ACTION
(Silver Chrome)**

Practical . . . . . . . . . . . . . . . . . . . . . . . . . . . . $570.95
Silver Chrome . . . . . . . . . . . . . . . . . . . . . . . . . 570.95
Also available:
**Model BPM-D** (Decocker) . . . . . . . . . . . . . . . . . 550.95
**Model BRM DAO** (Double Action Only) . . . . . . . . 550.95

# BROWNING AUTOMATIC PISTOLS

**MODEL
BDA-380**

## MODEL BDA-380

A high-powered, double-action semiautomatic pistol with fixed sights in 380 caliber.

**SPECIFICATIONS**
**Capacity:** 10 shots
**Barrel length:** 3$^{13}$/$_{16}$"
**Overall length:** 6.75"
**Weight:** 23 oz.
**Sights:** Fixed
**Grips:** Walnut
**Prices:**
Nickel Finish . . . . . . . . . . . . . . . . . . . . . . . . . . . . . $606.95
Blued Finish . . . . . . . . . . . . . . . . . . . . . . . . . . . . . . 563.95

## BUCK MARK SERIES

**BUCK MARK STANDARD**
**(5.5" Barrel)**

**BUCK MARK
PLUS NICKEL**

## BUCK MARK SPECIFICATIONS

| BUCK MARK MODELS | Mag. Cap. | Barrel Length | Overall Length | Weight | Overall Height | Sight Radius | Grips | Prices |
|---|---|---|---|---|---|---|---|---|
| **Standard** | 10 | 5.5" | 9.5" | 36 oz. | 5$^5$/$_8$" | 8" | Molded Composite, Ambidextrous | $256.95 |
| **Micro Standard** | 10 | 4" | 8" | 32 oz. | 5$^3$/$_8$" | 9$^9$/$_{16}$" | Molded Composite, Ambidextrous | 256.95 |
| **Nickel** | 10 | 5.5" | 9.5" | 36 oz. | 5$^3$/$_8$" | 8" | Molded Composite, Ambidextrous | 301.95 |
| **Micro Nickel** | 10 | 4" | 8" | 32 oz. | 5$^3$/$_8$" | 9$^9$/$_{16}$" | Molded Composite, Ambidextrous | 301.95 |
| **Plus Nickel** | 10 | 5.5" | 9.5" | 36 oz. | 5$^3$/$_8$" | 8" | Laminated Hardwood | 342.95 |
| **Micro Plus Nickel** | 10 | 4" | 8" | 32 oz. | 5$^3$/$_8$" | 9$^9$/$_{16}$" | Laminated Hardwood | 342.95 |
| **Plus** | 10 | 5.5" | 9.5" | 36 oz. | 5$^3$/$_8$" | 8" | Laminated Hardwood | 313.95 |
| **Micro Plus** | 10 | 4" | 8" | 32 oz. | 5$^3$/$_8$" | 9$^9$/$_{16}$" | Laminated Hardwood | 313.95 |

# BROWNING AUTOMATIC PISTOLS

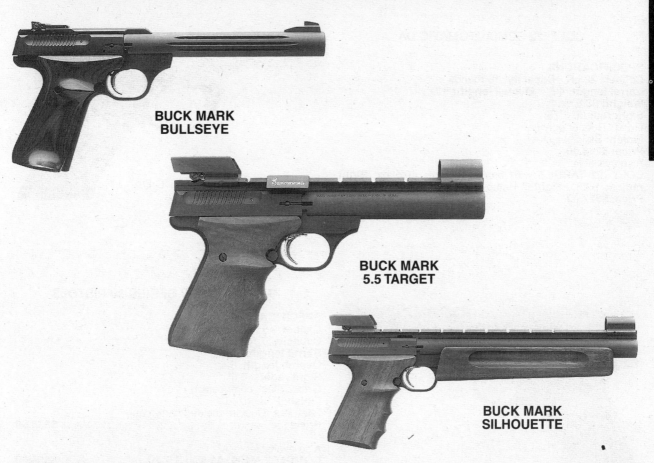

**BUCK MARK
BULLSEYE**

**BUCK MARK
5.5 TARGET**

**BUCK MARK
SILHOUETTE**

## BUCK MARK SPECIFICATIONS (cont.)

| BUCK MARK MODELS | Mag. Cap. | Barrel Length | Overall Length | Weight | Overall Height | Sight Radius | Grips | Prices |
|---|---|---|---|---|---|---|---|---|
| **Bullseye, Standard** | 10 | 7.25" | $11^5/_{16}$" | 36 oz. | $5^3/_8$" | $9^7/_8$" | Molded Composite, Ambidextrous | $376.95 |
| **Bullseye, Target** | 10 | 7.25" | $11^5/_{16}$" | 36 oz. | $5^3/_8$" | $9^7/_8$" | Contoured Rosewood | 484.95 |
| | 10 | 7.25" | $11^5/_{16}$" | 36 oz. | $5^3/_8$" | $9^7/_8$" | Wraparound fingergroove | 484.95 |
| **5.5 Field** | 10 | 5.5" | $9^5/_8$" | 35.5 oz. | $5^5/_{16}$" | 8.25" | Contoured walnut | 411.95 |
| | 10 | 5.5" | $9^5/_8$" | 35.5oz. | $5^5/_{16}$" | 8.25" | Wraparound fingergroove | 411.95 |
| **5.5 Target** | 10 | 5.5" | $9^5/_8$" | 35.5 oz. | $5^5/_{16}$" | 8.25" | Contoured walnut | 411.95 |
| | 10 | 5.5" | $9^5/_8$" | 35.5 oz. | $5^5/_{16}$" | 8.25" | Wraparound fingergroove | 411.95 |
| **5.5 Nickel Target** | 10 | 5.5" | $9^5/_8$" | 35.5 oz. | $5^5/_{16}$" | 8.25" | Contoured walnut | 462.95 |
| | 10 | 5.5" | $9^5/_8$" | 35.5 oz. | $5^5/_{16}$" | 8.25" | Wraparound fingergroove | 462.95 |
| **5.5 Gold Target** | 10 | 5.5" | $9^5/_8$" | 35.5 oz. | $5^5/_{16}$" | 8.25" | Contoured walnut | 462.95 |
| | 10 | 5.5" | $9^5/_8$" | 35.5 oz. | $5^5/_{16}$" | 8.25" | Wraparound fingergroove | 462.95 |
| **Silhouette** | 10 | $9^7/_8$" | 14" | 53 oz. | $5^5/_{16}$" | 13" | Contoured walnut | 434.95 |
| | 10 | $9^7/_8$" | 14" | 53 oz. | $5^5/_{16}$" | 13" | Wraparound fingergroove | 434.95 |
| **Unlimited Silhouette** | 10 | 14" | 14" | 64 oz. | $5^5/_{16}$" | 15" | Contoured walnut | 535.95 |
| | 10 | 14" | $18^{11}/_{16}$" | 64 oz. | $5^5/_{16}$" | 15" | Wraparound fingergroove | 535.95 |
| **Varmint** | 10 | $9^7/_8$" | 14" | 48 oz. | $5^5/_{16}$" | | Contoured walnut | 390.95 |
| | 10 | $9^7/_8$" | 14" | 48 oz. | $5^5/_{16}$" | | Wraparound fingergroove | 390.95 |
| **Extra Magazine** | | | | | | | | 24.95 |

# COLT AUTOMATIC PISTOLS

## COLT .22 SEMIAUTOMATIC DA

**SPECIFICATIONS**
**Caliber:** 22 LR  **Capacity:** 10 rounds
**Barrel length:** 4.5"  **Overall length:** $8^5/_8$"
**Weight:** 33.5 oz.
**Sight radius:** 5.75"
**Grips:** Rubber polymer
**Finish:** Stainless steel
**Price:** $248.00
Also available:
**COLT .22 TARGET** w/6" barrel. **Weight:** 40.5 oz. **Sight radius:** 9.25". **Sights:** Removable front, adjustable rear. **Price:** $377.00

**.22 SEMIAUTOMATIC DA**

## M1991A1 MKIV SERIES 80 PISTOLS

**SPECIFICATIONS**
**Caliber:** 45 ACP
**Capacity:** 7 rounds
**Barrel length:** 5"
**Overall length:** 8.5"
**Sight radius:** 6.5"
**Grips:** Black composition
**Finish:** Parkerized
**Features:** Custom-molded carry case
**Price:** .................................... $556.00

Also available:
**COMPACT M1991A1** with 3.5" barrel .......... $556.00
**COMMANDER M1991A1** with 4.25" barrel and
   7-round capacity ........................ 556.00
   Stainless (all models). .................... 610.00

**MODEL M1991A1**

## COMBAT COMMANDER MKIV SERIES 80

The semiautomatic Combat Commander, available in 45 ACP and 38 Super, features an all-steel frame that supplies the pistol with an extra measure of heft and stability. This Colt pistol also offers 3-dot high-profile sights, lanyard-style hammer and thumb and beavertail grip safety. Also available in lightweight version with alloy frame (45 ACP only). **Barrel length:** 4.25".

**SPECIFICATIONS**

| Caliber | Weight (ounces) | Overall Length | Magazine Rounds | Finish | Price |
|---------|-----------------|----------------|-----------------|--------|-------|
| 45 ACP | 36 | 7.75" | 8 | Stainless | $813.00 |
| 45 ACP LW | 27.5 | 7.75" | 8 | Blue | 735.00 |

Also available:
**Combat Target (45 ACP)** w/5" barrel (blue) ... $768.00
Stainless. .............................. 828.00

**COMBAT COMMANDER**
**4 1/4" barrel only**

# COLT AUTOMATIC PISTOLS

## MKIV SERIES 80

### GOLD CUP TROPHY

**SPECIFICATIONS**
**Caliber**: 45 ACP
**Capacity**: 7 and 8 rounds
**Barrel length**: 5"    **Overall length**: 8.5"
**Weight**: 39 oz.
**Sights**: Colt Elliason sights; adjustable rear for windage and elevation
**Hammer**: Serrated rounded hammer
**Stock**: Rubber combat
**Finish**: Colt blue, stainless or "Ultimate" bright stainless steel
**Prices**: $  840.00 Blue
         1116.00 Stainless steel

**GOLD CUP
TROPHY**

### GOVERNMENT MODEL
### MKIV SERIES 80 SEMIAUTOMATIC

These full-size automatic pistols with 5-inch barrels are available in 45 ACP and 38 Super. The Government Model's special features include high-profile 3-dot sights, grip and thumb safeties, and rubber combat stocks.

**SPECIFICATIONS**
**Calibers**: 38 Super and 45 ACP
**Capacity**: 9 rounds (38 Super); 8 rounds (45 ACP)
**Barrel length**: 5"    **Overall length**: 8.5"
**Weight**: 38 oz. (45 ACP), 39 oz. (38 Super)
**Prices**: $735.00 45 ACP blue
         813.00 45 ACP stainless
Also available in 9x23mm Win. . . . . . . . . . . . . . . $735.00

**GOVERNMENT MODEL**

### GOVERNMENT MODEL 380
### MKIV SERIES 80 SEMIAUTOMATIC
### (not shown)

This scaled-down version of the 1911A1 Colt Government Model does not include a grip safety. It incorporates the use of a firing-pin safety to provide for a safe method to carry a round in the chamber in a "cocked-and-locked" mode. Available in matte stainless-steel finish with black composition stocks.

**SPECIFICATIONS**
**Caliber**: 380 ACP
**Magazine capacity**: 7 rounds
**Barrel length**: 3.25"    **Overall length**: 6"
**Height**: 4.4"    **Weight**: 21.75 oz. (empty)
**Sights**: Fixed ramp blade front; fixed square-notched rear
**Grip**: Composition stocks
**Prices**: $474.00 Blue

# COLT AUTOMATIC PISTOLS

## MKIV SERIES 80 AND 90

### MUSTANG .380

This backup automatic has four times the knockdown power of most 25 ACP automatics. It is a smaller version of the 380 Government Model.

**SPECIFICATIONS**
**Caliber:** 380 ACP  **Capacity:** 6 rounds
**Barrel length:** 2.75"  **Overall length:** 5.5"
**Height:** 3.9"  **Weight:** 18.5 oz.
**Prices:** $462.00 Standard, blue
     508.00 Stainless steel
Also available:
**MUSTANG POCKETLITE 380** with aluminum alloy receiver; 12" shorter than standard Govt. 380; weighs only 12.5 oz. **Prices: $508.00.**
**MUSTANG PLUS II** features full grip length (Govt. 380 model only) with shorter compact barrel and slide (Mustang .380 model only). **Weight:** 20 oz. **$508.00** (Stainless Steel.)

**MUSTANG .380**

### GOVERNMENT 380 MKIV
### PONY SERIES 90 DA SEMIAUTO
### (Not shown)

**SPECIFICATIONS**
**Caliber:** 380
**Capacity:** 6 rounds
**Action:** DA only (Single in Mustang Pocketlite LW)
**Barrel length:** 2.75"
**Overall length:** 5.5"
**Weight:** 19 oz. (13 oz. in Pocketlite LW; 12.5 oz. in Mustang Pocketlite LW)
**Grips:** Black composition
**Sights:** Ramp front, fixed rear
**Finish:** Teflon and stainless steel
**Features:** Bobbed hammer; smooth combat trigger; firing pin safety; no-snag slim profile; locked breeches
**Price: $493.00**
(Pocketlite price to be determined)

**.380 MUSTANG
PLUS II**

### COLT OFFICER'S 45 ACP

**SPECIFICATIONS**
**Caliber:** 45 ACP  **Capacity:** 6 rounds
**Barrel length:** 3.5"  **Overall length:** 7.25"
**Weight:** 34 oz.
**Prices:** $813.00 Stainless steel
Also available:
**OFFICER'S LW** w/aluminum alloy frame (24 oz.) and blued finish. **Price: $735.00**

**OFFICER'S 45 ACP**

# COLT REVOLVERS

## KING COBRA DOUBLE ACTION

This "snake" revolver features a solid barrel rib, full-length ejector rod housing, red ramp front sight, white outline adjustable rear sight and "gripper" rubber combat grips.

### SPECIFICATIONS
**Calibers:** 357 Mag./38 Special   **Capacity:** 6 rounds
**Barrel length:** 4" or 6"
**Overall length:** 9" (4" bbl.); 11" (6" bbl.)
**Weight:** 42 oz. (4"); 46 oz. (6")
**Finish:** Stainless
**Price:** $468.00

**KING COBRA**

## SINGLE ACTION ARMY
### (Nickel Finish)

## SINGLE ACTION ARMY REVOLVER

Colt's Custom Gun Shop maintains the tradition of quality and innovation that Samuel Colt began more than a century and a half ago. Single Action Army revolvers continue to be highly prized collectible arms and are offered in full nickel finish or in Royal Blue with color casehardened frame, without engraving, unless otherwise specified by the purchaser. Grips are American walnut.
**Price:**. . . . . . . . . . . . . . . . . . . . . . . . . . . . . . $1213.00

### SINGLE ACTION ARMY SPECIFICATIONS

| Caliber | Bbl. Length (inches) | Finish | Approx. Weight (ozs.) | O.A. Length (inches) | Grips | Medallions |
|---|---|---|---|---|---|---|
| 45LC | 4.75 | CC/B | 40 | 10.25 | BCE | Gold |
| 45LC | 4.75 | N | 40 | 10.25 | BCE | Nickel |
| 45LC | 5.5 | CC/B | 42 | 11 | BCE | Gold |
| 45LC | 5.5 | N | 42 | 11 | BCE | Nickel |
| 45LC | 7.5 | CC/B | 43 | 13 | BCE | Gold |
| 45LC | 7.5 | N | 43 | 13 | BCE | Nickel |
| 44LC | 7.5 | CC/B | 43 | 13 | BCE | Gold |
| 44LC | 7.5 | N | 43 | 13 | BCE | Nickel |
| 44-40 | 4.75 | CC/B | 40 | 10.25 | BCE | Gold |
| 44-40 | 4.75 | N | 40 | 10.25 | BCE | Nickel |
| 44-40 | 5.5 | CC/B | 42 | 11 | BCE | Gold |
| 44-40 | 5.5 | N | 42 | 11 | BCE | Nickel |

N—Nickel  CC/B—Colorcase frame/Royal Blue cylinder & barrel  BCE—Black Composite Eagle

# COLT REVOLVERS

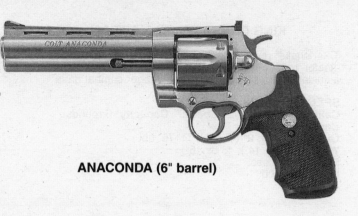

## ANACONDA DOUBLE ACTION

### SPECIFICATIONS
**Calibers:** 44 Magnum/44 Special and 45 Colt (6" and 8" barrel only)
**Capacity:** 6 rounds
**Barrel length:** 4", 6" or 8"
**Overall length:** 9⅝", 11⅝", 13⅝"
**Weight:** 47 oz. (4"), 53 oz. (6"), 59 oz. (8")
**Sights:** Red insert front; adjustable white outline rear
**Sight radius:** 5.75" (4"), 7.75" (6"), 9.75" (8")
**Grips:** Black neoprene combat-style with finger grooves
**Finish:** Matte stainless steel
**Price:** $629.00

**ANACONDA (6" barrel)**

**MODEL 38SF-VI**

## COLT MODEL 38 SF-VI

### SPECIFICATIONS
**Caliber:** 38 Special   **Capacity:** 6 rounds
**Barrel lengths:** 2" and 4"
**Overall length:** 7" w/4" bbl.
**Weight:** 21 oz.   **Sight radius:** 4"
**Grips:** Black composition
**Finish:** Stainless steel
**Price:** $408.00

## PYTHON ELITE

The Colt Python revolver, suitable for hunting, target shooting and police use, is chambered for the powerful 357 Magnum cartridge. Python features include ventilated rib, fast cocking, wide-spur hammer, trigger and rubber grips, adjustable rear and ramp-type front sights, grooved.

### SPECIFICATIONS
**Calibers:** 357 Mag./38 Special
**Barrel length:** 4" or 6"
**Overall length:** 9.5" and 11.5"
**Weight:** 38 oz. (4"); 43.5 oz. (6")
**Stocks:** Rubber combat (4") or rubber target (6")
**Finish:** Stainless steel or royal blue.
**Prices:** $  929.00 Royal Blue
          1018.00 Stainless steel

**PYTHON ELITE**

# COONAN ARMS

**357 MAGNUM PISTOL
5" Barrel (top)
6" Barrel (middle)
Compensated Barrel (bottom)**

## 357 MAGNUM PISTOL

### SPECIFICATIONS
**Caliber:** 357 Magnum
**Magazine capacity:** 7 rounds + 1
**Barrel length:** 5" (6" or Compensated barrel optional)
**Overall length:** 8.3"
**Weight:** 48 oz. (loaded)
**Height:** 5.6"
**Width:** 1.3"

**Sights:** Ramp front; fixed rear, adjustable for windage only
**Grips:** Smooth black walnut (checkered grips optional)
**Finish:** Stainless steel and alloy steel
**Features:** Linkless barrel; recoil-operated; extended slide catch and thumb lock
**Prices:**
With 5" barrel . . . . . . . . . . . . . . . . . . . . . . . . . . . $ 735.00
With 6" barrel . . . . . . . . . . . . . . . . . . . . . . . . . . . 768.00
With Compensated barrel . . . . . . . . . . . . . . . . . . 1015.00

## "CADET" COMPACT MODEL

### SPECIFICATIONS
**Caliber:** 357 Magnum
**Magazine capacity:** 6 rounds + 1
**Barrel length:** 3.9"
**Overall length:** 7.8"
**Weight:** 39 oz.
**Height:** 5.3"
**Width:** 1.3"
**Sights:** Ramp front; fixed rear, adjustable for windage only
**Grips:** Smooth black walnut
**Features:** Linkless bull barrel; full-length guide rod; recoil-operated (Browning falling-block design); extended slide catch and thumb lock for one-hand operation
**Price:** . . . . . . . . . . . . . . . . . . . . . . . . . . . . . . . . $855.00

**"CADET" COMPACT**

# DAEWOO PISTOLS

## MODEL DP51 (not shown)
### $415.00

**SPECIFICATIONS**
**Caliber:** 9mm Parabellum
**Capacity:** 10 rounds
**Barrel length:** 4.1"  **Overall length:** 7.5"
**Weight:** 28 oz.
**Muzzle velocity:** 1150 fps
**Sights:** Blade front (1/8"); square notch rear, drift adjustable
   with 3 self-luminous dots
**Safety:** Ambidextrous manual safety, automatic firing-pin
   block
**Feature:** Patented Fastfire action with light 5-6 lb. trigger
   pull for first-shot accuracy

## MODEL DP51C
## COMPACT

**MODEL DH380**

Also available:
**MODEL DP51C COMPACT. Barrel length:** 3.6". **Overall
length:** 7". **Weight:** 26 oz. **Height:** 4.5". **Price:** $445.00

## MODEL DH380
### $410.00

**SPECIFICATIONS**
**Caliber:** 380 ACP **Capacity:** 8 rounds
**Barrel length:** 3.8"  **Overall length:** 6.7"
**Weight:** 24 oz.  **Height:** 4.1"
**Width:** 1.2"

## MODEL DH40
### $450.00

**SPECIFICATIONS**
**Caliber:** 40 S&W
**Capacity:** 10 rounds
**Barrel length:** 4.1"  **Overall length:** 7.5"
**Weight:** 32 oz.  **Height:** 4.8"
**Width:** 1.38"
**Firing mode:** Double, single or FastFire, Tri-Action

## MODEL DP52 PISTOL
### $380.00

**SPECIFICATIONS**
**Caliber:** 22 LR
**Capacity:** 10 rounds
**Barrel length:** 3.8"  **Overall length:** 6.7"
**Weight:** 23 oz.  **Width:** 1.18"
**Sights:** 1/8" front blade; drift adjustable rear (3 white-dot
   system)

# DAVIS PISTOLS

**MODEL D-25 DERRINGER**

## D-SERIES DERRINGERS
### $75.00

**SPECIFICATIONS**
**Calibers:** 22 LR, 22 Mag., 25 Auto, 32 Auto
**Capacity:** 2 shot
**Barrel length:** 2.4"   **Overall length:** 4"
**Height:** 2.8"   **Weight:** 9.5 oz.
**Grips:** Laminated wood
**Finish:** Black teflon or chrome

## LONG BORE D-SERIES
### $104.00 ($110.00 9mm only)

**SPECIFICATIONS**
**Calibers:** 22 Mag., 9mm, 32 H&R Mag., 38 Special
**Capacity:** 2 rounds
**Barrel length:** 3.5"   **Overall length:** 5.4"
**Height:** 3.31"   **Weight:** 16 oz.

Also available:
**BIG BORE D-SERIES. Calibers:** 22 WMR, 9mm, 32 H&R Mag., 38 Special. **Barrel length:** 2.75". **Overall length:** 4.65". **Weight:** 14 oz. . . . . . . . $98.00 ($104.00 9mm only)

## MODEL P-32
### $87.50

**SPECIFICATIONS**
**Caliber:** 32 Auto
**Magazine capacity:** 6 rounds
**Barrel length:** 2.8"   **Overall length:** 5.4"
**Weight** (empty): 22 oz.   **Height:** 4"
**Grips:** Laminated wood
**Finish:** Black teflon or chrome

## MODEL P-380
### $98.00

**SPECIFICATIONS**
**Caliber:** 380 Auto
**Magazine capacity:** 5 rounds
**Barrel length:** 2.8"   **Overall length:** 5.4"
**Height:** 4"
**Weight:** 22 oz. (empty)

**LONG BORE D-SERIES**

**MODEL P-32**

**MODEL P-380**

# DOWNSIZER PISTOLS

### "WORLD'S SMALLEST PISTOL"
### $299.00

**SPECIFICATIONS**
**Action:** Single-shot double-action only
**Caliber:** 9mm, 40 S&W, 45 ACP, 357 Mag.
**Barrel length:** 2.1"; tip-up barrel w/o extractor
**Overall length:** 3.25"
**Weight:** 11 oz.  **Height:** 2.25"
**Width:** 9"
**Materials:** Stainless steel; CNC machined from solid bar stock

"WORLD'S SMALLEST PISTOL"

# EMF/DAKOTA REVOLVERS

## E.M.F. HARTFORD SINGLE-ACTION REVOLVERS

Hartford Single Action revolvers are the most authentic of all the Colt reproduction single actions. All parts are interchangeable with the original Colt 1st and 2nd generation revolvers.

### HARTFORD SCROLL-ENGRAVED SINGLE-ACTION REVOLVER
### $840.00  ($965.00 in Nickel)

**SPECIFICATIONS**
**Calibers:** 45 Long Colt, 357 Magnum, 44-40. **Barrel lengths:** 4 5/8", 5.5" and 7.5". **Features:** Classic original-type scroll engraving.

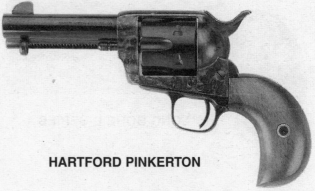

HARTFORD PINKERTON

### HARTFORD PINKERTON
### $455.00

**Caliber:** 45 LC. **Barrel length:** 4". Bird's-head grip with ejector tube.

### HARTFORD MODELS "CAVALRY COLT" AND "ARTILLERY"
### $700.00

The Model 1873 Government Model Cavalry revolver is an exact reproduction of the original Colt made for the U.S. Cavalry in caliber 45 Long Colt with barrel length of 7.5". The Artillery Model has 5.5" barrel.
Also available:
**Sheriff's Model** (3.5" barrel). . . . . . . . . . . . . . . **$600.00**

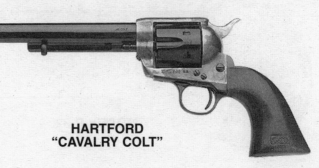

HARTFORD "CAVALRY COLT"

# EMF/DAKOTA REVOLVERS

## E.M.F. HARTFORD SINGLE ACTION REVOLVERS

1st and 2nd generations models available. Parts are interchangeable with the original Colts. Forged steel frames, case hardened, steel backstrap & triggerguard. Original blue finish, walnut grips. Barrel lengths: 4³/₄", 5¹/₂", 7¹/₂", 12" buntline

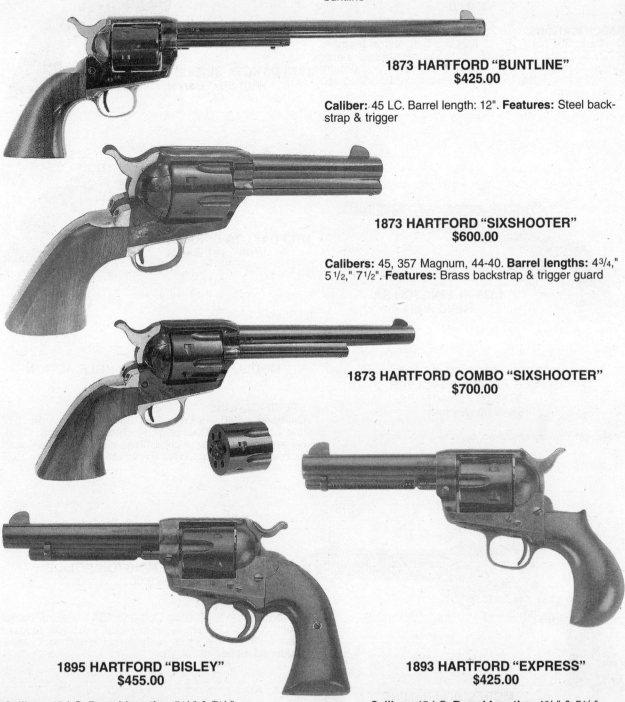

### 1873 HARTFORD "BUNTLINE"
### $425.00

**Caliber:** 45 LC. Barrel length: 12". **Features:** Steel backstrap & trigger

### 1873 HARTFORD "SIXSHOOTER"
### $600.00

**Calibers:** 45, 357 Magnum, 44-40. **Barrel lengths:** 4³/₄," 5¹/₂," 7¹/₂". **Features:** Brass backstrap & trigger guard

### 1873 HARTFORD COMBO "SIXSHOOTER"
### $700.00

### 1895 HARTFORD "BISLEY"
### $455.00

**Caliber:** 45 LC. **Barrel lengths:** 5¹/₂" & 7¹/₂".
**Features:** Steel backstrap & trigger guard

### 1893 HARTFORD "EXPRESS"
### $425.00

**Caliber:** 45 LC. **Barrel lengths:** 4³/₄" & 5¹/₂".
**Features**: Steel backstrap & trigger guard

# EMF/DAKOTA REVOLVERS

**1873 DAKOTA SINGLE ACTION**
**With 5¹/₂" Barrel**

### 1873 DAKOTA SINGLE ACTION
### $350.00

**SPECIFICATIONS**
**Calibers:** 357 Mag., 44-40, 45 Long Colt. **Barrel lengths:** 4.75", 5.5" and 7.5". **Finish:** Blued, casehardened frame. **Grips:** One-piece walnut. **Features:** Classic Colt design, set screw for cylinder pin release; black nickel backstrap and trigger design

**1873 DAKOTA SINGLE ACTION**
**With 7¹/₂" Barrel**

**1875 REMINGTON SA**
**REVOLVER**

### MODEL 1875 REMINGTON
### SINGLE ACTION REVOLVER
### $750.00 (Blued)
### $825.00 (Nickel)

**Features:** Factory engraved; casehardened frame

### MODEL 1875 "OUTLAW" SINGLE ACTION
### $550.00 (not shown)

**SPECIFICATIONS**
**Calibers:** 44-40, 45 Long Colt, 357. **Barrel length:** 5.5" and 7.5". **Finish:** Blued or nickel. **Special features:** Case-hardened frame, walnut grips; brass trigger guard; an exact replica of the Remington No. 3 revolver produced from 1875 to 1889.

**MODEL 1890 REMINGTON**
**POLICE**

### MODEL 1890 REMINGTON POLICE
### $570.00

**SPECIFICATIONS**
**Calibers:** 44-40, 45 Long Colt and 357 Magnum. **Barrel length:** 5.75". **Finish:** Blued or nickel. **Features:** Original design (1891–1894) with lanyard ring in buttstock; case-hardened frame; walnut grips.

# ERMA TARGET ARMS

**MODEL ESP 85A**

**MODEL ESP 85A JUNIOR**
**$1460.00  (22 LR)**

## MODEL ESP 85A AUTOLOADING COMPETITION PISTOLS

### SPECIFICATIONS
**Caliber:** 22 LR or 32 S&W Wadcutter
**Action:** Semiautomatic
**Capacity:** 5 cartridges (8 in 22 LR optional)
**Barrel length:** 6"
**Overall length:** 10"
**Weight:** 37 oz.
**Sight radius:** 7.8"
**Sights:** Micrometer rear sight; fully adjustable interchange-
able front and rear sight blade (.13/.16")
**Grip:** Checkered walnut grip with thumbrest

**Prices:**
**ESP 85A MATCH**  32 S&W . . . . . . . . . . . . . . . $2110.00
Target adjustable grip, **add** . . . . . . . . . . . . . . . . . . . 258.75
   Left hand, **add**. . . . . . . . . . . . . . . . . . . . . . . . . 302.25
**ESP 85A MATCH** 22 LR. . . . . . . . . . . . . . . . . . . . 1895.00
   In 32 S&W . . . . . . . . . . . . . . . . . . . . . . . . . . . . 2000.00
**ESP 85A CHROME MATCH** 22 LR . . . . . . . . . . . 2110.00
   In 32 S&W . . . . . . . . . . . . . . . . . . . . . . . . . . . . 2325.00
**ESP 85A SPORT PISTOL** 22 LR . . . . . . . . . . . . 1785.00
   In 32 S&W . . . . . . . . . . . . . . . . . . . . . . . . . . . . 2000.00
**ESP 85A CHROME SPORT PISTOL** 22 LR . . . . . 2000.00
   In 32 S&W . . . . . . . . . . . . . . . . . . . . . . . . . . . . 2215.00
**Conversion Units** 22 LR . . . . . . . . . . . . . . . . . . . 980.00
   In 32 S&W . . . . . . . . . . . . . . . . . . . . . . . . . . . . 1185.00
**Chrome Slide** 22 LR . . . . . . . . . . . . . . . . . . . . . 1185.00
   In 32 S&W . . . . . . . . . . . . . . . . . . . . . . . . . . . . 1390.00

# EUROPEAN AMERICAN ARMORY

**ASTRA MODEL A-75**

**SPECIFICATIONS**
**Calibers:** 9mm, 40 S&W and 45 ACP
**Capacity:** 8 rounds (7 in 45 ACP & 40 S&W)
**Barrel length:** 3.5" (3.7" in 45 ACP)
**Overall length:** 6.5" (6.75" in 45 ACP)
**Weight:** 31 oz.; 23.5 oz.(Featherweight Model); 34.4 oz.
 (45 ACP steel)
**Height:** 4.75" (5.1" in 45 ACP)
**Finish:** Blued, nickel or stainless steel
**Prices:**
Blue. . . . . . . . . . . . . . . . . . . . . . . . . . . . . . . . . . $357.00
**Nickel or Stainless Steel** . . . . . . . . . . . . . . . . . 380.00
40 S&W, Blue . . . . . . . . . . . . . . . . . . . . . . . . . 310.50
40 S&W, nickel . . . . . . . . . . . . . . . . . . . . . . . . 329.00
9mm, blue . . . . . . . . . . . . . . . . . . . . . . . . . . . . . 302.00
9mm, nickel. . . . . . . . . . . . . . . . . . . . . . . . . . . . 320.00

Also available:
**Lightweight 9mm** . . . . . . . . . . . . . . . . . . . . . . . . 323.00

**ASTRA MODEL A-75**
**Blued**

**ASTRA MODEL A-100**

**SPECIFICATIONS**
**Calibers:** 9mm, 40 S&W and 45 ACP
**Capacity:** 17 rounds (9mm); 10 rounds (40 S&W);
 9 rounds (45 ACP)
**Barrel length:** 3.8"
**Overall length:** 7.5"
**Weight:** 34 oz. (steel); 26.5 oz. (9mm)
**Finish:** Blued, nickel or stainless steel
**Prices:**
Blue. . . . . . . . . . . . . . . . . . . . . . . . . . . . . . . . . . $351.00
**Nickel** . . . . . . . . . . . . . . . . . . . . . . . . . . . . . . . 373.00

Also available:
**MODEL A-100 CARRY COMP.** Same specifications as
Model A-100 (w/o compensator) but with 1" compensator;
blued finish only. **Price:**. . . . . . . . . . . . . . . . . . . . $546.00

**ASTRA MODEL A-100**
**Blued**

# EUROPEAN AMERICAN ARMORY

## WITNESS DOUBLE-ACTION PISTOLS

### SPECIFICATIONS
**Calibers:** 9mm, 38 Super, 40 S&W and 45 ACP
**Capacity:** 10 rounds; 15 rounds (9mm)
**Barrel lengths:** 4.5" (38 Super, 45 ACP, 9mm); 3⅝" (40 S&W, 45ACP, 9mm)
**Overall length:** 8.1"
**Weight:** 33 oz.
**Finish:** Blued or Wonder Finish
**Prices:**
Blue . . . . . . . . . . . . . . . . . . . . . . . . . . . . . . . $351.00
Wonder Finish . . . . . . . . . . . . . . . . . . . . . . . . . 359.00

## WITNESS FAB-92

This all-steel semiautomatic pistol features a special ambidextrous hammer drop safety/decocker system now required by many law-enforcement agencies.

### SPECIFICATIONS
**Calibers:** 9mm, 40 S&W, 45 ACP (full size only)
**Capacity:** 10 rounds
**Barrel length:** 4.5" (3⅝" Compact)
**Overall length:** 8.1" (4.5" Compact)
**Weight:** 33 oz. (30 oz. Compact)
**Finish:** Blue
**Optional:** Tritium night sights; extended magazine release; rubber grips
**Prices:**
**9mm** Blue (full and Compact) . . . . . . . . . . . . . . . $395.00
**40 S&W** Blue (full and Compact) . . . . . . . . . . . . . 425.00
**45 ACP** Blue . . . . . . . . . . . . . . . . . . . . . . . . . . 475.00

## WITNESS SUBCOMPACT (not shown)

### SPECIFICATIONS
**Calibers:** 9mm, 40 S&W, 45 ACP. **Capacity:** 10 rounds (9mm); 9 rounds (40 S&W); 8 rounds (45 ACP). **Barrel length:** 3.66". **Overall length:** 7.24". **Weight:** 30 oz. **Finish:** Blued, chrome or stainless steel.
**Prices:**
Blue . . . . . . . . . . . . . . . . . . . . . . . . . . . . . . . $351.00
Wonder Finish . . . . . . . . . . . . . . . . . . . . . . . . . 359.00

### WITNESS GOLD TEAM

## WITNESS GOLD TEAM

### SPECIFICATIONS
**Calibers:** 9mm, 40 S&W, 38 Super, 9X21mm, 45 ACP
**Capacity:** 10 rounds; 16 rounds (9mm); 19 rounds (38 Super)
**Barrel length:** 5.25" **Overall length:** 10.5"
**Weight:** 38 oz.
**Finish:** Hard chrome

**Features:** Triple chamber comp, S/A trigger, extended safety competition hammer, checkered front strap and backstrap, low-profile competition grips, square trigger guard
**Price:** . . . . . . . . . . . . . . . . . . . . . . . . . . . . $2150.00
Also available:
**WITNESS SILVER TEAM.** Same calibers as above. Features double chamber compensator, competition hammer, extended safety & magazine release, blued finish. **O.A. length:** 9.75". **Weight:** 34 oz. **Price:** . . . . . . . . . . $967.45

# EUROPEAN AMERICAN ARMORY

## EUROPEAN SINGLE-ACTION COMPACT

**SPECIFICATIONS**
**Caliber:** 380 ACP
**Capacity:** 7 rounds
**Barrel length:** 3.2"  **Overall length:** 6.5"
**Weight:** 26 oz.
**Finish:** Blued or Wonder Finish
**Features:** All-steel construction; automatic ejection; single-action trigger; European wood grips; rear sight adj. for windage; positive sighting system
**Prices:**
Blued finish . . . . . . . . . . . . . . . . . . . . . . . . . . . $132.50
Wonder Finish . . . . . . . . . . . . . . . . . . . . . . . . . . 164.00

**EUROPEAN SA COMPACT**

## WINDICATOR DOUBLE ACTION (STANDARD GRADE)

**SPECIFICATIONS**
**Calibers:** 38 Special, 357 Mag.
**Capacity:** 6 rounds
**Barrel length:** 2" or 4"
**Finish:** Blued only
**Features:** Swing-out cylinder; black rubber grips; hammer block safety
**Prices:**
**38 Special** w/2" barrel . . . . . . . . . . . . . . . . . . . . . $168.50
**38 Special** w/4" barrel . . . . . . . . . . . . . . . . . . . . . 195.00
**357 Magnum** w/2" barrel . . . . . . . . . . . . . . . . . . 187.50
**357 Magnum** w/4" barrel . . . . . . . . . . . . . . . . . . 233.50

**WINDICATOR REVOLVER**

**BIG BORE
BOUNTY HUNTER
SINGLE ACTION**

**SPECIFICATIONS**
**Calibers:** 357 Mag., 45 Long Colt and 44 Mag.
**Capacity:** 6 rounds
**Barrel length:** 4.5" or 7.5"
**Sights:** Fixed
**Weight:** 2.45 lbs. (4.5" bbl.); 2.7 lbs. (7.5" bbl.)
**Finish:** Blued or color casehardened
**Features:** Transfer-bar safety, 3-position hammer; hammer-forged barrel; walnut grips
**Prices:**
Blued or color casehardened receiver . . . . . . . . . $281.00
Also available in 22 LR/WMR
(4.75" or 6.75" barrel) w/ blue finish . . . . . . . . . . . 185.50

## SMALL BORE BOUNTY HUNTER (not shown)

**SPECIFICATIONS**
**Caliber:** 22 LR/22 WMR
**Capacity:** 6 or 8 shots
**Action:** Single action
**Barrel length:** 4.75" or 6.75" (8 lands and grooves)
**Overall length:** 9.5" or 11.5"
**Height:** 5.25"  **Weight:** 38 oz.
**Grips:** European walnut
**Sights:** Fixed
**Finish:** Blue or nickel
**Features:** Transfer bar safety
**Price:** . . . . . . . . . . . . . . . . . . . . . . . . . . . . . . . . . . $185.50

# LUGER
REG. U.S. PAT. OFF.

## STAINLESS STEEL

# AMERICAN EAGLE

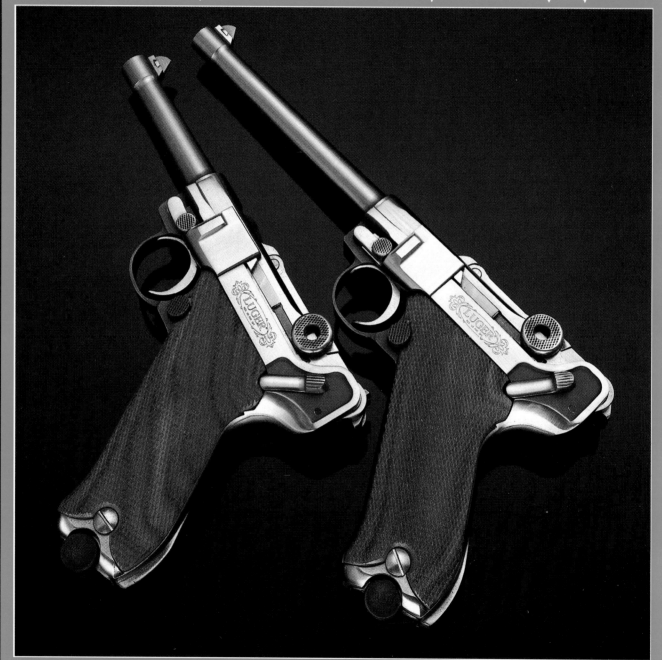

**YESTERDAY'S TRADITION - TODAY'S TECHNOLOGY**

# FEG/INTERARMS

## MARK II APK
## $269.00

### SPECIFICATIONS
**Caliber:** 380 ACP
**Capacity:** 7 rounds
**Action:** Single or double action
**Barrel length:** 3.4"
**Overall length:** 6.4"
**Height:** 4.7"  **Width:** 1.2"
**Weight:** 25 oz.
**Finish:** Blue
**Sights:** Windage-adjustable sights
**Features:** Grooved non-reflective integral sighting rib; safety acts as decocker; thumbrest target grip and field cleaning rod w/padded carrying case included

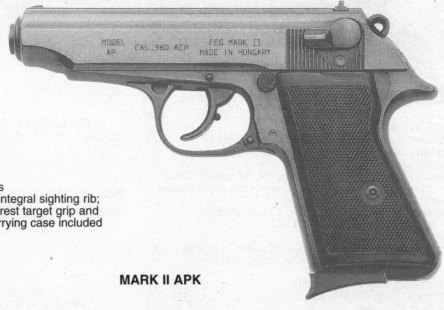

**MARK II APK**

## MARK II AP
## $269.00

### SPECIFICATIONS
**Caliber:** 380 ACP
**Capacity:** 7 rounds
**Action:** Single or double action
**Barrel length:** 3.9"
**Overall length:** 6.9"
**Height:** 4.7"  **Width:** 1.2"
**Weight:** 27 oz.
**Finish:** Blue
**Sights:** Windage-adjustable sights
**Features:** Same as Model APK

## MARK II AP22 (not shown)
## $269.00

### SPECIFICATIONS
**Caliber:** 22 LR
**Capacity:** 8 rounds
**Action:** Single or double action
**Barrel length:** 3.4"
**Overall length:** 6.3"
**Height:** 4.2"  **Width:** 1.28"
**Weight:** 23 oz.
**Finish:** Blue
**Sights:** Windage-adjustable sights
**Features:** Same as Model APK

**MARK II AP**

# FREEDOM ARMS

## MODEL 252 REVOLVER
### SILHOUETTE CLASS 10" BARREL

### 454 CASULL FIELD GRADE

**SPECIFICATIONS**
**Caliber:** 22 LR (optional 22 Magnum cylinder)
**Barrel lengths:** 5.13", 7.5" (Varmint Class) and 10"
(Silhouette Class)
**Sights:** Silhouette competition sights (Silhouette Class);
adjustable rear express sight; removable front express
blade; front sight hood
**Grips:** Black micarta (Silhouette Class); black and green
laminated hardwood (Varmint Class)
**Finish:** Stainless steel
**Features:** Dual firing pin; lightened hammer; pre-set trigger
stop; accepts all sights and/or scope mounts
**Prices:**
**Silhouette Class** (10" barrel) . . . . . . . . . . . . . . $1531.75
**Varmint Class** (5.13" & 7.5" barrels) . . . . . . . . . 1454.00
**22 Mag. Cylinder** . . . . . . . . . . . . . . . . . . . . . . . . 264.00

## SILHOUETTE/COMPETITION MODELS
### (not shown)

### MODEL 555
### PREMIER GRADE (50 AE)

**SPECIFICATIONS**
**Calibers:** 357 Magnum and 44 Rem. Mag.
**Barrel lengths:** 9" (357 Mag.) and 10" (44 Rem. Mag.)
**Sights:** Silhouette competition  **Grips:** Pachmayr
**Trigger:** Pre-set stop; trigger over travel screw
**Finish:** Field Grade
**Price:** . . . . . . . . . . . . . . . . . . . . . . . . . . . . . . . $1376.85

### MODEL 353 REVOLVER
### FIELD GRADE 7½" BARREL

**SPECIFICATIONS**
**Caliber:** 357 Magnum
**Action:** Single action  **Capacity:** 5 shots
**Barrel lengths:** 4.75", 6", 7.5", 9"
**Sights:** Removable front blade; adjustable rear
**Grips:** Pachmayr Presentation grips (Premier Grade has
impregnated hardwood grips
**Finish:** Nonglare Field Grade (standard model); Premier
Grade brushed finish (all stainless steel)
**Prices:**
**Field Grade** . . . . . . . . . . . . . . . . . . . . . . . . . $1269.00
**Premier Grade** . . . . . . . . . . . . . . . . . . . . . . . . 1673.00

### 454 CASULL & MODEL 555
### PREMIER & FIELD GRADES

**SPECIFICATIONS**
**Calibers:** 454 Casull, 44 Rem. Mag.
**Action:** Single action  **Capacity:** 5 rounds
**Barrel lengths:** 4.75", 6", 7.5", 10"
**Overall length:** 14" (w/7.5" barrel)
**Weight:** 3 lbs. 2 oz. (w/7.5" barrel)
**Safety:** Patented sliding bar
**Sights:** Notched rear; blade front (optional adjustable rear
and replaceable front blade)
**Grips:** Impregnated hardwood or rubber Pachmayr
**Finish:** Brushed stainless
**Features:** Patented interchangeable forcing cone bushing
(optional); ISGW silhouette, Millett competition and
express sights are optional; SSK T'SOB 3-ring scope
mount optional; optional cylinder in 454 Casull, 45 ACP,
45 Win. Mag. (**$311.50**)
**Prices:**
**MODEL FA-454AS Premier Grade**
W/adjustable sights . . . . . . . . . . . . . . . . . . . . . $1724.00
W/fixed sights . . . . . . . . . . . . . . . . . . . . . . . . . 1620.00
44 Remington w/adjustable sights . . . . . . . . . . . 1673.00
W/fixed sights . . . . . . . . . . . . . . . . . . . . . . . . . 1571.00
**MODEL FA-454FGAS Field Grade**
With stainless-steel matte finish, adj. sight,
Pachmayr presentation grips . . . . . . . . . . . . . 1328.00
W/fixed sights . . . . . . . . . . . . . . . . . . . . . . . . . 1218.00
44 Remington w/adjustable sights . . . . . . . . . . . 1269.00
**MODEL 555 Premier** 50 Action Express . . . . . . . 1724.00
**MODEL 555 Field** . . . . . . . . . . . . . . . . . . . . . . . 1328.00

# GLOCK

**MODEL 17L COMPETITION**

**MODEL 19 COMPACT**
**$646.00 (Fixed Sight)**

**SPECIFICATIONS**
**Caliber:** 9mm Parabellum
**Magazine capacity:** 10 rounds (15 and 17 rounds optional)*
**Barrel length:** 4" **Overall length:** 6.85" **Weight:** 21 oz.
Also available:
**MODEL 21. Caliber:** 45 ACP. **Capacity:** 10 rounds (13 rounds optional)*. **Price: $668.00** (Fixed Sight)

**MODEL 20**
**$668.00 (Fixed Sight)**

**SPECIFICATIONS**
**Caliber:** 10mm
**Magazine capacity:** 10 rounds (15 rounds optional)*
**Action:** Double action **Barrel length:** 4.6"
**Overall length:** 7.59" **Height:** 5.47" (w/sights)
**Weight:** 27.68 oz. (empty) **Sights:** Fixed
   (adjustable **$29.00 add'l**)
**Features:** 3 safeties, "safe-action" system, polymer frame

**MODEL 24 COMPETITON**
**$800.00 ($830.00 w/Compensated Barrel, Fixed Sights)**

**SPECIFICATIONS**
**Caliber:** 40 S&W **Capacity:** 10 rounds (15 rounds optional)*
**Barrel length:** 6.02" **Overall length:** 8.85"

*For law enforcement and military use only

**MODEL 17L COMPETITION**
**$800.00 (Fixed Sight)**

**SPECIFICATIONS**
**Caliber:** 9mm Parabellum
**Magazine capacity:** 10 rounds (17 and 19  rounds optional)*
**Barrel length:** 6.02" **Overall length:** 8.85"
**Weight:** 23.35 oz. (without magazine)
**Sights:** Fixed (adjustable rear sights **$28.00** add'l)

**MODEL 17 (Not Shown)**
**$616.00 (Fixed Sight)**

**SPECIFICATIONS**
**Caliber:** 9mm Parabellum
**Magazine capacity:** 10 rounds (17 and 19 rounds optional)*
**Barrel length:** 4.5" (hexagonal profile with right-hand twist)
**Overall length:** 7.32" **Weight:** 22 oz.
   (without magazine)
**Sights:** Fixed (adjustable rear sights **$28.00** add'l)

**MODEL 20**

**MODEL 24 COMPETITION**

**Weight:** 26.5 oz. (empty)
**Safety:** Manual trigger safety; passive firing block and drop safety
**Finish:** Matte (Tenifer process); nonglare

# GLOCK

## MODEL 23 COMPACT SPORT/SERVICE MODEL
## $606.00

**SPECIFICATIONS**
**Caliber:** 40 S&W
**Capacity:** 10 rounds (15 rounds optional)*
**Barrel length:** 4.5"
**Overall length:** 7.32"
**Weight:** 23 oz.

Also available:
**MODEL 22** (Sport and Service models). **Caliber:** 40 S&W. **Capacity:** 10 rounds (15 rounds optional)*. **Overall length:** 7.32". **Price: $616.00** (Fixed Sight)

## MODEL 26
## $616.00 (Fixed Sight)

**SPECIFICATIONS**
**Caliber:** 9mm  **Action:** DA
**Capacity:** 10 rounds
**Barrel length:** 3.47"
**Overall length:** 6.3"
**Weight:** 19.77 oz.
**Finish:** Matte (Tenifer process); nonglare
**Features:** 3 safeties; Safe Action trigger system; polymer frame

Also available:
**MODEL 27**. Same specifications as Model 26 but in .40 S&W. **Capacity:** 9 rounds. **Price: $616.00** (Fixed Sight)

## MODEL 29 SUBCOMPACT
## $668.00

**SPECIFICATIONS**
**Caliber:** 10mm auto
**Capacity:** 10 rounds
**Weight:** 24 oz. (approx.) **Height:** 4.5"
**Finish:** Matte (Tenifer process); nonglare
**Features:** Safe Action trigger system; two magazines provided; 6.7-inch slide

## MODEL 30 SUBCOMPACT
## $668.00

**SPECIFICATIONS**
**Caliber:** 45 ACP
**Capacity:** 10 rounds
**Weight:** 24 oz. (approx.) **Height:** 4.5"
**Finish:** Matte (Tenifer process); nonglare
**Features:** Safe Action trigger system; two magazines provided; magazine has an extended floorplate that serves as a finger rest; 6.7-inch slide

* For law enforcement and military use only.

# HÄMMERLI U.S.A. PISTOLS

## MODEL 160 FREE PISTOL
### $2085.00

**SPECIFICATIONS**
**Caliber:** 22 LR
**Barrel length:** 11.3"  **Overall length:** 17.5"
**Height:** 5.7"  **Weight:** 45 oz.
**Trigger action:** Infinitely variable set trigger weight; cocking lever located on left of receiver; trigger length variable along weapon axis
**Sights:** Sight radius 14.8"; micrometer rear sight adj. for windage and elevation
**Locking action:** Martini-type locking action w/side-mounted locking lever

**MODEL 160
FREE PISTOL**

**Barrel:** Free floating, cold swaged precision barrel w/low axis relative to the hand
**Ignition:** Horizontal firing pin (hammerless) in line w/barrel axis; firing pin travel 0.15"
**Grips:** Selected walnut w/adj. hand rest for direct arm to barrel extension

## MODEL 162 ELECTRONIC PISTOL
### $2295.00

**SPECIFICATIONS**
Same as **Model 160** except trigger action is electronic.
**Features:** Short lock time (1.7 milliseconds between trigger actuation and firing pin impact), light trigger pull, and extended battery life.

**MODEL 162
ELECTRONIC PISTOL**

## MODEL 208S STANDARD PISTOL
### $1925.00

**SPECIFICATIONS**
**Caliber:** 22 LR  **Capacity:** 8 rounds
**Action:** Single
**Barrel length:** 5.9"  **Overall length:** 10"
**Height:** 5.9"  **Weight:** 36.7 oz.
**Sight radius:** 8.2"
**Sights:** Micrometer rear sight w/notch width; adj. for windage & elevation; standard front blade
**Trigger:** Adj. for pull weight, travel, slackweight & creep
**Safety:** Rotating knob on rear of frame

**MODEL 208S
STANDARD PISTOL**

## MODEL 280 TARGET PISTOL
### $1565.00 ($1765.00 in 32 S&W)

**SPECIFICATIONS**
**Calibers:** 22 LR and 32 S&W
**Capacity:** 6 rounds (22 LR); 5 rounds (32 S&W)
**Action:** Single
**Barrel length:** 4.58"  **Overall length:** 11.8"
**Height:** 5.9"
**Weight:** (excluding counterweights) 34.6 oz. (22 LR); 41.8 oz. (32 S&W)
**Sight radius:** 8.7"  **Sights:** Micrometer adjustable
**Grips:** Orthopedic type; stippled walnut w/adj. palm shelf
**Features:** 3 steel & 3 carbon fiber barrel weight; combination tool; 4 Allen wrenches; dry fire plug; magazine loading tool; extra magazine
Also available:
**MODEL 280 TARGET PISTOL COMBO**
With carrying case . . . . . . . . . . . . . . . . . . . . . . $2595.00
Conversion Unit (22 LR) . . . . . . . . . . . . . . . . . . . . 765.00
In 32 S&W . . . . . . . . . . . . . . . . . . . . . . . . . . . . . 965.00

**MODEL 280
TARGET PISTOL**

# HARRINGTON & RICHARDSON

**MODEL 929 SIDEKICK**

## MODEL 929 SIDEKICK REVOLVER
### $159.95

**SPECIFICATIONS**
**Calibers:** 22 Short, Long, Long Rifle
**Action:** Single and double action
**Capacity:** 9 rounds
**Barrel length:** 6" (w/sighting rib)
**Weight:** 36 oz.
**Sights:** Fixed front; fully adjustable rear
**Grips:** Walnut finished hardwood; nickel medallion
**Finish:** High-polish blue

**MODEL 939 PREMIER
TARGET REVOLVER**

## MODEL 939 PREMIER
## TARGET REVOLVER
### $184.95

**SPECIFICATIONS**
**Calibers:** 22 Short, Long, Long Rifle
**Capacity:** 9 rounds
**Barrel length:** 6"
**Weight:** 36 oz.
**Grips:** Walnut hardwood; nickel medallion
**Sights:** Fully adjustable rear; fixed front
**Features:** Two-piece walnut-stained hardwood western-styled grip frame profile, transfer bar system; made of high-quality ferrous metals

## FORTY-NINER CLASSIC
## WESTERN REVOLVER
### $184.95

**SPECIFICATIONS**
**Calibers:** 22 Short, Long and Long Rifle
**Capacity:** 9 rounds
**Barrel length:** 5.5" or 7.5" (case colored)
**Weight:** 36 oz. (5.5" barrel); 38 oz. (7.5" barrel)
**Sights:** Fixed front; drift-adjustable rear
**Grips:** Two-piece walnut-stained hardwood; nickel medallion

**FORTY-NINER CLASSIC
WESTERN REVOLVER**

## SPORTSMAN 999 REVOLVER
### $279.95

**SPECIFICATIONS**
**Calibers:** 22 Short, Long, Long Rifle
**Action:** Single and double
**Capacity:** 9 rounds
**Barrel lengths:** 4" and 6" (both fluted)
**Weight:** 30 oz. (4" barrel); 34 oz. (6" barrel)
**Sights:** Windage adjustable rear; elevation adjustable front
**Grips:** Walnut-finished hardwood
**Finish:** Blued

**SPORTSMAN
999 REVOLVER**

# HECKLER & KOCH

**MODEL HK USP**

## MODEL HK USP

**SPECIFICATIONS**
**Calibers:** 9mm, 45 ACP and 40 S&W
**Capacity:** 10 + 1
**Operating system:** Short recoil, modified Browning action
**Barrel length:** 4.25"   **Overall length:** 7.64"
**Weight:** 1.74 lbs. (40 S&W); 1.66 lbs. (9mm)
**Height:** 5.35"   **Sights:** Adjustable 3-dot
**Grips:** Polymer receiver and integral grips
**Prices:**
9mm & 40 S&W . . . . . . . . . . . . . . . . . . . . . . . . . . **$636.00**
  W/control lever on right . . . . . . . . . . . . . . . . . . **656.00**
45 ACP . . . . . . . . . . . . . . . . . . . . . . . . . . . . . . . . **696.00**
  W/control lever on right. . . . . . . . . . . . . . . . . . **716.00**
Mark II Universal Tactical Pistol Light (UTL) . . . . . **267.00**

## MODEL USP45 UNIVERSAL SELF-LOADING PISTOL

**SPECIFICATIONS**
**Caliber:** 45 ACP   **Capacity:** 10 rounds
**Action:** DA/SA or DAO
**Barrel length:** 4.41"   **Overall length:** 7.87"
**Height:** 5.55"   **Weight:** 1.90 lbs.
**Grips:** Polymer frame & integral grips
**Prices:**
Variants* 1, 3, 5, 7, 9 . . . . . . . . . . . . . . . . . . . . . **$696.00**
Variants* 2, 4, 6, 10 . . . . . . . . . . . . . . . . . . . . . . **716.00**
Stainless steel, **add** . . . . . . . . . . . . . . . . . . . . . . **45.00**
* Variants refers to availabilty of control lever options for
  right- or left-hand shooters

Also available in 9mm and 40 S&W. **Barrel length:** 4.25".
**Overall length:** 7.64". **Weight:** 1.75 lbs. **Price: $681.00**
(**$701.00** w/control lever on right)

**MODEL USP45 UNIVERSAL SELF-LOADING PISTOL**

## HK USP COMPACT UNIVERSAL SELF-LOADING PISTOL

**SPECIFICATIONS**
**Calibers:** 9mm and 40 S&W
**Capacity:** 10 rounds
**Operating system:** Short recoil, modified Browning action
**Barrel length:** 3.58"   **Overall length:** 6.81"
**Weight:** 1.70 lbs. (40 S&W); 1.60 lbs. (9mm)
**Height:** 5"   **Sights:** Adjustable 3-dot
**Grips:** Polymer frame and integral grips
**Prices:**
9mm and 40 S&W . . . . . . . . . . . . . . . . . . . . . . . . **$665.00**
W/control lever on right. . . . . . . . . . . . . . . . . . . . . **685.00**

Also available:
**HK USP COMPACT UNIVERSAL
SELF-LOADING PISTOL.** Same specifications as above
but with stainless steel slide: **$710.00**; w/control lever
on right **$730.00**

**HK USP COMPACT UNIVERSAL SELF-LOADING PISTOL**

**HK USP45 MATCH PISTOL**

## HK USP45 MATCH PISTOL

**SPECIFICATIONS**
**Caliber:** 45 ACP
**Capacity:** 10 rounds
**Operating system:** Short recoil, modified Browning action
**Barrel length:** 6.02"
**Overall length:** 9.45"
**Weight:** 2.38 lbs.
**Height:** 5.90"
**Sights:** Adjustable 3-dot
**Grips & Stock:** Polymer frame and integral grips
**Prices:**
Blued . . . . . . . . . . . . . . . . . . . . . . . . . . . . . . . . . . . $1329.00
Stainless Steel . . . . . . . . . . . . . . . . . . . . . . . . . . . . 1399.00

## MARK 23 SPECIAL OPERATIONS PISTOL (SOCOM)

**SPECIFICATIONS**
**Caliber:** 45 ACP
**Capacity:** 10 rounds
**Operating system:** Short recoil, modified Browning action
**Barrel length:** 5.87"
**Overall length:** 9.65"
**Height:** 5.9"
**Weight:** 2.66 lbs.
**Sights:** 3-dot
**Grips:** Polymor frame & integral grips
**Price:** . . . . . . . . . . . . . . . . . . . . . . . . . . . . . $1995.00

**MARK 23 SPECIAL
OPERATIONS PISTOL (SOCOM)**

**MODEL P7M8**

## MODEL P7M8

**SPECIFICATIONS**
**Caliber:** 9mmX19 (Luger)
**Capacity:** 8 rounds
**Barrel length:** 4.13"
**Overall length:** 6.73"
**Weight:** 1.75 lbs. (empty)
**Sight radius:** 5.83"
**Sights:** Adjustable rear
**Grips:** Plastic
**Finish:** Blue or nickel
**Operating System:** Recoil-operated; retarded inertia slide
**Price:** . . . . . . . . . . . . . . . . . . . . . . . . . . . . . . . . $1187.00

# HERITAGE MANUFACTURING

**ROUGH RIDER SA**

## SENTRY DOUBLE ACTION

**SPECIFICATIONS**
**Caliber:** 38 Special  **Capacity:** 6 rounds
**Barrel length:** 2"  **Overall length:** 6.5"
**Weight:** 21 oz.
**Sights:** Ramped front, fixed rear
**Grips:** Black polymer  **Finish:** Blued or nickel
**Features:** Internal hammer block; additional safety plug in cylinder, transfer bar safety.
**Prices:**
Blued . . . . . . . . . . . . . . . . . . . . . . . . . . . . . . . . . **$129.95**
Nickel . . . . . . . . . . . . . . . . . . . . . . . . . . . . . . . . **139.95**

**SPECIFICATIONS**
**Caliber:** 22 LR or 22 LR/22 WMR
**Capacity:** 6 rounds  **Weight:** 31 to 38 oz.
**Barrel lengths:** 4.75", 6.5", 9" (regular grip); 2.75", 3.75", 4.75" (Bird's-Head grip)
**Sights:** Blade front, fixed rear
**Grips:** Exotic hardwood  **Finish:** Blued or nickel
**Features:** Rotating hammer block safety; brass accent screws
**Prices:**
**22 LR** (4.75", 6.5" bbl.) blued, regular grip . . . . . . **$109.95**
**22 LR/22 WMR**
W/blued finish, regular grip:
  4.75" & 6.5" barrels . . . . . . . . . . . . . . . . . . . . . **129.95**
  9" barrel . . . . . . . . . . . . . . . . . . . . . . . . . . . . . . **139.95**
W/nickel finish, regular grip:
  4.75" & 6.5" barrels . . . . . . . . . . . . . . . . . . . . . **149.95**
  9" barrel . . . . . . . . . . . . . . . . . . . . . . . . . . . . . . **169.95**
W/blued finish, bird's-head grip:
  2.75", 3.75" & 4.75" barrels . . . . . . . . . . . . . . . **129.95**
W/nickel finish: bird's-head grip:
  2.75", 3.75" & 4.75" barrels . . . . . . . . . . . . . . . **149.95**

## STEALTH COMPACT PISTOL

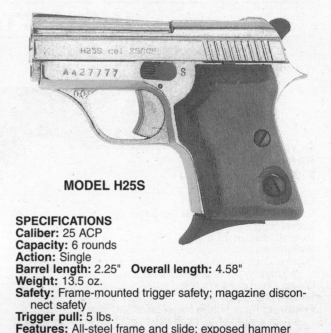

**MODEL H25S**

**SPECIFICATIONS**
**Caliber:** 9mm  **Capacity:** 10 rounds
**Barrel length:** 3.9"  **Overall length:** 6.3"
**Weight:** 20 oz.  **Height:** 4.2"
**Triggerpull:** 4 lbs.
**Frame:** Black polymer
**Styles:** Model C-1000 17-4 Stainless steel slide
       Model C-2000 17-4 Black chrome slide
       Model C-1010 17-4 Two-tone stainless steel/black chrome slide
**Features:** Striker-fire trigger; gas-delayed blow back action; frame-mounted ambidextrous trigger safety; drop safety; closed breech safety; magazine disconnect safety
**Price:** all styles. . . . . . . . . . . . . . . . . . . . . . . . . **$299.95**

**SPECIFICATIONS**
**Caliber:** 25 ACP
**Capacity:** 6 rounds
**Action:** Single
**Barrel length:** 2.25"  **Overall length:** 4.58"
**Weight:** 13.5 oz.
**Safety:** Frame-mounted trigger safety; magazine disconnect safety
**Trigger pull:** 5 lbs.
**Features:** All-steel frame and slide; exposed hammer
**Prices:**
Blued . . . . . . . . . . . . . . . . . . . . . . . . . . . . . . . . . **$149.95**
Nickel . . . . . . . . . . . . . . . . . . . . . . . . . . . . . . . . **159.95**

# HI-POINT FIREARMS

**MODEL 9mm**

**380 POLYMER**

### MODEL 9mm
### $139.95

**SPECIFICATIONS**
**Caliber:** 9mm Parabellum
**Capacity:** 9 shots
**Barrel length:** 4.5"
**Overall length:** 7.72"
**Weight:** 39 oz.
**Sights:** 3-dot type
**Features:** Quick on-off thumb safety; nonglare military black finish

### MODEL 380 POLYMER
### $79.95

**SPECIFICATIONS**
**Caliber:** 380 ACP
**Capacity:** 8 shots
**Barrel length:** 3.5"
Also available:
**MODEL 45** in 45 ACP. Same specifications as the 9mm, except w/7-shot capacity and two-tone Polymer finish.
**Price:**. . . . . . . . . . . . . . . . . . . . . . . . . . . . . . . . **$148.95**
**MODEL 40** in 40 S&W. Same specifications as the 45 ACP w/8-shot capacity. . . . . . . . . . . . . . . . . . . . . 148.95
**MODEL 9mm COMPACT** w/3.5" barrel. . . . . . . . . 124.95

# HIGH STANDARD

**OLYMPIC
RAPID FIRE
$1995.00**

**SPECIFICATIONS**
**Caliber:** 22 Short   **Capacity:** 5 rounds
**Barrel length:** 4"
**Overall length:** 11.5"
**Weight:** 46 oz.
**Sights:** Click-adjustable for windage and elevation (rear); mounted on vent aluminum rib
**Grips:** Special International
**Finish:** Matte blue
**Features:** Push-button barrel takedown system; trigger adj.for weight of pull and travel; gold-plated trigger, slide stop, safety and magazine release
Also available:
**OLYMPIC MILITARY** w/5.5" barrel . . . . . . . . . . . . **$562.00**

**OLYMPIC
RAPID FIRE**

# HIGH STANDARD

## SUPERMATIC CITATION
### $468.00

**SPECIFICATIONS**
**Caliber:** 22 LR  **Capacity:** 10 rounds
**Barrel length:** 5.5"  **Overall length:** 9.5"
**Weight:** 44 oz.
**Finish:** Blued or Parkerized
**Features:** Optional Universal Mount to replace open-sight rib (deduct $30.00)
Also available:
**SUPERMATIC CITATION MS**. Similar to Citation above, except 10" barrel (14" overall), 54 oz. weight, RPM sights click-adjustable for windage and elevation, checkered right-hand thumbrest and matte blue finish. . . . . . . . . **$632.00**
**TROPHY/CITATION 22 Short Conversion Kit** (incl. barrel w/sight, slide, 2 magazines) . . . . . . . . . . . . . . . . **$309.00**

## SUPERMATIC TROPHY
### $542.00 (5.5" Barrel)
### $587.00 (7.25" Barrel)

**SPECIFICATIONS**
**Caliber:** 22 LR  **Capacity:** 10 rounds
**Action:** Recoil-operated semiautomatic
**Barrel length:** 5.5" bull or 7.25" fluted
**Overall length:** 9.5 (w/5.5" bbl.) and 11.25" (w/7.25" bbl.)
**Weight:** 44 oz. (w/5.5" bbl.) and 46 oz. (w/7.25" bbl.)
**Sights:** Click-adjustable rear for windage/elevation; undercut ramp front
**Grips:** Checkered American walnut with right-hand thumbrest (left-hand optional)
**Features:** Gold-plated trigger; slide lock lever; push-button takedown system; magazine release
Also available:
**22 Short Conversion Kit** (see left)

## SUPERMATIC TOURNAMENT
### $468.00

**SPECIFICATIONS**
**Caliber:** 22 LR
**Capacity:** 10 rounds
**Barrel length:** 5.5"
**Overall length:** 9.5"
**Weight:** 44 oz.
**Finish:** Matte frame
**Features:** Fully adjustable rear sight; non-adjustable trigger

## VICTOR 22 LR
### $502.00 ($558.00 w/ 5.5" barrel)

**SPECIFICATIONS**
**Caliber:** 22 LR  **Capacity:** 10 rounds
**Barrel lengths:** 4.5" and 5.5"
**Overall length:** 8.5" and 9.5"
**Weight:** 45 oz. (w/4.5" bbl.); 46 oz. (w/5.5" bbl.)
**Finish:** Blued or Parkerized frame
**Features:** Optional steel rib; click-adjustable sights for windage and elevation; optional barrel weights and Universal Mount (to replace open-sight rib)
Also avaliable:
**22 Short Conversion Kit** 5.5" barrel w/vent rib, slide, two magazines . . . . . . . . . . . . . . . . . . . . . . . . . . . . . . **$397.00**

# ISRAEL ARMS

## KAREEN MK II COMPACT
### $450.00

**SPECIFICATIONS**
**Caliber:** 9mm, 40 S&W
**Capacity:** 10 rounds
**Barrel length:** 3.9"
**Overall length:** 6"
**Height:** 5.1"  **Weight:** 32.2 oz.
**Features:** Ambidextrous safety; rubberized grips; 41/40 steel; extended hammer protection: improved trigger guard
Also available:
**KAREEN MK II.** Single-action semiautomatic with the same specifications as the Kareen MK II Compact, except 4.6" barrel (7.78" overall) and weight 33.6 oz. . . . . . . . . **$410.50**

**KAREEN MKII**

## GAL 45 ACP
### $480.00

**SPECIFICATIONS**
**Caliber:** 45 ACP
**Capacity:** 8 rounds
**Barrel length:** 4.25"
**Overall length:** 6"
**Height:** 5.25"  **Weight:** 42 oz.
**Finish:** Blued and satin
**Sights:** Low-profile fixed three-dot configuration
**Features:** Slide grooved across top; competition trigger, hammer and slide stop; wraparound combat-style grips

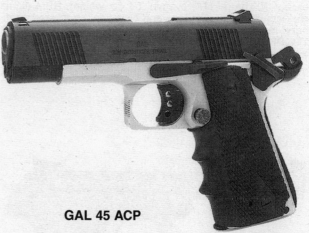

**GAL 45 ACP**

## GOLAN DA
### $649.50

**SPECIFICATIONS**
**Calibers:** 9mm, 40 S&W
**Capacity:** 10 rounds
**Barrel length:** 3.9"
**Overall length:** 7"
**Height:** 5.4"  **Weight:** 34 oz.
**Features:** Double action; forged steel slide; ambidextrous controls; drop proof safety; chromed barrel; internal automatic safety
Also available:
In 45 ACP, 8 shots, 4.25" barrel (7.75" overall), weight 36 oz. rubberized wraparound grip, forged-steel frame and slide, competition trigger, hammer, slide stop, standard two-tone.
**Price** . . . . . . . . . . . . . . . . . . . . . . . . . . . . . . . . **$525.00**

**GOLAN**

# JENNINGS FIREARMS

**J-22 TARGET PISTOL**
**$179.00**

**SPECIFICATIONS**
**Caliber:** 22  **Capacity:** 10 rounds
**Barrel length:** 5"
**Weight:** 28 oz.
**Sights:** Screw adjustable sights; red front
**Features:** Steel thumb safety on left grip blocks sear, locks side and becomes slide hold open after last round; red loaded chamber indicator; serrated trigger; quick magazine release

**LAZER NINE (not shown)**
**$249.00**

**SPECIFICATIONS**
**Caliber:** 9mm  **Capacity:** 7 shots
**Overall length:** 6"
**Height:** 4"  **Weight:** 14 oz.
**Sights:** Laser sights
**Features:** Polymer frame; slide hold open; locked breech; extra 7-shot magazine

**JENNINGS NINE (not shown)**
**$145.00**

**SPECIFICATIONS**
**Caliber:** 9mm
**Capacity:** 13 rounds (law enforcement only)
**Barrel length:** 6.7"
**Height:** 4.8"  **Weight:** 30 0z.
**Sights:** Red front sight
**Features:** Serrated target trigger; slide hold open (last round); internal drop safety; improved grip contour; loaded chamber indicator; screw adjustment sight; internal drop safety; quick magazine release

# KAHR ARMS

**MODEL K9 PISTOL**

All key components of the Kahr K9-frame, slide, barrel, etc.-mare made from 4140 steel, allowing the pistol to chamber reliably and fire virtually any commercial 9mm ammo, including +P rounds. The frame and sighting surfaces are matte blued, and the sides of the slide carry a polished blue finish. The grips are crafted from exotic wood.

The unique trigger system holds the striker in a partially cocked state; then, a pull of the trigger completes the cocking cycle and releases the striker. Recoil on firing partially cocks the striker for the next trigger pull. This design allows a lighter-than-normal "DA" pull that is consistent from shot to shot. A trigger-activated firing-pin block prevents accidental discharge. Like a double-action revolver, no other safeties are needed.

**SPECIFICATIONS**
**Caliber:** 9mm (9x19), 40 S&W
**Capacity:** 7 rounds (6 rounds 40 S&W)
**Barrel length:** 3.5"
**Overall length:** 6" (6.1" 40 S&W)
**Height:** 4.5" (4.55" 40 S&W)
**Weight (empty):** 25 oz.; 26 oz. (40 S&W)
**Grips:** Wraparound soft polymer
**Sights:** Drift-adjustable, low-profile white bar-dot combat sights
**Finish:** Nonglare matte black finish on slide, frame & sighting surfaces, electroless nickel, black titanium, satin hard chrome (matte black, electroless nickel only in 40 S&W)
**Features:** Trigger cocking safety; passive firing-pin block; no magazine disconnect; locked breech

**Prices: K9 PISTOL**
Matte black. . . . . . . . . . . . . . . . . . . . . . . . . $538.00
Matte black w/night sights. . . . . . . . . . . . . . . 624.00
Matte electroless nickel. . . . . . . . . . . . . . . . 612.00
Electroless nickle w/night sights . . . . . . . . . . . 699.00
Black titanium. . . . . . . . . . . . . . . . . . . . . . 638.00
Black titanium w/night sights. . . . . . . . . . . . . . 725.00

**Prices: LADY K9**
Lightened recoil spring, matte black . . . . . . . . . . 545.00
W/night sights. . . . . . . . . . . . . . . . . . . . . . 631.00
Satin electroless nickel . . . . . . . . . . . . . . . . 619.00
Electroless nickel w/night sights . . . . . . . . . . . . 706.00

# KBI PISTOLS

### FEG SMC-22 AUTO PISTOL
### $279.00

**SPECIFICATIONS**
**Calibers:** 22 LR and 380 ACP
**Capacity:** 6 rounds (380 ACP) or 8 rounds (22 LR)
**Barrel length:** 3.5"
**Overall length:** 6 1/8"
**Weight:** 18.5 oz.
**Stock:** Checkered composition w/thumbrest
**Sights:** Blade front; rear adjustable for windage
**Features:** Alloy frame; steel slide; double action; blue finish; two magazines and cleaning rod standard

**FEG SMC-22**

### FEG MODEL PJK-9HP
### $319.00

**SPECIFICATIONS**
**Caliber:** 9mm Luger Parabellum
**Magazine capacity:** 10 rounds
**Action:** Single
**Barrel length:** 4.75"
**Overall length:** 8"
**Weight:** 21 oz.
**Grips:** Hand-checkered walnut
**Safety:** Thumb safety
**Sights:** 3-dot system
**Finish:** Blue
**Features:** One 10-round magazine, cleaning rod

**FEG MODEL
PJK-9HP**

### FEG MODEL SMC-380
### $279.00

**SPECIFICATIONS**
**Calibers:** 22 LR, 380 ACP, 9mm Makarov (9X18)
**Capacity:** 6 rounds (10 rds in 22 LR)
**Action:** Double
**Barrel length:** 3.5"
**Overall length:** 6 1/8"
**Weight:** 18.5 oz.
**Safety:** Thumb safety w/decocking
**Grips:** Black composite
**Features:** High-luster blued steel slide; blue anodized aluminum alloy frame

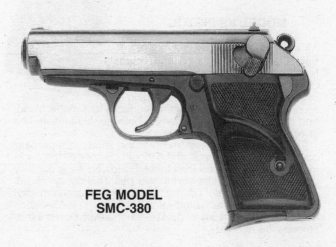

**FEG MODEL
SMC-380**

# KBI HANDGUNS

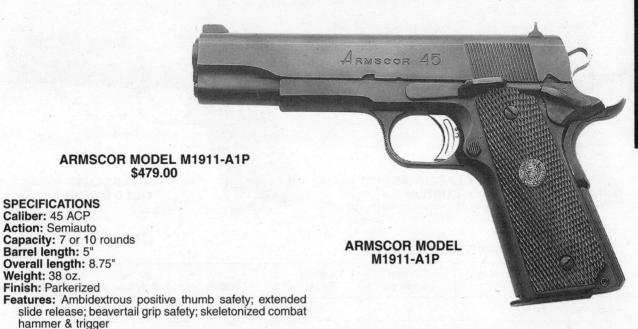

## ARMSCOR MODEL M1911-A1P
### $479.00

**SPECIFICATIONS**
**Caliber:** 45 ACP
**Action:** Semiauto
**Capacity:** 7 or 10 rounds
**Barrel length:** 5"
**Overall length:** 8.75"
**Weight:** 38 oz.
**Finish:** Parkerized
**Features:** Ambidextrous positive thumb safety; extended slide release; beavertail grip safety; skeletonized combat hammer & trigger

**ARMSCOR MODEL
M1911-A1P**

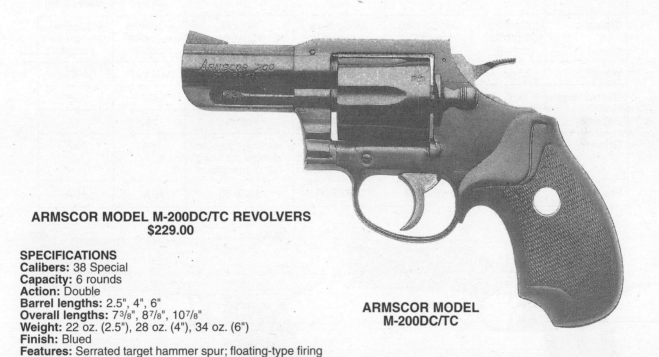

## ARMSCOR MODEL M-200DC/TC REVOLVERS
### $229.00

**SPECIFICATIONS**
**Calibers:** 38 Special
**Capacity:** 6 rounds
**Action:** Double
**Barrel lengths:** 2.5", 4", 6"
**Overall lengths:** $7^3/_8$", $8^7/_8$", $10^7/_8$"
**Weight:** 22 oz. (2.5"), 28 oz. (4"), 34 oz. (6")
**Finish:** Blued
**Features:** Serrated target hammer spur; floating-type firing pin (mounted in frame); transfer bar safety; full shroud; combat style rubber grips (Model M-200 DC) or checkered wood grips (Model M-200TC)

**ARMSCOR MODEL
M-200DC/TC**

# KIMBER ARMS

**CLASSIC .45
CUSTOM**

**CLASSIC .45
GOLD MATCH**

## SPECIFICATIONS KIMBER CLASSIC .45 ACP

| Model | Custom | Custom Stainless | Custom Royal | Gold Match | Matte Polymer | Stainless Polymer |
|---|---|---|---|---|---|---|
| **Barrel length** | 5" | 5" | 5" | 5" | 5" | 5" |
| **Finish** | Matte black oxide | Satin stainless steel | Highly polished blue | Highly polished blue | Matte black oxide (slide) | Satin stainless steel (slide) |
| **Sights** | McCormick low-profile combat | McCormick low-profile combat | McCormick low-profile combat | Kimber adjustable | McCormick low-profile combat | McCormick low-profile combat |
| **Weight** | 38 oz. | 38 oz. | 38 oz. | 38 oz. | 34.4 oz. | 34.4 oz. |
| **Overall length** | 8.5" | 8.5" | 8.5" | 8.5" | 8.75" | 8.75" |
| **Capacity** | 7 | 7 | 7(2) | 8/10 | 13 | 13 |
| **Grips** | Black synthetic | Black synthetic | Rosewood double diamond hand-checkered | Premium rosewood double diamond hand-checkered | N/A | N/A |
| **Prices** | $615.00 | $690.00 | $739.00 | $935.00 | N/A | N/A |

**CLASSIC .45
CUSTOM ROYAL**

**CLASSIC .45
CUSTOM STAINLESS**

# L.A.R. GRIZZLY

## MARK I GRIZZLY
### 45 Win Mag $1000.00    357 Magnum $1014.00

This semiautomatic pistol is a direct descendant of the tried and trusted 1911-type .45 automatic, but with the added advantage of increased caliber capacity.

**SPECIFICATIONS**
**Calibers:** 45 Win. Mag., 45 ACP, 357 Mag., 10mm
**Magazine capacity:** 7 rounds
**Barrel lengths:** 5.4" and 6.5"
**Overall length:** 10.5"
**Weight** (empty): 48 oz.
**Height:** 5.75"
**Sights:** Fixed, ramped blade (front); fully adjustable for elevation and windage (rear)

**Grips:** Checkered rubber, nonslip, combat-type
**Safeties:** Grip depressor, manual thumb, slide-out-of-battery disconnect
**Materials:** Mil spec 4140 steel slide and receiver with non-corrosive, heat-treated, special alloy steels for other parts. All models available in blue, Parkerized, chrome, two-tone or nickel.

Also available:
**Grizzly 44 Magnum Mark IV** w/adj. sights . . . . . **$1014.00**
**Grizzly Win Mag Conversion Units**
   In 45 Win. Mag., 45 ACP, 10mm . . . . . . . . . . . 233.00
   In 357 Magnum . . . . . . . . . . . . . . . . . . . . . . . 248.00
**Win Mag Compensator** . . . . . . . . . . . . . . . . . . . 119.00
   In 50 caliber . . . . . . . . . . . . . . . . . . . . . . . . . 130.00

**L.A.R.GRIZZLY
MARK I**

**L.A.R.GRIZZLY
MARK V**

## GRIZZLY 50 MARK 5
### $1152.00

**SPECIFICATIONS**
**Caliber:** 50 AE   **Capacity:** 6 rounds
**Barrel lengths:** 5.4" and 6.5"
**Overall length:** 10⅝"
**Weight:** 56 oz.   **Height:** 5.75"
**Sights:** Fixed front; fully adjustable rear
**Features:** Browning–type short recoil; locked breech

**L.A.R.GRIZZLY
MARK IV**

# LASERAIM TECHNOLOGIES

## LASERAIM SERIES I PISTOLS

### SPECIFICATIONS
**Calibers:** 45 ACP, 10mm
**Capacity:** 7+1 (45 ACP) and 8+1 (10mm)
**Barrel lengths:** 3⁷/₈" and 5.5"
**Overall length:** 8.75" (3⁷/₈") and 10.5"
**Weight:** 46 oz. (3 ⁷/₈") and 52 oz.
**Features:** Adjustable Millet sights, ambidextrous safety, beavertail tang, non-glare slide serration, beveled magazine well, extended slide release
**Price:**. . . . . . . . . . . . . . . . . . . . . . . . . . . . . . . . . . **$499.00**

Also available:
**DREAM TEAM** w/Laseraim Laser, fixed sights, HOTDOT . . . . . . . . . . . . . . . . . . . . . . . . . . . . . **$599.00**

The Series I pistol features a dual port compensated barrel and vented slide to reduce recoil and improve control. Other features include stainless-steel construction, ramped barrel, accurized barrel bushing and fixed sights (Laseraim's "HOT-DOT" sight or Auto Illusion electronic red dot sight available as options).

## LASERAIM SERIES III PISTOLS

## LASERAIM VELOCITY 357/400 HIGH SPEED SERIES

This all-stainless steel line of handguns features an extended slide release, skeletonized hammer and safety, and a serrated slide. These improvements lower overall weight and reduce action time. Available in ported full-size and non-ported compact versions in the popular 357 SIG and 400 COR-BON calibers.

The **Velocity 400** model features the new 400 COR-BON (a 45 ACP necked down to 40 S&W), adding to its speed and stopping power by 60 percent. The **Velocity 357** model offers the 357 SIG (a 40 caliber necked down to 357) in a lightweight package with the same speed and stopping power as the 400 CAR-BON. Both are available in 3⁵/₈" and 5" barrels.
**Prices:**
3⁵/₈" barrel . . . . . . . . . . . . . . . . . . . . . . . . . . . . . . **$399.00**
5" barrel . . . . . . . . . . . . . . . . . . . . . . . . . . . . . . . . . **449.00**

# LLAMA AUTOMATIC PISTOLS

**SMALL-FRAME 380 AUTOMATIC**

## LLAMA CLASSIC AUTOMATIC PISTOL SPECIFICATIONS (prices on following page)

| Type: | Small-Frame | Compact-Frame | Government Model |
|---|---|---|---|
| **Calibers:** | 380 Auto | 45 Auto | 45 Auto |
| **Frame:** | Precision machined from high-strength steel | Precision machined from high-strength steel | Precision machined from high-strength steel |
| **Trigger:** | Serrated | Serrated | Serrated |
| **Hammer:** | External; wide spur, serrated | External; military style | External; military style |
| **Operation:** | Straight blow-back | Locked breech | Locked breech |
| **Loaded Chamber Indicator:** | Yes | Yes | Yes |
| **Safeties:** | Extended manual & grip safeties | Extended manual & beavertail grip safeties | Extended manual & beavertail grip safeties |
| **Grips:** | Matte black polymer | Anatomically designed rubber grips | Anatomically designed rubber grips |
| **Sights:** | Patridge-type front; square-notch rear | 3-dot combat sight | 3-dot combat sights |
| **Sight Radius:** | 4 1/4" | 6 1/4" | 6 1/4" |
| **Magazine Capacity:** | 7 shots | 10 shots | 10 shots |
| **Weight:** | 23 oz. | 39 oz. | 41 oz. |
| **Barrel Length:** | 3 11/16" | 4 1/4" | 5 1/8" |
| **Overall Length:** | 6 1/2" | 7 7/8" | 8 1/2" |
| **Height:** | 4 3/8" | 5 7/16" | 5 5/16" |
| **Finish:** | Standard: High-polished, deep blue. Deluxe: Satin chrome | Non-glare combat matte | Non-glare combat matte |

# LLAMA PISTOLS

**MINIMAX-II 45**

## CLASSICS/MAX-I AUTO PISTOLS

**Matte Finish**
380 Auto 7-Shot SF . . . . . . . . . . . . . . . . . . . . . .$258.95
9mm Auto 8-Shot Mini Compact . . . . . . . . . . . . 374.95
40 S&W Auto 7-Shot Mini Compact . . . . . . . . . . 374.95
45 Auto 6-Shot Mini Compact . . . . . . . . . . . . . . 374.95
45 Auto 10-Shot Mini Compact . . . . . . . . . . . . . 398.95
45 Auto 7-Shot Gov't Model . . . . . . . . . . . . . . . 358.95
45 Auto 10-Shot Gov't Model . . . . . . . . . . . . . . 408.95
45 Auto 10-Shot Compact Model . . . . . . . . . . . . 408.95
**Satin Chrome Finish**
380 Auto 7-Shot SF . . . . . . . . . . . . . . . . . . . . . 291.95
9mm Auto 8-Shot Mini Compact . . . . . . . . . . . . 419.95
40 S&W Auto 7-Shot Mini Compact . . . . . . . . . . 419.95
45 Auto 6-Shot Mini Compact . . . . . . . . . . . . . . 419.95
45 Auto 10-Shot Mini Compact . . . . . . . . . . . . . 431.95
45 Auto 7-Shot Gov't Model . . . . . . . . . . . . . . . 408.95
45 Auto 10-Shot Gov't Model . . . . . . . . . . . . . . 424.95
45 Auto 10-Shot Compact Model . . . . . . . . . . . . 424.95
**Duo-Tone Finish**
45 Auto 7-Shot Gov't Model . . . . . . . . . . . . . . . 374.95
45 Auto 6-Shot Mini Compact Model . . . . . . . . . 391.95

| | MAX-I 9-SHOT 9mm | | MAXI-I 7-SHOT 45 Auto | |
|---|---|---|---|---|
| | **Compact Frame** | **Government Model** | **Compact Frame** | **Government Model** |
| **Calibers:** | 9mm | 9mm | 45 Auto | 45 Auto |
| **Mag. Capacity:** | 9 | 9 | 7 | 7 |
| **Action:** | Single | Single | Single | Single |
| **Operation:** | Locked breech | Locked breech | Locked breech | Locked breech |
| **Barrel Length:** | 4 1/4" | 5 1/8" | 4 1/4" | 5 1/8" |
| **Overall Length:** | 7 7/8" | 8 1/2" | 7 7/8" | 8 1/2" |
| **Weight:** | 34 oz. | 36 oz. | 34 oz. | 36 oz. |
| **Height:** | 5 7/16" | 5 7/16" | 5 7/16" | 5 5/16" |
| **Frame:** | Precision machined from high-strength steel | | Precision machined from high-strength steel | |
| **Trigger:** | Serrated | Serrated | Serrated | Serrated |
| **Hammer:** | Skeletonized combat-style | | Skeletonized combat-style | |
| **Loaded Chamber Indicator:** | Yes | Yes | Yes | Yes |
| **Safeties:** | Extended manual & beavertail grip safeties | | Extended manual & beavertail grip safeties | |
| **Sights:** | 3-dot combat sights | | 3-dot combat sights | |
| **Sight Radius:** | 6 1/4" | 6 1/4" | 6 1/4" | 6 1/4" |
| **Grips:** | Anatomically designed rubber grips | | Anatomically designed rubber grips | |
| **Finish:** | Non-Glare Combat Matte | | Non-Glare Combat Matte | |

# AMERICAN EAGLE LUGER

**AMERICAN EAGLE LUGER®**

## 9mm AMERICAN EAGLE LUGER®
## STAINLESS STEEL

It is doubtful that there ever was a pistol created that evokes the nostalgia or mystique of the Luger pistol. Since its beginnings at the turn of the 20th century, the name Luger® conjures memories of the past. Stoeger Industries is indeed proud to have owned the name Luger® since the late 1920s and is equally proud of the stainless-steel version that graces this page.

The "American Eagle" name was introduced around 1900 to capture the American marketplace. It served its purpose well, the name having become legendary along with the Luger® name. The "American Eagle" inscribed on a Luger® also distinguishes a firearm of exceptional quality over some inexpensive models that have been manufactured in the past.

Constructed entirely of stainless steel, the gun is available in 9mm Parabellum only, with either a 4" or 6"

barrel, each with deeply checkered American walnut grips.

The name Luger®, combined with Stoeger's reputation of selling only quality merchandise since 1918, assures the owner of complete satisfaction.

### SPECIFICATIONS
**Caliber:** 9mm Parabellum
**Capacity:** 7 + 1
**Barrel length:** 4" (P-08 Model); 6" (Navy Model)
**Overall length:** 8.25" (w/4" bbl.), 10.25" (w/6" bbl.)
**Weight:** 30 oz. w/4" barrel, 32 oz. w/6" barrel
**Grips:** Deeply checkered American walnut
**Features:** All stainless-steel construction
**Price:** . . . . . . . . . . . . . . . . . . . . . . . . . . . . . . . . . . **$699.00**
In matte black. . . . . . . . . . . . . . . . . . . . . . . . . . . . . . **789.00**

# MAGNUM RESEARCH

## MARK XIX COMPONENT SYSTEM

**The Mark XIX Component system allows for three caliber changes in two different barrel lengths.**

The Desert Eagle Pistol Mark XIX Component System is based on a single platform that transforms into six different pistols—three Magnum calibers, each with a 6-inch or 10-inch barrel. Changing calibers is a simple matter of switching barrels and magazines. (Converting to or from .357 Magnum also involves changing the bolt.)

The barrel design alone sports several improvements. Each barrel is now made of a single piece of steel instead of three. All six barrels, including the optional 10-inch barrels, have a 7/8" dovetailed design with cross slots to accommodate scope rings; no other scope mounts are required. The .50 A.E.'s new 10-inch barrel will fit existing .50s, as well as the new Mark XIX platform.

Hogue soft rubber grips are standard equipment on the new gun. The pistol's well-known gas operation, polygonal rifling, low recoil and safety features remain the same, as do the Mark VII adjustable trigger, slide release and safety levers.

## SPECIFICATIONS

**Calibers:** 357 Magnum, 44 Magnum and 50 A.E.
**Capacity:** 9 rounds (357 Mag.); 8 rounds (44 Mag.); 7 rounds (50 A.E.)
**Barrel lengths:** 6" and 10"
**Overall length:** 10.75" (w/6" bbl.); 14.75" (w/10" bbl.)
**Weight:** 4 lbs. 6.5 oz. (w/6" bbl.); 4 lbs. 15 oz. (w/10" bbl.)(empty)
**Height:** 6.25"   **Width:** 1.25"
**Finish:** Standard black
**Prices:**

| | |
|---|---|
| 357 Mag. w/6" barrel | $ 979.00 |
| 357 Mag. w/10" barrel | 1029.00 |
| 44 Mag. w/6" barrel | 999.00 |
| 44 Mag. w/10" barrel | 1049.00 |
| 50 A.E. w/6" barrel | 1049.00 |
| 50 A.E. w/10" barrel | 1099.00 |

**LONE EAGLE**

## LONE EAGLE SINGLE SHOT BARRELED ACTION
### $289.00

This specialty pistol is designed for hunters, silhouette enthusiasts, long-range target shooters and other marksmen. The pistol can fire 15 different calibers of ammo. Available w/interchangeable 14-inch barreled actions. Calibers: 22 Hornet, 22-250, 223 Rem., 243 Win., 30-06, 30-30, 308 Win., 35 Rem., 357 Maximum, 358 Win., 44 Mag., 444 Marlin, 7mm-08, 7mm Bench Rest., 7.62x39 Features ambidextrous grip, new cocking indicator and lever.

Also available:

| | |
|---|---|
| Barreled action w/ muzzle brake | $369.00 |
| Barreled action w/ chrome finish | 319.99 |
| Barreled action w/ chrome finish, muzzle brake | 399.00 |
| Ambidextrous grip assembly | 119.00 |

# MOA MAXIMUM PISTOLS

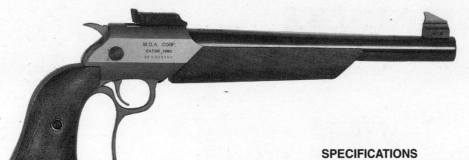

**MAXIMUM
SINGLE SHOT**

### MAXIMUM

This single-shot pistol with its unique falling-block action performs like a finely tuned rifle. The single-piece receiver of stainless steel is mated to a Douglas barrel for optimum accuracy and strength.

**SPECIFICATIONS**
**Calibers:** 22 Hornet to 358 Win.
**Barrel lengths:** 8.5", 10.5" and 14"
**Weight:** 3 lbs. 8 oz. (8.5" bbl.); 3 lbs. 13 oz. (10.5" bbl.);
   4 lbs. 3 oz. (14" bbl.)
**Prices:**
Stainless receiver, blued barrel . . . . . . . . . . . . . . $698.00
Stainless receiver and barrel . . . . . . . . . . . . . . . . 773.00
Extra barrels (blue) . . . . . . . . . . . . . . . . . . . . . . . 180.00
   Stainless . . . . . . . . . . . . . . . . . . . . . . . . . . . . . 244.00
Muzzle brake . . . . . . . . . . . . . . . . . . . . . . . . . . . 125.00

# NAVY ARMS REPLICAS

**1873 SINGLE ACTION**

### 1873 COLT-STYLE SA REVOLVER

The classic 1873 Single Action is the most famous of all the "six shooters." From its adoption by the U.S. Army in 1873 to the present, it still retains its place as America's most popular revolver. **Calibers:** 44-40 or 45 Long Colt. **Barrel lengths:** 3", 4.75", 5.5" or 7.5". **Overall length:** 10.75" (5.5" barrel). **Weight:** 2.25 lbs. **Sights:** Blade front; notch rear. **Grips:** Walnut.
**Price:** . . . . . . . . . . . . . . . . . . . . . . . . . . . . . . . $390.00

### 1873 U.S. CAVALRY MODEL
### (not shown)

An exact replica of the original U.S. Government issue Colt Single-Action Army, complete with Arsenal stampings and inspector's cartouche. **Caliber:** 45 Long Colt. **Barrel length:** 7.5". **Overall length:** 13.25". **Weight:** 2 lbs. 7 oz. **Sights:** Blade front; notch rear. **Grips:** Walnut.
**Price:** . . . . . . . . . . . . . . . . . . . . . . . . . . . . . . . $480.00

### "FLAT TOP" TARGET MODEL
### SA REVOLVER (not shown)

A fine replica of Colt's rare "Flat Top" Single Action Army revolver that was used for target shooting. **Caliber:** 45 Long Colt. **Barrel length:** 7.5". **Overall length:** 12.75", **Weight:** 2 lbs. 7 oz. **Sights:** Spring-loaded German silver Patridge front, adjustable notch rear. **Grips:** Walnut.
**Price:** . . . . . . . . . . . . . . . . . . . . . . . . . . . . . . . $445.00

**1873 "PINCHED FRAME"
SA REVOLVER**

### 1873 "PINCHED FRAME" SA REVOLVER

A replica of the early "pinched frame" Colt Peacemaker, the first run commercial Single Action manufactured in 1873. **Caliber:** 45 Long Colt. **Barrel length:** 7.5". **Overall length:** 13.75". **Weight:** 2 lbs. 13 oz. **Sights:** German siver blade front, U-shaped "pinched-frame" rear notch.
**Price:** . . . . . . . . . . . . . . . . . . . . . . . . . . . . . . . $405.00

# NAVY ARMS REPLICAS

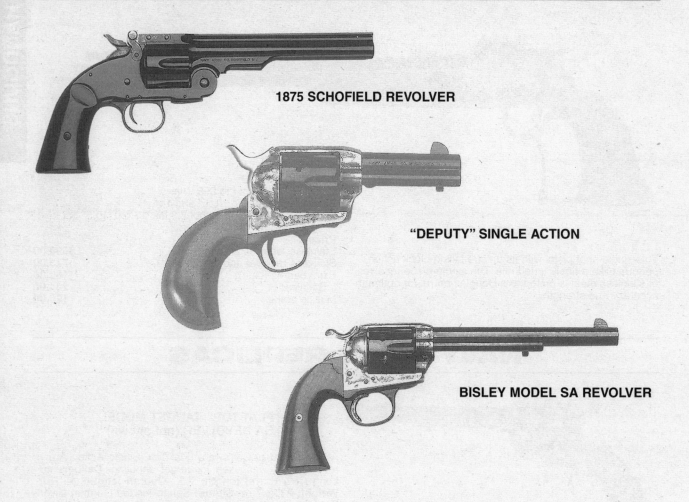

**1875 SCHOFIELD REVOLVER**

**"DEPUTY" SINGLE ACTION**

**BISLEY MODEL SA REVOLVER**

## 1875 SCHOFIELD REVOLVER

A favorite side arm of Jesse James and General George Armstrong, the 1875 Schofield revolver was one of the legendary handguns of the Old West. **Caliber:** 44-40, 45 LC. **Barrel lengths:** 5" (Wells Fargo Model) or 7" (U.S. Cavalry Model). **Overall length:** 10.75" or 12.75". **Weight:** 2 lbs. 7 oz. **Sights:** Blade front; notch rear. **Features:** Top-break, automatic ejector single action.
**Price:** . . . . . . . . . . . . . . . . . . . . . . . . . . . . . . . . $795.00

## "DEPUTY" SINGLE ACTION REVOLVER

The "Deputy" is a single-action reproduction of Colt's famous 1877 "Thunderer" double-action "bird's-head" grip revolver that was carried by Doc Holiday, John Wesley Hardin and Billy the Kid. **Calibers:** 44-40 or 45 Long Colt. **Barrel lengths:** 3.5", 4" and 4.75". **Sights:** Blade front, notch rear. **Grips:** Walnut **Features:** Color casehardened frame, ejecttors on all barrel lengths.
**Price:** . . . . . . . . . . . . . . . . . . . . . . . . . . . . . . . . $405.00

## BISLEY MODEL SINGLE ACTION REVOLVER

Introduced in 1894, Colt's "Bisley Model" was named after the Bisley shooting range in England. Most of these revolvers were sold in the United States and were popular sidearms in the American West at the turn of the century. This replica features the unique Bisley grip style, low-profile spur hammer, blued barrel and color casehardened frame. **Calibers:** 44-40 or 45 Long Colt. **Barrel lengths:** 4.75", 5.5" and 7.5". **Sights:** Blade front, notch rear. **Grips:** Walnut.
**Price:** . . . . . . . . . . . . . . . . . . . . . . . . . . . . . . . . $445.00

## 1895 U.S. ARTILLERY MODEL (not shown)

Same specifications as the U.S. Cavalry Model, but with a 5.5" barrel as issued to Artillery units. **Caliber:** 45 Long Colt
**Price:** . . . . . . . . . . . . . . . . . . . . . . . . . . . . . . . . $480.00

# NEW ENGLAND FIREARMS

## STANDARD REVOLVER
### $134.95 ($144.95 in Nickel)

**SPECIFICATIONS**
**Calibers:** 22 S, L or LR
**Capacity:** 9 shots
**Barrel lengths:** 2.5" and 4"
**Overall length:** 7" (2.5" barrel) and 8.5" (4" barrel)
**Weight:** 25 oz. (2.5" bbl.) and 28 (4" bbl.)
**Sights:** Blade front; fixed rear
**Grips:** American hardwood, walnut finish, NEF medallion
**Finish:** Blue or nickel

Also available:
In 5-shot, calibers 32 H&R Mag., 32 S&W, 32 S&W Long.
**Weight:** 23 oz. (2.5 barrel); 26 oz. (4" barrel). Other specifications same as above.
**Blued finish** . . . . . . . . . . . . . . . . . . . . . . . . . . $134.95
**Nickel finish** (2.5" bbl. only) . . . . . . . . . . . . . . . 144.95
**STARTER REVOLVER** (pull pin cylinder & lanyard ring) in 22 cal. **Capacity:** 5 and 9 shot. **Finish:** Blued.
**Price:** . . . . . . . . . . . . . . . . . . . . . . . . . . . . . . . . $104.95

**STANDARD MODEL**
**(22 LR, 2.5" Barrel)**

**ULTRA MAG.**

**ULTRA MODEL**
**(6" Barrel)**

## ULTRA AND ULTRA MAG. REVOLVERS
### $169.95

**SPECIFICATIONS**
**Calibers:** 22 Short, Long, Long Rifle (Ultra); 22 Win. Mag. (Ultra Mag.)
**Capacity:** 9 shots (22 LR); 6 shots (22 Win. Mag.)
**Barrel length:** 6"
**Overall length:** 10⅝"
**Weight:** 36 oz.
**Sights:** Blade on rib front; fully adjustable rear
**Grips:** American hardwood, walnut finish, NEF medallion

Also available:
**LADY ULTRA** in 5-shot 32 H&R Magnum. **Barrel length:** 3". **Overall length:** 7 1/4". **Weight:** 31 oz. **Price:** . $169.95

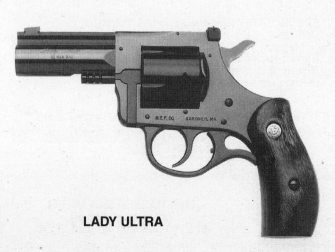

**LADY ULTRA**

# NORTH AMERICAN ARMS

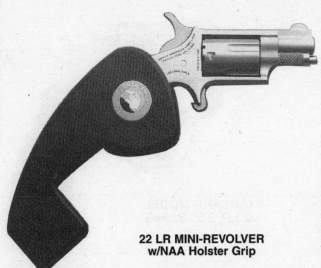

**22 LR MINI-REVOLVER**
**w/NAA Holster Grip**

## MINI-REVOLVERS

**SPECIFICATIONS** (Standard on all models)
**Calibers:** 22 Short (1⅛" bbl. only), 22 LR and 22 Magnum
**Capacity:** 5-shot cylinder **Grips:** Laminated rosewood
**Safety:** Half-cock safety
**Sights:** Blade front (integral w/barrel); fixed,[ql~notched rear
**Material:** Stainless steel **Finish:** Matte with brushed sides

### COMPANION CAP & BALL MINI-REVOLVER
### (Not Shown)
### $173.00 (1⅛" Barrel) $195.00 (1⅝"Barrel)

**SPECIFICATIONS**
**Calibers:** 22 LR and 22 Magnum (#11 percussion caps)
**Capacity:** 5-shot cylinder
**Barrel lengths:** 1⅛" (22 LR); 1⅝" (22 Mag.)
**Overall length:** 4⁵/₁₆" (22 LR); 5⁷/₁₆" (22 Mag.)
**Weight:** 5.12 oz. (22 LR); 7.02 oz. (22 Mag.)
**Finish:** Stainless steel
**Features:** Includes 50-30 gr. lead bullets; powder charge
measure; bullet seater; leather clip holster; lockable
gun rug

## SPECIFICATIONS: MINI-REVOLVERS & MINI-MASTER SERIES

| Model | Weight | Barrel Length | Overall Length | Overall Height | Overall Width | Price |
|---|---|---|---|---|---|---|
| NAA-MMT-M | 10.7 oz. | 4" | 7¾" | 3⅞" | ⅞" | **$292.00** |
| NAA-MMT-L | 10.7 oz. | 4" | 7¾" | 3⅞" | ⅞" | 292.00 |
| *NAA-BW-M | 8.8 oz. | 2" | 5⅞" | 3⅞" | ⅞" | 243.00 |
| *NAA-BW-L | 8.8 oz. | 2" | 5⅞" | 3⅞" | ⅞" | 243.00 |
| NAA-22LR** | 4.5 oz. | 1⅛" | 4¼" | 2⅜" | ¹³/₁₆" | 162.00 |
| NAA-22LLR** | 4.6 oz. | 1⅝" | 4¾" | 2⅜" | ¹³/₁₆" | 162.00 |
| *NAA-22MS | 5.9 oz. | 1⅛" | 5" | 2⅞" | ⅞" | 184.00 |
| *NAA-22M | 6.2 oz. | 1⅝" | 5⅜" | 2⅞" | ⅞" | 184.00 |

* Available with Conversion Cylinder chambered for 22 Long Rifle    ** Available with holster grip **($195.00)**

## MINI-MASTER SERIES

**SPECIFICATIONS** (Standard on all models)
**Calibers:** 22 LR (NAA-MMT-L, NAA-BW-L) and 22
Magnum (NAA-MMT-M, NAA-BW-M)
**Barrel:** Heavy vent
**Rifling:** 8 land and grooves, 1:12 R.H. button broach twist
**Grips:** Oversized black rubber

**Cylinder:** Bull
**Sights:** Front integral with barrel; rear Millett adjustable
white outlined (elevation only) or low-profile fixed

**MINI-MASTER NAA-MMT-M**
**(22 Mag. 4" Barrel)**
**$292.00 ($276.00 w/Fixed Sight)**

**MINI-MASTER NAA**
**BLACK WIDOW**
**$259.00 (adjustable sight)**
**$243.00 (fixed sight)**

# PARA-ORDNANCE

**MODEL P10·45ER**
(Black)

**MODEL P10·45TR**
(Duotone)

**MODEL P10·45SR**
(Stainless)

## P-SERIES PISTOL SPECIFICATIONS

| Model | Caliber | Barrel Length | Weight (Oz.) | Overall Length | Height (w/mag.) | Receiver Type | Matte Finish | Prices |
|-------|---------|---------------|--------------|----------------|-----------------|---------------|--------------|--------|
| P10·40ER | 40 S&W | 3" | 31 | $6^5/_8$" | $4^1/_2$" | Steel | Black | $750.00 |
| P10·40RR | 40 S&W | 3" | 23 | $6^5/_8$" | $4^1/_2$" | Alloy | Black | 705.00 |
| P10·40TR | 40 S&W | 3" | 31 | $6^5/_8$" | $4^1/_2$" | Stainless | Duotone | 785.00 |
| P10·40SR | 40 S&W | 3" | 31 | $6^5/_8$" | $4^1/_2$" | Stainless | Stainless | 799.00 |
| P10·45ER | 45 ACP | 3" | 31 | $6^5/_8$" | $4^1/_2$" | Steel | Black | 750.00 |
| P10·45RR | 45 ACP | 3" | 23 | $6^5/_8$" | $4^1/_2$" | Alloy | Black | 705.00 |
| P10·45TR | 45 ACP | 3" | 31 | $6^5/_8$" | $4^1/_2$" | Stainless | Duotone | 785.00 |
| P10·45SR | 45 ACP | 3" | 31 | $6^5/_8$" | $4^1/_2$" | Stainless | Stainless | 799.00 |
| P12·45ER | 45 ACP | 3.5" | 34 | $7^1/_8$" | 5" | Steel | Black | 750.00 |
| P12·45RR | 45 ACP | 3.5" | 26 | $7^1/_8$" | 5" | Alloy | Black | 705.00 |
| P12·45TR | 45 ACP | 3.5" | 34 | $7^1/_8$" | 5" | Stainless | Duotone | 785.00 |
| P12·45SR | 45 ACP | 3.5" | 34 | $7^1/_8$" | 5" | Stainless | Stainless | 799.00 |
| P13·45ER | 45 ACP | 4.25" | 36 | 7.75" | 5.25" | Steel | Black | 750.00 |
| P13·45RR | 45 ACP | 4.25" | 28 | 7.75" | 5.25" | Alloy | Black | 705.00 |
| P13·45TR | 45 ACP | 4.25" | 36 | 7.75" | 5.25" | Stainless | Duotone | 785.00 |
| P13·45SR | 45 ACP | 4.25" | 36 | 7.75" | 5.25" | Stainless | Stainless | 799.00 |

*For recreational purposes, magazine capacities are restricted to 10 rounds.*

# PARA-ORDNANCE

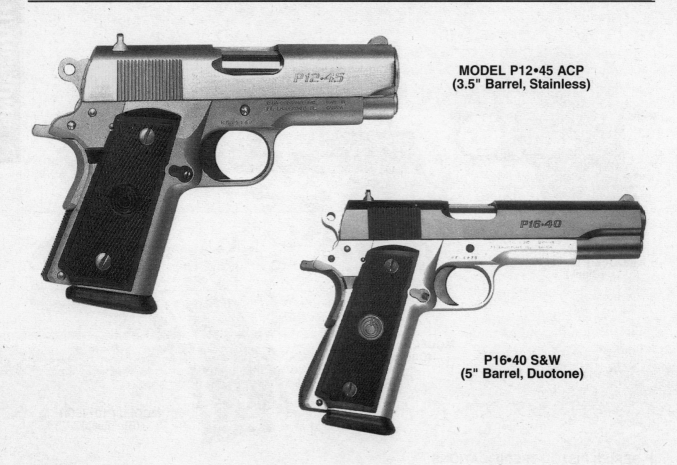

**MODEL P12•45 ACP**
**(3.5" Barrel, Stainless)**

**P16•40 S&W**
**(5" Barrel, Duotone)**

## P-SERIES PISTOL SPECIFICATIONS (cont.)

| Model | Caliber | Barrel Length | Weight (Oz.) | Overall Length | Height (w/mag.) | Receiver Type | Matte Finish | Prices |
|---|---|---|---|---|---|---|---|---|
| P14•45ER | 45 ACP | 5" | 40 | 8.5" | 5.75" | Steel | Black | $750.00 |
| P14•45RR | 45 ACP | 5" | 31 | 8.5" | 5.75" | Alloy | Black | 705.00 |
| P14•45TR | 45 ACP | 5" | 40 | 8.5" | 5.75" | Stainless | Duotone | 785.00 |
| P14•45SR | 45 ACP | 5" | 40 | 8.5" | 5.75" | Stainless | Stainless | 799.00 |
| P14•40ER | 40 S&W | 3.5" | 34 | 7 1/8" | 5" | Steel | Black | 750.00 |
| P14•40RR | 40 S&W | 3.5" | 26 | 7 1/8" | 5" | Alloy | Black | 705.00 |
| P14•40TR | 40 S&W | 3.5" | 34 | 7 1/8" | 5" | Stainless | Duotone | 785.00 |
| P14•40SR | 40 S&W | 3.5" | 34 | 7 1/8" | 5" | Stainless | Stainless | 799.00 |
| P15•40ER | 40 S&W | 4.25" | 36 | 7.75" | 5.25" | Steel | Black | 750.00 |
| P15•40RR | 40S&W | 4.25" | 28 | 7.75" | 5.25" | Alloy | Black | 705.00 |
| P15•40TR | 40 S&W | 4.25" | 36 | 7.75" | 5.25" | Stainless | Duotone | 785.00 |
| P15•40SR | 40 S&W | 4.25" | 36 | 7.75" | 5.25" | Stainless | Stainless | 799.00 |
| P16•40ER | 40 S&W | 5" | 40 | 8.5" | 5.75" | Steel | Black | 750.00 |
| P16•40TR | 40 S&W | 5" | 40 | 8.5" | 5.75" | Stainless | Duotone | 785.00 |
| P16•40SR | 40 S&W | 5" | 40 | 8.5" | 5.75" | Stainless | Stainless | 799.00 |

*For recreational purposes, magazine capacities are restricted to 10 rounds.*

# PRECISION SMALL ARMS

### TRADITIONAL MODEL PSA-25
### $249.00

**PSA-25**

**SPECIFICATIONS**
**Type:** Single action, self-loading, blow-back, semiautomatic; all-steel construction; manufactured in the U.S.
**Caliber:** 25 ACP  **Capacity:** 6+1 round in chamber
**Ignition system:** Striker fired
**Barrel length:** 2.13"
**Rifling:** 6 lands and grooves; right-hand twist
**Overall length:** 4.11"  **Height:** 2.88"
**Weight (unloaded):** 9.5 oz.
**Radius:** 3.54"
**Safety Systems:** Manual frame-mounted safety; magazine safety; cocking indicator
**Sights:** Blade front, 0.03" width (0.9mm); fixed V-notched rear
**Trigger:** Smooth faced, single stage, draw bar; 0.20" width; 5.25 lbs. pull weight
**Grips:** Composition; black polymer
**Finish:** Highly polished black oxide (traditional)
**Options:** Polished stainless-steel frame, slide and barrel; industrial hard chrome, chromium nitrate and gold finish; various grips; engraved limited editions

Also available:
**NOUVEAU MODEL** w/satin chrome finish over electroless nickel; black polymer grips . . . . . . . . **$298.00**

**FEATHERWEIGHT MODEL** w/polished chrome slide & magazine; aluminum frame; gold-plated trigger  . **$375.00**
**RENAISSANCE MODEL** w/engraved frame & slide; satin nickel finish; gold-plated trigger . . . . . . . . . . **975.00**
**IMPERIALE** w/gold scroll pattern; high-luster hot blued finish; gold-plated trigger; ivory grips, grip screw & bevel . . . . . . . . . . . . . . . . . . . . . . . . . . **1375.00**

# ROSSI REVOLVERS

### MODEL 68
### $225.00

### MODEL 88
### $255.00

**SPECIFICATIONS**
**Caliber:** 38 Special
**Capacity:** 5 rounds
**Barrel lengths:** 2" and 3"
**Overall length:** 6.5" (2" barrel); 7.5" (3" barrel)
**Weight:** 22 oz. (2" barrel); 23 oz. (3" barrel)
**Grips:** Wood or rubber
**Finish:** Blued or nickel
**Features:** Frames machined from chrome-molybdenum SAE 4140

**SPECIFICATIONS**
**Caliber:**  38 Special
**Capacity:** 5 rounds, swing-out cylinder
**Barrel lengths:** 2" and 3"
**Overall length:** 6.5" (2" barrel); 7.5" (3" barrel)
**Weight:** 22 oz. (2"); 23 oz. (3")
**Sights:** Ramp front, square-notched rear adjustable for windage
**Grips:** Wood or rubber (2" barrel only)
**Finish:** Stainless steel

# ROSSI REVOLVERS

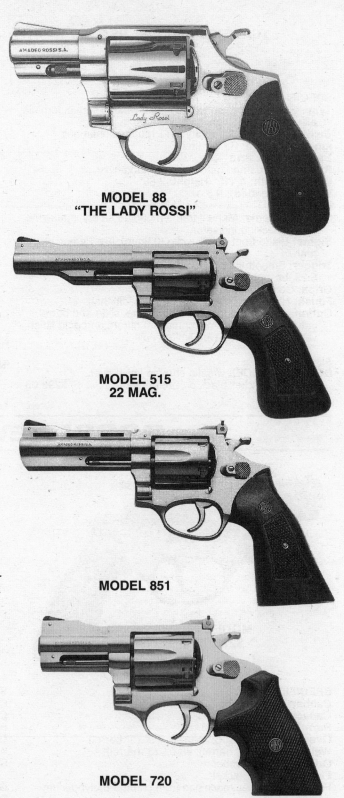

## MODEL 88 "THE LADY ROSSI"
### $285.00

**SPECIFICATIONS**
**Caliber:** 38 Special
**Capacity:** 5 rounds
**Barrel length:** 2"
**Overall length:** 6.5"
**Weight:** 21 oz.
**Grips:** Rosewood
**Finish:** Stainless steel
**Features:** Fixed sights, velvet bag

**MODEL 88
"THE LADY ROSSI"**

## MODELS 515/518
### $255.00 (22 LR, 518)
### $270.00 (22 Mag., 515)

**SPECIFICATIONS**
**Calibers:** 22 LR (Model 518) and 22 Mag. (Model 515)
**Capacity:** 6 rounds
**Barrel length:** 4"
**Overall length:** 9"
**Weight:** 30 oz.
**Grips:** Checkered wood and rubber wraparound supplied

**MODEL 515
22 MAG.**

## MODEL 851
### $255.00

**SPECIFICATIONS**
**Caliber:** 38 Special
**Capacity:** 6 rounds
**Barrel length:** 4"
**Overall length:** 7.5"
**Weight:** 31 oz.
**Frame:** Medium
**Grips:** Full-size checkered Brazilian hardwood
**Finish:** Stainless
**Features:** Ventilated rib; full-length ejector shroud; fully
   adjustable rear sight; red insert front sight; wide target-
   style hammer and trigger

**MODEL 851**

## MODEL 720
### $290.00

**SPECIFICATIONS**
**Caliber:** 44 S&W Special
**Capacity:** 5 shots
**Barrel length:** 3"
**Overall length:** 8"
**Weight:** 30 oz.  **Height:** 5.37"
**Sights:** Adjustable rear; red insert front
**Finish:** Stainless steel
**Features:** Rubber combat grips; full ejector rod shroud;
   available in hammerless mode

**MODEL 720**

# ROSSI REVOLVERS

## MODEL 877
## $290.00

**SPECIFICATIONS**
**Caliber:** 357 Magnum
**Capacity:** 6 rounds
**Barrel length:** 2" heavy
**Weight:** 26 oz.
**Grips:** Rubber  **Finish:** Stainless
**Features:** Fully enclosed ejector rod; serrated ramp front
   sight
Also available:
**Model 677** w/matte blued finish . . . . . . . . . . . . . $260.00

**MODEL 677 357 MAGNUM**

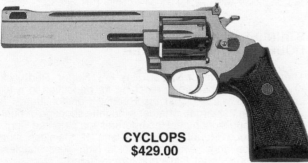

## CYCLOPS
## $429.00

**SPECIFICATIONS**
**Caliber:** 357 Magnum
**Capacity:** 6 rounds
**Barrel length:** 8" **Overall length:** 13.75"
**Height:** 5.75"  **Width:** 1.47"
**Weight:** 51 oz.
**Finish:** Stainless steel
**Grips:** Rubber
**Features:** Four recessed compensator ports on each side
   of muzzle, plus extra heavy barrel; mounts and rings
   included

**MODEL 877**

## MODEL 971 (not shown)
## $290.00 ($255.00 Blued)

**SPECIFICATIONS**
**Caliber:** 357 Magnum
**Capacity:** 6 rounds
**Barrel lengths:** 2.5", 3.25" 4" and 6"
**Overall length:** 7$\frac{1}{2}$", 8$\frac{1}{4}$", 9", 11"
**Weight:** 30.4 oz. (2.5"), 32 oz. (3.25"), 31.5 oz. (4"),
   35.4 oz. (4" w/rubber grips), 40.5 oz. (6")
**Finish:** Blued (4" barrel only) or stainless steel

Also available:
**MODEL 971 VRC.** In 357 Magnum, stainless, rubber grips.
**Weight:** 30.4 oz. (2.5"); 34.7 oz. (4"); 38.9 oz. (6").
**Price:** . . . . . . . . . . . . . . . . . . . . . . . . . . . . . . $340.00

**MODEL 971 VRC
357 MAG. STAINLESS**

# RUGER REVOLVERS

**REDHAWK REVOLVER**

**MODEL KRH-44
STAINLESS REDHAWK**

**STAINLESS REDHAWK
w/Scope (KRH-44R)**

**MODEL KSRH-9
SUPER REDHAWK STAINLESS**

## BLUED STEEL REDHAWK REVOLVER

The popular Ruger Redhawk® double-action revolver is available in an alloy steel model with blued finish or high-gloss standard steel in 44 Magnum caliber. Constructed of hardened chrome-moly and other alloy steels, this Redhawk is satin polished to a high luster and finished in a rich blue. **Capacity:** 6 rounds.

| Catalog Number | Caliber | Barrel Length | Overall Length | Approx. Weight (Ounces) | Price |
|---|---|---|---|---|---|
| **RUGER BLUED REDHAWK REVOLVER** | | | | | |
| RH-445 | 44 Mag. | 5.5" | 11" | 49 | **$490.00** |
| RH-44 | 44 Mag. | 7.5" | 13" | 54 | **490.00** |
| RH-44R* | 44 Mag. | 7.5" | 13" | 54 | **527.00** |

*Scope model, with Integral Scope Mounts, 1" Ruger Scope rings.

## STAINLESS REDHAWK DOUBLE-ACTION REVOLVER

There is no other revolver like the Ruger Redhawk. Knowledgeable sportsmen reaching for perfection in a big bore revolver will find that the Redhawk demonstrates its superiority at the target, whether silhouette shooting or hunting. The scope sight model incorporates the patented Ruger integral Scope Mounting System with 1" stainless steel Ruger scope rings. Available also in high-gloss stainless steel w/ scope model. Case and lock included.

| Catalog Number | Caliber | Barrel Length | Overall Length | Approx. Weight (Ounces) | Price |
|---|---|---|---|---|---|
| **RUGER STAINLESS REDHAWK REVOLVER** | | | | | |
| KRH-445 | 44 Mag. | 5.5" | 11" | 49 | **$547.00** |
| KRH-44 | 44 Mag. | 7.5" | 13" | 54 | **547.00** |
| KRH-44R* | 44 Mag. | 7.5" | 13" | 54 | **589.00** |

*Scope model, with Integral Scope Mounts, 1" Stainless Steel Ruger Scope rings.

## SUPER REDHAWK STAINLESS DOUBLE-ACTION REVOLVER

The Super Redhawk double-action revolver in stainless steel features a heavy extended frame with 7.5" and 9.5" barrels. Cushioned grip panels contain Goncalo Alves wood grip panel inserts to provide comfortable, nonslip hold. Comes with case and lock, integral scope mounts and 1" stainless steel Ruger scope rings.

**SPECIFICATIONS**
**Caliber:** 44 Magnum
**Barrel lengths:** 7.5" and 9.5"
**Overall length:** 13" w/7.5" bbl.; 15" w/9.5" bbl.
**Weight (empty):** 53 oz. (7.5" bbl.); 58 oz. (9.5" bbl.)
**Sight radius:** 9.5" (7.5" bbl.); 11.25" (9.5" bbl.)
**Finish:** Stainless steel; satin polished

KSRH-7 (7.5" barrel) . . . . . . . . . . . . . . . . . . . . . **$589.00**
KSRH-9 (9.5" barrel) . . . . . . . . . . . . . . . . . . . . . **589.00**
GKSRH-7 & 9 (high-gloss stainless steel) . . . . . . . **589.00**

# RUGER SINGLE-ACTION REVOLVERS

**VAQUERO SINGLE ACTION**
**$434.00 (All Models)**

## SPECIFICATIONS: VAQUERO SA

| Catalog Number | Caliber | Finish* | Barrel Length | Overall Length | Approx. Wt. (oz.) |
|---|---|---|---|---|---|
| BNV34 | 357 Mag.+ | CB | 4⁵/₈" | 10.25" | 39 |
| KBNV34 | 357 Mag.+ | SSG | 4⁵/₈" | 10.25" | 39 |
| BNV35 | 357 Mag.+ | CB | 5.5" | 11.5" | 40 |
| KBNV35 | 357 Mag.+ | SSG | 5.5" | 11.5" | 40 |
| BNV40 | 44-40 | CB | 4⁵/₈" | 10.25" | 39 |
| KBNV40 | 44-40 | SSG | 4⁵/₈" | 10.25" | 39 |
| BNV405 | 44-40 | CB | 5.5" | 11.5" | 40 |
| KBNV405 | 44-40 | SSG | 5.5" | 11.5" | 40 |
| BNV407 | 44-40 | CB | 7.5" | 13¹/₈" | 41 |
| KBNV407 | 44-40 | SSG | 7.5" | 13¹/₈" | 41 |
| BNV475 | 44 Mag. | CB | 5.5" | 11.5" | 40 |
| KBNV475 | 44 Mag. | SSG | 5.5" | 11.5" | 40 |
| BNV477 | 44 Mag | CB | 7.5" | 13¹/₈" | 41 |
| KBNV477 | 44 Mag. | SSG | 7.5" | 13¹/₈" | 41 |
| BNV44 | 45 Long Colt | CB | 4⁵/₈" | 10.25" | 39 |
| KBNV44 | 45 Long Colt | SSG | 4⁵/₈" | 10.25" | 39 |
| BNV455 | 45 Long Colt | CB | 5.5" | 11.5" | 40 |
| KBNV455 | 45 Long Colt | SSG | 5.5" | 11.5" | 40 |
| BNV45 | 45 Long Colt | CB | 7.5" | 13¹/₈" | 41 |
| KBNV45 | 45 Long Colt | SSG | 7.5" | 13¹/₈" | 41 |

*Finish: high-gloss stainless steel (SSG); "color-cased finish" on steel cylinder frame w/blued steel grip, barrel and cylinder (CB).   **With similated ivory grips: **$470.00**

## SPECIFICATIONS: NEW MODEL BLACKHAWK AND BLACKHAWK CONVERTIBLE*

| Cat. Number | Caliber | Finish** | Bbl. Length | O.A. Length | Weight (Oz.) | Price |
|---|---|---|---|---|---|---|
| BN34 | 357 Mag.++ | B | 4⁵/₈" | 10³/₈" | 40 | **$360.00** |
| KBN34 | 357 Mag.++ | SS | 4⁵/₈" | 10³/₈" | 40 | **443.00** |
| BN36 | 357 Mag.++ | B | 6.5" | 12.25" | 42 | **360.00** |
| KBN36 | 357 Mag.++ | SS | 6.5" | 12.5" | 42 | **443.00** |
| BN34X* | 357 Mag.++ | B | 4⁵/₈" | 10³/₈" | 40 | **380.00** |
| BN36X* | 357 Mag.++ | B | 6.5" | 12.25" | 42 | **380.00** |
| BN44 | 45 Long Colt | B | 4⁵/₈" | 10.25" | 39 | **360.00** |
| KBN44 | 45 Long Colt | SS | 4⁵/₈" | 10.25" | 39 | **443.00** |
| BN455 | 45 Long Colt | B | 5.5" | 11¹/₈" | 39 | **360.00** |
| BN45 | 45 Long Colt | B | 7.5" | 13¹/₈" | 41 | **360.00** |
| KBN45 | 45 Long Colt | SS | 7.5" | 13¹/₈" | 41 | **443.00** |

*Convertible: Designated by an X in the Catalog Number, this model comes with an extra interchangeable 9mm Parabellum cylinder; price includes extra cylinder.   **Finish: blued (B); stainless steel (SS); high-gloss stainless steel (HGSS); color-cased finish on the steel cylinder frame with blued steel grip, barrel, and cylinder (CB). **Also accept factory-loaded 38 Special cartridges.

# RUGER REVOLVERS

**NEW SUPER MODEL
BLACKHAWK
SINGLE-ACTION REVOLVER**

**NEW MODEL SUPER BLACKHAWK
SINGLE-ACTION REVOLVER**

## SPECIFICATIONS
**Caliber:** 44 Magnum; interchangeable with 44 Special
**Barrel lengths:** 4⅝", 5.5", 7.5", 10.5"
**Overall length:** 13⅜" (7.5" barrel)
**Weight:** 45 oz. (4⅝" bbl.), 46 oz. (5.5" bbl.), 48 oz. (7.5" bbl.) and 51 oz. (10.5" bbl.)
**Frame:** Chrome molybdenum steel or stainless steel
**Springs:** Music wire springs throughout
**Sights:** Patridge style, ramp front matted blade 18" wide; rear sight click-adjustable for windage and elevation
**Grip frame:** Chrome molybdenum or stainless steel, enlarged and contoured to minimize recoil effect
**Trigger:** Wide spur, low contour, sharply serrated for convenient cocking with minimum disturbance of grip

**Finish:** Polished and blued or brushed satin stainless steel
**Features:** Case and lock included
**Prices:**
**KS45N** 5.5" bbl., brushed or high-gloss
stainless . . . . . . . . . . . . . . . . . . . . . . . . . . . . . . $450.00
**KS458N** 4⅝" bbl., brushed or high-gloss
stainless . . . . . . . . . . . . . . . . . . . . . . . . . . . . . . 450.00
**KS47N** 7.5" bbl., brushed or high-gloss stainless. 450.00
**KS411N** 10.5" bull bbl., stainless steel . . . . . . . . 435.00
**S45N** 5.5" bbl., blued . . . . . . . . . . . . . . . . . . . . 413.00
**S458N** 4⅝" bbl., blued . . . . . . . . . . . . . . . . . . . . 413.00
**S47N** 7.5" bbl., blued . . . . . . . . . . . . . . . . . . . . 413.00
**S411N** 10.5" bull bbl., blued . . . . . . . . . . . . . . . . 398.00

**FIXED SIGHT
NEW MODEL SINGLE-SIX
(W/Extra Cylinder)**

**FIXED SIGHT
NEW MODEL SINGLE-SIX**

## SPECIFICATIONS
**Caliber:** 22 LR (fitted with 22 WMR cylinder)
**Barrel lengths:** 4⅝", 5.5", 6.5", 9.5"; stainless steel model in 5.5" and 6.5" lengths only
**Weight (approx.):** 33 oz. (with 5.5" barrel); 38 oz. (with 9.5" barrel)
**Sights:** Patridge-type ramp front sight; rear sight click adjustable for elevation and windage; protected by inte-

gral frame ribs. Fixed sight model available with 5.5" or 6.5" barrel (same prices as adj. sight models).
**Finish:** Blue or stainless steel
**Features:** Case and lock included
**Prices:**
In blue. . . . . . . . . . . . . . . . . . . . . . . . . . . . . . . . $313.00
In brushed steel (convertible 5.5" and 6.5"
barrels only) . . . . . . . . . . . . . . . . . . . . . . . . . 393.00

# RUGER REVOLVERS

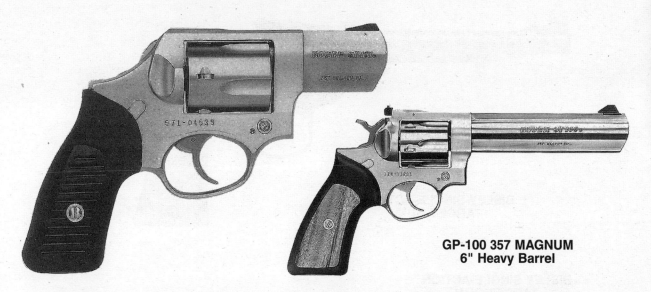

### GP-100 357 MAGNUM
### 6" Heavy Barrel

## MODEL SP101 SPURLESS DA
## $443.00

### GP-100 DA 357 MAGNUM

The GP-100 is designed for the unlimited use of 357 Magnum ammunition in all factory loadings; it combines strength and reliability with accuracy and shooting comfort. (Revolvers chambered for the 357 Magnum cartridge also accept the 38 Special cartridge.)

## SPECIFICATIONS SP101 REVOLVERS

| Catalog Number | Caliber | Cap.* | Sights | Barrel Length | Approx Wt.(Oz.) |
|---|---|---|---|---|---|
| KSP-221 | 22 LR | 6 | A | 2.25" | 32 |
| KSP-240 | 22 LR | 6 | A | 4" | 33 |
| KSP-241 | 22 LR | 6 | A | 4" | 34 |
| KSP-3231 | 32 Mag. | 6 | A | 3¹/₁₆" | 30 |
| KSP-3241 | 32 Mag. | 6 | A | 4" | 33 |
| KSP-921 | 9mmx19 | 5 | F | 2.25" | 25 |
| KSP-931 | 9mmx19 | 5 | F | 3¹/₁₆" | 27 |
| KSP-821 | 38+P | 5 | F | 2.25" | 25 |
| KSP-821 | L38+P | 5 | F | 2.25" | 26 |
| KSP-831 | 38+P | 5 | F | 3¹/₁₆" | 27 |
| KSP-321X** | 357 Mag. | 5 | F | 2.25" | 25 |
| KSP-321XL** | 357 Mag. | 5 | F | 2.25" | 25 |
| KSP-331X** | 357 Mag. | 5 | F | 3¹/₁₆" | 27 |

*Indicates cylinder capacity **Revolvers chambered for 357 Magnum also accept 38 Special cartridges.
 Model KSP-240 has short shroud; all others have full. Spurless hammer models are designated by "L" in catalog no. "G" before a catalog no. indicates high-gloss finish models.

## SPECIFICATIONS

| Catalog Number | Finish | Sights+ | Shroud++ | Barrel Length | Wt. (Oz.) | Price |
|---|---|---|---|---|---|---|
| GP-141 | B | A | F | 4" | 41 | $440.00 |
| GP-160 | B | A | S | 6" | 43 | 440.00 |
| GP-161 | B | A | F | 6" | 46 | 440.00 |
| GPF-331 | B | F | F | 3" | 36 | 423.00 |
| GPF-340 | B | F | S | 4" | 37 | 423.00 |
| GPF-341 | B | F | F | 4" | 38 | 423.00 |
| KGP-141 | SS | A | F | 4" | 41 | 474.00 |
| KGP-160 | SS | A | S | 6" | 43 | 474.00 |
| KGP-161 | SS | A | F | 6" | 46 | 474.00 |
| KGPF-330 | SS | F | S | 3" | 35 | 457.00 |
| KGPF-331 | SS | F | F | 3" | 36 | 457.00 |
| KGPF-340 | SS | F | S | 4" | 37 | 457.00 |
| KGPF-341 | SS | F | F | 4" | 38 | 457.00 |
| KGPF-840* | SS | F | S | 4" | 37 | 457.00 |
| GPF-841* | SS | F | F | 4" | 38 | 457.00 |

*38 Special only. B = blued; SS = stainless; SSG = high-gloss stainless. +A = adjustable; F = fixed. ++ F = full; S = short.

# RUGER REVOLVERS

**BISLEY SINGLE-ACTION
TARGET GUN**

## BISLEY SINGLE-ACTION TARGET GUN

The Bisley single-action was originally used at the British National Rifle Association matches held in Bisley, England, in the 1890s. Today's Ruger Bisleys are offered in two frame sizes, chambered from 22 LR to 45 Long Colt. These revolvers are the target-model versions of the Ruger single-action line.

   **Special features:** Unfluted cylinder rollmarked with classic foliate engraving pattern; hammer is low with smoothly curved, deeply checkered wide spur positioned for easy cocking.

**Prices:**
22 LR . . . . . . . . . . . . . . . . . . . . . . . . . . . . . . . $380.00
357 Mag., 44 Mag., 45 Long Colt . . . . . . . . . . . . 450.00

### BISLEY SPECIFICATIONS

| Catalog Number | Caliber | Barrel Length | Overall Length | Sights | Approx. Wt.(Oz.) |
|---|---|---|---|---|---|
| RB22AW | 22 LR | 6.5" | 11.5" | Adj. | 41 |
| RB35W | 357 Mag. | 7.5" | 13" | Adj. | 48 |
| RB44W | 44 Mag. | 7.5" | 13" | Adj. | 48 |
| RB45W | 45 LC | 7.5" | 13" | Adj. | 48 |

*Dovetail rear sight adjustable for windage only.

**THE NEW BEARCAT**

### THE NEW BEARCAT
### $320.00 (Blued)

Originally manufactured between 1958 and 1973, the 22-rimfire single-action Bearcat features an all-steel precision investment-cast frame and patented transfer-bar mechanism. The New Bearcat also has walnut grips with the Ruger medallion.

**SPECIFICATIONS**
**Caliber:** 22 LR
**Capacity:** 6 shots
**Barrel length:** 4"
**Grips:** Walnut
**Finish:** Blued chrome-moly steel

# RUGER P-SERIES PISTOLS

### MODEL P93 (not shown)

**SPECIFICATIONS:** (See also table below)
**Barrel length:** 3.9"   **Overall length:** 7.3"
**Height:** 5.75"         **Width:** 1.5"
**Weight:** 31 oz.
**Sights:** 3-dot system; square-notch rear, drift adjustable for windage; square post front (both sights have white dots)
**Mechanism:** Recoil-operated, double action, autoloading
**Features:** Oversized trigger guard with curved trigger-guard bow; slide stop activated automatically on last shot (w/magazine in pistol); all stainless steel models made with "Terhune Anticorro" steel for maximum corrosion resistance

**MODEL KP95DC**

### MODEL P94

**SPECIFICATIONS** (see also table below)
**Barrel length:** 4.5"
**Capacity:** 10 rounds
**Overall length:** 7.5"
**Weight:** 33 oz. (empty magazine)
**Height:** 5.5"  **Width:** 1.5"
**Sight radius:** 5"
**Sights:** 3-dot system
**Features:** See Model P93

**MODEL KP94 9mm**
**(4.5" Barrel)**

## SPECIFICATIONS P-SERIES PISTOLS

| Cat. Number | Model | Finish | Caliber | Mag. Cap. | Price |
|---|---|---|---|---|---|
| P89 | Manual Safety | Blued | 9mm | 10 | $410.00 |
| KP89 | Manual Safety | Stainless | 9mm | 10 | 452.00 |
| P89DC | Decock Only | Blued | 9mm | 10 | 410.00 |
| KP89DC | Decock Only | Stainless | 9mm | 10 | 452.00 |
| KP89DAO | Double-Action Only | Stainless | 9mm | 10 | 452.00 |
| KP90 | Manual Safety | Stainless | 45 ACP | 7 | 488.65 |
| KP90DC | Decock Only | Stainless | 45 ACP | 7 | 488.65 |
| KP93DC | Decock Only | Stainless | 9mm | 10 | 520.00 |
| KP93DAO | Double-Action Only | Stainless | 9mm | 10 | 520.00 |
| KP94 | Manual Safety | Stainless | 9mm | 10 | 520.00 |
| KP94DC | Decock Only | Stainless | 9mm | 10 | 520.00 |
| KP94DAO | Double-Action Only | Stainless | 9mm | 10 | 520.00 |
| KP944 | Manual Safety | Stainless | 40 Auto | 10 | 520.00 |
| KP944DC | Decock Only | Stainless | 40Auto | 10 | 520.00 |
| KP944DAO | Double-Action Only | Stainless | 40 Auto | 10 | 520.00 |
| KP95DC | Decock Only | Stainless | 9mm | 10 | 369.00 |
| KP95DAO | Double-Action Only | Stainless | 9mm | 10 | 369.00 |
| P95DC | Decock Only | Blued, Stainless Frame | 9mm | 10 | 351.00 |
| P95DAO | Double-Action Only | Blued, Stainless Frame | 9mm | 10 | 351.00 |

# RUGER 22 AUTOMATIC PISTOLS

**MK II STANDARD MODEL**

### MARK II STANDARD MODEL

The Ruger Mark II models represent continuing refinements of the original Ruger Standard and Mark I Target Model pistols. More than two million of this series of autoloading rimfire pistol have been produced since 1949.

The bolts on all Ruger Mark II pistols lock open automatically when the last cartridge is fired, if the magazine is in the pistol. The bolt can be operated manually with the safety in the "on" position for added security while loading and unloading. A bolt stop can be activated manually to lock the bolt open.

The Ruger Mark II pistol uses 22 Long Rifle ammunition in a detachable, 10-shot magazine (standard on all Mark II models except Model 22/45, whose 10-shot magazine is not interchangeable with other Mark II magazines). Designed for easy insertion and removal, the Mark II magazine is equipped with a magazine follower button for convenience in reloading.

For additional specifications, please see the chart on the next page.

**MARK II GOVERNMENT MODEL**

**MK II STANDARD MODEL**

# RUGER PISTOLS

**MODEL P-4 22/45**

**MARK II 22/45 w/Zytel Frame**

**22/45 TARGET MODEL P-512 (w/11-degree angle)**

## SPECIFICATIONS: RUGER 22 MARK II PISTOLS

| Catalog Number | Model* | Finish ** | Barrel Length | Overall Length | Approx. Wt. (Oz.) | Price |
|---|---|---|---|---|---|---|
| MK-4 | Std. | B | 4³/₄" | 8⁵/₁₆" | 35 | $252.00 |
| MK-4B | Bull | B | 4" | 8.25" | 38 | 336.50 |
| KMK-4 | Std. | SS | 4³/₄" | 8⁵/₁₆" | 35 | 330.25 |
| KP-4***22/45 | Std. | SS | 4³/₄" | 8¹³/₁₆" | 28 | 280.00 |
| P-4 | Bull | B | 4" | 8" | 31 | 237.50 |
| MK-6 | Std. | B | 6" | 10⁵/₁₆" | 37 | 252.00 |
| KMK-6 | Std. | SS | 6" | 10⁵/₁₆" | 37 | 330.25 |
| MK-678 | Target | B | 6⁷/₈" | 11¹/₈" | 42 | 310.50 |
| KMK-678 | Target | SS | 6⁷/₈" | 11¹/₈" | 42 | 389.00 |
| P-512*** 22/45 | Bull | B | 5.5" | 9³/₄" | 35 | 237.50 |
| MK-512 | Bull | B | 5.5" | 9³/₄" | 42 | 310.50 |
| KMK-512 | Bull | SS | 5.5" | 9³/₄" | 42 | 389.00 |
| KP-512***22/45 | Bull | SS | 5.5" | 9³/₄" | 35 | 330.00 |
| MK-10 | Bull | B | 10" | 14⁵/₁₆" | 51 | 294.50 |
| KMK-10 | Bull | SS | 10" | 14⁵/₁₆" | 51 | 373.00 |
| MK-678G | Bul | B | 6⁷/₈" | 11¹/₈" | 46 | 356.50 |
| KMK-678G | Bull | SS | 6⁷/₈" | 11¹/₈" | 46 | 427.25 |
| KMK-678GC | Bull | SS | 6⁷/₈" | 11¹/₈" | 45 | 441.00 |

*Model: Std.= standard **Finish: B = blued; SS = stainless steel ***22 cartridge, 45 grip angle and magazine latch

# SAFARI ARMS PISTOLS

### MATCHMASTER
### $725.00 (5" Barrel)
### $854.00 (6" Barrel)

**SPECIFICATIONS**
**Caliber:** 45 ACP
**Capacity:** 7 rounds
**Barrel length:** 5" or 6"
**Overall length:** 8.25"
**Weight:** 40.3 oz.
**Finish:** Stainless steel or black Parkerized carbon steel
**Features:** Extended safety & slide stop; wide beavertail grip safety; LPA fully adjustable rear sight; full-length recoil spring guide; squared trigger guide & finger-groove front strap frame; laser-etched walnut grips

### ENFORCER
### $750.00

**SPECIFICATIONS**
**Caliber:** 45 ACP
**Capacity:** 6 rounds
**Barrel length:** 3.8" conical
**Overall length:** 7.3"
**Height:** $4^7/_8$"
**Weight:** 36 oz.
**Sight radius:** 5.75"
**Finish:** Stainless steel or matte black Parkerized carbon steel
**Features:** Beavertail grip safety; extended thumb safety and slide release; smooth walnut stock w/laser-etched Black Widow logo

### COHORT
### $790.00

**SPECIFICATIONS**
**Caliber:** 45 ACP
**Capacity:** 7 rounds
**Barrel length:** 3.8" conical
**Overall length:** 8.5"
**Height:** 5.5"
**Weight:** 37 oz.
**Sights:** Ramped blade front, LPA adjustable rear
**Finish:** Stainless steel or black Parkerized carbon steel
**Features:** Beavertail grip safety; extended thumb safety and slide release; commander-style hammer; smooth walnut stock w/laser-etched Black Widow logo

# SIG-SAUER PISTOLS

**MODEL P220 "AMERICAN"**

## MODEL P220 "AMERICAN"

**SPECIFICATIONS**
**Calibers:** 38 Super, 45 ACP
**Capacity:** 9 rounds; 7 rounds in 45 ACP
**Barrel length:** 4.4"  **Overall length:** 7.79"
**Height:** 5.6"  **Width:** 1.4"
**Weight (empty):** 26.5 oz.; 25.7 oz. in 45 ACP
**Finish:** Blue, K-Kote or Two-tone
**Prices:**
Blued . . . . . . . . . . . . . . . . . . . . . . . . . . . . . . . . . . **$750.00**
  w/"Siglite" night sights . . . . . . . . . . . . . . . . . . . **845.00**
w/K-Kote finish . . . . . . . . . . . . . . . . . . . . . . . . . . . **795.00**
  w/K-Kote and "Siglite" night sights . . . . . . . . . . . **885.00**

## MODEL P210 (Not shown)

**SPECIFICATIONS**
Single-action 8-round pistol in 9mm Luger. **Barrel length:** 4.75". **Overall length:** 8.5". **Weight:** 32 oz. **Height:** 5.4". **Width:** 1.3". **Sights:** Blade front; notch rear (drift adjustable for windage). **Safety:** Thumb-operated manual safety lever; magazine safety. **Finish:** Blue only. Long Rifle conversion kit available (**add $600.00**). **Price:** . . . . . . . . . . . . . . **$2300.00**

## MODEL P225

**SPECIFICATIONS**
**Caliber:** 9mm Parabellum
**Capacity:** 8 rounds
**Action:** DA/SA or DA only
**Barrel length:** 3.9"
**Overall length:** 7.1"
**Weight (empty):** 26.1 oz.
**Height:** 5.2"  **Width:**1.3"
**Finish:** Blue, K-Kote or Two-tone
**Prices:**
Blued finish . . . . . . . . . . . . . . . . . . . . . . . . . **$725.00**
Blued w/"Siglite" night sights . . . . . . . . . . . . . . . . **830.00**
w/K-Kote . . . . . . . . . . . . . . . . . . . . . . . . . . . . . . **770.00**
w/K-Kote and "Siglite" night sights . . . . . . . . . . . . **860.00**

**MODEL P225**

## MODEL P226

**SPECIFICATIONS**
**Calibers:** 9mm Parabellum and 357 SIG
**Capacity:** 10 rounds  **Action:** DA/SA or DA only
**Barrel length:** 4.4"  **Overall length:** 7.7"
**Weight (empty):** 26.5 oz.; 30.1 oz. in 357 SIG
**Height:** 5.5"
**Finish:** Blue, K-Kote or Two-tone
**Prices:**
9mm, Blued finish. . . . . . . . . . . . . . . . . . . . . . . . **$750.00**
  Blued w/"Siglite" night sights . . . . . . . . . . . . . **845.00**
  w/K-Kote . . . . . . . . . . . . . . . . . . . . . . . . . . . . . **795.00**
  K-Kote w/"Siglite" night sights . . . . . . . . . . . . . **885.00**
357 SIG . . . . . . . . . . . . . . . . . . . . . . . . . . . . . . . **795.00**
  w/"Siglite" night sights . . . . . . . . . . . . . . . . . . . **885.00**
  w/nickel slide (DA only) . . . . . . . . . . . . . . . . . . **830.00**

**MODEL P226**

# SIG-SAUER PISTOLS

**MODEL P228**

## MODEL P228

**SPECIFICATIONS**
**Caliber:** 9mm
**Capacity:** 10 rounds
**Action:** DA/SA or DA only
**Barrel length:** 3.9"
**Overall length:** 7.1"
**Weight (empty):** 26.1 oz.
**Height:** 5.4"  **Width:** 1.5"
**Finish:** Blue, K-Kote or Two-tone
**Prices:**
Blued finish . . . . . . . . . . . . . . . . . . . . . . . . . . . . . **$750.00**
Blued w/"Siglite" night sights . . . . . . . . . . . . . . . . . 845.00
w/K-Kote . . . . . . . . . . . . . . . . . . . . . . . . . . . . . . . . 795.00
w/K-Kote and "Siglite" night sights . . . . . . . . . . . 885.00

## MODEL P232 (Not shown)

**SPECIFICATIONS**
**Calibers:** 9mm Short (380 ACP) and 32 ACP
**Action:** DA/SA or DAO
**Capacity:** 7 rounds (380 ACP); 8 rounds (32 ACP)
**Barrel length:** 3.6"  **Overall length:** 6.6"
**Weight (empty):** 16.2 oz.; (16.4 oz. in 32 ACP)
**Height:** 4.7"  **Width:** 1.2"
**Safety:** Automatic firing-pin lock
**Finish:** Blued or stainless steel
**Prices:**
Blued finish . . . . . . . . . . . . . . . . . . . . . . . . . . . . . **$485.00**
Stainless steel . . . . . . . . . . . . . . . . . . . . . . . . . . . . 525.00
  With Stainless slide . . . . . . . . . . . . . . . . . . . . . . 505.00

**MODEL P229**

**MODEL P239**

## MODEL P229

**SPECIFICATIONS**
**Calibers:** 9mm, 357 and 40 S&W
**Capacity:** 10 rounds
**Action:** DA/SA or DA only
**Barrel length:** 3.8"  **Overall Length:** 7.1"
**Weight (empty):** 27.5 oz.
**Height:** 5.4"  **Width:** 1.5"
**Finish:** Blackened stainless steel
**Features:** Stainless steel slide; automatic firing-pin lock;
    wood grips (optional); aluminum alloy frame
**Prices:**
Model P229 . . . . . . . . . . . . . . . . . . . . . . . . . . . . . **$795.00**
w/"Siglite" night sight. . . . . . . . . . . . . . . . . . . . . . 885.00
w/Nickel slide . . . . . . . . . . . . . . . . . . . . . . . . . . . . 830.00
w/Nickel slide/"Siglite" night sight . . . . . . . . . . . 925.00

## MODEL P239

**SPECIFICATIONS**
**Calibers:** 9mm Luger and 357 SIG
**Action:** DA/SA or DA only
**Capacity:** 7 rounds (357 SIG); 8 rounds (9mm)
**Barrel length:** 3.6"  **Overall length:** 6.6"
**Weight:** 25.2 oz.
**Height:** 5.1"  **Width:** 1.2"
**Finish:** Blackened stainless steel
**Features:** Mechanically locked, reoil-operated semiauto;
    automatic firing-pin lock
**Prices:** . . . . . . . . . . . . . . . . . . . . . . . . . . . . . . . **$595.00**
w/"Siglite" night sight. . . . . . . . . . . . . . . . . . . . . . 685.00

# SMITH & WESSON PISTOLS

## COMPACT SERIES

### MODEL 3900 COMPACT SERIES

**SPECIFICATIONS**
**Caliber:** 9mm Parabellum DA Autoloading Luger
**Capacity:** 8 rounds
**Barrel length:** 3.5"
**Overall length:** 6⁷/₈"
**Weight (empty):** 25 oz.
**Sights:** Post w/white dot front; fixed rear adj. for windage only w/2 white dots. Adjustable sight models include micrometer click, adj. for windage and elevation w/2 white dots. Deduct $25 for fixed sights.
**Finish:** Satin stainless
**Prices:**
MODEL 3913 . . . . . . . . . . . . . . . . . . . . . . . . . . $633.00
MODEL 3913 LADYSMITH (single slide) . . . . . . . 651.00
MODEL 3953 (double action only) . . . . . . . . . . . 633.00

### MODEL 4013 TACTICAL  (not shown)

**SPECIFICATIONS (MODEL 4013 TSW)**
**Caliber:** 40 S&W
**Capacity:** 9 rounds
**Action:** Traditional double action
**Barrel length:** 3.5"  **Overall length:** 6⁷/₈"
**Height:** 5"  **Width:** 1.4"
**Weight:** 26.4 oz.
**Sights:** White dot front; fixed w/2-dot rear
**Price:** . . . . . . . . . . . . . . . . . . . . . . . . . . . . . $788.00
Also available:
**MODEL 4056 TSW.** Double action only; weighs 36.5 oz.
**Price:** . . . . . . . . . . . . . . . . . . . . . . . . . . . . . $815.00

### MODEL 4500 COMPACT SERIES

**SPECIFICATIONS (MODEL 4516)**
**Caliber:** 45 ACP
**Capacity:** 7 rounds
**Barrel length:** 3.75"
**Overall length:** 7.25"
**Weight:** 36.5 oz.
**Sights:** White dot front; fixed w/2-dot rear
**Price:** . . . . . . . . . . . . . . . . . . . . . . . . . . . . . $787.00

### MODEL 6900 COMPACT SERIES

**SPECIFICATIONS**
**Caliber:** 9mm Parabellum; traditional DA autoloading Luger
**Capacity:** 12 rounds
**Barrel length:** 3.5"
**Overall length:** 6 7/8"
**Weight (empty):** 26.5 oz.
**Sights:** Post w/white dot front; fixed rear, adj. for windage only w/2 white dots
**Grips:** Curved backstrap
**Finish:** Blue (Model 6904); satin stainless (Model 6906)
**Prices:**
MODEL 6904 . . . . . . . . . . . . . . . . . . . . . . . . . . $625.00
MODEL 6906 . . . . . . . . . . . . . . . . . . . . . . . . . . 688.00
MODEL 6906 Fixed Novak night sight . . . . . . . . . 801.00
MODEL 6946 DA only, fixed sights . . . . . . . . . . . 688.00

**MODEL 3913 DA Stainless**

**MODEL 4516 COMPACT**

**MODEL 6906 DA Stainless**

# SMITH & WESSON PISTOLS

## FULL-SIZE DOUBLE-ACTION PISTOLS

Smith & Wesson's double-action semiautomatic Third Generation line includes the following features: fixed barrel bushing for greater accuracy • smoother trigger pull plus a slimmer, contoured grip and lateral relief cut where trigger guard meets frame • beveled magazine well • ambidextrous safety lever • low-glare bead-blasted finish.

**MODEL 4506**
**Adjustable Sight**

**MODEL 4006**
**With Fixed Sight**

**MODEL 4586**
**Fixed Sight**

**MODEL 4046**

### MODEL 4000 SERIES

**SPECIFICATIONS**
**Caliber:** 40 S&W **Capacity:** 11 rounds
**Barrel length:** 4" **Overall length:** 7.5"
**Weight:** 38.5 oz. (with fixed sights)
**Sights:** Post w/white dot front; fixed w/white 2-dot rear
**Grips:** Straight backstrap
**Finish:** Stainless steel
**Prices:**
**MODEL 4006** w/fixed sights . . . . . . . . . . . . . . . . $758.00
  Same as above w/adj. sights . . . . . . . . . . . . . . 788.00
  w/fixed night sight. . . . . . . . . . . . . . . . . . . . 870.00
**MODEL 4043** DA only (28 oz.) . . . . . . . . . . . . . . 739.00
**MODEL 4046** Fixed sights, DA only (39.5 oz.) . . . 758.00
  Double action only, fixed Tritium night sight . . . . . 870.00

### MODEL 4500 SERIES

**SPECIFICATIONS**
**Caliber:** 45 ACP Autoloading DA
**Capacity:** 8 rounds
**Barrel lengths:** 5" (Model 4506); 4.25" (Models 4566 & 4586)
**Overall length:** 8.5" (Model 4506)
**Weight (empty):** 40.5 oz. (Model 4506); 38.5 oz. (Model 4566)
**Sights:** Post w/white-dot front; fixed rear, adj. for windage only. Adj. sight incl. micrometer click, adj. for windage and elevation w/2 white dots. Add **$29.00** for adj. sights.
**Grips:** Delrin one-piece wraparound, arched backstrap, textured surface
**Finish:** Satin stainless
**Prices:**
**MODEL 4506** w/adj. sights, 5" bbl. . . . . . . . . . . . . $819.00
  With fixed sights . . . . . . . . . . . . . . . . . . . . . . 787.00
**MODEL 4516** DA, 3.75" bbl., fixed sights . . . . . . . 787.00
**MODEL 4566** w/4.25" bbl., fixed sights . . . . . . . . 787.00
**MODEL 4586** DA only, 4.25" bbl., 39.5 oz.,
  fixed 2-dot rear sight, white dot front. . . . . . . . . 787.00

# SMITH & WESSON PISTOLS

## FULL-SIZE DOUBLE-ACTION PISTOLS

### MODEL 5900 SERIES

**SPECIFICATIONS**
**Caliber:** 9mm Parabellum DA Autoloading Luger
**Capacity:** 15 rounds
**Barrel length:** 4"
**Overall length:** 7.5"
**Weight (empty):** 28 oz. (Models 5903, 5904); 37.5 oz. (Model 5906); 38 oz. (Model 5906 w/adj. sight)
**Sights:** Front, post w/white dot; fixed rear, adj. for windage only w/2 white dots. Adjustable sight models include micrometer click, adj. for windage and elevation w/2 white dots.
**Finish:** Blue (Model 5904); satin stainless (Models 5903 and 5906)

**Prices:**
| | |
|---|---|
| **MODEL 5903** Satin stainless | $701.00 |
| **MODEL 5904** Blue | 653.00 |
| **MODEL 5906** Satin stainless | 754.00 |
| With fixed sights | 719.00 |
| With Tritium night sight | 831.00 |
| **MODEL 5946** Double action only | 719.00 |

**MODEL 5906 DA
Stainless**

### MODEL 410

**SPECIFICATIONS**
**Caliber:** 40 S&W
**Capacity:** 10 rounds
**Barrel length:** 4"
**Overall length:** 7.5"
**Weight:** 28.5 oz.
**Sights:** 3-dot sights
**Grips:** Straight backstrap
**Features:** Right-hand slide-mounted manual safety; decocking lever; aluminum alloy frame; blue carbon steel slide; nonreflective matte blued finish; beveled edge slide
**Price:** $490.00

**MODEL 410**

### MODEL 900 SERIES (MODELS 908 & 910)

**SPECIFICATIONS**
**Caliber:** 9mm
**Capacity:** 8 rounds (Model 908); 10 rounds (Model 910)
**Barrel lengths:** 3.5" (Model 908); 4" (Model 910)
**Overall length:** 6¹³/₁₆" (Model 908); 7³/₈" (Model 910)
**Weight:** 28.8 oz. (Model 908); 28 oz. (Model 910)
**Sights:** White dot front; fixed 2- dot rear
**Grips:** Straight backstrap
**Safety:** External, single side
**Finish:** Matte blue
**Features:** Carbon steel slide; alloy frame
**Price:** $443.00

**MODEL 910**

# SMITH & WESSON PISTOLS

## SIGMA SERIES

Smith & Wesson's Sigma Series is the product of several years' effort to produce a series of pistols that has resulted in 12 patent applications. These pistols are a combination of traditional craftsmanship and the latest technological advances that allow the guns to be assembled without the usual "fitting" process required for other handguns, a method that results in complete interchangeability of parts.

The polymer frame design for the Sigma Series provides unprecedented comfort and pointability. The low barrel centerline combined with the ergonomic design means low muzzle flip and fast reaction for the next shot.

### SIGMA SERIES MODEL SW40F
### FULL SIZE DA

### SIGMA SERIES SW40C/SW40F
### FULL SIZE DA
### $531.00

SPECIFICATIONS
**Calibers:** 40 S&W
**Capacity:** 10 rounds
**Barrel length:** 4" (SW40C); 4.5" (SW40F)
**Overall length:** 6.9" (SW40C); 7.75" (SW40F)
**Weight (empty):** 24.4 oz. (SW40C); 26 oz. (SW40F)
**Sights:** 3-dot system (Tritium night sights available)
**Finish:** Satin black/Melonite

### SIGMA SERIES SW9V/SW40V
### $372.00

SPECIFICATIONS
**Caliber:** 9mm and 40 S&W
**Capacity:** 10 rounds
**Action:** Traditional double action
**Barrel length:** 4"
**Overall length:** 7.25"
**Weight:** 24.7 oz
**Finish:** Satin stainless
**Sights:** White dot front; fixed 2-dot rear
**Features:** Strike firing system; grips integral with frame; stainless steel slide

### SIGMA SERIES SW380
### COMPACT DA

### SIGMA SERIES SW380 COMPACT DA
### $308.00 (380 ACP)

SPECIFICATIONS
**Caliber:** 380 ACP
**Capacity:** 6 rounds
**Barrel length:** 3"  **Overall length:** 5.8"
**Weight:** 14 oz.
**Sights:** Post w/channel front; fixed channel rear
**Finish:** Satin black
**Features:** Lightweight polymer frame with integral thumbrest; two-piece trigger; corrosion-resistant steel slide
Also available:
**MODEL SW9M** in 9mm w/3.25" barrel (6.25" overall).
**Weight:** 17.9 oz. **Sights:** Post .060" front; fixed channel rear.
**Price:**. . . . . . . . . . . . . . . . . . . . . . . . . . . . . . . . . **$356.00**

### SIGMA SERIES SW40V

# SMITH & WESSON PISTOLS

**MODEL 457**

**MODEL NO. 41**

## MODEL 457
## $490.00

**SPECIFICATIONS**
**Caliber:** 45 ACP
**Capacity:** 7 rounds
**Barrel length:** 3.75"
**Overall length:** 7.25"
**Weight:** 29 oz.
**Grips:** Straight backstrap
**Sights:** White dot front; fixed 2-dot rear
**Finish:** Blued
**Features:** Carbon steel slide and alloy frame; .260"
bobbed hammer; single side external safety

## MODEL NO. 41 RIMFIRE
## $768.00 (Blue Only)

**SPECIFICATIONS**
**Caliber:** 22 LR  **Magazine capacity:** 12 rounds
**Barrel lengths:** 5.5" and 7"  **Weight:** 41 oz. (5.5" barrel)
**Overall length:** 10.5" (7" bbl.)
**Sights:** Front, 1/8" Patridge undercut; rear, S&W microme-
ter click sight adjustable for windage and elevation
**Grips:** Hardwood target
**Finish:** S&W Bright blue
**Trigger:** .365" width; S&W grooving, adj. trigger stop
**Features:** Carbon steel slide and frame

# TARGET PISTOLS

**MODEL 2213
"SPORTSMAN"**

**MODEL 22A SPORT (not shown)**
**$214.00 (4")   $237.00 (5.5")**
**$300.00 (5.5" Bull Barrel)   $270.00 (7")**

**SPECIFICATIONS**
**Caliber:** 22 LR
**Capacity:** 10 rounds
**Action:** Single
**Barrel lengths:** 4", 5.5" (standard or bull barrel) and 7"
**Overall length:** 8" (4"), 9.5" (5.5"), 11" (7")
**Grips:** Two-piece polymer (4"); 2-piece Soft Touch (5.5"
and 7")
**Weight:** 28 oz. (4"), 32 oz. (5.5"), 33 oz. (7")
**Sights:** Patridge front, adjustable rear
**Finish:** Blue
**Features:** Single slide external safety

**MODEL 2213/2214 RIMFIRE "SPORTSMAN"**
**$269.00 (Blue)   $314.00 (Stainless)**

**SPECIFICATIONS**
**Caliber:** 22 LR. **Capacity:** 8 rounds. **Barrel length:** 3".
**Overall length:** 6 1/8". **Weight:** 18 oz. **Finish:** Stainless
steel slide w/alloy frame (Model 2214 has blued carbon
steel slide w/alloy frame and blued finish)

# SMITH & WESSON REVOLVERS

## SMALL FRAME

**MODEL 60LS LADYSMITH
38 S&W Special**

### LADYSMITH HANDGUNS
### MODEL 36-LS $415.00 (Blue)
### MODEL 60-LS $469.00 (Stainless)

**SPECIFICATIONS**
**Calibers:** 38 S&W Special and 357 Magnum
**Capacity:** 5 shots
**Barrel lengths:** 2" (2¹/₈" 357 Magnum)
**Overall length:** 6⁵/₁₆"
**Weight:** 20 oz. (23 oz. 357 Magnum)
**Sights:** Serrated ramp front (black pinned ramp in 357 Mag.); fixed notch rear
**Grips:** Contoured laminated rosewood, round butt
**Finish:** Glossy deep blue or stainless
**Features:** Both models come with soft-side LadySmith carry case

**MODEL 37
CHIEFS SPECIAL AIRWEIGHT
38 S&W Special**

### MODEL 36
### 38 CHIEFS SPECIAL
### $384.00

**SPECIFICATIONS**
**Caliber:** 38 S&W Special  **Capacity:** 5 shots
**Barrel length:** 2"  **Overall length:** 6⁵/₁₆"
**Weight:** 20 oz.
**Sights:** Serrated ramp front; fixed, square-notch rear
**Grips:** Uncle Mike's Boot
**Finish:** S&W blued carbon steel; satin stainless Model 637
**Features:** .312" smooth combat-style trigger; .240" service hammer
**MODEL 37 CHIEFS SPECIAL AIRWEIGHT:** Same as Model 36, except finish is blue or nickel aluminum alloy.
**Price:** . . . . . . . . . . . . . . . . . . . . . . . . **$419.00**
**MODEL 637 CHIEFS SPECIAL AIRWEIGHT.** With 2" barrel, synthetic round butt, stainless finish. **Weight:** 13.5 oz.
**Price:** . . . . . . . . . . . . . . . . . . . . . . . . **$435.00**

**MODEL 60
38 CHIEFS SPECIAL
STAINLESS**

### MODEL 60
### 38 CHIEFS SPECIAL, STAINLESS
### $438.00 (2" Barrel)  $466.00 (3" Barrel)

**SPECIFICATIONS**
**Calibers:** 38 S&W Special and 357 Mag.
**Capacity:** 5 shots
**Barrel lengths:** 2¹/₈" (357 Mag.); 3" full lug (38 S&W Spec.)
**Overall length:** 6⁵/₁₆"(2¹/₈" bbl.); 7.5" (3" bbl.)
**Weight:** 23 oz. (2¹/₈" barrel); 24.5 oz. (3" full lug barrel)
**Sights:** Micrometer click rear, adj. for windage and elevation; pinned black front (3" full lug model only); standard sights as on Model 36
**Grips:** Uncle Mike's Combat
**Finish:** Satin stainless
**Features:** .312" smooth combat-style trigger

# SMITH & WESSON REVOLVERS

## SMALL FRAME

### 38 CENTENNIAL "AIRWEIGHT"
### MODEL 442
### $435.00

**SPECIFICATIONS**
**Caliber:** 38 S&W Special
**Capacity:** 5 rounds
**Barrel length:** 2"
**Overall length:** 6⁵/₁₆"
**Weight:** 15.8 oz.
**Sights:** Serrated ramp front; fixed, square-notch rear
**Finish:** Matte blue
Also available:
**MODEL 642 CENTENNIAL AIRWEIGHT.** Stainless steel w/2" barrel, synthetic round butt grip, double-action only.
  **Price:** . . . . . . . . . . . . . . . . . . . . . . . . . . . . . **$450.00**
  **LadySmith Model** (satin stainless) . . . . . . . . . **480.00**

**MODEL 442 38 SPECIAL**

### 38 BODYGUARD "AIRWEIGHT"
### MODEL 38 (not shown)
### $452.00 Blue

**SPECIFICATIONS**
**Caliber:** 38 S&W Special
**Capacity:** 5 rounds
**Barrel length:** 2"
**Overall length:** 6³/₈"
**Weight:** 14 oz.
**Sights:** Front serrated ramp; square-notch rear
**Grips:** Checkered walnut Service with S&W monograms
**Finish:** S&W blue
Also available:
**Model 638** in nickel aluminum alloy

### MODEL 317 AIRLITE
### $441.00
### ($475.00 w/Dymondwood Boot)

**SPECIFICATIONS**
**Caliber:** 22 Long Rifle
**Capacity:** 8 rounds
**Action:** Single or double action
**Barrel length:** 2"
**Overall length:** 6³/₁₆"
**Weight:** 9.9 oz.; 10.9 oz. w/Dymondwood Boot
**Sights:** Serrated ramp front; fixed notch rear

### MODEL 649 BODYGUARD
### $477.00

**SPECIFICATIONS**
**Caliber:** 38 S&W Special
**Capacity:** 5 rounds
**Barrel length:** 2¹/₈"
**Overall length:** 6⁵/₁₆"
**Weight:** 20 oz.
**Sights:** Black pinned ramp front; fixed, square-notch rear
**Grips:** Uncle Mike's Combat
**Finish:** Satin stainless

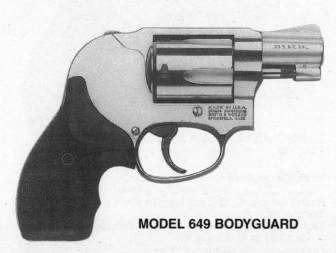

**MODEL 649 BODYGUARD**

### MODEL 696 (not shown)
### $499.00

**SPECIFICATIONS**
**Caliber:** 44 S&W Special  **Capacity:** 5 rounds
**Action:** Single or double action
**Barrel length:** 3"  **Overall length:** 8³/₁₆"
**Weight:** 48 oz.
**Sights:** Pinned ramp front; adjustable black rear
**Grips:** Hogue rubber
**Finish:** Satin stainless
**Features:** .500" target hammer; .400" smooth combat trigger

# SMITH & WESSON REVOLVERS

## SMALL FRAME

**MODEL 63**

### MODEL 63 22/32 KIT GUN
### $466.00 (2" Barrel)
### $470.00 (4" Barrel)

**SPECIFICATIONS**
**Caliber:** 22 Long Rifle  **Capacity:** 6 shots
**Barrel lengths:** 2" and 4"
**Overall length:** 6.25" (w/2" bbl.); 8 11/16 (w/4" bbl.)
**Weight:** 22 oz. (2" barrel); 24.5 oz. (4" barrel)
**Sights:** 1/8" red ramp front sight; rear sight is black stainless
steel S&W micrometer click, square-notch, adjustable for
windage and elevation
**Grips:** Synthetic round butt
**Finish:** Satin stainless

**MODEL 640**

### MODEL 640 CENTENNIAL
### $477.00

**SPECIFICATIONS**
**Calibers:** 357 Magnum and 38 S&W Special
**Action:** Double action only
**Capacity:** 5 rounds
**Barrel length:** 2 1/8"  **Overall length:** 6 3/4"
**Weight:** 25 oz.
**Sights:** Pinned black ramp front; fixed, square-notch rear
**Features:** Fully concealed hammer; smooth hardwood
service stock; satin stainless steel finish; round-butt
synthetic grips

### MODEL 940 CENTENNIAL
### $482.00

**SPECIFICATIONS**
**Caliber:** 9mm Parabellum  **Capacity:** 5 rounds
**Action:** Double action only
**Barrel length:** 2"  **Overall length:** 6 5/16"
**Weight:** 23 oz.
**Sights:** Serrated ramp front; fixed, square-notch rear
**Grips:** Synthetic round-butt grips
**Finish:** Satin stainless
**Feature:** Fully concealed hammer

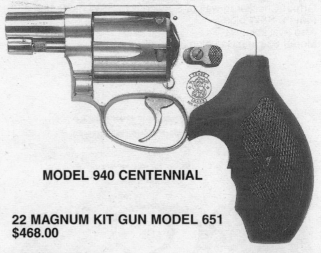

**MODEL 940 CENTENNIAL**

### 22 MAGNUM KIT GUN MODEL 651
### $468.00

**SPECIFICATIONS**
**Caliber:** 22 Magnum  **Capacity:** 6 shots
**Barrel length:** 4"  **Overall length:** 8 11/16"
**Weight:** 24.5 oz.
**Sights:** Red ramp front; micrometer click rear, adjustable
for windage and elevation
**Grips:** Synthetic round-butt grips
**Finish:** Satin stainless
**Features:** .375" hammer; .312" smooth combat trigger

**MODEL 651
22 MAGNUM KIT GUN**

# SMITH & WESSON REVOLVERS

## MEDIUM FRAME

**MODEL 10 HEAVY BARREL**

### 38 MILITARY & POLICE MODEL 10
### $397.00

**SPECIFICATIONS**
**Caliber:** 38 S&W Special  **Capacity:** 6 shots
**Barrel length:** 4" heavy barrel
**Overall length:** 9.25"
**Weight:** 33.5 oz.
**Sights:** Front, fixed 1/8" serrated ramp; square-notch rear
**Grips:** Uncle Mike's Combat
**Finish:** S&W blue

### 38 MILITARY & POLICE STAINLESS MODEL 64
### $422.00 (2" Bbl.)  $430.00 (3" & 4" Bbl.)

**SPECIFICATIONS**
**Caliber:** 38 S&W Special
**Capacity:** 6 shots
**Barrel lengths:** 4" heavy barrel, square butt; 3" heavy barrel, round butt; 2" regular barrel, round butt
**Overall length:** 9.25" w/4" bbl.; 7 7/8" w/3" bbl.; 6 7/8" w/2" barrel
**Weight:** 28 oz. w/2" barrel; 30.5 oz. w/3" bbl.; 33.5 oz. w/4" barrel
**Sights:** Fixed, 1/8" serrated ramp front; square-notch rear
**Grips:** Uncle Mike's Combat
**Finish:** Satin stainless

**MODEL 64**

### 357 MILITARY & POLICE MODEL 13 (HEAVY BARREL)
### $400.00

**SPECIFICATIONS**
**Calibers:** 357 Magnum and 38 S&W Special
**Capacity:** 6 shots
**Barrel lengths:** 3" and 4"
**Overall length:** 9.25" (w/4" bbl.) **Weight:** 30 oz. (w/4" bbl.)
**Sights:** Front, 1/8" serrated ramp; square-notch rear
**Grips:** Uncle Mike's Combat
**Finish:** S&W blue

**MODEL 13**

### 357 MILITARY & POLICE MODEL 65 (HEAVY BARREL)
### $435.00

**SPECIFICATIONS**
Same specifications as Model 13, except Model 65 is satin stainless steel.
Also available:
**MODEL 65 LADYSMITH.** Same specifications as **Model 65** but with 3" barrel only (weighs 31 oz.) and rosewood laminate stock; satin stainless finish, smooth combat wood grips.
**Price:** . . . . . . . . . . . . . . . . . . . . . . . . . . . . . . . . **$469.00**

**MODEL 65**

# SMITH & WESSON REVOLVERS

## MEDIUM FRAME

**K-38 MASTERPIECE
MODEL 14
$473.00**

**38 COMBAT MASTERPIECE
MODEL 15
$426.00**

### SPECIFICATIONS
**Caliber:** 38 S&W Special
**Barrel length:** 6" full lug barrel
**Overall length:** 11 1/8"
**Weight:** 47 oz.
**Sights:** Micrometer click rear, adjustable for windage and elevation; pinned black Patridge-style front
**Grips:** Synthetic square butt (on round-butt frame)
**Finish:** Blue carbon steel
**Features:** .500 target hammer; .312" smooth combat trigger

### SPECIFICATIONS
**Caliber:** 38 S&W Special   **Capacity:** 6 shots
**Barrel length:** 4"
**Overall length:** 9 5/16"
**Weight (loaded):** 32 oz.
**Sights:** Serrated ramp front; S&W micrometer click sight adjustable for windage and elevation
**Grips:** Uncle Mike's Combat
**Finish:** S&W blue
**Features:** .375" semi-target hammer; .312" smooth combat-style trigger
Also available:
**MODEL 67.** Same specifications as **Model 15** but with satin stainless finish, red ramp front sight and .375" semi-target hammer

**MODEL 17
$498.00**

**MODEL 617
$468.00 (4" Barrel)  $498.00 (6" Barrel)
$510.00 (8.75" Barrel)
$514.00 (6" Bbl. 10-Shot)**

### SPECIFICATIONS
**Caliber:** 22 LR   **Capacity:** 10 rounds
**Action:** Single/Double
**Barrel length:** 6"
**Overall length:** 11 1/8"
**Weight:** 42 oz.
**Sights:** Pinned Patridge front; adjustable black blade rear
**Grips:** Hogue rubber
**Finish:** Blued carbon steel
**Features:** .312" smooth combat trigger; .375" semi-target hammer

### SPECIFICATIONS
**Caliber:** 22 Long Rifle   **Capacity:** 6 shots
**Barrel length:** 4", 6" or 8 3/8"
**Overall length:** 9 1/8" (4" barrel); 11 1/8" (6" barrel); 13.5" (8 3/8" barrel)
**Weight (loaded):** 42 oz. with 4" barrel; 48 oz. with 6" barrel; 54 oz. with 8 3/8" barrel
**Sights:** Front pinned Patridge; rear, S&W micrometer click sight adjustable for windage and elevation
**Grips:** Hogue rubber, square butt
**Finish:** Satin stainless
**Features:** Target hammer and trigger; drilled and tapped for scope

## MEDIUM FRAME

**MODEL 19**

### 357 COMBAT MAGNUM
### MODEL 19
### $423.00 (2.5" Bbl.) $433.00 (4" Bbl.)

**SPECIFICATIONS**
**Caliber:** 357 S&W Magnum (actual bullet dia. 38 S&W Spec.)
**Capacity:** 6 shots
**Barrel lengths:** 2.5" and 4"
**Overall length:** 9.5" w/4" bbl.; 7.5" w/2.5" bbl.
**Weight:** 30.5 oz. (2.5" bbl.); 36 oz. (4" bbl.)
**Sights:** Serrated ramp front; adjustable black rear
**Grips:** Uncle Mike's Combat
**Finish:** S&W bright blue

**MODEL 66**

### 357 COMBAT MAGNUM
### MODEL 66
### $474.00 (2.5" Bbl.) $480.00 (4" Bbl.)

**SPECIFICATIONS**
**Caliber:** 357 Magnum (actual bullet dia. 38 S&W Spec.)
**Capacity:** 6 shots
**Barrel lengths:** 4" or 6" with square butt; 2.5" with round butt
**Overall length:** 7.5" w/2.5" bbl.; 9.5" w/4" bbl.; 11 3/8" w/6" bbl.
**Weight:** 30.5 oz. w/2.5" bbl.; 36 oz. w/4" bbl.; 39 oz. w/6" bbl.
**Sights:** Front, 1/8"; rear, S&W Red Ramp on ramp base, S&W Micrometer Click, adjustable for windage and elevation
**Grips:** Uncle Mike's Combat
**Trigger:** .312" Smooth Combat
**Finish:** Satin stainless

**MODEL 586**

### DISTINGUISHED COMBAT MAGNUM
### MODEL 586
### $469.00 (4" Bbl.) $474.00 (6" Bbl.)

**SPECIFICATIONS**
**Calibers:** 357 Magnum and 38 S&W Special
**Capacity:** 6 shots
**Barrel lengths:** 4" and 6"
**Overall length:** 9 9/16" w/4" bbl.; 11 15/16" w/6" bbl.
**Weight:** 41 oz. w/4" bbl.; 46 oz. w/6" bbl.
**Sights:** Front, S&W Red Ramp; rear, S&W Micrometer Click, adjustable for windage and elevation; white outline notch
**Grips:** Hogue rubber square butt
**Finish:** S&W Blue

# SMITH & WESSON REVOLVERS

## MEDIUM FRAME

### MODEL 686

### MODEL 686 POWERPORT

**MODEL 686 (2.5" Barrel)**
**$489.00-$539.00**

Same specifications as Model 586 (see preceding page), except also available with 2.5" barrel (35.5 oz.) and 8 3/8" barrel (53 oz.). All models have stainless steel finish, combat or target stock and/or trigger; adjustable sights optional.

**MODEL 686 POWERPORT**
**$537.00**

Same general specifications as the **Model 686**, except this revolver features 6" full lug barrel with integral compensator, Hogue rubber grips and black-pinned Patridge front sight. Also available:
**MODEL 686 PLUS DISTINGUISHED COMBAT MAGNUM** (Stainless). **Capacity:** 7 rounds. **Barrel lengths:** 2.5", 4" or 6" full lug. **Overall length:** 7.5"–11 15/16". **Weight:** 34.5 oz.–45 oz. **Prices:** **$508.00** (2.5" bbl.); **$516.00** (4" bbl.); **$524.00** (6" bbl.)

## LARGE FRAME

**MODEL 29**
**44 MAGNUM MODEL 29**
**$564.00 (6" Bbl.) $575.00 (8 3/8" Bbl.)**

### MODEL 625

**SPECIFICATIONS**
**Calibers:** 44 Magnum and 44 S&W Spec.
**Capacity:** 6 shots
**Barrel lengths:** 6" and 8 3/8"
**Overall length:** 11 3/8" with 6" bbl.; 13 7/8" with 8 3/8" bbl.
**Weight:** 47 oz. w/6" bbl.; 54 oz. w/8 3/8" bbl.
**Sights:** Front, Red Ramp on ramp base; rear, S&W Micrometer Click, adjustable for windage and elevation; white outline notch
**Grips:** Hogue rubber
**Hammer:** .500 " Target
**Trigger:** .400" serrated
**Finish:** Blued carbon steel

**MODEL 625**
**$607.00**

**SPECIFICATIONS**
**Caliber:** 45 ACP  **Capacity:** 6 shots
**Barrel length:** 5" full lug barrel  **Overall length:** 10 3/8"
**Weight (empty):** 45 oz.
**Sights:** Front, Patridge on ramp base; S&W Micrometer Click rear, adjustable for windage and elevation
**Grips:** Hogue rubber, round butt
**Finish:** Satin stainless

# SMITH & WESSON REVOLVERS

## LARGE FRAME

**MODEL 629**

### MODEL 629
### $597.00 (4" Bbl.)  $602.00 (6" Bbl.)
### $616.00 (8³/₈" Barrel)

**SPECIFICATIONS**
**Calibers:** 44 Magnum, 44 S&W Special
**Capacity:** 6 shots
**Barrel lengths:** 4", 6", 8³/₈"
**Overall length:** 9⁵/₈", 11³/₈", 13⁷/₈"
**Weight (empty):** 44 oz. (4" bbl.); 47 oz. (6" bbl.); 54 oz. (8³/₈" bbl.)
**Sights:** S&W Red Ramp front; white outline rear w/S&W Micro-[l]meter Click, adjustable for windage and elevation; drilled and tapped
**Grips:** Hogue rubber
**Finish:** Satin stainless steel
**Features:** Combat trigger, target hammer

### MODEL 629 CLASSIC
### $640.00 (5" & 6.5" Bbl.)
### $661.00 (8³/₈" Bbl.)

**SPECIFICATIONS**
**Calibers:** 44 Magnum, 44 S&W Special
**Capacity:** 6 rounds
**Barrel lengths:** 5", 6.5", 8³/₈"
**Overall length:** 10.5", 12", 13⁷/₈"
**Weight:** 51 oz. (5" bbl.); 52 oz. (6.5" bbl.); 54 oz.  (8³/₈" bbl.)
**Grips:** Hogue rubber

Also available:
**MODEL 629 CLASSIC DX.** Same features as the Model 629 Classic above, plus interchangeable front sights.
   With 6.5" barrel . . . . . . . . . . . . . . . . . . . . . . . **$825.00**
   With 8³/₈" barrel . . . . . . . . . . . . . . . . . . . . . . . **852.00**
**MODEL 629 POWERPORT** w/6.5" barrel (12" overall length), weighs 52 oz. Patridge front sight, adjustable black blade rear sight. **Price:** . . . . . . . . . . . . . . . . . . . . . **$640.00**

**MODEL 629 CLASSIC DX**

**MODEL 657**

### MODEL 657 STAINLESS
### $537.00

**SPECIFICATIONS**
**Caliber:** 41 Magnum
**Capacity:** 6 shots
**Barrel length:** 6"
**Overall length:** 11³/₈"
**Weight (empty):** 48 oz.
**Sights:** Front, pinned ramp on ramp base; black blade rear, adjustable for windage and elevation; drilled and tapped
**Grips:** Hogue rubber
**Finish:** Satin stainless steel
**Features:** Combat trigger, target hammer

# SPRINGFIELD PISTOLS

## MODEL 1911-A1 PISTOLS

### STANDARD MIL-SPEC 1911-A1

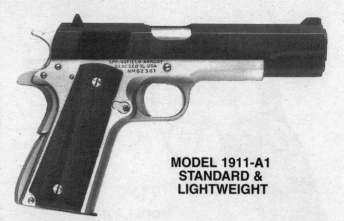

### MODEL 1911-A1 STANDARD & LIGHTWEIGHT

**SPECIFICATIONS**
**Calibers:** 45 ACP and 38 Super
**Capacity:** 7 rounds (45 ACP); 9 rounds (38 Super)
**Barrel length:** 5"  **Overall length:** 8⅝"
**Trigger pull:** 5-6.5 lbs.  **Sight radius:** 6.25"
**Weight:** 38.5 oz.  **Finish:** Parkerized
**Features:** Black plastic grips; military hammer; 3-dot fixed combat sights
**Price:**....................................$519.00

**SPECIFICATIONS**
**Calibers:** 45 ACP, 9mm and 38 Super
**Capacity:** 8 rounds (45 ACP), 9 rounds (9mm & 38 Super)
**Barrel length:** 5"  **Overall length:** 8⅝"
**Weight:** 38.5 oz. (31.5 oz. Lightweight)
**Features:** Walnut grips; Bo-Mar-type sights optional
**Prices:**

| | |
|---|---|
| 45 ACP Blued or Lightweight Matte............ | **$549.00** |
| 45 ACP Stainless................................ | **589.00** |
| 45 ACP Stainless Steel V-12 (ported).......... | **719.00** |
| 9mm Blued...................................... | **549.00** |
| 9mm Stainless.................................. | **599.00** |
| Long slide Stainless Steel w/Bo-Mar sights...... | **679.00** |
| 38 Super Blued................................. | **545.00** |
| 38 Super Stainless Steel........................ | **599.00** |

### MODEL 1911-A1 TROPHY MATCH BI-TONE

### TROPHY MATCH

**SPECIFICATIONS**
**Calibers:** 45 ACP and 9mm  **Capacity:** 7 rounds
**Barrel length:** 5"  **Overall length:** 8⅝"
**Weight:** 40 oz.
**Trigger pull:** 4–5.5 lbs.
**Sights:** Fully adjustable target sights  **Sight radius:** 6.75"
**Finish:** Blued, Bi-tone or stainless
**Features:** Match grade barrel; Videcki speed trigger; extended thumb safety; serrated front strap & top of slide
**Prices:**

| | |
|---|---|
| Blued...................................... | **$954.00** |
| Bi-Tone (w/fitted beavertail safety)............ | **940.00** |
| Stainless (w/fitted beavertail safety).......... | **985.00** |

### MODEL 1911-A1 HIGH-CAPACITY STANDARD (not shown)

**SPECIFICATIONS**
**Caliber:** 45 ACP
**Capacity:** 10 rounds (13-round & 17-round capacity available for law enforcement and military use only)
**Barrel length:** 5"  **Trigger pull:** 5-6.5 lbs.
**Sight radius:** 6.14"
**Finish:** Blued, stainless or Parkerized

| | |
|---|---|
| 45 ACP Parkerized........................ | **$659.00** |
| 45 ACP & 9mm Blued...................... | **679.00** |
| 45 ACP & 9mm Stainless................... | **709.00** |

In addition to the models listed above and in the following pages, Springfield Armory also produces a broad line of customized pistols (including the Super Tuned series described later). These include the following: Bullseye Wadcutter, National Match Hardball, PPC Auto, High Capacity Full House Racegun, and more. For additional information, contact: Springfield Custom (see Directory of Manufacturers and Suppliers).

# SPRINGFIELD PISTOLS

## MODEL 1911-A1 CHAMPION SERIES

### MODEL 1911-A1 CHAMPION

### MODEL 1911-A1 MIL-SPEC CHAMPION

**SPECIFICATIONS**
**Caliber:** 45 ACP   **Capacity:** 7 rounds
**Barrel length:** 4"   **Overall length:** 7.75"
**Weight:** 36.3 oz.
**Trigger pull:** 5-6.5"   **Sight radius:** 5.25"
**Sights:** 3-dot fixed combat sights
**Finish:** Blued or stainless
Blued . . . . . . . . . . . . . . . . . . . . . . . . . . . . . . . . . **$569.00**
Stainless . . . . . . . . . . . . . . . . . . . . . . . . . . . . . . **579.00**
Bi-tone . . . . . . . . . . . . . . . . . . . . . . . . . . . . . . . . **665.00**
V-10 (Ported) stainless w/ultra compact slide . . . . **749.00**

**SPECIFICATIONS**
**Caliber:** 45 ACP   **Capacity:** 7 rounds
**Barrel length:** 4"   **Overall length:** 7.75"
**Weight:** 36.3 oz.   **Sights:** 3-Dot Combat
**Finish:** Parkerized
**Price:** . . . . . . . . . . . . . . . . . . . . . . . . . . . . . . . . **$519.00**

### MODEL 1911A-1 MIL-SPEC CHAMPION ULTRA COMPACT

### MODEL 1911-A1 LIGHTWEIGHT COMPACT

**SPECIFICATIONS**
**Caliber:** 45 ACP   **Capacity:** 7 rounds
**Barrel length:** 4"   **Overall length:** 7.75"
**Weight:** 36.3 oz.
**Trigger pull:** 5-6.5 lbs.   **Sight radius:** 5.25"
**Sights:** 3-dot fixed Combat sights
**Finish:** Parkerized
**Price:** . . . . . . . . . . . . . . . . . . . . . . . . . . . . . . . . **$549.00**

**SPECIFICATIONS**
**Caliber:** 45 ACP   **Capacity:** 7 rounds
**Barrel length:** 4"   **Overall length:** 7.75"
**Weight:** 32 oz. (27 oz. alloy)
**Trigger pull:** 5-6.5"
**Sights:** 3-dot fixed combat sights
**Sight radius:** 5.25"
**Finish:** Matte
**Price:** . . . . . . . . . . . . . . . . . . . . . . . . . . . . . . . . **$669.00**

# SPRINGFIELD PISTOLS

## SUPER TUNED SERIES

**CHAMPION 1911-A1**

### CHAMPION 1911-A1

**SPECIFICATIONS**
**Caliber:** 45 ACP **Capacity:** 7 + 1
**Barrel length:** 4" **Overall length:** 7.75"
**Weight:** 36.3 oz. **Sight radius:** 5.25"
**Trigger pull:** 4.4-5.5 lbs. crisp
**Grips:** Lightweight combat **Finish:** Blue or Parkerized
**Sights:** Novak fixed low-mount; dovetailed serrated ramp
front
**Features:** Tuned and polished extractor and ejector; beavertail grip safety; polished feed ramp and throat barrel
**Prices:**
Parkerized . . . . . . . . . . . . . . . . . . . . . . . . . . . . . . **$959.00**
Blued . . . . . . . . . . . . . . . . . . . . . . . . . . . . . . . . . **989.00**
Also available:
**SUPER TUNED V10 1911-A1.** In stainless or Bi-tone w/3.5"
barrel. **$1119.00** (Stainless); **$1049.00** (Bi-Tone)
**SUPER TUNED STANDARD 1911-A1.** In Stainless w/5"
barrel. **$995.00**

## ULTRA COMPACT SERIES

### HIGH-CAPACITY
### ULTRA COMPACT MODELS (not shown)

**SPECIFICATIONS**
**Calibers:** 45 ACP and 9mm
**Capacity:** 10 rounds (11-round capacity available for law
enforcement and military use only)
**Barrel length:** 3.5" **Weight:** 33.6 oz.
**Sight radius:** 5.25" **Trigger pull:** 5-6.5 lbs.
**Finish:** Blued or stainless

**Features:** 3-dot fixed combat sights; flared ejection port;
beveled magazine well
**Prices:**
Blued . . . . . . . . . . . . . . . . . . . . . . . . . . . . . . . . . **$719.00**
Stainless . . . . . . . . . . . . . . . . . . . . . . . . . . . . . . . **759.00**
Mil-Spec Parkerized . . . . . . . . . . . . . . . . . . . . . . . **689.00**

**1911-A1 V-10
ULTRA COMPACT
BI-TONE**

**SPECIFICATIONS**
**Caliber:** 45 ACP **Capacity:** 7 rounds
**Barrel length:** 3.5" **Overall length:** 7.75"
**Weight:** 34.8 oz.
**Sights:** 3-dot fixed combat sights **Sight radius:** 5.25"
**Trigger pull:** 5-6.5 lbs.
**Finish:** Bi-Tone or stainless
**Prices:**
Bi-Tone. . . . . . . . . . . . . . . . . . . . . . . . . . . . . . . . **$675.00**
Stainless . . . . . . . . . . . . . . . . . . . . . . . . . . . . . . . **699.00**

**1911-A1
ULTRA COMPACT
BI-TONE**

**SPECIFICATIONS**
**Caliber:** 45 ACP **Capacity:** 7 rounds
**Barrel length:** 3.5" **Overall length:** 7¹/₈"
**Weight:** 31 oz.
**Finish:** Bi-Tone or Parkerized
**Prices:**
Bi-Tone. . . . . . . . . . . . . . . . . . . . . . . . . . . . . . . . **$629.00**
Parkerized . . . . . . . . . . . . . . . . . . . . . . . . . . . . . . **519.00**

# SPRINGFIELD PISTOLS

## MODEL 1911-A1 PDP SERIES

**CHAMPION COMP**

### CHAMPION COMP

**SPECIFICATIONS**
**Caliber:** 45 ACP   **Capacity:** 7 rounds
**Barrel length:** 4.5"   **Overall length:** 8"
**Weight:** 38.4 oz.   **Sights:** 3-Dot Combat
**Finish:** Blued
**Features:** Single port expansion chamber
**Price:**....................................$869.00

### LIGHTWEIGHT COMPACT COMP

**SPECIFICATIONS**
**Caliber:** 45 ACP   **Capacity:** 6 rounds
**Barrel length:** 4.5"   **Overall length:** 8"
**Weight:** 30.2 oz. (alloy frame)
**Finish:** Matte   **Sights:** 3-Dot fixed Combat
**Price:**....................................$869.00

**LIGHTWEIGHT COMPACT COMP**

### DEFENDER (not shown)

**SPECIFICATIONS**
**Caliber:** 45 ACP   **Capacity:** 8 rounds
**Barrel length:** 5"   **Overall length:** 9"
**Weight:** 42.2 oz.
**Sight radius:** 6 3/8"   **Sights:** 3-dot adjustable
**Finish:** Bi-Tone
**Features:** Videcki speed trigger, extended safety
**Price:**....................................$993.00

### FACTORY COMP (not shown)

**SPECIFICATIONS**
**Calibers:** 45 ACP and 38 Super
**Capacity:** 8 rounds (9 rounds 38 Super)
**Barrel length:** 5 5/8"   **Overall length:** 10"
**Weight:** 42.8 oz.   **Finish:** Blued
**Sights:** Adjustable 3-dot rear; ramp front
**Features:** Videcki speed trigger; checkered walnut grips;
   extended thumb safety; skeletonized hammer
**Prices:**
45 ACP ...............................$947.00
38 Super ...............................979.00

**HIGH-CAPACITY FACTORY COMP**

### HIGH-CAPACITY FACTORY COMP

**SPECIFICATIONS**
**Calibers:** 45 ACP and 38 Super
**Capacity:** 10 rounds (13 rounds and 17 rounds available for
   law-enforcement and military use only)
**Barrel length:** 5.5"   **Overall length:** 10"
**Weight:** 40 oz.   **Finish:** Blued
**Features:** Triple port comp, skeletonized hammer and grip
   safety; match barrel & bushing; extended thumb safety;
   lowered & flared ejection port
**Prices:**
45 ACP ...............................$1075.00
38 Super ...............................1099.00

# STAR AUTOMATIC PISTOLS

**M43 FIRESTAR**

## MODELS M40, M43 & M45 FIRESTAR
### 9mm Parabellum, 40 S&W or 45 ACP

This pocket-sized Firestar pistol features all-steel construction, a triple-dot sight system (fully adjustable rear) and ambidextrous safety. The Acculine barrel design reseats and locks the barrel after each shot. Checkered rubber grips.

### SPECIFICATIONS
**Capacity:** 7 rounds (9mm); 6 rounds
  (40 S&W and 45 ACP)
**Barrel lengths:** 3.39" (3.6" 45 ACP)
**Overall length:** 6.5" (6.85" 45 ACP)
**Weight:** 30 oz. (9mm); 31.2 oz. (40 S&W); 35 oz. (45 ACP)
**Height:** 4.62"; 4.75" (45 ACP)
**Width:** 1.35"; 1.41" (45 ACP)
**Prices:**

| | |
|---|---|
| **Firestar M40** Blued finish, 40 S&W | $445.00 |
| Starvel finish | 465.00 |
| **Firestar M43** Blued finish, 9mm | 430.00 |
| Starvel finish, 9mm | 450.00 |
| **Firestar M45** Blued finish, 45 ACP | 470.00 |
| Starvel finish, 45 ACP | 490.00 |

## FIRESTAR PLUS

**FIRESTAR PLUS**

The Firestar Plus features enlarged magazine capacity, lightweight alloy frame, fast-button-release magazine, large grip and ambidextrous safety. It also has a triple-dot sight system, tight-lock Acculine barrel for positive barrel/slide alignment and an all-steel slide that glides on internal rails machined inside the frame.

### SPECIFICATIONS
**Caliber:** 9mm Parabellum
**Capacity:** 10 rounds
**Barrel length:** 3.39"
**Overall length:** 6.6"
**Weight:** 24 oz.
**Height:** 4.8"   **Width:** 1.37"
**Finish:** Blued or Starvel
**Prices:**

| | |
|---|---|
| 9mm blued | $460.00 |
| Starvel finish | 485.00 |

## ULTRASTAR

**ULTRASTAR**

The Ultrastar features a slim profile, light weight and first-shot, double-action speed. The use of polymer frames makes this pistol exceptionally strong and durable. Other features include a triple-dot sight system, ambidextrous two-position manual safety (safe and safe decock), all-steel internal mechanism and barrel, slide-mounted on rails inside frame.

### SPECIFICATIONS
**Calibers:** 9mm Parabellum and 40 S&W
**Capacity:** 9 rounds (9mm); 8 rounds (40 S&W)
**Barrel length:** 3.5"   **Overall length:** 7"
**Weight:** 26 oz.
**Height:** 5.0"   **Width:** 1.33"
**Price:** ................................. $359.00

# STOEGER PISTOLS

## PRO SERIES 95

The PRO SERIES 95 are precision target pistols designed for the knowledgeable, advanced target shooter. Destined to be among the world's most popular competitive pistols, the PRO SERIES 95 features 10-round capacity in 22 Long Rifle caliber, plus:

• interchangeable barrels
• fully adjustable target sights
• trigger pull adjustment
• trigger travel adjustment
• automatic slide lock
• Pachmayr military-style rubber grips
• stainless-steel finish

The vent-rib model features a full-length vent rib that produces the most positive sighting plane for the advanced competitor.

The bull-barrel and fluted-barrel models feature the military bracket rear sight, acclaimed by many competitive shooters as the most reliable sighting system developed.

**Optional:**
Walnut target grips with thumbrest . . . . . . . . . . . . . **$55.00**
Stainless-steel magazine (10 rounds): . , . . . . . . . . . **42.00**

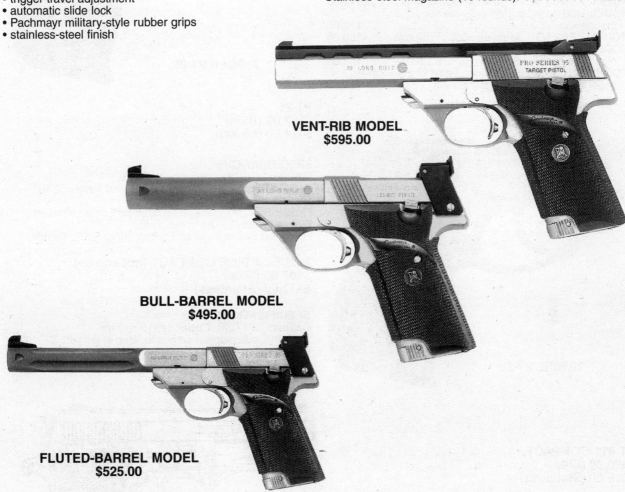

**VENT-RIB MODEL**
**$595.00**

**BULL-BARREL MODEL**
**$495.00**

**FLUTED-BARREL MODEL**
**$525.00**

## SPECIFICATIONS PRO SERIES 95

| MODEL | BBL. LGTH. | O.A. LGTH. | REAR SIGHT | SIGHT RADIUS | WT./OZ. |
|---|---|---|---|---|---|
| Vent Rib | 5¹/₂" | 9³/₄" | ON RIB | 8³/₄" | 47 |
| Bull Barrel | 5¹/₂" | 9³/₄" | ON BRACKET | 8³/₄" | 45 |
| Fluted Barrel | 7¹/₄" | 11³/₄" | ON BRACKET | 10" | 45 |

# TAURUS PISTOLS

## MODEL PT 22
**$162.00 (Blue)**
**$171.00 (Nickel)**

### SPECIFICATIONS
**Caliber:** 22 LR **Action:** Semiautomatic (DA only)
**Capacity:** 8 shots **Barrel length:** 2.75"
**Overall length:** 5.25" **Weight:** 12.3 oz.
**Sights:** Fixed **Safety:** Manual
**Grips:** Brazilian hardwood
**Finish:** Blue, nickel, duotone or gold trimmed
Also available:
**MODEL 22 NB3** w/blue slide on nickel frame . . . . **$171.00**
**MODEL B3R** w/finger groove & rosewood
  grip panels . . . . . . . . . . . . . . . . . . . . . . . . . . . . **172.00**
**MODEL PT 22 N3R** Same as above in nickel . . . . **180.00**
**MODEL 22NB3R** w/finger groove, rosewood grip panel,
  blue slide & nickel frame. . . . . . . . . . . . . . . . . **180.00**
**MODEL 22G3R** w/blue finish and gold or blue barrel,
  finger groove, rosewood grip panels . . . . . . . . **195.00**

**MODEL PT 22**

## PT-25
**$162.00 (Blue)**
**$171.00 (Nickel)**

### SPECIFICATIONS
**Caliber:** 25 ACP **Capacity:** 9 rounds
**Action:** Double action semiauto **Barrel length:** 2.75"
**Overall length:** 5.25" **Weight:** 12.3 oz.
**Finish:** Blue, stainless steel, duotone or gold trimmed
**Sights:** Fixed
**Features:** See options and prices under PT-22 listings

## MODEL PT-938 COMPACT (not shown)
**$397.00 (Blue)**
**$412.00 (Stainless)**

### SPECIFICATIONS
**Caliber:** 380 ACP **Capacity:** 10 rounds
**Action:** Double action semiauto **Barrel length:** 3"
**Overall length:** 6.75" **Weight:** 27 oz.
**Finish:** Blue or stainless steel
**Sights:** Fixed

**MODEL PT-25**

## PT 911 COMPACT
**$390.00 (Blue)**
**$399.00 (Stainless)**

### SPECIFICATIONS
**Caliber:** 9mm **Capacity:** 10 rounds
**Action:** Double action semiauto **Barrel length:** 3.75"
**Overall length:** 7" **Weight:** 28.2 oz.
**Safeties:** Manual, ambidextrous hammer drop; intercept
  notch; firing pin block; chamber load indicator
**Grips:** Santoprene II
**Sights:** Fixed 3-dot combat
**Finish:** Blue or stainless
**Features:** Floating firing pin

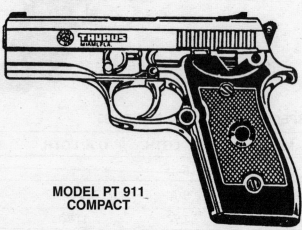

**MODEL PT 911
COMPACT**

# TAURUS PISTOLS

## MODEL PT-92

## MODEL PT-92 AF
### $449.00 (Blue)   $493.00 (Stainless)

**SPECIFICATIONS**
**Caliber:** 9mm Parabellum
**Action:** Semiautomatic double action
**Capacity:** 10 + 1
**Hammer:** Exposed
**Barrel length:** 5"   **Overall length:** 8.5"
**Height:** 5.39"   **Width:** 1.45"
**Weight:** 34 oz. (empty)
**Rifling:** R.H., 6 grooves
**Sights:** Front, fixed; rear, drift adjustable, 3-dot combat
**Safeties:** (a) Ambidextrous manual safety locking trigger mechanism and slide in locked position; (b) half-cock position; (c) inertia-operated firing pin; (d) chamber-loaded indicator
**Slide:** Hold open upon firing last cartridge
**Grips:** Smooth Brazilian walnut
**Finish:** Blue or stainless steel

Also available:
**MODEL PT-99.** Same specifications as Model PT 92, but has micrometer click-adjustable rear sight. **$471.00** Blue; **$518.00** Stainless
**MODEL PT-99AFD** Deluxe Shooter's Pak w/extra magazine & custom case. **$500.00** Blue; **$546.00** Stainless

## MODEL PT-99 STAINLESS

## MODEL PT-940 (not shown)
### $437.00 (Blue)   $452.00 (Stainless)

**SPECIFICATIONS**
**Caliber:** 40 S&W
**Action:** Semiautomatic double
**Capacity:** 10 rounds
**Barrel length:** 3.75"   **Overall length:** 7"
**Weight:** 28.2 oz.
**Grips:** Santoprene II
**Sights:** Low-profile 3-cot combat
**Finish:** Blue or stainless
**Features:** Factory porting standard

## MODEL PT-945

## MODEL PT-945
### $453.00 (Blue)
### $469.00 (Stainless)

**SPECIFICATIONS**
**Caliber:** 45 ACP   **Capacity:** 8 shots
**Action:** Semiautomatic double
**Barrel length:** 4.25"   **Overall length:** 7.48"
**Weight:** 29.5 oz.
**Sights:** Drift-adjustable front and rear; 3-dot combat
**Grips:** Santoprene II
**Safety features:** Manual safety; ambidextrous; chamber load indicator; intercept notch; firing-pin block; floating firing pin
**Finish:** Blue or stainless

Also available:
**MODEL 945C** w/factory porting (blue) . . . . . . . . . $492.00
   w/factory porting (stainless) . . . . . . . . . . . . . . 507.00
**MODEL 945D** Deluxe Shooter's Pak
   w/extra magazine and case (blue) . . . . . . . . . . 476.00
   w/extra magazine and case (stainless) . . . . . . . 498.00
   w/factory porting (blue). . . . . . . . . . . . . . . . . 515.00
   w/factory porting (stainless) . . . . . . . . . . . . . . 531.00

# TAURUS REVOLVERS

## MODEL 44

### SPECIFICATIONS
**Caliber:** 44 Mag.   **Capacity:** 6 rounds
**Barrel lengths:** 3" and 4" (heavy, solid); 6.5" and 8³/₈" (vent. rib)
**Weight:** 44 oz. (4"); 52.5 oz. (6.5"); 57.25 oz. (8³/₈")
**Sights:** Serrated ramp front; rear micrometer click, adjustable for windage and elevation
**Grips:** Santoprene I
**Finish:** Blue or stainless steel
**Features:** Compensated barrel; transfer bar safety
**Prices:**
| | |
|---|---|
| 3" barrel blue | **$447.00** |
| stainless steel | **608.00** |
| w/fixed sights, rosewood colored round butt grips, ported barrel | **554.00** |
| 4" barrel blue | **447.00** |
| stainless steel | **508.00** |
| 6.5" and 8³/₈" blue | **465.00** |
| stainless steel | **629.00** |

## MODEL 82
**$264.00 (Blue)**
**$313.00 (Stainless)**

### SPECIFICATIONS
**Caliber:** 38 Special
**Capacity:** 6 shot
**Action:** Double
**Barrel lengths:** 3", 4"
**Weight:** 34 oz. (4" barrel)
**Sights:** Notched rear; serrated ramp front
**Grips:** Brazilian hardwood
**Finish:** Blue or stainless

## MODEL 83
**$278.00 (Blue)**
**$324.00 (Stainless)**

### SPECIFICATIONS
**Caliber:** 38 Special
**Action:** Double
**Capacity:** 6 shot
**Barrel length:** 4"
**Weight:** 34 oz.
**Sights:** Serrated ramp front; micrometer-click rear adjustable for windage and elevation
**Grips:** Brazilian hardwood
**Finish:** Blue or stainless

## MODEL 85
**$239.00 (Blue)**
**$287.00 (Stainless Steel)**

### SPECIFICATIONS
**Caliber:** 38 Special
**Capacity:** 5 shot
**Action:** Double
**Barrel length:** 2" and 3"
**Weight:** 21 oz. (2" barrel)
**Sights:** Notched rear, serrated ramp front
**Grips:** Brazilian hardwood
**Finish:** Blue or stainless steel

Also available:
**MODEL 85CH.** Same specifications and prices as Model 85, except has concealed hammer and 2" barrel only.
**MODEL 85UL** w/2" barrel only and optional porting; weighs 17 oz. **$274.00** (Blue); **$304.00** (Stainless)

# TAURUS REVOLVERS

**MODEL 941**

## MODEL 94
### $308.00 (Blue)
### $356.00 (Stainless)

**SPECIFICATIONS**
**Caliber:** 22 LR
**Number of shots:** 9
**Action:** Double
**Barrel lengths:** 3", 4", and 5"
**Weight:** 25 oz. (w/4" barrel)
**Sights:** Serrated ramp front; rear micrometer click adjustable for windage and elevation
**Grips:** Brazilian hardwood
**Finish:** Blue or stainless steel

Also available:
**MODEL 941** in 22 Magnum, 8-shot capacity; 2" barrel available; ejector shroud.
In blue . . . . . . . . . . . . . . . . . . . . . . . . . . . . . . . **$331.00**
In stainless steel . . . . . . . . . . . . . . . . . . . . . . . 384.00

## MODEL 96
### $376.00

**SPECIFICATIONS**
**Caliber:** 22 LR
**Capacity:** 6 shot
**Action:** Double
**Barrel length:** 6"
**Weight:** 34 oz.
**Sights:** Patridge-type front; rear, micrometer click[qladjustable for windage and elevation
**Safety:** Transfer bar
**Grips:** Brazilian hardwood
**Finish:** Blue only
**Features:** Target hammer; adjustable target trigger

## MODEL 445 DOUBLE ACTION
### $270.00 (Blue) $319.00 (Stainless)

**SPECIFICATIONS**
**Caliber:** 44 Special  **Capacity:** 5 shots
**Barrel length:** 2"
**Weight:** 28.25 oz.
**Grips:** Santoprene I
**Sights:** Serrated ramp front; notched rear
**Finish:** Blue or stainless
**Features:** Optional porting; heavy solid rib barrel

Also available:
**MODEL 445CH.** Same specifications as Model 445 but features concealed hammer

## MODEL 605
### $262.00 (Blue)
### $312.00 (Stainless)

**SPECIFICATIONS**
**Caliber:** 357 Magnum
**Capacity:** 5 shot
**Barrel length:** 2"
**Weight:** 24.5 oz.
**Sights:** Notched rear; serrated ramp front
**Grips:** Santoprene I
**Safety:** Transfer bar
**Finish:** Blue or stainless
**Features:** Optional porting ($19.00 add'l.)

Also available:
**MODEL 605CH** w/concealed hammer and ported barrel

# TAURUS REVOLVERS

## MODEL 606 COMPACT
**$270.00 (2¹/₄" Blue)  $319.00 (2¹/₄" Stainless)**
**289.00 (2" Blue)       330.00 (2" Stainless)**

### SPECIFICATIONS
**Caliber:** 357 Magnum/38 Special
**Capacity:** 6 shots
**Action:** Double action
**Barrel lengths:** 2" and 2¹/₄"
**Weight:** 29 oz.
**Sights:** Notched rear; serrated ramp front
**Grips:** Santoprene I
**Finish:** Blue or stainless
**Features:** Transfer bar safety; heavy solid rib barrel; ejector shroud; floating firing pin; optional porting

Also available:
**MODEL 606CH.** Same specifications as Model 606, but with concealed hammer (**$20.00** additional)

## MODEL 608 DOUBLE ACTION
**$447.00 (3", 4" Blue)**
**508.00 (3", 4" Stainless)**
**465.00 (6¹/₂", 8³/₈" Blue)**
**529.00 (6¹/₂", 8³/₈" Stainless)**

### SPECIFICATIONS
**Caliber:** 357 Magnum    **Capacity:** 8 shots
**Barrel lengths:** 3" and 4" (heavy solid rib); 6¹/₂" and 8³/₈" (ejector shroud)
**Weight:** 51.5 oz. (6.5" barrel)
**Grips:** Santoprene I
**Sights:** Serrated ramp front w/red insert; micrometer click adjustable
**Finish:** Blue or stainless
**Features:** Compensated barrel; transfer bar safety; concealed hammer (3" barrel and stainless steel only **$46.00** additional)

## MODEL 669
**$344.00 (4" and 6" Blue)**
**$421.00 (4" and 6" Stainless)**

### SPECIFICATIONS
**Caliber:** 357 Magnum
**Capacity:** 6 shot
**Action:** Double
**Barrel lengths:** 4" and 6.5"
**Weight:** 37 oz. (4" barrel)
**Sights:** Serrated ramp front; rear, micrometer click adjustable for windage and elevation
**Grips:** Brazilian hardwood
**Finish:** Royal blue or stainless
**Optional feature:** Recoil compensator **$363.00** (Blue); **$442.00** (Stainless)

### MODEL 689 STAINLESS

## MODEL 689
**$358.00 (Blue)**
**$435.00 (Stainless)**

The Model 689 has the same specifications as the Model 669, except vent rib is featured. Recoil compensator not available.

# THOMPSON/CENTER

## CONTENDER HUNTER

## ENCORE PISTOL

### SPECIFICATIONS
**Calibers:** 7-30 Waters, 223 Rem., 30-30 Win., 35 Rem., 45-70 Government, 375 Win. and 44 Rem. Mag.
**Barrel length:** 14"  **Overall length:** 16"
**Weight:** 4 lbs. (approx.)
**Features:** T/C Muzzle Tamer (to reduce recoil); a mounted T/C Recoil Proof 2.5X scope w/lighted reticle, QD sling swivels and nylon sling, plus suede leather carrying case
**Prices:**
Blued Steel. . . . . . . . . . . . . . . . . . . . . . . . . . . . . . **$798.00**
Stainless . . . . . . . . . . . . . . . . . . . . . . . . . . . . .     829.00

### SPECIFICATIONS
**Calibers:** 22-250 Rem., 223 Rem., 243 Win., 270 Win., 7mm BR Rem., 7mm-08 Rem., 7.62X39mm, 308 Win., 30-06 Sprfld., 44 Rem. Mag., 444 Marlin
**Action:** Single break-open  **Barrel lengths:** 10" and 15"
**Overall length:** 14.5" (10" bbl.); 19.5" (15" bbl.)
**Weight:** 4 lbs. (10" bbl.); 4.5 lbs. (15" bbl.)
**Trigger:** Adjustable
**Safety:** Automatic hammerblock w/bolt interlock
**Grips:** Ambidextrous walnut pistol grip w/finger grooves and butt cap
**Sights:** Adjustable rear; ramp front sight blade
**Features:** Interchangeable barrels (**$215.00** 10" bbl., **$225.00** 15" bbl.); drilled and tapped for T/C scope mounts barrel lug welded by electronic beam process
**Prices:** 10" Barrel . . . . . . . . . . . . . . . . . . . . . . . **$485.00**
15" Barrel. . . . . . . . . . . . . . . . . . . . . . . . . . . .     495.00

## CONTENDER BULL BARREL MODELS

## CONTENDER SUPER "14" BULL BARREL MODELS

These pistols with 10-inch barrel feature fully adjustable Patridge-style iron sights. All stainless-steel models (including the Super "14" and Super "16") are equipped with Rynite finger-groove grip with rubber recoil cushion and matching Rynite forend, plus Cougar etching on the steel frame.
**Standard and Custom calibers available:** 22 LR, 22 Hornet, 223 Rem., 300 Whisper, 30-30 Win., 7mm T.C.U., 357 Mag., 44 Mag. and 45 Colt/.410
**Prices:**
Bull Barrel Blue . . . . . . . . . . . . . . . . . . . . . . **$463.50**
Bull Barrel Stainless . . . . . . . . . . . . . . . . . . . . .     494.00
 In 45/.410. . . . . . . . . . . . . . . . . . . . . . . . . . . .     499.00
Vent Rib Model Stainless . . . . . . . . . . . . . . . .     515.00
Match Grade Barrel (22 LR only, stainless) . . . . . .     505.00

**Calibers:** 22 LR, 22 LR Match Grade Chamber, 22 Hornet, 223 Rem., 7-30 Waters, 30-30 Win., 35 Rem., 375 Win. and 44 Mag. (Blued version also available in 17 Rem., 222 Rem., 300 Whisper, 357 Rem. Max.). **Barrel length:** 14" bull barrel. **Features:** Fully adjustable target rear sight and Patridge-style ramped front sight with 13.5-inch sight radius.
**Overall length:** 18.25" **Weight:** 3.5 lbs.
**Prices:**
Blued . . . . . . . . . . . . . . . . . . . . . . . . . . . . . . . **$473.80**
 Match Grade Chamber. . . . . . . . . . . . . . . . . .     484.00
 17 Rem.. . . . . . . . . . . . . . . . . . . . . . . . . . . . . .     504.70
Stainless . . . . . . . . . . . . . . . . . . . . . . . . . . . . .     504.70
14" Vent Rib Model in 45 Colt/.410, blue . . . . . . .     504.70
 Stainless . . . . . . . . . . . . . . . . . . . . . . . . . . . .     535.60

### CONTENDER SUPER "16" (Not Shown)

## CONTENDER OCTAGON BARREL MODELS (Not Shown)

This standard blued-steel barrel is interchangeable with any model listed here. Available in 22 LR 10-inch length, it is supplied with iron sights. Incl. Match Grade Chamber. No external choke. **Price:** . . . . . . . . . . . . . . . . . . . . . . . . . . . **$473.80**

**Calibers:** 223 Rem., 7-30 Waters, 30-30 Win., 45-70 (bull barrel)
**Prices:**
16" Tapered Barrel Blued finish . . . . . . . . . . . . . **$478.90**
Stainless finish . . . . . . . . . . . . . . . . . . . . . . . . .     509.00
45-70 bull barrel w/muzzle tamer . . . . . . . . . . . . .     530.50
16" Vent Rib Barrel Blued finish . . . . . . . . . . . . .     509.90
Stainless finish. . . . . . . . . . . . . . . . . . . . . . . . .     540.80

# UBERTI REPLICAS

## 1871 ROLLING BLOCK TARGET PISTOL
### $410.00

**SPECIFICATIONS**
**Calibers:** 22 LR, 22 Magnum, 22 Hornet and 357 Mag.
**Capacity:** Single shot
**Barrel length:** 9.5" (half-octagon/half-round or full round Navy Style)
**Overall length:** 14"
**Weight:** 2.75 lbs.
**Sights:** Fully adjustable rear; ramp front or open sight on Navy Style barrel
**Grip and forend:** Walnut
**Trigger guard:** Brass
**Frame:** Color casehardened steel

**1871 ROLLING BLOCK TARGET PISTOL**

## 1873 CATTLEMAN S.A.
### $410.00-475.00

**SPECIFICATIONS**
**Calibers:** 357 Magnum, 44-40, 45 L.C., 45 ACP
**Capacity:** 6 shots
**Barrel lengths:** 4.75", 5.5", 7.5" round, tapered; 18" (Buntline)
**Overall length:** 10.75" w/5.5" barrel
**Weight:** 2.42 lbs.
**Grip:** One-piece walnut
**Frame:** Color casehardened steel; also available in charcoal blue or nickel
Also available:
45 L.C./45 ACP Convertible . . . . . . . . . . . . . . . . $485.00

**1873 CATTLEMAN**

## 1875 "OUTLAW"/1890 POLICE
### $435.00

**SPECIFICATIONS**
**Calibers:** 357 Magnum, 44-40, 45 ACP, 45 Long Colt
**Capacity:** 6 shots
**Barrel lengths:** 5.5", 7.5" round, tapered
**Overall length:** 13.75"
**Weight:** 2.75 lbs.
**Grips:** Two-piece walnut
**Frame:** Color casehardened steel
Also available:
In nickel plate . . . . . . . . . . . . . . . . . . . . . . . . . . . $435.00
45 L.C./45 ACP Convertible . . . . . . . . . . . . . . . . 485.00

**1875 "OUTLAW"/1890 POLICE**

# UNIQUE PISTOLS

**MODEL DES 69U**

## MODEL DES 69U
## $1295.00

### SPECIFICATIONS
**Caliber:** 22 LR
**Capacity:** 5- or 6-shot magazine
**Barrel length:** 5.9"
**Overall length:** 11.2"
**Weight:** 40.2 oz. (empty)
**Height:** 5.5"
**Width:** 1.97"
**Sights:** Micrometric rear; lateral and vertical correction by clicks
**Safety:** Manual
**Features:** Orthopedic French walnut grip with adjustable hand rest; external hammer

Also available:
**Model DES 32U** in 32 S&W Long Wadcutter. Designed for centerfire U.I.T. and military rapid fire. Other specifications same as Model DES 69U. **Price:** . . . . . . . . . . . . . . **$1325.00**

**MODEL I.S. INTERNATIONAL**

## MODEL I.S. INTERNATIONAL SILHOUETTE
## $995.00

### SPECIFICATIONS
**Calibers:** 22 LR, 22 Magnum, 7mm TCU, 357 Magnum, 44 Magnum
**Barrel length:** 10"
**Overall length:** 14.5"
**Weight:** 38 oz.
**Height:** 6.5"
**Width:** 1.5"
**Sights:** Micrometric rear; lateral and vertical correction by clicks; interchangeable front sight; dovetailed grooves for scope
**Features:** French walnut grip; interchangeable shroud/barrel assembly; external hammer; firing adjustments

Also available:
**International Sport** w/light alloy frame in 22 LR and 22 Mag.
**Price:** . . . . . . . . . . . . . . . . . . . . . . . . . . . . . . . . . . . **$795.00**

**MODEL DES 2000U**

## MODEL DES 2000U
## $1375.00

### SPECIFICATIONS
**Caliber:** 22 Short
**Barrel length:** 5.9"
**Overall length:** 11.4"
**Weight:** 43.4 oz. (empty)
**Height:** 5.3"
**Width:** 1.97"
**Sights:** Micrometric rear; lateral and vertical correction by clicks
**Features:** French walnut grips with adjustable hand rest; left-hand grips available; external hammer; dry firing device; slide stop catch; antirecoil device

# WALTHER PISTOLS

The Walther double-action system combines the principles of the DA revolver with the advantages of the modern pistol without the disadvantages inherent in either design.

Models PPK and PPK/S differ only in the overall length of the barrel and slide. Both models offer the same features, including compact form, light weight, easy handling, and absolute safety. Both models can be carried with a loaded chamber and closed hammer, but ready to fire either single- or double-action. Both models are provided with a live round indicator pin to signal a loaded chamber. An automatic internal safety blocks the hammer to prevent accidental striking of the firing pin, except with a deliberate pull of the trigger. Sights are provided with white markings for high visibility in poor light. Rich Walther blue/black finish is standard, and each pistol is complete with an extra magazine with finger-rest extension.

## MODEL PPK & PPK/S

### MODEL PPK & PPK/S

**SPECIFICATIONS**
**Caliber:** 380 ACP
**Capacity:** 6 rounds (PPK), 7 rounds (PPK/S)
**Barrel length:** 3.35"
**Overall length:** 6.5"
**Weight:** 21 oz. (PPK); 23 oz. (PPK/S)
**Finish:** Walther blue or stainless steel
**Price:**. . . . . . . . . . . . . . . . . . . . . . . . . . . . . . $540.00

### MODEL PP DOUBLE ACTION

**SPECIFICATIONS**
**Calibers:** 32 ACP and 380 ACP
**Capacity:** 7 rounds
**Barrel length:** 3.8"
**Overall length:** 6.7"
**Weight:** 25 oz.
**Finish:** Walther blue
**Price:**. . . . . . . . . . . . . . . . . . . . . . . . . . . . . . $999.00

### MODEL PP

### MODEL TPH

### MODEL TPH DOUBLE ACTION

Walther's Model TPH is considered by government agents and professional lawmen to be one of the top of undercover/backup guns available. A scaled-down version Walther's PP-PPK series.

**SPECIFICATIONS**
**Calibers:** 22 LR and 25 ACP
**Capacity:** 6 rounds
**Barrel length:** 2.85"
**Overall length:** 5.5"
**Weight:** 14 oz.
**Finish:** Walther blue or stainless steel
**Price:**. . . . . . . . . . . . . . . . . . . . . . . . . . . . . . $440.00

# WALTHER PISTOLS

## MODEL P 88 COMPACT

The Walther P 88 Compact is a double-action, locked-breech, semiautomatic pistol with an external hammer. Its compact form, light weight and easy handling are combined with the superb performance of the 9mm Luger Parabellum cartridge. The P 88 Compact boasts target-grade accuracy, dual-function controls and comes with two 10-shot double-column magazines.

### SPECIFICATIONS
**Caliber:** 9mm Parabellum
**Capacity:** 10 rounds
**Barrel length:** 3.93"
**Overall length:** 7.5"
**Weight:** 28 oz.
**Finish:** Blue
**Price:**. . . . . . . . . . . . . . . . . . . . . . . . . . . . . . **$900.00**

**MODEL P 88 COMPACT**

## MODEL P 99

### SPECIFICATIONS
**Caliber:** 9mm Parabellum
**Capacity:** 10 rounds
**Barrel length:** 4"
**Overall length:** 7"
**Weight:** 25 oz.
**Height:** 5.37"  **Width:** 1.2"
**Sights:** Windage-adjustable micrometer rear; three inter-changeable front blades included
**Features:** Polymer frame; blued slide; customized back-strap; three automatic safeties; cocking and loaded chamber indicator; ambidextrous magazine release levers
**Price:**. . . . . . . . . . . . . . . . . . . . . . . . . . . . . . **$799.00**

**MODEL P 99**

# WICHITA ARMS PISTOLS

### SPECIFICATIONS
**Calibers:** 308 Win. F.L., 7mm IHMSA and 7mmX308
**Barrel length:** 14 15/16"
**Weight:** 4.5 lbs.
**Action:** Single-shot bolt action
**Sights:** Wichita Multi-Range Sight System
**Grips:** Right-hand center walnut grip or right-hand rear walnut grip
**Features:** Glass bedded; bolt ground to precision fit; adjustable Wichita trigger
Also available:
**WICHITA CLASSIC SILHOUETTE PISTOL. Barrel:** 11 1/4".
**Weight:** 3 lbs. 15 oz. **Grips:** AAA grade walnut, glass bedded . . . . . . . . . . . . . . . . . . . . . . . . . . . . . **$3450.00**
**Engraved Model** . . . . . . . . . . . . . . . . . . . . . . . . . . 4850.00

**SILHOUETTE PISTOL**
**(Right-Hand Rear Grip)**
**$1695.00**

### SPECIFICATIONS
**Calibers:** 7-30 Waters, 7mm Super Mag., 7R (30-30 Win. necked to 7mm), 30-30 Win., 357 Mag., 357 Super Mag., 32 H&H Mag., 22 RFM, 22 LR
**Barrel lengths:** 10" and 14" (10.5" for centerfire calibers)
**Weight:** 3 lbs. 2 oz. (10" barrel); 4 lbs. 7 oz. (14" barrel)
**Action:** Top-break, single-shot, single action only
**Sights:** Patridge front sight; rear sight adjustable for windage and elevation
**Grips and Forend:** Walnut
**Safety:** Crossbolt

**INTERNATIONAL PISTOL**
**$735.00 (10" Barrel)**
**$813.75 (14" Barrel)**

# WILDEY PISTOLS

### WILDEY PISTOLS

These gas-operated pistols are designed to meet the needs of hunters who want to use handguns for big game. The Wildey pistol includes such features as: •Ventilated rib •Reduced recoil •Double-action trigger mechanism •Patented hammer and trigger blocks and rebounding fire pin •Sights adjustable for windage and elevation •Stainless construction •Fixed barrel for increased accuracy •Increased action strength (with 3-lug and exposed face rotary bolt) •Selective single or autoloading capability •Ability to handle high-pressure loads

### SPECIFICATIONS
**Calibers:** 41 Wildey Mag., 45 Win. Mag., 44 Wildey Mag., 475 Wildey Mag., 475 Win. Mag.
**Capacity:** 7 shots
**Barrel lengths:** 5", 6", 7", 8", 10", 12", 14"
**Overall length:** 11" with 7" barrel
**Weight:** 64 oz. with 5" barrel
**Height:** 6"

**SURVIVOR AND GUARDSMAN** in 45 Win. Mag.  **Prices**
5", 6" or 7" barrels . . . . . . . . . . . . . . . . . . . . . . **$1295.00**
8", 10" or 12" barrels . . . . . . . . . . . . . . . . . . . . 1316.00
**SURVIVOR MODEL** in 475 Wildey Mag.
8", 10" or 12" barrels . . . . . . . . . . . . . . . . . . . . **$1316.00**
14" barrel . . . . . . . . . . . . . . . . . . . . . . . . . . . . . 1895.00

**HUNTER MODEL** in 45 Win. Mag.  **Prices**
5", 6" or 7" barrels . . . . . . . . . . . . . . . . . . . . . . **$1413.00**
8", 10" or 12" barrels . . . . . . . . . . . . . . . . . . . . 1435.00
**HUNTER MODEL** in 475 Wildey Mag.
8" or 10" barrels . . . . . . . . . . . . . . . . . . . . . . . . 1435.00
12" barrel . . . . . . . . . . . . . . . . . . . . . . . . . . . . . 1515.00
14" barrel . . . . . . . . . . . . . . . . . . . . . . . . . . . . . 2015.00
Also available:
Interchangeable barrel extension assemblies **$523.00** (5" barrel); **$648.95** (12" barrel); **$1148.00** (14" barrel).

# Rifles

For addresses and phone/fax numbers of manufacturers and distributors included in this section, please turn to DIRECTORY OF MANUFACTURERS AND SUPPLIERS on page 554.

# AMERICAN ARMS RIFLES

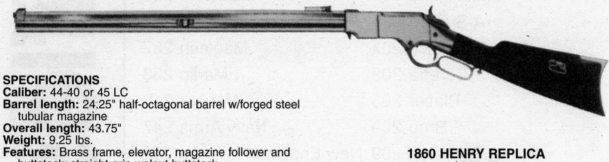

**SPECIFICATIONS**
**Caliber:** 44-40 or 45 LC
**Barrel length:** 24.25" half-octagonal barrel w/forged steel
tubular magazine
**Overall length:** 43.75"
**Weight:** 9.25 lbs.
**Features:** Brass frame, elevator, magazine follower and
buttstock; straight-grip walnut buttstock

**1860 HENRY REPLICA**
**$996.00**

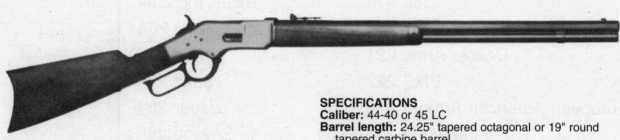

**1866 WINCHESTER REPLICA**
**$829.00  ($797.00 19" barrel)**

**SPECIFICATIONS**
**Caliber:** 44-40 or 45 LC
**Barrel length:** 24.25" tapered octagonal or 19" round
tapered carbine barrel
**Overall length:** 43.25"(w/24.25" barrel)
**Weight:** 8.15 lbs.
**Features:** Tubular magazine; brass frame, elevator and
buttplate; walnut buttstock and forend

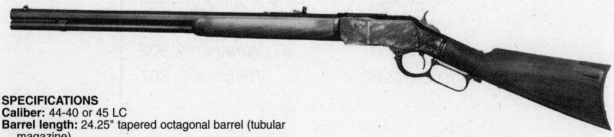

**SPECIFICATIONS**
**Caliber:** 44-40 or 45 LC
**Barrel length:** 24.25" tapered octagonal barrel (tubular
magazine)
**Features:** Color casehardened steel frame with ejection
port cover; brass elevator; walnut buttstock with steel
buttplate
Also available:
**DELUXE 1873 WINCHESTER REPLICA** w/pistol grip and
deluxe hand-checkered stock. **Price:** . . . . . . . . . **$1299.00**

**1873 WINCHESTER**
**$984.00**

# AMT RIFLES

**22 RIMFIRE MAGNUM**

## 22 MAGNUM HUNTER

AMT's rimfire magnum rifle delivers big-bore velocity with minimum cost ammunition. Jacketed bullets combine with magnum velocity to yield high impact. Greater power flattens trajectory and improves accuracy.

### SPECIFICATIONS
**Caliber:** 22 Rimfire Magnum
**Capacity:** 10 rounds
**Barrel length:** 20"
**Weight:** 6 lbs.
**Sights:** No sights; drilled and tapped for 87-A Weaver scope mount base
**Features:** Stainless steel construction
**Price:** (scope not included). . . . . . . . . . . . . . . . **$409.99**

## TARGET MODEL SEMIAUTOMATIC

### SPECIFICATIONS
**Caliber:** 22 LR
**Capacity:** 10 rounds
**Barrel length:** 20" target barrel .920 O.D.
**Weight:** 7.5 lbs.
**Features:** Button rifled barrel w/target crown; one-piece receiver w/built-in integral Weaver-style mount; left or right hand Fajen laminated Aristocrat-style stock or Hogue composite stock; cryogenic-treated barrel
**Prices:**. . . . . . . . . . . . . . . . . . . . . . . . . . . . . . **$549.00**
**With Fajen stock**. . . . . . . . . . . . . . . . . . . . . . . . **599.99**

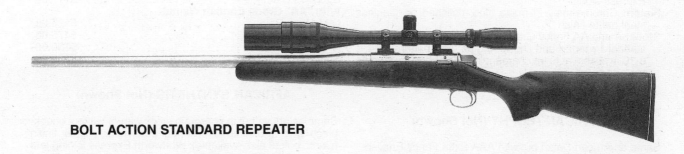

**BOLT ACTION STANDARD REPEATER**

## STANDARD RIFLES (Single Shot & Repeater)

### SPECIFICATIONS
**Calibers:** *Single Shot*—22 Hornet, 222, 223, 22-250, 243 Win., 243A, 22 PPC, 6 PPC, 6.5X08, 708, 308
*Repeaters*—223, 22-250, 243, 243A, 6 PPC, 25-06, 6.5X08, 270, 30-06, 308, 7mm Mag., 300 Win. Mag., 338 Win. Mag., 375 H&H, 416 Rem., 458 Win. Mag., 416 Rigby, 7.62X39, 7X57, 7.62mm
**Action:** Push feed post-64 Win. Type
**Magazine:** Mauser type
**Barrels:** Match grade up to 28" long #3
**Weight:** Approximately 8.5 lbs.
**Trigger:** Custom-type adjustable
**Safety:** Three position pre-64 Model 70-type
**Stock:** Classic Composite
**Pull:** 13.5" stock length

**Features:** Pillar bedding; sliding ejector 2/30° cone bolt; stainless and chrome moly steel; sights drilled and tapped for scope mount
Also available:
**DELUXE RIFLES (Single Shot & Repeater).** Same as Standard models, but action is Mauser type control feed and stock is custom Kevlar; also features plunger ejector and claw-type extractor
**Prices:**
**Standard Single Shot** . . . . . . . . . . . . . . . . . . . **$1109.99**
**Standard Repeater** . . . . . . . . . . . . . . . . . . . . . . **1109.99**
**Deluxe Single Shot**. . . . . . . . . . . . . . . . . . . . . . **2399.99**
**Deluxe Repeater** . . . . . . . . . . . . . . . . . . . . . . . **1595.99**
**Actions** (Left-Hand models available)
    **Single Shot**. . . . . . . . . . . . . . . . . . . . . . . . . . **550.00**
    **Repeater** . . . . . . . . . . . . . . . . . . . . . . . . . . . **650.00**
    **Magnum actions** . . . . . . . . . . . . . . . . . . . . . **690.00**

# ARNOLD ARMS RIFLES

## AFRICAN SERIES

Arnold Arms Company introduces a full line of rifles built on its "Apollo" action with the strongest and hardest chrome-moly and stainless steels available. Alignment of bolt face, receiver and barrel centerline axis results in optimum accuracy. Lapping the bolt lugs, squaring the bolt and truing the receiver are unnecessary—the Apollo action assures perpendicular alignment and equal pressure lock-up. A perfect mating of the receiver, recoil lug and stock, achieved only through the process of glass bedding, assures uniformity of recoil bearing points shot after shot. The revolutionary positive feed and extraction features designed and machined into the "Apollo" bolt face assure full extraction and ejection as well as next cartridge feeding with every complete bolt cycling. The 3-position positive-lock safety locks up the bolt and firing pin to prevent accidental discharge until the rifle is ready to fire.

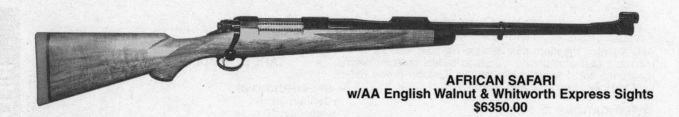

**AFRICAN SAFARI**
**w/AA English Walnut & Whitworth Express Sights**
**$6350.00**

## AFRICAN SAFARI

**SPECIFICATIONS**
**Calibers:** 243 to 458 Win. Magnum
**Barrel length:** 22" to 26" (Contours #2 to #7 C-M; #4 to #7 S.S.)
**Sights:** Scope mount standard or with optional M70 Express sights
**Finish:** Chrome-moly in matte blue, polished or stainless steel matte finish
**Stock:** A and AA Fancy Grade English walnut stock with #5 standard wraparound checkering pattern (patterns 1-4 & 6-10 available at extra charge.); includes ebony forend tip

**Prices:**
**With "A" Grade English Walnut**

| | |
|---|---|
| Matte Blue | $4987.00 |
| Std. Polish | 5337.00 |
| Hi-Luster | 5612.00 |
| Stainless Steel Matte | 5117.00 |

**With "AA" Grade English Walnut**

| | |
|---|---|
| C-M Matte Blue | 5125.00 |
| Std. Polish | 5475.00 |
| Hi-Luster | 5750.00 |
| Stainless Steel Matte | 5255.00 |

### AFRICAN TROPHY (Not Shown)

Same as African Safari but with AAA Extra Fancy English walnut stock with #9 checkering.
**Prices:**

| | |
|---|---|
| C-M Matte | $6072.00 |
| Std. Polish | 6422.00 |
| Hi-Luster | 6697.00 |
| Stainless Steel Matte | 6202.00 |

### AFRICAN SYNTHETIC (Not Shown)

Same as above but in fibergrain stock with or without cheekpiece and traditional checkering pattern or stipple finish (Camo colors also available); Whitworth Express folding leaf optional w/front hood sight.

**Prices:**

| | |
|---|---|
| C-M Matte | $3528.00 |
| Std. Polish | 3878.00 |
| Stainless Steel Matte | 3658.00 |

### GRAND AFRICAN (Not Shown)

Same as above but in calibers .338 Magnum to .458 Win. Mag. Other standard features include: Exhibition Grade stock with #10 checkering pattern; choice of ebony or Cape Buffalo forend tip; barrel band; scope mount w/Express sights w/front ring & hood. **Barrel length:** 24"-26".
**Prices:**

| | |
|---|---|
| C-M Hi-Luster Polish only | $8219.00 |
| Stainless Steel Matte | 7694.00 |

### SERENGETI SYNTHETIC (Not Shown)

Same as above but in calibers 243 to 300 Magnum; choice of classic or Monte Carlo cheekpiece; scope mount only. Barrel length: 22"-26" (Contours Featherweight to #5 C-M, #4 to #6S.S.)

**Prices:**

| | |
|---|---|
| C-M Matte | $3528.00 |
| Std. Polish | 3878.00 |
| Stainless Steel Matte | 3658.00 |

# ARNOLD ARMS RIFLES

## ALASKAN SERIES

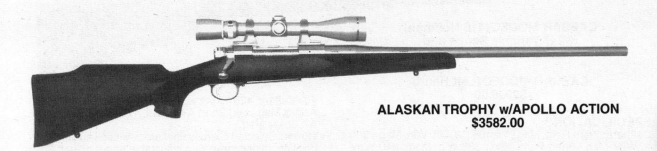

### ALASKAN TROPHY w/APOLLO ACTION
### $3582.00

## ALASKAN TROPHY

Features stainless steel or chrome-moly Apollo action with fibergrain or black synthetic stock;  barrel band (357 H&H and larger magnums); scope mount with Express sights standard. **Calibers:** 300 Magnum to 458 Win. Mag. **Barrel length:** 24"-26" (contours #4 to #7 C-M, #4 to #7 S.S.)

**Prices:**
| | |
|---|---|
| C-M Matte | $4064.00 |
| Std. Polish | 4414.00 |
| Stainless Steel Matte | 4194.00 |

## ALASKAN RIFLE (Not Shown)

Features stainless steel or chrome-moly Apollo action with black, woodland, or Artic camo stock; scope mount only. **Calibers:** 300 Magnum to 458 Win. Mag. **Barrel length:** 24"-26" (Contours #4 to #7 C-M, #4 to #7 S.S.)

**Prices:**
| | |
|---|---|
| C-M Matte | $3315.00 |
| Std. Polish | 3665.00 |
| Stainless Steel | 3445.00 |

## ALASKAN SYNTHETIC RIFLE (Not Shown)

Same as above but with fibergrain stock; scope mounts or Express sights optional. **Calibers:** 257 to 338 Magnum.

**Prices:**
| | |
|---|---|
| C-M Matte | $4110.00 |
| Std. Polish | 4460.00 |
| Stainless Steel Matte | 4240.00 |

## GRAND ALASKAN (Not Shown)

Same as above but with AAA fancy select or Exhibition grade English walnut,    barrel band and ebony forend; Express sights & scope mount standard. **Calibers:** 300 Magnum to 458 Win. Mag.

**Prices:**
**"AAA" Grade Select English Walnut**
| | |
|---|---|
| C-M Matte | $6667.00 |
| Std. Polish | 7017.00 |
| Stainless Steel Matte | 6797.00 |

**"Exhibition" Grade, Extra Fancy Select English Walnut**
| | |
|---|---|
| C-M Matte | $7594.00 |
| Std. Polish | 7944.00 |
| Hi-Luster | 8219.00 |
| Stainless Steel Matte | 7724.00 |

## ALASKAN GUIDE (Not Shown)

Same as above but with choice of either "A" English walnut or snythetic stock; scope mount only. **Calibers:** .257 to .338 Magnum. **Barrel length:** 22"-26" depending on caliber (Contours #4 to #6 C-M, #4 to #6 S.S.)

**Prices:**
| | |
|---|---|
| C-M Matte | $5031.00 |
| Std. Polish | 5381.00 |
| Stainless Steel Matte | 5161.00 |

# A-SQUARE RIFLES

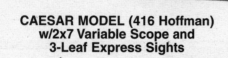

**CAESAR MODEL (416 Hoffman)
w/2x7 Variable Scope and
3-Leaf Express Sights**

**CAESAR MODEL (Left Hand)
$2995.00**

## SPECIFICATIONS
**Calibers:** 7mm Rem. Mag., 7mm STW, 300 Win. Mag., 300 Wby. Mag., 8mm Rem. Mag., 338 Win. Mag., 340 Wby. Mag., 338 A-Square Mag., 358 Norma, 358 STA, 9.3 X 64mm, 375 H&H, 375 Weatherby, 375 JRS, 375 A-Square Mag., 416 Taylor, 416 Hoffman, 416 Rem. Mag., 404 Jeffery, 425 Express, 458 Win. Mag., 458 Lott, 450 Ackley Mag., 460 Short A-Square, 470 Capstick and 495 A-Square Mag.

**Features:** Selected Claro walnut stock with oil finish; three-position safety; three-way adjustable target trigger; flush detachable swivels; leather sling; dual recoil lugs; coil spring ejector; ventilated recoil pad; premium honed barrels; contoured ejection port

**HANNIBAL MODEL
$2995.00**

**HANNIBAL MODEL (416 Rigby)
w/2xLER Scope and 3-Leaf
Express Sights**

## SPECIFICATIONS
**Calibers:** 300 Pegasus, 8mm Rem. Mag., 338 Win., 340 Wby., 338 A-Square Mag., 338 Excalibur, 358 Norma Mag., 358 STA, 9.3X64, 375 A-Square, 375 JRS, 375 H&H, 375 Wby., 378 Wby., 404 Jeffery, 416 Hoffman, 416 Rem., 416 Rigby, 416 Taylor, 416 Wby., 425 Express, 450 Ackley, 458 Lott, 458 Win., 460 Short A-Square, 460 Weatherby, 470 Capstick, 495 A-Square, 500 A-Square, 577 Tyrannosaur

**Barrel lengths:** 20" to 26"
**Length of pull:** 12" to 15.25"
**Finish:** Deluxe walnut stock; oil finish; matte blue
**Features:** Flush detachable swivels, leather sling, dual recoil lugs, coil spring ejector, ventilated recoil pad, premium honed barrels, contoured ejection port, three-way adjustable target-style trigger, Mauser-style claw extractor and controlled feed, positive safety

**HAMILCAR
$2995.00**

**Finish:** Deluxe walnut stock; oil finish; matte blue
**Features:** Flush detachable swivels; leather sling, coil spring ejector, vent. recoil pad; honed barrels; contoured ejection port; target-style adjustable trigger; Mauser-style claw extractor; controlled feed; positive safety
Also available:
**GENGHIS KHAN MODEL** in 22-250, 243 Win., 25 Souper, 6mm Rem., 25-06, 257 Wby., 6.5-06, 6.5-08, 264 Win. Features benchrest-quality heavy taper barrel and coil-chek stock. **Price:**. . . . . . . . . . . . . . . . . . . . . . $2895.00

## SPECIFICATIONS
**Calibers:** 25-06, 257 Wby., 6.5 X55 Swedish, 6.5-06, 264 Win., 270 Win., 270 Wby., 7X57 Mauser, 280 Rem., 7mm Rem., 7mm Wby., 7mm STW, 30-06, 300 Win., 300 Wby., 338-06, 9.3X62
**Barrel lengths:** 20" to 26"
**Length of pull:** 12" to 15.25"

# AUTO-ORDNANCE

## SEMIAUTOMATIC RIFLES

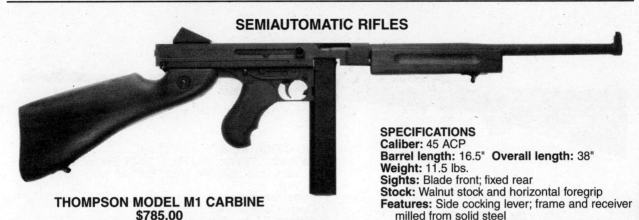

**THOMPSON MODEL M1 CARBINE**
**$785.00**

**SPECIFICATIONS**
**Caliber:** 45 ACP
**Barrel length:** 16.5"  **Overall length:** 38"
**Weight:** 11.5 lbs.
**Sights:** Blade front; fixed rear
**Stock:** Walnut stock and horizontal foregrip
**Features:** Side cocking lever; frame and receiver
milled from solid steel

**THOMPSON DELUXE MODEL 1927 A1**
**$795.00 (45 Cal.)**

**SPECIFICATIONS**
**Caliber:** 45 ACP
**Barrel length:** 16.5"   **Overall length:** 41"
**Weight:** 13 lbs.
**Sights:** Blade front; open rear adjustable
**Stock:** Walnut stock; vertical foregrip

Also available:
**THOMPSON 1927A1C LIGHTWEIGHT** (45 cal.). Same as
the 1927A1 model, but weighs only 9.5 lbs. **Price:** $795.00

**MODEL 1927A1 COMMANDO**
**$780.00**

**SPECIFICATIONS**
**Caliber:** 45 ACP
**Barrel length:** 16.5"   **Overall length:** 41"

**Weight:** 13 lbs.
**Sights:** Blade front; open rear (adjustable)
**Finish:** Black (stock and forend)

# BERETTA RIFLES

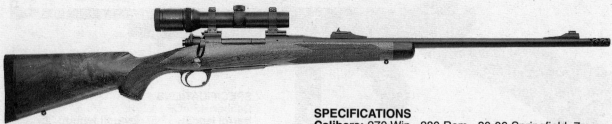

## MATO RIFLES

Beretta's new Mato (the Dakota Indian word for "bear") is designed for hunters. Based on the Mauser 98 action, it has a drop-out box magazine that releases quickly. The barrels are machined from high-grade chrome-moly steel. Other features include ergonomic bolt handle, adjustable trigger, wraparound hand checkering and three-position safety.

**SPECIFICATIONS**
**Calibers:** 270 Win., 280 Rem., 30-06 Springfield, 7mm Rem. Mag., 300 Win. Mag., 338 Win. Mag., 375 H&H Mag.
**Barrel length:** 23.6"
**Overall length:** 44.5"
**Weight:** 7.9 lbs. (Deluxe); 8 lbs. (Standard)
**Stock:** Matte grey composite synthetic (Standard); Triple-X Grade Claro walnut w/hand-rubbed satin oil finish and black forend tip (Deluxe)
**Length of pull:** 13.5"
**Drop at comb:** .56"   **Drop at heel:** .81"
**Twist:** 1:10" (1:12" 375 H&H Mag.)
**Prices:** Standard . . . . . . . . . . . . . . . . . . . . . . . . . . . **N/A**
Deluxe . . . . . . . . . . . . . . . . . . . . . . . . . . . . . . **N/A**

# BLASER RIFLES

## MODEL R 93

## MODEL R 93 BOLT ACTION

**SPECIFICATIONS**
**Calibers:** (interchangeable)
 **Standard:** 22-250, 243 Win., 270 Win., 30-06, 308 Win.
 **Magnum:** 257 Weatherby Mag., 264 Win. Mag., 7mm Rem. Mag., 300 Win. Mag., 300 Wby. Mag., 338 Win.Mag., 375 H&H, 416 Rem. Mag.
 **Varmint:** 222 Rem., 223
**Barrel lengths:** 22" (Standard) and 24" (Magnum)
**Overall length:** 40" (Standard) and 42" (Magnum)
**Weight:** (w/scope mounts) 7 lbs. (Standard) and 7.25 lbs. (Magnum)
**Safety:** Cocking slide
**Stock:** Two-piece Turkish walnut stock and forend; solid black recoil pad, hand-cut checkering (18 lines/inch, borderless)

**Length of pull:** 13.75"
**Prices:**
**Standard Model.** . . . . . . . . . . . . . . . . . . . . . . **$2800.00**
Interchangeable barrels . . . . . . . . . . . . . . . . . . **550.00**
**Deluxe Model** . . . . . . . . . . . . . . . . . . . . . . . . **3100.00**
**Super Deluxe Model** . . . . . . . . . . . . . . . . . . . . **3500.00**

Also available:
**SAFARI MODEL.** 375 H&H and 416 Rem. Mag. only. 24"heavy barrel (42" overall); open sights. **Weight:** 9.5 lbs. **$3300.00** (Standard); **$3600.00** (Deluxe); **$4000.00** (Super Deluxe)

# BRNO RIFLES

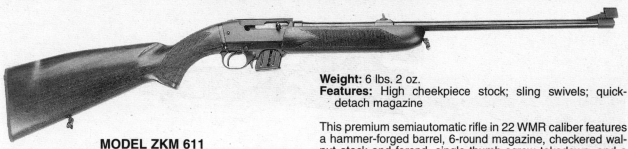

**Weight:** 6 lbs. 2 oz.
**Features:** High cheekpiece stock; sling swivels; quick-detach magazine

### MODEL ZKM 611
### $569.00

**SPECIFICATIONS**
**Caliber:** 22 WMR  **Capacity:** 6 rounds
**Barrel length:** 20"  **Overall length:** 37"

This premium semiautomatic rifle in 22 WMR caliber features a hammer-forged barrel, 6-round magazine, checkered walnut stock and forend, single thumb-screw takedown, and a grooved receiver for scope mounting. The rear sight is mid-mounted and the front sight is hooded. The action has a lightweight precision spring and large bolt to improve accuracy while practically eliminating felt recoil.

# BROWN PRECISION RIFLES

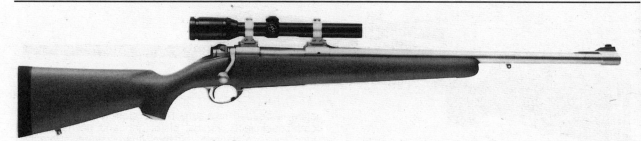

Designed for the serious game hunter or guide, this custom version of Brown Precision's Pro-Hunter rifle begins as a Winchester Model 70 Super Grade action with controlled feed claw extractor. The trigger is tuned to crisp let-off at each customer's specified weight. A Shilen Match Grade stainless-steel barrel is custom crowned and hand-fitted to the action.

The Pro-Hunter Elite features choice of express rear sight or custom Dave Talley removable peep sight and banded front ramp sight with European dovetail and replaceable brass bead. An optional flip-up white night sight is also available, as is a set of Dave Talley detachable T.N.T. scope mount rings and bases installed with Brown's Magnum Duty 8X40 screws. QD sling swivels are standard.

All metal parts are finished in either matte electroless nickel or black Teflon. The barreled action is glass bedded to a custom Brown Precision Alaskan-configuration fiberglass stock, painted according to customer choice and fitted w/premium 1" buttpad and Dave Talley trapdoor grip cap. Weight ranges from 7 to 15 lbs., depending on barrel length, coutour and options.

Optional equipment includes custom steel drop box magazine, KDF or Answer System muzzle brake, Mag-Na-Port, Zeiss, Swarovski or Leupold scope and Americase aluminum hard case.
**Price:** . . . . . . . . . . . . . . . . . . . . . . . . . . . . . . . . . **$3565.00**

### PRO-VARMINTER RIFLE

The standard Pro-Varminter is built on the Remington 700 or Remington 40X action (right or left hand) and features a hand-fitted Shilen Match Grade Heavy Benchrest stainless-steel barrel in bright or bead-blasted finish. The barreled action is custom-bedded in Brown Precision's Varmint Special Hunter Bench or 40X Benchrest-style custom fiberglass, Kevlar or graphite stock.

Other standard features include custom barrel length

and contour, trigger tuned for crisp pull to customer's specified weight, custom length of pull, and choice of recoil pad. Additional options include metal finishes, muzzle brakes, Leupold target or varmint scopes and others.
**Prices:**
Right-hand Model 700 Action . . . . . . . . . . . . . . . **$1965.00**
For Left-hand Model, **add** . . . . . . . . . . . . . . . . . . 120.00
40X Action . . . . . . . . . . . . . . . . . . . . . . . . . . . . . 2450.00

# BROWN PRECISION RIFLES

## HIGH COUNTRY YOUTH RIFLE

This custom rifle has all the same features as the standard High Country rifle, but scaled-down to fit the younger or smaller shooter. Based on the Remington Model 7 barreled action, it is available in calibers 223, 243, 7mm-08, 6mm and 308. The rifle features a shortened fiberglass, Kevlar or graphite stock, which can be lengthened as the shooter grows, a new recoil pad installed and the stock refinished. Custom features/options include choice of actions, custom barrels, chamberings, muzzle brakes, metal finishes, scopes and accessories.

All Youth Rifles include a deluxe package of shooting, reloading and hunting accessories and information to increase a young shooter's interest.

**Price: starts at** . . . . . . . . . . . . . . . . . . . . . . . . . **$1340.00**

## TACTICAL ELITE RIFLE

Brown Precision's Tactical Elite is built on a Remington 700 action and features a bead-blasted Shilen Select Match Grade Heavy Benchrest Stainless Steel barrel custom-chambered for 223 Rem., 308 Win., 300 Win. Mag. (or any standard or wildcat caliber). A nonreflective custom black Teflon metal finish on all metal surfaces ensures smooth bolt operation and 100 percent weatherproofing. The barreled action is bedded in a target-style stock with high rollover comb/cheekpiece, vertical pistol grip and palmswell. The stock is an advanced, custom fiberglass/Kevlar/graphite composite for maximum durability and rigidity, painted in flat black (camouflage patterns are also available). QD sling swivel studs and swivels are standard.

Other standard features include: three-way adjustable buttplate/recoil pad assembly with length of pull, vertical and cant angle adjustments, custom barrel length and contour, and trigger tuned for a crisp pull to customer's specifications. Options include muzzle brakes, Leupold or Kahles police scopes, and others, and are priced accordingly.

**Price:** . . . . . . . . . . . . . . . . . . . . . . . . . . . . . . . . . **$2750.00**

## CUSTOM TEAM CHALLENGER

This custom rifle was designed for use in the Chevy Trucks Sportsman's Team Challenge shooting event. It's also used in metallic silhouette competition as well as in the field for small game and varmints. Custom built on the Ruger 10/22 semiautomatic rimfire action, which features an extended magazine release, a simplified bolt release and finely tuned trigger, this rifle is fitted with either a Brown Precision fiber- glass or Kevlar stock with custom length of pull up to 15". The stock can be shortened at the butt and later relengthened and repainted to accommodate growing youth shooters. Stock color is also optional. To facilitate shooting with scopes, the lightweight stock has high-comb classic styling. The absence of a cheekpiece accommodates either right- or left-handed shooters, while the stock's flat-bottom, 1³/₄" forearm ensures maximum comfort in both offhand and rest shooting. Barrels are custom-length Shilen Match Grade .920" diameter straight or lightweight tapered.

**Prices:**

With blued action/barrel . . . . . . . . . . . . . . . . . . $ 975.00
With blued action/stainless barrel . . . . . . . . . . . . 1050.00
With stainless action/stainless barrel. . . . . . . . . . 1095.00

# BROWNING RIFLES

**MODEL BL-22 LEVER-ACTION RIFLE**

## RIMFIRE RIFLE SPECIFICATIONS

| Model | Caliber | Barrel Length | Sight Radius | Overall Length | Average Weight | Price |
|---|---|---|---|---|---|---|
| Semi-Auto 22 Grade I | 22 LR | 19 1/4" | 16 1/4" | 37" | 4 lbs. | $398.95 |
| Semi-Auto 22 Grade VI | 22 LR | 19 1/4" | 16 1/4" | 37" | 4 lbs. | 819.00 |
| BL-22 Grade I | 22 LR, Long, Short | 20" | 15 3/8" | 36 3/4" | 5 lbs. | 345.95 |
| BL-Grade II | 22 LR, Long, Short | 20" | 15 3/8" | 36 3/4" | 5 lbs. | 359.95 |

## STOCK DIMENSIONS

| | Semi-Auto | BL-22 |
|---|---|---|
| Length of Pull | 13 3/4" | 13 1/2" |
| Drop at Comb | 1 3/6" | 5/8" |
| Drop at Heel | 2 5/8" | 2 1/4" |

**GRADE VI ENGRAVED**
**(24-Karat Gold Plated)**

### 22 SEMIAUTOMATIC RIMFIRE RIFLES GRADES I AND VI
**(See table above for prices)**

**SPECIFICATIONS** (See also table above)
**Capacity:** 11 cartridges in magazine, 1 chamber
**Safety:** Cross-bolt type
**Trigger:** Grade I is blued; Grade VI is gold colored
**Sights:** Gold bead front, adjustable folding leaf ear; drilled and tapped for Browning scope mounts
**Stock & Forearm:** Grade I, select walnut with checkering (18 lines/inch); Grade VI, high-grade walnut with checkering (22 lines/inch).

# BROWNING RIFLES

### MODEL 1885 LOW WALL RIFLE
### $939.95 (High & Low Wall Models)

## SPECIFICATIONS MODEL 1885 LOW WALL or HIGH WALL

| Calibers | Barrel Length | Sight Radius | Overall Length | Approximate Weight | Rate of Twist (R. hand) |
|---|---|---|---|---|---|
| **HIGH WALL** | | | | | |
| 22-250 Rem. | 28" | — | 43½" | 8 lbs.13 oz. | 1 in 14" |
| 270 Win. | 28" | — | 43½" | 8 lbs.12 oz. | 1 in 10" |
| 30-06 Sprg. | 28" | — | 43½" | 8 lbs.12 oz. | 1 in 10" |
| 7mm Rem. Mag. | 28" | — | 43½" | 8 lbs.11 oz. | 1 in 9½" |
| 45-70 Govt. | 28" | 21½" | 43½" | 8 lbs.14 oz. | 1 in 20" |
| **LOW WALL** | | | | | |
| 22 Hornet | 24" | — | 39½" | 6 lbs. 4 oz. | 1 in 16" |
| 223 Rem. | 24" | — | 39½" | 6 lbs. 4 oz. | 1 in 12" |
| 243 Win. | 24" | — | 39½" | 6 lbs. 4 oz. | 1 in 10" |

### MODEL 1885 TRADITIONAL HUNTER
### $1149.95

### MODEL 1885 TRADITIONAL HUNTER

**SPECIFICATIONS**
**Calibers:** 30-30 Win., 38-55 Win., 45-70 Govt.
**Barrel length:** 28"
**Overall length:** 44¼"
**Weight:** 9 lbs.

Also available:
**Model 1885 BPCR Front Sight Card ($12.00)**

### MODEL 1885 BPCR
### (BLACK POWDER CARTRIDGE RIFLE)
### $1664.95

### MODEL 1885 BPCR
### (BLACK POWDER CARTRIDGE RIFLE)

**SPECIFICATIONS**
**Calibers:** 40-65, 45-70 Govt.
**Barrel length:** 30"  **Overall length:** 46⅛"
**Weight:** 11 lbs. (45-70 Govt.); 11 lbs. 7 oz. (40-65)
**Sight radius:** 34"
**Rate of twist:** 1 in 16" (R.H.).

### A-BOLT II HUNTER BOLT-ACTION CENTERFIRE RIFLES
### $606.85 w/BOSS, No Sights
### $545.35 (No Sights)

BOSS (Ballistic Optimizing Shooting System) is now optional on all A-Bolt II models (except standard on Varmint). BOSS adjusts barrel vibrations to allow a bullet to leave the rifle muzzle at the most advantageous point in the barrel oscillation, thereby fine-tuning accuracy with any brand of ammunition regardless of caliber.

This hard-working rifle features a practical grade of walnut and low-luster bluing ideal for rugged conditions. Includes the standard A-Bolt II fast-cycling bolt, crisp trigger, calibrated rear sights and ramp-style front sights. Optional BOSS.

**Scopes:** Closed. Clean tapered barrel. Receiver is drilled and tapped for a scope mount; or select **Hunter** model has open sights.

### A-BOLT II GOLD DEER HUNTER
### (with Cantilever Scope Mount) $798.95 (Rifled)
### $758.95 (Std. Invector w/Rifled Tube)

## A-BOLT II SPECIFICATIONS (See following page for additional A-Bolt II prices)

| Caliber | Twist (R.H.) | Magazine Capacity | Hunter | Gold Medal. | Medal. | Micro Medal. | Stainless Stalker | Comp Stalker | Varmint | Eclipse |
|---|---|---|---|---|---|---|---|---|---|---|
| **LONG ACTION MAGNUM CALIBERS** | | | | | | | | | | |
| 375 H&H | 1:12" | 3 | – | – | • | – | • | – | – | – |
| 338 Win. Mag. | 1:10" | 3 | • | • | • | – | • | • | – | – |
| 300 Win. Mag. | 1:10" | 3 | • | • | • | – | • | • | – | New |
| 7mm Rem. Mag. | 1:9½" | 3 | • | • | • | – | • | • | – | • |
| **LONG ACTION STANDARD CALIBERS** | | | | | | | | | | |
| 25-06 Rem. | 1:10" | 4 | • | – | • | – | • | • | – | – |
| 270 Win. | 1:10" | 4 | • | • | • | – | • | • | – | • |
| 280 Rem. | 1:10" | 4 | • | – | • | – | • | • | – | – |
| 30-06 Sprg. | 1:10" | 4 | • | • | • | – | • | • | – | • |
| **SHORT ACTION CALIBERS** | | | | | | | | | | |
| 243 Win. | 1:10" | 4 | • | – | • | • | • | • | – | • |
| 308 Win. | 1:12" | 4 | • | – | • | • | • | • | • | •+ |
| 7mm-08 Rem. | 1:9½" | 4 | • | – | • | • | • | • | – | – |
| 22-250 Rem. | 1:14" | 4 | • | – | • | • | • | • | • | •+ |
| 223 Rem. | 1:12" | 6* | • | – | • | • | • | • | • | + |
| 22 Hornet | 1:16" | 4 | – | – | – | • | – | – | – | – |

•Magazine capacity of 223 Rem. models is up to 5 rounds on Micro-Medallion (up to 6 on other models).
+ = also available in Varmint version of new Eclipse. •• New M-1000 Eclipse.

### A-BOLT II AVERAGE WEIGHTS

| Model | Long Action Magnum Calibers | Long Action Standard Calibers | Short Action Calibers |
|---|---|---|---|
| Composite/ Stainless Steel | 7 lbs. 3 oz. | 6 lbs. 11 oz. | 6 lbs. 4 oz. |
| Micro-Medal. | | | 6 lbs. 1 oz. |
| Gold Medal. | 7 lbs. 11 oz. | 7 lbs. 3 oz. | |
| Medallion & Hunter | 7 lbs. 3 oz | 6 lbs. 11 oz. | 6 lbs. 7 oz. |
| Varmint | | 9 lbs. | |
| Eclipse | 8 lbs. | 7 lbs. 8 oz. | 7 lbs. 10 oz. |
| Eclipse Varmint | | 9 lbs. 1 oz. | |
| M-1000 | 9 lbs. 13 oz. | | |

### A-BOLT II STOCK DIMENSIONS

| | Micro-Med. | Gold Medal. | Hunter | Varmint | Stalker | Eclipse | Eclipse Varmint M-1000 |
|---|---|---|---|---|---|---|---|
| Length of Pull | 13⁵/₁₆" | 13⁵/₈" | 13⁵/₈" | 13³/₄" | 13⁵/₈" | 14" | 14" |
| Drop at Comb | ³/₄" | ³/₄"-1" | ³/₄" | ⁹/₁₆" | ⁵/₈" | ⁷/₁₆" | ¹/₂" |
| Drop at Heel | 1¹/₈" | 1³/₄" | 1¹/₈" | ⁷/₁₆" | ¹/₂" | 1¹/₁₆" | 1" |

### A-BOLT II GENERAL DIMENSIONS

| Length | Overall Length | Barrel Length | Sight Radius* |
|---|---|---|---|
| Long Action Mag. Cal. | 46³/₄" | 26" | 18" |
| Long Action Std. Cal. | 42³/₄" | 22" | 18" |
| Short Action Cal. | 41³/₄" | 22" | 16" |
| Micro-Medallion | 39⁹/₁₆" | 20"** | – |
| Varmint Models | 44¹/₂" | 26" | 26" |

*Open sights available on A-Bolt Hunter and all models in 375 H&H.
**22 Hornet Micro-Medallion has a 22" barrel. BOSS equipped rifles have the same dimensions.

RIFLES

# BROWNING RIFLES

### NEW A-BOLT II M-1000 ECLIPSE
### 300 Win. Mag.

## A-BOLT II ECLIPSE MODELS
## WITH THUMBHOLE STOCK

Some of the most advanced, specialized developments of the A-Bolt II have evolved into the new A-Bolt II Eclipse Series. Each rifle is fitted with a newly designed thumbhole stock configuration. To hold accuracy under changing humidity and precipitation conditions the stock itself is crafted from rugged gray/black, multi-laminated hardwood. This gives the Eclipse a camouflaged look. The custom thumbhole-style stock provides a solid grip and secure feel that adds up to accuracy. The Eclipse is available in two versions: long and short action hunting model with standard A-Bolt II barrel, and a short action varmint version with a heavy barrel. All are BOSS equipped.

### A-BOLT II STAINLESS STALKER

The barrel, receiver and bolt are machined from solid stainless steel for a high level of corrosion and rust resistance and also to prolong the life of the rifle bore. The advanced graphite-fiberglass composite stock shrugs off wet weather and rough handling and isn't affected by humidity. A palm swell on both right- and left-hand models offers a better grip. A lower comb directs recoil away from the face. Barrel, receiver and stock have a durable matte finish. The BOSS is optional in all calibers.

### A-BOLT II VARMINT

The A-bolt II Varmint's heavy varmint/target-style barrel provides a steady hold and is less affected by breathing, cross winds and barrel vibrations. A flat forend provides a solid contact surface on a sandbag or bench. A palm swell helps position the hand and trigger finger. The laminated wood stock is stronger and less likely to warp than walnut. All Varmint Models are equipped with the BOSS accuracy device. Available with a satin or high-gloss finish.

| A-BOLT II SERIES | Prices |
|---|---|
| **Gold Medallion** no sights, BOSS | $916.45 |
| **Gold Medallion** no sights | 854.95 |
| **Medallion** no sights, BOSS | 697.95 |
| **Medallion** no sights | 636.25 |
| **Medallion** L.H., no sights, BOSS | 722.95 |
| **Medallion** L.H., no sights | 661.45 |
| **Medallion 375 H&H** no sights, BOSS | 798.95 |
| **Medallion 375 H&H** sights | 737.95 |
| **Medallion 375 H&H** L.H., no sights, BOSS | 823.75 |
| **Medallion 375 H&H** L.H., sights | 762.25 |
| **Micro Medallion** no sights | 636.25 |
| **Varmint**, hvy. bbl., BOSS, gloss or satin/matte | 819.25 |

| A-BOLT II SERIES | Prices |
|---|---|
| **Stainless Stalker** no sights, BOSS | $769.75 |
| **Stainless Stalker** no sights | 708.25 |
| **Stainless Stalker** L.H., no sights, BOSS | 792.25 |
| **Stainless Stalker** L.H., no sights | 730.75 |
| **Stainless Stalker 375 H&H**, BOSS | 893.00 |
| **Stainless Stalker 375 H&H**, open sights | 806.35 |
| **Stainless Stalker 375 H&H**, L.H., BOSS | 893.00 |
| **Stainless Stalker 375 H&H**, L.H., open sights | 831.55 |
| **Composite Stalker**, no sights, BOSS | 623.95 |
| **Composite Stalker**, no sights | 562.45 |
| **Eclipse** no sights, BOSS | 895.75 |
| **Eclipse Varmint** no sights, BOSS | 922.75 |
| **Eclipse M-1000**, w/BOSS | 922.75 |

# BROWNING RIFLES

## LIGHTNING BLR
### $576.95 (Short Action) $608.95 (Long Action)

**Barrel length:** *Long Action*—22"; 24" magnum calibers;
*Short Action*—20"
**Overall length:** *Long Action* 42 7/8"; 44 7/8" magnum calibers; *Short Action* - 39.5"
**Approximate weight:** *Long Action*—7 lbs. 4 oz.; 7 lbs. 12 oz. magnum calibers; *Short Action*—6 lbs. 8 oz.
**Sight radius:** 17 3/4"; 19 3/4" magnum calibers

## SPECIFICATIONS
**Calibers:** *Long Action*—270 Win., 30-06 Springfield; 7mm Rem. Mag.; *Short Action*—22-250 Rem., 243 Win., 7mm-08 Rem., 308 Win.
**Capacity:** 4 rounds; 3 in magnum calibers

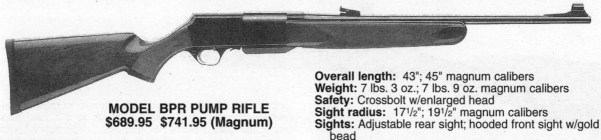

## MODEL BPR PUMP RIFLE
### $689.95 $741.95 (Magnum)

**Overall length:** 43"; 45" magnum calibers
**Weight:** 7 lbs. 3 oz.; 7 lbs. 9 oz. magnum calibers
**Safety:** Crossbolt w/enlarged head
**Sight radius:** 17 1/2"; 19 1/2" magnum calibers
**Sights:** Adjustable rear sight; hooded front sight w/gold bead
**Stock dimensions:** Length of pull; 13 7/8"; Drop at comb: 1 5/8"; Drop at heel: 2"
**Features:** Drilled and tapped for scope mounts; multiple lug rotating bolt locks directly into barrel; detachable box magazine w/hinged floorplate; single-stage trigger; recoil pad standard; full pistol grip

## SPECIFICATIONS
**Calibers:** 243 Win., 308 Win., 270 Win., 30-06 Springfield; 7mm Rem. Mag., 300 Win. Mag.
**Capacity:** 4 rounds; 3 in magnum calibers
**Action:** Pump action
**Barrel length:** 22"; 24" magnum calibers

## BAR MARK II SAFARI

## BAR MARK II SAFARI & LIGHTWEIGHT SEMIAUTOMATIC RIFLES

The BAR Mark II features an engraved receiver, a redesigned bolt release, new gas and buffeting systems, and a removable trigger assembly. Additional features include: crossbolt safety with enlarged head; hinged floorplate, gold trigger; select walnut stock and forearm with cut-checkering and swivel studs; 13 3/4" length of pull; 2" drop at heel; 1 5/8" drop at comb; and a recoil pad (magnum calibers only). The New Lightweight model features alloy receiver and shortened barrel. Open sights are standard.

### BAR MARK II SPECIFICATIONS
**Calibers:** Standard—22-250, 243 Win., 25-06, 270 Win.,, 308 Win.; Magnum—7mm Rem. Mag., 300 Win. Mag., 338 Win. Mag.; Lightweight—243 Win., 270 Win., 30-06 Springfield; 308 Win.
**Capacity:** 4 rounds; 3 in magnum
**Barrel length:** Standard—22"; Magnum—24"; Lightweight—20"
**Overall length:** Standard — 43"; Magnum—45"; Lightweight — 41"
**Average weight:** Standard—7 lbs. 9 oz. in 25-06, 270 Win., 308 Win. ; 7 lbs. 10 oz. in 22-250, 243 Win.; Magnum—8 lbs. 6 oz.; Lightweight—7 lbs. 2 oz.
**Sight radius:** Standard—17.5"; Magnum—19.5";

| BAR MARK II SAFARI | Prices |
|---|---|
| **Standard Calibers** | |
| No sights, BOSS | $811.95 |
| Open sights, no BOSS | 729.95 |
| No sights, no BOSS | 713.95 |
| | |
| **Magnum Calibers** | |
| No sights, BOSS | 863.95 |
| Open sights | 765.95 |
| No sights, no BOSS | 781.95 |
| | |
| **BAR MARK II LIGHTWEIGHT** | |
| Open sights, no BOSS | 729.95 |

# CHRISTENSEN ARMS

### CARBONCANNON SERIES
### $2750.00

Custom lightweight graphite barreled precision magnum big-game class rifle. All popular calibers available. Up to 28" long match-grade stainless steel barrel liner, head spaced minimum, accurized action, custom trigger, synthetic or wood stock and fitted for scope mounts. Bedded with graphite barrel free floating. **Weight:** 7.5 pounds (or less). **Accuracy:** 3 shots 1/2" or less at 100 yards (shoots straight when barrel is hot)

### CARBONCHALLENGE SERIES
### $1000.00-1200.00

Custom ultra-lightweight graphite barreled precision target and small-game rimfire-class rifle. Up to 20" long match-grade stainless steel barrel liner, semi-auto action, custom trigger, synthetic or wood stock and fitted for scope mounts. Bedded with action free floating. **Weight:** 3-5 pounds. **Accuracy:** 3 shots 1/2" or less at 50 yards.

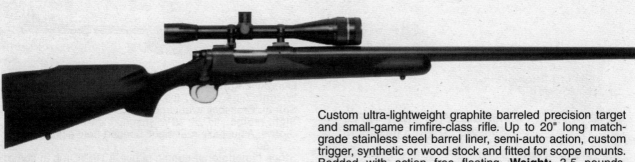

### CARBONTACTICAL SERIES
### $2750.00

Custom lightweight graphite, barreled precision tactical-class rifle. All popular calibers available. Up to 28" long match-grade stainless steel barrel liner, head spaced minimum, muzzle break optional, accurized action, custom trigger, synthetic or wood stock and fitted for scope mounts. Bedded with free-floating graphite barrel. **Weight:** 5-8 pounds. **Accuracy:** 3 shots 1/2" or less at 100 yards (shoots straight when barrel is hot).

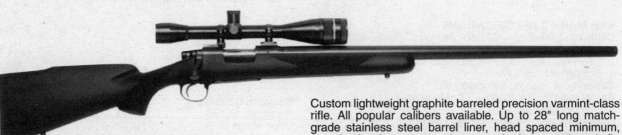

### CARBONONE SERIES
### $2750.00

Custom lightweight graphite barreled precision varmint-class rifle. All popular calibers available. Up to 28" long match-grade stainless steel barrel liner, head spaced minimum, accurized action, custom trigger, synthetic or wood stock; fitted for scope mounts. Bedded with free-floating graphite barrel. **Weight:** 6.5 pounds (or less). **Accuracy:** 3 shots 1/2" or less at 100 yards (shoots straight when barrel is hot).

# CHRISTENSEN ARMS

**CARBONLITE SERIES**
**$2750.00**

Custom ultra-lightweight graphite, barreled precision mountain-class rifle. All popular calibers available. Up to 28" long match-grade stainless steel barrel liner, head spaced minimum, accurized action, custom trigger, synthetic or wood stock and fitted for scope mounts. Bedded with free-floating graphite barrel. **Weight:** 5.5 pounds (or less). **Accuracy:** 3 shots 1/2" or less at 100 yards (shoots straight when barrel is hot).

**CARBONKING SERIES**
**$2750.00**

Custom lightweight graphite, barreled precision hunting-class rifle. All popular calibers available. Up to 28" long match-grade stainless steel barrel liner, head spaced minimum, accurized action, custom trigger, synthetic or wood stock and fitted for scope mounts. Bedded with free-floating graphite barrel. **Weight:** 7 pounds or less. **Accuracy:** 3 shots 1/2" or less at 100 yards (shoots straight when barrel

# CLIFTON ARMS

**SCOUT RIFLE**
**$3100.00**

Several years ago, in response to Colonel Jeff Cooper's concept of an all-purpose rifle, which he calls the "Scout Rifle," Clifton Arms developed the integral, retractable bipod and its accompanying state-of-the-art composite stock. Further development resulted in an integral butt magazine well for storage of cartridges inside the buttstock. These and other components make up the Clifton Scout Rifle.

**SPECIFICATIONS**
**Calibers:** 30-06, 308, 35 Whelen, 416 Rem.
**Barrel length:** 19" to 22" (longer or shorter lengths available; made with Shilen stainless premium match-grade steel)
**Weight:** 7 to 8 lbs.
**Sights:** Forward-mounted Burris 2³/₄X Scout Scope attached to integral scope base pedestals machined in the barrel; Warne rings; reserve iron sight is square post dovetailed into a ramp integral to the barrel, plus a large aperture "ghost ring" mounted on the receiver bridge.
**Features:** Standard action is Ruger 77 MKII stainless; metal finish options include Poly-T, NP3 and chrome sulphide; left-handed rifles available.

# COLT RIFLES

## LIGHTWEIGHTS

The Colt Match Target Lightweight semiautomatic rifle fires from a closed bolt, is easy to load and unload, and has a buttstock and pistol grip made of tough nylon. A round, ribbed handguard is fiberglass-reinforced to ensure better grip control. **Calibers:** 223 Rem., 7.62 X 39mm and 9mm. **Barrel length:** 16". **Overall length:** 34.5" (35.5" in 7.62 X 39mm). **Weight:** 7.1 lbs. (9mm). **Capacity:** 5 rounds (7.62 X 39mm); 8 rounds (223 Rem. and 9mm).
**Price:**....................................... **$987.00**

## COMPETITION H-BAR

## MATCH TARGET RIFLES

The Colt Target and H-Bar rifles are range-selected for top accuracy. They have a 3-9x rubber armored variable-power scope mount, carry handle with iron sight, Cordura nylon case and other accessories. **Caliber:** 223 Rem. **Barrel length:** 20" (16" H-BAR II). **O.A. length:** 39" (34.5" H-BAR II). **Weight:** 8.5 lbs. (Competition/Match H-Bar); 8 lbs. (Target H-BAR); 7.5 lbs. (Target); 7.1 lbs. (H-Bar II). **Capacity:** 8 rounds.
**Prices:**
MATCH TARGET ........................ **$1019.00**
MATCH TARGET H-BAR .................. 1067.00
COMPETITION H-BAR. .................. 1073.00
COMPETITION H-BAR II ................ 1044.00

## COLT ACCURIZED RIFLE
### (not shown)

**SPECIFICATIONS**
**Caliber:** 223 Rem.
**Capacity:** 8 rounds
**Action:** Semiauto; gas operated; locking bolt
**Barrel length:** 24" heavy
**Overall length:** 43"

**Weight:** 9.25 oz.
**Rifling twist:** 1 turn in 9", 6 grooves
**Trigger:** Smooth
**Finish:** Matte black w/matte stainless steel barrel
**Features:** Flattop upper receiver for low scope mount (1" rings)
**Price:**..................................... **$1295.00**

# COOPER ARMS RIFLES

## VARMINT EXTREME SERIES

**MODEL 21 VARMINT EXTREME**

### MODEL 21 VARMINT EXTREME

**SPECIFICATIONS**
**Calibers:** 17 Rem., 17 Mach IV, 221 Fireball, 222 Rem., 222 Rem. Mag., 22 PPC, 223
**Barrel length:** 24"

**Stock:** AAA Claro walnut; flared oval forearm
Other specifications same as Model 36 RF.
**Price** . . . . . . . . . . . . . . . . . . . . . . . . . . . . . . . . . . $1695.00

Also available:
**MODEL 21 CUSTOM CLASSIC** . . . . . . . . . . . . . $1895.00
**MODEL 21 WESTERN CLASSIC** . . . . . . . . . . . . 1995.00

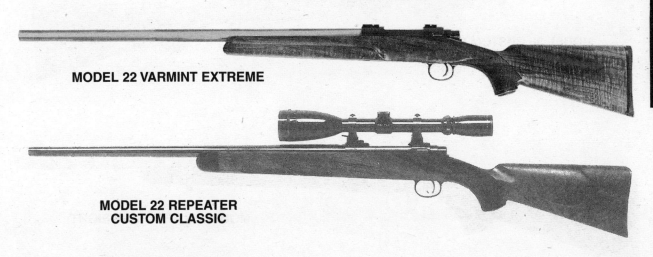

### MODEL 22 VARMINT EXTREME

### MODEL 22 REPEATER
CUSTOM CLASSIC

### MODEL 22 SINGLE SHOT
VARMINT EXTREME

**SPECIFICATIONS**
**Calibers:** 22-250, 220 Swift, 243, 25-06, 308, 6mm PPC
**Capacity:** Single shot
**Barrel length:** 24"
**Action:** 3 front locking lug; glass-bedded
**Trigger:** Single-stage Match, fully adjustable; Jewell 2-stage (optional)

**Stock:** McMillan black-textured synthetic, beaded, w/Monte Carlo cheekpiece; 4-panel checkering print; Pachmayr recoil pad
**Price:**
**MODEL 22 VARMINT EXTREME** . . . . . . . . . . . $1795.00
Also available:
**MODEL 22 BR-50 BENCH REST**
(w/Jewell Trigger) . . . . . . . . . . . . . . . . . . . . . . . 2195.00
**MODEL 22 REPEATER CUSTOM CLASSIC** . . . 2675.00

### MODEL 22 BR-50 SINGLE SHOT

# COOPER ARMS RIFLES

## COMPETITION SERIES

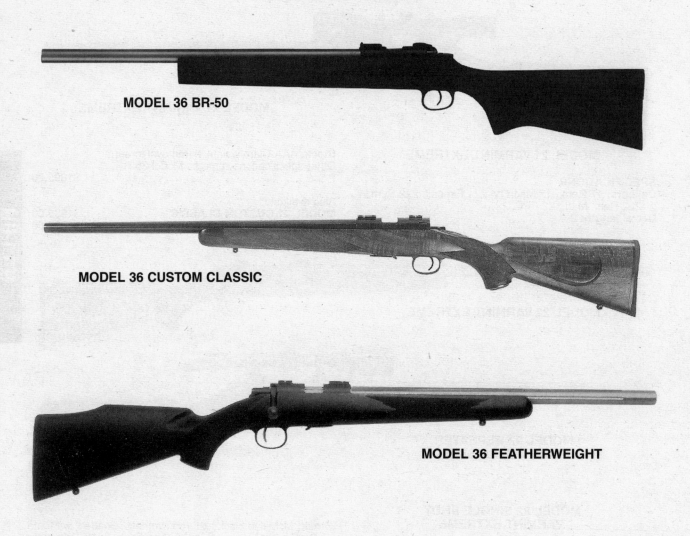

MODEL 36 BR-50

MODEL 36 CUSTOM CLASSIC

MODEL 36 FEATHERWEIGHT

## MODEL 36 CLASSIC

**SPECIFICATIONS**
**Caliber:** 22 LR   **Capacity:** 5-shot magazine
**Action:** bolt-action repeater
**Barrel length:** 23.75" (chrome moly); free-floated barrel w/competition step crown
**Stock:** AAA Claro, side panel checkering, Pachmayr recoil pad, steel grip cap (Classic Model); AAA Claro, wrap-around custom checkering, beaded cheekpiece, ebony tip, steel grip cap (Custom Classic)
**Features:** Glass-bedded adjustable trigger; bases and rings optional;  3 mid-locking lugs

**Prices:**
CUSTOM CLASSIC . . . . . . . . . . . . . . . . . . . . . . $1795.00
WESTERN CLASSIC . . . . . . . . . . . . . . . . . . . . . 1995.00
VARMINT EXTREME . . . . . . . . . . . . . . . . . . . . . 1695.00

Also available:
**MODEL 36 RF/CF FEATHERWEIGHT:** Same specifications as Model 36 RF, but weighs 6.5 lbs. . . . . . $1695.00
**MODEL 36 RF BR-50:** Same specifications as Model 36 RF, but w/22" stainless steel bbl. 6.8 lbs. . . . . . . . 1895.00
**MODEL IR 50/50** . . . . . . . . . . . . . . . . . . . . . . . . 1895.00

# DAKOTA ARMS

## DAKOTA 76 AFRICAN GRADE

## DAKOTA 76 RIFLES

### SPECIFICATIONS
**Calibers:**
  **Safari Grade:** 338 Win. Mag., 300 Mag., 375 H&H Mag., 458 Win. Mag.

  **Classic Grade:** 22-250, 257 Roberts, 270 Win., 280 Rem., 30-06, 7mm Rem. Mag., 338 Win. Mag., 300 Win. Mag., 375 H&H Mag., 458 Win. Mag.

  **African Grade:** 404 Jeffery, 416 Dakota, 416 Rigby, 450 Dakota

  **Varmint Grade:** 22 Hornet, 22 PPC, 22-250, 220 Swift, 222 Rem. Mag., 223, 6mm PPC

**Barrel lengths:** 21" or 23" (Classic); 23" only (Safari); 24" (Varmint and African)

**Weight:** 7.5 lbs. (Classic); 9.5 lbs. (African); 8.5 lbs. (Safari)

**Safety:** Three-position striker-blocking safety allows bolt operation with safety on

**Sights:** Ramp front sight; standing-leaf rear

**Stock:** Choice of X grade oil-finished English, Bastogne or Claro walnut (Classic); choice of XXX grade oil-finished English or Bastogne walnut w/ebony forent tip (Safari)

**Prices:**

| | |
|---|---|
| **Varmint Grade** (semifancy walnut) . . . . . . . . . . | **$2500.00** |
| **Classic Grade** . . . . . . . . . . . . . . . . . . . . . . . . . | 2995.00 |
| **Safari Grade** . . . . . . . . . . . . . . . . . . . . . . . . . . | 3995.00 |
| **African Grade** . . . . . . . . . . . . . . . . . . . . . . . . . | 4495.00 |
| **Barreled actions:** | |
|   Classic Grade . . . . . . . . . . . . . . . . . . . . . . . | 2000.00 |
|   Varmint Grade . . . . . . . . . . . . . . . . . . . . . . . | 1950.00 |
|   Safari Grade . . . . . . . . . . . . . . . . . . . . . . . . | 2350.00 |
|   African Grade . . . . . . . . . . . . . . . . . . . . . . . | 2950.00 |
| **Actions:** | |
|   Classic Grade . . . . . . . . . . . . . . . . . . . . . . . | 1750.00 |
|   Varmint Grade . . . . . . . . . . . . . . . . . . . . . . . | 1650.00 |
|   Safari Grade . . . . . . . . . . . . . . . . . . . . . . . . | 1900.00 |
|   African Grade . . . . . . . . . . . . . . . . . . . . . . . | 2500.00 |

## DAKOTA 10 SINGLE SHOT

### SPECIFICATIONS
**Calibers:** Most rimmed/rimless commercially loaded types

**Barrel length:** 23"   **Overall length:** 39.5"   **Weight:** 6 lbs.

**Features:** Receiver and rear of breech block are solid steel without cuts or holes for maximum lug area (approx. 8 times more bearing area than most bolt rifles); crisp, clean trigger pull; removable trigger plate allows action to adapt to single-set triggers; straight-line coil-spring action and short hammer fall combine for fast lock time; smooth, quiet top tang safety blocks the striker forward of the main spring; strong, positive extractor and manual ejector adapted to rimmed/rimless cases. XX grade oil-finished English, Bastogne or Claro walnut stock.

| | |
|---|---|
| **Price:** . . . . . . . . . . . . . . . . . . . . . . . . . . . . . . . | **$2995.00** |
| **Barreled actions** . . . . . . . . . . . . . . . . . . . . . . . | 2000.00 |
| **Actions only** . . . . . . . . . . . . . . . . . . . . . . . . . . | 1675.00 |
| Also available: | |
| **DAKOTA 10 MAGNUM SINGLE SHOT** . . . . . . . . | **$3295.00** |
|   Barreled actions . . . . . . . . . . . . . . . . . . . . . | 2050.00 |
|   Actions only . . . . . . . . . . . . . . . . . . . . . . . . | 1775.00 |

## DAKOTA 22 LR SPORTER

### SPECIFICATIONS
**Calibers:** 22 LR   **Capacity:** 5-round clip

**Barrel length:** 22" (chrome-moly, 1 turn in 16")

**Weight:** 6.5 lbs.

**Stock:** X Claro or English walnut with hand-cut checkering

**Features:** Plain bolt handle; swivels and single screw studs; 1/2-inch black pad; 13 5/8" length of pull

**Price:** . . . . . . . . . . . . . . . . . . . . . . . . . . . . . . . **$1795.00**

# EMF REPLICA RIFLES

### 1860 HENRY RIFLE
### $1110.00

**SPECIFICATIONS**
**Calibers:** 44-40 and 45 LC
**Barrel length:** 24.25"; upper half-octagonal w/magazine tube in one-piece steel

**Overall length:** 43.75"  Weight: 9.25 lbs.
**Stock:** Varnished American walnut wood
**Features:** Polished brass frame; brass buttplate

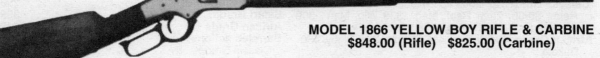

### MODEL 1866 YELLOW BOY RIFLE & CARBINE
### $848.00 (Rifle)   $825.00 (Carbine)

These exact reproductions of guns used over 100 years ago are available in 45 Long Colt, 38 Special and 44-40. Both carbine and rifle are offered with blued finish, walnut stock and brass frame.

### MODEL 1873 SPORTING RIFLE
### $1050.00

**SPECIFICATIONS**
**Calibers:** 357, 44-40, 45 Long Colt
**Barrel length:** 24.25" octagonal   **Overall length:** 43.25"
**Weight:** 8.16 lbs.
**Features:** Magazine tube in blued steel; frame is casehardened steel; stock and forend are walnut wood

Also available:
**MODEL 1873 CARBINE.** Same features as the 1873 Sporting Rifle, except in 45 Long Colt only with 19" barrel, overall length 38.25" and weight 7.38 lbs. **Price: $1050.00; $1050.00** Casehardened
**MODEL 1873 SHORT RIFLE** in 45 LC, 20" barrel **$1050.00**

# EUROPEAN AMERICAN AMORY

### HW 660 WEIHRAUCH RIMFIRE TARGET RIFLE (SINGLE SHOT)
### $881.50

**SPECIFICATIONS**
**Caliber:** 22 LR  **Barrel length:** 26"
**Overall length:** 45.33"
**Weight:** 10.8 lbs.  **Finish:** Blue
**Stock:** European walnut w/adjustable black rubber buttplate and comb

**Features:** Adjustable match trigger; left-handed stock available; aluminum adjustable sling swivel; adj. vertical and lateral cheekpiece; rear sight click-adjustable for windage and elevation; aluminum forend rail; polished feed ramp; external thumb safety

# FRANCOTTE RIFLES

August Francotte rifles are available in all calibers for which barrels and chambers are made. All guns are custom made to the customer's specifications; there are no standard models. Most bolt-action rifles use commercial Mauser actions; however, the magnum action is produced by Francotte exclusively for its own production. Side-by-side and mountain rifles use either boxlock or sidelock action. Francotte system sidelocks are back-action type. Options include gold and silver inlay, special engraving and exhibition and museum grade wood. Francotte rifles are distributed in the U.S. by Armes de Chasse (*see* Directory of Manufacturers and Distributors for details).

**BOLT-ACTION RIFLE**

## SPECIFICATIONS
**Calibers:** 17 Bee, 7×64, 30-06, 270, 222R, 243W, 308W,
   375 H&H, 416 Rigby, 460 Weatherby, 505 Gibbs
**Barrel length:** To customer's specifications
**Weight:** 8 to 12 lbs., or to customer's specifications
**Stock:** A wide selection of wood in all possible styles according to customer preferences; prices listed below do not include engraving or select wood
**Engraving:** Per customer specifications
**Sights:** All types of sights and scopes

## BOLT-ACTION RIFLES                                Prices
Standard Bolt Action (30-06, 270, 7×64,
   etc.) .................................. $7000.00
Short Bolt Action (222R, 243W, etc.) ......... 8500.00
Magnum Action (300 WM, 338 WM, 375 H&H,
   458 WM ................................ 8000.00

## BOXLOCK SIDE-BY-SIDE DOUBLE RIFLES          Prices
Std. boxlock double rifle (9.3×74R, 8×57JRS,
   7×65R, etc.)......................... $14,000.00
Std. boxlock double (Magnum calibers) ...... 19,000.00
Optional sideplates, **add**................... 1,400.00

## SIDELOCK S/S DOUBLE RIFLES
Std. sidelock double rifle (9.3×74R, 8×57JRS,
   7×65R, etc.).......................... $28,000.00
Std. sidelock double (Magnum calibers)...... 33,000.00
Special safari sidelock ..............**Price on request**

## MOUNTAIN RIFLES
Standard boxlock .........................$12,000.00
Std. boxlock (Mag. & rimless calibers)... **Price on request**
Optional sideplates, **add**................... 1,400.00
Standard sidelock ....................... 25,000.00

**MOUNTAIN RIFLE
w/Elaborate Engraving**

# HARRINGTON & RICHARDSON

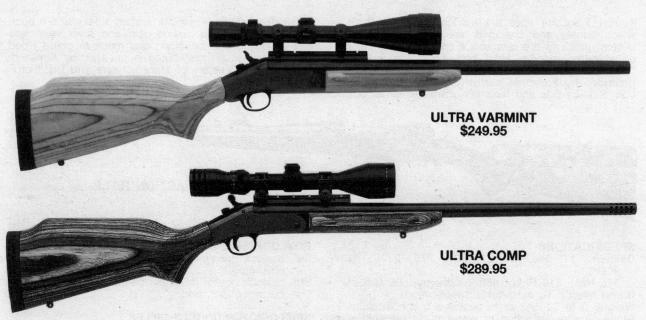

**ULTRA VARMINT**
**$249.95**

**ULTRA COMP**
**$289.95**

## ULTRA SINGLE-SHOT RIFLES

**SPECIFICATIONS**
**Calibers:** 223 Rem. (Varmint), 25-06, 308 Win. and 357 Rem. Max.
**Action:** Break-open; side lever release; positive ejection
**Barrel length:** 22″ (308 Win., 357 Rem. Max.); 22″ bull barrel (223 Rem. Varmint); 26″ (25-06)
**Weight:** 7 to 8 lbs.
**Sights:** None (scope mount included)
**Length of pull:** 14¼″
**Drop at comb:** 1¼″    **Drop at heel:** 1⅛″

**Forend:** Semibeavertail
**Stock:** Monte Carlo; hand-checkered curly maple; Varmint model has light laminate stock
**Features:** Sling swivels on stock and forend; patented transfer bar safety; automatic ejection; hammer extension; rebated muzzle
Also available:
**ULTRA COMP** in 30-06 and 270 Win. **Barrel length:** 24″. **Weight:** 7–8 lbs. Camo laminate stock.

**WHITETAILS UNLIMITED
1997 COMMEMORATIVE**

## WHITETAILS UNLIMITED
### 1997 COMMEMORATIVE RIFLE
**$289.95**

This new Harrington & Richardson 45-70 Government commemorative edition features hand-checkered American black walnut stock and forend. Included is a heat investment-cast steel frame, high-polish blue action and barrel, pistol-grip stock with sling swivel studs and a premium recoil pad. A special laser engraving of the WTU logo and a legend indicating the status as part of the 1997 limited edition are included.

**SPECIFICATIONS**
**Caliber:** 45-70 Government
**Action:** Break-open; side lever release; positive ejection
**Barrel length:** 22″   **Weight:** 7 lbs.
**Length of pull:** 14″
**Drop at comb:** 1½″   **Drop at heel:** 2⅛″
**Stock:** Hand-checkered American black walnut
**Sights:** Ramp front; fully adjustable rear

# HARRIS GUNWORKS RIFLES

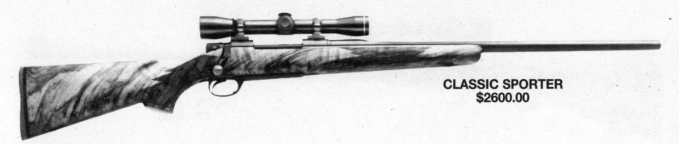

### CLASSIC SPORTER
### $2600.00

**SPECIFICATIONS**
**Calibers:**

**Model SA:** 22-250, 243, 6mm Rem., 6mm BR, 7mm BR, 7mm-08, 284, 308, 350 Rem. Mag.
**Model LA:** 25-06, 270, 280 Rem., 30-06
**Model MA:** 7mm STW, 7mm Rem. Mag., 300 Win. Mag., 300 Weatherby, 300 H&H, 338 Win. Mag., 340 Weatherby, 375 H&H, 416 Rem.

**Capacity:** 4 rounds; 3 rounds in magnum calibers
**Weight:** 7 lbs; 7 lbs. 9 oz. in long action
**Barrel lengths:** 22″, 24″, 26″
**Options:** Wooden stock, optics, 30mm rings, muzzle brakes, steel floor plates, iron sights

### STAINLESS SPORTER
### $2800.00

Same basic specifications as the Classic and Standard Sporters, but with stainless steel action and barrel. It is designed to withstand the most adverse weather conditions. Accuracy is guaranteed (3 shot in ½″ at 100 yards). Choice of wood, laminate or Gunworks fiberglass stock.

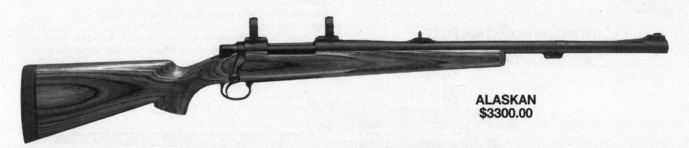

### ALASKAN
### $3300.00

**SPECIFICATIONS**
**Calibers:**

**Model LA:** 270, 280, 30-06
**Model MA:** 7mm Rem. Mag., 300 Win. Mag., 300 H&H, 300 Weatherby, 358 Win., 340 Weatherby, 375 H&H, 416 Rem.

Other specifications same as the Classic Sporter, except Harris action is fitted to a match-grade barrel, complete with single-leaf rear sight, barrel band front sight, 1″ detachable rings and mounts, steel floorplate, electroless nickel finish. Monte Carlo stock features cheekpiece, palm swell and special recoil pad.
Also available: Stainless Steel Receiver, **add** . . . . . **$150.00**

# HARRIS GUNWORKS RIFLES

**TALON SPORTER**
**$2600.00**

The all-new action of this model is designed and engineered specifically for the hunting of dangerous (African-type) game animals. Patterned after the renowned pre-64 Model 70, the Talon features a cone breech, controlled feed, claw extractor, positive ejection and three-position safety. Action is available in chromolybdenum and stainless steel. Drilled and tapped for scope mounting in long, short or magnum, left or right hand.

Same basic specifications as Harris Signature series, but offered in the following **calibers:**
**Standard Action:** 22-250, 243, 6mm Rem., 6mm BR, 7mm BR, 7mm-08, 284, 308, 350 Rem. Mag.
**Long Action:** 25-06, 270, 280 Rem., 30-06
**Magnum Action:** 7mm STW, 7mm Rem. Mag., 300 Win. Mag., 300 Weatherby, 300 H&H, 338 Win. Mag., 340 Weatherby, 375 H&H, 416 Rem.

**VARMINTER**
**$2600.00**

**SPECIFICATIONS**
**Calibers:** 223, 22-250, 220 Swift, 243, 6mm Rem., 25-06, 7mm-08, 308, 350 Rem. Mag.
Other specifications same as the Classic Sporter, except the Super Varminter comes with heavy contoured barrel, adjustable trigger, field bipod and hand-bedded fiberglass stock.

**TITANIUM MOUNTAIN RIFLE**
**$3200.00**
**$3600.00 w/Titanium Barrel**

**SPECIFICATIONS**
**Calibers:**
　**Model LA:** 270, 280 Rem., 30-06
　**Model MA:** 7mm Rem. Mag., 300 Win. Mag.
**Weight:** 5 1/2 lbs.
Other specifications same as the Classic Sporter, except barrel is made of chrome-moly (titanium alloy light contour match-grade barrel is available at additional cost of **$500.00**).

**.300 PHOENIX**
**$2600.00**

**Caliber:** 300 Phoenix. **Barrel length:** 27 1/2″. **Weight:** 12 1/2 lbs. **Stock:** Fiberglass with adjustable cheekpiece. **Feature:** Available in left-hand action.

# HARRIS GUNWORKS RIFLES

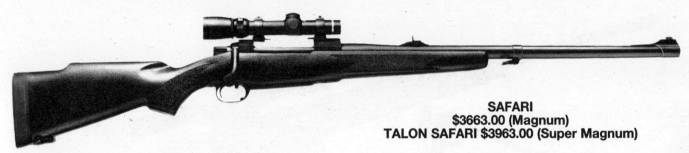

## SAFARI
### $3663.00 (Magnum)
### TALON SAFARI $3963.00 (Super Magnum)

**SPECIFICATIONS**
**Calibers:**
   **Magnum:** 300 Win. Mag., 300 Weatherby, 300 H&H, 338 Win. Mag., 340 Weatherby, 375 H&H, 404 Jeffrey, 416 Rem., 458 Win.
   **Super Magnum:** 300 Phoenix, 338 Lapua, 378 Wby., 416 Rigby, 416 Wby., 460 Wby.

Other specifications same as the Classic Sporter, except for match-grade barrel, positive extraction Harris Safari action, quick detachable 1" scope mounts, positive locking steel floorplate, multi-leaf express sights, barrel band ramp front sight, barrel band swivels, and Harris Safari stock.

## NATIONAL MATCH RIFLE
### $2600.00

**SPECIFICATIONS**
**Calibers:** 308, 7mm-08    **Mag. Capacity:** 5 rounds
**Weight:** Approx. 11 lbs. (12½ lbs. w/heavy contour barrel)
Available for right-hand shooters only. Features Harris fiberglass stock with adjustable buttplate, stainless steel match barrel with barrel band and Tompkins front sight; Harris repeating bolt action with clip shot and Canjar trigger. Barrel twist is 1:12".

## LONG RANGE RIFLE
### $2600.00

**SPECIFICATIONS**
**Calibers:** 300 Win. Mag., 300 Phoenix, 7mm Mag., 338 Lapua
**Barrel length:** 26"   **Weight:** 14 lbs.
Available in right-hand only. Features a fiberglass stock with adjustable butt plate and cheekpiece. Stainless steel match barrel comes with barrel band and Tompkins front sight. Harris solid bottom single-shot action and Canjar trigger. Barrel twist is 1:12".

## HARRIS BENCHREST RIFLE
### $2600.00 (not shown)

**SPECIFICATIONS**
**Calibers:** 6mm PPC, 243, 6mm BR, 6mm Rem., 308
Built to individual specifications to be competitive in hunter, light varmint and heavy varmint classes. Features solid bottom or repeating bolt action, Canjar trigger, fiberglass stock with recoil pad, stainless steel match-grade barrel and reloading dies. Right- or left-hand models.

# HECKLER & KOCH RIFLES

**MODEL HK PSG-1 HIGH PRECISION
MARKSMAN'S RIFLE
$10,811.00**

**SPECIFICATIONS**
**Caliber:** 308 (7.62mm)
**Capacity:** 5 rounds
**Barrel length:** 25.6″
**Overall length:** 47.5″
**Rifling:** 4 groove, polygonal
**Twist:** 12″, right hand

**Weight:** 17.8 lbs.  **Height:** 8.26 lbs.
**Sights:** Hensoldt 6×42 telescopic
**Stock:** Matte black, high-impact plastic
**Finish:** Matte black, phosphated
**Features:** Aluminum case; tripod; sling; adj. buttstock and
contoured grip

# HENRY REPEATING ARMS

**HENRY RIFLE**

**HENRY RIFLE
$229.95**

**SPECIFICATIONS**
**Calibers:** 22 S, L, LR
**Capacity:** 15 rounds (22 LR); 17 rds. (22 L); 21 rds. (22 S)

**Barrel length:** 18.25″
**Overall length:** 36.5″
**Weight:** 5.5 lbs.
**Stock:** American walnut
**Sights:** Adjustable rear; hooded front
**Features:** Grooved receiver for scope mount

# HOWA LIGHTNING RIFLES

### LIGHTNING BOLT-ACTION RIFLE

**SPECIFICATIONS**
**Calibers:** 22-250, 223, 243, 270, 308, 30-06, 300 Win. Mag., 338 Win. Mag., 7mm Rem. Mag.
**Capacity:** 5 rounds (3 in Magnum)
**Barrel length:** 22″ (24″ in Magnum)
**Overall length:** 42″
**Weight:** 7.5 lbs. (7.75 lbs. in Magnum)
**Price:**
**Standard Model** . . . . . . . . . . . . . . . . . . . . . . . . . . . . **$425.00**
   In Magnum calibers . . . . . . . . . . . . . . . . . . . . . . . 445.00
**Barreled Actions** . . . . . . . . . . . . . . . . . . . . . . . . . . . 325.00
   In Magnum calibers . . . . . . . . . . . . . . . . . . . . . . . 345.00

The rugged mono-bloc receivers on all Howa rifles are machined from a single billet of high carbon steel. The machined steel bolt boasts dual-opposed locking lugs and triple relief gas ports. Actions are fitted with a button-release hinged floorplate for fast reloading. Premium steel sporter-weight barrels are hammer-forged. A silent sliding thumb safety locks the trigger for safe loading or clearing the chamber. The stock is ultra-tough polymer.

# JARRETT CUSTOM RIFLES

### MODEL NO. 1
### $2850.00

Jarrett's Standard Hunting Rifle uses McMillan's fiberglass stock and is made primarily for hunters of big game and varmints.

Also available:
**MODEL NO. 3 Coup de Grace.** Same specifications as the Standard model, but can use a Remington or Winchester receiver. Includes a muzzlebreak kit (Serial No. 1-100) and weatherproofing metal finish. Model 70-style bolt release installed on a Rem. 700.
**Price:** . . . . . . . . . . . . . . . . . . . . . . . . . . . . . . . . . . **$3495.00**

**MODEL NO. 2**

### MODEL NO. 2
### $2850.00

This lightweight rifle—called the "Walkabout"—is based on Remington's Model 7 (or Short 700) receiver. It is available in any short-action caliber and is pillar-bedded into a McMillan Model 7-style or Mountain stock.

### MODEL NO. 4 (not shown)
### $6000.00

This model—the "Professional Hunter"—is based on a Winchester controlled round-feed Model 70. It features a quarter rib and iron sights and comes with two Leupold scopes with quick-detachable scope rings. A handload is developed for solids and soft points (40 rounds each). It is then pillar-bedded into a McMillan fiberglass stock. Available in any Magnum caliber. Comes with takedown rifle case.

# KBI ARMSCOR RIFLES

**MODEL M-2000SC SUPER CLASSIC
SEMIAUTOMATIC**

**MODEL M-1800S CLASSIC
BOLT ACTION**

**SUPER CLASSIC
MODELS M-1400SC, M-1500SC, M-1800SC,
M-2000SC**

## SPECIFICATIONS
**Calibers:** 22 LR, 22 Mag. RF, 22 Hornet
**Action:** Bolt and semiauto
**Capacity:** 10 rounds (22 LR); 5 rounds (22 Mag. RF and 22 Hornet)
**Barrel length:** 22⅝"; 20¾" in semiauto
**Overall length:** 41¼"; 40½" in semiauto)
**Weight:** 6.4 lbs. (semiauto); 6.5 lbs. (22 Mag. RF); 6.6 lbs. (22 Hornet); 6.7 lbs. (22 LR)
**Finish:** Blue
**Features:** Oil-finished American walnut stock w/hardwood grip cap & forend tip; checkered Monte Carlo comb and cheekpiece, high polish blued barreled action w/damascened bolt; dovetailed receiver and iron sights (ramp front sight, fully adjustable rear sight); recoil pad; QD swivel posts

**Prices:**
| | |
|---|---|
| **22 Long Rifle** | **$355.00** |
| **22 Mag. Rimfire** | 379.00 |
| **22 Hornet** | 486.00 |
| **22 LR Semiauto** | 340.00 |

Also available:
**CLASSIC 22 LR.** Same specifications as the Super Classic but with walnut-finished hardwood stock and cut checkering.
**Prices:**
| | |
|---|---|
| **M-1400S 22 LR Bolt Action** | **$224.00** |
| **M-1500S 22 MRF** | 236.00 |
| **M-1800S 22 Hornet** | 358.00 |
| **M-2000S Semiauto 22 LR** | 213.00 |

**STANDARD M-20P SEMIAUTOMATIC**

**MODEL M-12Y YOUTH BOLT ACTION**

**STANDARD 22 RIFLES
$129.00**

## SPECIFICATIONS
**Caliber:** 22 Long Rifle
**Action:** Bolt and semiauto
**Capacity:** 10 rounds
**Barrel length:** 20¾" (Model M-20P); 22⅝" (Model M-14P)
**Overall length:** 40½" (Model M-20P); 41" (Model M-14P)
**Weight:** 6 lbs. 3 oz. (Model M-20P); 6 lbs. 8 oz. (Model M-14P)

**Finish:** Blue
**Features:** Walnut-finished hardwood stocks; dovetailed receiver; iron sights (hooded front and leaf-adjustable rear)

Also available:
**MODEL M-12Y YOUTH RIFLE.** Single shot. **Barrel length:** 17½". **Overall length:** 34⅜". **Weight:** 4 lbs. 13 oz. **$122.00.**
Also available w/ 10-shot capacity: **$126.00**

# KIMBER RIFLES

**MODEL 82C 22 LR CLASSIC**

## MODEL 82C 22 LR SPECIFICATIONS

| Model: | Model 82C Classic | Model 82C Stainless Classic | Model 82C SVT | Model 82C SuperAmerica | Model 82C Custom Match |
|---|---|---|---|---|---|
| **Weight:** | 6.5 lbs. | 6.5 lbs. | 7.5 lbs. | 6.5 lbs. | 6.75 lbs. |
| **Overall length:** | 40.5″ | 40.5″ | 36.5″ | 40.5″ | 40.5″ |
| **Action Type:** | Rear Locking Repeater | Rear Locking Repeater | Rear Locking Single Shot | Rear Locking Repeater | Rear Locking Repeater |
| **Capacity:** | 4-Shot Clip 5 & 10 Shot (opt.) | 4-Shot Clip 5 & 10 Shot (opt.) | | 4-Shot Clip 5 & 10 Shot (opt.) | 4-Shot Clip 5 & 10 Shot (opt.) |
| **Trigger:**   Pressure: | Fully Adjustable Set at 2.5 lbs. | Fully Adjustable Set at 2.5 lbs. | Fully Adjustable Set at 2.5 lbs. | Fully Adjustable Set at 2.5 lbs. | Fully Adjustable Set at 2.5 lbs. |
| **Barrel Length:**   Grooves   Twist | 22″ 6 16″ | 22″ 6 16″ | 18″ Fluted 6 16″ | 22″ 6 16″ | 22″ 6 16″ |
| **Stock:**   Grade Walnut   Checkering (LPI)   Coverage | A Claro 18 Side Panel | A Claro 18 Side Panel | A Claro None NA | AAA Claro 22 Full Coverage Wrap Around | AA French 22 Full Coverage Wrap Around |
| **Length of Pull:** | 13⅝″ | 13⅝″ | 13⅝″ | 13⅝″ | 13⅝″ |
| **Metal Finish:** | Polished & Blued | Stainless steel bbl. Matte blued action | Stainless steel bbl. Matte blued action | Polished & Blued | Matte "rust" type blue |

**MODEL 82C 22 LR**          **Prices**
Classic . . . . . . . . . . . . . . . . . . . . . . . . . . . . . $ 810.00
Stainless Classic . . . . . . . . . . . . . . . . . . . . . . 899.00
SVT (Short/Varmint/Target) . . . . . . . . . . . . . . 825.00

HS (Hunter Silhouette) . . . . . . . . . . . . . . . . . . . . $ 655.00
Varmint Stainless (Ltd. Ed.) . . . . . . . . . . . . . . . . 925.00
SuperAmerica . . . . . . . . . . . . . . . . . . . . . . . . . . 1326.00
Custom Match . . . . . . . . . . . . . . . . . . . . . . . . . . 2075.00

**MODEL 82C 22LR SVT**
**(Short/Varmint/Target)**

# KIMBER RIFLES

## MODEL 84 C SINGLE SHOT VARMINT

### MODEL 84C

The Kimber Model 84C is a scaled-down mini-Mauser with controlled round feeding. Like other Kimber rifles, the 84C action is machined from solid steel. Designed for the .223 Rem. family of cartridges, it is available in both single shot and repeater versions. Every Model 84C is test-fired for accuracy at the factory. Each rifle must shoot a 5-shot group measuring .400" or less center-to-center at 50 yards.

| MODEL 84C | Prices |
|---|---|
| Single Shot Varmint | $ 999.00 |
| Classic | 1145.00 |
| SuperAmerica | 1595.00 |
| Varmint Stainless | 1250.00 |

## MODEL 84C SPECIFICATIONS

| Model: | Model 84C Single Shot Varmint | Model 84C Classic | Model 84C SuperAmerica | Model 84C Varmint Stainless |
|---|---|---|---|---|
| Calibers: | 17 Rem., 223 Rem. | 222 Rem., 223 Rem. | 17 Rem., 222 Rem. 223 Rem. | 223 Rem. |
| Weight: | 7.5 lbs. | 6.75 lbs. | 6.75 lbs. | 7.5 lbs. |
| Overall Length: | 43.5" | 40.5" | 40.5" | 42.5" |
| Action Type: | Front Locking Single Shot | Front Locking Controlled Feed Repeater Hinged floorplate 5-shot box magazine | Front Locking Controlled Feed Repeater Hinged floorplate 5-shot box magazine | Front Locking Controlled Feed Repeater Hinged floorplate 5-shot box magazine |
| Trigger: Pressure | Fully Adjustable Set at 2.5 lbs. | Fully Adjustable Set at 2.5 lbs. | Fully Adjustable Set at 2.5 lbs. | Fully Adjustable Set at 2.5 lbs. |
| Barrel Length: Grooves: Twist: | 25" (Fluted) 6 17 Rem.-10"/223 Rem.-12" | 22" 6 222 Rem.-12"/223 Rem.-12" | 22" 6 17 Rem.-10"/222 Rem.-12" 223 Rem.-12" | 24" (Fluted) 6 12" |
| Stock: Grade Walnut Checkering (LPI) Coverage | A Claro 18 Side Panel | A Claro 18 Side Panel | AAA Claro 22 Full Coverage Wrap Around | A Claro 18 Side Panel |
| Length of Pull: | 13⅝" | 13⅝" | 13⅝" | 13⅝" |
| Metal Finish: | Stainless steel barrel, Matte blue action | Polished & Blued | Polished & Blued | Stainless steel barrel, Matte blue action |

### MODEL 84C SUPERAMERICA REPEATER

# KIMBER RIFLES

**SWEDISH MAUSER 96 SPORTER**

**SWEDISH MAUSER 96**

## SPECIFICATIONS
**Calibers:** *Sporters*—243 Win., 6.5×55mm, 7mm-08, 308 Win.; *Heavy Barrel Models*—22-250 and 308 Win. (SS Varmint)
**Capacity:** 5 shots
**Action:** Mauser, front-locking bolt action, cock on closing
**Barrel length:** 22″ (Sporters); 25″ (Heavy barrel models)
**Overall length:** 41.5″ (Sporters); 44.5″ (Heavy barrel models)
**Weight:** 7.25 lbs. (Sporters); 8.25 lbs. (SS Varmint)
**Trigger:** Two-stage military trigger
**Stock:** Ramline™ Syn-Tech™ synthetic plastic "krinkle" finish; lifetime guarantee; length of pull 13.5″

**Finish:** Satin silver or matte blue (Sporters); stainless barrel w/matte blue action (SS Varmint)
**Prices:**
**SPORTERS**

| | |
|---|---|
| 243, 7mm-08 or 308 (matte blue). | $415.00 |
| Same as above in satin silver. | 465.00 |
| 6.5×55mm matte blue. | 340.00 |
| Same as above in satin silver. | 370.00 |
| **HEAVY BARREL MODELS** | |
| 22-250 SS Varmint. | 505.00 |
| 308 SS Fluted. | 520.00 |

**MAUSER 98 SPORTER**

**MAUSER 98 SPORTER**

The Mauser 98 Sporter features a new match-grade stainless steel fluted barrel with a heavy sporter contour. To compliment the barrel finish, the action is finished in a deep matte blue. Each rifle also incorporates a high- quality synthetic stock with a 1″ recoil pad and comes with scope mounts.00 To permit proper scope mounting, Kimber installs a new steel

Buehler-style safety and repositions the bolt handle. Claro walnut stock also available (**$100.**add'l). **Calibers:** 270 Win., 30-06 Spfd., 7mm Rem. Mag., 300 Win. Mag., 338 Win. Mag. **Barrel length:** 24″ (25″ in magnum calibers). **Overall length:** 46″ (47″ magnum calibers). **Weight:** 7.5 lbs.
**Prices:**

| | |
|---|---|
| Standard calibers. | $535.00 |
| Magnum calibers. | 560.00 |

**K770 CLASSIC**

**MODEL K770 BOLT ACTION**

The Kimber K770 is a new repeater version of a single-shot target rifle designed by Jack Warne, co-founder of Kimber of Oregon. The K770 design contains several features that enhance accuracy. The front-locking improved bolt has three lugs that lock directly into the barrel breech instead of the receiver. This provides cartridge alignment and support, thus increasing accuracy. Each K770 is test-fired for accuracy at the factory. Five-shot group size of .500″ or less center-to-center at 50 yards is required.

**Calibers:** 270 Win., 30-06 Springfield, 7mm Rem. Mag., 300 Win. Mag., 338 Win. Mag. **Barrel length:** 24″. The **Classic** model has a rich claro-walnut stock, 18 LPI side panel hand-cut checkering, polished steel grip cap and hinged floorplate. **Overall length:** 45″ (46″ magnum calibers). **Weight:** 7.75 lbs. **Length of pull:** 13⅝″. The **SuperAmerica** model features a AAA claro-walnut stock with ebony forend tip and beaded cheekpiece (22 LPI full coverage wraparound checkering). Both are finished in matte blue and have two-position Model 70-type safeties.
**Prices:**

| | |
|---|---|
| Classic. | $ 745.00 |
| SuperAmerica. | 1260.00 |

# KONGSBERG RIFLES

**MODEL 393 CLASSIC**

## HUNTER 393 MODELS

**SPECIFICATIONS**
**Calibers:** 243 Win., 6.5mm×55 Swedish, 270 Win., 30-06, 308 Win., 7mm Rem. Mag., 300 Win. Mag., 338 Win. Mag.
**Capacity:** 4 rounds (3 rounds in Magnum calibers)
**Barrel length:** 22.8″ (26″ in Magnum calibers)
**Muzzle diameter:** 0.63″ (0.69″ in Magnum calibers)
**Weight:** 7.5 lbs.
**Stock:** Turkish walnut; Select and Deluxe Models have Monte Carlo stock

**Prices:**
**Select (Standard) Model** . . . . . . . . . . . . . . . . . . $ 980.00
  Left Hand . . . . . . . . . . . . . . . . . . . . . . . 1118.00
  In Magnum calibers . . . . . . . . . . . . . . . . . . . . 1093.00
**Classic Model** . . . . . . . . . . . . . . . . . . . . . . . . . . . 995.00
  In Magnum calibers . . . . . . . . . . . . . . . . . . . . 1109.00
**Deluxe Model** . . . . . . . . . . . . . . . . . . . . . . . . . . 1124.00
  Left Hand . . . . . . . . . . . . . . . . . . . . . . . 1261.00
  In Magnum calibers . . . . . . . . . . . . . . . . . . . . 1236.00

**SPORTER 393 THUMBHOLE**

## SPORTER 393 THUMBHOLE MODEL

**SPECIFICATIONS**
**Calibers:** 308 Win.
**Capacity:** 4 rounds
**Barrel length:** 22.4″
**Muzzle diameter:** 0.75″

**Weight:** 9 lbs.
**Stock:** American walnut thumbhole stock
**Features:** Adjustable comb, release in front of bolt handle for easy bolt removal
**Price:** (scope not included) . . . . . . . . . . . . . . . . . $1579.00

# KRIEGHOFF DOUBLE RIFLES

### CLASSIC SIDE-BY-SIDE DOUBLE RIFLE
### $7850.00 (Standard)
### $9450.00 (Magnum)

Kreighoff's new Classic Side-by-Side offers many standard features, including: Schnabel forearm . . . classic English-style stock with rounded cheekpiece . . . UAS anti-doubling device . . . extractors . . . 1" quick- detachable sling swivels . . . decelerator recoil pad . . . short opening angle for fast loading . . . compact action with reinforced sidewalls . . . sliding, self-adjusting wedge for secure bolt . . . large underlugs . . . automatic hammer safety . . . horizontal firing-pin placement . . . Purdey-style extension between barrels.

**SPECIFICATIONS**
**Calibers:** *Standard*—7×65R, 308 Win., 30-06, 8×57JRS, 8×75RS, 9.3×74R; *Magnum*—375 Flanged Mag. N.E., 470 N.E., 500 N.E., 500/.416 N.E.

**Action:** Cocking device for optimum safety
**Barrel length:** 23.5"
**Trigger:** Double triggers with steel trigger guard
**Weight:** 7.5 to 11 lbs. (depending on caliber and wood density)
**Options:** 21.5" barrel; engraved sideplates
**Prices:**
**STANDARD** . . . . . . . . . . . . . . . . . . . . . . . . . . . . . . $7850.00
Interchangeable barrels (installed, w/extra forearm) . . . . . . . . . . . . . . . . . . . . . . . . . . . . . . 4500.00
**MAGNUM** . . . . . . . . . . . . . . . . . . . . . . . . . . . . . 9450.00
Interchangeable barrels . . . . . . . . . . . . . . . . . . . . . 5500.00

# L.A.R. GRIZZLY RIFLE

### BIG BOAR COMPETITOR

**SPECIFICATIONS**
**Caliber:** 50 BMG
**Capacity:** Single shot
**Action:** Bolt action, bull pup, breechloading
**Barrel length:** 36"
**Overall length:** 45 1/2"
**Weight:** 30.4 lbs.
**Safety:** Thumb safety
**Features:** All-steel construction; receiver made of 4140 alloy steel, heat-treated to 42 R/C; bolt made of 4340 alloy steel; low recoil (like 12 ga. shotgun)

### BIG BOAR COMPETITOR
### $2570.00
### $2670.00 (Parkerized)
### $2820.00 (Nickel Frame)
### $2920.00 (Full Nickel)

# LAZZERONI RIFLES

These new, state-of-the-art rifles feature 4340 chrome-moly steel receivers with two massive locking lugs, a match-grade 416R stainless steel barrel, fully adjustable benchrest-style trigger and a Lazzeroni-designed synthetic or wood stock that is hand-bedded using aluminum pillar blocks. Included is a precision-machined floorplate/triggerguard assembly.

### MODEL L2000ST-F
### $3695.00   $4195.00 Meteor

**SPECIFICATIONS**
**Calibers:** 6.53 (.257) Scramjet™; 7.21 (.284) Firehawk™; 7.82 (.308) Warbird™; 8.59 (.338) Titan™ ; 10.57 (.416) Meteor
**Capacity:** 3 rounds (1 in chamber)
**Barrel length:** 27″ (24″ in 10.57 Meteor)
**Overall length:** 47.5″
**Weight:** 8.1 lbs. (10 lbs. in I0.57 Meteor)
**Stock:** Lazzeroni fiberglass sporter; right or left hand available; "fibergrain" finish on Meteor stock

### MODEL L2000ST-W
### $4795.00

**SPECIFICATIONS**
**Calibers:** 6.53 (.257) Scramjet™; 7.21 (.284) Firehawk™; 7.82 (.308) Warbird™; 8.59 (.338) Titan™
**Capacity:** 3 rounds (1 in chamber)
**Barrel length:** 27″
**Overall length:** 47.5″
**Weight:** 9.5 lbs.
**Stock:** Lazzeroni black laminated wood sporter: right or left hand available

### MODEL L2000SP-F
### $3695.00

**SPECIFICATIONS**
**Calibers:** 6.53 (.257) Scramjet™; 7.21 (.284) Firewhawk™; 7.82 (.308) Warbird™; 8.59 (.338) Titan™
**Capacity:** 3 rounds (1 in chamber)
**Barrel length:** 23″
**Overall length:** 43.5″
**Weight:** 7.8 lbs.
**Stock:** Lazzeroni fiberglass thumbhole; available right hand only

# MAGNUM RESEARCH

**MOUNTAIN EAGLE**

**VARMINT MODEL**
**w/Stainless Steel Krieger Barrel**

## MOUNTAIN EAGLE BOLT-ACTION RIFLE
### $1499.00    $1549.00 Left Hand
### $1799.00 in 375 H&H Mag. and 416 Rem. Mag.

**SPECIFICATIONS**
**Calibers:** 270 Win., 280 Rem., 30-06 Springfield, 7mm Mag., 300 Wby. Mag., 300 Win. Mag., 338 Win. Mag., 340 Wby. Mag., 375 H&H Mag., 416 Rem. Mag.
**Capacity:** 5-shot magazine (long action); 4-shot (Magnum action)
**Action:** Sako-built to MRI specifications
**Barrel length:** 24″ with .004″ headspace tolerance
**Overall length:** 44″    **Weight:** 7 lbs. 13 oz.
**Sights:** None
**Stock:** Fiberglass composite    **Length of pull:** 13⅝″

**Features:** Adjustable trigger; high comb stock (for mounting and scoping); one-piece forged bolt; free-floating, match-grade, cut-rifles, benchrest barrel; recoil pad and sling swivel studs; Platform Bedding System front lug; pillar-bedded rear guard screw; lengthened receiver ring; solid steel hinged floorplate
Also available:
**VARMINT EDITION.** In 222 Rem. and 223 Rem. with stainless steel Krieger barrel . . . . . . . . . . . . . . . . . . $1629.00
**SPORTER** . . . . . . . . . . . . . . . . . . . . . . . . . . . . 1499.00
    **Left Hand** . . . . . . . . . . . . . . . . . . . . . . . . . . 1549.00

# MAGTECH RIFLES

**MODEL MT 122.2R**

## MODEL MT 122.2S/R/T BOLT-ACTION RIFLE
### $100.00

**SPECIFICATIONS**
**Calibers:** 22 Short, Long, Long Rifle
**Capacity:** 6- or 10-shot clip
**Action:** Bolt action
**Barrel length:** 25″ (8-groove rifling), free-floating
**Overall length:** 43″    **Weight:** 6.5 lbs.
**Safety:** Double locking bolt, red cocking indicator, safety lever (disconnects trigger from firing mechanism in "safe" position)
**Finish:** Brazilian hardwood

**Features:** Double extractors; beavertail forearm; sling swivels. No mechanical sight (for mounting scope or sight later) on Model 122.2S.
Also available:
**MODEL MT 122.2R.** With adjustable rear sight and post front sight. **Price: $115.00**
**MODEL MT 122.2T.** With adjustable micrometer-type rear sight and ramp front sight; positive click stops for precise adjustment. **Price: $120.00**

# MARLIN 22 RIFLES

## MODEL 60
### $158.50

**SPECIFICATIONS**
**Caliber:** 22 Long Rifle
**Capacity:** 14-shot tubular magazine with patented closure system

**Barrel length:** 22"
**Overall length:** 40½"
**Weight:** 5½ lbs.
**Sights:** Ramp front sight with brass bead and Wide-Scan hood; adjustable open rear, receiver grooved for scope mount
**Action:** Self-loading; side ejection;

manual and automatic "last-shot" hold-open devices; receiver top has serrated, nonglare finish; crossbolt safety
**Stock:** One-piece Maine birch Monte Carlo stock, press-checkered, with full pistol grip; Mar-Shield® finish

## MODEL 60SS
### $255.00

**SPECIFICATIONS**
**Caliber:** 22 Long Rifle
**Capacity:** 14 rounds
**Barrel length:** 22"

**Overall length:** 40½"
**Weight:** 5½ lbs.
**Sights:** Adjustable folding semibuckhorn rear; ramp front sight with high-visibility post and removable Wide Scan™ hood

**Stock:** Laminated two-tone Maine birch with nickel-plated swivel studs and rubber rifle buttpad
**Features:** Micro-Groove® rifling; side ejection; manual bolt hold-open; automatic last-shot bolt hold-open; crossbolt safety

## MODEL 70PSS "PAPOOSE"
### $259.00

**SPECIFICATIONS**
**Caliber:** 22 Long Rifle
**Capacity:** 7-shot clip
**Barrel length:** 16¼"
**Overall length:** 35¼"

**Weight:** 3¼ lbs.
**Action:** Self-loading; side ejection; manual bolt hold-open; crossbolt safety; stainless-steel breech bolt and barrel

**Sights:** Screw adjustable open rear; ramp front; receiver grooved for scope mount
**Stock:** Black fiberglass-filled synthetic with abbrev. forend, nickel-plated swivel studs and molded-in checkering

## MODEL 7000
### $213.00

**SPECIFICATIONS**
**Caliber:** 22 LR
**Capacity:** 10 shots
**Action:** Self-loading; side ejection
**Barrel length:** 18" heavy target; recessed muzzle (12 grooves)

**Overall length:** 37"
**Weight:** 5.5 lbs.
**Stock:** Monte Carlo black fiberglass-filled synthetic
**Sights:** No sights; receiver grooved for scope mount (1" scope ring mounts standard)

**Features:** Manual bolt hold-open; cross-bolt safety; steel charging handle
**Also available: MODEL 795.** Same specifications as above but w/ screw-adjustable open rear sight w/ brass bead; barrel has 16 grooves; **Weight:** 5 lbs. . . . . . . . . . **$151.00**

# MARLIN RIFLES

## MODEL 922 MAGNUM
## $423.00

**SPECIFICATIONS**
**Caliber:** 22 Win. Mag. Rimfire
**Capacity:** 7-shot clip magazine
**Barrel length:** 20¹/₂″

**Overall length:** 39³/₄″
**Weight:** 6¹/₂ lbs.
**Sights:** Adjustable semibuckhorn rear; ramp front sight with brass bead and removable Wide-Scan hood™

**Stock:** Monte Carlo checkered American black walnut with rubber rifle buttpad and swivel studs
**Features:** Side ejection; manual bolt hold-open; automatic last-shot bolt hold-open; magazine safety; Garand-type safety; Micro-Groove® rifling

## MODEL 995SS
## $247.00

**SPECIFICATIONS**
**Caliber:** 22 Long Rifle
**Action:** Self-loading
**Capacity:** 7-shot nickel-plated clip magazine
**Barrel:** 18″ stainless steel with Micro-Groove® rifling (16 grooves)

**Overall length:** 37″
**Weight:** 5 lbs.
**Stock:** Black fiberglass-filled synthetic with nickel-plated swivel studs and molded-in checkering

**Sights:** Screw-adjustable open rear; ramp front with high-visibility orange post; cutaway Wide-Scan™ hood
**Features:** Receiver grooved for tip-off scope mount; stainless-steel breechbolt and barrel; crossbolt safety

## MODEL MR-7
## $638.00

**SPECIFICATIONS:**
**Calibers:** 25-06 Rem., 270 Win., 30-06 Sprfd.
**Action:** Bolt action
**Capacity:** 4-shot detachable box magazine

**Barrel length:** 22″ (6-groove rifling), recessed muzzle
**Overall length:** 43″
**Weight:** 7¹/₂ lbs.
**Sights:** Rear, optional Williams streamlined ramp w/brass bead; front, Williams blade

**Stock:** American black walnut w/cut checkering; Mar-Shield™ finish
**Features:** 3-position safety; shrouded striker; red cocking indicator; drilled and tapped receiver, rubber recoil pad

# MARLIN BOLT-ACTION RIFLES

**MARLIN 15YN "LITTLE BUCKAROO™" Single Shot 22 Beginner's Rifle**
**$179.00**

**SPECIFICATIONS**
**Caliber:** 22 Short, Long or Long Rifle
**Capacity:** Single shot
**Action:** Bolt action; easy-load feed throat; thumb safety; red cocking indicator

**Barrel length:** 16¼" (16 grooves)
**Overall length:** 33¼"
**Weight:** 4¼ lbs.
**Sights:** Adjustable open rear; ramp front sight

**Stock:** One-piece walnut-finished press-checkered Maine birch Monte Carlo w/full pistol grip; tough Mar-Shield® finish

**MODEL 25MN**
**$207.00**

**SPECIFICATIONS**
**Caliber:** 22 WMR (not interchangeable w/other 22 cartridges)
**Capacity:** 7-shot clip magazine

**Barrel length:** 22" with Micro-Groove® rifling
**Overall length:** 41"
**Weight:** 6 lbs.

**Sights:** Adjustable open rear, ramp front sight; receiver grooved for scope mount
**Stock:** One-piece walnut-finished press-checkered Maine birch Monte Carlo w/full pistol grip; Mar-Shield® finish

**MODEL 25N**
**$181.00**

Same specifications as Model 25MN, except **caliber** 22 LR and **weight** 5½ pounds.

**MARLIN 880**
**$251.00**

**Sights:** Adj. folding semibuckhorn rear; ramp front w/Wide-Scan™ hood; receiver grooved for scope mount
**Overall length:** 41"  **Weight:** 5½ lbs.
**Stock:** Checkered Monte Carlo American black walnut with full pistol grip; Mar-Shield® finish; rubber buttpad; swivel studs

**SPECIFICATIONS**
**Caliber:** 22 Long Rifle
**Capacity:** 7-shot clip magazine
**Action:** Bolt action; positive thumb safety; red cocking indicator
**Barrel:** 22" with Micro-Groove® rifling (16 grooves)

Also available:
**MODEL 880SS.** Same as Model 880, in stainless steel. **Weight:** 6 lbs. **$270.00**
**MODEL 881.** Same as Model 880, except w/tubular mag.; holds 17 22-LR rounds. **Weight:** 6 lbs. **$261.00**
**MODEL 880SQ SQUIRREL RIFLE.** With heavy 22" barrel, recessed muzzle; black synthetic stock w/ molded-in checkering, swivel studs; no sights. **Weight:** 7 lbs. **$284.00**

# MARLIN BOLT-ACTION RIFLES

## MODEL 882
## $277.00

**SPECIFICATIONS**
**Caliber:** 22 WMR
**Action:** Bolt action; thumb safety; red cocking indicator
**Capacity:** 7-shot clip
**Barrel length:** 22″

**Overall length:** 41″ **Weight:** 6 lbs.
**Sights:** Adj. semibuckhorn folding rear; ramp front w/brass bead and Wide-Scan™ front sight hood
**Stock:** Monte Carlo American black walnut with swivel studs; full pistol grip; classic cut-checkering; rubber rifle buttpad

Also available:
**MODEL 882SS.** Same as Model 882, except stainless-steel barrel, receiver front breechbolt striker knob and trigger stud; orange front sight post; black fiberglass-filled synthetic stock w/nickel-plated swivel studs and molded-in checkering. **$294.00**
**MODEL 882SSV** w/thumb safety with red cocking indicator; stainless barrel; black synthetic stock. **$289.00**

## MODEL 882L
## $293.00

**SPECIFICATIONS**
**Caliber:** 22 WMR (not interchangeable with other 22 cartridges)

**Capacity:** 7-shot clip magazine
**Barrel length:** 22″ Micro-Groove®
**Overall length:** 41″ **Weight:** 6¼ lbs.
**Sights:** Ramp front w/brass bead and removable Wide-Scan™ hood; adj. folding semibuckhorn rear

**Stock:** Laminated hardwood Monte Carlo w/Mar-Shield® finish
**Features:** Swivel studs; rubber rifle butt pad; receiver grooved for scope mount; positive thumb safety; red cocking indicator

## MODEL 883
## $288.00

**SPECIFICATIONS**
**Caliber:** 22 WMR (not interchangeable with other 22 cartridges)
**Capacity:** 12-shot tubular magazine with patented closure system

**Action:** Bolt action; positive thumb safety; red cocking indicator
**Barrel length:** 22″ with Micro-Groove® rifling (20 grooves)
**Overall length:** 41″ **Weight:** 6 lbs.
**Sights:** Adjustable folding semibuckhorn rear; ramp front with Wide-

Scan™ hood; receiver grooved for scope mount
**Stock:** Checkered Monte Carlo American black walnut with full pistol grip; rubber buttpad; swivel studs; tough Mar-Shield® finish

## MODEL 883SS (Stainless Steel)
## $306.00

Same as Model 883, except with stainless barrel and receiver, laminated two-tone brown Maine birch stock with nickel-plated swivel studs and rubber rifle buttpad.

# MARLIN RIFLES

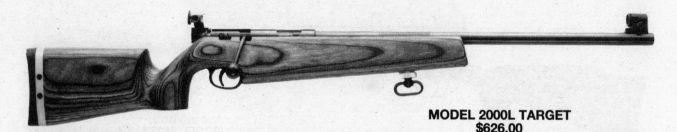

### MODEL 2000L TARGET
### $626.00

**SPECIFICATIONS**
**Caliber:** 22 Long Rifle
**Capacity:** Single-shot; 5-shot Summer Biathlon adapter kit available
**Action:** Bolt action, 2-stage target trigger, red cocking indicator

**Barrel length:** Heavy 22" Micro-Groove w/match chamber, recessed muzzle
**Overall length:** 41"   **Weight:** 8 lbs.
**Sights:** Hooded Lyman front sight with 10 aperture inserts; fully adjustable Lyman target rear peep sight

**Stock:** Laminated black/grey w/ambidextrous pistol grip; buttplate adjustable for length of pull, height and angle; aluminum forearm rail w/forearm stop and quick-detachable swivel

### MODEL 9 CAMP CARBINE
### $432.00

**SPECIFICATIONS**
**Caliber:** 9mm
**Capacity:** 10-shot clip (12-shot avail.)
**Action:** Self-loading. Manual bolt hold-open. Garand-type safety, magazine safety, loaded chamber indicator.

Solid-top, machined steel receiver is sandblasted to prevent glare, and is drilled/tapped for scope mounting.
**Barrel length:** 16¹/₂" with Micro-Groove® rifling
**Overall length:** 35¹/₂"   **Weight:** 6³/₄ lbs.

**Sights:** Adjustable folding rear, ramp front sight with high-visibility, orange front sight post; Wide-Scan™ hood.
**Stock:** Press-checkered walnut-finished hardwood w/pistol grip; tough Mar-Shield™ finish; rubber rifle buttpad; swivel studs

### MODEL 45
### $438.00

**SPECIFICATIONS**
**Caliber:** 45 Auto
**Capacity:** 7-shot clip
**Barrel length:** 16¹/₂"

**Overall length:** 35¹/₂"
**Weight** 6.75 lbs.
**Sights:** Adjustable folding rear; ramp front sight with high-visibility, orange

front sight post; Wide-Scan™ hood
**Stock:** Press-checkered walnut-finished Maine birch with pistol grip; rubber rifle buttpad; swivel studs

# MARLIN LEVER-ACTION CARBINES

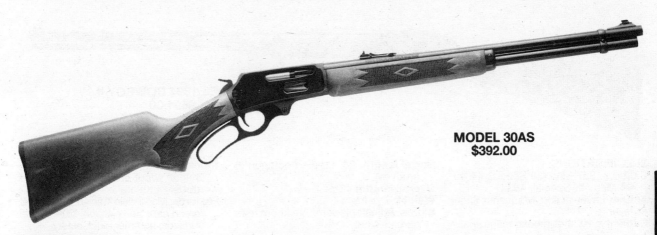

**MODEL 30AS**
**$392.00**

## SPECIFICATIONS
**Caliber :** 30-30
**Capacity:** 6-shot tubular magazine
**Action:** Lever w/hammer block safety; solid top receiver w/side ejection

**Barrel length:** 20″ w/Micro-Groove®
**Overall length:** 38¼″   **Weight:** 7 lbs.
**Sights:** Tapped for scope mount and receiver sight; also available in com-

bination w/4x, 32mm, 1″ scope
**Stock:** Walnut-finished Maine birch stock w/pistol grip; pressed checkering; Mar-Shield® finish

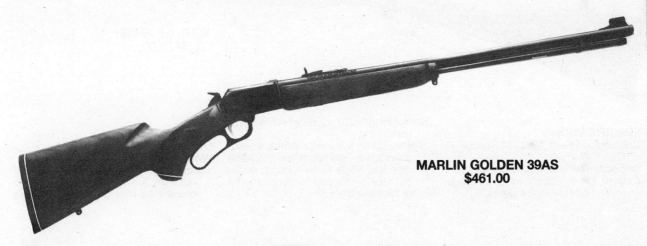

**MARLIN GOLDEN 39AS**
**$461.00**

Introduced in 1891, the Marlin lever-action 22 is the oldest shoulder gun still being manufactured.

**Solid Receiver Top.** You can easily mount a scope on your Marlin 39 by screwing on the machined scope adapter base provided. The screw-on base is a neater, more versatile method of mounting a scope on a 22 sporting rifle. The solid top receiver and scope adapter base provide a maximum in eye relief adjustment. If you prefer iron sights, you'll find the 39 receiver clean, flat and sandblasted to prevent glare. Exclusive brass magazine tube

**Micro-Groove® Barrel.** Marlin's famous rifling system of multi-grooving has consistently produced fine accuracy because the system grips the bul

let more securely, minimizes distortion, and provides a better gas seal.

And the Model 39 maximizes accuracy with the heaviest barrels available on any lever-action 22.

## SPECIFICATIONS
**Caliber:** 22 Short, Long and Long Rifle
**Capacity:** Tubular magazine holds 26 Short, 21 Long and 19 LR cartridges
**Action:** Lever; solid top receiver; side ejection; one-step takedown; deeply blued metal surfaces; receiver top sandblasted to prevent glare; hammer block safety; rebounding hammer

**Barrel:** 24″ with Micro-Groove® rifling (16 grooves)
**Overall length:** 40″   **Weight:** 6½ lbs.
**Sights:** Adjustable folding semibuckhorn rear, ramp front sight with Wide-Scan™ hood; solid top receiver tapped for scope mount or receiver sight; scope adapter base; offset hammer spur for scope use—works right or left
**Stock:** Two-piece cut-checkered American black walnut w/fluted comb; full pistol grip and forend; blued-steel forend cap; swivel studs; grip cap; white butt and pistol-grip spacers; Mar-Shield® finish; rubber buttpad

# MARLIN LEVER-ACTION CARBINES

**MODEL 1894 COWBOY II**
**$691.00**

**SPECIFICATIONS:**
**Calibers:** 357 Mag./38 Special, 44-40, 44 Mag./44 Special, 45 LC
**Action:** Lever action w/squared finger lever
**Capacity:** 10-shot tubular magazine

**Barrel length:** 24″ tapered octagon (6 grooves)
**Overall length:** 41 1/2″
**Weight:** 7 1/2 lbs.
**Sights:** Adjustable semi-buckhorn rear; carbine front

**Stock:** Straight-grip American black walnut w/cut-checkering and hard rubber buttplate
**Features:** Mar-Shield™ finish; blued steel forend cap; side ejection; blued metal surfaces; hammer block safety

**MARLIN 1894S**
**$477.00**

**SPECIFICATIONS**
**Calibers:** 44 Rem. Mag./44 Special, 45 Colt
**Capacity:** 10-shot tubular magazine
**Action:** Lever action w/square finger lever; hammer block safety

**Barrel length:** 20″ w/ deep-cut Ballard-type rifling
**Sights:** Ramp front sight w/brass bead; adjustable semibuckhorn folding rear and Wide-Scan™ hood; solid-top receiver tapped for scope mount or receiver sight

**Overall length:** 37 1/2″
**Weight:** 6 lbs.
**Stock:** Checkered American black walnut stock w/Mar-Shield™ finish; blued steel forend cap; swivel studs

**MARLIN 1894CS 357 MAGNUM**
**$477.00**

**SPECIFICATIONS**
**Calibers:** 357 Magnum, 38 Special
**Capacity:** 9-shot tubular magazine
**Action:** Lever action w/square finger lever; hammer block safety; side ejection; solid top receiver; deeply blued metal surfaces; receiver top sandblasted to prevent glare

**Barrel length:** 18 1/2″ w/deep-cut Ballard-type rifling (12 grooves)
**Sights:** Adjustable semibuckhorn folding rear, ramp front w/brass bead and Wide-Scan™ hood; solid top receiver tapped for scope mount or receiver sight; offset hammer spur for scope use—adjustable for right or left hand

**Overall length:** 36″
**Weight:** 6 lbs.
**Stock:** Cut-checkered straight-grip two-piece American black walnut Mar-Shield® finish; swivel studs; rubber rifle buttpad

# MARLIN LEVER-ACTION CARBINES

**MARLIN 1895SS**
**$543.00**

### SPECIFICATIONS
**Caliber:** 45-70 Government
**Capacity:** 4-shot tubular magazine
**Action:** Lever action; hammer block safety; receiver top sandblasted to prevent glare

**Barrel:** 22″ w/deep-cut Ballard-type rifling
**Sights:** Ramp front sight w/brass bead; adjustable semibuckhorn folding rear and Wide-Scan™ hood; receiver tapped for scope mount or receiver sight

**Overall length:** 40¹/₂″
**Weight:** 7¹/₂ lbs.
**Stock:** Checkered American black walnut pistol-grip stock w/rubber rifle buttpad and Mar-Shield® finish; white pistol grip, butt spacers; swivel studs

**MARLIN 336CS**
**$459.00**

### SPECIFICATIONS
**Calibers:** 30-30 Win., and 35 Rem.
**Capacity:** 6-shot tubular magazine
**Action:** Lever action w/hammer block safety; deeply blued metal surfaces; receiver top sandblasted to prevent glare

**Barrel:** 20″ Micro-Groove® barrel
**Sights:** Adjustable folding semibuckhorn rear; ramp front sight w/brass bead and Wide-Scan™ hood; tapped for receiver sight and scope mount; offset hammer spur for scope use (works right or left)

**Overall length:** 38¹/₂″
**Weight:** 7 lbs.
**Stock:** Checkered American black walnut pistol-grip stock w/fluted comb and Mar-Shield® finish; rubber rifle buttpad; swivel studs

**MODEL 444SS**
**$543.00**

### SPECIFICATIONS
**Caliber:** 444 Marlin
**Capacity:** 5-shot tubular magazine
**Barrel:** 22″ Micro-Groove®

**Overall length:** 40¹/₂″
**Weight:** 7¹/₂ lbs.
**Stock:** Checkered American black walnut pistol grip stock with rubber rifle buttpad; swivel studs

**Sights:** Ramp front sight with brass bead and Wide-Scan® hood; adjustable semibuckhorn folding rear; receiver tapped for scope mount or receiver sight

# MARLIN LEVER-ACTION CARBINES

**MODEL 1897 CENTURY LIMITED**
**$1055.00**

In celebration of the first high-quality lever-action takedown 22 rifle, Marlin introduces this new model that remains much the same as the one Annie Oakley used.

**SPECIFICATIONS**
**Calibers:** 22 Short, Long, Long Rifle
**Capacity:** 19 Short, 15 Long, 13 Long Rifle
**Action:** Lever action
**Barrel length:** 24″ half-round/half-octagon
**Overall length:** 40″

**Weight:** 6.5 lbs.
**Stock:** American black walnut w/cut checkering; full pistol grip and forend; hard rubber buttplate
**Finish:** Marshield™ finish
**Sights:** Adjustable marble semi-buckhorn rear; marble carbine front

# MAUSER RIFLES

**MODEL 96 BOLT ACTION**

**MODEL 96**
**$699.00**
**SPECIFICATIONS**
**Calibers:** 25-06, 270 Win., 30-06 S'fld, 308 Win., 7mm Rem. Mag., 300 Win. Mag.
**Capacity:** 5 rounds
**Action:** Sliding bolt action
**Barrel length:** 22″ (24″ magnum)
**Overall length:** 42″
**Weight:** 6.25 lbs.
**Safety:** Rear tang, 3-position
**Trigger:** Single
**Stock:** Checkered walnut

**Sights:** None; drilled and tapped for Rem. 700 scope mounts and bases
**Features:** Quick-detachable 1″ sling swivels; 16 locking lugs

Also available:
**MODEL SR 86** w/28.75″ barrel in 308 Win. w/muzzle brake; adjustable black laminated thumbhold stock w/bipod rail. **Weight:** 13 lbs. . . . . . . . . . . . . . . . . . . . . . . . .**$11,795.00**
**MODEL M94** w/22″ barrel (24″ magnum) in 243 Win., 308 Win., 270 Win., 30-06 S'fld, 7mm Rem. Mag., 300 Win Mag. Features aluminum bedding block, interchangeable barrels (**$799.00**), combo or single-set trigger, detachable mag., walnut stock. **Weight:** 7.25 lbs. . . . . . . . **$2295.00**

# NAVY ARMS REPLICA RIFLES

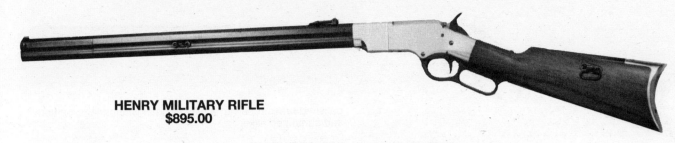

### HENRY MILITARY RIFLE
### $895.00

This Civil War replica features a highly polished brass frame and blued barrel; sling swivels to the original specifications are located on the left side.

**SPECIFICATIONS**
**Caliber:** 44-40 **Capacity:** 13 rounds
**Barrel length:** 24″ **Overall length:** 43″
**Weight:** 9¼ lbs.
**Stock:** Walnut

### IRON FRAME HENRY
### $945.00

**SPECIFICATIONS**
**Caliber:** 44-40 **Capacity:** 13 rounds
**Barrel length:** 24″ **Overall length:** 43″
**Weight:** 9 lbs.

**Stock:** Walnut
**Finish:** Blued or casehardened
**Feature:** Iron frame

### HENRY CARBINE
### $875.00

The arm first utilized by the Kentucky Cavalry, with blued finish and brass frame.

**SPECIFICATIONS**
**Caliber:** 44-40 **Capacity:** 11 rounds
**Barrel length:** 22″ **Overall length:** 41″
**Weight:** 8¾ lbs.

### HENRY TRAPPER MODEL
### $875.00

This short, lightweight lever-action arm is ideal for the hunter.

**SPECIFICATIONS**
**Caliber:** 44-40 **Capacity:** 8 rounds

**Barrel length:** 16½″
**Overall length:** 34½″
**Weight:** 7 lbs. 7 oz.

# NAVY ARMS REPLICA RIFLES

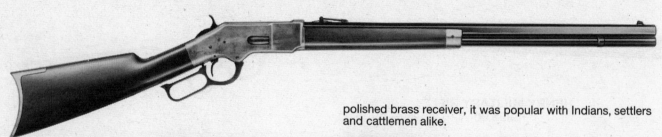

## 1866 "YELLOWBOY" RIFLE
## $680.00

The 1866 model was Oliver Winchester's improved version of the Henry rifle. Called the " Yellowboy" because of its polished brass receiver, it was popular with Indians, settlers and cattlemen alike.

**SPECIFICATIONS**
**Caliber:** 44-40
**Barrel length:** 24″ full octagon    **Overall length:** 42½″
**Weight:** 8¼ lbs.
**Sights:** Blade front; open ladder rear
**Stock:** Walnut

## 1866 "YELLOWBOY" CARBINE
## $670.00

This is the "saddle gun" variant of the rifle described above.

**SPECIFICATIONS**
**Caliber:** 44-40
**Barrel length:** 19″ round    **Overall length:** 38¼″
**Weight:** 7¼ lbs.
**Sights:** Blade front; open ladder rear
**Stock:** Walnut

## 1873 WINCHESTER SPORTING RIFLE
## $960.00 (30″ Barrel)    $930.00 (24″ Barrel)

This replica of the state-of-the-art Winchester 1873 Sporting Rifle features a checkered pistol grip, buttstock, casehardened receiver and blued octagonal barrel.

**SPECIFICATIONS**
**Caliber:** 44-40 or 45 LC
**Barrel length:** 24″ or 30″
**Overall length:** 48¾″ (w/30″ barrel)
**Weight:** 8 lbs. 14 oz.
**Sights:** Blade front; buckhorn rear

## 1873 WINCHESTER-STYLE RIFLE
## $820.00

Known as "The Gun That Won the West," the 1873 was the most popular lever-action rifle of its time. This fine replica features a casehardened receiver.

**SPECIFICATIONS**
**Caliber:** 44-40 or 45 Long Colt
**Barrel length:** 24″    **Overall length:** 43″
**Weight:** 8¼ lbs.
**Sights:** Blade front; open ladder rear
**Stock:** Walnut
Also available: **1873 WINCHESTER-STYLE CARBINE**
(19″ barrel) . . . . . . . . . . . . . . . . . . . . . . . . . . . . . . $800.00

# NAVY ARMS REPLICA RIFLES

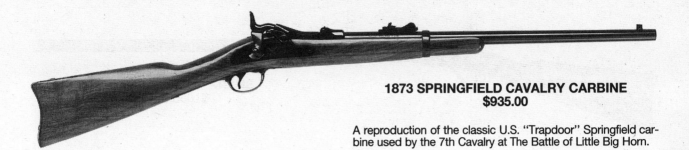

## 1873 SPRINGFIELD CAVALRY CARBINE
### $935.00

A reproduction of the classic U.S. "Trapdoor" Springfield carbine used by the 7th Cavalry at The Battle of Little Big Horn.

**SPECIFICATIONS**
**Caliber:** 45-70 Government
**Barrel length:** 22"
**Overall length:** 40½"
**Weight:** 7 lbs.

**Sights:** Blade front, military ladder rear
**Stock:** Walnut
**Features:** Saddle bar with ring
Also available:
**1873 SPRINGFIELD INFANTRY Rifle** (32.5" bbl.) **$1060.00**

## 1874 SHARPS CAVALRY CARBINE
### $935.00

This cavalry carbine version of the Sharps rifle features a side bar and saddle ring.

**SPECIFICATIONS**
**Caliber:** 45-70 percussion
**Barrel length:** 22"   **Overall length:** 39"

**Weight:** 7¾ lbs.
**Sights:** Blade front; military ladder rear
**Stock:** Walnut

## 1874 SHARPS SNIPER RIFLE
### $1115.00

This replica of the 1874 three-band sharpshooter's rifle was a popular target rifle at the Creedmoor military matches and was the issue longarm of the New York State Militia.
**SPECIFICATIONS**
**Caliber:** 45-70
**Barrel length:** 30"   **Overall length:** 46¾"

**Weight:** 8 lbs. 8 oz.   **Stock:** Walnut
**Features:** Double-set triggers; casehardened receiver; patchbox and furniture

Also available:
**SINGLE TRIGGER INFANTRY MODEL** . . . . . . . . $1060.00

# NAVY ARMS REPLICA RIFLES

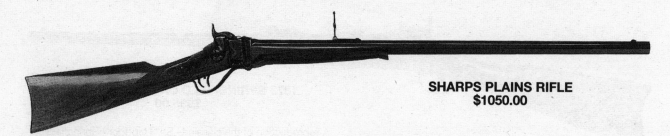

### SHARPS PLAINS RIFLE
### $1050.00

**SPECIFICATIONS**
**Caliber:** 45-70
**Barrel length:** 32″ octagonal   **Overall length:** 49″
**Weight:** 9 lbs. 8 oz.
**Sights:** Blade front, ladder rear (optional tang sight avail.)

**Stock:** Walnut
**Features:** Color casehardened receiver and furniture; double-set triggers
Also available:
**DELUXE ENGRAVED MODEL** . . . . . . . . . . . . . . . $3200.00

### SHARPS BUFFALO RIFLE
### $1080.00

**SPECIFICATIONS**
**Caliber:** 45-70 or 45-90
**Barrel length:** 28″ octagonal   **Overall length:** 46″
**Weight:** 10 lbs. 10 oz.
**Sights:** Blade front, ladder rear (tang sight optional w/set triggers only—**$65.00**)

**Stock:** Walnut
**Features:** Color casehardened receiver and furniture; double-set trigger
Also available:
**DELUXE ENGRAVED MODEL** . . . . . . . . . . . . . . . $3215.00

### KODIAK MK IV DOUBLE RIFLE
### $3125.00

**SPECIFICATIONS**
**Caliber:** 45-70
**Barrel length:** 24″   **Overall length:** 39³/₄″
**Weight:** 10 lbs. 3 oz.
**Sights:** Bead front, folding-leaf express rear
**Stock:** Checkered European walnut

**Features:** Color casehardened locks, breech and hammers; semi-regulated barrels
Also available:
**DELUXE KODIAK MK IV DOUBLE RIFLE** with browned barrels and hand-engraving on satin frame and fittings.
**Price:** . . . . . . . . . . . . . . . . . . . . . . . . . . . . . . . $4000.00

# NAVY ARMS REPLICA RIFLES

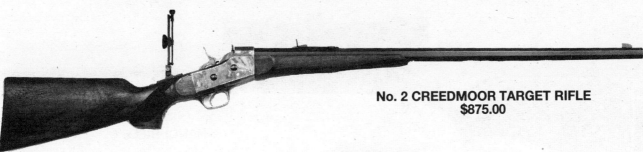

### No. 2 CREEDMOOR TARGET RIFLE
### $875.00

**SPECIFICATIONS**
**Caliber:** 45-70
**Barrel length:** 30″, tapered   **Overall length:** 46″
**Weight:** 9 lbs.
**Sights:** Globe front, adjustable Creedmoor rear
**Stock:** Checkered walnut stock and forend
Also available:
**ENGRAVED MODEL**........................$1875.00

This reproduction of the Remington No. 2 Creedmoor Rifle features a color casehardened receiver and steel trigger guard, tapered octagon barrel, and walnut forend and butt-stock with checkered pistol grip.

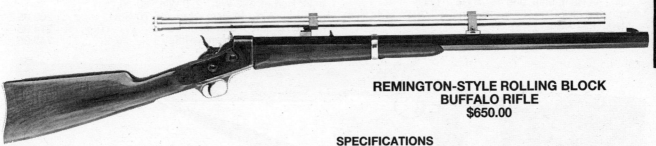

### REMINGTON-STYLE ROLLING BLOCK
### BUFFALO RIFLE
### $650.00

**SPECIFICATIONS**
**Caliber:** 45-70
**Barrel length:** 26″ or 30″; full octagon or half-round
**Sights:** Blade front, open notch rear
**Stock:** Walnut stock and forend
**Feature:** Shown with optional 32½″ Model 1860 brass tel-
escopic sight **$210.00**; Compact Model (18″): **$200.00**
Also available:
With casehardened steel (no brass furniture)......**$745.00**

This replica of the rifle used by buffalo hunters and plainsmen of the 1800s features a casehardened receiver, solid brass trigger guard and walnut stock and forend. The tang is drilled and tapped to accept the optional Creedmoor sight.

### GREENER LIGHT MODEL
### HARPOON GUN
### $995.00

**SPECIFICATIONS**
**Caliber:** 38 Special (blank)
**Barrel length:** 20″   **Overall length:** 36″
**Weight:** 6 lbs. 5 oz.   **Stock:** Walnut

Designed for large game fish, the Greener Harpoon gun utilizes the time-proven Martini action. The complete outfit consists of gun, harpoons, harpoon lines, line release frames, blank cartridges and cleaning kit—all housed in a carrying case.

RIFLES

# NEW ENGLAND FIREARMS RIFLES

**HANDI-RIFLE**

## SPECIFICATIONS
**Calibers:** 22 Hornet, 223 Rem., 223 Rem. Bull Barrel, 243 Win., 270 Win., 280 Rem., 30-06, 30-30 Win., 45-70 Govt., 44 Rem. Mag.
**Action:** Break-open; side lever release; positive ejection
**Barrel length:** 22"   **Weight:** 7 lbs.
**Sights:** Scope mounts; no iron sights; ramp front; fully adjustable rear; tapped for scope mounts (22 Hornet, 30-30 Win., 44 Rem. Mag. and 45-70 Govt. only)
**Length of pull:** 14 1/4"; (14" in 22 Hornet, 30-30 Win., 44 Rem. Mag., 45-70 Govt.)
**Drop at comb:** 1 1/2" (1 1/4" in Monte Carlo)

**Drop at heel:** 2 1/8" (1 1/8" in Monte Carlo)
**Stock:** American hardwood, walnut finish; full pistol grip
**Features:** Semi-beavertail forend; patented transfer bar safety; automatic ejection; rebated muzzle; hammer extension; sling swivel studs on stock and forend
**Prices:**
In 223 Rem., blued.............................. $209.95
In 223 Rem., Bull barrel, blued................. 209.95
In 22 Hornet, 243 Win., 270 Win., 30-06,
   30-30 Win., 44 Rem. Mag., 45-70 Govt. ...... 209.95
In 280 Rem. (26" barrel), blued.................. 214.95
**10th Anniversary Handi-Rifle**................. 749.95

**SURVIVOR RIFLE**
**$219.95 (Blued)   $234.95 (Nickel)**

## SPECIFICATIONS
**Calibers:** 223 Rem. and 357 Mag. (3" chamber)
**Action:** Break action   **Capacity:** Single shot
**Barrel length:** 22"   **Overall length:** 36"
**Weight:** 6 lbs.

**Stock:** High-density polymer thumbhole stock with beavertail forend
**Finish:** Matte blue or electroless matte nickel
**Features:** Fully adjustable rifle sights; drilled and tapped for scope; transfer bar safety

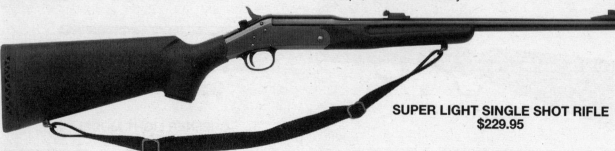

**SUPER LIGHT SINGLE SHOT RIFLE**
**$229.95**

## SPECIFICATIONS
**Calibers:** 22 Hornet (Model SB2-SL4); 223 Rem. (Model SB2-SL4)
**Action:** Break open; side lever release; single shot
**Barrel length:** 20" (rebated muzzle)   **Overall length:** 36"
**Weight:** 5.5 lbs.   **Length of pull:** 14.25"

**Drop at comb:** 1.5"   **Drop at heel:** 2 1/8"
**Stock:** Black polymer
**Sights:** No sights (SB2-SL3); ramp front, fully adjustable rear (SB2-SL4)
**Features:** Semi-beavertail forend; sling swivel and recoil pad; transfer bar system; automatic shell ejector

# PEDERSOLI REPLICA RIFLES

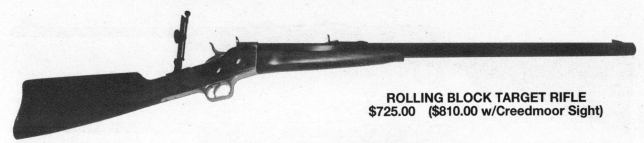

### ROLLING BLOCK TARGET RIFLE
### $725.00   ($810.00 w/Creedmoor Sight)

**SPECIFICATIONS**
**Calibers:** 45-70 and 357
**Barrel length:** 30″ octagonal (blued)
**Weight:** 9¹/₂ lbs. (45-70); 10 lbs. (357)

**Sights:** Adjustable rear sight; tunnel modified front (all models designed for fitting of Creedmoor sight)
Also available:
**Cavalry, Infantry, Long Range**
**Creedmoor** . . . . . . . . . . . . . . . . . . . . . . **$650.00–$875.00**

### SHARPS CARBINE MODEL 766
### $885.00 w/Patchbox

**SPECIFICATIONS**
**Caliber:** 54
**Barrel length:** 22″ round (6 grooves)
**Overall length:** 39″
**Weight:** 7¹/₂ lbs.

**Sights:** Fully adjustable rear; fixed front
Also available:
**Sharps 1859 Military Rifle** (set trigger, 30″ barrel, 8.4 lbs.).
**Price:** . . . . . . . . . . . . . . . . . . . . . . . . . . . . . . . . **$1095.00**

### KODIAK MARK IV DOUBLE RIFLE
### $2495.00

**SPECIFICATIONS**
**Calibers:** 45-70, 9.3×74R, 8×57JSR
**Barrel length:** 22″ (24″ 45-70)
**Overall length:** 39″ (40¹/₂″ 45-70)

**Weight:** 8.24 lbs. (9.7 lbs. 45/70)
Also available:
**Kodiak Mark IV** w/interchangeable 20-gauge barrel
**Price:** . . . . . . . . . . . . . . . . . . . . . . . . . . . . . . . . **$4125.00**

# PRAIRIE GUN WORKS

### MODEL M-15 ULTRA LITE (Not shown)
### $1750.00

**SPECIFICATIONS**
**Caliber:** Most Short Action calibers
**Action:** Remington 700 Short Action
**Barrel length:** 22″ Douglas Match Grade
**Length of pull:** 13.5″
**Weight:** 4.5–5.25 lbs.
**Stock:** Fiberglass-Kevlar composite w/integral recoil lug; recoil pad installed

**Finish:** Black or grey textured finish
**Sights:** Custom aircraft-grade aluminum scope mounts
**Features:** Trigger set and polished for 3 lb. pull; bolt fluted, hollowed and tapped w/Ultra Lite custom firing pin and bolt shroud

Also available:
**MODEL M-18.** Same specifications and price as Model M-15, except chambered for long-action calibers (up to 340 Weatherby)

# REMINGTON BOLT-ACTION RIFLES

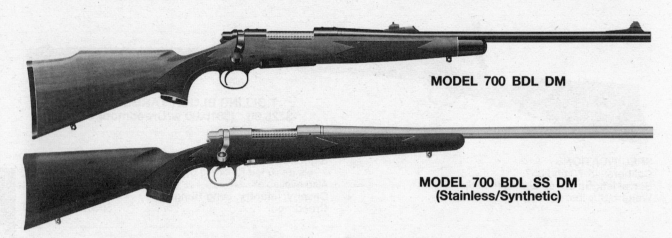

**MODEL 700 BDL DM**

**MODEL 700 BDL SS DM**
**(Stainless/Synthetic)**

## MODEL 700 BDL DM
### $702.00 ($729.00 Magnum)

The **Model 700 DM** (Detachable Magazine) models feature detachable 4-shot magazines (except the 3-shot magnum-caliber models), stainless-steel latches, latch springs and magazine boxes. **Model 700 BDL DM** rifles feature the standard Remington BDL barrel contour with 22″ barrels on standard-caliber models and 24″ barrels on magnum-caliber rifles. All barrels have a hooded

front sight and adjustable rear sight. Additional features include polished blued-metal finish, high-gloss, Monte Carlo-style cap, white line spacers, 20 lines-per-inch skipline checkering, recoil pad and swivel studs. All models now feature fine-line engraving on receiver front rings, rear bridges, non-ejection receiver sides and floorplates. **Calibers:** Standard—25-06 Rem., 243 Win., 260 Rem., 280 Rem., 7mm-08 Rem., 30-06, 308 Win.; Magnum—7mm Rem. Mag., 7mm STW, 300 Win. Mag., 338 Win. Mag.

**MODEL 700 BDL SS**

## MODEL 700 BDL

Now available in 338 Win. Mag., this Model 700 features the Monte Carlo American walnut stock finished to a high gloss with fine-cut skipline checkering. Also includes a hinged floorplate, sling swivels studs, hooded ramp front sight and adjustable rear sight. Also available in stainless synthetic version (Model 700 BDL SS) with stainless-steel barrel, receiver and bolt plus synthetic stock for maximum weather resistance; now in 338 Win. Mag. and 375 H&H Mag. For additional specifications, see Model 700 table.

| Model 700 BDL | Prices |
|---|---|
| In 17 Rem., 7mm Rem. Mag., 300 Win. Mag. | $609.00 |
| In 222 Rem., 22-250 Rem., 223 Rem., 243 Win., 25-06 Rem., 270 Win., 30-06 | 583.00 |
| In 338 Win. Mag. | 609.00 |
| Left Hand in 270 Win., 30-06 | 609.00 |
| Left Hand in 7mm Rem. Mag. | 636.00 |
| **Model BDL SS (Stainless Synthetic)** in 270 Win. 30-06 | 641.00 |
| In 7mm Rem. Mag., 300 Win. Mag. | 668.00 |
| In 338 Win. Mag. and 375 H&H Mag. | 668.00 |

## MODEL 700 BDL SS DM-B
### $789.00

Available in **calibers:** 7mm Rem. Mag., 7mm STW, 300 Win. Mag., 300 Wby. Mag. and 338 Win. Mag. **Barrel length:** 25¹/₂″ (magnum contour barrel). Stainless synthetic detachable magazine with muzzle brake.

# REMINGTON BOLT-ACTION RIFLES

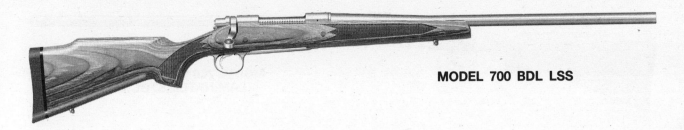

### MODEL 700 BDL LSS

## MODEL 700 BDL LSS

The Model 700 BDL LSS features a stainless barrel, laminated synthetic stock, hinged magazine floorplate and sling swivel studs. **Barrel length:** 24″. **Overall length:** 44½″. **Weight:** 7½ lbs. (Magnum); 7⅜ lbs. (Long Action). **Length of pull:** 13⅜″. **Drop at comb:** ½″. **Drop at heel:** ⅜″

### MODEL 700 "SENDERO SPECIAL"

## MODEL 700 SENDERO

Remington's Sendero rifle combines the accuracy features of the Model 700 Varmint Special with long action and magnum calibers for long-range hunting. The 26-inch barrel has a heavy varmint profile and features a spherical concave crown. For additional specifications, see table on the following page.

### MODEL 700 SENDERO SF

## MODEL 700 SENDERO SF
## (STAINLESS FLUTED)

This version of the Model 700 Sendero features satin-finished stainless steel receiver and bolt and a 26-inch heavy stainless barrel with six longitudinal flutes designed to improve heat dissipation and reduce gun weight (8½ lbs.). A spherical, concave crown protects the muzzle. Other features include a composite synthetic fiberglass stock, graphite reinforced by du Pont Kevlar, and a full-length aluminum bedding block.

## MODEL 700 ADL (not shown)

Synthetic model has a fiberglass-reinforced synthetic stock, positive checkering, straight comb, raised cheekpiece and black rubber recoil pad. Stock and blued metalwork have a non-reflective black matte finish.

*(See also table on the following page for prices, calibers and additional specifications)*

# REMINGTON BOLT-ACTION RIFLES

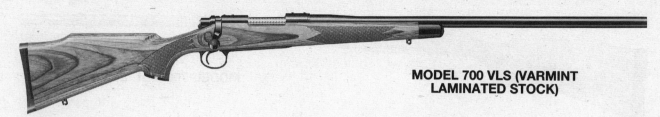

**MODEL 700 VLS (VARMINT LAMINATED STOCK)**

## MODEL 700/Calibers — Prices

**Mountain** 243 Win., 25-06, 270 Win., 280 Rem., 7mm-08, 30-06 .............. $636.00
**Sendero** 25-06, 270 Win. ................ 705.00
 7mm-08 Rem., 300 Win. Mag. ........... 732.00

**Sendero SF** 25-06 ........................ $852.00
 7mm Rem. Mag., 7mm STW, 300 Win. Mag., 300 Wby. Mag. ....................... 879.00
**BDL SS DM** 243 Win., 25-06 Rem., 260 Rem., 270 Win., 280 Rem., 7mm-08, 30-06, 308 Win. .... 702.00
 300 Win. Mag. and 300 Wby. Mag. ........... 729.00

## MODEL 700™ CENTERFIRE RIFLE SPECIFICATIONS

| Calibers | Magazine Capacity | Barrel Length | Twist (R–H) 1 Turn In | Mountain Rifle (DM) | Sendero (26″ Bbl. only) | Sendero SF (26″ Bbl. only) | BDL Stainless Synthetic DM | BDL SS | DM-B | BDL LSS |
|---|---|---|---|---|---|---|---|---|---|---|
| 17 Rem. | 5 | 24″ | 9″ | | | | | | | |
| 220 Swift | 4 | 26″ | 14″ | | | | | | | |
| 222 Rem. | 5 | 24″ | 14″ | | | | | | | |
| 22-250 Rem. | 4 | 24″ | 14″ | | | | | | | |
| 223 Rem. | 5 | 24″ | 12″ | | | | | | | |
| 243 Win. | 4 | 22″ | 9⅛″ | ● | | | | | | |
|  | 4 | 24″ | 9⅛″ | | | | New | | | |
| 25-06 Rem. | 4 | 24″ | 10″ | ● | ● | ● | New | | | |
|  | 4 | 22″ | 10″ | ● | | | | | | |
| 260 Rem. | 4 | 24″ | 9″ | | | | New | | | |
| 270 Win. | 4 | 22″ | 10″ | ● | | | | | | |
|  | 4 | 22″ | 10″ | | | | | | | |
|  | 4 | 24″ | 10″ | | ● | | New | ● | | |
| 280 Rem. | 4 | 22″ | 9¼″ | ● | | | | | | |
|  | 4 | 24″ | 9¼″ | | | | New | | | |
| 7mm-08 Rem. | 4 | 22″ | 9¼″ | ● | | | | | | |
|  | 4 | 24″ | 9¼″ | | | | New | | | |
| 7mm Rem. Mag. | 3 | 24″ | 9¼″ | | ● | ● | | ● | New | ● |
|  | 3 | 24″ | 9¼″ | | | | | | | |
| 7mm STW | 3 | 24″ | 9½″ | | | ● | | | New | |
| 30-06 | 4 | 22″ | 10″ | ● | | | | ● | ● | |
|  | 4 | 22″ | 10″ | | | | New | | | |
| 308 Win. | 4 | 22″ | 10″ | | | | | | | |
|  | 4 | 24″ | 12″ | | | | New | New | | |
| 300 Win. Mag. | 3 | 24″ | 10″ | New | New | New | New | | | ● |
|  | 3 | 24″ | 12″ | | | | | New | New | |
| 300 Wby. Mag. | 3 | 24″ | 12″ | | | New | | New | New | |
| 338 Win. Mag. | 3 | 24″ | 10″ | | | | New | New | New | |
| 375 H&H Mag. | 3 | 24″ | 12″ | | | | | | | |

All Model 700™ rifles come with sling swivel studs. The BDL, ADL, and Seven™ are furnished with sights. The BDL Stainless Synthetic, LSS, Mountain Rifle, Classic, Sendero and Varmint guns have clean barrels. All Remington CF rifles drilled and tapped for scope mounts.

## MODEL 700/Calibers (cont.)                                    Prices

**BDL SS DM-B** 7mm Rem. Mag., 7mm STW, 300 Win. Mag., 300 Wby. Mag., 338 Win. Mag. . . . . . . . . . . . . . . . . . . . . . . . . . . . . . . . . . . . . **$789.00**
**BDL Stainless Synthetic** 270 Win., 30-06 . . . . . . . 641.00
7mm Rem. Mag., 300 Win. Mag., 375 H&H Mag. . . . . . . . . . . . . . . . . . . . . . . . . . . . . . . . . . . . 668.00
**BDL LSS** 7mm Rem. Mag., 300 Win. Mag. . . . . . . . 714.00
**BDL** 222 Rem., 270 Win. LH, 7mm Rem. Mag., 30-06 LH, 300 Win. Mag., 338 Win. Mag. . . . . . . 609.00
222 Rem., 22-250, 223 Rem., 243 Win., 25-06, 270 Win., 30-06 . . . . . . . . . . . . . . . . . . 583.00
7mm Rem. Mag. LH . . . . . . . . . . . . . . . . . . . . . . 636.00

**BDL DM** 243 Win., 25-06 Rem., 270 Win., 280 Rem., 7mm-08 Rem., 30-06 . . . . . . . . . . . **$636.00**
270 Win. LH . . . . . . . . . . . . . . . . . . . . . . . . . . . . . . 663.00
7mm Rem. Mag. LH, 300 Win. Mag. LH . . . . . . . 689.00
**ADL** 243 Win., 270 Win., 30-06, 308 Win. . . . . . . . . 485.00
7mm Rem. Mag. . . . . . . . . . . . . . . . . . . . . . . . . . . 512.00
**ADL Synthetic** 243 Win., 270 Win., 30-06, 308 Win. 425.00
7mm Rem. Mag. . . . . . . . . . . . . . . . . . . . . . . . . . . 452.00
**VLS** 22-250 Rem., 223 Rem., 243 Win., 7mm-08 Rem., 308 Win. . . . . . . . . . . . . . . . . . . . . . . . . . . . 625.00
**VS** w/26" Heavy Barrel in 222 Rem., 223 Rem., 243 Win., 308 Win. . . . . . . . . . . . . . . . . . . . . . . . 705.00
w/26" Fluted Barrel in 220 Swift, 22-250 Rem., 223 Rem., 308 Win. . . . . . . . . . . . . . . . . . . . . . . 852.00

## MODEL 700™ CENTERFIRE RIFLE SPECIFICATIONS (cont.)

| Calibers | Magazine Capacity | Barrel Length | Twist (R–H) 1 Turn In | BDL | BDL (DM) | ADL | ADL Synthetic | VLS* (26" Heavy BBL) | VS (Varmint Synthetic) (26" Heavy BBL) | VS (Varmint Synthetic) (26" Stainless Fluted BBL) |
|---|---|---|---|---|---|---|---|---|---|---|
| 17 Rem. | 5 | 24" | 9" | New | | | | | | |
| 220 Swift | 4 | 26" | 14" | | | | | | | ● |
| 222 Rem. | 5 | 24" | 14" | New | | | | | | |
| 22-250 Rem. | 4 | 24" | 14" | New | | | | ● | ● | ● |
| 223 Rem. | 5 | 24" | 12" | New | | | | ● | ● | ● |
| 243 Win. | 4 | 22" | 9⅛" | New | New | ● | ● | | New | |
|  | 4 | 24" | 9⅛" | | | | | New | | |
| 25-06 Rem. | 4 | 24" | 10" | New | New | | | | | |
|  | 4 | 22" | 10" | | | | | | | |
| 260 Rem. | 4 | 24" | 9" | | | | | | | |
| 270 Win. | 4 | 22" | 10" | New | New | ● | ● | | | |
|  | 4 | 22" | 10" | ● | ● | | | | | |
|  | 4 | 24" | 10" | | | | | | | |
| 280 Rem. | 4 | 22" | 9¼" | | New | | | | | |
|  | 4 | 24" | 9¼" | | | | | | | |
| 7mm-08 Rem. | 4 | 22" | 9¼" | | New | | | | | |
|  | 4 | 24" | 9¼" | | | | | New | | |
| 7mm Rem. Mag. | 3 | 24" | 9¼" | New | New | ● | ● | | | |
|  | 3 | 24" | 9¼" | ● | ● | | | | | |
| 7mm STW | 3 | 24" | 9½" | | | | | | | |
| 30-06 | 4 | 22" | 10" | New | New | ● | ● | | | |
|  | 4 | 22" | 10" | ● | ● | | | | | |
| 308 Win. | 4 | 22" | 10" | | | ● | ● | | | |
|  | 4 | 24" | 12" | | | | | ● | ● | ● |
| 300 Win. Mag. | 3 | 24" | 10" | New | New | | | | | |
|  | 3 | 24" | 12" | | ● | | | | | |
| 300 Wby. Mag. | 3 | 24" | 12" | | | | | | | |
| 338 Win. Mag. | 3 | 24" | 10" | New | | | | | | |
| 375 H&H Mag. | 3 | 24" | 12" | | | | | | | |

\* Varmint Laminated Stock

RIFLES

# REMINGTON BOLT-ACTION RIFLES

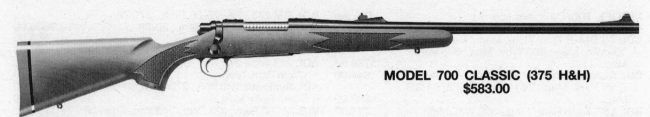

### MODEL 700 CLASSIC (375 H&H)
### $583.00

Since Remington's series of Model 700 Classics began in 1981, the company has offered this model in a special chambering each year. The 300 Win. Mag. was introduced in 1963 for the Model 70 bolt-action rifle following the development of the 338 Win. Mag., 30-338 Wildcat and 308 Norma Mag. The 300 Win. Mag. has a slightly longer body and a shorter neck than its predecessors and is recommended for all North American big-game hunting. The 375 H&H shown above was introduced in 1996.

The Model 700 Classic features an American walnut, straight-comb stock without a cheekpiece for rapid mounting, better sight alignment and reduced felt recoil. A hinged magazine floorplate, sling swivel studs and satin wood finish with cut-checkering are standard, along with 22″ barrel and 1:10″ twist (no sights). Receiver drilled/tapped for scope mounts.

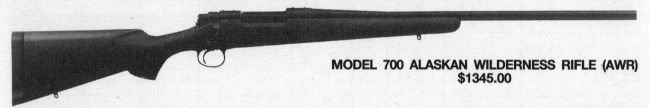

### MODEL 700 MOUNTAIN DM
### (DETACHABLE MAGAZINE) RIFLE
### $636.00

The Remington Model 700 MTN DM rifle features the traditional mountain rifle-styled stock with a pistol grip pitched lower to position the wrist for a better grip. The cheekpiece is designed to align the eye for quick, accurate sighting. The American walnut stock has a hand-rubbed oil finish and comes with a brown recoil pad

and deep-cut checkering. The Model 700 MTN DM also features a lean contoured 22″ barrel that helps reduce total weight to 6.75 pounds. (no sights). All metalwork features a glass bead-blasted, blued-metal finish. **Calibers:** 243 Win., 25-06 Rem., 270 Win., 7mm-08 Rem., 280 Rem and 30-06 Springfield.

### MODEL 700 ALASKAN WILDERNESS RIFLE (AWR)
### $1345.00

This custom-built rifle has the same rate of twist and custom magnum barrel contour as the African Plains Rifle below, but features a Kevlar-reinforced composite stock. **Calibers:** 7mm Rem. Mag., 300 Win. Mag., 300

Wby. Mag., 338 Win. Mag., 375 H&H Mag. **Capacity:** 3 shots. **Barrel length:** 24″. **Overall length:** 44 1/2″. **Weight:** 6 lbs. 12 oz.

### MODEL 700 AFRICAN PLAINS RIFLE (APR)
### $1466.00

The custom-built Model 700 APR rifle has a laminated classic wood stock and the following specifications. **Calibers:** 7mm Rem. Mag., 300 Win. Mag., 300 Wby. Mag., 338 Win. Mag., 375 H&H Mag. **Capacity:** 3

shots. **Barrel length:** 26″. **Overall length:** 46 1/2″. **Weight:** 7 3/4 lbs. **Rate of twist:** R.H. 1 turn in 9 1/4″ (7mm Rem. Mag.); 10″ (300 Win. Mag. and 338 Win. Mag.); 12″ (300 Wby. Mag. and 375 H&H Mag.).

# REMINGTON BOLT-ACTION RIFLES

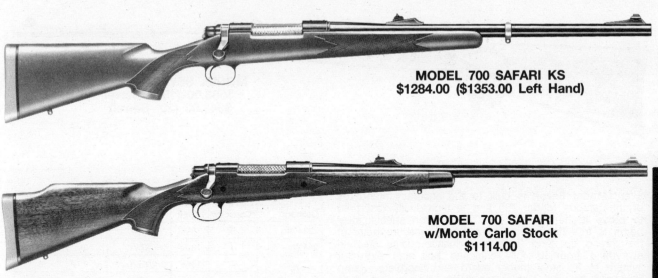

**MODEL 700 SAFARI KS**
$1284.00 ($1353.00 Left Hand)

**MODEL 700 SAFARI**
**w/Monte Carlo Stock**
$1114.00

**Model 700™ Safari Grade** bolt-action rifles provide big-game hunters with a choice of either wood or synthetic stocks. Model 700 Safari Monte Carlo (with Monte Carlo comb and cheekpiece) and Model 700 Safari Classic (with straight-line classic comb and no cheekpiece) are the satin-finished wood-stock models. Both are decorated with hand-cut checkering 18 lines to the inch and fitted with two reinforcing crossbolts covered with rosewood plugs. The Monte Carlo model also has

rosewood pistol-grip and forend caps. All models are fitted with sling swivel studs and 24″ barrels. Synthetic stock has simulated wood-grain finish, reinforced with Kevlar® (KS). **Calibers:** 8mm Rem. Mag., 375 H&H Magnum, 416 Rem. Mag. and 458 Win. Mag. **Capacity:** 3 rounds. **Avg. weight:** 9 lbs. **Overall length:** 44½″. **Rate of twist:** 10″ (8mm Rem. Mag.); 12″ (375 H&H Mag.); 14″ (416 Rem. Mag., 458 Win. Mag.).

**MODEL 40-XR KS SPORTER**
**Target Rimfire Position Rifle w/Kevlar Stock**
$1409.00

**Action:** Bolt action, single shot
**Caliber:** 22 Long Rifle rimfire  **Capacity:** Single loading
**Barrel:** 24″ medium weight target barrel countersunk at muzzle. Drilled and tapped for target scope blocks. Fitted with front sight base
**Bolt:** Artillery style with lockup at rear; 6 locking lugs, double extractors
**Overall length:** 43½″  **Average weight:** 10½ lbs.
**Sights:** Optional at extra cost; Williams Receiver No. FPTK and Redfield Globe front match sight
**Safety:** Positive serrated thumb safety
**Receiver:** Drilled and tapped for receiver sight
**Trigger:** Adjustable from 2 to 4 lbs.

**Stock:** Position style with Monte Carlo, cheekpiece and thumb groove; five-way adj. buttplate and full-length guide rail
Also available:
**MODEL 40-XR BR** with 22″ stainless-steel barrel (heavy contour), 22 LR match chamber and bore dimensions. Receiver and barrel drilled and tapped for scope mounts (mounted on green, Du Pont Kevlar reinforced fiberglass benchrest stock. Fully adjustable trigger (2 oz. trigger optional).
**Price:** . . . . . . . . . . . . . . . . . . . . . . . . . . . . . . . $1500.00
(Additional target rifles are available through Remington's Custom Shop.)

RIFLES

# REMINGTON BOLT-ACTION RIFLES

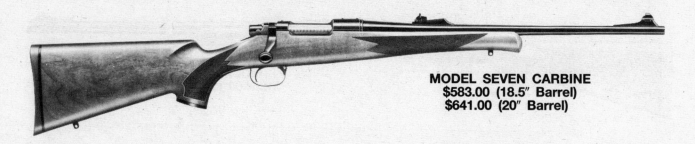

**MODEL SEVEN CARBINE**
**$583.00 (18.5″ Barrel)**
**$641.00 (20″ Barrel)**

## MODEL SEVEN RIFLES

Every **Model Seven** is built to the accuracy standards of the famous Model 700 and is individually test fired to prove it. Its tapered 18½″ Remington special steel barrel is free floating out to a single pressure point at the forend tip. And there is ordnance-quality steel in everything from its fully enclosed bolt and extractor system to its steel trigger guard and floorplate. Ramp front and fully adjustable rear sights, sling swivel studs are standard. The Youth Model features a hardwood stock that is 1 inch shorter for easy ontrol. Chambered in 243 Win. and 7mm-08 for less recoil. See table at right for additional specifications.

## SPECIFICATIONS MODEL SEVEN™

| Calibers | Clip Mag. Capacity | Barrel Length | Overall Length | Twist R-H 1 Turn In | Avg. Wt. (lbs.) |
|---|---|---|---|---|---|
| 223 Rem. | 5 | 18½″ | 37¾″ | 12″ | 6¼ |
| 243 Win. | 4 | 18½″ | 37¾″ | 9⅛″ | 6¼ |
| | 4 | 18½″ | 36¾″ (Youth) | 9⅛″ | 6 |
| | 4 | 20″ | 39¼″ | 9⅛″ | 6¼ |
| 260 Rem. | 4 | 18½″ | 37¾″ | 9″ | 6¼ |
| 7mm-08 Rem. | 4 | 18½″ | 37¾″ | 9¼″ | 6¼ |
| | 4 | 18½″ | 36¾″ (Youth) | 9¼″ | 6 |
| | 4 | 20″ | 39¼″ | 9¼″ | 6¼ |
| 308 Win. | 4 | 18½″ | 37¾″ | 10″ | 6¼ |
| | 4 | 20″ | 39¼″ | 10″ | 6¼ |

Stock Dimensions: 13³⁄₁₆″ length of pull, ⁹⁄₁₆″ drop at comb, ⁵⁄₁₆″ drop at heel. Youth gun has 12½″ length of pull. 17. Rem. provided without sights.
*Note:* New Model Seven Mannlicher and Model Seven KS versions are available from the Remington Custom Shop through your local dealer.

**MODEL SEVEN YOUTH**
**$479.00 (243 Win., 7mm-08 Rem.)**

**MODEL SEVEN SS**
**(STAINLESS SYNTHETIC 20″ Bbl.)**
**$623.00 (243 Win., 260 Rem., 7mm-08 Rem.,**
**308 Win.)**

# REMINGTON REPEATING RIFLES

**MODEL 7400 (High Gloss Stock)**
**$573.00**

**Calibers:** 243 Win., 270 Win., 280 Rem., 30-06, 308 Win.
**Capacity:** 5 centerfire cartridges (4 in the magazine, 1 in the chamber); extra 4-shot magazine available
**Action:** Gas-operated; receiver drilled and tapped for scope mounts
**Barrel lengths:** 22″ (18¹/₂″ in 30-06 Carbine)
**Weight:** 7¹/₂ lbs. (7¹/₄ lbs. in 30-06 Carbine)
**Overall length:** 42″

**Sights:** Standard blade ramp front; sliding ramp rear
**Stock:** Satin or high-gloss (270 Win. and 30-06 only) walnut stock and forend; curved pistol grip; also available with Special Purpose nonreflective finish (270 Win. and 30-06 only)
**Length of pull:** 13³/₈″
**Drop at heel:** 2¹/₄″   **Drop at comb:** 1¹³/₁₆″

**MODEL 7600 (High Gloss Stock)**
**$540.00**

The Model 7600 shares nearly the same specifications as the Model 7400 featured above, except the 7600 is pump action.
**Drop at heel:** ¹⁵/₁₆″. **Drop at comb:** ⁹/₁₆″.

Also available:
**Limited Edition "Buckmasters" ADF** (American Deer Foundation) in 30-06 Springfield. Features include fine-line en-

graving on both sides of receiver panel; Monte Carlo stocks in American walnut w/cut-checkering on buttstocks and for-ends.

Model 7600 Ltd. Ed. . . . . . . . . . . . . . . . . . . . . . . $567.00
Model 7400 Ltd. Ed. . . . . . . . . . . . . . . . . . . . . . .   600.00

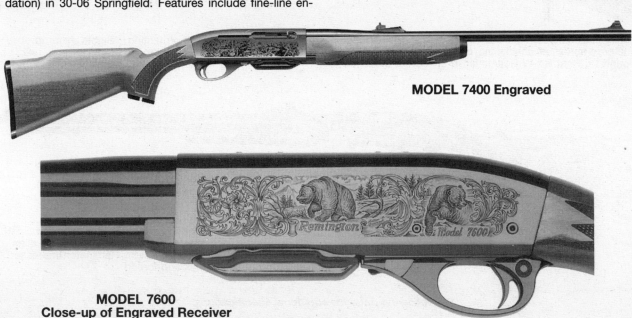

**MODEL 7400 Engraved**

**MODEL 7600**
**Close-up of Engraved Receiver**

# REMINGTON RIMFIRE RIFLES

**MODEL 522 VIPER (22 LR)**
**$152.00**

Remington's autoloading rimfire rifle utilizes a strong light-weight stock of PET resin that is impervious to changing temperatures and humidity. The receiver is made of a du Pont high-tech synthetic. All exposed metalwork, including barrel, breech bolt and trigger guard, have a nonglare, black matte finish. Stock shape with slim pistol grip and semibeavertail forend is proportioned to fit the size and stature of younger or smaller shooters. Other features include: factory-installed centerfire-type iron sights, detachable clip magazine, safety features, primary and secondary sears in trigger mechanism and a protective ejection port shield.

**MODEL 541-T BOLT ACTION**
**$455.00**
**$481.00 (Heavy Barrel)**
**$239.00 (Model 581-S)**

**MODEL 552 BDL DELUXE SPEEDMASTER**
**$340.00**

The rimfire semiautomatic 552 BDL Deluxe sports Remington custom-impressed checkering on both stock and forend. Tough Du Pont RK-W lifetime finish brings out the lustrous beauty of the walnut while protecting it. Sights are ramp-style in front and rugged big-game type fully adjustable in rear.

**MODEL 572 BDL DELUXE FIELDMASTER**
**$353.00**

Features of this rifle with big-game feel and appearance are: Du Pont's tough RK-W finish; centerfire-rifle-type rear sight fully adjustable for both vertical and horizontal sight alignment; big-game style ramp front sight; Remington impressed checkering on both stock and forend.

*See following page for additional specifications.*

# REMINGTON RIMFIRE RIFLES

## MODEL 597 SERIES

Remington's new autoloading rimfire rifles—the Model 597™ Series—are made for those outdoorsmen who view rimfire shooting as a serious activity. They are available in three versions, offering a choice of carbon or stainless steel barreled actions, synthetic or laminated wood stocks, and chambering for either standard 22 Long Rifle or 22 Magnum ammo. All three M597™ rifles feature beavertail-style forends rounded with finger grooves for hand-filling control. The top of the receiver blends into the pistol grip, creating a rimfire autoloader that points like a shotgun but aims like a rifle. Features include a bolt guidance system of twin steel rails for smooth bolt travel and functional reliability. The 20-inch barrels are free-floated for consistent accuracy with all types of rimfire ammunition. A new trigger design creates crisp let-off for autoloading rifles. Bolts on the two 22 LR versions are nickel-plated. The magnum-version bolt is constructed of a special alloy steel to provide controlled, uniform function with magnum cartridges. All receivers are grooved for standard tip-off mounts and are also drilled and tapped for Weaver-type bases. Adjustable open sights and one-piece scope mount rails are standard, as are spare magazine clips.

## RIMFIRE RIFLE SPECIFICATIONS

| Model | Action | Barrel Length | Overall Length | Average Wt. (lbs.) | Magazine Capacity |
|---|---|---|---|---|---|
| 597™ | Auto | 20″ | 40″ | 5½ | 10-Shot Clip |
| 597™LSS | Auto | 20″ | 40″ | 5½ | 10-Shot Clip |
| 597™ Mag. | Auto | 20″ | 40″ | 5½ | 8-Shot Clip |
| 522 Viper | Auto | 20″ | 40″ | 4⅝ | 10-Shot Clip |
| 541-T | Bolt | 24″ | 42½″ | 5⅞* | 5-Shot Clip |
| 541-T HB Heavy Barrel | Bolt | 24″ | 42½″ | 6½* | 5-Shot Clip |
| 552 BDL Deluxe Speedmaster | Auto | 21″ | 40″ | 5¾ | 15 Long Rifle |
| 572 BDL Deluxe Fieldmaster | Pump | 21″ | 40″ | 5½ | 15 Long Rifle |
| 581-S | Bolt | 24″ | 42½″ | 5⅞ | 5-Shot Clip |

**MODEL 597 (22 LR CARBON STEEL)**
**$159.00**

The M597™ is chambered for 22 Long Rifle ammunition and matches Remington's carbon steel barrel with a strong, lightweight, alloy receiver. All metal has a non-reflective, matte black finish. The rifle is housed in a one-piece, dark gray synthetic stock.

**MODEL 597™ LSS**
**$265.00**

The M597™ LSS (Laminated Stock Stainless) has a satin-finished stainless steel barrel and matching, gray-toned alloy receiver. Also chambered for 22 LR cartridges, its stock is of laminated wood in light and dark brown tones.

**MODEL 597™ MAGNUM**
**$292.00**

Chambered for 22 Win. Mag. rimfire cartridges, the M597™ MAGNUM features a carbon steel barrel, alloy receiver and black synthetic stock.

RIFLES

# RIFLES, INC.

## CUSTOM RIFLES

### CLASSIC MODEL

### CLASSIC MODEL
### $1550.00

**SPECIFICATIONS**

**Calibers:** Customized for varmint, target or hunter specifications, up to 375 H&H

**Action:** Remington or Winchester stainless steel Control-round with lapped bolt

**Barrel length:** 26"–28" depending on caliber; stainless-steel match grade, lapped

**Weight:** 6$^{1}/_{2}$ lbs. (approx.)

**Stock:** Pillar glass bedded; laminated fiberglass, finished with textured epoxy

**Features:** Fine-tuned and adjustable trigger; hinged floorplate trigger guard

### SAFARI MODEL

### SAFARI MODEL
### $1950.00   ($2970.00 with Options)

**SPECIFICATIONS**

**Action:** Winchester Model 70 Control-round feed; hand lapped and honed bolt; drilled and tapped for 8×40 base screws

**Barrel length:** 23"–25" depending on caliber; stainless-steel match grade, lapped

**Weight:** 9 lbs. (approx.)

**Muzzle break:** Stainless Quiet Slimbrake

**Metal finish:** Matte stainless or black Teflon

**Stock:** Pillar glass bedded; double reinforced laminated fiberglass/graphite; finished with textured epoxy

**Features:** Fine-tuned and adjustable trigger; hinged floorplate

**Options:** Drop box for additional rounds; express sights; barrel band; quarter ribs

### LIGHTWEIGHT STRATA STAINLESS

### LIGHTWEIGHT STRATA STAINLESS MODEL
### $2150.00

**SPECIFICATIONS**

**Calibers:** Up to 375 H&H

**Action:** Stainless Remington; fluted, tapped and handle-hollowed bolt; aluminum bolt shroud

**Barrel length:** 22"–24" depending on caliber; stainless-steel match grade

**Weight:** 4.75 lbs. (approx.)

**Stock:** Pillar glass bedded; laminated Kevlar/Boron/Graphite, finished with textured epoxy

**Features:** Matte stainless metal finish; aluminum blind or hinged floorplate trigger guard; custom Protektor pad

# ROSSI RIFLES

## PUMP-ACTION GALLERY GUNS

**MODEL M62 SAC CARBINE**
**$240.00    ($250.00 Nickel)**

**SPECIFICATIONS**
**Caliber:** 22 LR   **Capacity:** 12 rounds
**Barrel length:** 16$1/2$″   **Overall length:** 32$3/4$″
**Weight:** 4$1/4$″
**Finish:** Blue or nickel

**MODEL M62 SA**
**$240.00    ($250.00 Nickel)**
**$250.00 (w/Octagonal Bbl.)**

**SPECIFICATIONS**
**Caliber:** 22 LR   **Capacity:** 13 rounds
**Barrel length:** 23″   **Overall length:** 39$1/4$″
**Weight:** 5.2 lbs.
**Finish:** Blue or nickel
Also available:
**Model 59** 22 Magnum (10 rds., blue only)........ $280.00

## LEVER-ACTION OLD WEST CARBINES

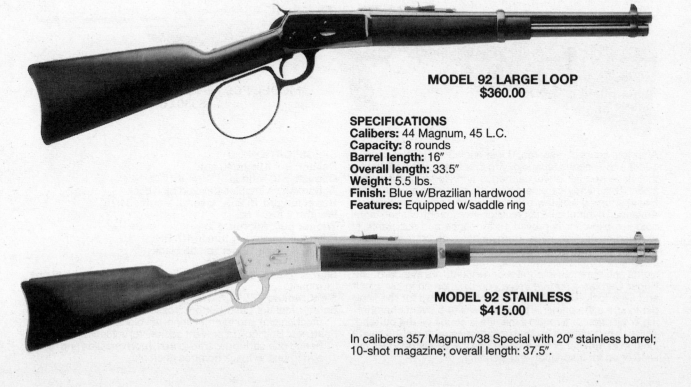

**MODEL 92 LARGE LOOP**
**$360.00**

**SPECIFICATIONS**
**Calibers:** 44 Magnum, 45 L.C.
**Capacity:** 8 rounds
**Barrel length:** 16″
**Overall length:** 33.5″
**Weight:** 5.5 lbs.
**Finish:** Blue w/Brazilian hardwood
**Features:** Equipped w/saddle ring

**MODEL 92 STAINLESS**
**$415.00**

In calibers 357 Magnum/38 Special with 20″ stainless barrel;
10-shot magazine; overall length: 37.5″.

# ROSSI RIFLES

## LEVER-ACTION OLD WEST CARBINES

**MODEL M92 SRC**
**$415.00**

### SPECIFICATIONS
**Caliber:** 38 Special or 357 Magnum
**Capacity:** 10 rounds
**Barrel length:** 20″   **Overall length:** 37″
**Weight:** 6 lbs.
**Finish:** Blue

Also available:
**Model M92 SRC** in 45 LC w/24″ half-
octagonal barrel. . . . . . . . . . . . . . . . . . . . . . . . **$429.00**
**Model M92 SRS** in 38 Spec., 357 Mag. & 44 Mag.
w/16″ barrel, 8-shot magazine. **Overall length:**
33″. **Weight:** 5.75 lbs. . . . . . . . . . . . . . . . . . .    360.00
**Model M92 Carbine** w/16″ barrel, 8-shot
magazine. **Weight:** 5.5 lbs.  . . . . . . . . . . . . . .    366.00

# RUGER CARBINES

**MODEL PC9 AUTOLOADING CARBINE**
**$550.00**

After four years of research, Ruger engineers have combined 10/22 and P-series technology to create an autoloading rifle that uses popular pistol cartridges and Ruger pistol magazines. This handy carbine meets the needs of personal defense, sporting use, law enforcement and security agencies. Advanced synthetics and precision investment-casting technologies allow for improved performance and substantially reduced costs. The Ruger Carbine has a chrome-moly steel barrel, receiver, slide and recoil springs, and features a checkered Zytel stock with rubber buttplate. Adjustable open sights and patented integral scope mounts are standard. The Ruger Carbine also features a combination firing-pin block and slide lock. Trigger engagement is required for the firing pin to strike the primer. The slide locks to prevent chambering or ejection of a round if the rifle is struck on the buttpad. This safety system is backed up by a manual crossbolt safety located at the rear of the trigger guard. A slide stop locks the slide open for inspection and cleaning.

### SPECIFICATIONS
**Caliber:** 9 × 19mm/40 auto
**Capacity:** 10 rounds
**Action:** Mass impulse delayed blowback
**Barrel length:** 15.25″   **Overall length:** 34.75″
**Weight:** 6 lbs. 4 oz.
**Trigger pull:** Approx. 6 lb.
**Rifling:** 6 grooves, 1 turn in 10″ RH
**Stock:** du Pont "Zytel" matte black
**Finish:** Matte black oxide
**Sights:** Blade front, open rear plus provision for scope mounts
**Sight radius:** 12.65″
**Safety:** Manual push-button crossbolt safety (locks trigger mechanism) and internal firing-pin block safety
**Features:** Bolt lock to prevent accidental unloading or chambering of a cartridge; steel barrel, receiver, slide and recoil spring unit w/black composite stock

# RUGER CARBINES

**RUGER MINI-14/5**

**Mechanism:** Gas-operated, semiautomatic. **Materials:** Heat-treated chrome molybdenum and other alloy steels as well as music wire coil springs are used throughout the mechanism to ensure reliability under field-operating conditions. **Safety:** The safety blocks both the hammer and sear. The slide can be cycled when the safety is on. The safety is mounted in the front of the trigger guard so that it may be set to Fire position without removing finger from trigger guard. **Firing pin:** The firing pin is retracted mechanically during the first part of the unlocking of the bolt. The rifle can only be fired when the bolt is safely locked. **Stock:** One-piece American hardwood reinforced with steel liner at stressed areas. Sling swivels standard. Handguard and forearm separated by air space from barrel to promote cooling under rapid-fire conditions. **Field stripping:** The Carbine can be field-stripped to its eight (8) basic sub-assemblies in a matter of seconds and without use of special tools.

**MINI-14 SPECIFICATIONS**
**Caliber:** 223 (5.56mm). **Barrel length:** 18¹/₂″. **Overall length:** 37¹/₄″. **Weight:** 6 lbs. 8 oz. **Magazine:** 5-round, detachable box magazine. **Sights:** Rear adj. for windage/elevation.
**Prices:**
Mini-14/5 Blued............................$516.00
K-Mini-14/5 Stainless Steel..................569.00
(Scopes rings not included)

**MINI-14/5R RANCH RIFLE**

**SPECIFICATIONS**
**Caliber:** 223 (5.56mm). **Barrel length:** 18¹/₂″. **Overall length:** 37¹/₄″. **Weight:** 6 lbs. 8 oz. **Magazine:** 5-round detachable box magazine. **Sights:** Fold-down rear sight; 1″ scope rings

**Prices:**
Mini-14/5R Blued...........................$556.00
K-Mini-14/5R Stainless Steel ................609.00

**MINI-THIRTY**

This modified version of the Ruger Ranch rifle is chambered for the 7.62 × 39mm Soviet service cartridge. Designed for use with telescopic sights, it features low, compact scope-mounting for greater accuracy and carrying ease, and a buffer in the receiver. Sling swivels are standard.

**SPECIFICATIONS**
**Caliber:** 7.62×39mm. **Barrel length:** 18¹/₂″. **Overall length:** 37¹/₈″. **Weight:** 6 lbs. 14 oz. (empty). **Magazine capacity:** 5 shots. **Rifling:** 6 grooves, R.H. twist, 1:10″. **Finish:** Blued or stainless. **Stock:** One-piece American hardwood w/steel liners in stressed areas. **Sights:** Blade front; peep rear.
**Prices:**
Blue .......................................$556.00
Stainless steel ............................609.00

# RUGER CARBINES

**STANDARD 10/22 CARBINE**

**MODEL K10/22RP "ALL WEATHER"**

**MODEL K10/22RBI INTERNATIONAL CARBINE STAINLESS**

**MODEL 10/22T TARGET**

## MODEL 10/22 CARBINE 22 LONG RIFLE

Construction of the 10/22 Carbine is rugged and follows the Ruger design practice of building a firearm from integrated sub-assemblies. For example, the trigger housing assembly contains the entire ignition system, which employs a high-speed, swinging hammer to ensure the shortest possible lock time. The barrel is assembled to the receiver by a unique dual-screw dovetail system that provides unusual rigidity and strength—and accounts, in part, for the exceptional accuracy of the 10/22.

### SPECIFICATIONS
**Mechanism:** Blow-back, semiautomatic. **Caliber:** 22 LR, high-speed or standard-velocity loads. **Magazine:** 10-shot capacity, exclusive Ruger rotary design; fits flush into stock. **Barrel:** 18 1/2", assembled to the receiver by dual-screw dovetail mounting for added strength and rigidity. **Overall length:** 37 1/4". **Weight:** 5 lbs. **Sights:** 1/16" brass bead front; single folding-leaf rear, adjustable for elevation; receiver drilled and tapped for scope blocks or tip-off mount adapter (included). **Trigger:** Curved finger surface, 3/8" wide. **Safety:**
Sliding cross-button type; safety locks both sear and hammer and cannot be put in safe position unless gun is cocked. **Stocks:** 10/22 RB is birch; 10/22 SP Deluxe Sporter is American walnut. **Finish:** Polished all over and blued or anodized or brushed satin bright metal.

**Prices:**

| | |
|---|---|
| **Model 10/22 RB Standard** (Birch carbine stock) . . . . | **$213.00** |
| **Model 10/22 DSP Deluxe** (Hand-checkered American walnut) . . . . . . . . . . . . . . . . . . . . . . . . . | **274.00** |
| **Model K10/22 RB Stainless** . . . . . . . . . . . . . . . . . | **255.00** |
| **Model K10/22 RBI International Carbine** w/full-length hardwood stock, stainless-steel bbl. . . . . | **282.00** |
| **MODEL 10/22 RBI International Carbine** w/blued barrel . . . . . . . . . . . . . . . . . . . . . . . . . . | **262.00** |
| **MODEL 10/22T TARGET** (no sights) Hammer-forged barrel, laminated target-style stock . . . . . . | **392.50** |
| **MODEL K10/22RP** stainless "All Weather" w/synthetic stock . . . . . . . . . . . . . . . . . . . . . . . . | **255.00** |

# RUGER SINGLE-SHOT RIFLES

The following illustrations show the variations currently offered in the Ruger No. 1 Single-Shot Rifle Series. Ruger No. 1 rifles have a Farquharson-type falling-block action and select American walnut stocks. Pistol grip and forearm are hand-checkered to a borderless design. Price for any listed model is **$688.00** (except the No. 1 RSI International Model: **$699.00**). Barreled Actions (blued only): **$465.00**

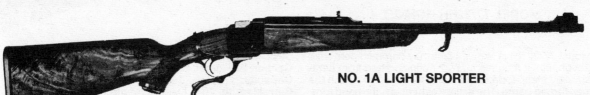

### NO. 1A LIGHT SPORTER

**Calibers:** 243 Win., 270 Win., 30-06, 7×57mm. **Barrel length:** 22″. **Sights:** Adjustable folding-leaf rear sight mounted on quarter rib with ramp front sight base and dovetail-type gold bead front sight; open. **Weight:** 7¼ lbs.

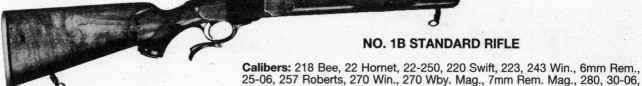

### NO. 1S MEDIUM SPORTER

**Calibers:** 218 Bee, 7mm Rem. Mag., 300 Win. Mag., 338 Win. Mag., 45-70. **Barrel length:** 26″ (22″ in 45-70). **Sights:** (same as above). **Weight:** 8 lbs. (7¼ lbs. in 45-70).

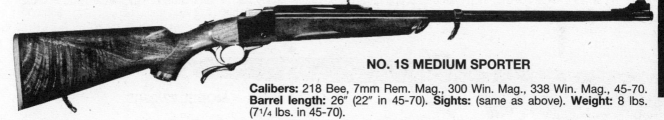

### NO. 1B STANDARD RIFLE

**Calibers:** 218 Bee, 22 Hornet, 22-250, 220 Swift, 223, 243 Win., 6mm Rem., 25-06, 257 Roberts, 270 Win., 270 Wby. Mag., 7mm Rem. Mag., 280, 30-06, 300 Win. Mag., 300 Wby. Mag., 338 Win. Mag. **Barrel:** 26″. **Sights:** Ruger 1″ steel tip-off scope rings. **Weight:** 8 lbs.

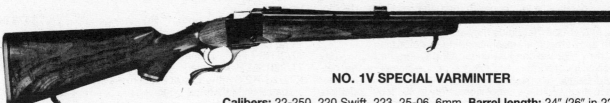

### NO. 1V SPECIAL VARMINTER

**Calibers:** 22-250, 220 Swift, 223, 25-06, 6mm. **Barrel length:** 24″ (26″ in 220 Swift). **Sights:** Ruger target scope blocks, heavy barrel and 1″ tip-off scope rings. **Weight:** 9 lbs.

Also available:
**NO. 1H TROPICAL RIFLE** (24″ heavy barrel) in 375 H&H Mag., 458 Win. Mag., 416 Rigby and 416 Rem. Mag.
**NO 1. RSI INTERNATIONAL** (20″ lightweight barrel) in 243 Win., 270 Win., 30-06 and 7×57mm

# RUGER BOLT-ACTION RIFLES

### MODEL 77/22RH HORNET
### $489.00   ($499.00 w/Sights)

The Model 77/22RH is Ruger's first truly compact centerfire bolt-action rifle. It features a 77/22 action crafted from heat-treated alloy steel. Exterior surfaces are blued to match the hammer-forged barrel. The action features a right-hand turning bolt with a 90-degree bolt throw, cocking on opening. Fast lock time (2.7 milliseconds) adds to accuracy. A three-position swing-back safety locks the bolt; in its center position firing is blocked, but bolt operation and safe loading and unloading are permitted. When fully forward, the rifle is ready to fire. The American walnut stock has recoil pad, grip cap and sling swivels installed. One-inch diameter scope rings fit integral bases.

**SPECIFICATIONS**
**Caliber:** 22 Hornet
**Capacity:** 6 rounds (detachable rotary magazine)
**Barrel length:** 20″   **Overall length:** 40″
**Weight:** 6 lbs. (unloaded)
**Sights:** Single folding-leaf rear; gold bead front
**Length of pull:** 13¾″
**Drop at heel:** 2⅜″   **Drop at comb:** 2″
**Finish:** Polished and blued, matte, nonglare receiver top
**Also available: MODEL K77/22VHZ Varmint** w/stainless-steel heavy barrel, laminated American hardwood stock.
   **Price:** (w/o sights) . . . . . . . . . . . . . . . . . . . . . . . $535.00

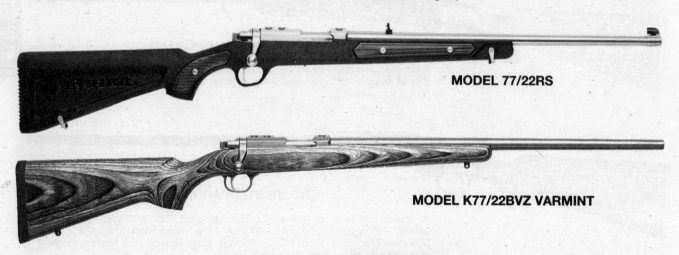

### MODEL 77/22RS

### MODEL K77/22BVZ VARMINT

### MODEL 77/22 RIMFIRE RIFLE

The Ruger 22-caliber rimfire 77/22 bolt-action rifle has been built especially to function with the patented Ruger 10-Shot Rotary Magazine concept. The magazine throat, retaining lips, and ramps that guide the cartridge into the chamber are solid alloy steel that resists bending or deforming.

The 77/22 weighs just under six pounds. Its heavy-duty receiver incorporates the integral scope bases of the patented Ruger Scope Mounting System, with 1-inch Ruger scope rings. With the 3-position safety in its "lock" position, a dead bolt is cammed forward, locking the bolt handle down. In this position the action is locked closed and the handle cannot be raised.

All metal surfaces are finished in nonglare deep blue or satin stainless. Stock is select straight-grain American walnut, hand checkered and finished with durable polyurethane.

An All-Weather, all-stainless steel **MODEL K77/22RS** features a stock made of glass-fiber reinforced Zytel. **Weight:** Approx. 6 lbs.

**SPECIFICATIONS**
**Calibers:** 22 LR and 22 Magnum. **Barrel length:** 20″. **Overall length:** 39¼″. **Weight:** 6 lbs. (w/o scope, magazine empty). **Feed:** Detachable 10-Shot Ruger Rotary Magazine.
**Prices:**
**77/22R** Blue, w/o sights, 1″ Ruger rings . . . . . . . . . $473.00
**77/22RM** Blue, walnut stock, plain barrel,
   no sights, 1″ Ruger rings, 22 Mag. . . . . . . . . . . . 473.00
**77/22RS** Blue, sights included, 1″ Ruger rings . . . . 481.00
**77/22RSM** Blue, American walnut, iron sights . . . . 481.00
**K77/22-RP** Synthetic stock, stainless steel, plain
   barrel with 1″ Ruger rings . . . . . . . . . . . . . . . . . . 473.00
**K77/22-RMP** Synthetic stock, stainless steel,
   plain barrel, 1″ Ruger rings . . . . . . . . . . . . . . . . 473.00
**K77/22-RSP** Synthetic stock, stainless steel, gold
   bead front sight, folding-leaf rear, Ruger 1″
   rings. . . . . . . . . . . . . . . . . . . . . . . . . . . . . . . . . . . 481.00
**K77/22RSMP** Synthetic stock, metal sights,
   stainless. . . . . . . . . . . . . . . . . . . . . . . . . . . . . . . . . 481.00
**K77/22VBZ Varmint** Laminated stock, scope
   rings, heavy barrel, stainless . . . . . . . . . . . . . . . . 499.00

# RUGER BOLT-ACTION RIFLES

## MARK II SERIES

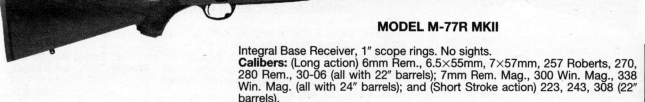

### MODEL M-77R MKII

Integral Base Receiver, 1″ scope rings. No sights.
**Calibers:** (Long action) 6mm Rem., 6.5×55mm, 7×57mm, 257 Roberts, 270, 280 Rem., 30-06 (all with 22″ barrels); 7mm Rem. Mag., 300 Win. Mag., 338 Win. Mag. (all with 24″ barrels); and (Short Stroke action) 223, 243, 308 (22″ barrels).
**Weight:** Approx. 7 lbs.
**Price:** .............................................................. **$574.00**

Also available: **M-77LR MKII** (Left Hand).
**Calibers:** 270, 30-06, 7mm Rem. Mag., 300 Win. Mag. ........... **574.00**

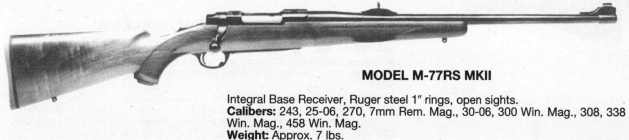

### MODEL M-77RS MKII

Integral Base Receiver, Ruger steel 1″ rings, open sights.
**Calibers:** 243, 25-06, 270, 7mm Rem. Mag., 30-06, 300 Win. Mag., 308, 338 Win. Mag., 458 Win. Mag.
**Weight:** Approx. 7 lbs.
**Price:** .............................................................. **$635.00**

### MODEL M-77RL MKII ULTRA LIGHT

This big-game, bolt-action rifle encompasses the traditional features that have made the Ruger M-77 one of the most popular centerfire rifles in the world. It includes a sliding top tang safety, a one-piece bolt with Mauser-type extractor and diagonal front mounting system. American walnut stock is hand-checkered in a sharp diamond pattern. A rubber recoil pad, pistol-grip cap and studs for mounting quick detachable sling swivels are standard. Available in both long- and short-action versions, with Integral Base Receiver and 1″ Ruger scope rings.
**Calibers:** 223, 243, 257, 270, 30-06, 308.
**Barrel length:** 20″. **Weight:** Approx. 6 lbs.
**Price:** .............................................................. **$610.00**

# RUGER BOLT-ACTION RIFLES

## MARK II SERIES

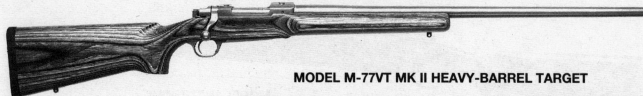

### MODEL M-77VT MK II HEAVY-BARREL TARGET

Features Mark II stainless-steel bolt action, gray matte finish, two-stage adjustable trigger. No sights.
**Calibers:** 22-250, 220 Swift, 223, 243, 25-06 and 308. **Barrel length:** 26″, hammer-forged, free-floating stainless steel. **Weight:** 9³/₄ lbs. **Stock:** Laminated American hardwood with flat forend.
**Price: KM-77VT MK II** . . . . . . . . . . . . . . . . . . . . . . . . . . . . . . . . . . . . . $684.00

### M-77 II MARK II ALL-WEATHER

**KM-77RP MK II ALL-WEATHER** Receiver w/integral dovetails to accommodate Ruger 1″ rings, no sights, stainless steel, synthetic stock.
**Calibers:** 223, 22-250, 243, 270, 280, 30-06, 7mm Rem. Mag., 300 Win. Mag., 308,
338 Win. Mag. . . . . . . . . . . . . . . . . . . . . . . . . . . . . . . . . . . . . . . . . . . . **$574.00**
**KM-77RSP MK II ALL-WEATHER** Receiver w/integral dovetails to accommodate Ruger 1″ rings, metal sights, stainless steel, synthetic stock.
**Calibers:** 243, 270, 7mm Rem. Mag., 30-06, 300 Win. Mag.,
338 Win. Mag. . . . . . . . . . . . . . . . . . . . . . . . . . . . . . . . . . . . . . . . . . **635.00**

### RUGER 77RSM MK II MAGNUM RIFLE

This "Bond Street" quality African safari hunting rifle features a sighting rib machined from a single bar of steel; Circassian walnut stock with black forend tip; steel floorplate and latch; a new Ruger Magnum trigger guard with floorplate latch designed flush with the contours of the trigger guard (to eliminate accidental dumping of cartridges); a three-position safety mechanism; Express rear sight; and front sight ramp with gold bead sight. Also available in Express Model (long action, no heavy barrel).
**Calibers:** 375 H&H, 416 Rigby. **Capacity:** 4 rounds (375 H&H) and 3 rounds (416 Rigby). **Barrel length:** 22″. **Overall length:** 42¹/₈″. **Barrel thread diameter:** 1¹/₈″. **Weight:** 9¹/₄ lbs. (375 H&H); 10¹/₄ lbs. (416 Rigby).
**Price:** . . . . . . . . . . . . . . . . . . . . . . . . . . . . . . . . . . . . . . . . . . . . . . . . . . **$1550.00**

# RUGER BOLT-ACTION RIFLES

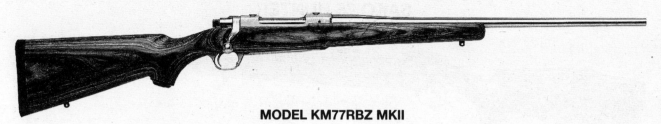

### MODEL KM77RBZ MKII

Stainless steel, laminated stock, scope rings, no sights.
**Price:** . . . . . . . . . . . . . . . . . . . . . . . . . . . . . . . . . . . . . . . . . . . . . . $606.00

### MODEL KM77RSBZ MKII

Stainless steel, laminated stock, scope rings, open sights.
**Price:** . . . . . . . . . . . . . . . . . . . . . . . . . . . . . . . . . . . . . . . . . . . . $667.00

Also available:
**MODEL KM77RSP MKII**
Stainless steel, synthetic stock, scope rings, open sights.
**Price:** . . . . . . . . . . . . . . . . . . . . . . . . . . . . . . . . . . . . . . . . . . . . $635.00

### MODEL M-77RSI INTERNATIONAL MANNLICHER

Mannlicher-type stock, Integral Base Receiver, open sights, Ruger 1″ steel
rings. **Calibers:** 243, 270, 30-06, 308. **Barrel length:** 18.5″. **Weight:** Approx. 6
lbs.
**Price** . . . . . . . . . . . . . . . . . . . . . . . . . . . . . . . . . . . . . . . . . . . . . . $642.00

# SAKO RIFLES

## SAKO 75 HUNTER

**SAKO 75 HUNTER**

The New SAKO 75 Hunter is the first rifle to offer an action furnished with both a bolt with three locking lugs and a mechanical ejector. This combination results in unprecedented smoothness and reliability. The sturdy receiver helps to zero the rifle with different bullets and loads. The new bolt provides a solid, well-balanced platform for the cartridge. The traditional safety catch is either on or off. Cartridge removal or loading is done by pressing a separate bolt release button in front of the safety. No need to touch the safety to remove a cartridge and then disengage it by mistake under difficult or stressful conditions. The new cold hammer-forged barrel is manufactured in an advanced custom-built robotic cell. The New SAKO features a totally free-floating barrel. Instead of checkering, this all-stainless, all-weather model has soft rubbery grips molded in the stock to provide a firmer, more comfortable hold than with conventional synthetic stocks. The selected moisture stabilized high-grade walnut ensures quality and craftsmanship.

Other features include:

- Five bolt sliding guides
- 70° bolt lift
- Totally free-floating cold hammer-forged barrel
- Positive safety system with separate bolt release button for safe unloading

- Top-loading hinged floorplate
- Detachable staggered 5-round magazine
- Single-shot version
- Five (5) action sizes for perfect cartridge match
- All-Stainless metal parts and All-Weather synthetic stock with special grips
- Selected moisture stabilized walnut stock with hand-crafted checkering
- Integral scope rails

**Prices:**
**SAKO 75 HUNTER**
22" barrel (22-250 Rem., 243 Win., 7mm-08, 308 Win., 25-06 Rem., 270 Win., 280 Win., 30-06) . . . . . . . . . . . . . . . . . . . . . . . . . . . . . . . **$1055.00**
24" barrel (7mm Rem. Mag., 300 Win. Mag., 338 Win. Mag., 375 H&H Mag., 416 Rem. Mag. . . . . . . . . . . . . . . . . . . . . . . . . . . . . . . . **1085.00**
26" barrel (270 Wby. Mag., 7mm STW, 7mm Wby. Mag., 300 Wby. Mag., 340 Wby.) . . . . **1085.00**

Also available:
**SAKO 75 STAINLESS SYNTHETIC**
22" barrel (22-250 Rem., 243 Win., 308 Win., 25-06 Rem., 270 Win., 30-06) . . . . . . . . . . **$1148.00**
24" barrel (7mm Rem. Mag., 300 Win. Mag. . . . . . . . . . . . . . . . . . . . . . . . . . . . . . . . **1178.00**

**SAKO 75 STAINLESS SYNTHETIC**

# SAKO RIFLES

**FINNFIRE
22 LONG RIFLE**

**FINNFIRE
HEAVY BARREL**

### FINNFIRE 22 LR BOLT-ACTION RIFLE
### $732.00   $815.00 (Heavy Barrel)

Sako of Finland, acclaimed as the premier manufacturer of bolt-action centerfire rifles, presents its 22 Long Rifle Finnfire. Designed by engineers who use only state-of-the-art technology to achieve both form and function and produced by craftsmen to exacting specifications, this premium grade bolt-action rifle exceeds the requirements of even the most demanding firearm enthusiast.

The basic concept in the design of the Finnfire was to make it as similar to its "big brothers" as possible—just scaled down. For example, the single-stage adjustable trigger is a carbon copy of the trigger found on any other big-bore hunting model. The 22-inch barrel is cold-hammered to ensure superior accuracy.

**Overall length:** 39 1/2″. **Weight:** 5 1/4 lbs.; 7 1/2 lbs. (w/ heavy barrel). **Rate of twist:** 16 1/2″.

Other outstanding features include:
- European walnut stock
- Luxurious matte lacquer finish
- 50° bolt lift
- Free-floating barrel
- Integral 11mm dovetail for scope mounting
- Two-position safety that locks the bolt
- Cocking indicator
- Five-shot detachable magazine
- Ten-shot magazine available
- Available with open sights

*COMMITMENT TO EXCELLENCE — A SAKO TRADITION*

# SAKO RIFLES

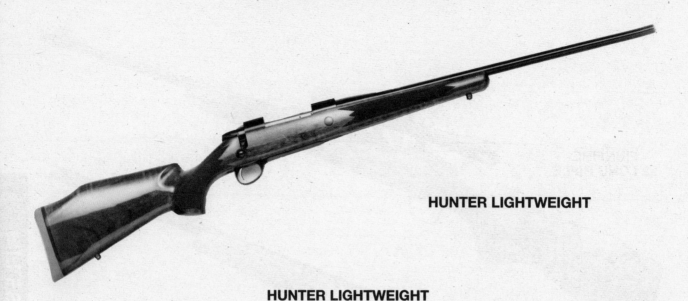

**HUNTER LIGHTWEIGHT**

## HUNTER LIGHTWEIGHT

Here's one case of less being more. SAKO has taken its famed bolt-action, centerfire rifle, redesigned the stock and trimmed the barrel contour. In fact, in any of the short action (S 491-1) calibers—17 Rem., 222 or 223 Rem.—the Hunter weighs in at less than 7 pounds, making it one of the lightest wood stock production rifles in the world.

The same cosmetic upgrading and weight reduction have been applied to the entire Hunter line in all calibers and action lengths, standard and magnum. All the precision, quality and accuracy for which this Finnish rifle has been so justly famous are still here. Now it just weighs less.

The SAKO trigger is a rifleman's delight—smooth, crisp and fully adjustable. If these were the only SAKO features, it would still be the best rifle available. But the real test that sets SAKO apart from all others is its truly outstanding accuracy.

While many factors can affect a rifle's accuracy, 90 percent of any rifle's accuracy potential lies in its barrel. And the creation of superbly accurate barrels is where SAKO excels.

The care that SAKO takes in the cold-hammer processing of each barrel is unparalleled in the industry. For example, after each barrel blank is drilled, it is diamond-lapped and then optically checked for microscopic flaws. This extra care affords the SAKO owner lasting accuracy and a finish that will stay "new" season after season.

You can't buy an unfired SAKO. Every gun is test-fired using special overloaded proof cartridges. This test ensures the SAKO owner total safety and uncompromising accuracy. Every barrel must group within SAKO specifications or it's scrapped. Not recycled. Not adjusted. Scrapped. Either a SAKO barrel delivers SAKO accuracy, or it never leaves the factory.

And hand-in-hand with SAKO accuracy is SAKO beauty. Pistol-grip stocks are of genuine European walnut, flawlessly finished and checkered by hand. Also available with a matte lacquer finish. For Left-handed Models, see page 281.

**Prices:**
**Short Action (S 491-1)**
In 17 Rem., 222 Rem., 223 Rem. . . . . . . . . . . . . **$1050.00**
**Medium Action (M 591)**
In 22-250 Rem., 7mm-08, 243 Win. &
   308 Win. . . . . . . . . . . . . . . . . . . . . . . . . . . . . 1050.00
**Long Action (L 691)**
In 25-06 Rem., 270 Win., 280 Rem., 30-06 . . . . . 1085.00
In 7mm Rem. Mag., 300 Win. Mag.,
   338 Win. Mag. . . . . . . . . . . . . . . . . . . . . . . . . 1100.00
In 270 Wby. Mag., 300 Wby. Mag., 7mm Wby.
   Mag., 340 Wby. Mag, 375 H&H Mag.,
   416 Rem. Mag. . . . . . . . . . . . . . . . . . . . . . . . 1120.00

**LEFT-HANDED MODELS** (Matte Lacquer Finish)
**Medium Action (M 591)**
In 22-250 Rem., 7mm-08, 243 Win. and
   308 Win. . . . . . . . . . . . . . . . . . . . . . . . . . . . **$1135.00**
**Long Action (L 691)**
In 25-06 Rem., 270 Win., 280 Rem., 30-06 . . . . . 1165.00
In 7mm Rem. Mag., 300 Win. Mag.,
   338 Win. Mag. . . . . . . . . . . . . . . . . . . . . . . . . 1180.00
In 300 Wby. Mag., 375 H&H Mag.,
   416 Rem. Mag. . . . . . . . . . . . . . . . . . . . . . . . 1200.00

# SAKO RIFLES

**DELUXE
BOLT-ACTION RIFLE**

## DELUXE BOLT-ACTION RIFLE

All the fine-touch features you expect of the deluxe grade SAKO are here—beautifully grained French walnut, superbly done high-gloss finish, hand-cut checkering, deep rich bluing and rosewood forend tip and grip cap. And of course the accuracy, reliability and superior field performance for which SAKO is so justly famous are still here too. It's all here—it just weighs less than it used to. Think of it as more for less.

In addition, the scope mounting system on these SAKOs is among the strongest in the world. Instead of using separate bases, a tapered dovetail is milled into the receiver, to which the scope rings are mounted. A beautiful system that's been proven by over 20 years of use. SAKO Original Scope Mounts and SAKO scope rings are available in short/medium, and high in one-inch and 30mm.

**Prices:**
**Short Action (S 491)**
In 17 Rem., 222 Rem. & 223 Rem. . . . . . . . . . . . **$1475.00**
**Medium Action (M 591)**
In 22-250 Rem., 243 Win., 7mm-08
   and 308 Win. . . . . . . . . . . . . . . . . . . . . . . . **1475.00**
**Long Action (L 691)**
In 25-06 Rem., 270 Win., 280 Rem., 30-06 . . . . . **1510.00**
In 7mm Rem. Mag., 300 Win. Mag. and
   338 Win. Mag. . . . . . . . . . . . . . . . . . . . . . . . **1525.00**
In 300 Wby. Mag., 375 H&H Mag.,
   416 Rem. Mag. . . . . . . . . . . . . . . . . . . . . . . . **1545.00**

## SUPER DELUXE

SAKO offers the Super Deluxe for the most discriminating gun buyer. This one-of-a-kind beauty is available on special order.

**SUPER DELUXE** . . . . . . . . . . . . . . . . . . . . . . **$3100.00**

# SAKO RIFLES

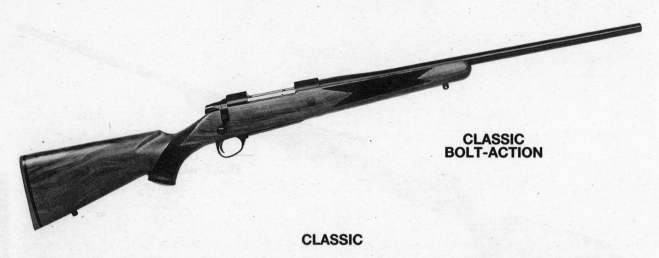

**CLASSIC
BOLT-ACTION**

## CLASSIC

Classic elegance best describes one of Sako's latest models—the CLASSIC—designed for discriminating shooters who demand quality and the traditional clean, graceful lines of the classic style. Available in two action lengths and the most popular calibers (see below). Also available in a left-handed model.

### SPECIFICATIONS
**Calibers:** 243 Win., 270 Win., 30-06, 7mm Rem. Mag.
**Barrel length:** 22″ and 24″ (Magnum action only)
**Capacity:** 5 rounds (Medium and Long action); 3 rounds (Magnum action)

**Overall length:** 42″ and 44″ (Magnum action only)
**Weight:** 6⅞ lbs. (243 Win.); 7 lbs. (270 Win. and 30-06); 7¼ lbs. (7mm Rem. Mag.)
**Finish:** Matte lacquer

**Prices:**
**Medium Action (M 591)**
In 243 Win. ............................... $1050.00
**Long Action (L 691)**
In 270 Win., 30-06 ...................... 1085.00
In 7mm Rem. Mag. ...................... 1100.00

**LONG-RANGE HUNTER**

## LONG-RANGE HUNTING MODELS

Proudly acclaimed as the premier manufacturer of bolt-action rifles, Sako offers its long-range hunting rifle with 26-inch free-floating heavy barrel. The barrel is fluted to reduce weight while maintaining rigidity. Sako designed a wide beavertail forend for additional stability and support. The European walnut stock features Sako's custom recoil-pad spacer system. A fixed magazine with hinged floorplate has a 4-plus-1 round magazine capacity in 25-06 and 270, while the magnum calibers have a 3-plus-1 capacity. Trigger pull is adjustable from 2 to 4 pounds. Other standard features include mechanical ejection, integral dovetailed scope mount rails, one-piece forged bolt and a matte lacquer stock with palm swell.

**Prices:**
25-06, 270 Win. .......................... $1275.00
7mm Rem. Mag., 300 Win. Mag. ............ 1290.00

# SAKO RIFLES/CARBINES

**SAFARI GRADE**

Crafted in the tradition of the classic British express rifles, Safari Grade is truly a professional's rifle. Every feature has been carefully thought out and executed with one goal in mind: performance. The magazine allows four belted magnums to be stored inside (instead of the usual three). The steel floorplate straddles the front of the trigger guard bow for added strength and security.

An express-style quarter rib provides a rigid, non-glare base for the rear sight, which consists of a fixed blade. The front swivel is carried by a contoured barrel band to keep the stud away from the off-hand under the recoil of big calibers. The front sight assembly is also a barrel-band type for maximum strength. The blade sits on a non-glare ramp, protected by a steel hood.

The Safari's barreled action carries a subtle semi-matte blue, which lends an understated elegance to this eminently practical rifle. The functional, classic-style stock is of European walnut selected especially for its strength of grain orientation as well as for its color and figure. A rosewood forend tip, rosewood pistol grip cap with metal insert suitable for engraving, an elegant, beaded cheekpiece and presentation-style recoil pad complete the stock embellishments.

In **Calibers:** 338 Win. Mag., 375 H&H Mag. and 416 Rem. Mag. See also Specifications Table on page 282.

**Price:** . . . . . . . . . . . . . . . . . . . . . . . . . . . . . . . **$2765.00**

**MANNLICHER-STYLE CARBINE**

SAKO's Mannlicher-style Carbine combines the handiness and carrying qualities of the traditional, lever-action "deer rifle" with the power of modern, high-performance cartridges. An abbreviated 18½-inch barrel trims the overall length of the Carbine to just over 40 inches in the Long Action (L 691) calibers, and 38 inches in the Medium Action (M 591) calibers. Weight is a highly portable 7 pounds and 6½ pounds, respectively (except in the 338 and 375 H&H calibers, which measure 7½ pounds).

As is appropriate for a rifle of this type, the Carbine is furnished with an excellent set of open sights; the rear is fully adjustable for windage, while the front is a non-glare, serrated ramp with protective hood.

The Mannlicher Carbine is available in the traditional wood stock of European walnut done in a contemporary Monte Carlo style with hand-rubbed oil finish. Hand-finished checkering is standard. The Mannlicher-style full stock Carbine wears SAKO's exclusive two-piece forearm, which joins beneath the barrel band and also features an oil finish. This independent forward section of the forearm eliminates the bedding problems normally associated with the full forestock. A blued steel muzzle cap puts the finishing touches on this European-styled Carbine.

**Prices:**
**Medium Action (M 591)**
In 243 Win. and 308 Win. . . . . . . . . . . . . . . . . . **$1275.00**
**Long Action (L 691)**
In 270 Win. and 30-06 . . . . . . . . . . . . . . . . . . . . . **1310.00**
In 338 Win. Mag. . . . . . . . . . . . . . . . . . . . . . . . . . **1335.00**
In 375 H&H Mag. . . . . . . . . . . . . . . . . . . . . . . . . . **1350.00**

# SAKO RIFLES

**MODEL TRG-21**
**$4265.00**

SAKO, known for manufacturing the finest and most accurate production sporting rifles available today, presents the ultimate in sharpshooting systems: the sleek **TRG-21 Target Rifle.** Designed for use when nothing less than total precision is demanded, this new SAKO rifle features a cold-hammer forged receiver, "resistance-free" bolt, stainless-steel barrel and a fully adjustable polyurethane stock. Chambered in .308 Win. A wide selection of optional accessories is also available. Designed, crafted and manufactured in Finland. For additional specifications, see the table on page 282.

• Cold-hammer forged receiver
• "Resistance-free" bolt
• Cold-hammer forged, stainless steel barrel
• Three massive locking lugs
• 60° bolt lift
• Free-floating barrel

• Detachable 10-round magazine
• Fully adjustable cheekpiece
• Infinitely adjustable buttplate
• Adjustable two-stage trigger pull
• Trigger adjustable for both length and pull
• Trigger also adjustable for horizontal or vertical pitch
• Safety lever inside the trigger guard
• Reinforced polyurethane stock

**Optional features:**
• Muzzle brake
• Quick-detachable one-piece scope mount base
• Available with 1″ or 30mm rings
• Collapsible and removable bipod rest
• Quick-detachable sling swivels
• Wide military-type nylon sling

Also available:
**TRG-41** in 338 Lapua Mag. . . . . . . . . . . . . . . **$4825.00**

**MODEL TRG-S**
**$790.00 (Standard Calibers)**
**$830.00 (Magnum Calibers**

The TRG-S has been crafted and designed around SAKO's highly sophisticated and extremely accurate TRG-21 Target Rifle (above). The "resistance-free" bolt and precise balance of the TRG-S, plus its three massive locking lugs and short 60-degree bolt lift, are among the features that attract the shooter's attention. Also of critical importance is the cold-hammer forged receiver—unparalleled for strength and durability. The detachable 5-round magazine fits securely into the polyurethane stock. The stock, in turn, is molded around a synthetic skeleton that provides additional support and maximum rigidity. **Calibers:** *Standard*— 25-06 Rem., 270 Win., 6.5×55, 30-06; *Magnum*— 7mm Rem. Mag., 7mm STW, 270 Wby. Mag., 300 Win. Mag., 300 Wby., 338 Win. Mag., 338 Lapua Mag., 340 Wby. Mag., 375 H&H Mag., 416 Rem. Mag.

For additional specifications, see page 282.

# SAKO RIFLES

## FIBERCLASS MODEL

In answer to the increased demand for SAKO quality and accuracy in a true "all-weather" rifle, this fiberglass-stock version of the renowned SAKO barreled action has been created. Long since proven on the bench rest circuit to be the most stable material for cradling a rifle, fiberglass is extremely strong, light in weight, and unaffected by changes in weather. Because fiberglass is inert, it does not absorb or expel moisture; hence, it cannot swell, shrink or warp. It is impervious to the high humidity of equatorial jungles, the searing heat of arid deserts or the rain and snow of the high mountains. Not only is this rifle lighter than its wood counterpart, it also appeals to the performance-oriented hunter who seeks results over appearance.

**Prices:**
**Long Action (L 691)**
In 25-06 Rem., 270 Win., 280 Rem., 30-06 . . . . . **$1388.00**
In 7mm Rem. Mag., 300 Win. Mag. and
    338 Win. Mag. . . . . . . . . . . . . . . . . . . . . . . . . . 1405.00
In 375 H&H Mag., 416 Rem. Mag. . . . . . . . . . . . 1425.00

## LEFT-HANDED MODELS

SAKO's Left-Handed models are based on mirror images of the right-handed models SAKO owners have enjoyed for years; the handle, extractor and ejection port all are located on the port side. Naturally, the stock is also reversed, with the cheekpiece on the opposite side and the palm swell on the port side of the grip.

Otherwise, these guns are identical to the right-handed models. That means hammer-forged barrels, one-piece bolts with integral locking lugs and handles, integral scope mount rails, adjustable triggers and Mauser-type inertia ejectors.

SAKO's Left-Handed rifles are available in all Long Action models, while the Hunter grade is available in both Medium and Long Action. The Hunter Grade carries a durable matte lacquer finish with generous-size panels of hand-cut checkering, a presentation-style recoil pad and sling swivel studs installed. The Deluxe model is distinguished by its rosewood forend tip and grip cap, its skip-line checkering and gloss lacquer finish atop a select-grade of highly figured European walnut. The metal work carries a deep, mirror-like blue that looks more like black chrome.

**Prices:**
**Hunter Lightweight (Medium Action)**
In 22-250 Rem. 243 Win., 308 Win., 7mm-08 . . . **$1135.00**
**Hunter Lightweight (Long Action)**
In 25-06, 270 Win., 280 Rem. & 30-06 . . . . . . . . 1165.00
In 7mm Rem. Mag., 300 Win. Mag. and
    338 Win. Mag. . . . . . . . . . . . . . . . . . . . . . . . . 1180.00
In 300 Wby. Mag., 375 H&H Mag. and
    416 Rem. Mag. . . . . . . . . . . . . . . . . . . . . . . . . 1200.00

## VARMINT

The SAKO Varmint is specifically designed with a prone-type stock for shooting from the ground or bench. The forend is extra wide to provide added steadiness when rested on sandbags or makeshift field rests.

**Calibers:**
    Short Action—17 Rem., 222 Rem., 223 Rem.
    Medium Action—22-250, 243 Win., 7mm-08,
    308 Win.
**Price:** . . . . . . . . . . . . . . . . . . . . . . . . . . . . . . . . **$1240.00**

# SAKO RIFLES

| | Finnfire* | Hunter** | Classic | Deluxe | TRG-S | TRG-S*** Magnum | Fiberclass | Varmint | Carbine Mannlicher Style | Safari | TRG-21**** | Super Deluxe | Long Range Hunting | Category |
|---|---|---|---|---|---|---|---|---|---|---|---|---|---|---|
| **Action** | | S491, M591, L691, L691, L691 | M591, L691 | S491, M591, L691, L691, L691 | * | * | L691, L691, L691 | S491, M591, L691 | M591, L691, L691 | L691 | * | S491, M591, L691, L691, L691 | L691 | Model |
| **Left-handed** | | ■ | ■ | ■ | | | | | | | | | | |
| **Total length (inches)** | 39½ | 41½, 42½, 44, 46, 46 | 42½, 44 | 41½, 42½, 44, 46, 46 | 45½ | 47½ | 44, 46, 46 | 43½, 43½ | 39½, 40½, 40½ | 44 | 46½ | 41½, 42½, 44, 46, 46 | 48 | Dimensions |
| **Barrel length (inches)** | 22 | 21¼, 21¾, 22, 24, 24 | 21¾, 24 | 21¼, 21¾, 22, 24, 24 | 22 | 24 | 22, 24, 24 | 23, 23 | 18½, 18½, 18½ | 23½ | 25¾ | 21¼, 21¾, 22, 24, 24 | 26 | |
| **Weight (lbs)** | 5¼ | 6¼, 6½, 7¾, 8¼ | 7½ | 6¼, 6½, 7¾, 8¼ | 7¾ | 7¾ | 7¼, 7¼, 8 | 8½, 8½ | 6, 7¼, 7¾ | 8¼ | 10½ | 6¼, 6½, 7¾, 8¼ | 9½ | |
| **17 Rem/10″** | ■ | | | ■ | | | | ■ | | | | ■ | | Caliber/Rate of Twist |
| **22 LR/16.5″ (Finnfire)** | ■ | | | | | | | | | | | | | |
| **222 Rem/14″** | ■ | | | ■ | | | | ■ | | | | ■ | | |
| **223 Rem/12″** | ■ | | | ■ | | | | ■ | | | | ■ | | |
| **22-250 Rem/14″** | ■ | | | ■ | | | | ■ | | | | ■ | | |
| **243 Win/10″** | ■ | | ■ | ■ | | | | | ■ | | | ■ | | |
| **308 Win/12″** | ■ | | | ■ | | | | | ■ | | ■ | ■ | | |
| **7mm-08/9½″** | ■ | | | ■ | | | | ■ | | | | ■ | | |
| **25-06 Rem/10″** | | ■ | | | ■ | | ■ | | | | | ■ | ■ | |
| **270 Win/10″** | | ■ | ■ | ■ | | | | | | | | ■ | ■ | |
| **280 Rem/10″** | | ■ | | ■ | | | ■ | | | | | ■ | | |
| **30-06/10″** | | ■ | ■ | ■ | ■ | | ■ | ■ | | | | ■ | | |
| **7mm/Rem Mag/9½″** | | ■ | | ■ | | | ■ | | | | | ■ | ■ | |
| **300 Win Mag/10″** | | ■ | | ■ | | | ■ | | | | | ■ | ■ | |
| **300 Wby Mag/10″** | | ■ | | ■ | | | ■ | | | | | ■ | | |
| **338 Win Mag/10″** | | ■ | | ■ | | | ■ | | | ■ | | ■ | | |
| **338 Lapua/12″** | | | | | | | | | | | ■ | | | |
| **375 H&H Mag/12″** | | ■ | | ■ | ■ | | ■ | | ■ | ■ | | ■ | | |
| **416 Rem Mag/14″** | | ■ | | | ■ | | | | | ■ | | ■ | ■ | |
| **Lacquered** | | ■ | | ■■■■■ | | | | | | | | ■■■■■ | | Stock Finish |
| **Matte Lacquered** | ■ | ■■■■■ | ■■ | | | | | | | | | | ■ | |
| **Oiled** | | | | | | | | ■■ | ■■■ | ■ | | | | |
| **Reinforced polyurethane** | | | | | ■ | ■ | | | | | ■ | | | |
| **Without sights** | ■ | ■■■■■ | ■■ | ■■■■■ | | | ■■■ | ■■ | | | | ■■■■■ | ■ | Sights |
| **Open sights** | ■ | ■■ | | | | | | | ■■■ | ■ | | | | |
| **Scope mount rails** | ■ | ■■■■■ | ■ | ■■■■■ | ■ | ■ | ■■■ | ■ | ■ | ■ | | ■■■■■ | ■ | |
| **Magazine capacity** | 5*** | 6, 5, 5, 4, 4 | 5, 4 | 4, 4, 5, 5, 6 | 5 | ** | 4, 5, 6 | 5, 6 | 5, 5, 6 | 4 | 10 | 4, 4, 5, 6 | | Mag. |
| **Rubber recoil pad** | ■ | ■■■■■ | ■ | ■■■■■ | | | ■■■ | ■ | ■ | ■ | | ■■■■■ | ■ | Buttplate |

*Also available w/heavy barrel (weight: 7½ lbs.).  
**Also available in 270 Wby. Mag., 7mm Wby. Mag, 340 Wby. Mag.  
***Also available in 6.5 × 55, 270 Wby. Mag., 7mm Wby. Mag., 340 Wby. Mag., 7mm STW (26″ barrel)  
****Available in 338 Lapua Mag. (as Model TRG-41)

# SAKO ACTIONS

Only by building a rifle around a SAKO action do shooters enjoy the choice of three different lengths, each scaled to a specific family of cartridges. The S 491-1 (Short) action is miniaturized in every respect to match the 222 family, which includes everything from 17 Remington to 223 Remington. The M 591 (Medium) action is scaled down to the medium-length cartridges of standard bolt face—22-250, 243, 308, 7mm-08 or similar length cartridges. The L 691 (Long) action is offered in either standard or Magnum bolt face and accommodates cartridges of up to 3.65 inches in overall length, including rounds like the 300 Weatherby and 375 H&H Magnums. **For left-handers, the Medium and Long actions are offered in either standard or Magnum bolt face.** All actions are furnished in-the-white only.

**S 491 SHORT ACTION** (formerly AI-1)
$544.00
CALIBERS:
17 Rem., 222 Rem.
222 Rem. Mag.
223 Rem.

**S 491-PPC SHORT ACTION**
HUNTER: $544.00
$620.00 SINGLE SHOT
CALIBERS:
22 PPC
6 PPC

**M 591 MEDIUM ACTION** (formerly AII-1)
$544.00
CALIBERS:
22-250 Rem. (M 591-3)
243 Win.
308 Win.
7mm-08

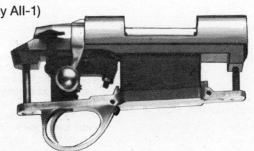

**L 691 LONG ACTION** (formerly AV-4)
$544.00
CALIBERS:
25-06 Rem. (L 691-1)
270 Win. (L 691-1)
280 Rem. (L 691-1)
30-06 (L 691-1)
7mm Rem. Mag. (L 691-4)
300 Win. Mag. (L 691-4)
300 Wby. Mag. (L 691-4)
338 Win. Mag. (L 691-4)
375 H&H Mag. (L 691-4)
416 Rem. Mag. (L 691-4)

Also available:
**LEFT-HANDED ACTIONS**
Medium and Long: $582.00

# SAUER RIFLES

**MODEL 90**

## MODEL 90
### $1595.00 (Standard)   $1649.00 (Magnum)

**SPECIFICATIONS**
**Calibers:** 243 Win., 25-06, 270, 30-06, 308 Win.; *Supreme Magnum calibers:* 7mm Rem. Mag., 300 Win. Mag., 300 Wby. Mag. and 375 H&H
**Barrel length:** 23.6"; 26" (Supreme Magnum)
**Overall length:** 42.5"; 46.5" (Supreme Magnum)
**Weight:** 7.5 lbs.; 7.7 lbs. (Supreme Magnum)
**Sights:** None furnished; drilled and tapped for scope mount

**Stock:** Monte Carlo cut with sculptured cheekpiece, hand-checkered pistol grip and forend, rosewood pistol grip cap and forend tip, black rubber recoil pad, and fully in-letted sling swivel studs.
**Features:** Rear bolt cam-activated locking lug action; jeweled bolt with an operating angle of 65°; fully adjustable gold-plated trigger; chamber loaded signal pin; cocking indicator; tang-mounted slide safety with button release; bolt release button (to operate bolt while slide safety is engaged); detachable 3 or 4-round box magazine; sling side scope mounts; leather sling (extra)

**MODEL 90 ENGRAVING #2**

## MODEL 202 BOLT ACTION (not shown)
### $950.00   $1050.00 (Magnum)

**SPECIFICATIONS**
**Calibers:** 243 Win., 270 Win., 308., 30-06 S'field; *Supreme Magnum calibers:* 7mm Rem. Mag., 300 Win. Mag., 375 Win. Mag.
**Action:** Bolt takedown
**Capacity:** 3 rounds
**Barrel lengths:** 23.6"; 26" (Supreme Magnum)
**Overall length:** 44.3"; 46" (Supreme Magnum)

**Weight:** 7.7 lbs.; 8.4 lbs. (Supreme Magnum)
**Stock:** Select American claro walnut with high-gloss epoxy finish and rosewood forend and grip caps; Monte Carlo comb with checkpiece; 22 line-per- inch diamond pattern, hand-cut checking
**Sights:** Drilled and tapped for sights and scope bases
**Features:** Adjustable two-stage trigger; polished and jeweled bolt; quick-change barrel; tapered bore; QD sling swivel studs; black rubber recoil pad; Wundhammer palm swell; dual release safety; six locking lugs on bolt head; removable box magazine; fully enclosed bolt face; three gas relief holes; firing-pin cocking indicator on bolt rear

**SAUER .458 SAFARI**

## SAUER .458 SAFARI

The Sauer .458 Safari features a rear bolt cam-activated locking-lug action with a low operating angle of 65°. It has a gold plated trigger, jeweled bolt, oil finished bubinga stock and deep luster bluing. Safety features include a press bottom slide safety that engages the trigger sear, toggle joint and bolt. The bolt release feature allows the sportsman to unload the rifle while the safety remains engaged to the trigger sear and toggle joint. The Sauer Safari is equipped with a chamber loaded signal pin for positive identification. Specifications include: **Barrel Length:** 24" (heavy barrel contour). **Overall length:** 44". **Weight:** 10 lb. 6 oz. **Sights:** Williams open sights (sling swivels included). **$1995.00**

# SAVAGE RIFLES

## MODEL 93 FSS "ALL WEATHER"
### $175.00

**SPECIFICATIONS**
**Caliber:** 22 WMR. **Capacity:** 5 shots. **Barrel length:** 20.75" (1 in 16 twist). **Overall length:** 39.5". **Weight:** 5.5 lbs. **Sights:** Front bead sight; sporting rear sight w/step elevator. **Fea-** tures: Precision button-rifled, free-floated barrel; black graphite/polymer filled stock w/positive checkering on grip and forend; corrosion and rust-resistant stainless steel barreled action.

## MODEL 93G MAGNUM
### $145.00

**SPECIFICATIONS**
**Caliber:** 22 WMR. **Capacity:** 5-shot clip. **Barrel length:** 20 3/4". **Overall length:** 39 1/2". **Weight:** 5 3/4 lbs. **Stock:** Cut- checkered walnut-stained hardwood. **Sights:** Bead front; sporting rear with step elevator. **Feature:** Free-floated precision button rifling.

## MODEL 99C LEVER ACTION
### $665.00

Clip magazine allows for the chambering of pointed, high-velocity big-bore cartridges. **Calibers:** 243 Win., 308 Win. **Action:** Hammerless, lever action, top tang safety. **Magazine:** Detachable clip; holds 4 rounds plus 1 in the chamber. **Stock:** Select walnut with high Monte Carlo and deep-fluted comb. Cut-checkered stock and forend with swivel studs. Recoil pad and pistol grip cap. **Sights:** Detachable hooded ramp front sight, bead front sight on removable ramp adjustable rear sight. Tapped for top mount scopes. **Barrel length:** 22". **Overall length:** 42 3/4". **Weight:** 7 3/4 lbs.

## MODEL 110 FP TACTICAL
### $429.00

**SPECIFICATIONS**
**Calibers:** 223 Rem., 25-06 Rem., 30-06 Spfd., 308 Win., 7mm Rem. Mag., 300 Win. Mag.
**Capacity:** 5 rounds (1 in chamber)
**Barrel length:** 24" (w/recessed target-style muzzle)
**Overall length:** 45 1/2"
**Weight:** 8 1/2 lbs.
**Sights:** None; drilled and tapped for scope mount
**Features:** Black matte nonreflective finish on metal parts; bolt coated with titanium nitride; stock made of black graphite/fiberglass-filled composite with positive checkering; left-hand model available
Also available:
**MODEL 110CY. Calibers:** 223 Rem., 243 Win., 270 Win., 308 Win. **Capacity:** 5 rounds (1 in chamber); top-loading internal magazine. **Barrel length:** 22" blued. **Overall length:** 42 1/2". **Weight:** 6 3/8 lbs. **Sights:** Adjustable: drilled and tapped for scope mounts. **Stock:** High comb, walnut-stained hardwood w/cut checkering and short pull.
**Price:** . . . . . . . . . . . . . . . . . . . . . . . . . . . . . . . . . **$360.00**

# SAVAGE RIFLES

### MODEL 111GC CLASSIC HUNTER
### $410.00

**SPECIFICATIONS**
**Calibers:** 270 Win., 30-06 Springfield, 7mm Rem. Mag., 300 Win. Mag.
**Capacity:** 5 rounds (4 rounds in Magnum calibers)
**Overall length:** 43$\frac{1}{2}$" (45$\frac{1}{2}$" Magnum calibers)
**Weight:** 6$\frac{3}{8}$–7 lbs.

**Sights:** Adjustable
**Stock:** American-style walnut-finished hardwood; cut checkering
**Features:** Detachable staggered box-type magazine; left-hand model available

### MODEL 111FC CLASSIC HUNTER
### $420.00

Same specifications as Classic Hunter above, except stock is lightweight graphite/fiberglass-filled composite w/positive checkering. Left-hand model available. **Calibers:** 270 Win., 30-06 Spfld., 7mm Rem. Mag. and 300 Win. Mag.

### MODEL 111G CLASSIC HUNTER
### $360.00

Same specifications as Model 111GC Classic Hunter, except available also in **calibers** 22-250 Rem., 223 Rem., 243 Win., 25-06, 270 Win., 7mm-08, 7mm Rem. Mag., 30-06 Sprgfld., 300 Win. Mag., 308. Stock is American-style walnut-finished hardwood with cut-checkering. Lef-hand model available.

### MODEL 111F CLASSIC HUNTER
### $380.00

Same specifications as Model 111G Classic Hunter, except stock is black nonglare graphite/fiberglass-filled polymer with positive checkering. Left-hand model available.

# SAVAGE CENTERFIRE RIFLES

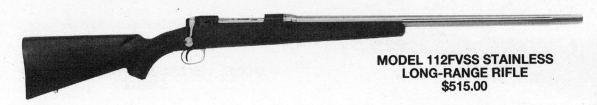

### MODEL 112FVSS STAINLESS LONG-RANGE RIFLE
### $515.00

### MODEL 112BVSS VARMINT
### $535.00 (not shown)

**SPECIFICATIONS**
**Calibers:** 22-250 Rem., 223 Rem., 25-06 Rem., 30-06, 308 Win., 7mm Rem. Mag., 300 Win. Mag. (single-shot model available in 220 Swift, 22-250, 223 Rem., 300 Win. Mag.)
**Capacity:** 4+1
**Barrel length:** 26″ fluted, stainless steel
**Overall length:** 47 1/2″
**Weight:** 8 7/8 lbs.
**Sights:** Graphite/fiberglass-filled composite w/positve checkering
Also available:
**MODEL 112FV** in 223 Rem. and 22-250 only w/blued barrel

**SPECIFICATIONS**
**Calibers:** 22-250 Rem., 223 Rem., 25-06, 7mm Rem. Mag., 300 Win Mag., 30-06 Sprgfld., 308 Win. (single-shot model also available in 220 Swift, 22-250, 223 Rem., 300 Win. Mag.)
**Capacity:** 4+1
**Barrel length:** 26″ fluted heavy barrel, stainless steel
**Overall length:** 47 1/2″    **Weight:** 10 lbs. (approx.)
**Sights:** None; drilled and tapped
**Stock:** Laminated hardwood w/high comb; ambidextrous grip

### MODEL 112FV VARMINT
### w/Graphite Fiberglass Polymer Stock
### $410.00

### MODEL 112 BT COMPETITION GRADE
### $1000.00

**SPECIFICATIONS**
**Calibers:** 223 Rem. and 308 Win. Mag. (single-shot available in 300 Win. Mag.)
**Capacity:** 5+1

**Barrel length:** 26″; blackened stainless steel w/recessed target-style muzzle
**Overall length:** 47 1/2″   **Weight:** 10 7/8 lbs.
**Stock:** Laminated brown w/straight comb

### MODEL 114CE "CLASSIC EUROPEAN"
### $600.00

**SPECIFICATIONS**
**Calibers:** 270 Win., 30-06 Sprgfld., 7mm Rem. Mag., 300 Win. Mag.
**Capacity:** 3 rounds (magnum); 4 rounds (standard); plus 1 in each chamber
**Barrel length:** 22″ (standard); 24″ (magnum)
**Overall length:** 43 1/2″ (standard); 45 1/2″ (magnum)

**Weight:** 7 1/8 lbs. (approx.)
**Finish:** Oil-finished walnut stock w/schnabel tip, cheekpiece and French skip-line checkering on grip and forend
**Features:** Rubber recoil pad; pistol-grip cap with gold medallion; high-luster blued finish on receiver barrel and bolt handle; side button release; adjustable metal sights; precision rifled barrel; drilled and tapped

**RIFLES**

# SAVAGE CENTERFIRE RIFLES

### MODEL 116FSS "WEATHER WARRIOR"
### $495.00

Savage Arms combines the strength of a black graphite fiberglass polymer stock and the durability of a stainless-steel barrel and receiver in this bolt-action rifle. Major components are made from stainless steel, honed to a low reflective satin finish. Drilled and tapped for scope mounts. Left-hand model available.

**SPECIFICATIONS**
**Calibers:** 223, 243, 270, 30-06, 308 Win., 7mm Rem Mag., 300 Win. Mag., 338 Win. Mag.
**Capacity:** 4 (7mm Rem. Mag., 300 Win. Mag., 338 Win. Mag.); 5 (223, 243, 270, 30-06)
**Barrel length:** 22" (223, 243, 270, 30-06); 24" (7mm Rem. Mag., 300 Win. Mag., 338 Win. Mag.)
**Overall length:** 43 1/2"–45 1/2"   **Weight:** 6 1/2 lbs.

### MODEL 116FCS "WEATHER WARRIOR"
### $560.00

**Calibers:** 270, 30-06, 300 Win. Mag. This bolt-action rifle has the same quality features as the Model 116FSS plus a removable box magazine with recessed push-button release for ease in loading and unloading. Left-hand model available.

### MODEL 116SE SAFARI EXPRESS
### $900.00

**SPECIFICATIONS**
**Calibers:** 300 Win. Mag., 338, 458 Win. Mag.
**Capacity:** 4 rounds (1 in chamber)
**Barrel length:** 24" stainless steel w/AMB
**Overall length:** 45 1/2"   **Weight:** 8 1/2 lbs.

**Sights:** 3-leaf express
**Stock:** Classic-style select-grade walnut w/cut checkering; ebony tip; stainless-steel crossbolts; internally vented recoil pad

### MODEL 116FSK "WEATHER WARRIOR"
### $554.00

Features a compact barrel with "shock suppressor" that reduces average linear recoil by more than 30% without loss of Magnum stopping power. Left-hand model available.

**SPECIFICATIONS**
**Calibers:** 270 Win., 30-06 Sprg., 7mm Rem. Mag., 300 Win. Mag., 338 Win. Mag.

**Capacity:** 5 rounds (4 in Magnum)
**Barrel length:** 22"   **Overall length:** 43 1/2"
**Weight:** 7 lbs.

Also available:
**MODEL 116FSAK.** Same specifications as above except includes adj. muzzle brake. **Price:** . . . . . . . . . . . . . $585.00

# SAVAGE SPORTING RIFLES

**MODEL 900S SILHOUETTE**

## SPECIFICATIONS

| MODEL | 900B BIATHLON | 900S SILHOUETTE |
|---|---|---|
| **Caliber** | 22 Long Rifle Only | 22 Long Rifle |
| **Capacity** | 5-shot metal magazine | 5-shot metal magazine |
| **Action** | Self-cocking bolt action, thumb-operated rotary safety | Self-cocking bolt action, thumb-operated rotary safety |
| **Stock** | One-piece target-type stock with natural finish hardwood; comes with clip holder, carrying & shooting rails, butt hook and hand stop | One-piece high comb, target-type with walnut finish hardwood |
| **Barrel Length** | 21″ w/snow cover | 21″ |
| **Sights** | Receiver peep sights with 1/4 min. click micrometer adjustments; target front sight with inserts | None (receiver drilled and tapped for scope base) |
| **Overall Length** | 39⁵/₈″ | 39⁵/₈″ |
| **Approx. Weight** | 8¼ lbs. | 8 lbs. |
| **Price** | **$498.00** | **$346.00** |

**MODEL 64F SEMIAUTO**
**$145.00**

**SPECIFICATIONS**
**Caliber:** 22 LR
**Capacity:** 10 shots
**Action:** Semiautomatic side-ejecting
**Barrel length:** 20.25″ (1 in 16″ twist)
**Overall length:** 40″

**Weight:** 5.5 lbs.
**Sights:** Front bead; adjustable open rear
**Finish:** Matte blue
**Stock:** Black graphite/polymer synthetic
**Features:** Detachable clip magazine; free-floated precision button-rifled barrel;

**MODEL 64G SEMIAUTO**
**$123.00**

**SPECIFICATIONS**
**Caliber:** 22 LR
**Capacity:** 10-shot clip
**Action:** Semiautomatic side-ejecting
**Barrel length:** 20.25″    **Overall length:** 40″
**Weight:** 5.5 lbs.

**Sights:** Open bead front; adjustable rear
**Stock:** One-piece, walnut-finish hardwood, Monte Carlo buttstock w/full pistol grip; checkered pistol grip and for-end
**Features:** Bolt hold-open device; thumb-operated rotary safety

# SAVAGE SPORTING RIFLES

## MARK SERIES

**MARK I-G SINGLE SHOT**
**$119.00**

**SPECIFICATIONS**
**Caliber:** 22 Short, Long or LR
**Capacity:** Single shot
**Action:** Self-cocking bolt action, thumb-operated rotary safety
**Barrel length:** 20.75"
**Overall length:** 39.5"
**Weight:** 5.5 lbs.

**Sights:** Open bead front; adjustable rear
**Stock:** One-piece, walnut-finish hardwood, Monte Carlo buttstock w/full pistol grip; checkered pistol grip and forend
**Features:** Receiver grooved for scope mounting
Also available:
**MARK I-G "Smoothbore"** (20³/₄" barrel) . . . . . . . . **$119.00**
**MARK I-G Youth** (19" barrel). . . . . . . . . . . . . . . . . 119.00

**MARK II-FSS**
**$150.00**

**SPECIFICATIONS**
**Caliber:** 22 LR
**Capacity:** 10-shot clip
**Barrel length:** 20.75" (1 in 16" twist)
**Overall length:** 39.5"
**Weight:** 5 lbs.
**Stock:** Synthetic
**Sights:** Bead front sight; adjustable open rear
**Features:** Stainless steel barreled action

Also available:
**MARK II-G** w/one-piece walnut-finished Monte Carlo-style hardwood stock, blued steel bolt-action receiver, bead front sight . . . . . . . . . . . . . . . . . . . . . . . . . . . . . **$126.00**
**MARK II-GY LADIES/YOUTH** w/19" barrel (37" overall).
Weight: 5 lbs. . . . . . . . . . . . . . . . . . . . . . . . . . . . 126.00
**MARK II-GXP** w/4×15mm scope (LH model avail.) . . . . . . . . . . . . . . . . . . . . . . . . . . . . . . . . . 131.00

**MARK II-LV**
**$200.00**

**SPECIFICATIONS**
**Caliber:** 22 LR
**Capacity:** 10-shot
**Barrel length:** 21" heavy barrel (1 in 16" twist)
**Overall length:** 39.75"

**Weight:** 6.5 lbs.
**Stock:** Grey laminated hardwood stock; cut-checkered
**Features:** Precision button rifled with recessed target-style muzzle; machined blued steel barreled action; dovetailed for scope mounting

# SAVAGE SPORTING RIFLES

## MODEL 900TR TARGET REPEATER
### $415.00

**SPECIFICATIONS**
**Caliber:** 22 Long Rifle
**Capacity:** 5-shot clip magazine
**Action:** Self-cocking bolt action, thumb-operated rotary safety
**Overall Length:** 43⅝″

**Approx. Weight:** 8 lbs.
**Stock:** One-piece, target-type with walnut finish hardwood; comes with shooting rail and hand stop
**Sights:** Receiver peep sights with ¼ min. click micrometer adjustments, target front sight with inserts

## SAVAGE MODEL 24F COMBINATION RIFLE/SHOTGUN
### $400.00

## SPECIFICATIONS MODEL 24F COMBINATION RIFLE/SHOTGUN

| O/U Comb. Model | Gauge/ Caliber | Choke | Chamber | Barrel Length | O.A. Length | Twist R.H. | Stock |
|---|---|---|---|---|---|---|---|
| 24F-20 24F-12 | 20/22 LR | 20 gauge: Modified Barrel 12 gauge: 3 Chokes | 3″ | 24″ | 40½″ | 1 in 14″ | Black Graphite Fiberglass Polymer |
| | 12 or 20/22 Hornet | | | | | 1 in 14″ | |
| | 12 or 20/223 | | | | | 1 in 14″ | |
| | 12 or 20/30-30 | | | | | 1 in 12″ | |

# SPRINGFIELD RIFLES

**M1A STANDARD**

### SPECIFICATIONS
**Calibers:** 308 Win./7.62mm NATO (243 or 7mm-08 optional)
**Capacity:** 5- or 10-round box magazine
**Barrel length:** 22"  **Rifling:** 6 groove, RH twist, 1 turn in 11"
**Overall length:** 44¹/₃"  **Weight:** 9.2 lbs.
**Sights:** Military square post front; military aperture rear, adjustable for windage and elevation
**Sight radius:** 26³/₄"
**Prices:**
Standard w/walnut stock . . . . . . . . . . . . . . . . . . . **$1381.00**
w/Brown laminated stock. . . . . . . . . . . . . . . . . . **1466.00**

w/Black laminated stock . . . . . . . . . . . . . . . . . . . **$1440.00**
w/Camo fiberglass stock . . . . . . . . . . . . . . . . . . **1249.00**

Also available:
**BASIC M1A RIFLE** w/painted black fiberglass stock, caliber 308 only. **$1199.00**; w/bipod and stabilizer **$1381.00**
**M1A SCOUT RIFLE** w/scope mount and handguard, black fiberglass stock . . . . . . . . . . . . . . . . . . . . . . **$1459.00**
w/Walnut stock. . . . . . . . . . . . . . . . . . . . . . . . . . **1479.00**
w/G.I. collector stock . . . . . . . . . . . . . . . . . . . . . **1449.00**
w/Black laminated stock . . . . . . . . . . . . . . . . . . . **1499.00**

**M1A NATIONAL MATCH**

### SPECIFICATIONS
**Caliber:** 308 Win.
**Barrel length:** 22"
**Overall length:** 44.375"
**Trigger pull:** 4¹/₂ lbs.
**Weight:** 10.8 lbs.
**Features:** Comes with National Match barrel, flash suppressor, gas cylinder, special glass-bedded walnut stock and match-tuned trigger assembly.
**Price:** . . . . . . . . . . . . . . . . . . . . . . . . . . . . . . . . . . **$1729.00**
Also available:
**M1A SUPER MATCH.** Heavy match barrel and permanently attached figure-8-style operating rod guide, plus heavy walnut match stock, longer pistol grip and contoured area behind rear sight for better grip; 11.2 lbs. . . . . . . . . . **$2050.00**

**M1A-A1 BUSH RIFLE**

### SPECIFICATIONS
**Calibers:** 308 Win./7.62mm
**Barrel length:** 18" (w/o flash suppressor)
**Overall length:** 40.5"
**Weight:** 8.9 lbs.  **Sight radius:** 22.75"

**Prices:**
w/Walnut stock. . . . . . . . . . . . . . . . . . . . . . . . . . **$1410.00**
w/Black fiberglass stock . . . . . . . . . . . . . . . . . . . **1396.00**
w/Black laminated stock . . . . . . . . . . . . . . . . . . . **1466.00**

# SPRINGFIELD RIFLES

## MODEL SAR-8 SPORTER RIFLE
### $1204.00

**SPECIFICATIONS**
**Caliber:** 7.62mm
**Barrel length:** 18″ (1:12″ twist, 4-groove)
**Overall length:** 40.38″
**Weight:** 10.6 lbs.

**Sights:** Protected front post; rotary-style adjustable rear aperture
**Features:** Recoil-operated w/delayed roller-lock locking system; synthetic thumbhole stock
Also available:
**SAR-8 HEAVY BARREL TACTICAL RIFLE** . . . . . **$1610.00**

## MODEL SAR-4800 SPORTER RIFLE
### $1249.00

**SPECIFICATIONS**
**Caliber:** 7.62mm, 5.56mm
**Barrel length:** 21″ (7.62mm); 18″ (5.56mm)
**Overall length:** 43.3″ (7.62mm); 38.25″ (5.56mm)
**Weight:** 11.1 lbs. (7.62mm); 10.45 lbs. (5.56mm)

**Sights:** Protected front post; adjustable rear
**Features:** Forged receiver and bolt; hammer-forged chrome-lined barrel; adjustable gas system; synthetic thumbhole stock

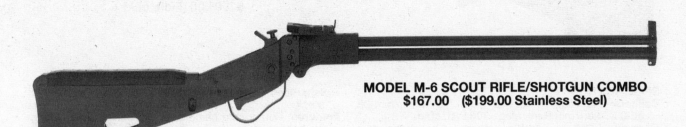

## MODEL M-6 SCOUT RIFLE/SHOTGUN COMBO
### $167.00   ($199.00 Stainless Steel)

**SPECIFICATIONS**
**Calibers:** 22 LR/.410 and 22 Hornet/.410
**Barrel length:** 18.25″ (1:15″ R.H. twist in 22 LR; 1:13″ R.H. twist in 22 Hornet)
**Overall length:** 32″

**Weight:** 4 lbs.
**Finish:** Parkerized or stainless steel
**Features:** .410 shotgun barrel (2¹/₂″ or 3″ chamber) choked Full; drilled and tapped for scope mount with Weaver base; lockable plastic carry case (**$24.00**)

# STEYR-MANNLICHER RIFLES

**STEYR SSG-PI**

**SSG-PII (w/26″ Barrel)**

The Steyr SSG features a black synthetic Cycolac stock (walnut optional), heavy Parkerized barrel, five-round standard (and optional 10-round) staggered magazine, heavy-duty milled receiver. **Calibers:** 243 Win. and 308 Win. **Barrel length:** 26″. **Overall length:** 44.5″. **Weight:** 8.5 lbs. **Sights:** Iron sights; hooded ramp front with blade adjustable for elevation; rear standard V-notch adjustable for windage. **Features:** Sliding safety; 1″ swivels.

**Prices:**
**Model SSG-PI** Cycolac half-stock (26″ bbl. with sights in 308 Win.) . . . . . . . . . . . . . . . . . . . . . . **$2195.00**
**Model SSG-PII** (20″ or 26″ heavy bbl. in 308 Win.) . . . . . . . . . . . . . . . . . . . . . . . . . . . . . . . . 2195.00
**Model SSG P-IV Urban** in 308 Win. w/16³/₄″ heavy barrel . . . . . . . . . . . . . . . . . . . . . . 2660.00
**Model SSG Scope Mount** (1″) . . . . . . . . . . . . . . . 244.00

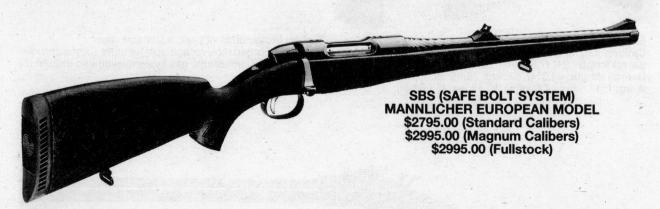

**SBS (SAFE BOLT SYSTEM)
MANNLICHER EUROPEAN MODEL**
**$2795.00** (Standard Calibers)
**$2995.00** (Magnum Calibers)
**$2995.00** (Fullstock)

**SPECIFICATIONS**
**Calibers:** 243 Win., 25-06, 308 Win., 270 Win., 7mm-08, 30-06 S'fld, 7mm Rem. Mag., 300 Win. Mag.
**Capacity:** 4 rounds; detachable staggered box magazine
**Barrel lengths:** 23.6″; 26″ (magnum calibers); 20″ (fullstock standard calibers)
**Overall length:** 40″
**Weight:** 7 lbs.
**Safety:** 3-position roller safety
**Trigger:** Single adjustable trigger
**Sights:** Ramp front w/black adjustment for elevations; rear standard V-notch adjustable for windage; drilled and tapped for mounts

**Finish:** Blued; hand-checkered fancy European oiled walnut stock
**Features:** Rotary cold hammer-forged barrel; front locking lug bolt

Also available:
**Steyr SBS Prohunter** in 243 Win., 25-06, 7mm-08 Rem., 308 Win. w/synthetic half stock; no sights . . . . . . . . . . . . . . . . . . . . . . . . . . . . . . . . . . . . **$799.00**
**Steyr Magnum Model** in 300 Win. Mag. only w/25.6″ barrel . . . . . . . . . . . . . . . . . . . . . . . . . . . . 899.00
**Steyr SBS Forester** in 243 Win, 25-06, 270 Win., 7mm-08 Rem., 308 Win., 30-06 w/23.6″ bbl. . . . 929.00

**THE CONTENDER CARBINE**
**$460.00**

Available in 7 **calibers:** 17 Rem., 22 LR Match, 22 Hornet, 223 Rem., 7×30 Waters, 30-30 Win. and 375 Win. **Barrels:** 21 inches, interchangeable. Adjustable iron sights; tapped and drilled for scope mounts. **Weight:** 5 lbs. 3 oz.
Also available:
**Contender Vent Rib Carbine**
With standard walnut stock in 22 Hornet, 223 Rem. 7×30 Waters, 30-30 Win., 375 Win. . . . . . . . . . **$515.00**

**Contender Vent Rib Carbine (cont.)**
With 21″ 17 Rem. barrel . . . . . . . . . . . . . . . . . . . . . **$546.00**
In .410 smoothbore . . . . . . . . . . . . . . . . . . . . . . 535.60
**Contender Youth Model Carbine**
22 LR & 223 Rem., 16¼″ bbl., walnut Youth
stock . . . . . . . . . . . . . . . . . . . . . . . . . . . . . . . . . . **479.00**
**Contender Carbine**
With Match Grade 22 LR barrel . . . . . . . . . . . . . . . 525.00

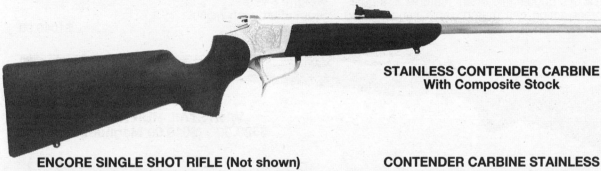

**STAINLESS CONTENDER CARBINE**
**With Composite Stock**

**ENCORE SINGLE SHOT RIFLE (Not shown)**

Available in **calibers:** 22-250 Rem., 223 Rem., 243 Win., 270 Win., 7mm-08 Rem., 30-06, 308 Win., 7mm Rem. Mag., 300 Win. Mag. **Barrels:** 24″; 26″ heavy barrel. **Overall length:** 38.5″ (w/24″ barrel). **Weight:** 6 lbs. 12 oz. (7mm-08 w/24″ barrel). **Stock:** Monte Carlo-style American walnut w/pistol grip. **Finish:** Blued. . . . . . . . . . . . . . . . . . . . . . . . . . **$535.00**
Barrel only . . . . . . . . . . . . . . . . . . . . . . . . . . . . . . 235.00

**CONTENDER CARBINE STAINLESS**

Available in 22 LR Match, 22 Hornet, 223 Rem., 7×30 Waters, 30-30 Win., 375 Win., and .410 bore. Same specifications as standard model, with walnut or composite stock. All stainless-steel components interchange readily with blued components (barrels and frames can be mixed or matched).
**Prices:**
**Stainless Carbine, Standard** . . . . . . . . . . . . . . . . . **$509.00**
In 22 LR Match . . . . . . . . . . . . . . . . . . . . . . . . . . . . . 520.00
**Stainless Carbine w/vent rib** (.410 ga.) . . . . . . . . . 535.50

**CONTENDER CONVERSION KIT**
**(Pistol-to-Carbine)**

Available in 22 LR Match, 22 Hornet, 223 Rem., 30-30 Win. and .410 smoothbore. Each kit contains a buttstock, blued 21″ barrel, forend and sights.
**Prices:**
**Walnut stock** . . . . . . . . . . . . . . . . . . . . . . . . . . . . **$309.00**

In 22 LR Match . . . . . . . . . . . . . . . . . . . . . . . . . . . . . **$319.50**
**Composite stock,** stainless steel barrel . . . . . . . . . 329.50
In 22 LR Match . . . . . . . . . . . . . . . . . . . . . . . . . . . . . 340.00
In .410 smoothbore . . . . . . . . . . . . . . . . . . . . . . . . . 355.50

# TIKKA RIFLES

## MODEL 512S DOUBLE RIFLE
### $1890.00

The renowned Valmet 512S line of fine firearms is now being produced under the TIKKA brand name and is being manufactured to the same specifications as the former Valmet. As a result of a joint venture entered into by SAKO Ltd., the production facilities for these firearms are now located in Italy. The manufacture of the 512S series is controlled under the rigid quality standards of SAKO Ltd., with complete interchangeability of parts between firearms produced in Italy and Finland. TIKKA's double rifle offers features and qualities no other action can match: rapid handling and pointing qualities and the silent, immediate availability of a second shot. As such, this model overcomes the two major drawbacks usually associated with this type of firearm: price and accuracy. Automatic ejectors on 9.3×74R only.

**SPECIFICATIONS**
**Calibers:** 308 Win., 30-06, 9.3×74R
**Barrel length:** 24″
**Overall length:** 40″
**Weight:** 8½ lbs.
**Stock:** European walnut
**Barrel sets only:** ......................... **$1040.00**

## WHITETAIL HUNTER
### $589.00    ($619.00 Magnum)

**SPECIFICATIONS**
**Calibers:** 22-250, 223, 243, 308 (Medium); 25-06, 270, 30-06 (Long); 7mm Mag., 300 Win. Mag., 338 Win. Mag.
**Capacity:** 3 rounds (5 rounds optional); detachable magazine
**Barrel length:** 22½″ (24½″ Magnum)
**Overall length:** 42″ (Medium); 42½″ (Long); 44½″ (Magnum)

**Weight:** 7 lbs. (Medium); 7¼ lbs. (Long); 7½ lbs. (Magnum)
**Sights:** No sights; integral scope mount rails; drilled and tapped
**Safety:** Locks trigger and bolt handle
**Features:** Oversized trigger guard; short bolt throw; customized spacer system; walnut stock with palm swell and matte lacquer finish; cold hammer-forged barrel

## WHITETAIL HUNTER SYNTHETIC
### $589.00   $619.00 (Magnum)

Same specifications as the standard Whitetail Hunter, except with All-Weather synthetic stock.

Also available:
**WHITETAIL HUNTER STAINLESS SYNTHETIC.**
Same specifications as above, except with stainless steel receiver, barrel and bolt .............. **$649.00**
In Magnum calibers ...................... 679.00

# TIKKA RIFLES

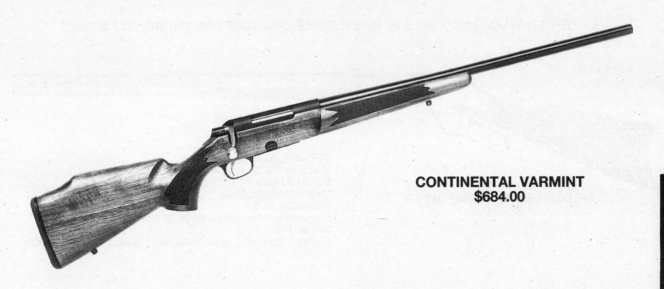

## CONTINENTAL VARMINT
### $684.00

**SPECIFICATIONS**
**Calibers:** 22-250, 223, 308
**Capacity:** 3 rounds (5 rounds optional)
**Barrel length:** 26″
**Overall length:** 46″
**Weight:** 8 lbs. 10 oz.

**Finish:** Matte lacquer walnut stock w/palm swell
**Features:** Recoil pad spacer system; quick-release detachable magazine; beavertail forend; cold hammer-forged barrel; integral scope mount rails; adjustable trigger

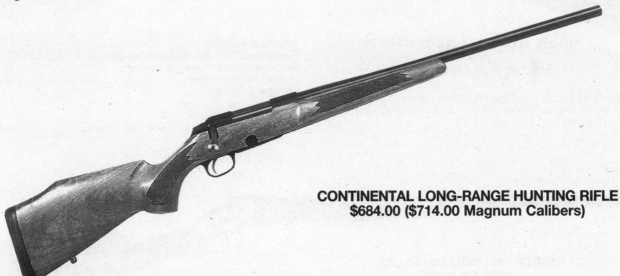

## CONTINENTAL LONG-RANGE HUNTING RIFLE
### $684.00 ($714.00 Magnum Calibers)

**SPECIFICATIONS**
**Calibers:** 25-06 Rem., 270 Win., 7mm Rem. Mag., 300 Win. Mag.
**Capacity:** 3 rounds (5 rounds in standard calibers, 4 rounds in magnum calibers)

**Barrel length:** 26″ heavy barrel
**Overall length:** 46.5″
**Weight:** 8 lbs. 12 oz.
**Finish:** Matte lacquer walnut stock w/palm swell
**Features:** Same as Continental Varmint model

# UBERTI REPLICAS

ALL UBERTI FIREARMS AVAILABLE IN SUPER GRADE, PRESTIGE AND ENGRAVED FINISHES

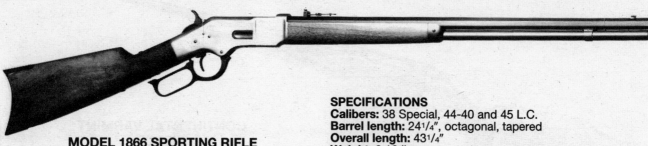

### MODEL 1866 SPORTING RIFLE
### $840.00

**SPECIFICATIONS**
**Calibers:** 38 Special, 44-40 and 45 L.C.
**Barrel length:** 24¹/₄", octagonal, tapered
**Overall length:** 43¹/₄"
**Weight:** 8.16 lbs.
**Frame:** Elevator and buttplate in brass
**Stock:** Walnut
**Sights:** Vertically adjustable rear; horizontally adjustable front

### MODEL 1866 YELLOWBOY CARBINE
### $760.00
### $820.00 in 22 LR or 22 Mag.

The first gun to carry the Winchester name, this model was born as the 44-caliber rimfire cartridge Henry and is now chambered for 22 LR and 44-40.

**SPECIFICATIONS**
**Calibers:** 22 LR, 22 Magnum, 38 Special, 44-40, 45 L.C.
**Barrel length:** 19", round, tapered
**Overall length:** 38¹/₄"
**Weight:** 7.380 lbs.
**Frame:** Brass
**Stock and forend:** Walnut
**Sights:** Vertically adjustable rear; horizontally adjustable front

### MODEL 1871 ROLLING BLOCK
### BABY CARBINE
### $490.00

**SPECIFICATIONS**
**Calibers:** 22 LR, 22 Hornet, 22 Magnum, 357 Magnum
**Barrel length:** 22"
**Overall length:** 35¹/₂"
**Weight:** 4.85 lbs.

**Stock & forend:** Walnut
**Trigger guard:** Brass
**Sights:** Fully adjustable rear; ramp front
**Frame:** Color-casehardened steel

# UBERTI REPLICAS

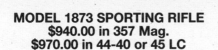

### MODEL 1873 SPORTING RIFLE
**$940.00 in 357 Mag.**
**$970.00 in 44-40 or 45 LC**

**SPECIFICATIONS**
**Calibers:** 357 Magnum, 44-40 and 45 LC. Hand-checkered.
    Other specifications same as Model 1866 Sporting Rifle.
    Also available with 24¼″ or 30″ octagonal barrel and pis-
    tol-grip stock (extra).
Also available with pistol grip. . . . . . . . . . . . . . . . . $1020.00
    With pistol grip and 30″ barrel . . . . . . . . . . . . .  **1050.00**

### 1873 CARBINE
**$920.00 in 357 Mag.**
**$900.00 in 44-40 or 45 LC**

**SPECIFICATIONS**
**Calibers:** 357 Mag., 44-40, 45 LC
**Barrel length:** 19″ round, tapered
**Overall length:** 38¼″
**Weight:** 7.38 lbs.
**Sights:** Fixed front; vertically adjustable rear

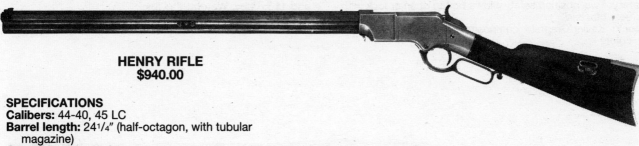

### HENRY RIFLE
**$940.00**

**SPECIFICATIONS**
**Calibers:** 44-40, 45 LC
**Barrel length:** 24¼″ (half-octagon, with tubular
    magazine)
**Overall length:** 43¾″
**Weight:** 9.26 lbs.
**Frame:** Brass
**Stock:** Varnished American walnut

### HENRY CARBINE (not shown)
**$950.00**

**SPECIFICATIONS**
**Caliber:** 44-40  **Capacity:** 12 shots
**Barrel length:** 22¼″  **Weight:** 9.04 lbs.

Also available:
**HENRY TRAPPER. Barrel length:** 16¼″ or 18″. **Overall
    length:** 35¾″ or 37¾″. **Weight:** 7.383 lbs. or 7.934 lbs.
    **Capacity:** 8 or 9 shots. **Price: $950.00**
**HENRY RIFLE w/Steel Frame** (24¼″ barrel; 44/40 cal.).
    **Price: $995.00**

**RIFLES**

# ULTRA LIGHT ARMS

**MODEL 20
MOUNTAIN RIFLE**

**MODEL 28**

## MODEL 20 SERIES
### $2500.00  ($2600.00 Left Hand)

**SPECIFICATIONS**
**Calibers (Short Action):** 6mm Rem., 17 Rem., 22 Hornet, 222 Rem., 222 Rem. Mag., 22-250 Rem., 223 Rem., 243 Win., 250-3000 Savage, 257 Roberts, 257 Ackley, 7×57 Mauser, 7×57 Ackley, 7mm-08 Rem., 284 Win., 300 Savage, 308 Win., 358 Win.
**Barrel length:** 22″
**Weight:** 4.75 lbs.
**Safety:** Two-position safety allows bolt to open or lock with sear blocked
**Stock:** Kevlar/Graphite composite; choice of 7 or more colors

Also available:
**MODEL 24 SERIES** (Long Action) in 270 Win., 30-06, 25-06, 7mm Express **Weight:** 5¼ lbs.
    **Barrel length:** 22″ . . . . . . . . . . . . . . . . . . . . . . .$2600.00
    Same as above in Left-Hand Model . . . . . . . . 2700.00
**MODEL 28 SERIES** (Magnum Action) in 264 Win., 7mm Rem., 300 Win., 338 **Weight:** 5¾ lbs.
    **Barrel length:** 24″ . . . . . . . . . . . . . . . . . . . . . . 2900.00
    Same as above in Left-Hand Model . . . . . . . . 3000.00
**MODEL 40 SERIES** (Magnum Action) in 300 Wby. and 416 Rigby. **Weight:** 7½ lbs.
    **Barrel length:** 26″ . . . . . . . . . . . . . . . . . . . . . . 2900.00
    Same as above in Left-Hand Model . . . . . . . . 3000.00

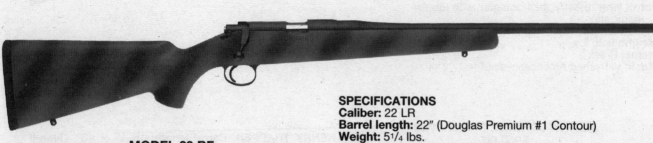

## MODEL 20 RF
### $800.00 (Single Shot)   $850.00 (Repeater)

**SPECIFICATIONS**
**Caliber:** 22 LR
**Barrel length:** 22″ (Douglas Premium #1 Contour)
**Weight:** 5¼ lbs.
**Sights:** None (drilled and tapped for scope)
**Stock:** Composite
**Features:** Recoil pad; sling swivels; fully adjustable Timney trigger; 3-function safety; color options

# UNIQUE RIFLES

### MODEL T DIOPTRA SPORTER
### $795.00

**SPECIFICATIONS**
**Caliber:** 22 LR or 22 Magnum bolt action
**Capacity:** 5 or 10 shots (5 shots only in 22 Mag.)
**Barrel length:** 23.6"   **Overall length:** 41.1"
**Weight:** 6.4 lbs.
**Sights:** Adjustable rear; lateral and vertical correction; dovetailed grooves for scope or Micro-Match target sight
**Features:** French walnut Monte Carlo stock; firing adjustment safety (working in firing pin)

### MODEL T UIT STANDARD RIFLE
### $1695.00

**SPECIFICATIONS**
**Caliber:** 22 LR
**Barrel length:** 25.6"   **Overall length:** 44.1"
**Weight:** 10.4 lbs.
**Sights:** Micro-Match target sight
**Stock:** French walnut
**Features:** Adjustable buttplate and cheek rest; fully adjustable firing; left-hand stock and action available

### MODEL T/SM SILHOUETTE
### $895.00

**SPECIFICATIONS**
**Caliber:** 22 LR or 22 Magnum
**Capacity:** 5- or 10-shot magazine (5-shot only in 22 Mag.)
**Barrel length:** 20.5"   **Overall length:** 38.4"
**Weight:** 6.6 lbs.
**Sights:** Dovetailed grooves on receiver for scope or Micro-Match target sight
**Stock:** French walnut Monte Carlo stock (left-hand stock available)

### MODEL TGC CENTERFIRE
### $1295.00

**SPECIFICATIONS**
**Calibers:** 243 Win., 270 Win., 7mm-08, 7mm Rem. Mag., 308 Win., 30-06, 300 Win. Mag.
**Capacity:** 3- or 5-shot magazine
**Barrel length:** 24" bolt action (interchangeable barrel)
**Overall length:** 44.8"   **Weight:** 8.4 lbs.
**Sights:** Dovetailed grooves on receiver for scope
**Stock:** French walnut Monte Carlo stock (left-hand stock available)

# WEATHERBY MARK V RIFLES

**MARK V DELUXE**

## MARK V DELUXE

The Mark V Deluxe stock is made of hand-selected American walnut with skipline checkering, traditional diamond-shaped inlay, rosewood pistol-grip cap and forend tip. Monte Carlo design with raised cheekpiece properly positions the shooter while reducing felt recoil. The action and hammer-forged barrel are hand-bedded for accuracy, then deep blued to a high-luster finish. See also specifications tables below and on the following page.

**Calibers**
**26″ Barrel:**
In 257 Wby. Mag., 270 Wby. Mag., 7mm Wby. Mag., 300 Wby. Mag. and 340 Wby. Mag. . . . . . . . . . $1499.00
In 378 Wby. Mag. . . . . . . . . . . . . . . . . . . . . . . . . . 1586.00
In 416 Wby. Mag. . . . . . . . . . . . . . . . . . . . . . . . . . 1736.00
In 460 Wby. Mag. . . . . . . . . . . . . . . . . . . . . . . . . . 2034.00

## SPECIFICATIONS MARK V MAGNUM RIFLES

| Caliber | Model | Barrelled Action | Weight * | Overall Length | Magazine Capacity | Barrel Length/ Contour | Rifling | Length of Pull | Drop at Comb | Monte Carlo | Drop at Heel |
|---|---|---|---|---|---|---|---|---|---|---|---|
| .257 Wby. Mag. | Mark V Sporter | RH 26" | 8 1/2 lbs. | 46 5/8" | 3+1 in chamber | 26" #2 | 1-10" twist | 13 5/8" | 1" | 1/2" | 1 5/8" |
| | Eurosport | RH 26" | 8 1/2 lbs. | 46 5/8" | 3+1 in chamber | 26" #2 | 1-10" twist | 13 5/8" | 1" | 1/2" | 1 5/8" |
| | Mark V Deluxe | RH 26" | 8 1/2 lbs. | 46 5/8" | 3+1 in chamber | 26" #2 | 1-10" twist | 13 5/8" | 7/8" | 3/8" | 1 3/8" |
| | Euromark | RH 26" | 8 1/2 lbs. | 46 5/8" | 3+1 in chamber | 26" #2 | 1-10" twist | 13 5/8" | 7/8" | 3/8" | 1 3/8" |
| | Lazermark | RH 26" | 8 1/2 lbs. | 46 5/8" | 3+1 in chamber | 26" #2 | 1-10" twist | 13 5/8" | 7/8" | 3/8" | 1 3/8" |
| | Synthetic | RH 26" | 8 lbs. | 46 5/8" | 3+1 in chamber | 26" #2 | 1-10" twist | 13 5/8" | 7/8" | 1/2" | 1 1/8" |
| | Fluted Synthetic | RH 26" | 7 1/2 lbs. | 46 5/8" | 3+1 in chamber | 26" #2 | 1-10" twist | 13 5/8" | 7/8" | 1/2" | 1 1/8" |
| | Stainless | RH 26" | 8 lbs. | 46 5/8" | 3+1 in chamber | 26" #2 | 1-10" twist | 13 5/8" | 7/8" | 1/2" | 1 1/8" |
| | Fluted Stainless | RH 26" | 7 1/2 lbs. | 46 5/8" | 3+1 in chamber | 26" #2 | 1-10" twist | 13 5/8" | 7/8" | 1/2" | 1 1/8" |
| | Accumark | RH 26" | 8 1/2 lbs. | 46 5/8" | 3+1 in chamber | 26" #3 | 1-10" twist | 13 5/8" | 1" | 9/16" | 1 1/2" |
| | SLS | RH 26" | 8 1/2 lbs. | 46 5/8" | 3+1 in chamber | 26" #2 | 1-10" twist | 13 5/8" | 1" | 1/2" | 1 5/8" |
| .270 Wby. Mag. | Mark V Sporter | RH 26" | 8 1/2 lbs. | 46 5/8" | 3+1 in chamber | 26" #2 | 1-10" twist | 13 5/8" | 1" | 1/2" | 1 5/8" |
| | Eurosport | RH 26" | 8 1/2 lbs. | 46 5/8" | 3+1 in chamber | 26" #2 | 1-10" twist | 13 5/8" | 1" | 1/2" | 1 5/8" |
| | Mark V Deluxe | RH 26" | 8 1/2 lbs. | 46 5/8" | 3+1 in chamber | 26" #2 | 1-10" twist | 13 5/8" | 7/8" | 3/8" | 1 3/8" |
| | Euromark | RH 26" | 8 1/2 lbs. | 46 5/8" | 3+1 in chamber | 26" #2 | 1-10" twist | 13 5/8" | 7/8" | 3/8" | 1 3/8" |
| | Lazermark | RH 26" | 8 1/2 lbs. | 46 5/8" | 3+1 in chamber | 26" #2 | 1-10" twist | 13 5/8" | 7/8" | 3/8" | 1 3/8" |
| | Synthetic | RH 26" | 8 lbs. | 46 5/8" | 3+1 in chamber | 26" #2 | 1-10" twist | 13 5/8" | 7/8" | 1/2" | 1 1/8" |
| | Fluted Synthetic | RH 26" | 7 1/2 lbs. | 46 5/8" | 3+1 in chamber | 26" #2 | 1-10" twist | 13 5/8" | 7/8" | 1/2" | 1 1/8" |
| | Stainless | RH 26" | 8 lbs. | 46 5/8" | 3+1 in chamber | 26" #2 | 1-10" twist | 13 5/8" | 7/8" | 1/2" | 1 1/8" |
| | Fluted Stainless | RH 26" | 7 1/2 lbs. | 46 5/8" | 3+1 in chamber | 26" #2 | 1-10" twist | 13 5/8" | 7/8" | 1/2" | 1 1/8" |
| | Accumark | RH 26" | 8 1/2 lbs. | 46 5/8" | 3+1 in chamber | 26" #3 | 1-10" twist | 13 5/8" | 1" | 9/16" | 1 1/2" |
| | SLS | RH 26" | 8 1/2 lbs. | 46 5/8" | 3+1 in chamber | 26" #2 | 1-10" twist | 13 5/8" | 1" | 1/2" | 1 5/8" |
| 7mm Rem. Mag. | Mark V Sporter | RH 24" | 8 lbs. | 44 5/8" | 3+1 in chamber | 24" #2 | 1-9 1/2" twist | 13 5/8" | 1" | 1/2" | 1 5/8" |
| | Eurosport | RH 24" | 8 lbs. | 44 5/8" | 3+1 in chamber | 24" #2 | 1-9 1/2" twist | 13 5/8" | 1" | 1/2" | 1 5/8" |
| | Synthetic | RH 24" | 8 lbs. | 44 5/8" | 3+1 in chamber | 24" #2 | 1-9 1/2" twist | 13 5/8" | 7/8" | 1/2" | 1 1/8" |
| | Fluted Synthetic | RH 24" | 7 1/2 lbs. | 44 5/8" | 3+1 in chamber | 24" #2 | 1-9 1/2" twist | 13 5/8" | 7/8" | 1/2" | 1 1/8" |
| | Stainless | RH 24" | 8 lbs. | 44 5/8" | 3+1 in chamber | 24" #2 | 1-9 1/2" twist | 13 5/8" | 7/8" | 1/2" | 1 1/8" |
| | Fluted Stainless | RH 24" | 7 1/2 lbs. | 44 5/8" | 3+1 in chamber | 24" #2 | 1-9 1/2" twist | 13 5/8" | 7/8" | 1/2" | 1 1/8" |
| | Accumark | RH 26" | 8 1/2 lbs. | 46 5/8" | 3+1 in chamber | 26" #3 | 1-9 1/2" twist | 13 5/8" | 1" | 9/16" | 1 1/2" |
| | SLS | RH 24" | 8 1/2 lbs. | 44 5/8" | 3+1 in chamber | 24" #2 | 1-9 1/2" twist | 13 5/8" | 1" | 1/2" | 1 5/8" |
| 7mm Wby. Mag. | Mark V Sporter | RH 26" | 8 1/2 lbs. | 46 5/8" | 3+1 in chamber | 26" #2 | 1-10" twist | 13 5/8" | 1" | 1/2" | 1 5/8" |
| | Eurosport | RH 26" | 8 1/2 lbs. | 46 5/8" | 3+1 in chamber | 26" #2 | 1-10" twist | 13 5/8" | 1" | 1/2" | 1 5/8" |
| | Mark V Deluxe | RH 26" | 8 1/2 lbs. | 46 5/8" | 3+1 in chamber | 26" #2 | 1-10" twist | 13 5/8" | 7/8" | 3/8" | 1 3/8" |
| | Euromark | RH 26" | 8 1/2 lbs. | 46 5/8" | 3+1 in chamber | 26" #2 | 1-10" twist | 13 5/8" | 7/8" | 3/8" | 1 3/8" |
| | Lazermark | RH 26" | 8 1/2 lbs. | 46 5/8" | 3+1 in chamber | 26" #2 | 1-10" twist | 13 5/8" | 7/8" | 3/8" | 1 3/8" |
| | Synthetic | RH 26" | 8 lbs. | 46 5/8" | 3+1 in chamber | 26" #2 | 1-10" twist | 13 5/8" | 7/8" | 1/2" | 1 1/8" |
| | Fluted Synthetic | RH 26" | 7 1/2 lbs. | 46 5/8" | 3+1 in chamber | 26" #2 | 1-10" twist | 13 5/8" | 7/8" | 1/2" | 1 1/8" |
| | Stainless | RH 26" | 8 lbs. | 46 5/8" | 3+1 in chamber | 26" #2 | 1-10" twist | 13 5/8" | 7/8" | 1/2" | 1 1/8" |
| | Fluted Stainless | RH 26" | 7 1/2 lbs. | 46 5/8" | 3+1 in chamber | 26" #2 | 1-10" twist | 13 5/8" | 7/8" | 1/2" | 1 1/8" |
| | Accumark | RH 26" | 8 1/2 lbs. | 46 5/8" | 3+1 in chamber | 26" #3 | 1-10" twist | 13 5/8" | 1" | 9/16" | 1 1/2" |
| | SLS | RH 26" | 8 1/2 lbs. | 46 5/8" | 3+1 in chamber | 26" #2 | 1-10" twist | 13 5/8" | 1" | 1/2" | 1 5/8" |

# WEATHERBY MARK V RIFLES

**MARK V SPORTER**

**MARK V SPORTER**

**Calibers**
**26″ Barrel:**
In 257 Wby. Mag., 270 Wby. Mag., 7mm Wby. Mag.,
300 Wby. Mag. and 340 Wby. Mag. . . . . . . . . . . **$949.00**

**24″ Barrel:**
In 7mm Rem. Mag., 300 Win. Mag.,
338 Win. Mag. and 375 H&H Mag. . . . . . . . . . . **$949.00**
Also available:
**EUROSPORT.** Same specifications and prices but with hand-rubbed satin oil finish.

## SPECIFICATIONS MARK V MAGNUM RIFLES (CONT.)

| Caliber | Model | Barrelled Action | Weight * | Overall Length | Magazine Capacity | Barrel Length/ Contour | Rifling | Length of Pull | Drop at Comb | Monte Carlo | Drop at Heel |
|---|---|---|---|---|---|---|---|---|---|---|---|
| .300 Win Mag. | Mark V Sporter | RH 24″ | 8 lbs. | 44 5/8″ | 3+1 in chamber | 24″ #2 | 1-10″ twist | 13 5/8″ | 1″ | 1/2″ | 1 5/8″ |
| | Eurosport | RH 24″ | 8 lbs. | 44 5/8″ | 3+1 in chamber | 24″ #2 | 1-10″ twist | 13 5/8″ | 1″ | 1/2″ | 1 5/8″ |
| | Synthetic | RH 24″ | 8 lbs. | 44 5/8″ | 3+1 in chamber | 24″ #2 | 1-10″ twist | 13 5/8″ | 7/8″ | 1/2″ | 1 1/8″ |
| | Fluted Synthetic | RH 24″ | 7 1/2 lbs. | 44 5/8″ | 3+1 in chamber | 24″ #2 | 1-10″ twist | 13 5/8″ | 7/8″ | 1/2″ | 1 1/8″ |
| | Stainless | RH 24″ | 8 lbs. | 44 5/8″ | 3+1 in chamber | 24″ #2 | 1-10″ twist | 13 5/8″ | 7/8″ | 1/2″ | 1 1/8″ |
| | Fluted Stainless | RH 24″ | 7 1/2 lbs. | 44 5/8″ | 3+1 in chamber | 24″ #2 | 1-10″ twist | 13 5/8″ | 7/8″ | 1/2″ | 1 1/8″ |
| | Accumark | RH 26″ | 8 1/2 lbs. | 46 5/8″ | 3+1 in chamber | 26″ #3 | 1-10″ twist | 13 5/8″ | 1″ | 9/16″ | 1 1/2″ |
| | SLS | RH 24″ | 8 1/2 lbs. | 44 5/8″ | 3+1 in chamber | 24″ #2 | 1-10″ twist | 13 5/8″ | 1″ | 1/2″ | 1 5/8″ |
| .300 Wby. Mag. | Mark V Sporter | RH 26″ | 8 1/2 lbs. | 46 5/8″ | 3+1 in chamber | 26″ #2 | 1-10″ twist | 13 5/8″ | 1″ | 1/2″ | 1 5/8″ |
| | Eurosport | RH 26″ | 8 1/2 lbs. | 46 5/8″ | 3+1 in chamber | 26″ #2 | 1-10″ twist | 13 5/8″ | 1″ | 1/2″ | 1 5/8″ |
| | Mark V Deluxe | RH 26″ | 8 1/2 lbs. | 46 5/8″ | 3+1 in chamber | 26″ #2 | 1-10″ twist | 13 5/8″ | 7/8″ | 3/8″ | 1 3/8″ |
| | Euromark | RH 26″ | 8 1/2 lbs. | 46 5/8″ | 3+1 in chamber | 26″ #2 | 1-10″ twist | 13 5/8″ | 7/8″ | 3/8″ | 1 3/8″ |
| | Lazermark | RH 26″ | 8 1/2 lbs. | 46 5/8″ | 3+1 in chamber | 26″ #2 | 1-10″ twist | 13 5/8″ | 7/8″ | 3/8″ | 1 3/8″ |
| | Synthetic | RH 26″ | 8 lbs. | 46 5/8″ | 3+1 in chamber | 26″ #2 | 1-10″ twist | 13 5/8″ | 7/8″ | 1/2″ | 1 1/8″ |
| | Fluted Synthetic | RH 26″ | 7 1/2 lbs. | 46 5/8″ | 3+1 in chamber | 26″ #2 | 1-10″ twist | 13 5/8″ | 7/8″ | 1/2″ | 1 1/8″ |
| | Stainless | RH 26″ | 8 lbs. | 46 5/8″ | 3+1 in chamber | 26″ #2 | 1-10″ twist | 13 5/8″ | 7/8″ | 1/2″ | 1 1/8″ |
| | Fluted Stainless | RH 26″ | 7 1/2 lbs. | 46 5/8″ | 3+1 in chamber | 26″ #2 | 1-10″ twist | 13 5/8″ | 7/8″ | 1/2″ | 1 1/8″ |
| | Accumark | RH 26″ | 8 1/2 lbs. | 46 5/8″ | 3+1 in chamber | 26″ #3 | 1-10″ twist | 13 5/8″ | 1″ | 9/16″ | 1 1/2″ |
| | SLS | RH 26″ | 8 1/2 lbs. | 46 5/8″ | 3+1 in chamber | 26″ #2 | 1-10″ twist | 13 5/8″ | 1″ | 1/2″ | 1 5/8″ |
| .338 Win Mag. | Mark V Sporter | RH 24″ | 8 lbs. | 44 5/8″ | 3+1 in chamber | 24″ #2 | 1-10″ twist | 13 5/8″ | 1″ | 1/2″ | 1 5/8″ |
| | Eurosport | RH 24″ | 8 lbs. | 44 5/8″ | 3+1 in chamber | 24″ #2 | 1-10″ twist | 13 5/8″ | 1″ | 1/2″ | 1 5/8″ |
| | Synthetic | RH 24″ | 8 lbs. | 44 5/8″ | 3+1 in chamber | 24″ #2 | 1-10″ twist | 13 5/8″ | 7/8″ | 1/2″ | 1 1/8″ |
| | Stainless | RH 24″ | 8 lbs. | 44 5/8″ | 3+1 in chamber | 24″ #2 | 1-10″ twist | 13 5/8″ | 7/8″ | 1/2″ | 1 1/8″ |
| | SLS | RH 24″ | 8 1/2 lbs. | 44 5/8″ | 3+1 in chamber | 24″ #2 | 1-10″ twist | 13 5/8″ | 1″ | 1/2″ | 1 5/8″ |
| .340 Wby. Mag. | Mark V Sporter | RH 26″ | 8 1/2 lbs. | 46 5/8″ | 3+1 in chamber | 26″ #2 | 1-10″ twist | 13 5/8″ | 1″ | 1/2″ | 1 5/8″ |
| | Eurosport | RH 26″ | 8 1/2 lbs. | 46 5/8″ | 3+1 in chamber | 26″ #2 | 1-10″ twist | 13 5/8″ | 1″ | 1/2″ | 1 5/8″ |
| | Mark V Deluxe | RH 26″ | 8 1/2 lbs. | 46 5/8″ | 3+1 in chamber | 26″ #2 | 1-10″ twist | 13 5/8″ | 7/8″ | 3/8″ | 1 3/8″ |
| | Euromark | RH 26″ | 8 1/2 lbs. | 46 5/8″ | 3+1 in chamber | 26″ #2 | 1-10″ twist | 13 5/8″ | 7/8″ | 3/8″ | 1 3/8″ |
| | Lazermark | RH 26″ | 8 1/2 lbs. | 46 5/8″ | 3+1 in chamber | 26″ #2 | 1-10″ twist | 13 5/8″ | 7/8″ | 3/8″ | 1 3/8″ |
| | Synthetic | RH 26″ | 8 lbs. | 46 5/8″ | 3+1 in chamber | 26″ #2 | 1-10″ twist | 13 5/8″ | 7/8″ | 1/2″ | 1 1/8″ |
| | Stainless | RH 26″ | 8 lbs. | 46 5/8″ | 3+1 in chamber | 26″ #2 | 1-10″ twist | 13 5/8″ | 7/8″ | 1/2″ | 1 1/8″ |
| | Accumark | RH 26″ | 8 1/2 lbs. | 46 5/8″ | 3+1 in chamber | 26″ #3 | 1-10″ twist | 13 5/8″ | 1″ | 9/16″ | 1 1/2″ |
| | SLS | RH 26″ | 8 1/2 lbs. | 46 5/8″ | 3+1 in chamber | 26″ #2 | 1-10″ twist | 13 5/8″ | 1″ | 1/2″ | 1 5/8″ |
| .375 H&H Mag. | Mark V Sporter | RH 24″ | 8 1/2 lbs. | 44 5/8″ | 3+1 in chamber | 24″ #3 | 1-12″ twist | 13 5/8″ | 1″ | 1/2″ | 1 5/8″ |
| | Eurosport | RH 24″ | 8 1/2 lbs. | 44 5/8″ | 3+1 in chamber | 24″ #3 | 1-12″ twist | 13 5/8″ | 1″ | 1/2″ | 1 5/8″ |
| | Euromark | RH 24″ | 8 lbs. | 44 5/8″ | 3+1 in chamber | 24″ #3 | 1-12″ twist | 13 5/8″ | 1″ | 1/2″ | 1 5/8″ |
| | Synthetic | RH 24″ | 8 lbs. | 44 5/8″ | 3+1 in chamber | 24″ #3 | 1-12″ twist | 13 5/8″ | 7/8″ | 1/2″ | 1 1/8″ |
| | Stainless | RH 24″ | 8 lbs. | 44 5/8″ | 3+1 in chamber | 24″ #3 | 1-12″ twist | 13 5/8″ | 7/8″ | 1/2″ | 1 1/8″ |
| **.30-378 Wby. Mag. | Accumark | RH 26″ | 8 1/2 lbs. | 46 5/8″ | 2+1 in chamber | 26″ #3 | 1-10″ twist | 13 5/8″ | 1″ | 9/16″ | 1 1/2″ |
| .378 Wby. Mag. | Mark V Deluxe | RH 26″ | 9 1/2 lbs. | 46 5/8″ | 2+1 in chamber | 26″ #3 | 1-12″ twist | 13 7/8″ | 7/8″ | 3/8″ | 1 3/8″ |
| | Euromark | RH 26″ | 9 1/2 lbs. | 46 5/8″ | 2+1 in chamber | 26″ #3 | 1-12″ twist | 13 7/8″ | 7/8″ | 3/8″ | 1 3/8″ |
| | Lazermark | RH 26″ | 9 1/2 lbs. | 46 5/8″ | 2+1 in chamber | 26″ #3 | 1-12″ twist | 13 7/8″ | 7/8″ | 3/8″ | 1 3/8″ |
| **.416 Wby. Mag. | Mark V Deluxe | RH 26″ | 9 1/2 lbs. | 46 3/4″ | 2+1 in chamber | 26″ #3 | 1-14″ twist | 13 7/8″ | 7/8″ | 3/8″ | 1 3/8″ |
| | Euromark | RH 26″ | 9 1/2 lbs. | 46 3/4″ | 2+1 in chamber | 26″ #3 | 1-14″ twist | 13 7/8″ | 7/8″ | 3/8″ | 1 3/8″ |
| | Lazermark | RH 26″ | 9 1/2 lbs. | 46 3/4″ | 2+1 in chamber | 26″ #3 | 1-14″ twist | 13 7/8″ | 7/8″ | 3/8″ | 1 3/8″ |
| **.460 Wby. Mag. | Mark V Deluxe | RH 26″ | 10 1/2 lbs. | 46 3/4″ | 2+1 in chamber | 26″ #4 | 1-16″ twist | 14″ | 7/8″ | 3/8″ | 1 3/8″ |
| | Lazermark | RH 26″ | 10 1/2 lbs. | 46 3/4″ | 2+1 in chamber | 26″ #4 | 1-16″ twist | 14″ | 7/8″ | 3/8″ | 1 3/8″ |

# WEATHERBY MARK V RIFLES

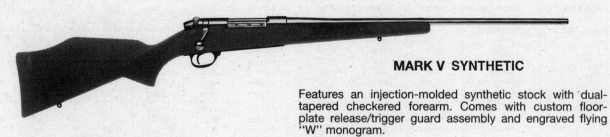

## LAZERMARK

**LAZERMARK**

| | Prices |
|---|---|
| **LAZERMARK** | |
| **26" Barrel** | |
| In Weatherby Magnum calibers 257, 270, 7mm, | |
| 300 and 340 . . . . . . . . . . . . . . . . . . . . . . . . | **$1599.00** |
| In 378 Wby. Mag. . . . . . . . . . . . . . . . . . . . . | **1701.00** |
| In 416 Wby. Mag. . . . . . . . . . . . . . . . . . . . . | **1847.00** |
| In 460 Wby. Mag. . . . . . . . . . . . . . . . . . . . . | **2174.00** |

## MARK V STAINLESS

**MARK V STAINLESS**

Features 400 Series stainless steel. The action is hand-bedded to a lightweight, injection-molded synthetic stock. A custom floorplate on stainless-steel trigger guard with engraved flying "W" monogram is standard.

| | Prices |
|---|---|
| **MARK V STAINLESS** | |
| **26" Barrel** | |
| In Weatherby Magnum calibers 257, 270, 7mm, | |
| 300 and 340 . . . . . . . . . . . . . . . . . . . . . . . . | **$ 999.00** |
| **24" Barrel** | |
| In 7mm Rem. Mag., 300 Win. Mag., | |
| 338 Win. Mag. and 375 H&H Mag. . . . . . . . . | **999.00** |
| Also available: | |
| **MODEL SLS (Stainless Laminated Sporter)** . . . | **1249.00** |
| **FLUTED STAINLESS** . . . . . . . . . . . . . . . . . . . . | **1149.00** |
| **FLUTED SYNTHETIC** . . . . . . . . . . . . . . . . . . . . | **949.00** |

## MARK V SYNTHETIC

**MARK V SYNTHETIC**

Features an injection-molded synthetic stock with dual-tapered checkered forearm. Comes with custom floorplate release/trigger guard assembly and engraved flying "W" monogram.

| | Prices |
|---|---|
| **MARK V SYNTHETIC** | |
| **26" Barrel** | |
| In Weatherby Magnum calibers 257, 270, 7mm, | |
| 300 and 340 . . . . . . . . . . . . . . . . . . . . . . . . | **$799.00** |
| **24" Barrel** | |
| In 7mm Rem. Mag., 300 Win. Mag., | |
| 338 Win. Mag. and 375 H&H Mag. . . . . . . . . | **799.00** |

*FOR COMPLETE SPECIFICATIONS ON THE ABOVE RIFLES, PLEASE SEE THE TABLES ON THE PRECEDING PAGES.*

# WEATHERBY MARK V RIFLES

**MARK V EUROMARK**

## MARK V EUROMARK

The Euromark features a hand-rubbed oil finish and Monte Carlo stock of American walnut, plus custom grade, hand-cut checkering with an ebony pistol-grip cap and forend tip.

**26" Barrel**
In Weatherby Magnum calibers 257, 270, 7mm,
  300 and 340 ............................ $1499.00
In 378 Wby. Mag. ......................... 1586.00
In 416 Wby. Mag. ......................... 1736.00
**24" Barrel**
In 7mm Rem. Mag., 300 Win. Mag.,
  338 Win. Mag. and 375 H&H Mag. ......... 1499.00

**ACCUMARK**

## ACCUMARK
### $1299.00

The Accumark joins the ranks of other legendary Weatherby Mark V rifles, featuring the flat-shooting hard-hitting performance and accuracy that is the Weatherby trademark.

Built on the proven performance of the Mark V action, the Accumark is a composite of several field-tested features that help make it the utmost in accuracy, including a specially designed, hand-laminated raised-comb Monte Carlo synthetic stock by H-S Precision (a combination of Kevlar, unidirectional fibers and fiberglass). There's also a molded-in, CNC-machined aluminum bedding plate that stiffens the receiver area of the rifle when the barreled action is secured to the block, providing a solid platform for the action. To give the Accumark stock a distinctive look, a matte black gel coat finish is accented with faint grey "spider web" patterning.

The Accumark also features a cold hammer-forged, heavy contour stainless steel barrel with a special longitudinal fluting system and a .705 diameter muzzle with recessed target crown. The flutes deliver 40% more barrel surface to help dissipate heat, while the recessed target crown assures pinpoint accuracy. The custom trigger assembly ranks among the finest. Each trigger is fully adjustable with sear engagement preset at between .012 to .015 and a letoff weight of 4 lbs.

The Accumark is available in Weatherby Magnum calibers from 257 through 340, 7mm Rem. Mag. and .300 Win. Mag.

Please see the specifications on the previous pages for additional information.

## Accuracy

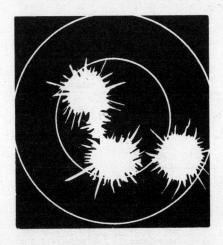

## Guarantee

# WEATHERBY MARK V RIFLES

## NEW MARK V LIGHTWEIGHT RIFLES

Virtually identical in design to the Mark V magnum action, Weatherby's new lightweight version is shorter, narrower and lighter than the original. It accommodates up to 30-06 length cartridges, including the 240 Weatherby Magnum. For complete specifications, see table below.

**Prices:**
**LIGHTWEIGHT SYNTHETIC**
22-250 to 308 Win. Mag. . . . . . . . . . . . . . . . . . . . **$699.00**
  Carbine Model (20″ in 243 Win., 7mm-08 Rem.,
  308 Win.) . . . . . . . . . . . . . . . . . . . . . . . . . . . . . . **699.00**
**LIGHTWEIGHT STAINLESS** . . . . . . . . . . . . . . . . **899.00**
**LIGHTWEIGHT SPORTER** . . . . . . . . . . . . . . . . . **849.00**

### MARK V LIGHTWEIGHT SPORTER

### MARK V LIGHTWEIGHT CARBINE

## SPECIFICATIONS MARK V LIGHTWEIGHT RIFLES

| Caliber | Model | Barrelled Action | Weight * | Overall Length | Magazine Capacity | Barrel Length/ Contour | Rifling | Length of Pull | Drop at Comb | Monte Carlo | Drop at Heel |
|---|---|---|---|---|---|---|---|---|---|---|---|
| .240 Wby. Mag. | Mark V Sporter | RH 24" | 6 3/4 lbs | 44" | 5+1 in chamber | 24" #1 | 1-10" twist | 13 5/8" | 3/4" | 3/8" | 1 1/8" |
| | Mark V Stainless | RH 24" | 6 1/2 lbs | 44" | 5+1 in chamber | 24" #1 | 1-10" twist | 13 5/8" | 3/4" | 3/8" | 1 1/8" |
| | Mark V Synthetic | RH 24" | 6 1/2 lbs | 44" | 5+1 in chamber | 24" #1 | 1-10" twist | 13 5/8" | 3/4" | 3/8" | 1 1/8" |
| .22-250 Rem. | Mark V Sporter | RH 24" | 6 3/4 lbs | 44" | 5+1 in chamber | 24" #1 | 1-14" twist | 13 5/8" | 3/4" | 3/8" | 1 1/8" |
| | Mark V Stainless | RH 24" | 6 1/2 lbs | 44" | 5+1 in chamber | 24" #1 | 1-14" twist | 13 5/8" | 3/4" | 3/8" | 1 1/8" |
| | Mark V Synthetic | RH 24" | 6 1/2 lbs | 44" | 5+1 in chamber | 24" #1 | 1-14" twist | 13 5/8" | 3/4" | 3/8" | 1 1/8" |
| .243 Winchester | Mark V Sporter | RH 24" | 6 3/4 lbs | 44" | 5+1 in chamber | 24" #1 | 1-10" twist | 13 5/8" | 3/4" | 3/8" | 1 1/8" |
| | Mark V Stainless | RH 24" | 6 1/2 lbs | 44" | 5+1 in chamber | 24" #1 | 1-10" twist | 13 5/8" | 3/4" | 3/8" | 1 1/8" |
| | Mark V Synthetic | RH 24" | 6 1/2 lbs | 44" | 5+1 in chamber | 24" #1 | 1-10" twist | 13 5/8" | 3/4" | 3/8" | 1 1/8" |
| | Mark V Carbine | RH 20" | 6 lbs | 40" | 5+1 in chamber | 20" #1 | 1-10" twist | 13 5/8" | 3/4" | 3/8" | 1 1/8" |
| 7mm-08 Rem. | Mark V Sporter | RH 24" | 6 3/4 lbs | 44" | 5+1 in chamber | 24" #1 | 1-9 1/2" twist | 13 5/8" | 3/4" | 3/8" | 1 1/8" |
| | Mark V Stainless | RH 24" | 6 1/2 lbs | 44" | 5+1 in chamber | 24" #1 | 1-9 1/2" twist | 13 5/8" | 3/4" | 3/8" | 1 1/8" |
| | Mark V Synthetic | RH 24" | 6 1/2 lbs | 44" | 5+1 in chamber | 24" #1 | 1-9 1/2" twsis | 13 5/8" | 3/4" | 3/8" | 1 1/8" |
| | Mark V Carbine | RH 20" | 6 lbs | 40" | 5+1 in chamber | 20" #1 | 1-9 1/2" twist | 13 5/8" | 3/4" | 3/8" | 1 1/8" |
| .308 Winchester | Mark V Sporter | RH 24" | 6 3/4 lbs | 44" | 5+1 in chamber | 24" #1 | 1-12" twist | 13 5/8" | 3/4" | 3/8" | 1 1/8" |
| | Mark V Stainless | RH 24" | 6 1/2 lbs | 44" | 5+1 in chamber | 24" #1 | 1-12" twist | 13 5/8" | 3/4" | 3/8" | 1 1/8" |
| | Mark V Synthetic | RH 24" | 6 1/2 lbs | 44" | 5+1 in chamber | 24" #1 | 1-12" twist | 13 5/8" | 3/4" | 3/8" | 1 1/8" |
| | Mark V Carbine | RH 20" | 6 lbs | 40" | 5+1 in chamber | 20" #1 | 1-12" twist | 13 5/8" | 3/4" | 3/8" | 1 1/8" |
| .25-06 Rem. | Mark V Sporter | RH 24" | 6 3/4 lbs | 44" | 5+1 in chamber | 24" #1 | 1-10" twist | 13 5/8" | 3/4" | 3/8" | 1 1/8" |
| | Mark V Stainless | RH 24" | 6 1/2 lbs | 44" | 5+1 in chamber | 24" #1 | 1-10" twist | 13 5/8" | 3/4" | 3/8" | 1 1/8" |
| | Mark V Synthetic | RH 24" | 6 1/2 lbs | 44" | 5+1 in chamber | 24" #1 | 1-10" twist | 13 5/8" | 3/4" | 3/8" | 1 1/8" |
| .270 Winchester | Mark V Sporter | RH 24" | 6 3/4 lbs | 44" | 5+1 in chamber | 24" #1 | 1-10" twist | 13 5/8" | 3/4" | 3/8" | 1 1/8" |
| | Mark V Stainless | RH 24" | 6 1/2 lbs | 44" | 5+1 in chamber | 24" #1 | 1-10" twist | 13 5/8" | 3/4" | 3/8" | 1 1/8" |
| | Mark V Synthetic | RH 24" | 6 1/2 lbs | 44" | 5+1 in chamber | 24" #1 | 1-10" twist | 13 5/8" | 3/4" | 3/8" | 1 1/8" |
| .280 Rem. | Mark V Sporter | RH 24" | 6 3/4 lbs | 44" | 5+1 in chamber | 24" #1 | 1-10" twist | 13 5/8" | 3/4" | 3/8" | 1 1/8" |
| | Mark V Stainless | RH 24" | 6 1/2 lbs | 44" | 5+1 in chamber | 24" #1 | 1-10" twist | 13 5/8" | 3/4" | 3/8" | 1 1/8" |
| | Mark V Synthetic | RH 24" | 6 1/2 lbs | 44" | 5+1 in chamber | 24" #1 | 1-10" twist | 13 5/8" | 3/4" | 3/8" | 1 1/8" |
| .30-06 Springfield | Mark V Sporter | RH 24" | 6 3/4 lbs | 44" | 5+1 in chamber | 24" #1 | 1-10" twist | 13 5/8" | 3/4" | 3/8" | 1 1/8" |
| | Mark V Stainless | RH 24" | 6 1/2 lbs | 44" | 5+1 in chamber | 24" #1 | 1-10" twist | 13 5/8" | 3/4" | 3/8" | 1 1/8" |
| | Mark V Synthetic | RH 24" | 6 1/2 lbs | 44" | 5+1 in chamber | 24" #1 | 1-10" twist | 13 5/8" | 3/4" | 3/8" | 1 1/8" |

# WINCHESTER BOLT-ACTION RIFLES

**MODEL 70 CUSTOM
SHARPSHOOTER**

## MODEL 70 CUSTOM CLASSICS

The Model 70 Ultimate Classic features a stock configuration with slimmer, classic styling and special rounded forend. The design offers ideal eye-to-scope alignment without using a Monte Carlo or cheekpiece configuration. The fluted barrel option gives the barrel the stiffness of that of a larger diameter barrel with greatly reduced weight. Both blued steel or all- stainless-steel versions are offered. Other options include:

- Pre-'64 type action
- Choice of round, round fluted, half-octagon, half-round or full- tapered octagon barrels
- Fancy Grade American walnut stock

- Hand-crowned, match-grade barrel
- Special Custom Shop serial numbers and proof stamp
- Inletted swivel bases
- Red 1/2" or 1" recoil pad, depending on caliber
- 70-point cut-checkering
- Hard case

For additional specifications, see table below.

**Prices:**
Ultimate Classic (Right or left hand)............ **$2386.00**
**Custom Express** ............................. 2612.00
**Sharpshooter II** (Stainless steel).............. 1994.00
**Sporting Sharpshooter II** .................... 1875.00

## SPECIFICATIONS MODEL 70 CUSTOM

| Caliber | Maga-zine Capacity* | Barrel Length | Overall Length | Nominal Length of Pull | Nominal Drop at Comb | Heel | Nominal Weight (lbs.) | Rate of Twist 1 turn in | BOSS Option** | Features |
|---|---|---|---|---|---|---|---|---|---|---|
| **ULTIMATE CLASSIC** | | | | | | | | | | |
| 25-06 Rem. | 5 | 24" | 44³/4" | 13³/4" | 5/8" | 9/16" | 7¹/2" | 10" | YES | B&R |
| 264 Win. Mag. | 3 | 26 | 46³/4 | 13³/4 | 5/8 | 9/16 | 7³/4 | 9 | YES | B&R |
| 270 Win. | 5 | 24 | 44³/4 | 13³/4 | 5/8 | 9/16 | 7¹/2 | 10 | YES | B&R |
| 30-06 Spfld. | 5 | 24 | 44³/4 | 13³/4 | 5/8 | 9/16 | 7¹/2 | 10 | YES | B&R |
| 7mm Rem. Mag. | 3 | 26 | 46³/4 | 13³/4 | 5/8 | 9/16 | 7³/4 | 9¹/2 | YES | B&R |
| 7mm STW | 3 | 26 | 46³/4 | 13³/4 | 5/8 | 9/16 | 7³/4 | 10 | YES | |
| 300 Win. Mag. | 3 | 26 | 46³/4 | 13³/4 | 5/8 | 9/16 | 7³/4 | 10 | YES | B&R |
| 300 H&H | 3 | 26 | 46³/4 | 13³/4 | 5/8 | 9/16 | 7³/4 | 10 | N/A | |
| 300 Weath. Mag. | 3 | 26 | 46³/4 | 13³/4 | 5/8 | 9/16 | 7³/4 | 10 | YES | |
| 338 Win. Mag. | 3 | 26 | 46³/4 | 13³/4 | 5/8 | 9/16 | 7³/4 | 10 | YES | B&R |
| **CLASSIC CUSTOM EXPRESS** | | | | | | | | | | |
| 375 H&H | 3 | 24" | 44³/4" | 13³/4" | 9/16" | 13/16" | 10 | 12" | N/A | Express Sights |
| 416 Rem. Mag. | 3 | 24 | 44³/4 | 13³/4 | 9/16 | 13/16 | 10 | 14 | N/A | Express Sights |
| 458 Win. Mag. | 3 | 22 | 42³/4 | 13³/4 | 9/16 | 13/16 | 10 | 14 | N/A | Express Sights |
| **CLASSIC CUSTOM SPORTING SHARPSHOOTER II** | | | | | | | | | | |
| 7mm STW | 3 | 26" | 46³/4" | 13¹/2" | 11/16" | 7/8" | 8¹/2" | 10" | N/A | Pillar Plus Accu Block |
| 300 Win. Mag. | 3 | 26 | 46³/4 | 13¹/2 | 11/16 | 7/8 | 8¹/2 | 10 | N/A | Pillar Plus Accu Block |
| **CLASSIC CUSTOM SHARPSHOOTER II (Stainless Steel)** | | | | | | | | | | |
| 22-250 Rem. | 5 | 26" | 46³/4" | 13¹/2" | 3/8" | 1/8" | 11¹/4" | 14" | N/A | Pillar Plus Accu Block |
| 308 Win. | 5 | 24 | 44³/4 | 13¹/2 | 3/8 | 1/8 | 11 | 12 | N/A | Pillar Plus Accu Block |
| 30-06 Spfld. | 5 | 26 | 46³/4 | 13¹/2 | 11/16 | 7/8 | 11¹/4 | 10 | N/A | Pillar Plus Accu Block |
| 300 Win. Mag. | 3 | 26 | 46³/4 | 13¹/2 | 3/8 | 1/8 | 11¹/4 | 10 | N/A | Pillar Plus Accu Block |

\* For additional capacity, add one round in chamber. \*\*BOSS available on round barrel models only. Drops are measured from center line of bore. Twist is right hand. Certain combinations of barrel type, stainless steel option, and stock grade vary with models. Details are available on request. B&R = Bases and rings included. N/A = BOSS accuracy system not available. Code numbers and specifications in red indicate a new product or new specification for 1997.

# WINCHESTER BOLT-ACTION RIFLES

## SPECIFICATIONS MODEL 70 CLASSIC FEATHERWEIGHT

| Model | Caliber | Magazine Capacity* | Barrel Length | Overall Length | Nominal Length Of Pull | Nominal Drop At Comb | Nominal Drop At Heel | Nominal Weight (Lbs.) | Rate of Twist 1 Turn In |
|---|---|---|---|---|---|---|---|---|---|
| CLASSIC FEATHERWEIGHT (Walnut Stock) $620.00 | 22-250 Rem. | 5 | 22" | 42" | 13 1/2" | 9/16" | 7/8" | 7 | 14" |
| | 243 Win. | 5 | 22 | 42 | 13 1/2 | 9/16 | 7/8 | 7 | 10 |
| | 6.5×55mmSwed. | 5 | 22 | 42 | 13 1/2 | 9/16 | 7/8 | 7 | 8 |
| | 308 Win. | 5 | 22 | 42 | 13 1/2 | 9/16 | 7/8 | 7 | 12 |
| | 7mm-08 Rem. | 5 | 22 | 42 | 13 1/2 | 9/16 | 7/8 | 7 | 10 |
| | 270 Win. | 5 | 22 | 42 1/2 | 13 1/2 | 9/16 | 7/8 | 7 1/4 | 10 |
| | 280 Rem. | 5 | 22 | 42 1/2 | 13 1/2 | 9/16 | 7/8 | 7 1/4 | 10 |
| | 30-06 Spfld. | 5 | 22 | 42 1/2 | 13 1/2 | 9/16 | 7/8 | 7 1/4 | 10 |
| CLASSIC FEATHERWEIGHT STAINLESS (Walnut Stock) $716.00 | 22-250 Rem. | 5 | 22" | 42" | 13 1/2" | 9/16" | 7/8" | 7 | 14" |
| | 243 Win. | 5 | 22 | 42 | 13 1/2 | 9/16 | 7/8 | 7 | 10 |
| | 308 Win. | 5 | 22 | 42 | 13 1/2 | 9/16 | 7/8 | 7 | 12 |
| | 270 Win. | 5 | 22 | 42 1/2 | 13 1/2 | 9/16 | 7/8 | 7 1/4 | 10 |
| | 30-06 Spfld. | 5 | 22 | 42 1/2 | 13 1/2 | 9/16 | 7/8 | 7 1/4 | 10 |
| | 7mm Rem. Mag. | 3 | 24 | 44 1/2 | 13 1/2 | 9/16 | 7/8 | 7 1/2 | 9 1/2 |
| | 300 Win. Mag. | 3 | 24 | 44 1/2 | 13 1/2 | 9/16 | 7/8 | 7 1/2 | 10 |
| CLASSIC FEATHERWEIGHT ALL-TERRAIN™ (Composite Stock) $672.00 | 270 Win. | 5 | 22 | 42 3/4 | 13 3/4 | 9/16 | 13/16 | 7 | 10 |
| | 30-06 Spfld. | 5 | 22 | 42 3/4 | 13 3/4 | 9/16 | 13/16 | 7 | 10 |
| | 7mm Rem. Mag. | 3 | 24 | 44 3/4 | 13 3/4 | 9/16 | 13/16 | 7 1/4 | 9 1/2 |
| | 300 Win. Mag | 3 | 24 | 44 3/4 | 13 3/4 | 9/16 | 13/16 | 7 1/4 | 10 |

* For additional capacity, add one round in chamber when ready to fire. Drops are measured from center line of bore. Rate of twist: RH.

**CLASSIC FEATHERWEIGHT ALL-TERRAIN**

## MODEL 70 CLASSIC STAINLESS (Synthetic Composite Stock)   $672.00 ($724.00 in 375 H&H Mag.)

| Caliber | Magazine Capacity | Barrel Length | Overall Length | Nominal Length Of Pull | Nominal Drop At Comb | Nominal Drop At Heel | Nominal Weight (Lbs.) | Rate of Twist 1 Turn In | Bases & Rings or Sights |
|---|---|---|---|---|---|---|---|---|---|
| 22-250 Rem. | 5 | 22" | 42 1/4" | 13 3/4" | 9/16" | 13/16" | 6 3/4 | 14" | — |
| 243 Win. | 5 | 22 | 42 1/4 | 13 3/4 | 9/16 | 13/16 | 6 3/4 | 10 | — |
| 308 Win. | 5 | 22 | 42 1/4 | 13 3/4 | 9/16 | 13/16 | 6 3/4 | 12 | — |
| 270 Win.* | 5 | 24 | 44 3/4 | 13 3/4 | 9/16 | 13/16 | 7 1/4 | 10 | — |
| 30-06 Spfld.* | 5 | 24 | 44 3/4 | 13 3/4 | 9/16 | 13/16 | 7 1/4 | 10 | — |
| 270 Wby. Mag.* | 3 | 26 | 46 3/4 | 13 3/4 | 9/16 | 13/16 | 7 1/2 | 10 | — |
| 7mm Rem. Mag.* | 3 | 26 | 46 3/4 | 13 3/4 | 9/16 | 13/16 | 7 1/2 | 9 1/2 | — |
| 300 Win. Mag.* | 3 | 26 | 46 3/4 | 13 3/4 | 9/16 | 13/16 | 7 1/2 | 10 | — |
| 300 Wby. Mag.* | 3 | 26 | 46 3/4 | 13 3/4 | 9/16 | 13/16 | 7 1/2 | 10 | — |
| 338 Win. Mag.* | 3 | 26 | 46 3/4 | 13 3/4 | 9/16 | 13/16 | 7 1/2 | 10 | — |
| 375 H&H Mag. | 3 | 24 | 44 3/4 | 13 3/4 | 9/16 | 13/16 | 7 1/4 | 12 | Sights |

* Available with BOSS System ($788.00)

# WINCHESTER BOLT-ACTION RIFLES

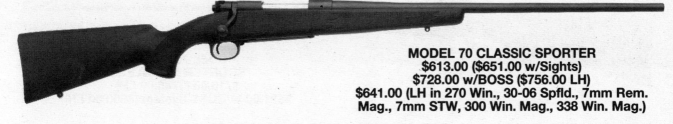

### MODEL 70 CLASSIC SPORTER
$613.00 ($651.00 w/Sights)
$728.00 w/BOSS ($756.00 LH)
$641.00 (LH in 270 Win., 30-06 Spfld., 7mm Rem.
Mag., 7mm STW, 300 Win. Mag., 338 Win. Mag.)

## SPECIFICATIONS MODEL 70 CLASSIC SPORTER (Walnut Stock)

| Caliber | Magazine Capacity A | Barrel Length | Overall Length | Nominal Length Of Pull | Nominal Drop At Comb | Nominal Drop At Heel | Nominal Weight (Lbs.) | Rate of Twist 1 Turn In | Sights |
|---|---|---|---|---|---|---|---|---|---|
| 25-06 Rem. | 5 | 24" | 44³/4" | 13³/4" | 9/16" | 13/16" | 7³/4 | 10" | |
| 264-Win. Mag. | 3 | 26 | 46³/4 | 13³/4 | 9/16 | 13/16 | 8 | 9 | |
| 270 Win. | 5 | 24 | 44³/4 | 13³/4 | 9/16 | 13/16 | 7³/4 | 10 | Sights |
| 270 Win.* | 5 | 24 | 44³/4 | 13³/4 | 9/16 | 13/16 | 7³/4 | 10 | |
| 270 Wby. Mag. | 3 | 26 | 46³/4 | 13³/4 | 9/16 | 13/16 | 8 | 10 | |
| 30-06 Spfld. | 5 | 24 | 44³/4 | 13³/4 | 9/16 | 13/16 | 7³/4 | 10 | Sights |
| 30-06 Spfld.* | 5 | 24 | 44³/4 | 13³/4 | 9/16 | 13/16 | 7³/4 | 10 | |
| 7mm STW* | 3 | 26 | 46³/4 | 13³/4 | 9/16 | 13/16 | 8 | 9¹/2 | |
| 7mm Rem. Mag. | 3 | 26 | 46³/4 | 13³/4 | 9/16 | 13/16 | 8 | 9¹/2 | Sights |
| 7mm Rem. Mag.* | 3 | 26 | 46³/4 | 13³/4 | 9/16 | 13/16 | 8 | 9¹/2 | |
| 300 Win. Mag. | 3 | 26 | 46³/4 | 13³/4 | 9/16 | 13/16 | 8 | 10 | Sights |
| 300 Win. Mag.* | 3 | 26 | 46³/4 | 13³/4 | 9/16 | 13/16 | 8 | 10 | |
| 300 Wby. Mag. | 3 | 26 | 46³/4 | 13³/4 | 9/16 | 13/16 | 8 | 10 | |
| 338 Win. Mag. | 3 | 26 | 46³/4 | 13³/4 | 9/16 | 13/16 | 8 | 10 | Sights |
| 338 Win. Mag.* | 3 | 26 | 46³/4 | 13³/4 | 9/16 | 13/16 | 8 | 10 | |

* Available w/BOSS system.

### MODEL 70 HEAVY BARREL VARMINT
w/Composite Stock/Matte Finish

## SPECIFICATIONS MODEL 70 HEAVY BARREL VARMINT RIFLE  $764.00 ($894.00 w/Fluted Barrel)

| Caliber | Magazine Capacity (A) | Barrel Length | Overall Length | Nominal Length Of Pull | Nominal Drop Comb | Nominal Drop Heel | Nominal Weight (Lbs.) | Rate of Twist 1 Turn In | Sights |
|---|---|---|---|---|---|---|---|---|---|
| 220 Swift | 5 | 26" | 46" | 13¹/2" | 3/4" | 1/2" | 10³/4 | 14" | * |
| 22-250 Rem. | 5 | 26 | 46 | 13¹/2 | 3/4 | 1/2 | 10³/4 | 14 | * |
| 222 Rem. | 6 | 26 | 46 | 13¹/2 | 3/4 | 1/2 | 10³/4 | 14 | * |
| 223 Rem. | 6 | 26 | 46 | 13¹/2 | 3/4 | 1/2 | 10³/4 | 9 | * |
| 243 Win. | 5 | 26 | 46 | 13¹/2 | 3/4 | 1/2 | 10³/4 | 10 | * |
| 308 Win. | 5 | 26 | 46 | 13¹/2 | 3/4 | 1/2 | 10³/4 | 12 | * |

(A) For add'l. capacity, add one round in chamber when ready to fire. Drops measured from center line of bore. R.H. rate of twist. * Pillar Plus Accu Block

# WINCHESTER BOLT-ACTION RIFLES

**MODEL 70 CLASSIC
SPORTER STAINLESS
$716.00 ($745.00 LH)
$831.00 w/BOSS System ($860.00 LH)**

## SPECIFICATIONS MODEL 70 CLASSIC SPORTER STAINLESS/SUPER GRADE

| Caliber | Magazine Capacity | Barrel Length | Overall Length | Nominal Length Of Pull | Nominal Drop At Comb | Nominal Drop At Heel | Nominal Weight (Lbs.) | Rate of Twist 1 Turn In | Features |
|---|---|---|---|---|---|---|---|---|---|
| **CLASSIC SUPER GRADE (Selected Walnut Stock)** | | | | | | | | | |
| 270 Win. | 5 | 24″ | 44³/₄″ | 13³/₄″ | 9/16″ | 13/16″ | 7³/₄ | 10″ | B&R |
| 30-06 Spfld. | 5 | 24 | 44³/₄ | 13³/₄ | 9/16 | 13/16 | 7³/₄ | 10 | B&R |
| 7mm Rem. Mag. | 3 | 26 | 46³/₄ | 13³/₄ | 9/16 | 13/16 | 8 | 9¹/₂ | B&R |
| 300 Win. Mag. | 3 | 26 | 46³/₄ | 13³/₄ | 9/16 | 13/16 | 8 | 10 | B&R |
| 338 Win. Mag. | 3 | 26 | 46³/₄ | 13³/₄ | 9/16 | 13/16 | 8 | 10 | B&R |
| **BOSS · CLASSIC SUPER GRADE (Selected Walnut Stock)** | | | | | | | | | |
| 270 Win. | 5 | 24″ | 44³/₄″ | 13³/₄″ | 9/16″ | 13/16″ | 7³/₄ | 10″ | B&R |
| 30-06 Spfld. | 5 | 24 | 44³/₄ | 13³/₄ | 9/16 | 13/16 | 7³/₄ | 10 | B&R |
| 7mm Rem. Mag. | 3 | 26 | 46³/₄ | 13³/₄ | 9/16 | 13/16 | 8 | 9¹/₂ | B&R |
| 300 Win. Mag. | 3 | 26 | 46³/₄ | 13³/₄ | 9/16 | 13/16 | 8 | 10 | B&R |
| 338 Win. Mag. | 3 | 26 | 46³/₄ | 13³/₄ | 9/16 | 13/16 | 8 | 10 | B&R |
| **CLASSIC SUPER EXPRESS (Walnut Stock)** | | | | | | | | | |
| 375 H&H Mag. | 3 | 24″ | 44³/₄″ | 13³/₄″ | 9/16″ | 15/16″ | 8¹/₂ | 12″ | Sights |
| 416 Rem. Mag. | 3 | 24 | 44³/₄ | 13³/₄ | 9/16 | 15/16 | 8¹/₂ | 14 | Sights |
| 458 Win. Mag. | 3 | 22 | 42³/₄ | 13³/₄ | 9/16 | 15/16 | 8¹/₄ | 14 | Sights |
| **CLASSIC SPORTER STAINLESS (Walnut Stock)** | | | | | | | | | |
| 270 Win. | 5 | 24″ | 44³/₄″ | 13³/₄″ | 9/16″ | 13/16″ | 7³/₄ | 10″ | — |
| 30-06 Spfld. | 5 | 24 | 44³/₄ | 13³/₄ | 9/16 | 13/16 | 7³/₄ | 10 | — |
| 7mm Rem. Mag. | 3 | 26 | 46³/₄ | 13³/₄ | 9/16 | 13/16 | 8 | 9¹/₂ | — |
| 300 Win. Mag. | 3 | 26 | 46³/₄ | 13³/₄ | 9/16 | 13/16 | 8 | 10 | — |
| 338 Win. Mag. | 3 | 26 | 46³/₄ | 13³/₄ | 9/16 | 13/16 | 8 | 10 | — |
| **BOSS · CLASSIC SPORTER STAINLESS (Walnut Stock)** | | | | | | | | | |
| 270 Win. | 5 | 24 | 44³/₄ | 13³/₄ | 9/16 | 13/16 | 7³/₄ | 10″ | — |
| 30-06 Spfld. | 5 | 24 | 44³/₄ | 13³/₄ | 9/16 | 13/16 | 7³/₄ | 10 | — |
| 7mm Rem. Mag. | 3 | 26 | 46³/₄ | 13³/₄ | 9/16 | 13/16 | 8 | 9¹/₂ | — |
| 300 Win. Mag. | 3 | 26 | 46³/₄ | 13³/₄ | 9/16 | 13/16 | 8 | 10 | — |
| 338 Win. Mag. | 3 | 26 | 46³/₄ | 13³/₄ | 9/16 | 13/16 | 8 | 10 | — |

**MODEL 70 CLASSIC SUPER GRADE
$840.00   $956.00 w/BOSS Option
$865.00 CLASSIC SUPER EXPRESS**

# WINCHESTER BOLT-ACTION RIFLES

## MODEL 70 CLASSIC LAREDO
### $764.00   $879.00 w/BOSS

Features heavy 26″ barrel H-S Precision gray synthetic stock with full-length "Pillar Plus Accu-Block." **Calibers:** 7mm Rem. Mag., 7mm STW, 300 Win. Mag. **Overall length:** 46.75″. 3-shot capacity.

## WINCHESTER RANGER®
### BOLT-ACTION CENTERFIRE RIFLE
### $482.00

The Ranger Bolt-Action Rifle comes with an American hardwood stock, a wear-resistant satin walnut finish, ramp beadpost front sight, steel barrel, hinged steel magazine floorplate, three-position safety and engine-turned, anti-bind bolt.

The receiver is drilled and tapped for scope mounting; accuracy is enhanced by thermoplastic bedding of the receiver. Barrel and receiver are brushed and blued.

## WINCHESTER RANGER®
### LADIES'/YOUTH BOLT-ACTION CARBINE
### $482.00

Scaled-down design to fit the younger, smaller shooter, this carbine features anti-bind bolt design, jeweled bolt, three-position safety, contoured recoil pad, ramped bead front sight, semibuckhorn folding-leaf rear sight, hinged steel magazine floorplate, and sling swivels. Receiver is drilled and tapped for scope mounting.

## SPECIFICATIONS RANGER & LADIES' YOUTH RIFLES (Hardwood Stock)

| Model | Caliber | Magazine Capacity | Barrel Length | Overall Length | Nominal Length Of Pull | Nominal Drop Comb | Nominal Drop Heel | Nominal Weight (Lbs.) | Rate of Twist 1 Turn in | Bases & Rings/ Sights |
|---|---|---|---|---|---|---|---|---|---|---|
| **RANGER** | 223 Rem. | 6 | 22″ | 42″ | 13$\frac{1}{2}$″ | $\frac{9}{16}$″ | $\frac{7}{8}$″ | 6$\frac{3}{4}$ | 12″ | Sights |
| | 243 Win. | 5 | 22 | 42 | 13$\frac{1}{2}$ | $\frac{9}{16}$ | $\frac{7}{8}$ | 6$\frac{3}{4}$ | 10 | Sights |
| | 270 Win. | 5 | 22 | 42$\frac{1}{2}$ | 13$\frac{1}{2}$ | $\frac{9}{16}$ | $\frac{7}{8}$ | 7 | 10 | Sights |
| | 30-06 Spfld. | 5 | 22 | 41$\frac{1}{2}$ | 13$\frac{1}{2}$ | $\frac{9}{16}$ | $\frac{7}{8}$ | 7 | 10 | Sights |
| | 7mm Rem. Mag. | 3 | 24 | 44$\frac{1}{2}$ | 13$\frac{1}{2}$ | $\frac{9}{16}$ | $\frac{7}{8}$ | 7$\frac{1}{2}$ | 9$\frac{1}{2}$ | Sights |
| **RANGER LADIES/ YOUTH** | 223 Rem. | 6 | 22 | 41 | 12$\frac{1}{2}$ | $\frac{3}{4}$ | 1 | 6$\frac{1}{2}$ | 12 | Sights |
| | 243 Win. | 5 | 22 | 41 | 12$\frac{1}{2}$ | $\frac{3}{4}$ | 1 | 6$\frac{1}{2}$ | 10 | Sights |
| | 7mm 08 Rem. | 5 | 22 | 41 | 12$\frac{1}{2}$ | $\frac{3}{4}$ | 1 | 6$\frac{1}{2}$ | 10 | Sights |
| | 308 Win. | 5 | 22 | 41 | 12$\frac{1}{2}$ | $\frac{3}{4}$ | 1 | 6$\frac{1}{2}$ | 12 | Sights |

For add'l. capacity, add one round in chamber when ready to fire. Drops are measured from center line of bore. R.H. rate of twist.

# WINCHESTER RIFLES

## LEVER-ACTION CARBINES/RIFLES

### MODEL 94 STANDARD WALNUT RIFLE

The top choice for lever-action styling and craftsmanship. Metal surfaces are highly polished and blued. American wal-nut stock and forearm have a protective stain finish with precise-cut wraparound checkering. It has a 20-inch barrel with hooded blade front sight and semibuckhorn rear sight.
**Prices:**
30-30 Win., checkered . . . . . . . . . . . . . . . . . . . . . . . **$393.00**
  w/o checkering . . . . . . . . . . . . . . . . . . . . . . . . . . . **363.00**

### MODEL 94 WALNUT TRAPPER CARBINE

With 16-inch short-barrel lever action and straight forward styling. Compact and fast handling in dense cover, it has a 5-shot magazine capacity (9 in 45 Colt or 44 Rem. Mag./44 S&W Special). **Calibers:** 30-30 Win., 357 Mag., 45 Colt, and 44 Rem. Mag./44 S&W Special.
**Prices:**
30-30 Winchester . . . . . . . . . . . . . . . . . . . . . . . . . . . **$363.00**
357 Mag., 45 Colt, 44 Rem. Mag./44 S&W Spec. . . . **384.00**

### MODEL 94 WRANGLER
$384.00 (30-30 Win.)   $404.00 (44 Rem.)

## MODEL 94 SPECIFICATIONS

| Model | Caliber | Magazine Capacity (A) | Barrel Length | Overall Length | Nominal Length Of Pull | Nominal Drop Comb | Nominal Drop Heel | Nominal Weight (Lbs.) | Rate of Twist 1 Turn in | Fea-tures |
|---|---|---|---|---|---|---|---|---|---|---|
| WALNUT (Checkered) | 30-30 Win. | 6 | 20" | 38 1/8" | 13 1/2" | 1 1/8" | 1 7/8" | 6 1/4 | 12" | RS/SL |
| WALNUT (Standard) | 30-30 Win. | 6 | 20 | 38 1/8 | 13 1/2 | 1 1/8 | 1 7/8 | 6 1/4 | 12 | RS/SL |
| BIG BORE | 307 Win. | 6 | 20 | 38 1/8 | 13 1/2 | 1 1/8 | 1 7/8 | 6 1/2 | 12 | RS/SL |
| | 356 Win. | 6 | 20 | 38 1/8 | 13 1/2 | 1 1/8 | 1 7/8 | 6 1/2 | 12 | RS/SL |
| TRAPPER | 30-30 Win. | 5 | 16 | 34 1/4 | 13 1/2 | 1 1/8 | 1 7/8 | 6 | 12 | RS/SL |
| | 357 Mag. | 9 | 16 | 34 1/4 | 13 1/2 | 1 1/8 | 1 7/8 | 6 | 16 | RS/SL |
| | 44 Rem. Mag. | 9 | 16 | 34 1/4 | 13 1/2 | 1 1/8 | 1 7/8 | 6 | 38 | RS/SL |
| | 45 Colt | 9 | 16 | 34 1/4 | 13 1/2 | 1 1/8 | 1 7/8 | 6 | 38 | RS/SL |
| WRANGLER | 30-30 Win. | 5 | 16 | 34 1/4 | 13 1/2 | 1 1/8 | 1 7/8 | 6 | 12 | RS/LL |
| | 44 Rem. Mag. | 9 | 16 | 34 1/4 | 13 1/2 | 1 1/8 | 1 7/8 | 6 | 38 | RS/LL |
| RANGER | 30-30 Win. | 6 | 20 | 38 1/8 | 13 1/2 | 1 1/8 | 1 7/8 | 6 1/4 | 12 | RS/LL* |

(A) For additional capacity, add one round in chamber when ready to fire. Drops measured from center line of bore. RH rate of twist. RS/SL = rifle sights/standard loop; RS/LL = rifle sights/large loop. * Bushnell 4×32 scope and see-thru mounts available.

# WINCHESTER RIFLES

## LEVER ACTION

### MODEL 94 RANGER
### $320.00   ($376.00 with Scope)

**Model 94 Ranger** is an economical version of the Model 94. Lever action is smooth and reliable. In 30-30 Winchester, the rapid-firing six-shot magazine capacity provides two more shots than most other centerfire hunting rifles. See also Specifications table on previous page.

### MODEL 94 BIG-BORE WALNUT
### $404.00

Winchester's powerful 307 and 356 hunting calibers combined with maximum lever-action power and angled ejection provide hunters with improved performance and economy. See also Specifications table on previous page.

### MODEL 94 TRAILS END
### $398.00 (Standard Loop Lever)
### $420.00 (Large Loop Lever)

**Calibers:** 357 Mag., 44 Rem. Mag., 45 Colt. **Capacity:** 11 shot magazine. **Barrel length:** 20″. **Overall length:** 38 1/8″. **Weight:** 6.5 lbs. Features include rifle sights and standard loop or large loop.

### MODEL 94 LEGACY
### Standard Loop Lever
### $420.00

**Calibers:** 30-30 Win., 357 Mag., 44 Rem. Mag., 45 Colt. **Capacity:** 6 shots (30-30 Win.); 11 shots (other calibers); add 1 shot for 24″ barrel. **Barrel length:** 20″ or 24″. **Overall length:** 38 1/8″ w/20″ barrel. **Weight:** 6.5 lbs. w/20″ bbl.; 6 3/4 w/24″ bbl. Features include pistol-grip stock, rifle sights and standard loop lever.

# WINCHESTER RIFLES

## MODEL 9422 LEVER-ACTION RIMFIRE RIFLES

Positive lever action and bolt design ensure feeding and chambering from any shooting position. The bolt face is T-slotted to guide the cartridge with complete control from magazine to chamber. Receivers are grooved for scope mounting. Stock and forearm are checkered American walnut with high-luster finish and straight-grip design. Internal parts are carefully finished for smoothness of action.

### MODEL 9422 WALNUT
### $407.00

Considered one of the world's finest production sporting arms, this lever-action holds 21 Short, 17 Long or 15 Long Rifle rimfire cartridges. **Barrel length:** 20.5″. **Overall length:** 37 1/8″. **Weight:** 6.25 lbs. Features rifle sights.

**Model 9422 Walnut Magnum** gives exceptional accuracy at longer ranges than conventional 22 rifles. It is designed specifically for the 22 WMR and holds 11 cartridges. Otherwise same basic specifications as the 9422 Walnut..... **$424.00**

**Model 9422 WinCam™ Magnum** features laminated non-glare, green-shaded stock and forearm. American hardwood stock is bonded to withstand all climates. Holds 11 22 WMR cartridges and has same basic specifications as the 9422 Walnut Magnum. ............................**$424.00**

### MODEL 9422 WINTUFF™ RIFLE
### $404.00

Includes all features and specifications of standard Model 94 plus tough laminated hardwood styled for the brush-gunning hunter who wants good concealment and a carbine that can stand up to all kinds of weather. In standard and magnum rimfire.

### MODEL 9422 TRAPPER
### $407.00

Same basic specifications as the 9422 Walnut, except with 16.5″ barrel, 33 1/8″ overall length and 5.75 lbs. weight. Holds 15 Short, 12 Long and 11 Long Rifle cartridges.

Also available:
**25th ANNIVERSARY EDITION** of the Model 9422 in Grade I and High Grade versions (for a limited time only).
**Grade I** ...................................... $ 606.00
**High Grade** .............................. 1348.00

**Shotguns**

For addresses and phone/fax numbers of manufacturers and distributors included in this section, please turn to DIRECTORY OF MANUFACTURERS AND SUPPLIERS on page 554.

# AMERICAN ARMS SHOTGUNS

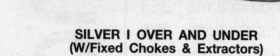

### SILVER I OVER AND UNDER
**(W/Fixed Chokes & Extractors)**

Features polished white frame w/outline engraving; blued trigger guard, top lever and forward latch; radiused rubber recoil pad

### SILVER II
**(W/Choke Tubes & Automatic Selective Ejectors)**

Same features as Silver I, but with more refined engraving. Models in 16, 20 and .410 gauge have fixed chokes.

### SILVER SPORTING
**(Ported, w/Choke Tubes)**

## SPECIFICATIONS

| Model | Gauge | Bbl. Length | Chamber | Chokes | Avg. Weight | Prices |
|---|---|---|---|---|---|---|
| **Silver I** | 12 | 26"–28" | 3" | IC/M-M/F | 6 lbs. 15 oz. | **$625.00** |
| | 20 | 26"–28" | 3" | IC/M-M/F | 6 lbs. 12 oz. | |
| | 28 | 26" | 2³/₄" | IC/M | 5 lbs. 14 oz. | 650.00 |
| | .410 | 26" | 3" | IC/M | 6 lbs. 6 oz. | |
| **Silver II** | 12 | 26"–28" | 3" | CT-3 | 6 lbs. 15 oz. | |
| | 16 | 26" | 2³/₄" | IC/M | 6 lbs. 13 oz. | 750.00 |
| | 20 | 26" | 3" | CT-3 | 6 lbs. 12 oz. | |
| | 28 | 26" | 2³/₄" | IC/M | 5 lbs. 14 oz. | 775.00 |
| | .410 | 26" | 3" | IC/M | 6 lbs. 6 oz. | |
| **Sporting** | 12 | 28"–30" | 2³/₄" | CTS | 7 lbs. 6 oz. | 925.00 |
| | 20 | 28" | 3" | CTS | 7 lbs. 3 oz. | |

CT-3 Choke Tubes IC/M/F        Cast Off = ³/₈"        CTS = SK/SK/IC/M
Silver I and II: Pull = 14¹/₈"; Drop at Comb = 1³/₈"; Drop at Heel = 2³/₈"
Silver Sporting: Pull = 14¹/₄"; Drop at Comb = 1¹/₂"; Drop at Heel = 2¹/₂"

# AMERICAN ARMS SHOTGUNS

## BRITTANY SIDE-BY-SIDE

### $860.00

**SPECIFICATIONS**
**Gauges:** 12, 20
**Chamber:** 3″   **Chokes:** CT-3
**Barrel length:** 26″
**Weight:** 6 lbs. 7 ozs. (20 ga.); 6 lbs. 15 oz. (12 ga.)

**Features:** Engraved case-colored frame; single selective trigger with top tang selector; automatic selective ejectors; manual safety; hard chrome-lined barrels; walnut English-style straight stock and semi-beavertail forearm w/cut checkering and oil-rubbed finish; ventilated rubber recoil pad; and choke tubes with key

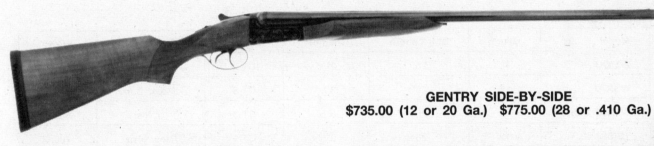

## GENTRY SIDE-BY-SIDE
### $735.00 (12 or 20 Ga.)   $775.00 (28 or .410 Ga.)

Features boxlocks with engraved English-style scrollwork on side plates; one-piece, steel-forged receiver; chrome barrels; manual thumb safety; independent floating firing pin.

**SPECIFICATIONS**
**Gauges:** 12, 20, 28, .410
**Chambers:** 3″ (except 28 gauge, 2¾″)

**Barrel lengths:** 26″, choked IC/M (all gauges); 28″, choked M/F (12 and 20 gauges)
**Weight:** 6 lbs. 15 oz. (12 ga.); 6 lbs. 7 oz. (20 and .410 ga.); 6 lbs. 5 oz. (28 ga.)
**Drop at comb:** 1³/₈″   **Drop at heel:** 2³/₈″
**Other features:** Fitted recoil pad; flat matted rib; walnut pistol-grip stock and beavertail forend with hand-checkering; gold front sight bead

## MODEL 610 VARIOPRESS SYSTEM
### $750.00 ($795.00 w/Engraved Receiver)

**SPECIFICATIONS**
**Gauge:** 12 ga. semiauto gas-operated
**Barrel lengths:** 26″ and 28″
**Overall length:** 47.5″ (26″ barrel)
**Weight:** 7 lbs. 2 oz.
**Length of pull:** 14.25″

**Drop at comb:** 1.5″   **Drop at heel:** 2.5″
**Finish:** Alloy frame w/non-glare finish
**Features:** Patented Variopress System; shoots all shotshells up to 3″; chrome-lined barrel w/Franchoke system (IC-M-F); pistol-grip stock

**SHOTGUNS**

# AMERICAN ARMS SHOTGUNS

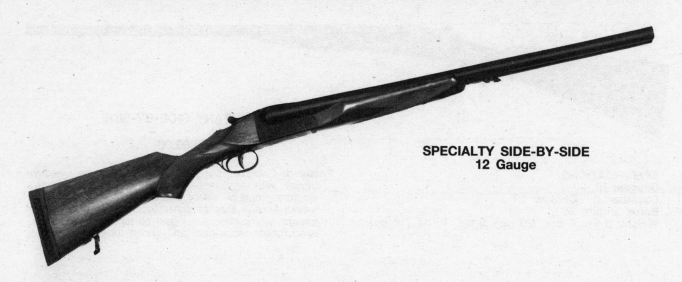

**SPECIALTY SIDE-BY-SIDE**
**12 Gauge**

## SPECIFICATIONS

| Model | Gauge | Bbl. Length | Chamber | Chokes | Avg. Wgt. | Prices |
|-------|-------|-------------|---------|--------|-----------|--------|
| WT/OU | 10 | 26" | 3½" | CT-2 | 9 lbs. 10 oz. | $995.00 |
| WS/OU | 12 | 28" | 3½" | CT-3 | 7 lbs. 2 oz. | 775.00 |
| WT/OU Camo | 12 | 26" | 3½" | CT-3 | 7 lbs. | 850.00 |
| TS/SS | 12 | 26" | 3½" | CT-3 | 7 lbs. 6 oz. | 785.00 |

CT-3 = Choke tubes IC/M/F.  CT-2 = Choke tubes F/F.  Drop at Comb = 1⅛".  Drop at Heel = 2⅜".

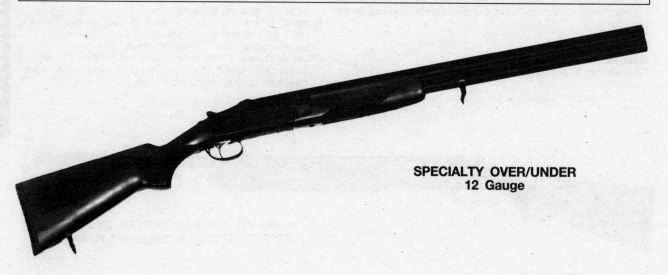

**SPECIALTY OVER/UNDER**
**12 Gauge**

# AMERICAN ARMS/FRANCHI

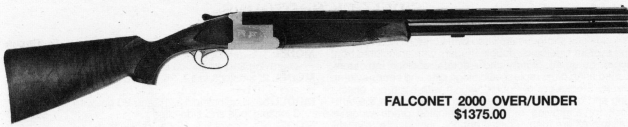

## FALCONET 2000 OVER/UNDER
### $1375.00

**SPECIFICATIONS**
**Gauge:** 12 ga. (2³/₄″ chamber)
**Barrel length:** 26″  **Overall length:** 43¹/₈″
**Weight:** 6 lbs. 2 oz.
**Length of pull:** 14¹/₄″
**Drop at comb:** 1¹/₂″  **Drop at heel:** 2¹/₂″

**Finish:** Select European walnut stock and forend w/fine-line checkering
**Features:** Gold-plated gamebird scene engraved on frame; chrome- lined barrels w/Franchoke system; safety and barrel selector on top tang; ventilated top rib and separated barrels; hard case standard

## SPORTING 2000
### $1495.00

**SPECIFICATIONS**
**Gauge:** 12 ga.
**Choke:** Franchoke (F-1M-M-1C-SK)
**Barrel length:** 28″  **Overall length:** 45³/₈″
**Length of pull:** 14¹/₄″
**Drop at comb:** 1³/₈″  **Drop at heel:** 2¹/₄″

**Weight:** 7 lbs. 12 oz.
**Stock:** Select European walnut stock and forend w/fine-line checkering
**Features:** Target vent rib; single selective trigger; auto-selective ejectors; hard case standard; ventilated 10mm rib w/white bead front sight

## MODEL 48/AL
### Recoil Operated Semiautomatic
### $649.00 ($725.00 in 20 ga./28″ and 28 ga./26″)

**SPECIFICATIONS**
**Gauges:** 12/20; 28 gauge (26″ barrel only)
**Action:** Single Action  **Chamber:** 2³/₄″
**Barrel lengths:** 24″, 26″, 28″
**Choke:** Multi chokes (IC-M-F) all gauges

**Weight:** 6 lbs. 9 oz. (12 ga.); 6 lbs. 8 oz. (20 ga.); 5 lbs. 6 oz. (28 ga.)
**Length of pull:** 14¹/₄″
**Drop at comb:** 1⁵/₈″  **Drop at heel:** 2¹/₂″

## ALCIONE 2000 SX O/U (not shown)
### $1895.00

**SPECIFICATIONS**
**Gauge:** 12 ga. (2³/₄″ chamber)
**Choke:** Franchoke (F-M-1C)
**Barrel length:** 28″  **Overall length:** 45¹/₈″

**Weight:** 7 lbs. 4 oz.  **Length of pull:** 14¹/₄″
**Drop at comb:** 1¹/₂″  **Drop at heel:** 2¹/₂″
**Stock:** Select European walnut stock and forend w/fine-line checkering
**Features:** Engraved chrome steel frame; chrome-lined barrels; safety and barrel selector on top tang; ventilated 10mm top rib and separated barrels

**SHOTGUNS**

# AYA SHOTGUNS

## SIDELOCK SHOTGUNS

AYA sidelock shotguns are fitted with London Holland & Holland system sidelocks, double triggers with articulated front trigger, automatic safety and ejectors, cocking indicators, bushed firing pins, replaceable hinge pins and chopper lump barrels. Stocks are of figured walnut with hand-cut checkering and oil finish, complete with a metal oval on the buttstock for engraving of initials. Exhibition grade wood is available as are many special options, including a true left-hand version and self-opener. Available from Armes de Chasse (*see* Directory of Manufacturers and Suppliers).

**Barrel lengths:** 26″, 27″, 28″, 29″ and 32 ″. **Weight:** 5 to 7 pounds, depending on gauge.

| Model | Prices |
|---|---|
| **MODEL 1:** Sidelock in 12 and 20 ga. w/special engraving and exhibition quality wood | $7500.00 |
| **MODEL 2:** Sidelock in 12, 16, 20, 28 ga. and .410 bore | 3500.00 |
| **MODEL 53:** Sidelock in 12, 16 and 20 ga. with 3 locking lugs and side clips | 5000.00 |
| **MODEL 56:** Sidelock in 12 ga. only with 3 locking lugs and side clips | 8000.00 |
| **MODEL XXV/SL:** Sidelock in 12 and 20 ga. only w/Churchill-type rib | 4000.00 |

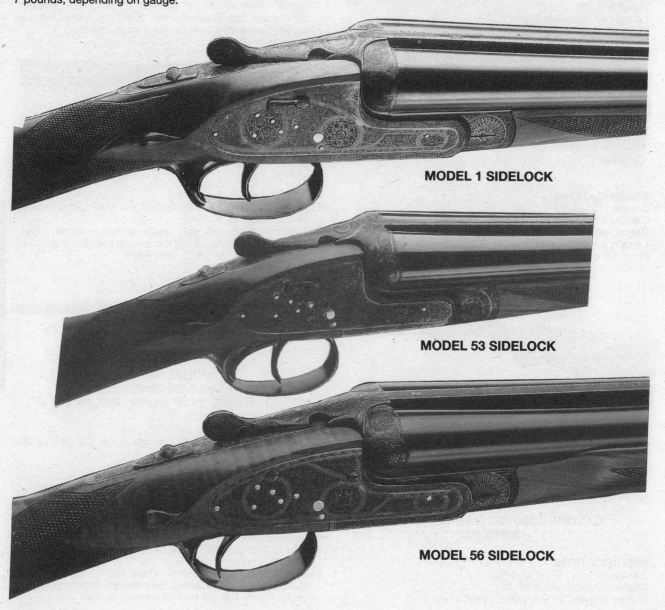

**MODEL 1 SIDELOCK**

**MODEL 53 SIDELOCK**

**MODEL 56 SIDELOCK**

# AYA SHOTGUNS

## BOXLOCK SHOTGUNS

AYA boxlocks use the Anson & Deeley system with double locking lugs, incorporating detachable cross pin and separate plate to allow easy access to the firing mechanism. Barrels are chopper lump, firing pins are bushed, plus automatic safety and ejectors and metal oval for engraving of initials. Other features include disc set strikers, replaceable hinge pin, split bottom plate.

**Barrel lengths:** 26″, 27″ and 28″. **Weight:** 5 to 7 pounds, depending on gauge.

| Model | Price |
|---|---|
| **MODEL XXV BOXLOCK:** 12 and 20 gauge only | $ 3,100.00 |
| **MODEL 4 BOXLOCK:** 12, 16, 20, 28, .410 ga. | 2,000.00 |
| **MODEL 4 DELUXE BOXLOCK:** Same gauges as above | 3,000.00 |
| **MODEL 37 SUPER A** (12 gauge only) | 15,000.00 |
| **MODEL AUGUSTA** (12 gauge only) | 28,000.00 |

**MODEL XXV BOXLOCK**
**(Close-up)**

**MODEL XXV BOXLOCK**

**MODEL 4 BOXLOCK**

# BENELLI SHOTGUNS

### BLACK EAGLE COMPETITION
### $1229.00

Benelli's Black Eagle Competition shotgun combines the best technical features of the Montefeltro Super 90 and the classic design of the old SL 80 Series. It comes standard with a specially designed two-piece receiver of steel and aluminum, adding to its reliability and resistance to wear. A premium high-gloss walnut stock and gold-plated trigger are included, along with a Montefeltro rotating bolt. The Black Eagle Competition has no complex cylinders and pistons to maintain. Features include etched receiver, competition stock and mid-rib bead.

### SUPER BLACK EAGLE
### $1199.00 (24″ or 26″ barrel)
### $1213.00 (28″ barrel)

Benelli's Super Black Eagle shotgun offers the advantage of owning one 12-gauge auto that fires every type of 12 gauge currently available. It has the same balance, sighting plane and fast-swinging characteristics whether practicing on the sporting clays course with light target loads or touching off a 3¹/₂″ Magnum steel load at a high-flying goose.

The Super Black Eagle also features a specially strengthened steel upper receiver mated to the barrel to endure the toughest shotgunning. The alloy lower receiver keeps the overall weight low, making this model as well balanced and point-able as possible. Distinctive high-gloss or satin walnut stocks and a choice of dull finish or blued metal add up to a universal gun for all shotgun hunting and sports.

**Stock:** Satin walnut (28″) with drop adjustment kit; high-gloss walnut (26″) with drop adjustment kit; or synthetic stock

**Finish:** Matte black finish on receiver, barrel and bolt (28″); blued finish on receiver and barrel (26″) with bolt mirror polished

**Features:** Montefeltro rotating bolt with dual locking lugs For additional specifications, *see* table on previous page.

Also available:
**Custom Slug Gun** with 24″ E.R. Shaw rifled barrel for sabot-type slugs and polymer stock. **Price:** .......... **$1243.00**

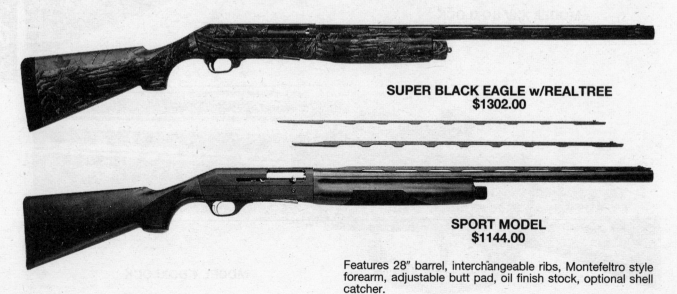

### SUPER BLACK EAGLE w/REALTREE
### $1302.00

### SPORT MODEL
### $1144.00

Features 28″ barrel, interchangeable ribs, Montefeltro style forearm, adjustable butt pad, oil finish stock, optional shell catcher.

# BENELLI SHOTGUNS

## MODEL M1 SUPER 90 SERIES

*See table on the following page for all Benelli specifications.*

### M1 SUPER 90 FIELD W/REALTREE

The M1 Field 12-gauge shotgun combines the M1 Super 90 receiver with a choice of polymer or walnut stocks, including a camouflaged model with an Xtra Brown pattern sealed onto the matte finish metal and polymer stock. Available in 24″, 26″ or 28″ barrels with vent rib.
**M1 Super 90 Field w/Realtree**
Camo finish, camo polymer buttstock and forearm . . . . . . . . . . . . . . . $992.00

### MODEL M1 SUPER 90 FIELD
**$916.00 (26″ and 28″ barrels w/wood stock)**

Also available:
**Model M1 Super 90 Sporting Special**
   with 18½″ barrel . . . . . . . . . . . . . . . . . . . . . . . . . . . . . . . . . . . . . . $ 924.00
**Model M1 Super 90 Tactical** w/18½″ bbl. . . . . . . . . . . . . . . . . 873.00–916.00
   With pistol-grip stock, ghost ring sights . . . . . . . . . . . . . . . . . . . . . . 951.00
**Model M1 Super 90 Field** (polymer stock) w/21″, 24″, 26″, 28″ bbl. . . . . . . 902.00
**Model M3 Super 90 Pump/Auto Series**
   Standard stock, 19¾″ barrel . . . . . . . . . . . . . . . . . . . . . . . . . . . . . 1040.00
   w/Ghost Ring Sight and standard stock . . . . . . . . . . . . . . . . . . . . . 1081.00

### MONTEFELTRO SUPER 90 VENT RIB
**$923.00 (12 Ga.—21″, 24″, 26″, or 28″ Barrel)**
**(20 ga.—24″ or 26″ barrel only)**
**$943.00 (Left Hand w/26″ or 28″ Barrel)**

# BENELLI SHOTGUNS

### EXECUTIVE TYPE III

## EXECUTIVE SERIES

These special-order firearms are designed and manufactured with the best materials available. Each Executive Series Shotgun with vent rib has an all-steel tower receiver hand-engraved with gold inlay by Bottega Incisione di Cesare Giovanelli, one of Italy's finest engravers. The highest grade of walnut wood stocks is selected, and each can be custom-fitted with Benelli's drop adjustment kit. The Executive Series is engineered with all the features found on the Black Eagle Series Shotguns plus its many luxury features, including Montefeltro rotating bolt with dual locking lugs.

**Prices:**
**EXECUTIVE TYPE I** with 5 screw-in choke tubes and
   21″, 24″, 26″, 28″ vent-rib barrels . . . . . . . . . . . . **$4950.00**
**EXECUTIVE TYPE II** . . . . . . . . . . . . . . . . . . . . . . . 5659.00
**EXECUTIVE TYPE III** . . . . . . . . . . . . . . . . . . . . . 6577.00

## BENELLI SHOTGUN SPECIFICATIONS

| | Gauge (Chamber) | Operation | Magazine Capacity* | Barrel Length | Overall Length | Weight (in lbs.) | Choke | Receiver Finish | Stock | Sights |
|---|---|---|---|---|---|---|---|---|---|---|
| Super Black Eagle | 12 (3½ in.) | semi-auto inertia recoil | 3 | 28 in. | 49⅝ in. | 7.3 | S,IC,M,IM,F** | matte | satin walnut or polymer | front & mid rib bead |
| Super Black Eagle | 12 (3½ in.) | semi-auto inertia recoil | 3 | 26 in. | 47⅝ in. | 7.1 | S,IC,M,IM,F** | matte or blued | satin walnut or polymer | front & mid rib bead |
| Super Black Eagle | 12 (3½ in.) | semi-auto inertia recoil | 3 | 24 in. | 45⅝ in. | 7.0 | S,IC,M,IM,F** | matte | polymer | front & mid rib bead |
| Super Black Eagle Custom Slug | 12 (3 in.) | semi-auto inertia recoil | 3 | 24 in. | 45½ in. | 7.6 | rifled barrel | matte | satin walnut or polymer | scope mount base |
| Black Eagle Competition Gun | 12 (3 in.) | semi-auto inertia recoil | 4 | 28/26 in. | 49⅝ in. or 47⅝ in. | 7.3/7 | S,IC,M,IM,F** | blued with etched receiver | satin walnut | front & mid rib bead |
| Black Eagle Executive I, II, III | 12 (3 in.) | semi-auto inertia recoil | 4 | 26 in. | 47⅝ in | 7.3/7 | S,IC,M,IM,F** | engraved & gold inlaid rec. | satin high grade walnut | front & mid rib bead |
| Montefeltro Super 90 | 12 (3 in.) | semi-auto inertia recoil | 4 | 28/26 in. | 49½ in. or 47½ in. | 7.4/7 | S,IC,M,IM,F** | blued | satin walnut | bead |
| Montefeltro Super 90 | 12 (3 in.) | semi-auto inertia recoil | 4 | 24/21 in. | 45½ in. or 42½ in. | 6.9/6.7 | S,IC,M,IM,F** | blued | satin walnut | bead |
| Montefeltro Left Hand | 12 (3 in.) | semi-auto inertia recoil | 4 | 28/26 in. | 49½ in. or 47½ in. | 7.4/7 | S,IC,M,IM,F** | blued | satin walnut | bead |
| Montefeltro 20 Gauge | 20 (3 in.) | semi-auto inertia recoil | 4 | 26/24 in. | 47½ or 45½ in. | 5.75/5.5 | S,IC,M,IM,F** | blued | satin walnut | front & mid rib bead |
| Montefeltro 20 Gauge Limited Edition | 20 (3 in.) | semi-auto inertia recoil | 4 | 26 in. | 47½ in. | 5.75 | S,IC,M,IM,F** | nickel with gold | satin walnut | front & mid rib bead |
| M1 Super 90 Field | 12 (3 in.) | semi-auto inertia recoil | 3 | 28 in. | 49½ in. | 7.4 | S,IC,M,IM,F** | matte | polymer standard or satin walnut | bead |
| M1 Super 90 Field | 12 (3 in.) | semi-auto inertia recoil | 3 | 26 in. | 47½ in. | 7.3 | S,IC,M,IM,F** | matte | polymer standard or satin walnut | bead |
| M1 Super 90 Field | 12 (3 in.) | semi-auto inertia recoil | 3 | 24 in. | 45½ in. | 7.2 | S,IC,M,IM,F** | matte | polymer standard | bead |
| M1 Super 90 Field | 12 (3 in.) | semi-auto inertia recoil | 3 | 21 in. | 42½ in. | 7 | S,IC,M,IM,F** | matte | polymer standard | bead |
| M1 Sporting Special | 12 (3 in.) | semi-auto inertia recoil | 3 | 18½ in. | 39¾ in. | 6.5 | IC,M,F** | matte | polymer standard | ghost ring |
| M1 Super 90 Tactical | 12 (3 in.) | semi-auto inertia recoil | 5 | 18½ in. | 39¾ in. | 6.5 | IC,M,F** | matte | polymer pistol grip*** or polymer standard | rifle or ghost ring |
| M1 Super 90 Slug | 12 (3 in.) | semi-auto inertia recoil | 5 | 18½ in. | 39¾ in. | 6.5 | Cylinder | matte | polymer standard | rifle or ghost ring |
| M1 Super 90 Defense | 12 (3 in.) | semi-auto inertia recoil | 5 | 18½ in. | 39¾ in. | 6.8 | Cylinder | matte | polymer pistol grip*** | rifle or ghost ring |
| M1 Super 90 Entry | 12 (3 in.) | semi-auto inertia recoil | 5 | 14 in. | 35½ in. | 6.3 | Cylinder | matte | polymer pistol grip*** or polymer standard | rifle or ghost ring |
| M3 Super 90 Pump/Auto | 12 (3 in.) | semi-auto/pump inertia recoil | 7 | 19¾ in. | 41 in. | 7.9 | Cylinder | matte | polymer standard | rifle or ghost ring |

*Magazine capacity given for 2¾ inch shells, size variations among some brands may result in less capacity.   **Skeet, Improved Cylinder, Modified, Improved Modified, Full
***CAUTION: Increasing magazine capacity to more than five rounds on M1 shotguns with pistol grip stocks violates provisions of the 1994 Crime Bill.

# BERETTA SHOTGUNS

## COMPETITION TRAP, SKEET & SPORTING

### SERIES 682 GOLD COMPETITION TRAP OVER/UNDER

These 12 gauge Model 682 Trap guns feature adjustable gold-plated, single-selective sliding trigger; fluorescent competition front sight; step-up top rib; Greystone finish (an ultralite, durable, wear-resistant finish in gunmetal grey w/gold accents); low-profile improved boxlock action; manual safety w/barrel selector; 2³/₄" chambers; auto ejector; competition recoil pad buttplate; hand-checkered walnut stock with silver oval for initials; silver inscription inlaid on trigger guard; handsome fitted case. **Weight:** Approx. 8 lbs. The **682 Gold "Live Bird"** features MC4 choke, leather-covered recoil pad, single selective trigger, 30" barrel.

**Barrel lengths/Chokes** 30" Imp. Mod./Full (Black)
30" or 32" Mobilchoke® (Black)
Top Single 32" or 34" Mobilchoke®
"Live Bird" (Flat rib, Silver)
Combo.: 30" or 32" Mobilchoke® (Top)
        30" IM/F (Top)
        32" Mobilchoke® (Mono)
        30" or 32" Mobilchoke® ported

| | |
|---|---|
| Model 682 Gold Trap | $2910.00 |
| Model 682 Gold Trap Combo | 3845.00 |
| Model 682 Gold Super Trap Top Combo | 4040.00 |
| Model 682 Gold "Live Bird" | 2910.00 |

### MODEL 682 GOLD COMPETITION SKEET O/U

This 12-gauge skeet gun sports a hand-checkered premium walnut stock w/silver oval for initials, forged and hardened receiver w/Greystone finish, manual safety with trigger selector, auto ejector, silver inlaid on trigger guard.
**Action:** Low-profile hard chrome-plated boxlock
**Trigger:** Single adjustable sliding trigger

**Barrels:** 28" blued barrels with 2³/₄" chambers
**Stock dimensions:** Length of pull 14³/₄"; drop at comb 1³/₈"; drop at heel 2¹/₄"
**Sights:** Fluorescent front and metal middle bead
**Weight:** Approx. 7¹/₂ lbs.
**Price:** (incl. fitted case) . . . . . . . . . . . . . . . . . . . . . $2850.00

### MODEL 682 GOLD SPORTING

## MODELS 682 and 686 SPORTING CLAYS

These competition-style sporting clays features 28" or 30" barrels with four flush-mounted screw-in choke tubes (Full, Modified, Improved Cylinder and Skeet), plus hand-checkered stock and forend of fine walnut, 2³/₄" or 3" chambers and adjustable trigger. **Model 682 Gold** features Greystone finish—an ultra-durable finish in gunmetal grey w/gold accents. **Model 682 Continental Course Sporting** has tapered rib and schnabel forend. **Model 686 Onyx Sporting** has black matte receiver and **Model 686 Silver Pigeon Sporting** has coin silver receiver with scroll engraving.

| Models | Prices |
|---|---|
| 682 Gold Sporting | $2910.00 |
|     Ported | 3035.00 |
| 682 Continental Course Sporting | 2345.00 |
| 682 Gold Sporting (ported) | 3035.00 |
| 686 Onyx Sporting | 1450.00 |
| 686 Silver Pigeon Sporting | 1760.00 |
|     Combo | 2210.00 |

# BERETTA SHOTGUNS

## MODEL 686 ONYX

**SPECIFICATIONS**
**Gauges:** 12, 20   **Chambers:** 3″ and 3½″
**Barrel lengths:** 26″ and 28″
**Chokes:** Mobilchoke® screw-in system

**Weight:** 6 lbs. 12 oz. (12 ga.); 6.2 lbs. (20 ga.)
**Stock:** American walnut with recoil pad (English stock available)
**Features:** Automatic ejectors; matte black finish on barrels and receiver to reduce glare
**Price:** . . . . . . . . . . . . . . . . . . . . . . . . . . . . . . . . . . . . . . **$1420.00**

## MODEL 686 SILVER ESSENTIAL

**SPECIFICATIONS**
**Gauge:** 12 (2¾″ and 3″ chambers)
**Choke:** MC3 Mobilchoke® (F, M, IC)
**Barrel length:** 26″ or 28″   **Overall length:** 45.7″
**Weight:** 6.7 lbs.

**Stock:** American walnut
**Drop at comb:** 1.4″   **Drop at heel:** 2.2″
**Length of pull:** 14½″
**Features:** Satin chrome receiver
**Price:** . . . . . . . . . . . . . . . . . . . . . . . . . . . . . . . . . . . . . **$1005.00**

## MODEL 686 SILVER PIGEON FIELD

**SPECIFICATIONS**
**Gauges:** 12, 20 and 28
**Barrels/chokes:** 26″ and 28″ with Mobilchoke® screw-in choke tubes
**Action:** Low-profile, improved boxlock
**Weight:** 6.8 lbs.
**Trigger:** Selective single trigger, auto safety
**Extractors:** Auto ejectors

**Stock:** Choice walnut, hand-checkered and hand-finished with a tough gloss finish
**Prices:**
**Standard** . . . . . . . . . . . . . . . . . . . . . . . . . . . . . . . **$1695.00**
**Combo 20 or 28 gauge** . . . . . . . . . . . . . . . . . . . . 2350.00
Also available:
**Model 686 Silver Pigeon Trap & Skeet O/U.** In 12 gauge, w/30″ barrels, 7.7 lbs. weight, matte finish
**Price:** . . . . . . . . . . . . . . . . . . . . . . . . . . . . . . . . . . . . **$1760.00**

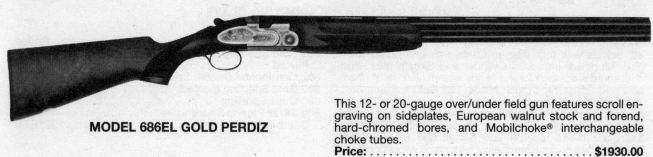

## MODEL 686EL GOLD PERDIZ

This 12- or 20-gauge over/under field gun features scroll engraving on sideplates, European walnut stock and forend, hard-chromed bores, and Mobilchoke® interchangeable choke tubes.
**Price:** . . . . . . . . . . . . . . . . . . . . . . . . . . . . . . . . . . . . **$1930.00**

# BERETTA SHOTGUNS

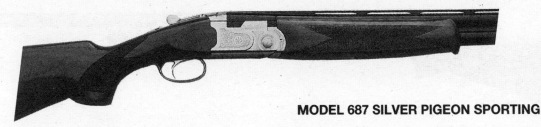

## MODEL 687 SILVER PIGEON SPORTING

This sporting over/under features enhanced engraving pattern, schnabel forend and an electroless nickel finished receiver. **Chamber:** 3″. Mobilchoke® screw-in tube system. **Gauges:** 12, 20 and 28 (Field Models)

**Prices:**
**Model 687 Silver Pigeon Sporting** . . . . . . . . . . $2575.00
**Model 687 Silver Pigeon Sporting Combo** . . . . 3395.00

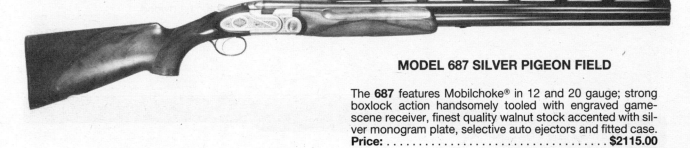

## MODEL 687 SILVER PIGEON FIELD

The **687** features Mobilchoke® in 12 and 20 gauge; strong boxlock action handsomely tooled with engraved game-scene receiver, finest quality walnut stock accented with silver monogram plate, selective auto ejectors and fitted case.
**Price:** . . . . . . . . . . . . . . . . . . . . . . . . . . . . . . . . . $2115.00

## MODEL 687EL GOLD PIGEON FIELD
### (not shown)

Features game-scene engraving on receiver with gold highlights. Available in 12, 20 gauge (28 ga. and .410 in small frame).

**SPECIFICATIONS**
**Barrels/chokes:** 26″ and 28″ with Mobilchoke®
**Action:** Low-profile improved boxlock
**Weight:** 6.8 lbs. (12 ga.)
**Trigger:** Single selective with manual safety
**Extractors:** Auto ejectors
**Prices:**
**Model 687EL** (12, 20, 28 ga.; 26″ or 28″ bbl.) . . . . $3595.00
**Model 687EL Small Frame** (28 ga./.410) . . . . . . . 3760.00

## MODEL 687EELL DIAMOND PIGEON
### $4999.00 (not shown)
### Model 687EELL Combo (20 and 28 ga.) $5777.00

In 12, 20 or 28 ga., this model features the Mobilchoke® choke system, a special premium walnut stock and exquisitely engraved sideplate with game-scene motifs.
Also available:
**Model EELL Diamond Pigeon Trap**
   **Top Mono (Full)** . . . . . . . . . . . . . . . . . . . . . . . . . $5055.00
**Diamond Pigeon Trap O/U** . . . . . . . . . . . . . . . . . 4815.00

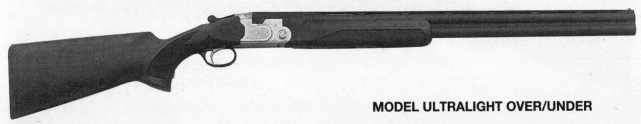

**SPECIFICATIONS**
**Gauge:** 12   **Chambers:** 2³/₄″
**Barrel length:** 28″   **Choke:** MC3
**Weight:** 5.75 lbs.

## MODEL ULTRALIGHT OVER/UNDER

**Stock:** Select walnut
**Features:** Nickel finish receiver w/game scene engraving; black rubber recoil pad; single selective trigger
**Price:** . . . . . . . . . . . . . . . . . . . . . . . . . . . . . . . . . $1795.00

# BERETTA SHOTGUNS

**PINTAIL**

This 12-gauge semiautomatic shotgun with short-recoil operation is available with 24″ or 26″ barrels and Mobilchoke®. Finish is nonreflective matte on all exposed wood and metal surfaces; receiver is aluminum alloy.

**SPECIFICATIONS**
**Barrel lengths:** 24″, 26″; 24″ Slug
**Weight:** 7.3 lbs.
**Stock:** Checkered selected hardwood
**Sights:** Bead front
**Price:** . . . . . . . . . . . . . . . . . . . . . . . . . . . . . . . . . . . . . $780.00

**MODEL ASE GOLD SKEET**

**SPECIFICATIONS**
**Barrel lengths:**
   28″ (Gold Sporting, Gold Skeet)
   30″ (Gold Sporting, Gold Trap)
   31″ (Gold Sporting)
   30″/32″ (Gold Trap)
   30″/34″ (Gold Trap)

**Chokes:** MC4 (Gold Sporting); SK/SK (Gold Skeet); MCT (Gold Trap)
**Prices:**
Model ASE Gold Skeet. . . . . . . . . . . . . . . . . . .$12,060.00
Model ASE Gold Sporting Clays . . . . . . . . . . . 12,145.00
Model ASE Gold Trap. . . . . . . . . . . . . . . . . . . . 12,145.00
Model ASE Gold Trap Combo . . . . . . . . . . . . . 16,055.00

**MODEL 1201 FP RIOT**
**$745.00 ($830.00 w/Tritium Sights)**

This all-weather semiautomatic shotgun features an adjustable space-age technopolymer stock and forend with recoil pad. Lightweight, it sports a unique weather-resistant matte black finish to reduce glare, resist corrosion and aid in heat dispersion; short recoil action for light and heavy loads. **Gauge:** 12. **Chamber:** 3″. **Capacity:** 6 rounds. **Choke:** Cylinder (fixed). **Barrel length:** 18″. **Weight:** 6.3 lbs. **Sights:** Blade front; adjustable rear.

# BERETTA SHOTGUNS

## FIELD GRADE SEMIAUTOMATICS

**MODEL AL390 SILVER MALLARD**

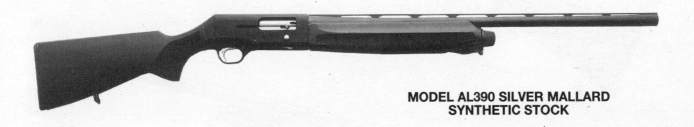

**MODEL AL390 SILVER MALLARD SYNTHETIC STOCK**

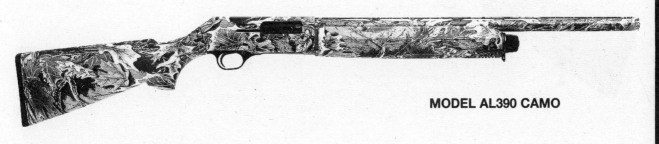

**MODEL AL390 CAMO**

## SPECIFICATIONS

**Gauges:** 12; Silver Mallard 12 and 20; Youth 20 ga. only; 3" chamber

**Chokes:** Mobilchoke® tubes; CL (Cylinder choke on Silver Mallard Slug only); fixed chokes available on request

**Barrel lengths:** 24", 26", 28", 30" (22" and 24" Silver Mallard Slug only)

**Overall length:** 41.7" (22" Slug model only); 44.1" w/24" Youth bbl.; 47.6" w/28" bbl.

**Weight:** 6.4 lbs. (Youth); 6.8 lbs. (Slug); 7.2–7.5 lbs. (other 12 ga. models)

**Features:** All models equipped with vent, field-type rib, except Slug model, which has no rib. **Silver Mallard** is available w/matte, satin finish & cut checkering on stock & forend. **Silver Mallard Slug** comes w/special rifle sights and shorter barrels. **Camo (new)** has Advantage camouflage w/eight different earth tones, natural shapes and open areas to produce four patterns in one (limb, leaf, bark, sky)

| FIELD GRADE MODELS | Prices |
| --- | --- |
| AL390 Silver Mallard (12 or 20 ga.) . . . . . . . . . . . | $ 860.00 |
| AL390 Silver Mallard—Matte, Black Synthetic or Slug (12 ga. only) . . . . . . . . . . . . . . . . . . . . . | 860.00 |
| AL390 Gold Mallard (12 ga. only) . . . . . . . . . . . . | 1025.00 |
| AL390 Camo (12 ga. only) . . . . . . . . . . . . . . . . . . | TBA |
| AL390 Youth (20 ga. only) . . . . . . . . . . . . . . . . . | 860.00 |

# BERETTA SHOTGUNS

## COMPETITION, TRAP, SKEET & SPORTING

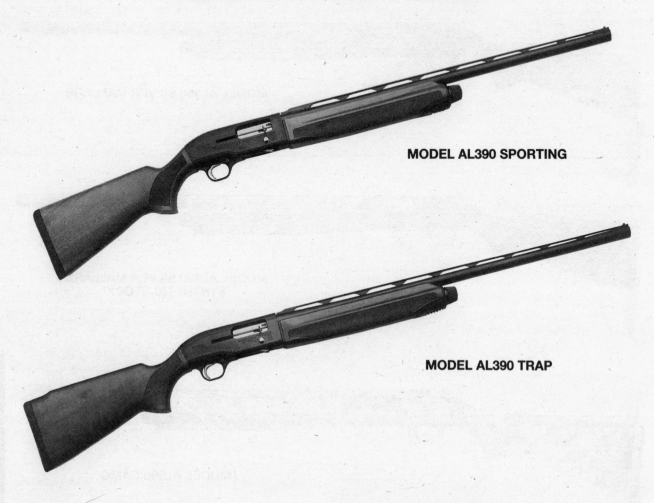

**MODEL AL390 SPORTING**

**MODEL AL390 TRAP**

**SPECIFICATIONS**

**Gauges:** 12 and 20 (Sporting and Gold Sporting); 12 ga. only (Trap and Skeet); 20 ga. only (Youth/Collection); 3″ chamber

**Chokes:** Mobilchoke® tubes; MC/Fixed on Trap; Fixed on Skeet

**Barrel lengths:** 26″ (Youth only); 26″ and 28″ (Skeet); 28″ and 30″ (Sporting, Gold Sporting & Trap); 32″ avail. on Trap only

**Overall length:** 47.8″ w/28″ bbl.

**Weight:** 7.6 lbs. (approx.)

**Features:** All models equipped with wide vent rib. **Trap** has white front and mid-rib bead sights, Monte Carlo stock, special trap recoil pad. **Skeet** has Skeet stock, interchangeable rubber skeet pad. **Sporting** has slim competition stock, rounded receiver, interchangeable rubber sporting-type recoil pad. **Gold Sporting** has engraved receiver w/gold-filled game scenes, ''PB'' logo, satin black or silver side panels.

| COMPETITION TRAP MODELS | Prices |
|---|---|
| AL390 Trap (MCT) | $ 900.00 |
|    Full Choke | 890.00 |
|    Ported (MCT) | 1005.00 |
| AL390 Super Trap | 1215.00 |

| COMPETITION SKEET MODELS | |
|---|---|
| AL390 Skeet | 860.00 |
|    Ported | 995.00 |
| AL390 Super Skeet | 1160.00 |

| COMPETITION SPORTING | |
|---|---|
| AL390 Sporting | 900.00 |
|    Ported | 995.00 |
| AL390 Gold Sporting | 1115.00 |
| AL390 Youth | 900.00 |
| AL390 Youth Collection | TBA |

# BERNARDELLI SHOTGUNS

Bernardelli shotguns are the creation of the Italian firm of Vincenzo Bernardelli, known for its fine quality firearms and commitment to excellence for more than a century. Most of the long arms featured below can be built with a variety of options, customized for the discriminating sportsman. With the exceptions indicated for each gun respectively, options include choice of barrel lengths and chokes; pistol or straight English grip stock; single selective or non-selective trigger; long tang trigger guard; checkered butt; beavertail forend; hand-cut rib; automatic safety; custom stock dimensions; standard or English recoil pad; extra set of barrels; choice of luggage gun case. Engravings are available in three grades.

### MODEL 112 12 GAUGE
**$1770.00 (Single Trigger)**
**$1625.00 (Double Trigger)**
**$2135.00 (Ejector & Multichoke)**

Features extractors or automatic ejectors, English or half pistol-grip stock and splinter forend. **Barrel length:** 26³/4″ (3″ chamber). **Choke:** Improved Cylinder and Improved Modified. **Safety:** Manual. **Weight:** 6¹/2 lbs.

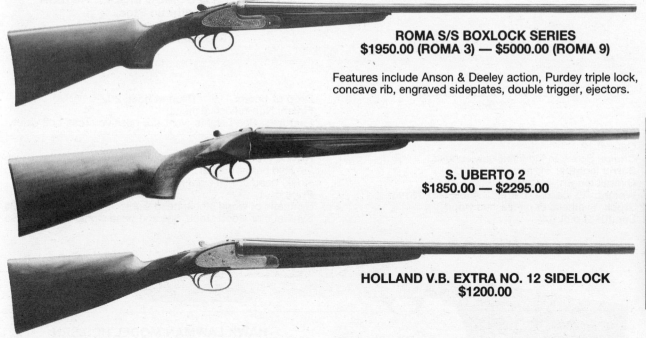

### ROMA S/S BOXLOCK SERIES
**$1950.00 (ROMA 3) — $5000.00 (ROMA 9)**

Features include Anson & Deeley action, Purdey triple lock, concave rib, engraved sideplates, double trigger, ejectors.

### S. UBERTO 2
**$1850.00 — $2295.00**

### HOLLAND V.B. EXTRA NO. 12 SIDELOCK
**$1200.00**

This 12-gauge Holland & Holland-style side-by-side feature sidelocks with double safety levers, reinforced breech, three-round Purdey locks, automatic ejectors, single or double triggers, right trigger folding, striker retaining plates, best-quality walnut stock and finely chiseled English scroll engraving.

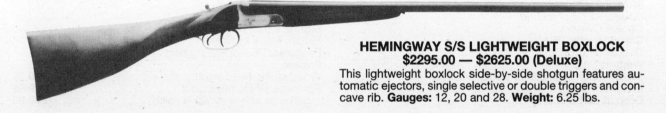

### HEMINGWAY S/S LIGHTWEIGHT BOXLOCK
**$2295.00 — $2625.00 (Deluxe)**
This lightweight boxlock side-by-side shotgun features automatic ejectors, single selective or double triggers and concave rib. **Gauges:** 12, 20 and 28. **Weight:** 6.25 lbs.

# BROLIN SHOTGUNS

**HAWK FIELD MODEL HF24WB**
Wood Stock, Bead Sights
24″ Barrel

**HAWK FIELD COMBO MODEL HC28SR**
Synthetic Stock
28″ Barrel/Bead Sights
18¹/₂″ Barrel/Rifle Sights

## HAWK FIELD SERIES
### $269.95

**SPECIFICATIONS**
**Gauge:** 12
**Choke:** Screw-in Modified Hawk choke
**Barrel lengths:** 24″ and 28″
**Overall length:** 44″ and 48″
**Weight:** 7.3 lbs. (24″ barrel); 7.4 lbs. (28″ barrel)
**Stock:** Synthetic or oil-finished wood
**Length of pull:** 14″

**Drop at comb:** 1¹/₂″   **Drop at heel:** 2¹/₂″
**Finish:** Non-reflective metal
**Features:** Bead sights, vent rib, positive cross-bolt safety, swivel studs
Also available:
**HAWK FIELD COMBO.** Combines 18¹/₂″ short barrel with 28″ field barrel; choice of oil-finished wood or black synthetic stock; bead or rifle sights on shorter barrel only
**Prices:**
Synthetic or wood stock, bead sights . . . . . . . . . . **$299.95**
Synthetic or wood stock, rifle and bead sights . . . .  319.95

**HAWK LAWMAN MODEL HL18SRN**
Synthetic Stock, Rifle Sights
Nickel Finish

## HAWK LAWMAN SERIES

**SPECIFICATIONS**
**Gauge:** 12 (3″ chamber)
**Choke:** Cylinder
**Barrel length:** 18¹/₂″
**Overall length:** 38¹/₂″
**Weight:** 7 lbs.
**Stock:** Black synthetic or wood
**Length of pull:** 14″
**Drop at comb:** 1¹/₂″

**Drop at heel:** 2¹/₂″
**Sights:** Bead, rifle or ghost ring sights
**Finish:** Matte or nickel
**Features:** Dual operating bars
**Prices:**
Wood stock, bead sights . . . . . . . . . . . . . . . . . . . . . **$249.95**
Synthetic stock, rifle sights . . . . . . . . . . . . . . . . . .  259.95
  Same as above w/nickel finish . . . . . . . . . . . . . .  269.95

# BROWNING AUTOMATIC SHOTGUNS

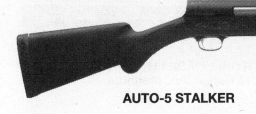

**AUTO-5 STALKER**

## SPECIFICATIONS AUTO-5 SHOTGUNS

| Model | Chamber | Barrel Length | Overall Length | Average Weight | Chokes Available |
|---|---|---|---|---|---|
| **12 GAUGE** Light | 2³/₄″ | 30″ | 49¹/₂″ | 8 lbs. 7 oz. | Invector-Plus |
| Light | 2³/₄″ | 28″ | 47¹/₂″ | 8 lbs. 4 oz. | Invector-Plus |
| Light | 2³/₄″ | 26″ | 45¹/₂″ | 8 lbs. 1 oz. | Invector-Plus |
| Lt. Buck Special | 2³/₄″ | 24″ | 43¹/₂″ | 8 lbs. | Slug/buckshot |
| Light | 2³/₄″ | 22″ | 41¹/₂″ | 7 lbs. 13 oz. | Invector-Plus |
| Magnum | 3″ | 32″ | 51¹/₄″ | 9 lbs. 2 oz. | Invector-Plus |
| Magnum | 3″ | 30″ | 49¹/₄″ | 8 lbs. 13 oz. | Invector-Plus |
| Magnum | 3″ | 28″ | 47¹/₄″ | 8 lbs. 11 oz. | Invector-Plus |
| Magnum | 3″ | 26″ | 45¹/₄″ | 8 lbs. 9 oz. | Invector-Plus |
| Mag. Buck Special | 3″ | 24″ | 43¹/₄″ | 8 lbs. 8 oz. | Slug/buckshot |
| Light Stalker | 2³/₄″ | 28″ | 47¹/₂″ | 8 lbs. 4 oz. | Invector-Plus |
| Light Stalker | 2³/₄″ | 26″ | 45¹/₂″ | 8 lbs. 1 oz. | Invector-Plus |
| Magnum Stalker | 3″ | 32″ | 51¹/₄″ | 8 lbs. 15 oz. | Invector-Plus |
| Magnum Stalker | 3″ | 30″ | 49¹/₄″ | 8 lbs. 13 oz. | Invector-Plus |
| Magnum Stalker | 3″ | 28″ | 47¹/₄″ | 8 lbs. 11 oz. | Invector-Plus |
| **20 GAUGE** Light | 2³/₄″ | 28″ | 47¹/₈″ | 6 lbs. 10 oz. | Invector-Plus |
| Light | 2³/₄″ | 26″ | 45¹/₄″ | 6 lbs. 8 oz. | Invector-Plus |

| AUTO-5 MODELS | Prices |
|---|---|
| Light 12, Hunting & Stalker, Invector Plus | **$839.95** |
| Light 20, Hunting, Invector Plus | 839.95 |
| 3″ Magnum 12, Hunting & Stalker, Invector Plus | 865.95 |
| 3″ Magnum 12, Hunting, Invector Plus | 865.95 |
| Light 12, Buck Special | 828.95 |
| 3″ Magnum 12 ga. Buck Special | 854.95 |
| Extra Barrels | **$296.95–307.95** |

## GOLD HUNTER & STALKER SEMIAUTOMATIC SHOTGUNS
### $734.95   $759.95 (Sporting Clays)

## SPECIFICATIONS GOLD 12 AND 20

| Gauge | Model | Barrel Length | Overall Length | Average Weight | Chokes Available |
|---|---|---|---|---|---|
| 12 | Hunting | 30″ | 50½″ | 7 lbs. 9 oz. | Invector-Plus |
| 12 | Hunting | 28″ | 48½″ | 7 lbs. 6 oz. | Invector-Plus |
| 12 | Hunting | 26″ | 46½″ | 7 lbs. 3 oz. | Invector-Plus |
| 20 | Hunting | 28″ | 48¼″ | 6 lbs. 14 oz. | Invector |
| 20 | Hunting | 26″ | 46¼″ | 6 lbs. 12 oz. | Invector |

## SPECIFICATIONS GOLD 10 $1007.95

| Chamber | Barrel Length | Overall Length | Average Weight | Chokes |
|---|---|---|---|---|
| 3½″ | 30″ | 52″ | 10 lbs. 13 oz. | Standard Invector |
| 3½″ | 28″ | 50″ | 10 lbs. 10 oz. | Standard Invector |
| 3½″ | 26″ | 48″ | 10 lbs. 7 oz. | Standard Invector |

Extra barrels are available for **$261.95** (10 ga.); **$272.95** (12 and 20 ga.) and **$258.95**.

## GOLD SPORTING CLAYS
### 12 Gauge

## GOLD DEER HUNTER (12 Gauge) (not shown) $798.95

Features 5″ rifled choke tube, special cantilever scope mount, sling posts, magazine cap, select walnut forearm and stock w/vented recoil pad, non-glare black finish on receiver, satin-finish 22″ barrel, 42.5″ overall length; weighs 7 lbs. 12 oz.

# BROWNING CITORI SHOTGUNS

### CITORI GRADE I HUNTING
### 12 Gauge 3¹/₂″ Magnum

**Grade I** = Blued steel w/scroll engraving
**Grade III** = Grayed steel w/light relief

**Grade VI** = Blued or grayed w/engraved ringneck pheasants and mallard ducks
**GL (Gran Lightning)** = High-grade wood w/satin finish

## CITORI PRICES (all Invector-Plus chokes unless noted otherwise)

**HUNTING MODELS** (w/pistol-grip stock, beavertail forearm, high-gloss finish)

12 ga., 3.5″ Mag., 28″ & 30″ barrels . . . . . . . . . . . . . . **$1418.00**
Same as above in 12 & 20 ga. w/3″ chamber
26″, 28″, 30″ barrels . . . . . **1334.00**

**LIGHTNING MODELS** (w/classic rounded pistol grip, Lightning-style forearm)

Grade I, 12 & 20 ga., 3″ chamber 26″ & 28″ barrels . . . . . . . . . . . . . . **1376.00**
Same as above in Grade GL **1869.00**
Grade III . . . . . . . . . . . . . . **2006.00**
Grade VI . . . . . . . . . . . . . . **2919.00**

**MICRO LIGHTNING MODEL** (20 Ga.)

Grade I, 2.75″ chamber, 24″ barrel . . . . . . . . . . . . . . **1428.00**

**SUPERLIGHT MODELS** (w/straight-grip stock, slimmed-down Schnabel forearm; 2.75″ chamber, 12 or 20 ga.)

Grade I . . . . . . . . . . . . . . . . **1376.00**
Grade III . . . . . . . . . . . . . . **2006.00**
Grade VI . . . . . . . . . . . . . . **2919.00**

**CITORI MODELS** w/Standard Invector chokes (Lightning models only, 28 and .410 ga., 2.75″ chamber, 26″ & 28″ barrels)

Grade I . . . . . . . . . . . . . . . . **1418.00**
Grade GL . . . . . . . . . . . . . . **1969.00**
Grade III . . . . . . . . . . . . . . **2242.00**
Grade VI . . . . . . . . . . . . . . **3145.00**

## SPECIFICATIONS CITORI FIELD MODELS

| Gauge | Model | Chamber* | Barrel Length | Overall Length | Average Weight | Chokes Available[1] | Grades Available |
|---|---|---|---|---|---|---|---|
| 12 | Hunting | 3 1/2″ Mag. | 30″ | 47″ | 8 lbs. 10 oz. | Invector-Plus | I |
| 12 | Hunting | 3 1/2″ Mag. | 28″ | 45″ | 8 lbs. 9 oz. | Invector-Plus | I |
| 12 | Hunting | 3″ | 30″ | 47″ | 8 lbs. 4 oz. | Invector-Plus | I |
| 12 | Hunting | 3″ | 28″ | 45″ | 8 lbs. 1 oz. | Invector-Plus | |
| 12 | Hunting | 3″ | 26″ | 43″ | 7 lbs. 15 oz. | Invector-Plus | |
| 12 | Lightning | 3″ | 28″ | 45″ | 8 lbs. 1 oz. | Invector-Plus | I, GL, III, VI |
| 12 | Lightning | 3″ | 26″ | 43″ | 7 lbs. 15 oz. | Invector-Plus | I, GL III, VI |
| 12 | Superlight | 2 3/4″ | 28″ | 45″ | 6 lbs. 12 oz. | Invector-Plus | I, III, VI |
| 12 | Superlight | 2 3/4″ | 26″ | 43″ | 6 lbs. 10 oz. | Invector-Plus | I, III, VI |
| 12 | Upland Special | 2 3/4″ | 24″ | 41″ | 6 lbs. 11 oz. | Invector-Plus | I |
| 20 | Hunting | 3″ | 28″ | 45″ | 6 lbs. 12 oz. | Invector-Plus | |
| 20 | Hunting | 3″ | 26″ | 43″ | 6 lbs. 10 oz. | Invector-Plus | |
| 20 | Lightning | 3″ | 28″ | 45″ | 6 lbs. 14 oz. | Invector-Plus | I, GL, III, VI |
| 20 | Lightning | 3″ | 26″ | 43″ | 6 lbs. 9 oz. | Invector-Plus | I, GL, III, VI |
| 20 | Lightning | 3″ | 24″ | 41″ | 6 lbs. 6 oz. | Invector-Plus | I |
| 20 | Micro Lightning | 2 3/4″ | 24″ | 41″ | 6 lbs. 3 oz. | Invector-Plus | |
| 20 | Superlight | 2 3/4″ | 26″ | 43″ | 6 lbs. | Invector-Plus | I, III, VI |
| 20 | Upland Special | 2 3/4″ | 24″ | 41″ | 6 lbs. | Invector-Plus | I |
| 28 | Lightning | 2 3/4″ | 28″ | 45″ | 6 lbs. 11 oz. | Invector | I |
| 28 | Lightning | 2 3/4″ | 26″ | 43″ | 6 lbs. 10 oz. | Invector | I, GL, III, VI |
| 28 | Superlight | 2 3/4″ | 26″ | 43″ | 6 lbs. 10 oz. | Invector | I, III, VI |
| .410 | Lightning | 3″ | 28″ | 45″ | 7 lbs. | Invector | I |
| .410 | Lightning | 3″ | 26″ | 43″ | 6 lbs. 14 oz. | Invector | I, GL, III, VI |
| .410 | Superlight | 3″ | 28″ | 45″ | 6 lbs. 14 oz. | Invector | I |
| .410 | Superlight | 3″ | 26″ | 43″ | 6 lbs. 13 oz. | Invector | I, III, VI |

[1]Full & Modified Choke installed; Improved Cylinder and wrench included. GL=Gran Lightning grade.

**STANDARD INVECTOR** (28 & .410 ga.)
Grade I . . . . . . . . . . . . . . . . **$1418.00**
Grade III . . . . . . . . . . . . . . **2242.00**   **UPLAND SPECIAL** (12 & 20 ga.)
Grade VI . . . . . . . . . . . . . . **3145.00**   Grade I only, 24″ barrel . . . . . **$1386.00**

### RECOILLESS TRAP
### $1995.00

## SPECIFICATIONS
**Gauge:** 12, Standard or Micro; Invector-Plus choke
**Chamber:** 2³/₄″
**Barrel length:** 27″ or 30″
**Overall length:** 48⁵/₈″ (27″ barrel); 51⁵/₈″ (30″ barrel)
**Weight:** 8 lbs. 10 oz.; 8 lbs. 8 oz. (30″ barrel)

# BROWNING CITORI SHOTGUNS

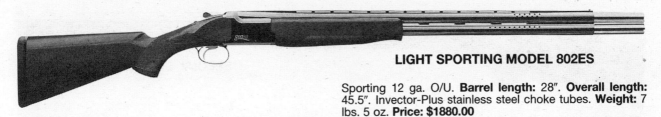

## LIGHT SPORTING MODEL 802ES

Sporting 12 ga. O/U. **Barrel length:** 28". **Overall length:** 45.5". Invector-Plus stainless steel choke tubes. **Weight:** 7 lbs. 5 oz. **Price: $1880.00**

## CITORI MODEL 425 SPORTING CLAYS

### MODELS 425 AND ULTRA SPORTER (Not shown)
(all Invector-Plus)

**MODEL 425** (12 & 20 Ga.)
Grade I, 28", 30", 32" bbls.   **$1775.00**
Grade GC (Golden Clays) . . .   **3308.00**
For adjustable comb, **add** . . .   **210.00**

**MODEL WSSF**
12 Ga. only, 28" barrel,
   walnut stock . . . . . . . . . . .   **1775.00**

**ULTRA SPORTER** (12 Ga. only)
Grade I, Blue or Gray, 28", 30",
   32" bbls. . . . . . . . . . . . .   **1722.00**
Grade GC 28", 30", 32"
   barrels . . . . . . . . . . . . . .   **3203.00**
For adjustable comb, **add** . . .   **210.00**
* WSSF = Women's Shooting Sports
Foundation

## 425 & ULTRA SPORTER SPECIFICATIONS

| Model | Chamber | Barrel Length | Overall Length | Average Weight | Chokes Available | Grades Available |
|---|---|---|---|---|---|---|
| **425** | | | | | | |
| 12 ga. | 2 3/4" | 32" | 49 1/2" | 7 lbs. 15 oz. | Invector-Plus | Gr.I, Golden Clays |
| 12 ga. | 2 3/4" | 30" | 47 1/2" | 7 lbs. 14 oz. | Invector-Plus | Gr.I, Golden Clays |
| 12 ga. | 2 3/4" | 28" | 45 1/2" | 7 lbs. 13 oz. | Invector-Plus | Gr.I, Golden Clays |
| 20 ga. | 2 3/4" | 30" | 47 1/2" | 6 lbs. 13 oz. | Invector-Plus | Gr.I, Golden Clays |
| 20 ga. | 2 3/4" | 28" | 45 1/2" | 6 lbs. 12 oz. | Invector-Plus | Gr.I, Golden Clays |
| WSSF 12 ga. | 2 3/4" | 28" | 45 1/2" | 7 lbs. 4 oz. | Invector-Plus | Custom WSSF Exclusive |
| **Ultra Sporter** | | | | | | |
| 12 ga. Sporter | 2 3/4" | 32" | 49" | 8 lbs. 4 oz. | Invector-Plus | Gr.I, Golden Clays |
| 12 ga. Sporter | 2 3/4" | 30" | 47" | 8 lbs. 2 oz. | Invector-Plus | Gr.I, Golden Clays |
| 12 ga. Sporter | 2 3/4" | 28" | 45" | 8 lbs. | Invector-Plus | Gr.I, Golden Clays |

*Sporting Clays models: One modified, one Improved Cylinder and one Skeet tube supplied.*
*Other chokes available as accessories.*

## SPECIFICATIONS SPECIAL SPORTING CLAYS, TRAP & SKEET AND LIGHTNING SPORTING (Add'l prices on following page)

| Gauge | Model | Chamber | Barrel Length | Overall Length | Average Weight | Chokes | Grades Available |
|---|---|---|---|---|---|---|---|
| **SPECIAL*** | | | | | | | |
| 12 | Sporting Clays | 2 3/4" | 32" | 49" | 8 lbs. 5 oz. | Invector-Plus | I, Golden Clays |
| 12 | Sporting Clays | 2 3/4" | 30" | 47" | 8 lbs. 3 oz. | Invector-Plus | I, Golden Clays |
| 12 | Sporting Clays | 2 3/4" | 28" | 45" | 8 lbs. 1 oz. | Invector-Plus | I, Golden Clays |
| 12 | Trap (Conv.) | 2 3/4" | 32" | 49" | 8 lbs. 11 oz. | Invector-Plus | I, III, Golden Clays |
| 12 | Trap (Monte Carlo) | 2 3/4" | 32" | 49" | 8 lbs. 10 oz. | Invector-Plus | I, III, Golden Clays |
| 12 | Trap (Conv.) | 2 3/4" | 30" | 47" | 8 lbs. 7 oz. | Invector-Plus | I, III, Golden Clays |
| 12 | Trap (Monte Carlo) | 2 3/4" | 30" | 47" | 8 lbs. 6 oz. | Invector-Plus | I, III, Golden Clays |
| 12 | Skeet | 2 3/4" | 28" | 45" | 8 lbs. | Invector-Plus | I, III, Golden Clays |
| 12 | Skeet | 2 3/4" | 26" | 43" | 7 lbs. 15 oz. | Invector-Plus | I, III, Golden Clays |
| 20 | Skeet | 2 3/4" | 28" | 45" | 7 lbs. 4 oz. | Invector-Plus | I, III, Golden Clays |
| 20 | Skeet | 2 3/4" | 26" | 43" | 7 lbs. 1 oz. | Invector-Plus | I, III, Golden Clays |
| 28 | Skeet | 2 3/4" | 28" | 45" | 6 lbs. 15 oz. | Invector | I, III, Golden Clays |
| 28 | Skeet | 2 3/4" | 26" | 43" | 6 lbs. 10 oz. | Invector | I, III, Golden Clays |
| .410 | Skeet | 3" | 28" | 45" | 7 lbs. 6 oz. | Invector | I, III, Golden Clays |
| .410 | Skeet | 3" | 26" | 43" | 7 lbs. 3 oz. | Invector | I, III, Golden Clays |
| **LIGHTNING SPORTING** | | | | | | | |
| 12 | Sporting Clays | 3" | 30" | 47" | 8 lbs. 8 oz. | Invector-Pus | I, Golden Clays |
| 12 | Sporting Clays | 3" | 28" | 45" | 8 lbs. 6 oz. | Invector-Plus | I, Golden Clays |

# BROWNING CITORI SHOTGUNS

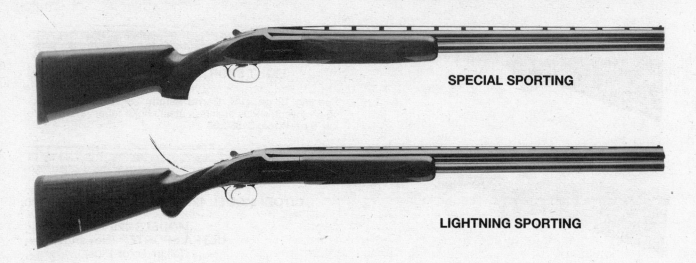

**SPECIAL SPORTING**

**LIGHTNING SPORTING**

## CITORI SPECIAL SPORTING AND LIGHTNING SPORTING

**Prices:**
**Special Sporting**
Grade I, ported barrels . . . . . . . . . . . . . . . . . . . . . . $1565.00
Grade I, ported bbls., adj. comb . . . . . . . . . . . . 1775.00
Golden Clays, ported barrels . . . . . . . . . . . . . . . 3203.00
Golden Clays, adj. comb . . . . . . . . . . . . . . . . . . . 3413.00
**Lightning Sporting**
Grade I, high rib, ported bbl., 3″. . . . . . . . . . . . . 1565.00

**Lightning Sporting (cont.)**
Grade I, high rib, adj. comb . . . . . . . . . . . . . . . . . $1775.00
Grade I, low rib, ported bbls., 3″ . . . . . . . . . . . . . 1496.00
Grade I, low rib, adj. comb. . . . . . . . . . . . . . . . . . . 1706.00
Golden Clays, low rib, ported bbls., 3″ . . . . . . . . 3092.00
Golden Clays, low rib, adj. comb . . . . . . . . . . . . . 3302.00
Golden Clays, high rib, ported bbls., 3″ . . . . . . . . 3203.00
Golden Clays, high rib, adj. comb . . . . . . . . . . . . . 3413.00

*(See previous page for specifications)*

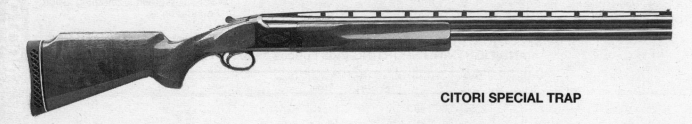

**CITORI SPECIAL TRAP**

## SPECIAL TRAP MODELS

| 12 Gauge, Invector-Plus, Ported Barrels | Prices |
| --- | --- |
| Grade I, Monte Carlo stock . . . . . . . . . . . . . . . | $1586.00 |
| Grade I, adj. comb . . . . . . . . . . . . . . . . . . . . | 1796.00 |
| Grade III, Monte Carlo stock . . . . . . . . . . . . . | 2179.00 |
| Grade III, adj. comb . . . . . . . . . . . . . . . . . . . . | 2389.00 |
| Golden Clays, Monte Carlo stock . . . . . . . . . . | 3239.00 |
| Golden Clays, adj. comb . . . . . . . . . . . . . . . . . | 3449.00 |

## SPECIAL SKEET MODELS

| 12 and 20 Gauge, Invector Plus, Ported Barrels | Prices |
| --- | --- |
| Grade I, high post rib . . . . . . . . . . . . . . . . . . . . | $1586.00 |
| Grade I, high post rib, adj. comb . . . . . . . . . . . . | 1796.00 |
| Grade III, high post rib . . . . . . . . . . . . . . . . . . . | 2179.00 |
| Grade III, high post rib, adj. comb . . . . . . . . . . . | 2389.00 |
| Golden Clays, high post rib . . . . . . . . . . . . . . . . | 3239.00 |
| Golden Clays, high post rib, adj. comb . . . . . . . . | 3449.00 |
| **28 Ga. and .410 Bore Std. Invector** | |
| Grade I, high post rib . . . . . . . . . . . . . . . . . . . . | 1586.00 |
| Grade III, high post rib . . . . . . . . . . . . . . . . . . . | 2179.00 |
| Golden Clays, high post rib . . . . . . . . . . . . . . . . | 3239.00 |

# BROWNING SHOTGUNS

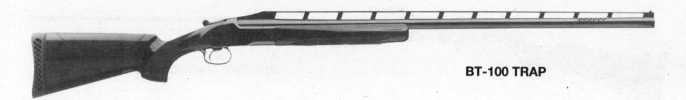

**BT-100 TRAP**

## SPECIFICATIONS BT-100

| Gauge | Model | Chamber | Barrel Length | Overall Length | Average Weight | Chokes | Grades Available |
|---|---|---|---|---|---|---|---|
| 12 | BT-100 | 2 3/4" | 34" | 50 1/2" | 8 lbs. 10 oz. | Invector Plus[1] | I, Stainless |
| 12 | BT-100 | 2 3/4" | 32" | 48 1/2" | 8 lbs. 9 oz. | Invector Plus[1] | I, Stainless |
| 12 | BT-100 Monte Carlo | 2 3/4" | 34" | 50 1/2" | 8 lbs. 10 oz. | Invector Plus | I, Stainless |
| 12 | BT-100 Monte Carlo | 2 3/4" | 32" | 48 1/2" | 8 lbs. 9 oz. | Invector Plus | I, Stainless |
| 12 | BT-100 Thumbhole | 2 3/4" | 34" | 50 3/4" | 8 lbs. 8 oz. | Invector Plus | I, Stainless |
| 12 | BT-100 Thumbhole | 2 3/4" | 32" | 48 3/4" | 8 lbs. 6 oz. | Invector Plus | I, Stainless |

*F=Full, M=Modified, IM=Improved Modified, S=Skeet, Invector=Invector Choke System — Invector-Plus Trap models: Full, Improved Modified, Modified, and wrench included.*
*[1] Also available with conventional full choke barrel.*

## STOCK DIMENSIONS BT-100

| | Adjustable Conventional | Thumbhole | Monte Carlo |
|---|---|---|---|
| Length of Pull | 14 3/8" | 14 3/8" | 14 3/8" |
| Drop at Comb | Adj.* | 1 3/4" | 1 9/16" |
| Drop at Monte Carlo | — | 1 1/4" | 1 7/16" |
| Drop at Heel | Adj.* | 2 1/8" | 2" |

*Adjustable Drop at Comb and Heel.*

### BT-100 SINGLE BARREL TRAP
**Grade I, Invector-Plus**
| | |
|---|---|
| Monte Carlo stock | $1995.00 |
| Adjustable comb | 2205.00 |
| Full choke barrel | 1948.00 |
| Full choke barrel, adj. comb | 2158.00 |
| Thumbhole stock | 2270.00 |
| Full choke barrel | 2225.00 |

**Stainless, Invector-Plus**
| | |
|---|---|
| Monte Carlo stock | 2415.00 |
| Adjustable comb | 2625.00 |
| Full choke barrel | 2368.00 |
| Full choke barrel, adj. comb | 2578.00 |
| Thumbhole stock | 2690.00 |
| Full choke barrel | 2645.00 |

**Trigger Assembly Replacement** .......... 525.00

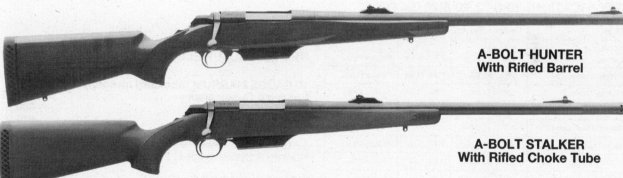

**A-BOLT HUNTER**
**With Rifled Barrel**

**A-BOLT STALKER**
**With Rifled Choke Tube**

## A-BOLT SHOTGUNS   Prices
**Hunter**
| | |
|---|---|
| With choke tube | $828.95 |
| Without sights | 804.95 |
| With rifled barrel | 881.95 |
| Without sights | 856.95 |

**Stalker**
| | |
|---|---|
| With choke tube | 744.95 |
| Without sights | 719.95 |
| With rifled barrel | 797.95 |
| Without sights | 772.95 |

## SPECIFICATIONS A-BOLT SHOTGUNS

| Model | Chamber | Magazine Capacity | Barrel Length | Overall Length | Average Weight | Choke/Barrel Available |
|---|---|---|---|---|---|---|
| Hunter/Choke Tube | 3" | 2[1] | 23" | 44 3/4" | 7 lbs. 2 oz. | Standard Invector* |
| Hunter/Rifled Barrel | 3" | 2[1] | 22" | 43 3/4" | 7 lbs. | Fully rifled barrel |
| Stalker/Choke Tube | 3" | 2[1] | 23" | 44 3/4" | 7 lbs. 2 oz. | Standard Invector* |
| Stalker/Rifled Barrel | 3" | 2[1] | 22" | 43 3/4" | 7 lbs. | Fully rifled barrel |

*Standard Invector interchangeable choke tube system: One rifled choke tube and one X-Full Turkey choke tube included.*
*[1] Total capacity is 2 shells in magazine, one in chamber.*

# BROWNING SHOTGUNS

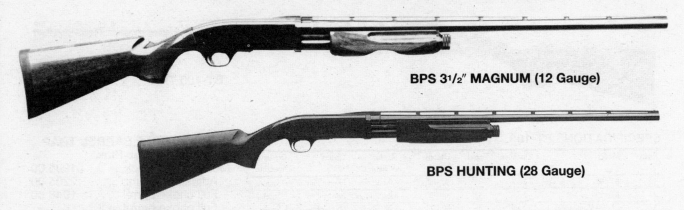

**BPS 3¹/₂″ MAGNUM (12 Gauge)**

**BPS HUNTING (28 Gauge)**

## SPECIFICATIONS BPS MAGNUMS (Capacity: 4 rounds)

| Gauge | Model | Chamber Length | Barrel Length | Overall Weight | Average Available | Chokes |
|---|---|---|---|---|---|---|
| 10 Magnum | Hunting & Stalker | 3¹/₂″ | 30″ | 51³/₄″ | 9 lbs. 8 oz. | Invector |
| 10 Magnum | Hunting & Stalker | 3¹/₂″ | 28″ | 49³/₄″ | 9 lbs. 6 oz. | Invector |
| 10 Magnum | Hunting & Stalker | 3¹/₂″ | 26″ | 47³/₄″ | 9 lbs. 4 oz. | Invector |
| 10 Magnum | Hunting & Stalker | 3¹/₂″ | 24″ | 45³/₄″ | 9 lbs. 4 oz. | Invector |
| 10 Magnum | Hunting Buck Special | 3¹/₂″ | 24″ | 45³/₄″ | 9 lbs. 2 oz. | Slug/Buckshot |
| 12, 3¹/₂″ Mag | Hunting & Stalker | 3¹/₂″ | 30″ | 51³/₄″ | 8 lbs. 12 oz. | Invector-Plus |
| 12, 3¹/₂″ Mag | Hunting & Stalker | 3¹/₂″ | 28″ | 49³/₄″ | 8 lbs. 9 oz. | Invector-Plus |
| 12, 3¹/₂″ Mag | Hunting & Stalker | 3¹/₂″ | 26″ | 47³/₄″ | 8 lbs. 6 oz. | Invector-Plus |
| 12, 3¹/₂″ Mag | Hunting & Stalker | 3¹/₂″ | 24″ | 45³/₄″ | 8 lbs. 3 oz. | Invector-Plus |

## SPECIFICATIONS BPS 12, 20 & 28 Ga. (3″)

| Model | Barrel Length | Overall Length | Average Weight | Chokes Available |
|---|---|---|---|---|
| **12 GAUGE** Hunting | 32″ | 52¹/₂″ | 7 lbs. 14 oz. | Invector-Plus |
| Hunting, Stalker | 30″ | 50³/₄″ | 7 lbs. 12 oz. | Invector-Plus |
| Hunting, Stalker | 28″ | 48³/₄″ | 7 lbs. 11 oz. | Invector-Plus |
| Hunting, Stalker | 26″ | 46³/₄″ | 7 lbs. 10 oz. | Invector-Plus |
| Standard Buck Special | 24″ | 44³/₄″ | 7 lbs. 10 oz. | Slug/Buckshot |
| Upland Special | 22″ | 42³/₄″ | 7 lbs. 8 oz. | Invector-Plus |
| Hunting, Stalker | 22″ | 42¹/₂″ | 7 lbs. 7 oz. | Invector-Plus |
| Game Gun Turkey Special | 20¹/₂″ | 40⁷/₈″ | 7 lbs. 7 oz. | Invector |
| Game Gun Deer Special* | 20¹/₂″ | 40⁷/₈″ | 7 lbs. 7 oz. | Special Inv./Rifled |
| **20 GAUGE** Hunting | 28″ | 48³/₄″ | 7 lbs. 1 oz. | Invector-Plus |
| Hunting | 26″ | 46³/₄″ | 7 lbs. | Invector-Plus |
| Youth/Ladies | 22″ | 41³/₄″ | 6 lbs. 11 oz. | Invector-Plus |
| Upland Special | 22″ | 42³/₄″ | 6 lbs. 12 oz. | Invector-Plus |
| **28 GAUGE** Hunting** | 28″ | 48³/₄″ | 7 lbs. 1 oz. | Invector |
| Hunting** | 26″ | 46³/₄″ | 7 lbs. | Invector |

\* Smooth or rifled   \*\* 2³/₄″ chamber

## BPS MAGNUM/FIELD GUNS                                Prices

**10 GAUGE MAGNUM (Standard Invector)**
Hunting & Stalker grades . . . . . . . . . . . . . . . . . . . . . $671.95
Waterfowl . . . . . . . . . . . . . . . . . . . . . . . . . . . . . . . . 860.95
Buck Special (cyl. bore) . . . . . . . . . . . . . . . . . . . . . 676.95

**12 GAUGE 3.5″ MAGNUM (Invector Plus)**
Hunting & Stalker grades . . . . . . . . . . . . . . . . . . . . . 676.95

**FIELD MODELS (12 Ga. Invector Plus)**
Hunting & Stalker grades . . . . . . . . . . . . . . . . . . . . . 534.95
Pigeon grade . . . . . . . . . . . . . . . . . . . . . . . . . . . . . . 713.95
Upland Special grade . . . . . . . . . . . . . . . . . . . . . . . . 534.95
Buck Special grade (cyl. bore) . . . . . . . . . . . . . . . . . 519.95

**GAME GUN MODELS (12 Ga. Standard Invector)**
Deer Special grade (gloss finish w/polished
   metal) . . . . . . . . . . . . . . . . . . . . . . . . . . . . . . . . . . 603.95
Turkey Special . . . . . . . . . . . . . . . . . . . . . . . . . . . . . 571.95

**20 & 28 GAUGE FIELD MODELS (Std./Invector-Plus)**
Hunting/Youth & Ladies . . . . . . . . . . . . . . . . . . . . . . 534.95

# COUNTY SHOTGUNS

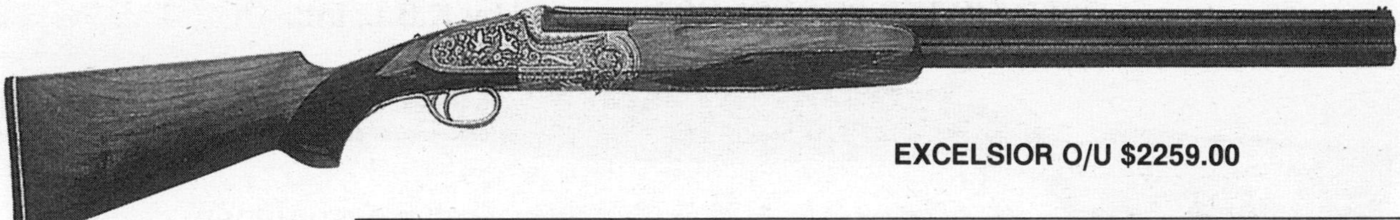

**EXCELSIOR O/U $2259.00**

| Gauge | Barrel Lenght | Chamber | Chokes | Rib | Ejector | Trigger | Frame Finish | Stock | Stock Lenght of pull | Dimensions Drop Comb | Dimensions At Heel | Average Weight lb | Average Weight oz |
|---|---|---|---|---|---|---|---|---|---|---|---|---|---|
| 12 | 28"-26" | 3" | MULTI. | 1/4" | ASE | ST | OS | FPG | 14⅛" | 1⅜" | 2⅜" | 7 | 3 |
| 20 | 26" | 3" | MULTI. | 1/4" | ASE | ST | OS | FPG | 14⅛" | 1⅜" | 2⅜" | 6 | 15 |

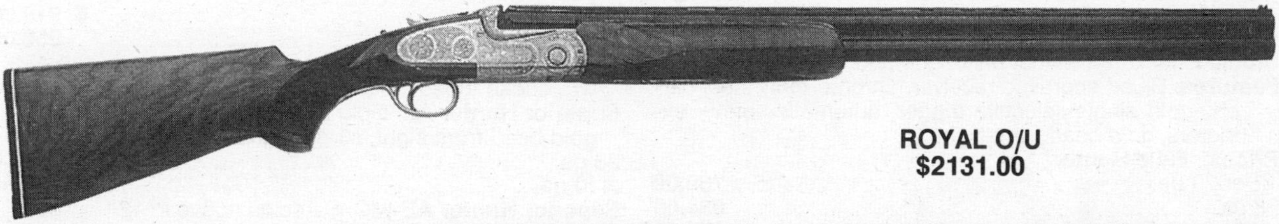

**ROYAL O/U**
**$2131.00**

| Gauge | Barrel Lenght | Chamber | Chokes | Rib | Ejector | Trigger | Frame Finish | Stock | Stock Lenght of pull | Dimensions Drop Comb | Dimensions At Heel | Average Weight lb | Average Weight oz |
|---|---|---|---|---|---|---|---|---|---|---|---|---|---|
| 12 | 28"-26" | 3" | MULTI. | 1/4" | ASE | ST | OS | FPG | 14⅛" | 1⅜" | 2⅜" | 7 | 3 |
| 20 | 26" | 3" | MULTI. | 1/4" | ASE | ST | OS | FPG | 14⅛" | 1⅜" | 2⅜" | 6 | 15 |

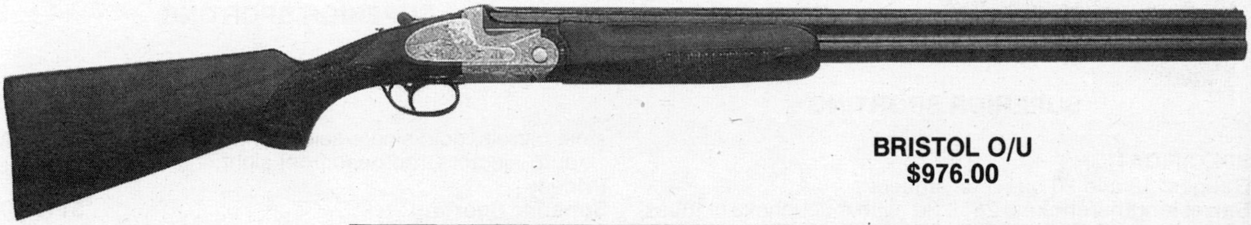

**BRISTOL O/U**
**$976.00**

| Gauge | Barrel Lenght | Chamber | Chokes | Rib | Ejector | Trigger | Frame Finish | Stock | Stock Lenght of pull | Dimensions Drop Comb | Dimensions At Heel | Average Weight lb | Average Weight oz |
|---|---|---|---|---|---|---|---|---|---|---|---|---|---|
| 12 | 28"-26" | 3" | M/F-IC/M MULTI. | 1/4" | ASE | SST | OS | FPG | 14⅛" | 1⅜" | 2⅜" | 7 | 1 |
| 20 | 26" | 3" | M/F-IC/M MULTI. | 1/4" | ASE | SST | OS | FPG | 14⅛" | 1⅜" | 2⅜" | 6 | 12 |

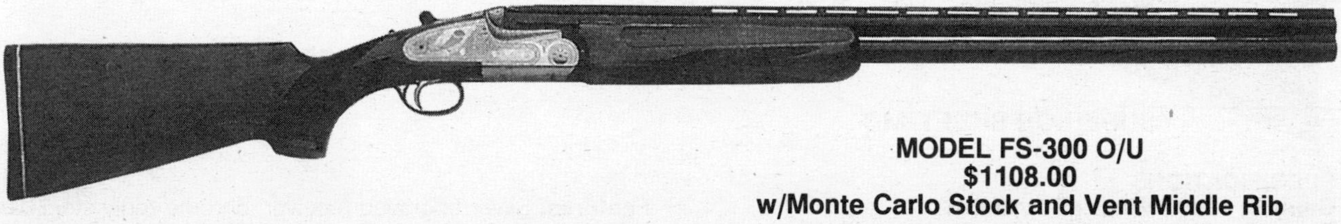

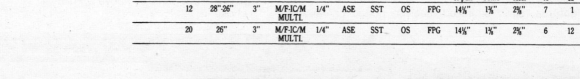

**MODEL FS-300 O/U**
**$1108.00**
**w/Monte Carlo Stock and Vent Middle Rib**

| Gauge | Barrel Lenght | Chamber | Chokes | Rib | Ejector | Trigger | Frame Finish | Stock | Stock Lenght of pull | Dimensions Drop Comb | Dimensions At Heel | Average Weight lb | Average Weight oz |
|---|---|---|---|---|---|---|---|---|---|---|---|---|---|
| 12 | 30" | 2¾" | IM/F | 3/8" | ASE | ST | OS | FPG | 14 5/16" | 1⅜" | 1½" | 8 | 2 |

# CHARLES DALY SHOTGUNS

## OVER/UNDER SHOTGUNS Imported by K.B.I., Inc.

**FIELD OVER/UNDER**

### FIELD HUNTER

**SPECIFICATIONS**
**Gauges:** 12, 20, 28 and .410 (3″ chambers); 28 ga. (2³/₄″)
**Barrel lengths/chokes:** 28″ Mod./Full; 26″ IC/Mod.; .410 ga. Full/Full
**Weight:** Approx. 7 lb.
**Stock:** Checkered walnut pistol grip and forend
**Features:** Blued engraved receiver, chrome-moly steel barrels, gold single-selective trigger, automatic safety, extractors, gold bead front sight
**Prices:  Field Hunter**

| | |
|---|---:|
| 12 or 20 ga. | $   769.00 |
| 28 ga. | 834.00 |
| .410 ga. | 874.00 |

**Field Hunter AE.** Same as above w/auto-ejectors (not available in 12 or 20 ga.)

| | |
|---|---:|
| 28 ga. | $   919.00 |
| .410 ga. | 959.00 |

**Field Hunter AE-MC.** Same as Field Hunter but w/5 choke tubes (12 and 20 ga. only) ........ 979.00
**Superior Hunter AE.** Gold single-selective trigger, gold bead front sight, silver engraved receiver

| | |
|---|---:|
| 28 ga. | 1099.00 |
| .410 ga. | 1139.00 |

**Superior Hunter AE-MC.** Same as above in 12 and 20 ga. w/5 choke tubes................ 1199.00

**SUPERIOR SPORTING**

### SUPERIOR SPORTING

**SPECIFICATIONS**
**Gauges:** 12 and 20 ga.; 3″ chambers
**Barrel lengths/chokes:** 28″ & 30″ with multi-choke (5 tubes)
**Weight:** Approx. 7 lb.
**Stock:** Checkered walnut pistol-grip buttstock w/semibeavertail forend
**Features:** Silver engraved receiver, ported chrome-moly

steel barrels, gold single-selective trigger, automatic safety, auto-ejectors, red bead front sight
**Prices:**
**Superior Sporting**......................$1179.00
**Superior Trap-MC.** Same as above in 12 ga. only (2³/₄″ chamber) 30″ bbl. only............... 1299.00
**Superior Trap.** Same as above w/Full/Full choke.................................. 1179.00

**SUPERIOR SKEET**

### SUPERIOR SKEET-MC

**SPECIFICATIONS**
**Gauges:** 12 and 20 ga.; 3″ chambers
**Barrel length/choke:** 26″ with multi-choke (5 choke tubes)
**Weight:** Approx. 7 lb.
**Sights:** Red bead front; metal bead center
**Stock:** Checkered walnut pistol-grip w/semibeavertail forend

**Features:** Silver engraved receiver, chrome-moly steel barrels, gold single-selective trigger, automatic safety, auto-ejectors, recoil pad
**Prices:**
**Superior Skeet-MC.**......................$1239.00
**Superior Skeet** w/SK1 & SK2 chokes.......... 1109.00

# CHARLES DALY SHOTGUNS

## OVER/UNDER SHOTGUNS Imported by K.B.I., Inc.

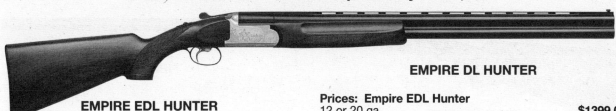

### EMPIRE DL HUNTER

### EMPIRE EDL HUNTER

**SPECIFICATIONS**
**Gauges:** 12, 20, .410 ga. (3″ chambers); 28 ga. (2³/₄″)
**Barrel lengths/chokes:** 26″ & 28″—5 multi-choke tubes in
 12 & 20 ga.; 26″ IC/M in 28 ga.; 26″ Full/Full in .410 ga.
**Weight:** Approx. 7 lb.
**Sights:** Red bead front; metal bead center
**Stock:** Checkered walnut pistol-grip buttstock w/semibeav-
 ertail forend
**Features:** Silver engraved receiver, full sideplate, chrome-
 moly steel barrels, gold single-selective trigger, automatic
 safety, auto-ejector, recoil pad

**Prices:  Empire EDL Hunter**

| | |
|---|---:|
| 12 or 20 ga. | $1399.00 |
| 28 ga. | 1469.00 |
| .410 ga. | 1519.00 |
| **Empire DL Hunter** w/o full sideplate (12 or 20 ga.) | 1229.00 |
| .410 ga. | 1349.00 |
| **Empire Sporting.** 12 and 20 ga. only, w/30″ and 28″ ported barrels, no metal bead center sight | 1389.00 |
| **Empire Trap-MC.** 12 ga. w/30″ bbl. (unported) metal bead center sight, recoil pad | 1469.00 |
| **Empire Trap.** Same as above w/Full/Full choke | 1349.00 |
| **Empire Skeet-MC.** 12 and 20 ga. w/26″ barrel (multi-choke) | 1399.00 |
| **Empire Skeet.** w/SK1 & SK2 chokes | 1249.00 |

### DIAMOND GTX EDL HUNTER

### DIAMOND GTX EDL HUNTER

**SPECIFICATIONS**
**Gauges:** 12, 20, .410 ga. (3″ chambers); 28 ga. (2³/₄″)
**Barrel lengths/chokes:** 30″, 28″ & 26″ multi-choke (5 tubes)
 in 12 & 20 ga.; 26″ IC/M in 28 ga.; 26″ Full/Full in .410 ga.
**Weight:** Approx. 8.5 lb.
**Stock:** Select fancy European walnut stock w/24 lines-per-
 inch hand-checkering and hand-rubbed oil finish; hand-
 engraved scrollwork and game scene with dog and birds
 and three gold inlays
**Features:** Boss-type action with internal side lugs, milled
 from steel bars and forged solid billets; GTX detachable

single-selective trigger system with coil springs, automatic
 safety, auto-ejectors, red blade front sight

**Prices:  Diamond GTX EDL Hunter**

| | |
|---|---:|
| 12 or 20 ga. | $15,999.00 |
| 28 ga. | 16,179.00 |
| .410 ga. | 16,219.00 |
| **Diamond GTX DL Hunter.** w/26″ & 28″ barrels, recoil pad, chrome-moly steel barrels (no gold inlays) | |
| 12 or 20 ga. | 12,399.00 |
| 28 ga. | 12,489.00 |
| .410 ga. | 12,529.00 |

### DIAMOND REGENT DL HUNTER

### DIAMOND REGENT GTX EDL HUNTER

**SPECIFICATIONS**
**Gauges:** 12, 20, .410 ga. (3″ chambers); 28 ga. (2³/₄″)
**Barrel lengths:** 30″, 28″ & 26″ w/5 multi-choke tubes in 12 &
 20 ga.; 26″ IC/M in 28 ga.; 26″ Full/Full in .410 ga.
**Weight:** Approx. 7 lb.
**Sights:** White bead front; metal bead center
**Stock:** Extra-select fancy European walnut w/finest hand-
 engraved scrollwork and game scene by Italian masters

**Features:** Same as Diamond GTX above, plus chrome-moly
 barrels, auto safety
**Prices:  Diamond Regent GTX EDL Hunter**

| | |
|---|---:|
| 12 or 20 ga. | $26,249.00 |
| 28 ga. | 26,499.00 |
| .410 ga. | 26,549.00 |
| **Diamond Regent GTX DL Hunter.** Same as above w/o gold inlays in 12 & 20 ga. | 22,299.00 |
| 28 ga. | 22,369.00 |
| .410 ga. | 22,419.00 |

# CHARLES DALY SHOTGUNS

## SIDE BY SIDE SHOTGUNS Imported by K.B.I., Inc.

**FIELD S/S**

**FIELD HUNTER**

### SPECIFICATIONS
**Gauges:** 10, 12, 20 and .410 (3″ chambers); 28 ga. (2³/₄″)
**Barrel lengths/chokes:** 32″ Mod./Mod.; 30″ Mod./Full; 28″ Mod./Full; 26″ IC/Mod.; .410 ga. Full/Full
**Weight:** Approx. 6 lbs.–11.4 lbs.
**Stock:** Checkered walnut pistol-grip and forend
**Features:** Silver engraved receiver; gold single-selective trigger in 10, 12 and 20 ga.; double trigger in 28 and 410 ga.; automatic safety, extractors, gold bead front sight. Imported from Spain.

**Prices:**
| | |
|---|---|
| 10 ga. ................................................. | $ 979.00 |
| 12 or 20 ga. ...................................... | 799.00 |
| 28 or .410 ga. ................................... | 849.00 |
| **Field Hunter-MC** (5 multi-choke tubes) | |
| 10 ga. ................................................. | 1089.00 |
| 12 or 20 ga. ...................................... | 929.00 |

## SUPERIOR HUNTER (not shown)

### SPECIFICATIONS
**Gauges:** 12 and 20; 3″ chambers
**Barrel lengths/chokes:** 28″ Mod./Full; 26″ IC/Mod.
**Weight:** Approx. 7 lb.
**Stock:** Checkered walnut pistol-grip buttstock and splinter forend
**Features:** Silver engraved receiver, chrome-lined steel barrels, gold single trigger, automatic safety, extractors, gold bead front sight
**Prices:**
| | |
|---|---|
| **Superior Hunter** .......................... | $ 989.00 |
| **Empire Hunter.** Same as above w/hand-checkered stock auto ejectors, game scene engraved receiver. .... | 1339.00 |

## DIAMOND DL (not shown)

### SPECIFICATIONS
**Gauges:** 12, 20, .410 ga. (3″ chambers); 28 ga. (2³/₄″)
**Barrel lengths/chokes:** 28″ Mod./Full; 26″ IC/Mod.; 26″ Full/Full in .410 ga.
**Weight:** Approx. 5–7 lbs.
**Stock:** Select fancy European walnut, English-styled, beavertail forend, hand-checkered, hand-rubbed oil finish
**Features:** Fine steel drop-forged action with gas escape valves; fine steel demiblock barrels w/concave rib; selective auto ejectors, hand- detachable double safety sidelocks w/hand-engraved rose and scrollwork; front-hinged trigger, casehardened receiver. Imported from Spain.
**Prices:**
| | |
|---|---|
| **Diamond DL** 12 or 20 ga. ................. | $6799.00 |
| 28 or .410 ga. ................................... | 7229.00 |

## RIFLE/SHOTGUN COMBINATION GUNS

**SUPERIOR COMBINATION**

### SPECIFICATIONS
**Gauge/Calibers:** 12/22 Hornet, 22-250, 223 Rem., 243 Win., 270 Win., 308 Win., 30-06 Sprgfld.
**Barrel length/choke:** 23.5″, shotgun choke IC
**Weight:** Approx. 7.5 lbs.
**Stock:** Checkered walnut pistol-grip buttstock and semi-beavertail forend

**Features:** Silver engraved receiver forged and milled from a solid block of high-strength steel; chrome-moly steel barrels, double trigger, extractors, sling swivels, gold bead front sight
**Prices:**
| | |
|---|---|
| **Superior Combination** ...................... | $1229.00 |
| **Empire Combination.** Same as above w/deluxe walnut European-style comb/cheekpiece, slim forend ............................................. | 1649.00 |

# DAKOTA ARMS INC.

**DAKOTA ARMS AMERICAN LEGEND**

The new Dakota American Legend 20-gauge side-by-side double shotgun is built in the United States and reflects the best fit and finish found on game guns the world over. Cased in a Marvis Huey oak and leather trunk case, only 100 of these world-class double guns will be made. These limited-edition shotguns will be offered on a first come, first served basis, with each purchaser having the opportunity to reserve a serial number in the 20-gauge offering, as well as in the 12-gauge and .410/28-gauge set to follow.

Made from bar stock steel and special selection English walnut, this shotgun features precision-machined receiver and intricate hand checkering. Standard features include custom-fitted stock, full-coverage hand engraving, gold in-

lays, straight-hand grip, double triggers, selective ejectors, 24-lines-per-inch hand checkering, French gray receiver, concave rib, splinter forend, checkered butt and ivory beads. Options include a single trigger, leather-covered pad, skeleton butt, semi-beavertail forend and screw-in chokes.
**Barrel length:** 27″  **Weight:** 6 lbs.
**Price:** . . . . . . . . . . . . . . . . . . . . . . . . . . . . . . . . .**$18,000.00**
Also available:
**CLASSIC GRADE** features hard rubber buttplate w/logo, game rib with gold bead, double triggers, and hand-rubbed oil finish . . . . . . . . . . . . . . . . . . . . . . . . . . . . . . . . **$7950.00**
**PREMIER GRADE** w/50% engraving coverage, Exhibition English walnut, 14¼″ length of pull . . . . . . . . . . **$9950.00**

# A.H. FOX SHOTGUNS

**DE GRADE ENGRAVED SHOTGUN**

## CUSTOM BOXLOCKS

### SPECIFICATIONS
**Gauges:** 16, 20, 28 and .410
**Barrel:** Any barrel lengths and chokes; rust blued Chromox or Krupp steel barrels
**Weight:** 5 /to 6 /lbs.
**Stock:** Custom stock dimensions including cast; hand-checkered Turkish Circassian walnut stock and forend with hand-rubbed oil finish; straight grip, full pistol grip (with cap), or semi-pistol grip; splinter, schnabel or beavertail forend; traditional pad, hard rubber plate, checkered, or skeleton butt
**Features:** Boxlock action with automatic ejectors; scalloped, rebated and color casehardened receiver; double or Fox

single selective trigger; hand-finished and hand-engraved. This is the same gun that was manufactured between 1905 and 1930 by the A.H. Fox Gun Company of Philadelphia, PA, now manufactured in the U.S. by the Connecticut Shotgun Mfg. Co. (New Britain, CT).
**Prices:***
CE Grade . . . . . . . . . . . . . . . . . . . . . . . . . . . . .$ 9,500.00
XE Grade . . . . . . . . . . . . . . . . . . . . . . . . . . . . . 11,000.00
DE Grade . . . . . . . . . . . . . . . . . . . . . . . . . . . . . 13,500.00
FE Grade . . . . . . . . . . . . . . . . . . . . . . . . . . . . . 18,500.00
Exhibition Grade. . . . . . . . . . . . . . . . . . . . . . . . . 26,000.00

* Grades differ in engraving and inlay, grade of wood and amount of hand finishing needed.

**SHOTGUNS**

# FRANCOTTE SHOTGUNS

**CLOSE-UP OF BOXLOCK S6**

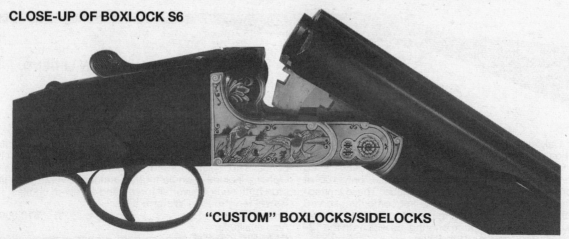

**"CUSTOM" BOXLOCKS/SIDELOCKS**

There are no standard Francotte models, since every shotgun is custom made in Belgium to the purchaser's individual specifications. Features and options include Anson & Deeley boxlocks or Auguste Francotte system sidelocks. All guns have custom-fitted stocks. Available are exhibition-grade stocks as well as extensive engraving and gold inlays. U.S. agent for Auguste Francotte of Belgium is Armes de Chasse (*see* Directory of Manufacturers and Distributors).

**SPECIFICATIONS**
**Gauges:** 12, 16, 20, 28, .410; also 24 and 32

**Chambers:** 2¹/₂″, 2³/₄″ and 3″
**Barrel length:** To customer's specifications
**Forend:** To customer's specifications
**Stock:** Deluxe to exhibition grade; pistol, English or half-pistol grip
**Prices:**
Basic Boxlock . . . . . . . . . . . . . . . . . . . . . . . . . . . . . .$12,000.00
Basic Boxlock (28 & .410 ga.) . . . . . . . . . . . . . . 13,500.00
Optional sideplates, add . . . . . . . . . . . . . . . . . . . 1,400.00
Basic Sidelock . . . . . . . . . . . . . . . . . . . . . . . . . . . 27,000.00
Basic Sidelock (28 & .410 ga.) . . . . . . . . . . . . . . 30,000.00

# GARBI SIDELOCK SHOTGUNS

**MODEL 100 SIDELOCK**
**$4700.00**

Like this Model 100 shotgun, all Spanish-made Garbi models are Holland & Holland pattern sidelock ejector guns with chopper lump (demibloc) barrels. They are built to English gun standards with regard to design, weight, balance and proportions, and all have the characteristic "feel" associated with the best London guns. Models offer fine 24-line hand-checkering, with outstanding quality wood-to-metal and

metal-to-metal fit. The Model 100 is available in 12, 16, 20 and 28 gauge and sports Purdey-style fine scroll and rosette engraving, partly done by machine. Also available:
Model 101 . . . . . . . . . . . . . . . . . . . . . . . . . . . . . . . $6000.00
Model 103A . . . . . . . . . . . . . . . . . . . . . . . . . . . . . . . 7250.00
Model 103B . . . . . . . . . . . . . . . . . . . . . . . . . . . . . . . 9950.00

**MODEL 200**
**$9500.00**

The **Model 200** double is available in 12, 16, 20 or 28 gauge; features Holland-pattern stock ejector design, heavy-duty locks, heavy proof, Continental-style floral and scroll engraving, walnut stock.

# HARRINGTON & RICHARDSON

## SINGLE-BARREL SHOTGUNS

**.410 TAMER SHOTGUN**
**$124.95**

This barreled .410 snake gun features single-shot action, transfer-bar safety and high-impact synthetic stock and forend. Stock has a thumbhole design that sports a full pistol grip and a recessed open side, containing a holder for storing ammo. Forend is modified beavertail configuration. Other features include a matte, electroless nickel finish. **Weight:** 5–6 lbs. **Barrel length:** 20″ (3″ chamber). **Choke:** Full.

**ULTRA SLUG HUNTER**
**$209.95**

**Features:** 12-gauge 24″ barrel, 3″ chamber, fully rifled heavy slug barrel (1:35″ twist); Monte Carlo stock and forend of American hardwood w/dark walnut stain; matte black receiver; transfer-bar safety system; scope rail, swivels and sling; ventilated recoil pad.

**ULTRA SLUG HUNTER DELUXE**
**$209.95**

**SPECIFICATIONS**
**Gauge:** 20 rifled slug (3″ chamber)
**Action:** 12 gauge action
**Barrel length:** 24″ heavy target-style
**Rate of twist:** 1:35″
**Finish:** Low-luster blue
**Stock:** Select hand-checkered camo laminate wood
**Features:** Transfer-bar safety system, scope rail, vent recoil pad, matte black receiver, swivels and black nylon sling

Also available:
**ULTRA YOUTH SLUG HUNTER.** Features 12-gauge barrel blank underbored to 20 gauge and shortened to 22″; factory-mounted Weaver-style scope base; reduced Monte Carlo stock of American hardwood with dark walnut stain; vent recoil pad, sling swivels and black nylon sling. **Price: $209.95**

# HARRINGTON & RICHARDSON

## SINGLE-BARREL SHOTGUNS

### TOPPER MODEL 098
### $114.95

**Chokes:** Modified (12 and 20 ga.); Full (.410 ga.)
**Barrel lengths:** 26″ and 28″ **Weight:** 5 to 6 lbs.
**Action:** Break-open; side lever release; automatic ejection
**Stock:** Full pistol grip; American hardwood; black finish with white buttplate spacer
**Length of pull:** 14 1/2″

**SPECIFICATIONS**
**Gauges:** 12, 20 and .410 (3″ chamber); 16 and 28 ga. (2 3/4″ chamber)

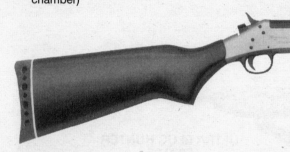

### TOPPER JR. YOUTH
### $119.95

**Barrel length:** 22″ **Weight:** 5 to 6 lbs.
**Stock:** Full pistol grip; American hardwood; black finish; white line spacer; recoil pad
**Finish:** Satin nickel frame; blued barrel

**SPECIFICATIONS**
**Gauges:** 20 and .410 (3″ chamber)
**Chokes:** Modified (20 ga.); Full (.410 ga.)

### TOPPER JUNIOR CLASSIC
### $144.95

Same specifications as the Standard Topper, but with 22″ barrel, American black walnut stock and 12 1/2″ pull.

### TOPPER DELUXE MODEL 098
### $134.95

with semibeavertail forend; white line spacer; ventilated recoil pad
**Finish:** Satin nickel frame; blued barrel
**Also available: TOPPER DELUXE RIFLED SLUG GUN.** In gauges 12, 20 and 20 Youth; 24″ compensated choke barrel, 3″ chamber (1:35″ twist); nickel frame; black finished American hardwood stock w/recoil pad and swivel studs; fully adjustable rifle sights; transfer-bar safety system. **Price: $169.95**

**SPECIFICATIONS**
**Gauge:** 12 (3 1/2″ chamber)
**Chokes:** Screw-in Modified (Full, Extra-Full Turkey and Steel Shot also available)
**Action:** Break-open; side lever release; positive ejection
**Barrel length:** 28″ **Weight:** 5 to 6 lbs.
**Stock:** American hardwood, black finish, full pistol-grip stock

# ITHACA SHOTGUNS

### MODEL 37 DEERSLAYER DELUXE

**SPECIFICATIONS**
**Gauge:** 12 or 20 (3″ chamber)    **Capacity:** 5 rounds
**Barrel lengths:** 26″, 28″ and 30″
**Choke:** Cation Tightshot

**Weight:** 7 lbs.
**Stock:** Cut-checkered walnut stock and forend
**Price:** . . . . . . . . . . . . . . . . . . . . . . . . . . . . . . . . . . . . $529.95

### MODEL 37 DEERSLAYER II

### MODEL 37 TURKEYSLAYER

### MODEL 37 DEERSLAYER II

**SPECIFICATIONS**
**Gauge:** 12 or 20 (3″ chamber)
**Barrel lengths:** 20″ and 25″
**Choke/Bore:** Rifled Bore Deer Bore
**Capacity:** 5 rounds
**Weight:** 6.75 lbs. (7 lbs.)

**Stock:** Monte Carlo
**Features:** Integral barrel and receiver; uses sabot slugs
**Prices:**
**Deerslayer II** . . . . . . . . . . . . . . . . . . . . . . . . . . . . . . $549.95
    **Smooth Bore Deluxe.** . . . . . . . . . . . . . . . . . . . . .   499.95
Also available:
**Turkeyslayer** w/22″ barrel; Cation Tightshot choke tube;
4 camouflage options. . . . . . . . . . . . . . . . . . . . . . . .   549.95

### MODEL 37 DELUXE FIELD GUN

**SPECIFICATIONS**
**Gauge:** 12 or 20 (3″ chamber)
**Barrel lengths:** 26″, 28″ and 30″

**Choke/Bore:** 3 Cation Tightshot choke tubes
**Capacity:** 5 rounds
**Weight:** 7 lbs.
**Price:** . . . . . . . . . . . . . . . . . . . . . . . . . . . . . . . . . . . . $529.95

# KBI SHOTGUNS

**ARMSCOR MODEL M-30F FIELD**

## ARMSCOR FIELD PUMP SHOTGUN

**SPECIFICATIONS**
**Gauge:** 12 (3″ chamber)
**Capacity:** 6 shot
**Choke:** Modified (Model M-30F); 2 ICT (Model M-30F/MC)
**Barrel length:** 28″
**Overall length:** 47 1/2″

**Weight:** 7.6 lbs.
**Stock:** Walnut-finished hardwood buttstock and forend
**Features:** Double slide-action bars; damascened bolt
**Prices:**
Model M-30F . . . . . . . . . . . . . . . . . . . . . . . . . . . . . . . $254.00
Model M-30F/MC . . . . . . . . . . . . . . . . . . . . . . . . . . . 289.00

**ARMSCOR MODEL M-30R8**

## ARMSCOR MODELS M-30R8/M-30R6 RIOT PUMP SHOTGUNS

**SPECIFICATIONS**
**Gauge:** 12 (3″ chamber)
**Choke:** Cylinder
**Capacity:** 6-shot (M-30R6); 8-shot (M-30R8)
**Barrel lengths:** 18 1/2″ (M-30R6); 20″ (M-30R8)
**Overall length:** 37 3/4″ and 39 3/4″

**Weight:** 7 lbs. and 7.2 lbs.
**Stock:** Walnut finished hardwood buttstock and forend
**Features:** Double-action slide bar; damascened bolt; blued finish
**Prices:**
M-30R6 . . . . . . . . . . . . . . . . . . . . . . . . . . . . . . . . . . $229.00
M-30R8 . . . . . . . . . . . . . . . . . . . . . . . . . . . . . . . . . . 245.00

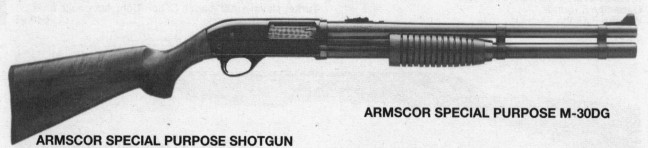

**ARMSCOR SPECIAL PURPOSE M-30DG**

## ARMSCOR SPECIAL PURPOSE SHOTGUN

**SPECIFICATIONS**
**Gauge:** 12 (3″ chamber)   **Choke:** Cylinder
**Barrel length:** 20″   **Overall length:** 39 1/4″
**Weight:** 7 1/2 lbs.
**Stock:** Walnut-finished hardwood (Model 30SAS has speed-feed 4-shot capacity buttstock and synthetic forend)

**Features:** Double-action slide bar; damascened bolt; **Model M-30DG** has 7-shot magazine in traditional stocked/blued pump shotgun with iron sights; **Model M-30SAS** has ventilated shroud and parkerized finish
**Prices:**
Model M-30DG . . . . . . . . . . . . . . . . . . . . . . . . . . . . $279.00
Model M-30SAS . . . . . . . . . . . . . . . . . . . . . . . . . . . 319.00

# KRIEGHOFF SHOTGUNS

(*See* following page for additional Specifications and Prices)

## MODEL K-80 SPORTING CLAY

## MODEL K-80 TRAP, SKEET, SPORTING CLAY AND LIVE BIRD

**Barrels:** Made of Boehler steel; free-floating bottom barrel with adjustable point of impact; standard Trap and Live Pigeon ribs are tapered step; standard Skeet, Sporting Clay and International ribs are tapered or parallel flat.
**Receivers:** Hard satin-nickel finish; casehardened; blue finish available as special order
**Triggers:** Wide profile, single selective, position adjustable.
**Weight:** 8$1/2$" lbs. (Trap); 8 lbs. (Skeet)
**Ejectors:** Selective automatic

**Sights:** White pearl front bead and metal center bead
**Stocks:** Hand-checkered and epoxy-finished Select European walnut stock and forearm; stocks available in seven different styles and dimensions
**Safety:** Push button safety located on top tang.

Also available:
**SKEET SPECIAL.** 28″ and 30″ barrel; tapered flat or 8mm rib; 5 choke tubes. **Price:** Standard . . . . . . . . $7575.00

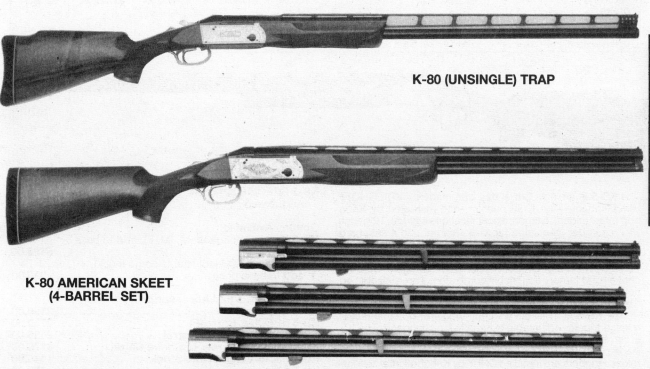

## K-80 (UNSINGLE) TRAP

## K-80 AMERICAN SKEET (4-BARREL SET)

# KRIEGHOFF SHOTGUNS

## SPECIFICATIONS AND PRICES MODEL K-80 (*see also preceding page*)

| Model | Description | Bbl. Length | Choke | Standard | Bavaria | Danube | Gold Target | Extra Barrels |
|---|---|---|---|---|---|---|---|---|
| **TRAP** | Over & Under | 30"/32" | IM/F | $ 7,375.00 | $12,525.00 | $23,625.00 | $27,170.00 | $2900.00 |
| | | 30"/32" | CT/CT | 8,025.00 | 13,175.00 | 24,275.00 | 27,820.00 | 3550.00 |
| | Unsingle | 32"/34" | Full | 7,950.00 | 13,100.00 | 24,200.00 | 27,745.00 | 3575.00 |
| | Combo | 30" + 34" | IM/F&F | 10,475.00 | 15,625.00 | 26,725.00 | 30,270.00 | |
| | (Top Single) | 32" + 34" | CT/CT&CT | 11,550.00 | 16,700.00 | 27,800.00 | 31,345.00 | |
| | | 30" + 32" | | | | | | |
| | Combo | 30" + 34" | IM/F+F | 9,975.00 | 15,125.00 | 26,225.00 | 29,770.00 | 2950.00 |
| | (Unsingle) | | | | | | | |
| | | 32" + 34" | CT/CT&CT | 11,050.00 | 16,200.00 | 27,300.00 | 30,845.00 | 3375.00 |
| **Optional Features:** | | | | | | | | |
| Screw-in chokes (Top or Unsingle) | | **$425.00** | | | | | | |
| Single factory release | | **425.00** | | | | | | |
| Double factory release | | **750.00** | | | | | | |
| **SKEET** | 4-Barrel Set | 28"/12 ga. | Tula | | | | | $2990.00 |
| | | 28"/20 ga. | Skeet | | | | | 2880.00 |
| | | 28"/28 ga. | Skeet | $16,950.00 | $22,100.00 | $33,200.00 | $36,745.00 | 2990.00 |
| | | 28"/.410 ga. | Skeet | | | | | 2880.00 |
| | 2-Barrel Set | 28"/12 ga. | Tula | 11,840.00 | 18,990.00 | 28,090.00 | 31,685.00 | 4150.00 |
| | Lightweight | 28" + 30"/12 ga. | Skeet | 6,900.00 | N/A | N/A | N/A | 2650.00 |
| | 1-Barrel Set | 28" | Skeet | 8,825.00 | 13,975.00 | 25,075.00 | 28,620.00 | 4150.00 |
| | International | 28"/12 ga. | Tula | 7,825.00 | 12,975.00 | 24,075.00 | 27,620.00 | 2990.00 |
| | Skeet Special | | | 7,575.00 | 12,725.00 | 23,825.00 | 27,370.00 | 3300.00 |
| **SPORTING CLAYS** | Over/Under w/screw-in tubes (5) | 28" + 30" + 32"/ 12 ga. 30" Semi-Light | Tubes IC/ICTF | $8,150.00 | $13,300.00 | $24,400.00 | $27,945.00 | $2900.00 |

Optional engravings:  Super Scroll  **$1995.00**; Gold Super Scroll  **$4450.00**; Parcours  **$2100.00**; Parcours Special  **$3950.00**

## MODEL KS-5

The KS-5 is a single barrel trap gun made by KRIEGHOFF, Ulm/Germany—the K-80 people—and marketed by Krieghoff International. Standard specifications include: 12 gauge, 2³/₄" chamber, ventilated tapered step rip, and a casehardened receiver (satin gray finished in electroless nickel). The KS-5 features an adjustable point of impact from 50/50 to 70/30 by means of different optional fronthangers. Screw-in chokes and factory adjustable comb stocks are available options. An adjustable rib (AR) and comb stock (ADJ) are standard features.

The KS-5 is available with pull trigger or optional factory release trigger, adjustable externally for poundage. The KS-5 can be converted to release by the installation of the release parts. To assure consistency and proper functioning, release triggers are installed ONLY by Krieghoff International. Release parts are NOT available separately. These shotguns are available in Standard grade only. Engraved models can be special ordered.

**Prices:**
KS-5 32" or 34" barrel, Full choke, case . . . . . . . . **$3695.00**
KS-5 SPECIAL 32" or 34" barrel, Full choke, AR, ADJ, cased . . . . . . . . . . . . . . . . . . . . . . . . . . . . . . 4695.00

**Options Available:**
KS-5 Screw-in chokes (M, IM, F), **add** to base price . . . . . . . . . . . . . . . . . . . . . . . . . . . . . . . . . . . **$425.00**
KS-5 Factory ADJ (adjustable comb stock), **add** to base price . . . . . . . . . . . . . . . . . . . . . . . 395.00

**Other Features and Accessories:**
KS-5 Regular Barrel . . . . . . . . . . . . . . . . . . . . . . . **$2100.00**
KS-5 SPECIAL Barrel(F) . . . . . . . . . . . . . . . . . . . . . 2750.00
KS-5 Screw-In Choke Barrel . . . . . . . . . . . . . . . . . 2525.00
KS-5 SPECIAL Screw-In Choke Barrel . . . . . . . . 3175.00
KS-5 Factory Adjustable Stock . . . . . . . . . . . . . . . 1145.00
KS-5 Stock . . . . . . . . . . . . . . . . . . . . . . . . . . . . . . . . 750.00
KS-5 Forearm . . . . . . . . . . . . . . . . . . . . . . . . . . . . . . 290.00
KS-5 Release Trigger (installed) . . . . . . . . . . . . . 295.00
KS-5 Fronthanger . . . . . . . . . . . . . . . . . . . . . . . . . . . 70.00
KS-5 Aluminum Case . . . . . . . . . . . . . . . . . . . . . . . 425.00
KS-5 Individual Choke Tubes . . . . . . . . . . . . . . . 75.00

# MAGTECH SHOTGUNS

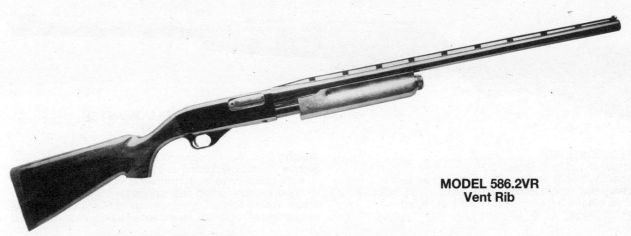

## MODEL 586.2VR
### Vent Rib

## MODEL 586.2VR SERIES

The Magtech 586.2VR Series 12-gauge pump shotguns handle 2³/₄" and 3" magnum shells interchangeably and give the shooter custom features, including: • ordnance-grade, deep-blued steel receiver • double-action slide bars • hand-finished Brazilian Embuia wood stock and forearm • hammer-forged chrome-moly barrel • high-profile steel rib • brass mid-bead and ivory-colored front sight • chrome-plated bolt • screw-in Magchokes in IC, Mod. and Full • crossbolt safety • special magazine release for unloading without cycling round through the chamber.

**SPECIFICATIONS**
**Gauge:** 12 (2³/₄" or 3" shells)
**Capacity:** 5 rounds (8 in Model 586.2P)
**Chokes:** Magchokes in IC, Mod. & Full (IC only in Model 586.2P)
**Barrel:** 26" and 28", vent rib (19" plain in Model 586.2P)
**Overall length:** 46¹/₄" and 48¹/₄" (39¹/₄" in Model 586.2P)
**Sights** Two beads (one bead in Model 586.2P)
**Prices:**
MODEL 586.2VR26 and 586.2VR28 . . . . . . . . . . . . $255.00
MODEL 586.2P . . . . . . . . . . . . . . . . . . . . . . . . . . . 235.00

# MARLIN SHOTGUNS

## MODEL 512DL SLUGMASTER

## MODEL 512DL SLUGMASTER
### $372.00

**SPECIFICATIONS**
**Gauge:** 12 (up to 3" shells)
**Capacity:** 2-shot box magazine (+1 in chamber)
**Action:** Bolt action; thumb safety; red cocking indicator

**Barrel length:** 21" rifled (1:28" right-hand twist)
**Overall length:** 44.75"
**Weight:** 8 lbs. (w/o scope and mount)
**Sights:** Adjustable folding semi-buckhorn rear; ramp front with brass bead and removable cutaway Wide-Scan® hood; receiver drilled and tapped for scope mount
**Stock:** Black fiberglass-filled synthetic w/molded-in checkering and padded black nylon sling

# MARLIN SHOTGUNS

## MODEL 512 SLUGMASTER
## $356.00

### SPECIFICATIONS
**Gauge:** 12 (up to 3" shells)
**Capacity:** 2-shot box magazine (+1 in chamber)
**Action:** Bolt action; thumb safety; red cocking indicator
**Barrel length:** 21" rifled (1:28" right-hand twist)
**Overall length:** 44.75"

**Weight:** 8 lbs. (w/o scope and mount)
**Sights:** Adjustable folding semi-buckhorn rear; ramp front with brass bead and removable cutaway Wide-Scan® hood; receiver drilled and tapped for scope mount
**Stock:** Walnut finished, press-checkered Maine birch w/pistol grip and Mar-Shield® finish, swivel studs, vent. recoil pad

## MODEL 50DL
## $322.00

## MODEL 50DL

### SPECIFICATIONS
**Gauge:** 12 ga. (2³/₄" or 3" chamber)
**Capacity:** 2-shot clip

**Action:** Bolt action
**Barrel length:** 28" (Modified choke)
**Overall length:** 48.25"
**Weight:** 7.5 lbs.
**Sights:** Brass bead front; U-groove rear
**Stock:** Black synthetic w/ventilated rubber recoil pad
**Features:** Thumb safety; red cocking indicator; swivel studs

## MARLIN MODEL 55GDL GOOSE GUN
## $372.00

High-flying ducks and geese are the Goose Gun's specialty. The Marlin Goose Gun has an extra-long 36-inch full-choked barrel and Magnum capability, making it the perfect choice for tough shots at wary waterfowl. It also features a quick-loading 2-shot clip magazine, a convenient leather carrying strap and a quality ventilated recoil pad.

### SPECIFICATIONS
**Gauge:** 12; 2³/₄" Magnum, 3" Magnum or 2³/₄" regular shells (also handles rifled slugs and buckshot)

**Choke:** Full
**Capacity:** 2-shot detachable box magazine
**Action:** Bolt action; positive thumb safety; red cocking indicator
**Barrel length:** 36"   **Overall length:** 56³/₄"
**Weight:** 8 lbs.
**Sights:** Bead front sight and U-Groove rear sight
**Stock:** Black fiberglass-filled synthetic stock w/molded-in checkering

# MAROCCHI SHOTGUNS

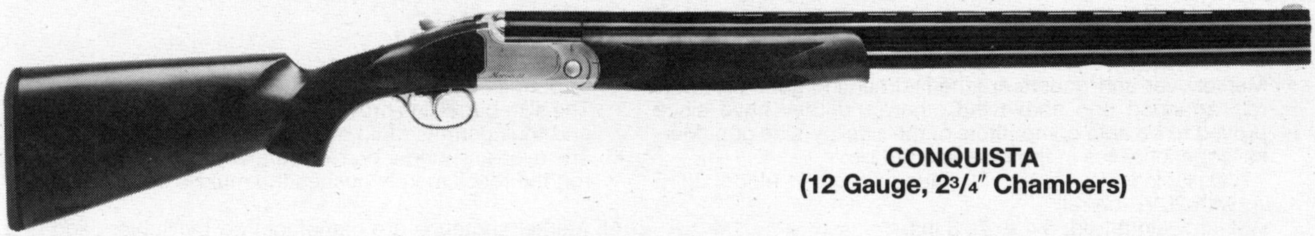

CONQUISTA
(12 Gauge, 2 3/4" Chambers)

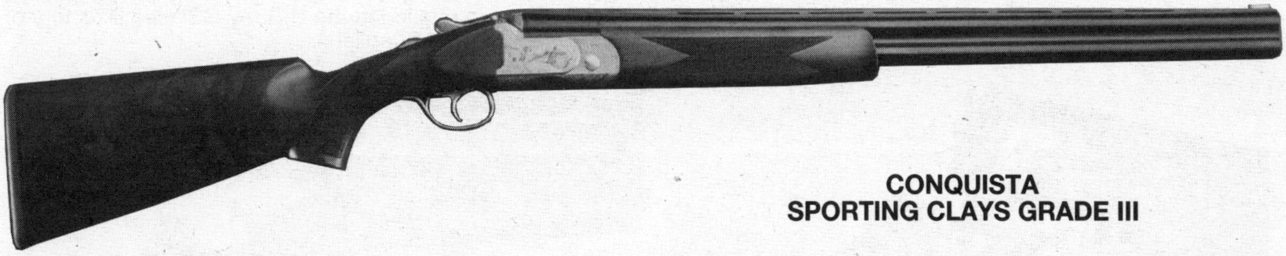

CONQUISTA
SPORTING CLAYS GRADE III

The Marocchi shotguns listed below all feature 10mm concave ventilated upper rib; Clasic middle rib (Classic Doubles has vent middle rib); competition white front sight and automatic extractors/ejectors.

| **Models** | **Prices** |
|---|---|
| **Conquista Sporting** | **$1995.00–3599.00** |
| **Sporting Left** | **$2120.00–3995.00** |
| **Sporting Light** | **TBA** |
| **Lady Sport** | **2199.00–2300.00** |
| **Conquista Trap** | **1995.00–3599.00** |
| **Conquista Skeet** | **1995.00–3599.00** |
| **Classic Doubles** | **1598.00** |

**SPECIFICATIONS CONQUISTA SHOTGUNS (all 12 Gauge)**

| | CONQUISTA SPORTING | SPORTING LEFT | SPORTING LIGHT | LADY SPORT | CONQUISTA TRAP | CONQUISTA SKEET | CLASSIC DOUBLES |
|---|---|---|---|---|---|---|---|
| **BARRELS:** | | | | | | | |
| Gauge | 12 | 12 | 12 | 12 | 12 | 12 | 12 |
| Chamber | 2 3/4" | 2 3/4" | 2 3/4" | 2 3/4" | 2 3/4" | 2 3/4" | 3" |
| Barrel Length | 28", 30", 32" | 28", 30", 32" | 28", 30" | 28", 30" | 29", 30" | 28" | 30" |
| Chokes | Contrechokes | Contrechokes | Contrechokes | Contrechokes | Full/Full | Skeet/Skeet | Contre Plus |
| **TRIGGER:** | | | | | | | |
| Trigger type | Instajust Selective | Instajust Selective | Instajust Selective | Instajust Selective | Instajust | Instajust Selective | Instajust Selective |
| Trigger Pull (Weight) | 3.5 - 4.0 lbs. | 3.5 - 4.0 lbs. | 3.5 - 4.0 lbs. | 3.5 - 4.0 lbs. | 3.5 - 4.0 lbs. | 3.5 - 4.0 lbs. | 3.5 - 4.0 lbs. |
| Trigger Pull (Length) | 14 1/2" - 14 7/8" | 14 1/2" - 14 7/8" | 13 7/8" - 14 1/4" | 13 7/8" - 14 1/4" | 14 1/2" - 14 7/8" | 14 1/2" - 14 7/8" | 14 1/4" - 14 5/8" |
| **STOCK:** | | | | | | | |
| Drop at comb | 1 7/16" | 1 7/16" | 1 11/32" | 1 11/32" | 1 9/32" | 1 1/2" | 1 3/8" |
| Drop at heel | 2 3/16" | 2 3/16" | 2 9/32" | 2 9/32" | 1 11/16" | 2 3/16" | 2 1/8" |
| Cast at heel | 3/16" Off | 3/16" On | 3/16" Off | 3/16" Off | 3/16" Off | 3/16" Off | N/A |
| Cast at toe | 3/8" Off | 3/8" On | 3/8" Off | 3/8" Off | 5/16" Off | 3/16" Off | N/A |
| Stock | | | | Select Walnut | | | |
| Checkering | 20 lines/inch | 20 lines/inch | 20 lines/inch | 20 lines/inch | 20 lines/inch | 20 lines/inch | 18 lines/inch |
| **OVERALL:** | | | | | | | |
| Length Overall | 45" - 49" | 45" - 49" | 44 3/8" - 46 3/8" | 44 3/8" - 46 3/8" | 47" - 49" | 45" | 47" |
| Weight Approx.* | 7 7/8 lbs. | 7 7/8 lbs. | 7 1/2 lbs. | 7 1/2 lbs. | 8 1/4 lbs. | 7 3/4 lbs. | 8 1/8 lbs. |

# MERKEL SHOTGUNS

## OVER/UNDER SHOTGUNS

Merkel over-and-unders are the first hunting guns with barrels arranged one above the other, and they have since proved to be able competitors of the side-by-side gun. Merkel superiority lies in the following details:

- Available in 12, 16 and 20 gauge (28 ga. in Model 201E with 26³/₄″ barrel)
- Lightweight from 6.4 to 7.28 lbs.
- The high, narrow forend protects the shooter's hand from the barrel in hot or cold climates
- The forend is narrow and therefore lies snugly in the hand

to permit easy and positive swinging
- The slim barrel line provides an unobstructed field of view and thus permits rapid aiming and shooting
- The over-and-under barrel arrangement reduces recoil error; the recoil merely pushes the muzzle up vertically

All Merkel shotguns are manufactured by Suhler Jagd und Sport-waffen GmbH, Suhl, Thuringia, Germany; imported, distributed and retailed in the U.S. by GSI (see Directory of Manufacturers and Suppliers).

**MODEL 201E BOXLOCK**

**MODEL 203E SIDELOCK**

### MERKEL OVER/UNDER SHOTGUN SPECIFICATIONS
**Gauges:** 12, 16, 20, 28
**Barrel lengths:** 26³/₄″ and 28″
**Weight:** 6.4 to 7.28 lbs.
**Stock:** English or pistol grip in European walnut
**Features:** Model 201E is a boxlock; Models 202E, 203E and 303E are sidelocks. All models include three-piece forearm, automatic ejectors, Kersten double crossbolt lock, Blitz action and single selective or double triggers.

**Prices:**
**BOXLOCKS**
**MODEL 201E** 12 or 16 ga. 28″ IC/Mod, Mod/
Full . . . . . . . . . . . . . . . . . . . . . . . . . . . . . . . .$ 5,805.00

**MODEL 201E** 20 ga. 26³/₄″ IC/Mod, Mod/
Full . . . . . . . . . . . . . . . . . . . . . . . . . . . . . . . . $6,495.00
**MODEL 201E** 28 ga. 26³/₄″ IC/Mod, Mod/
Full . . . . . . . . . . . . . . . . . . . . . . . . . . . . . . . . . 6,495.00
**MODEL 202E** 12 or 16 ga., 28″ IC/Mod,
Mod/Full . . . . . . . . . . . . . . . . . . . . . . . . . . . . . 9,995.00
**SIDELOCKS**
**MODEL 203E** 12 or 16 ga., 28″ IC/Mod, Mod/Full
(w/English-style engraving) . . . . . . . . . . . . . . 14,595.00
**MODEL 303E** 12 or 16 ga., 28″ IC/Mod, Mod/Full,
English-style arabesque engraving in large
scrolls on silver-gray sidelocks . . . . . . . . . . . .19,995.00

Also available:
**MERKEL O/U SHOTGUN/RIFLE COMBINATIONS.**
  Models 210E, 211E, 213E, 313E: 12, 16 and 20 gauge.
  Price: . . . . . . . . . . . . . . . . . . . . . . . . . . . . .$22,795.00

**MODEL 203E**

# MERKEL SHOTGUNS

## SIDE-BY-SIDE SHOTGUNS

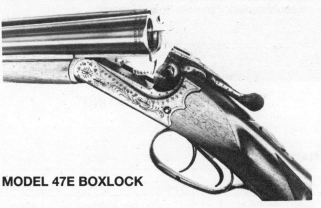

**MODEL 47E BOXLOCK**

**MODEL 147E BOXLOCK**

**SPECIFICATIONS**
**Gauges:** 12 and 20 (28 ga. in Models 147E and 147S)
**Barrel lengths:** 26″ and 28″ (25½″ in Models 47S and 147S)
**Weight:** 6 to 7 lbs.
**Stock:** English or pistol grip in European walnut
**Features:** Models 47E and 147E are boxlocks; Models 47S and 147S are sidelocks. All guns have cold hammer-forged barrels, double triggers, double lugs and Greener crossbolt locking systems and automatic ejectors.

| Models | Prices |
|---|---|
| **MODEL 47E** (Holland & Holland ejectors) . . . . . . | $2695.00 |
| **MODEL 122** (H&H ejectors, engraved hunting scenes) . . . . . . . . . . . . . . . . . . . . | 4995.00 |
| **MODEL 147** (H&H ejectors) . . . . . . . . . . . . . . . . | 2995.00 |
| **MODEL 147E** (engraved hunting scenes) | |
| 12, 16 & 20 ga. . . . . . . . . . . . . . . . . . . . . . . . | 3195.00 |
| 28 ga. . . . . . . . . . . . . . . . . . . . . . . . . . . . . . . | 3895.00 |
| **MODEL 47S Sidelock** (H&H ejectors) . . . . . . . . . | 5295.00 |
| **MODEL 147S Sidelock** | |
| 12, 16 & 20 ga. . . . . . . . . . . . . . . . . . . . . . . . | 6695.00 |
| 28 ga. . . . . . . . . . . . . . . . . . . . . . . . . . . . . . . | 6995.00 |
| **MODEL 247S** (English-style engraving) . . . . . . . . | 6995.00 |
| **MODEL 347S** (H&H ejectors) . . . . . . . . . . . . . . . | 7895.00 |
| **MODEL 447S** . . . . . . . . . . . . . . . . . . . . . . . . . . | 8995.00 |

**MODEL 47S SIDE-BY-SIDE**

**MODEL 247S SIDELOCK**

# MOSSBERG PUMP SHOTGUNS

## MODEL 500 SPORTING

All Mossberg Model 500 pump-action shotguns feature 3″ chambers, Milspec tough, lightweight alloy receivers with "top thumb safety." Standard models include 6-shot capacity with 2¾″ shells, cut-checkered stocks, Quiet Carry fore-arms, gold trigger, engraved receiver, blued Woodland Camo or Marinecote metal finish and the largest selection of accessory barrels. Ten-year limited warranty.

**MODEL 500 SPORTING**

## SPECIFICATIONS & PRICES MODEL 500 CROWN GRADE

| Ga. | Stock # | Bbl. Length | Barrel Type | Sights | Chokes | Stock | Length O/A | Wt. | Q.D. Studs | Notes | Prices |
|---|---|---|---|---|---|---|---|---|---|---|---|
| 12 | 54220 | 28″ | Vent rib, ported | 2 Beads | Accu-Choke | Walnut Finish | 48″ | 7.2 | | IC, Mod. & Full Tubes | $301.00 |
| 12 | 54116 | 26″ | Vent rib, ported | 2 Beads | Accu-Choke | Walnut Finish | 46″ | 7.1 | | IC & Mod. Tubes | 301.00 |
| 20 | 54132 | 22″ | Vent Rib | 2 Beads | Accu-Choke | Walnut Finish | 42″ | 6.9 | | Mod. Tube Only, Bantam Stock | 301.00 |
| 20 | 54136 | 26″ | Vent Rib | 2 Beads | Accu-Choke | Walnut Finish | 46″ | 7.0 | | IC, Mod. & Full Tubes | 301.00 |
| .410 | 50149 | 24″ | Plain | 2 Beads | Full | Synthetic | 43″ | 6.8 | | Fixed Choke, Bantam Stock | 290.00 |
| .410 | 58104 | 24″ | Vent Rib | 2 Beads | Full | Walnut Finish | 44″ | 6.8 | | Fixed Choke | 297.00 |
| 12 | 54232 | 24″ | Trophy Slugster™, Ported | Scope Mount | Rifled Bore | Walnut Finish | 44″ | 7.3 | Y | Dual-Comb™ Stock | 369.00 |
| 12 | 54244 | 24″ | Slugster, ported | Rifle | Rifled Bore | Walnut Finish | 44″ | 7.0 | Y | | 341.00 |
| 12 | 58245 | 24″ | Slugster, ported | Rifle | Cyl. Bore | Walnut Finish | 44″ | 7.0 | Y | | 308.00 |
| 20 | 54233 | 24″ | Trophy Slugster™, Ported | Scope Mount | Rifled Bore | Walnut Finish | 44″ | 6.9 | Y | Dual-Comb™ Stock | 369.00 |
| 20 | 54251 | 24″ | Slugster, ported | Rifle | Rifled Bore | Walnut Finish | 44″ | 6.9 | Y | | 341.00 |
| 20 | 58252 | 24″ | Slugster | Rifle | Rifled Bore | Walnut Finish | 44″ | 6.9 | Y | Bantam Stock | 341.00 |

## SPECIFICATIONS MODEL 500 COMBOS

| Ga. | Stock # | Bbl. Length | Barrel Type | Sights | Chokes | Stock | Length O/A | Wt. | Q.D. Studs | Notes | Prices |
|---|---|---|---|---|---|---|---|---|---|---|---|
| 12 | 54243 | 28″ 24″ | Vent rib, ported Trophy Slugster™, ported | 2 Beads Scope Mount | Accu-Choke Rifled Bore | Walnut Finish | 48″ | 7.2 | Y | IC, Mod. & Full Tubes Dual-Comb™ Stock | $401.00 |
| 12 | 54264 | 28″ 24″ | Vent rib, ported Slugster, ported | 2 Beads Rifle | Accu-Choke Rifled Bore | Walnut Finish | 48″ | 7.2 | Y | IC, Mod. & Full Tubes | 385.00 |
| 12 | 58483 | 28″ 18.5″ | Plain Plain | Bead Bead | Modified Cyl. Bore | Walnut Finish | 48″ | 7.2 | | Fixed Choke, Pistol Grip Kit | 321.00 |
| 20 | 54282 | 26″ 24″ | Vent Rib Slugster, ported | 2 Beads Rifle | Accu-Choke Rifled Bore | Walnut Finish | 46″ | 7.0 | Y | IC, Mod. & Full Tubes | 371.00 |
| 12 | 54158 | 28″ 24″ | Vent rib, ported Slugster, ported | 2 Beads Rifle | Accu-Choke Cyl. Bore | Walnut Finish | 48″ | 7.2 | | IC, Mod. & Full Tubes | 353.00 |
| 12 | 54169 | 28″ 18.5″ | Vent rib, ported Plain | 2 Beads Bead | Accu-Choke Cyl. Bore | Walnut Finish | 48″ | 7.2 | | IC, Mod. & Full Tubes, Pistol Grip Kit | 338.00 |
| .410 | 58456 | 24″ 18.5″ | Vent Rib Plain | 2 Beads Bead | Full Cyl. Bore | Walnut Finish | 44″ | 6.8 | | Fixed Choke, Pistol Grip Kit | 345.00 |
| 20 | 54283 | 26″ 24″ | Vent Rib Trophy Slugster™, Ported | 2 Beads Scope Mount | Accu-Choke Rifled Bore | Walnut Finish | 46″ | 7.0 | | IC, Mod. & Full Tubes Dual-Comb Stock | 401.00 |
| 20 | 54188 | 22″ 24″ | Vent Rib Slugster, ported | 2 Beads Rifle | Accu-Choke Rifled Bore | Walnut Finish | 42″ | 7.0 | | IC, Mod. & Full Tubes Bantam Stock & Forearm | 363.00 |

# MOSSBERG PUMP SHOTGUNS

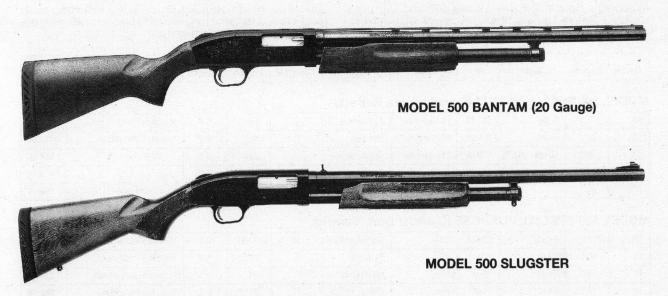

**MODEL 500 BANTAM (20 Gauge)**

**MODEL 500 SLUGSTER**

## SPECIFICATIONS MODEL 500 WOODLAND CAMO (6-shot)

| 12 | 52193 | 28″ | Vent rib, ported | 2 Beads | Accu-Choke | Synthetic | 48″ | 7.2 | Y | IC, Mod. & Full Tubes | $325.00 |
|----|-------|-----|------------------|---------|------------|-----------|-----|-----|---|-----------------------|---------|
| 12 | 50195 | 24″ | Vent Rib | 2 Beads | Accu-Choke | Synthetic | 44″ | 7.1 | Y | IC, Mod., Full & X-Full Tubes | 324.00 |
| 20 | 58135 | 22″ | Vent Rib | 2 Beads | Accu-Choke | Synthetic | 42″ | 6.8 | Y | X-Full Tubes only | 309.00 |
| 12 | 52213 | 28″ 24″ | Vent Rib, Ported Slugster, Ported | 2 Beads Rifle | Accu-Choke Rifled Bore | Synthetic | 48″ | 7.2 | Y | IC, Mod. & Full Tubes | 409.00 |
| 12 | 58143 | 24″ 24″ | Vent Rib, Ported Slugster, Ported | 2 Beads Scope Base | Accu-Choke Rifled Bore | Synthetic | 46″ | 6.9 | Y | X-Full Tube Dual-Combo Stock | 444.00 |

**MODEL 500 OFM WOODLAND CAMO**

## MODEL 500 AMERICAN FIELD (Pressed Checkered, Blued Barrel)

| 12 | 50117 | 28″ | Vent Rib | 2 Beads | Accu-Choke | Walnut Finish | 48″ | 7.2 | | Mod. Tube Only | $287.00 |
|----|-------|-----|----------|---------|------------|---------------|-----|-----|---|----------------|---------|
| 20 | 50137 | 26″ | Vent Rib | 2 Beads | Accu-Choke | Walnut Finish | 46″ | 7.1 | | Mod. Tube Only | 287.00 |
| .410 | 50104 | 24″ | Vent Rib | 2 Beads | Full | Walnut Finish | 44″ | 7.0 | | Fixed Choke | 291.00 |
| 12 | 50044 | 24″ | Slugster, Ported | Rifle | Rifled Bore | Walnut Finish | 44″ | 7.0 | Y | | 325.00 |

# MOSSBERG PUMP SHOTGUNS

## MODEL 500/590 SPECIAL PURPOSE

Mossberg's Special Purpose Models 500 and 590 pump shotguns feature lightweight alloy receivers with ambidextrous "top thumb safety" button, walnut-finished wood or durable synthetic stocks with Quiet Carry™ forearms, rubber recoil pads, dual extractors, two slide bars and twin cartridge stops. Ten-year limited warranty.

| Gauge | Barrel Length | Sight | Stock # | Finish | Stock | Capacity | Overall Length | Weight | Notes | Price |
|-------|--------------|-------|---------|--------|-------|----------|----------------|--------|-------|-------|

### MODEL 500/590 MARINER™ (Cylinder Bore Barrels)

| Gauge | Barrel Length | Sight | Stock # | Finish | Stock | Capacity | Overall Length | Weight | Notes | Price |
|-------|--------------|-------|---------|--------|-------|----------|----------------|--------|-------|-------|
| 12 | 18.5″ | Bead | 50273 | Marinecote™ | Synthetic | 6 | 38.5″ | 6.8 | Includes Pistol Grip | $404.00 |
| 12 | 20″ | Bead | 50299 | Marinecote™ | Synthetic | 9 | 40″ | 7.0 | Includes Pistol Grip | 416.00 |
| 12 | 18.5″ | Ghost Ring™ | 50276 | Marinecote™ | Synthetic | 6 | 38.5″ | 6.8 | | 460.00 |
| 12 | 20″ | Ghost Ring™ | 50296 | Marinecote™ | Synthetic | 9 | 40″ | 7.0 | | 472.00 |
| 12 | 20″ | — | 50298 | Marinecote™ | Synthetic | — | 40″ | 9.0 | Line Launcher | 899.00 |

### MODEL 500 SPECIAL PURPOSE (Cylinder Bore Barrels)

| Gauge | Barrel Length | Sight | Stock # | Finish | Stock | Capacity | Overall Length | Weight | Notes | Price |
|-------|--------------|-------|---------|--------|-------|----------|----------------|--------|-------|-------|
| 12 | 18.5″ | Bead | 50404 | Blue | Walnut Finish | 6 | 38.5″ | 6.8 | Includes Pistol Grip | $282.00 |
| 12 | 18.5″ | Bead | 50411 | Blue | Synthetic | 6 | 38.5″ | 6.8 | Includes Pistol Grip | 282.00 |
| 12 | 18.5″ | Bead | 50440 | Blue | Pistol Grip | 6 | 28″ | 5.6 | Includes Heat Shield | 274.00 |
| 20 | 18.5″ | Bead | 50451 | Blue | Walnut Finish | 6 | 38.5″ | 6.8 | Includes Pistol Grip | 282.00 |
| 20 | 18.5″ | Bead | 50452 | Blue | Synthetic | 6 | 38.5″ | 6.8 | Includes Pistol Grip | 281.00 |
| 20 | 18.5″ | Bead | 50450 | Blue | Pistol Grip | 6 | 28″ | 5.6 | | 274.00 |
| .410 | 18.5″ | Bead | 50455 | Blue | Pistol Grip | 6 | 28″ | 5.3 | | 281.00 |
| 12 | 20″ | Bead | 50564 | Blue | Walnut Finish | 8 | 40″ | 7.0 | Includes Pistol Grip | 282.00 |
| 12 | 20″ | Bead | 50579 | Blue | Synthetic | 8 | 40″ | 7.0 | Includes Pistol Grip | 282.00 |
| 12 | 20″ | Bead | 50580 | Blue | Pistol Grip | 8 | 40″ | 7.0 | | 274.00 |
| 20 | 21″ | Bead | 50581 | Blue | Synthetic | 8 | 38.5″ | 6.9 | Includes Pistol Grip | 281.00 |
| 20 | 21″ | Bead | 50582 | Blue | Pistol Grip | 8 | 28.5″ | 5.6 | | 274.00 |

### MODEL 590 SPECIAL PURPOSE (Cylinder Bore Barrels)

| Gauge | Barrel Length | Sight | Stock # | Finish | Stock | Capacity | Overall Length | Weight | Notes | Price |
|-------|--------------|-------|---------|--------|-------|----------|----------------|--------|-------|-------|
| 12 | 20″ | Bead | 50645 | Blue | Synthetic | 9 | 40″ | 7.2 | w/Acc. Lug & Heat Shield | $331.00 |
| 12 | 20″ | Bead | 50650 | Blue | Speed Feed | 9 | 40″ | 7.2 | w/Acc. Lug & Heat Shield | 363.00 |
| 12 | 20″ | Bead | 50660 | Parkerized | Synthetic | 9 | 40″ | 7.2 | w/Acc. Lug & Heat Shield | 381.00 |
| 12 | 20″ | Bead | 50665 | Parkerized | Speed Feed | 9 | 40″ | 7.2 | w/Acc. Lug & Heat Shield | 413.00 |

### MODEL 500/590 GHOST RING™ (Cylinder Bore Barrels)

| Gauge | Barrel Length | Sight | Stock # | Finish | Stock | Capacity | Overall Length | Weight | Notes | Price |
|-------|--------------|-------|---------|--------|-------|----------|----------------|--------|-------|-------|
| 12 | 18.5″ | Ghost Ring™ | 50402 | Blue | Synthetic | 6 | 38.5″ | 6.8 | | $332.00 |
| 12 | 18.5″ | Ghost Ring™ | 50517 | Parkerized | Synthetic | 6 | 38.5″ | 6.8 | | 385.00 |
| 12 | 20″ | Ghost Ring™ | 50652 | Blue | Synthetic | 9 | 40″ | 7.2 | w/Acc. Lug | 381.00 |
| 12 | 20″ | Ghost Ring™ | 50663 | Parkerized | Synthetic | 9 | 40″ | 7.2 | w/Acc. Lug | 434.00 |
| 12 | 20″ | Ghost Ring™ | 50668 | Parkerized | Speed Feed | 9 | 40″ | 7.2 | w/Acc. Lug | 466.00 |

### HS 410 HOME SECURITY (Spreader Choke)

| Gauge | Barrel Length | Sight | Stock # | Finish | Stock | Capacity | Overall Length | Weight | Notes | Price |
|-------|--------------|-------|---------|--------|-------|----------|----------------|--------|-------|-------|
| .410 | 18.5″ | Bead | 50359 | Blue | Synthetic | 6 | 39.5″ | 6.6 | Includes Vertical Foregrip | $294.00 |

# MOSSBERG PUMP SHOTGUNS

## MODEL 835 ULTI-MAG

Mossberg's Model 835 Ulti-Mag pump action shotgun has a 3¹/₂″ 12-gauge chamber but can also handle standard 2³/₄″ and 3″ shells. Field barrels are overbored and ported for optimum patterns and felt recoil reduction. Cut-checkered walnut and walnut-finished stocks and Quiet Carry™ forearms are standard, as are gold triggers and engraved receivers. Camo models are drilled and tapped for scope and feature detachable swivels and sling. All models include a Cablelock™ and 10-year limited warranty.

**MODEL 835 ULTI-MAG**

**MODEL 835 ULTI-MAG**
**Mossy Oak™ Camo Finish**

## SPECIFICATIONS AND PRICES MODEL 835 ULTI-MAG (12 Gauge, 6 Shot)

| Ga. | Stock No. | Barrel Length | Type | Sights | Choke | Finish | Stock | O.A. Length | Wt. | Studs | Notes | Price |
|---|---|---|---|---|---|---|---|---|---|---|---|---|
| **ULTI-MAG™ 835 CROWN GRADE** | | | | | | | | | | | | |
| 12 | 64110 | 28″ | Vent Rib, Ported | 2 Beads | Accu-Mag | Blue | Walnut | 48.5″ | 7.7 | | 4 Tubes* & Dual-Comb™ Stock | $428.00 |
| 12 | 68232 | 24″ | Trophy Slugster™, Ported | Scope Mount | Rifled Bore | Blue | Walnut | 44.5″ | 7.3 | Y | Dual-Comb™ Stock | 381.00 |
| 12 | 61120 | 28″ | Vent Rib, Ported | 2 Beads | Accu-Mag | Blue | Walnut Finish | 48.5″ | 7.7 | | Mod. Tube | 325.00 |
| 12 | 68220 | 28″ | Vent Rib, Ported | 2 Beads | Accu-Mag | Blue | Walnut Finish | 48.5″ | 7.7 | | Mod. Tube Only | 328.00 |
| 12 | 68225 | 24″ | Vent Rib, Ported | 2 Beads | Accu-Mag | Matte | Walnut Finish | 44.5″ | 7.3 | | X-Full Tube | 331.00 |
| 12 | 68244 | 28″ 24″ | Vent Rib, Ported Trophy Slugster™ Ported | 2 Beads Scope Mount | Accu-Mag Rifled Bore | Blue | Walnut | 48.5″ | 7.7 | | Mod. Tube only Dual-Comb™ Stock | 440.00 |
| 12 | 68223 | 28″ 24″ | Vent Rib, Ported Slugster, Ported | 2 Beads Rifle | Accu-Mag Rifled Bore | Blue | Walnut | 48.5″ | 7.7 | | Mod. Tube only | 410.00 |
| 12 | 68260 | 28″ 24″ | Vent Rib, Ported Slugster | 2 Beads Rifle | Accu-Mag Cyl. Bore | Blue | Walnut Finish | 48.5″ | 7.7 | | Mod. Tube Only | 393.00 |
| **ULTI-MAG™ 835 CAMO** | | | | | | | | | | | | |
| 12 | 61134 | 24″ | Vent Rib, Ported | 2 Beads | Accu-Mag | Realtree® A.P. | Synthetic | 44.5″ | 7.3 | Y | 4 Tube w/Turkey | $515.00 |
| 12 | 61434 | 24″ | Vent Rib, Ported | 2 Beads | Accu-Mag | Mossy Oak® | Synthetic | 44.5″ | 7.3 | Y | 4 Tube w/Turkey | 515.00 |
| 12 | 62035 | 28″ | Vent Rib, Ported | 2 Beads | Accu-Mag | Realtree® A.P. | Synthetic | 48.5″ | 7.7 | | 4 Tubes | 515.00 |
| 12 | 68235 | 28″ | Vent Rib, Ported | 2 Beads | Accu-Mag | OFM Woodland | Synthetic | 48.5″ | | | Mod. Tube | 359.00 |
| 12 | 68230 | 24″ | Vent Rib, Ported | 2 Beads | Accu-Mag | OFM Woodland | Synthetic | 44.5″ | 7.3 | Y | X-Full Tube Only | 359.00 |
| 12 | 61247 | 24″ 24″ | Vent Rib, Ported Slugster, Ported | 2 Beads Rifle | Accu-Mag Rifled Bore | Realtree® A.P. | Synthetic | 44.5″ | 7.3 | Y | 4 Tube w/Turkey Includes Hard Case | 640.00 |
| 12 | 62148 | 28″ 24″ | Vent Rib, Ported Slugster, Ported | 2 Beads Rifle | Accu-Mag Rifled Bore | OFM Woodland | Wood/ Synthetic | 48.5″ | 7.7 | Y | 4 Tubes Dual-Comb™ Stock | 554.00 |

# MOSSBERG SHOTGUNS

## MODEL 9200 AUTOLOADERS

All Mossberg Model 9200 autoloader shotguns handle light 2³/₄″ and heavy 3″ magnum loads. Features include cut-checkered walnut stock and forearm, gold trigger, engraved receiver, top thumb safety, light weight and easy shooting. All models include a Cablelock™ and a Lifetime Limited Warranty.

**MODEL 9200 w/Vent Rib**

## SPECIFICATIONS AND PRICES MODEL 9200 (12 Gauge, 5 Shot)

| Ga. | Stock # | Bbl. Length | Barrel Type | Sights | Choke | Finish | Stock | Length O.A. | Wt. | Q.D. Studs | Notes | Prices |
|---|---|---|---|---|---|---|---|---|---|---|---|---|
| **MODEL 9200 CROWN GRADE** | | | | | | | | | | | | |
| 12 | 49420 | 28″ | Vent Rib, Ported | 2 Beads | Accu-Choke | Blue | Walnut | 48″ | 7.7 | | IC, Mod. & Full Tubes | $503.00 |
| 12 | 49432 | 24″ | Trophy Slugster™ | Scope Mount | Rifled Bore | Blue | Walnut | 44″ | 7.3 | Y | Dual-Comb™ Stock | 524.00 |
| 12 | 49444 | 24″ | Slugster | Rifle | Rifled Bore | Blue | Walnut | 44″ | 7.3 | | | 501.00 |
| 12 | 49403 | 26″ | Vent Rib | 2 Beads | Accu-Choke | Blue | Walnut | 46″ | 7.5 | | USST, IC, Mod., Full & Skeet | 502.00 |
| 12 | 49406 | 18.5″ | Plain | Bead | Mod. | Matte Blue | Synthetic | 39.5″ | 7.0 | Y | Fixed Choke | 410.00 |
| 12 | 49435 | 22″ | Vent Rib | 2 Beads | Accu-Choke | Blue | Walnut | 42″ | 7.2 | | IC/Mod., Full Bantam | 501.00 |

**MODEL 9200 OFM WOODLAND CAMO**

## MODEL 9200 CAMO

| Ga. | Stock # | Bbl. Length | Barrel Type | Sights | Choke | Finish | Stock | Length O.A. | Wt. | Q.D. Studs | Notes | Prices |
|---|---|---|---|---|---|---|---|---|---|---|---|---|
| 12 | 49434 | 24″ | Vent Rib | 2 Beads | Accu-Choke | Mossy Oak® | Synthetic | 44″ | 7.3 | Y | IC, Mod., Full & X-Full Tubes | $579.00 |
| 12 | 49134 | 24″ | Vent Rib | 2 Beads | Accu-Choke | Realtree® A.P. | Synthetic | 44″ | 7.3 | Y | IC, Mod., Full & X-Full Tubes | 579.00 |
| 12 | 49491 | 28″ | Vent Rib | 2 Beads | Accu-Choke | OFM Woodland | Synthetic | 48″ | 7.7 | Y | IC, Mod. & Full Tubes | 487.00 |
| 12 | 49430 | 24″ | Vent Rib | 2 Beads | Accu-Choke | OFM Woodland | Synthetic | 44″ | 7.3 | Y | X-Full Tubes Only | 445.00 |
| 12 | 49466 | 28″ 24″ | Vent Rib Slugster | 2 Beads Rifle | Accu-Choke Rifled Bore | OFM Woodland OFM Woodland | Synthetic | 48″ | 7.7 | Y | IC, Mod. & Full Tubes | 562.00 |
| 12 | 49443 | 28″ 24″ | Vent Rib Trophy Slugster™ | 2 Beads Scope Mount | Accu-Choke Rifled Bore | Blued | Walnut | 48″ | 7.7 | | IC, Mod. & Full Tubes Dual-Comb™ Stock | 590.00 |
| 12 | 49464 | 28″ 24″ | Vent Rib Slugster | 2 Beads Rifle | Accu-Choke Rifled Bore | Blued | Walnut | 48″ | 7.7 | | IC, Mod., & Full Tubes | 572.00 |

# MOSSBERG SHOTGUNS

### MODEL 695 BOLT ACTION

The 3-inch chambered 12-gauge Model 695 bolt-action shotgun features a 22-inch barrel and rugged synthetic stock. This combination delivers the fast handling and fine balance of a classic sporting rifle. Every Model 695 comes with a two-round detachable magazine and Weaver-style scope bases to give hunters the advantage of today's specialized slug and turkey optics.

Mossberg's fully rifled slug barrels are specially "ported" to help soften the recoil and reduce muzzle jump. Mossberg's pioneering involvement with turkey hunting has generated the development of the special Extra-full Accu-Choke Tube. The Model 695 Turkey Gun provides the precise pattern placement to make the most of this remarkably tight patterning choke tube. Non-rotating dual claw extractors ensure reliable ejection and feeding. Ten-year limited warranty.

**MOSSBERG MODEL 695 BOLT ACTION**

**MOSSBERG MODEL 695 OFM CAMO**

| Gauge | Model No. | Barrel Length | Barrel Type | Sights | Finish | Stock | Choke | Price |
|---|---|---|---|---|---|---|---|---|
| 12 | 59001 | 22″ | Rifled Ported | Rifle | Matte | Black Synthetic | Cyl. Bore | $307.00 |
| 12 | 59005 | 22″ | Plain | Bead | Woodland Camo | Synthetic | X-Full Turkey Accu-Choke | 276.00 |
| 12 | 59011 | 22″ | Rifled Ported | Rifle | Matte | Black Synthetic | Cyl. Bore | 429.00* |

* Includes Bushnell 1.5X-4.5X scope and Protecto case

**MOSSBERG LINE LAUNCHER**
**$899.00    ($599.00 Launcher Kit)**

The Line Launcher is the first shotgun devoted to rescue and personal safety. It provides an early self-contained rescue opportunity for boaters, police and fire departments, salvage operations or whenever an extra-long throw of line is the safest alternative. This shotgun uses a 12-gauge blank cartridge to propel a convertible projectile with a line attached. With a floating head attached, the projectile will travel 250 to 275 feet. Removing the floating head increases the projectile range to approx. 700 feet.

# MOSSBERG SHOTGUNS

## VIKING SERIES

**VIKING SERIES
12 Gauge Pump Action**

Mossberg's Viking Series shotguns are available in Models 500 and 835 pump actions or as a Model 9200 Autoloader

Viking models are identified by their "Moss-Green" synthetic stocks and matte-metal finish.

| Model | Model No. | Gauge | Barrel length | Barrel Type | Choke/Features | Overall length | Weight | Price |
|---|---|---|---|---|---|---|---|---|
| 9200 Autoloader | 47420 | 12 | 28" | Vent Rib | Accu-choke w/3 tubes | 48" | 7.7 lbs. | $429.00 |
| 835 Ulti-Mag | 67220 | 12 | 28" | Vent Rib, Ported | Mod. Tube | 48" | 7.7 lbs. | 316.00 |
| 500 Pump | 57418 | 12 | 28" | Vent Rib, Ported | 3 Tubes | 48" | 7.2 lbs. | 287.00 |
| | 57125 | 12 | 24" | Vent Rib, Ported | Turkey Tube | 44" | 7.1 lbs. | 274.00 |
| | 57437 | 20 | 26" | Vent Rib | Accu-choke w/3 Tubes | 46" | 7.1 lbs. | 287.00 |
| | 57244 | 12 | 24" | Rifled, Ported | Rifle sights | 44" | 7.1 lbs. | 326.00 |
| Scope Combo | 57432 | 12 | 24" | Rifled, Ported | Scope base w/bore-sighted scope and Protecto case | 44" | 7.2 lbs. | 394.00 |

# MAVERICK BY MOSSBERG

**MAVERICK MODEL 31017
12 Gauge**

Maverick 12-gauge-only shotguns feature durable synthetic stocks and forearms and a crossbolt safety located in front of the trigger. All models have a 3" chamber and a 6-shot capacity with 2³/₄" shells. Barrels are interchangeable with Mossberg brand barrels.

**Model 31002** features 28" barrel, Mod. choke, 48" overall length, bead sight, weighs 7.2 lbs. . . . . . . . . . . . . **$221.00**
**Model 31017** features 24" barrel with rifle sights, Cyl. Bore, 44" overall length and weight of 7.1 lbs. . . . . . . . . . **235.00**
**Model 31023** features the shorter 18¹/₂" barrel with bead sight and Cyl. Bore, overall length of 39" and weight of 6.9 pounds. . . . . . . . . . . . . . . . . . . . . . . . . . . . . . . . . **213.00**

# NEW ENGLAND FIREARMS

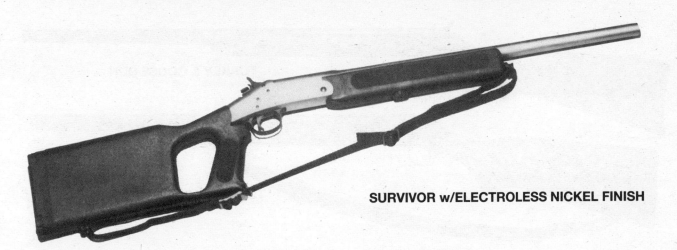

**SURVIVOR w/ELECTROLESS NICKEL FINISH**

## SURVIVOR SERIES

This new series of survival arms is available in 12 and 20 ga. with either a blued or electroless nickel finish. All shotguns feature the New England Firearms action with a patented transfer bar safety and high-impact, synthetic stock and forend. The stock is a modified thumbhole design with a full and secure pistol grip. The buttplate is attached at one end with a large thumbscrew for access to a large storage compartment holding a wide variety of survival gear or extra ammunition. The forend, which has a hollow cavity for storing three rounds of ammunition, is accessible by removing a thumbscrew (also used for takedown).

### SPECIFICATIONS
**Action:** Break open, side-lever release, automatic ejection
**Gauge:** 12, 20, .410/45 Colt (Combo)
**Barrel length:** 22"  **Choke:** Modified
**Chamber:** 3" (Combo also available w/2½" chamber)
**Overall length:** 36"  **Weight:** 6 lbs.
**Sights:** Bead
**Stock:** High-density polymer, black matte finish, sling swivels
**Prices:**
Blued finish. . . . . . . . . . . . . . . . . . . . . . . . . . . . . . **$129.95**
Nickel finish . . . . . . . . . . . . . . . . . . . . . . . . . . . . . **145.95**
.410/45 Colt Combo, blued . . . . . . . . . . . . . . . . . . **145.95**
　Nickel. . . . . . . . . . . . . . . . . . . . . . . . . . . . . . . . **164.95**

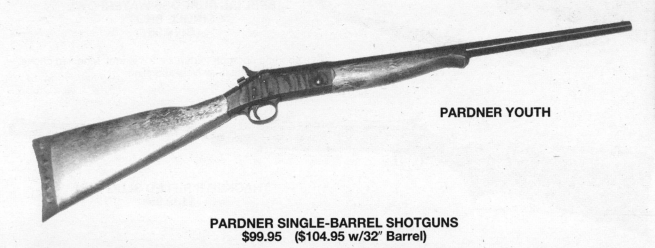

**PARDNER YOUTH**

### PARDNER SINGLE-BARREL SHOTGUNS
**$99.95    ($104.95 w/32" Barrel)**

### SPECIFICATIONS
**Gauges:** 12, 16, 20, 28 and .410
**Barrel lengths:** 22" (Youth); 26" (20, 28, .410);
　28" (12 and 16 ga.), 32" (12 ga.)
**Chokes:** Full (all gauges, except 28);
　Modified (12, 20 and 28 ga.)

**Chamber:** 2¾" (16 and 28 ga.); 3" (all others)
Also available:
**PARDNER YOUTH.** With 22" barrel in gauges 20, 28 and .410.
　**Price:** . . . . . . . . . . . . . . . . . . . . . . . . . . . . . . . **$109.95**

# NEW ENGLAND FIREARMS

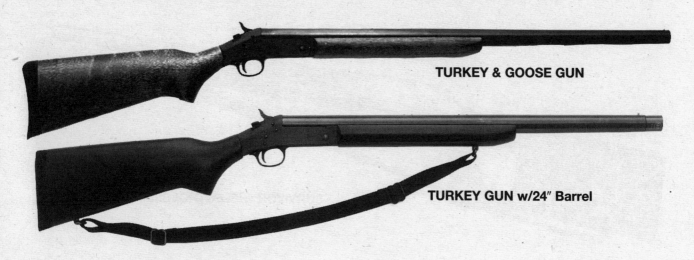

**TURKEY & GOOSE GUN**

**TURKEY GUN w/24" Barrel**

### TURKEY & GOOSE GUN
### $149.95
### ($159.95 w/Camo Paint, Swivels & Sling)
**SPECIFICATIONS**
**Gauge:** 10 (3¹/₂" chamber)   **Choke:** Full
**Barrel length:** 28"   **Overall length:** 44"

**Weight:** 9¹/₂ lbs.
**Sights:** Bead sights
**Stock:** American hardwood; walnut or camo finish; full pistol grip; ventilated recoil pad.   **Length of pull:** 14¹/₂"
Also available:
**TURKEY GUN.** With 24" screw-in barrel, turkey Full choke, black matte finish, swivels and sling. **Price: $184.95**

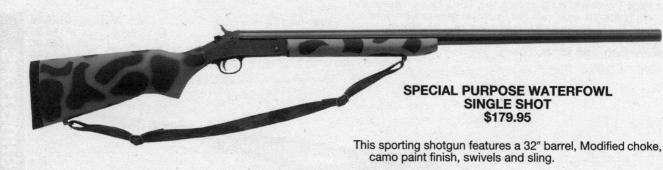

### SPECIAL PURPOSE WATERFOWL
### SINGLE SHOT
### $179.95

This sporting shotgun features a 32" barrel, Modified choke, camo paint finish, swivels and sling.

### TRACKER II RIFLED SLUG GUN
### $139.95

**SPECIFICATIONS**
**Gauges:** 12 and 20 (3" chamber)   **Choke:** Rifled bore
**Barrel length:** 24"   **Overall length:** 40"
**Weight:** 6 lbs.
**Sights:** Adjustable rifle sights

**Length of pull:** 14¹/₂"
**Stock:** American hardwood; walnut or camo finish; full pistol grip; recoil pad; sling swivel studs
Also available:
**TRACKER SLUG GUN** w/Cylinder Bore: . . . . . . . . **$129.95**

# PARKER REPRODUCTIONS

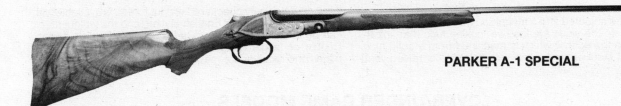

**PARKER A-1 SPECIAL**

Recognized by the shooting fraternity as the finest American shotgun ever produced, the Parker A-1 Special is again available. Exquisite engraving and rare presentation-grade French walnut distinguish the A-1 Special from any other shotguns in the world. Currently offered in 12 and 20 gauge, each gun is custom-fitted in its own oak and leather trunk case. Two models are offered: Hand Engraved and Custom Engraved. Also available in D Grade.

**Standard features:** Automatic safety, selective ejectors, skeleton steel butt plate, splinter forend, engraved snap caps, fitted leather trunk case, canvas and leather case cover, chrome barrel interiors, hand-checkering. The A-1 Special also features a 24k gold initial plate or pistol cap, 32 lines-per-inch checkering, selected wood and fine hand-engraving. Choose from single or double trigger, English or pistol grip stock (all models). Options include beavertail forend, additional barrels.

In addition to the A-1 Special, the D-Grade is available in 12, 20, 16/20 and 28 gauge. A 16-gauge, 28" barrel can be ordered with a 20-gauge one or two-barrel set. The two-barrel sets come in a custom leather cased with a fitted over cover.

**Prices: D-GRADE**
| | |
|---|---|
| One Barrel—12, 20, 28 gauge | $3370.00 |
| Two-barrel set | 4200.00 |
| 16/20 Combo | 4870.00 |
| 20/20/16 Combo | 5630.00 |

## SPECIFICATIONS

| Gauge | Barrel Length | Chokes | Chambers | Drop At Comb | Drop At Heel | Length of Pull | Nominal Weight (lbs.) | Overall Length |
|---|---|---|---|---|---|---|---|---|
| 12 | 26" | Skeet I & II or IC/M | 2¾" | 1³/₈" | 2³/₁₆" | 14¹/₈" | 6¾ | 42⁵/₈" |
| 12 | 28" | IC/M or M/F | 2¾ & 3" | 1³/₈" | 2³/₁₆" | 14¹/₈" | 6¾ | 44⁵/₈" |
| 20 | 26" | Skeet I & II or IC/M | 2¾" | 1³/₈" | 2³/₁₆" | 14³/₈" | 6½ | 42³/₈" |
| 20 | 28" | M/F | 3" | 1³/₈" | 2³/₁₆" | 14³/₈" | 6½ | 44⁵/₈" |
| 16 on 20 frame | 28" | Skeet I & II, IC/M or M/F | 2¾" | 1³/₈" | 2³/₁₆" | 14³/₈" | 6¼ | 44⁵/₈" |
| 28 | 26" | Skeet I & II or IC/M | 2¾" | 1³/₈" | 2³/₁₆" | 14³/₈" | 5¹/₃ | 42⁵/₈" |
| 28 | 28" | M/F | 2¾ & 3" | 1³/₈" | 2³/₁₆" | 14³/₈" | 5¹/₃ | 44⁵/₈" |

*\* Note: The 16-gauge barrels are lighter than the 20-gauge barrels.*

# PERAZZI SHOTGUNS

The heart of the Perazzi line is the classic over/under, whose barrels are soldered into a monobloc that holds the shell extractors. At the sides are the two locking lugs that link the barrels to the action, which is machined from a solid block of forged steel. Barrels come with flat, step or raised ventilated rib. The finely checkered walnut forend is available with schnabel, beavertail or English styling, and the walnut stock can be of standard, Monte Carlo, Skeet or English design. Double or single nonselective or selective triggers. Sideplates and receiver are masterfully engraved.

## OVER/UNDER GAME MODELS

### GAME MODEL MX20C

### GAME MODELS MX8, MX12, MX20, MX8/20, MX28 & MX410

**SPECIFICATIONS**
**Gauges:** 12, 20, 28 & .410
**Chambers:** 2³/₄"; also available in 3"
**Barrel lengths:** 26" and 27¹/₂"
**Weight:** 6 lbs. 6 oz. to 7 lbs. 4 oz.
**Trigger group:** Nondetachable with coil springs and selective trigger

**Stock:** Interchangeable and custom; schnabel forend
**Prices:**
Standard Grade . . . . . . . . . . . . . . $ 8,330.00–$16,650.00
SC3 Grade. . . . . . . . . . . . . . . . . . 14,110.00– 22,430.00
SCO Grade . . . . . . . . . . . . . . . . . 24,030.00– 32,410.00
SCO Gold Grades . . . . . . . . . . . . . 27,110.00– 35,430.00

## AMERICAN TRAP SINGLE BARREL MODELS

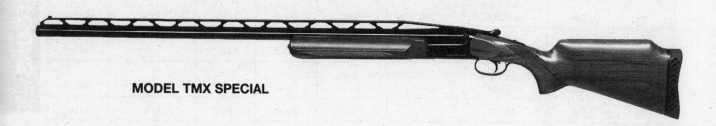

### MODEL TMX SPECIAL

### AMERICAN TRAP SINGLE-BARREL MODELS MX15 & TMX SPECIAL

**SPECIFICATIONS**
**Gauge:** 12
**Chamber:** 2³/₄"
**Barrel lengths:** 32" and 34"
**Weight:** 8 lbs. 6 oz.
**Choke:** Full

**Trigger group:** Detachable and interchangeable with coil springs
**Stock:** Interchangeable and custom made
**Forend:** Beavertail
**Prices:**
TMX Special . . . . . . . . . . . . . . . . . . . . . . . . . . . . . . $6790.00
MX15 . . . . . . . . . . . . . . . . . . . . . . . . . . . . . . . . . . . 7080.00

# PERAZZI SHOTGUNS

## COMPETITION OVER/UNDER SHOTGUNS
### OLYMPIC, DOUBLE TRAP, SKEET, PIGEON & ELECTROCIBLES

**MODEL MX10**

**MODEL DB81 TRAP**

**MX8 SKEET**

**MIRAGE SPORTING**

**SPECIFICATIONS STANDARD GRADE**
**Gauges:** 12 and 20
**Barrel lengths:** 27$\frac{1}{2}$", 28$\frac{3}{8}$", 29$\frac{1}{2}$", 30$\frac{3}{4}$", 31$\frac{1}{2}$"
**Prices:**
**MX8-MIRAGE** 12 ga., removable trigger group
   29$\frac{1}{2}$", 30$\frac{3}{4}$" and 31$\frac{1}{2}$" barrels . . . . . . . . . . .$ 8,330.00
**MX8-MIRAGE SPECIAL** 12 ga., removable trigger group
   29$\frac{1}{2}$", 30$\frac{3}{4}$" and 31$\frac{1}{2}$" barrels . . .   8,830.00–9,430.00
**MX10** 12 & 20 ga. w/adj. stock and rib
   29$\frac{1}{2}$", 30$\frac{3}{4}$" and 31$\frac{1}{2}$" bbl. . . . .   10,610.00–11,670.00
**MX11** 12 ga., removable trigger group
   29$\frac{1}{2}$", 30$\frac{3}{4}$" and 31$\frac{1}{2}$" bbl. . . . .   7,850.00–10,450.00
**MX8/20** 20 ga., removable trigger group
   26$\frac{3}{4}$", 27$\frac{1}{2}$", 28$\frac{3}{8}$", 29$\frac{1}{2}$", 30$\frac{3}{4}$" and
   31$\frac{1}{2}$" barrels . . . . . . . . . . . . . . . .   8,830.00–9,430.00
**MIRAGE SPECIAL** 12 ga. w/adj. trigger,
   28$\frac{3}{8}$", 29$\frac{1}{2}$", 31$\frac{1}{2}$" barrels . . . . . . . . . . . . . .   8,830.00
**MIRAGE SPECIAL SPORTING** 12 ga. w/external
   selector and 5 chokes; 27$\frac{1}{2}$", 28$\frac{3}{8}$", 29$\frac{1}{2}$"
   and 31$\frac{1}{2}$" barrels . . . . . . . . . . .   9,430.00
**MIRAGE SPORTING CLASSIC** 12 ga. . . . . . . . .   10,500.00

**MX8 SPECIAL** 12 ga. w/adjustable trigger
   29$\frac{1}{2}$" and 31$\frac{1}{2}$" barrels . . . . . . . . . . . . . . . .$ 8,830.00
**DB81 SPECIAL** w/adjustable trigger
   29$\frac{1}{2}$", 30$\frac{3}{4}$" and 31$\frac{1}{2}$" barrels . . . . . . . . . . .   10,610.00

*NOTE:* **PIGEON & ELECTROCIBLE MODELS** available in MX1B, Mirage, Mirage Special, MX10 & MX11 only w/27$\frac{1}{2}$", 28$\frac{3}{8}$", 29$\frac{1}{2}$" & 31$\frac{1}{2}$" barrels . . . . . . . . . . . . . . . . . . . . . .$7,850.00–$10,610.00

Also available:
**SC3 Grade** (Models MX8, MX10, MX10/20,
   MX8/20, MX8 Special, Mirage
   Spec., DB81 Spec.) . . . . . . . . . .   $14,110.00–$16,070.00
**SCO Grade** (same models as SC3
   Grade) . . . . . . . . . . . . . . . . .   24,030.00–  25,390.00
**SCO GOLD Grade** (same models
   as above) . . . . . . . . . . . . . . .   27,110.00–  28,270.00
**SCO Grade Sideplates** (same
   models as above) . . . . . . . . . .   36,860.00–  37,370.00
**SCO GOLD Grade Sideplates** (same
   models above) . . . . . . . . . . . . .   42,800.00–  43,300.00

# PIOTTI SHOTGUNS

One of Italy's top gunmakers, Piotti limits its production to a small number of hand-crafted, best-quality double-barreled shotguns whose shaping, checkering, stock, action and barrel work meets or exceeds the standards achieved in London before WWII. All of the sidelock models exhibit the same overall design, materials and standards of workmanship; they differ only in the quality of the wood, shaping and sculpturing of the action, type of engraving and gold inlay work and other details. The Model Piuma differs from the other shotguns only in its Anson & Deeley boxlock design. Piotti's new over/under model appears below.

**SPECIFICATIONS**
**Gauges:** 10, 12, 16, 20, 28, .410
**Chokes:** As ordered
**Barrels:** 12 ga., 25" to 32"; other gauges, 25" to 30"; chopper lump (demi-bloc) barrels with soft-luster blued finish; level, file-cut rib or optional concave
**Action:** Boxlock, Anson & Deeley; Sidelock, Holland & Holland pattern; both have automatic ejectors, double triggers with yielding front trigger (non-selective single trigger optional); coin finish or optional color casehardening
**Stock:** Hand-rubbed oil finish on straight grip stock with checkered butt (pistol grip optional)
**Forend:** Classic (splinter); optional beavertail
**Weight:** 5 lbs. 4 oz. (.410 ga.) to 8 lbs. 4 oz. (12 ga.)

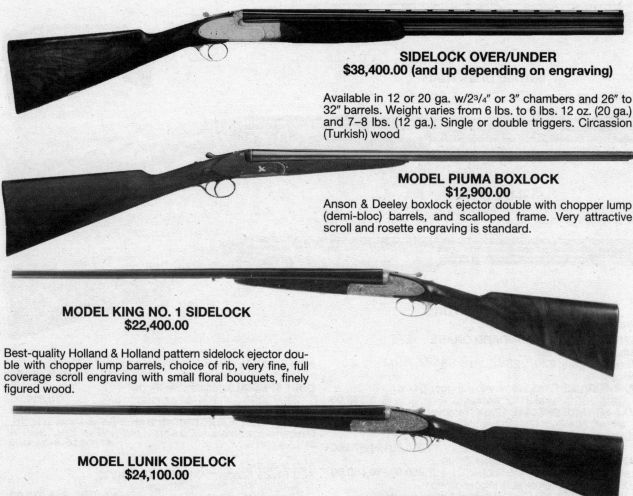

### SIDELOCK OVER/UNDER
### $38,400.00 (and up depending on engraving)

Available in 12 or 20 ga. w/2³/₄" or 3" chambers and 26" to 32" barrels. Weight varies from 6 lbs. to 6 lbs. 12 oz. (20 ga.) and 7–8 lbs. (12 ga.). Single or double triggers. Circassion (Turkish) wood

### MODEL PIUMA BOXLOCK
### $12,900.00
Anson & Deeley boxlock ejector double with chopper lump (demi-bloc) barrels, and scalloped frame. Very attractive scroll and rosette engraving is standard.

### MODEL KING NO. 1 SIDELOCK
### $22,400.00

Best-quality Holland & Holland pattern sidelock ejector double with chopper lump barrels, choice of rib, very fine, full coverage scroll engraving with small floral bouquets, finely figured wood.

### MODEL LUNIK SIDELOCK
### $24,100.00

Best-quality Holland & Holland pattern sidelock ejector double with chopper lump (demi-bloc) barrels, choice of rib, Renaissance-style, large scroll engraving in relief, finely figured wood.

### MODEL KING EXTRA (not shown)
### $31,700.00 (and up depending on engraving)

Best-quality Holland & Holland pattern sidelock ejector double with chopper lump barrels, choice of rib and bulino game-scene engraving or game-scene engraving with gold inlays; engraved and signed by a master engraver.

# REMINGTON SHOTGUNS

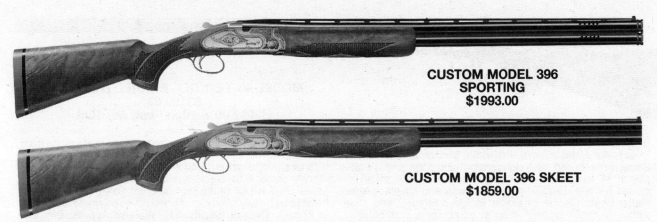

**CUSTOM MODEL 396
SPORTING
$1993.00**

**CUSTOM MODEL 396 SKEET
$1859.00**

## CUSTOM MODEL 396 OVER/UNDER SHOTGUN (SKEET AND SPORTING CLAYS)

The Model 396 is produced in 12-gauge Skeet and Sporting Clays versions. Chrome-moly barrels in both versions have lengthened forcing cones, are fitted with side ribs, and have a flat 10-millimeter-wide parallel vent rib. Barrel lengths are 28″ or 30″. All barrels are fitted for the interchangeable Rem Choke system. Skeet and Improved Skeet choke tubes are supplied for the Model 396 Skeet, and four choke tubes—Skeet, Improved Skeet, Improved Cylinder and Modified configurations—for the Model 396 Sporting. The Sporting Clays version also features factory porting on both barrels.

Barrels and side ribs are finished with high-polished deep bluing. The receiver and sideplates, trigger guard, top lever and forend metal are finished with gray nitride coloring.

Extensive scroll work appears on the receiver, trigger guard, tang, hinge pins and forend metal. The sideplates include detailed renditions of a pointer and setter on the left and right sides, respectively. Identifying individual versions of the Model 396 on both sideplates are the words "Sporting" or "Skeet" in script lettering. Additional scroll work, the Remington logo and the model designation appear on the floorplate.

Stocks on both models are selected from fancy American walnut and given a soft satin finish. Several stock design features are specifically adapted to clay target shooting, including a wider, target-style forend, a comb with larger radius and a universal palm swell on the pistol grip.

### SPECIFICATIONS
**Gauge:** 12 **Chamber:** 2³/₄″
**Choke:** Rem Choke
**Length of pull:** 14³/₁₆″
**Drop at comb:** 1¹/₂″ **Drop at heel:** 2¹/₄″
**Barrel lengths:** 28″ and 30″
**Overall length:** 45″ and 47″
**Weight:** 7¹/₂ lbs. and 7³/₈ lbs.

**PEERLESS OVER/UNDER SHOTGUN
w/Vent Rib and Engraved Sideplates
$1092.00**

Practical, lightweight, well-balanced and affordable are the attributes of this Remington shotgun. Features include an all-steel receiver, boxlock action and removable sideplates (engraved with a pointer on one side and a setter on the other). The bottom of the receiver has the Remington logo, plus the words "Peerless, Field" and the serial number. Cut-checkering appears on both pistol grip and forend (shaped with finger grooves and tapered toward the front). The American walnut stock is fitted w/black, vented recoil pad.

### SPECIFICATIONS
**Gauge:** 12 (3″ chamber)
**Chokes:** REM Choke System (1 Full, 1 Mod., 1 Imp. Cyl.)

**Barrel lengths:** 26″, 28″, 30″ with vent rib
**Overall length:** 43″ (26″ barrel); 45″ (28″ barrel); 47″ (30″ barrel)
**Weight:** 7¹/₄ lbs. (26″); 7³/₈ lbs. (28″); 7¹/₂ lbs. (30″)
**Trigger:** Single, selective, gold-plated
**Safety:** Automatic safety
**Sights:** Target gun style with mid-bead and Bradley-type front bead
**Length of pull:** 14³/₁₆″
**Drop at comb:** 1¹/₂″ **Drop at heel:** 2¹/₄″
**Features:** Solid, horseshoe-shaped locking bar with two rectangular lug extensions on either side of the barrel's mid-bore; fast lock time (3.28 milliseconds)

# REMINGTON SHOTGUNS

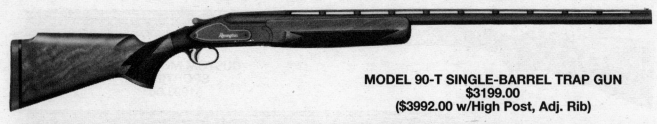

## MODEL 90-T SINGLE-BARREL TRAP GUN
### $3199.00
### ($3992.00 w/High Post, Adj. Rib)

Remington's **Model 90-T Single-Barrel Trap** features a top-lever release and internal, full-width, horizontal bolt lockup. Barrel is overbored, with elongated forcing cone, and is available in 34" length. A medium-high, tapered, ventilated rib includes a white, Bradley-type front bead and stainless-steel center bead. Choice of stocks includes Monte Carlo style with 1³/₈", 1¹/₂" or 1¹/₄" drop at comb, or a conventional straight stock with 1¹/₂" drop. Standard length of pull is 14³/₈". Stocks and modified beavertail forends are made from semifancy American walnut. Wood finish is low-luster satin with positive, deep-cut checkering 20 lines to the inch. All stocks come with black, vented-rubber recoil pads. The Model 90-T HPAR offers four different rib elevations. Comb height can be adjusted simultaneously to retain desired point of impact. **Overall length:** 51". **Weight:** Approx. 8³/₄ lbs. **Choke:** Full.

## MODEL 870 EXPRESS "YOUTH" GUN
### 20-Gauge Lightweight
### $292.00    $325.00 (w/Deer Barrel)

The **Model 870 Express "Youth" Gun** has been specially designed for youths and smaller-sized adults. It's a 20-gauge lightweight with a 1-inch shorter stock and 21-inch barrel. Yet it is still all 870, complete with REM Choke and ventilated rib barrel. Also available with a 20" fully rifled, rifle-sighted deer barrel. **Barrel length:** 21". **Stock Dimensions:** Length of pull 12¹/₂" (including recoil pad); drop at heel; 2¹/₂" drop at comb 1⁵/₈". **Overall length:** 39" (40¹/₂" w/deer barrel). **Average Weight:** 6 lbs. **Choke:** REM Choke-Mod. (vent-rib version).

## MODEL 870 EXPRESS
## SYNTHETIC HOME DEFENSE
### $292.00

This shotgun is designed specifically for home defense use. The 12-gauge pump-action shotgun features an 18" barrel with Cylinder choke and front bead sight. Barrel and action have the traditional Express-style metal finish. The synthetic stock and forend have a textured black, nonreflective finish and feature positive checkering. **Capacity:** 4 rounds.

# REMINGTON PUMP SHOTGUNS

**MODEL 870 EXPRESS**

## MODEL 870 EXPRESS
### $292.00 (12 & 20 GA.)
### ($299.00 w/Black Synthetic Stock & Forend)

**Model 870 Express** features the same action as the Wingmaster and is available with 3″ chamber and 26″ or 28″ vent-rib barrel. It has a hardwood stock with low-luster finish and solid buttpad. Choke is Modified REM Choke tube and wrench. **Overall length:** 48¹/₂″ (28″ barrel). **Weight:** 7¹/₄ lbs (26″ barrel).

**MODEL 870 EXPRESS TURKEY GUN**
**$305.00**

The **Model 870 Express Turkey Gun** boasts all the same features as the Model 870 Express, except has 21″ vent-rib barrel and Turkey Extra-Full REM Choke.

**MODEL 870 EXPRESS DEER GUN**
**$287.00 With Rifle Sights**
**($325.00 Fully Rifled)**

This 12-gauge, pump-action deer gun is for hunters who prefer open sights. Features a 20″ barrel, quick-reading iron sights, fixed Imp. Cyl. choke and Monte Carlo stock. Also available with fully rifled barrel.

### MODEL 870 EXPRESS COMBO (Not Shown)
### $383.00

The **Model 870 Express** in 12 and 20 gauge offers all the features of the standard Model 870, including twin-action bars, quick-changing 28″ barrels, REM Choke and vent rib plus low-luster, checkered hardwood stock and no-shine finish on barrel and receiver. The Model 870 Combo is packaged with an extra 20″ deer barrel, fitted with rifle sights and fixed, Improved Cylinder choke (additional REM chokes can be added for special applications). The 3-inch chamber handles all 2³/₄″ and 3″ shells without adjustment. **Weight:** 7¹/₂ lbs.

Also available w/26″ REM choke barrel w/vent rib and 20″ fully rifled deer barrel w/rifle sights (12 and 20 ga.). **Weight:** 7.5 lbs. **Price: $421.00**

# REMINGTON PUMP SHOTGUNS

## SPECIAL PURPOSE

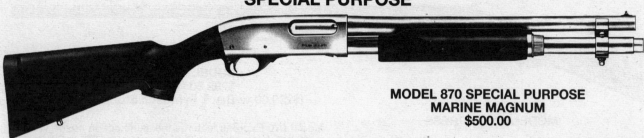

### MODEL 870 SPECIAL PURPOSE MARINE MAGNUM
### $500.00

Remington's **Model 870 Special Purpose Marine Magnum** is a versatile, multipurpose security gun featuring a rugged synthetic stock and extensive, electroless nickel plating on all metal parts. This new shotgun utilizes a standard 12-gauge Model 870 receiver with a 7-round magazine extension tube and an 18″ cylinder barrel (38 1/2″ overall) with bead front sight. The receiver, magazine extension and barrel are protected (inside and out) with heavy-duty, corrosion-resistant nickel plating. The synthetic stock and forend reduce the effects of moisture. The gun is supplied with a black rubber recoil pad, sling swivel studs, and positive checkering on both pistol grip and forend. **Weight:** 7 1/2 lbs.

### MODEL 870 SPS-CAMO
### $496.00

This Mossy Oak Bottomland™ Camo version of Model 11-87 and Model 870 Special Purpose Synthetic shotguns features a durable camo finish and synthetic stocks that are immune to the effects of ice, snow and mud. Available with a 26″ vent-rib barrel with twin bead sights and Imp. Cyl., Modified, and Full REM Choke tubes.

### MODEL 870 SPST ALL BLACK TURKEY GUN
### $425.00

Same as the Model 870 SPS above, except with a 21″ vent-rib turkey barrel and Extra-Full REM Choke tube. Also available:

Mossy Oak Greenleaf Camo finish. . . . . . . . . . . . . **$511.00**
20″ fully rifled cantilever deer barrel (All Black) . . . . **496.00**

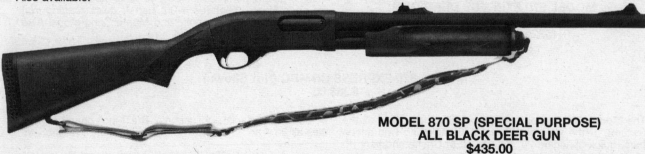

### MODEL 870 SP (SPECIAL PURPOSE) ALL BLACK DEER GUN
### $435.00

**Gauge:** 12. **Choke:** Fully rifled with rifle sights, recoil pad. **Barrel length:** 20″. **Overall length:** 40 1/2.″ **Average weight:** 7 lbs.

# REMINGTON SHOTGUNS

### MODEL 870 WINGMASTER
### 12 Gauge, Light Contour Barrel
### $519.00

This restyled **870 "Wingmaster"** pump has cut-checkering on its satin-finished American walnut stock and forend for confident handling, even in wet weather. Also available in Hi-Gloss finish. An ivory bead "Bradley"-type front sight is included. Rifle is available with 26″, 28″ and 30″ barrel with REM Choke and handles 3″ and 2³/₄″ shells interchangeably.

**Overall length:** 46¹/₂ (26″ barrel), 48¹/₂″ (28″ barrel), 50¹/₂ (30″ barrel). **Weight:** 7¹/₄ lbs. (w/26″ barrel).
Also available:
**MODEL 870 WINGMASTER.** 20 Ga. Lightweight (6¹/₂ lbs.), American walnut stock and forend. **Price:** ....... **$492.00**

### MODEL 870 WINGMASTER
### CANTILEVER SCOPE MOUNT DEER GUN
### (12 & 20 Ga.)
### $599.00 (Fully Rifled, American Walnut Stock)

Also available:
Engraved **Model 870 Wingmaster** in Grade D. Price on request.

### MODEL 11-87 SPORTING CLAYS
### $745.00 ($793.00 Nickel Plated)

Remington's **Model 11-87 Premier Sporting Clays** features a target-grade, American walnut competition stock with a length of pull that is ³/₁₆″ longer and ¹/₄″ higher at the heel. The tops of the receiver, barrel and rib have a nonreflective matte finish. The rib is medium high with a stainless mid-bead and ivory front bead. The barrel (26″ or 28″) has a lengthened forcing cone to generate greater pattern uniformity; and there are 5 REM choke tubes—Skeet, Improved Skeet, Improved Cylinder, Modified and Full. All sporting clays choke tubes have a knurled end extending .45″ beyond the muzzle for fast field changes. Both the toe and heel of the buttpad are rounded. **Weight:** 7¹/₂ lbs. (26″); 7⁵/₈ lbs. (28″)

**SHOTGUNS**

# REMINGTON AUTO SHOTGUNS

### MODEL 11-87 PREMIER AUTOLOADER
**$684.00 (Light Contour Barrel)**
**$734.00 (Left Hand, 28″ Barrel)**

Remington's redesigned 12-gauge **Model 11-87 Premier Autoloader** features new, light-contour barrels that reduce both barrel weight and overall weight (more than 8 ounces). The shotgun has a standard 3-inch chamber and handles all 12-gauge shells interchangeably—from 2 3/4″ field loads to 3″ Magnums. The gun's interchangeable REM choke system includes Improved Cylinder, Modified and Full chokes. Select

American walnut stocks with fine-line, cut-checkering in satin or high-gloss finish are standard. Right-hand models are available in 26″, 28″ and 30″ barrels (left-hand models are 28″ only). A two-barrel gun case is supplied.
Also available:
**Model 11-87 Premier SC** (Sporting Clays) . . . . . . **$745.00**
**Model 11-87 SC NP** (Nickel Plated) . . . . . . . . . . . . **793.00**

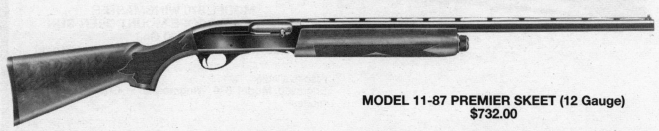

### MODEL 11-87 PREMIER TRAP (12 Gauge)
**$754.00 with Monte Carlo Stock**

A 30″ trap barrel (50 1/2″ overall) offers trap shooters a REM Choke system with three interchangeable choke constrictions: trap full, trap extra full, and trap super full. **Weight:** 8 3/4 lbs.

### MODEL 11-87 PREMIER SKEET (12 Gauge)
**$732.00**

This model features American walnut wood and distinctive cut checkering with satin finish, plus new two-piece butt-plate. REM Choke system includes option of two skeet chokes—skeet and improved skeet. Trap and skeet guns are

designed for 12-gauge target loads and are set to handle 2 3/4″ shells only. **Barrel length:** 26″. **Overall length:** 46″. **Weight:** 8 1/8 lbs.

### MODEL 11-87 PREMIER DEER GUN
**With Cantilever Scope Mount and**
**Fully Rifled 21″ Barrel**
**$749.00 (Satin Finish)**

# REMINGTON AUTO SHOTGUNS

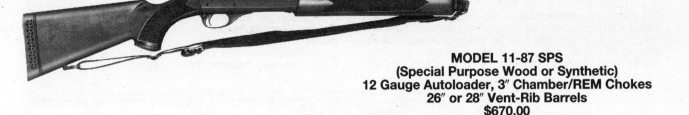

**MODEL 11-87 SPS**
**(Special Purpose Wood or Synthetic)**
**12 Gauge Autoloader, 3″ Chamber/REM Chokes**
**26″ or 28″ Vent-Rib Barrels**
**$670.00**

**MODEL 11-87 SPST TURKEY GUN**
**12 Gauge Autoloader, 3″ Chamber**
**All-Black Synthetic Stock**
**Extra-Full REM Choke Turkey Tube**
**$684.00**
**$757.00 w/Mossy Oak Break-Up Camo Finish**

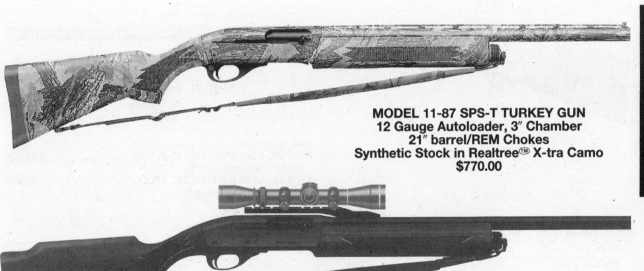

**MODEL 11-87 SPS-T TURKEY GUN**
**12 Gauge Autoloader, 3″ Chamber**
**21″ barrel/REM Chokes**
**Synthetic Stock in Realtree™ X-tra Camo**
**$770.00**

**MODEL 11-87 SPS SPECIAL PURPOSE**
**SYNTHETIC ALL-BLACK DEER GUN**
**$692.00 (3″ Magnum)**
**$752.00 (Fully Rifled Cantilever)**

Features the same finish as other SP models plus a padded, camo-style carrying sling of Cordura nylon with QD sling swivels. Barrel is 21″ (41″ overall) with rifle sights and rifled and IC choke (handles all 2³/₄″ and 3″ rifled slug and buckshot loads as well as high-velocity field and magnum loads; does not function with light 2³/₄″ field loads). **Weight:** 8¹/₂ lbs.

# REMINGTON AUTO SHOTGUNS

### MODEL 1100 AUTOLOADING SHOTGUNS

The Remington **Model 1100** is a 5-shot gas-operated auto-loader with a gas-metering system designed to reduce recoil. This design enables the shooter to use 2¾-inch standard velocity "Express" and 2¾-inch Magnum loads without gun adjustments. Barrels, within gauge and versions, are inter-changeable. All 12- and 20-gauge versions include REM™ Choke; interchangeable choke tubes in 26″ and 28″ (12 gauge only) barrels. American walnut stocks come with fleur-de-lis design fine-line checkering and a scratch-resistant finish. See table below for specifications.

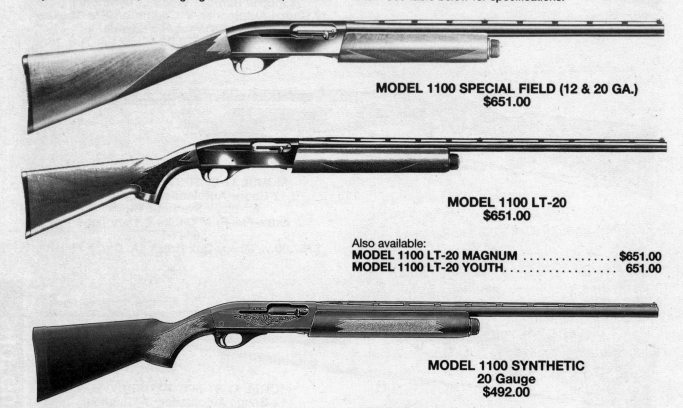

### MODEL 1100 SPECIAL FIELD (12 & 20 GA.)
### $651.00

### MODEL 1100 LT-20
### $651.00

Also available:
**MODEL 1100 LT-20 MAGNUM** . . . . . . . . . . . . . . . $651.00
**MODEL 1100 LT-20 YOUTH** . . . . . . . . . . . . . . . . . 651.00

### MODEL 1100 SYNTHETIC
### 20 Gauge
### $492.00

Also available:
**MODEL 1100 SYNTHETIC FR RS** . . . . . . . . . . . . . $475.00
(fully rifled, rifle sights)
**MODEL 1100 SYNTHETIC FR CL** . . . . . . . . . . . . . 585.00
(fully rifled, cantilever)

## SPECIFICATIONS MODEL 1100™

| Model | Gauge | Barrel Length | Overall Length | Average Wt.(lbs.) | Length of Pull | Drop Comb | Drop Heel |
|---|---|---|---|---|---|---|---|
| 1100 Special Field | 12 | 23″ | 43½″ | 7¼ | 14″ | 1½″ | 2½″ |
| | 20 | 23″ | 43½″ | 6½ | 14″ | 1½″ | 2½″ |
| 1100 LT-20 | 20 | 28″ | 48″ | 7 | 14″ | 1½″ | 2½″ |
| | 20 | 26″ | 46″ | 6¾ | 14″ | 1½″ | 2½″ |
| 1100 LT-20 Magnum | 20 | 28″ | 48″ | 7 | 14″ | 1½″ | 2½″ |
| 1100 LT-20 Youth | 20 | 21″ | 40½″ | 6½ | 13″ | 1½″ | 2½″ |
| 1100 Synthetic | 12 | 28″ | 48″ | 7½ | 14″ | 1½″ | 2½″ |
| | 20 | 26″ | 46″ | 7 | 14″ | 1½″ | 2½″ |
| 1100 Synthetic FR RS | 20 | 21″ | 41″ | 7 | 14″ | 1½″ | 2½″ |
| 1100 Synthetic FR CL | 12 | 21″ | 41½″ | 7½ | 14″ | 1½″ | 2½″ |

# REMINGTON AUTO SHOTGUNS

**MODEL 1100 SYNTHETIC**
**12 Gauge**
**$492.00**

See table on previous page for specifications.

**MODEL 11-96 EURO LIGHTWEIGHT**
**$862.00**

Based on the Model 11-87™ action, the new Model 11-96™ features modifications to the 11-87 action to reduce the overall weight of the 26″ barrel version (from 7⅝ lbs. to just 6⅞ lbs.). These modifications include changing the profile of the receiver and shortening the magazine assembly (capacity of 3 shells).

This new shotgun is available with 26″ or 28″ barrels and features Remington's pressure-compensated, low-recoil gas system, which handles both 2¾″ field and 3″ magnum shells interchangeably; three flush-fitting REM™ chokes (for steel or lead shot) are supplied. Each gun has fine-line embellishments on the receivers and cut-checkered, Claro walnut stocks and forends. Barrels are chrome-moly steel with chrome-plated bores and 6mm vent ribs.

**SP-10 MAGNUM SHOTGUN**
**$1054.00**

Remington's **SP-10 Magnum** is the only gas-operated semi-automatic 10-gauge shotgun made today. Engineered to shoot steel shot, the SP-10 delivers up to 34 percent more pellets to the target than standard 12-gauge shotgun and steel shot combinations. This autoloader features a vented, noncorrosive, stainless-steel gas system, in which the cylinder moves—not the piston. This reduces felt recoil energy by spreading the recoil over a longer time. The receiver is machined from a solid billet of ordnance steel for total integral strength. The SP-10 has a ⅜″ vent rib with mid and front sights for a better sight plane. The American walnut stock and forend have a protective, low-gloss satin finish for reduced glare, and positive deep-cut checkering. The receiver and barrel have a matte finish, and the stainless-steel breech bolt features a non-reflective finish. The SP-10 also has a brown-vented recoil pad and a padded camo sling of Cordura nylon. **Barrel lengths/choke:** 26″ or 30″/REM Choke. **Overall length:** 51½″ (30″ barrel) and 47½″ (26″ barrel). **Weight:** 11 lbs. (30″ barrel) and 10¾ lbs. (26″ barrel).

**MODEL SP-10 MAGNUM CAMO**
**10-Gauge Autoloader**
**with 23″ Vent-Rib Barrel**
**and Mossy Oak Break-Up Camo Pattern**
**$1145.00**

# RIZZINI SHOTGUNS

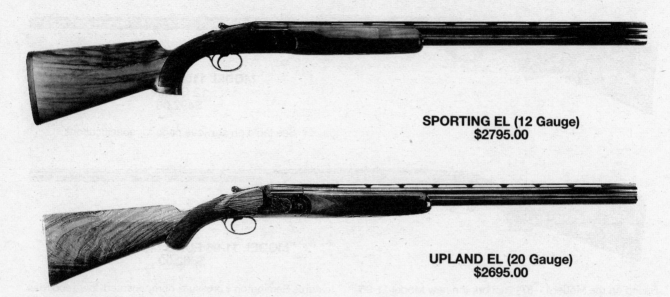

**SPORTING EL (12 Gauge)**
**$2795.00**

**UPLAND EL (20 Gauge)**
**$2695.00**

Rizzini builds a well-finished boxlock ejector over/under that is available in all gauges and in many different configurations. Rizzini guns are manufactured in Marcheno, Italy, in the famous Val Trompia gunmaking region. All Rizzini guns have special steel barrels that are proof-tested at 1200 Bars, as well as pattern-tested at the factory. The guns are built in field, sporting clays and express rifle configurations.

The **Artemis** and **Premier** are production guns built to standard specifications. The EL models, which include the Upland EL, the Sporting EL and the High Grades feature higher grade wood, checkering and hand finishing.

**Field** guns are available with case-colored or coin-finish actions with straight grips or round knob semi-pistol grips.

Also available are multi-gauge field sets with .410, 28 or 20 gauge barrels in any combination. These sets are available in EL or High Grade level guns. On custom orders, stock dimensions, chokes and barrel length may be specified. Screw-in chokes are available on 12 and 20 gauge guns.

**Sporting** guns, in 12 and 20 gauge only, feature heavier weight and a target-style rib, stock and forearm. The Sporting models are available in three versions: Premier Sporting, Sporting EL and S790EL.

High Grade models, built with or without sideplates, are available in four engraving styles, including game scenes and gold inlays.

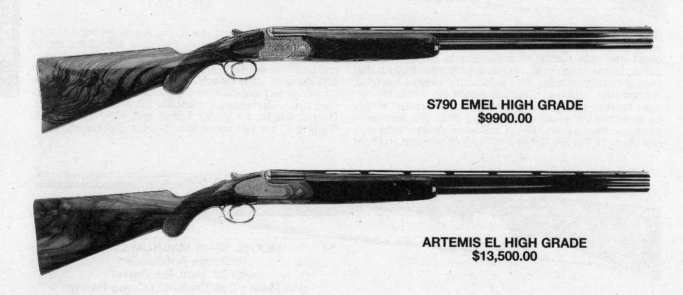

**S790 EMEL HIGH GRADE**
**$9900.00**

**ARTEMIS EL HIGH GRADE**
**$13,500.00**

# ROTTWEIL SHOTGUNS

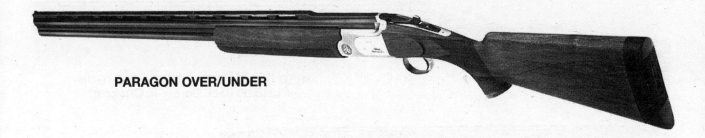

**PARAGON OVER/UNDER**

## ROTTWEIL PARAGON

This concept in shotgun systems, trap, skeet and sporting clays includes the following features: Detachable and interchangeable trigger action with super-imposed hammers • Safety action on trigger and sears • Spring-loaded self-adjusting wedges • Ejector can be turned on and off at will • Top lever convertible for right- and left-handed shooters • Interchangeable firing pins (without disassembly) • Length and weight of barrels selected depending on application (see below) • Module system: Fully interchangeable receiver, barrels, stocks trigger action and forends • Select walnut stocks

**Barrel lengths:**

| | | | |
|---|---|---|---|
| Field & Skeet | 27½" | Sporting | 28½" |
| American Skeet | 28" | Trap | 29" & 30" |
| Parcours | 28³/₈" | American Trap Single | 32" & 34" |

**Prices:** . . . . . . . . . . . . . . . . . . . . . . . . . . . . . . . . . . . . . . . . . **on request**

**PARAGON**
**(Close-up Open)**

# RUGER OVER/UNDER SHOTGUNS

**RED LABEL OVER/UNDER SHOTGUN**
**$1215.00 (Incl. Screw-in Chokes)**

**SPORTING CLAYS OVER/UNDER**
**MODEL KRL-2036 (20 Ga. shown above)**
**$1349.00 (w/Screw-in Chokes)**

## SPECIFICATIONS RED LABEL AND SPORTING CLAYS OVER/UNDERS

| Catalog Number | Gauge | Chamber | Choke* | Barrel Length | Overall Length | Length Pull | Drop Comb | Drop Heel | Sights** | Approx. Wt. (lbs.) | Type Stock |
|---|---|---|---|---|---|---|---|---|---|---|---|
| KRL-1226 | 12 | 3" | F,M,IC,S+ | 26" | 43" | 14 1/8" | 1 1/2" | 2 1/2" | GBF | 7 3/4 | Pistol Grip |
| KRL-1227 | 12 | 3" | F,M,IC,S+ | 28" | 45" | 14 1/8" | 1 1/2" | 2 1/2" | GBF | 8 | Pistol Grip |
| KRLS-1226 | 12 | 3" | F,M,IC,S+ | 26" | 43" | 14 1/8" | 1 1/2" | 2 1/2" | GBF | 7 1/2 | Straight |
| KRLS-1227 | 12 | 3" | F,M,IC,S+ | 28" | 45" | 14 1/8" | 1 1/2" | 2 1/2" | GBF | 7 3/4 | Straight |
| KRL-1236 | 12 | 3" | M,IC,S+ | 30" | 47" | 14 1/8" | 1 1/2" | 2 1/2" | GBF/GBM | 7 3/4 | Pistol Grip |
| KRL-2029 | 20 | 3" | F,M,IC,S+ | 26" | 43" | 14 1/8" | 1 1/2" | 2 1/2" | GBF | 7 | Pistol Grip |
| KRL-2030 | 20 | 3" | F,M,IC,S+ | 28" | 45" | 14 1/8" | 1 1/2" | 2 1/2" | GBF | 7 1/4 | Pistol Grip |
| KRLS-2029 | 20 | 3" | F,M,IC,S+ | 26" | 43" | 14 1/8" | 1 1/2" | 2 1/2" | GBF | 6 3/4 | Straight |
| KRLS-2030 | 20 | 3" | F,M,IC,S+ | 28" | 45" | 14 1/8" | 1 1/2" | 2 1/2" | GBF | 7 | Straight |
| KRL-2036 | 20 | 3" | M,IC,S+ | 30" | 47" | 14 1/8" | 1 1/2" | 2 1/2" | GBF/GBM | 7 | Pistol Grip |
| KRLS-2826 | 28 | 2 3/4" | F,M,IC,S+ | 26" | 43" | 14 1/8" | 1 1/2" | 2 1/2" | GBF | 5 7/8 | Straight |
| KRLS-2827 | 28 | 2 3/4" | F,M,IC,S+ | 28" | 45" | 14 1/8" | 1 1/2" | 2 1/2" | GBF | 6 | Straight |
| KRL-2826 | 28 | 2 3/4" | F,M,IC,S+ | 26" | 43" | 14 1/8" | 1 1/2" | 2 1/2" | GBF | 6 | Pistol Grip |
| KRL-2827 | 28 | 2 3/4" | F,M,IC,S+ | 28" | 45" | 14 1/8" | 1 1/2" | 2 1/2" | GBF | 6 1/8 | Pistol Grip |

*F-Full, M-Modified, IC-Improved Cylinder, S-Skeet. +Two skeet chokes standard with each shotgun.
**GBF-Gold-Bead Front Sight, GBM-Gold-Bead Middle

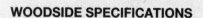

## WOODSIDE SPECIFICATIONS

| Catalog Number | Gauge | Choke* | Barrel Length | Overall Length | Approx. Wt. | Stock |
|---|---|---|---|---|---|---|
| KWS-1226 | 12 | F, M, IC, S | 26" | 43" | 7 3/4 lbs. | Pistol |
| KWS-1227 | 12 | F, M, IC, S | 28" | 45" | 8 lbs. | Pistol |
| KWS-1226 | 12 | F, M, IC, S | 26" | 43" | 7 1/2 lbs. | Straight |
| KWS-1227 | 12 | F, M, IC, S | 28" | 45" | 7 3/4 lbs. | Straight |
| KWS-1236 | 12 | F, M, IC, S | 30" | 47" | 7 3/4 lbs. | Pistol |

**WOODSIDE OVER/UNDER SHOTGUN**
**(w/Screw-in Chokes)**
**$1675.00**

# SAVAGE SHOTGUNS

### MODEL 210FT "MASTER SHOT" SHOTGUN
### $440.00

**SPECIFICATIONS**
**Gauge:** 12
**Choke:** Full choke tube
**Barrel length:** 24″
**Overall length:** 43.5″
**Weight:** 7.5 lbs.

**Finish:** Advantage™ camo pattern
**Features:** Barrel threaded for interchangeable Winchester-style choke tubes; drilled and tapped for scope mounting; positive checkering; ventilated rubber recoil pad and swivel studs; bead front sight with U-notch blade rear; short lift 60° bolt rotation, controlled round feed; triple front locking lugs

### MODEL 210F SLUG GUN

Also available:
**210F "MASTER SHOT" SLUG GUN** (12 gauge). Features full-length baffle; 24″ barrel chambered for 2³/₄″ or 3″ shells; three-position, top tang rifle-style safety; no sights; 1 in 35″ twist (8-groove precision button rifled). **Price:** ..... **$380.00**

# SIGARMS SHOTGUNS

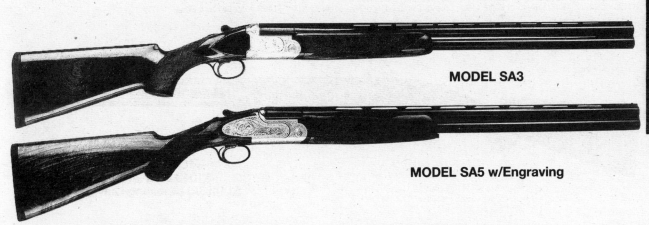

### MODEL SA3

### MODEL SA5 w/Engraving

### MODEL SA3 OVER/UNDER

**SPECIFICATIONS**
**Gauge:** 12 (3″ chamber)
**Choke:** Full, Modified & Improved Cylinder
**Action:** Automatic ejectors w/single selective trigger
**Barrel lengths:** 26″ and 27″
**Weight:** 7 lbs.
**Length of pull:** 14.5″

**Drop at comb:** 1.5″   **Drop at heel:** 2.5″
**Stock:** Medium gloss select-grade walnut
**Finish:** Low-luster nickel
**Features:** Hand-checkering (18 lines per inch); chrome-lined bores; screw-in multi-choke system; hardened monobloc; rolled game scenes on receiver
**Prices:**
**MODEL SA3** ............................... $1425.00
**MODEL SA5** w/elaborately engraved receiver ... 3052.00

# SKB SHOTGUNS

## MODEL 385 SIDE-BY-SIDE
### $1769.00 ($2499.00 Field Set)

Model 385 features silver nitride receiver with engraved scroll and game scene design; solid boxlock action w/double locking lugs; single selective trigger; selective automatic ejectors; automatic safety; sculpted American walnut stock; pistol or English straight grip; semi-beavertail forend; stock and forend finished w/18-line fine checkering; standard series choke tube system; solid rib w/flat matte finish and metal front bead. For additional specifications, see table below. Also available:

**MODEL 485 SERIES.** Features engraved upland game scene; semi-fancy American walnut stock and beavertail forend; raised vent rib with flat matte finish. **Price: $2369.00**

## SPECIFICATIONS MODEL 385

| GAUGE | CHAMBER | BARREL LENGTH | OVERALL LENGTH | INTER-CHOKE** | SIGHTS | RIB WIDTH | STOCK | AVERAGE WEIGHT* | MFR. I.D. |
|-------|---------|---------------|----------------|---------------|--------|-----------|-------|-----------------|-----------|
| 20 | 3" | 26" | 42½" | STND | MFB | 5/16" | PISTOL | 6 lbs. 10 oz. | A3806CFP |
| 20 | 3" | 26" | 42½" | STND | MFB | 5/16" | ENGLISH | 6 lbs. 10 oz. | A3806CFE |
| 28 | 2¾" | 26" | 42½" | STND | MFB | 5/16" | PISTOL | 6 lbs. 13 oz. | A3886CFP |
| 28 | 2¾" | 26" | 42½" | STND | MFB | 5/16" | ENGLISH | 6 lbs. 13 oz. | A3886CFE |

* Weights may vary due to wood density. Specifications may vary.
** INTER-CHOKE SYSTEMS: STANDARD SERIES Imp. Cyl., Mod., Skeet
STOCK DIMENSIONS: Length of Pull - 14⅛"; Drop at Comb - 1½"; Drop at Heel - 2½". MFB = Metal Front Bead

## MODEL 505
### $1049.00 (Field)
### $1149.00 (Sporting Clays)

| 505 FIELD OVER AND UNDERS | | | | | | | | |
|-------|---------|---------------|----------------|--------------|--------|-----------|-----------------|----------------------|
| GAUGE | CHAMBER | BARREL LENGTH | OVERALL LENGTH | INTER CHOKE | SIGHTS | RIB WIDTH | AVERAGE WEIGHT* | MANUFACTURES ID NUMBER |
| 12 | 3" | 28" | 45 3/8" | STND-A | MFB | 3/8" | 7 lb. 12 oz. | N528CFP |
| 12 | 3" | 26" | 43 3/8" | STND-B | MFB | 3/8" | 7 lb. 11 oz. | N526CFP |
| 20 | 3" | 26" | 43 3/8" | STND-B | MFB | 3/8" | 6 lb. 10 oz. | N506CFP |

# SKB SHOTGUNS

## MODEL 585 and 785 SERIES

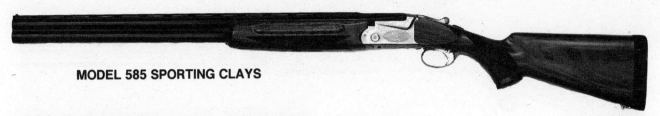

**MODEL 585 SPORTING CLAYS**

### FIELD MODELS

| GAUGE | CHAMBER | BARREL LENGTH | OVERALL LENGTH | INTER CHOKE | SIGHTS | RIB WIDTH | AVERAGE WEIGHT * 785 | AVERAGE WEIGHT * 585 |
|---|---|---|---|---|---|---|---|---|
| 12 | 3" | 28" | 45 3/8" | COMP. | MFB | 3/8" | 8 lb. 0 oz. | 7 lb. 12 oz. |
| 12 | 3" | 26" | 43 3/8" | COMP. | MFB | 3/8" | 8 lb. 0 oz. | 7 lb. 11 oz. |
| 20 | 3" | 28" | 45 3/8" | STND-A | MFB | 5/16" | 7 lb. 4 oz. | 6 lb. 12 oz. |
| 20 | 3" | 26" | 43 3/8" | STND-B | MFB | 5/16" | 7 lb. 3 oz. | 6 lb. 10 oz. |
| 28 | 2 3/4" | 28" | 45 3/8" | STND-A | MFB | 5/16" | 7 lb. 4 oz. | 6 lb. 14 oz. |
| 28 | 2 3/4" | 26" | 43 3/8" | STND-B | MFB | 5/16" | 7 lb. 3 oz. | 6 lb. 13 oz. |
| 410 | 3" | 28" | 45 3/8" | M / F | MFB | 5/16" | 7 lb. 4 oz. | 7 lb. 0 oz. |
| 410 | 3" | 26" | 43 3/8" | IC / M | MFB | 5/16" | 7 lb. 3 oz. | 6 lb. 14 oz. |

### 2 BARREL FIELD SETS

| GAUGE | CHAMBER | BARREL LENGTH | OVERALL LENGTH | INTER CHOKE | SIGHTS | RIB WIDTH | AVERAGE WEIGHT * 785 | AVERAGE WEIGHT * 585 |
|---|---|---|---|---|---|---|---|---|
| 12 | 3" | 28" | 45 3/8" | COMP. | MFB | 3/8" | 8 lb. 1 oz. | 7 lb. 11 oz. |
| 20 | 3" | 28" | 43 3/8" | STND-B | MFB | 3/8" | 8 lb. 4 oz. | 7 lb. 12 oz. |
| 20 | 3" | 28" | 45 3/8" | STND-A | MFB | 5/16" | 7 lb. 5 oz. | 7 lb. 2 oz. |
| 28 | 2 3/4" | 28" | 45 3/8" | STND-A | MFB | 5/16" | 7 lb. 5 oz. | 7 lb. 1 oz. |
| 20 | 3" | 26" | 43 3/8" | STND-B | MFB | 5/16" | 7 lb. 3 oz. | 7 lb. 1 oz. |
| 28 | 2 3/4" | 26" | 43 3/8" | STND-B | MFB | 5/16" | 7 lb. 3 oz. | 7 lb. 0 oz. |
| 28 | 2 3/4" | 28" | 45 3/8" | STND-A | MFB | 5/16" | 7 lb. 6 oz. | 7 lb. 1 oz. |
| 410 | 3" | 26" | 43 3/8" | IC / M | MFB | 5/16" | 7 lb. 5 oz. | 7 lb. 0 oz. |

*Weights may vary due to wood density. Specifications may vary.
*INTER-CHOKE SYSTEMS
   COMP. - Competition series includes Mod., Full, Imp. Cyl.
   STND A - Standard series includes Mod., Full, Imp. Cyl.
   STND B - Standard series includes Imp. Cyl., Mod., Skeet

STOCK DIMENSIONS
Length of Pull - 14 1/8"
Drop at Comb - 1 1/2"
Drop at Heel - 2 3/16"

✓ MFB - Metal Front Bead

| MODEL 585 | Prices |
|---|---|
| **Field/Youth** (12 & 20 ga.) . . . . . . . . . . . . . . . . . . | **$1329.00** |
| **Field** (28 or .410 ga.) . . . . . . . . . . . . . . . . . . . . . . | 1379.00 |
| **Two-Barrel Field Set** (12 & 20 ga.) . . . . . . . . . . . | 2129.00 |
|    20/28 ga. or 28/.410 ga. . . . . . . . . . . . . . . . . . . . | 1989.00 |
| **Skeet** (12 or 20 ga.) . . . . . . . . . . . . . . . . . . . . . . . | 1429.00 |
|    28 or .410 ga. . . . . . . . . . . . . . . . . . . . . . . . . . . . | 1479.00 |
|    3-Bbl. Set (20, 28, & .410 ga.) . . . . . . . . . . . . . . | 3329.00 |
| **Sporting Clays** (12 or 20 ga.) . . . . . . . . . . . . . . . | 1479.00 |
|    28 gauge. . . . . . . . . . . . . . . . . . . . . . . . . . . . . . . | 1529.00 |
| **Trap** (Monte Carlo or Std.). . . . . . . . . . . . . . . . . . | 1429.00 |
|    2-Barrel Trap Combo . . . . . . . . . . . . . . . . . . . . . . | 2129.00 |
| **Upland** . . . . . . . . . . . . . . . . . . . . . . . . . . . . . . . . . | 1379.00 |

### SPORTING CLAY MODELS

| GAUGE | CHAMBER | BARREL LENGTH | OVERALL LENGTH | INTER CHOKE | SIGHTS | RIB WIDTH | AVERAGE WEIGHT * 785 | AVERAGE WEIGHT * 585 |
|---|---|---|---|---|---|---|---|---|
| 12 | 3" | 32" | 49 3/8" | COMP. | CP/WFB | 15/32" CH/STP | 8 lb. 14 oz. | 8 lb. 7 oz. |
| 12 | 3" | 30" | 47 3/8" | COMP. | CP/WFB | 15/32" CH/STP | 8 lb. 12 oz. | 8 lb. 5 oz. |
| 12 | 3" | 30" | 47 3/8" | COMP. | CP/WFB | 3/6" SW | 8 lb. 9 oz. | 8 lb. 1 oz. |
| 12 | 3" | 45 3/8" | 45 3/8" | COMP. | CP/WFB | 15/32" CH/STP | 8 lb. 8 oz. | 8 lb. 1 oz. |
| 12 | 3" | 28" | 45 3/8" | COMP. | CP/WFB | 3/8" SW | 8 lb. 5 oz. | 7 lb. 14 oz. |
| 20 | 3" | 28" | 45 3/8" | STND-B | CP/WFB | 15/32" CH/STP | 7 lb. 6 oz. | 6 lb. 14 oz. |
| 28 | 2 3/4" | 28" | 45 3/8" | STND-B | CP/WFB | 5/16" SW | 7 lb. 4 oz. | 6 lb. 14 oz. |

### 2 BARREL SPORTING CLAY SET

| GAUGE | CHAMBER | BARREL LENGTH | OVERALL LENGTH | INTER CHOKE | SIGHTS | RIB WIDTH | AVERAGE WEIGHT 785 | 585 |
|---|---|---|---|---|---|---|---|---|
| 12 | 3" | 30" | 47 3/8" | COMP. | CP/WFB | 15/32" CH/STP | 8 lb. 14 oz. | |
| 20 | 3" | 28" | 45 3/8" | STND-B | CP/WFB | 15/32" CH/STP | 8 lb. 10 oz. | |

*Weights may vary due to wood density. Specifications may vary.
*INTER-CHOKE SYSTEMS
   COMP. - Competition series includes SK II/SC III,
   SK I/SC I and MOD/SC IV
   STND B - Standard series includes Mod., Imp. Cyl., Skeet

STOCK DIMENSIONS
Length of Pull - 14 1/4"
Drop at Comb - 1 7/16"
Drop at Heel - 1 7/8"

✓ CP/WFB - Center Post White Front Bead
✓ CH/STP - Center Channeled, Semi Wide Step Up Rib
SW - Semi Wide Step Up Rib

**MODEL 585 UPLAND**

SHOTGUNS

# SKB SHOTGUNS

## MODEL 585 and 785 SERIES

### MODEL 785 OVER/UNDER

The SKB 785 Series features chrome-lined oversized chambers and bores, lengthened forcing cones, chrome-plated ejectors and competition choke tube system.

**MODEL 785** — **Prices**

| | |
|---|---|
| **Field** (12 & 20 ga.) . . . . . . . . . . . . . . . . . . . . . . . . | **$1949.00** |
| 28 or .410 ga. . . . . . . . . . . . . . . . . . . . . . . . . . . . . . | 2029.00 |
| **Two-Barrel Field Set** (12 & 20 ga.) . . . . . . . . . . . | 2829.00 |
| 20/28 ga. or 28/.410 ga. . . . . . . . . . . . . . . . . . | 2929.00 |
| **Skeet** (12 or 20 ga.) . . . . . . . . . . . . . . . . . . . . . . | 2029.00 |
| 28 or .410 ga. . . . . . . . . . . . . . . . . . . . . . . . . . | 2069.00 |
| 3-Bbl. Set (20, 28, & .410 ga.) . . . . . . . . . . . . | 4089.00 |
| **Sporting Clays** (12 or 20 ga.) . . . . . . . . . . . . . . | 2099.00 |
| 28 gauge . . . . . . . . . . . . . . . . . . . . . . . . . . . . | 2169.00 |
| 2-Barrel Set (12 & 20 ga.) . . . . . . . . . . . . . . . | 2999.00 |
| **Trap** (Monte Carlo or Std.) . . . . . . . . . . . . . . . . . | 2029.00 |
| 2-Barrel Trap Combo . . . . . . . . . . . . . . . . . . . . | 2829.00 |

### TRAP MODELS

| GAUGE | STOCK | BARREL LENGTH | OVERALL LENGTH | INTER CHOKE | SIGHTS | 785 RIB WIDTH | 585 RIB WIDTH | AVERAGE WEIGHT * 785 | 585 | MANUFACTURES ID # 785 | 585 |
|---|---|---|---|---|---|---|---|---|---|---|---|
| 12 | STND | 30" | 47 3/8" | COMP-A | CP/WFB | 15/32" CH/STP | 3/8" STP | 8 lb. 15 oz. | 8 lb. 7 oz. | A7820CVTN | A5820CVTN |
| 12 | MONTE | 30" | 47 3/8" | COMP-A | CP/WFB | 15/32" CH/STP | 3/8" STP | 9 lb. 0 oz. | 8 lb. 7 oz. | A7820CVTM | A5820CVTM |
| 12 | STND | 32" | 49 3/8" | COMP-A | CP/WFB | 15/32" CH/STP | 3/8" STP | 9 lb. 1 oz. | 8 lb. 10 oz. | A7822CVTN | A5822CVTN |
| 12 | MONTE | 32" | 49 3/8" | COMP-A | CP/WFB | 15/32" CH/STP | 3/8" STP | 9 lb. 1 oz. | 8 lb. 9 oz. | A7822CVTM | A5822CVTM |

### TRAP COMBO'S — STANDARD

| GAUGE | STOCK | BARREL LENGTH | OVERALL LENGTH | INTER CHOKE | SIGHTS | 785 RIB WIDTH | 585 RIB WIDTH | AVERAGE WEIGHT * 785 | 585 | MANUFACTURES ID # 785 | 585 |
|---|---|---|---|---|---|---|---|---|---|---|---|
| 12 | STND | O/U-30" | 47 3/8" | COMP. | CP/WFB | 15/32" CH/STP | 3/8" STP | 8 lb. 15 oz. | 8 lb. 6 oz. | A7820TN / 7822 | A5820TN / 5822 |
| 12 | STND | S/O-32" | 49 3/8" | COMP. | CP/WFB | 15/32" CH/STP | 3/8" STP | 9 lb. 0 oz. | 8 lb. 6 oz. | | |
| 12 | STND | O/U-30" | 47 3/8" | COMP. | CP/WFB | 15/32" CH/STP | 3/8" STP | 9 lb. 0 oz. | 8 lb. 4 oz. | A7820TN / 7824 | A5820TN / 5824 |
| 12 | STND | S/O-34" | 51 3/8" | COMP. | CP/WFB | 15/32" CH/STP | 3/8" STP | 9 lb. 1 oz. | 8 lb. 6 oz. | | |
| 12 | STND | O/U-32" | 49 3/8" | COMP. | CP/WFB | 15/32" CH/STP | 3/8" STP | 9 lb. 0 oz. | 8 lb. 7 oz. | A7822TN / 7824 | A5822TN / 5824 |
| 12 | STND | S/O-34" | 51 3/8" | COMP. | CP/WFB | 15/32" CH/STP | 3/8" STP | 9 lb. 1 oz. | 8 lb. 8 oz. | | |

### TRAP COMBO'S — MONTE CARLO

| 12 | MONTE | O/U-30" | 47 3/8" | COMP. | CP/WFB | 15/32" CH/STP | 3/8" STP | 8 lb. 15 oz. | 8 lb. 6 oz. | A7820TM / 7822 | A5820TM / 5822 |
|---|---|---|---|---|---|---|---|---|---|---|---|
| 12 | MONTE | S/O-32" | 49 3/8" | COMP. | CP/WFB | 15/32" CH/STP | 3/8" STP | 9 lb. 0 oz. | 8 lb. 6 oz. | | |
| 12 | MONTE | O/U-30" | 47 3/8" | COMP. | CP/WFB | 15/32" CH/STP | 3/8" STP | 8 lb. 15 oz. | 8 lb. 4 oz. | A7820TM / 7824 | A5820TM / 5824 |
| 12 | MONTE | S/O-34" | 51 3/8 | COMP. | CP/WFB | 15/32" CH/STP | 3/8" STP | 9 lb. 1 oz. | 8 lb. 6 oz. | | |
| 12 | MONTE | O/U-32" | 49 3/8" | COMP. | CP/WFB | 15/32" CH/STP | 3/8" STP | 9 lb. 0 oz. | 8 lb. 7 oz. | A7822TM / 7824 | A5822TM / 5824 |
| 12 | MONTE | S/O-34" | 51 3/8 | COMP. | CP/WFB | 15/32" CH/STP | 3/8" STP | 9 lb. 1 oz. | 8 lb. 9 oz. | | |

*Weights may vary due to wood density. Specifications may vary.
*INTER-CHOKE SYSTEMS
   COMP. - Competition series includes Full, Mod, Imp. Cyl.
   STND. B - Standard series includes Imp. Cyl, Mod. and Skeet

STOCK DIMENSIONS
Length of Pull - 13 1/2"
Drop at Comb - 1 1/2"
Drop at Heel - 2 1/4"
✓ MFB - Metal Front Bead

### YOUTH & LADIES

| GAUGE | CHAMBER | BARREL LENGTH | OVERALL LENGTH | INTER CHOKE | SIGHTS | RIB WIDTH | AVERAGE WEIGHT * 785 | 585 | MANUFACTURES ID # 785 | 585 |
|---|---|---|---|---|---|---|---|---|---|---|
| 12 | 3" | 28" | 44 1/2" | COMP. | MFB | 3/8" | | 7 lb. 11 oz. | | A5828CFY |
| 12 | 3" | 26" | 42 1/2" | COMP. | MFB | 3/8" | | 7 lb. 9 oz. | | A5826CFY |
| 20 | 3" | 26" | 42 1/2" | STND-B | MFB | 3/8" | | 6 lb. 7 oz. | | A5806CFY |

### SKEET MODELS

| GAUGE | CHAMBER | BARREL LENGTH | OVERALL LENGTH | INTER CHOKE | SIGHTS | RIB WIDTH | AVERAGE WEIGHT * 785 | 585 | MANUFACTURES ID # 785 | 585 |
|---|---|---|---|---|---|---|---|---|---|---|
| 12 | 3" | 30" | 47 1/4" | COMP. | CP/WFB | 3/8" | 8 lb. 9 oz. | 8 lb. 1 oz. | A7820CV | A5820CV |
| 12 | 3" | 28" | 45 1/4" | COMP. | CP/WFB | 3/8" | 8 lb. 6 oz. | 7 lb. 12 oz. | A7828CV | A5828CV |
| 20 | 3" | 28" | 45 1/4" | STND. | CP/WFB | 5/16" | 7 lb. 2 oz. | 6 lb. 15 oz. | A7808CV | A5808CV |
| 28 | 2 3/4" | 28" | 45 1/4" | STND. | CP/WFB | 5/16" | 7 lb. 5 oz. | 6 lb. 15 oz. | A7888CV | A5888CV |
| 410 | 3" | 28" | 45 1/4" | SK/SK | CP/WFB | 5/16" | 7 lb. 5 oz. | 7 lb. 0 oz. | A7848V | A5848V |

### 3 BARREL SKEET SETS

| 20 | 3" | 28" | 45 1/4" | STND. | CP/WFB | 5/16" | 7 lb. 2 oz. | 6 lb. 15 oz. | | |
|---|---|---|---|---|---|---|---|---|---|---|
| 28 | 2 3/4" | 28" | 45 1/4" | STND. | CP/WFB | 5/16" | 7 lb. 5 oz. | 7 lb. 0 oz. | A7808B | A5808B |
| 410 | 3" | 28" | 45 1/4" | SK/SK | CP/WFB | 5/16" | 7 lb. 5 oz. | 7 lb. 0 oz. | | |

*Weights may vary due to wood density. Specifications may vary.
*INTER-CHOKE SYSTEMS
   COMP. - Competition series includes 2-SKI/SCI, 1-Mod/SC,IV
   STND. - Standard series includes Skeet, Skeet and Imp. Cyl.

STOCK DIMENSIONS
Length of Pull - 14 1/8"
Drop at Comb - 1 1/2"
Drop at Heel - 2 3/16"
✓ CP/WFB - Center Post/White Front Bead

NOTE: 785's Are Equipped With Step-Up Style Ribs

# STOEGER IGA SHOTGUNS

*See table on page 388 for additional specifications*

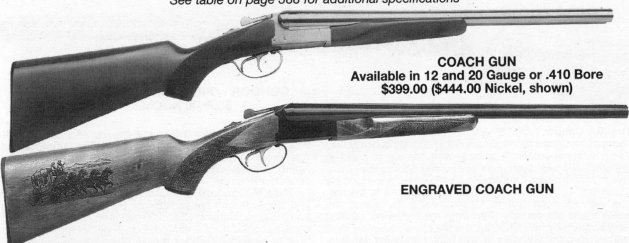

**COACH GUN**
**Available in 12 and 20 Gauge or .410 Bore**
**$399.00 ($444.00 Nickel, shown)**

**ENGRAVED COACH GUN**

The **IGA CLASSIC SIDE-BY-SIDE COACH GUN** sports a 20-inch barrel. Lightning fast, it is the perfect shotgun for hunting upland game in dense brush or close quarters. This endurance-tested workhorse of a gun is designed from the ground up to give you years of trouble-free service. Two massive underlugs provide a super-safe, vise-tight locking system for lasting strength and durability. The mechanical extraction of spent shells and double-trigger mechanism assures reliability. The automatic safety is actuated whenever the action is opened, whether or not the gun has been fired.

The polish and blue is deep and rich, and the solid sighting rib is matte-finished for glare-free sighting. Chrome-moly steel barrels with micro-polished bores give dense, consistent patterns. Nickel finish is now available. The classic stock and forend are of durable hardwood . . . oil finished, hand-rubbed and hand-checkered.

Improved Cylinder/Modified choking and its short barrel make the IGA coach gun the ideal choice for hunting in close quarters, security and police work. Three-inch chambers.

Also available with Engraved Stagecoach scene on the stock: . . . . . . . . . . . . . . . . . . . . . . . . . . . . . . . . . . . **$459.00**

**UPLANDER LADIES SIDE-BY-SIDE**
**$464.00**

**UPLANDER IGA SIDE-BY-SIDE (not shown)**
**Available also in 12, 20, 28 Gauge or .410 Bore**
**$414.00**
**$454.00 (12 and 20 Gauge w/Choke Tubes)**

Crafted specifically with women in mind, IGA's new model features a lightweight 20 gauge with 24″ barrel and is equipped with IC/M choke tubes. The durable 13″ Brazilian hardwood stock is fitted with a ventilated pad to reduce recoil. Standard features include extractors, double triggers and automatic safety.

**UPLANDER YOUTH SIDE-BY-SIDE (not shown)**
**$424.00**

IGA's new Youth gun is a lightweight .410 gauge with 24″ barrels bored modified and full. Both barrels will handle 2¹/₂″ or 3″ shells. The 13″ Brazilian hardwood stock includes a recoil pad. Standard features include double triggers, extractors and an automatic safety (activated when the gun is open). This shotgun is easy to load, light to carry and safe to handle with a second shot available when needed.

The **IGA SIDE-BY-SIDE** is a rugged shotgun, endurance-tested and designed to give years of trouble-free service. A vise-tight, super-safe locking system is provided by two massive underlugs for lasting strength and durability. Two design features that make the IGA a standout for reliability are its positive mechanical extraction of spent shells and its traditional double-trigger mechanism. The safety is automatic in that every time the action is opened, whether or not the gun has been fired, the safety is actuated. The polish and bluing are deep and rich. The solid sighting rib carries a machined-in matte finish for glare-free sighting. Barrels are of chrome-moly steel with micro-polished bores to give dense, consistent patterns. The stock and forend are available with either traditional stock or the legendary English-style stock. Both are of durable Brazilian hardwood, oil-finished, hand-rubbed and hand-checkered.

Also available with English stock w/choke tubes (IC/M) and fixed (M/M).

**SHOTGUNS**

# STOEGER IGA SHOTGUNS

*See table on page 388 for additional specifications*

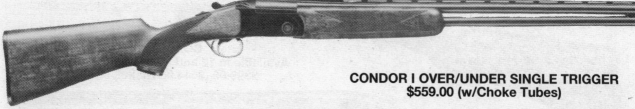

## CONDOR I OVER/UNDER SINGLE TRIGGER
### $559.00 (w/Choke Tubes)

The **IGA Condor I O/U Single Trigger** is a workhorse of a shotgun, designed for maximum dependability in heavy field use. The super-safe lock-up system makes use of a sliding underlug, the best system for over/under shotguns. A massive monobloc joins the barrel in a solid one-piece assembly at the breech end. Reliability is assured, thanks to the mechanical extraction system. Upon opening the breech, the spent shells are partially lifted from the chamber, allowing easy removal by hand. IGA barrels are of chrome-moly steel with micro-polished bores to give tight, consistent patterns. They are specifically formulated for use with steel shot where

Federal migratory bird regulations require. Atop the barrel is a sighting rib with an anti-glare surface. The buttstock and forend are of durable hardwood, hand-checkered and finished with an oil-based formula that takes dents and scratches in stride.

The IGA **Condor I** over/under shotgun is available in 12 and 20 gauge with 26- and 28-inch barrels with choke tubes and 3-inch chambers; 12 and 20 gauge with 26- and 28-inch barrels choked IC/M and Mod./Full, 3-inch chambers.

Also available: **Condor II O/U** 12 gauge, double trigger, 26" barrel IC/M or 28" barrel M/F. **Price:** . . . . . . . . . **$459.00**

## CONDOR SUPREME
### $629.00

The **IGA Condor Supreme** truly complements its name. The stock is selected from upgraded Brazilian walnut, and the hand-finished checkering is sharp and crisp. A matte-laquered finish provides a soft warm glow, while maintaining a high resistance to dents and scratches.

A massive monoblock joins the barrel in a solid one-piece assembly at the breech end. Upon opening the breech, the

automatic ejectors cause the spent shells to be thrown clear of the gun. The barrels are of moly-chrome steel with micro-polished bores to give tight, consistent patterns; they are specifically formulated for use with steel shot. Choke tubes are provided. Atop the barrel is a sighting rib with an anti-glare surface with both mid- and front bead.

## SIDE-BY-SIDE TURKEY MODEL
### $559.00

## OVER/UNDER WATERFOWL MODEL
### $729.00

The 12-gauge **Side-by-Side Turkey Model** features IGA's new Advantage™ camouflage finish, plus double triggers, 3" chamber with 24" barrel and wide beavertail forend. The 26" barrel over/under **Waterfowl Model** also features the new

Advantage™ camouflage pattern on the barrel, stock and forend, plus single trigger, automatic ejector and Full/Full flush-mounted choke tubes and ventilated recoil pad.

# STOEGER IGA SHOTGUNS

*See table on page 388 for additional specifications*

### DELUXE UPLANDER SIDE-BY-SIDE
### $559.00

Offered in 12 and 20 gauge with internal choke tubes along with 28 and .410 gauge with 26″ fixed chokes; semi-fancy American walnut stock and forend; wood is finished in matte lacquer and stocks are fitted with a soft black recoil pad; front and mid-rib bead sight, gold double trigger and positive extractor are standard.

### DELUXE HUNTER CLAY
### $699.00

Features include a matte lacquer finish, select grade semi-fancy American walnut stock and forend with a black target-style recoil pad. Also red bead front and mid-rib beads ensure accuracy. Over/under barrels are 28 inches long with 3″ chambers.

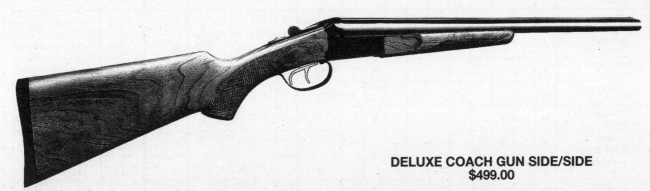

### DELUXE COACH GUN SIDE/SIDE
### $499.00

The Deluxe version of the Coach Gun featured earlier, this 12-gauge only side-by-side features 20″ barrels with 3″ chambers, IC/M chokes, gold double trigger, vented rubber recoil pad; weighs 6.75 lbs.

# STOEGER IGA SHOTGUNS

| | GAUGE | | | | | BARREL LENGTH | | | | | CHOKES | | SPECIFICATIONS | | | | | SAFETY | | BUTT-PLATES | | DIMENSIONS | | | |
|---|---|---|---|---|---|---|---|---|---|---|---|---|---|---|---|---|---|---|---|---|---|---|---|---|---|
| | 12 | 16 | 20 | 28 | .410 | 20" | 22" | 24" | 26" | 28" | Fixed | Choke Tubes | Chamber | Weight (lbs.) | Extractors | Ejectors | Triggers | Manual | Automatic | Molded | Rubber-Ventilated | Length of pull | Drop of comb | Drop of heel | Overall length |
| COACH GUN Side by Side | ■ | | ■ | | ■ | ■ | | | | | IC/M | | 3" | 6 3/4 | ■ | | D.T. | | ■ | ■ | | 14 1/2" | 1 1/2" | 2 1/2" | 36 1/2" |
| COACH GUN Nickel | ■ | | ■ | | ■ | ■ | | | | | IC/M | | 3" | 6 3/4 | ■ | | D.T. | | ■ | ■ | | 14 1/2" | 1 1/2" | 2 1/2" | 36 1/2" |
| COACH GUN Engraved | ■ | | ■ | | ■ | ■ | | | | | IC/M | | 3" | 6 3/4 | ■ | | D.T. | | ■ | ■ | | 14 1/2" | 1 1/2" | 2 1/2" | 36 1/2" |
| COACH GUN Deluxe | ■ | | | | | ■ | | | | | IC/M | | 3" | 6 3/4 | ■ | | D.T. | | ■ | | ■ | 14 1/2" | 1 1/2" | 2 1/2" | 36 1/2" |
| UPLANDER Side by Side | ■ | | ■ | | | | | | ■ | | IC/M | | 3" | 6 3/4 | ■ | | D.T. | | ■ | ■ | | 14 1/2" | 1 1/2" | 2 1/2" | 42" |
| UPLANDER Side by Side | ■ | | ■ | | | | | | | ■ | M/F | | 3" | 6 3/4 | ■ | | D.T. | | ■ | ■ | | 14 1/2" | 1 1/2" | 2 1/2" | 42" |
| UPLANDER Side by Side | | ■ | | ■ | | | | | ■ | | IC/M | | 23/4" | 6 3/4 | ■ | | D.T. | | ■ | ■ | | 14 1/2" | 1 1/2" | 2 1/2" | 42" |
| UPLANDER Side by Side | ■ | | ■ | | | | | | | ■ | M/F | | 3" | 6 3/4 | ■ | | D.T. | | ■ | ■ | | 14 1/2" | 1 1/2" | 2 1/2" | 45 1/2" |
| UPLANDER Side by Side | ■ | | ■ | | | | | | ■ | | IC/M | | 3" | 6 3/4 | ■ | | D.T. | | ■ | ■ | | 14 1/2" | 1 1/2" | 2 1/2" | 42" |
| UPLANDER Side by Side | | | | ■ | | | | | ■ | | F/F | | 3" | 6 3/4 | ■ | | D.T. | | ■ | ■ | | 14 1/2" | 1 1/2" | 2 1/2" | 42" |
| UPLANDER English | | | ■ | | | | | ■ | | | IC/M | | 3" | 6 3/4 | ■ | | D.T. | | ■ | ■ | | 14 1/2" | 1 1/2" | 2 1/2" | 40" |
| UPLANDER English | | | | ■ | | | | ■ | | | M/M | | 3" | 6 3/4 | ■ | | D.T. | | ■ | ■ | | 14 1/2" | 1 1/2" | 2 1/2" | 40" |
| UPLANDER Ladies | | | ■ | | | | | ■ | | | IC/M | | 3" | 6 3/4 | ■ | | D.T. | | ■ | | ■ | 13" | 1 1/2" | 2 1/2" | 40" |
| UPLANDER Youth | | | | ■ | | | | ■ | | | M/F | | 3" | 6 3/4 | ■ | | D.T. | | ■ | | ■ | 13" | 1 1/2" | 2 1/2" | 40" |
| UPLANDER Deluxe | ■ | | | | | | | | | ■ | M/F | | 3" | 6 3/4 | ■ | | D.T. | | ■ | | ■ | 14 1/2" | 1 1/2" | 2 1/2" | 44" |
| UPLANDER Deluxe | | | ■ | | | | | | ■ | | IC/M | | 3" | 6 3/4 | ■ | | D.T. | | ■ | | ■ | 14 1/2" | 1 1/2" | 2 1/2" | 42" |
| UPLANDER Deluxe | | | | ■ | | | | | ■ | | IC/M | | 23/4" | 6 3/4 | ■ | | D.T. | | ■ | | ■ | 14 1/2" | 1 1/2" | 2 1/2" | 42" |
| UPLANDER Deluxe | | | | ■ | | | | | ■ | | M/F | | 3" | 6 3/4 | ■ | | D.T. | | ■ | | ■ | 14 1/2" | 1 1/2" | 2 1/2" | 42" |
| CONDOR I Over / Under | ■ | | ■ | | | | | | ■ | | IC/M | | 3" | 8 | ■ | | S.T. | ■ | | | ■ | 14 1/2" | 1 1/2" | 2 1/2" | 43 1/2" |
| CONDOR I Over / Under | ■ | | ■ | | | | | | | ■ | M/F | | 3" | 8 | ■ | | S.T. | ■ | | | ■ | 14 1/2" | 1 1/2" | 2 1/2" | 45 1/2" |
| CONDOR II Over / Under | ■ | | | | | | | | ■ | | IC/M | | 3" | 8 | ■ | | D.T. | ■ | | ■ | | 14 1/2" | 1 1/2" | 2 1/2" | 43 1/2" |
| CONDOR II Over / Under | ■ | | | | | | | | | ■ | M/F | | 3" | 8 | ■ | | D.T. | ■ | | ■ | | 14 1/2" | 1 1/2" | 2 1/2" | 45 1/2" |
| CONDOR Supreme | ■ | | ■ | | | | | | ■ | | IC/M | | 3" | 8 | | ■ | S.T. | | | | ■ | 14 1/2" | 1 1/2" | 2 1/2" | 43 1/2" |
| CONDOR Supreme | ■ | | ■ | | | | | | | ■ | M/F | | 3" | 8 | | ■ | S.T. | ■ | | | ■ | 14 1/2" | 1 1/2" | 2 1/2" | 45 1/2" |
| UPLANDER Camo | ■ | | | | | | | ■ | | | F/F | | 3" | 6 3/4 | ■ | | D.T. | | | ■ | ■ | 14 1/2" | 1 1/2" | 2 1/2" | 40" |
| CONDOR Supreme Camo | ■ | | | | | | | | ■ | | F/F | | 3" | 8 | | ■ | S.T. | ■ | | | ■ | 14 1/2" | 1 1/2" | 2 1/2" | 45 1/2" |
| HUNTERS-CLAYS | ■ | | | | | | | | | ■ | IC M/F | | 3" | 8 | | ■ | S.T. | ■ | | | ■ | 14 1/2" | 1 1/2" | 2 1/2" | 45 1/2" |

# TIKKA SHOTGUNS

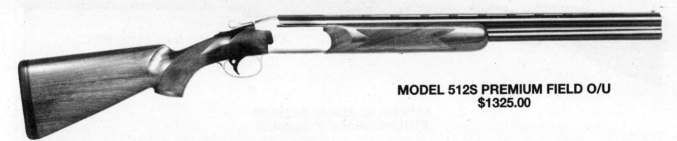

## MODEL 512S PREMIUM FIELD O/U
## $1325.00

Designed for the experienced hunter, TIKKA's 512S represents the pride and skill of "Old World" European craftsmanship. Features include: Chrome-lined barrels w/wide vent rib, stainless steel choke tubes, single selective trigger, auto ejectors, large trigger-guard opening, auto safety, cocking indicators, polished blue forged-steel receiver, semifancy European walnut stock and forearm of superior design, sliding locking bolt, changeability from O/U shotgun to shotgun/rifle, trap, skeet or double rifle.

### SPECIFICATIONS
**Gauge:** 12  **Chambers:** 3″
**Weight:** 7¼ lbs. w/26″ barrels; 7½ lbs. w/28″ barrels
**Barrel lengths/chokes:**
  26″, 5 chokes (F, M, IM, IC & Skeet)
  28″, 5 chokes (F, M, IM, IC & Skeet)

## TIKKA 512S SHOTGUN/RIFLE
## $1770.00

TIKKA's unique 512S Shotgun/Rifle combo's features are identical to the 512S Field Grade over/under shotguns, including strong steel receiver, superior sliding locking mechanism with automatic safety, cocking indicators, mechanical triggers and two-piece firing pin. Plus receiver will accommodate TIKKA's over/under shotgun barrels and double-rifle barrels with minor initial fitting. European walnut semi-Monte Carlo stock is equipped with quick-detachable sling swivels; length or pitch adjustable with factory spacers.

### SPECIFICATIONS
**Gauge/Caliber:** 12/222, 12/30-06, 12/308 and 12/9.3×74R
**Chamber:** 3″ with Improved Modified choke
**Barrel length:** 24″  **Overall length:** 40″
**Weight:** 8 lbs.
**Stock:** European walnut with semi-Monte Carlo design
**Extra Barrel Sets:**

| | |
|---|---:|
| Over/Under | $ 745.00 |
| Shotgun/Rifle | 810.00 |
| Double Rifle | 1040.00 |
| Sporting Clays | 765.00 |

## SPORTING CLAYS SHOTGUN (not shown)
## $1360.00

The Sporting Clays shotgun features a specially designed American walnut stock with a double palm swell finished with a soft satin lacquer for maximum protection with minimum maintenance. Available in 12 gauge with a selection of 5 recessed choke tubes. Other features include a 3″ chamber, manual safety, customized sporting clay recoil pad, single selective trigger, blued receiver and 28″ and 30″ barrel with ventilated side and top rib with two iridescent beads. Furnished with an attractive carrying case.

Manufactured in Italy, TIKKA is designed and crafted by SAKO of Finland, which has enjoyed international acclaim for the manufacture of precision sporting firearms since 1918.

**SHOTGUNS**

# WEATHERBY SHOTGUNS

**ATHENA GRADE V CLASSIC FIELD**

**ATHENA GRADE IV  $2259.00**
**ATHENA GRADE V  $2599.00**

The Athena receiver houses a boxlock action, sidelock-type plates with fine floral engraving. The hinge pivots are made of high-strength steel alloy. The locking system employs the Greener crossbolt design. The single selective trigger is mechanically operated for a fully automatic switchover, allowing the second barrel to be fired on a subsequent trigger pull, even during a misfire. The selector lever, located in front of the trigger, enables the shooter to fire the lower barrel or upper barrel first.

The breech block is hand-fitted to the receiver. Every Athena is equipped with a matted, ventilated rib and bead front sight. Ejectors are fully automatic. The safety is a slide type located on the upper tang atop pistol grip. Each stock is carved from Claro walnut, with fine line hand-checkering and high-luster finish. Trap model has Monte Carlo stock only.

*See* the Athena and Orion table on the following page for additional information and specifications.

**GRADE IV CHOKES**
**Fixed Choke**
Field, .410 Gauge
Skeet, 12 or 20 Gauge
**IMC Multi-Choke**
Field, 12, 20 or 28 Gauge
Trap, 12 Gauge
Trap, single barrel, 12 Gauge
Trap Combo, 12 Gauge

**ORION GRADE II CLASSIC FIELD**

**ORION GRADES I, II & III OVER/UNDERS**

For greater versatility, the Orion incorporates the integral multichoke (IMC) system. Available in Extra-full, Full, Modified, Improved Modified, Improved Cylinder and Skeet, the choke tubes fit flush with the muzzle without detracting from the beauty of the gun. Three tubes are furnished with each gun. The precision hand-fitted monobloc and receiver are machined from high-strength steel with a highly polished finish. The boxlock design uses the Greener cross-bolt locking system and special sears maintain hammer engagement. Pistol grip stock and forearm are carved of Claro walnut with hand-checkered diamond inlay pattern and high-gloss finish. Chrome-moly steel barrels, and the receiver, are deeply blued. The Orion also features selective automatic ejectors, single selective trigger, front bead sight and ventilated rib. The trap model boasts a curved trap-style recoil pad and is available with Monte Carlo stock only. **Weight:** 12 ga. Field, 7$\frac{1}{2}$ lbs.; 20 ga. Field, 7$\frac{1}{2}$ lbs.; Trap, 8 lbs.

*See* following page for prices and additional specifications.

**ORION CHOKES**
**Grade I**
IMC Multi-Choke, Field, 12 or 20 Gauge
**Grade II**
Fixed Choke, Field, .410 Gauge
Fixed Choke, Skeet, 12 or 20 Gauge
IMC Multi-Choke, Field, 12, 20 or 28 Gauge
IMC Multi-Choke, Trap, 12 Gauge
**Grade II Sporting Clays**
12 Gauge only
**Grade III**
IMC Multi-Choke, Field, 12 or 20 Gauge

# WEATHERBY SHOTGUNS

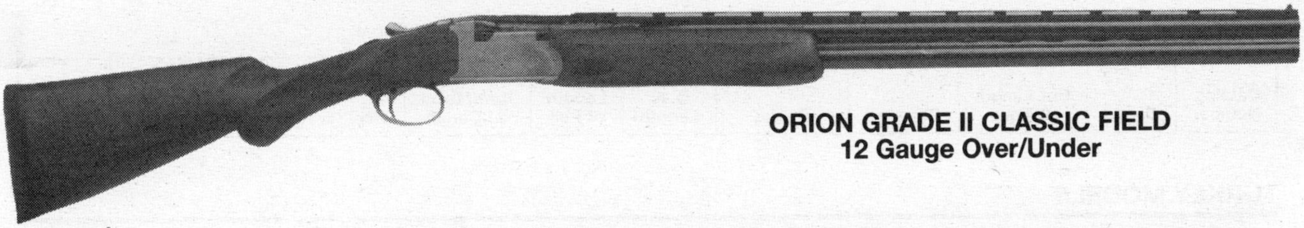

**ORION GRADE II CLASSIC FIELD**
**12 Gauge Over/Under**

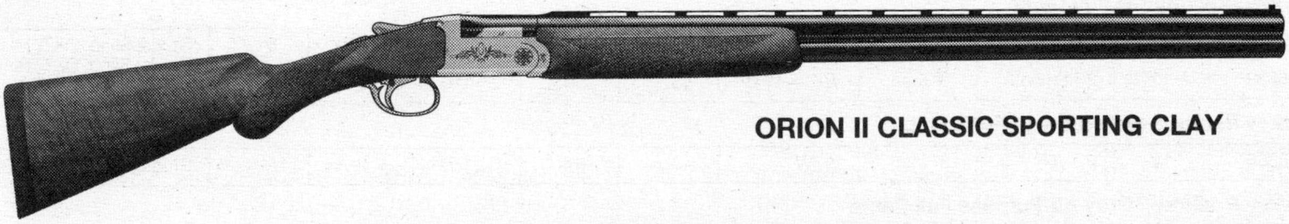

**ORION II CLASSIC SPORTING CLAY**

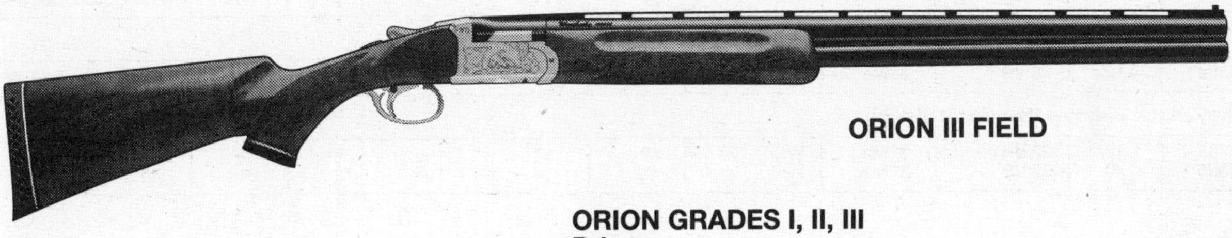

**ORION III FIELD**

**ORION GRADES I, II, III**
**Prices:**
**Orion I . . . . . . . . . . . . . . . . . . . . . . . . . . . . . . . . . $1329.00**
**Orion II Classic Field . . . . . . . . . . . . . . . . . . . . 1399.00**
**Orion II Sporting Clays. . . . . . . . . . . . . . . . . . . 1499.00**
**Orion III Field & Classic Field. . . . . . . . . . . . . . 1699.00**



## WEATHERBY SHOTGUN SPECIFICATIONS

| Model | Gauge | Chamber | Barrel Length | Overall Length | Length of Pull | Drop at Heel | Drop at Comb | Bead Sight | Approx. Weight (lbs.) |
|---|---|---|---|---|---|---|---|---|---|
| Athena Grade V Classic Field | 12<br>20 | 3″<br>3″ | 28″ or 26″<br>28″ or 26″ | 45″ or 43″<br>45″ or 43″ | 14¼″<br>14¼″ | 2.25″<br>2.25″ | 1.5″<br>1.5″ | Brilliant front<br>Brilliant front | 6½–8<br>6½–8 |
| Athena Grade IV Field | 12<br>20 | 3″<br>3″ | 28″ or 26″<br>28″ or 26″ | 45″ or 43″<br>45″ or 43″ | 14¼″<br>14¼″ | 2.5″<br>2.5″ | 1.5″<br>1.5″ | Brilliant front<br>Brilliant front | 6½–8<br>6½–8 |
| Orion Grade III Classic Field | 12<br>20 | 3″<br>3″ | 28″ or 26″<br>28″ or 26″ | 45″ or 43″<br>45″ or 43″ | 14¼″<br>14¼″ | 2.25″<br>2.25″ | 1.5″<br>1.5″ | Brilliant front<br>Brilliant front | 6½–8<br>6½–8 |
| Orion Grade III English Field | 12<br>20 | 3″<br>3″ | 28″<br>28″ or 26″ | 45″<br>45″ or 43″ | 14¼″<br>14¼″ | 2.5″<br>2.5″ | 1.5″<br>1.5″ | Brilliant front<br>Brilliant front | 7–7½<br>6½–7 |
| Orion Grade III Field | 12<br>20 | 3″<br>3″ | 28″ or 26″<br>28″ or 26″ | 45″ or 43″<br>45″ or 43″ | 14¼″<br>14¼″ | 2.25″<br>2.25″ | 1.5″<br>1.5″ | Brilliant front<br>Brilliant front | 6½–8<br>6½–8 |
| Orion Grade II Classic Field | 12<br>20<br>28 | 3″<br>3″<br>2¾″ | 30″, 28″ or 26″<br>28″ or 26″<br>26″ | 47″, 45″ or 43″<br>45″ or 43″<br>43″ | 14¼″<br>14¼″<br>14¼″ | 2.25″<br>2.25″<br>2.25″ | 1.5″<br>1.5″<br>1.5″ | Brilliant front<br>Brilliant front<br>Brilliant front | 6½–8<br>6½–8<br>6½–8 |
| Orion Grade I Field | 12<br>20 | 3″<br>3″ | 30″, 28″ or 26″<br>28″ or 26″ | 47″, 45″ or 43″<br>45″ or 43″ | 14¼″<br>14¼″ | 2.5″<br>2.5″ | 1.5″<br>1.5″ | Brilliant front<br>Brilliant front | 6½–8<br>6½–8 |
| Orion Grade II Classic Sporting | 12 | 3″ | 30″ or 28″ | 47″ or 45″ | 14¼″ | 2.25″ | 1.5″ | Midpoint w/white front | 7½–8 |
| Orion Grade II Sporting | 12 | 3″ | 30″ or 28″ | 47″ or 45″ | 14¼″ | 2.25″ | 1.5″ | Midpoint w/white front | 7½–8 |

Weight varies due to wood density.

## MODEL 1300 SPECIFICATIONS (see following page for prices)*

| Catalog Number | Gauge | Bbl. Length & Type | Chamber | Choke | Nom. O. A. Length | Nom. Length of Pull | Nom. Drop at Comb | Heel | Weight (lbs.) | Features |
|---|---|---|---|---|---|---|---|---|---|---|
| **TURKEY MODELS** | | | | | | | | | | |
| **Turkey Advantage® Full Camo** | | | | | | | | | | |
| 16372 | 12 | 22" VR | 3" Mag. | W3W | 43 | 14" | 1½" | 2½" | 6¾" | Studs, Sling, D&T, MBF |
| 16289 | 12 | 22 Smooth | 3" Mag. | WIC & WXF | 43 | 14 | 1½ | 2½ | 6¾ | Studs, Sling, D&T, Rifle Sights |
| **Turkey Realtree® All-Purpose Full Camo** | | | | | | | | | | |
| 16366 | 12 | 22 VR | 3" Mag. | W3W | 43 | 14 | 1½ | 2½ | 6¾ | Studs, Sling, D&T, MBF |
| **Turkey Realtree® Gray All-Purpose Full Camo** | | | | | | | | | | |
| 16374 | 12 | 22 VR | 3" Mag. | W3W | 43 | 14 | 1½ | 2½ | 6¾ | Studs, Sling, D&T, MBF |
| **Turkey Realtree® All-Purpose Pattern (Matte Metal)** | | | | | | | | | | |
| 16364 | 12 | 22 VR | 3" Mag. | W3W | 43 | 14 | 1½ | 2½ | 6¾ | Studs, Sling, D&T, MBF |
| **Turkey Black Shadow (Synthetic Stock)** | | | | | | | | | | |
| 16335 | 12 | 22 VR | 3" Mag. | WXF | 43 | 14 | 1½ | 2½ | 6¾ | D&T, MBF |
| 16336 | 20 | 22 VR | 3" Mag. | WIF | 43 | 14 | 1½ | 2½ | 6⅝ | D&T, MBF |
| **DEER MODELS** | | | | | | | | | | |
| **Deer (Walnut Stock)** | | | | | | | | | | |
| 16205 | 12 | 22" Rifled | 3" Mag. | Rifled Barrel | 42¾" | 14" | 1½" | 2½" | 6⅞" | Studs, B&R, D&T, Rifle Sights |
| **Deer Black Shadow (Synthetic Stock)** | | | | | | | | | | |
| 16275 | 12 | 22" Smooth | 3" Mag. | W1C | 43 | 14 | 1½ | 2½ | 6¾ | D&T, Rifle Sights |
| 16278 | 12 | 22" Rifled | 3" Mag. | Rifled Barrel | 42¾ | 14 | 1½ | 2½ | 6¾ | D&T, Rifle Sights |
| **Deer Advantage® Full Camo Pattern** | | | | | | | | | | |
| 16285 | 12 | 22" Rifled | 3" Mag. | Rifled Barrel | 42¾" | 14 | 1½ | 2½ | 6¾ | Studs, Sling, D&T, Rifle Sights |
| 16289 | 12 | 22 Smooth | 3" Mag. | WIC & WXF | 43 | 14 | 1½ | 2½ | 7¼ | Studs, Sling, D&T, Rifle Sights |
| **Black Shadow Deer Combo (Cylinder Deer Barrel and 12 Ga. Extra Vent Rib Barrel)** | | | | | | | | | | |
| 16611 | 12 | 22" Smooth | 3" Mag. | Cyl | 42¾ | 14 | 1½ | 2½ | 6¾ | Studs, MBF |
| **FIELD MODELS** | | | | | | | | | | |
| **Walnut** | | | | | | | | | | |
| 16015 | 12 | 28" VR | 3" Mag. | W3 | 49" | 14" | 1½" | 2½" | 7⅜ | Walnut Stock, MBF |
| 16072 | 12 | 26 VR | 3" Mag. | W3 | 47 " | 14 | 1½ | 2½ | 7⅛ | Walnut Stock, MBF |
| **Black Shadow (Synthetic Stock)** | | | | | | | | | | |
| 16339 | 12 | 28 VR | 3" Mag. | WIM | 49 | 14 | 1½ | 2½ | 7 | MBF |
| 16341 | 12 | 26 VR | 3" Mag. | WIM | 47 | 14 | 1½ | 2½ | 7 | MBF |
| 16340 | 20 | 28 VR | 3" Mag. | WIM | 49 | 14 | 1½ | 2½ | 7⅛ | MBF |
| 16342 | 20 | 26 VR | 3" Mag. | WIM | 47 | 14 | 1½ | 2½ | 6⅞ | MBF |
| **Advantage® Full Camo** | | | | | | | | | | |
| 16370 | 12 | 28 VR | 3" Mag. | W3 | 49 | 14 | 1½ | 2½ | 7¼ | MBF |

* Five-shot shell capacity, incl. 1 in chamber.

# WINCHESTER SHOTGUNS

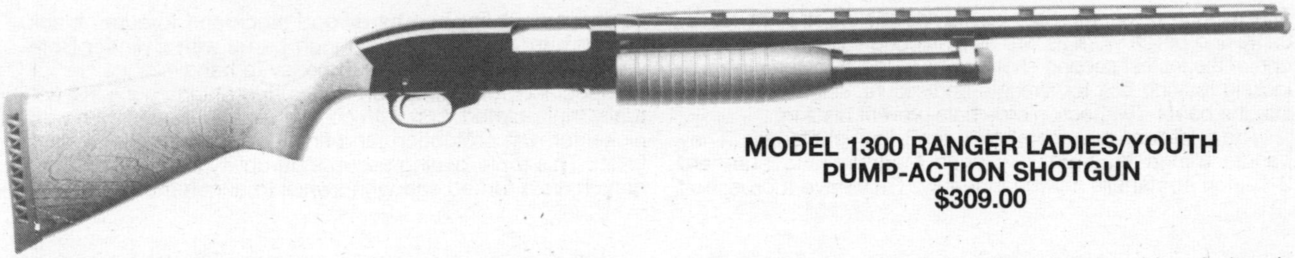

**MODEL 1300 RANGER LADIES/YOUTH PUMP-ACTION SHOTGUN**
**$309.00**

**Gauge:** 20 gauge only; 3″ chamber; 5-shot magazine. **Barrel:** 22″ barrel w/vent rib; Winchoke (Full, Modified, Improved Cylinder). **Weight:** 6 1/2 lbs. **Length:** 41 5/8″. **Stock:** Walnut or American hardwood with ribbed forend. **Sights:** Metal bead front. **Features:** Crossbolt safety; black rubber buttpad; twin-action slide bars; front-locking rotating bolt; removable segmented magazine plug to limit shotshell capacity for training purposes

**MODEL 1300 FIELD**
16015 .................. **$340.00**
16072 .................. **340.00**
16339 .................. **296.00**
16340 .................. **296.00**
16342 .................. **296.00**
16370 .................. **432.00**

**MODEL 1300 DEER**
16205 .................. **$404.00**
16275 .................. **296.00**
16278 .................. **$317.00**
16285 .................. **432.00**
16289 .................. **410.00**
16611 .................. **366.00**
16519 .................. **309.00**
16568 .................. **309.00**
17111 .................. **309.00**
16610 .................. **379.00**
16630 .................. **401.00**
16717 .................. **309.00**
16660 .................. **$379.00**
16372 .................. **432.00**

**MODEL 1300 TURKEY**
16289 .................. **$410.00**
16366 .................. **432.00**
16374 .................. **432.00**
16364 .................. **370.00**
16335 .................. **296.00**
16336 .................. **296.00**

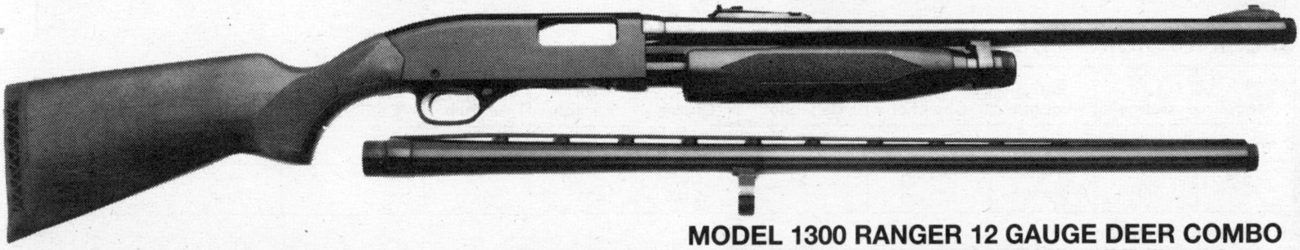

**MODEL 1300 RANGER 12 GAUGE DEER COMBO**
**22″ Rifled w/Sights & 28″ Vent-Rib Barrels**
**$401.00**

## 1300 RANGER MODELS (Five-shot shell capacity)

| Catalog Number | Gauge | Bbl. Length & Type | Chamber | Choke | Nom. O. A. Length | Nom. Length of Pull | Nom. Drop at Comb | Heel | Weight (Lbs.) | Features |
|---|---|---|---|---|---|---|---|---|---|---|
| **Ranger** | | | | | | | | | | |
| 16519 | 12 | 28″ VR | 3″ Mag. | W3 | 40″ | 14″ | 1 1/2″ | 2 1/2″ | 7 3/8 | MBF |
| 16568 | 20 | 28″ VR | 3″ Mag. | W3 | 49 | 14″ | 1 1/2″ | 2 1/2″ | 7 1/8″ | MBF |
| **Ranger Ladies/Youth** | | | | | | | | | | |
| 17111 | 20 | 22″ VR | 3″ Mag. | W3 | 42 | 13″ | 1 1/2″ | 2 3/8″ | 6 5/8 | UP, MBF |
| **Ranger Deer Combo (Cylinder Deer Barrel and Extra Vent Rib Barrel)** | | | | | | | | | | |
| 16610 | 12<br>12 | 22″ Smooth<br>28 VR | 3″ Mag.<br>3″ Mag. | Cyl.<br>W3 | 42 3/4″<br>49 | 14″<br>14″ | 1 1/2″<br>1 1/2″ | 2 1/2″<br>2 1/2″ | 6 7/8<br>7 3/8 | SB, D&T, Rifle Sights<br>MBF |
| **Ranger Deer Combo (Rifled Deer Barrel and Extra Vent Rib Barrel)** | | | | | | | | | | |
| 16630 | 12<br>12 | 22″ Rifled<br>28″ VR | 3″ Mag.<br>3″ Mag. | Rifled<br>W3 | 42 3/4″<br>49 | 14″<br>14″ | 1 1/2″<br>1 1/2″ | 2 1/2″<br>2 1/2″ | 6 7/8<br>7 3/8 | SB, D&T, Rifle Sights<br>MBF |
| **Ranger Deer Combo Cylinder Deer Barrel and Extra Vent Rib Barrel** | | | | | | | | | | |
| 16660 | 20<br>20 | 22″ Smooth<br>28″ VR | 3″ Mag.<br>3″ Mag. | Cyl.<br>W3 | 42 3/4″<br>49 | 14″<br>14″ | 1 1/2″<br>1 1/2″ | 2 1/2″<br>2 1/2″ | 6 3/4<br>7 1/4 | SB, D&T, Rifle Sights<br>MBF |
| **Ranger Deer** | | | | | | | | | | |
| 16717 | 12 | 22″ Smooth | 3″ Mag. | Cyl. | 42 3/4″ | 14″ | 1 1/2″ | 2 1/2″ | 6 7/8 | B&R, D&T, Rifle Sights |

# WINCHESTER SECURITY SHOTGUNS

These tough 12-gauge shotguns provide backup strength for security and police work as well as all-around utility. The action is one of the fastest second-shot pumps made. It features a front-locking rotating bolt for strength and secure, single-unit lockup into the barrel. Twin-action slide bars prevent binding.

The shotguns are chambered for 3-inch shotshells. They handle 3-inch Magnum, 2¾-inch Magnum and standard 2¾-inch shotshells interchangeably. They have a crossbolt safety, walnut-finished hardwood stock and forearm, black rubber buttpad and plain 18-inch barrel with Cylinder Bore choke. All are ultra-reliable and easy to handle.

Special chrome finish on Police and Marine guns are actually triple-plated: first with copper for adherence, then with nickel for rust protection, and finally with chrome for a hard finish. This triple-plating assures durability and quality. Both guns have a forend cap with swivel to accommodate sling.

**MODEL 1300 DEFENDER**
**$290.00 (8-Shot Wood Model Shown)**
**$393.00 DEFENDER/FIELD COMBO**
**$460.00 STAINLESS MARINE DEFENDER**

## SPECIFICATIONS MODEL 1300 DEFENDER

| Model | Gauge | Barrel Length | Chamber | Capacity* | Choke | Overall Length | Length of Pull | Drop At Comb/Heel | | Weight (Lbs.) | Sights |
|---|---|---|---|---|---|---|---|---|---|---|---|
| **Combo, Hardwood Stock and Synthetic Pistol Grip, 5 Shot** | | | | | | | | | | | |
| 17814 | 12 | 18" | 3" Mag | 5 | Cyl. | 29⅛" | — | — | — | 5⅝" | Studs, MBF |
| | 12 | 28" VR | 3" Mag | 5 | W1M | 49 | 14" | 1½" | 2½" | 7⅜" | Studs, MBF |
| **Hardwood Stock, 8 Shot** | | | | | | | | | | | |
| 17566 | 12 | 18" | 3" Mag | 8** | Cyl. | 39½" | 14" | 1½" | 2½" | 6½" | Studs, MBF |
| 31427 | 12 | 24 | 3" Mag | 8** | Cyl. | 44¾ | 14 | 1½ | 2½ | 6¾" | Studs, MBF |
| **Synthetic Pistol Grip, 8 Shot** | | | | | | | | | | | |
| 17616 | 12 | 18" | 3" Mag | 8** | Cyl. | 29⅛" | — | — | — | 5½" | Studs |
| **Synthetic Stock, 8 Shot** | | | | | | | | | | | |
| 17632 | 12 | 18" | 3" Mag | 8** | Cyl. | 39½" | 14" | 1½" | 2½" | 6⅜" | Studs, MBF |
| 31435 | 12 | 24" | 3" Mag | 8** | Cyl. | 44¾" | 14". | 1½" | 2½" | 6¾" | Studs, MBF |
| **Lady Defender, Synthetic Stock, 8 Shot** | | | | | | | | | | | |
| 17690 | 20 | 18" | 3" Mag | 8** | Cyl. | 39½" | 14" | 1½" | 2½" | 6¼" | Studs, MBF |
| **Lady Defender, Synthetic Pistol Grip, 8 Shot** | | | | | | | | | | | |
| 17685 | 20 | 18" | 3" Mag | 8** | Cyl. | 29⅛" | — | — | — | 5⅜" | Studs, MBF |
| **Stainless Marine, Synthetic Stock** | | | | | | | | | | | |
| 17475 | 12 | 18" | 3" Mag | 7** | Cyl. | 39½" | 14" | 1½" | 2½" | 6⅜" | Studs, MBF |
| **Stainless Marine, Pistol Grip Stock** | | | | | | | | | | | |
| 17483 | 12 | 18" | 3" Mag | 7** | Cyl. | 29⅛" | — | — | — | 5½" | Studs, MBF |

* Includes one shotshell in chamber. ** Subtract one for 3-inch shells. VR = Ventilated rib. MBF = Metal bead front. Rifle = Rifle-type front and rear sights. W3W = WinChoke, Extra Full, Full and Modified Tubes. W3 = WinChoke, Full, Modified and Improved Cylinder Tubes. Cyl. = Non-WinChoke, choked Cylinder Bore. W1M = Modified Tube. W1C = Cylinder Choke Tube. WF = Full Choke Tube. WXF = Extra Full Tube.
SB = Scope Bases Included. B&R = Scope, Bases and Rings included. D&T = Drilled and topped to accept scope bases. Studs = Buttstock and magazine cap sling studs provided (sling loop on pistol grip models).
All model 1300s except Defender models are supplied with a removable plug that limits magazine capacity to two shells. UP = Ladies/Youth models are supplied with universal plug for limigint magazine capacity to one, two, or three shells.
All WinChoke equipped guns are supplied with a special spanner wrench for removing and installing choke tubes.

# Blackpowder

For addresses and phone/fax numbers of manufacturers and distributors included in this section, please turn to DIRECTORY OF MANUFACTURERS AND SUPPLIERS on page 554.

# AMERICAN ARMS

## 1851 COLT NAVY
### $165.00 (Brass Frame)  $195.00 (Steel Frame)

This replica of the most famous revolver of the percussion era was used extensively during the Civil War and on the Western frontier.

**SPECIFICATIONS**
**Caliber:** 36
**Capacity:** 6 shots
**Barrel length:** 7½″ octagonal w/hinged loading lever
**Overall length:** 13″
**Weight:** 44 oz.
**Features:** Solid brass frame, trigger guard and backstrap; one-piece walnut grip; engraved blued steel cylinder

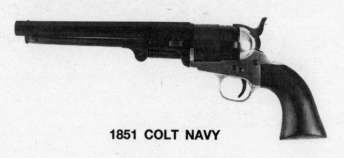

**1851 COLT NAVY**

**1858 ARMY
STAINLESS STEEL TARGET**

**1858 REMINGTON ARMY**

## 1858 REMINGTON ARMY
### $179.00 (Brass Frame)  $225.00 (Steel Frame)

This replica of the last of Remington's percussion revolvers saw extensive use in the Civil War.

**SPECIFICATIONS**
**Caliber:** 44
**Capacity:** 6 shots
**Barrel length:** 8″ octagonal w/creeping loading lever

**Overall length:** 13″  **Weight:** 38 oz.
**Features:** Two-piece walnut grips
Also available:
**1858 ARMY STAINLESS STEEL TARGET.** Same specifications as 1858 Remington, but with adjustable rear trigger sight and blade front sight; stainless steel frame, barrel and cylinder. **Price:** .......... $375.00

## 1860 COLT ARMY
### $179.00 (Brass Frame)  $225.00 (Steel Frame)

Union troops issued this sidearm during the Civil War and subsequent Indian Wars.

**SPECIFICATIONS**
**Caliber:** 44
**Capacity:** 6 shots
**Barrel length:** 8″ round w/creeping loading lever
**Overall length:** 13½″
**Weight:** 44 oz.
**Features:** Solid brass or steel frame, trigger guard and backstrap; one-piece walnut grip; engraved blued steel cylinder

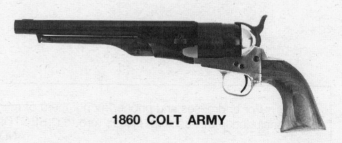

**1860 COLT ARMY**

# AMERICAN FRONTIER FIREARMS

### RICHARDS 1851 MODEL NAVY CONVERSION
### $695.00

Available in 38 and 44 calibers with non-rebated cylinder, 4.75", 5.5" & 7.5" octagon barrels, colorcase hardened hammer and trigger, ramrod and plunger, blued steel backstrap and trigger guard; walnut varnished navy-sized grips (*Note:* No ejector rod assembly on this model)

**RICHARDS 1851 MODEL
NAVY CONVERSION**

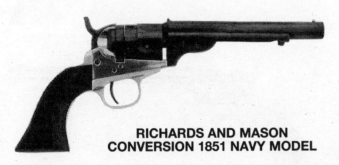

**RICHARDS AND MASON
CONVERSION 1851 NAVY MODEL**

### RICHARDS AND MASON CONVERSION 1851 NAVY MODEL
### $695.00

Available in 38 and 44 calibers with Mason ejector assembly and non-rebated cylinder, 4.75", 5.5" and 7.5" octagon barrels, high-polish blued steel parts, colorcase hammer and trigger, blued steel backstrap and trigger guard with ejector rod; varnished walnut grips.

**POCKET RICHARDS AND MASON
NAVY CONVERSION**

### POCKET RICHARDS AND MASON NAVY CONVERSION
### $495.00 (and up)

Available in 32 caliber, non-rebated cylinder, five shot, high-polish blued steel parts, silver-plated brass backstrap and trigger guard with ejector assembly, colorcase hardened hammer and trigger, varnished walnut grips.

### RICHARDS 1860 ARMY MODEL CONVERSION
### $695.00

Available in 38 or 44 caliber with rebated cylinder with or without ejector assembly; 4.75", 5.5" and 7.5" round barrels, standard finishes are high-polish blued steel parts (including backstrap); trigger guard is silver- plated brass; colorcase hardened hammer and trigger, walnut varnished army-sized grips.

### RICHARDS 1861 MODEL NAVY CONVERSION
### $695.00 (Not shown)

Same as 1860 Model, except with non-rebated cylinder and navy-sized grips.

**RICHARDS 1860 ARMY MODEL
CONVERSION**

# AMERICAN FRONTIER FIREARMS

**1871-2 OPEN-TOP FRONTIER MODEL**

### 1871-2 OPEN-TOP FRONTIER MODEL
### $795.00

Available in 38 or 44 caliber with non-rebated cylinder, 7.5″ and 8″ round barrels; standard-finish high-polish blued steel parts, silver-plated brass backstrap and trigger guard, color-case hardened hammer and walnut varnished navy-sized grips.

### 1871-2 OPEN-TOP TIFFANY MODEL
### $995.00

Available in 38 and 44 calibers, non-rebated cylinder, 4.75″, 5.5″, 7.5″ and 8″ round barrels; Tiffany grips; silver and gold finish with engraving.

**1871-2 OPEN-TOP TIFFANY MODEL**

### REMINGTON NEW ARMY CAVALRY MODEL
### $795.00

Available in 38, 44 and 45 calibers with 5.5″, 7.5″ and 8″ barrels; high-polish blued finish, colorcase hardened hammer. Comes with an ejector assembly, loading gate and government inspector's cartouche on left grip and sub-inspector's initials on various other parts.

**REMINGTON NEW ARMY CAVALRY MODEL**

### POCKET REMINGTON
### $495.00 (and up)

Available in 22, 32 and 38 calibers with 3.5″ barrel, with or without ejector rod or gate, high-polish blued steel parts, colorcase hardened hammer, varnished walnut grips.

**POCKET REMINGTON**

# AUSTIN & HALLECK RIFLES

**MODEL 320 LR/SS**

**MODEL 420 LR CLASSIC**

**MODEL 420 LR MONTE CARLO**

## MODEL 420 LR (MONTE CARLO & CLASSIC)

**Caliber:** 50
**Action:** In-line percussion (removable weather shroud)
**Barrel Length:** 26″ (1:28″); 8 lands & grooves; 3/4″ tapered round
**Overall length:** 47 1/2″
**Weight:** 7 7/8 lbs.
**Length of pull:** 13 1/2″
**Stock:** Select grade tiger-striped curly maple (Classic model has filled-grain luster finish w/steel pistol grip; Monte

Carlo has filled-grain high-gloss finish)
**Features:** Timney-adjustable target triggers w/sear block safety; 1″ recoil pad; shadow line (optional); scope not included
**Prices:**

| | |
|---|---|
| **MODEL 420 LR MONTE CARLO & CLASSIC** | **$599.00** |
| Hand Select | 669.00 |
| **MODEL 320 LR BLU w/Synthetic Stock** | 449.00 |
| **MODEL 320 LR S/S** | 469.00 |

**MOUNTAIN RIFLE**

### MOUNTAIN RIFLE

**Caliber:** 50 percussion or flintlock
**Barrel length:** 32″ (1:66″); 1″ octagonal; slow rust brown finish
**Overall length:** 49″    **Weight:** 7 1/2 lbs.

**Stock:** Select grade tiger-striped curly maple; filled-grain luster finish
**Sights:** Fixed buckhorn rear; silver blade brass bead front
**Features:** Double throw adjustable set triggers

| | |
|---|---|
| **Price:** | **$412.00** |
| Hand Select | 502.00 |

# CABELA'S RIFLES

### HAWKEN RIFLE
### $174.99 ($184.99 Left Hand)

Traditional "plains rifle" styling with American walnut stock, brass furniture including patch box, and color-casehardened lockplate. Adjustable double-set trigger, hardened coil-spring three-stage lock with hardened steel sear and tumbler. Screw adjustable rear sight with bead and ramp front. **Calibers:** 45, 50 and 54 percussion (R.H./L.H.); flintlock (R.H. only). **Barrel length:** 28" (1:48" twist and 12 grooves in

45 cal.; 1:48" twist, 6 grooves in 50 cal.; 1:48" twist with 5 grooves in 54 caliber).
Also available:
**SPORTERIZED HAWKEN.** Same as standard percussion model except blued steel furniture and fittings, rubber recoil pad, checkered walnut stock and leather sling. Also in carbine and synthetic stock carbine versions (right- and left-hand except in synthetic). **Price: $184.99 ($194.99 LH)**

### S. HAWKEN PLAINS RIFLE
### $1349.00

A true reproduction of a later model rifle built by the legendary Samuel Hawken. The Hawken-style breech plug has an enlarged flash channel for better iginition. Double-set triggers adjust to 3-lb. pull. **Barrel:** 34" match-grade chrome-moly steel tapers from 1" at the breech to 7/8" at the muzzle; 7

lands/grooves cut to .012 with 1:60" twist. **Overall length:** 52". **Weight:** 9 lbs. **Stock:** Premium-grade curly maple with tapered hickory ramrod. **Sights:** Rear has hidden, modern screw adjustment for windage and elevation; front is German silver blade on copper base. "S. Hawken St. Louis" stamped on top barrel flat.

### ROLLING BLOCK MUZZLELOADER
### $339.99

American walnut stock w/sling swivel studs. **Calibers:** 50 and 54. **Overall length:** 43 1/2". **Weight:** 8 1/2 lbs.
Also available:
**ROLLING BLOCK CARBINE.** Same as above, but with 22 1/4" round barrel, screw-adj. rear sight and front blade/bead sight, rubber butt pad. **Overall length:** 38 3/4". **Weight:** 7 3/4 lbs. **Price: $319.99**

The breechblock/firing-pin mechanism on this model completely shrouds the nipple area, keeping caps dry and secure. Features include black engraved receiver, tapered 26 1/2" barrel with 1:24" twist. Block, hammer and buttplate are color-casehardened steel; breech plug is easily removable.

### KODIAK EXPRESS DOUBLE RIFLE
### $549.99

Early explorers of Africa and Asia often had to rely on large-bore express rifles like this handsome sidelock replica featuring oil-finished, hand-checkered European walnut stock with casehardened steel buttplate. Ramp-mounted, adjust-

able folding double rear sights, ramp front sight, drilled and tapped for folding tang sight. Color-casehardened lock, blued top tang and trigger guard are all polished and engraved. **Calibers:** 50, 52, 54. **Barrels:** 28" with 1:48" twist (regulated at 75 yards); blued. **Overall length:** 45 1/4". **Weight:** 9.3 lbs.

# COLT BLACKPOWDER ARMS

## SIGNATURE SERIES

### COLT 1847 WALKER
### $525.00

**SPECIFICATIONS**
**Caliber:** 44
**Barrel length:** 9″   **Overall length:** 15.5″
**Weight:** 73 oz. (empty)
**Sights:** Fixed blade front sight   **Sight radius:** 12.25″
**Stock:** One-piece walnut
**Finish:** Colt blue with color casehardened frame; hammer, lever and plunger

### COLT WALKER
### 150th ANNIVERSARY MODEL
### $675.00

**SPECIFICATIONS**
**Caliber:** 44
**Weight:** 4 lbs. 9 oz.
**Barrel length:** 9″
**Cylinder length:** 2⁷/₁₆″
**Finish:** Color casehardened frame and hammer; smooth wooden grips
**Features:** Colt's Signature Series 150th anniversary re-issue carries the identical markings as the original 1847 Walker. "U.S. 1847" appears above the barrel wedge, exactly as on the Walkers produced for service in the Mexican War. The cylinder has a battle scene depicting 15 Texas Rangers defeating a Comanche war party using the first revolver invented by Sam Colt. This Limited Edition features original A Company No. 1 markings embellished in gold. Serial numbers begin with #221, a continuation of A Company numbers.

### COLT THIRD MODEL
### DRAGOON
### $525.00

**SPECIFICATIONS**
**Caliber:** 44 percussion
**Barrel length:** 7.5″   **Overall length:** 13.75″
**Weight:** 66 oz. (empty)
**Sight:** Fixed blade front   **Sight radius:** 10.75″
**Stock:** One-piece walnut
**Finish:** Colt blue with color casehardened frame; hammer, lever and plunger
Also available with steel backstrap and fluted cylinder: **$540.00**

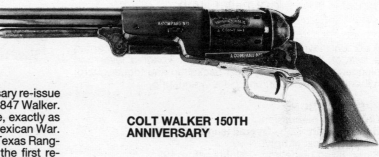

### COLT WALKER 150TH
### ANNIVERSARY

### COLT 1849 POCKET
### REVOLVER
### $487.50

**SPECIFICATIONS**
**Caliber:** 31
**Barrel length:** 4″   **Overall length:** 9.5″
**Weight :** 24 oz. (empty)
**Stock:** One-piece walnut
**Finish:** Colt blue and color casehardened frame

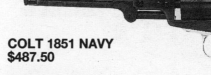

### COLT 1851 NAVY
### $487.50

**SPECIFICATIONS**
**Caliber:** 36
**Barrel length:** 7.5″   **Overall Length:** 13¹/₈″
**Weight:** 40.5 oz. (empty)
**Sights:** Fixed blade front
**Sight Radius:** 10″
**Stock:** Oiled American walnut
**Finish:** Colt blue and color casehardened frame

**BLACK POWDER**

# COLT BLACKPOWDER ARMS

## SIGNATURE SERIES

### COLT 1860 ARMY
### $487.50

A continuation in production of the famous cap-and-ball revolver used by the U.S. Cavalry with color casehardened frame, hammer and loading lever. Blued backstrap and brass trigger guard, roll-engraved cylinder and one-piece walnut grips

**SPECIFICATIONS**
**Caliber:** 44
**Barrel length:** 8"    **Overall length:** 13.75"
**Weight:** 42 oz. (empty)
**Sights:** Fixed blade front    **Sight radius:** 10.5"
**Stock:** One-piece walnut
**Finish:** Colt blue with color casehardened frame; hammer, lever and plunger

### COLT 1861 NAVY
### $487.50

A personal favorite of George Armstrong Custer, who carried a pair of them during the Civil War. Loading lever and plunger; blued barrel, cylinder backstrap and trigger guard; roll-engraved cylinder; one-piece walnut grip.

**SPECIFICATIONS**
**Caliber:** 36 percussion
**Barrel length:** 7.5"    **Overall length:** 13¹/₈"
**Weight:** 42 oz. (empty)
**Sight:** Fixed blade front    **Sight radius:** 10"
**Stock:** One-piece walnut
**Finish:** Colt blue with color casehardened frame; hammer, lever and plunger

### COLT CAVALRY MODEL 1860 ARMY
### FLUTED CYLINDER
### $487.50

The first Army revolvers shipped from Hartford were known as the "Cavalry Model"—with fluted cylinder, hardened frame, hammer, loading lever and plunger. Features blued barrel, backstrap and cylinder; brass trigger guard, fluted cylinder, one-piece walnut grip and a 4-screw frame (cut for optional shoulder stock)

**SPECIFICATIONS**
**Caliber:** 44 percussion
**Barrel length:** 8"    **Overall length:** 13.75"
**Weight:** 42 oz. (empty)
**Sight:** Fixed blade front    **Sight radius:** 10.5"
**Stock:** One piece walnut
**Finish:** Colt blue with color casehardened frame; hammer, lever and plunger

### COLT 1861 NAVY

### TRAPPER MODEL 1862 POCKET POLICE
### $487.50

The first re-issue of the rare and highly desirable Pocket Police "Trapper Model." The Trapper's 3¹/₂" barrel without attached loading lever makes it an ideal backup gun, as well as a welcome addition to any gun collection. Color casehardened frame and hammer; silver-plated backstrap and trigger guard; blued semifluted cylinder and barrel; one-piece walnut grip. Separate 4⁵/₈" brass ramrod.

**SPECIFICATIONS**
**Caliber:** 36
**Barrel length:** 3.5"    **Overall length:** 8.5"
**Weight:** 20 oz. (empty)
**Sight:** Fixed blade front    **Sight radius:** 6"
**Stock:** One-piece walnut
**Finish:** Colt blue with color casehardened frame and hammer

### TRAPPER MODEL 1862
### POCKET POLICE

# COLT BLACKPOWDER ARMS

### COLT MODEL 1861 MUSKET
### $615.00

Manufactured to original specifications using modern steels, this re-issue has the authentic Colt markings of its Civil War predecessor. Plus triangular bayonet.

**SPECIFICATIONS**
**Caliber:** 58
**Barrel length:** 40″

**Overall length:** 56″
**Weight:** 9 lbs. 3 oz. (empty)
**Sights:** Folding leaf rear; steel blade front
**Sight Radius:** 36″
**Stock:** One piece
**Finish:** Bright steel lockplate, hammer, buttplate, bands, ramrod and nipple; blued rear sight

### COLT GAMEMASTER .50

### COLT GAMEMASTER .50

This Colt rifle is a direct reproduction of the highly prized and rare 1861 Artillery Model, which was produced in limited numbers during the Civil War. It carries a 50-caliber barrel with 1:28″ twist and it features Colt's hunter-designed aperature peep sight system, removable Pachmayr recoil pad and redesigned ignition (allows use of musket caps five times the ignition power of standard percussion caps).
**Price:** . . . . . . . . . . . . . . . . . . . . . . . . . . . . . . . . . . . . . . . **$799.95**

# CUMBERLAND MOUNTAIN ARMS

### PLATEAU RIFLE

### PLATEAU RIFLE
### $1295.00

**SPECIFICATIONS**
**Calibers:** 40-65, 45-70 (and others as requested)
**Action:** CMA falling block; 4140 heat-treated steel (regular blue)
**Barrel length:** Up to 32″ (round)
**Weight:** 10½ lbs.
**Sights:** Marble
**Stock:** Grade #1 walnut stock with lacquer finish; smooth semibeavertail forearm; crescent buttplate

| Also available: | Prices |
|---|---|
| Half-round or half-octagonal barrel . . . . . . . . . . . . . | $210.00 |
| Octagonal barrel. . . . . . . . . . . . . . . . . . . . . . . . . . . . . . | 210.00 |
| Standard checkering pattern . . . . . . . . . . . . . . . . . . | 170.00 |
| Deluxe wood . . . . . . . . . . . . . . . . . . . . . . . . . . . . . . . . | 200.00 |
| Action (unblued) . . . . . . . . . . . . . . . . . . . . . . . . . . . . | 633.00 |
| Barreled action . . . . . . . . . . . . . . . . . . . . . . . . . . . . . . | 999.00 |
| Action kits. . . . . . . . . . . . . . . . . . . . . . . . . . . . . . . . . . | 465.00 |
| Ebony forend tip. . . . . . . . . . . . . . . . . . . . . . . . . . . . . | 100.00 |
| Double set triggers. . . . . . . . . . . . . . . . . . . . . . . . . . . | 157.00 |
| Case coloring . . . . . . . . . . . . . . . . . . . . . . . . . . . . . . . | 125.00 |

# CVA REVOLVERS/PISTOLS

**1851 NAVY REVOLVER
BRASS FRAME**

**1858 ARMY REVOLVER**

## SPECIFICATIONS
**Caliber:** 44
**Barrel length:** 7¹/₂″ octagonal; hinged-style loading lever
**Overall length:** 13″
**Weight:** 44 oz.
**Cylinder:** 6-shot, engraved
**Sights:** Post front; hammer notch rear
**Grip:** One-piece walnut
**Finish:** Solid brass frame, trigger guard and backtrap; blued barrel and cylinder; color casehardened loading lever and hammer
**Price:** . . . . . . . . . . . . . . . . . . . . . . . . . . . . . . . . **$139.95**

## SPECIFICATIONS
**Caliber:** 44
**Cylinder:** 6-shot, engraved
**Barrel length:** 8″ octagonal
**Overall length:** 13″
**Weight:** 38 oz.
**Sights:** Blade front; adjustable target
**Grip:** Two-piece walnut
**Prices:**
Brass Frame. . . . . . . . . . . . . . . . . . . . . . . . . . . . . . **$149.95**
Also available:
**1860 ARMY** w/8″ barrel (13¹/₂″ overall). **Weight:** 44 oz.
**Price:** Brass Frame . . . . . . . . . . . . . . . . . . . . . . . . **$139.95**
Steel Frame . . . . . . . . . . . . . . . . . . . . . . . . . . . . . . **194.95**

**KENTUCKY PISTOL**

**HAWKEN PISTOL**

## SPECIFICATIONS
**Caliber:** 50 percussion
**Barrel:** 9³/₄″, rifled, octagonal
**Overall length:** 15¹/₂″
**Weight:** 40 oz.
**Finish:** Blued barrel, brass hardware
**Sights:** Brass blade front; fixed open rear
**Stock:** Select hardwood
**Ignition:** Engraved, color casehardened percussion lock, screw adjustable sear engagement
**Accessories:** Brass-tipped, hardwood ramrod; stainless-steel nipple or flash hole liner
**Prices:**
Finished . . . . . . . . . . . . . . . . . . . . . . . . . . . . . . . . . . **$149.95**
Percussion Kit . . . . . . . . . . . . . . . . . . . . . . . . . . . . . **109.95**

## SPECIFICATIONS
**Caliber:** 50 percussion
**Barrel length:** 9³/₄″, octagonal
**Overall length:** 16¹/₂″
**Weight:** 50 oz.
**Trigger:** Early-style brass
**Sights:** Beaded steel blade front; fully adjustable rear (click adj. screw settings lock into position)
**Stock:** Select hardwood
**Finish:** Solid brass wedge plate, nose cap, ramrod thimbles, trigger guard and grip cap
**Prices:**
Finished . . . . . . . . . . . . . . . . . . . . . . . . . . . . . . . . . . **$149.95**
Kit. . . . . . . . . . . . . . . . . . . . . . . . . . . . . . . . . . . . . . . **109.95**
Laminated stock. . . . . . . . . . . . . . . . . . . . . . . . . . . . **159.95**

# CVA RIFLES/SHOTGUNS

**ST. LOUIS HAWKEN RIFLE**

**Calibers:** 50 and 54 percussion or flintlock (50 cal. only)
**Barrel:** 28″ octagonal ¹⁵/₁₆″ across flats; hooked breech; rifling one turn in 66″, 8 lands and deep grooves
**Overall length:** 44″
**Weight:** 8 lbs.
**Sights:** Dovetail, beaded blade front; adjustable open hunting-style dovetail rear
**Stock:** Select hardwood with beavertail cheekpiece
**Triggers:** Double set; fully adjustable trigger pull
**Finish:** Solid brass wedge plates, nose cap, ramrod thimbles, trigger guard and patchbox

**Prices:**
50 Caliber Flintlock . . . . . . . . . . . . . . . . . . . . . . . . . . . **$234.95**
50 Caliber Flintlock Left Hand (finished) . . . . . . . . . 249.95
50 Caliber Flintlock Kit . . . . . . . . . . . . . . . . . . . . . . . 169.95

Also available:
**PLAINSMAN** (Flintlock Rifle) w/26″ barrel. **Caliber:** 50.
    **Weight:** 6¹/₂ lbs. **Price:** . . . . . . . . . . . . . . . . . . . **$159.95**

**TRAPPER SINGLE-BARREL SHOTGUN**

**Gauge:** 12 percussion
**Barrel length:** 28″ round, chrome-lined bore; hooked breech
**Choke:** European Modified
**Overall length:** 46″   **Weight:** 6 lbs.
**Trigger:** Early-style steel
**Lock:** Color casehardened; engraved with V-type mainspring, bridle and fly

**Sights:** Brass bead front (no rear sight)
**Stock:** Select hardwood
**Features:** Color casehardened engraved lockplate; ventilated recoil pad, fiberglass ramrod and rear sling swivel
**Price:** . . . . . . . . . . . . . . . . . . . . . . . . . . . . . . . . . . **$239.95**

**CLASSIC TURKEY
DOUBLE-BARREL SHOTGUN**

**Gauge:** 12 percussion
**Barrel length:** 28″ round, chrome-lined bore; double button-style breech
**Choke:** European Modified
**Overall length:** 45″   **Weight:** 9 lbs.
**Triggers:** Hinged, gold-tone double triggers
**Lock:** Color casehardened; engraved with V-type mainspring, bridle and fly

**Sights:** Brass bead front (no rear sight)
**Stock:** Select hardwood; wraparound forearm with bottom screw attachment
**Features:** Ventilated recoil pad; rear sling swivel; fiberglass ramrod
**Price:** . . . . . . . . . . . . . . . . . . . . . . . . . . . . . . . . . . **$459.95**

**BLACK POWDER**

# CVA RIFLES

## IN-LINE MUZZLELOADING RIFLES

### ACCUBOLT PRO

**Caliber:** 50
**Barrel length:** 24"
**Rifling:** 1:28"
**Weight:** 7 1/2 lbs.
**Price:** . . . . . . . . . . . . . . . . . . . . . . . . . . . . **$449.95**
Also available:
Same model as above w/hammer forged barrel . . . **$334.95**

### APOLLO ECLIPSE

**Calibers:** 50 and 54
**Barrel length:** 24", round (1:32")
**Overall length:** 42"
**Weight:** 7 lbs.
**Features:** Weatherproof Dura-Grip synthetic stock; sling swivel studs; sporter adjustable rear sight
**Price:** . . . . . . . . . . . . . . . . . . . . . . . . . . . . **$207.95**

### APOLLO BROWN BEAR

**Calibers:** 50 and 54 (Left Hand only)
**Barrel length:** 24" round (1:32"); one-piece octagonal receiver
**Overall length:** 42"
**Weight:** 8 lbs.
**Sights:** Blued steel beaded blade front; Williams "Hunter" sight rear

**Stock:** Select hardwood w/pistol grip
**Features:** Moulded oversized black trigger guard; bottom screw barrel attachment and swivel studs; black synthetic ramrod w/black tips
**Price:** . . . . . . . . . . . . . . . . . . . . . . . . . . . . **$223.95**
Left Hand . . . . . . . . . . . . . . . . . . . . . . . . . . . . 237.95

# CVA RIFLES

## IN-LINE MUZZLELOADING RIFLES

### ELK MASTER/ELK HUNTER RIFLES

Both of these rifles are furnished with Bell & Carlson custom composite stocks with Realtree X-TRA Grey camouflage and bronze Rocky Mountain Elk Foundation Medallion inset. Choose between thumbhole stock (Elk Master) or traditional style (Elk Hunter). Other features include: Parkerized barrels, sling swivel studs, oversized trigger guard, recoil pad and removable breech plug; plus CVA's Illuminator™ Fiber Optic

### ELK MASTER w/Thumbhole Stock

sights. Standard accessories: breech plug/nipple wrench, synthetic ramrod, cleaning jag, Allen wrench and instructions.
**Caliber:** 54
**Barrel length:** 24" (Parkerized)
**Rifling:** 1:32"  **Weight:** 7½ lbs.
**Prices:**
Elk Master . . . . . . . . . . . . . . . . . . . . . . . . . . . . . **$416.95**
Elk Hunter . . . . . . . . . . . . . . . . . . . . . . . . . . . . . **371.95**

### FIREBOLT™ SERIES

**Calibers:** 50 (1:28" rifling)) and 54 (1:38")
**Barrel length:** 24"
**Weight:** 7 lbs.
**Finish:** Matte blue or stainless

### FIREBOLT™ w/Advantage Camo

**Stock:** Synthetic, Synthetic w/Advantage Camo, Thumbhole
**Prices:**
Synthetic Stock w/stainless barrel . . . . . . . . . . . **$329.95**
Synthetic Stock w/matte blue bbl. . . . . . . . . . . . **269.95**
Synthetic Stock Advantage Camo/matte
  blue . . . . . . . . . . . . . . . . . . . . . . . . . . . . . . . . . **329.95**
Thumbhole Stock w/matte blue . . . . . . . . . . . . . . **299.95**

**Calibers:** 50 and 54
**Lock:** In-line chrome-plated percussion bolt
**Barrel length:** 24" round (1.32"); blued steel w/one-piece
  receiver

### BUCKMASTER STAG HORN RIFLE

**Overall length:** 42"  **Weight:** 7 lbs.
**Sights:** Blued steel beaded blade front; Williams "Hunter"
  sight rear
**Stock:** Dura-Grip synthetic stock w/Advantage camo
**Price:** . . . . . . . . . . . . . . . . . . . . . . . . . . . . . . . . . **$246.95**

**Calibers:** 50 and 54
**Lock:** In-line chrome-plated steel percussion bolt
**Barrel length:** 24" round (1:32")
**Overall length:** 42"  **Weight:** 7 lbs.
**Sights:** Blued steel beaded blade front; Williams "Hunter"

### STAG HORN RIFLE

sight rear
**Stock:** Synthetic Dura-Grip stock w/pistol grip
**Features:** Removable breech plug; moulded oversized black
  trigger guard; bottom screw barrel attachment; black syn-
  thetic ramrod w/black tips
**Price:** . . . . . . . . . . . . . . . . . . . . . . . . . . . . . . . . . **$184.95**

# DIXIE

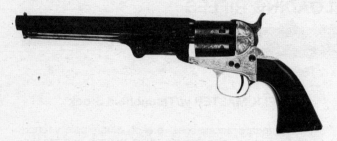

### 1851 NAVY BRASS-FRAME REVOLVER
### Plain Model $135.00
### Kit $114.00

This 36-caliber revolver was a favorite of the officers of the Civil War. Although called a Navy type, it is somewhat misnamed since many more of the Army personnel used it. Made in Italy; uses .376 mold or ball to fit and number 11 caps. Blued steel barrel and cylinder with brass frame.

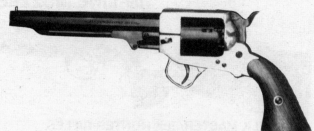

### SPILLER & BURR 36 CALIBER
### BRASS-FRAME REVOLVER
### $149.95   Kit $129.95

The 36-caliber octagonal barrel on this revolver is 7 inches long. The six-shot cylinder chambers mike .378, and the hammer engages a slot between the nipples on the cylinder as an added safety device. It has a solid brass trigger guard and frame with backstrap cast integral with the frame, two-piece walnut grips and Whitney-type casehardened loading lever.

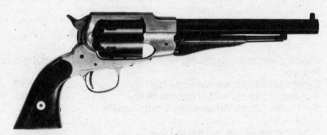

### REMINGTON 44 ARMY REVOLVER
### $169.95

All steel external surfaces finished bright blue, including 8" octagonal barrel (hammer is casehardened). Polished brass guard and two-piece walnut grips are standard.

### DIXIE 1860 ARMY REVOLVER
### $169.95

The Dixie 1860 Army has a half-fluted cylinder and its chamber diameter is .447. Use .451 round ball mold to fit this 8-inch barrel revolver. Cut for shoulder stock.

### "WYATT EARP" REVOLVER
### $130.00

This 44-caliber revolver has a 12-inch octagon rifled barrel and rebated cylinder. Highly polished brass frame, backstrap and trigger guard. The barrel and cylinder have a deep blue luster finish. Hammer, trigger, and loading lever are casehardened. Walnut grips. Recommended ball size is .451.

### RHO200 WALKER REVOLVER
### $225.00   Kit $210.00

This 4½-pound, 44-caliber pistol is the largest ever made. Steel backstrap; guard is brass with Walker-type rounded-to-frame walnut grips; all other parts are blued. Chambers measure .445 and take a .450 ball slightly smaller than the originals.

# DIXIE

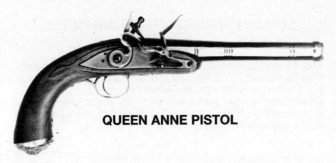

**QUEEN ANNE PISTOL**

## QUEEN ANNE PISTOL
### $195.00    ($169.95 Kit)

Named for the Queen of England (1702–1714), this flintlock pistol has a 7¹/₂″ barrel that tapers from rear to front with a cannon-shaped muzzle. The brass trigger guard is fluted and the brass butt on the walnut stock features a grotesque mask worked into it. **Overall length:** 13″. **Weight:** 2¹/₄ lbs.

**PEDERSOLI ENGLISH DUELING PISTOL**

## PEDERSOLI ENGLISH DUELING PISTOL
### $366.45 (Flint)    $309.95 (Percussion)

This reproduction of an English percussion dueling pistol, created by Charles Moore of London, features a European walnut halfstock with oil finish and checkered grip. The 45-caliber octagonal barrel is 11″ with 12 grooves and a twist of 1 in 15″. Nose cap and thimble are silver. Barrel is blued; lock and trigger guard are color casehardened.

**PEDERSOLI MANG TARGET PISTOL**

## PEDERSOLI MANG TARGET PISTOL
### $786.00

Designed specifically for the precision target shooter, this 38-caliber pistol has a 10⁷/₁₆″ octagonal barrel with 7 lands and grooves. Twist is 1 in 15″. **Sights:** Blade front dovetailed into barrel; rear mounted on breechplug tang, adjustable for windage. **Overall length:** 17¹/₄″. **Weight:** 2¹/₂ lbs.

**SCREW BARREL PISTOL**

## SCREW BARREL (FOLDING TRIGGER) PISTOL
### $120.75    ($89.25 Kit)

This little gun, only 6¹/₂″ overall, has a unique loading system that eliminates the need for a ramrod. The barrel is loosened with a barrel key, then unscrewed from the frame by hand. The recess is then filled with 10 grains of FFFg black powder, the .445 round ball is seated in the dished area, and the barrel is then screwed back into place. The .245×32 nipple uses #11 percussion caps. The pistol also features a sheath trigger that folds into the frame, then drops down for firing when the hammer is cocked. Comes with color casehardened frame, trigger and center-mounted hammer.

**BLACK POWDER**

# DIXIE

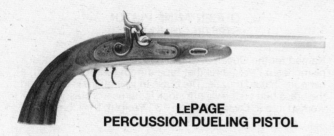

**LePAGE
PERCUSSION DUELING PISTOL**

## LePAGE PERCUSSION DUELING PISTOL
### $259.95

This 45-caliber percussion pistol features a blued 10″ octagonal barrel with 12 lands and grooves; a brass-bladed front sight with open rear sight dovetailed into the barrel; polished silver-plated trigger guard and butt cap. Right side of barrel is stamped ''LePage á Paris.'' Double-set triggers are single screw adjustable. **Overall length:** 16″. **Weight:** 2¹/₂ lbs.

## DIXIE PENNSYLVANIA PISTOL
### Percussion $174.95   Kit $135.00
### Flintlock $183.75   Kit $173.25

Available in 44-caliber percussion or flintlock. The bright luster blued barrel measures 10″ long; rifled, ⁷/₈-inch octagonal and takes .430 ball; barrel is held in place with a steel wedge and tang screw; brass front and rear sights. The brass trigger guard, thimbles, nose cap, wedge plates and side plates are highly polished. Locks are fine quality with early styling. Plates measure 4³/₄ inches × ⁷/₈ inch. Percussion hammer is engraved and both plates are left in the white. The flint is an excellent style lock with the gooseneck hammer having an early wide thumbpiece. The stock is walnut stained and has a wide bird's-head-type grip.

**DIXIE PENNSYLVANIA PISTOL**

## DOUBLE-BARREL MAGNUM MUZZLELOADING SHOTGUN (Not Shown)

A full 10, 12 or 20 gauge, high-quality, double-barreled percussion shotgun with 30-inch browned barrels. Will take the plastic shot cups for better patterns. Bores are Choked, Modified and Full. Lock, barrel tang and trigger are casehardened in a light gray color and are nicely engraved.

| | |
|---|---:|
| 12 Gauge | $449.00 |
| 12 Gauge Kit | 375.00 |
| 10 Gauge Magnum (double barrel—right-hand = cyl. bore, left-hand = Mod.) | 495.00 |
| 10 Gauge Magnum Kit | 375.00 |
| 20 Gauge | 495.00 |

## THE KENTUCKIAN RIFLE
### Flintlock $269.95
### Percussion $259.95

This 45-caliber rifle, in flintlock or percussion, has a 33¹/₂-inch blued octagonal barrel that is ¹³/₁₆ inch across the flats. The bore is rifled with 6 lands and grooves of equal width and about .006″ deep. Land-to-land diameter is .453 with groove-to-groove diameter of .465. Ball size ranges from .445 to .448.

The rifle has a brass blade front sight and a steel open rear sight. The Kentuckian is furnished with brass buttplate, trigger guard, patchbox, sideplate, thimbles and nose cap plus casehardened and engraved lock plate. Highly polished and finely finished stock in European walnut. **Overall length:** 48″. **Weight:** Approx. 6¹/₄ lbs.

# DIXIE

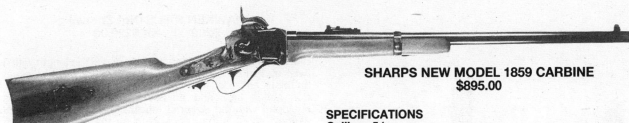

### SHARPS NEW MODEL 1859 CARBINE
### $895.00

About 115,000 Sharps New Model 1859 carbines and its variants were made during the Civil War. Characterized by durability and accuracy, they became a favorite of cavalrymen on both sides. Made in Italy by David Pedersoli & Co.

**SPECIFICATIONS**
**Caliber:** 54
**Barrel length:** 22″ (1 in 48″ twist); blued, round barrel has 7-groove rifling
**Overall length:** 37¹/₂″  **Weight:** 7³/₄ lbs.
**Sights:** Blade front; adjustable rear
**Stock:** Oil-finished walnut
**Features:** Barrel band, hammer, receiver, saddle bar and ring all color casehardened

### SHARPS NEW MODEL 1859 MILITARY RIFLE
### $895.00

Initially used by the First Connecticut Volunteers, this rifle is associated mostly with the 1st U.S. (Berdan's) Sharpshooters. There were 6,689 made with most going to the Sharpshooters (2,000) and the U.S. Navy (2,780). Made in Italy by David Pedersoli & Co.
**SPECIFICATIONS**
**Caliber:** 54
**Barrel length:** 30″ (1 in 48″ twist)

**Overall length:** 45¹/₂″
**Weight:** 9 lbs.
**Sights:** Blade front; rear sight adjustable for elevation and windage
**Features:** Buttstock and forend straight-grained and oilfinished walnut; three barrel bands, receiver, hammer, nose cap, lever, patchbox cover and butt are all color casehardened; sling swivels attached to middle band and butt

### 1874 SHARPS LIGHTWEIGHT TARGET/
### HUNTER RIFLE    $995.00

This Sharps rifle in 45-70 Government caliber has a 30″ octagon barrel with blued matte finish (1:18″ twist). It also features an adjustable hunting rear sight and blade front, making it ideal for blackpowder hunters. The tang is drilled and threaded for tang sights. The oil-finished military-style buttstock has a blued metal buttplate. Double-set triggers. Color casehardened receiver and hammer. **Overall length:** 49¹/₂″. **Weight:** 10 lbs.

### 1874 SHARPS SILHOUETTE MODEL
### $995.00

This rifle in .40-65 and .45-70 caliber has a shotgun-style buttstock with a pistol grip and a metal buttplate. The 30-inch tapered octagon barrel is blued and has a 1 in 18″ twist. The receiver, hammer, lever and buttplate are color casehardened. Ladder-type hunting rear and blade front sights are standard. Four screw holes are in the tang: two with 10 x 28 threads, two with metric threads, for attaching tang sights. Double set triggers are standard. **Weight** is 10 lbs. 3 oz. without target sights. **Overall length:** 47¹/₂″. Also available in .45-70

# DIXIE RIFLES

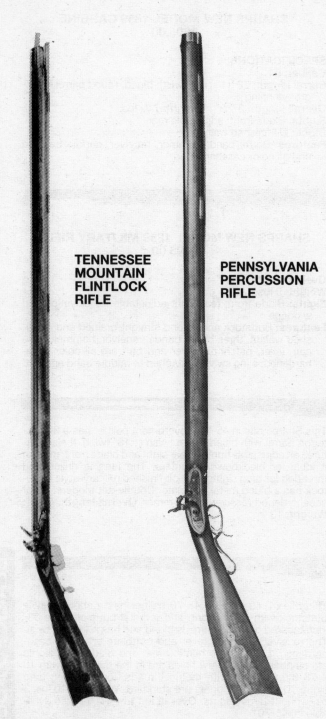

**TENNESSEE MOUNTAIN FLINTLOCK RIFLE**

**PENNSYLVANIA PERCUSSION RIFLE**

### HAWKEN RIFLE (Not Shown)
### $250.00    Kit $220.00

Blued barrel is 15/16″ across the flats and 30″ in length with a twist of 1 in 64″. Stock is of walnut with a steel crescent buttplate, halfstock with brass nosecap. Double-set triggers, front-action lock and adjustable rear sight. Ramrod is equipped with jag. **Overall length:** 46 1/2″. Average actual **weight:** about 8 lbs., depending on the caliber; shipping weight is 10 lbs. Available in either finished gun or kit. **Calibers:** 45, 50 and 54.

### DIXIE TENNESSEE MOUNTAIN RIFLE
### $575.00 Percussion or Flintlock

This 50-caliber rifle features double-set triggers with adjustable set screw, bore rifled with 6 lands and grooves, barrel of 15/16 inch across the flats, brown finish and cherry stock. **Overall length:** 41 1/2 inches. Right- and left-hand versions in flint or percussion. **Kit:**. . . . . . . . . . . . . . . . . . **$495.00**

### DIXIE TENNESSEE SQUIRREL RIFLE
### $575.00    (not shown)

In 32-caliber flint or percussion, right hand only, cherry stock. **Kit:**. . . . . . . . . . . . . . . . . . . . . . . . . . . . . . **$495.00**

### PENNSYLVANIA RIFLE
### Percussion or Flintlock $450.00
### Kit (Flint or Perc.) $395.00

A lightweight at just 8 pounds, the 41 1/2″ blued rifle barrel is fitted with an open buckhorn rear sight and front blade. The walnut one-piece stock is stained a medium darkness that contrasts with the polished brass buttplate, toe plate, patchbox, sideplate, trigger guard, thimbles and nose cap. Featuring double-set triggers, the rifle can be fired by pulling only the front trigger, which has a normal trigger pull of 4 to 5 pounds; or the rear trigger can first be pulled to set a spring-loaded mechanism that greatly reduces the amount of pull needed for the front trigger to kick off the sear in the lock. The land-to-land measurement of the bore is an exact .450: the recommended ball size is .445. **Overall length:** 51 1/2″.

### PEDERSOLI WAADTLANDER RIFLE (Not Shown)
### $1412.00

This authentic re-creation of a Swiss muzzleloading target rifle features a heavy octagonal barrel (31″) that has 7 lands and grooves. **Caliber:** 45. Rate of twist is 1 turn in 48″. Double-set triggers are multilever type and are easily removable for adjustment. Sights are fitted post front and tang-mounted Swiss-type diopter rear. Walnut stock, color casehardened hardware, classic buttplate and curved trigger guard complete this reproduction. The original was made between 1839 and 1860 by Marc Bristlen, Morges, Switzerland.

# DIXIE

### MISSISSIPPI RIFLE
### $495.00

Commonly called the U.S. Rifle Model 1841, this Italian-made replica is rifled in a .58 caliber to use a round ball or a Minie ball; 3 grooves and regulation sights; solid brass furniture; casehardened lock.

### 1863 SPRINGFIELD CIVIL WAR MUSKET
### $595.00    Kit $525.00

This exact copy of the Model 1863 Springfield was the last of the regulation muzzleloading rifles. The barrel on this .58-caliber gun measures 40 inches. The action and all-metal furniture is finished bright. The oil-finished walnut-stained stock is 53 inches long. **Overall length:** 56". **Weight:** 9 1/2 lbs.

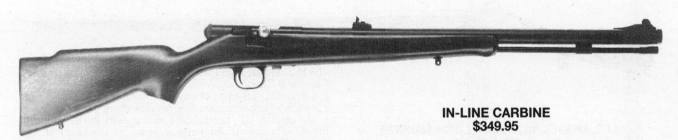

### IN-LINE CARBINE
### $349.95

Made in Italy by D. Pedersoli, this rifle in 50 or 54 caliber features a sliding "bolt" that completely encloses cap and nipple, making it the most weatherproof muzzleloader available. **Barrel length:** 24". **Overall length:** 41". **Weight:** 6 1/2 lbs. **Sights:** Ramp front with red insert; rear sight adjustable for windage and elevation. **Stock:** Walnut-colored wood with Monte Carlo comb and black plastic buttplate. Features include fully adj. trigger, automatic slide safety, and chromed bolt and handle.

### TRYON CREEDMOOR RIFLE (Not Shown)
### $682.00

This Tryon rifle features a high-quality back-action lock, double-set triggers, steel buttplate, patchbox, toe plate and curved trigger guard. **Caliber:** 45. **Barrel:** 32 3/4", octagonal, with 1 twist in 20.87". **Sights:** Hooded post front fitted with replaceable inserts; rear is tang-mounted and adjustable for windage and elevation.

# DIXIE

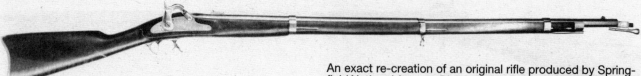

### U.S. MODEL 1861 SPRINGFIELD PERCUSSION RIFLE-MUSKET
### $595.00    Kit $525.00

An exact re-creation of an original rifle produced by Springfield National Armory, Dixie's Model 1861 Springfield .58-caliber rifle features a 40″ round, tapered barrel with three barrel bands. Sling swivels are attached to the trigger guard bow and middle barrel band. The ramrod has a trumpet-shaped head with swell; sights are standard military rear and bayonet-attachment lug front. The percussion lock is marked "1861" on the rear of the lockplate with an eagle motif and "U.S. Springfield" in front of the hammer. "U.S." is stamped on top of buttplate. All furniture is "National Armory Bright." **Overall length:** 55$^{13}/_{16}$″. **Weight:** 8 lbs.

### 1862 THREE-BAND ENFIELD RIFLED MUSKET
### $495.00    Kit $425.00

One of the finest reproduction percussion guns available, the 1862 Enfield was widely used during the Civil War in its original version. This rifle follows the lines of the original almost exactly. The .58-caliber musket features a 39-inch barrel and walnut stock. Three steel barrel bands and the barrel itself are blued; the lockplate and hammer are case colored and the remainder of the furniture is highly polished brass. The lock is marked, "London Armory Co." **Weight:** 10$^{1}/_{2}$ lbs. **Overall length:** 55″.

### U.S. MODEL 1816 FLINTLOCK MUSKET
### $725.00

The U.S. Model 1816 Flintlock Musket was made by Harpers Ferry and Springfield Arsenals from 1816 until 1864. It had the highest production of any U.S. flintlock musket and after conversion to percussion saw service in the Civil War. It has a .69-caliber, 42″ smoothbore barrel held by three barrel bands with springs. All metal parts are finished in "National Armory Bright." The lockplate has a brass pan and is marked "Harpers Ferry" vertically behind the hammer, with an American eagle placed in front of the hammer. The bayonet lug is on top of the barrel and the steel ramrod has a button-shaped head. Sling swivels are mounted on trigger guard and middle barrel band. **Overall length:** 56$^{1}/_{2}$″. **Weight:** 9$^{3}/_{4}$ lbs.

### 1858 TWO-BAND ENFIELD RIFLE
### $475.00

This 33-inch barrel version of the British Enfield is an exact copy of similar rifles used during the Civil War. The .58-caliber rifle sports a European walnut stock, deep blue-black finish on the barrel, bands, breech-plug tang and bayonet mount. The percussion lock is color casehardened and the rest of the furniture is brightly polished brass.

# EMF HARTFORD REVOLVERS

**SHERIFF'S MODEL 1851**

### SHERIFF'S MODEL 1851 REVOLVER
### $140.00 (Brass)   $192.00 (Steel)

**SPECIFICATIONS**
**Caliber:** 44 Percussion
**Ball diameter:** .376 round or conical, pure lead
**Barrel length:** 5″
**Overall length:** 10¹/₂″
**Weight:** 39 oz.
**Sights:** V-notch groove in hammer (rear); truncated cone in front
**Percussion cap size:** #11

### MODEL 1860 ARMY REVOLVER
### $160.00 (Brass Frame)

**SPECIFICATIONS**
**Caliber:** 44 Percussion
**Barrel length:** 8″
**Overall length:** 13⁵/₈″
**Weight:** 41 oz.
**Frame:** Casehardened
**Finish:** High-luster blue with walnut grips
Also available:
**Cased set** with steel frame, wood case, flask
and mould . . . . . . . . . . . . . . . . . . . . . . . . . . . . . **$360.00**
   Engraved cased set (brass frame only) . . . . . . . . 325.00
**Fluted cylinder model** (steel frame only) . . . . . . . . 375.00

**MODEL 1860 ARMY**

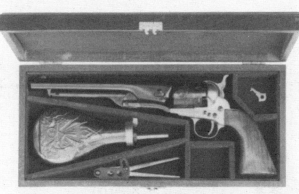

**1860 ARMY BRASS FRAME
CASED SET
$225.00**

### HARTFORD MODEL
### 1862 POLICE REVOLVER
### $248.00 (Steel)   $184.00 (Brass)

**SPECIFICATIONS**
**Caliber:** 36 Percussion   **Capacity:** 5-shot
**Barrel length:** 6¹/₂″

### HARTFORD 1863 TEXAS DRAGOON
### $370.00

**SPECIFICATIONS**
**Caliber:** 44
**Barrel length:** 7″ (round)
**Overall length:** 14″
**Weight:** 4 lbs.
**Finish:** Steel casehardened frame

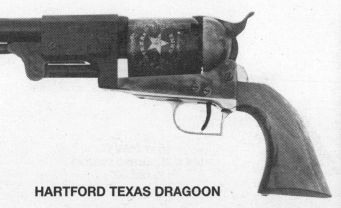

**HARTFORD TEXAS DRAGOON**

# EMF HARTFORD REVOLVERS

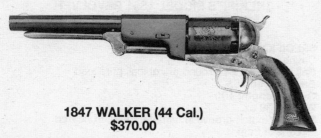

**1847 WALKER (44 Cal.)**
**$370.00**

**1851 NAVY (36 or 44 Cal.)**
**$230.00**

**1848 DRAGOON (44 Cal.)**
**$330.00**

**1858 REMINGTON ARMY**
**(44 Cal., Steel Frame)**
**$168.00**

Six-shot, 8″ octagonal barrel, one-piece walnut grip.

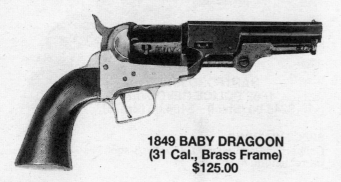

**1849 BABY DRAGOON**
**(31 Cal., Brass Frame)**
**$125.00**

**1858 REMINGTON ARMY**
**44 CAL. STEEL FRAME**
**$130.00**

**1851 NAVY**
**(44 Cal., Brass Frame)**
**$125.00**

**1860 ARMY (44 Cal.)**
**$270.00**

# Let The Drooling Begin.

## Introducing the Model 700 ML & MLS Muzzleloaders.

One glance and it hits you immediately. This is like no muzzleloader you've ever seen before. For good reason. It's the first muzzleloader ever crafted on a totally-modern, totally-proven bolt action centerfire design. In fact, the most popular bolt

*At typical hunting distances, the Model 700 Muzzleloader is capable of accuracy rivaling many centerfire rifles.*

*The only in-line with a true bolt action design. Lock time is an astonishing 3 milliseconds, the fastest of any muzzleloader available.*

action centerfire ever produced: the Remington® Model 700.™ In fit, feel and function it is Model 700 through and through. The same cocking action. The same trigger mechanism. The same lock time. The same legendary out-of-the-box accuracy. Shoulder it once and you realize that it is, without question, the easiest-to-use, most advanced black powder rifle ever created. It should be. It's a Remington Model 700.

*For a complete guide to Remington black powder rifles, ammunition and accessories, see your Remington retailer today.*

## Remington®
### C O U N T R Y

# PRO SERIES 95

## MATCH GRADE TARGET PISTOLS

# EUROARMS OF AMERICA

## COOK & BROTHER CONFEDERATE CARBINE
### Model 2300: $447.00

**COOK & BROTHER
CONFEDERATE CARBINE**

Classic re-creation of the rare 1861, New Orleans-made Artillery Carbine. The lockplate is marked "Cook & Brother N.O. 1861" and is stamped with a Confederate flag at the rear of the hammer.

**SPECIFICATIONS**
**Caliber:** 58 percussion
**Barrel length:** 24"  **Overall length:** 40 1/3"
**Weight:** 7 1/2 lbs.
**Sights:** Fixed blade front and adjustable dovetailed rear

**Ramrod:** Steel
**Finish:** Barrel is antique brown; buttplate, trigger guard, barrel bands, sling swivels and nose cap are polished brass; stock is walnut
**Recommended ball sizes:** .575 r.b., .577 Minie and .580 maxi; uses musket caps

Also available:
**MODEL 2301 COOK & BROTHER FIELD** with 33" barrel
**Price:** . . . . . . . . . . . . . . . . . . . . . . . . . . . . . . . . . . $480.00

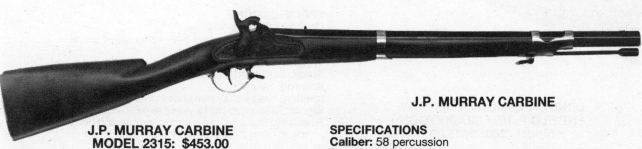

## J.P. MURRAY CARBINE
### MODEL 2315: $453.00

**J.P. MURRAY CARBINE**

Replica of an extremely rare CSA Cavalry Carbine based on an 1841 design of parts and lock.

**SPECIFICATIONS**
**Caliber:** 58 percussion
**Barrel length:** 23"
**Features:** Brass barrel bands and buttplate; oversized trigger guard; sling swivels

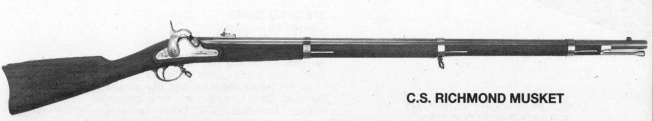

## C.S. RICHMOND MUSKET
### MODEL 2370: $530.00

**C.S. RICHMOND MUSKET**

**SPECIFICATIONS**
**Caliber:** 58 percussion. **Barrel length:** 40" with three bands.

# EUROARMS OF AMERICA

### LONDON ARMORY COMPANY
### ENFIELD P-1858
### 2-BAND RIFLE MUSKET
#### Model 2270: $470.00

**SPECIFICATIONS**
**Caliber:** 58 percussion
**Barrel length:** 33", blued and rifled
**Overall length:** 49"
**Weight:** 8 1/2 to 8 3/4 lbs., depending on wood density
**Stock:** One-piece walnut; polished "bright" brass buttplate, trigger guard and nose cap; blued barrel bands
**Sights:** Inverted 'V' front sight; Enfield folding ladder rear
**Ramrod:** Steel

### LONDON ARMORY COMPANY
### ENFIELD P-1861 MUSKETOON
#### Model 2280: $415.00

**SPECIFICATIONS**
**Caliber:** 58; Minie ball
**Barrel length:** 24"; round high-luster blued barrel
**Overall length:** 40 1/2"
**Weight:** 7 to 7 1/2 lbs., depending on density of wood
**Stock:** Seasoned walnut stock with sling swivels
**Ramrod:** Steel
**Ignition:** Heavy-duty percussion lock
**Sights:** Graduated military-leaf sight
**Furniture:** Brass trigger guard, nose cap and buttplate; blued barrel bands, lock plate, and swivels

### LONDON ARMORY COMPANY
### 3-BAND ENFIELD P-1853
### RIFLED MUSKET
#### Model 2260: $480.00

**SPECIFICATIONS**
**Caliber:** 58 percussion
**Barrel length:** 39", blued and rifled
**Overall length:** 54"
**Weight:** 9 1/2 to 9 3/4 lbs., depending on wood density
**Stock:** One-piece walnut; polished "bright" brass buttplate, trigger guard and nose cap; blued barrel bands
**Ramrod:** Steel; threaded end for accessories
**Sights:** Traditional Enfield folding ladder rear sight; inverted 'V' front sight
Also available:
**MODEL 2261** w/white barrel, satin finish . . . . . . . . $520.00

# EUROARMS OF AMERICA

### U.S. 1803 HARPERS FERRY FLINTLOCK RIFLE
**Model 2305: $640.00**

**SPECIFICATIONS**
**Caliber:** 54 Flintlock
**Barrel length:** 35", octagonal
**Features:** Walnut half stock with cheekpiece; browned barrel

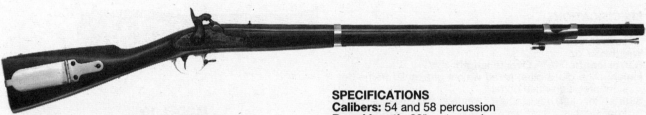

### U.S. 1841 MISSISSIPPI RIFLE
**Model 2310: $500.00**

**SPECIFICATIONS**
**Calibers:** 54 and 58 percussion
**Barrel length:** 33", octagonal
**Features:** Walnut stock; brass barrel bands and buttplate; sling swivels

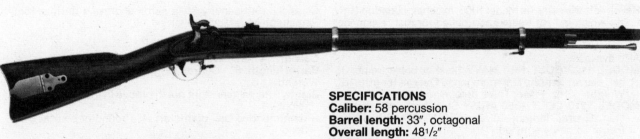

### U.S. MODEL 1863 REMINGTON ZOUAVE RIFLE (2-Barrel Bands)
**Model 2255: $430.00**

**SPECIFICATIONS**
**Caliber:** 58 percussion
**Barrel length:** 33", octagonal
**Overall length:** 48 1/2"
**Weight:** 9 1/2 to 9 3/4 lbs.
**Sights:** U.S. Military 3-leaf rear; blade front
**Features:** Two brass barrel bands; brass buttplate and nose cap; sling swivels

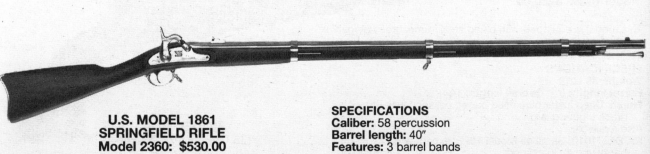

### U.S. MODEL 1861 SPRINGFIELD RIFLE
**Model 2360: $530.00**

**SPECIFICATIONS**
**Caliber:** 58 percussion
**Barrel length:** 40"
**Features:** 3 barrel bands

**BLACK POWDER**

# EUROARMS OF AMERICA

**MODEL 1005**

## ROGERS & SPENCER ARMY REVOLVER
### Model 1006 (Target): $239.00

**SPECIFICATIONS**
**Caliber:** 44; takes .451 round or conical lead balls; #11 percussion cap
**Weight:** 47 oz.
**Barrel length:** 7¹/₂″  **Overall length:** 13³/₄″
**Finish:** High gloss blue; flared walnut grip; solid frame design; precision-rifled barrel
**Sights:** Rear fully adjustable for windage and elevation; ramp front sight

## ROGERS & SPENCER REVOLVER
## LONDON GRAY (Not shown)
### Model 1007: $245.00

Revolver is the same as Model 1005, except for London Gray finish, which is heat treated and buffed for rust resistance; same recommended ball size and percussion caps.

Also available:
**MODEL 1120 COLT 1851 NAVY** Steel or brass frame. 36 cal. **Barrel length:** 7¹/₂″ octagonal. **Overall length:** 13″. **Weight:** 42 oz. **Price:** To be determined.
**MODEL 1210 COLT 1860 ARMY** Steel frame. 44 percussion. **Overall length:** 10⁵/₈″ or 13⁵/₈″. **Weight:** 41 oz. **Price:** To be determined.

## REMINGTON 1858
## NEW MODEL ARMY REVOLVER
### Model 1020: $200.00

This model is equipped with blued steel frame, brass trigger guard in 44 caliber.

**SPECIFICATIONS**
**Weight:** 40 oz.
**Barrel length:** 8″  **Overall length:** 14³/₄″
**Finish:** Deep luster blue rifled barrel; polished walnut stock; brass trigger guard.
Also available:
**MODEL 1010.** Same as Model 1020, except w/6¹/₂″ barrel and in 36 caliber: . . . . . . . . . . . . . . . . . . **$200.00**

## ROGERS & SPENCER REVOLVER
### Model 1005: $227.00

**SPECIFICATIONS**
**Caliber:** 44 Percussion; #11 percussion cap
**Barrel length:** 7¹/₂″  **Overall length:** 13³/₄″
**Weight:** 47 oz.
**Sights:** Integral rear sight notch groove in frame; brass truncated cone front sight
**Finish:** High gloss blue; flared walnut grip; solid frame design; precision-rifled barrel
**Recommended ball diameter:** .451 round or conical, pure lead

**MODEL 1006**

## REMINGTON 1858
## NEW MODEL ARMY ENGRAVED (Not shown)
### Model 1040: $275.00

Classical 19th-century style scroll engraving on this 1858 Remington New Model revolver.

**SPECIFICATIONS**
**Caliber:** 44 Percussion; #11 cap
**Barrel length:** 8″  **Overall length:** 14³/₄″
**Weight:** 41 oz.
**Sights:** Integral rear sight notch groove in frame; blade front sight
**Recommended ball diameter:** .451 round or conical, pure lead

**MODEL 1010**
**(36 Cal. w/6¹/₂″ barrel)**

# GONIC ARMS

**MODEL 87 MAG RIFLE**
**$870.00 (Open Sights)**

**SPECIFICATIONS**
**Calibers:** 45 and 50 Mag.
**Barrel length:** 26″  **Overall length:** 43″
**Weight:** 6½ lbs.
**Sights:** Bead front; open rear (adjustable for windage and elevation); drilled and tapped for scope bases

**Stock:** American walnut  **Length of pull:** 14″
**Trigger:** Single stage (4-lb. pull)
**Mechanism type:** Closed-breech muzzleloader
**Features:** Ambidextrous safety; nonglare satin finish; newly designed loading system; all-weather performance guaranteed; faster lock time

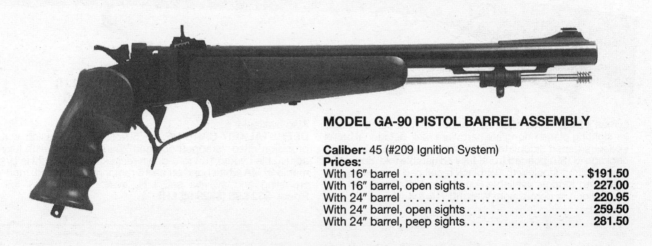

**MODEL GA-90 PISTOL BARREL ASSEMBLY**

**Caliber:** 45 (#209 Ignition System)
**Prices:**
With 16″ barrel . . . . . . . . . . . . . . . . . . . . . . . . . . $191.50
With 16″ barrel, open sights. . . . . . . . . . . . . . . . . . 227.00
With 24″ barrel . . . . . . . . . . . . . . . . . . . . . . . . . . . 220.95
With 24″ barrel, open sights. . . . . . . . . . . . . . . . . . 259.50
With 24″ barrel, peep sights. . . . . . . . . . . . . . . . . . 281.50

**MODEL 93 MAGNUM RIFLE**
**$500.00 (Open Sights)**
**$603.00 (Stainless w/Open Sights)**

Gonic Arms's blackpowder rifle has a unique loading system that produces better consistency and utilizes the full powder charge of the specially designed penetrator bullet (ballistics = 2,650 foot-pounds at 1,600 fps w/465-grain .500 bullet).

**SPECIFICATIONS**
**Caliber:** 50 Magnum
**Barrel length:** 26″  **Overall length:** 43″
**Weight:** 6 to 6½ lbs.

**Sights:** Open hunting sights (adjustable)
**Features:** Walnut-stained hardwood stock; adjustable trigger; nipple wrench; drilled and tapped for scope bases; ballistics and instruction manual

Also available:
**MODEL 93 SAFARI RIFLE** w/classic walnut stock,
open sights . . . . . . . . . . . . . . . . . . . . . . . . . . . $1560.00

**BLACK POWDER**

# LYMAN RIFLES

### COUGAR IN-LINE RIFLE
### $299.95

The new Lyman Cougar In-Line rifle is designed for the serious blackpowder hunter who wants a rugged and accurate muzzleloader with the feel of a centerfire bolt-action rifle. The Cougar In-Line is traditionally styled with a walnut stock and blued barrel and action. Available in 50 and 54 caliber. Features include a 22″ barrel with 1:24″ twist and shallow rifling grooves; dual safety system (equipped with a bolt safety notch in receiver and a sliding thumb safety that disables the trigger mechanism); drilled and tapped for Lyman 57 WTR receiver sight; fully adjustable trigger; sling swivel studs installed; unbreakable Derlin ramrod; modern folding-leaf rear and bead front sights; rubber recoil pad.

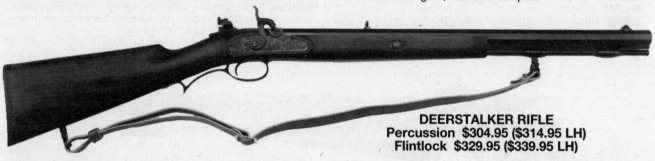

### DEERSTALKER RIFLE
### Percussion $304.95 ($314.95 LH)
### Flintlock $329.95 ($339.95 LH)

Lyman's Deerstalker rifle incorporates • higher comb for better sighting plane • nonglare hardware • 24″ octagonal barrel • casehardened sideplate • Q.D. sling swivels • Lyman sight package (37MA beaded front; fully adjustable fold-down 16A rear) • walnut stock with 1/2″ black recoil pad • single trigger. Left-hand models available (same price). **Calibers:** 50 and 54, flintlock or percussion. **Weight:** 7 1/2 lbs.

Also available:
**DEERSTALKER CARBINE.** In .50-caliber percussion w/a precision-rifled "stepped octagon" barrel (1:24″ twist); fully adjustable Lyman 16A fold-down rear sight; front sight is Lyman's 37MA white bead on an 18 ramp; nylon ramrod, modern sling and swivels set. L.H. avail. **Weight:** 6 3/4 lbs. **Price: $324.95 ($329.95 LH)**

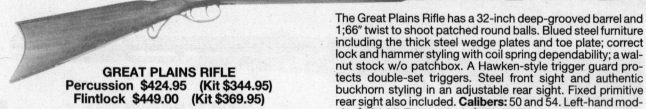

### GREAT PLAINS RIFLE
### Percussion $424.95 (Kit $344.95)
### Flintlock $449.00 (Kit $369.95)

The Great Plains Rifle has a 32-inch deep-grooved barrel and 1;66″ twist to shoot patched round balls. Blued steel furniture including the thick steel wedge plates and toe plate; correct lock and hammer styling with coil spring dependability; a walnut stock w/o patchbox. A Hawken-style trigger guard protects double-set triggers. Steel front sight and authentic buckhorn styling in an adjustable rear sight. Fixed primitive rear sight also included. **Calibers:** 50 and 54. Left-hand models: **$434.95** (Percussion); **$459.95** (Flint)

### LYMAN TRADE RIFLE
### Percussion $299.95
### Flintlock $324.95

The Lyman Trade Rifle features a 28-inch octagonal barrel, rifled 1 turn at 48 inches, designed to fire both patched round balls and the popular maxistyle conical bullets. Polished brass furniture with blued finish on steel parts; walnut stock; hook breech; single spring-loaded trigger; coil-spring percussion lock; fixed steel sights; adjustable rear sight for elevation also included. Steel barrel rib and ramrod ferrrule. **Caliber:** 50 or 54 percussion and flint. **Overall length:** 45″.

# MARLIN MUZZLELOADERS

### MLS-50/MLS-54
### Stainless Barrel/Black Rynite Stock

### MODELS MLS-50 & MLS-54

Marlin's new in-line muzzleloaders—the MLS-50 and MLS-54—feature stainless steel one-piece barrel/receiver construction, automatic tang safety and an ambidextrous cocking handle that disengages from the hammer for added safety. The open breech features a shrouded hammer and standard nipple. Both models come equipped with an aluminum ramrod and black Rynite stocks with molded-in checkering and swivel studs.

**Calibers:** 50 (MLS-50) and 54 (MLS-54)
**Barrel length:** 22"; 1:28" rifling twist (Right hand)
**Overall length:** 41"    **Weight:** 6½ lbs.
**Sights:** Adjustable Marble semi-buckhorn rear; ramp front w/brass beads
**Price:** . . . . . . . . . . . . . . . . . . . . . . . . . . . . . . . . . . . . . **$411.00**

# MODERN MUZZLELOADING

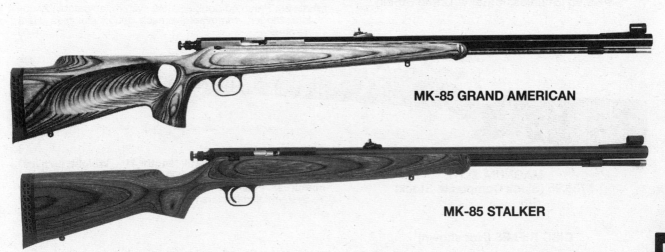

### MK-85 GRAND AMERICAN

### MK-85 STALKER

### MK-85 KNIGHT RIFLES

The MK-85 muzzleloading rifles (designed by William A. "Tony" Knight) are handcrafted, lightweight rifles capable of 1½-inch groups at 100 yards. They feature a one-piece, in-line bolt assembly, patented double-safety system, Timney featherweight deluxe trigger system, recoil pad, and Green Mountain barrels (1 in 28" twist in 50 and 54 caliber).

**Calibers:** 50 and 54
**Barrel length:** 24"    **Overall length:** 43"
**Weight:** 6 to 7¼ lbs.

**Sights:** Adjustable high-visibility open sights
**Stock:** Classic walnut, laminated or composite
**Features:** Swivel studs installed; hard anodized aluminum ramrod; combo tool; hex keys; and more.
**Prices:**
**MK-85 HUNTER** (Walnut) . . . . . . . . . . . . . . . . . . . $ 549.95
**MK-85 KNIGHT HAWK** (Blued barrel). . . . . . . . . 769.95
**MK-85 PREDATOR** (Stainless) . . . . . . . . . . . . . 649.95
**MK-85 STALKER** (Laminated). . . . . . . . . . . . . . . 619.95
**MK-85 GRAND AMERICAN** (Blued barrel,
   Shadow brown or black) . . . . . . . . . . . . . . . . . . 995.95
   In Stainless Steel . . . . . . . . . . . . . . . . . . . . . . 1095.95

# MODERN MUZZLELOADING

## MODEL LK-93 WOLVERINE
### $269.95 (Blued)   $349.95 (Stainless)

**Calibers:** 50 and 54
**Barrel length:** 22"; blued rifle-grade steel (1:28" twist)
**Overall length:** 41"   **Weight:** 6 lbs.
**Sights:** Adjustable high-visibility rear sight; drilled and tapped for scope mount

**Stock:** Lightweight Fiber-Lite molded stock
**Features:** Patented double-safety system; adjustable Accu-Lite trigger; removable breechplug; stainless-steel hammer

## LK-93 THUMBHOLE WOLVERINE
### $319.95 (Blued w/Black Stock)
### $369.95 (Blued w/Camo Stock)
### $399.95 (Stainless Steel w/Black Stock)
### $449.95 (Stainless Steel w/Camo Stock)

## LK-93 THUMBHOLE WOLVERINE
## w/MOSSY OAK CAMO

**SPECIFICATIONS**
**Calibers:** 50 and 54
**Barrel length:** 22" rifle-grade steel (1:28" twist)
**Overall length:** 41"
**Weight:** 6 lbs. 4 oz.
**Features:** Patented double safety system; adjustable Accu-Lite trigger; removable breech plug; stainless steel hammer

## MAGNUM ELITE
### $739.95 (Black Composite Stock)

**Calibers:** 50 and 54
**Barrel length:** 24"   **Overall length:** 41"   **Weight:** 6.75 lbs.
**Sights:** Adjustable high-visibility open sights
**Features:** "Posi-Fire" ignition system; Knight Double-Safety System; aluminum ramrod; sling swivel studs

## DISC RIFLES (Not shown)

**Caliber:** 50 only (1:28" twist)
**Barrel length:** 22"   **Overall length:** 41"
**Weight:** 6 lbs. 14 oz.
**Stock:** Black composite, Advantage, Realtree X-tra Brown, Mossy Oak Treestand or Break-Up
**Sights:** Fully adjustable rear sight; front ramp
**Features:** Removable stainless steel breech plug; checkered forearm and palm swell pistol grip; solid rubber recoil pad; sling swivels; drilled and tapped for scope mounting; adjustable trigger, in-line ignition system; removable bolt assembly
Also available:
**DISC DELUXE RIFLE.** Same specifications as standard model but with adjustable metallic high-visibility hunting sight w/front ramp and high-visibility bead; double safety system; metallic trigger guard and ramrod guide.

**Prices:**
**DISC RIFLE**
| | |
|---|---|
| Blued w/black composite | $399.95 |
| Blued w/camo stock | 449.95 |
| Stainless w/black composite | 469.95 |
| Stainless w/camo stock | 519.95 |

**DISC DELUXE**
| | |
|---|---|
| Blued w/black composite | 469.95 |
| Blued w/camo stock | 519.95 |
| Stainless w/black composite | 539.95 |
| Stainless w/camo stock | 589.95 |

# NAVY ARMS REVOLVERS

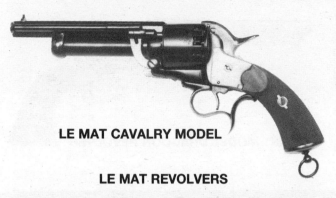

**LE MAT CAVALRY MODEL**

**LE MAT NAVY MODEL**

## LE MAT REVOLVERS

Once the official sidearm of many Confederate cavalry offi-cers, this 9-shot .44-caliber revolver with a central single-shot barrel of approx. 65 caliber gave the cavalry man 10 shots to use against the enemy. **Barrel length:** 7⁵/₈″. **Overall length:** 14″. **Weight:** 3 lbs. 7 oz.

| | |
|---|---|
| Cavalry Model . . . . . . . . . . . . . . . . . . . . . . . . . . . | $ 595.00 |
| Navy Model . . . . . . . . . . . . . . . . . . . . . . . . . . . . . | 595.00 |
| Army Model . . . . . . . . . . . . . . . . . . . . . . . . . . . . . | 595.00 |
| 18th Georgia (engraving on cylinder, display case) . . . . . . . . . . . . . . . . . . . . . . . . . | 795.00 |
| Beauregard (hand-engraved cylinder and frame; display case and mold) . . . . . . . . . . . . . . . . . . | 1000.00 |

**LE MAT ARMY MODEL**

**1862 NEW MODEL POLICE**

This is the last gun manufactured by the Colt plant in the percussion era. It encompassed all the modifications of each gun, starting from the early Paterson to the 1861 Navy. It was favored by the New York Police Dept. for many years. One-half fluted and rebated cylinder, 36 cal., 5 shot. This replica features brass trigger guard and backstrap. Casehardened frame, loading lever and hammer. **Barrel length:** 5¹/₂″.

| | |
|---|---|
| 1862 Police . . . . . . . . . . . . . . . . . . . . . . . . . . . . . | $290.00 |
| Law and Order Set . . . . . . . . . . . . . . . . . . . . . . . . . | 365.00 |

## ROGERS & SPENCER REVOLVER

This revolver features a six-shot cylinder, octagonal barrel, hinged-type loading lever assembly, two-piece walnut grips, blued finish and casehardened hammer and lever. **Caliber:** 44. **Barrel length:** 7¹/₂″. **Overall length:** 13³/₄″. **Weight:** 3 lbs.

| | |
|---|---|
| Rogers & Spencer . . . . . . . . . . . . . . . . . . . . . . . . . | $245.00 |
|   London Gray | 270.00 |
|   Target Model (w/adjustable sights) . . . . . . . . . . | 270.00 |

**COLT 1847 WALKER**

The 1847 Walker replica comes in 44 caliber with a 9-inch barrel. **Weight:** 4 lbs. 8 oz. Well suited for the collector as well as the blackpowder shooter. Features include: rolled cyl-inder scene; blued and casehardened finish; and brass guard. Proof tested.

| | |
|---|---|
| Colt 1847 Walker . . . . . . . . . . . . . . . . . . . . . . . . . | $275.00 |
| Single Cased Set . . . . . . . . . . . . . . . . . . . . . . . . . | 405.00 |
| Deluxe Cased Set . . . . . . . . . . . . . . . . . . . . . . . . . | 505.00 |

**ROGERS & SPENCER REVOLVER**

# NAVY ARMS REVOLVERS

### FIRST MODEL DRAGOON REVOLVER

An improved version of the 1847 Walker, the First Model has a shorter barrel and cylinder as well as a loading lever latch. Used extensively during the Civil War. **Caliber:** 44. **Barrel length:** 7.5″. **Overall length:** 13.75″. **Weight:** 4 lbs. **Sights:** Blade front, notch rear. **Grip:** Walnut.
**First Model Dragoon** . . . . . . . . . . . . . . . . . . . . . . . $275.00
Also available:
**THIRD MODEL DRAGOON** w/oval trigger guard and cylinder stop . . . . . . . . . . . . . . . . . . . . . . . . . . . . . . . $275.00

**FIRST MODEL DRAGOON REVOLVER**

**1851 NAVY "YANK"**

A favorite of "Wild Bill" Hickok, the 1851 Navy was originally manufactured by Colt from 1850 through 1876. This model was the most popular of the Union revolvers, mostly because it was lighter and easier to handle than the Dragoon. **Barrel length:** 7¹/₂″. **Overall length:** 14″. **Weight:** 2 lbs. **Rec. ball diam.:** .375 R.B. (.451 in 44 cal) **Calibers:** 36 and 44. **Capacity:** 6 shot. **Features:** Steel frame, octagonal barrel, cylinder roll-engraved with Naval battle scene, backstrap and trigger guard are polished brass.

| | |
|---|---|
| **1851 Navy "Yank"** . . . . . . . . . . . . . . . . . . . . . . . . | **$155.00** |
| **Kit**. . . . . . . . . . . . . . . . . . . . . . . . . . . . . . . . . . . . . | 125.00 |
| **Single Cased Set** . . . . . . . . . . . . . . . . . . . . . . . . | 280.00 |
| **Double Cased Set**. . . . . . . . . . . . . . . . . . . . . . . . | 455.00 |

### REB MODEL 1860

A modern replica of the confederate Griswold & Gunnison percussion Army revolver. Rendered with a polished brass frame and a rifled steel barrel finished in a high-luster blue with genuine walnut grips. All Army Model 60s are completely proof-tested by the Italian government to the most exacting standards. **Calibers:** 36 and 44. **Barrel length:** 7¹/₄″. **Overall length:** 13″. **Weight:** 2 lbs. 10 oz.–11 oz. **Features:** Brass frame, backstrap and trigger guard, round barrel.

| | |
|---|---|
| **Reb Model 1860** . . . . . . . . . . . . . . . . . . . . . . . . . . | **$115.00** |
| **Single Cased Set** . . . . . . . . . . . . . . . . . . . . . . . . | 235.00 |
| **Double Cased Set**. . . . . . . . . . . . . . . . . . . . . . . . | 365.00 |
| **Kit**. . . . . . . . . . . . . . . . . . . . . . . . . . . . . . . . . . . . . | 90.00 |

### 1860 ARMY

The 1860 Army satisfied the Union Army's need for a more powerful .44-caliber revolver. The cylinder on this replica is roll engraved with a polished brass trigger guard and steel strap cut for shoulder stock. The frame, loading lever and hammer are finished in high-luster color case-hardening. Walnut grips. **Weight:** 2 lbs. 9 oz. **Barrel length:** 8″. **Overall length:** 13⁵/₈″. **Caliber:** 44. **Finish:** Brass trigger guard, steel backstrap, round barrel, creeping lever, rebated cylinder, engraved Navy scene.

| | |
|---|---|
| **1860 Army** . . . . . . . . . . . . . . . . . . . . . . . . . . . . . . | **$175.00** |
| **Single Cased Set** . . . . . . . . . . . . . . . . . . . . . . . . | 290.00 |
| **Double Cased Set**. . . . . . . . . . . . . . . . . . . . . . . . | 480.00 |
| **Kit**. . . . . . . . . . . . . . . . . . . . . . . . . . . . . . . . . . . . . | 155.00 |

# NAVY ARMS REVOLVERS

## 1858 NEW MODEL ARMY REMINGTON-STYLE, STAINLESS STEEL

Exactly like the standard 1858 Remington (below) except that every part except for the grips and trigger guard is manufactured from corrosion-resistant stainless steel. This gun has all the style and feel of its ancestor with all of the conveniences of stainless steel. **Caliber:** 44.

1858 Remington Stainless . . . . . . . . . . . . . . . . . . . . $270.00
**Single Cased Set** . . . . . . . . . . . . . . . . . . . . . . . . . . 395.00
**Double Cased Set.** . . . . . . . . . . . . . . . . . . . . . . . . 680.00

## 1858 TARGET MODEL

Based on the Army Model, the target gun has target sights for controlled accuracy. Ruggedly built from modern steel and proof tested.

**1858 Target Model** . . . . . . . . . . . . . . . . . . . . . . . . $205.00

## 1858 NEW MODEL ARMY REMINGTON-STYLE REVOLVER

## 1858 NEW MODEL ARMY REMINGTON-STYLE REVOLVER

This rugged, dependable, battle-proven Civil War veteran with its top strap and rugged frame was considered the Magnum of C.W. revolvers, ideally suited for the heavy 44 charges. Blued finish. **Caliber:** 44. **Barrel length:** 8″. **Overall length:** 14¼″. **Weight:** 2 lbs. 8 oz.

**New Model Army Revolver** . . . . . . . . . . . . . . . . . . $170.00
**Single Cased Set** . . . . . . . . . . . . . . . . . . . . . . . . . . 290.00
**Double Cased Set.** . . . . . . . . . . . . . . . . . . . . . . . . 480.00
**Kit.** . . . . . . . . . . . . . . . . . . . . . . . . . . . . . . . . . . . . . 150.00

Also available:
**Brass Frame** . . . . . . . . . . . . . . . . . . . . . . . . . . . . . $125.00
**Brass Frame Kit** . . . . . . . . . . . . . . . . . . . . . . . . . . 115.00
**Single Cased Set** . . . . . . . . . . . . . . . . . . . . . . . . . . 250.00
**Double Cased Set.** . . . . . . . . . . . . . . . . . . . . . . . . 395.00

## REB 60 SHERIFF'S MODEL

A shortened version of the Reb Model 60 Revolver. The Sheriff's model version became popular because the shortened barrel was fast out of the leather. This is actually the original snub nose, the predecessor of the detective specials or belly guns designed for quick-draw use. **Calibers:** 36 and 44.

**Reb 60 Sheriff's Model.** . . . . . . . . . . . . . . . . . . . . $115.00
**Kit.** . . . . . . . . . . . . . . . . . . . . . . . . . . . . . . . . . . . . . 90.00
**Single Cased Set** . . . . . . . . . . . . . . . . . . . . . . . . . . 235.00
**Double Cased Set.** . . . . . . . . . . . . . . . . . . . . . . . . 365.00

## DELUXE NEW MODEL 1858 REMINGTON-STYLE 44 CALIBER (not shown)

Built to the exact dimensions and weight of the original Remington 44, this model features an 8″ barrel with progressive rifling, adjustable front sight for windage, all-steel construction with walnut stocks and silver-plated trigger guard. Steel is highly polished and finished in rich blue. **Barrel length:** 8″. **Overall length:** 14¼″. **Weight:** 2 lbs. 14 oz.

**Deluxe New Model 1858** . . . . . . . . . . . . . . . . . . . . $415.00

# NAVY ARMS PISTOLS

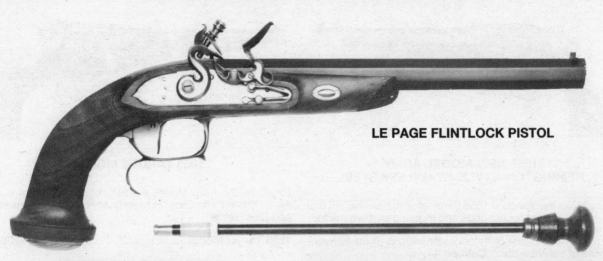

**LE PAGE FLINTLOCK PISTOL**

## LE PAGE FLINTLOCK PISTOL
### (44 Caliber)

The Le Page pistol is a beautifully hand-crafted reproduction featuring hand-checkered walnut stock with hinged buttcap and carved motif of a shell at the forward portion of the stock. Single-set trigger and highly polished steel lock and furniture together with a brown-finished rifled barrel make this a highly desirable target pistol. **Barrel length:** 10½". **Overall length:** 17". **Weight:** 2 lbs. 2 oz.

**Le Page Flintlock** (rifled or smoothbore) . . . . . . . . $625.00

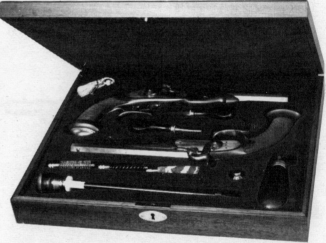

## CASED LE PAGE PISTOL SETS

The case is French-fitted and the accessories are the finest quality to match.

**Double Cased Sets**
French-fitted double cased set comprising two Le Page pistols, turn screw, nipple key, oil bottle, cleaning brushes, leather covered flask and loading rod. Rifled or smoothbore barrel.

**Double Cased Flintlock Set** . . . . . . . . . . . . . . . . . $1575.00
**Double Cased Percussion Set** . . . . . . . . . . . . . . 1300.00

**Single Cased Sets**
French-fitted single cased set comprising one Le Page pistol, turn screw, nipple key, oil bottle, cleaning brushes, leather covered flask and loading rod. Rifled or smoothbore barrel.

**Single Cased Flintlock Set** . . . . . . . . . . . . . . . . . $900.00
**Single Cased Percussion Set** . . . . . . . . . . . . . . . 775.00

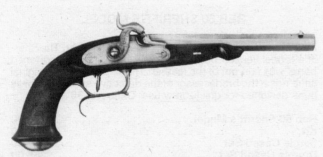

## LE PAGE PERCUSSION PISTOL
### (44 Caliber)

The tapered octagonal rifled barrel is in the traditional style with 7 lands and grooves. Fully adjustable single-set trigger. Engraved overall with traditional scrollwork. The European walnut stock is in the Boutet style. Spur-style trigger guard. Fully adjustable elevating rear sight. Dovetailed front sight adjustable for windage. **Barrel length:** 9". **Overall length:** 15". **Weight:** 2 lbs. 2 oz. **Rec. ball diameter:** 420 R.B.

**Le Page Percussion** . . . . . . . . . . . . . . . . . . . . . . $500.00

# NAVY ARMS

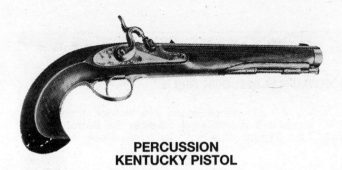

**PERCUSSION
KENTUCKY PISTOL**

**FLINTLOCK
KENTUCKY PISTOL**

## KENTUCKY PISTOLS

The Kentucky Pistol is truly a historical American gun. It was carried during the Revolution by the Minutemen and was the sidearm of "Andy" Jackson in the Battle of New Orleans. Navy Arms Company has conducted extensive research to manufacture a pistol representative of its kind, with the balance and handle of the original for which it became famous.

| | |
|---|---|
| Flintlock. . . . . . . . . . . . . . . . . . . . . . . . . . . . . . . . | $225.00 |
| Single Cased Flintlock Set. . . . . . . . . . . . . . . . . . | 350.00 |
| Double Cased Flintlock Set. . . . . . . . . . . . . . . . | 580.00 |
| Percussion . . . . . . . . . . . . . . . . . . . . . . . . . . . . . | 215.00 |
| Single Cased Percussion Set . . . . . . . . . . . . . . | 335.00 |
| Double Cased Percussion Set. . . . . . . . . . . . . . | 550.00 |

**1806 HARPERS FERRY
FLINTLOCK PISTOL**

### 1806 HARPERS FERRY PISTOL

Of all the early American martial pistols, Harpers Ferry is one of the best known and was carried by both the Army and the Navy. Navy Arms Company has authentically reproduced the Harper's Ferry to the finest detail, providing a well-balanced and well-made pistol. **Weight:** 2 lbs. 9 oz. **Barrel length:** 10″. **Overall length:** 16″. **Caliber:** 58. **Finish:** Walnut stock; case-hardened lock; brass-mounted browned barrel.

| | |
|---|---|
| Harpers Ferry . . . . . . . . . . . . . . . . . . . . . . . . . . . | $310.00 |
| Single Cased Set . . . . . . . . . . . . . . . . . . . . . . . . . | 355.00 |

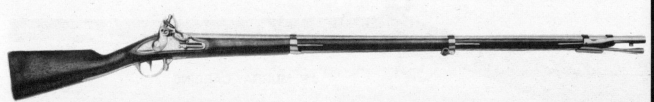

### 1816 M.T. WICKHAM MUSKET

This version of the French 1777 Charleville musket was chosen by the U.S. Army in 1816 to replace the 1808 Springfield. Manufactured in Philadelphia by M.T. Wickham, it was one of the last contract models. **Caliber:** 69. **Barrel length:** 44½″. **Overall length:** 56¼″. **Weight:** 10 lbs. **Sights:** Brass blade front. **Stock:** European walnut. **Feature:** Brass flash-pan.

**1816 M.T. Wickham Musket** . . . . . . . . . . . . . . . . $810.00

**BLACK POWDER**

# NAVY ARMS RIFLES

### MORTIMER FLINTLOCK RIFLE

This big-bore flintlock rifle, a replica of the Mortimer English-style flintlock smoothbore, features a waterproof pan, roller frizzen and external safety. **Caliber:** 54. **Barrel length:** 36″. **Overall length:** 53″. **Weight:** 7 lbs. **Sights:** Blade front; notch rear. **Stock:** Walnut.

**Mortimer Flintlock Rifle** . . . . . . . . . . . . . . . . . . . . . . . . . . . . . . . . . . . . . . . . . . . . . . **$780.00**
   12-gauge drop-in barrel . . . . . . . . . . . . . . . . . . . . . . . . . . . . . . . . . . . . . . . . . . . 340.00

### MORTIMER FLINTLOCK MATCH RIFLE

This is the sleek match version of the large-bore rifle above. **Caliber:** .54. **Barrel length:** 36″. **Overall length:** 52¼″. **Weight:** 9 lbs. **Sights:** Precision aperture match rear; globe-style front. **Stock:** Walnut with cheekpiece, checkered wrist, sling swivels. **Features:** Waterproof pan; roller frizzen; external safety.

**Mortimer Flintlock Match Rifle** . . . . . . . . . . . . . . . . . . . . . . . . . . . . . . . . . . . . . . . **$900.00**

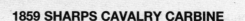

### 1859 SHARPS CAVALRY CARBINE

This percussion version of the Sharps is a copy of the popular breechloading Cavalry Carbine of the Civil War. It features a patchbox and bar and saddle ring on left side of the stock. **Caliber:** 54. **Barrel length:** 22″. **Overall length:** 39″. **Weight:** 7¾ lbs. **Sights:** Blade front; military ladder rear.
**Stock:** Walnut.

**Sharps Cavalry Carbine** . . . . . . . . . . . . . . . . . . . . . . . . . . . . . . . . . . . . . . . . . . . **$ 885.00**
Also available:
**1859 Sharps Infantry Rifle** (54 cal.) . . . . . . . . . . . . . . . . . . . . . . . . . . . . . . . . . . 1030.00

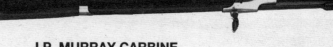

### J.P. MURRAY CARBINE

Popular with the Confederate Cavalry, the J.P. Murray percussion carbine was originally manufactured in Columbus, Georgia, during the Civil War. **Caliber:** 58. **Barrel length:** 23½″. **Overall length:** 39¼″. **Weight:** 8 lbs. 5 oz.
**Finish:** Walnut stock with polished brass.

**J.P. Murray Carbine** . . . . . . . . . . . . . . . . . . . . . . . . . . . . . . . . . . . . . . . . . . . . . . . **$405.00**

# NAVY ARMS RIFLES

### 1853 ENFIELD RIFLE MUSKET

The Enfield Rifle Musket marked the zenith in design and manufacture of the military percussion rifle, and this perfection has been reproduced by Navy Arms Company. This and other Enfield muzzleloaders were the most coveted rifles of the Civil War, treasured by Union and Confederate troops alike for their fine quality and deadly accuracy. **Caliber:** 58. **Barrel length:** 39″. **Weight:** 10 lbs. 6 oz. **Overall length:** 55″. **Sights:** Fixed front; graduated rear. **Stock:** Seasoned walnut with solid brass furniture.

1853 Enfield Rifle Musket . . . . . . . . . . . . . . . . . . . . . . . . . . . . . . . . . . . . . . . . . . . . . $480.00

### 1858 ENFIELD RIFLE

In the late 1850s the British Admiralty, after extensive experiments, settled on a pattern rifle with a 5-groove barrel of heavy construction, sighted to 1,100 yards, designated the Naval rifle, Pattern 1858. **Caliber:** 58. **Barrel length:** 33″. **Weight:** 9 lbs. 10 oz. **Overall length:** 48.5″. **Sights:** Fixed front; graduated rear. **Stock:** Seasoned walnut w/solid brass furniture.

1858 Enfield Rifle . . . . . . . . . . . . . . . . . . . . . . . . . . . . . . . . . . . . . . . . . . . . . . . . . . . . $450.00

### 1861 MUSKETOON

The 1861 Enfield Musketoon was the favorite long arm of the Confederate Cavalry. **Caliber:** 58. **Barrel length:** 24″. **Weight:** 7 lbs. 8 oz. **Overall length:** 40.25″. **Sights:** Fixed front; graduated rear. **Stock:** Seasoned walnut with solid brass furniture.

1861 Musketoon . . . . . . . . . . . . . . . . . . . . . . . . . . . . . . . . . . . . . . . . . . . . . . . . . . . . . $405.00
Kit . . . . . . . . . . . . . . . . . . . . . . . . . . . . . . . . . . . . . . . . . . . . . . . . . . . . . . . . . . . . . . . . 365.00

### ITHACA/NAVY HAWKEN RIFLE

Features a 31½″ octagonal browned barrel crowned at the muzzle with buckhorn-style rear sight, blade front sight. Color casehardened percussion lock is fitted on walnut stock. **Calibers:** 50 and 54.

Ithaca/Navy Hawken Rifle . . . . . . . . . . . . . . . . . . . . . . . . . . . . . . . . . . . . . . . . . . . . . $445.00

# NAVY ARMS RIFLES

## MISSISSIPPI RIFLE MODEL 1841

This historic percussion weapon gained its name because of its performance in the hands of Jefferson Davis' Mississippi Regiment during the heroic stand at the Battle of Buena Vista. Also known as the "Yager" (a misspelling of the German Jaeger), this was one of the first percussion rifles adopted by Army Ordnance. The Mississippi is handsomely furnished in brass, including patchbox for tools and spare parts. **Weight:** 9½ lbs. **Barrel length:** 32½". **Overall length:** 48½". **Calibers:** 54 and 58. **Finish:** Walnut finish stock, brass mounted.

**Mississippi Rifle Model 1841** . . . . . . . . . . . . . . . . . . . . . . . . . . . . . . . . . . . . . . . . **$465.00**

## SMITH CARBINE

The Smith Carbine was considered one of the finest breechloading carbines of the Civil War period. The hinged breech action allowed fast reloading for cavalry units. Available in either the **Cavalry Model** (with saddle ring and bar) or **Artillery Model** (with sling swivels). **Caliber:** 50. **Barrel length:** 21½". **Overall length:** 39". **Weight:** 7¾ lbs. **Sights:** Brass blade front; folding ladder rear. **Stock:** American walnut.

**Smith Carbine** . . . . . . . . . . . . . . . . . . . . . . . . . . . . . . . . . . . . . . . . . . . . . . . . . **$600.00**

## 1861 SPRINGFIELD RIFLE

One of the most popular Union rifles of the Civil War, the 1861 used the 1855-style hammer. The lockplate on this replica is marked "1861, U.S. Springfield." **Caliber:** 58. **Barrel length:** 40". **Overall length:** 56". **Weight:** 10 lbs. **Finish:** Walnut stock with polished metal lock and stock fitting.

**1861 Springfield Rifle** . . . . . . . . . . . . . . . . . . . . . . . . . . . . . . . . . . . . . . . . . . . **$550.00**

## 1863 SPRINGFIELD RIFLE

An authentically reproduced replica of one of America's most historical firearms, the 1863 Springfield rifle features a full-size, three-band musket and precision-rifled barrel. **Caliber:** 58. **Barrel length:** 40". **Overall length:** 56". **Weight:** 9½ lbs. **Finish:** Walnut stock with polished metal lock and stock fittings. Casehardened lock available upon request.

**1863 Springfield Rifle** . . . . . . . . . . . . . . . . . . . . . . . . . . . . . . . . . . . . . . . . . . . **$550.00**

# NAVY ARMS

## PENNSYLVANIA LONG RIFLE

This new version of the Pennsylvania Rifle is an authentic reproduction of the original model. Its classic lines are accented by the long, browned octagon barrel and polished lockplate. **Caliber:** 32 or 45 (flint or percussion. **Barrel length:** 40½″. **Overall length:** 56½″. **Weight:** 7½ lbs. **Sights:** Blade front; adjustable Buckhorn rear. **Stock:** Walnut.

**Pennsylvania Long Rifle** Flintlock . . . . . . . . . . . . . . . . . . . . . . . . . . . . . . . . . . . . . **$475.00**
    Percussion . . . . . . . . . . . . . . . . . . . . . . . . . . . . . . . . . . . . . . . . . . . . . . . . . . 460.00

## BROWN BESS MUSKET

Used extensively in the French and Indian War, the Brown Bess Musket proved itself in the American Revolution as well. This fine replica of the "Second Model" is marked "Grice" on the lockplate. **Caliber:** 75. **Barrel length:** 42″. **Overall length:** 59″. **Weight:** 9½ lbs. **Sights:** Lug front. **Stock:** Walnut.

**Brown Bess Musket** . . . . . . . . . . . . . . . . . . . . . . . . . . . . . . . . . . . . . . . . . . . . . . **$750.00**
**Kit** . . . . . . . . . . . . . . . . . . . . . . . . . . . . . . . . . . . . . . . . . . . . . . . . . . . . . . . . . . 625.00

Also available:
**Brown Bess Carbine**
**Caliber:** 75. **Barrel length:** 30″. **Overall length:** 47″. **Weight:** 7¾ lbs.
**Price**. . . . . . . . . . . . . . . . . . . . . . . . . . . . . . . . . . . . . . . . . . . . . . . . . . . . . . . . . **$750.00**

## 1803 HARPERS FERRY RIFLE

This 1803 Harpers Ferry rifle was carried by Lewis and Clark on their expedition to explore the Northwest territory. This replica of the first rifled U.S. Martial flintlock features a browned barrel, casehardened lock and a brass patchbox. **Caliber:** 54. **Barrel length:** 35″. **Overall length:** 50½″. **Weight:** 8½ lbs.

**1803 Harpers Ferry Rifle** . . . . . . . . . . . . . . . . . . . . . . . . . . . . . . . . . . . . . . . . . . **$615.00**

## "BERDAN" 1859 SHARPS RIFLE

A replica of the Union sniper rifle used by Col. Hiram Berdan's First and Second U.S. Sharpshooters Regiments during the Civil War. **Caliber:** 54. **Barrel length:** 30″. **Overall length:** 46¾″. **Weight:** 8 lbs. 8 oz. **Sights:** Military-style ladder rear; blade front. **Stock:** Walnut. **Features:** Double-set triggers, casehardened receiver; patchbox and furniture.

**"Berdan" 1859 Sharps Rifle** . . . . . . . . . . . . . . . . . . . . . . . . . . . . . . . . . . . . . . . **$1095.00**
Also available:
**Single Trigger Infantry Model** . . . . . . . . . . . . . . . . . . . . . . . . . . . . . . . . . . . . . . 1030.00

**BLACK POWDER**

# NAVY ARMS RIFLES

## 1862 C.S. RICHMOND RIFLE

This model was manufactured by the Confederacy at the Richmond Armory utilizing 1855 Rifle Musket parts captured from the Harpers Ferry Arsenal. This replica features the unusual 1855 lockplate, stamped "1862 C.S. Richmond, V.A." **Caliber:** 58. **Barrel length:** 40″. **Overall length:** 56″. **Weight:** 10 lbs. **Finish:** Walnut stock with polished metal lock and stock fittings.

**1862 C.S. Richmond Rifle** . . . . . . . . . . . . . . . . . . . . . . . . . . . . . . . . . . . . . . . . . . **$550.00**

## TRYON CREEDMOOR RIFLE

This replica of the Tryon Creedmoor match rifle won a Gold Medal at the 13th World Shoot in Germany. It features a blued octagonal heavy match barrel, hooded target front sight, adjustable Vernier tang sight, double-set triggers, sling swivels and a walnut stock. **Caliber:** 451. **Barrel length:** 33″. **Overall length:** 48¼″. **Weight:** 9½ lbs.

**Tryon Creedmoor Rifle** . . . . . . . . . . . . . . . . . . . . . . . . . . . . . . . . . . . . . . . . . . . . . **$780.00**

## KODIAK DOUBLE RIFLE

The powerful double-barreled Kodiak percussion rifle has fully adjustable sights mounted on blued steel barrels. The lockplates are engraved and highly polished. **Calibers:** 50, 54 and 58. **Barrel length:** 28½″. **Overall length:** 45″. **Weight:** 11 lbs. **Sights:** Folding notch rear; ramp bead front. **Stock:** Hand-checkered walnut.

**Kodiak Double Rifle** . . . . . . . . . . . . . . . . . . . . . . . . . . . . . . . . . . . . . . . . . . . . . . . **$775.00**

## "COUNTRY BOY" IN-LINE RIFLE
### $165.00   $175.00 (w/Satin Chrome Finish)

The Navy Arms "Country Boy" incorporates a trap in the buttstock for storage of a takedown tool for removing the breech plug or nipple in the field. It is also capable of replacing the #11 nipple with the hotter musket type. **Caliber:** 50. **Barrel length:** 24″ (rate of twist 1:32). **Overall length:** 41″. **Weight:** 8 lbs. **Sights:** Bead front, adjustable rear. **Features:** Chrome-lined barrel; weather-resistant synthetic stock; drilled and tapped for scope mount.

# NAVY ARMS SHOTGUNS

### MORTIMER FLINTLOCK SHOTGUN

This replica of the Mortimer Shotgun features a browned barrel, casehardened furniture, sling swivels and checkered walnut stock. The lock contains waterproof pan, roller frizzen and external safety. **Gauge:** 12. **Barrel length:** 36″. **Overall length:** 53″. **Weight:** 7 lbs.

**Mortimer Flintlock Shotgun** . . . . . . . . . . . . . . . . . . . . . . . . . . . . . . . . . . . . . . . . . . . $735.00

### STEEL SHOT MAGNUM SHOTGUN

This shotgun, designed for the hunter who must use steel shot, features engraved polished lockplates, English-style checkered walnut stock (with cheekpiece) and chrome-lined barrels. **Gauge:** 10. **Barrel length:** 28″. **Overall length:** 45½″. **Weight:** 7 lbs. 9 oz. **Choke:** Cylinder/Cylinder.

**Steel-Shot Magnum Shotgun** . . . . . . . . . . . . . . . . . . . . . . . . . . . . . . . . . . . . . . . . . . $560.00

### FOWLER SHOTGUN

A traditional side-by-side percussion field gun, this fowler model features blued barrels and English-style straight stock design. It also sports a hooked breech, engraved and color casehardened locks, double triggers and checkered walnut stock. **Gauge:** 12. **Chokes:** Cylinder/Cylinder. **Barrel length:** 28″. **Overall length:** 44½″. **Weight:** 7½ lbs.

**Fowler Shotgun** . . . . . . . . . . . . . . . . . . . . . . . . . . . . . . . . . . . . . . . . . . . . . . . . . . . . $340.00
**Kit** . . . . . . . . . . . . . . . . . . . . . . . . . . . . . . . . . . . . . . . . . . . . . . . . . . . . . . . . . . . . . . . . 310.00

### T & T SHOTGUN

This Turkey and Trap side-by-side percussion shotgun, choked Full/Full, features a genuine walnut stock with checkered wrist and oil finish, color casehardened locks and blued barrels. **Gauge:** 12. **Barrel length:** 28″. **Overall length:** 44″. **Weight:** 7½ lbs.

**T & T Shotgun** . . . . . . . . . . . . . . . . . . . . . . . . . . . . . . . . . . . . . . . . . . . . . . . . . . . . . $540.00

**BLACK POWDER**

# PEIFER RIFLES

**MODEL TS-93**

**MODEL TS-93BA**

### MODELS TS-93/93BA

## SPECIFICATIONS
**Calibers:** 45 and 50
**Barrel length:** 24″ (8 lands/grooves); 1:20″ twist (45 cal.); 1:28″ twist (50 cal.)
**Overall length:** 43.25″
**Weight:** 7 lbs.
**Trigger:** Single acting, adjustable (2.5–5 lbs. pull)
**Safety:** Automatic on, push-to-release tang thumb lever; primer holder SAFE or FIRE position
**Sights:** Williams adjustable rear and gold bead hooded front; drilled and tapped for scope mounts; dovetailed for rear peep sight

**Stock:** Synthetic wood grain; 3 camo patterns or black composite; pistol grip; recoil pad; checkering
**Lock:** In-line, 45# spring; 2″ hammer travel; 416 SS hardened hammer; ambidextrous action; 10:1 power cocking lever operates left or right; ignition by 209 shotshell primer in removable primer holder
**Features:** Extra primer holder; MSM Super-rod ramrod w/ cleaning jag; sling mounts; Allen wrench; breech plug tool
**Prices:**
Models BW, BC and SB . . . . . . . . . . . . . . . . . . . . . $803.00
Models SW & SC Stainless Steel . . . . . . . . . . . . . 876.00
Model BB . . . . . . . . . . . . . . . . . . . . . . . . . . . . . . . . 730.00

# RUGER

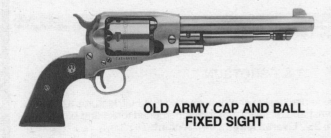

**OLD ARMY CAP AND BALL
FIXED SIGHT**

### OLD ARMY CAP AND BALL
### $413.00    ($495.00 Stainless Steel)

This Old Army cap-and-ball revolver with fixed sights is reminiscent of the Civil War era martial revolvers and those used by the early frontiersmen in the 1800s. This Ruger model comes in both blued and stainless-steel finishes and features modern materials, technology and design throughout, including steel music-wire coil springs. Fixed or adjustable sights. Also available with ivory grips.

## SPECIFICATIONS
**Caliber:** 45 (.443″ bore; .45″ groove)
**Barrel length:** 7 1/2″    **Weight:** 2 7/8 lbs.
**Rifling:** 6 grooves, R.H. twist (1:16″)
**Sights:** Fixed, ramp front; topstrap channel rear
**Percussion cap nipples:** Stainless steel (#11)

# PRAIRIE RIVER ARMS

**PRA BULLPUP RIFLE**

## SPECIFICATIONS
**Calibers:** 50 and 54
**Barrel length:** 28″ (1:28″ twist)  **Overall length:** 31¹/₂″
**Weight:** 7¹/₂ lbs.
**Stock:** Hardwood or Black All Weather
**Sights:** Blade front, open adjustable rear

**Features:** Bullpup design, thumbhole stock; patented internal percussion ignition system; left-hand model available. Dovetailed for scope mount; two built-in safety positions; introduced 1995. Made in the U.S.A.
**Prices:**

| | |
|---|---|
| 4140 Alloy barrel, hardwood stock | $375.00 |
| 4140 Alloy barrel, black stock | 390.00 |
| Stainless barrel, hardwood stock | 425.00 |
| Stainless barrel, black stock | 440.00 |

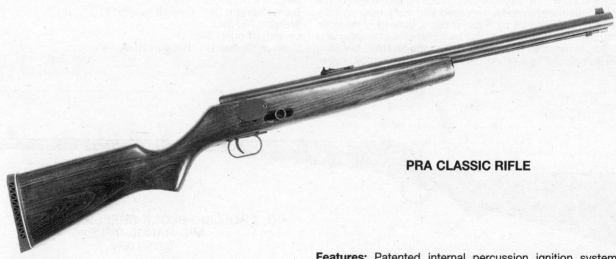

**PRA CLASSIC RIFLE**

## PRA CLASSIC RIFLE

## SPECIFICATIONS
**Calibers:** 50 and 54
**Barrel length:** 26″ (1:28″ twist)  **Overall length:** 40¹/₂″
**Stock:** Hardwood or Black All Weather
**Sights:** Blade front, open adjustable rear

**Features:** Patented internal percussion ignition system; drilled and tapped for scope mount. Only two moving parts; flexible ramrod from hard anodized aluminum; sling swivel studs installed; one screw takedown; introduced 1995. Made in the U.S.A.
**Prices:**

| | |
|---|---|
| 4140 Alloy barrel, hardwood stock | $375.00 |
| 4140 Alloy barrel, black stock | 390.00 |
| Stainless barrel, hardwood stock | 425.00 |
| Stainless barrel, black stock | 440.00 |

**BLACK POWDER**

# REMINGTON RIFLES

**MODEL 700 ML**

**MODEL 700 MLS STAINLESS**

## MODEL 700 ML AND MLS IN-LINE MUZZLELOADING RIFLES
### $372.00 (MODEL ML)   $469.00 (MODEL MLS STAINLESS)

Remington began building flintlock muzzleloaders in 1816. These two in-line muzzleloading rifles have the same cocking action and trigger mechanism as the original versions. The difference comes from a modified bolt and ignition system. The Model 700 ML has a traditionally blued carbon-steel barreled action. On the Model 700 MLS the barrel, receiver and bolt are made of 416 stainless steel with a non-reflective, satin finish. Each is set in a fiberglass-reinforced synthetic stock fitted with a Magnum-style recoil pad. One end of the solid aluminum ramrod is recessed into the forend and the outer end is secured by a barrel band. Instead of an open chamber, the breech is closed by a stainless-steel plug and nipple. In the internal structure of the modified bolt, the firing pin is replaced by a cylindrical rod that is cocked by normal bolt lift. It is released by pulling the trigger to strike a #11 percussion cap seated on the nipple. Lock time is 3.0 milli-seconds. Barrels are rifled with a 1 in 28" twist. The barrels are fitted with standard adjustable iron sights; receivers are drilled and tapped for short-action scope mounts.

Also available w/Mossy Oak Break-Up camo stock: **$405.00 ($503.00** in stainless steel).

**SPECIFICATIONS**
**Barrel length:** 24"   **Overall length:** 44 1/2"
**Weight:** 7 3/4 lbs.
**Length of pull:** 13 3/8"
**Drop at Comb:** 1/2"   **Drop at Heel:** 3/8"

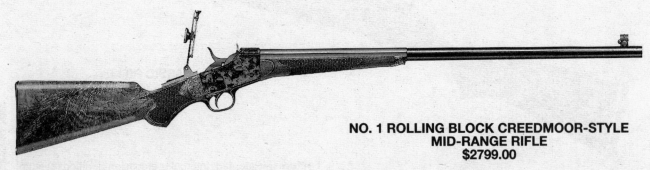

## NO. 1 ROLLING BLOCK CREEDMOOR-STYLE MID-RANGE RIFLE
### $2799.00

Remington's **No. 1 Rolling Block Mid-Range Rifle** is not a replica, but a reintroduction of the original design that was produced from 1875 to 1890. It features a 30-inch, half-octagon, half-round tapered barrel chambered for the 45-70 Government round, with 1:18" twist and six-groove rifling. A case-colored receiver extends through the integral trigger guard at the bottom. The steel forend tip is also case-colored. The trigger and rolling-block breech bolt and hammer are niter-blued and the barrel is finished with standard bluing (all barrel, receiver and metalwork markings duplicate those of original production). Sights include a rear, tang-mounted vernier sight and a front globe sight with four interchangeable inserts and traditional spirit lever. A single set trigger completes the action. The original stock is fancy American walnut with extensive cut-checkering on forend and pistol grip. A hard case with interior fitted compartments of green billiard felt and outside appointments of duck canvas with genuine leather end trip are standard.

# SHILOH SHARPS

## MODEL 1874 BUSINESS RIFLE
### $1210.00

**Calibers:** 45-70, 45-90, 45-120, 50-70 and 50-90.
**Barrel:** 28-inch heavy-tapered round; dark blue.
**Features:** Double-set triggers adjustable set. Blade-front sight with sporting-leaf rear. Buttstock is straight grip rifle buttplate, forend sporting schnabel style. Receiver group and buttplate case-colored; wood is American walnut oil-finished.
**Weight:** 9 lbs. 8 oz.
Other **Model 1874 Black Powder Metallic Cartridge Rifles** available:
THE HARTFORD . . . . . . . . . . . . . . . . . . . . . . . . . . . . . . . . . . . . . . . . . . . . . $1374.00
THE SADDLE RIFLE . . . . . . . . . . . . . . . . . . . . . . . . . . . . . . . . . . . 1262.00

## MODEL 1874 SPORTING RIFLE NO. 1
### $1308.00

**Calibers:** 45-70, 45-90, 45-120, 50-70 and 50-90.
**Features:** 30-inch tapered octagon barrel. Double-set triggers with adjustable set, blade front sight, sporting rear with elevation leaf and sporting tang sight adjustable for elevation and windage. Buttstock is pistol grip, shotgun butt, sporting forend style. Receiver group and buttplate case colored. Barrel is high-finish blue-black; wood is American walnut oil finish.

## MODEL 1874 SPORTING RIFLE NO. 3
### $1204.00

**Calibers:** 45-70, 45-90, 45-120, 50-70 and 50-90.
**Barrel:** 30-inch tapered octagonal; with high finish blue-black.
**Features:** Double-set triggers with adjustable set, blade front sight, sporting rear with elevation leaf and sporting tang sight adjustable for elevation and windage. Buttstock is straight grip with rifle buttplate; trigger plate is curved and checkered to match pistol grip. Forend is sporting schnabel style. Receiver group and buttplate are case colored. Wood is oil-finished American walnut, and may be upgraded in all rifles.
**Weight:** 9 lbs. 8 oz.
Also available:
MODEL 1874 LONG-RANGE EXPRESS . . . . . . . . . . . . . . . . . . . . $1334.00
MODEL 1874 MONTANA ROUGHRIDER . . . . . . . . . . . . . . . . . . . . 1204.00
HARTFORD MODEL . . . . . . . . . . . . . . . . . . . . . . . . . . . . . . . . . . . . 1374.00

CUSTOM RIFLES:
CREEDMOOR TARGET RIFLE (32″ Barrel) . . . . . . . . . . . . . . . . . . . $2374.00
MIDRANGE RIFLE (30″ Barrel) . . . . . . . . . . . . . . . . . . . . . . . . . . . . 2224.00
SCHUETZEN RIFLE (28″ Half-octagon) . . . . . . . . . . . . . . . . . . . . . 2062.00
QUIGLEY RIFLE (34″ Heavy Barrel) . . . . . . . . . . . . . . . . . . . . . . . . 2660.00

**BLACK POWDER**

# THOMPSON/CENTER

### PENNSYLVANIA HUNTER FLINTLOCK RIFLE

The 31″ barrel on this model is cut rifled (.010″ deep) with 1 turn in 66″ twist. Its outer contour is stepped from octagon to round. Sights are fully adjustable for both windage and elevation. Stocked with select American black walnut; metal hardware is blued steel. Features a hooked breech system and coil-spring lock, plus T/C's QLA™ Muzzle System for improved accuracy and easier reloading. **Caliber:** 50. **Overall length:** 48″. **Weight:** Approx. 7.6 lbs.

**Pennsylvania Hunter Flintlock** . . . . . . . . . . . . . . . . . . . . . . . . . . . . . $375.00
Also available:
**Pennsylvania Match Rifle.** Caplock w/tang-style peep sight and
    globe front sight . . . . . . . . . . . . . . . . . . . . . . . . . . . . . . . . . . . . . . 400.00

### PENNSYLVANIA HUNTER FLINTLOCK CARBINE

Thompson/Center's Pennsylvania Hunter Flintlock Carbine is 50-caliber with 1:66″ twist and cut-rifling. It was designed specifically for the hunter who uses patched round balls only and hunts in thick cover or brush. The 21″ barrel is stepped from octagonal to round. Features T/C's QLA™ Muzzle System. **Overall length:** 38″. **Weight:** 6½ lbs. **Sights:** Fully adjustable open hunting-style rear with bead front. **Stock:** Select American walnut. **Trigger:** Single hunting-style trigger. **Lock:** Color cased, coil spring, with floral design.

**Pennsylvania Hunter Flintlock Carbine** . . . . . . . . . . . . . . . . . . . . . . . $365.00

### THE NEW ENGLANDER RIFLE

This percussion rifle features a 26″ round, 50- or 54-caliber rifled barrel (1 in 48″ twist). Contains T/C's QLA™ Muzzle System. **Weight:** 7 lbs. 15 oz.

**New Englander Rifle** . . . . . . . . . . . . . . . . . . . . . . . . . . . . . . . . . . . . . $310.00
**Left-Hand Model** . . . . . . . . . . . . . . . . . . . . . . . . . . . . . . . . . . . . . . . . 330.00

### THE NEW ENGLANDER SHOTGUN

This 12-gauge muzzleloading percussion shotgun weighs only 6 lbs. 8 oz. It features a 27-inch (screw-in IC choke) round barrel and is stocked with select American black walnut. Additional choke tubes available in Modified and Full.

**New Englander Shotgun** . . . . . . . . . . . . . . . . . . . . . . . . . . . . . . . . . . . $330.00
    12-Gauge Accessory Barrel, IC Choke . . . . . . . . . . . . . . . . . . . . . . 170.00

# THOMPSON/CENTER

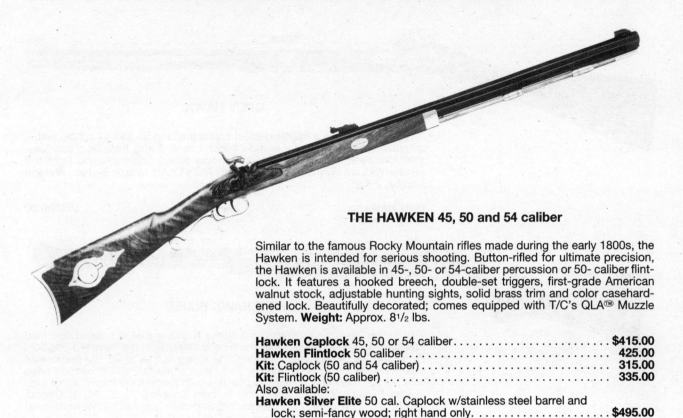

### THE HAWKEN 45, 50 and 54 caliber

Similar to the famous Rocky Mountain rifles made during the early 1800s, the Hawken is intended for serious shooting. Button-rifled for ultimate precision, the Hawken is available in 45-, 50- or 54-caliber percussion or 50- caliber flintlock. It features a hooked breech, double-set triggers, first-grade American walnut stock, adjustable hunting sights, solid brass trim and color casehardened lock. Beautifully decorated; comes equipped with T/C's QLA™ Muzzle System. **Weight:** Approx. 8½ lbs.

**Hawken Caplock** 45, 50 or 54 caliber. . . . . . . . . . . . . . . . . . . . . . . $415.00
**Hawken Flintlock** 50 caliber . . . . . . . . . . . . . . . . . . . . . . . . . . . 425.00
**Kit:** Caplock (50 and 54 caliber) . . . . . . . . . . . . . . . . . . . . . . . . . . 315.00
**Kit:** Flintlock (50 caliber) . . . . . . . . . . . . . . . . . . . . . . . . . . . . . 335.00
Also available:
**Hawken Silver Elite** 50 cal. Caplock w/stainless steel barrel and
    lock; semi-fancy wood; right hand only. . . . . . . . . . . . . . . . . . $495.00

### THE RENEGADE

Available in 50- or 54-caliber percussion, the Renegade was designed to provide maximum accuracy and maximum shocking power. It is constructed of superior modern steel with investment cast parts fitted to an American walnut stock, featuring a precision-rifled (26-inch carbine-type) octagonal barrel, hooked-breech system, coil spring lock, double-set triggers, adjustable hunting sights and steel trim. Features T/C's QLA™ Muzzle System. **Overall length:** 42½". **Weight:** Approx. 8 lbs.

**Renegade Caplock** 50 and 54 caliber. . . . . . . . . . . . . . . . . . . . $360.00

**BLACK POWDER**

# THOMPSON/CENTER

### GREY HAWK

T/C's Grey Hawk is a stainless-steel caplock rifle in 50 and 54 caliber with a composite buttstock and a round 24-inch barrel. It also features a stainless-steel lockplate, hammer, thimble and trigger guard. Adjustable rear sight and bead-style front sight are blued. Includes T/C's QLA™ Muzzle System. **Weight:** Approx. 7 lbs.

**Grey Hawk** . . . . . . . . . . . . . . . . . . . . . . . . . . . . . . . . . . . . . . . . . . . . . . . . $330.00

### FIRE HAWK BLUED

This in-line ignition muzzleloader features a striker that is cocked and held rearward, locked in place when the thumb safety is in the rearward position. By sliding the thumb safety forward, the striker is free to fire the percussion cap when the trigger is pulled. The Fire Hawk's free-floated 24″ barrel is rifled with a 1:38″ twist and is designed for use with modern conical or sabot projectiles. Features T/C's QLA™ Muzzle System. **Calibers:** 32, 50, 54, 58. **Overall length:** 41³/₄″. **Weight:** 7 lbs. **Sights:** Adj. leaf-style rear; ramp-style white bead front. **Stock:** American black walnut or Composite.
Also available:
| | |
|---|---|
| **Blued** w/walnut stock in all calibers . . . . . . . . . . . . . . . . . . . . . . . . . | $365.00 |
| **Blued** w/thumbhole composite stock. . . . . . . . . . . . . . . . . . . . . . . | 385.00 |
| **Blued** w/Advantage camo composite stock . . . . . . . . . . . . . . . . . | 395.00 |
| **Stainless Steel** w/composite stock . . . . . . . . . . . . . . . . . . . . . . . . | 395.00 |
| **Stainless Steel** w/walnut stock . . . . . . . . . . . . . . . . . . . . . . . . . . . | 405.00 |
| **Stainless Steel** w/thumbhole composite stock . . . . . . . . . . . . . . . | 425.00 |
| **Deluxe SST** w/walnut stock in 50 and 54 cal. . . . . . . . . . . . . . . . . | 535.00 |
| **Deluxe blued** w/walnut in 50 and 54 cal. . . . . . . . . . . . . . . . . . . . | 495.00 |
| **Bantam** (21″ barrel) w/walnut stock . . . . . . . . . . . . . . . . . . . . . . . | 365.00 |

### FIRE HAWK DELUXE BLUED

### FIRE HAWK ADVANTAGE™ CAMO MODEL

### SCOUT RIFLE, CARBINE & PISTOL

**SCOUT CARBNIE with Rynite Stock**

Thompson/Center's Scout Carbine & Pistol use the in-line ignition system with a special vented breechplug that produces constant pressures from shot to shot, thereby improving accuracy. The patented trigger mechanism consists of only two moving parts—the trigger and the hammer—thus providing ease of operation and low maintenance. Features T/C's QLA™ Muzzle System. Both the carbine and pistol are available in 50 and 54 caliber. The carbine's 21″ (round) and 24″ (stepped) barrels and the pistol's 12-inch barrel (overall length: 17″) are easily removable for cleaning. Their lines are reminiscent of the saddle guns and pistols of the "Old West," combining modern-day engineering with the flavor of the past. Both are suitable for left- or right--handed shooters.

**Scout Rifle** w/walnut stock . . . . . . . . . . . . . . . . . . . . . . . . . . . . . . . . **$435.00**
   With Composite stock . . . . . . . . . . . . . . . . . . . . . . . . . . . . . . . . . . 360.00
**Scout Carbine** w/walnut stock . . . . . . . . . . . . . . . . . . . . . . . . . . . . . . 425.00
   With composite stock. . . . . . . . . . . . . . . . . . . . . . . . . . . . . . . . . . . 345.00
**Scout Pistol** (50 and 54 cal.) . . . . . . . . . . . . . . . . . . . . . . . . . . . . . . . 350.00

### THUNDER HAWK

**THUNDER HAWK**

Thompson/Center's in-line caplock rifle, the Thunder Hawk, combines the features of an old-time caplock with the look and balance of a modern bolt-action rifle. The in-line ignition system ensures fast, positive ignition, plus an adjustable trigger for a crisp trigger pull. The 21-inch and 24-inch barrels have an adjustable rear sight and bead-style front sight (barrel is drilled and tapped to accept T/C's Thunder Hawk scope rings, Weaver-style base and rings, or Quick-Release Mounting System). The stock is American black walnut with rubber recoil pad and sling swivel studs. Rifling is 1:38″ twist, designed to fire patched round balls, conventional conical projectiles and sabot bullets. Includes T/C's QLA™ Muzzle System. **Weight:** Approx. 6¾ lbs. **Calibers:** 50, 54.

**Thunder Hawk** w/21″ barrel, blued w/walnut stock. . . . . . . . . . . . . . . **$315.00**
   Stainless steel w/composite stock. . . . . . . . . . . . . . . . . . . . . . . . . . 335.00
**Thunder Hawk** w/24″ barrel
   Stainless steel with composite stock. . . . . . . . . . . . . . . . . . . . . . . . 345.00
   Blued steel with Advantage Camo composite stock. . . . . . . . . . . . 305.00
   Blued steel with walnut stock . . . . . . . . . . . . . . . . . . . . . . . . . . . . . 325.00

### THUNDERHAWK SHADOW

**SST THUNDERHAWK SHADOW**

These 50 and 54 caliber rifles are also available w/21″ or 24″ barrels and several combinations of finishes.

**Advantage Camo composite stock, blued barrel** . . . . . . . . . . . . . . **$305.00**
w/Value Pack (includes powder measure, nipple wrench, T-handle short starter, Break-O-Way sabots, Star-7 capper, cleaning kit). . . . . . . . . 349.00
   Same as above w/Advantage Camo stock (21″ barrel) . . . . . . . . . 379.00
**SST ThunderHawk Shadow** stainless steel barrel
w/composite stock (21″ barrel) . . . . . . . . . . . . . . . . . . . . . . . . . . . . . 306.00
   Same as above w/24″ barrel . . . . . . . . . . . . . . . . . . . . . . . . . . . . . . 315.00
w/Value Pack (24″ barrel only) . . . . . . . . . . . . . . . . . . . . . . . . . . . . . 389.00

**BLACK POWDER**

# TRADITIONS PISTOLS

**PIONEER PISTOL**

### PIONEER PISTOL
### $140.00   ($116.25 Kit)

**SPECIFICATIONS**
**Caliber:** 45 percussion
**Barrel length:** $9^5/8''$ octagonal with tenon; $13/16''$ across flats, rifled 1 in 16''; fixed tang breech
**Overall length:** 15''   **Weight:** 1 lb. 15 oz.
**Sights:** Blade front; fixed rear
**Trigger:** Single
**Stock:** Beech, rounded
**Lock:** V-type mainspring
**Features:** German silver furniture; blackened hardware

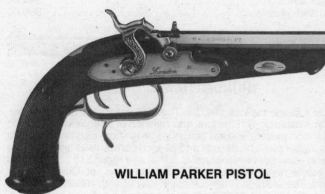

**WILLIAM PARKER PISTOL**

### WILLIAM PARKER PISTOL
### $250.00

**SPECIFICATIONS**
**Caliber:** 50 percussion (1:20'')
**Barrel length:** $10^3/8''$ octagonal ($15/16''$ across flats)
**Overall length:** $17^1/2''$   **Weight:** 2 lbs. 5 oz.
**Sights:** Brass blade front; fixed rear
**Stock:** Walnut, checkered at wrist
**Triggers:** Double set; will fire set and unset
**Lock:** Adjustable sear engagement with fly and bridle; V-type mainspring
**Features:** Brass percussion cap guard; polished hardware, brass inlays and separate ramrod

**TRAPPER PISTOL**

### TRAPPER PISTOL
### $175.00 Percussion   ($131.00 Percussion Kit)
### $189.50 Flintlock

**SPECIFICATIONS**
**Caliber:** 50 percussion or flintlock (1:20'')
**Barrel length:** $9^3/4''$; octagonal ($7/8''$ across flats) with tenon
**Overall length:** $15^1/2''$   **Weight:** 2 lbs. 14 oz.
**Stock:** Beech
**Lock:** Adjustable sear engagement with fly and bridle
**Triggers:** Double set, will fire set and unset
**Sights:** Primitive-style adjustable rear; brass blade front
**Furniture:** Solid brass; blued steel on assembled pistol

# TRADITIONS PISTOLS

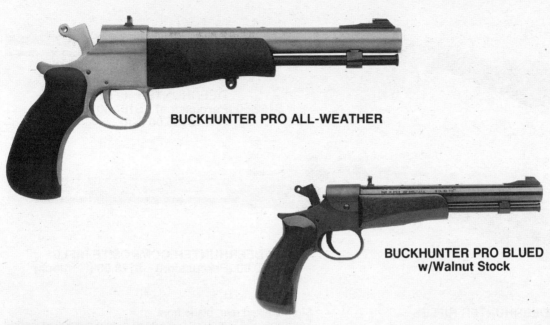

**BUCKHUNTER PRO ALL-WEATHER**

**BUCKHUNTER PRO BLUED**
w/Walnut Stock

## BUCKHUNTER PRO IN-LINE PISTOLS
### $219.00   ($233.75 w/All-Weather Stock)

**SPECIFICATIONS**
**Calibers:** 50 and 54 Percussion
**Barrel length:** 10″ round (removable breech plug); 1:20″ twist
**Overall length:** 14″ or 16½″ (also available w/12″ barrel in wood)
**Weight:** 3 lbs.
**Trigger:** Single
**Sights:** Fold-down adjustable rear; beaded blade front
**Stock:** Walnut or All-Weather
**Features:** Blued or C-Nickel furniture; PVC ramrod; drilled and tapped for scope mounting; coil mainspring; thumb safety

## BUCKSKINNER PISTOL (not shown)
### $145.50

**SPECIFICATIONS**
**Caliber:** 50 percussion (1:20″)
**Barrel length:** 10″ octagonal (⅞″ across flats)
**Overall length:** 15 ½″
**Weight:** 2 lbs. 9 oz.
**Trigger:** Single
**Sights:** Fixed rear; blade front
**Stock:** Beech
**Features:** Blackened furniture; PVC ramrod

**KENTUCKY PISTOL**
$131.00   ($101.25 Kit)

**SPECIFICATIONS**
**Caliber:** 50 Percussion (1:20″)
**Barrel length:** 10″ octagon (⅞″ flats); fixed tang breech; 1:20″ twist
**Overall length:** 15″
**Weight:** 2 lbs. 8 oz.
**Trigger:** Single
**Sights:** Fixed rear; blade front
**Stock:** Beechwood
**Features:** Brass furniture; wood ramrod; kit available

**BLACK POWDER**

# TRADITIONS

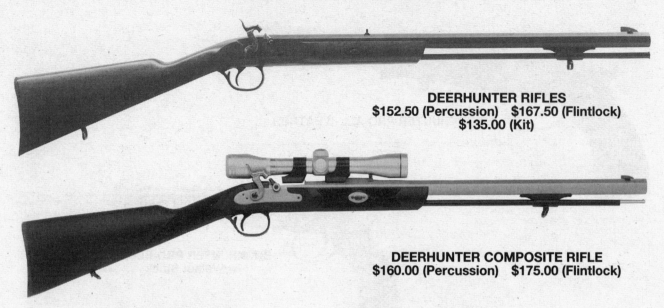

**DEERHUNTER RIFLES**
$152.50 (Percussion)    $167.50 (Flintlock)
$135.00 (Kit)

**DEERHUNTER COMPOSITE RIFLE**
$160.00 (Percussion)    $175.00 (Flintlock)

## DEERHUNTER RIFLES

**SPECIFICATIONS**
**Calibers:** 32, 50 and 54 percussion
**Barrel length:** 24″ octagonal
**Rifling twist:** 1:48″ (percussion only); 1:66″ (flint or percussion)
**Overall length:** 40″
**Weight:** 6 lbs. (6 lbs. 3 oz. in Small Game rifle)
**Trigger:** Single

**Sights:** Fixed rear; blade front
**Features:** PVC ramrod; blackened furniture; inletted wedge plates

Also available:
**COMPOSITE STOCK MODELS**
Percussion w/blued barrel . . . . . . . . . . . . . . . . . . . . . $131.00
Percussion w/nickel barrel . . . . . . . . . . . . . . . . . . . . . 152.50
Flintlock w/nickel barrel and 1:66″ twist. . . . . . . . . . 175.00
**SMALL GAME RIFLE** w/aluminum ramrod. . . . . . . 152.50

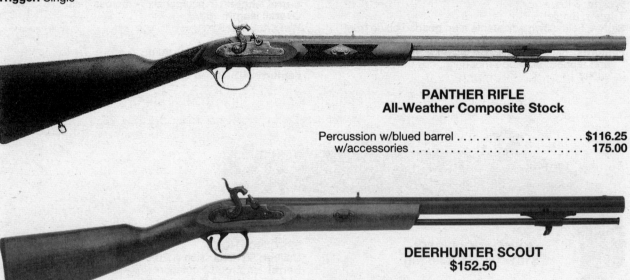

**PANTHER RIFLE**
**All-Weather Composite Stock**

Percussion w/blued barrel . . . . . . . . . . . . . . . . . . . . . $116.25
w/accessories . . . . . . . . . . . . . . . . . . . . . . . . . . . 175.00

**DEERHUNTER SCOUT**
$152.50

**SPECIFICATIONS**
**Caliber:** 50 percussion
**Barrel length:** 22″ octagonal
**Twist:** 1:48″
**Overall length:** 36½″
**Weight:** 5 lbs. 10 oz.

# TRADITIONS

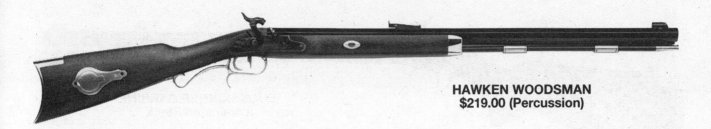

### HAWKEN WOODSMAN
### $219.00 (Percussion)

**SPECIFICATIONS**
**Calibers:** 50 and 54 percussion
**Barrel length:** 28" (octagonal); hooked breech; rifled 1 turn in 48" (1 turn in 66" in 50 caliber also available)
**Overall length:** 44½"
**Weight:** 7 lbs. 11 oz.
**Triggers:** Double set; will fire set or unset
**Lock:** Adjustable sear engagement with fly and bridle

**Stock:** Beech
**Sights:** Beaded blade front; hunting-style rear, fully screw adjustable for windage and elevation
**Furniture:** Solid brass, blued steel or blackened (50 cal. only); unbreakable ramrod
Also available:
Left-Hand model w/1:48" twist . . . . . . . . . . . . . . . $233.75

### PENNSYLVANIA RIFLE
### $463.00 (Flintlock)    $454.00 (Percussion)

**SPECIFICATIONS**
**Caliber:** 50
**Barrel length:** 40¼"; octagonal (⅞" across flats) with 3 pins; rifled 1 turn in 66"
**Overall length:** 57"    **Weight:** 8 lbs. 8 oz.

**Lock:** Adjustable sear engagement with fly and bridle
**Stock:** Walnut, beavertail style
**Triggers:** Double set; will fire set and unset
**Sights:** Primitive-style adjustable rear; brass blade front
**Furniture:** Solid brass, blued steel

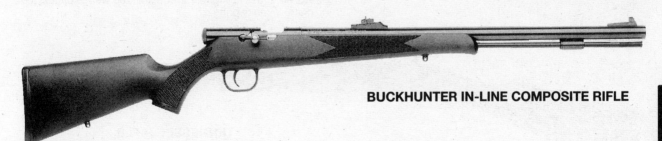

### BUCKHUNTER IN-LINE COMPOSITE RIFLE

**SPECIFICATIONS**
**Calibers:** 50 (1:32") and 54 (2:48") percussion
**Barrel length:** Blued 24" round
**Overall length:** 42"
**Weight:** 7 lbs. 6 oz.
**Stock:** All-Weather Composite (matte black)
**Sights:** Beaded blade front; fully adjustable rear
**Features:** Blackened furniture; PVC ramrod; stainless steel removable breech plug; optional Redi-Pak (includes com-

posite powder flask with valve dispenser, powder measure, two universal fast loaders, 5-in-1 loader, cleaning jab and patches, ball puller, 20 conical bullets, in-line nipple wrench
**Prices:**
Standard 50p or 54p . . . . . . . . . . . . . . . . . . . . . . $160.00
 w/Redi-Pak . . . . . . . . . . . . . . . . . . . . . . . . . . . .   219.00
 w/Redi-Pak plus Pyrodex and percussion
 caps . . . . . . . . . . . . . . . . . . . . . . . . . . . . . . . .   233.75

**BLACK POWDER**

# TRADITIONS

### BUCKSKINNER CARBINE
### Laminated Stock

### BUCKSKINNER CARBINE
**$189.50 (Percussion)   $204.00 (Flintlock)**
**$256.00 (Laminated Stock, Percussion)**
**$277.50 (Laminated Stock, Flintlock)**

**SPECIFICATIONS**
**Caliber:** 50 percussion or flintlock
**Barrel length:** 21″ octagonal-to-round with tenon; 15/16″ across flats; 1:66″ twist (flintlock) and 1:20″ (percussion)

**Overall length:** 36 1/4″   **Weight:** 5 lbs. 15 oz.
**Sights:** Hunting-style, click adjustable rear; beaded blade front with white dot
**Trigger:** Single
**Features:** Blackened furniture; German silver ornamentation; sling swivels; unbreakable ramrod
Also available:
**BUCKSKINNER CARBINE DELUXE**
Percussion w/nickel barrel . . . . . . . . . . . . . . . . . . . $277.50

### KENTUCKY RIFLE

### KENTUCKY RIFLE
**$219.00   ($175.00 Kit)**

**SPECIFICATIONS**
**Caliber:** 50 percussion
**Barrel length:** 33 1/2″ octagon (7/8″ flats); fixed tang; 1:66″ twist

**Overall length:** 49″
**Weight:** 7 lbs.
**Trigger:** Single
**Tenons:** 2 pins
**Stock:** Beechwood
**Sights:** Fixed rear; blade front
**Features:** Brass furniture; ramrod; inletted wedge plates; toe plate; V-mainspring

### TENNESSEE RIFLE

### TENNESSEE RIFLE
**$285.00 (Flintlock)   $270.00 (Percussion)**

**SPECIFICATIONS**
**Caliber:** 50 flintlock or percussion
**Barrel length:** 24″ octagon (7/8″ across flats); hooked breech; 1:32″ twist (percussion) and 1:66″ (flintlock)

**Overall length:** 40 1/2″
**Weight:** 6 lbs.
**Sights:** Fixed rear; blade front
**Stock:** Beechwood
**Features:** Brass furniture; ramrod; inletted wedge plate; stock inlays; toe plate; V-mainspring

# TRADITIONS

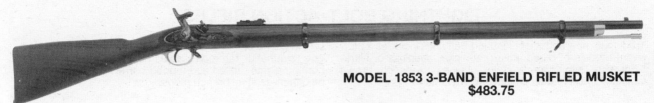

## MODEL 1853 3-BAND ENFIELD RIFLED MUSKET
### $483.75

Carried by Northern and Southern troops alike, the 1853 Enfield was noted for its ability to shoot straight and hard. This fine replica captures all the features of the original, from its full-length walnut stock and color casehardened lock to the solid brass buttplate, trigger guard and nose cap. The 1:48″ rifling and V-spring lock mechanism team with the military sights to make this as much a solid shooter today as the original was in its day. Approved by the North-South Skirmish Association.

**SPECIFICATIONS**
**Caliber:** 58 percussion
**Barrel length:** 39″ round; 1:48″ twist; blued finish; 3 barrel bands
**Overall length:** 55″
**Weight:** 10 lbs.
**Sights:** Military
**Stock:** Walnut
**Features:** Brass furniture; steel ramrod; sling swivels; V-mainspring

## MODEL 1861 U.S. SPRINGFIELD RIFLED MUSKET
### $513.00

The Model 1861 Springfield rifled musket was the principal firearm of the Civil War. By the end of 1863, most Federal infantrymen were armed with either this musket or the Enfield 58-caliber rifled barrel. This faithful replica glows "in the white" as was the original, with a full-length walnut military stock. The authentic sidelock action is accented by markings of "1861 U.S. Springfield" to complement the steel buttplate, wide trigger guard, barrel bands and sling hardware. The steel ramrod, like the original, is of the swelled design. Military-style sights and a long sighting plane make this an accurate long gun approved for use by the North-South Skirmish Association.

**SPECIFICATIONS**
**Caliber:** 58 percussion
**Barrel length:** 40″ round; 1:66″ twist; white steel finish; 3 barrel bands
**Overall length:** 56″
**Weight:** 10 lbs.
**Trigger:** Single
**Sights:** Military
**Stock:** Walnut
**Features:** Steel furniture and ramrod; sling swivels; V-mainspring

## SHENANDOAH RIFLE
### $336.25 (Flintlock)
### $322.00 (Percussion)

The Shenandoah Rifle captures the frontier styling and steady performance of Tradition's Pennsylvania Rifle in a slightly shorter length and more affordable price. Choice of engraved and color casehardened flintlock or percussion V-type mainspring lock with double-set triggers. The full-length stock in walnut finish is accented by a solid brass curved buttplate, inletted patch box, nose cap, thimbles, trigger guard and decorative furniture.

**SPECIFICATIONS**
**Caliber:** 50 (1:66″) flint or percussion
**Barrel length:** 33½″ octagon
**Overall length:** 49½″
**Weight:** 7 lbs. 3 oz.
**Sights:** Buckhorn rear, blade front
**Stock:** Beech

**BLACK POWDER**

# TRADITIONS

## LIGHTNING BOLT-ACTION RIFLES

Traditions' new series of Lightning Bolt rifles includes 21 different models of blued, chemical-nickel, stainless or Ultra-Coat with Teflon barrels. Stock choices are beech, brown laminated, All-Weather Composite, Advantage™ Camo, X-tra brown Camo or Break-up Camo. All models come with rugged synthetic ramrods, adjustable triggers, adjustable hunting sights, drilled and tapped barrels and field-removable stainless steel breech plugs.

**LIGHTNING w/Walnut Stock**

**LIGHTNING w/All-Weather composite Stock**

**LIGHTNING w/Advantage™ Camo Composite Stock**

## SPECIFICATIONS LIGHTNING BOLT ACTION RIFLES

| | | Standard | Laminated | A-W Composite | Stainless Steel | Camo Composite | TEFLON |
|---|---|---|---|---|---|---|---|
| Lock: | action | bolt | bolt | bolt | bolt | bolt | bolt |
| | | in-line percussion | in-line percussion | in-line percussion | in-line percussion | in-line percussion | in-line percussion |
| Stock: | | beech | brown laminated | A-W Composite | A-W Composite | Advantage X-tra Brown, Break-Up | A-W Composite X-tra Brown, Break-Up |
| Caliber. | rifling/twist | .50p (1:32") .54p (1:48") | .50p (1:32") | .50p (1:32") .54p (1:48") | .50p (1:32") .54p (1:48") | .50p (1:32") .54p (1:48") | .50p (1:32") .54p (1:48") |
| Barrel: | length/shape | 24" round | 24" round | 24" round | 24" round | 24" round | 24" round |
| | finish | blued | stainless steel | blued/C-Nickel | stainless steel | blued | TEFLON |
| | breech plug | SS removable | SS removable | SS removable | SS removable | SS removable | SS removable |
| Sights: | rear | fully adjustable | fully adjustable | fully adjustable | fully adjustable | fully adjustable | fully adjustable |
| | front | beaded blade | beaded blade | beaded blade | beaded blade | beaded blade | beaded blade |
| Features: | ramrod | PVC | PVC | PVC | PVC | PVC | PVC |
| Overall length: | | 43" | 43" | 43" | 43" | 43" | 43" |
| Weight: | | 7 lbs., 4 oz. | 7 lbs., 12 oz. | 7 lbs. | 7 lbs. | 7 lbs. | 7 lbs. |
| Models/prices: | | R60002 .50p $277.50 R60048 .54p $277.50 | R62802 .50p $380.00 | R61002 .50p B $262.50 R61048 .54p B $262.50 R61102 .50p N $277.50 R61148 .54p N $277.50 | R61802 .50p SS $307.50 R61848 .54p SS $307.50 | R610022 .50p A $307.50 R610482 .54p A $307.50 R610025 .50p BU $307.50 R610485 .54p BU $307.50 R610024 .50p XB $307.50 R610484 .54p XB $307.50 | R61202 .50p Bl $307.50 R61248 .54p Bl $307.50 R612024 .50p XB $351.25 R612484 .54p XB $351.25 R612025 .50p BU $351.25 R612485 .54p BU $351.25 |

All models are drilled and tapped. N denotes C-Nickel. SS denotes stainless steel. B denotes blued.

Bl denotes matte black All-Weather Composite. A denotes Advantage camouflage. XB denotes X-tra Brown camouflage. BU denotes Break-Up camouflage.

# TRADITIONS

## BUCKHUNTER PRO™ IN-LINE RIFLES/SHOTGUNS

**BUCKHUNTER PRO™ IN-LINE RIFLE**
**w/Walnut-Stained Stock**

**BUCKHUNTER PRO™ IN-LINE RIFLE**
**w/Black Composite Stock, Stainless Barrel,**
**Optional Scope**

Traditions has upgraded its Buckhunter In-Line ignition rifles and shotguns with the new Buckhunter Pro series. The new guns feature an adjustable trigger, thumb safety and a choice of Ultracoat Teflon, C-Nickel, blued or stainless steel barrels. New slimmed-down matte black composite stocks are available as are two camouflage patterns, laminated, thumbhole or walnut-stained stocks. All Buckhunter Pros have field-removable stainless steel breech plugs and improved adjustable hunting sights. The Buckhunter Pro rifles are available in 50 caliber (1:32″) or 54 caliber (1:48″) for use with conical and saboted bullets.

## SPECIFICATIONS AND PRICES

| | | Standard | Laminated | A-W Composite | Thumbhole | TEFLON | Shotgun | Rifle |
|---|---|---|---|---|---|---|---|---|
| Lock: | ignition | in-line | in-line | in-line | in-line | in-line | in-line | in-line |
| | | percussion | percussion | percussion | percussion | percussion | percussion | percussion |
| Stock: | | beech | laminated | A-W Composite | A-W Composite | A-W Composite | A-W Composite | A-W Composite |
| | | | | | Advantage | X-tra Brown, Break-Up | Advantage, Break-Up | |
| Caliber: | rifling/twist | .50p (1:32″) | .50p (1:32″) | .50p (1:32″) | .50p (1:32″) | .50p (1:32″) | 12 Ga | .50p (1:32″) |
| | | | | .54p (1:48″) | | .54p (1:48″) | smoothbore | .54P (1:48″) |
| Barrel: | length/shape | 24″ tapered round | 24″ tapered round | 24″ tapered round | 24″ tapered round | 24″ tapered round | 24″ round | 24″ round |
| | finish | blued | blued/C-Nickel | blued/C-Nickel/SS | blued | TEFLON | matte blued | blued |
| | breech plug | SS removable | SS removable | SS removable | SS removable | SS removable | SS removable | SS removable |
| Sights: | rear | fully adjustable | fully adjustable | fully adjustable | fully adjustable | fully adjustable | n/a | fully adjustable |
| | front | beaded blade | beaded blade | beaded blade | beaded blade | beaded blade | bead | beaded blade |
| Features: | ramrod | PVC | PVC | PVC | PVC | PVC | PVC | PVC |
| Overall length: | | 42″ | 42″ | 42″ | 42½″ | 42″ | 43″ | 42″ |
| Weight: | | 7 lbs., 10 oz. | 7 lbs., 10 oz. | 7 lbs., 5 oz. | 7 lbs., 8 oz. | 7 lbs., 5 oz. | 6 lbs., 4 oz. | 7 lbs., 5 oz. |
| Models/prices: | | R50002 .50p $211.²⁵ | R50202 .50p Bk $315.⁰⁰ | R50102 .50p N $211.²⁵ | R52202 .50p Bl $307.⁵⁰ | R51162 .50p Bl $233.⁷⁵ | S5202 Bl $285.⁰⁰ | R42102 .50p $160.⁰⁰ |
| | | | R50302 .50p Br $292.⁵⁰ | R50148 .54p N $211.²⁵ | R52902 .50p A $336.²⁵ | R51168 .54p Bl $233.⁷⁵ | S5402 A $329.⁰⁰ | R42148 .54p $160.⁰⁰ |
| | | | | R50802 .50p SS $262.⁵⁰ | | R511624 .50p XB $270.⁰⁰ | S5502 BU $329.⁰⁰ | RP42102 .50p $233.⁷⁵ |
| | | | | R51102 .50p B $196.²⁵ | | R511684 .54p XB $270.⁰⁰ | | RP42148 .54p $233.⁷⁵ |
| | | | | R51148 .54p B $196.²⁵ | | R511625 .50p BU $270.⁰⁰ | | RS42102 .50p $219.⁰⁰ |
| | | | | R51302* .50p B $175.⁰⁰ | | R511685 .54p BU $270.⁰⁰ | | RS42148 .54p $219.⁰⁰ |
| | | | | R51302S** .50p B $226.²⁵ | | | | |

All models are drilled and tapped. *No sights option. **Scope & mount option. Br denotes brown laminated/blued. Bk denotes black laminated/C-Nickel. N denotes C-Nickel. SS denotes stainless steel. B denotes blued. Bl denotes matte black All-Weather Composite. A denotes Advantage camouflage. XB denotes X-tra Brown camouflage. BU denotes Break-Up camouflage. RP denotes Redi-Pak™ with Pyrodex® and caps. RS denotes Redi-Pak™ without powder or caps.

**BUCKHUNTER PRO™ IN-LINE**
**12 GAUGE SHOTGUN**

The Buckhunter Pro Series 12 Gauge Shotgun for bird and turkey hunters has the same field-removable stainless steel breech plug, thumb safety and slimmed down stock as the Buckhunter Pro In-Line Rifles. The shotgun's 24″ round blued barrel is furnished with a full screw-in choke tube. All shotguns come drilled and tapped, with adjustable trigger and rubber buttpad. Option of matte black composite, Breakup or Advantage™ Camo stock.

BLACK POWDER

# UBERTI REVOLVERS

### PATERSON REVOLVER
### $399.00
### ($435.00 w/Lever)

Manufactured at Paterson, New Jersey, by the Patent Arms Manufacturing Company from 1836 to 1842, these were the first revolving pistols created by Samuel Colt. All early Patersons featured a five-shot cylinder, roll-engraved with one or two scenes, octagon barrel and folding trigger that extends when the hammer is cocked.

**SPECIFICATIONS**
**Caliber:** 36
**Capacity:** 5 shots (engraved cylinder)
**Barrel length:** 7¹/₂″ octagonal
**Overall length:** 11¹/₂″
**Weight:** 2.552 lbs.
**Frame:** Color casehardened steel
**Grip:** One-piece walnut

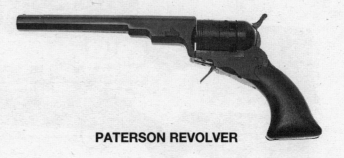

**PATERSON REVOLVER**

### 1st MODEL DRAGOON REVOLVER
### $325.00

**SPECIFICATIONS**
**Caliber:** 44
**Capacity:** 6 shots
**Barrel length:** 7¹/₂″ round forward of lug
**Overall length:** 13¹/₂″
**Weight:** 4 lbs.
**Frame:** Color casehardened steel
**Grip:** One-piece walnut
Also available:
**2nd Model Dragoon** w/square cylinder bolt shot   **$325.00**
**3rd Model Dragoon** w/loading lever latch, steel
  backstrap, cut for shoulder stock . . . . . . . . . . . .   **335.00**
**Whitney Dragoon** w/7¹/₂″ barrel . . . . . . . . . . . . . .   **360.00**

**1st MODEL DRAGOON**

### WALKER REVOLVER
### $370.00

**SPECIFICATIONS**
**Caliber:** 44
**Barrel length:** 9″ (round in front of lug)
**Overall length:** 15³/₄″
**Weight:** 4.41 lbs.
**Frame:** Color casehardened steel
**Backsstrap:** Steel
**Cylinder:** 6 shots (engraved with "Fighting Dragoons" scene)
**Grip:** One-piece walnut

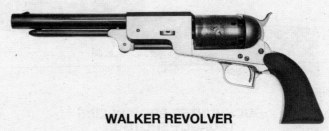

**WALKER REVOLVER**

# UBERTI REVOLVERS

## 1851 NAVY REVOLVER
### $295.00

**SPECIFICATIONS**
**Caliber:** 36
**Barrel length:** 7¹/₂″ (octagonal, tapered)
**Cylinder:** 6 shots (engraved)
**Overall length:** 13″
**Weight:** 2³/₄ lbs.
**Frame:** Color casehardened steel
**Backstrap and trigger guard:** Brass
**Grip:** One-piece walnut
Also available:
**1851 Squareback or Oval**................... $270.00

**1851 NAVY REVOLVER**

**1858 REMINGTON NEW ARMY
TARGET MODEL**

## 1858 REMINGTON NEW ARMY
## 44 REVOLVER

**Prices:**
8″ barrel, open sights ........................ $295.00
With stainless steel and open sights ............ 420.00
**Target Model** w/black finish ................. 330.00
**Target Model** w/stainless steel............... 420.00

Also available:
**1858 New Navy** (36 cal.) ..................... 270.00
**1858 New Army Revolving Carbine** (18″ bbl.).... 420.00

## 1860 ARMY REVOLVER
### $270.00

**SPECIFICATIONS**
**Caliber:** 44
**Barrel length:** 8″ (round, tapered)
**Overall length:** 13³/₄″
**Weight:** 2.65 lbs.
**Frame:** One-piece, color casehardened steel
**Trigger guard:** Brass
**Cylinder:** 6 shots (engraved)
**Grip:** One-piece walnut
Also available:
**1860 Army Fluted** ......................... $295.00

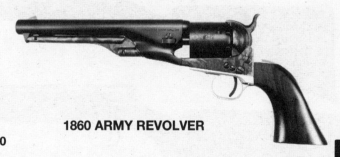

**1860 ARMY REVOLVER**

## 1861 NAVY REVOLVER
### $270.00

**SPECIFICATIONS**
**Caliber:** 36
**Capacity:** 6 shots
**Barrel length:** 7¹/₂″
**Overall length:** 13″
**Weight:** 2.75 lbs.
**Grip:** One-piece walnut
**Frame:** Color casehardened steel

**1861 NAVY REVOLVER**

# WHITE SYSTEMS

## G & W SERIES RIFLES

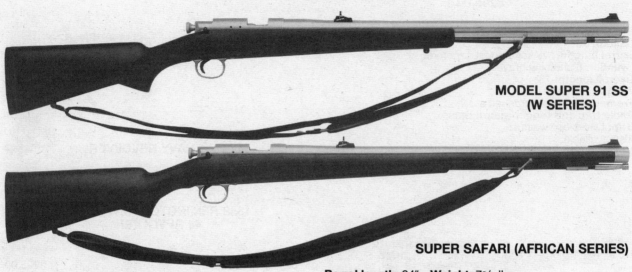

**MODEL SUPER 91 SS
(W SERIES)**

**SUPER SAFARI (AFRICAN SERIES)**

### MODEL SUPER 91

This modern muzzleloading system features the following: Ordnance-grade stainless-steel construction • Fast twist, shallow groove rifling • Stainless-steel nipple and breechplug • Side swing safety (locks the striker, not just the trigger) • Classic stock configuration (fits right- or left-handed shooters • Fast second shot and easy access to nipple from either side for quick capping • Fully adjustable trigger
**Calibers:** 41, 45 and 50

**Barrel length:** 24″    **Weight:** 7³⁄₄ lbs.
**Rifling:** 1 in 20″ (45 cal.); 1 in 24″ (50 cal.)
**Sights:** Fully adjustable Williams sights
**Prices:**
Stainless Steel . . . . . . . . . . . . . . . . . . . . . . . . . . . . . . **$659.95**
    w/Black Laminate stock . . . . . . . . . . . . . . . . . . . . **699.95**
Also available:
**A SERIES SUPER SAFARI SS TAPERED** (African Series)
41, 45, 50 caliber Mannlicher. . . . . . . . . . . . . . . . . . **$799.00**
**GRAND ALASKAN SS**
54 caliber, black laminate . . . . . . . . . . . . . . . . . . . . **799.95**

**WHITETAIL SS (G SERIES)**

**BISON BLUE (G SERIES)**

### WHITETAIL AND BISON MUZZLELOADING RIFLES

White's "G Series" rifles feature straight-line action with easy no-tool takedown in the field. A stainless-steel hammer system has an ambidextrous cocking handle that doubles as a sure-safe hammer-lock safety. Other features include the "Insta-Fire" one-piece nipple/breechplug system (with standard #11 percussion caps); fully adjustable open hunting sights; 22″ bull barrel with integrated ramrod guide and swivel studs.
**Calibers:** 41, 45, 50 and 54 (Bison only)
**Prices:**
**Bison** (50 and 54 cal.) Blued . . . . . . . . . . . . . . . . . . **$399.95**
**Whitetail** (45 and 50 cal.)
Blued . . . . . . . . . . . . . . . . . . . . . . . . . . . . . . . . . . . . **399.00**
Stainless steel . . . . . . . . . . . . . . . . . . . . . . . . . . . . . . **499.00**
    w/Black Laminate stock . . . . . . . . . . . . . . . . . . . . **529.95**
Also available:
**JAVELINA SS PISTOL** w/14″ Barrel
41, 45 and 50 caliber . . . . . . . . . . . . . . . . . . . . . . . . **$499.95**

**sights & scopes**

For addresses and phone/fax numbers of manufacturers and distributors included in this section, please turn to DIRECTORY OF MANUFACTURERS AND SUPPLIERS on page 554.

# AIMPOINT SIGHTS

## AIMPOINT 5000 SIGHT
## $277.00

**SPECIFICATIONS**
**System:** Parallax free
**Optical:** Anti-reflex coated lenses
**Adjustment:** 1 click = 1/4-inch at 100 yards
**Length:** 5 1/2″
**Weight:** 5.8 oz.
**Objective diameter:** 36mm
**Mounting system:** 30mm rings
**Magnification:** 1X
**Material:** Anodized aluminum; black or stainless finish
**Diameter of dot:** 3″ at 100 yds. or Mag Dot reticle, 10″ at 100 yards.

## SERIES 3000 UNIVERSAL
## $232.00 (Black or Stainless)

**SPECIFICATIONS**
**System:** 100% parallax free
**Weight:** 5.8 oz.
**Length:** 6.15″
**Magnification:** 1X
**Scope attachment:** 3X
**Eye relief:** Unlimited
**Battery choices:** 2X Mercury SP 675 1X Lithium or DL 1/3N
**Material:** Anodized aluminum, black or stainless finish
**Mounting:** 1″ Rings (Medium or High)

## AIMPOINT COMP
## $308.00

**SPECIFICATIONS**
**System:** 100% Parallax free
**Optics:** Anti-reflex coated lenses
**Eye relief:** Unlimited
**Batteries:** 3 × Mercury SP 675
**Adjustment:** 1 click = 1/4-inch at 100 yards
**Length:** 4 3/8″
**Weight:** 4.75 oz.
**Objective diameter:** 36mm
**Dot diameter:** 2″ at 30 yds. (7 MOA); 3″ at 30 yds. (10 MOA)
**Mounting system:** 30mm rings
**Magnification:** 1X
**Material:** Black, blue or stainless finish
Also available with 3-minute Dot with Flip Up lens covers and captive metal adjustment covers.

## AIMPOINT 5000 2-POWER
## $367.00

**SPECIFICATIONS**
**System:** Parallax free
**Optical:** Anti-reflex coated lens
**Adjustment:** clock = 1/4″ at 100 yards
**Length:** 7″
**Weight:** 9 oz.
**Objective diameter:** 46mm
**Diameter of dot:** 1 1/2″ at 100 yards
**Mounting system:** 30mm rings
**Magnification:** 2X
**Material:** Anodized aluminum; blue finish

# BAUSCH & LOMB RIFLESCOPES

## ELITE™ 3000 RIFLESCOPES

| Model | Special Feature | Actual Magni-fication | Obj. Lens Aperature (mm) | Field of View @100yds (ft.) | Weight (oz) | Length | Eye Relief (in.) | Exit Pupil (mm) | Click Value @100yds (in.) | Adjust Range @100yds (in.) | Selection | Suggested Retail |
|-------|-----------------|-----------------------|--------------------------|------------------------------|-------------|--------|------------------|-----------------|---------------------------|-----------------------------|-----------|------------------|
| 30-1545M | Matte Finish | 1.5x-4.5x | 32 | 63-20 | 13 | 12.5 | 3.3 | 21-7 | .25 | 100 | Low power variable ideal for brush, medium range slug gun hunting | $433.95 |
| 30-1642E | European Reticle, Matte finish | 1.5x-6x | 42 | 57.7-15 | 21 | 14.4 | 3 | 17.6-7 | .36 | 60 | Large exit pupil & 30mm, tube for max. brightness. | $640.95 |
| 30-2632G | Handgun (30-2632S Silver Finish) | 2x-6x | 32 | 10-4 | 10 | 9 | 20 | 16-5.3 | .25 | 50 | Constant 20" eye relief at all powers w/max. recoil resistance | $417.95 |
| 30-2732G | (30-2732M Matte Finish) | 2x-7x | 32 | 44.6-12.7 | 12 | 11.6 | 3 | 12.2-4.6 | .25 | 50 | Compact variable for close-in brush ormed. range shooting .Excellent for shotguns | $303.95 |
| 30-3940G | (30-3940M Matte Finish, 30-3940S Silver Finish) | 3x-9x | 40 | 33.8-11.5 | 13 | 12.6 | 3 | 13.3-4.4 | .25 | 50 | For the full range of hunting. From varmint to big game. Tops in versatility. | $319.95 |
| 30-3950G | (30-3950M Matte Finish) | 3x-9x | 50 | 31.5-10.5 | 19 | 15.7 | 3 | 16-5.6 | .25 | 50 | All purpose variable with extra brightness. | $382.95 |
| 30-3955E | European Reticle Matte Finish | 3x-9x | 50 | 31.5-10.5 | 22 | 15.6 | 3 | 16-5.6 | .36 | 70 | Large exit pupil and 30mm tube for max. brightness. | $592.95 |
| 30-4124A | Adjustable Objective | 4x-12x | 40 | 26.9-9 | 15 | 13.2 | 3 | 10-3.33 | .25 | 50 | Medium to long-range variable makes a superb choice for varmint or big game. | $417.95 |

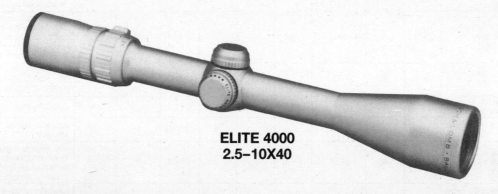

**ELITE 4000**
**2.5–10X40**

## ELITE™ 4000 RIFLESCOPES

| Model | Special Feature | Actual Magni-fication | Obj. Lens Aperature (mm) | Field of View @100yds (ft.) | Weight (oz) | Length | Eye Relief (in.) | Exit Pupil (mm) | Click Value @100yds (in.) | Adjust Range @100yds (in.) | Selection | Suggested Retail |
|-------|-----------------|-----------------------|--------------------------|------------------------------|-------------|--------|------------------|-----------------|---------------------------|-----------------------------|-----------|------------------|
| 40-1040 | Ranging reticle 30mm body tube | 10x | 40 | 10.5 | 22.1 | 13.8 | 3.6 | 4@10x | .25 | 120 | The ultimate for precise pinpoint accuracy w/parallax focus & target adj. knobs- | $1858.00 |
| 40-1636G | (40-1636M Matte Finish) | 1.5x-6x | 36 | 61.8-16.1 | 15.4 | 12.8 | 3 | 14.6-6 | .25 | 60 | Compact wide angle for close-in & brush hunting. Max. brightness. Execel. for shotguns | $528.95 |
| 40-2104G | (40-2104M Matte Finish, 40-2104S Silver Finish) | 2.5x-10x | 40 | 41.5-10.8 | 16 | 13.5 | 3 | 15.6-4 | .25 | 50 | All purpose hunting scope w/4x zoom range for close-in brush & long range shooting | $560.95 |
| 40-3640A | Adjustable Objective | 36x | 40 | 3 | 17.6 | 15 | 3.2 | 1.1 | .125 | 30 | Ideal benchrest scope. | $850.95 |
| 40-4165M | Matte Finish | 4x-16x | 50 | 26-7.2 | 22 | 15.6 | 3 | 12.5-3.1 | .25 | 50 | The ultimate varmint, airgun and precision shooting scope. Parallax focus from 10 meter to infinity. | $738.95 |
| 40-6244A | Adjustable Objective, Sunshade (40-6244M Matte Finish) | 6x-24x | 40 | 18-4.5 | 20.2 | 16.9 | 3 | 6.7-1.7 | .125 | 26 | Varmint, target & silhouette long range shooting and airgun. Parallax focus adjust. for pinpoint accuracy. Parallax focus from 10 meter to infinity. | $640.95 |

# BAUSCH & LOMB/BUSHNELL

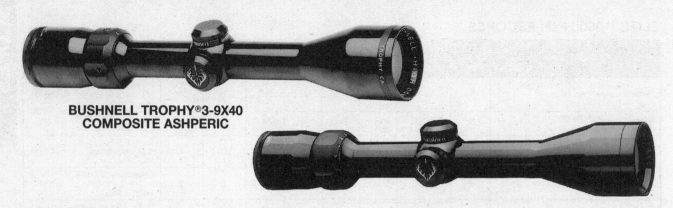

**BUSHNELL TROPHY® 3-9X40
COMPOSITE ASHPERIC**

**3X-9X (40mm) TROPHY®
WIDE ANGLE RIFLESCOPE**

## BUSHNELL TROPHY® RIFLESCOPES

| Model | Special Feature | Actual Magni-fication | Obj. Lens Aperature (mm) | Field of View @100yds (ft.) | Weight (oz) | Length | Eye Relief (in.) | Exit Pupil (mm) | Click Value @100yds (in.) | Adjust Range @100yds (in.) | Selection | Suggested Retail |
|---|---|---|---|---|---|---|---|---|---|---|---|---|
| 73-1500 | Wide angle | 1.75x-5x | 32 | 68-23 | 12.3 | 10.8 | 3.5 | 18.3@1.75x | .25 | 120 | Shotgun, black powder or center-fire Close-in brush hunting. | $243.95 |
| 73-3940 | Wide angle (73-3940S Silver, 73-3948 Matte) | 3x-9x | 40 | 42/14-14/5 | 13.2 | 11.7 | 3 | 13.3-4.44 | .25 | 60 | All purpose variable, excellent for use from close to long range. Circular view provides a definite advantage over "TV screen" type scopes for running game-uphill or down. | $159.95 |
| 73-3941 | Illuminated reticle with back-up crosshairs | 3x-9x | 40 | 37-12.5 | 16 | 13 | 3 | 13.3-4.4 | .25 | 70 | Variable intensity light control Battery Sony CR 2032 or equivalent | $410.95 |
| 73-3942 | Long mounting length de-signed for long-action rifles | 3x-9x | 42 | 42-14 | 13.8 | 12 | 3 | 14-4.7 | .25 | 40 | 7" mounting length. | $164.95 |
| 73-3949 | Wide angle with Circle-x™ Reticle | 3x-9x | 40 | 42-14 | 13.2 | 11.7 | 3 | 13.3-4.4 | .25 | 60 | Matte finish, Ideal low light reticle. | $170.95 |
| 73-4124 | Wide angle, adjustable objective (73-4124M Matte) | 4x-12x | 40 | 32-11 | 16.1 | 12.6 | 3 | 10-3.3 | .25 | 60 | Medium to long range variable for varmint and big game. Range focus adjustment. Excellent air riflescope. | $285.95 |
| 73-6184 | Semi-turret target adjustments, adjustable objective | 6x-18x | 40 | 17.3-6 | 17.9 | 14.8 | 3 | 6.6-2.2 | .125 | 40 | Long-range varmint centerfire or short range air rifle target precision accuracy. | $360.95 |
| TROPHY® CA SCOPES | | | | | | | | | | | | |
| 73-3947 | CA design (Matte) | 3x-9x | 40 | 44-14 | 13 | 12 | 4 | 13.3-4.4 | .25 | 60 | Superb optics. | $225.95 |
| TROPHY® HANDGUN SCOPES | | | | | | | | | | | | |
| 73-0232 | (73-0232S Silver) | 2x | 32 | 20 | 7.7 | 8.7 | 9 | 16 | .25 | 90 | Designed for target and short to med.range hunting. Magnum recoil resistant. | $20295 $218.95(S) |
| 73-2632 | (73-2632S Silver) | 2x-6x | 32 | 11-4 | 10.9 | 9.1 | 18 | 16-5.3 | .25 | 50 | 18 inches of eye relief at all powers. | $268.95 $284.95(S) |
| TROPHY® SHOTGUN/HANDGUN SCOPES | | | | | | | | | | | | |
| 73-1420 | Turkey Scope with Circle-x™ Reticle | 1.75x-4x | 32 | 73-30 | 10.9 | 10.8 | 3.5 | 18-8 | .25 | 120 | Ideal for turkey hunting, slug guns or blackpowder guns. Matte finish. | $237.95 |
| 73-1421 | Brush Scope with Circle-x™ Reticle | 1.75x-4x | 32 | 73-30 | 10.9 | 10.8 | 3.5 | 18-8 | .25 | 120 | Ideal for turkey hunting, slug guns or blackpowder guns. Matte finish. | $237.95 |
| TROPHY® AIR RIFLESCOPES | | | | | | | | | | | | |
| 73-4124 | Wide angle, adjustable objective (73-4124M Matte) | 4x-12x | 40 | 32-11 | 16.1 | 12.6 | 3 | 10-3.3 | .25 | 60 | Medium to long range variable for varmint and big game. Range focus adjustment. Excellent air riflescope. | $285.95 |
| 73-6184 | Semi-turret target adjustments, adjustable objective | 6x-18x | 40 | 17-6 | 17.9 | 14.8 | 3 | 6.6-2.2 | .125 | 40 | Long-range varmint centerfire or short range air rifle target precision accuracy. | $369.95 |

# BAUSCH & LOMB/BUSHNELL

## BUSHNELL SPORTVIEW PLUS RIFLESCOPES

| Model | Special Feature | Actual Magni-fication | Obj. Lens Aperature (mm) | Field of View @100yds (ft.) | Weight (oz) | Length | Eye Relief (in.) | Exit Pupil (mm) | Click Value @100yds (in.) | Adjust Range @100yds (in.) | Selection | Suggested Retail |
|---|---|---|---|---|---|---|---|---|---|---|---|---|
| 79-0412 | Adjustable objective | 4x-12x | 40 | 27-9 | 14.6 | 13.1 | 3.2 | 10-3.3 | .25 | 60 | Long range. | $141.95 |
| 79-1393 | (79-1398 Matte) (79-1393S Matte Silver) | 3x-9x | 32 | 38-14 | 10 | 11.75 | 3.5 | 10.7-3.6 | .25 | 50 | All purpose variable. | $68.95 |
| 79-1403 | (79-1403S Silver) | 4x | 32 | 29 | 9.2 | 11.75 | 4 | 8 | .25 | 60 | General purpose. | $56.95 |
| 79-1404 | Black powder | 4x | 32 | 29 | 9.2 | 11.75 | 4 | 8 | .25 | 60 | For black powder guns. | $56.95 |
| 79-1545 | | 1.5x-4.5x | 21 | 69-24 | 8.6 | 10.7 | 3 | 14-4.7 | .25 | 60 | Low power variable ideal for close-in brush or medium range shooting. | $86.95 |
| 79-2243 | | 4x | 32 | 24 | 9.75 | 9.75 | 5 | 8 | .25 | 60 | All purpose .22 scope. | $88.95 |
| 79-3145 | Larger objective | 3.5x-10x | 45 | 36-13 | 13.9 | 12.75 | 3 | 12.9-4.5 | .25 | 60 | Large objective for low light use. | $154.95 |
| 79-3938 | Wide angle | 3x-9x | 38 | 42-14 | 12.5 | 12.7 | 3 | 12.7-4.2 | .25 | 50 | Excellent for use at any range. | $88.95 |
| 79-3940 | Wide angle | 3x-9x | 40 | 42-15 | 12.5 | 12 | 3 | 4.4 | .25 | 50 | Excellent for use at any range. | $91.95 |
| 79-3942 | Built-in bullet drop compensator | 3x-9x | 40 | 40-13 | 12 | 12.25 | 3 | 13.3-4.4 | .25 | 45 | All purpose. BDC adjusts for target range. | $102.95 |
| 79-6184* | Adjustable objective | 6x-18x | 40 | 19.1-6.8 | 15.9 | 14.5 | 3 | 6.7-2.2 | .25 | 50 | Excellent varmint scope. | $170.95 |
| | SPORTVIEW® AIR RIFLE SERIES | | | | | | | | | | | |
| 79-0004 | Adjustable objective, with rings | 4x | 32 | 31 | 11.2 | 11.7 | 4 | 8 | .25 | 50 | General pupose for air rifle and rimfire. With range focus & target adjustments. | $97.95 |
| 79-0039 | Adjustable objective, with rings | 3x-9x | 32 | 38-13 | 11.2 | 10.75 | 3.5 | 10.6-3.5 | .25 | 60 | Air rifle, rimfire with range focus adjustments and target adjustments | $116.95 |
| | SPORTVIEW® RIMFIRE SERIES | | | | | | | | | | | |
| 79-1416 | 3/4" tube | 4x | 15 | 17 | 3.6 | 10.7 | 3.5 | 3.8 | Friction | 60 | General purpose. | $11.95 |
| 79-3720 | 3/4" tube | 3x-7x | 20 | 23-11 | 5.7 | 11.3 | 2.6 | 6.7-2.9 | Friction | 50 | All purpose variable. | $36.95 |
| | .22 VARMINT™ WITH RINGS | | | | | | | | | | | |
| 79-0428 | With rings | 4x | 28 | 25 | 8.5 | 7.6 | 3 | 7 | .5 | 52 | Compact for .22's. | $75.95 |

* We recommend Trophy® airgun scopes for adult spring-loaded airguns which achieve over 800 FPS velocity

## BUSHNELL BANNER RIFLESCOPES

| Model | Special Feature | Actual Magni-fication | Obj. Lens Aperature (mm) | Field of View @100yds (ft.) | Weight (oz) | Length | Eye Relief (in.) | Exit Pupil (mm) | Click Value @100yds (in.) | Adjust Range @100yds (in.) | Selection | Suggested Retail |
|---|---|---|---|---|---|---|---|---|---|---|---|---|
| 71-1545 | Wide Angle | 1.5x-4.5x | 32 | 67-23 | 10.5 | 10.5 | 3.5 | 17-7 | .25 | 60 | Ideal Shotgun and median to short range scope. | $116.95 |
| 71-3944 | Black powder scope w/ extended eye relief and Circle-x™ reticle | 3x-9x | 40 | 36-13 | 12.5 | 11.5 | 4 | 13-4.4 | .25 | 60 | Specifically designed for black powder and shotguns | $120.95 |
| 71-3948 | Ideal scope for multi purpose guns | 3x-9x | 40 | 40-74 | 13 | 12 | 3 | 13.3-4.4 | .25 | 60 | General purpose. | $113.95 |
| 71-3950 | Large objective for extra brightness in low light | 3x-9x | 50 | 31-10 | 19 | 16 | 3 | 16-5.6 | .25 | 50 | Low light conditions. | $205.95 |
| 71-4124 | Adjustable objective | 4x-12x | 40 | 29-11 | 15 | 12 | 3 | 10-3.3 | .25 | 60 | Ideal scope for long-range shooting. | $157.95 |
| 71-6185 | Adjustable objective | 6x-18x | 50 | 17-6 | 18 | 16 | 3 | 8.3-2.8 | .25 | 40 | Long range varmint and target scope. | $209.95 |

# BAUSCH & LOMB/BUSHNELL

## BUSHNELL® HOLOsight®

The BUSHNELL® HOLOsight® is a revolutionary break-through in optical sighting systems. It delivers instant target acquisition, improved accuracy, and can be tailored to virtually any shooting discipline. How does it work? A hologram of a reticle pattern is recorded on a heads-up display window. When illuminated by laser (coherent) light, a holographic image becomes visible at the target plane - where it remains in focus with the target. Critical eye alignment is not required and multi-plane focusing error is eliminated. With the BUSHNELL® HOLOsight®, simply look through the window, place the reticle image on the target and shoot. The use of holographic technology allows the creation of virtually any image as a reticle pattern, in either two or three dimensions. Shooters have the flexibility to design reticles in any geometric shape, size and in any dimension to enhance a specific shooting discipline. Since no light is cast on the target, use of the BUSHNELL® HOLOsight® is completely legal in most hunting, target and competition areas.

**BUSHNELL® HOLOsight®**

## BUSHNELL HOLOSIGHT® SPECIFICATIONS

| Optics | Magni-fication @ 100 yds. | Field of View ft @100 yds | Weight (oz/g) | Length (in/mm) | Eye Relief (in/mm) | Batteries | Windage Click Value in@100yds mm@100m | Elevation Click Value in@100yds mm@100m | Brightness adjustment settings |
|---|---|---|---|---|---|---|---|---|---|
| Holographic | 1x | Unlimited | 8.7/247 | 6/152 | 1/2" to 10 ft. 13 to 3048 mm | 2 Type N 1.5 Volt | .25 M.O.A./ 7mm@100m | .5 M.O.A./ 14mm@100m | 20 levels |

| Model | | Description | Suggested Retail |
|---|---|---|---|
| 50-0021 | HOLOsight Model 400 | HOLOsight with mounts for Weaver rail and standard reticle. | $638.95 |
| 50-0020 | HOLOsight Model 400 (without reticle) | HOLOsight with mounts for Weaver rail and no reticle. Reticle must be purchased separately. | $524.95 |
| 50-0310 | HOLOsight Comp Model 430 | HOLOsight with diamond reticle and integrated 1911 No-hole pattern mount. | $800.95 |
| 50-0315 | HOLOsight Comp Model 430 | HOLOsight with diamond reticle and integrated 1911 5-hole pattern mount. | $800.95 |
| 50-0360 | HOLOsight Comp Model 430 | HOLOsight with diamond reticle and integrated STI No-hole pattern mount. | $800.95 |
| 50-0364 | HOLOsight Comp Model 430 | HOLOsight with diamond reticle and integrated STI 5-hole pattern mount. | $800.95 |

| Model | Reticle | Description | Uses | |
|---|---|---|---|---|
| HOLOsight® RETICLES | | | | |
| Included w/50-0021 | Standard | 2-Dimensional 65 M.O.A. ring with one M.O.A. dot and tick marks. | General all-purpose handguns, rifles, slug guns, and wing shooting. | $136.95 |
| 50-0122 | Dual Rings | 2-Dimensional design with two rings (20 M.O.A. & 90 M.O.A.) | Wing shooting, 20" IPSC targets, slug and turkey guns. | $136.95 |
| 50-0123 | Open Crosshairs | 2-Dimensional all-purpose design which does not cover up the target area. Inner circle covers 30" at 100 yards. | General all purpose handguns, short range rifles, slug guns and wing shooting. | $136.95 |
| 50-0124 | Diamond | 20 M.O.A. Diamond | IPSC Shooting, and hand gun steel. | $136.95 |
| 50-0125 | Dot | 1 M.O.A. Dot | Precision rifle, handgun, and slug gun shooting. | $136.95 |
| 50-0126 | 10 MOA Ring | 10 M.O.A. See-Thru Ring | All purpose handguns, slug guns, wing shooting, and rifles. | $136.95 |
| 50-0127 | 20 MOA Ring | 20 M.O.A. See-Thru Ring | All purpose handguns, slug guns, wing shooting, and rifles. | $136.95 |
| 50-0131 | 3D Tracer Dot | 3-Dimensional tracer line appears to come out of the gun barrel and ends in 1 M.O.A. dot under one half of a standard reticle. | Rifles, handguns and slug guns. | $136.95 |
| 50-0132 | 3-D Crosshairs | 140 M.O.A. ring at 5 feet, 30 M.O.A. open crosshair at 50 yards. | All purpose handguns, rifles and shotguns. | $136.95 |

# BURRIS SCOPES

## SIGNATURE SERIES

All models in the Signature Series have **Hi-Lume** (multi-coated) lenses for maximum light transmission. Also features **Posi-Lock** to prevent recoil and protect against rough hunting use and temperature change. Allows the shooter to lock the internal optics of the scope in position after the rifle has been sighted in.

| Models | Prices |
|---|---|
| 4X-16X Fine Plex Parallax Adjustment (matte) | $684.00 |
| 4X-16X Fine Plex Parallax Adjustment (black) | 666.00 |
| 4X-16X Plex Parallax Adjustment (black) | 666.00 |
| 4X-16X Plex Parallax Adjustment (matte) | 684.00 |
| 4X-16X Plex Posi-Lock Parallax Adjustment (black) | 710.00 |
| 4X-16X Plex Posi-Lock Parallax Adjustment (matte) | 728.00 |

**8X-32X SIGNATURE**

**6X-24X**

| Models | Prices |
|---|---|
| 4X Plex (black) | $359.00 |
| 6X Plex (black) | 378.00 |
| 6X Plex (matte) | 396.00 |
| 1.5X-6X Plex (black) | 440.00 |
| 1.5X-6X Plex (matte) | 460.00 |
| 1.5X-6X Plex Posi-Lock (black) | 483.00 |
| 1.5X-6X Plex Posi-Lock (matte) | 501.00 |
| 2X-8X Plex (black) | 512.00 |
| 2X-8X Plex (matte) | 530.00 |
| 2X-8X Plex Posi-Lock (black) | 552.00 |
| 2X-8X Plex Posi-Lock (matte) | 570.00 |
| 2.5X-10X Plex Posi-Lock Parallax Adjustment (black) | 636.00 |
| 2.5X-10X Plex Posi-Lock Parallax Adjustment (matte) | 654.00 |
| 2.5X-10X Plex Posi-Lock Parallax Adjustment (nickel) | 654.00 |
| 3X-9X Plex (black) | 523.00 |
| 3X-9X Plex (matte) | 541.00 |
| 3X-9X Plex Posi-Lock (black) | 573.00 |
| 3X-9X Plex Posi-Lock (matte) | 591.00 |
| 3X-9X Plex Posi-Lock (nickel) | 590.00 |
| 3X-9X LDPX* (black) | 614.00 |
| 3X-9X LDPX* (matte) | 633.00 |
| 3X-9X LDPX* Posi-Lock (black) | 661.00 |
| 3X-9X LDPX* Posi-Lock (matte) | 679.00 |
| 3X-9X-50mm Plex Posi-Lock (matte) | 644.00 |
| 3X-9X-50mm Mil-Dot Posi-Lock (matte) | 778.00 |
| 3X-12X Plex Parallax Adjustment (matte) | 671.00 |
| 3X-12X Plex Posi-Lock Parallax Adjustment (black) | 697.00 |
| 3X-12X Plex Posi-Lock Parallax Adjustment (matte) | 715.00 |

| Models | Prices |
|---|---|
| 6X-24X Plex Parallax Adjustment (black) | $680.00 |
| 6X-24X Plex Parallax Adjustment (matte) | 701.00 |
| 6X-24X Fine Flex Target (black) | 706.00 |
| 6X-24X Fine Plex Target (matte) | 724.00 |
| 6X-24X Fine Plex Target (nickel) | 724.00 |
| 6X-24X Mil Dot Target | 858.00 |
| 6X-24X Plex Posi-Lock Parallax Adjustment (black) | 724.00 |
| 6X-24XP Plex Posi-Lock Parallax Adjustment (matte) | 742.00 |
| 6X-24X LDPX* Parallax Adjustment (black) | 772.00 |
| 6X-24X LDPX* Parallax Adjustment (matte) | 792.00 |
| 8X-32X Fine Plex Target (black) | 745.00 |
| 8X-32X Fine Plex Target (matte) | 765.00 |
| 8X-32X Fine Plex Target (nickel) | 765.00 |
| 8X-32X Peep Plex Target (black) | 756.00 |
| 8X-32X Fine Plex Posi-Lock Parallax Adjustment (black) | 808.00 |
| 8X-32X Fine Plex Posi-Lock Parallax Adjustment (matte) | 826.00 |

*LDPXlectro-Dot Plex

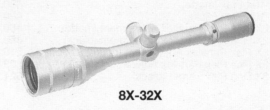

**8X-32X**

**4X-16X**

**8X-32X**

SCOPES

# BURRIS SCOPES

## FULLFIELD SCOPES
### Fixed Power with Hi-Lume Lenses

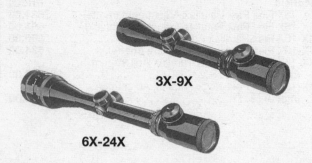

**3X-9X**

**6X-24X**

| Models | Prices |
|---|---|
| 1X XER Plex (camo) | $302.00 |
| 1X XER Plex (matte) | 275.00 |
| 1¹/₂X Plex (matte) | 284.00 |
| 2¹/₂X Plex (camo) | 320.00 |
| 4X Plex (black) | 293.00 |
| 4X Plex (matte) | 317.00 |
| 6X Plex (black) | 319.00 |
| 6X Plex (matte) | 339.00 |
| 12X Fine Plex Target (black) | 433.00 |
| 1X-4X XER Plex (matte) | 360.00 |
| 1.75X-5X Plex (black) | 348.00 |
| 1.75X-5X Plex (matte) | 369.00 |
| 2X-7X Plex (black) | 374.00 |
| 2X-7X Plex (matte) | 392.00 |
| 3X-9X Plex (black) | 339.00 |
| 3X-9X Plex (matte) | 366.00 |
| 3X-9X Plex (nickel) | 366.00 |
| 3X-9X CHD, RAC (matte) | 433.00 |
| 3X-9X Electro-Dot Plex (black) | 462.00 |
| 3X-9X Electro-Dot Plex (matte) | 470.00 |
| 3X-9X-40mm Plex (black) | 372.00 |
| 3X-9X-40mm Plex (matte) | 391.00 |
| 3X-9X-40mm Electro-Dot Plex (black) | 464.00 |
| 3X-9X-40mm Electro-Dot Plex (matte) | 483.00 |
| 3.5X-10X Plex (black) | 462.00 |
| 3.5X-10X Plex (matte) | 480.00 |
| 3.5X-10X Plex (nickel) | 480.00 |
| 4X-12X Fine Plex Parallex Adjustment (matte) | 488.00 |
| 4X-12X Fine Plex Parallex Adjustment (black) | 468.00 |
| 6X-18X Plex Parallax Adjustment (matte) | 510.00 |
| 6X-18X Fine Plex Parallax Adjustment (black) | 492.00 |
| 6X-18X Fine Plex Target (black) | 521.00 |

### 2.7X SCOUT SCOPE
#### W/Precision Clock Adjustments

## COMPACT SCOPES

| Models | Prices |
|---|---|
| 1X XER Plex (matte) | $275.00 |
| 1X XER Plex (camo) | 302.00 |
| 1X-4X XER Plex (matte) | 360.00 |
| 4X Plex (black) | 246.00 |
| 4X Plex (nickel) | 263.00 |
| 6X Plex (black) | 260.00 |
| 6X Plex Parallax Adjustment (black) | 301.00 |
| 6X HBR Fine Plex Target (black) | 337.00 |
| 6X HBR .375 Dot Target (black) | 358.00 |
| 6X HBR Peep Plex Target (matte) | 377.00 |
| 2X-7X Plex (black) | 336.00 |
| 2X-7X Plex (matte) | 356.00 |
| 3X-9X Plex (black) | 343.00 |
| 3X-9X Plex (matte) | 363.00 |
| 3X-9X Plex (nickel) | 363.00 |
| 4X-12X Plex Parallax Adjustment (black) | 453.00 |
| 4X-12X Plex Target (black) | 482.00 |

## HANDGUN LONG EYE RELIEF SCOPE
### with Plex Reticle:

**3X-9X HANDGUN SCOPE**

| Models | Prices |
|---|---|
| 1X XER Plex (matte) | $275.00 |
| 1X XER Plex (camo) | 302.00 |
| 2X Plex Posi-Lock (nickel) | 293.00 |
| 2X Plex Posi-Lock (black) | 275.00 |
| 2X Plex Posi-Lock (matte) | 293.00 |
| 4X Plex Posi-Lock (black) | 302.00 |
| 10X Plex Target (black) | 398.00 |
| 1.5X-4X Plex Posi-Lock (black) | 352.00 |
| 1.5X-4X Plex Posi-Lock (nickel) | 370.00 |
| 2X-7X Plex Posi-Lock (black) | 411.00 |
| 2X-7X Plex Posi-Lock (nickel) | 429.00 |
| 3X-9X Plex Posi-Lock (black) | 456.00 |
| 3X-9X Plex Posi-Lock (nickel) | 474.00 |

## SCOUT SCOPES

Made for hunters who need a 7- to 14-inch eye relief to mount just in front of the ejection port opening, allowing hunters to shoot with both eyes open. The 15-foot field of view and 2³/₄X magnification are ideal for brush guns and handgunners. Also ideal for the handgunner that uses a "two-handed hold." Rugged, reliable and 100% fog proof.

| Models | Prices |
|---|---|
| 1X XER Plex (matte) | $275.00 |
| 1X XER Plex (camo) | 302.00 |
| 1.5X Heavy Plex (matte) | 264.00 |
| 2.75X Plex (black) | 240.00 |
| 2.75X Heavy Plex (matte) | 270.00 |

# DOCTER OPTIC RIFLESCOPES

## VARIABLE POWER

**MODEL 1-4X24**
**$1129.00**

This is a compact, low-power riflescope ideal for close-range shooting.

**3-10X40 RIFLESCOPE**
**$798.00**

Made with high-quality multi-coated optics, the 3-10X40 is ideal for late afternoon and early morning hunting. Its rugged design handles recoil from large-caliber rifles and, with a full three inches of eye relief, it protects the shooter's eye. The extended eye relief also allows those who wear eyeglasses or sunglasses to take full advantage of the scope's capabil- ities. Its one-inch tube and large area for mounting rings are easily mounted on all popular sporting rifles. The European-style diopter adjustment system simplifies focusing with or without glasses. It also features 1/4-inch audible click adjustments and generous elevation and windage adjustments. **Weight:** 18 oz. Field-tested in the Alaskan wilderness.

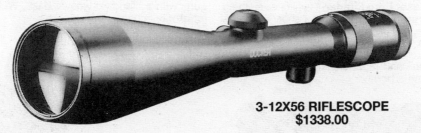

**3-12X56 RIFLESCOPE**
**$1338.00**

With its 56mm objective lens and 30mm tube, the 3-12X56M Rifle Scope has excellent light transmission properties. Its adjustable magnification factor allows shooters to zoom out for wide-field viewing or zoom in for precise bullet placement. A floating diopter makes focusing quick and easy.

**VZF 2.5-10X48**
**$1299.00**

Docter Optic's VZF 2.5-10X48M variable riflescope delivers high-power performance yet weighs less than 19 ounces. Designed for long-range hunting and target shooting, its rugged, die-cast aluminum body and shock-proof optical system alignment have been tested and are guaranteed recoil-resistant with most rifle calibers. The VHF 2.5-10X48M also features special multi-level coating of all glass-to-air surfaces. Its large field of view extends to approx. 33 feet at 2.5X power. The focusing mechanism provides smooth, silent adjustment of the zoom range. A special sealing element ensures that the optical system is protected against all weather conditions, dust and dirt.

# LASERAIM TECHNOLOGIES

### MODEL LA16
### HOTDOT MIGHTY SIGHT
### $169.00

Ten times brighter than other laser sights, Laseraim's Hotdot Lasersights include a rechargeable NICad battery and in-field charger. Produce a 2″ dot at 100 yards with a 500-yard range. **Length:** 2″. **Diameter:** .75″. Can be used with handguns, rifles, shotguns and bows. Fit all Laseraim mounts. Available in black or satin.

### LA70 SHOTLESS LASER BORE SIGHTER™
### $169.00 (Not shown)

The **LA70 Shotless Laser Bore Sighter**™ facilitates sighting to near perfect accuracy without wasting a shot. To check the center of the bore, simimply rotate the laser on axis of the gun bore. The LA70 is equipped with a rotational **Laseraim**™ with constant ON switch and six arbors fitting caibers 22 thru 45, 12-gauge shotguns and muzzleloders (50 and 54 cal.). **Length:** 8″ (w/laser and arbor).

### GI HOT CUSTOM LASERS
### $299.00

The GI HOT (Hotdot® laser) has been custom-designed for Glock models 17 to 30. It allows a two-handed shooting grip by locating the laser close to the bottom of the frame. This patented system internalizes the wires, leaving a clean, easy-to-use laser that conforms to the pistol and makes sighting a breeze. A pressure-sensitive pad turns the laser on and off. Four button-cell batteries power it up to one hour continuously. The Easy-lock™ windage & elevation system makes sighting quick and reliable. GI HOT range = 500 yds. **Length:** 1.5″. **Weight:** 2 oz.

### LA3XHD™ HOTDOT®
### $249.00

This electronic red dot/laser combo can be used in all light conditions—the electronic red dot sight in bright light and the laser in low light conditions. The three-piece sighting system offers the newest technology in red dot scopes and a versatile laser. The 30mm objective lens gives an increased field of view over traditional 1″ scopes and zero eye relief makes sighting a breeze. The 4 m.o.a. (about 4″ at 100 yards) dot size is ideal for hunting and target. The laser projects a 2″ dot at 100 yards, has up to a 500 yd. range, and gives pinpoint accuracy with Laseraim's new Easy Lock™ windage & elevation system. The LA3XHD™ HOTDOT® Dualdot™ laser is 10 times brighter. Fits all rifles, bows, shotguns and handguns with a standard weaver base. **Weight:** 12 oz. **Overall length:** 6 inches.

### LA93 ILLUSION III™
### RED DOT SCOPE
### $169.00

This two-piece design offers more flexibility in mounting with less added overall weight. The 30mm objective lens gives an increased field of view over traditional 1″ scopes and zero eye relief. The 4 m.o.a. (about 4″ at 100 yards) dot size is ideal for hunting and target. Fits all rifles, bows, shotguns and handguns with a standard weaver base (sold separately). **Weight:** 5 oz. **Overall length:** 6 inches. Black or satin finish.

# LEUPOLD RIFLESCOPES

## VARI-X III LINE

The Vari-X III scopes feature a power-changing system that is similar to the sophisticated lens systems in today's finest cameras. Improvements include an extremely accurate internal control system and a sharp sight picture. All lenses are coated with **Multicoat 4**. Reticles are the same apparent size throughout the power range and stay centered during elevation/windage adjustments. Eyepieces are adjustable and fog-free. Reticles are also available in German #1, German #1 European, German #4, Post and Duplex, and Leupold Dot.

### VARI-X III 1.75-6X32mm E
### (Extended Version)
### $596.50

### VARI-X III 1.5-5X20mm
This selection of hunting powers is for ranges varying from very short to those at which big game is normally taken. The field at 1.5X lets you get on a fast-moving animal quickly. With magnification at 5X, medium and big game can be hunted around the world at all but the longest ranges. Duplex or Heavy Duplex: **$573.20**. In black matte finish: **$594.60**. Also available:
**VARI-X III 1.75-6X32mm: $598.20.** Matte finish: **$619.60**

### VARI-X III 2.5-8X36mm
This is an excellent range of powers for almost any kind of game, including varmints. The top magnification provides resolution for practically any situation. Duplex: **$617.90**. In matte or silver finish: **$639.30**.

### VARI-X III 3.5-10X40mm
The extra power range makes these scopes the optimum choice for year-around big game and varmint hunting. The adjustable objective model, with its precise focusing at any range beyond 50 yards, also is an excellent choice for some forms of target shooting. Duplex: **$641.10**. With matte or silver finish: **$662.50**.

### VARI-X III 3.5-10X50mm
The hunting scope is designed specifically for low-light situations. The 3.5X10–50mm scope, featuring lenses coated with Multicoat 4, is ideal for twilight hunting (especially whitetail deer) because of its efficient light transmission. The new scope delivers maximum available light through its large 50mm objective lens, which translates into an exit pupil that transmits all the light the human eye can handle in typical low-light circumstances, even at the highest magnification. Duplex or Heavy Duplex: **$739.30**. With matte or silver finish: **$760.70**. With Leupold Dot: **$792.90.**

### VARI-X III 4.5-14X40mm (Adj. Objective)
This model has enough range to double as a hunting scope and as a varmint scope.
Duplex or Heavy Duplex. . . . . . . . . . . . . . . . . . . . . **$717.90**
  With matte finish . . . . . . . . . . . . . . . . . . . . . . . . 739.30
Same as above with 50mm adj. obj., Duplex or
  Heavy Duplex; matte finish only . . . . . . . . . . . . 837.50

### VARI-X III 6.5-20X50mm
### Target Long Range

### VARI-X III 6.5-20X40mm (Adj. Objective)
This scope has a wide range of power settings, with magnifications useful to hunters of all types of varmints. Can be used for any kind of big-game hunting where higher magnifications are an aid. Gloss finish: **$748.20**. With matte or silver finish: **$769.60**
Also available:
**6.5-20X50mm Adj. Obj.** w/duplex matte finish . . . $ **867.90**
**6.5-20X50mm Adj. Obj.** w/European duplex
  matte finish . . . . . . . . . . . . . . . . . . . . . . . . . . . . . 1126.80
**6.5-20X50mm Adj. Obj.** Long Range Duplex
  finish . . . . . . . . . . . . . . . . . . . . . . . . . . . . . . . . . 1073.20

### VARI-X III 8.5-25X40mm

### VARI-X III 8.5-25X40mm (Adj. Objective)
Features one-piece main tube of T-6061 aluminum, 1/4-minute click adjustments, Multicoat 4™ lens coating. With matte finish: **$801.80**. Target Model: **$855.40**

# LEUPOLD

## VARI-X II 1-4X20mm DUPLEX
This scope, the smallest of Leupold's VARI-X II line, is noted for its large field of view: 70 feet at 100 yards. Gloss finish only: **$375.00**

## VARI-X II 3-9X40mm DUPLEX
A wide selection of powers offers the right combination of field of view and magnification to fit most hunting conditions. Many hunters use the 3X or 4X setting most of the time, cranking up to 9X for positive identification of game or for extremely long shots. The adjustable objective eliminates parallax and permits precise focusing on any object from less than 50 yards to infinity for extra-sharp definition. Gloss finish: **$410.70**. In matte or silver: **$432.10**. Tactical Model (Matte): **$510.70**

## VARI-X II 2-7X33mm DUPLEX
A compact scope, no larger than the Leupold M8-4X, offering a wide range of power. It can be set at 2X for close ranges in heavy cover or zoomed to maximum power for shooting or identifying game at longer ranges: **$407.10**

## VARI-X II 4-12X40mm (Adj. Objective)
The ideal answer for big game and varmint hunters alike. At 12.25 inches, the 4X12 is virtually the same length as Vari-X II 3X9. Gloss finish: **$564.30**. Matte or silver finish: **$585.70**

## VARI-X II 3-9X50mm
This LOV scope delivers a 5.5mm exit pupil for low-light visibility: **$489.30**. Matte finish (Tactical): **$510.70**. 3.5-10X40mm (Tactical): **$741.10**

### VARI-X II 6-18X40mm
### Adj. Obj. Target

## VARI-X II 6-18X40mm Adj. Obj. Target
Features target-style click adjustments, fully coated lenses, adj. objective for parallax-free shooting from 50 yards to infinity.

| | |
|---|---:|
| In matte | **$675.00** |
| Tactical Model (Matte) | 510.70 |
| Target Dot Model | 728.60 |

# LEUPOLD SCOPES

## LEUPOLD PREMIER SCOPES (LPS)

This new premier line of "Golden Ring" riflescopes was developed to exceed the optical and mechanical performance characteristics currently available to hunters and shooters. Two products are currently available, a 1.5-6X42mm and 3.5-14X52mm. Both products have a black satin hard anodized finish and feature a new advanced scratch-resistant, multi-layer and anti-reflective coating, called "DiamondCoat™," which provides 99.65% light transmission per lens surface.

The LPS also features a 30mm one-piece main tube, which allows for a full 60 inches of windage and elevation adjustment at 100 yards. The main tube also provides more field-of-view than most scopes with a similar range. The power selector and adjustable objective have easy-to-grip rubber surfaces that allow for smooth adjustments. Additionally, the markings on these adjustments are angled for easy reading even in shooting positions. Low-profile windage and elevation dials are finger-adjustable. Once sighted in, pull-up/push-down dials can be reset to zero.

LPS 1.5-6x42mm (satin finish). . . . . . . . . . . . . . . . $1426.80
LPS 3.5-14x52mm (adjustable objective) . . . . . . . 1516.10

**LPS™ 3.5-14X52mm Adj. Obj.**

## SHOTGUN SCOPES (not shown)

Leupold shotgun scopes are parallax-adjusted to deliver precise focusing at 75 yards. Each scope features a special Heavy Duplex reticle that is more effective against heavy, brushy backgrounds. All scopes have matte finish.

Prices:
Vari-X II 1-4X20mm Model Heavy Duplex . . . . . . $396.40
M8-4X33mm Heavy Duplex . . . . . . . . . . . . . . . . . . 371.40
Vari-X III 2-7X33mm Heavy Duplex. . . . . . . . . . . . 428.60

## COMPACT SCOPES

### M8-4X28mm COMPACT & 4X RF SPECIAL
The 4X RF Special is focused to 75 yards and has a Duplex reticle with finer crosshairs. . . . . . . . . . . . . . . . . . . $350.00

**4X COMPACT & 4X RF SPECIAL**

### 2-7X28mm COMPACT RF SPECIAL
Two ounces lighter and an inch shorter than its full-size counterpart, this 2-X7 is one of the most compact variable power scopes available for today's trend toward smaller and lighter rifles. . . . . . . . . . . . . . . . . . . . . . . . . . . . . . . . . . . . $437.50

**2-7 COMPACT**

### 3-9X28mm COMPACT
The 3X9 Compact is 3 1/2 ounces lighter and 1.3 inches shorter than a standard 3-9 . . . . . . . . . . . . . . . . . . $453.60
In black matte finish or silver . . . . . . . . . . . . . . . . . 475.00

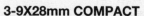

**3-9 COMPACT SILVER**

# LEUPOLD SCOPES

## 6X42mm TACTICAL SCOPE

The new Leupold 6X42mm features ¼-minute click target-style adjustments for precise corrections in the field. Adjustment travel for windage or elevation is 76 inches. The combination of an exact 6X magnification, adjustable objective and target-style adjustments make it an excellent choice for Hunter Benchrest Competitions as well. Leupold's exclusive Multicoat 4 lens coating is applied to all air-to-glass surfaces to provide the 6X42mm maximum light transmission. **Length:** 12″. **Weight:** 11.5 ounces. Two reticles styles: classic Duplex or a ¾-minute Military Dot. Black matte finish.

Matte finish. . . . . . . . . . . . . . . . . . . . . . . . . . . . . . . . . . . **$600.00**
With ¾-minute Military Dot . . . . . . . . . . . . . . . . . . . . . 733.00

## FIXED POWER SCOPES

### M8-4X

The 4X delivers a widely used magnification and a generous field of view. . . . . . . . . . . . . . . . . . . . . . . . . . . . . . . . . . . . . . . . . . . **$350.00**
In black matte finish . . . . . . . . . . . . . . . . . . . . . . . . . . . . . . 371.40

### M8-6X

The 6X extends the range for big-game hunting and doubles in some cases as a varmint scope. . . . . . . . . . . . . . . . . . . . . . . . . . . . . . . . . . . **$373.20**

### M8-6X42mm

Large 42mm objective lens features increased light-gathering capability and a 7mm exit pupil. Recommended for varmint shooting at night. Duplex or Heavy Duplex: . . . . . . . . . . . . . . . . . . . . . . . . . . . . . . . . . . . . . . . . **$462.50**
In matte finish . . . . . . . . . . . . . . . . . . . . . . . . . . . . . . . . . . . 483.90

## VARMINT SCOPES

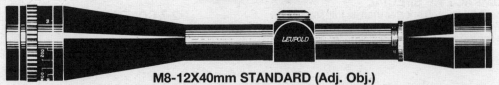

### M8-12X40mm STANDARD (Adj. Obj.)

Outstanding optical qualities, resolution and magnification make the 12X a natural for the varmint shooter. Adjustable objective is standard for parallax-free focusing.
Duplex: . . . . . . . . . . . . . . . . . . . . . . . . . . . . . . . . . . . . . . . **$517.90**
With CPC reticle or Dot: . . . . . . . . . . . . . . . . . . . . . . . . . . . . 571.40
Also available:
**VARI-X III 6.5-20X40mm VARMINT** (Adj. Obj.) Target Dot w/Multicoat 4 (matte only): . . . . . . . . . . . . . . . . . . . . . . . . . . . . . . . . . . . . . . . . . . **$850.00**

# NIKON SCOPES

## MONARCH™ UCC SCOPES

6.5-20X44 AO

2-7X32

### RIFLESCOPES

| | |
|---|---|
| **Model 6500** 4x40 Lustre | $284.00 |
| **Model 6505** 4x40 Matte | 304.00 |
| **Model 6510** 2-7x32 Lustre | 367.00 |
| **Model 6515** 2-7x32 Matte | 387.00 |
| **Model 6520** 3-9x40 Lustre | 371.00 |
| **Model 6525** 3-9x40 Matte | 391.00 |
| **Model 6530** 3.5-10x50 Lustre | 554.00 |

| | |
|---|---|
| **Model 6535** 3.5-10x50 Matte | $572.00 |
| **Model 6540** 4-12x40 AO Lustre | 476.00 |
| **Model 6545** 4-12x40 AO Matte | 496.00 |
| **Model 6550** 6.5-20x44 AO Lustre | 591.00 |
| **Model 6555** 6.5-20x44 AO Matte | 612.00 |

### HANDGUN SCOPES

| | |
|---|---|
| **Model 6560** 2x20 EER Black Lustre | $213.00 |
| **Model 6565** 2x20 EER Silver | 233.00 |

## MONARCH™ UCC RIFLESCOPE SPECIFICATIONS

| Model | 4x40 | 2-7x32 | 3-9x40 | 3.5-10x50 | 4-12x40 AO | 6.5-20x44 AO | 2x20 EER |
|---|---|---|---|---|---|---|---|
| **Lustre** | #6500 | #6510 | #6520 | #6530 | #6540 | #6550 | #6560 |
| **Matte** | #6505 | #6515 | #6525 | #6535 | #6545 | #6555 | - |
| **Silver** | - | - | - | - | - | - | #6565 |
| **Actual Magnification** | 4x | 2x-7x | 3x-9x | 3.5x-10x | 4x-12x | 6.5x-19.46x | 1.75x |
| **Objective Diameter** | 40mm | 32mm | 40mm | 50mm | 40mm | 44mm | 20mm |
| **Exit Pupil** | 10mm | 16-4.6mm | 13.3-4.4mm | 14.3-5mm | 10-3.3mm | 6.7-2.2mm | 10mm |
| **Eye Relief** | 89mm 3.5 in. | 101-93mm 3.9-3.6 in. | 93-90mm 3.6-3.5 in. | 100-98mm 3.9-3.8 in. | 92-87mm 3.6-3.4 in. | 89-81mm 3.5-3.1 in. | 670-267mm 26.4-10.5 in. |
| **Field of View at 100 yards** | 26.9 ft. | 44.5-12.7 ft. | 33.8-11.3 ft. | 25.5-8.9 ft. | 25.6-8.5 ft. | 16.1-5.4 ft. | 22.0 ft. |
| **Tube Diameter** | 25.4mm 1 in. | 25.4mm 1 in. | 25.4mm 1 in. | 25.4mm 1 in. | 25.4mm 1 in. | 25.4mm 1 in. | 25.4mm 1 in. |
| **Objective Tube Diameter** | 47.3mm 1.86 in. | 39.3mm 1.5 in | 47.3mm 1.86 in. | 57.3mm 2.2 in. | 53.1mm 2.09 in. | 54mm 2.13 in. | 25.4mm 1 in. |
| **Eyepiece O.D. Diameter** | 38mm 1.5 in. | 38mm 1.5 in. | 38mm 1.5 in. | 38mm 1.5 in. | 38mm 1.5 in. | 38mm 1.5 in. | 35.5mm 1.4 in. |
| **Length** | 297mm 11.7 in. | 283mm 11.1 in. | 312mm 12.3 in. | 350mm 13.7 in. | 348.5mm 13.7 in. | 373mm 14.6 in. | 207mm 8.1 in. |
| **Weight** | 315 g. 11.2 oz. | 315 g. 11.2 oz. | 355 g. 12.6 oz. | 435 g. 15.5 oz. | 475 g. 16.9 oz. | 565 g. 20.1 oz. | 185 g. 6.6 oz. |
| **Adjustment Graduation** | ¼:1 Click ½:1 Div. | ¼:1 Click ¼:1 Div. | ¼:1 Click ¼:1 Div. | ¼:1 Click ¼:1 Div. | ¼:1 Click ¼:1 Div. | ⅛:1 Click ⅛:1 Div. | ¼:1 Click ½:1 Div. |
| **Max. Internal Adjustment (moa)** | 120 | 70 | 55 | 45 | 45 | 38 | 120 |
| **Parallax Setting (yards)** | 100 | 100 | 100 | 100 | 50 to infinity | 50 to infinity | 100 |

# PENTAX RIFLESCOPES

## LIGHTSEEKER RIFLESCOPES

**3X-9X LIGHTSEEKER**
Electroless Nickel Finish
$608.00

**8.5X-32X LIGHTSEEKER**
$900.00 (Fine Plex)

## LIGHTSEEKER RIFLESCOPE SPECIFICATIONS

| Model | Objective Diameter (mm) | Eyepiece Diameter (mm) | Exit Pupil (mm) | Eye Relief (in.) | Field of View (ft 100 yd) | Adjustment Graduation (in 100 yd) | Maximum Adjustment (in 100yd) | Length (in.) | Weight (oz.) | Reticle* | Recommended Use** | Prices: |
|---|---|---|---|---|---|---|---|---|---|---|---|---|
| Lightseeker 1.75X-6X | 35 | 36 | 15.3-5 | 3.5-4.0 | 71-20 | 1/2 | 110 | 10.75 | 13.0 | HP | BG,DG,SG/P | **$504.00** |
| Lightseeker 2X-8X | 39 | 36 | 11.0-4.0 | 3.5-4.0 | 53-17 | 1/3 | 80 | 11.7 | 14.0 | P | BG,DG,SG/P | 550.00 |
| Lightseeker 3X-9X | 43 | 36 | 12.0-5.0 | 3.5-4.0 | 36-14 | 1/4 | 50 | 12.7 | 15.0 | P or HP | BG | **574.00** |
| Lightseeker 3X-11X AO | 43 | 36 | 11.0-3.5 | 3.5-4.0 | 38.5-13 | 1/4 | 50 | 13.3 | 19.0 | P | BG,V | 700.00 |
| Lightseeker 3.5X-10X | 50 | 36 | 11.0-5.0 | 3.5-4.0 | 29.5-11 | 1/4 | 50 | 14.0 | 19.5 | P or HP | BG,V | 610.00 |
| Lightseeker 4X-16X AO | 44 | 36 | 10.4-2.8 | 3.5-4.0 | 33-9 | 1/4 | 35 | 15.4 | 23.7 | FP or HP | T,V,BG | 780.00 |
| Lightseeker 6X-24X AO | 44 | 36 | 6.9-2.3 | 3.5-4.0 | 18-5.5 | 1/8 | 26 | 16.0 | 22.7 | FP or D | T,V | 820.00 |
| Lightseeker 8.5X-32X AO | 44 | 36 | 5.0-1.4 | 3.5-4.0 | 13-3.8 | 1/8 | 26 | 17.2 | 24.0 | FP or MD | T,V | 900.00 |
| Lightseeker 2.5X SG Plus | 25 | 36 | 7.0 | 3.5-4.0 | 55 | 1/2 | 60 | 10.0 | 9.0 | DW | BG,DG,TK | 304.00 |
| Lightseeker Zero-X SG Plus | 27 | 35 | 19.5 | 4.5-15 | 51 | 1/2 | 196 | 8.9 | 7.9 | DW | BG,DG,TK | 340.00 |
| Lightseeker Zero-X/V SG Plus | 27 | 35 | 19.5-5.5 | 3.5-7 | 53.8-15 | 1/2 | 129 | 8.9 | 10.3 | HP | BG,DG,TK | 420.00 |

All scope tubes measure 1 inch in diameter. Scopes are available in high-gloss black, matte black, satin chrome or camouflage, depending on model. *P = Penta-Plex  FP = Fine-Plex  DW = Deepwoods Plex  D = Dot  HP = Heavy Plex  MD = Mil Dot  **BG = Big Game  SG/P = Small Game/Plinking  V = Varmint  DG = Dangerous Game  T = Target  TK = Turkey  Add **$20** for matte finish

# PENTAX SCOPES

## LIGHTSEEKER II RIFLESCOPES

**4X-16XAO LIGHTSEEKER II**
$804.00 (Glossy)    $828.00 (Matte)

**3X-9X LIGHTSEEKER II**
$624.00 (Glossy)    $648.00 (Matte)

**6X-24XAO LIGHTSEEKER II**
$836.00 (Glossy)    $860.00 (Matte)
$884.00 (Satin Chrome)

**Features:**
• **Scratch-resistant outer tube.** Under ordinary wear and tear, the outer tube is almost impossible to scratch.
• **High Quality cam zoom tube.** No plastics are used. The tube is made of a bearing-type brass with precision machined cam slots. The zoom control screws are precision-ground to 1/2 of one thousandth tolerance.

• **Leak Prevention.** The power rings are sealed on a separate precision-machined seal tube. The scopes are then filled with nitrogen and double-sealed with heavy-duty "O" rings, making them leak-proof and fog-proof.
• **Excellent eyepieces.** The eyepiece lenses have a greater depth of field than most others. Thus, a more focused target at 100, 200 or 500 yards is attainable. Most Pentax Riflescopes are available in High Gloss, Matte or Satin Chrome finish.

Also available:

## LIGHTSEEKER PISTOLSCOPE SPECIFICATIONS

| Model | Objective Diameter (mm) | Eyepiece Diameter (mm) | Exit Pupil (mm) | Eye Relief (in.) | Field of View (ft 100 yd) | Adjustment Graduation (in 100 yd) | Maximum Adjustment (in 100yd) | Length (in.) | Weight (oz.) | Reticle* | Prices |
|---|---|---|---|---|---|---|---|---|---|---|---|
| 2X | 22 | 30 | 12.9 | 10-24 | 21 | 1/2 | 70 | 8.8 | 6.8 | P | $230.00 ($260.00 Satin Chrome) |
| 1.5X-4X | 22 | 30 | 16.9-7.3 | 11-25/11-18 | 16-11 | 1/4 | 55 | 10.0 | 11.0 | P | 350.00 ($380.00 Satin Chrome) |
| 2.5X-7X | 36 | 30 | 15.1-5.7 | 11-28/9-14 | 12-7.5 | 1/6 | 40 | 12.0 | 12.5 | P | 370.00 ($390.00 Satin Chrome) |

# QUARTON BEAMSHOT SIGHTS

**1000 (PLUS RV2 MOUNT)**

## BEAMSHOT 1000 ULTRA/SUPER

**SPECIFICATIONS**
**Size:** $3/4'' \times 2^3/5''$ (overall length)
**Weight:** 3.8 oz. (incl. battery & mount)
**Construction:** Aluminum 6061 T6
**Finish:** Black anodized
**Cable length:** 5″
**Range:** 500 yards
**Power:** <5mW Class IIIA Laser
**Wave length:** 650nm (Beamshot 1000U-635nm)
**Power supply:** 3V Lithium battery
**Battery life:** Approx. 20 hrs. (continuous)
**Dot size:** 5″ at 10 yds.; 4″ at 100 yds.
**Prices:**
Standard . . . . . . . . . . . . . . . . . . . . . . . . . . . . . . . $50.00
Super . . . . . . . . . . . . . . . . . . . . . . . . . . . . . . . . . . 60.00
Ultra . . . . . . . . . . . . . . . . . . . . . . . . . . . . . . . . . . . 80.00

Bore Sight Arbor 1 (.22-.264 diam.) . . . . . . . . . . 99.00
Bore Sight Arbor 2 (.264-.308 diam.) . . . . . . . . . 99.00
Bore Sight Arbor 3 (.308-.35 diam.) . . . . . . . . . . 99.00

**1000 (PLUS P1A MOUNT)**

## BEAMSHOT 3000

**SPECIFICATIONS**
**Size:** $3/5'' \times 2''$ (overall length)
**Weight:** 2 oz. (incl. battery)
**Construction:** Aluminum 6061 T6
**Finish:** Black
**Cable length:** 5″
**Range:** 300 yards
**Power:** <5mW Class IIIA Laser
**Wave length:** 670nm
**Power supply:** 3 SR44 silver oxide watch battery
**Battery life:** Approx. 4 hrs. (continuous)
**Dot size:** 0.5″ at 10 yds.; 4″ at 100 yds.
**Prices:**
Super . . . . . . . . . . . . . . . . . . . . . . . . . . . . . . . . . $60.00
Ultra . . . . . . . . . . . . . . . . . . . . . . . . . . . . . . . . . . 80.00

**Also available:**
**BEAMSHOT 2000 SUPER** for semiautomatic pistols only.
Uses a 6 volt battery. Measures $1^1/4''$ x $2^1/2''$ overall
length . . . . . . . . . . . . . . . . . . . . . . . . . . . . . . . . . . $58.00

**3000 (PLUS P4 MOUNT)**

# REDFIELD SCOPES

## LOW PROFILE WIDEFIELD

The Widefield®, with 25% more field of view than conventional scopes, lets you spot game quicker, stay with it and see other animals that might be missed.

The patented Low Profile design means a low mounting on the receiver, allowing you to keep your cheek tight on the stock for a more natural and accurate shooting stance, especially when swinging on running game.

The one-piece, fog-proof tube is machined with high tensile strength aluminum alloy and is anodized to a lustrous finish that's rust-free and virtually scratch-proof. Available in seven models.

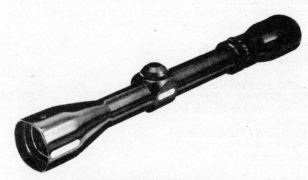

### LOW PROFILE WIDEFIELD 3X-9X VARIABLE

### WIDEFIELD LOW PROFILE SCOPES

1³/₄X-5X Low Profile Black Matte Variable Power
113807 1³/₄X-5X 4 Plex . . . . . . . . . . . . . . . . . . . . . . . $397.95
1³/₄X-5X Low Profile Variable Power
113806 1³/₄X-5X 4 Plex . . . . . . . . . . . . . . . . . . . . . . 389.95
2X-7X Low Profile Variable Power
111806 2X-7X 4 Plex . . . . . . . . . . . . . . . . . . . . . . . . 400.95
3X-9X Low Profile Variable Power
112806 3X-9X 4 Plex . . . . . . . . . . . . . . . . . . . . . . . . 442.95
3X-9X Low Profile Accu-Trac Variable Power
112810 3X-9X 4 Plex AT . . . . . . . . . . . . . . . . . . . . . 511.95
2³/₄X Low Profile Fixed Power
141807 2³/₄X 4 Plex . . . . . . . . . . . . . . . . . . . . . . . . . 283.00
4X Low Profile Fixed Power
143806 4X 4 Plex . . . . . . . . . . . . . . . . . . . . . . . . . . 316.95
6X Low Profile Fixed Power
146806 6X 4 Plex . . . . . . . . . . . . . . . . . . . . . . . . . . 340.95
3X-9X Low Profile Nickel Matte Variable Power
112814 4 Plex . . . . . . . . . . . . . . . . . . . . . . . . . . . . 460.95
3X-9X Low Profile Black Matte Variable Power
112812 4 Plex . . . . . . . . . . . . . . . . . . . . . . . . . . . . 452.95

### GOLDEN FIVE STAR TARGET ADJUST KNOBS (6X-18X)

### GOLDEN FIVE STAR SCOPES

This series of seven scopes incorporates the latest variable and fixed power scope features, including multi-coated and magnum recoil-resistant optical system, plus maximum light-gathering ability. Positive quarter-minute click adjustments for ease of sighting and optimum accuracy. Anodized finish provides scratch-resistant surface.

**Golden Five Star Scopes:**
4X Fixed Power . . . . . . . . . . . . . . . . . . . . . . . . . . . . $257.95
6X Fixed Power . . . . . . . . . . . . . . . . . . . . . . . . . . . . 281.95
6X Fixed Power Matte . . . . . . . . . . . . . . . . . . . . . . . 290.95
1X-4X Variable Power. . . . . . . . . . . . . . . . . . . . . . . . 316.95
1X-4X Black Matte Variable Power . . . . . . . . . . . . . 325.95
2X-7X Variable Power. . . . . . . . . . . . . . . . . . . . . . . . 331.95
3X-9X Variable Power. . . . . . . . . . . . . . . . . . . . . . . . 356.95
3X-9X Black Matte Variable Power . . . . . . . . . . . . . 366.95
3X-9X Nickel Matte Variable Power . . . . . . . . . . . . . 377.95
3X-9X Accu-Trac Variable Power. . . . . . . . . . . . . . . 407.95
4X-12X Variable Power (Adj. Objective) . . . . . . . . . . 453.95
4X-12X Black Matte . . . . . . . . . . . . . . . . . . . . . . . . . 460.95
4X-12X w/Target Knob (AO). . . . . . . . . . . . . . . . . . . 477.95
4X-12X Black Matte Target Knob . . . . . . . . . . . . . . . 477.95
4X-12X Accu-Trac (AO) . . . . . . . . . . . . . . . . . . . . . . 510.95
4X-12X Accu-Trac (AO) . . . . . . . . . . . . . . . . . . . . . . 508.95
6X-18X Accu-Trac Black Matte . . . . . . . . . . . . . . . . 536.95
6X-18X Variable Power (Adj. Objective) . . . . . . . . . . 481.95
6X-18X Accu-Trac Variable Power (Adj. Obj.) . . . . . 508.95
6X-18X Black Matte (AO) . . . . . . . . . . . . . . . . . . . . . 490.95
6X-18X w/Target Knob (AO). . . . . . . . . . . . . . . . . . . 500.95
6X-18X Black Matte w/Target Knob (AO). . . . . . . . . 508.95

**50mm Golden Five Star Scopes:**
3X-9X 50mm Five Star Variable
116500 4 Plex . . . . . . . . . . . . . . . . . . . . . . . . . . . . $429.95
3X-9X 50mm Five Star Matte Finish
116508 4 Plex . . . . . . . . . . . . . . . . . . . . . . . . . . . . 440.95
3X-9X 50mm Five Star Nickel Matte Finish
116900 4 Plex . . . . . . . . . . . . . . . . . . . . . . . . . . . . 394.95

### 50mm GOLDEN FIVE STAR SCOPE

# REDFIELD SCOPES

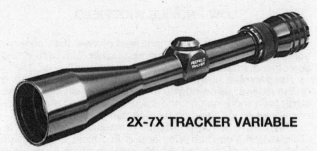

**3X-9X WIDEFIELD® ILLUMINATOR**
**w/Nickel Matte Finish**

**2X-7X TRACKER VARIABLE**

## THE ILLUMINATOR

With the Illuminator series, you can add precious minutes to morning and evening hunting. These scopes actually compensate for the low light, letting you "see" contrasts between field and game.

Optimum resolution, contrast, color correction, flatness of field, edge-to-edge sharpness and absolute fidelity are improved by the unique air-spaced, triplet objective, and the advanced 5-element erector lens system.

The Illuminators also feature a zero tolerance nylon cam follower and thrust washers to provide absolute point of impact hold through all power ranges. The one-piece tube construction is virtually indestructible, tested at 1200g acceleration forces, and fog-free through the elimination of potential leak paths.

Offered in both the Traditional and Widefield® variable power configurations, the Illuminator is also available with the Accu-Trac® feature.

Also offered in 30mm 3X-12X with a 56mm adj. obj.

## THE TRACKER

The Tracker series brings you a superior combination of price and value. It provides the same superb quality, precision and strength of construction found in all Redfield scopes, but at an easily affordable price. Features include the tough, one-piece tube, machined and hand-fitted internal parts, excellent optical quality and traditional Redfield styling.

**TRACKER SCOPES:**
**2X-7X Tracker Variable Power**
122300 2X-7X 4 Plex . . . . . . . . . . . . . . . . . . . . . . . . $240.95
**3X-9X Tracker Variable Power**
123300 3X-9X 4 Plex . . . . . . . . . . . . . . . . . . . . . . . 268.95
**3X-9X Tracker Nickel Matte Variable Power**
123320 4 Plex . . . . . . . . . . . . . . . . . . . . . . . . . . . 290.95
**4X Tracker Fixed Power**
135300 4X 4 Plex . . . . . . . . . . . . . . . . . . . . . . . . . 188.95
**4X40mm Black**
135310 4 Plex . . . . . . . . . . . . . . . . . . . . . . . . . . . 199.95
**4X40mm Tracker Black Matte Fixed Power**
135320 4 Plex . . . . . . . . . . . . . . . . . . . . . . . . . . . 207.95
**6X Tracker Fixed Power**
135600 6X 4 Plex . . . . . . . . . . . . . . . . . . . . . . . . . 216.95
**8X40mm Black**
135800 . . . . . . . . . . . . . . . . . . . . . . . . . . . . . . . 237.95
**Matte Finish**
122308 2X-7X 4 Plex . . . . . . . . . . . . . . . . . . . . . . . 249.95
123308 3X-9X 4 Plex . . . . . . . . . . . . . . . . . . . . . . . 277.95
135608 6X 4 Plex . . . . . . . . . . . . . . . . . . . . . . . . . 226.95
135308 4X 32mm . . . . . . . . . . . . . . . . . . . . . . . . . 199.95
135808 8X 40mm . . . . . . . . . . . . . . . . . . . . . . . . . 247.95

**ILLUMINATOR SCOPES**
**2X-7X Widefield Variable Power**
112910 4 Plex . . . . . . . . . . . . . . . . . . . . . . . . $539.95
**3X-9X Widefield Variable Power**
112886 3X-9X 4 Plex . . . . . . . . . . . . . . . . . . . . . 609.95
**3X-9X Widefield Accu-Trac Variable Power**
112880 3X-9X 4 Plex . . . . . . . . . . . . . . . . . . . . . 665.95
**3X9 Widefield Var. Power Black Matte Finish**
112888 . . . . . . . . . . . . . . . . . . . . . . . . . . . . . . . 619.95
**3X-9X Widefield Nickel Matte Variable Power**
112892 4 Plex AT . . . . . . . . . . . . . . . . . . . . . . . . 629.95
**3X-9X Widefield Accu-Trac Black Matte Variable**
112890 4 Plex AT . . . . . . . . . . . . . . . . . . . . . . . . 590.95
**3X-10X Widefield 50mm Black**
112700 . . . . . . . . . . . . . . . . . . . . . . . . . . . . . . . 681.95
**3X-10X 50mm Black Matte** . . . . . . . . . . . . . . . . 689.95

## GOLDEN FIVE STAR EXTENDED EYE RELIEF HANDGUN SCOPES

**2X Fixed**
140002 4 Plex . . . . . . . . . . . . . . . . . . . . . . . . $222.95
**2X Nickel Plated Fixed**
140003 4 Plex . . . . . . . . . . . . . . . . . . . . . . . . 240.95
**4X Fixed**
140005 4 Plex . . . . . . . . . . . . . . . . . . . . . . . . 222.95
**4X Nickel Plated Fixed**
140006 4 Plex . . . . . . . . . . . . . . . . . . . . . . . . 240.95
**2-1/2X-7X Variable**
140008 4 Plex . . . . . . . . . . . . . . . . . . . . . . . . 303.95
**2-1/2X-7X Nickel Plated Variable**
140009 4 Plex . . . . . . . . . . . . . . . . . . . . . . . . 319.95
**2-1/2X-7X Black Matte Variable**
140010 4 Plex . . . . . . . . . . . . . . . . . . . . . . . . 319.95

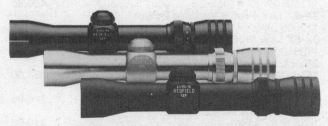

**VARIABLE GOLDEN FIVE STAR**
**(2½X-7X) HANDGUN SCOPES**
**(Black, Nickel, Black Matte)**

# SAKO SCOPE MOUNTS

**"ORIGINAL" SCOPE MOUNTS**

### "ORIGINAL" SCOPE MOUNTS

SAKO's "Original" scope mounts are designed and engineered to exacting specifications, which is traditional to all SAKO products. The dovetail mounting system provides for a secure and stable system that is virtually immovable. Unique to this Sako mount is a synthetic insert that provides maximum protection against possible scope damage. It also affords additional rigidity by compressing itself around the scope. Manufactured in Finland.

**Prices:**
**1″ Low, Medium & High** (Short, Medium
   & Long Action) . . . . . . . . . . . . . . . . . . . . . . . . **$ 94.00**
**30mm Low, Medium & High** (Short, Medium
   & Long Action) . . . . . . . . . . . . . . . . . . . . . . . . **113.00**
**1″ Medium & High Extended Base Scope
   Mounts** . . . . . . . . . . . . . . . . . . . . . . . . . . . . . . . **140.00**

### SCOPE MOUNTS

These SAKO scope mounts are lighter, yet stronger than ever. Tempered steel allows the paring of every last gram of unnecessary weight without sacrificing strength. Like the original mount, these rings clamp directly to the tapered dovetails on Sako rifles, thus eliminating the need for separate bases. Grooves inside the rings preclude scope slippage even under the recoil of the heaviest calibers. Nicely streamlined and finished in a rich blue-black to complement any Sako rifle.

**Prices:**
Low, medium, or high (1″) . . . . . . . . . . . . . . . . . . **$68.00**
Medium or high (30mm) . . . . . . . . . . . . . . . . . . . **84.00**

**"NEW" SCOPE MOUNTS**

# SCHMIDT & BENDER RIFLE SCOPES

## VARIABLE POWER

### 2¹/₂-10X56 VARIABLE POWER SCOPE
### $1298.00

Also available:
1¹/₄-4X20 Variable Power Scope............. $ 980.00
1¹/₂-6X42 Variable Power Scope............. 1073.00
3-12X42 Variable Power Scope.............. 1222.00
3-12X50 Variable Power Scope.............. 1262.00
*Note:* All variable power scopes have glass
reticles and are available in steel and aluminum

### SAFARI 1.25-4X20 (Not shown)
### $980.00

The Safari is designed for use on magnum rifles and for hunting large game. A newly designed ocular results in a longer eye relief, providing a wide field of view (31.5 yards at 100 yards).
**Magnification:** 1.25-4X
**Objective lens diameter:** 12.7-20mm
**Field of view at 100m:** 32m-10m; at 100 yards: 96'-16'
**Objective housing diameter:** 30mm
**Scope tube diameter:** 30mm
**Twilight factor:** 3,7-8,9
**Lenses:** Hard multi-coating
**Click value 1 click @100 meters:** 15mm; @100 yards: .540"

## FIXED POWER

### 4X36 FIXED POWER SCOPE
### (Steel Tube w/o Mounting Rail)
### $725.00

Also available:
**6X42 Fixed Power Scope**
Steel Tube w/o Mounting Rail ................ $795.00
**8X56 Fixed Power Scope**
Steel Tube w/o Mounting Rail ................ 915.00
**10X42 Fixed Power Scope**
Steel Tube w/o Mounting Rail ................ 910.00

### "VARMINT" (Not shown)
### Price to be announced

Designed for long-range target shooters and varmint hunters, Schmidt & Bender 4-16X50 "Varmint" riflescope features a precise parallax adjustment located in a third turret on the left side of the scope, making setting adjustments quick and convenient. The fine crosshairs of Reticle No. 6 cover only 1.5mm at 100 meters (.053" at 100 yards) throughout the entire magnification range.
**Magnification:** 4-16X
**Objective lens diameter:** 50mm
**Field of view at 100m:** 7.5-2.5m; at 100 yards: 22.5'-7.5'
**Objective housing diameter:** 57mm
**Scope tube diameter:** 30mm
**Twilight factor:** 14-28
**Lenses:** Hard multi-coating
**Click value 1 click @100 meters:** 10mm; @100 yards: .360"

## POLICE/MARKSMAN RIFLESCOPES

This line of riflescopes was designed specifically to meet the needs of the precision sharpshooter. It includes fixed-power scopes in 6X42 and 10X42 magnifications and variable-power scopes in 1.5-6X42, 3-12X42 and 3-12X50 configurations. The 3-12X50 is available in two models: Standard (for shooting to 500 yards) and a military version (MIL) designed for ranges up to 1000 yards. Each scope is equipped with two elevation adjustment rings: a neutral ring with ¹/₄" 100-yard clicks, which can be matched to any caliber and

### POLICE/MARKSMAN
### 3.12X50mm w/Detachable
### Rubber Sunshade and
### Bryant P-Rangefinding Reticle

bullet weight, and a second ring calibrated for the .308 caliber bullet. The 1.5-6X42 is calibrated for the 150-grain bullet, while all other rings are calibrated for the 168-grain bullet. The military elevation adjustment ring has 1" @100-yard clicks. Windage adjustment rings are set for ¹/₄" @100-yard clicks, except for the MIL scope which has ¹/₂" @100-yard clicks.

6X42........................................ $ 900.00
10X42....................................... 950.00
1.5-6X42.................................... 1200.00
3-12X42.................................... 1360.00
3-12X50.................................... 1400.00

# SIMMONS SCOPES

## AETEC
### MODELS 2100/2101/2102
### 2.8-10X44 WA
**Field of view:** 44'-14'
**Eye relief:** 5"
**Length:** 11.9"
**Weight:** 15.5 oz.
**Reticle:** Truplex
**Price:** $349.95

**AETEC SCOPE**
**2.8-10x44 WA Aspherical Lens System**
**w/Sunshade, Black Matte**

Also available:
**Model 2104**
**3.8-12X44 WA/AO**
Aspherical Lens System w/
  sunshade, black matte
**Price: $364.95**

**Model 2107**
**6-20X44mm AO**
**Price: $389.95**

**Model 2113**
**6-20X50mm AO**
**Price: $399.95**

## 44 MAG RIFLESCOPES

### MODEL M1044
### 3-10X44mm
**Field of view:** 34'-10.5'
**Eye relief:** 3"
**Length:** 12.8"
**Weight:** 16.9 oz.
**Price:** $259.95

### MODEL M1050DM
### 44 DIAMOND MAG

| | |
|---|---|
| 3.8-12X44mm | **Length:** 13.2" |
| **Field of view:** 30'-9.5' | **Weight:** 18.25 oz. |
| **Eye relief:** 3" | **Price:** $299.95 |

### MODEL M1045
### 4-12X44mm
**Field of view:** 30'-10'
**Eye relief:** 3"
**Length:** 12.8"
**Weight:** 19.5 oz.
**Price:** $279.95

### MODEL M1047
### 6.5-20X44mm
**Field of view:** 16'-6'
**Eye relief:** 2.6"-3.4"
**Length:** 12.8"
**Weight:** 19½ oz.
**Price:** $289.95

Also available:
**MODEL M1048**
6.5-20X44 Target Turrets
Black Matte (1/8" MOA)
  **$329.95**
  with Sunshade: **$344.90**

### MODEL M3044
### 3-10X44mm
**Field of view:** 34'-11'
**Eye relief:** 3"
**Length:** 13.1"
**Weight:** 16.4 oz.
**Price:** $269.95

## PROHUNTER RIFLESCOPES

### MODEL 7710

### MODEL 7710
### 3-9X40mm Wide Angle Riflescope
**Field of view:** 36'-13'
**Eye relief:** 3"
**Length:** 12.6"
**Weight:** 13.5 oz.
**Features:** Truplex reticle; silver matte finish
**Price:** $179.95 (Same in black matte or black polish, Models
  7711 and 7712)

Also available:
| Model 7700 2-7X32 Black Matte or Black Polish | $169.95 |
|---|---|
| **Model 7716** 4-12X40 Black Matte | 199.95 |
| **Model 7720** 6-18X40 (adj. obj. Black) | 224.95 |
| **Model 7721** 6-18X40 AO Black Matte | 224.95 |
| **Model 7740** 6X40 Black Matte | 144.95 |

# SIMMONS SCOPES

## WHITETAIL CLASSIC RIFLESCOPES

Simmons' Whitetail Classic Series features fully coated lenses and glare-proof BlackGranite finish. The Mono-Tube construction means that front bell and tube, saddle and rear tube are all turned from one piece of aircraft aluminum. This system eliminates 3 to 5 joints found in most other scopes in use today, making the Whitetail Classic up to 400 times stronger than comparably priced scopes.

**MODEL WTC9**
**3X28** Lighted Reticle Black Granite
**Field of view:** 11.5'
**Eye relief:** 11"-20"
**Length:** 9"
**Weight:** 9.2 oz.
**Price:** $329.95

**MODEL WTC11**

**MODEL WTC11**
**1.5-5X20mm**
**Field of view:** 75'-23'
**Eye relief:** 3.5"
**Length:** 9½"
**Weight:** 9.9 oz.
**Price:** $184.95

**MODEL WTC12**

**MODEL WTC12**
**2.5-8X36mm**
**Field of view:** 48'-14.8'
**Eye relief:** 3"
**Length:** 11.3"
**Weight:** 12.9 oz.
**Price:** $199.95

**MODEL WTC13**

**MODEL WTC13**
**3.5-10X40mm**
**Field of view:** 35'-12'
**Eye relief:** 3"
**Length:** 12.4"
**Weight:** 12.75 oz.
**Price:** $219.95

**MODEL WTC16**
**4X40** Black Granite
**Field of view:** 36.8'
**Eye relief:** 4"
**Length:** 9.9"
**Weight:** 12 oz.
**Price:** $149.95

**MODEL WTC33**
**3.5-10X40 Silver**
Same specifications as
Model WTC23
**Price:** $219.95

**MODEL WTC15/35**
**3.5-10X50 Black**
or Silver Granite
**Field of view:** 30.3'-11.3'
**Eye relief:** 3.2"
**Length:** 12.75"
**Weight:** 13.6 oz.
**Price:** $329.95

**MODEL WTC23**
**3.5-10X40**
**Field of view:** 34'-11.5'
**Eye relief:** 3.2"
**Length:** 12.4"
**Weight:** 12.8 oz.
**Price:** $219.95

**MODEL WTC45**
**4.5-14X40 AO**
**Field of view:** 22.5'-8.6'
**Eye relief:** 3.2"
**Length:** 13.2"
**Weight:** 14 oz.
**Price:** $269.95

# SIMMONS SCOPES

## GOLD MEDAL SILHOUETTE/VARMINT SERIES

Simmons Gold Medal Silhouette/Varmint Riflescopes are made of state-of-the-art drive train and erector tube design, a new windage and elevation indexing mechanism, camera-quality 100% multicoated lenses, and a super smooth ob-jective focusing device. High silhouette-type windage and elevation turrets house ⅛ minute click adjustments. The scopes have a black matte finish and crosshair reticle and are fogproof, waterproof and shockproof.

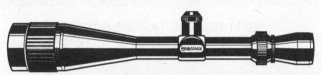

**MODEL 23002**

**MODEL 3007 V-TAC RIFLESCOPE**

**MODEL #23002**
**6-20X44mm**
**Field of view:** 17.4'-5.4'
**Eye relief:** 3"
**Length:** 14.5"
**Weight:** 18.3 oz.
**Feature:** Truplex reticle, 100% Multi-Coat Lens System, black matte finish, obj. focus
**Price:** $529.95 (Crosshair)
          529.95 (Dot Reticle)

**MODEL 3006V-TAC**
**3-9x40 Black Matte ProDiamond**
**Field of view:** 33'-14.5'
**Eye relief:** 4.1"-3.0"
**Length:** 12.5"
**Weight:** 17 oz.
**Price:** $699.95
Also available:
4.5-14X44 AO w/range-calculating reticle **$749.99**

## GOLD MEDAL HANDGUN SERIES

Simmons gold medal handgun scopes offer long eye relief, no tunnel vision, light weight, high resolution, non-critical head alignment, compact size and durability to withstand the heavy recoil of today's powerful handguns. In black and silver finishes, all have fully multicoated lenses and a Truplex reticle.

**MODEL 22001**

**MODEL #22001**
**2.5-7X28mm**
**Field of view:** 11'-4'
**Eye relief:** 15.7"-19.7"
**Length:** 9.2"
**Weight:** 9 oz.
**Feature:** Truplex reticle, 100% Multi-Coat Lens System, black polished finish.
**Price:** $329.95

**MODEL #22002**
**2.5-7X28mm**
**Field of view:** 11'-4'
**Eye relief:** 15.7"-19.7"
**Length:** 9.2"
**Weight:** 9 oz.
**Feature:** Truplex reticle, 100% Multi-Coat Lens System, black polished finish.
**Price:** $329.95

Also Available:
**MODEL #22003**
2X20 . . . . . . . . . . . . . . . . . . . $229.95
**MODEL #22004**
2X20 . . . . . . . . . . . . . . . . . . . 229.95
1.5-4X28 (black matte)
2208 . . . . . . . . . . . . . . . . . . . 299.95

# SIMMONS SCOPES

## 1022T RIMFIRE TARGET SCOPE
### $199.95

**Magnification:** 3-9X32mm AO
**Finish:** Black matte
**Features:** Adjustable for windage and elevation; parallax-free focus at 50 yards

Also available:
**1022** 4X32 black matte w/22 rings . . . . . . . . . . . . . **$ 74.95**
**1032** 4X28 22 Mag Mini silver matte w/22 rings . . . **96.95**
**1033** 4X32 silver matte w/22 rings. . . . . . . . . . . . . **79.95**
**1037** 3-9X32 silver matte w/22 rings . . . . . . . . . . . **109.95**
**1039** 3-9X32 black matte w/22 rings . . . . . . . . . . . **119.95**

**1022T RIMFIRE TARGET SCOPE**

## BLACKPOWDER SCOPES

**MODEL BP2732M**

**MODELS BP2732M/2732S**
**Magnification:** 2-7X32
**Finish:** Black or silver matte
**Field of view:** 57.7'-16.6'
100 yards
**Eye relief:** 3"   **Reticle:** Truplex
**Length:** 11.6"   **Weight:** 12.4 oz.
**Price: $129.95**

Also available:
**MODELS BP400M/400S**
**4X20 Black Matte or Silver Matte,**
**Long Body**
**Field of view:** 28"   **Eye relief:** 5.0"
**Length:** 10.25"   **Weight:** 8.7 oz.
**Reticle:** Truplex
**Price: $79.95**

**MODELS BP0420M/420S**
**4x20 Octagon Body**
**Field of view:** 19.5'
**Eye relief:** 4"
**Length:** 7.5"   **Weight:** 8.3 oz.
**Reticle:** Truplex
**Price: $169.95**

## SHOTGUN SCOPES

**MODELS 21004/7790D**
**Magnification:** 4X32
**Finish:** Black matte
**Field of view:** 16' (Model 21004); 17' (Model 7790D)
**Eye relief:** 5.5"
**Reticle:** Truplex (Model 21004); Pro-Diamond (Model 7790D)
**Length:** 8.5" (8.8" Model 21004)
**Weight:** 8.75 oz. (9.1 oz. Model 7790D)
**Prices:**
**Model 21004** . . . . . . . . . . . . . **$109.95**
**Model 7790D** . . . . . . . . . . . . . **139.95**

**MODEL 7790D**

Also available:
**Model 21005** 2.5X20 Black matte (Truplex reticle). . . . . . . . . . . . . . . **$ 99.95**
**Model 7789D** 2X32 Black matte (ProDiamond reticle). . . . . . . . . . . . **129.95**
**Model 7791D** 1.5-5X20 WA Black matte (ProDiamond reticle) . . . . . . **139.95**

# SWAROVSKI RIFLESCOPES

## HUNTER PH SERIES

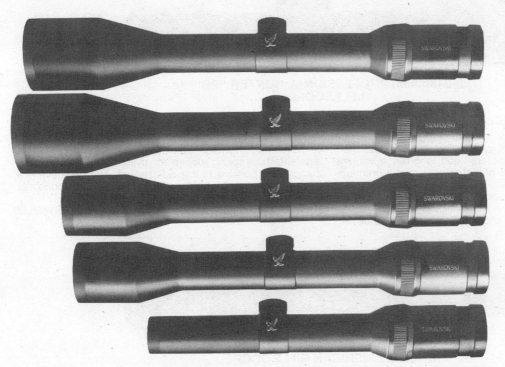

**3-12X50  $1376.65**
**($1698.89 Illuminated)**

**2.5-10X56  $1398.95**
**($1765.55 Illuminated)**

**2.5-10X42  $1298.95**

**1.5-6X42  $1132.25**

**1.25-4X24  $998.95**

## SPECIFICATIONS HUNTER PH SERIES (*see* following page for additional PH Models)

| Type | Maintube | Magnification | Max. effective objective lens ø in/mm | Exit pupil ø in/mm | Exit pupil distance in/mm | Field of view ft/100yds m/100 m | Twilight performance acc. to DIN 58388 | Middle tube ø standard in/mm a | Objective lens tube ø in/mm b | Total length in/mm c | 1 click in/100 yds mm/100 m | Max. adjustment range in/100 yds m/100 m | Weight S/LS (approx.) oz/g | Licencenumber |
|---|---|---|---|---|---|---|---|---|---|---|---|---|---|---|
| 1.25-4x24 | S L LS | 1.25-4 | 0.94 24 | 0.49-0.24 12.5-6 | 3.15 80 | 10.8-3.5 32.8-10.4 | 3.5-9.8 | 1.18 30 | 1.18 30 | 10.6 270 | 0.54 15 | 119 3.3 | 450 350 385 | 15.9 12.3 13.6 |
| 1.5-6x42 | S L LS | 1.5-6 | 1.65 42 | 0.52-0.28 13.1-7 | 3.15 80 | 7.3-2.3 21.8-7 | 4.2-15.9 | 1.18 30 | 1.89 48 | 13.0 330 | 0.36 10 | 79 2.2 | 580 450 485 | 20.5 15.9 17.1 |
| 2.5-10x42 | S L LS | 2.5-10 | 1.65 42 | 0.52-0.17 13.1-4.2 | 3.15 80 | 4.4-1.4 13.2-4.1 | 7.1-20.5 | 1.18 30 | 1.89 48 | 13.2 336 | 0.36 10 | 47 1.3 | 550 420 455 | 19.4 14.8 16.0 |
| 2.5-10x56 | S L LS | 2.5-10 | 2.20 56 | 0.52-0.22 13.1-5.6 | 3.15 80 | 4.4-1.4 13.2-4.1 | 7.1-23.7 | 1.18 30 | 2.44 62 | 14.7 374 | 0.36 10 | 47 1.3 | 690 520 560 | 24.3 18.3 19.8 |
| 3-12x50 | S L LS | 3-12 | 1.97 50 | 0.52-0.17 13.1-4.2 | 3.15 80 | 3.7-1.2 11-3.5 | 8.5-24.5 | 1.18 30 | 2.20 56 | 14.3 364 | 0.36 10 | 40 1.1 | 625 470 510 | 22.0 16.6 18.0 |

S = steel body, L = light alloy body, LS = light alloy body with mounting rail

# SWAROVSKI RIFLESCOPES

## 6-24X50mm PROFESSIONAL HUNTER "PH" RIFLESCOPE

Swarovski's 6-24X50mm "PH" riflescope was developed for long-range target, big-game and varmint shooting. Its waterproof parallax adjustment system should be popular with White Tail "Bean Field Shooters" and long-range varmint hunters looking for a choice of higher powers in a premium rifle scope and still deliver accuracy. The new scope will also appeal to many bench rest shooters who compete in certain classes where power and adjustment are limited. A non-magnifying, fine plex reticle and an all-new fine crosshair reticle with $1/8$" MOA dot are available in the 6-24X50mm scope. Reticle adjustment clicks are $1/6$" (minute) by external, waterproof "target turrets." The internal optical system features a patented coil spring suspension system for dependable accuracy and positive reticle adjustment. The objective bell, 30mm middle tube, turret housing and ocular bell connection are machined from one solid bar of aluminum.

**Price:** . . . . . . . . . . . . . . . . . . . . . . . . . . . . . . . . . . . . . . **$1665.50**

## 3-10X42 AMERICAN RIFLE SCOPE

Swarovski's 3-10X42mm American style riflescope is an addition to the company's one-inch "A" line of lightweight riflescopes. It offers greater magnification and a larger objective lens for better light gathering ability needed for twilight and "black timber" hunting. Encased in a special one-piece aluminum alloy tube, this scope is waterproof/submersible, shockproof and carries a limited lifetime warranty. As in all Swarovski's fixed-power scopes, the 3-10X42 variable riflescope features a variety of popular style reticles, laser-aligned optics and fully multi-coated optics for maximum light transmission and brilliant images

**Price:** . . . . . . . . . . . . . . . . . . . . . . . . . . . . . . . . . . . . . . **$776.65**

**8X50 (30mm)**

**8X56 (30mm)**

## FIXED POWER PH RIFLESCOPES

Swarovski's fixed-power models—the 1" 6X42 and 30mm 8X50 and 8X56—were added to the 10 variable-power models introduced in 1994. Among the features of these additions are an objective bell, 30mm middle tube, turret housing and ocular bell connection machined out of one solid piece of bar stock. The internal optical system uses a patented coil spring suspension that helps to insure dependable accuracy and positive reticle adjustment. All scopes are purged with nitrogen and tested for accuracy. The scopes come with a wide choice of reticles and an unconditional lifetime warranty.

**Prices:**

| | |
|---|---|
| 6X42 . . . . . . . . . . . . . . . . . . . . . . . . . . . . . . . . . . . . . . | **$921.00** |
| 8X50 . . . . . . . . . . . . . . . . . . . . . . . . . . . . . . . . . . . . . . | 954.50 |
| 8X56 . . . . . . . . . . . . . . . . . . . . . . . . . . . . . . . . . . . . . . | 998.95 |

# SWAROVSKI RIFLESCOPES

**KAHLES Z-95 (6X42)**

## KAHLES TACTICAL RIFLESCOPES

Both reticles on the Kahles riflescopes (6X42 and 10X42) have a range- finding capability and include a .308 caliber Ballistic Cam Adjustment System. This allows the shooter to estimate range, using known object sizes, downrange. The shooter then dials in a fairly accurate range measurement with the ballistic cam adjustment for predicted bullet drop at that distance. The mil-dot reticle used was developed by the U.S. Marine Corps in the late 1970s. The mil-dots are spaced one mil apart and equal 36″ at 1,000 yards or 18″ at 500 yds.

The dots above and below the cross-hair can be used for holdover estimating, while the dots to the right and left can be used to lead a moving target or to compensate for wind drift. The ZF-95 scopes have 1″ steel tubes, a Parkerized matte black finish and externally adjusted turrets.

**Prices:**

| | |
|---|---|
| Z-95 6X42 | $1198.95 |
| Z-95 10X42 | 1221.00 |

**KAHLES 30mm RIFLESCOPE**

## KAHLES 30mm RIFLESCOPE

Three variable-power Kahles riflescopes have been introduced by Swarovski Optik as additions to their "Value Class Optics" line. Produced in Austria, these scopes offer optimum optical clarity and brightness from a 30mm tube using large diameter lenses throughout. The scope selection includes 1.5-6X42, 2.2-9X42 and 3-12X56 models. the optical components are fully multi-coated and the scope tubes are

purged with nitrogen. All are shockproof, waterproof and come with an unconditional lifetime warranty.

**Prices:**

| | |
|---|---|
| S-6X42 | $776.65 |
| Illuminated | 127.65 |
| 2.2-9X42 | 943.35 |
| 3-12X56 | 998.95 |

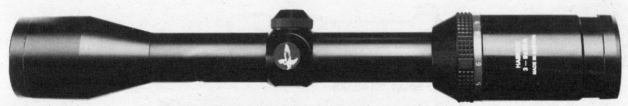

**AMERICAN LIGHTWEIGHT RIFLESCOPE**

This model features precision ground, coated and aligned optics sealed in a special aluminum alloy tube to withstand heavy recoil. Eye relief is 85mm and the recoiling eyepiece protects the eye. Positive click adjustments for elevation and windage change the impact point (approx. ¼″) per click at 100 yards, with parallax also set at 100 yards. Weight is only 13 ounces.

**Prices:**

| | |
|---|---|
| 1.5-4.5X20 with duplex reticle | $665.56 |
| 4X32 with duplex reticle | 554.50 |
| 6X36 with duplex reticle | 610.00 |
| 3-9X36 with duplex reticle | 698.89 |
| 3-10X42 with duplex reticle | 776.65 |

# SWIFT RIFLESCOPES

**MODEL 650 $80.00**

**MODEL 653 $104.00**
**(Matte $106.00  Silver $106.50)**

## RIFLESCOPE SPECIFICATIONS

| MODEL# | DESCRIPTION | FIELD OF VIEW AT 100 YDS. (FT') | ZERO PARALLAX AT | EYE RELIEF (INCH) | TUBE DIAMETER (INCH) | CLICK ADJUSTMENT (INCH) | LENGTH (INCH) | WEIGHT (OZ.) |
|---|---|---|---|---|---|---|---|---|
| 650 | 4x,32mm | 26' | 100 YDS. | 4 | 1" | 1/4" | 12" | 9.1 |
| 653 | 4x,40mm, W.A. | 35' | 100 YDS. | 4 | 1" | 1/4" | 12.2" | 12.6 |
| 660 | 4x,20mm | 25' | 35 YDS. | 4 | 1" | 1/4" | 11.8" | 9 |
| 668 | 4x,32mm | 25' | 100 YDS. | 4 | 1" | 1/4" | 10" | 8.9 |
| 666 | 1x,20mm | 113' | - | 3.2 | 1" | 1/4" | 7.5" | 9.6 |
| 657 | 6x,40mm | 28' | 100 YDS. | 4" | 1" | 1/4" | 12.6" | 10.4 |
| 654 | 3-9x,32mm | 35' @ 3x 12' @ 9x | 100 YDS. | 3.4 @ 3x 2.9 @ 9x | 1" | 1/4" | 12" | 9.8 |
| 656 | 3-9x,40mm, W.A. | 40' @ 3x 14' @ 9x | 100 YDS. | 3.4 @ 3x 2.8 @ 9x | 1" | 1/4" | 12.6" | 12.3 |
| 664R | 4-12x,40mm | 27' / 9' | Adjustable | 3.0 / 2.8 | 1" | 1/4" | 13.3" | 14.8 |
| 665 | 1.5-4.5x,21mm | 69' / 24.5' | 100 YDS. | 3.5 / 3.0 | 1" | 1/4" | 10.9" | 9.6 |
| 659 | 3.5-10x,44mm, W.A. | 34' @ 3.5x 12' @ 10x | 100 YDS. | 3.0 / 2.8 | 1" | 1/4" | 12.8" | 13.5 |
| 669 | 6-18x,44mm | 18' @ 6x 6.5' @ 18x | Adjustable | 2.8 | 1" | 1/4" | 14.5" | 17.6 |
| 649 | 4-12x,50mm, W.A. | 30' @ 4x 10' @ 12x | 100 YDS. | 3.2 / 3.0 | 1" | 1/4" | 13.2" | 14.6 |
| 658 | 2-7x,40mm, W.A. | 55' @ 2x 18' @ 7x | 100 YDS. | 3.3 / 3.0 | 1" | 1/4" | 11.6" | 12.5 |
| 667 | FIRE-FLY, 1x,30mm | 40' | 100 YDS. | Unlimited | 30mm | 1/2" | 5 3/8" | 5 |

Also available:
| | |
|---|---|
| **Model 649** | **$218.00** |
| **Model 649M** | 220.00 |
| **Model 654** | 102.00 |
| **Model 656** | 112.00 |
|     Matte | 114.00 |
|     Silver | 114.50 |
| **Model 657** 6X, 40mm | 102.00 |
| **Model 658** | 140.00 |
|     Matte | 142.00 |
| **Model 659** | 215.00 |
|     Matte | 216.00 |
|     Silver | 217.00 |

**PISTOLS SCOPES**
| | |
|---|---|
| **Model 661** 4X32 | **$118.00** |
| **Model 663B** 2X20 | 118.00 |
| **Model 670M** 2.5-7X28 | 155.00 |

**MODEL 664R $146.00**
**(Matte $147.00  Silver $148.00)**

**MODEL 668**
**COMPACT RIFLESCOPE**
**$99.00**

484 SHOOTER'S BIBLE 1998

# TASCO SCOPES

## MODEL 1.75X-5X

### WORLD CLASS™ WIDE-ANGLE® RIFLESCOPES

**Features:**
- 25% larger field of view
- Exceptional optics

- Fully coated for maximum light transmission
- Waterproof, shockproof, fogproof
- Non-removable eye bell
- Free haze filter lens caps
- TASCO's unique World Class Lifetime Warranty

The Model 1.75X-5X member of Tasco's World Class Wide Angle line offers a wide field of view—72 feet at 1.75X and 24 feet at 5X—and quick sighting without depending on a critical view. The scope is ideal for hunting deer and dangerous game, especially in close quarters or in heavily wooded and poorly lit areas. Other features include ¼-minute positive click stops, fully coated lenses (including Supercon process), nonremovable eyebell and windage/elevation screws. Length: 10″, with 1″ diameter tube. Weight: 10 ounces.

## WORLD CLASS, WIDE-ANGLE VARIABLE ZOOM RIFLESCOPES

| Model No. | Power | Objective Diameter | Finish | Reticle | Field of View @100 Yds. | Eye Relief | Tube Diameter | Scope Length | Scope Weight | Price |
|---|---|---|---|---|---|---|---|---|---|---|
| WA4X40 | 4X | 40mm | Black Gloss | 30/30 | 36′ | 3″ | 1″ | 13″ | 11.5 oz. | $135.85 |
| WA6X40 | 6X | 40mm | Black Gloss | 30/30 | 23′ | 3″ | 1″ | 12.75″ | 11.5 oz. | 144.30 |
| WA1.755X20 | 1.75X-5X | 20mm | Black Gloss | 30/30 | 72′-24′ | 3″ | 1″ | 10.5″ | 10 oz. | 152.80 |
| DWC39X40 | 3X-9X | 40mm | Black Matte | 30/30 | 41′-15′ | 3″ | 1″ | 12.75″ | 13 oz. | 198.45 |
| WA39X40 | 3X-9X | 40mm | Black Gloss | 30/30 | 41′-15′ | 3″ | 1″ | 12.75″ | 13 oz. | 198.65 |
| WA39X40TV | 3X-9X | 40mm | Black Gloss | 30/30 TV | 41′-15′ | 3″ | 1″ | 12.75″ | 13 oz. | 198.65 |
| WA39X40ST | 3X-9X | 40mm | Stainless | 30/30 | 41′-15′ | 3″ | 1″ | 12.75″ | 13 oz. | 198.65 |

## WORLD CLASS™ 1″ PISTOL SCOPES

Built to withstand the most punishing recoil, these scopes feature a 1″ tube that provides long eye relief to accommodate all shooting styles safely, along with fully coated optics for a bright, clear image and shot-after-shot durability. The 2X22 model is recommended for target shooting, while the 4X28 model and 1.25X-4X28 are used for hunting as well. All are fully waterproof, fogproof, shockproof and include haze filter caps.

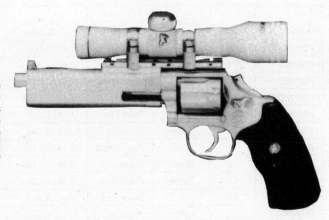

## SPECIFICATIONS

| Model | Power | Objective Diameter | Finish | Reticle | Field of View @ 100 Yds | Eye Relief | Tube Diam. | Scope Length | Scope Weight | Prices |
|---|---|---|---|---|---|---|---|---|---|---|
| PWC2X22 | 2X | 22mm | Blk Gloss | 30/30 | 25′ | 11″–20″ | 1″ | 8.75″ | 7.3 oz. | $288.60 |
| PWC2X22MA | 2X | 22mm | Matte Alum. | 30/30 | 25′ | 11″–20″ | 1″ | 8.75″ | 7.3 oz. | 288.60 |
| PWC4X28 | 4X | 28mm | Blk Gloss | 30/30 | 8′ | 12″–19″ | 1″ | 9.45″ | 7.9 oz. | 399.55 |
| PWC4X28MA | 4X | 28mm | Matte Alum. | 30/30 | 8′ | 12″–19″ | 1″ | 9.45″ | 7.9 oz. | 339.55 |
| P1.254X28 | 1.25X-4X | 28mm | Blk Gloss | 30/30 | 23′-9′ | 15″-23″ | 1″ | 9.25″ | 8.2 oz. | 339.55 |
| P1.254X28MA | 1.25X-4X | 28mm | Matte Alum. | 30/30 | 23′-9′ | 15″-23″ | 1″ | 9.25″ | 8.2 oz. | 285.45 |

# TASCO SCOPES

## PROPOINT PLUS PDP3CMP

**TASCO LUMINA
MODEL 11-6x40wa-1**

## PROPOINT™ MULTI-PURPOSE SCOPES

Tasco's ProPoint is a true 1X-30mm scope with electronic red dot reticle that features unlimited eye relief, enabling shooters to shoot with both eyes open. It is available with a 3X booster and also has application for rifle, shotgun, bow and black powder. The compact version (PDP2) houses a lithium battery pack, making it 1¼ inches narrower than previous models and lighter as well (5.5 oz.). A mercury battery converter is provided for those who prefer standard batteries. Tasco's 3X booster with crosshair reticle weighs 6.1 oz. and is 5½ inches long. Specifications and prices are listed below.

## LUMINA™ RIFLESCOPES
### $84.95–152.95

Tasco's line of Lumina riflescopes with Rubicon™ ruby coated objective lenses filter out red light for crisp daylight viewing and are especially suited for use over snow and in other bright conditions. The line offers fixed power and variable scopes: 4X21mm, 6X40mm, 3X-12X40mm (all with 30/30 reticles) and a 3X-9X40mm model with a standard round reticle or TV reticle.

## SPECIFICATIONS PROPOINT SCOPES

| Model | Power | Objective Diameter | Finish | Reticle | Field of View @ 100 Yds. | Eye Relief | Tube Diam. | Scope Length | Scope Weight | Prices |
|---|---|---|---|---|---|---|---|---|---|---|
| PDP2 | 1X | 25mm | Black Matte | 5 M.O.A.Dot | 40' | Unlimited | 30mm | 5" | 5.5 oz. | $254.65 |
| PDP2ST | 1X | 25mm | Stainless | 5 M.O.A. Dot | 40' | Unlimited | 30mm | 5" | 5.5 oz. | 254.65 |
| PDP2BD | 1X | 25mm | Black Matte | 10 M.O.A. Dot | 40' | Unlimited | 30mm | 5" | 5.5 oz. | 254.65 |
| PDP2BDST | 1X | 25mm | Stainless | 10 M.O.A. Dot | 40' | Unlimited | 30mm | 5" | 5.5 oz. | 254.65 |
| PDP3 | 1X | 25mm | Black Matte | 5 M.O.A. Dot | 52' | Unlimited | 30mm | 5" | 5.5 oz. | 305.60 |
| PDP3ST | 1X | 25mm | Stainless | 5 M.O.A. Dot | 52' | Unlimited | 30mm | 5" | 5.5 oz. | 305.60 |
| PDP3BD | 1X | 25mm | Black Matte | 10 M.O.A. Dot | 52' | Unlimited | 30mm | 5" | 5.5 oz. | 305.60 |
| PDP3BDST | 1X | 25mm | Stainless | 10 M.O.A. Dot | 52' | Unlimited | 30mm | 5" | 5.5 oz. | 305.60 |
| PDP3CMP | 1X | 30mm | Black Matte | 10 M.O.A. Dot | 68' | Unlimited | 33mm | 4.75" | 5.4 oz. | 390.45 |
| PDP405 | 1X | 40mm | Black Matte | 5 M.O.A. Dot | 82' | Unlimited | 45mm | 4.8" | 6.1 oz. | 407.45 |
| PDP45ST | 1X | 40mm | Stainless | 5 M.O.A. Dot | 82' | Unlimited | 45mm | 4.8" | 6.1 oz. | 407.45 |
| PDP410 | 1X | 40mm | Black Matte | 10 M.O.A. Dot | 82' | Unlimited | 45mm | 4.8" | 6.1 oz. | 407.45 |
| PDP410ST | 1X | 40mm | Stainless | 10 M.O.A. Dot | 82' | Unlimited | 45mm | 4.8" | 6.1 oz. | 407.45 |
| PDP415 | 1X | 40mm | Black Matte | 15 M.O.A. Dot | 82' | Unlimited | 45mm | 4.8" | 6.1 oz. | 407.45 |
| PDP415ST | 1X | 40mm | Stainless | 15 M.O.A. Dot | 82' | Unlimited | 45mm | 4.8" | 6.1 oz. | 407.45 |
| PDP420 | 1X | 40mm | Black Matte | 20 M.O.A. Dot | 82' | Unlimited | 45mm | 4.8" | 6.1 oz. | 407.45 |
| PDP420ST | 1X | 40mm | Stainless | 20 M.O.A. Dot | 82' | Unlimited | 45mm | 4.8" | 6.1 oz. | 407.45 |
| PDP420SG | 1X | 40mm | Black Matte | 20 M.O.A. Dot | 82' | Unlimited | 45mm | 4.8" | 6.1 oz. | 407.45 |
| PDP5SCMP | 1X | 45mm | Black Matte | 4, 8, 12, 16 MOA | 82' | Unlimited | 45mm | 4" | 8.0 oz. | 407.45 |

# TASCO RIFLESCOPES

## WORLD CLASS PLUS RIFLESCOPES

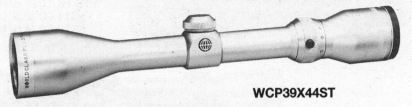

**WCP39X44ST**

## SPECIFICATIONS WORLD CLASS PLUS RIFLESCOPES

| Model | Power | Objective Diameter | Finish | Reticle | Field of View @ 100 Yds. | Eye Relief | Tube Diam. | Scope Length | Scope Weight | Prices |
|---|---|---|---|---|---|---|---|---|---|---|
| WCP4X44 | 4X | 44mm | Black Gloss | 30/30 | 32' | 3¼" | 1" | 12.75" | 13.5 oz. | $392.50 |
| WCP6X44 | 6X | 44mm | Black Gloss | 30/30 | 21' | 3¼" | 1" | 12.75" | 13.6 oz. | 407.45 |
| WCP39X44 | 3X-9X | 44mm | Black Gloss* | 30/30 | 39'-14' | 3½" | 1" | 12.75" | 15.8 oz. | 407.45 |
| DWCP39X44 | 3X-9X | 44mm | Black Matte | 30/30 | 39'-14' | 3½" | 1" | 12.75" | 15.8 oz. | 407.45 |
| WCP39X44ST | 3X-9X | 44 mm | Stainless | 30/30 | 39'-14' | 3½" | 1" | 12.75" | 15.8 oz. | 407.45 |
| WCP3.510X50 | 3.5X-10X | 50mm | Black Gloss | 30/30 | 30'-10.5' | 3¾" | 1" | 13" | 17.1 oz. | 492.35 |
| DWCP3.510X50 | 3.5X-10X | 50mm | Black Matte | 30/30 | 30'-10.5' | 3¾" | 1" | 13" | 17.1 oz. | 492.35 |
| DWCP832X50 | 8X-32X | 50mm | Black Matte | Crosshair* | 13'-4' | 3" | 1" | 14.5 " | 25.1 oz. | 560.00 |
| DWCP1040X50 | 10X-40X | 50mm | Black Matte | Crosshair* | 13'-4' | 3" | 1" | 14.5" | 25.3 oz. | 611.00 |

\* With 10 M.O.A.

## RUBBER ARMORED SCOPES

| Model | Power | Objective Diameter | Finish | Reticle | Field of View @ 100 Yards | Eye Relief | Tube Diam. | Scope Length | Scope Weight | Price |
|---|---|---|---|---|---|---|---|---|---|---|
| RC39X40 | 3-9X | 40mm | Black Rubber | 30/30 | 35'-12' | 3¼" | 1" | 12.5" | 14.3 oz. | $254.65 |

"A" fits standard dove tail base.    "B" fits ³⁄₈" grooved receivers—most 22 cal. and airguns.

## MAG IV™ RIFLESCOPES (not shown)

MAG IV scopes yield four times magnification range in a standard size riflescope and one-third more zooming range than most variable scopes. Features include: Fully coated optics and large objective lens to keep target in low light . . . Nonremovable eye bell . . . ¼-minute positive click stops. . . Nonremovable windage and elevation screws. . . Opticentered 30/30 rangefinding reticle . . . Waterproof, fogproof, shockproof.

## SPECIFICATIONS

| Model | Power | Objective Diameter | Finish | Reticle | Field of View @ 100 Yds. | Eye Relief | Tube Diam. | Scope Length | Scope Weight | Price |
|---|---|---|---|---|---|---|---|---|---|---|
| W312X40 | 3–12 | 40mm | Black | 30/30 | 35'–9' | 3⅛" | 1" | 12³⁄₁₆" | 12 oz. | $152.80 |
| W416X40† | 4–16 | 40mm | Black | 30/30 | 26'–6' | 3⅛" | 1" | 14⅛" | 15.6 oz. | 203.75 |
| W624X40† | 6–24 | 40mm | Black | 30/30 | 17'–4' | 3" | 1" | 15⅜" | 16.75 oz. | 254.65 |

† Indicates focusing objective.    \* Also available: **Model V416X40ST**in stainless. $203.75

# TASCO RIFLESCOPES

### BIG HORN® RIFLESCOPES
### $611.00 (2.5-10X50mm)
### $679.00 (4.5-18X50mm)

## BIG HORN® RIFLESCOPES

Tasco's line of Big Horn® riflescopes features two high-quality models—the 2.5-10X50mm and a 4.5X-18X50mm—with the latter offering a big 18 power and wide-angle optics for fast sighting of running game. Designed with a one-piece body tube for strength and durability, the Big Horn scopes are equipped with 50mm objective lenses that offer greater light transmission for hunting at dawn and dusk when game is most active. Multi-coating on the objective lens and ocular lenses, plus fully coated optics throughout, provide the hunter with sharp detailed images. Big Horn scopes also feature parallax adjustment rings on the objective tube.

### MAG-IV
### 4X-16X50mm

## MAG-IV-50™ RIFLESCOPES
### $390.00–$475.00

Tasco's MAG-IV™ riflescopes feature large 50mm objective lenses that transmit even more light than the MAG-IV with 40mm objectives and are especially designed for dawn and dusk use. The additions to the MAG-IV line include three high-quality variable scopes: the 4X-16X50mm, the 5X-20X50mm and the 5X-20X50mm with bullet drop compensation. All three models have Super-Con® multi-layered lens coating and fully coated optics.

These MAG-IV scopes feature windage and elevation adjustments with $\frac{1}{4}$-minute clickstops and an Opti-Centered® 30/30 range-finding reticle. This adjustment system allows the reticle to remain centered in the field of view (an "image moving" system as opposed to a "reticle moving" system). Finished in black matte.
Also available:
**MAG-IV Riflescopes 3X-12X40mm, 4X-16X40mm,**
**6X-24X40mm . . . . . . . . . . . . . . . . . . . . . . . . . . . . . $254.65**

## TITAN™ RIFLESCOPES
### $594.00 (1.25-4.5X26mm)
### $645.00 (3X-9X42mm)
### $679.00 (1.5X-6X42mm)
### $763.95 (3X-12X52mm)

Tasco's Titan™ riflescopes are equipped with unusually large 42mm and 52mm objective lenses that can transmit more light than standard 40mm lenses for dim early morning and dusk conditions. Three variable scopes—the 1.5X-6X42mm, the 3X-9X42mm and the 3X-12X52mm—are available with 30/30 reticles and feature lenses with five-layer multi-coating for greater image contrast and clarity. Titan scopes also have finger-adjustable windage and elevation controls along with fast focusing eyebells. Waterproof, shockproof and fogproof, these scopes feature all-weather lubrication of each moving part for smooth functioning in any climate condition. Finished in matte black.

Now available in 1.25-4.5X26mm for close range hunting; features a German reticle and 5-layer multi-coating, long eye relief and wide field of view.

# WEAVER SCOPES

### QWIK-POINT 45mm SCOPE

### QUIK-POINT 30mm SCOPE

## QWIK-POINT™ SCOPE 45MM

The 45mm Quick-Point red dot scope provides a large field of view for shotgun and pistol hunting. A straight-cut objective protects the lens from fragments and powder residue. The objective lock ring keeps lenses aligned and fixed in place. Offers quick MOA dot adjustment, shockproof and waterproof. An 11-setting light adjustment dot for selecting light intensity.

**Prices:**
**49962** Qwik-Point 45mm 4 MOA Silver . . . . . . . . . $296.25
**49963** Qwik-Point 45mm 12 MOA Silver . . . . . . . . . 296.25
**49964** Qwik-Point 45mm Variable silver . . . . . . . . . 383.00
**49968** Qwik-Point 45mm Variable Matte . . . . . . . . 383.00
**49966** Qwik-Point 45mm 12 MOA Matte . . . . . . . . 296.25

## QWIK-POINT SCOPE 30MM

The 30mm Qwik-Point red dot scope offers shooters the speed and accuracy of point-and-shoot target recognition. The red dot (powered by a low cost camera battery) can be adjusted to 11 different light intensities and is available in 4 or 12 minute-of- angle dot size. Click type windage and elevation adjustments make zeroing easy. The multi-coated optics provide sharp images and the nitrogen filled 30mm tube is fogproof, waterproof and shockproof. Scopes are one power magnification.

**Prices:**
**49960** Qwik-Point 30mm 4 MOA . . . . . . . . . . . . . . $235.95
**49961** Qwik-Point 30mm 12 MOA . . . . . . . . . . . . . 235.95
Also available:
**33mm** Variable Qwik-Point Scope
Silver . . . . . . . . . . . . . . . . . . . . . . . . . . . . . . . . . . . . $383.00
Matte . . . . . . . . . . . . . . . . . . . . . . . . . . . . . . . . . . . . 382.25

### RIMFIRE 4X MATTE SCOPE

## RIMFIRE SCOPE 2.5-7X

Lenses are multi-coated for bright, clear low-light performance and the one-piece tube design is shockproof and waterproof.

**Prices:**
**49622** 2.5-7x Rimfire Matte . . . . . . . . . . . . . . . . . . . $176.75
**49623** 2.5-7x Rimfire Silver . . . . . . . . . . . . . . . . . . 178.50

## RIMFIRE SCOPE 4X

Fixed 4x scope is ideal for a variety of shooting applications. It's durable, light-weight and waterproof.

**Prices:**
**49620** 4x Rimfire Matte . . . . . . . . . . . . . . . . . . . . . . $153.75
**49621** 4x Rimfire Silver . . . . . . . . . . . . . . . . . . . . . . 156.75

# WEAVER SCOPES

## T-SERIES MODEL T-6 RIFLESCOPE
## $409.00

Weaver's T-6 competition rifle scope is only 12.7 inches long and weighs less than 15 ounces. Magnification is six-power. All optical surfaces are fully multi-coated for maximum clarity and light transmission. The T-6 features Weaver's Micro-Trac precision adjustments in 1/8-minute clicks to ensure parallel tracking. The protected target-style turrets are a low-profile configuration combining ease of adjustment with weight re-duction. A 40mm adjustable objective permits parallax correction from 50 feet to infinity without shifting the point of impact. A special AO lock ring eliminates bell vibration or shift. The T-6 comes with screw-in metal lens caps and features a competition matte black finish. Also available with matte silver finish.

## V24 6X24 VARMINT SCOPE
## AND V24 6X24 RIFLESCOPE
## $444.00

Weaver's V24 Varmint scope is the big brother of the V16, one of Weaver's most popular scopes. The V24 zooms from 6 to 24 power, has a 42mm adjustable objective and a special varmint reticle. Reticle adjustments are in precise, 1/8-minute clicks for precision positioning. One-piece tube design and intelligent engineering make the V24 lighter than comparable high-quality scopes. Like the V16, the new scope has generous eye relief, multi-coated optics for maximum light transmission, and comes with a matte black finish. An optional 4-inch sun shade is available for shooting in critical light conditions.

## MODEL SV6 SHOTGUN SCOPE
## $199.00

Weaver's variable shotgun scope, the SV6, has a 1.5 to 6X zoom range and parallax correction preset to 75 yards. It has a one-inch tube and a 28mm objective to allow low mounting on most popular shotguns. The finish is matte black. The SV6 is recommended for short-range rifles (carbines or muzzle-loaders) as well as slug guns.

# WILLIAMS SIGHTS

**MODEL WSKS APERTURE SIGHT**

### MODEL WSKS RIFLE SIGHT
**$22.75 (Open Sight)**
**$24.75 (Aperture Sight)**

The WSKS replaces the military rear sight on SKS 7.62X39 rifles. No drilling and tapping required. Fully adjustable for elevation and windage. Open sight comes with 1/4" U blade. Aperture sight includes a special target hole aperture (R 3/8X.150 for enhanced field of view).

**MODEL FP RECEIVER SIGHT**

### FP RECEIVER SIGHTS SERIES
**$59.95    $71.25 with Target Knobs**

Internal micrometer adjustments have positive internal locks. Alloy used has a tensile strength of 85,000 pounds, yet sights weigh only 1.5 ounces each. Target knobs are available. Options include standard, blade, shotgun/big game aperture. Model shown mounted on a Knight MK-85 (Modern Muzzle-loading).

### WGRS RECEIVER SIGHTS SERIES
**$30.95**

These sights (22 in all) offer a compact low profile and in most cases utilize dovetail or existing screws on top of receiver for installation. Made from aluminum alloy (stronger than most steel). Positive windage and elevation locks. Rustproof. Can be converted to open sights by installing a 1/4" WGOS blade (in place of aperture holder).

**MODEL WGRS-KN RECEIVER SIGHT**

### WGOS OPEN SIGHT BASES (Not Shown)
**$16.50**

Made from high tensile-strength, rustproof aluminum. Streamlined and lightweight with tough anodized finish. Dovetailed windage and elevation. Interchangeable blades available in four heights and styles. All parts milled.

### "SLUGGER" SIGHTS (Not Shown)
**$34.95**

Williams' own concept in front and rear combinations for ribbed shotgun barrels. Made from tough aircraft aluminum. Fully adjustable rear sight for windage and elevation. No drilling and tapping—installs in minutes without harming gun. 1/4" sight fits most Browning Auto-5's. 5/16" fits most Remington 870, 1100 and 11/87s, Browning BPS, and more. 3/8" fits most Winchester 1200, 1300 and 1400 models.

# ZEISS RIFLESCOPES

## "THE "Z" SERIES"

**DIAVARI-C 3-9X36**
**$625.00**
**New lighter version of the German-made scope now built in the U.S.A.**

**DIAVARI-C 3-9X36T (not shown)**
**$815.00 ($845.00 Silver)**

**DIATAL-Z 6X42 T**
**$955.00**

**DIAVARI-Z 1.5-6X42 T**
**$1240.00**

**DIATAL-Z 3-12X56 T**
**$1575.00**
**($1810.00 w/Illuminated #8 Reticle)**

**DIAVARI-Z 2.5-10X48 T**
**(not shown)**
**$1465.00**

**DIATAL-Z 8X56 T**
**$1135.00**

**DIAVARI-Z 1.25-4×24**
**(not shown)**
**$1085.00**

## ZM/Z SERIES RIFLESCOPE SPECIFICATIONS

| Model | Diatal-ZM/Z 6X42 T | Diavari-ZM/Z 1.5-6X42 T | Diavari-ZM/Z 3-12X56 T | Diatal-ZM/Z 8X56 T | Diavari-ZM/Z 2.5-10X48 T | Diavera-ZM/Z 1.25-4X24 | Diavari-C 3-9X36 |
|---|---|---|---|---|---|---|---|
| Magnification | 6X | 1.5X 6X | 3X 12X | 8X | 2.5X-10X | 1.25-4X | 3X 9X |
| Effective obj. diam. | 42mm/1.7" | 19.5/0.8" 42/1.7" | 38/1.5" 56/2.2" | 56mm/2.2" | 33/1.30" 48/1.89" | NA | 30.0/1.2" 36.0/1.4" |
| Diameter of exit pupil | 7mm | 13mm 7mm | 12.7mm 4.7mm | 7mm | 13.2mm 4.8mm | 12.6mm 6.3mm | 10.0 4.0mm |
| Twilight factor | 15.9 | 4.2 15.9 | 8.5 25.9 | 21.2 | 7.1 21.9 | 3.54 9.6 | 8.5 18.0 |
| Field of view at 100 m/ ft. at 100 yds. | 6.7m/20.1' | 18/54.0' 6.5/19.5' | 9.2/27.6' 3.3/9.9' | 5m/15.0' | 11.0/33.0 3.9/11.7 | 32 10 | 12.0/36.0 4.3/12.9 |
| Approx. eye relief | 8cm/3.2" | 8cm/3.2" | 8cm/3.2" | 8cm/3.2" | 8cm/3.2" | 8cm/3.2" | 3.5" |
| Click-stop adjustment 1 click = (cm at 100 m)/ (inch at 100 yds.) | 1cm/0.36" | 1cm/0.36" | 1cm/0.36" | 1cm/0.36" | 1cm/0.36" | 1cm/0.36" | 107/0.25" |
| Max. adj. (elev./wind.) at 100 m (cm)/at 100 yds. | 187 | 190 | 95 | 138 | 110/39.6 | 300 | 135/49 |
| Center tube dia. | 25.4mm/1" | 30mm/1.18" | 30mm/1.18" | 25.4mm/1" | 30mm/1.18" | 30mm/1.18" | 25.4/1.0" |
| Objective bell dia. | 48mm/1.9" | 48mm/1.9" | 62mm/2.44" | 62mm/2.44" | 54mm/2.13" | NA | 44.0/1.7 |
| Ocular bell dia. | 40mm/1.57" | 40mm/1.57" | 40mm/1.57" | 40mm/1.57" | 40mm/1.57" | NA | 42.5/1.8 |
| Length | 324mm/12.8" | 320mm/12.6" | 388mm/15.3" | 369mm/14.5" | 370mm/14.57" | 290mm/11.46" | |
| Approx. weight: ZM | 350g/15.3 oz. | 586g/20.7 oz. | 765g/27.0 oz. | 550g/19.4 oz. | 715g/25.2 oz. | 490g/17.3 oz. | NA |
| Z | 400g/14.1 oz. | 562g/19.8 | 731g/25.8 oz. | 520g/18.3 oz. | 680g/24 oz. | NA | 430g/15.2 oz. |

# Ammunition

For addresses and phone/fax numbers of manufacturers and distributors included in this section, please turn to DIRECTORY OF MANUFACTURERS AND SUPPLIERS on page 554.

# FEDERAL AMMUNITION

Federal's new pistol and rifle cartridges for 1997–98 are featured below. For a complete listing of Federal ammunition, call or write the Federal Cartridge Company (see Directory of Manufacturers and Suppliers in the Reference section for address and phone number). See also Federal ballistics tables.

### NEW PREMIUM® TUNGSTEN

Federal Tungsten-iron is 32% denser than steel—actually 94% as dense as lead—delivering the speed and energy needed to reach large ducks and geese. Combines the pellet energy of lead for better penetration than either steel or lead. This new non-toxic Tungsten-iron load has been approved by the U.S. Fish and Wildlife Service. Six-petal wad (patent pending) controls shot alignment and provides tighter patterns as well as barrel protection. Shells are headstamped "Tungsten" for easy identification in the field and are triple sealed to keep out moisture.

### PREMIUM® HIGH VELOCITY LEAD

Federal's new High Velocity Lead loads provide velocities up to 1400 fps (150 fps faster than standard loads). This increased speed offers more pellet energy so loads are effective at longer ranges. Federal's special hard shot, combined with an exclusive Triple Plus wad column, deliver tighter patterns and better downrange penetration.

### BALLISTICLEAN™ NON-TOXIC

As the world's first lead-free, non-toxic cartridges, Federal's patented BallistiClean line is the only ammunition that eliminates airborne lead, lead exposure from target impact and range disposal problems. Meets all EPA and OSHA environmental standards. Also meets the accuracy standards of match and range shooters. BallistiClean is available in popular centerfire pistol calibers and 22 rimfire.

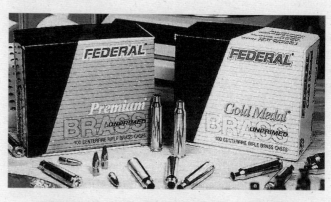

### PREMIUM AND GOLD MEDAL® BRASS

Federal brass is now available in two brands: Premium for hunters and Gold Medal for match shooters, both offering a wide variety of rifle calibers.

### PREMIUM® PERSONAL DEFENSE™

Federal's Personal Defense ammunition starts with muzzle velocities 15–10% faster than conventional loads for maximum stopping power. Hydra-Shok® bullet's unique center-post design expands to double caliber. Recoil is still 10% lower than conventional loads.

# HORNADY AMMUNITION

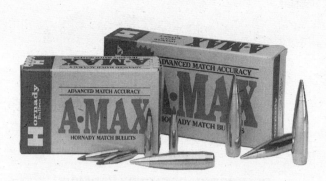

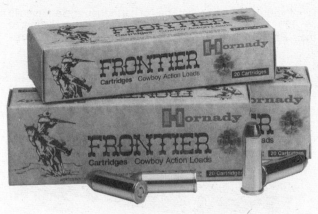

### A-MAX MATCH AMMUNITION

Hornady Match ammunition is now available in two popular service rifle calibers: 223 Rem/75 BTHP and 308 Win/168 A-MAX. Hornady's ultra-precise match cartridges are loaded with Hornady A-MAX and Hornady BTHP match bullets, featuring brass cartridges carefully selected for proper case wall concentricity. Early match results have confirmed the accuracy of this ammo.

### FRONTIER COWBOY AMMUNITION AND BULLETS

Hornady introduces Frontier Cowboy ammunition loaded to appropriate velocities in 45 Colt and 44-40 calibers. The 45 Colt round is loaded with a traditionally designed swaged 255-grain lead bullet, while the 44-40 is loaded with a similarly designed 205-grain lead bullet. Velocities are appropriate for use in both handguns and lever-action rifles. Each round of Frontier Cowboy ammo is loaded with Hornady brass cases with the Hornady headstamp. Frontier Cowboy ammo features specially designed swaged bullets with a diamond-knurl bearing surface dipped in hot wax for total lubrication. Frontier Cowboy ammo is also loaded at the correct velocity for competition shooting and plinking.

### VARMINT EXPRESS AMMUNITION

Hornady has expanded its line of Varmint Express ammunition. The 50-grain V-MAX is now loaded in both 22-250 and 220 Swift. The lightweight 6MM/58-grain V-MAX is available in a high-velocity 243 Winchester load.

### MUZZLE LOADING ADDITIONS

Five new loadings make up Hornady's new line of Sabots with XTP bullets designed for faster muzzle velocity and flatter trajectory at normal muzzleloading distances. Hornady also introduces three new weights of Great Plains lead conical bullets, pre-lubricated with Great Plains All Natural Lube.

Remington's new or recent lines of cartridges and shotshells for 1997–98 are featured below. For a complete listing of their ammunition products, call or write Remington whose address/phone no. is listed in the Directory of Manufacturers and Suppliers in the reference section. *See also* Ballistics Section.

## 22 WIN. MAG. RIMFIRE AMMUNITION

In conjunction with its new Model 597™ autoloading rimfire rifle, Remington has introduced a new line of 22 WMR ammunition, including a choice of three different bullet styles designed for a variety of rimfire shooting and small-game hunting situations. This new Remington Premier specification provides flatter trajectory and greater energy at 100 to 150 yards than any other super-high velocity 22 rimfire magnum. The rapid break-up characteristics of the new polymer-tipped bullets also eliminate any potential ricochet at all ranges.

## REMINGTON PREMIER® BUCKSHOT

With the continued expansion of shotgun-only deer-hunting zones, the effective performance of buckshot loads has become increasingly important. Remington's new 12-gauge buck loads encase the pellets in a Remington Power Piston shotcup/wad to reduce pellet deformation from the impact of firing and contact with the barrel. Encasing the pellets in a shotcup/wad creates even greater roundness and truer flight of the buck pellets. For example: All Remington 12- and 20-gauge Premier buckshot is specially hardened with 3% antimony and then nickel-plated for additional hardness. It is the only buckshot available to receive this dual hardening treatment. Also, in-between pellet spaces are packed with a polymer buffering filler that cushions the pellets against each other. The sum of this combined protection produces patterns that are 25% tighter than those of normal buck loads. The 12-gauge Remington Premier buckshot, all in 00 buck sizes, is available in 3-inch magnum, 2³⁄₄-inch magnum, and standard 2³⁄₄-inch loadings. The 20-gauge, #3 Buck specification is offered in a standard 2³⁄₄-inch loading.

## REMINGTON PREMIER® VARMINT

Remington's new "Premier Varmint" line provides accuracy, retained high velocity, flat trajectory and explosive break-up. The line includes four of the most popular 22-caliber cartridges—the 222 Rem., 223 Rem., 22-250 Rem. and the 220 Swift. These new rounds feature a 50-grain polymer-tipped boattail bullet. The secant ogive profile, coupled with a boattail base, create an exceptionally high ballistic coefficient that retains higher downrange velocities and flatter trajectories than other 22-caliber varmint-style bullets. Each Remington Premier Varmint round delivers straighter-line, flatter trajectory out to 500 yards than standard loadings of the same caliber.

## REMINGTON 7MM STW

Remington has added a factory-loaded version of the powerful 7mm STW (Shooting Times Westerner). It is based on the original 8mm Remington Magnum case necked down to 7mm (28 caliber). The new Remington 7mm STW is loaded with a 140-grain Pointed Soft Point Core-Lokt® bullet at 3325 feet per second. With its large case capacity, the 7mm STW outperforms any other 7mm Magnum cartridge now produced.

## 260 REMINGTON CARTRIDGE

Remington has created a medium-bore cartridge of moderate recoil for serious shooting competition. It has, when matched with game bullets, the potential for a highly effective medium-game round for use in lightweight short-action rifles. The result is a 26-caliber round of .264-inch bullet diameter and loaded with a 140-grain pointed softpoint Remington Core-Lokt® bullet. A muzzle velocity of 2750 feet per second produces comfortably moderate recoil. The 26-caliber bullet creates downrange velocity and energy, however, nearly duplicating that of a .270 Win. cartridge with a 130-grain bullet.

# SAKO AMMUNITION

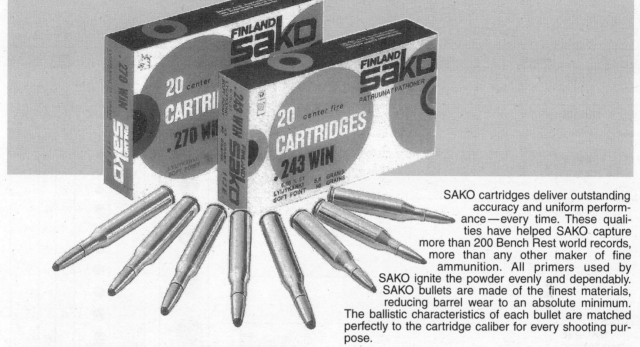

SAKO cartridges deliver outstanding accuracy and uniform performance—every time. These qualities have helped SAKO capture more than 200 Bench Rest world records, more than any other maker of fine ammunition. All primers used by SAKO ignite the powder evenly and dependably. SAKO bullets are made of the finest materials, reducing barrel wear to an absolute minimum. The ballistic characteristics of each bullet are matched perfectly to the cartridge caliber for every shooting purpose.

## SAKO PREMIUM PISTOL & REVOLVER CARTRIDGES

| Calibers | Bullet Weight Gr. | Bullet Type | Suggested Retail Price |
|----------|-----------|-------------|------------------------|
| 380 ACP | 95 | FMJ | $34.70 |
| 30 Luger | 92 | FMJ | 31.65 |
| 9mm Luger | 115 | FMJ | 34.70 |
| 9mm Luger | 114 | FMJ | 60.35 |
| 32 W&W Long | 98 | WC | 27.75 |
| 38 Special | 148 | WC | 30.65 |
| 38 Special | 158 | SWC | 30.65 |

## SAKO PREMIUM CENTERFIRE RIFLE CARTRIDGES

| Calibers | Bullet Weight Gr. | Bullet Type | Suggested Retail Price |
|----------|-----------|-------------|------------------------|
| 22 Hornet | 45 | SP | $15.95 |
| 22 Hornet | 40 | HP | 19.25 |
| 222 Remington | 50 | SP | 17.25 |
| 222 Remington | 55 | SP | 17.65 |
| 222 Remington SM | 52 | HP | 20.50 |
| 222 Rem. Mag. | 50 | SP | 18.00 |
| 222 Rem. Mag. | 55 | SP | 18.50 |
| 223 Remington | 50 | SP | 18.00 |
| 223 Remington | 55 | SP | 18.50 |
| 22 PPC USA | 52 | HP | 37.90 |
| 22-250 Remington | 50 | SP | 25.85 |
| 22-250 Remington | 55 | SP | 27.00 |
| 6 PPC USA | 70 | HP | 37.90 |
| 243 Winchester | 90 | SP | 23.75 |
| 6.5 X 55 | 139 | SP | 24.95 |
| 6.5 X 55 | 155 | SP | 26.90 |
| 270 Winchester | 156 | SP | 25.35 |

## SAKO PREMIUM CENTERFIRE RIFLE CARTRIDGES

| Calibers | Bullet Weight Gr. | Bullet Type | Suggested Retail Price |
|----------|-----------|-------------|------------------------|
| 7 X 33 Sako | 78 | SP | $38.75 |
| 7mm Rem. Mag. | 170 | SP | 34.00 |
| 7.62 X 39 | 123 | SP | 25.85 |
| 308 Winchester | 123 | SP | 22.50 |
| 308 Winchester | 156 | SP | 24.60 |
| 308 Winchester | 180 | SP | 23.75 |
| 308 Winchester | 200 | SP | 23.75 |
| 308 Winchester | 180 | SHH | 24.95 |
| 308 Win. SM | 168 | HP | 25.40 |
| 308 Win. SM | 190 | HP | 25.80 |
| 7.62 X 53R | 156 | SP | 25.00 |
| 7.62 X 53R | 180 | SP | 24.15 |
| 7.62 X 53R | 200 | SP | 24.40 |
| 7.62 X 53R | 180 | SHH | 25.55 |
| 30-06 | 123 | SP | 22.90 |
| 30-06 | 156 | SP | 25.80 |
| 30-06 | 180 | SHH | 25.95 |
| 300 Win. Mag. | 156 | SHH | 41.65 |
| 300 Win. Mag. | 180 | HH | 41.00 |
| 300 Win. Mag. | 168 | HP | 42.80 |
| 8.2 X 53R | 200 | SP | 24.20 |
| 8 X 57 J.S. | 200 | SP | 25.80 |
| 338 Win. Mag. | 250 | SP | 35.65 |
| 9.3 X 53R Finish | 257 | SP | 13.50 |
| 9.3 X 62 | 250 | SPC | 48.15 |
| 9.3 X 74R | 250 | SPC | 59.65 |
| 375 H & H | 270 | SPC | 64.00 |

# WINCHESTER AMMUNITION

## SHOTSHELL GUIDE

### SHOTSHELL GAME GUIDE

| | SHELL | SHOT SIZE | CHOKE | GAUGE |
|---|---|---|---|---|
| **GEESE** | STEEL: Super-X® Drylok<br>Super Steel™ | T, BBB, BB,<br>1, 2 | Mod.<br>Mod., Imp. Mod. | 10,12<br>10, 12 |
| **DUCKS** | STEEL: Super-X® Drylok<br>Super Steel™ | 1, 2, 3, 4, 6 | Imp. Cyl. Mod., Imp. Mod. | 10, 12, 20 |
| **TURKEY** | LEAD: Super-X® | 4, 5, 6 | Full | 12, 16, 20 |
| | Double X® | 4, 5, 6 | Full | 10, 12, 16, 20 |
| **PHEASANT** | LEAD: Super-X® | 4, 5, 6, 7½ | Imp. Cyl., Mod., Imp. Mod. | 12, 16, 20 |
| | Double X® | 4, 6 | Imp. Cyl., Mod., Imp. Mod. | 12, 16, 20 |
| | Upland Heavy Field Load | 4, 6 | Imp. Cyl., Mod., Imp. Mod. | 12, 16, 20 |
| | AA® Super Pigeon® | 7½ | Full, Imp. Mod., Mod. | 12 |
| | STEEL: Super-X® Drylok<br>Super Steel™ | 4, 6, 7 | Mod., Imp. Mod. | 12, 20 |
| **GROUSE PARTRIDGE** | LEAD: Super-X® | 5, 6, 7½, 8 | Imp. Cyl., Mod. | 12, 16, 20, 28 |
| | Upland Heavy Game Load | 6, 7½, 8 | Imp. Cyl., Mod. | 12, 20 |
| **WOODCOCK SNIPE RAIL** | LEAD: Super-X® | 6, 7½, 8 | Imp. Cyl., Mod. | 12, 16, 20, 28 |
| | Upland Heavy Game Load | 7½, 8 | Imp. Cyl., Mod. | 12, 20 |
| | STEEL: Super-X® Drylok<br>Super Steel™ | 4, 6 | Imp. Cyl., Mod. | 12, 16, 20 |
| **QUAIL** | LEAD: Super-X® | 7½, 8, 9 | Imp. Cyl., Mod. | 12, 16, 20, 28 |
| | Upland Heavy Game Load | 7½, 8 | Imp. Cyl., Mod. | 12, 20 |
| **DOVE** | LEAD: Super-X® | 7½, 8, 9 | Imp. Cyl., Mod., Imp. Mod. | 12, 16, 20, 28 |
| | Upland Heavy Game Load | 7½, 8 | Imp. Cyl., Mod., Imp. Mod. | 12, 20 |
| | STEEL: Super-X® Drylok<br>Super Steel™ | 6 | Imp. Cyl., Mod., Imp. Mod. | 12, 16, 20 |
| | AA® Steel | 7 | Imp. Cyl., Mod., Imp. Mod. | 12 |
| **RABBIT** | LEAD: Super-X® | 4, 5, 6, 7½ | Imp. Cyl., Mod. | 12, 16, 20, 28, 410 |
| | Upland Heavy Game Load | 6, 7½ | Imp. Cyl., Mod. | 12, 20 |
| **SQUIRREL** | LEAD: Super-X® | 4, 5, 6 | Mod., Imp. Mod., Full | 12, 16, 20, 28, 410 |
| | Upland Heavy Game Load | 6, 7½ | Mod., Imp. Mod., Full | 12, 20 |

### STANDARD SHOT SIZES

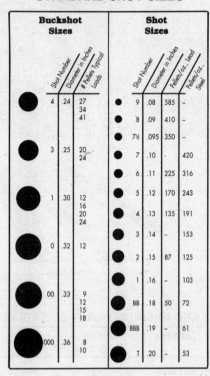

**Buckshot Sizes**

| Shot Number | Diameter in Inches | # Pellets Typical Loads |
|---|---|---|
| 4 | .24 | 27, 34, 41 |
| 3 | .25 | 20, 24 |
| 1 | .30 | 12, 16, 20, 24 |
| 0 | .32 | 12 |
| 00 | .33 | 9, 12, 15, 18 |
| 000 | .36 | 8, 10 |

**Shot Sizes**

| Shot Number | Diameter in Inches | Pellets/oz., Lead | Pellets/oz., Steel |
|---|---|---|---|
| 9 | .08 | 585 | – |
| 8 | .09 | 410 | – |
| 7½ | .095 | 350 | – |
| 7 | .10 | - | 420 |
| 6 | .11 | 225 | 316 |
| 5 | .12 | 170 | 243 |
| 4 | .13 | 135 | 191 |
| 3 | .14 | – | 153 |
| 2 | .15 | 87 | 125 |
| 1 | .16 | – | 103 |
| BB | .18 | 50 | 72 |
| BBB | .19 | – | 61 |
| T | .20 | – | 53 |

### LEAD VS. STEEL

**COMPARISON CHART***

| Shot Type | Wt. | Shot Size | No. Pellets | Muzzle Velocity (FPS) | Retained Energy Per Pellet (Ft. Lbs.) 40 Yds. | 60 Yds. |
|---|---|---|---|---|---|---|
| Lead | 1¼ | 6 | 281 | 1330 | 2.3 | 1.3 |
| Steel | 1⅛ | 4 | 215 | 1365 | 2.5 | 1.4 |
| Lead | 1¼ | 4 | 169 | 1330 | 4.4 | 2.7 |
| Steel | 1⅛ | 2 | 141 | 1365 | 4.4 | 2.6 |
| Lead | 1½ | 4 | 202 | 1260 | 4.1 | 2.6 |
| Steel | 1¼ | 2 | 156 | 1275 | 4.1 | 2.4 |
| Lead | 1½ | 2 | 130 | 1260 | 7.0 | 4.6 |
| Steel | 1¼ | BB | 90 | 1275 | 8.3 | 5.2 |

*Source: SAAMI Exterior Ballistics Tables Adopted 4/23/81
NOTE: Steel shot pellets two sizes larger than lead deliver comparable down range energy.

# Ballistics

# FEDERAL RIFLE BALLISTICS

## PREMIUM HIGH ENERGY RIFLE

| USAGE | FEDERAL LOAD NO. | CALIBER | BULLET GRAINS | WGT. IN GRAMS | BULLET STYLE | FACTORY PRIMER NO. | VELOCITY IN FEET PER SECOND (TO NEAREST 10 FPS) | | | | | | ENERGY IN FOOT-POUNDS (TO NEAREST 5 FOOT-POUNDS) | | | | | |
|---|---|---|---|---|---|---|---|---|---|---|---|---|---|---|---|---|---|---|
| | | | | | | | MUZZLE | 100 YDS. | 200 YDS. | 300 YDS. | 400 YDS. | 500 YDS. | MUZZLE | 100 YDS. | 200 YDS. | 300 YDS. | 400 YDS. | 500 YDS. |
| [2] NEW P270T3 | 270 Win. | 140 | 9.07 | Trophy Bonded Bear Claw | 210 | 3100 | 2860 | 2620 | 2400 | 2200 | 2000 | 2990 | 2535 | 2140 | 1795 | 1500 | 1240 |
| [3] P308T2 | 308 Win. (7.62x51mm) | 165 | 10.69 | Trophy Bonded Bear Claw | 210 | 2870 | 2600 | 2350 | 2120 | 1890 | 1690 | 3020 | 2485 | 2030 | 1640 | 1310 | 1040 |
| [3] P308G | 308 Win. (7.62x51mm) | 180 | 11.66 | Nosler Partition | 210 | 2740 | 2550 | 2370 | 2200 | 2030 | 1870 | 3000 | 2600 | 2245 | 1925 | 1645 | 1395 |
| [3] P3006T3 | 30-06 Spring (7.62x63mm) | 180 | 11.66 | Trophy Bonded Bear Claw | 210 | 2880 | 2630 | 2380 | 2160 | 1940 | 1740 | 3315 | 2755 | 2270 | 1855 | 1505 | 1210 |
| [3] P3006R | 30-06 Spring (7.62x63mm) | 180 | 11.66 | Nosler Partition | 210 | 2880 | 2690 | 2500 | 2320 | 2150 | 1980 | 3315 | 2880 | 2495 | 2150 | 1845 | 1570 |
| [3] P300WT3 | 300 Win. Mag. | 180 | 11.66 | Trophy Bonded Bear Claw | 215 | 3100 | 2830 | 2580 | 2340 | 2110 | 1900 | 3840 | 3205 | 2660 | 2190 | 1790 | 1445 |
| [3] P300WE | 300 Win. Mag. | 200 | 12.96 | Nosler Partition | 215 | 2930 | 2740 | 2550 | 2370 | 2200 | 2030 | 3810 | 3325 | 2885 | 2495 | 2145 | 1840 |
| [3] NEW P300WBT3 | 300 Weatherby Magnum | 180 | 11.66 | Nosler Partition | 215 | 3330 | 3080 | 2850 | 2750 | 2410 | 2210 | 4430 | 3795 | 3235 | 2750 | 2320 | 1950 |
| [3] NEW P300WBB | 300 Weatherby Magnum | 180 | 11.66 | Nosler Partition | 215 | 3330 | 3110 | 2910 | 2710 | 2520 | 2340 | 4430 | 3875 | 3375 | 2935 | 2540 | 2190 |
| [3] P338T2 | 338 Win. Mag. | 225 | 14.58 | Trophy Bonded Bear Claw | 215 | 2940 | 2690 | 2450 | 2230 | 2010 | 1810 | 4320 | 3610 | 3000 | 2475 | 2025 | 1640 |
| [3] P338D | 338 Win. Mag | 250 | 16.20 | Nosler Partition | 215 | 2800 | 2610 | 2420 | 2250 | 2080 | 1920 | 4350 | 3775 | 3260 | 2805 | 2395 | 2035 |

Usage Key: [1] =Varmints, predators, small game  [2] =Medium game  [3] =Large, heavy game  [4] =Dangerous game  [5] =Target shooting, training, practice

## PREMIUM HUNTING RIFLE

| USAGE | FEDERAL LOAD NO. | CALIBER | BULLET GRAINS | WGT. IN GRAMS | BULLET STYLE* | FACTORY PRIMER NO. | VELOCITY IN FEET PER SECOND (TO NEAREST 10 FPS) | | | | | | ENERGY IN FOOT-POUNDS (TO NEAREST 5 FOOT-POUNDS) | | | | | |
|---|---|---|---|---|---|---|---|---|---|---|---|---|---|---|---|---|---|---|
| | | | | | | | MUZZLE | 100 YDS. | 200 YDS. | 300 YDS. | 400 YDS. | 500 YDS. | MUZZLE | 100 YDS. | 200 YDS. | 300 YDS. | 400 YDS. | 500 YDS. |
| [1] P223E | 223 Rem. (5.56x45mm) | 55 | 3.56 | Sierra GameKing BTHP | 205 | 3240 | 2770 | 2340 | 1950 | 1610 | 1330 | 1280 | 935 | 670 | 465 | 315 | 215 |
| [1] P22250B | 22-250 Rem. | 55 | 3.56 | Sierra GameKing BTHP | 210 | 3680 | 3280 | 2920 | 2590 | 2280 | 1990 | 1655 | 1315 | 1040 | 815 | 630 | 480 |
| [2] P243C | 243 Win. (6.16x51mm) | 100 | 6.48 | Sierra GameKing BTSP | 210 | 2960 | 2760 | 2570 | 2380 | 2210 | 2040 | 1950 | 1690 | 1460 | 1260 | 1080 | 925 |
| [1] P243D | 243 Win. (6.16x51mm) | 85 | 5.50 | Sierra GameKing BTHP | 210 | 3320 | 3070 | 2830 | 2600 | 2380 | 2180 | 2080 | 1770 | 1510 | 1280 | 1070 | 890 |
| [1] P243F | 243 Win. (6.16x51mm) | 70 | 4.54 | Nosler Ballistic Tip | 210 | 3400 | 3070 | 2760 | 2470 | 2200 | 1950 | 1795 | 1465 | 1185 | 950 | 755 | 590 |
| [2] P6C | 6mm Rem. | 100 | 6.48 | Nosler Partition | 210 | 3100 | 2860 | 2640 | 2420 | 2220 | 2020 | 2135 | 1820 | 1545 | 1300 | 1090 | 910 |
| [2] P257B | 257 Roberts (High-Velocity + P) | 120 | 7.77 | Nosler Partition | 210 | 2780 | 2560 | 2360 | 2160 | 1970 | 1790 | 2060 | 1750 | 1480 | 1240 | 1030 | 855 |
| [2] P257WBA | 257 Weatherby Magnum | 115 | 7.45 | Nosler Partition | 210 | 3150 | 2900 | 2660 | 2440 | 2220 | 2020 | 2535 | 2145 | 1810 | 1515 | 1260 | 1040 |
| [2] P257WBT1 | 257 Weatherby Magnum | 115 | 7.45 | Trophy Bonded Bear Claw | 210 | 3150 | 2890 | 2640 | 2400 | 2180 | 1970 | 2535 | 2125 | 1775 | 1470 | 1210 | 990 |
| [2] P2506C | 25-06 Rem. | 117 | 7.58 | Sierra GameKing BTSP | 210 | 2990 | 2770 | 2570 | 2370 | 2190 | 2000 | 2320 | 2000 | 1715 | 1465 | 1240 | 1045 |
| [2] P2506D | 25-06 Rem. | 100 | 6.48 | Nosler Ballistic Tip | 210 | 3210 | 2960 | 2720 | 2490 | 2280 | 2070 | 2290 | 1940 | 1640 | 1380 | 1150 | 955 |
| [2] P2506E | 25-06 Rem. | 115 | 7.45 | Nosler Partition | 210 | 2990 | 2750 | 2520 | 2300 | 2100 | 1900 | 2285 | 1930 | 1620 | 1350 | 1120 | 915 |
| [2] P2506T1 | 25-06 Rem. | 115 | 7.45 | Trophy Bonded Bear Claw | 210 | 2990 | 2740 | 2500 | 2270 | 2050 | 1850 | 2285 | 1910 | 1590 | 1310 | 1075 | 870 |
| [2] P270C | 270 Win. | 150 | 9.72 | Sierra GameKing BTSP | 210 | 2850 | 2660 | 2480 | 2300 | 2130 | 1970 | 2705 | 2355 | 2040 | 1760 | 1510 | 1290 |
| [2] P270D | 270 Win. | 130 | 8.42 | Sierra GameKing BTSP | 210 | 3060 | 2830 | 2620 | 2410 | 2220 | 2030 | 2700 | 2320 | 1980 | 1680 | 1420 | 1190 |
| [2] P270E | 270 Win. | 150 | 9.72 | Nosler Partition | 210 | 2850 | 2590 | 2340 | 2100 | 1880 | 1670 | 2705 | 2225 | 1815 | 1470 | 1175 | 930 |
| [2] P270F | 270 Win. | 130 | 8.42 | Nosler Partition | 210 | 3060 | 2840 | 2630 | 2430 | 2230 | 2050 | 2700 | 2325 | 1990 | 1700 | 1440 | 1210 |
| [2] P270T1 | 270 Win. | 140 | 9.07 | Trophy Bonded Bear Claw | 210 | 2940 | 2700 | 2480 | 2260 | 2060 | 1860 | 2685 | 2270 | 1905 | 1590 | 1315 | 1080 |
| [2] P270T2 | 270 Win. | 130 | 8.42 | Trophy Bonded Bear Claw | 210 | 3060 | 2810 | 2570 | 2340 | 2130 | 1930 | 2705 | 2275 | 1905 | 1585 | 1310 | 1070 |
| [2] P270WBA | 270 Weatherby Magnum | 130 | 8.42 | Nosler Partition | 210 | 3200 | 2960 | 2740 | 2520 | 2320 | 2120 | 2955 | 2530 | 2160 | 1835 | 1550 | 1300 |
| [2] P270WBT1 | 270 Weatherby Magnum | 140 | 9.07 | Trophy Bonded Bear Claw | 210 | 3100 | 2840 | 2600 | 2370 | 2150 | 1950 | 2990 | 2510 | 2100 | 1745 | 1440 | 1175 |
| [2] P730A | 7-30 Waters | 120 | 7.77 | BTSP | 210 | 2700 | 2300 | 1930 | 1600 | 1330 | 1140 | 1940 | 1405 | 990 | 685 | 470 | 345 |
| [2] P7C | 7mm Mauser (7x57mm Mauser) | 140 | 9.07 | Nosler Partition | 210 | 2660 | 2450 | 2260 | 2070 | 1890 | 1730 | 2200 | 1865 | 1585 | 1330 | 1110 | 930 |
| [2] P708A | 7mm-08 Rem. | 140 | 9.07 | Nosler Partition | 210 | 2800 | 2590 | 2390 | 2200 | 2020 | 1840 | 2435 | 2085 | 1775 | 1500 | 1265 | 1060 |
| [2] P708B | 7mm-08 Rem. | 140 | 9.07 | Nosler Ballistic Tip | 210 | 2800 | 2610 | 2430 | 2260 | 2100 | 1940 | 2440 | 2135 | 1840 | 1590 | 1360 | 1165 |
| [2] P764A | 7x64 Brenneke | 160 | 10.37 | Nosler Partition | 210 | 2650 | 2480 | 2310 | 2150 | 2000 | 1850 | 2495 | 2180 | 1895 | 1640 | 1415 | 1215 |
| [2] P280A | 280 Rem. | 150 | 9.72 | Nosler Partition | 210 | 2890 | 2620 | 2370 | 2140 | 1910 | 1710 | 2780 | 2295 | 1875 | 1520 | 1215 | 970 |
| [2] P280T1 | 280 Rem. | 140 | 9.07 | Trophy Bonded Bear Claw | 210 | 2990 | 2630 | 2310 | 2040 | 1730 | 1480 | 2770 | 2155 | 1655 | 1250 | 925 | 680 |
| [2] P7RD | 7mm Rem. Magnum | 150 | 9.72 | Sierra GameKing BTSP | 215 | 3110 | 2920 | 2750 | 2580 | 2410 | 2250 | 3220 | 2850 | 2510 | 2210 | 1930 | 1690 |
| [3] P7RE | 7mm Rem. Magnum | 165 | 10.69 | Sierra GameKing BTSP | 215 | 2950 | 2800 | 2650 | 2510 | 2370 | 2230 | 3190 | 2865 | 2570 | 2300 | 2050 | 1825 |
| [3] P7RF | 7mm Rem. Magnum | 160 | 10.37 | Nosler Partition | 215 | 2950 | 2770 | 2590 | 2420 | 2250 | 2090 | 3090 | 2715 | 2375 | 2075 | 1800 | 1555 |
| [3] P7RG | 7mm Rem. Magnum | 140 | 9.07 | Nosler Partition | 215 | 3150 | 2930 | 2710 | 2510 | 2320 | 2130 | 3085 | 2660 | 2290 | 1960 | 1670 | 1415 |
| [2] P7RH | 7mm Rem. Magnum | 150 | 9.72 | Nosler Ballistic Tip | 215 | 3110 | 2910 | 2720 | 2540 | 2370 | 2200 | 3220 | 2825 | 2470 | 2150 | 1865 | 1610 |
| [3] P7RT1 | 7mm Rem. Magnum | 175 | 11.34 | Trophy Bonded Bear Claw | 215 | 2860 | 2600 | 2350 | 2120 | 1900 | 1700 | 3180 | 2625 | 2150 | 1745 | 1400 | 1120 |
| [3] P7RT2 | 7mm Rem. Magnum | 160 | 10.37 | Trophy Bonded Bear Claw | 215 | 2940 | 2660 | 2390 | 2140 | 1900 | 1680 | 3070 | 2505 | 2025 | 1620 | 1280 | 1005 |
| [3] P7WBA | 7mm Weatherby Magnum | 160 | 10.37 | Nosler Partition | 215 | 3050 | 2850 | 2650 | 2470 | 2290 | 2120 | 3305 | 2880 | 2505 | 2165 | 1865 | 1600 |
| [3] P7WBT1 | 7mm Weatherby Magnum | 160 | 10.37 | Trophy Bonded Bear Claw | 215 | 3050 | 2730 | 2420 | 2140 | 1880 | 1640 | 3305 | 2640 | 2085 | 1630 | 1255 | 955 |
| [2] P3030D | 30-30 Win. | 170 | 11.01 | | 210 | 2200 | 1900 | 1620 | 1380 | 1190 | 1060 | 1830 | 1355 | 990 | 720 | 535 | 425 |
| [2] P308C | 308 Win. (7.62x51mm) | 165 | 10.69 | Sierra GameKing BTSP | 210 | 2700 | 2520 | 2330 | 2160 | 1990 | 1830 | 2670 | 2310 | 1990 | 1700 | 1450 | 1230 |
| [3] P308E | 308 Win. (7.62x51mm) | 180 | 11.66 | Nosler Partition | 210 | 2620 | 2430 | 2240 | 2060 | 1890 | 1730 | 2745 | 2355 | 2005 | 1700 | 1430 | 1200 |
| [2] P308F | 308 Win. (7.62x51mm) | 150 | 9.72 | Nosler Ballistic Tip | 210 | 2820 | 2610 | 2410 | 2220 | 2040 | 1860 | 2650 | 2270 | 1935 | 1640 | 1380 | 1155 |
| [3] P308T1 | 308 Win. (7.62x51mm) | 165 | 10.69 | Trophy Bonded Bear Claw | 210 | 2700 | 2440 | 2200 | 1970 | 1760 | 1570 | 2670 | 2185 | 1775 | 1425 | 1135 | 900 |
| [2] P3006D | 30-06 Spring (7.62x63mm) | 165 | 10.69 | Sierra GameKing BTSP | 210 | 2800 | 2610 | 2420 | 2240 | 2070 | 1910 | 2870 | 2490 | 2150 | 1840 | 1580 | 1340 |
| [2] P3006F | 30-06 Spring (7.62x63mm) | 180 | 11.66 | Nosler Partition | 210 | 2700 | 2500 | 2320 | 2140 | 1970 | 1810 | 2915 | 2510 | 2150 | 1830 | 1550 | 1350 |
| [2] P3006G | 30-06 Spring (7.62x63mm) | 150 | 9.72 | Sierra GameKing BTSP | 210 | 2910 | 2690 | 2480 | 2270 | 2070 | 1880 | 2820 | 2420 | 2040 | 1710 | 1430 | 1180 |
| [3] P3006L | 30-06 Spring (7.62x63mm) | 180 | 11.66 | Sierra GameKing BTSP | 210 | 2700 | 2540 | 2380 | 2220 | 2080 | 1930 | 2915 | 2570 | 2260 | 1975 | 1720 | 1495 |
| [2] P3006P | 30-06 Spring (7.62x63mm) | 150 | 9.72 | Nosler Partition | 210 | 2910 | 2700 | 2490 | 2300 | 2110 | 1940 | 2820 | 2420 | 2070 | 1760 | 1485 | 1245 |
| [2] P3006Q | 30-06 Spring (7.62x63mm) | 165 | 10.69 | Nosler Ballistic Tip | 210 | 2800 | 2610 | 2430 | 2250 | 2080 | 1920 | 2870 | 2495 | 2155 | 1855 | 1585 | 1350 |
| [3] P3006T1 | 30-06 Spring (7.62x63mm) | 165 | 10.69 | Trophy Bonded Bear Claw | 210 | 2800 | 2540 | 2290 | 2050 | 1830 | 1630 | 2870 | 2360 | 1915 | 1545 | 1230 | 975 |
| [3] P3006T2 | 30-06 Spring (7.62x63mm) | 180 | 11.66 | Trophy Bonded Bear Claw | 210 | 2700 | 2460 | 2220 | 2000 | 1800 | 1610 | 2915 | 2410 | 1975 | 1605 | 1290 | 1035 |
| [3] P300WC | 300 Win. Magnum | 200 | 12.96 | Sierra GameKing BTSP | 215 | 2830 | 2680 | 2530 | 2380 | 2240 | 2110 | 3560 | 3180 | 2830 | 2520 | 2230 | 1970 |
| [3] P300WT4 | 300 Win. Magnum | 150 | 9.72 | Trophy Bonded Bear Claw | 215 | 3280 | 2980 | 2700 | 2430 | 2190 | 1950 | 3570 | 2950 | 2420 | 1970 | 1590 | 1270 |
| [3] P35WT1 | 35 Whelen | 225 | 14.58 | Trophy Bonded Bear Claw | 215 | 2500 | 2300 | 2110 | 1930 | 1770 | 1610 | 3120 | 2650 | 2235 | 1870 | 1560 | 1290 |

Usage Key: [1] =Varmints, predators, small game  [2] =Medium game  [3] =Large, heavy game  [4] =Dangerous game  [5] =Target shooting, training, practice

# FEDERAL RIFLE BALLISTICS

| USAGE | FEDERAL LOAD NO. | CALIBER | BULLET GRAINS | WGT. IN GRAMS | BULLET STYLE** | FACTORY PRIMER NO. | VELOCITY IN FEET PER SECOND (TO NEAREST 10 FPS) | | | | | | ENERGY IN FOOT-POUNDS (TO NEAREST 5 FOOT-POUNDS) | | | | | |
|---|---|---|---|---|---|---|---|---|---|---|---|---|---|---|---|---|---|---|
| | | | | | | | MUZZLE | 100 YDS. | 200 YDS. | 300 YDS. | 400 YDS. | 500 YDS. | MUZZLE | 100 YDS. | 200 YDS. | 300 YDS. | 400 YDS. | 500 YDS. |
| 1 | P223F | 223 Rem. (5.56x45mm) | 55 | 3.56 | Nosler Ballistic Tip | 205 | 3240 | 2870 | 2530 | 2220 | 1920 | 1660 | 1280 | 1005 | 780 | 600 | 450 | 335 |
| 1 | P223V | 223 Rem. (5.56x45mm) | 40 | 2.59 | Sierra Varminter HP | 205 | 3650 | 3010 | 2450 | 1950 | 1530 | 1210 | 1185 | 805 | 535 | 340 | 205 | 130 |
| 1 | *P22250V | 22-250 Rem. | 40 | 2.59 | Sierra Varminter HP | 210 | 4000 | 3320 | 2720 | 2200 | 1740 | 1360 | 1420 | 980 | 660 | 430 | 265 | 165 |
| 1 | P220V | 220 Swift | 52 | 3.37 | Sierra MatchKing BTHP | 210 | 3825 | 3370 | 2960 | 2600 | 2230 | 1910 | 1690 | 1310 | 1010 | 770 | 575 | 420 |
| 1 | P243V | 243 Win. (6.16x51mm) | 60 | 3.89 | Sierra Varminter HP | 210 | 3600 | 3110 | 2660 | 2260 | 1890 | 1560 | 1725 | 1285 | 945 | 680 | 475 | 325 |
| 1 | P2506V | 25-06 Rem. | 90 | 5.83 | Sierra GameKing BTHP | 210 | 3440 | 3040 | 2680 | 2340 | 2030 | 1750 | 2365 | 1850 | 1435 | 1100 | 825 | 610 |

Usage Key: 1 = Varmints, predators, small game  2 = Medium game  3 = Large, heavy game  4 = Dangerous game  5 = Target shooting, training, practice
* Also available in 50 round pack P22250V1  **BTHP = Boat-Tail Hollow Point  HP = Hollow Point
Sierra MatchKing and Varminter are registered trademarks of Sierra Bullets.

| WIND DRIFT IN INCHES 10 MPH CROSSWIND | | | | | HEIGHT OF BULLET TRAJECTORY IN INCHES ABOVE OR BELOW LINE OF SIGHT IF ZEROED AT ⊕ YARDS. SIGHTS 1.5 INCHES ABOVE BORE LINE | | | | | | | | | | TEST BARREL LENGTH INCHES | FEDERAL LOAD NO. |
|---|---|---|---|---|---|---|---|---|---|---|---|---|---|---|---|---|
| | | | | | AVERAGE RANGE | | | | LONG RANGE | | | | | | | |
| 100 YDS. | 200 YDS. | 300 YDS. | 400 YDS. | 500 YDS. | 50 YDS. | 100 YDS. | 200 YDS. | 300 YDS. | 50 YDS. | 100 YDS. | 200 YDS. | 300 YDS. | 400 YDS. | 500 YDS. | | |
| 1.3 | 5.8 | 14.2 | 27.7 | 47.6 | -0.3 | ⊕ | -2.7 | -10.8 | +0.4 | +1.4 | ⊕ | -6.7 | -20.5 | -43.4 | 24 | P223E |
| 0.8 | 3.6 | 8.4 | 15.8 | 26.3 | -0.4 | ⊕ | -1.7 | -7.6 | 0.0 | +0.9 | ⊕ | -5.0 | -15.1 | -32.0 | 24 | P22250B |
| 0.6 | 2.6 | 6.1 | 11.3 | 18.4 | -0.2 | ⊕ | -3.1 | -11.4 | +0.6 | +1.5 | ⊕ | -6.8 | -19.8 | -39.9 | 24 | P243C |
| 0.7 | 2.7 | 6.3 | 11.6 | 18.8 | -0.3 | ⊕ | -2.2 | -8.8 | +0.2 | +1.1 | ⊕ | -5.5 | -16.1 | -32.8 | 24 | P243D |
| 0.8 | 3.4 | 8.1 | 15.2 | 25.1 | -0.3 | ⊕ | -2.2 | -9.0 | +0.2 | +1.1 | ⊕ | -5.7 | -17.1 | -35.7 | 24 | P243F |
| 0.7 | 2.9 | 6.7 | 12.5 | 20.4 | -0.3 | ⊕ | -2.8 | -10.5 | +0.4 | +1.4 | ⊕ | -6.3 | -18.7 | -38.1 | 24 | P6C |
| 0.8 | 3.3 | 7.7 | 14.3 | 23.5 | -0.1 | ⊕ | -3.8 | -14.0 | +0.8 | +1.9 | ⊕ | -8.2 | -24.0 | -48.9 | 24 | P257B |
| 0.7 | 3.0 | 6.9 | 12.9 | 21.1 | -0.3 | ⊕ | -2.7 | -10.2 | +0.4 | +1.3 | ⊕ | -6.2 | -18.4 | -37.5 | 24 | P257WBA |
| 0.7 | 3.1 | 7.3 | 13.7 | 22.4 | -0.3 | ⊕ | -2.7 | -10.4 | +0.4 | +1.4 | ⊕ | -6.3 | -18.8 | -38.5 | 24 | P257WBT1 |
| 0.7 | 2.8 | 6.5 | 12.0 | 19.6 | -0.2 | ⊕ | -3.0 | -11.4 | +0.5 | +1.5 | ⊕ | -6.8 | -19.9 | -40.4 | 24 | P2506C |
| 0.7 | 2.9 | 6.7 | 12.4 | 20.2 | -0.3 | ⊕ | -2.5 | -9.7 | +0.3 | +1.2 | ⊕ | -6.0 | -17.5 | -35.8 | 24 | P2506D |
| 0.8 | 3.2 | 7.4 | 13.9 | 22.6 | -0.2 | ⊕ | -3.1 | -11.7 | +0.6 | +1.6 | ⊕ | -7.0 | -20.8 | -42.2 | 24 | P2506E |
| 0.8 | 3.4 | 7.9 | 14.8 | 21.4 | -0.2 | ⊕ | -3.2 | -11.9 | +0.6 | +1.6 | ⊕ | -7.2 | -21.1 | -43.2 | 24 | P2506T1 |
| 0.7 | 2.7 | 6.3 | 11.6 | 18.9 | -0.2 | ⊕ | -3.4 | -12.5 | +0.7 | +1.7 | ⊕ | -7.4 | -21.4 | -43.0 | 24 | P270C |
| 0.7 | 2.8 | 6.6 | 12.1 | 19.7 | -0.2 | ⊕ | -2.8 | -10.7 | +0.5 | +1.4 | ⊕ | -6.5 | -19.0 | -38.5 | 24 | P270D |
| 0.9 | 3.9 | 9.2 | 17.3 | 28.5 | -0.2 | ⊕ | -3.7 | -13.8 | +0.8 | +1.9 | ⊕ | -8.3 | -24.4 | -50.5 | 24 | P270E |
| 0.7 | 2.7 | 6.4 | 11.9 | 19.3 | -0.2 | ⊕ | -2.8 | -10.7 | +0.5 | +1.4 | ⊕ | -6.5 | -18.8 | -38.2 | 24 | P270F |
| 0.8 | 3.2 | 7.6 | 14.2 | 23.0 | -0.2 | ⊕ | -3.3 | -12.2 | +0.6 | +1.6 | ⊕ | -7.3 | -21.5 | -43.7 | 24 | P270T1 |
| 0.7 | 3.2 | 7.4 | 13.9 | 22.5 | -0.2 | ⊕ | -2.9 | -11.1 | +0.5 | +1.5 | ⊕ | -6.7 | -19.8 | -40.5 | 24 | P270T2 |
| 0.7 | 2.7 | 6.3 | 11.7 | 19.0 | -0.3 | ⊕ | -2.5 | -9.6 | +0.3 | +1.2 | ⊕ | -5.9 | -17.3 | -35.1 | 24 | P270WBA |
| 0.8 | 3.1 | 7.4 | 13.7 | 22.5 | -0.3 | ⊕ | -2.8 | -10.8 | +0.4 | +1.4 | ⊕ | -6.6 | -19.3 | -39.6 | 24 | P270WBT1 |
| 1.6 | 7.2 | 17.7 | 34.5 | 58.1 | 0.0 | ⊕ | -5.2 | -19.8 | +1.2 | +2.6 | ⊕ | -12.0 | -37.6 | -81.7 | 24 | P730A |
| 1.3 | 3.2 | 8.2 | 15.4 | 23.4 | -0.1 | ⊕ | -4.3 | -15.4 | +1.0 | +2.1 | ⊕ | -9.0 | -26.1 | -52.9 | 24 | P7C |
| 0.8 | 3.1 | 7.3 | 13.5 | 21.8 | -0.2 | ⊕ | -3.7 | -13.5 | +0.8 | +1.8 | ⊕ | -8.0 | -23.1 | -46.6 | 24 | P708A |
| 0.7 | 2.7 | 6.4 | 11.9 | 19.1 | -0.2 | ⊕ | -3.6 | -13.1 | +0.7 | +1.8 | ⊕ | -7.7 | -14.1 | -44.5 | 24 | P708B |
| 0.7 | 2.8 | 6.6 | 12.3 | 19.5 | -0.1 | ⊕ | -4.2 | -14.9 | +0.9 | +2.1 | ⊕ | -8.7 | -24.9 | -49.4 | 24 | P764A |
| 0.9 | 3.8 | 9.0 | 16.8 | 27.8 | -0.2 | ⊕ | -3.6 | -13.4 | +0.7 | +1.8 | ⊕ | -8.0 | -23.8 | -49.2 | 24 | P280A |
| 1.2 | 4.9 | 11.8 | 22.5 | 37.8 | -0.2 | ⊕ | -3.5 | -13.7 | +0.7 | +1.6 | ⊕ | -8.4 | -25.4 | -54.3 | 24 | P280T1 |
| 0.5 | 2.2 | 5.1 | 9.3 | 15.0 | -0.3 | ⊕ | -2.6 | -9.8 | +0.4 | +1.3 | ⊕ | -5.9 | -17.0 | -34.2 | 24 | P7RD |
| 0.5 | 2.0 | 4.6 | 8.4 | 13.5 | -0.2 | ⊕ | -3.0 | -10.9 | +0.5 | +1.5 | ⊕ | -6.4 | -18.4 | -36.6 | 24 | P7RE |
| 0.6 | 2.5 | 5.6 | 10.4 | 16.9 | -0.2 | ⊕ | -3.1 | -11.3 | +0.6 | +1.5 | ⊕ | -6.7 | -19.4 | -39.0 | 24 | P7RF |
| 0.6 | 2.6 | 6.0 | 11.1 | 18.2 | -0.3 | ⊕ | -2.6 | -9.9 | +0.4 | +1.3 | ⊕ | -6.0 | -17.5 | -35.6 | 24 | P7RG |
| 0.5 | 2.3 | 5.4 | 9.9 | 16.2 | -0.3 | ⊕ | -2.6 | -9.9 | +0.4 | +1.3 | ⊕ | -6.0 | -17.4 | -35.0 | 24 | P7RH |
| 1.0 | 3.8 | 9.1 | 16.7 | 27.9 | -0.2 | ⊕ | -3.6 | -13.6 | +0.7 | +1.8 | ⊕ | -8.2 | -24.0 | -49.8 | 24 | P7RT1 |
| 1.0 | 3.9 | 9.4 | 17.5 | 29.3 | -0.2 | ⊕ | -3.4 | -13.0 | +0.7 | +1.7 | ⊕ | -7.9 | -23.3 | -48.7 | 24 | P7RT2 |
| 0.6 | 2.5 | 5.9 | 10.7 | 17.3 | -0.2 | ⊕ | -3.2 | -10.5 | +0.4 | +1.4 | ⊕ | -6.3 | -18.4 | -37.1 | 24 | P7WBA |
| 1.0 | 4.2 | 10.1 | 19.1 | 31.9 | -0.2 | ⊕ | -3.2 | -12.4 | +0.6 | +1.6 | ⊕ | -7.6 | -22.7 | -47.8 | 24 | P7WBT1 |
| 0.9 | 8.0 | 19.4 | 36.7 | 59.8 | -0.3 | ⊕ | -8.3 | -29.8 | +2.4 | +4.1 | ⊕ | -17.4 | -52.4 | -109.4 | 24 | P3030D |
| 0.7 | 3.0 | 7.0 | 13.0 | 21.1 | -0.1 | ⊕ | -4.0 | -14.4 | +0.9 | +2.0 | ⊕ | -8.4 | -24.3 | -49.0 | 24 | P308C |
| 0.8 | 3.3 | 7.7 | 14.3 | 23.3 | -0.1 | ⊕ | -4.4 | -15.8 | +1.0 | +2.2 | ⊕ | -9.2 | -26.5 | -53.6 | 24 | P308E |
| 0.7 | 3.1 | 7.2 | 13.3 | 21.7 | -0.2 | ⊕ | -3.6 | -13.2 | +0.7 | +1.8 | ⊕ | -7.8 | -22.7 | -46.0 | 24 | P308F |
| 1.0 | 4.2 | 10.0 | 18.7 | 31.1 | -0.1 | ⊕ | -4.4 | -15.9 | +1.0 | +2.2 | ⊕ | -9.4 | -27.7 | -57.5 | 24 | P308T1 |
| 0.7 | 2.8 | 6.6 | 12.3 | 19.9 | -0.2 | ⊕ | -3.6 | -13.2 | +0.8 | +1.8 | ⊕ | -7.8 | -22.4 | -45.2 | 24 | P3006D |
| 0.7 | 3.0 | 7.3 | 13.4 | 27.7 | -0.1 | ⊕ | -4.0 | -14.6 | +0.9 | +2.0 | ⊕ | -8.6 | -24.6 | -49.6 | 24 | P3006F |
| 0.7 | 3.0 | 7.1 | 13.4 | 22.0 | -0.2 | ⊕ | -3.3 | -12.4 | +0.6 | +1.7 | ⊕ | -7.4 | -21.5 | -43.7 | 24 | P3006G |
| 0.6 | 2.6 | 6.0 | 11.0 | 17.8 | -0.1 | ⊕ | -3.9 | -13.9 | +0.9 | +1.9 | ⊕ | -8.1 | -23.1 | -46.1 | 24 | P3006L |
| 0.7 | 2.9 | 6.8 | 12.7 | 20.7 | -0.2 | ⊕ | -3.3 | -12.2 | +0.6 | +1.6 | ⊕ | -7.3 | -21.1 | -42.8 | 24 | P3006P |
| 0.7 | 2.8 | 6.6 | 12.1 | 19.7 | -0.2 | ⊕ | -3.6 | -13.2 | +0.7 | +1.8 | ⊕ | -7.7 | -22.3 | -45.0 | 24 | P3006Q |
| 1.0 | 4.0 | 9.6 | 17.8 | 29.7 | -0.1 | ⊕ | -3.9 | -14.5 | +0.8 | +2.0 | ⊕ | -8.7 | -25.4 | -53.1 | 24 | P3006T1 |
| 0.9 | 4.0 | 9.4 | 17.7 | 29.4 | -0.1 | ⊕ | -4.3 | -15.6 | +1.0 | +2.2 | ⊕ | -9.2 | -27.0 | -56.1 | 24 | P3006T2 |
| 0.5 | 2.2 | 5.0 | 9.2 | 14.9 | -0.2 | ⊕ | -3.4 | -12.2 | +0.7 | +1.7 | ⊕ | -7.1 | -20.4 | -40.5 | 24 | P300WC |
| 0.8 | 3.3 | 7.8 | 14.6 | 24.0 | -0.3 | ⊕ | -2.4 | -9.6 | +0.3 | +1.2 | ⊕ | -6.0 | -17.9 | -37.1 | 24 | P300WT4 |
| 0.9 | 3.8 | 8.6 | 16.1 | 26.6 | 0.0 | ⊕ | -5.1 | -17.9 | +1.3 | +2.6 | ⊕ | -10.2 | -29.9 | -61.0 | 24 | P35WT1 |

# FEDERAL BALLISTICS

## CLASSIC CENTERFIRE RIFLE

| USAGE | FEDERAL LOAD NO. | CALIBER | BULLET GRAINS | WGT. IN GRAMS | BULLET STYLE** | FACTORY PRIMER NO. | VELOCITY IN FEET PER SECOND (TO NEAREST 10 FPS) | | | | | | ENERGY IN FOOT-POUNDS (TO NEAREST 5 FOOT-POUNDS) | | | | | |
|---|---|---|---|---|---|---|---|---|---|---|---|---|---|---|---|---|---|---|
| | | | | | | | MUZZLE | 100 YDS. | 200 YDS. | 300 YDS. | 400 YDS. | 500 YDS. | MUZZLE | 100 YDS. | 200 YDS. | 300 YDS. | 400 YDS. | 500 YDS. |
| 1 | 222A | 222 Rem. (5.56x43mm) | 50 | 3.24 | Hi-Shok Soft Point | 205 | 3140 | 2600 | 2120 | 1700 | 1350 | 1110 | 1095 | 750 | 500 | 320 | 200 | 135 |
| 5 | 222B | 222 Rem. (5.56x43mm) | 55 | 3.56 | Hi-Shok FMJ Boat-Tail | 205 | 3020 | 2740 | 2480 | 2230 | 1990 | 1780 | 1115 | 915 | 750 | 610 | 485 | 385 |
| 1 | 223A | 223 Rem. (5.56x45mm) | 55 | 3.56 | Hi-Shok Soft Point | 205 | 3240 | 2750 | 2300 | 1910 | 1550 | 1270 | 1280 | 920 | 650 | 445 | 295 | 195 |
| 5 | 223B | 223 Rem. (5.56x45mm) | 55 | 3.56 | Hi-Shok FMJ Boat-Tail | 205 | 3240 | 2950 | 2670 | 2410 | 2170 | 1940 | 1280 | 1060 | 875 | 710 | 575 | 460 |
| 1 | 22250A | 22-250 Rem. | 55 | 3.56 | Hi-Shok Soft Point | 210 | 3680 | 3140 | 2660 | 2220 | 1830 | 1490 | 1655 | 1200 | 860 | 605 | 410 | 270 |
| 1 | 243AS | 243 Win. (6.16x51mm) | 80 | 5.18 | Sierra Pro-Hunter SP | 210 | 3350 | 2960 | 2590 | 2260 | 1950 | 1670 | 1995 | 1550 | 1195 | 905 | 675 | 495 |
| 2 | 243B | 243 Win. (6.16x51mm) | 100 | 6.48 | Hi-Shok Soft Point | 210 | 2960 | 2700 | 2450 | 2220 | 1990 | 1790 | 1945 | 1615 | 1330 | 1090 | 880 | 710 |
| 1 | 6AS | 6mm Rem. | 80 | 5.18 | Sierra Pro-Hunter SP | 210 | 3470 | 3060 | 2690 | 2350 | 2040 | 1750 | 2140 | 1665 | 1290 | 980 | 735 | 540 |
| 2 | 6B | 6mm Rem. | 100 | 6.48 | Hi-Shok Soft Point | 210 | 3100 | 2830 | 2570 | 2330 | 2100 | 1890 | 2135 | 1775 | 1470 | 1205 | 985 | 790 |
| 2 | 2506BS | 25-06 Rem. | 117 | 7.58 | Sierra Pro-Hunter SP | 210 | 2990 | 2730 | 2480 | 2250 | 2030 | 1830 | 2320 | 1985 | 1645 | 1350 | 1100 | 885 |
| 2 | 270A | 270 Win. | 130 | 8.42 | Hi-Shok Soft Point | 210 | 3060 | 2800 | 2560 | 2330 | 2110 | 1900 | 2700 | 2265 | 1890 | 1565 | 1285 | 1045 |
| 2 | 270B | 270 Win. | 150 | 9.72 | Hi-Shok Soft Point RN | 210 | 2850 | 2500 | 2180 | 1890 | 1620 | 1390 | 2705 | 2085 | 1585 | 1185 | 870 | 640 |
| 2 | NEW | 270GS | 270 Win. | 130 | 8.42 | Sierra Pro-Hunter SP | 210 | 3060 | 2830 | 2600 | 2390 | 2190 | 2000 | 2705 | 2305 | 1960 | 1655 | 1390 | 1155 |
| 2 | 7A | 7mm Mauser (7x57mm Mauser) | 175 | 11.34 | Hi-Shok Soft Point RN | 210 | 2440 | 2140 | 1860 | 1600 | 1380 | 1200 | 2315 | 1775 | 1340 | 1000 | 740 | 565 |
| 2 | 7B | 7mm Mauser (7x57mm Mauser) | 140 | 9.07 | Hi-Shok Soft Point | 210 | 2660 | 2450 | 2260 | 2070 | 1890 | 1730 | 2200 | 1865 | 1585 | 1330 | 1110 | 930 |
| 2 | NEW | 70BCS | 7mm-08 Rem. | 150 | 9.72 | Sierra Pro-Hunter SP | 210 | 2650 | 2440 | 2230 | 2040 | 1860 | 1690 | 2340 | 1980 | 1660 | 1390 | 1150 | 950 |
| 2 | 280B | 280 Rem. | 150 | 9.72 | Hi-Shok Soft Point | 210 | 2890 | 2670 | 2460 | 2260 | 2060 | 1880 | 2780 | 2370 | 2015 | 1695 | 1420 | 1180 |
| 2 | NEW | 280CS | 280 Rem. | 140 | 9.07 | Sierra Pro-Hunter SP | 210 | 2990 | 2740 | 2500 | 2270 | 2060 | 1860 | 2770 | 2325 | 1940 | 1605 | 1320 | 1070 |
| 2 | 7RA | 7mm Rem. Magnum | 150 | 9.72 | Hi-Shok Soft Point | 215 | 3110 | 2830 | 2570 | 2320 | 2090 | 1870 | 3220 | 2670 | 2200 | 1790 | 1450 | 1160 |
| 2 | 7RB | 7mm Rem. Magnum | 175 | 11.34 | Hi-Shok Soft Point | 215 | 2860 | 2650 | 2440 | 2240 | 2060 | 1880 | 3180 | 2720 | 2310 | 1960 | 1640 | 1370 |
| 3 | NEW | 7RJS | 7mm Rem. Magnum | 160 | 10.37 | Sierra Pro-Hunter SP | 215 | 2940 | 2730 | 2520 | 2320 | 2140 | 1960 | 3070 | 2640 | 2260 | 1920 | 1620 | 1360 |
| 1 | 30CA | 30 Carbine (7.62x33mm) | 110 | 7.13 | Hi-Shok Soft Point RN | 205 | 1990 | 1570 | 1240 | 1040 | 920 | 840 | 965 | 600 | 375 | 260 | 210 | 175 |
| 2 | 76239B | 7.62x39mm Soviet | 123 | 7.97 | Hi-Shok Soft Point | 210 | 2300 | 2030 | 1780 | 1550 | 1350 | 1200 | 1445 | 1125 | 860 | 655 | 500 | 395 |
| 2 | 3030A | 30-30 Win. | 150 | 9.72 | Hi-Shok Soft Point FN | 210 | 2390 | 2020 | 1680 | 1400 | 1180 | 1040 | 1900 | 1355 | 945 | 650 | 460 | 355 |
| 2 | 3030B | 30-30 Win. | 170 | 11.01 | Hi-Shok Soft Point RN | 210 | 2200 | 1900 | 1620 | 1380 | 1190 | 1060 | 1830 | 1355 | 990 | 720 | 535 | 425 |
| 1 | 3030C | 30-30 Win. | 125 | 8.10 | Hi-Shok Hollow Point | 210 | 2570 | 2090 | 1660 | 1320 | 1080 | 960 | 1830 | 1210 | 770 | 480 | 320 | 260 |
| 2 | NEW | 3030FS | 30-30 Win. | 170 | 11.01 | Sierra Pro-Hunter SP | 210 | 2200 | 1820 | 1500 | 1240 | 1060 | 960 | 1830 | 1255 | 845 | 575 | 425 | 345 |
| 2 | 300A | 300 Savage | 150 | 9.72 | Hi-Shok Soft Point | 210 | 2630 | 2350 | 2100 | 1850 | 1630 | 1430 | 2305 | 1845 | 1460 | 1145 | 885 | 685 |
| 2 | 300B | 300 Savage | 180 | 11.66 | Hi-Shok Soft Point | 210 | 2350 | 2140 | 1940 | 1750 | 1570 | 1410 | 2205 | 1825 | 1495 | 1215 | 985 | 800 |
| 2 | 308A | 308 Win. (7.62x51mm) | 150 | 9.72 | Hi-Shok Soft Point | 210 | 2820 | 2530 | 2260 | 2010 | 1770 | 1560 | 2650 | 2140 | 1705 | 1345 | 1050 | 810 |
| 2 | 308B | 308 Win. (7.62x51mm) | 180 | 11.66 | Hi-Shok Soft Point | 210 | 2620 | 2390 | 2180 | 1970 | 1780 | 1600 | 2745 | 2290 | 1895 | 1555 | 1270 | 1030 |
| 2 | NEW | 308HS | 308 Win. (7.62x51mm) | 180 | 11.66 | Sierra Pro-Hunter SP | 210 | 2620 | 2410 | 2200 | 2010 | 1820 | 1650 | 2745 | 2315 | 1940 | 1610 | 1330 | 1090 |
| 2 | 3006A | 30-06 Springfield (7.62x63mm) | 150 | 9.72 | Hi-Shok Soft Point | 210 | 2910 | 2620 | 2340 | 2080 | 1840 | 1620 | 2820 | 2280 | 1825 | 1445 | 1130 | 875 |
| 3 | 3006B | 30-06 Springfield (7.62x63mm) | 180 | 11.66 | Hi-Shok Soft Point | 210 | 2700 | 2470 | 2250 | 2040 | 1850 | 1660 | 2915 | 2435 | 2025 | 1665 | 1360 | 1105 |
| 1 | 3006CS | 30-06 Springfield (7.62x63mm) | 125 | 8.10 | Sierra Pro-Hunter SP | 210 | 3140 | 2780 | 2450 | 2140 | 1850 | 1600 | 2735 | 2145 | 1660 | 1270 | 955 | 705 |
| 3 | 3006HS | 30-06 Springfield (7.62x63mm) | 220 | 14.25 | Sierra Pro-Hunter SP RN | 210 | 2410 | 2130 | 1870 | 1630 | 1420 | 1250 | 2835 | 2215 | 1705 | 1300 | 985 | 760 |
| 3 | 3006JS | 30-06 Springfield (7.62x63mm) | 180 | 11.66 | Sierra Pro-Hunter SP RN | 210 | 2700 | 2350 | 2020 | 1730 | 1470 | 1250 | 2915 | 2200 | 1630 | 1190 | 860 | 620 |
| 2 | NEW | 3006SS | 30-06 Springfield (7.62x63mm) | 150 | 9.72 | Sierra Pro-Hunter SP | 210 | 2910 | 2640 | 2380 | 2130 | 1900 | 1690 | 2820 | 2315 | 1880 | 1515 | 1205 | 950 |
| 2 | NEW | 3006TS | 30-06 Springfield (7.62x63mm) | 165 | 10.69 | Sierra Pro-Hunter SP | 210 | 2800 | 2560 | 2340 | 2130 | 1920 | 1730 | 2875 | 2410 | 2005 | 1655 | 1360 | 1100 |
| 3 | 300WBS | 300 Win. Magnum | 180 | 11.66 | Sierra Pro-Hunter SP | 215 | 2960 | 2750 | 2540 | 2340 | 2160 | 1980 | 3500 | 3010 | 2580 | 2195 | 1860 | 1565 |
| 2 | 300WGS | 300 Win. Magnum | 150 | 9.72 | Sierra Pro-Hunter SP | 215 | 3280 | 3030 | 2800 | 2570 | 2360 | 2160 | 3570 | 3055 | 2600 | 2205 | 1860 | 1560 |
| 2 | 303AS | 303 British | 180 | 11.66 | Sierra Pro-Hunter SP | 210 | 2460 | 2230 | 2020 | 1820 | 1630 | 1460 | 2420 | 1995 | 1625 | 1315 | 1060 | 850 |
| 2 | 303B | 303 British | 150 | 9.72 | Hi-Shok Soft Point | 210 | 2690 | 2440 | 2210 | 1980 | 1780 | 1590 | 2400 | 1980 | 1620 | 1310 | 1055 | 840 |
| 2 | 32A | 32 Win. Special | 170 | 11.01 | Hi-Shok Soft Point | 210 | 2250 | 1920 | 1630 | 1370 | 1180 | 1040 | 1910 | 1395 | 1000 | 710 | 520 | 410 |
| 2 | *8A | 8mm Mauser (8x57mm JS Mauser) | 170 | 11.01 | Hi-Shok Soft Point | 210 | 2360 | 1970 | 1620 | 1330 | 1120 | 1000 | 2100 | 1465 | 995 | 670 | 475 | 375 |
| 3 | NEW | 338ES | 338 Win Magnum | 225 | 14.58 | Sierra Pro-Hunter SP | 215 | 2780 | 2570 | 2360 | 2170 | 1980 | 1800 | 3860 | 3290 | 2780 | 2340 | 1960 | 1630 |
| 2 | 357G | 357 Magnum | 180 | 11.66 | Hi-Shok Hollow Point | 100 | 1550 | 1160 | 980 | 860 | 770 | 680 | 960 | 535 | 385 | 295 | 235 | 185 |
| 2 | 35A | 35 Rem. | 200 | 12.96 | Hi-Shok Soft Point | 210 | 2080 | 1700 | 1380 | 1140 | 1000 | 910 | 1920 | 1280 | 840 | 575 | 445 | 370 |
| 3 | 375A | 375 H&H Magnum | 270 | 17.50 | Hi-Shok Soft Point | 215 | 2690 | 2420 | 2170 | 1920 | 1700 | 1500 | 4340 | 3510 | 2810 | 2220 | 1740 | 1355 |
| 4 | 375B | 375 H&H Magnum | 300 | 19.44 | Hi-Shok Soft Point | 215 | 2530 | 2270 | 2020 | 1790 | 1580 | 1400 | 4265 | 3425 | 2720 | 2135 | 1665 | 1295 |
| 2 | 44A | 44 Rem. Magnum | 240 | 15.55 | Hi-Shok Hollow Point | 150 | 1760 | 1380 | 1090 | 950 | 860 | 790 | 1650 | 1015 | 640 | 485 | 395 | 330 |
| 2 | 4570AS | 45-70 Government | 300 | 19.44 | Sierra Pro-Hunter HP FN | 210 | 1880 | 1650 | 1430 | 1240 | 1110 | 1010 | 2355 | 1815 | 1355 | 1015 | 810 | 680 |

Usage Key: 1 =Varmints, predators, small game  2 =Medium game  3 =Large, heavy game  4 = Dangerous game  5 =Target shooting, training, practice
* Only for use in barrels intended for .323 inch diameter bullets. Do not use in 8x57mm J Commission Rifles (M1888) or in sporting or other military arms of .318 inch bore diameter.  **RN = Round Nose  SP = Soft Point  FN = Flat Nose  FMJ = Full Metal Jacket  HP = Hollow Point

## CLASSIC CENTERFIRE RIFLE (cont.)

| 100 YDS. | 200 YDS. | 300 YDS. | 400 YDS. | 500 YDS. | 50 YDS. | 100 YDS. | 200 YDS. | 300 YDS. | 50 YDS. | 100 YDS. | 200 YDS. | 300 YDS. | 400 YDS. | 500 YDS. | TEST BARREL LENGTH INCHES | FEDERAL LOAD NO. |
|---|---|---|---|---|---|---|---|---|---|---|---|---|---|---|---|---|
| 1.7 | 7.3 | 18.3 | 36.4 | 63.1 | -0.2 | ⊕ | -3.7 | -15.3 | +0.7 | +1.9 | ⊕ | -9.7 | -31.6 | -71.3 | 24 | 222A |
| 0.9 | 3.4 | 8.5 | 16.8 | 26.3 | -0.2 | ⊕ | -3.1 | -12.0 | +0.6 | +1.6 | ⊕ | -7.3 | -21.5 | -44.6 | 24 | 222B |
| 1.4 | 6.1 | 15.0 | 29.4 | 50.8 | -0.3 | ⊕ | -3.2 | -12.9 | +0.5 | +1.6 | ⊕ | -8.2 | -26.1 | -58.3 | 24 | 223A |
| 0.8 | 3.3 | 7.8 | 14.5 | 24.0 | -0.3 | ⊕ | -2.5 | -9.9 | +0.3 | +1.3 | ⊕ | -6.1 | -18.3 | -37.8 | 24 | 223B |
| 1.2 | 5.2 | 12.5 | 24.4 | 42.0 | -0.4 | ⊕ | -2.1 | -9.1 | +0.1 | +1.0 | ⊕ | -6.0 | -19.1 | -42.6 | 24 | 22250A |
| 1.0 | 4.3 | 10.4 | 19.8 | 33.3 | -0.3 | ⊕ | -2.5 | -10.2 | +0.3 | +1.3 | ⊕ | -6.4 | -19.7 | -42.2 | 24 | 243AS |
| 0.9 | 3.6 | 8.4 | 15.7 | 25.8 | -0.2 | ⊕ | -3.3 | -12.4 | +0.6 | +1.6 | ⊕ | -7.5 | -22.0 | -45.4 | 24 | 243B |
| 1.0 | 4.1 | 9.9 | 18.8 | 31.6 | -0.3 | ⊕ | -2.2 | -9.3 | +0.2 | +1.1 | ⊕ | -5.9 | -18.2 | -39.0 | 24 | 6AS |
| 0.8 | 3.3 | 7.9 | 14.7 | 24.1 | -0.3 | ⊕ | -2.9 | -11.0 | +0.5 | +1.4 | ⊕ | -6.7 | -19.8 | -40.6 | 24 | 6B |
| 0.8 | 3.4 | 8.1 | 15.1 | 24.9 | -0.2 | ⊕ | -3.2 | -12.0 | +0.6 | +1.6 | ⊕ | -7.2 | -21.4 | -44.0 | 24 | 2506BS |
| 0.8 | 3.2 | 7.6 | 14.2 | 23.3 | -0.2 | ⊕ | -2.9 | -11.2 | +0.5 | +1.5 | ⊕ | -6.8 | -20.0 | -41.1 | 24 | 270A |
| 1.2 | 5.3 | 12.8 | 24.5 | 41.3 | -0.1 | ⊕ | -4.1 | -15.5 | +0.9 | +2.0 | ⊕ | -9.4 | -28.6 | -61.0 | 24 | 270B |
| 0.8 | 3.0 | 6.9 | 12.8 | 20.7 | +0.3 | ⊕ | -2.8 | -10.7 | +0.5 | +1.4 | ⊕ | -6.4 | -19.0 | -38.5 | 24 | 270GS |
| 1.5 | 6.2 | 15.0 | 28.7 | 47.8 | -0.1 | ⊕ | -5.2 | -22.6 | +1.6 | +3.1 | ⊕ | -13.3 | -40.1 | -84.6 | 24 | 7A |
| 1.3 | 3.2 | 8.2 | 15.4 | 23.4 | -0.1 | ⊕ | -4.3 | -15.4 | +1.0 | +2.1 | ⊕ | -9.0 | -26.1 | -52.9 | 24 | 7B |
| 0.9 | 3.6 | 8.4 | 15.6 | 25.5 | -0.1 | ⊕ | -4.4 | -15.7 | +1.0 | +2.2 | ⊕ | -9.2 | -26.7 | -54.4 | 24 | 708CS |
| 0.7 | 3.1 | 7.2 | 13.4 | 21.9 | -0.2 | ⊕ | -3.4 | -12.6 | +0.7 | +1.7 | ⊕ | -7.5 | -21.8 | -44.3 | 24 | 280B |
| 0.9 | 3.4 | 7.9 | 14.7 | 23.9 | -0.2 | ⊕ | -3.1 | -11.7 | +0.6 | +1.6 | ⊕ | -7.0 | -20.8 | -42.6 | 24 | 280CS |
| 0.8 | 3.4 | 8.1 | 15.1 | 24.9 | -0.3 | ⊕ | -2.9 | -11.0 | +0.5 | +1.4 | ⊕ | -6.7 | -19.9 | -40.4 | 24 | 7RA |
| 0.7 | 3.1 | 7.2 | 13.3 | 21.7 | -0.2 | ⊕ | -3.5 | -12.8 | +0.7 | +1.7 | ⊕ | -7.6 | -22.1 | -44.9 | 24 | 7RB |
| 0.7 | 2.9 | 6.8 | 12.5 | 20.4 | -0.2 | ⊕ | -3.2 | -11.9 | +0.6 | +1.6 | ⊕ | -7.1 | -20.6 | -42.2 | 24 | 7RJS |
| 3.4 | 15.0 | 35.5 | 63.2 | 96.7 | +0.6 | ⊕ | -12.8 | -46.9 | +3.9 | +6.4 | ⊕ | -27.7 | -81.8 | -167.8 | 18 | 30CA |
| 1.5 | 6.4 | 15.2 | 28.7 | 47.3 | +0.2 | ⊕ | -7.0 | -25.1 | +1.9 | +3.5 | ⊕ | -14.5 | -43.4 | -90.6 | 20 | 76239B |
| 2.0 | 8.5 | 20.9 | 40.1 | 66.1 | +0.2 | ⊕ | -7.2 | -26.7 | +1.9 | +3.6 | ⊕ | -15.9 | -49.1 | -104.5 | 24 | 3030A |
| 1.9 | 8.0 | 19.4 | 36.7 | 59.8 | +0.3 | ⊕ | -8.3 | -29.8 | +2.4 | +4.1 | ⊕ | -17.4 | -52.4 | -109.4 | 24 | 3030B |
| 2.2 | 10.1 | 25.4 | 49.4 | 81.6 | +0.1 | ⊕ | -6.6 | -26.0 | +1.7 | +3.3 | ⊕ | -16.0 | -50.9 | -109.5 | 24 | 3030C |
| 2.7 | 10.9 | 25.9 | 48.3 | 76.5 | +0.3 | ⊕ | -9.1 | -33.6 | +2.6 | +4.5 | ⊕ | -20.0 | -63.5 | -137.4 | 24 | 3030FS |
| 1.1 | 4.8 | 11.6 | 21.9 | 36.3 | 0.0 | ⊕ | -4.8 | -17.6 | +1.2 | +2.4 | ⊕ | -10.4 | -30.9 | -64.4 | 24 | 300A |
| 1.1 | 4.6 | 10.9 | 20.3 | 33.3 | +0.1 | ⊕ | -6.1 | -21.6 | +1.7 | +3.1 | ⊕ | -12.4 | -36.1 | -73.8 | 24 | 300B |
| 1.0 | 4.4 | 10.4 | 19.7 | 32.7 | -0.1 | ⊕ | -3.9 | -14.7 | +0.8 | +2.0 | ⊕ | -8.8 | -26.3 | -54.8 | 24 | 308A |
| 0.9 | 3.9 | 9.2 | 17.2 | 28.3 | -0.1 | ⊕ | -4.6 | -16.5 | +1.1 | +2.3 | ⊕ | -9.7 | -28.3 | -57.8 | 24 | 308B |
| 1.0 | 3.9 | 8.9 | 16.4 | 26.8 | -0.1 | ⊕ | -4.5 | -16.0 | +1.1 | +2.3 | ⊕ | -9.3 | -27.1 | -55.8 | 24 | 308HS |
| 1.0 | 4.2 | 9.9 | 18.7 | 31.2 | -0.2 | ⊕ | -3.6 | -13.6 | +0.7 | +1.8 | ⊕ | -8.2 | -24.4 | -50.9 | 24 | 3006A |
| 0.9 | 3.7 | 8.8 | 16.5 | 27.1 | -0.1 | ⊕ | -4.2 | -15.3 | +1.0 | +2.1 | ⊕ | -9.0 | -26.4 | -54.0 | 24 | 3006B |
| 1.1 | 4.5 | 10.8 | 20.5 | 34.4 | -0.3 | ⊕ | -3.0 | -11.9 | +0.5 | +1.5 | ⊕ | -7.3 | -22.3 | -47.5 | 24 | 3006CS |
| 1.4 | 6.0 | 14.3 | 27.2 | 45.0 | -0.1 | ⊕ | -5.2 | -22.4 | +1.7 | +3.1 | ⊕ | -13.1 | -39.3 | -82.2 | 24 | 3006HS |
| 1.5 | 6.4 | 15.7 | 30.4 | 51.2 | -0.1 | ⊕ | -4.9 | -18.3 | +1.1 | +2.4 | ⊕ | -11.0 | -33.6 | -71.9 | 24 | 3006JS |
| 1.1 | 4.0 | 9.5 | 17.5 | 29.0 | -0.2 | ⊕ | -3.4 | -13.1 | +0.7 | +1.7 | ⊕ | -7.9 | -23.3 | -48.7 | 24 | 3006SS |
| 0.9 | 3.6 | 8.4 | 15.7 | 25.7 | -0.1 | ⊕ | -3.8 | -14.0 | +0.8 | +1.9 | ⊕ | -8.3 | -24.3 | -49.8 | 24 | 3006TS |
| 0.7 | 2.8 | 6.6 | 12.3 | 20.0 | -0.2 | ⊕ | -3.1 | -11.7 | +0.6 | +1.6 | ⊕ | -7.0 | -20.3 | -41.1 | 24 | 300WBS |
| 0.7 | 2.7 | 6.3 | 11.5 | 18.8 | -0.3 | ⊕ | -2.3 | -9.1 | +0.3 | +1.1 | ⊕ | -5.6 | -16.4 | -33.6 | 24 | 300WGS |
| 1.1 | 4.5 | 10.6 | 19.9 | 32.7 | 0.0 | ⊕ | -5.5 | -19.6 | +1.4 | +2.8 | ⊕ | -11.3 | -33.2 | -68.1 | 24 | 303AS |
| 1.0 | 4.1 | 9.6 | 18.1 | 29.9 | -0.1 | ⊕ | -4.4 | -15.9 | +1.0 | +2.2 | ⊕ | -9.4 | -27.6 | -56.8 | 24 | 303B |
| 1.9 | 8.4 | 20.3 | 38.6 | 63.0 | +0.3 | ⊕ | -8.0 | -29.2 | +2.3 | +4.0 | ⊕ | -17.2 | -52.3 | -109.8 | 24 | 32A |
| 2.1 | 9.3 | 22.9 | 43.9 | 71.7 | +0.2 | ⊕ | -7.6 | -28.5 | +2.1 | +3.8 | ⊕ | -17.1 | -52.9 | -111.9 | 24 | *8A |
| 0.8 | 3.3 | 7.6 | 14.1 | 23.1 | -0.1 | ⊕ | -3.8 | -13.8 | +0.8 | +1.9 | ⊕ | -8.2 | -23.7 | -48.2 | 24 | 338ES |
| 5.8 | 21.7 | 45.2 | 76.1 | NA | ⊕ | -3.4 | -29.7 | -88.2 | +1.7 | ⊕ | -22.8 | -77.9 | -173.8 | -321.4 | 18 | 357G |
| 2.7 | 12.0 | 29.0 | 53.3 | 83.3 | +0.5 | ⊕ | -10.7 | -39.3 | +3.2 | +5.4 | ⊕ | -23.3 | -70.0 | -144.0 | 24 | 35A |
| 1.1 | 4.5 | 10.8 | 20.3 | 33.7 | -0.4 | ⊕ | -5.5 | -18.4 | +1.0 | +2.4 | ⊕ | -10.9 | -33.3 | -71.2 | 24 | 375A |
| 1.2 | 5.0 | 11.9 | 22.4 | 37.1 | +0.5 | ⊕ | -6.3 | -21.2 | +1.3 | +2.6 | ⊕ | -11.2 | -33.3 | -69.1 | 24 | 375B |
| 4.2 | 17.8 | 39.8 | 68.3 | 102.5 | ⊕ | -2.2 | -21.7 | -67.2 | +1.1 | ⊕ | -17.4 | -50.7 | -136.0 | -250.2 | 20 | 44A |
| 1.7 | 7.6 | 18.6 | 35.7 | NA | ⊕ | -1.3 | -14.1 | -43.7 | +0.7 | ⊕ | -11.5 | -39.7 | -89.1 | -163.1 | 24 | 4570AS |

# FEDERAL BALLISTICS

## CLASSIC REVOLVER

| USAGE | FEDERAL LOAD NO. | CALIBER | BULLET WGT. GRAINS | WGT. IN GRAMS | BULLET STYLE** | FACTORY PRIMER NO. | VELOCITY IN FEET PER SECOND (TO NEAREST 10 FPS) MUZZLE | 25 YDS. | 50 YDS. | 75 YDS. | 100 YDS. | ENERGY IN FOOT-POUNDS (TO NEAREST 5 FOOT-POUNDS) MUZZLE | 25 YDS. | 50 YDS. | 75 YDS. | 100 YDS. | MID-RANGE TRAJECTORY 25 YDS. | 50 YDS. | 75 YDS. | 100 YDS. | BARREL LENGTH INCHES |
|---|---|---|---|---|---|---|---|---|---|---|---|---|---|---|---|---|---|---|---|---|---|
| [4] | 32LA | 32 S&W Long | 98 | 6.35 | Lead Wadcutter | 100 | .780 | 700 | 630 | 560 | 500 | 130 | 105 | 85 | 70 | 55 | 0.5 | 2.2 | 5.6 | 11.1 | 4 |
| [4] | 32LB | 32 S&W Long | 98 | 6.35 | Lead Round Nose | 100 | 710 | 690 | 670 | 650 | 640 | 115 | 105 | 100 | 95 | 90 | 0.6 | 2.3 | 5.3 | 9.6 | 4 |
| [3] | 32HRA | 32 H&R Magnum | 95 | 6.15 | Lead Semi-Wadcutter | 100 | 1030 | 1000 | 940 | 930 | 900 | 225 | 210 | 195 | 185 | 170 | 0.3 | 1.1 | 2.5 | 4.7 | 4½ |
| [3] | 32HRB | 32 H&R Magnum | 85 | 5.50 | Hi-Shok JHP | 100 | 1100 | 1050 | 1020 | 970 | 930 | 230 | 210 | 195 | 175 | 165 | 0.2 | 1.0 | 2.3 | 4.3 | 4½ |
| [4] | 38B | 38 Special | 158 | 10.23 | Lead Round Nose | 100 | 760 | 740 | 720 | 710 | 690 | 200 | 190 | 185 | 175 | 170 | 0.5 | 2.0 | 4.6 | 8.3 | 4-V |
| [3],[4] | 38C | 38 Special | 158 | 10.23 | Lead Semi-Wadcutter | 100 | 760 | 740 | 720 | 710 | 690 | 200 | 190 | 185 | 175 | 170 | 0.5 | 2.0 | 4.6 | 8.3 | 4-V |
| [1],[3] | 38E | 38 Special (High-Velocity+P) | 125 | 8.10 | Hi-Shok JHP | 100 | 950 | 920 | 900 | 880 | 860 | 250 | 235 | 225 | 215 | 205 | 0.3 | 1.3 | 2.9 | 5.4 | 4-V |
| [1],[3] | 38F | 38 Special (High-Velocity+P) | 110 | 7.13 | Hi-Shok JHP | 100 | 1000 | 960 | 930 | 900 | 870 | 240 | 225 | 210 | 195 | 185 | 0.3 | 1.2 | 2.7 | 5.0 | 4-V |
| [1],[3] | 38G | 38 Special (High-Velocity+P) | 158 | 10.23 | Semi-Wadcutter HP | 100 | 890 | 870 | 860 | 840 | 820 | 280 | 265 | 260 | 245 | 235 | 0.3 | 1.4 | 3.3 | 5.9 | 4-V |
| [3],[4] | 38H | 38 Special (High-Velocity+P) | 158 | 10.23 | Lead Semi-Wadcutter | 100 | 890 | 870 | 860 | 840 | 820 | 270 | 265 | 260 | 245 | 235 | 0.3 | 1.4 | 3.3 | 5.9 | 4-V |
| [1],[3] | 38J | 38 Special (High-Velocity+P) | 125 | 8.10 | Hi-Shok JSP | 100 | 950 | 920 | 900 | 880 | 860 | 250 | 235 | 225 | 215 | 205 | 0.3 | 1.3 | 2.9 | 5.4 | 4-V |
| [2],[3] | 357A | 357 Magnum | 158 | 10.23 | Hi-Shok JSP | 100 | 1240 | 1160 | 1100 | 1060 | 1020 | 535 | 475 | 430 | 395 | 365 | 0.2 | 0.8 | 1.9 | 3.5 | 4-V |
| [1],[3] | 357B | 357 Magnum | 125 | 8.10 | Hi-Shok JHP | 100 | 1450 | 1350 | 1240 | 1160 | 1100 | 580 | 495 | 430 | 370 | 335 | 0.1 | 0.6 | 1.5 | 2.8 | 4-V |
| [4] | 357C | 357 Magnum | 158 | 10.23 | Lead Semi-Wadcutter | 100 | 1240 | 1160 | 1100 | 1060 | 1020 | 535 | 475 | 430 | 395 | 365 | 0.2 | 0.8 | 1.9 | 3.5 | 4-V |
| [1],[3] | 357D | 357 Magnum | 110 | 7.13 | Hi-Shok JHP | 100 | 1300 | 1180 | 1090 | 1040 | 990 | 410 | 340 | 290 | 260 | 235 | 0.2 | 0.8 | 1.9 | 3.5 | 4-V |
| [2],[3] | 357E | 357 Magnum | 158 | 10.23 | Hi-Shok JHP | 100 | 1240 | 1160 | 1100 | 1060 | 1020 | 535 | 475 | 430 | 395 | 365 | 0.2 | 0.8 | 1.9 | 3.5 | 4-V |
| [2] | 357G | 357 Magnum | 180 | 11.66 | Hi-Shok JHP | 100 | 1090 | 1030 | 980 | 930 | 890 | 475 | 425 | 385 | 350 | 320 | 0.2 | 1.0 | 2.4 | 4.5 | 4-V |
| [2],[3] | 357H | 357 Magnum | 140 | 9.07 | Hi-Shok JHP | 100 | 1360 | 1270 | 1200 | 1130 | 1080 | 575 | 500 | 445 | 395 | 360 | 0.2 | 0.7 | 1.6 | 3.0 | 4-V |
| [1],[3] | 41A | 41 Rem. Magnum | 210 | 13.60 | Hi-Shok JHP | 150 | 1300 | 1210 | 1130 | 1070 | 1030 | 790 | 680 | 595 | 540 | 495 | 0.2 | 0.7 | 1.8 | 3.3 | 4-V |
| [1],[3] | 44SA | 44 S&W Special | 200 | 12.96 | Semi-Wadcutter HP | 150 | 900 | 860 | 830 | 800 | 770 | 360 | 330 | 305 | 285 | 260 | 0.3 | 1.4 | 3.4 | 6.3 | 6½-V |
| [2],[3] | 44A | 44 Rem. Magnum | 240 | 15.55 | Hi-Shok JHP | 150 | 1180 | 1080 | 1010 | 1050 | 1010 | 740 | 675 | 625 | 580 | 550 | 0.2 | 0.9 | 2.0 | 3.7 | 6½-V |
| [1],[2] | 44B* | 44 Rem. Magnum | 180 | 11.66 | Hi-Shok JHP | 150 | 1610 | 1480 | 1370 | 1270 | 1180 | 1035 | 875 | 750 | 640 | 555 | 0.1 | 0.5 | 1.2 | 2.3 | 6½-V |
| [1],[3] | 45LCA | 45 Colt | 225 | 14.58 | Semi-Wadcutter HP | 150 | 900 | 880 | 860 | 840 | 820 | 405 | 385 | 370 | 355 | 340 | 0.3 | 1.4 | 3.2 | 5.8 | 5½ |

Usage Key: [1] = Varmints, predators, small game  [2] = Medium game  [3] = Self-defense  [4] = Target shooting, training, practice  *Also available in 20-round box (A44B20).  **JHP = Jacketed Hollow Point  HP = Hollow Point  JSP = Jacketed Soft Point
+ P ammunition is loaded to a higher pressure. Use only in firearms so recommended by the gun manufacturer.  "V" indicates vented barrel to simulate service conditions.

## CLASSIC .22 MAGNUM

| USAGE | FEDERAL LOAD NO. | CARTRIDGE PER BOX | CALIBER | BULLET WGT. IN GRAINS | BULLET STYLE* | VELOCITY IN FEET PER SECOND MUZZLE | 50 YDS. | 100 YDS. | 150 YDS. | ENERGY IN FOOT-POUNDS MUZZLE | 50 YDS. | 100 YDS. | 150 YDS. | WIND DRIFT 10 MPH 50 YDS. | 100 YDS. | 150 YDS. | TRAJECTORY (zero set 1) 50 YDS. | 100 YDS. | 150 YDS. | (zero set 2) 50 YDS. | 100 YDS. | 150 YDS. |
|---|---|---|---|---|---|---|---|---|---|---|---|---|---|---|---|---|---|---|---|---|---|---|
| [1],[4] | 757 | 50 | 22 Win. Magnum | 50 | Jacketed HP | 1650 | 1450 | 1280 | 1150 | 300 | 235 | 180 | 145 | 1.1 | 4.5 | 10.3 | ⊕ | -3.6 | -12.5 | +1.3 | ⊕ | -6.5 |
| [1],[4] | 737 | 50 | 22 Win. Magnum | 40 | Full Metal Jacket | 1910 | 1600 | 1330 | 1140 | 325 | 225 | 155 | 115 | 1.3 | 5.7 | 13.4 | ⊕ | -2.9 | -10.7 | +1.0 | ⊕ | -5.8 |
| [1],[4] | 767 | 50 | 22 Win. Magnum | 30 | Jacketed HP | 2200 | 1760 | 1400 | 1130 | 325 | 205 | 130 | 85 | 1.4 | 6.3 | 15.4 | ⊕ | -1.3 | -7.3 | +0.7 | ⊕ | -5.2 |

Usage Key: [1] = Varmints, predators, small game  [2] = Medium game  [3] = Self-defense  [4] = Target shooting, training, practice
*HP = Hollow Point  These trajectory tables were calculated by computer using the best available data for each load. Trajectories are representative of the nominal behavior of each load at standard conditions (59°F temperature; barometric pressure of 29.53 inches; altitude at sea level).

## CLASSIC AUTOMATIC PISTOL

| USAGE | FEDERAL LOAD NO. | CALIBER | BULLET WGT. GRAINS | WGT. IN GRAMS | BULLET STYLE* | FACTORY PRIMER NO. | VELOCITY (TO NEAREST 10 FPS) MUZZLE | 25 YDS. | 50 YDS. | 75 YDS. | 100 YDS. | ENERGY MUZZLE | 25 YDS. | 50 YDS. | 75 YDS. | 100 YDS. | MID-RANGE TRAJECTORY 25 YDS. | 50 YDS. | 75 YDS. | 100 YDS. | BARREL LENGTH INCHES |
|---|---|---|---|---|---|---|---|---|---|---|---|---|---|---|---|---|---|---|---|---|---|
| [3],[4] | 25AP | 25 Auto (6.35mm Browning) | 50 | 3.24 | Full Metal Jacket | 200 | 760 | 750 | 730 | 720 | 700 | 65 | 60 | 60 | 55 | 55 | 0.5 | 1.9 | 4.5 | 8.1 | 2 |
| [3],[4] | 32AP | 32 Auto (7.65mm Browning) | 71 | 4.60 | Full Metal Jacket | 100 | 910 | 880 | 860 | 830 | 810 | 130 | 120 | 115 | 110 | 105 | 0.3 | 1.4 | 3.2 | 5.9 | 4 |
| [3],[4] | 380AP | 380 Auto (9x17mm Short) | 95 | 6.15 | Full Metal Jacket | 100 | 960 | 910 | 870 | 830 | 790 | 190 | 175 | 160 | 145 | 130 | 0.3 | 1.3 | 3.1 | 5.8 | 3¾ |
| [3] | 380BP | 380 Auto (9x17mm Short) | 90 | 5.83 | Hi-Shok JHP | 100 | 1000 | 940 | 890 | 840 | 800 | 200 | 175 | 160 | 140 | 130 | 0.3 | 1.2 | 2.9 | 5.5 | 3¾ |
| [3] NEW | 9MKB | 9mm Makarov (9x18 Makarov) | 90 | 5.83 | Hi-Shok JHP | 100 | 990 | 950 | 910 | 880 | 850 | 195 | 180 | 165 | 155 | 145 | 0.3 | 1.2 | 2.9 | 5.3 | 3½ |
| [3],[4] | 9AP | 9mm Luger (9x19mm Parabellum) | 124 | 8.03 | Full Metal Jacket | 100 | 1120 | 1070 | 1030 | 990 | 960 | 345 | 315 | 290 | 270 | 255 | 0.2 | 0.9 | 2.2 | 4.1 | 4 |
| [3] | 9BP | 9mm Luger (9x19mm Parabellum) | 115 | 7.45 | Hi-Shok JHP | 100 | 1160 | 1100 | 1060 | 1020 | 990 | 345 | 310 | 285 | 270 | 250 | 0.2 | 0.9 | 2.1 | 3.8 | 4 |
| [3] | 9MS | 9mm Luger (9x19mm Parabellum) | 147 | 9.52 | Hi-Shok JHP | 100 | 980 | 950 | 920 | 900 | 880 | 310 | 295 | 285 | 265 | 255 | 0.3 | 1.2 | 2.8 | 5.1 | 4 |
| [3] | 357S2 | 357 Sig | 125 | 8.10 | Truncated FMJ | 100 | 1350 | 1270 | 1190 | 1130 | 1080 | 510 | 445 | 395 | 355 | 325 | 0.2 | 0.7 | 1.6 | 3.1 | 4 |
| [3] | 40SWA | 40 S&W | 180 | 11.66 | Hi-Shok JHP | 100 | 990 | 960 | 930 | 910 | 890 | 390 | 365 | 345 | 330 | 315 | 0.3 | 1.2 | 2.8 | 5.0 | 4 |
| [3] | 40SWB | 40 S&W | 155 | 10.04 | Hi-Shok JHP | 100 | 1140 | 1080 | 1030 | 990 | 950 | 445 | 400 | 365 | 335 | 315 | 0.2 | 0.9 | 2.2 | 4.1 | 4 |
| [3] | 10C | 10mm Auto | 180 | 11.66 | Hi-Shok JHP | 150 | 1030 | 1000 | 970 | 950 | 920 | 425 | 400 | 375 | 360 | 340 | 0.3 | 1.1 | 2.5 | 4.7 | 5 |
| [3] | 10E | 10mm Auto | 155 | 10.04 | Hi-Shok JHP | 150 | 1330 | 1230 | 1140 | 1080 | 1030 | 605 | 515 | 450 | 400 | 360 | 0.2 | 0.7 | 1.8 | 3.3 | 5 |
| [3] | 45A | 45 Auto | 230 | 14.90 | Full Metal Jacket | 150 | 850 | 830 | 810 | 790 | 770 | 370 | 350 | 335 | 320 | 305 | 0.4 | 1.6 | 3.6 | 6.6 | 5 |
| [3] | 45C | 45 Auto | 185 | 11.99 | Hi-Shok JHP | 150 | 950 | 920 | 900 | 880 | 860 | 370 | 350 | 335 | 315 | 300 | 0.3 | 1.3 | 2.9 | 5.3 | 5 |
| [3] | 45D | 45 Auto | 230 | 14.90 | Hi-Shok JHP | 150 | 850 | 830 | 810 | 790 | 770 | 370 | 350 | 335 | 320 | 300 | 0.4 | 1.6 | 3.7 | 6.7 | 5 |

Usage Key: [1] = Varmints, predators, small game  [2] = Medium game  [3] = Self-defense  [4] = Target shooting, training, practice  *JHP = Jacketed Hollow Point  FMJ = Full Metal Jacket

## GOLD MEDAL RIMFIRE

| USAGE | TYPE | FEDERAL LOAD NO. | CARTRIDGE PER BOX | CALIBER | BULLET WGT. IN GRAINS | BULLET STYLE | VELOCITY MUZZLE | 25 YDS. | 50 YDS. | 75 YDS. | 100 YDS. | ENERGY MUZZLE | 25 YDS. | 50 YDS. | 75 YDS. | 100 YDS. | WIND DRIFT 10 MPH 25 | 50 | 75 | 100 | TRAJECTORY 25 YDS. | 50 YDS. | 75 YDS. | 100 YDS. |
|---|---|---|---|---|---|---|---|---|---|---|---|---|---|---|---|---|---|---|---|---|---|---|---|---|
| [4] | UltraMatch | 1000A | 50 | 22 Long Rifle | 40 | Solid | 1140 | 1090 | 1040 | 1000 | 970 | 115 | 105 | 95 | 90 | 80 | 0.3 | 1.2 | 2.6 | 4.5 | 0.2 | ⊕ | -2.2 | -6.6 |
| [4] NEW | UltraMatch | 1000B | 50 | 22 Long Rifle | 40 | Solid | 1080 | 1030 | 1000 | 960 | 930 | 105 | 95 | 90 | 80 | 75 | 0.3 | 1.1 | 2.3 | 4.1 | 0.3 | ⊕ | -2.4 | -7.2 |
| [4] | Match | 900A* | 50 | 22 Long Rifle | 40 | Solid | 1140 | 1090 | 1040 | 1000 | 970 | 115 | 105 | 95 | 90 | 80 | 0.3 | 1.2 | 2.6 | 4.5 | 0.2 | ⊕ | -2.2 | -6.6 |
| [4] NEW | Match | 900B | 50 | 22 Long Rifle | 40 | Solid | 1080 | 1030 | 1000 | 960 | 930 | 105 | 95 | 90 | 80 | 75 | 0.3 | 1.1 | 2.3 | 4.1 | 0.3 | ⊕ | -2.4 | -7.2 |
| [4] | Target | 711 | 50 | 22 Long Rifle | 40 | Solid | 1150 | 1090 | 1045 | 1005 | 970 | 115 | 105 | 95 | 90 | 80 | 0.3 | 1.2 | 2.6 | 4.5 | 0.2 | ⊕ | -2.2 | -6.4 |

Usage Key: [1] = Varmints, predators, small game  [2] = Medium game  [3] = Self-defense  [4] = Target shooting, training, practice  *Formerly 900  These ballistic specifications were derived from test barrels 24 inches in length.

# HORNADY BALLISTICS

## BALLISTICS INFORMATION

| STANDARD AMMO | MUZZLE VELOCITY | VELOCITY FEET PER SECOND | | | | | ENERGY FOOT - POUNDS | | | | | | TRAJECTORY TABLES | | | | |
|---|---|---|---|---|---|---|---|---|---|---|---|---|---|---|---|---|---|
| RIFLE CALIBER | Muzzle | 100 yds. | 200 yds. | 300 yds. | 400 yds. | 500 yds. | Muzzle | 100 yds. | 200 yds. | 300 yds. | 400 yds. | 500 yds. | 100 yds. | 200 yds. | 300 yds. | 400 yds. | 500 yds. |
| 223 Rem., 53 gr. HP | 3330 | 2882 | 2477 | 2106 | 1710 | 1475 | 1305 | 978 | 722 | 522 | 369 | 356 | +1.7 | -0- | -7.4 | -22.7 | -49.1 |
| 223 Rem., 60 gr. SP | 3150 | 2782 | 2442 | 2127 | 1837 | 1575 | 1322 | 1031 | 795 | 603 | 450 | 331 | +1.6 | -0- | -7.5 | -22.5 | -48.1 |
| 223 Rem., 75 gr. BTHP MATCH | 2790 | 2554 | 2330 | 2119 | 1926 | 1744 | 1296 | 1086 | 904 | 747 | 617 | 506 | 2.37 | -0- | -8.75 | -25.06 | -50.80 |
| 22-250 Rem., 53 gr. HP | 3680 | 3185 | 2743 | 2341 | 1974 | 1646 | 1594 | 1194 | 886 | 645 | 459 | 319 | +1.0 | -0- | -5.7 | -17.8 | -38.8 |
| 22-250 Rem., 60 gr. SP | 3600 | 3195 | 2826 | 2485 | 2169 | 1878 | 1727 | 1360 | 1064 | 823 | 627 | 470 | +1.0 | -0- | -5.4 | -16.3 | -34.8 |
| 220 Swift, 50 gr. SP | 3850 | 3327 | 2862 | 2442 | 2060 | 1716 | 1645 | 1228 | 909 | 662 | 471 | 327 | +0.8 | -0- | -5.1 | -16.1 | -35.3 |
| 220 Swift, 60 gr. HP | 3600 | 3199 | 2824 | 2475 | 2156 | 1868 | 1727 | 1364 | 1063 | 816 | 619 | 465 | +1.0 | -0- | -5.4 | -16.3 | -34.8 |
| 243 Win., 75 gr. HP | 3400 | 2970 | 2578 | 2219 | 1890 | 1595 | 1926 | 1469 | 1107 | 820 | 595 | 425 | +1.2 | -0- | -6.5 | -20.3 | -43.8 |
| 243 Win., 100 gr. BTSP | 2960 | 2728 | 2508 | 2299 | 2099 | 1910 | 1945 | 1653 | 1397 | 1174 | 979 | 810 | +1.6 | -0- | -7.2 | -21.0 | -42.8 |
| 6MM Rem., 100 gr. BTSP | 3100 | 2861 | 2634 | 2419 | 2231 | 2018 | 2134 | 1818 | 1541 | 1300 | 1068 | 904 | +1.3 | -0- | -6.5 | -18.9 | -38.5 |
| 257 Roberts, 117 gr. BTSP | 2780 | 2550 | 2331 | 2122 | 1925 | 1740 | 2007 | 1689 | 1411 | 1170 | 963 | 787 | +1.9 | -0- | -8.3 | -24.4 | -49.9 |
| 25-06 117 gr. BTSP | 2990 | 2749 | 2520 | 2302 | 2096 | 1900 | 2322 | 1962 | 1649 | 1377 | 1141 | 938 | +1.6 | -0- | -7.0 | -20.7 | -42.2 |
| 270 Win, 130 gr. SP | 3060 | 2800 | 2560 | 2330 | 2110 | 1900 | 2700 | 2265 | 1890 | 1565 | 1285 | 1045 | +1.8 | -0- | -7.1 | -20.6 | -42.0 |
| 270 Win, 140 gr. BTSP | 2940 | 2747 | 2562 | 2385 | 2214 | 2050 | 2688 | 2346 | 2041 | 1769 | 1524 | 1307 | +1.6 | -0- | -7.0 | -20.2 | -40.3 |
| 270 Win, 150 gr. SP | 2800 | 2684 | 2478 | 2284 | 2100 | 1927 | 2802 | 2400 | 2046 | 1737 | 1469 | 1237 | +1.7 | -0- | -7.4 | -21.6 | -43.9 |
| 7 x 57 Mau, 139 gr. BTSP | 2700 | 2504 | 2316 | 2137 | 1965 | 1802 | 2251 | 1936 | 1656 | 1410 | 1192 | 1002 | +2.0 | -0- | -8.5 | -24.9 | -50.3 |
| 7MM Rem. Mag., 139 gr. BTSP | 3150 | 2933 | 2727 | 2530 | 2341 | 2160 | 3063 | 2656 | 2296 | 1976 | 1692 | 1440 | +1.2 | -0- | -6.1 | -17.7 | -35.5 |
| 7MM Rem. Mag., 154 gr. SP | 3035 | 2814 | 2604 | 2404 | 2212 | 2029 | 3151 | 2708 | 2319 | 1977 | 1674 | 1408 | +1.3 | -0- | -6.7 | -19.3 | -39.3 |
| 7MM Rem. Mag., 162 gr. BTSP | 2940 | 2757 | 2582 | 2413 | 2251 | 2094 | 3110 | 2735 | 2399 | 2095 | 1823 | 1578 | +1.6 | -0- | -6.7 | -19.7 | -39.3 |
| 7MM Rem. Mag., 175 gr. SP | 2860 | 2650 | 2440 | 2240 | 2060 | 1880 | 3180 | 2720 | 2310 | 1960 | 1640 | 1370 | +2.0 | -0- | -7.9 | -22.7 | -45.8 |
| 7MM Wby. Mag., 154 gr. SP | 3200 | 2971 | 2753 | 2546 | 2348 | 2159 | 3501 | 3017 | 2592 | 2216 | 1885 | 1593 | +1.2 | -0- | -6.8 | -17.0 | -34.5 |
| 7MM Wby. Mag., 175 gr. SP | 2910 | 2709 | 2516 | 2331 | 2154 | 1985 | 3290 | 2850 | 2459 | 2111 | 1803 | 1531 | +1.6 | -0- | -7.1 | -20.6 | -41.7 |
| 30-30 Win., 150 gr. RN | 2390 | 1973 | 1605 | 1303 | 1095 | 974 | 1902 | 1296 | 858 | 565 | 399 | 316 | -0- | -8.2 | -30.0 | | |
| 30-30 Win., 170 gr. FP | 2200 | 1895 | 1619 | 1381 | 1191 | 1064 | 1827 | 1355 | 989 | 720 | 535 | 425 | -0- | -8.9 | -31.1 | | |
| 308 Win., 150 gr. BTSP | 2820 | 2560 | 2315 | 2084 | 1866 | 1644 | 2648 | 2183 | 1785 | 1447 | 1160 | 922 | +2.0 | -0- | -8.5 | -25.2 | -51.8 |
| 308 Win., 165 gr. BTSP | 2700 | 2496 | 2301 | 2115 | 1937 | 1770 | 2670 | 2283 | 1940 | 1639 | 1375 | 1148 | +2.0 | -0- | -8.7 | -25.2 | -51.0 |
| 308 Win., 168 gr. BTHP MATCH | 2700 | 2524 | 2354 | 2191 | 2035 | 1885 | 2720 | 2377 | 2068 | 1791 | 1545 | 1326 | +2.0 | -0- | -8.4 | -23.9 | -48.0 |
| 308 Win., 168 gr. A-MAX MATCH | 2620 | 2446 | 2280 | 2120 | 1972 | 1831 | 2560 | 2232 | 1939 | 1677 | 1450 | 1251 | 2.60 | -0- | -9.23 | -25.65 | -51.92 |
| 308 Win., 180 gr. A-MAX MATCH | 2550 | 2397 | 2249 | 2106 | 1974 | 1848 | 2598 | 2295 | 2021 | 1773 | 1557 | 1364 | 2.71 | -0- | -9.49 | -26.22 | -52.95 |
| 30-06 150 gr. SP | 2910 | 2617 | 2342 | 2083 | 1843 | 1622 | 2820 | 2281 | 1827 | 1445 | 1131 | 876 | +2.1 | -0- | -8.5 | -25.0 | -51.8 |
| 30-06 150 gr. BTSP | 2910 | 2683 | 2467 | 2262 | 2066 | 1880 | 2820 | 2397 | 2027 | 1706 | 1421 | 1177 | +2.0 | -0- | -7.7 | -22.2 | -44.9 |
| 30-06 165 gr. BTSP | 2800 | 2591 | 2392 | 2202 | 2020 | 1848 | 2873 | 2460 | 2097 | 1777 | 1495 | 1252 | +1.8 | -0- | -8.0 | -23.3 | -47.0 |
| 30-06 168 gr. BTHP MATCH | 2790 | 2620 | 2447 | 2280 | 2120 | 1966 | 2925 | 2561 | 2234 | 1940 | 1677 | 1442 | +1.7 | -0- | -7.7 | -22.2 | -44.3 |
| 30-06 180 gr. SP | 2700 | 2469 | 2258 | 2042 | 1846 | 1663 | 2913 | 2436 | 2023 | 1666 | 1362 | 1105 | +2.4 | -0- | -9.3 | -27.0 | -54.9 |
| 300 Wby. Mag., 180 gr. SP | 3120 | 2891 | 2673 | 2466 | 2268 | 2079 | 3890 | 3340 | 2856 | 2430 | 2055 | 1727 | +1.3 | -0- | -6.2 | -18.1 | -36.8 |
| 300 Win. Mag., 150 gr. BTSP | 3275 | 2988 | 2718 | 2464 | 2224 | 1998 | 3573 | 2974 | 2461 | 2023 | 1648 | 1330 | +1.2 | -0- | -6.0 | -17.8 | -36.5 |
| 300 Win. Mag., 165 gr. BTSP | 3100 | 2877 | 2665 | 2462 | 2269 | 2084 | 3522 | 3033 | 2603 | 2221 | 1887 | 1592 | +1.3 | -0- | -6.5 | -18.5 | -37.3 |
| 300 Win. Mag., 180 gr. SP | 2960 | 2745 | 2540 | 2344 | 2157 | 1979 | 3501 | 3011 | 2578 | 2196 | 1859 | 1565 | +1.9 | -0- | -7.3 | -20.9 | -41.9 |
| 300 Win. Mag., 190 gr. BTSP | 2900 | 2711 | 2529 | 2355 | 2187 | 2026 | 3549 | 3101 | 2699 | 2340 | 2018 | 1732 | +1.6 | -0- | -7.1 | -20.4 | -41.0 |
| 303 British, 150 gr. SP | 2685 | 2441 | 2210 | 1992 | 1787 | 1598 | 2401 | 1984 | 1627 | 1321 | 1064 | 500 | +2.2 | -0- | -9.3 | -27.4 | -56.5 |
| 303 British, 174 gr. RN | 2500 | 2181 | 1886 | 1669 | 1387 | 1201 | 2414 | 1837 | 1374 | 1012 | 743 | 557 | +2.9 | -0- | -12.8 | -39.0 | -83.4 |

Barrel length is 24" except for 30-30 Win., which is 20."

| LIGHT MAGNUM™ | MUZZLE VELOCITY | VELOCITY FEET PER SECOND | | | | | ENERGY FOOT - POUNDS | | | | | | TRAJECTORY TABLES | | | | |
|---|---|---|---|---|---|---|---|---|---|---|---|---|---|---|---|---|---|
| RIFLE CALIBER | Muzzle | 100 yds. | 200 yds. | 300 yds. | 400 yds. | 500 yds. | Muzzle | 100 yds. | 200 yds. | 300 yds. | 400 yds. | 500 yds. | 100 yds. | 200 yds. | 300 yds. | 400 yds. | 500 yds. |
| 6MM Rem., 100 gr. BTSP LM | 3250 | 2997 | 2756 | 2528 | 2311 | 2105 | 2345 | 1995 | 1687 | 1418 | 1186 | 984 | 1.59 | -0- | -6.33 | -18.25 | -36.51 |
| 243 Win., 100 gr. BTSP LM | 3100 | 2839 | 2592 | 2358 | 2138 | 1936 | 2133 | 1790 | 1491 | 1235 | 1014 | 832 | +1.5 | -0- | -6.81 | -19.8 | -40.2 |
| 257 Roberts, 117 gr. BTSP LM | 2940 | 2694 | 2460 | 2240 | 2031 | 1844 | 2245 | 1885 | 1572 | 1303 | 1071 | 883 | +1.7 | -0- | -7.6 | -21.8 | -44.7 |
| 25-06, 117 gr. BTSP LM | 3110 | 2855 | 2613 | 2384 | 2168 | 1968 | 2512 | 2117 | 1774 | 1476 | 1220 | 1006 | 1.81 | -0- | -7.08 | -20.28 | -40.35 |
| 7 x 57 Mau, 139 gr. BTSP LM | 2830 | 2620 | 2450 | 2250 | 2070 | 1910 | 2475 | 2135 | 1835 | 1565 | 1330 | 1115 | +1.8 | -0- | -7.6 | -22.1 | -45.0 |
| 7 x 57MM, 139 gr. SP LM-E | 2950 | 2736 | 2532 | 2337 | 2152 | 1979 | 2686 | 2310 | 1978 | 1686 | 1429 | 1209 | 2.02 | -0- | -7.60 | -21.51 | -42.25 |
| 7MM-08, 139 gr. BTSP LM | 3000 | 2790 | 2590 | 2399 | 2216 | 2041 | 2777 | 2403 | 2071 | 1776 | 1515 | 1285 | +1.5 | -0- | -6.7 | -19.4 | -39.2 |
| 308 Win., 150 gr. SP LM | 2980 | 2703 | 2442 | 2195 | 1964 | 1748 | 2959 | 2433 | 1986 | 1606 | 1285 | 1018 | +1.6 | -0- | -7.5 | -22.2 | -46.0 |
| 308 Win., 165 gr. BTSP LM | 2870 | 2658 | 2456 | 2283 | 2078 | 1903 | 3019 | 2589 | 2211 | 1877 | 1583 | 1327 | +1.7 | -0- | -7.5 | -21.8 | -44.1 |
| 308 Win., 168 gr. BTHP LM MATCH | 2840 | 2630 | 2429 | 2238 | 2056 | 1892 | 3008 | 2579 | 2201 | 1868 | 1577 | 1335 | 1.84 | -0- | -7.83 | -22.38 | -45.23 |
| 30-06 150 gr. SP LM | 3100 | 2815 | 2548 | 2295 | 2058 | 1835 | 3200 | 2639 | 2161 | 1755 | 1410 | 1121 | +1.4 | -0- | -6.8 | -20.3 | -42.0 |
| 30-06 165 gr. BTSP LM | 3015 | 2790 | 2575 | 2370 | 2176 | 1994 | 3330 | 2850 | 2428 | 2058 | 1734 | 1496 | 1.55 | -0- | -6.96 | -20.11 | -39.77 |
| 30-06 180 gr. BTSP LM | 2880 | 2676 | 2480 | 2293 | 2114 | 1943 | 3316 | 2862 | 2459 | 2102 | 1786 | 1509 | +1.7 | -0- | -7.3 | -21.3 | -43.1 |
| 303 British, 150 gr. SP LM | 2830 | 2570 | 2325 | 2094 | 1884 | 1690 | 2667 | 2199 | 1800 | 1461 | 1185 | 952 | +2.0 | -0- | -8.4 | -24.6 | -50.3 |
| 6.5 x 55MM, 129 gr. SP LM | 2770 | 2561 | 2361 | 2171 | 1994 | 1830 | 2197 | 1878 | 1597 | 1350 | 1138 | 959 | 1.98 | -0- | -8.25 | -23.16 | -47.95 |
| 6.5 x 55, 140 gr. SP LM-E | 2740 | 2541 | 2351 | 2169 | 1999 | 1842 | 2333 | 2006 | 1717 | 1463 | 1242 | 1054 | 2.40 | -0- | -8.71 | -24.02 | -49.33 |
| 270 Win., 140 gr. BTSP LM | 3100 | 2894 | 2697 | 2508 | 2327 | 2155 | 2987 | 2604 | 2261 | 1955 | 1684 | 1443 | 1.37 | -0- | -6.32 | -18.30 | -36.61 |
| 300 Win. Mag., 180 gr. BTSP HM | 3100 | 2879 | 2668 | 2467 | 2275 | 2092 | 3840 | 3313 | 2845 | 2431 | 2068 | 1749 | 1.39 | -0- | -6.45 | -18.72 | -37.51 |
| 338 Win. Mag., 225 gr. SP HM | 2920 | 2678 | 2449 | 2232 | 2027 | 1843 | 4259 | 3583 | 2996 | 2489 | 2053 | 1697 | 1.75 | -0- | -7.65 | -22.01 | -45.05 |
| 375 H&H, 270 gr. SP HM | 2870 | 2620 | 2385 | 2162 | 1957 | 1767 | 4937 | 4116 | 3406 | 2802 | 2296 | 1871 | 2.24 | -0- | -8.39 | -23.87 | -48.79 |
| 375 H&H, 300 gr. FMJ-RN HM | 2705 | 2376 | 2072 | 1804 | 1560 | 1355 | 4873 | 3760 | 2861 | 2167 | 1621 | 1222 | 2.73 | -0- | -10.81 | -32.13 | -68.38 |

Barrel length is 24" except for 30-30 Win., which is 20."

| BARREL LENGTH | PISTOL AMMO | MUZZLE VELOCITY | VELOCITY FT. PER SECOND | | ENERGY | | |
|---|---|---|---|---|---|---|---|
| | Caliber | Muzzle | 50 yds. | 100 yds. | Muzzle | 50 yds. | 100 yds. |
| 2" | 25 Auto, 35 gr. JHP/XTP | 900 | 813 | 742 | 63 | 51 | 43 |
| 4" | 32 ACP, 60 gr. HP/XTP | 1000 | 917 | 849 | 133 | 112 | 96 |
| 4" | 32 Auto, 71 gr. FMJ | 900 | 845 | 797 | 128 | 112 | 100 |
| 3 3/4" | 380 Auto, 90 gr. JHP/XTP | 1000 | 902 | 823 | 200 | 163 | 135 |
| 4" | 9MM Luger, 115 gr. JHP/XTP | 1155 | 1047 | 971 | 341 | 280 | 241 |
| 4" | 9MM Luger, 124 gr. JHP/XTP | 1110 | 1030 | 971 | 339 | 292 | 259 |
| 4" | 9MM Luger, 124 gr. FMJ V | 1110 | 1038 | 981 | 339 | 297 | 265 |
| 4" | 9MM Luger, 147 gr. JHP/XTP | 975 | 935 | 899 | 310 | 285 | 264 |
| 4" | 9 x 18 Makarov, 95 gr. JHP/XTP | 1000 | 930 | 874 | 211 | 182 | 161 |
| 4"V | 38 Special, 125 gr. JHP/XTP | 900 | 856 | 817 | 225 | 203 | 185 |
| 4"V | 38 Special, 140 gr. JHP/XTP | 900 | 850 | 806 | 252 | 225 | 202 |
| 4"V | 38 Special, 148 gr. HBWC | 800 | 697 | 610 | 210 | 160 | 122 |
| 4"V | 38 Special, 158 gr. JHP/XTP | 800 | 765 | 731 | 225 | 205 | 188 |
| 4" | 357 SIG, 124 gr. JHP/XTP | 1350 | 1208 | 1108 | 502 | 405 | 338 |
| 4" | 357 SIG, 147 gr. JHP/XTP | 1225 | 1138 | 1072 | 490 | 422 | 375 |
| 8"V | 357 Mag., 125 gr. JHP/XTP | 1500 | 1314 | 1166 | 624 | 479 | 377 |
| 8"V | 357 Mag., 125 gr. JFP/XTP | 1500 | 1311 | 1161 | 624 | 477 | 374 |
| 8"V | 357 Mag., 140 gr. JHP/XTP | 1400 | 1249 | 1130 | 609 | 485 | 397 |
| 8"V | 357 Mag., 158 gr. JHP/XTP | 1250 | 1150 | 1073 | 548 | 464 | 404 |
| 8"V | 357 Mag., 158 gr. JFP | 1250 | 1147 | 1068 | 548 | 461 | 400 |

| BARREL LENGTH | PISTOL AMMO | MUZZLE VELOCITY | VELOCITY FT. PER SECOND | | ENERGY | | |
|---|---|---|---|---|---|---|---|
| | Caliber | Muzzle | 50 yds. | 100 yds. | Muzzle | 50 yds. | 100 yds. |
| 5" | 10MM Auto, 155 gr. JHP/XTP | 1265 | 1119 | 1020 | 551 | 431 | 358 |
| 5" | 10MM Auto, 180 gr. JHP/XTP Full | 1180 | 1077 | 1004 | 556 | 464 | 403 |
| 5" | 10MM Auto, 200 gr. JHP/XTP | 1050 | 994 | 948 | 490 | 439 | 399 |
| 4" | 40 S&W, 155 gr. JHP/XTP | 1180 | 1061 | 980 | 479 | 388 | 331 |
| 4" | 40 S&W, 180 gr. JHP/XTP | 950 | 903 | 862 | 361 | 326 | 297 |
| 4" | 40 S&W, 180 gr. FMJ V | 950 | 906 | 865 | 361 | 328 | 299 |
| 4 3/4"V | 44-40, 205 gr. Cowboy | 725 | 697 | 670 | 239 | 221 | 204 |
| 7 1/2"V | 44 Special, 180 gr. JHP/XTP | 1000 | 935 | 882 | 400 | 350 | 311 |
| 7 1/2"V | 44 Rem. Mag., 180 gr. JHP/XTP | 1550 | 1340 | 1173 | 960 | 717 | 550 |
| 7 1/2"V | 44 Rem. Mag., 200 gr. JHP/XTP | 1500 | 1284 | 1128 | 999 | 732 | 565 |
| 7 1/2"V | 44 Rem. Mag., 240 gr. JHP/XTP | 1350 | 1188 | 1078 | 971 | 753 | 619 |
| 7 1/2"V | 44 Rem. Mag., 300 gr. JHP/XTP | 1150 | 1084 | 1031 | 881 | 782 | 708 |
| 4 3/4"V | 45 Long Colt, 255 gr. Cowboy | 725 | 692 | 660 | 298 | 271 | 247 |
| 5" | 45 ACP, 185 gr. JHP/XTP | 950 | 880 | 819 | 371 | 318 | 276 |
| 5" | 45 ACP, 200 gr. JHP/XTP | 900 | 855 | 815 | 358 | 325 | 295 |
| 5" | 45 ACP+P, 200 gr. HP/XTP | 1055 | 982 | 925 | 494 | 428 | 380 |
| 5" | 45 ACP+P, 230 gr. HP/XTP | 950 | 904 | 865 | 462 | 418 | 382 |
| 5" | 45 ACP, 230 gr. FMJ/RN | 850 | 809 | 771 | 369 | 334 | 304 |
| 5" | 45 ACP, 230 gr. FMJ/FP | 850 | 809 | 771 | 369 | 334 | 304 |
| 5" | 45 ACP, 230 gr. FMJ-FP V | 850 | 814 | 779 | 369 | 338 | 310 |

# REMINGTON BALLISTICS

## CENTERFIRE RIFLE BALLISTICS

These tables were calculated by computer. A standard scientific technique was used to predict trajectories from the best available data for each round. Trajectories shown typify the ammunition's performance at sea level, but note that they may vary due to atmospheric conditions, and the equipment.

All velocity and energy figures in these charts have been derived by using test barrels of indicated lengths.

Ballistics shown are for 24″ barrels, except those for 30 carbine, 350 Rem. Mag. and .44 Rem. Mag., which are for 20″ barrels, and the 6mm BR Remington and 7mm BR Remington which have a 15″ barrel. These barrel lengths were chosen as representative, as it's impractical to show performance figures for all barrel lengths.

The muzzle velocities, muzzle energies and trajectory data in these tables represent the approximate performance expected of each specified loading. Differences in barrel lengths, internal firearm dimensions, temperature and test procedures can produce actual velocities that vary from those given here.

Specifications are nominal. Ballistics figures established in test barrels. Individual rifles may vary from test-barrel specifications.

* Inches above or below line of sight. Hold low for positive numbers, high for negative numbers.

† 280 Rem. and 7mm Express Rem. are interchangeable.

‡ Interchangeable in 244 Rem.

§ Subject to stock on hand

[1] Bullet does not rise more than 1″ above line of sight from muzzle to sighting in range.

[2] Bullet does not rise more than 3″ above line of sight from muzzle to sighting in range.

*Note:* 0.0 indicates yardage at which rifle was sighted in.

| Caliber | Order No. | Wt. (grs.) | Bullet Style | Primer No. | Muzzle | 100 yds. | 200 yds. | 300 yds. | 400 yds. | 500 yds. |
|---|---|---|---|---|---|---|---|---|---|---|
| .17 Remington | R17REM | 25 | Hollow Point Power-Lokt® | 7½ | 4040 | 3284 | 2644 | 2086 | 1606 | 1235 |
| .22 Hornet | R22HN1 | 45 | Pointed Soft Point | 6½ | 2690 | 2042 | 1502 | 1128 | 948 | 840 |
| | R22HN2 | 45 | Hollow Point | 6½ | 2690 | 2042 | 1502 | 1128 | 948 | 840 |
| .220 Swift | R220S1 | 50 | Pointed Soft Point | 9½ | 3780 | 3158 | 2617 | 2135 | 1710 | 1357 |
| | PRV220SA ★ | 50 | Polymer Tip Boat Tail | 9½ | 3780 | 3321 | 2908 | 2532 | 2185 | 1866 |
| .222 Remington | R222R1 | 50 | Pointed Soft Point | 7½ | 3140 | 2602 | 2123 | 1700 | 1350 | 1107 |
| | R222R3 | 50 | Hollow Point Power-Lokt® | 7½ | 3140 | 2635 | 2182 | 1777 | 1432 | 1172 |
| | PRV222RA ★ | 50 | Polymer Tip Boat Tail | 7½ | 3140 | 2744 | 2380 | 2045 | 1740 | 1471 |
| .222 Remington Mag. | R222M1 | 55 | Pointed Soft Point | 7½ | 3240 | 2748 | 2305 | 1906 | 1556 | 1272 |
| .223 Remington | PRV223RA ★ | 50 | Polymer Tip Boat Tail | 7½ | 3300 | 2889 | 2514 | 2168 | 1851 | 1568 |
| | R223R1 | 55 | Pointed Soft Point | 7½ | 3240 | 2747 | 2304 | 1905 | 1554 | 1270 |
| | R223R2 | 55 | Hollow Point Power-Lokt® | 7½ | 3240 | 2773 | 2352 | 1969 | 1627 | 1341 |
| | R223R3 | 55 | Metal Case | 7½ | 3240 | 2759 | 2326 | 1933 | 1587 | 1301 |
| | R223R6 ★ | 62 | Hollow Point Match | 7½ | 3025 | 2572 | 2162 | 1792 | 1471 | 1217 |
| .22-250 Remington | R22501 | 55 | Pointed Soft Point | 9½ | 3680 | 3137 | 2656 | 2222 | 1832 | 1493 |
| | R22502 | 55 | Hollow Point Power-Lokt® | 9½ | 3680 | 3209 | 2785 | 2400 | 2046 | 1725 |
| | PRV2250A ★ | 50 | Polymer Tip Boat Tail | 9½ | 3725 | 3272 | 2864 | 2491 | 2147 | 1832 |
| .243 Win. | R243W1 | 80 | Pointed Soft Point | 9½ | 3350 | 2955 | 2593 | 2259 | 1951 | 1670 |
| | R243W2 | 80 | Hollow Point Power-Lokt® | 9½ | 3350 | 2955 | 2593 | 2259 | 1951 | 1670 |
| | R243W3 | 100 | Pointed Soft Point Core-Lokt® | 9½ | 2960 | 2697 | 2449 | 2215 | 1993 | 1786 |
| | ER243WA | 105 | Extended Range | 9½ | 2920 | 2689 | 2470 | 2261 | 2062 | 1874 |
| 6mm Remington | R6MM1 ‡ | 80 | Pointed Soft Point | 9½ | 3470 | 3064 | 2694 | 2352 | 2036 | 1747 |
| | R6MM4 | 100 | Pointed Soft Point Core-Lokt® | 9½ | 3100 | 2829 | 2573 | 2332 | 2104 | 1889 |
| .25-20 Win. | R25202 | 86 | Soft Point | 6½ | 1460 | 1194 | 1030 | 931 | 858 | 797 |
| .250 Savage | R250SV | 100 | Pointed Soft Point | 9½ | 2820 | 2504 | 2210 | 1936 | 1684 | 1461 |
| .257 Roberts | R257 | 117 | Soft Point Core-Lokt® | 9½ | 2650 | 2291 | 1961 | 1663 | 1404 | 1199 |
| .25-06 Remington | R25062 | 100 | Pointed Soft Point Core-Lokt® | 9½ | 3230 | 2893 | 2580 | 2287 | 2014 | 1762 |
| | R25063 | 120 | Pointed Soft Point Core-Lokt® | 9½ | 2990 | 2730 | 2484 | 2252 | 2032 | 1825 |
| | ER2506A | 122 | Extended Range | 9½ | 2930 | 2706 | 2492 | 2289 | 2095 | 1911 |
| 6.5x55 Swedish | R65SWE1 | 140 | Pointed Soft Point Core-Lokt® | 9½ | 2550 | 2353 | 2164 | 1984 | 1814 | 1654 |
| .260 Remington | R260R1 ★ | 140 | Pointed Soft Point Core-Lokt® | 9½ | 2750 | 2544 | 2347 | 2158 | 1979 | 1812 |
| .264 Win. Mag. | R264W2 | 140 | Pointed Soft Point Core-Lokt® | 9½ M | 3030 | 2782 | 2548 | 2326 | 2114 | 1914 |
| .270 Win. | R270W1 | 100 | Pointed Soft Point | 9½ | 3320 | 2924 | 2561 | 2225 | 1916 | 1636 |
| | R270W2 | 130 | Pointed Soft Point Core-Lokt® | 9½ | 3060 | 2776 | 2510 | 2259 | 2022 | 1801 |
| | R270W3 | 130 | Bronze Point™ | 9½ | 3060 | 2802 | 2559 | 2329 | 2110 | 1904 |
| | R270W4 | 150 | Soft Point Core-Lokt® | 9½ | 2850 | 2504 | 2183 | 1886 | 1618 | 1385 |
| | RS270WA | 140 | Swift A-Frame™ PSP | 9½ | 2925 | 2652 | 2394 | 2152 | 1923 | 1711 |
| | ER270WA | 140 | Extended Range Boat Tail | 9½ | 2960 | 2749 | 2548 | 2355 | 2171 | 1995 |
| 7mm Mauser (7 x 57) | R7MSR1 | 140 | Pointed Soft Point Core-Lokt® | 9½ | 2660 | 2435 | 2221 | 2018 | 1827 | 1648 |
| 7 x 64 | R7X642 | 175 | Pointed Soft Point Core-Lokt® | 9½ | 2650 | 2445 | 2248 | 2061 | 1883 | 1716 |
| 7mm-08 Remington | R7M081 | 140 | Pointed Soft Point Core-Lokt® | 9½ | 2860 | 2625 | 2402 | 2189 | 1988 | 1798 |
| | R7M083 | 120 | Hollow Point | 9½ | 3000 | 2725 | 2467 | 2223 | 1992 | 1778 |
| | ER7M08A | 154 | Extended Range | 9½ | 2715 | 2510 | 2315 | 2128 | 1950 | 1781 |
| .280 Remington | R280R3 † | 140 | Pointed Soft Point Core-Lokt® | 9½ | 3000 | 2758 | 2528 | 2309 | 2102 | 1905 |
| | R280R1 † | 150 | Pointed Soft Point Core-Lokt® | 9½ | 2890 | 2624 | 2373 | 2135 | 1912 | 1705 |
| | R280R2 † | 165 | Soft Point Core-Lokt® | 9½ | 2820 | 2510 | 2220 | 1950 | 1701 | 1479 |
| | ER280RA † | 165 | Extended Range | 9½ | 2820 | 2623 | 2434 | 2253 | 2080 | 1915 |
| 7mm Remington Mag. | R7MM2 | 150 | Pointed Soft Point Core-Lokt® | 9½ M | 3110 | 2830 | 2568 | 2320 | 2085 | 1866 |
| | R7MM3 | 175 | Pointed Soft Point Core-Lokt® | 9½ M | 2860 | 2645 | 2440 | 2244 | 2057 | 1879 |
| | R7MM4 | 140 | Pointed Soft Point Core-Lokt® | 9½ M | 3175 | 2923 | 2684 | 2458 | 2243 | 2039 |
| | RS7MMA | 160 | Swift A-Frame™ PSP | 9½ M | 2900 | 2659 | 2430 | 2212 | 2006 | 1812 |
| | ER7MMA | 165 | Extended Range | 9½ M | 2900 | 2699 | 2507 | 2324 | 2147 | 1979 |
| 7mm Wby. Mag. | R7MWB2 | 175 | Pointed Soft Point Core-Lokt® | 9½ M | 2910 | 2693 | 2486 | 2288 | 2098 | 1918 |
| 7mm STW | R7MSTW1 ★ | 140 | Pointed Soft Point Core-Lokt® | 9½ M | 3325 | 3064 | 2818 | 2585 | 2364 | 2153 |
| .30 Carbine | R30CAR | 110 | Soft Point | 6½ | 1990 | 1567 | 1236 | 1035 | 923 | 842 |
| .30 Remington | R30REM § | 170 | Soft Point Core-Lokt® | 9½ | 2120 | 1822 | 1555 | 1328 | 1153 | 1036 |
| .30-30 Win. Accelerator® | R3030A | 55 | Soft Point | 9½ | 3400 | 2693 | 2085 | 1570 | 1187 | 986 |
| .30-30 Win. | R30301 | 150 | Soft Point Core-Lokt® | 9½ | 2390 | 1973 | 1605 | 1303 | 1095 | 974 |
| | R30302 | 170 | Soft Point Core-Lokt® | 9½ | 2200 | 1895 | 1619 | 1381 | 1191 | 1061 |
| | R30303 | 170 | Hollow Point Core-Lokt® | 9½ | 2200 | 1895 | 1619 | 1381 | 1191 | 1061 |
| | ER3030A | 160 | Extended Range | 9½ | 2300 | 1997 | 1719 | 1473 | 1268 | 1116 |
| .300 Savage | R30SV3 | 180 | Soft Point Core-Lokt® | 9½ | 2350 | 2025 | 1728 | 1467 | 1252 | 1098 |
| | R30SV2 | 150 | Pointed Soft Point Core-Lokt® | 9½ | 2630 | 2354 | 2095 | 1853 | 1631 | 1432 |

★ NEW FOR 1997

# REMINGTON BALLISTICS

☐ = Extended Range ▦ = Safari Grade

| Muzzle | Energy (ft-lbs.) | | | | | Short-range[1] Trajectory° | | | | | | Long-range[1] Trajectory° | | | | | | | Barrel Length |
|---|---|---|---|---|---|---|---|---|---|---|---|---|---|---|---|---|---|---|---|
| | 100 yds. | 200 yds. | 300 yds. | 400 yds. | 500 yds. | 50 yds. | 100 yds. | 150 yds. | 200 yds. | 250 yds. | 300 yds. | 100 yds. | 150 yds. | 200 yds. | 250 yds. | 300 yds. | 400 yds. | 500 yds. | |
| 906 | 599 | 388 | 242 | 143 | 85 | 0.1 | 0.5 | 0.0 | -1.5 | -4.2 | -8.5 | 2.1 | 2.5 | 1.9 | 0.0 | -3.4 | -17.0 | -44.3 | 24" |
| 723 | 417 | 225 | 127 | 90 | 70 | 0.3 | 0.0 | -2.4 | -7.7 | -16.9 | -31.3 | 1.6 | 0.0 | -4.5 | -12.8 | -26.4 | -75.6 | -163.4 | 24" |
| 723 | 417 | 225 | 127 | 90 | 70 | 0.3 | 0.0 | -2.4 | -7.7 | -16.9 | -31.3 | 1.6 | 0.0 | -4.5 | -12.8 | -26.4 | -75.6 | -163.4 | |
| 1586 | 1107 | 760 | 506 | 325 | 204 | 0.2 | 0.5 | 0.0 | -1.6 | -4.4 | -8.8 | 1.3 | 1.2 | 0.0 | -2.5 | -6.5 | -20.7 | -47.0 | 24" |
| 1586 | 1224 | 939 | 711 | 530 | 387 | 0.1 | 0.5 | 0.0 | -1.4 | -3.7 | -7.3 | 1.1 | 1.0 | 0.0 | -2.0 | -5.3 | -16.0 | -34.1 | 24" |
| 1094 | 752 | 500 | 321 | 202 | 136 | 0.5 | 0.9 | 0.0 | -2.5 | -6.9 | -13.7 | 2.2 | 1.9 | 0.0 | -3.8 | -10.0 | -32.3 | -73.8 | 24" |
| 1094 | 771 | 529 | 351 | 228 | 152 | 0.5 | 0.9 | 0.0 | -2.4 | -6.6 | -13.1 | 2.1 | 1.8 | 0.0 | -3.6 | -9.5 | -30.2 | -68.1 | |
| 1094 | 836 | 629 | 464 | 336 | 240 | 0.5 | 0.8 | 0.0 | -2.1 | -5.8 | -11.3 | 1.9 | 1.6 | 0.0 | -3.1 | -8.1 | -24.5 | -52.6 | 24" |
| 1282 | 922 | 649 | 444 | 296 | 198 | 0.4 | 0.8 | 0.0 | -2.2 | -6.0 | -11.8 | 1.9 | 1.6 | 0.0 | -3.3 | -8.5 | -26.7 | -59.5 | 24" |
| 1209 | 927 | 701 | 522 | 380 | 273 | 0.4 | 0.7 | 0.0 | -1.9 | -5.2 | -10.0 | 1.6 | 1.4 | 0.0 | -2.8 | -7.2 | -21.8 | -46.7 | 24" |
| 1282 | 921 | 648 | 443 | 295 | 197 | 0.4 | 0.8 | 0.0 | -2.2 | -6.0 | -11.8 | 1.9 | 1.6 | 0.0 | -3.3 | -8.5 | -26.7 | -59.6 | |
| 1282 | 939 | 675 | 473 | 323 | 220 | 0.4 | 0.8 | 0.0 | -2.1 | -5.8 | -11.4 | 1.8 | 1.6 | 0.0 | -3.2 | -8.2 | -25.5 | -56.0 | 24" |
| 1282 | 929 | 660 | 456 | 307 | 207 | 0.4 | 0.8 | 0.0 | -2.1 | -5.9 | -11.6 | 1.9 | 1.6 | 0.0 | -3.2 | -8.4 | -26.2 | -57.9 | |
| 1260 | 911 | 643 | 442 | 298 | 204 | 0.6 | 1.0 | 0.0 | -2.5 | -6.9 | -13.5 | 2.2 | 1.9 | 0.0 | -3.7 | -9.7 | -30.5 | -67.4 | 24" |
| 1654 | 1201 | 861 | 603 | 410 | 272 | 0.2 | 0.5 | 0.0 | -1.6 | -4.4 | -8.7 | 2.3 | 2.6 | 1.9 | 0.0 | -3.4 | -15.9 | -38.9 | 24" |
| 1654 | 1257 | 947 | 703 | 511 | 363 | 0.2 | 0.5 | 0.0 | -1.5 | -4.1 | -8.0 | 2.1 | 2.5 | 1.8 | 0.0 | -3.1 | -14.1 | -33.4 | |
| 1540 | 1188 | 910 | 689 | 512 | 372 | 0.1 | 0.5 | 0.0 | -1.4 | -3.9 | -7.6 | 2.0 | 2.3 | 1.7 | 0.0 | -2.9 | -13.2 | -31.0 | 24" |
| 1993 | 1551 | 1194 | 906 | 676 | 495 | 0.3 | 0.7 | 0.0 | -1.8 | -4.9 | -9.4 | 2.6 | 2.9 | 2.1 | 0.0 | -3.6 | -16.2 | -37.9 | |
| 1993 | 1551 | 1194 | 906 | 676 | 495 | 0.3 | 0.7 | 0.0 | -1.8 | -4.9 | -9.4 | 2.6 | 2.9 | 2.1 | 0.0 | -3.6 | -16.2 | -37.9 | 24" |
| 1945 | 1615 | 1332 | 1089 | 882 | 708 | 0.5 | 0.9 | 0.0 | -2.2 | -5.8 | -11.0 | 1.9 | 1.6 | 0.0 | -3.1 | -7.8 | -22.6 | -46.3 | |
| 1988 | 1686 | 1422 | 1192 | 992 | 819 | 0.5 | 0.9 | 0.0 | -2.2 | -5.8 | -11.0 | 2.0 | 1.6 | 0.0 | -3.1 | -7.7 | -22.2 | -44.8 | |
| 2139 | 1667 | 1289 | 982 | 736 | 542 | 0.3 | 0.6 | 0.0 | -1.6 | -4.5 | -8.7 | 2.4 | 2.7 | 1.9 | 0.0 | -3.3 | -14.9 | -35.0 | 24" |
| 2133 | 1777 | 1470 | 1207 | 983 | 792 | 0.4 | 0.8 | 0.0 | -1.9 | -5.2 | -9.9 | 1.7 | 1.5 | 0.0 | -2.8 | -7.0 | -20.4 | -41.7 | |
| 407 | 272 | 203 | 165 | 141 | 121 | 0.0 | -4.1 | -14.4 | -31.8 | -57.3 | -92.0 | 0.0 | -8.2 | -23.5 | -47.0 | -79.6 | -175.9 | -319.4 | 24" |
| 1765 | 1392 | 1084 | 832 | 630 | 474 | 0.2 | 0.0 | -1.6 | -4.7 | -9.6 | -16.5 | 2.3 | 2.0 | 0.0 | -3.7 | -9.5 | -28.3 | -59.5 | 24" |
| 1824 | 1383 | 999 | 718 | 512 | 373 | 0.3 | 0.0 | -1.9 | -5.8 | -11.9 | -20.7 | 2.9 | 2.4 | 0.0 | -4.7 | -12.0 | -36.7 | -79.2 | 24" |
| 2316 | 1858 | 1478 | 1161 | 901 | 689 | 0.4 | 0.7 | 0.0 | -1.9 | -5.0 | -9.7 | 1.6 | 1.4 | 0.0 | -2.7 | -6.9 | -20.5 | -42.7 | |
| 2382 | 1985 | 1644 | 1351 | 1100 | 887 | 0.5 | 0.8 | 0.0 | -2.1 | -5.6 | -10.7 | 1.9 | 1.6 | 0.0 | -3.0 | -7.5 | -22.0 | -44.8 | 24" |
| 2325 | 1983 | 1683 | 1419 | 1189 | 989 | 0.5 | 0.9 | 0.0 | -2.2 | -5.7 | -10.8 | 1.9 | 1.6 | 0.0 | -3.0 | -7.5 | -21.7 | -43.9 | |
| 2021 | 1720 | 1456 | 1224 | 1023 | 850 | 0.3 | 0.0 | -1.8 | -5.4 | -10.8 | -18.2 | 2.7 | 2.2 | 0.0 | -4.1 | -10.1 | -29.1 | -58.7 | 24" |
| 2351 | 2011 | 1712 | 1448 | 1217 | 1021 | 0.7 | 1.0 | 0.0 | -2.5 | -6.5 | -12.3 | 2.2 | 1.8 | 0.0 | -3.4 | -8.6 | -24.6 | -48.1 | |
| 2854 | 2406 | 2018 | 1682 | 1389 | 1139 | 0.5 | 0.8 | 0.0 | -2.0 | -5.4 | -10.2 | 1.8 | 1.5 | 0.0 | -2.9 | -7.2 | -20.8 | -42.2 | 24" |
| 2448 | 1898 | 1456 | 1099 | 815 | 594 | 0.3 | 0.7 | 0.0 | -1.8 | -5.0 | -9.7 | 2.7 | 3.0 | 2.2 | 0.0 | -3.7 | -16.6 | -39.1 | |
| 2702 | 2225 | 1818 | 1472 | 1180 | 936 | 0.5 | 0.8 | 0.0 | -2.0 | -5.5 | -10.4 | 1.8 | 1.5 | 0.0 | -2.9 | -7.4 | -21.6 | -44.3 | |
| 2702 | 2267 | 1890 | 1565 | 1285 | 1046 | 0.4 | 0.8 | 0.0 | -2.0 | -5.3 | -10.1 | 1.8 | 1.5 | 0.0 | -2.8 | -7.1 | -20.6 | -42.0 | 24" |
| 2705 | 2087 | 1587 | 1185 | 872 | 639 | 0.7 | 1.0 | 0.0 | -2.6 | -7.1 | -13.6 | 2.3 | 2.0 | 0.0 | -3.8 | -9.7 | -29.2 | -62.2 | |
| 2859 | 2186 | 1782 | 1439 | 1150 | 910 | 0.6 | 0.9 | 0.0 | -2.3 | -6.0 | -11.5 | 2.0 | 1.7 | 0.0 | -3.2 | -8.1 | -23.8 | -48.9 | |
| 2723 | 2349 | 2018 | 1724 | 1465 | 1237 | 0.5 | 0.8 | 0.0 | -2.1 | -5.5 | -10.3 | 1.9 | 1.5 | 0.0 | -2.9 | -7.2 | -20.7 | -41.6 | |
| 2199 | 1843 | 1533 | 1266 | 1037 | 844 | 0.2 | 0.0 | -1.7 | -5.0 | -10.0 | -17.0 | 2.5 | 2.0 | 0.0 | -3.8 | -9.6 | -27.7 | -56.3 | 24" |
| 2728 | 2322 | 1964 | 1650 | 1378 | 1144 | 0.2 | 0.0 | -1.7 | -4.9 | -9.9 | -16.8 | 2.5 | 2.0 | 0.0 | -3.9 | -9.4 | -26.9 | -54.3 | 24" |
| 2542 | 2142 | 1793 | 1490 | 1228 | 1005 | 0.6 | 0.9 | 0.0 | -2.3 | -6.1 | -11.6 | 2.1 | 1.7 | 0.0 | -3.2 | -8.1 | -23.5 | -47.7 | |
| 2398 | 1979 | 1621 | 1316 | 1058 | 842 | 0.5 | 0.8 | 0.0 | -2.1 | -5.7 | -10.8 | 1.9 | 1.6 | 0.0 | -3.0 | -7.6 | -22.3 | -45.8 | 24" |
| 2520 | 2155 | 1832 | 1548 | 1300 | 1085 | 0.7 | 1.0 | 0.0 | -2.5 | -6.7 | -12.6 | 2.3 | 1.9 | 0.0 | -3.5 | -8.8 | -25.3 | -51.0 | |
| 2797 | 2363 | 1986 | 1657 | 1373 | 1128 | 0.5 | 0.8 | 0.0 | -2.1 | -5.5 | -10.4 | 1.8 | 1.5 | 0.0 | -2.9 | -7.3 | -21.1 | -42.9 | |
| 2781 | 2293 | 1875 | 1518 | 1217 | 968 | 0.6 | 0.9 | 0.0 | -2.3 | -6.2 | -11.8 | 2.1 | 1.7 | 0.0 | -3.3 | -8.3 | -24.2 | -49.7 | |
| 2913 | 2308 | 1805 | 1393 | 1060 | 801 | 0.2 | 0.0 | -1.5 | -4.6 | -9.5 | -16.4 | 2.3 | 1.9 | 0.0 | -3.7 | -9.4 | -28.1 | -58.8 | 24" |
| 2913 | 2520 | 2171 | 1860 | 1585 | 1343 | 0.6 | 0.9 | 0.0 | -2.3 | -6.1 | -11.4 | 2.1 | 1.7 | 0.0 | -3.2 | -8.0 | -22.8 | -45.6 | |
| 3221 | 2667 | 2196 | 1792 | 1448 | 1160 | 0.4 | 0.8 | 0.0 | -1.9 | -5.2 | -9.9 | 1.7 | 1.5 | 0.0 | -2.8 | -7.0 | -20.5 | -42.1 | |
| 3178 | 2718 | 2313 | 1956 | 1644 | 1372 | 0.6 | 0.9 | 0.0 | -2.3 | -6.0 | -11.3 | 2.0 | 1.7 | 0.0 | -3.2 | -7.9 | -22.7 | -45.8 | 24" |
| 3133 | 2655 | 2240 | 1878 | 1564 | 1292 | 0.4 | 0.7 | 0.0 | -1.8 | -4.8 | -9.1 | 2.6 | 2.9 | 2.0 | 0.0 | -3.4 | -14.5 | -32.6 | |
| 2987 | 2511 | 2097 | 1739 | 1430 | 1168 | 0.6 | 0.9 | 0.0 | -2.2 | -5.9 | -11.3 | 2.0 | 1.7 | 0.0 | -3.2 | -7.9 | -23.0 | -46.7 | |
| 3081 | 2669 | 2303 | 1978 | 1689 | 1434 | 0.5 | 0.9 | 0.0 | -2.1 | -5.7 | -10.7 | 1.9 | 1.6 | 0.0 | -3.0 | -7.5 | -21.4 | -42.9 | |
| 3293 | 2818 | 2401 | 2033 | 1711 | 1430 | 0.5 | 0.9 | 0.0 | -2.2 | -5.7 | -10.8 | 1.9 | 1.6 | 0.0 | -3.0 | -7.6 | -21.8 | -44.0 | 24" |
| 3436 | 2918 | 2468 | 2077 | 1737 | 1441 | 0.8 | 0.6 | 0.0 | -1.6 | -4.3 | -8.2 | 2.3 | 2.6 | 1.8 | 0.0 | -3.0 | -13.1 | -29.5 | 24" |
| 967 | 600 | 373 | 262 | 208 | 173 | 0.9 | 0.0 | -4.5 | -13.5 | -28.3 | -49.9 | 0.0 | -4.5 | -13.5 | -28.3 | -49.9 | -118.6 | -228.2 | 20" |
| 1696 | 1253 | 913 | 666 | 502 | 405 | 0.7 | 0.0 | -3.3 | -9.7 | -19.6 | -33.8 | 2.2 | 0.0 | -5.3 | -14.1 | -27.2 | -69.0 | -136.9 | |
| 1412 | 836 | 521 | 301 | 172 | 119 | 0.4 | 0.8 | 0.0 | -2.4 | -6.7 | -13.8 | 2.0 | 1.8 | 0.0 | -3.8 | -10.2 | -35.0 | -84.4 | 24" |
| 1902 | 1296 | 858 | 565 | 399 | 316 | 0.5 | 0.0 | -2.7 | -8.2 | -17.0 | -30.0 | 1.8 | 0.0 | -4.6 | -12.5 | -24.6 | -65.3 | -134.9 | |
| 1827 | 1355 | 989 | 720 | 535 | 425 | 0.6 | 0.0 | -3.0 | -8.9 | -18.0 | -31.1 | 2.0 | 0.0 | -4.8 | -13.0 | -25.1 | -63.6 | -126.7 | 24" |
| 1827 | 1355 | 989 | 720 | 535 | 425 | 0.6 | 0.0 | -3.0 | -8.9 | -18.0 | -31.1 | 2.0 | 0.0 | -4.8 | -13.0 | -25.1 | -63.6 | -126.7 | |
| 1879 | 1416 | 1050 | 771 | 571 | 442 | 0.5 | 0.0 | -2.7 | -7.9 | -16.1 | -27.6 | 1.8 | 0.0 | -4.3 | -11.6 | -22.3 | -56.3 | -111.9 | |
| 2207 | 1639 | 1193 | 860 | 626 | 482 | 0.5 | 0.0 | -2.6 | -7.7 | -15.6 | -27.1 | 1.7 | 0.0 | -4.2 | -11.3 | -21.9 | -55.8 | -112.0 | 24" |
| 2303 | 1845 | 1462 | 1143 | 806 | 685 | 0.3 | 0.0 | -1.8 | -5.4 | 11.0 | 18.8 | 2.7 | 2.2 | 0.0 | -4.2 | -10.7 | -31.5 | -65.6 | |

# REMINGTON BALLISTICS

**CENTERFIRE RIFLE BALLISTICS (Cont.)**

| Caliber | Order No. | Wt. (grs.) | Bullet Style | Primer No. | Muzzle | 100 yds. | 200 yds. | 300 yds. | 400 yds. | 500 yds. |
|---|---|---|---|---|---|---|---|---|---|---|
| .30-40 Krag | R30402 | 180* | Pointed Soft Point Core-Lokt® | 9½ | 2430 | 2213 | 2007 | 1813 | 1632 | 1468 |
| .308 Win. | R308W1 | 150 | Pointed Soft Point Core-Lokt® | 9½ | 2820 | 2533 | 2263 | 2009 | 1774 | 1560 |
| | R308W2 | 180 | Soft Point Core-Lokt® | 9½ | 2620 | 2274 | 1955 | 1666 | 1414 | 1212 |
| | R308W3 | 180 | Pointed Soft Point Core-Lokt® | 9½ | 2620 | 2393 | 2178 | 1974 | 1782 | 1604 |
| | R308W7 | 168 | Boat Tail HP Match | 9½ | 2680 | 2493 | 2314 | 2143 | 1979 | 1823 |
| | ER308WA | 165 | Extended Range Boat Tail | 9½ | 2700 | 2497 | 2303 | 2117 | 1941 | 1773 |
| .30-06 Springfield | R30061 | 125 | Pointed Soft Point | 9½ | 3140 | 2780 | 2447 | 2138 | 1853 | 1595 |
| | R30062 | 150 | Pointed Soft Point Core-Lokt® | 9½ | 2910 | 2617 | 2342 | 2083 | 1843 | 1622 |
| | R30063 | 150 | Bronze Point™ | 9½ | 2910 | 2656 | 2416 | 2189 | 1974 | 1773 |
| | R3006B | 165 | Pointed Soft Point Core-Lokt® | 9½ | 2800 | 2534 | 2283 | 2047 | 1825 | 1621 |
| | R30064 | 180 | Soft Point Core-Lokt® | 9½ | 2700 | 2348 | 2023 | 1727 | 1466 | 1251 |
| | R30065 | 180 | Pointed Soft Point Core-Lokt® | 9½ | 2700 | 2469 | 2250 | 2042 | 1846 | 1663 |
| | R30066 | 180 | Bronze Point™ | 9½ | 2700 | 2485 | 2280 | 2084 | 1899 | 1725 |
| | R30067 | 220 | Soft Point Core-Lokt® | 9½ | 2410 | 2130 | 1870 | 1632 | 1422 | 1246 |
| | RS3006A | 180 | Swift A-Frame™ PSP | 9½ | 2700 | 2465 | 2243 | 2032 | 1833 | 1646 |
| | ER3006B | 165 | Extended Range Boat Tail | 9½ | 2800 | 2592 | 2394 | 2204 | 2023 | 1852 |
| .300 H&H Mag. | R300HH § | 180 | Pointed Soft Point Core-Lokt® | 9½ M | 2880 | 2640 | 2412 | 2196 | 1990 | 1798 |
| .300 Win. Mag. | R300W1 | 150 | Pointed Soft Point Core-Lokt® | 9½ M | 3290 | 2951 | 2636 | 2342 | 2068 | 1813 |
| | R300W2 | 180 | Pointed Soft Point Core-Lokt® | 9½ M | 2960 | 2745 | 2540 | 2344 | 2157 | 1979 |
| | RS300WA | 200 | Swift A-Frame™ PSP | 9½ M | 2825 | 2595 | 2376 | 2167 | 1970 | 1783 |
| | ER300WB | 190 | Extended Range Boat Tail | 9½ M | 2885 | 2691 | 2506 | 2327 | 2156 | 1993 |
| .300 Wby. Mag. | R300WB1 | 180 | Pointed Soft Point Core-Lokt® | 9½ M | 3120 | 2866 | 2627 | 2400 | 2184 | 1979 |
| | ER30WBB | 190 | Extended Range Boat Tail | 9½ M | 3030 | 2830 | 2638 | 2455 | 2279 | 2110 |
| | RS300WBB | 200 | Swift A-Frame™ PSP | 9½ M | 2925 | 2690 | 2467 | 2254 | 2052 | 1861 |
| .303 British | R303B1 | 180 | Soft Point Core-Lokt® | 9½ | 2460 | 2124 | 1817 | 1542 | 1311 | 1137 |
| 7.62 x 39mm | R762391 | 125 | Pointed Soft Point | 7½ | 2365 | 2062 | 1783 | 1533 | 1320 | 1154 |
| .32-20 Win. | R32201 | 100 | Lead | 6½ | 1210 | 1021 | 913 | 834 | 769 | 712 |
| | R32202 | 100 | Soft Point | 6½ | 1210 | 1021 | 913 | 834 | 769 | 712 |
| .32 Win. Special | R32WS2 | 170 | Soft Point Core-Lokt® | 9½ | 2250 | 1921 | 1626 | 1372 | 1175 | 1044 |
| 8mm Mauser | R8MSR | 170 | Soft Point Core-Lokt® | 9½ | 2360 | 1969 | 1622 | 1333 | 1123 | 997 |
| .338 Win. Mag. | R338W1 | 225 | Pointed Soft Point Core-Lokt® | 9½ M | 2780 | 2572 | 2374 | 2184 | 2003 | 1832 |
| | R338W2 | 250 | Pointed Soft Point Core-Lokt® | 9½ M | 2660 | 2456 | 2261 | 2075 | 1898 | 1731 |
| | RS338WA | 225 | Swift A-Frame™ PSP | 9½ M | 2785 | 2517 | 2266 | 2029 | 1806 | 1605 |
| .35 Remington | R35R1 | 150 | Pointed Soft Point Core-Lokt® | 9½ | 2300 | 1874 | 1506 | 1218 | 1039 | 934 |
| | R35R2 | 200 | Soft Point Core-Lokt® | 9½ | 2080 | 1698 | 1376 | 1140 | 1001 | 911 |
| .350 Remington Mag. | R350M1 § | 200 | Pointed Soft Point Core-Lokt® | 9½ M | 2710 | 2410 | 2130 | 1870 | 1631 | 1421 |
| .35 Whelen | R35WH1 | 200 | Pointed Soft Point | 9½ M | 2675 | 2378 | 2100 | 1842 | 1606 | 1399 |
| | R35WH3 | 250 | Pointed Soft Point | 9½ M | 2400 | 2197 | 2005 | 1823 | 1652 | 1496 |
| .375 H&H Mag. | R375M1 | 270 | Soft Point | 9½ M | 2690 | 2420 | 2166 | 1928 | 1707 | 1507 |
| | RS375MA | 300 | Swift A-Frame™ PSP | 9½ M | 2530 | 2245 | 1979 | 1733 | 1512 | 1321 |
| .416 Remington Mag. | R416R2 | 400 | Swift A-Frame™ PSP | 9½ M | 2400 | 2175 | 1962 | 1763 | 1579 | 1414 |
| .44-40 Win. | R4440W | 200 | Soft Point | 2½ | 1190 | 1006 | 900 | 822 | 756 | 699 |
| .44 Remington Mag. | R44MG2 | 240 | Soft Point | 2½ | 1760 | 1380 | 1114 | 970 | 878 | 806 |
| | R44MG3 | 240 | Semi-Jacketed Hollow Point | 2½ | 1760 | 1380 | 1114 | 970 | 878 | 806 |
| | R44MG6 | 210 | Semi-Jacketed Hollow Point | 2½ | 1920 | 1477 | 1155 | 982 | 880 | 802 |
| | RH44MGA | 275 | JHP Core-Lokt® | 2½ | 1580 | 1293 | 1093 | 976 | 896 | 832 |
| .444 Mar. | R444M | 240 | Soft Point | 9½ | 2350 | 1815 | 1377 | 1087 | 941 | 846 |
| .45-70 Government | R4570G | 405 | Soft Point | 9½ | 1330 | 1168 | 1055 | 977 | 918 | 869 |
| | R4570L | 300 | Jacketed Hollow Point | 9½ | 1810 | 1497 | 1244 | 1073 | 969 | 895 |
| .458 Win. Mag. | RS458WA | 450 | Swift A-Frame™ PSP | 9½ M | 2150 | 1901 | 1671 | 1465 | 1289 | 1150 |

# REMINGTON BALLISTICS

☐ = Extended Range     ▨ = Safari Grade

| Energy (ft.-lbs.) | | | | | | Short-range[1] Trajectory* | | | | | | Long-range[2] Trajectory* | | | | | | | Barrel |
| Muzzle | 100 yds. | 200 yds. | 300 yds. | 400 yds. | 500 yds. | 50 yds. | 100 yds. | 150 yds. | 200 yds. | 250 yds. | 300 yds. | 100 yds. | 150 yds. | 200 yds. | 250 yds. | 300 yds. | 400 yds. | 500 yds. | Length |
|---|---|---|---|---|---|---|---|---|---|---|---|---|---|---|---|---|---|---|---|
| 2360 | 1957 | 1610 | 1314 | 1064 | 861 | 0.4 | 0.0 | -2.1 | -6.2 | -12.5 | -21.1 | 1.4 | 0.0 | -3.4 | -8.9 | -16.8 | -40.9 | -78.1 | 24" |
| 2648 | 2137 | 1705 | 1344 | 1048 | 810 | 0.2 | 0.0 | -1.5 | -4.5 | -9.3 | -15.9 | 2.3 | 1.9 | 0.0 | -3.6 | -9.1 | -26.9 | -55.7 | |
| 2743 | 2066 | 1527 | 1109 | 799 | 587 | 0.3 | 0.0 | -2.0 | -5.9 | -12.1 | -20.9 | 2.9 | 2.4 | 0.0 | -4.7 | -12.1 | -36.9 | -79.1 | |
| 2743 | 2288 | 1896 | 1557 | 1269 | 1028 | 0.2 | 0.0 | -1.8 | -5.2 | -10.4 | -17.7 | 2.6 | 2.1 | 0.0 | -4.0 | -9.9 | -28.9 | -58.8 | 24" |
| 2678 | 2318 | 1998 | 1713 | 1460 | 1239 | 0.2 | 0.0 | -1.6 | -4.7 | -9.4 | -15.9 | 2.4 | 1.9 | 0.0 | -3.5 | -8.9 | -25.3 | -50.6 | |
| 2670 | 2284 | 1942 | 1642 | 1379 | 1152 | 0.2 | 0.0 | -1.6 | -4.7 | -9.4 | -16.0 | 2.3 | 1.9 | 0.0 | -3.5 | -8.9 | -25.6 | -51.5 | |
| 2736 | 2145 | 1662 | 1269 | 953 | 706 | 0.4 | 0.8 | 0.0 | -2.1 | -5.6 | -10.7 | 1.8 | 1.5 | 0.0 | -3.0 | -7.7 | -23.0 | -48.5 | |
| 2820 | 2281 | 1827 | 1445 | 1131 | 876 | 0.6 | 0.9 | 0.0 | -2.3 | -6.3 | -12.0 | 2.1 | 1.8 | 0.0 | -3.3 | -8.5 | -25.0 | -51.8 | |
| 2820 | 2349 | 1944 | 1596 | 1298 | 1047 | 0.6 | 0.9 | 0.0 | -2.2 | -6.0 | -11.4 | 2.0 | 1.7 | 0.0 | -3.2 | -8.0 | -23.3 | -47.5 | |
| 2872 | 2352 | 1909 | 1534 | 1220 | 963 | 0.7 | 1.0 | 0.0 | -2.5 | -6.7 | -12.7 | 2.3 | 1.9 | 0.0 | -3.6 | -9.0 | -26.3 | -54.1 | |
| 2913 | 2203 | 1635 | 1192 | 859 | 625 | 0.2 | 0.0 | -1.8 | -5.5 | -11.2 | -19.5 | 2.7 | 2.3 | 0.0 | -4.4 | -11.3 | -34.4 | -73.7 | |
| 2913 | 2436 | 2023 | 1666 | 1362 | 1105 | 0.2 | 0.0 | -1.6 | -4.8 | -9.7 | -16.5 | 2.4 | 2.0 | 0.0 | -3.7 | -9.3 | -27.0 | -54.9 | 24" |
| 2913 | 2468 | 2077 | 1736 | 1441 | 1189 | 0.2 | 0.0 | -1.6 | -4.7 | -9.6 | -16.2 | 2.4 | 2.0 | 0.0 | -3.6 | -9.1 | -26.2 | -53.0 | |
| 2837 | 2216 | 1708 | 1301 | 988 | 758 | 0.4 | 0.0 | -2.3 | -6.8 | -13.8 | -23.6 | 1.5 | 0.0 | -3.7 | -9.9 | -19.0 | -47.4 | -93.1 | |
| 2913 | 2429 | 2010 | 1650 | 1343 | 1085 | 0.2 | 0.0 | -1.6 | -4.8 | -9.8 | -16.6 | 2.4 | 2.0 | 0.0 | -3.7 | -9.4 | -27.2 | -55.3 | |
| 2872 | 2482 | 2100 | 1780 | 1500 | 1256 | 0.6 | 1.0 | 0.0 | -2.4 | -6.2 | -11.8 | 2.1 | 1.8 | 0.0 | -3.3 | -8.2 | -23.6 | -47.5 | |
| 3315 | 2785 | 2325 | 1927 | 1583 | 1292 | 0.6 | 0.9 | 0.0 | -2.3 | -6.0 | -11.5 | 2.1 | 1.7 | 0.0 | -3.2 | -8.0 | -23.3 | -47.4 | 24" |
| 3605 | 2900 | 2314 | 1827 | 1424 | 1095 | 0.3 | 0.7 | 0.0 | -1.8 | -4.8 | -9.3 | 2.6 | 2.9 | 2.1 | 0.0 | -3.5 | -15.4 | -35.5 | |
| 3501 | 3011 | 2578 | 2196 | 1859 | 1565 | 0.5 | 0.8 | 0.0 | -2.1 | -5.5 | -10.4 | 1.9 | 1.6 | 0.0 | -2.9 | -7.3 | -20.9 | -41.9 | 24" |
| 3544 | 2989 | 2506 | 2086 | 1722 | 1412 | 0.6 | 1.0 | 0.0 | -2.4 | -6.3 | -11.9 | 2.1 | 1.8 | 0.0 | -3.3 | -8.3 | -24.0 | -48.8 | |
| 3511 | 3055 | 2648 | 2285 | 1961 | 1675 | 0.5 | 0.9 | 0.0 | -2.2 | -5.7 | -10.7 | 1.9 | 1.6 | 0.0 | -3.0 | -7.5 | -21.4 | -42.9 | |
| 3890 | 3284 | 2758 | 2301 | 1905 | 1565 | 0.4 | 0.7 | 0.0 | -1.9 | -5.0 | -9.5 | 2.7 | 3.0 | 2.1 | 0.0 | -3.5 | -15.2 | -34.2 | |
| 3873 | 3378 | 2936 | 2542 | 2190 | 1878 | 0.4 | 0.8 | 0.0 | -1.9 | -5.1 | -9.6 | 1.7 | 1.4 | 0.0 | -2.7 | -6.7 | -19.2 | -38.4 | 24" |
| 3799 | 3213 | 2701 | 2256 | 1870 | 1538 | 0.5 | 0.9 | 0.0 | -2.2 | -5.8 | -11.0 | 3.2 | 3.5 | 2.4 | 0.0 | -4.0 | -17.4 | -39.0 | |
| 2418 | 1803 | 1319 | 950 | 687 | 517 | 0.4 | 0.0 | -2.3 | -6.9 | -14.1 | -24.4 | 1.5 | 0.0 | -3.8 | -10.2 | -19.8 | -50.5 | -101.5 | 24" |
| 1552 | 1180 | 882 | 652 | 483 | 370 | 0.4 | 0.0 | -2.5 | -7.3 | -14.3 | -25.7 | 1.7 | 0.0 | -4.8 | -10.8 | -20.7 | -52.3 | -104.0 | 24" |
| 325 | 231 | 185 | 154 | 131 | 113 | 0.0 | -6.3 | -20.9 | -44.9 | -79.3 | -125.1 | 0.0 | -11.5 | -32.3 | -63.8 | -106.3 | -230.3 | -413.3 | 24" |
| 325 | 231 | 185 | 154 | 131 | 113 | 0.0 | -6.3 | -20.9 | -44.9 | -79.3 | -125.1 | 0.0 | -11.5 | -32.3 | -63.6 | -106.3 | -230.3 | -413.3 | |
| 1911 | 1393 | 998 | 710 | 521 | 411 | 0.6 | 0.0 | -2.9 | -8.6 | -17.6 | -30.5 | 1.9 | 0.0 | -4.7 | -12.7 | -24.7 | -63.2 | -126.9 | 24" |
| 2102 | 1463 | 993 | 671 | 476 | 375 | 0.5 | 0.0 | -2.7 | -8.2 | -17.0 | -29.8 | 1.8 | 0.0 | -4.5 | -12.4 | -24.3 | -63.8 | -130.7 | 24" |
| 3860 | 3305 | 2815 | 2383 | 2004 | 1676 | 0.6 | 1.0 | 0.0 | -2.4 | -6.3 | -12.0 | 2.2 | 1.8 | 0.0 | -3.3 | -8.4 | -24.0 | -48.4 | |
| 3927 | 3348 | 2837 | 2389 | 1999 | 1663 | 0.2 | 0.0 | -1.7 | -4.9 | -9.8 | -16.8 | 2.4 | 2.0 | 0.0 | -3.7 | -9.3 | -26.6 | -53.6 | 24" |
| 3871 | 3185 | 2605 | 2057 | 1633 | 1286 | 0.2 | 0.0 | -1.5 | -4.6 | -9.4 | -16.0 | 2.3 | 1.9 | 0.0 | -3.6 | -9.1 | -26.7 | -54.9 | |
| 1762 | 1169 | 755 | 494 | 359 | 291 | 0.6 | 0.0 | -3.0 | -9.2 | -19.1 | -33.9 | 2.0 | 0.0 | -5.1 | -14.1 | -27.8 | -74.0 | -152.3 | 24" |
| 1921 | 1280 | 841 | 577 | 445 | 369 | 0.8 | 0.0 | -3.8 | -11.3 | -23.5 | -41.2 | 2.5 | 0.0 | -6.3 | -17.1 | -33.6 | -87.7 | -176.4 | |
| 3261 | 2579 | 2014 | 1553 | 1181 | 897 | 0.2 | 0.0 | -1.7 | -5.1 | -10.4 | -17.9 | 2.6 | 2.1 | 0.0 | -4.0 | -10.3 | -30.5 | -64.0 | 20" |
| 3177 | 2510 | 1958 | 1506 | 1145 | 869 | 0.2 | 0.0 | -1.8 | -5.3 | -10.8 | -18.5 | 2.6 | 2.2 | 0.0 | -4.2 | -10.6 | -31.5 | -65.9 | |
| 3197 | 2680 | 2230 | 1844 | 1515 | 1242 | 0.4 | 0.0 | -2.2 | -6.3 | -12.6 | -21.3 | 1.4 | 0.0 | -3.4 | -9.0 | -17.0 | -41.0 | -77.8 | |
| 4337 | 3510 | 2812 | 2228 | 1747 | 1361 | 0.2 | 0.0 | -1.7 | -5.1 | -10.3 | -17.6 | 2.5 | 2.1 | 0.0 | -3.9 | -10.0 | -29.4 | -60.7 | 24" |
| 4262 | 3357 | 2608 | 2001 | 1523 | 1163 | 0.3 | 0.0 | -2.0 | -6.0 | -12.3 | -21.0 | 3.0 | 2.5 | 0.0 | -4.7 | -12.0 | -35.6 | -74.5 | |
| 5115 | 4201 | 3419 | 2760 | 2214 | 1775 | 0.4 | 0.0 | -2.2 | -6.5 | -13.0 | -22.0 | 1.5 | 0.0 | -3.5 | -9.3 | -17.6 | -42.9 | -82.2 | 24" |
| 629 | 449 | 360 | 300 | 254 | 217 | 0.0 | -6.5 | -21.6 | -46.3 | -81.8 | -129.1 | 0.0 | -11.8 | -33.3 | -65.5 | -109.5 | -237.4 | -426.2 | 24" |
| 1650 | 1015 | 661 | 501 | 411 | 346 | 0.0 | -2.7 | -10.0 | -23.0 | -43.0 | -71.2 | 0.0 | -5.9 | -17.6 | -36.3 | -63.1 | -145.5 | -273.0 | |
| 1650 | 1015 | 661 | 501 | 411 | 346 | 0.0 | -2.7 | -10.0 | -23.0 | -43.0 | -71.2 | 0.0 | -5.9 | -17.6 | -36.3 | -63.1 | -145.5 | -273.0 | 20" |
| 1719 | 1017 | 622 | 450 | 361 | 300 | 0.0 | -2.2 | -8.3 | -19.7 | -37.6 | -63.2 | 0.0 | -5.1 | -15.4 | -32.1 | -56.7 | -134.0 | -256.2 | |
| 1524 | 1020 | 730 | 582 | 490 | 422 | 1.7 | 0.0 | -6.9 | -20.0 | -40.1 | -68.7 | 0.0 | -6.9 | -20.0 | -40.1 | -68.7 | -153.8 | -283.0 | |
| 2942 | 1755 | 1010 | 630 | 472 | 381 | 0.6 | 0.0 | -3.2 | -9.9 | -21.3 | -38.5 | 2.1 | 0.0 | -5.6 | -15.9 | -32.1 | -87.8 | -182.7 | 24" |
| 1590 | 1227 | 1001 | 858 | 758 | 679 | 0.0 | -4.7 | -15.8 | -34.0 | -60.0 | -94.5 | 0.0 | -8.7 | -24.6 | -48.2 | -80.3 | -172.4 | -305.9 | 24" |
| 2182 | 1492 | 1031 | 767 | 625 | 533 | 0.0 | -2.3 | -8.5 | -19.4 | -35.9 | -59.0 | 0.0 | -5.0 | -14.8 | -30.1 | -52.1 | -119.5 | — | |
| 4618 | 3609 | 2789 | 2144 | 1659 | 1321 | 0.6 | 0.0 | -3.0 | -8.8 | -17.6 | -30.1 | 2.0 | 0.0 | -4.8 | -12.6 | -24.0 | -59.5 | -115.7 | 24" |

# REMINGTON BALLISTICS

## PISTOL AND REVOLVER

☐ = Golden Saber™   ▨ = Core-Lokt® Hunting   ▨ = LeadLess™

| Caliber | Order No. | Primer No. | Weight (grs.) | Bullet Style | Velocity (ft./sec.) Muzzle | 50 yds. | 100 yds. | Energy (ft.-lbs.) Muzzle | 50 yds. | 100 yds. | Mid-range Trajectory 50 yds. | 100 yds. | B.L. |
|---|---|---|---|---|---|---|---|---|---|---|---|---|---|
| .221 Rem. Fireball | R221F | 7½ | 50 | Pointed Soft Point | 2650 | 2380 | 2130 | 780 | 630 | 505 | 0.2" | 0.8" | 10" |
| .25 (6.35mm) Auto. Pistol | R25AP | 1½ | 50 | Metal Case | 760 | 707 | 659 | 64 | 56 | 48 | 2.0" | 8.7" | 2" |
| 6mm BR Rem. | R6MMBR | 7½ | 100 | Pointed Soft Point | Refer to Remington CF Ballistics Charts | | | | | | | | |
| 7mm BR Rem. | R7MMBR | 7½ | 140 | Pointed Soft Point | Refer to Remington CF Ballistics Charts | | | | | | | | |
| .32 S&W | R32SW | 1½ | 88 | Lead | 680 | 645 | 610 | 90 | 81 | 73 | 2.5" | 0.5" | 3" |
| .32 S&W Long | R32SWL | 1½ | 98 | Lead | 705 | 670 | 635 | 115 | 98 | 88 | 2.3" | 10.5" | 4" |
| .32 (7.65mm) Auto. Pistol | R32AP | 1½ | 71 | Metal Case | 905 | 855 | 810 | 129 | 115 | 97 | 1.4" | 5.8" | 4" |
| .357 MAG. Vented Barrel Ballistics | R357M7 | 5½ | 110 | Semi-Jacketed Hollow Point | 1295 | 1094 | 975 | 410 | 292 | 232 | 0.8" | 3.5" | 4" |
| | R357M1 | 5½ | 125 | Semi-Jacketed Hollow Point | 1450 | 1240 | 1090 | 583 | 427 | 330 | 0.6" | 2.8" | 4" |
| | GS357MA | 5½ | 125 | Brass-Jacketed Hollow Point | 1220 | 1095 | 1009 | 413 | 333 | 283 | 0.8" | 3.5" | 4" |
| | RH357MA | 5½ | 165 | JHP Core-Lokt® | 1290 | 1189 | 1108 | 610 | 518 | 450 | 0.7" | 3.1" | 8½" |
| | LL357MB | 5½ | 130 | TEMC, Lead-Lokt™ | 1400 | 1239 | 1116 | 566 | 443 | 360 | 0.6" | 2.8" | 4" |
| | LL357MD | 5½ | 158 | TEMC, Lead-Lokt™ | 1200 | 1081 | 999 | 505 | 410 | 350 | 0.9" | 4.0" | 4" |
| Refer to Remington CF Ballistics Charts for test details | R357M2 | 5½ | 158 | Semi-Jacketed Hollow Point | 1235 | 1104 | 1015 | 535 | 428 | 361 | 0.8" | 3.5" | 4" |
| | R357M3 | 5½ | 158 | Soft Point | 1235 | 1104 | 1015 | 535 | 428 | 361 | 0.8" | 3.5" | 4" |
| | R357M5 | 5½ | 158 | Semi-Wadcutter | 1235 | 1104 | 1015 | 535 | 428 | 361 | 0.8" | 3.5" | 4" |
| | R357M10 | 5½ | 180 | Semi-Jacketed Hollow Point | 1145 | 1053 | 985 | 524 | 443 | 388 | 0.9" | 3.9" | 8½" |
| .357 Rem. Maximum* | 357MX1 § | 7½ | 158 | Semi-Jacketed Hollow Point | 1825 | 1588 | 1381 | 1168 | 885 | 669 | 0.4" | 1.7" | 10" |
| 9mm Luger Auto. Pistol | R9MM1 | 1½ | 115 | Jacketed Hollow Point | 1155 | 1047 | 971 | 341 | 280 | 241 | 0.9" | 3.9" | 4" |
| | R9MM10 | 1½ | 124 | Jacketed Hollow Point | 1120 | 1030 | 960 | 346 | 291 | 254 | 1.0" | 4.1" | 4" |
| | R9MM2 | 1½ | 124 | Metal Case | 1110 | 1030 | 971 | 339 | 292 | 259 | 1.0" | 4.1" | 4" |
| | R9MM3 | 1½ | 115 | Metal Case | 1135 | 1041 | 973 | 329 | 277 | 242 | 0.9" | 4.0" | 4" |
| | R9MM6 | 1½ | 115 | Jacketed Hollow Point (+P)‡ | 1250 | 1113 | 1019 | 399 | 316 | 265 | 0.8" | 3.5" | 4" |
| | R9MM8 | 1½ | 147 | Jacketed Hollow Point (Subsonic) | 990 | 941 | 900 | 320 | 289 | 264 | 1.1" | 4.9" | 4" |
| | R9MM9 | 1½ | 147 | Metal Case (Match) | 990 | 941 | 900 | 320 | 289 | 264 | 1.1" | 4.9" | 4" |
| | LL9MMA | 1½ | 115 | TEMC, Lead-Lokt™ | 1135 | 1041 | 973 | 329 | 277 | 242 | 0.9" | 4.0" | 4" |
| | LL9MMB | 1½ | 124 | TEMC, Lead-Lokt™ | 1110 | 1030 | 971 | 339 | 292 | 259 | 1.0" | 4.1" | 4" |
| | LL9MC | 1½ | 147 | TEMC, Lead-Lokt™ | 990 | 941 | 900 | 320 | 289 | 264 | 1.1" | 4.9" | 4" |
| | GS9MMB | 1½ | 124 | Brass-Jacketed Hollow Point | 1125 | 1031 | 963 | 349 | 293 | 255 | 1.0" | 4.0" | 4" |
| | GS9MMC | 1½ | 147 | Brass-Jacketed Hollow Point | 990 | 941 | 900 | 320 | 289 | 264 | 1.1" | 4.9" | 4" |
| | GS9MMD | 1½ | 124 | Brass-Jacketed Hollow Point (+P)‡ | 1180 | 1089 | 1021 | 384 | 327 | 287 | 0.8" | 3.8" | 4" |
| .380 Auto. Pistol | R380AP | 1½ | 95 | Metal Case | 955 | 865 | 785 | 190 | 160 | 130 | 1.4" | 5.9" | 4" |
| | R380A1 | 1½ | 88 | Jacketed Hollow Point | 990 | 920 | 868 | 191 | 165 | 146 | 1.2" | 5.1" | 4" |
| | GS380B | 1½ | 102 | Brass-Jacketed Hollow Point | 940 | 901 | 866 | 200 | 184 | 170 | 1.2" | 5.1" | 4" |
| | LL380B | 1½ | 95 | TEMC, Lead-Lokt™ | 955 | 865 | 785 | 190 | 160 | 130 | 1.4" | 5.9" | 4" |
| .38 Super Auto. Colt Pistol (A) | R38SU1 | 1½ | 115 | Jacketed Hollow Point (+P)‡ | 1300 | 1147 | 1041 | 431 | 336 | 277 | 0.7" | 3.3" | 5" |
| .38 S&W | R38SW | 1½ | 146 | Lead | 685 | 650 | 620 | 150 | 135 | 125 | 2.4" | 10.0" | 4" |
| .38 Special Vented Barrel Ballistics | R38S10 | 1½ | 110 | Semi-Jacketed Hollow Point (+P)‡ | 995 | 926 | 871 | 242 | 210 | 185 | 1.2" | 5.1" | 4" |
| | R38S18 | 1½ | 110 | Semi-Jacketed Hollow Point | 950 | 890 | 840 | 220 | 194 | 172 | 1.4" | 5.4" | 4" |
| | R38S2 | 1½ | 125 | Semi-Jacketed Hollow Point (+P)‡ | 945 | 898 | 858 | 248 | 224 | 204 | 1.3" | 5.4" | 4" |
| | LL38SB | 1½ | 130 | TEMC, Lead-Lokt™ | 950 | 901 | 859 | 261 | 235 | 213 | 1.4" | 5.0" | 4" |
| | LL38SD | 1½ | 158 | TEMC, Lead-Lokt™ | 755 | 723 | 692 | 200 | 183 | 168 | 2.0" | 8.3" | 4" |
| | GS38SB | 1½ | 125 | Brass-Jacketed Hollow Point (+P)‡ | 975 | 929 | 885 | 264 | 238 | 218 | 1.0" | 5.2" | 4" |
| | R38S3 | 1½ | 148 | Targetmaster® Lead WC Match | 710 | 634 | 566 | 166 | 132 | 105 | 2.4" | 10.8" | 4" |
| | R38S5 | 1½ | 158 | Lead (Round Nose) | 755 | 723 | 692 | 200 | 183 | 168 | 2.0" | 8.3" | 4" |
| | R38S14 | 1½ | 158 | Semi-Wadcutter (+P)‡ | 890 | 855 | 823 | 278 | 257 | 238 | 1.4" | 6.0" | 4" |
| | R38S6 | 1½ | 158 | Semi-Wadcutter | 755 | 723 | 692 | 200 | 183 | 168 | 2.0" | 8.3" | 4" |
| | R38S12 | 1½ | 158 | Lead Hollow Point (+P)‡ | 890 | 855 | 823 | 278 | 257 | 238 | 1.4" | 6.0" | 4" |
| .38 Short Colt | R38SC | 1½ | 125 | Lead | 730 | 685 | 645 | 150 | 130 | 115 | 2.2" | 9.4" | 6" |
| 10mm Auto. | R10MM3 | 2½ | 180 | Jacketed Hollow Point (Subsonic) | 1055 | 997 | 951 | 445 | 397 | 361 | 1.0" | 4.6" | 5" |
| | R10MM4 | 2½ | 180 | Jacketed Hollow Point (High-Vel.) | 1160 | 1079 | 1017 | 538 | 465 | 413 | 0.9" | 3.8" | 5" |
| .357 Sig. | R357SI | 5½ | 125 | Jacketed Hollow Point | 1350 | 1157 | 1032 | 506 | 372 | 296 | 0.7" | 3.2" | 4" |
| 40 S&W | R40SW1 | 5½ | 155 | Jacketed Hollow Point | 1205 | 1095 | 1017 | 499 | 413 | 356 | 0.8" | 3.6" | 4" |
| | R40SW2 | 5½ | 180 | Jacketed Hollow Point | 1015 | 960 | 914 | 412 | 368 | 334 | 1.3" | 4.5" | 4" |
| | LL40SWB | 5½ | 180 | TEMC, Lead-Lokt™ | 985 | 936 | 893 | 388 | 350 | 319 | 1.4" | 5.0" | 4" |
| | GS40SWA | 5½ | 165 | Brass-Jacketed Hollow Point | 1150 | 1040 | 964 | 485 | 396 | 340 | 1.0" | 4.0" | 4" |
| | GS40SWB | 5½ | 180 | Brass-Jacketed Hollow Point | 1015 | 960 | 914 | 412 | 368 | 334 | 1.3" | 4.5" | 4" |
| .41 Rem. Mag. Vented Barrel Ballistics | R41MG1 | 2½ | 210 | Soft Point | 1300 | 1162 | 1062 | 788 | 630 | 526 | 0.7" | 3.2" | 4" |
| | R41MG3 | 2½ | 170 | Semi-Jacketed Hollow Point | 1420 | 1166 | 1014 | 761 | 513 | 388 | 0.7" | 3.2" | 4" |
| .44 Rem. Mag. Vented Barrel Ballistics | R44MG5 | 2½ | 180 | Semi-Jacketed Hollow Point | 1610 | 1365 | 1175 | 1036 | 745 | 551 | 0.5" | 2.3" | 4" |
| | R44MG2 | 2½ | 240 | Soft Point | 1180 | 1081 | 1010 | 741 | 623 | 543 | 0.9" | 3.7" | 4" |
| | R44MG3 | 2½ | 240 | Semi-Jacketed Hollow Point | 1180 | 1081 | 1010 | 741 | 623 | 543 | 0.9" | 3.7" | 4" |
| | R44MG6 | 2½ | 210 | Semi-Jacketed Hollow Point | 1495 | 1312 | 1167 | 1042 | 803 | 634 | 0.6" | 2.5" | 6½" |
| | RH44MGA | 2½ | 275 | JHP Core-Lokt® | 1235 | 1142 | 1070 | 931 | 797 | 699 | 0.8" | 3.3" | 8½" |
| .44 S&W Special | R44SW | 2½ | 246 | Lead | 755 | 725 | 695 | 310 | 285 | 265 | 2.0" | 8.3" | 6" |
| | R44SW1 | 2½ | 200 | Semi-Wadcutter | 1035 | 938 | 866 | 476 | 391 | 333 | 1.1" | 4.9" | 6" |
| .45 Colt | R45C | 2½ | 250 | Lead | 860 | 820 | 780 | 410 | 375 | 340 | 1.6" | 6.6" | 5" |
| | R45C1 | 2½ | 225 | Semi-Wadcutter (Keith) | 960 | 890 | 832 | 460 | 395 | 346 | 1.3" | 5.5" | 5" |
| .45 Auto. | R45AP1 | 2½ | 185 | Targetmaster® MC WC Match | 770 | 707 | 650 | 244 | 205 | 174 | 2.0" | 8.7" | 5" |
| | R45AP2 | 2½ | 185 | Jacketed Hollow Point | 1000 | 939 | 889 | 411 | 362 | 324 | 1.1" | 4.9" | 5" |
| | R45AP4 | 2½ | 230 | Metal Case | 835 | 800 | 767 | 356 | 326 | 300 | 1.6" | 6.8" | 5" |
| | R45AP6 | 2½ | 185 | Jacketed Hollow Point (+P)‡ | 1140 | 1040 | 971 | 534 | 445 | 387 | 0.9" | 4.0" | 5" |
| | R45AP7 | 2½ | 230 | Jacketed Hollow Point (Subsonic) | 835 | 800 | 767 | 356 | 326 | 300 | 1.6" | 6.8" | 5" |
| | LL45APB | 2½ | 230 | TEMC, Lead-Lokt™ | 835 | 800 | 767 | 356 | 326 | 300 | 1.6" | 6.8" | 5" |
| | GS45APA | 2½ | 185 | Brass-Jacketed Hollow Point | 1015 | 951 | 899 | 423 | 372 | 332 | 1.1" | 4.5" | 5" |
| | GS45APB | 2½ | 230 | Brass-Jacketed Hollow Point | 875 | 833 | 795 | 391 | 355 | 323 | 1.5" | 6.1" | 5" |
| | GS45APC | 2½ | 185 | Brass-Jacketed Hollow Point (+P)‡ | 1140 | 1042 | 971 | 534 | 446 | 388 | 1.0" | 4.0" | 5" |

# SAKO RIFLE BALLISTICS

| Caliber | Bullet weight/type | | Velocity in feet per second | | | | | | Energy in foot-pounds | | | | | | Trajectory Inches / Yards | | | | | | Box | |
|---|---|---|---|---|---|---|---|---|---|---|---|---|---|---|---|---|---|---|---|---|---|---|
| | Grs | Type | Muzzle | 100 y | 200 y | 300 y | 400 y | 500 y | Muzzle | 100 y | 200 y | 300 y | 400 y | 500 y | Muzzle | 100 y | 200 y | 300 y | 400 y | 500 y | pcs | |
| 22 Hornet | 45 | SPEEDHEAD FMJ | 2300 | 1724 | 1291 | 1069 | 944 | 861 | 524 | 295 | 165 | 114 | 89 | 74 | -1.5 | 0 | -14.3 | -47.1 | -108.9 | -203.5 | 20 | |
| | 45 | SOFT POINT RN | 2300 | 1724 | 1291 | 1069 | 944 | 861 | 524 | 295 | 165 | 114 | 89 | 74 | -1.5 | 0 | -14.3 | -47.1 | -108.9 | -203.5 | 20 | |
| | 42 | HOLLOW POINT | 2700 | 2193 | 1764 | 1419 | 1161 | 1011 | 652 | 428 | 277 | 179 | 120 | 91 | -1,5 | 0 | -6.6 | -24.5 | -60.1 | -120.9 | 20 | |
| 22 PPC USA | 52 | HPBT MATCH | 3400 | 2990 | 2613 | 2255 | 1920 | 1616 | 1342 | 1040 | 795 | 592 | 429 | 304 | -1.5 | 1.2 | 0 | -6.0 | -19.1 | -41.8 | 20 | |
| 222 Remington | 50 | SPEEDHEAD FMJ | 3200 | 2663 | 2182 | 1776 | 1447 | 1192 | 1135 | 786 | 528 | 350 | 232 | 158 | -1.5 | 1.7 | 0 | -10.3 | -31.1 | -67.3 | 20 | |
| | 50 | SOFT POINT P | 3200 | 2663 | 2182 | 1776 | 1447 | 1192 | 1135 | 786 | 528 | 350 | 232 | 158 | -1.5 | 1.7 | 0 | -10.3 | -31.1 | -67.3 | 20 | |
| | 55 | SOFT POINT P | 3280 | 2800 | 2372 | 1978 | 1637 | 1350 | 1312 | 958 | 686 | 477 | 326 | 222 | -1.5 | 1.4 | 0 | -8.0 | -24.8 | -54.5 | 20 | |
| | 52 | HPBT MATCH | 3035 | 2613 | 2235 | 1894 | 1589 | 1333 | 1072 | 795 | 581 | 417 | 294 | 207 | -1.5 | 1.8 | 0 | -9.0 | -27.9 | -60.7 | 20 | |
| 222 Remington Mag | 50 | SPEEDHEAD FMJ | 3230 | 2690 | 2207 | 1798 | 1466 | 1207 | 1159 | 803 | 540 | 359 | 238 | 161 | -1.5 | 1.6 | 0 | -10.0 | -30.3 | -67.0 | 20 | |
| | 50 | SOFT POINT P | 3230 | 2690 | 2207 | 1798 | 1466 | 1207 | 1159 | 803 | 540 | 359 | 238 | 161 | -1.5 | 1.6 | 0 | -10.0 | -30.3 | -67.0 | 20 | |
| | 55 | SOFT POINT P | 3330 | 2848 | 2414 | 2016 | 1671 | 1378 | 1352 | 989 | 710 | 495 | 340 | 231 | -1.5 | 1.4 | 0 | -7.7 | -23.8 | -51.9 | 20 | |
| 223 Remington | 50 | SPEEDHEAD FMJ | 3230 | 2690 | 2207 | 1798 | 1466 | 1207 | 1159 | 803 | 540 | 359 | 238 | 161 | -1.5 | 1.6 | 0 | -10.0 | -30.3 | -67.0 | 20 | |
| | 50 | SOFT POINT P | 3230 | 2690 | 2207 | 1798 | 1466 | 1207 | 1159 | 803 | 540 | 359 | 238 | 161 | -1.5 | 1.6 | 0 | -10.0 | -30.3 | -67.0 | 20 | |
| | 55 | SOFT POINT P | 3330 | 2848 | 2414 | 2016 | 1671 | 1378 | 1352 | 989 | 710 | 495 | 340 | 231 | -1.5 | 1.4 | 0 | -7.7 | -23.8 | -51.9 | 20 | |
| 22-250 Remington | 50 | SPEEDHEAD FMJ | 3770 | 3168 | 2639 | 2168 | 1751 | 1396 | 1579 | 1113 | 773 | 522 | 340 | 216 | -1.5 | 1.0 | 0 | -6.0 | -19.5 | -44.0 | 20 | |
| | 50 | SOFT POINT P | 3770 | 3168 | 2639 | 2168 | 1751 | 1396 | 1579 | 1113 | 773 | 522 | 340 | 216 | -1.5 | 1.0 | 0 | -6.0 | -19.5 | -44.0 | 20 | |
| | 55 | SOFT POINT P | 3660 | 3146 | 2681 | 2255 | 1871 | 1533 | 1631 | 1206 | 876 | 620 | 426 | 286 | -1.5 | 1.0 | 0 | -5.9 | -18.7 | -41.3 | 20 | |
| 6PPC USA | 70 | HPBT MATCH | 3100 | 2740 | 2407 | 2090 | 1793 | 1527 | 1481 | 1156 | 892 | 673 | 495 | 359 | -1.5 | 1.5 | 0 | -7.2 | -22.8 | -49.2 | 20 | |
| 243 Winchester | 90 | SPEEDHEAD FMJ | 2855 | 2587 | 2340 | 2110 | 1895 | 1693 | 1618 | 1329 | 1087 | 884 | 713 | 569 | -1.5 | 1.9 | 0 | -8.2 | -24.3 | -49.9 | 20 | |
| | 90 | SOFT POINT P | 3130 | 2850 | 2587 | 2343 | 2114 | 1898 | 1949 | 1612 | 1329 | 1090 | 887 | 715 | -1.5 | 1.5 | 0 | -6.5 | -19.5 | -40.2 | 20 | |
| 6.5x55 Swedish | 100 | SPEEDHEAD FMJ | 2625 | 2270 | 1946 | 1651 | 1397 | 1196 | 1533 | 1147 | 842 | 606 | 434 | 319 | -1.5 | 2.6 | 0 | -11.9 | -36.0 | -76.8 | 20 | |
| | 139 | HPBT MATCH | 2790 | 2648 | 2512 | 2381 | 2252 | 2129 | 2396 | 2161 | 1945 | 1746 | 1563 | 1396 | -1.5 | 1.7 | 0 | -7.2 | -20.5 | -40.7 | 20 | |
| | 156 | SOFT POINT RN | 2625 | 2384 | 2156 | 1941 | 1740 | 1554 | 2382 | 1966 | 1607 | 1303 | 1047 | 835 | -1.5 | 2.3 | 0 | -9.8 | -28.9 | -59.7 | 20 | |
| 270 Winchester | 130 | SPEEDHEAD FMJ | 2820 | 2506 | 2212 | 1938 | 1687 | 1463 | 2290 | 1805 | 1407 | 1080 | 818 | 616 | -1.5 | 2.0 | 0 | -9.2 | -27.5 | -58.3 | 20 | |
| | 156 | HAMMERHEAD | 2755 | 2470 | 2208 | 1967 | 1743 | 1538 | 2626 | 2111 | 1685 | 1338 | 1051 | 818 | -1.5 | 2.2 | 0 | -9.3 | -27.6 | -57.5 | 20 | NEW |
| 7x33 Sako | 78 | SPEEDHEAD FMJ | 2430 | 1920 | 1500 | 1190 | 1013 | 906 | 1029 | 643 | 392 | 247 | 179 | 143 | -1.5 | 0 | -8.5 | -31.0 | -78.8 | -158.0 | 50 | |
| | 78 | SOFT POINT SP | 2430 | 1920 | 1500 | 1190 | 1013 | 906 | 1029 | 643 | 392 | 247 | 179 | 143 | -1.5 | 0 | -8.5 | -31.0 | -78.8 | -158.0 | 50 | |
| 7 mm Mauser (7x57) | 78 | SPEEDHEAD FMJ | 2950 | 2324 | 1783 | 1362 | 1090 | 950 | 1522 | 943 | 555 | 324 | 208 | 158 | -1.5 | 2.6 | 0 | -14.9 | -50.4 | -112.2 | 20 | |
| | 170 | SOFT POINT SP | 2495 | 2283 | 2086 | 1901 | 1728 | 1567 | 2342 | 1962 | 1638 | 1361 | 1125 | 925 | -1.5 | 2.6 | 0 | -10.8 | -31.1 | -63.3 | 20 | |
| 7x64 | 120 | SOFT POINT P | 3100 | 2816 | 2545 | 2296 | 2069 | 1856 | 2567 | 2117 | 1730 | 1408 | 1143 | 920 | -1.5 | 1.4 | 0 | -7.3 | -20.9 | -42.6 | 20 | |
| | 170 | HAMMERHEAD | 2790 | 2563 | 2351 | 2154 | 1967 | 1791 | 2929 | 2473 | 2081 | 1747 | 1458 | 1208 | -1.5 | 1.9 | 0 | -8.2 | -23.9 | -48.6 | 20 | |
| 7x65R | 170 | HAMMERHEAD | 2625 | 2409 | 2208 | 2019 | 1839 | 1670 | 2594 | 2186 | 1836 | 1535 | 1274 | 1050 | -1.5 | 2.3 | 0 | -9.4 | -27.4 | -55.6 | 20 | NEW |
| 7 mm Remington Mag | 170 | HAMMERHEAD | 2970 | 2734 | 2512 | 2303 | 2108 | 1924 | 3320 | 2814 | 2376 | 1996 | 1674 | 1394 | -1.5 | 1.6 | 0 | -7.2 | -21.0 | -42.5 | 20 | NEW |
| 7.62x39 Russian | 123 | SPEEDHEAD FMJ | 2345 | 2096 | 1863 | 1651 | 1466 | 1305 | 1507 | 1203 | 951 | 747 | 589 | 466 | -1.5 | 0 | -6.5 | -23.6 | -53.2 | -98.5 | 30 | |
| | 123 | SPEEDHEAD FMJ | 2345 | 2096 | 1863 | 1651 | 1466 | 1305 | 1507 | 1203 | 951 | 747 | 589 | 466 | -1.5 | 0 | -6.5 | -23.6 | -53.2 | -98.5 | 250 | NEW |
| | 123 | SOFT POINT P | 2345 | 2096 | 1863 | 1651 | 1466 | 1305 | 1507 | 1203 | 951 | 747 | 589 | 466 | -1.5 | 0 | -6.5 | -23.6 | -53.2 | -98.5 | 30 | |
| 30-30 Winchester | 93 | SPEEDHEAD FMJ | 2970 | 2354 | 1818 | 1400 | 1126 | 976 | 1811 | 1138 | 679 | 403 | 260 | 196 | -1.5 | 0 | -4.9 | -21.8 | -56.7 | -117.3 | 20 | |
| | 150 | SOFT POINT FP | 2310 | 1982 | 1681 | 1439 | 1240 | 1096 | 1777 | 1304 | 938 | 688 | 510 | 400 | -1.5 | 0 | -8.1 | -28.3 | -65.6 | -125.6 | 20 | |
| 308 Winchester | 93 | SPEEDHEAD FMJ | 2970 | 2354 | 1818 | 1400 | 1126 | 976 | 1811 | 1138 | 679 | 403 | 260 | 196 | -1.5 | 0 | -4.9 | -21.8 | -56.7 | -117.3 | 20 | |
| | 123 | SPEEDHEAD FMJ | 2920 | 2622 | 2347 | 2097 | 1868 | 1654 | 2335 | 1883 | 1509 | 1205 | 955 | 749 | -1.5 | 1.8 | 0 | -8.4 | -24.5 | -50.7 | 20 | |
| | 123 | SOFT POINT P | 3035 | 2734 | 2455 | 2194 | 1958 | 1738 | 2523 | 2047 | 1650 | 1318 | 1050 | 827 | -1.5 | 1.6 | 0 | -7.6 | -22.4 | -46.2 | 20 | |
| | 156 | S - HAMMERHEAD | 2790 | 2563 | 2353 | 2158 | 1973 | 1800 | 2689 | 2271 | 1914 | 1610 | 1346 | 1120 | -1.5 | 2.0 | 0 | -8.2 | -23.9 | -48.9 | 20 | |
| | 180 | HAMMERHEAD | 2610 | 2382 | 2169 | 1971 | 1786 | 1612 | 2725 | 2273 | 1885 | 1556 | 1277 | 1041 | -1.5 | 2.4 | 0 | -9.9 | -28.6 | -58.1 | 20 | |
| | 180 | S - HAMMERHEAD | 2610 | 2400 | 2204 | 2017 | 1839 | 1672 | 2725 | 2310 | 1946 | 1629 | 1355 | 1119 | -1.5 | 2.3 | 0 | -9.5 | -27.5 | -55.8 | 20 | NEW |
| | 200 | HAMMERHEAD | 2445 | 2210 | 1990 | 1782 | 1588 | 1415 | 2660 | 2172 | 1762 | 1414 | 1122 | 891 | -1.5 | 2.8 | 0 | -11.3 | -33.7 | -70.1 | 20 | |
| | 123 | RANGE | 2950 | 2652 | 2378 | 2126 | 1895 | 1679 | 2388 | 1927 | 1549 | 1238 | 983 | 772 | -1.5 | 1.8 | 0 | -8.0 | -23.7 | -49.0 | 50 | |
| | 102 | SUPER RANGE | 3120 | 2712 | 2342 | 2003 | 1695 | 1428 | 2195 | 1662 | 1240 | 907 | 649 | 461 | -1.5 | 1.6 | 0 | -8.0 | -24.7 | -53.7 | 50 | NEW |
| | 168 | HPBT MATCH | 2690 | 2500 | 2321 | 2159 | 2004 | 1857 | 2701 | 2328 | 2010 | 1739 | 1499 | 1286 | -1.5 | 2.3 | 0 | -8.5 | -24.5 | -49.1 | 20 | |
| | 190 | HPBT MATCH | 2525 | 2372 | 2224 | 2080 | 1940 | 1806 | 2688 | 2369 | 2082 | 1822 | 1585 | 1373 | -1.5 | 2.4 | 0 | -9.0 | -26.3 | -52.9 | 20 | |
| 7.62x53R | 93 | SPEEDHEAD FMJ | 2970 | 2354 | 1818 | 1400 | 1126 | 976 | 1811 | 1138 | 679 | 403 | 260 | 196 | -1.5 | 0 | -4.9 | -21.8 | -56.7 | -117.3 | 20 | |
| | 123 | SPEEDHEAD FMJ | 2920 | 2622 | 2347 | 2097 | 1868 | 1654 | 2335 | 1883 | 1509 | 1205 | 955 | 749 | -1.5 | 1.8 | 0 | -8.4 | -24.5 | -50.7 | 20 | |
| | 156 | S - HAMMERHEAD | 2790 | 2563 | 2353 | 2158 | 1973 | 1800 | 2689 | 2271 | 1914 | 1610 | 1346 | 1120 | -1.5 | 2.0 | 0 | -8.2 | -23.9 | -48.9 | 20 | |
| | 180 | HAMMERHEAD | 2610 | 2382 | 2169 | 1971 | 1786 | 1612 | 2725 | 2273 | 1885 | 1556 | 1277 | 1041 | -1.5 | 2.4 | 0 | -9.9 | -28.6 | -58.1 | 20 | |
| | 180 | S - HAMMERHEAD | 2610 | 2400 | 2204 | 2017 | 1839 | 1672 | 2725 | 2310 | 1946 | 1629 | 1355 | 1119 | -1.5 | 2.3 | 0 | -9.5 | -27.5 | -55.8 | 20 | NEW |
| | 200 | HAMMERHEAD | 2445 | 2210 | 1990 | 1782 | 1588 | 1415 | 2660 | 2172 | 1762 | 1414 | 1122 | 891 | -1.5 | 2.8 | 0 | -11.3 | -33.7 | -70.1 | 20 | |
| | 123 | RANGE | 2950 | 2652 | 2378 | 2126 | 1895 | 1679 | 2388 | 1927 | 1549 | 1238 | 983 | 772 | -1.5 | 1.8 | 0 | -8.0 | -23.7 | -49.0 | 50 | |
| 30-06 Springfield | 123 | SPEEDHEAD FMJ | 2920 | 2622 | 2347 | 2097 | 1868 | 1654 | 2335 | 1883 | 1509 | 1205 | 955 | 749 | -1.5 | 1.8 | 0 | -8.4 | -24.5 | -50.7 | 20 | |
| | 123 | SOFT POINT P | 3120 | 2800 | 2510 | 2250 | 2010 | 1786 | 2661 | 2148 | 1726 | 1385 | 1106 | 873 | -1.5 | 1.6 | 0 | -7.3 | -21.3 | -43.9 | 20 | |
| | 156 | S - HAMMERHEAD | 2900 | 2670 | 2454 | 2255 | 2070 | 1893 | 2915 | 2466 | 2083 | 1759 | 1481 | 1240 | -1.5 | 1.8 | 0 | -7.8 | -22.2 | -44.7 | 20 | |
| | 180 | HAMMERHEAD | 2700 | 2465 | 2242 | 2042 | 1857 | 1682 | 2935 | 2433 | 2013 | 1670 | 1381 | 1133 | -1.5 | 2.3 | 0 | -9.4 | -27.0 | -54.5 | 20 | |
| | 180 | S - HAMMERHEAD | 2700 | 2500 | 2295 | 2100 | 1920 | 1750 | 2935 | 2495 | 2105 | 1768 | 1475 | 1223 | -1.5 | 2.1 | 0 | -8.7 | -25.3 | -51.3 | 20 | NEW |
| | 220 | HAMMERHEAD | 2410 | 2200 | 2000 | 1826 | 1664 | 1517 | 2847 | 2369 | 1963 | 1632 | 1356 | 1126 | -1.5 | 3.3 | 0 | -12.4 | -34.7 | -69.6 | 20 | |
| | 123 | RANGE | 2950 | 2652 | 2378 | 2126 | 1895 | 1679 | 2388 | 1927 | 1549 | 1238 | 983 | 772 | -1.5 | 1.8 | 0 | -8.0 | -23.7 | -49.0 | 50 | |
| 300 Winchester Mag | 156 | S - HAMMERHEAD | 3150 | 2905 | 2673 | 2453 | 2243 | 2044 | 3430 | 2918 | 2470 | 2080 | 1740 | 1445 | -1.5 | 1.3 | 0 | -6.1 | -18.1 | -37.0 | 20 | |
| | 180 | HAMMERHEAD | 2950 | 2700 | 2467 | 2243 | 2031 | 1833 | 3493 | 2926 | 2438 | 2015 | 1653 | 1345 | -1.5 | 1.6 | 0 | -7.4 | -21.7 | -44.4 | 20 | |
| | 180 | S - HAMMERHEAD | 2950 | 2730 | 2517 | 2314 | 2121 | 1938 | 3493 | 2983 | 2537 | 2144 | 1801 | 1504 | -1.5 | 1.6 | 0 | -7.1 | -20.7 | -42.0 | 20 | NEW |
| | 168 | HPBT MATCH | 3020 | 2816 | 2622 | 2438 | 2260 | 2090 | 3400 | 2959 | 2566 | 2217 | 1905 | 1630 | -1.5 | 1.5 | 0 | -6.5 | -18.8 | -38.0 | 20 | |
| 8.2x53R | 127 | SPEEDHEAD FMJ | 2625 | 2143 | 1715 | 1373 | 1141 | 1003 | 1934 | 1290 | 826 | 529 | 365 | 283 | -1.5 | 0 | -6.1 | -26.2 | -64.2 | -128.0 | 20 | |
| | 200 | HAMMERHEAD | 2525 | 2215 | 1927 | 1675 | 1462 | 1281 | 2841 | 2184 | 1653 | 1248 | 951 | 731 | -1.5 | 2.8 | 0 | -13.5 | -38.6 | -79.8 | 20 | |
| 8x57IS (8.2x57) | 127 | SPEEDHEAD FMJ | 2625 | 2143 | 1715 | 1373 | 1141 | 1003 | 1934 | 1290 | 826 | 529 | 365 | 283 | -1.5 | 0 | -6.1 | -26.2 | -64.2 | -128.0 | 20 | |
| | 200 | HAMMERHEAD | 2525 | 2215 | 1927 | 1675 | 1462 | 1281 | 2841 | 2184 | 1653 | 1248 | 951 | 731 | -1.5 | 2.8 | 0 | -13.5 | -38.6 | -79.8 | 20 | |
| 8x57JRS | 200 | HAMMERHEAD | 2395 | 2093 | 1815 | 1563 | 1347 | 1176 | 2553 | 1949 | 1465 | 1087 | 807 | 616 | -1.5 | 3.3 | 0 | -13.9 | -42.0 | -89.7 | 20 | NEW |
| 338 Winchester Mag | 250 | HAMMERHEAD | 2675 | 2413 | 2169 | 1946 | 1742 | 1554 | 3966 | 3229 | 2608 | 2101 | 1683 | 1339 | -1.5 | 2.3 | 0 | -10.0 | -29.1 | -59.7 | 20 | |
| 9.3x53R Finnish | 256 | SOFT POINT RN | 2330 | 2000 | 1695 | 1439 | 1236 | 1091 | 3010 | 2211 | 1593 | 1148 | 847 | 660 | -1.5 | 3.6 | 0 | -16.9 | -50.3 | -107.0 | 20 | |
| 9.3x62 | 250 | POWERHEAD BARNES | 2500 | 2300 | 2106 | 1927 | 1758 | 1599 | 3465 | 2932 | 2461 | 2060 | 1714 | 1419 | -1.5 | 2.6 | 0 | -10.4 | -30.2 | -61.3 | 20 | NEW |
| 9.3x74R | 250 | POWERHEAD BARNES | 2360 | 2170 | 1988 | 1815 | 1652 | 1503 | 3095 | 2612 | 2192 | 1828 | 1514 | 1253 | -1.5 | 3.0 | 0 | -11.8 | -34.2 | -69.4 | 10 | NEW |
| 375 H&H Mag | 270 | POWERHEAD BARNES | 2720 | 2535 | 2354 | 2181 | 2015 | 1857 | 4440 | 3848 | 3319 | 2848 | 2432 | 2066 | -1.5 | 1.9 | 0 | -8.3 | -23.8 | -48.0 | 10 | NEW |

SPEEDHEAD= FMJ = Full Metal Jacket
HP = Hollow Point, Varmint, Precision
SP FP = Soft Point Flat Point
HAMMERHEAD = Soft Point Bonded Core
S - HAMMERHEAD = SUPER HAMMERHEAD = Hollow Point Bonded Core
POWERHEAD BARNES = Hollow Point Solid Copper
HP BT = Hollow Point Boat Tail, Precision
RANGE = Full Metal Jacket
SUPER RANGE = HPBT, Varmint, Precision
SP P = Soft Point Pointed
SP SP = Soft Point Semi Pointed
SP RN = Soft Point Round Nose

# WEATHERBY BALLISTICS

| SUGGESTED USAGE | CARTRIDGE | BULLET Weight Grains | BULLET Bullet Type | BALLISTIC COEFFICIENT | VELOCITY in Feet per Second Muzzle | 100 Yards | 200 Yards | 300 Yards | 400 Yards | 500 Yards | ENERGY in Foot-Pounds Muzzle | 100 Yards | 200 Yards | 300 Yards | 400 Yards | 500 Yards | PATH OF BULLET 100 Yards | 200 Yards | 300 Yards | 400 Yards | 500 Yards |
|---|---|---|---|---|---|---|---|---|---|---|---|---|---|---|---|---|---|---|---|---|---|
| V | .224 Wby. | 55 | Pt-Ex | .235 | 3650 | 3192 | 2780 | 2403 | 2056 | 1741 | 1627 | 1244 | 944 | 705 | 516 | 370 | 2.8 | 3.7 | 0.0 | -9.8 | -27.9 |
| V | .240 Wby. | 87 | Pt-Ex | .327 | 3523 | 3199 | 2898 | 2617 | 2352 | 2103 | 2397 | 1977 | 1622 | 1323 | 1069 | 855 | 2.7 | 3.4 | 0.0 | -8.4 | -23.3 |
|  |  | 90 | Barnes-X | .382 | 3500 | 3222 | 2962 | 2717 | 2484 | 2264 | 2448 | 2075 | 1753 | 1475 | 1233 | 1024 | 2.6 | 3.3 | 0.0 | -8.0 | -21.6 |
| M |  | 100 | Pt-Ex | .381 | 3406 | 3134 | 2878 | 2637 | 2408 | 2190 | 2576 | 2180 | 1839 | 1544 | 1287 | 1065 | 2.8 | 3.5 | 0.0 | -8.4 | -23.0 |
|  |  | 100 | Partition | .384 | 3406 | 3136 | 2882 | 2642 | 2415 | 2199 | 2576 | 2183 | 1844 | 1550 | 1294 | 1073 | 2.8 | 3.5 | 0.0 | -8.4 | -22.9 |
| V | .257 Wby. | 87 | Pt-Ex | .322 | 3825 | 3472 | 3147 | 2845 | 2563 | 2297 | 2826 | 2328 | 1913 | 1563 | 1269 | 1019 | 2.1 | 2.8 | 0.0 | -7.1 | -19.5 |
| M |  | 100 | Pt-Ex | .357 | 3602 | 3298 | 3016 | 2750 | 2500 | 2264 | 2881 | 2416 | 2019 | 1680 | 1388 | 1138 | 2.4 | 3.1 | 0.0 | -7.7 | -21.0 |
|  |  | 115 | Barnes-X | .429 | 3400 | 3158 | 2929 | 2711 | 2504 | 2306 | 2952 | 2546 | 2190 | 1877 | 1601 | 1358 | 2.7 | 3.4 | 0.0 | -8.1 | -21.7 |
|  |  | 117 | Rn-Ex | .243 | 3402 | 2984 | 2595 | 2240 | 1921 | 1639 | 3007 | 2320 | 1742 | 1302 | 956 | 690 | 3.38 | 4.31 | 0.0 | -11.12 | -31.92 |
|  |  | 120 | Partition | .391 | 3305 | 3046 | 2801 | 2570 | 2350 | 2141 | 2910 | 2472 | 2091 | 1760 | 1471 | 1221 | 3.0 | 3.7 | 0.0 | -8.9 | -24.3 |
| V | .270 Wby. | 100 | Pt-Ex | .307 | 3760 | 3396 | 3061 | 2751 | 2462 | 2190 | 3139 | 2560 | 2081 | 1681 | 1346 | 1065 | 2.3 | 3.0 | 0.0 | -7.6 | -21.0 |
| M |  | 130 | Pt-Ex | .409 | 3375 | 3123 | 2885 | 2659 | 2444 | 2240 | 3288 | 2815 | 2402 | 2041 | 1724 | 1448 | 2.8 | 3.5 | 0.0 | -8.4 | -22.6 |
|  |  | 130 | Partition | .416 | 3375 | 3127 | 2892 | 2670 | 2458 | 2256 | 3288 | 2822 | 2415 | 2058 | 1744 | 1470 | 2.8 | 3.5 | 0.0 | -8.3 | -22.4 |
|  |  | 140 | Barnes-X | .462 | 3250 | 3032 | 2825 | 2628 | 2438 | 2257 | 3283 | 2858 | 2481 | 2146 | 1848 | 1583 | 3.0 | 3.7 | 0.0 | -8.7 | -23.2 |
|  |  | 150 | Pt-Ex | .462 | 3245 | 3028 | 2821 | 2623 | 2434 | 2253 | 3507 | 3053 | 2650 | 2292 | 1973 | 1690 | 3.0 | 3.7 | 0.0 | -8.7 | -23.3 |
|  |  | 150 | Partition | .465 | 3245 | 3029 | 2823 | 2627 | 2439 | 2259 | 3507 | 3055 | 2655 | 2298 | 1981 | 1699 | 3.0 | 3.7 | 0.0 | -8.7 | -23.2 |
| M | 7MM Wby. | 139 | Pt-Ex | .392 | 3340 | 3079 | 2834 | 2601 | 2380 | 2170 | 3443 | 2926 | 2478 | 2088 | 1748 | 1453 | 2.9 | 3.6 | 0.0 | -8.7 | -23.7 |
|  |  | 140 | Partition | .434 | 3303 | 3069 | 2847 | 2636 | 2434 | 2241 | 3391 | 2927 | 2519 | 2159 | 1841 | 1562 | 2.9 | 3.6 | 0.0 | -8.5 | -23.1 |
|  |  | 150 | Barnes-X | .488 | 3100 | 2901 | 2710 | 2527 | 2352 | 2183 | 3200 | 2802 | 2446 | 2127 | 1842 | 1588 | 3.3 | 4.0 | 0.0 | -9.4 | -25.3 |
|  |  | 154 | Pt-Ex | .433 | 3260 | 3028 | 2807 | 2597 | 2397 | 2206 | 3634 | 3134 | 2694 | 2307 | 1964 | 1663 | 3.0 | 3.7 | 0.0 | -8.8 | -23.8 |
|  |  | 160 | Partition | .475 | 3200 | 2991 | 2791 | 2600 | 2417 | 2241 | 3638 | 3177 | 2767 | 2401 | 2075 | 1784 | 3.1 | 3.8 | 0.0 | -8.9 | -23.8 |
| B |  | 175 | Pt-Ex | .462 | 3070 | 2861 | 2662 | 2471 | 2288 | 2113 | 3662 | 3181 | 2753 | 2373 | 2034 | 1735 | 3.5 | 4.2 | 0.0 | -9.9 | -26.5 |
| M | .300 Wby. | 150 | Pt-Ex | .338 | 3600 | 3286 | 2980 | 2700 | 2435 | 2189 | 4316 | 3588 | 2960 | 2423 | 1975 | 1589 | 2.4 | 3.2 | 0.0 | -8.02 | -21.7 |
|  |  | 150 | Partition | .387 | 3600 | 3319 | 3057 | 2809 | 2575 | 2352 | 4316 | 3669 | 3111 | 2628 | 2208 | 1843 | 2.3 | 3.0 | 0.0 | -7.5 | -20.1 |
|  |  | 165 | Pt-Ex | .387 | 3450 | 3185 | 2929 | 2690 | 2450 | 2230 | 4361 | 3700 | 3123 | 2630 | 2186 | 1820 | 2.67 | 3.38 | 0.0 | -8.27 | -22.2 |
| B |  | 180 | Pt-Ex | .425 | 3300 | 3061 | 2835 | 2620 | 2415 | 2219 | 4352 | 3745 | 3212 | 2743 | 2331 | 1968 | 2.9 | 3.6 | 0.0 | -8.6 | -23.3 |
|  |  | 180 | Barnes-X | .511 | 3250 | 3053 | 2864 | 2683 | 2510 | 2343 | 4221 | 3724 | 3278 | 2878 | 2518 | 2193 | 2.9 | 3.6 | 0.0 | -8.4 | -22.2 |
|  |  | 180 | Partition | .474 | 3300 | 3085 | 2881 | 2686 | 2499 | 2319 | 4352 | 3804 | 3317 | 2882 | 2495 | 2149 | 2.8 | 3.5 | 0.0 | -8.4 | -22.2 |
|  |  | 220 | Rn-Ex | .300 | 2905 | 2599 | 2312 | 2045 | 1795 | 1570 | 4122 | 3299 | 2612 | 2042 | 1574 | 1205 | 4.6 | 5.6 | 0.0 | -13.9 | -39.0 |
| B | .340 Wby. | 200 | Pt-Ex | .361 | 3260 | 2983 | 2722 | 2476 | 2244 | 2023 | 4719 | 3951 | 3291 | 2723 | 2235 | 1818 | 3.2 | 3.9 | 0.0 | -9.6 | -26.2 |
|  |  | 210 | Partition | .400 | 3250 | 3000 | 2763 | 2538 | 2325 | 2122 | 4925 | 4195 | 3559 | 3004 | 2520 | 2099 | 3.1 | 3.8 | 0.0 | -9.2 | -25.0 |
|  |  | 225 | Pt-Ex | .307 | 3105 | 2792 | 2500 | 2226 | 1969 | 1732 | 4816 | 3894 | 3122 | 2475 | 1938 | 1499 | 3.9 | 4.7 | 0.0 | -11.8 | -32.6 |
|  |  | 225 | Barnes | .482 | 3040 | 2841 | 2651 | 2468 | 2293 | 2125 | 4617 | 4032 | 3510 | 3043 | 2626 | 2255 | 3.5 | 4.2 | 0.0 | -9.9 | -26.6 |
|  |  | 250 | Pt-Ex | .431 | 3002 | 2780 | 2570 | 2378 | 2189 | 2008 | 5002 | 4283 | 3650 | 3900 | 2625 | 2200 | 3.8 | 4.5 | 0.0 | -10.6 | -28.7 |
|  |  | 250 | Partition | .473 | 2980 | 2780 | 2589 | 2405 | 2229 | 2061 | 4929 | 4290 | 3720 | 3211 | 2759 | 2358 | 3.7 | 4.4 | 0.0 | -10.5 | -28.1 |
| MB | .30-378 Wby. | 180 | Barnes-X | .511 | 3450 | 3243 | 3046 | 2858 | 2678 | 2504 | 4757 | 4204 | 3709 | 3264 | 2865 | 2506 | 2.4 | 3.1 | 0.0 | -7.4 | -19.6 |
|  |  |  |  |  |  |  |  |  |  |  |  |  |  |  |  |  | 4.3 | 6.8 | 5.6 | 0.0 | -10.3 |
| B | .378 Wby. | 270 | Pt-Ex | .380 | 3180 | 2921 | 2677 | 2445 | 2225 | 2017 | 6062 | 5115 | 4295 | 3583 | 2968 | 2438 | 1.3 | 0.0 | -6.1 | -18.1 | -37.1 |
|  |  | 270 | Barnes-X | .503 | 3150 | 2954 | 2767 | 2587 | 2415 | 2249 | 5948 | 5232 | 4589 | 4013 | 3495 | 3031 | 1.2 | 0.0 | -5.8 | -16.7 | -33.7 |
|  |  | 300 | Rn-Ex | .250 | 2925 | 2558 | 2220 | 1908 | 1627 | 1383 | 5699 | 4360 | 3283 | 2424 | 1764 | 1274 | 1.9 | 0.0 | -9.0 | -27.8 | -60.0 |
|  |  | 300 | FMJ | .275 | 2925 | 2591 | 2280 | 1991 | 1725 | 1489 | 5699 | 4470 | 3461 | 2640 | 1983 | 1476 | 1.8 | 0.0 | -8.6 | -26.1 | -55.4 |
| A | .416 Wby. | 350 | Barnes-X | .521 | 2850 | 2673 | 2503 | 2340 | 2182 | 2031 | 6312 | 5553 | 4870 | 4253 | 3700 | 3204 | 1.7 | 0.0 | -7.2 | -20.9 | -41.8 |
|  |  | 400 | Swift A | .391 | 2650 | 2426 | 2213 | 2011 | 1820 | 1644 | 6237 | 5227 | 4350 | 3592 | 2941 | 2399 | 2.2 | 0.0 | -9.3 | -27.1 | -56.0 |
|  |  | 400 | Rn-Ex | .311 | 2700 | 2417 | 2152 | 1903 | 1676 | 1470 | 6474 | 5189 | 4113 | 3216 | 2493 | 1918 | 2.3 | 0.0 | -9.7 | -29.3 | -61.2 |
|  |  | 400 | **Mono | .304 | 2700 | 2411 | 2140 | 1887 | 1656 | 1448 | 6474 | 5162 | 4068 | 3161 | 2435 | 1861 | 2.3 | 0.0 | -9.8 | -29.7 | -62.1 |
| A | .460 Wby. | 450 | Barnes-X | .488 | 2700 | 2518 | 2343 | 2175 | 2013 | 1859 | 7284 | 6333 | 5482 | 4725 | 4050 | 3452 | 2.0 | 0.0 | -8.4 | -24.1 | -48.2 |
|  |  | 500 | RNSP | .287 | 2600 | 2301 | 2022 | 1764 | 1533 | 1333 | 7504 | 5877 | 4539 | 3456 | 2608 | 1972 | 2.6 | 0.0 | -11.1 | -33.5 | -71.1 |
|  |  | 500 | FMJ | .295 | 2600 | 2309 | 2037 | 1784 | 1557 | 1357 | 7504 | 5917 | 4605 | 3534 | 2690 | 2046 | 2.5 | 0.0 | -10.9 | -33.0 | -69.6 |
| M | .270 WIN | 130 | Barnes-X | .428 | 3100 | 2873 | 2658 | 2453 | 2257 | 2072 | 2774 | 2383 | 2039 | 1736 | 1470 | 1236 | 3.5 | 4.2 | 0.0 | -10.0 | -26.9 |
| M | .30-06 | 150 | Barnes-X | .386 | 2980 | 2736 | 2505 | 2285 | 2077 | 1879 | 2958 | 2493 | 2090 | 1740 | 1437 | 1176 | 3.9 | 4.7 | 0.0 | -11.5 | -30.8 |
| MB | 7MM REM MAG | 150 | Barnes-X | .488 | 3040 | 2843 | 2655 | 2475 | 2301 | 2135 | 3078 | 2692 | 2348 | 2040 | 1764 | 1518 | 3.5 | 4.2 | 0.0 | -9.9 | -26.5 |
| MB | .300 WIN MAG | 180 | Barnes-X | .511 | 3070 | 2881 | 2699 | 2525 | 2357 | 2196 | 3767 | 3316 | 2912 | 2548 | 2221 | 1928 | 3.4 | 4.1 | 0.0 | -9.5 | -25.4 |
| B | .338 WIN. MAG | 225 | Barnes-X | .482 | 2750 | 2563 | 2384 | 2213 | 2048 | 1890 | 3778 | 3283 | 2840 | 2446 | 2095 | 1784 | 4.6 | 5.4 | 0.0 | -12.5 | -33.0 |
|  |  |  |  |  |  |  |  |  |  |  |  |  |  |  |  |  | 1.9 | 0.0 | -8.1 | -23.2 | -46.4 |
| BA | .375 H&H MAG. | 270 | Barnes-X | .503 | 2750 | 2571 | 2399 | 2234 | 2075 | 1922 | 4533 | 3963 | 3450 | 2991 | 2581 | 2215 | 4.5 | 5.3 | 0.0 | -12.3 | -32.4 |
|  |  |  |  |  |  |  |  |  |  |  |  |  |  |  |  |  | 1.9 | 0.0 | -8.0 | -22.9 | -45.7 |

**LEGEND:** PT-EX = Pointed Expanding    Rn-Ex = Round Nose-Expanding    FMJ = Full Metal Jacket    A = Divided Lead Cavity or "H" Type    Barnes = Barnes "X" Flat Base

**NOTE:** These tables were calculated by computer using a standard modern scientific technique to predict trajectories and recoil energies from the best available data for each cartridge. The figures shown are expected to be reasonably accurate of ammunition behavior under standard conditions. However, the shooter is cautioned that performance will vary because of variations in rifles, ammunition, atmospheric conditions and altitude.

**USAGE:** V-Varmint    M-Medium Game (Deer, Sheep, Pronghorn, Black Bear)    B-Big Game (Elk, Moose, Grizzly)    A-African Big Game (Elephant, Cape Buffalo, Rhino, Lion)

# WINCHESTER BALLISTICS

## CENTERFIRE PISTOL/REVOLVER

### SUPREME®

| Cartridge | Symbol | Bullet Wt. Grs. | Type | User Guide | Velocity (fps) Muzzle | 50 Yds. | 100 Yds. | Energy (ft-lbs.) Muzzle | 50 Yds. | 100 Yds. | Mid Range Traj. (In.) 50 Yds. | 100 Yds. | Barrel Length In. |
|---|---|---|---|---|---|---|---|---|---|---|---|---|---|
| 380 Automatic SXT® | S380 | 95 | SXT | PP | 955 | 889 | 835 | 192 | 167 | 147 | 1.3 | 5.5 | 3-3/4 |
| 38 Special + P # SXT | S38SP | 130 | SXT | PP | 925 | 887 | 852 | 247 | 227 | 210 | 1.3 | 5.5 | 4V |
| 9mm Luger SXT | S9 | 147 | SXT | PP | 990 | 947 | 909 | 320 | 293 | 270 | 1.2 | 4.8 | 4 |
| 40 Smith & Wesson SXT | S401 | 165 | SXT | PP | 1110 | 1020 | 960 | 443 | 381 | 338 | 1.0 | 4.2 | 4 |
| 40 Smith & Wesson SXT | S40 | 180 | SXT | PP | 1015 | 959 | 912 | 412 | 367 | 333 | 1.1 | 4.7 | 4 |
| 45 Automatic SXT | S45 | 230 | SXT | PP | 880 | 846 | 816 | 396 | 366 | 340 | 1.5 | 6.1 | 5 |
| NEW 357 Magnum # Partition Gold™ | S357P | 180 | Partition Gold™ | H | 1180 | 1088 | 1020 | 557 | 473 | 416 | 0.8 | 3.6 | 8V |
| NEW 44 Magnum # Partition Gold™ | S44MP | 250 | Partition Gold™ | H | 1230 | 1132 | 1057 | 840 | 711 | 620 | 0.8 | 2.9 | 6.5V |

### SUPER-X®

| Cartridge | Symbol | Bullet Wt. Grs. | Type | User Guide | Velocity (fps) Muzzle | 50 Yds. | 100 Yds. | Energy (ft-lbs.) Muzzle | 50 Yds. | 100 Yds. | Mid Range Traj. (In.) 50 Yds. | 100 Yds. | Barrel Length In. |
|---|---|---|---|---|---|---|---|---|---|---|---|---|---|
| 25 Automatic | X25AXP | 45 | Expanding Point** | PP | 815 | 729 | 655 | 66 | 53 | 42 | 1.8 | 7.7 | 2 |
| 25 Automatic | X25AP | 50 | Full Metal Jacket | T | 760 | 707 | 659 | 64 | 56 | 48 | 2.0 | 8.7 | 2 |
| 30 Luger (7.65mm) | X30LP | 93 | Full Metal Jacket | T | 1220 | 1110 | 1040 | 305 | 255 | 225 | 0.9 | 3.5 | 4-1/2 |
| 30 Carbine | X30M1 | 110 | Hollow Soft Point | H | 1790 | 1601 | 1430 | 783 | 626 | 500 | 0.4 | 1.7 | 10 |
| 32 Smith & Wesson | X32SWP | 85 | Lead-Round Nose | T | 680 | 645 | 610 | 90 | 81 | 73 | 2.5 | 10.5 | 3 |
| 32 Smith & Wesson Long | X32SWLP | 98 | Lead-Round Nose | T | 705 | 670 | 635 | 115 | 98 | 88 | 2.3 | 10.5 | 4 |
| 32 Short Colt | X32SCP | 80 | Lead-Round Nose | T | 745 | 665 | 590 | 100 | 79 | 62 | 2.2 | 9.9 | 4 |
| 32 Automatic | X32ASHP | 60 | Silvertip® Hollow Point | PP | 970 | 895 | 835 | 125 | 107 | 93 | 1.3 | 5.4 | 4 |
| 32 Automatic | X32AP | 71 | Full Metal Jacket | T | 905 | 855 | 810 | 129 | 115 | 97 | 1.4 | 5.8 | 4 |
| 38 Smith & Wesson | X38SWP | 145 | Lead-Round Nose | T | 685 | 650 | 620 | 150 | 135 | 125 | 2.4 | 10.0 | 4 |
| 380 Automatic | X380ASHP | 85 | Silvertip Hollow Point | PP | 1000 | 921 | 860 | 189 | 160 | 140 | 1.2 | 5.1 | 3-3/4 |
| 380 Automatic | X380AP | 95 | Full Metal Jacket | T | 955 | 865 | 785 | 190 | 160 | 130 | 1.4 | 5.9 | 3-3/4 |
| 38 Special | X38S9HP | 110 | Silvertip Hollow Point | PP | 945 | 894 | 850 | 218 | 195 | 176 | 1.3 | 5.4 | 4V |
| 38 Special Super Unleaded™ | X38SSU | 130 | Full Metal Jacket Encapsulated | T | 775 | 743 | 712 | 173 | 159 | 146 | 1.9 | 7.9 | 4V |
| 38 Special Super Match® | X38SMRP | 148 | Lead-Wad Cutter | T | 710 | 634 | 566 | 166 | 132 | 105 | 2.4 | 10.8 | 4V |
| 38 Special | X38S1P | 158 | Lead-Round Nose | T | 755 | 723 | 693 | 200 | 183 | 168 | 2.0 | 8.3 | 4V |
| 38 Special | X38WCPSV | 158 | Lead-Semi Wad Cutter | T | 755 | 721 | 689 | 200 | 182 | 167 | 2.0 | 8.4 | 4V |
| 38 Special + P | X38SSHP | 95 | Silvertip Hollow Point | PP | 1100 | 1002 | 932 | 255 | 212 | 183 | 1.0 | 4.3 | 4V |
| 38 Special + P # | X38S6PH | 110 | Jacketed Hollow Point | PP | 995 | 926 | 871 | 242 | 210 | 185 | 1.2 | 5.1 | 4V |
| 38 Special + P # | X38S7PH | 125 | Jacketed Hollow Point | PP | 945 | 898 | 858 | 248 | 224 | 204 | 1.3 | 5.4 | 4V |
| 38 Special + P # | X38S8HP | 125 | Silvertip Hollow Point | PP | 945 | 898 | 858 | 248 | 224 | 204 | 1.3 | 5.4 | 4V |
| 38 Special + P Subsonic® | XSUB38S | 147 | Jacketed Hollow Point | PP | 860 | 830 | 802 | 241 | 225 | 210 | 1.5 | 6.3 | 4V |
| 38 Special +P Super Unleaded | X38SSU1 | 158 | Full Metal Jacket-Encapsulated | T | 890 | 864 | 839 | 278 | 262 | 249 | 1.4 | 5.8 | 4V |
| 38 Special + P | X38SPD | 158 | Lead-Semi Wad Cutter Hollow Point | PP | 890 | 855 | 823 | 278 | 257 | 238 | 1.4 | 6.0 | 4V |
| 38 Special + P | X38WCP | 158 | Lead-Semi Wad Cutter | T | 890 | 855 | 823 | 278 | 257 | 238 | 1.4 | 6.0 | 4V |
| 9mm Luger Super Unleaded | X9MMSU | 115 | Full Metal Jacket Encapsulated | T | 1155 | 1047 | 971 | 341 | 280 | 241 | 0.9 | 3.9 | 4 |
| 9mm Luger | X9LP | 115 | Full Metal Jacket | T | 1155 | 1047 | 971 | 341 | 280 | 241 | 0.9 | 3.9 | 4 |
| 9mm Luger | X9MMSHP | 115 | Silvertip Hollow Point | PP | 1225 | 1095 | 1007 | 383 | 306 | 259 | 0.8 | 3.6 | 4 |
| 9mm Luger Super Unleaded | X9MMSU2 | 147 | Full Metal Jacket-Encapsulated | T | 990 | 945 | 907 | 320 | 292 | 268 | 1.2 | 4.8 | 4 |
| 9mm Luger Subsonic | XSUB9MM | 147 | Jacketed Hollow Point | PP | 990 | 945 | 907 | 320 | 292 | 268 | 1.2 | 4.8 | 4 |
| 9mm Luger | X9MMST147 | 147 | Silvertip Hollow Point | PP | 1010 | 962 | 921 | 333 | 302 | 277 | 1.1 | 4.7 | 4 |
| 9mm Luger Super Match | X9MMTCM | 147 | Full Metal Jacket-Truncated Cone-Match | T | 990 | 945 | 907 | 320 | 292 | 268 | 1.2 | 4.8 | 4 |
| 38 Super Automatic + P* | X38ASHP | 125 | Silvertip Hollow Point | T/PP | 1240 | 1130 | 1050 | 427 | 354 | 306 | 0.8 | 3.4 | 5 |
| 38 Super Automatic + P* | X38A1P | 130 | Full Metal Jacket | T | 1215 | 1099 | 1017 | 426 | 348 | 298 | 0.8 | 3.6 | 5 |
| NEW 9 X 23 Winchester | X923W | 125 | Silvertip Hollow Point | T/PP | 1450 | 1249 | 1103 | 583 | 433 | 338 | 0.6 | 2.8 | 5 |
| 357 Magnum # | X3573P | 110 | Jacketed Hollow Point | PP | 1295 | 1095 | 975 | 410 | 292 | 232 | 0.8 | 3.5 | 4V |
| 357 Magnum # | X3576P | 125 | Jacketed Hollow Point | PP | 1450 | 1240 | 1090 | 583 | 427 | 330 | 0.6 | 2.8 | 4V |
| 357 Magnum # | X357SHP | 145 | Silvertip Hollow Point | PP | 1290 | 1155 | 1060 | 535 | 428 | 361 | 0.8 | 3.5 | 4V |
| 357 Magnum | X3571P | 158 | Lead-Semi Wad Cutter** | T | 1235 | 1104 | 1015 | 535 | 428 | 361 | 0.8 | 3.5 | 4V |
| 357 Magnum # | X3574P | 158 | Jacketed Hollow Point | H/PP | 1235 | 1104 | 1015 | 535 | 428 | 361 | 0.8 | 3.5 | 4V |
| 357 Magnum # | X3575P | 158 | Jacketed Soft Point | H/PP | 1235 | 1104 | 1015 | 535 | 428 | 361 | 0.8 | 3.5 | 4V |
| 40 Smith & Wesson | X40SWSTHP | 155 | Silvertip Hollow Point | PP | 1205 | 1096 | 1018 | 500 | 414 | 357 | 0.8 | 3.6 | 4 |
| 40 Smith & Wesson Super Match | X40SWTCM | 155 | Full Metal Jacket-Truncated Cone-Match | T | 1125 | 1046 | 986 | 436 | 377 | 335 | 0.9 | 3.9 | 4 |
| 40 Smith & Wesson Super Unleaded | X40SWSU1 | 165 | Full Metal Jacket-Encapsulated | T | 1110 | 1020 | 960 | 443 | 381 | 338 | 1.0 | 4.2 | 4 |
| 40 Smith & Wesson Super Unleaded | X40SWSU | 180 | Full Metal Jacket-Encapsulated | T | 990 | 933 | 886 | 392 | 348 | 314 | 1.2 | 5.0 | 4 |
| 40 Smith & Wesson Subsonic | XSUB40SW | 180 | Jacketed Hollow Point | PP | 1010 | 954 | 909 | 408 | 364 | 330 | 1.1 | 4.8 | 4 |
| 10mm Automatic | X10MMSTHP | 175 | Silvertip Hollow Point | PP | 1290 | 1141 | 1037 | 649 | 506 | 418 | 0.7 | 3.3 | 5-1/2 |
| 10mm Automatic Subsonic | XSUB10MM | 180 | Jacketed Hollow Point | PP | 990 | 936 | 891 | 390 | 350 | 317 | 1.2 | 4.9 | 5 |
| 41 Remington Magnum # | X41MSTHP2 | 175 | Silvertip Hollow Point | H/PP | 1250 | 1120 | 1029 | 607 | 488 | 412 | 0.8 | 3.4 | 4V |
| 41 Remington Magnum # | X41MHP2 | 210 | Jacketed Hollow Point | H | 1300 | 1162 | 1062 | 788 | 630 | 526 | 0.7 | 3.2 | 4V |
| 44 Smith & Wesson Special # | X44STHPS2 | 200 | Silvertip Hollow Point | PP | 900 | 860 | 822 | 360 | 328 | 300 | 1.4 | 5.9 | 6-1/2 |
| 44 Smith & Wesson Special | X44SP | 246 | Lead-Round Nose | T | 755 | 725 | 695 | 310 | 285 | 265 | 2.0 | 8.3 | 6-1/2 |
| 44 Remington Magnum # | X44MS | 210 | Silvertip Hollow Point | H/PP | 1250 | 1106 | 1010 | 729 | 570 | 475 | 0.8 | 3.5 | 4V |
| 44 Remington Magnum # | X44MHSP2 | 240 | Hollow Soft Point | H | 1180 | 1081 | 1010 | 741 | 623 | 543 | 0.9 | 3.7 | 4V |
| 45 Automatic | X45ASHP2 | 185 | Silvertip Hollow Point | PP | 1000 | 938 | 888 | 411 | 362 | 324 | 1.2 | 4.9 | 5 |
| 45 Automatic Super Match | X45AWCP | 185 | Full Metal Jacket - Semi Wad Cutter | T | 770 | 707 | 650 | 244 | 205 | 174 | 2.0 | 8.7 | 5 |
| 45 Automatic Super Unleaded | X45ASU | 230 | Full Metal Jacket - Encapsulated | T | 835 | 800 | 767 | 356 | 326 | 300 | 1.6 | 6.8 | 5 |
| 45 Automatic Subsonic | XSUB45A | 230 | Jacketed Hollow Point | PP | 880 | 842 | 808 | 396 | 363 | 334 | 1.5 | 6.1 | 5 |
| 45 Automatic | X45A1P2 | 230 | Full Metal Jacket | T | 835 | 800 | 767 | 356 | 326 | 300 | 1.6 | 6.8 | 5 |
| 45 Colt # | X45CSHP2 | 225 | Silvertip Hollow Point | PP | 920 | 877 | 839 | 423 | 384 | 352 | 1.4 | 5.6 | 5-1/2 |
| 45 Colt | X45CP2 | 255 | Lead-Round Nose | T | 860 | 820 | 780 | 420 | 380 | 345 | 1.5 | 6.1 | 5-1/2 |
| 45 Winchester Magnum # | X45WMA | 260 | Full Metal Jacket | H | 1250 | 1137 | 1053 | 902 | 746 | 640 | 0.8 | 3.3 | 5 |
| NEW 454 Casull® # | X454C1 | 260 | Jacketed Flat Point | H | 1800 | 1577 | 1381 | 1871 | 1436 | 1101 | 0.4 | 1.8 | 7.5V |
| NEW 454 Casull® # | X454C2 | 300 | Jacketed Flat Point | H | 1625 | 1451 | 1308 | 1759 | 1413 | 1141 | 0.5 | 2.0 | 7.5V |

### USER GUIDE

PP: PERSONAL PROTECTION

H: HUNTING

T: TARGET/RANGE

+P Ammunition with (+P) on the case head stamp is loaded to higher pressure. Use only in firearms designated for this cartridge and so recommended by the gun manufacturer.

V-Data is based on velocity obtained from vented test barrels for revolver cartridges (38 Special, 357 Magnum, 41 Rem. Mag. and 44 Rem. Mag.)
Specifications are nominal. Test barrels are used to determine ballistics figures. Individual firearms may differ from test barrel statistics.

# WINCHESTER RIFLE BALLISTICS

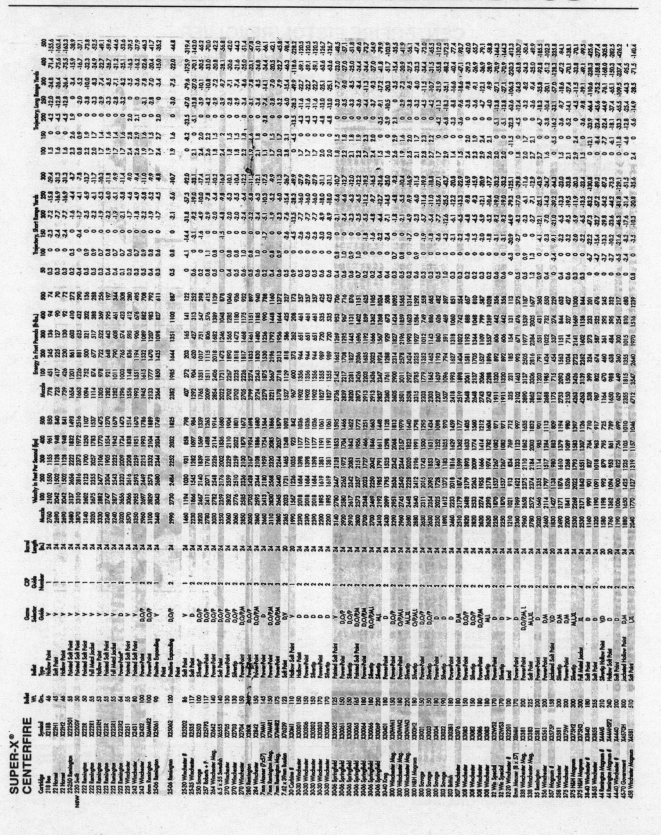

# Reloading

For addresses and phone/fax numbers of manufacturers and distributors included in this section, please turn to DIRECTORY OF MANUFACTURERS AND SUPPLIERS on page 554.

# HORNADY RIFLE BULLETS

## V-MAX BULLETS

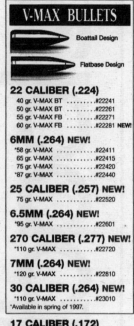

Boattail Design

Flatbase Design

### 22 CALIBER (.224)
40 gr. V-MAX BT ........#22241
50 gr. V-MAX BT ........#22261
55 gr. V-MAX FB ........#22271
60 gr. V-MAX FB ........#22281 NEW!

### 6MM (.264) NEW!
*58 gr. V-MAX ...........#22411
65 gr. V-MAX ...........#22415
75 gr. V-MAX ...........#22420
*87 gr. V-MAX ...........#22440

### 25 CALIBER (.257) NEW!
75 gr. V-MAX ...........#22520

### 6.5MM (.264) NEW!
*95 gr. V-MAX ...........#22601

### 270 CALIBER (.277) NEW!
*110 gr. V-MAX ..........#22720

### 7MM (.264) NEW!
*120 gr. V-MAX ..........#22810

### 30 CALIBER (.264) NEW!
*110 gr. V-MAX ..........#23010
*Available in spring of 1997.

### 17 CALIBER (.172)
25 gr. HP
#1710

### 22 CALIBER (.222)
40 gr. Jet
#2210

### 22 CALIBER (.223)
45 gr. Hornet
#2220

### 22 CALIBER (.224)

45 gr. Bee
#2229

45 gr. Hornet
#2230

50 gr. SXSP
#2240

50 gr. SP
#2245

55 gr. SXSP
#2260

55 gr. SP
#2265

55 gr. SP w/c
#2266

55 gr. FMJ-BT w/c
#2267

60 gr. SP
#2270

60 gr. HP
#2275

## MATCH BULLETS

### 22 CALIBER (.224)
52 gr. BTHP #2249

53 gr. HP #2250

68 gr. BTHP #2278 NEW!

75 gr. BTHP #2279 NEW!

### 22 CALIBER A-MAX (.224) NEW!
52 gr. A-MAX #22492*
75 gr. A-MAX #22792*

### 6MM A-MAX NEW!
105 gr. A-MAX #24562*

### 6.5MM BTHP
140 gr. BTHP #2633

### 6.5MM A-MAX NEW!
140 gr. A-MAX #26322

### 7MM
162 gr. A-MAX #28402

### 30 CALIBER BTHP
168 gr. BTHP    190 gr. BTHP
#30501        #3080
180 gr. BTHP
#30711

### 30 CALIBER A-MAX NEW!
150 gr. A-MAX    180 gr. A-MAX
#30312*         #30712*
168 gr. A-MAX
#30502*

### 50 CALIBER (.510)

**750 gr. A-MAX UHC #5165

*Available in spring of 1997.    **Packaged 20 per box.

### 22 CALIBER (.227)
70 gr. SP
#2280

### 6MM (.243)
70 gr. SP
#2410

70 gr. SXSP
#2415

75 gr. HP
#2420

## 6MM (.243)
80 gr. FMJ
#2430

80 gr. SP
Single Shot Pistol
#2435
InterLock

87 gr. SP
#2440

87 gr. BTHP
#2442

100 gr. SP
#2450
InterLock

100 gr. BTSP
#2453
InterLock

100 gr. RN
#2455
InterLock

## 25 CALIBER (.257)
60 gr. FP
#2510

75 gr. HP
#2520

87 gr. SP
#2530

100 gr. SP
#2540
InterLock

117 gr. RN
#2550
InterLock

117 gr. BTSP
#2552
InterLock

120 gr. HP
#2560
InterLock

## 6.5MM (.264)
100 gr. SP
#2610

129 gr. SP
#2620
InterLock

140 gr. SP
#2630
InterLock

160 gr. RN
#2640
InterLock

# HORNADY RIFLE BULLETS

## 270 CALIBER (.277)

100 gr. SP
#2710

110 gr. HP
#2720

130 gr. SP
#2730
InterLock

140 gr. BTSP
#2735
InterLock

150 gr. SP
#2740
InterLock

150 gr. RN
#2745
InterLock

## 7MM (.284)

100 gr. HP
#2800

120 gr. SP
#2810

120 gr. SP
Single Shot Pistol
#2811
InterLock

120 gr. HP
#2815

139 gr. SP
#2820
InterLock

139 gr. FP
#2822
InterLock

139 gr. BTSP
#2825
InterLock

154 gr. SP
#2830
InterLock

154 gr. RN
#2835
InterLock

162 gr. BTSP
#2845
InterLock

175 gr. SP
#2850
InterLock

175 gr. RN
#2855
InterLock

## 30 CALIBER (.308)

100 gr. SJ
#3005

110 gr. SP
#3010

110 gr. RN
#3015

110 gr. FMJ
#3017

130 gr. SP
#3020

130 gr. SP
Single Shot Pistol
#3021
InterLock

150 gr. SP
#3031
InterLock

150 gr. BTSP
#3033
InterLock

150 gr. RN (30-30)
#3035
InterLock

150 gr. FMJ-BT
#3037

165 gr. SP
#3040
InterLock

165 gr. BTSP
#3045
InterLock

170 gr. FP (30-30)
#3060
InterLock

180 gr. SP
#3070
InterLock

180 gr. BTSP
#3072
InterLock

180 gr. RN
#3075
InterLock

190 gr. BTSP
#3085
InterLock

220 gr. RN
#3090
InterLock

## 7.62 X 39 (.310)

123 gr. SP
#3140

123 gr. FMJ
#3147

## 303 CAL. AND 7.7 JAP (.312)

150 gr. SP
#3120
InterLock

174 gr. RN
#3130
InterLock

174 gr. FMJ-BT
#3131 NEW!

## 32 SPECIAL (.321)

170 gr. FP
#3210
InterLock

## 8MM (.323)

125 gr. SP
#3230

150 gr. SP
#3232
InterLock

170 gr. RN
#3235
InterLock

220 gr. SP
#3238
InterLock

## 338 CALIBER (.338)

200 gr. SP
#3310
InterLock

200 gr. FP
(33 Win)
#3315
InterLock

225 gr. SP
#3320
InterLock

250 gr. RN
#3330
InterLock

250 gr. SP
#3335
InterLock

## 348 CALIBER (.348)

200 gr. FP
#3410
InterLock

# HORNADY BULLETS

## RIFLE BULLETS

### 35 CALIBER (.358)

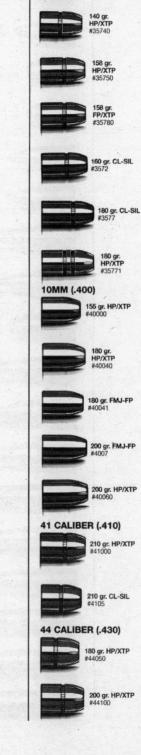

180 gr. SP
Single Shot Pistol
#3505
InterLock

200 gr. SP
#3510
InterLock

200 gr. RN
#3515
InterLock

### 375 CALIBER (.375)

220 gr. FP
(375 Win.)
#3705
InterLock

*270 gr. SP
#3710
InterLock

*270 gr. RN
#3715
InterLock

*300 gr. RN
#3720
InterLock

*300 gr. BTSP
#3725
InterLock

*300 gr. FMJ-RN
#3727

### 416 CALIBER (.416)

*400 gr. RN
#4165
InterLock

*400 gr. FMJ-RN
#4167

### 44 CALIBER (.430)

265 gr. FP
#4300
InterLock

### 45 CALIBER (.458)

*300 gr. HP
#4500

*350 gr. RN
#4502
InterLock

*500 gr. RN
#4504
InterLock

*500 gr. FMJ-RN
#4507

* Packed 50 per box. All others packed 100 per box.

## PISTOL BULLETS

### 25 CALIBER (.251)

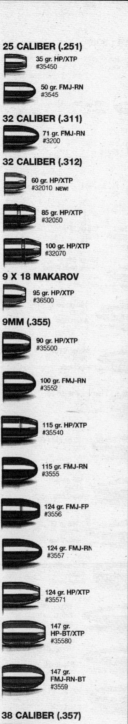

35 gr. HP/XTP
#35450

50 gr. FMJ-RN
#3545

### 32 CALIBER (.311)

71 gr. FMJ-RN
#3200

### 32 CALIBER (.312)

60 gr. HP/XTP
#32010 NEW!

85 gr. HP/XTP
#32050

100 gr. HP/XTP
#32070

### 9 X 18 MAKAROV

95 gr. HP/XTP
#36500

### 9MM (.355)

90 gr. HP/XTP
#35500

100 gr. FMJ-RN
#3552

115 gr. HP/XTP
#35540

115 gr. FMJ-RN
#3555

124 gr. FMJ-FP
#3556

124 gr. FMJ-RN
#3557

124 gr. HP/XTP
#35571

147 gr.
HP-BT/XTP
#35580

147 gr.
FMJ-RN-BT
#3559

### 38 CALIBER (.357)

110 gr.
HP/XTP
#35700

125 gr.
HP/XTP
#35710

125 gr.
FP/XTP
#35730

140 gr.
HP/XTP
#35740

158 gr.
HP/XTP
#35750

158 gr.
FP/XTP
#35780

160 gr. CL-SIL
#3572

180 gr. CL-SIL
#3577

180 gr.
HP/XTP
#35771

### 10MM (.400)

155 gr. HP/XTP
#40000

180 gr.
HP/XTP
#40040

180 gr. FMJ-FP
#40041

200 gr. FMJ-FP
#4007

200 gr. HP/XTP
#40060

### 41 CALIBER (.410)

210 gr. HP/XTP
#41000

210 gr. CL-SIL
#4105

### 44 CALIBER (.430)

180 gr. HP/XTP
#44050

200 gr. HP/XTP
#44100

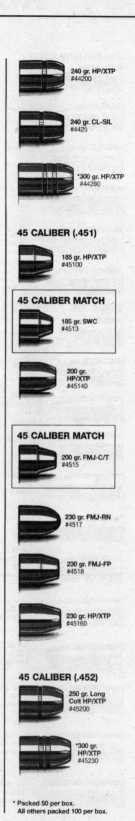

240 gr. HP/XTP
#44200

240 gr. CL-SIL
#4425

*300 gr. HP/XTP
#44280

### 45 CALIBER (.451)

185 gr. HP/XTP
#45100

### 45 CALIBER MATCH

185 gr. SWC
#4513

200 gr.
HP/XTP
#45140

### 45 CALIBER MATCH

200 gr. FMJ-C/T
#4515

230 gr. FMJ-RN
#4517

230 gr. FMJ-FP
#4518

230 gr. HP/XTP
#45160

### 45 CALIBER (.452)

250 gr. Long
Colt HP/XTP
#45200

*300 gr.
HP/XTP
#45230

* Packed 50 per box.
All others packed 100 per box.

# NOSLER BULLETS

## PISTOL AND REVOLVER BULLETS

| Cal. Dia. | HANDGUN Auto | BULLET WEIGHT AND STYLE | SECT. DENS. | BAL. COEF. | PART# |
|---|---|---|---|---|---|
| 9mm .355" | | 90 GR. HOLLOW POINT | .102 | .086 | 42050 |
| | | 115 GR. FULL METAL JACKET | .130 | .103 | 42059 |
| | | 115 GR. HOLLOW POINT 250 QUANTITY BULK PACK | .130 | .110 | 43009 44848 |
| 38 .357" | | 115 GR. HOLLOW POINT PRACTICAL PISTOL™ Formerly IPSC® | .129 | .110 | 44835 |
| | | 135 GR. PRACTICAL PISTOL™ Formerly IPSC® | .151 | .149 | 44836 |
| | | 150 GR. PRACTICAL PISTOL™ Formerly IPSC® | .168 | .157 | 44839 |
| 10mm .400" | | 135 GR. HOLLOW POINT 250 QUANTITY BULK PACK | .121 | .093 | 44838 44852 |
| | | 150 GR. HOLLOW POINT | .134 | .106 | 44849 |
| | | 170 GR. HOLLOW POINT | .152 | .137 | 44844 |
| | | 180 GR. HOLLOW POINT | .161 | .147 | 44837 |
| 45 .451" | | 185 GR. HOLLOW POINT 250 QUANTITY BULK PACK | .130 | .142 | 42062 44847 |
| | | 230 GR. FULL METAL JACKET | .162 | .183 | 42064 |

| Cal. Dia. | HANDGUN Revolver | BULLET WEIGHT AND STYLE | SECT. DENS. | BAL. COEF. | PART# |
|---|---|---|---|---|---|
| 38 .357" | | 125 GR. HOLLOW POINT 250 QUANTITY BULK PACK | .140 | .143 | 42055 44840 |
| | | 150 GR. SOFT POINT | .168 | .153 | 42056 |
| | | 158 GR. HOLLOW POINT 250 QUANTITY BULK PACK | .177 | .182 | 42057 44841 |
| | | 180 GR. SILHOUETTE 250 QUANTITY BULK PACK | .202 | .210 | 42058 44851 |
| 41 .410" | | 210 GR. HOLLOW POINT | .178 | .170 | 43012 |
| 44 .429" | | 200 GR. HOLLOW POINT 250 QUANTITY BULK PACK | .155 | .151 | 42060 44846 |
| | | 240 GR. HOLLOW POINT 250 QUANTITY BULK PACK | .186 | .173 | 42061 44842 |
| | | 240 GR. SOFT POINT | .186 | .177 | 42068 |
| | | 300 GR. HOLLOW POINT | .233 | .206 | 42069 |
| 45 Colt .451" | | 250 GR. HOLLOW POINT | .176 | .177 | 43013 |

# NOSLER BULLETS

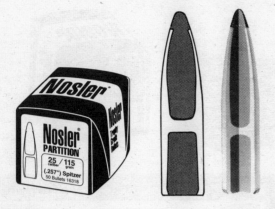

## Nosler Partition® Bullets

The Nosler Partition® bullet earned its reputation among professional guides and serious hunters for one reason: it doesn't fail. The patented Partition® design offers a dual core that is unequalled in mushrooming, weight retention and hydrostatic shock.

| Cal. Dia. | PARTITION® | BULLET WEIGHT AND STYLE | SECT. DENS. | BAL. COEF. | PART# |
|---|---|---|---|---|---|
| 270 .277" | | 130 GR. SPITZER | .242 | .416 | 16322 |
| | | 150 GR. SPITZER | .279 | .465 | 16323 |
| | | 160 GR. SEMI SPITZER | .298 | .434 | 16324 |
| 7mm .284" | | 140 GR. SPITZER | .248 | .434 | 16325 |
| | | 150 GR. SPITZER | .266 | .456 | 16326 |
| | | 160 GR. SPITZER | .283 | .475 | 16327 |
| | | 175 GR. SPITZER | .310 | .519 | 35645 |
| 30 .308" | | 150 GR. SPITZER | .226 | .387 | 16329 |
| | | 165 GR. SPITZER | .248 | .410 | 16330 |
| | | 170 GR. ROUND NOSE | .256 | .252 | 16333 |
| | | 180 GR. SPITZER | .271 | .474 | 16331 |
| | | 180 GR. PROTECTED POINT | .271 | .361 | 25396 |
| | | 200 GR. SPITZER | .301 | .481 | 35626 |
| | | 220 GR. SEMI SPITZER | .331 | .351 | 16332 |
| 8mm .323" | | 200 GR. SPITZER | .274 | .426 | 35277 |
| 338 .338" | | 210 GR. SPITZER | .263 | .400 | 16337 |
| | | 225 GR. SPITZER | .281 | .454 | 16336 |
| | | 250 GR. SPITZER | .313 | .473 | 35644 |
| 35 .358" | | 225 GR. SPITZER | .251 | .430 | 44800 |
| | | 250 GR. SPITZER | .279 | .446 | 44801 |
| 375 .375" | | 260 GR. SPITZER | .264 | .314 | 44850 |
| | | 300 GR. SPITZER | .305 | .398 | 44845 |

| Cal. Dia. | PARTITION® | BULLET WEIGHT AND STYLE | SECT. DENS. | BAL. COEF. | PART# |
|---|---|---|---|---|---|
| 6mm .243" | | 85 GR. SPITZER | .206 | .315 | 16314 |
| | | 95 GR. SPITZER | .230 | .365 | 16315 |
| | | 100 GR. SPITZER | .242 | .384 | 35642 |
| 25 .257" | | 100 GR. SPITZER | .216 | .377 | 16317 |
| | | 115 GR. SPITZER | .249 | .389 | 16318 |
| | | 120 GR. SPITZER | .260 | .391 | 35643 |
| 6.5mm .264" | | 125 GR. SPITZER | .256 | .449 | 16320 |
| | | 140 GR. SPITZER | .287 | .490 | 16321 |

# NOSLER BULLETS

## Nosler Ballistic Tip® Hunting Bullets

Nosler has replaced the familiar lead point of the Spitzer with a tough polycarbonate tip. The purpose of this new Ballistic Tip® is to resist deforming in the magazine and feed ramp of many rifles. The Solid Base® design produces controlled expansion for excellent mushrooming and exceptional accuracy.

| Cal. Dia. | SOLID BASE® BALLISTIC TIP® *Varmint* | BULLET WEIGHT AND STYLE | SECT. DENS. | BAL. COEF. | PART# |
|---|---|---|---|---|---|
| | | 40 GR. SPITZER (ORANGE TIP) | .114 | .221 | 39510 |
| *new* ➤ 22 .224" | | 45 GR. HORNET (SOFT LEAD TIP) | .128 | .144 | 35487 |
| | | 50 GR. SPITZER (ORANGE TIP) | .142 | .238 | 39522 |
| | | 55 GR. SPITZER (ORANGE TIP) | .157 | .267 | 39526 |
| *new* ➤ 6mm .243" | | 55 GR. SPITZER (PURPLE TIP) | .133 | .220 | 24055 |
| | | 70 GR. SPITZER (PURPLE TIP) | .169 | .310 | 39532 |
| 25 .257" | | 85 GR. SPITZER (BLUE TIP) | .183 | .331 | 43004 |

| Cal. Dia. | SOLID BASE® BALLISTIC TIP® *Hunting* | BULLET WEIGHT AND STYLE | SECT. DENS. | BAL. COEF. | PART# |
|---|---|---|---|---|---|
| 6mm .243" | | 95 GR. SPITZER (PURPLE TIP) | .230 | .379 | 24095 |
| 25 .257" | | 100 GR. SPITZER (BLUE TIP) | .216 | .393 | 25100 |
| 6.5mm .264" | | 100 GR. SPITZER (BROWN TIP) | .205 | .350 | 26100 |
| | | 120 GR. SPITZER (BROWN TIP) | .246 | .458 | 26120 |
| 270 .277" | | 130 GR. SPITZER (YELLOW TIP) | .242 | .433 | 27130 |
| | | 140 GR. SPITZER (YELLOW TIP) | .261 | .456 | 27140 |
| | | 150 GR. SPITZER (YELLOW TIP) | .279 | .496 | 27150 |
| *new* ➤ | | 120 GR. FLAT POINT (SOFT LEAD TIP) | .213 | .195 | 28121 |
| 7mm .284" | | 120 GR. SPITZER (RED TIP) | .213 | .417 | 28120 |
| | | 140 GR. SPITZER (RED TIP) | .248 | .485 | 28140 |
| | | 150 GR. SPITZER (RED TIP) | .266 | .493 | 28150 |
| 30 .308" | | 125 GR. SPITZER (GREEN TIP) | .188 | .366 | 30125 |
| | | 150 GR. SPITZER (GREEN TIP) | .226 | .435 | 30150 |
| | | 165 GR. SPITZER (GREEN TIP) | .248 | .475 | 30165 |
| | | 180 GR. SPITZER (GREEN TIP) | .271 | .507 | 30180 |
| 338 .338" | | 200 GR. SPITZER (MAROON TIP) | .250 | .414 | 33200 |

Also available:
25 caliber 150 grain
338 caliber 180 grain
35 caliber 225 grain (Whelen)

# SAKO BULLETS

## PISTOL AND REVOLVER BULLETS

**WC (Wad Cutter)**
An accurate, highly popular bullet for target shooting that makes a hole that is easy to interpret. Low recoil.

**SWC (Semi Wad Cutter)**
Has greater speed and energy than the WC. Also intended for target shooting.

**FMJ (Full Metal Jacket)**
Good penetration and excellent feeding characteristics with semiautomatic weapons.

**KPO**
Contact-opening special bullet with jacket reliability when feeding from magazine. Electrolytic core will not separate

**SPEEDHEAD FMJ**
Intended chiefly for shooting game, the full-metal-jacket bullet is characterized by high accuracy.

**SP (Soft Point)**
Sako's semijacketed soft-point bullet is the most popular type of bullet for hunting. On hitting the prey the bullet spreads rapidly, immediately producing a fatal shock effect.

**HP (Hollow Point)**
The ballistic characteristics of the hollow-point bullet make it the ideal choice for target shooting. This bullet is also fast, making it well suited to varmint shooting.

**HAMMERHEAD**
The Sako Hammerhead is a heavy, lead-tipped bullet especially designed for moose hunting and other big game.

## RIFLE BULLETS

**SUPER HAMMERHEAD**
The famous Hammerhead is designed in a light version for long-range hunting with better ballistic characteristics.

**POWERHEAD (Hollow Point Copper)**
An all-copper opening hollow-point bullet for big-game hunting without fear of core separation.

SP P = Soft Point Pointed
SP SP = Soft Point SemiPointed
SP RN = Soft Point Round Nose
SP FP = Soft Point Flat Point
HP = Hollow Point
HP BT = Hollow Point Boat Tail
HAMMERHEAD = Soft Point Bonded Core
SUPER HH = Hollow Point Bonded Core
POWERHEAD = Hollow Point Solid Copper

# SIERRA BULLETS

## RIFLE BULLETS

### .22 Caliber Hornet
**(.223/5.66MM Diameter)**

40 gr. Hornet
Varminter #1100

45 gr. Hornet
Varminter #1110

### .22 Caliber Hornet
**(.224/5.69MM Diameter)**

40 gr. Hornet
Varminter #1200

45 gr. Hornet
Varminter #1210

### .22 Caliber
**(.224/5.69MM Diameter)**

40 gr. HP
Varminter #1385

45 gr. SMP
Varminter #1300

45 gr. SPT
Varminter #1310

50 gr. SMP
Varminter #1320

50 gr. SPT
Varminter #1330

50 gr. Blitz
Varminter #1340

52 gr. HPBT
MatchKing #1410

53 gr. HP
MatchKing #1400

55 gr. Blitz
Varminter #1345

55 gr. SMP
Varminter #1350

55 gr. FMJBT
GameKing #1355

55 gr. SPT
Varminter #1360

55 gr. SBT
GameKing #1365

55 gr. HPBT
GameKing #1390

60 gr. HP
Varminter #1375

63 gr. SMP
Varminter #1370

69 gr. HPBT
MatchKing #1380
*7"-10" TWST BBLS*

### 6MM .243 Caliber
**(.243/6.17MM Diameter)**

60 gr. HP
Varminter #1500

70 gr. HPBT
MatchKing #1505

75 gr. HP
Varminter #1510

**80 gr. Blitz
Varminter #1515**

85 gr. SPT
Varminter #1520

85 gr. HPBT
GameKing #1530

90 gr. FMJBT
GameKing #1535

100 gr. SPT
Pro-Hunter #1540

100 gr. SMP
Pro-Hunter #1550

100 gr. SBT
GameKing #1560

107 gr. HPBT
MatchKing #1570
*7"-8" TWST BBLS*

### .25 Caliber
**(.257/6.53MM Diameter)**

75 gr. HP
Varminter #1600

87 gr. SPT
Varminter #1610

90 gr. HPBT
GameKing #1615

100 gr. SPT
Pro-Hunter #1620

100 gr. SBT
GameKing #1625

117 gr. SBT
GameKing #1630

117 gr. SPT
Pro-Hunter #1640

120 gr. HPBT
GameKing #1650

### 6.5MM .264 Caliber
**(.264/6.71MM Diameter)**

85 gr. HP
Varminter #1700

100 gr. HP
Varminter #1710

120 gr. SPT
Pro-Hunter #1720

120 gr. HPBT
MatchKing #1725

### 6.5MM .264 Caliber (cont.)
**(.264/6.71MM Diameter)**

140 gr. SBT
GameKing #1730

140 gr. HPBT
MatchKing #1740

160 gr. SMP
Pro-Hunter #1750

### .270 Caliber
**(.277/7.04MM Diameter)**

90 gr. HP
Varminter #1800

110 gr. SPT
Pro-Hunter #1810

130 gr. SBT
GameKing #1820

130 gr. SPT
Pro-Hunter #1830

**135 gr. HPBT
MatchKing #1833**

140 gr. HPBT
GameKing #1835

140 gr. SBT
GameKing #1845

150 gr. SBT
GameKing #1840

150 gr. RN
Pro-Hunter #1850

### 7MM .284 Caliber
**(.284/7.21MM Diameter)**

100 gr. HP
Varminter #1895

120 gr. SPT
Pro-Hunter #1900

140 gr. SBT
GameKing #1905

140 gr. SPT
Pro-Hunter #1910

150 gr. SBT
GameKing #1913

150 gr. HPBT
MatchKing #1915

160 gr. SBT
GameKing #1920

160 gr. HPBT
GameKing #1925

168 gr. HPBT
MatchKing #1930

170 gr. RN
Pro-Hunter #1950

175 gr. SBT
GameKing #1940

# SIERRA BULLETS

## RIFLE BULLETS

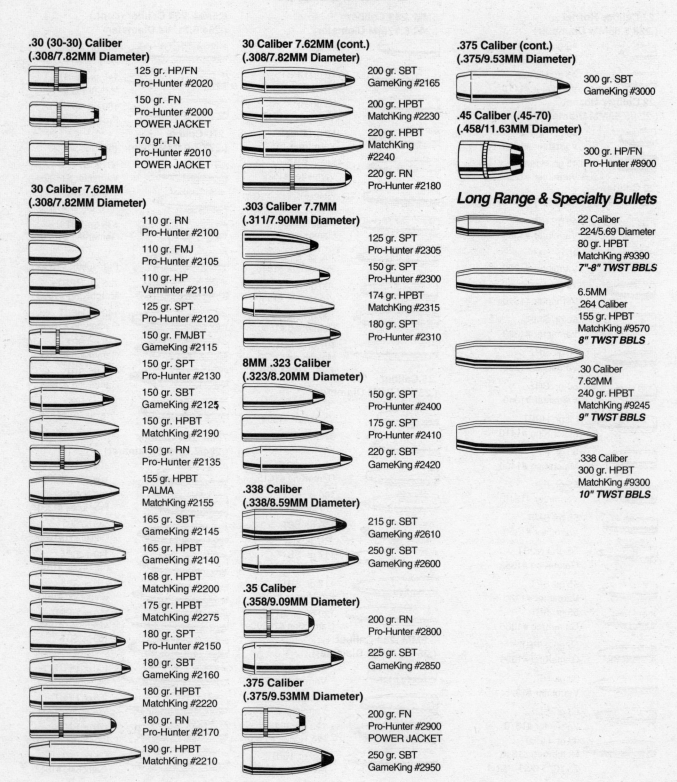

**.30 (30-30) Caliber (.308/7.82MM Diameter)**

125 gr. HP/FN
Pro-Hunter #2020

150 gr. FN
Pro-Hunter #2000
POWER JACKET

170 gr. FN
Pro-Hunter #2010
POWER JACKET

**30 Caliber 7.62MM (.308/7.82MM Diameter)**

110 gr. RN
Pro-Hunter #2100

110 gr. FMJ
Pro-Hunter #2105

110 gr. HP
Varminter #2110

125 gr. SPT
Pro-Hunter #2120

150 gr. FMJBT
GameKing #2115

150 gr. SPT
Pro-Hunter #2130

150 gr. SBT
GameKing #2125

150 gr. HPBT
MatchKing #2190

150 gr. RN
Pro-Hunter #2135

155 gr. HPBT
PALMA
MatchKing #2155

165 gr. SBT
GameKing #2145

165 gr. HPBT
GameKing #2140

168 gr. HPBT
MatchKing #2200

175 gr. HPBT
MatchKing #2275

180 gr. SPT
Pro-Hunter #2150

180 gr. SBT
GameKing #2160

180 gr. HPBT
MatchKing #2220

180 gr. RN
Pro-Hunter #2170

190 gr. HPBT
MatchKing #2210

**30 Caliber 7.62MM (cont.) (.308/7.82MM Diameter)**

200 gr. SBT
GameKing #2165

200 gr. HPBT
MatchKing #2230

220 gr. HPBT
MatchKing #2240

220 gr. RN
Pro-Hunter #2180

**.303 Caliber 7.7MM (.311/7.90MM Diameter)**

125 gr. SPT
Pro-Hunter #2305

150 gr. SPT
Pro-Hunter #2300

174 gr. HPBT
MatchKing #2315

180 gr. SPT
Pro-Hunter #2310

**8MM .323 Caliber (.323/8.20MM Diameter)**

150 gr. SPT
Pro-Hunter #2400

175 gr. SPT
Pro-Hunter #2410

220 gr. SBT
GameKing #2420

**.338 Caliber (.338/8.59MM Diameter)**

215 gr. SBT
GameKing #2610

250 gr. SBT
GameKing #2600

**.35 Caliber (.358/9.09MM Diameter)**

200 gr. RN
Pro-Hunter #2800

225 gr. SBT
GameKing #2850

**.375 Caliber (.375/9.53MM Diameter)**

200 gr. FN
Pro-Hunter #2900
POWER JACKET

250 gr. SBT
GameKing #2950

**.375 Caliber (cont.) (.375/9.53MM Diameter)**

300 gr. SBT
GameKing #3000

**.45 Caliber (.45-70) (.458/11.63MM Diameter)**

300 gr. HP/FN
Pro-Hunter #8900

### *Long Range & Specialty Bullets*

22 Caliber
.224/5.69 Diameter
80 gr. HPBT
MatchKing #9390
*7"-8" TWST BBLS*

6.5MM
.264 Caliber
155 gr. HPBT
MatchKing #9570
*8" TWST BBLS*

.30 Caliber
7.62MM
240 gr. HPBT
MatchKing #9245
*9" TWST BBLS*

.338 Caliber
300 gr. HPBT
MatchKing #9300
*10" TWST BBLS*

# SIERRA BULLETS

## HANDGUN

### Single Shot Pistol Bullets

6MM .243 Dia. 80 gr. SPT
Pro-Hunter #7150

7MM .284 Dia. 130 gr. SPT
Pro-Hunter #7250

.30 Cal. .308 Dia. 135 gr. SPT
Pro-Hunter #7350

### .25 Caliber (.251/6.38MM Diameter)

50 gr. FMJ
Tournament Master #8000

### .32 Caliber 7.65MM (.312/7.92MM Diameter)

71 gr. FMJ
Tournament Master #8010

### .32 Mag. (.312/7.92MM Diameter)

90 gr. JHC
Sports Master #8030
POWER JACKET

### 9MM .355 Caliber (.355/9.02MM Diameter)

90 gr. JHP
Sports Master #8100
POWER JACKET

95 gr. FMJ
Tournament Master #8105

115 gr. JHP
Sports Master #8110
POWER JACKET

115 gr. FMJ
Tournament Master #8115

125 gr. JHP Sports Master
#8125 POWER JACKET

125 gr. FMJ
Tournament Master #8120

130 gr. FMJ
Tournament Master #8345

### .38 Super (.356/9.04MM Diameter)

150 gr. FPJ Match
Tournament Master #8250

### .38 Caliber (.357/9.07MM Diameter)

110 gr. JHC Blitz
Sports Master #8300
POWER JACKET

125 gr. JSP
Sports Master #8310

125 gr. JHC
Sports Master #8320
POWER JACKET

140 gr. JHC
Sports Master #8325
POWER JACKET

### .38 Caliber (cont.) (.357/9.07MM Diameter)

158 gr. JSP
Sports Master #8340

158 gr. JHC
Sports Master #8360
POWER JACKET

170 gr. JHC
Sports Master #8365
POWER JACKET

170 gr. FMJ Match
Tournament Master #8350

180 gr. FPJ Match
Tournament Master #8370

### 9MM Makarov (.363/9.22MM Diameter)

95 gr. JHP
Sports Master #8200
POWER JACKET

100 gr. FPJ
Tournament Master #8210

### 10MM .400 Caliber (.400/10.16MM Diameter)

135 gr. JHP
Sports Master #8425
POWER JACKET

150 gr. JHP
Sports Master #8430
POWER JACKET

165 gr. JHP
Sports Master #8445
POWER JACKET

180 gr. JHP
Sports Master #8460
POWER JACKET

190 gr. FPJ
Tournament Master #8480

### .41 Caliber (.410/10.41MM Diameter)

170 gr. JHC
Sports Master #8500
POWER JACKET

210 gr. JHC
Sports Master #8520
POWER JACKET

220 gr. FPJ Match
Tournament Master #8530

### .44 Caliber (.4295/10.91MM Diameter)

180 gr. JHC
Sports Master #8600
POWER JACKET

210 gr. JHC
Sports Master #8620
POWER JACKET

### .44 Caliber (cont.) (.4295/10.91MM Diameter)

220 gr. FPJ Match
Tournament Master #8605

240 gr. JHC
Sports Master #8610
POWER JACKET

250 gr. FPJ Match
Tournament Master #8615

300 gr. JSP
Sports Master #8630

### .45 Caliber (.4515/11.47MM Diameter)

185 gr. JHP
Sports Master #8800
POWER JACKET

185 gr. FPJ Match
Tournament Master #8810

200 gr. FPJ Match
Tournament Master #8825

230 gr. JHP
Sports Master #8805
POWER JACKET

230 gr. FMJ Match
Tournament Master #8815

240 gr. JHC
Sports Master #8820
POWER JACKET

300 gr. JSP
Sports Master #8830

# SPEER RIFLE BULLETS

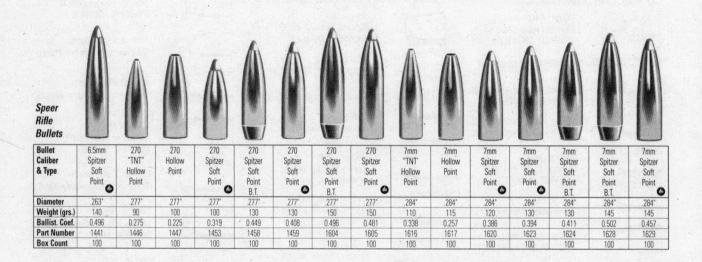

**Speer Rifle Bullets**

| Bullet Caliber & Type | Diameter | Weight (grs.) | Ballist. Coef. | Part Number | Box Count |
|---|---|---|---|---|---|
| 22 Spire Soft Point | .223" | 40 | 0.145 | 1005 | 100 |
| 22 Spitzer Soft Point | .223" | 45 | 0.166 | 1011 | 100 |
| 22 Spire Soft Point | .224" | 40 | 0.144 | 1017 | 100 |
| 22 Spitzer Soft Point | .224" | 45 | 0.167 | 1023 | 100 |
| 22 218 Bee Flat Soft Point w/Cann. | .224" | 46 | 0.094 | 1024 | 100 |
| 22 Spitzer Soft Point | .224" | 50 | 0.231 | 1029 | 100 |
| 22 "TNT" Hollow Point | .224" | 50 | 0.223 | 1030 | 100 |
| 22 Hollow Point | .224" | 52 | 0.225 | 1035 | 100 |
| 22 Hollow Point B.T. Match | .224" | 52 | 0.253 | 1036 | 100 |
| 22 FMJ B.T. w/Cann. | .224" | 55 | 0.269 | 1044 | 100 |
| 22 Spitzer Soft Point | .224" | 55 | 0.255 | 1047 | 100 |
| 22 Spitzer S.P. w/Cann. | .224" | 55 | 0.241 | 1049 | 100 |
| 22 FMJ B.T. w/Cann. | .224" | 62 | 0.307 | 1050 | 100 |
| 22 Semi-Spitzer Soft Point | .224" | 70 | 0.214 | 1053 | 100 |
| 6mm "TNT" Hollow Point | .243" | 70 | 0.282 | 1206 | 100 |

**Speer Rifle Bullets**

| Bullet Caliber & Type | Diameter | Weight (grs.) | Ballist. Coef. | Part Number | Box Count |
|---|---|---|---|---|---|
| 6.5mm Spitzer Soft Point | .263" | 140 | 0.496 | 1441 | 100 |
| 270 "TNT" Hollow Point | .277" | 90 | 0.275 | 1446 | 100 |
| 270 Hollow Point | .277" | 100 | 0.225 | 1447 | 100 |
| 270 Spitzer Soft Point | .277" | 100 | 0.319 | 1453 | 100 |
| 270 Spitzer Soft Point B.T. | .277" | 130 | 0.449 | 1458 | 100 |
| 270 Spitzer Soft Point | .277" | 130 | 0.408 | 1459 | 100 |
| 270 Spitzer Soft Point B.T. | .277" | 150 | 0.496 | 1604 | 100 |
| 270 Spitzer Soft Point | .277" | 150 | 0.481 | 1605 | 100 |
| 7mm "TNT" Hollow Point | .284" | 110 | 0.338 | 1616 | 100 |
| 7mm Hollow Point | .284" | 115 | 0.257 | 1617 | 100 |
| 7mm Spitzer Soft Point | .284" | 120 | 0.386 | 1620 | 100 |
| 7mm Spitzer Soft Point | .284" | 130 | 0.394 | 1623 | 100 |
| 7mm Spitzer Soft Point B.T. | .284" | 130 | 0.411 | 1624 | 100 |
| 7mm Spitzer Soft Point B.T. | .284" | 145 | 0.502 | 1628 | 100 |
| 7mm Spitzer Soft Point | .284" | 145 | 0.457 | 1629 | 100 |

**Speer Rifle Bullets**

| Bullet Caliber & Type | Diameter | Weight (grs.) | Ballist. Coef. | Part Number | Box Count |
|---|---|---|---|---|---|
| 30 Spitzer Soft Point B.T. | .308" | 150 | 0.423 | 2022 | 100 |
| 30 Spitzer Soft Point | .308" | 150 | 0.389 | 2023 | 100 |
| 30 Mag-Tip™ Soft Point | .308" | 150 | 0.301 | 2025 | 100 |
| 30 Round Soft Point | .308" | 165 | 0.274 | 2029 | 100 |
| 30 Spitzer Soft Point B.T. | .308" | 165 | 0.477 | 2034 | 100 |
| 30 Spitzer Soft Point | .308" | 165 | 0.433 | 2035 | 100 |
| 30 Match Hollow Point B.T. | .308" | 168 | 0.480 | 2040 | 100 |
| 30 Flat Soft Point | .308" | 170 | 0.304 | 2041 | 100 |
| 30 Round Soft Point | .308" | 180 | 0.304 | 2047 | 100 |
| 30 Spitzer Soft Point B.T. | .308" | 180 | 0.540 | 2052 | 100 |
| 30 Spitzer Soft Point | .308" | 180 | 0.483 | 2053 | 100 |
| 30 Mag-Tip™ Soft Point | .308" | 180 | 0.352 | 2059 | 100 |
| 30 Match Hollow Point B.T. | .308" | 190 | 0.540 | 2080 | 50 |
| 30 Spitzer Soft Point | .308" | 200 | 0.556 | 2211 | 50 |
| 303 Spitzer Soft Point w/Cann. | .311" | 125 | 0.292 | 2213 | 100 |

# SPEER RIFLE BULLETS

| 6mm Hollow Point | 6mm Spitzer Soft Point | 6mm Spitzer Soft Point B.T. | 6mm Spitzer Soft Point | 6mm Spitzer Soft Point B.T. | 6mm Round Soft Point | 6mm Spitzer Soft Point | 25-20 Win. Flat Soft Point w/Cann. | 25 Spitzer Soft Point | 25 "TNT" Hollow Point | 25 Hollow Point | 25 Spitzer Soft Point | 25 Spitzer Soft Point B.T. | 25 Spitzer Soft Point B.T. | 25 Spitzer Soft Point | 6.5mm Spitzer Soft Point |
|---|---|---|---|---|---|---|---|---|---|---|---|---|---|---|---|
| .243" | .243" | .243" | .243" | .243" | .243" | .243" | .257" | .257" | .257" | .257" | .257" | .257" | .257" | .257" | .263" |
| 75 | 80 | 85 | 90 | 105 | 105 | 105 | 75 | 87 | 87 | 100 | 100 | 100 | 120 | 120 | 120 |
| 0.234 | 0.365 | -0.404 | 0.385 | 0.430 | 0.207 | 0.443 | 0.133 | 0.300 | 0.310 | 0.369 | 0.255 | 0.393 | 0.435 | 0.41 | 0.433 |
| 1205 | 1211 | 1213 | 1217 | 1220 | 1223 | 1229 | 1237 | 1241 | 1246 | 1405 | 1407 | 1408 | 1410 | 1411 | 1435 |
| 100 | 100 | 100 | 100 | 100 | 100 | 100 | 100 | 100 | 100 | 100 | 100 | 100 | 100 | 100 | 100 |

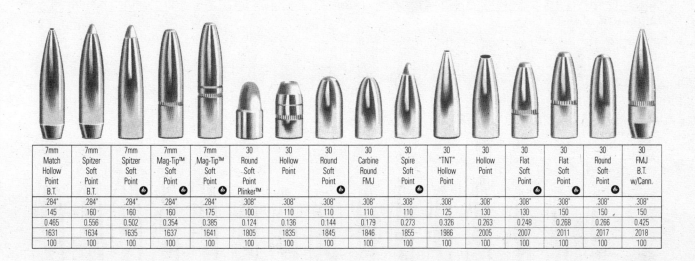

| 7mm Match Hollow Point B.T. | 7mm Spitzer Soft Point B.T. | 7mm Spitzer Soft Point | 7mm Mag-Tip™ Soft Point | 7mm Mag-Tip™ Soft Point | 30 Round Soft Point Plinker™ | 30 Hollow Point | 30 Round Soft Point | 30 Carbine Round FMJ | 30 Spire Soft Point | 30 "TNT" Hollow Point | 30 Hollow Point | 30 Flat Soft Point | 30 Flat Soft Point | 30 Round Soft Point | 30 FMJ B.T. w/Cann. |
|---|---|---|---|---|---|---|---|---|---|---|---|---|---|---|---|
| .284" | .284" | .284" | .284" | .284" | .308" | .308" | .308" | .308" | .308" | .308" | .308" | .308" | .308" | .308" | .308" |
| 145 | 160 | 160 | 160 | 175 | 100 | 110 | 110 | 110 | 110 | 125 | 130 | 130 | 150 | 150 | 150 |
| 0.465 | 0.556 | 0.502 | 0.354 | 0.385 | 0.124 | 0.136 | 0.144 | 0.179 | 0.273 | 0.326 | 0.263 | 0.248 | 0.268 | 0.266 | 0.425 |
| 1631 | 1634 | 1635 | 1637 | 1641 | 1805 | 1835 | 1845 | 1846 | 1855 | 1986 | 2005 | 2007 | 2011 | 2017 | 2018 |
| 100 | 100 | 100 | 100 | 100 | 100 | 100 | 100 | 100 | 100 | 100 | 100 | 100 | 100 | 100 | 100 |

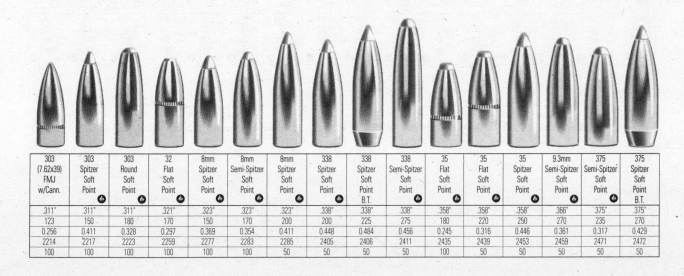

| 303 (7.62x39) FMJ w/Cann. | 303 Spitzer Soft Point | 303 Round Soft Point | 32 Flat Soft Point | 8mm Spitzer Soft Point | 8mm Semi-Spitzer Soft Point | 8mm Spitzer Soft Point | 338 Spitzer Soft Point | 338 Spitzer Soft Point | 338 Semi-Spitzer Soft Point B.T. | 35 Flat Soft Point | 35 Flat Soft Point | 35 Spitzer Soft Point | 9.3mm Semi-Spitzer Soft Point | 375 Semi-Spitzer Soft Point | 375 Spitzer Soft Point B.T. |
|---|---|---|---|---|---|---|---|---|---|---|---|---|---|---|---|
| .311" | .311" | .311" | .321" | .323" | .323" | .323" | .338" | .338" | .338" | .358" | .358" | .358" | .366" | .375" | .375" |
| 123 | 150 | 180 | 170 | 150 | 170 | 200 | 200 | 225 | 275 | 180 | 220 | 250 | 270 | 235 | 270 |
| 0.256 | 0.411 | 0.328 | 0.297 | 0.369 | 0.354 | 0.411 | 0.448 | 0.484 | 0.456 | 0.245 | 0.316 | 0.446 | 0.361 | 0.317 | 0.429 |
| 2214 | 2217 | 2223 | 2259 | 2277 | 2283 | 2285 | 2405 | 2406 | 2411 | 2435 | 2439 | 2453 | 2459 | 2471 | 2472 |
| 100 | 100 | 100 | 100 | 100 | 100 | 50 | 50 | 50 | 50 | 100 | 50 | 50 | 50 | 50 | 50 |

# SPEER RIFLE BULLETS

## Speer Rifle Bullets (cont.)

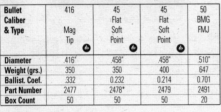

| Bullet Caliber & Type | 416 Mag Tip | 45 Flat Soft Point | 45 Flat Soft Point | 50 BMG FMJ |
|---|---|---|---|---|
| Diameter | .416" | .458" | .458" | .510" |
| Weight (grs.) | 350 | 350 | 400 | 647 |
| Ballist. Coef. | .332 | 0.232 | 0.214 | 0.701 |
| Part Number | 2477 | 2478* | 2479 | 2491 |
| Box Count | 50 | 50 | 50 | 20 |

*Not intended for lever-action rifles

## Speer African Grand Slam®

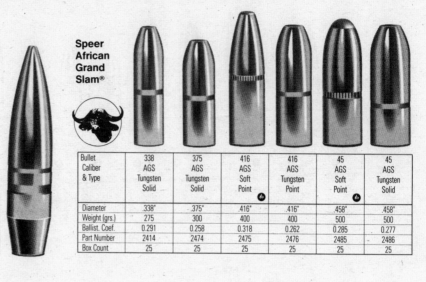

| Bullet Caliber & Type | 338 AGS Tungsten Solid | 375 AGS Tungsten Solid | 416 AGS Soft Point | 416 AGS Tungsten Point | 45 AGS Soft Point | 45 AGS Tungsten Solid |
|---|---|---|---|---|---|---|
| Diameter | .338" | .375" | .416" | .416" | .458" | .458" |
| Weight (grs.) | 275 | 300 | 400 | 400 | 500 | 500 |
| Ballist. Coef. | 0.291 | 0.258 | 0.318 | 0.262 | 0.285 | 0.277 |
| Part Number | 2414 | 2474 | 2475 | 2476 | 2485 | 2486 |
| Box Count | 25 | 25 | 25 | 25 | 25 | 25 |

## Speer Grand Slam®

| Bullet Caliber & Type | 6mm GS Soft Point | 25 GS Soft Point | 270 GS Soft Point | 270 GS Soft Point | 7mm GS Soft Point | 7mm GS Soft Point | 7mm GS Soft Point | 30 GS Soft Point | 30 GS Soft Point | 30 GS Soft Point | 30 GS Soft Point | 311 GS Soft Point | 338 GS Soft Point | 35 GS Soft Point | 375 GS Soft Point |
|---|---|---|---|---|---|---|---|---|---|---|---|---|---|---|---|
| Diameter | .243" | .257" | .277" | .277" | .284" | .284" | .284" | .308" | .308" | .308" | .308" | .311" | .338" | .358" | .375" |
| Weight (grs.) | 100 | 120 | 130 | 150 | 145 | 160 | 175 | 150 | 165 | 180 | 200 | 200 | 250 | 250 | 285 |
| Ballist. Coef. | 0.351 | 0.328 | 0.345 | 0.385 | 0.327 | 0.387 | 0.465 | 0.305 | 0.393 | 0.416 | 0.448 | 0.441 | 0.431 | 0.335 | 0.354 |
| Part Number | 1222 | 1415 | 1465 | 1608 | 1632 | 1638 | 1643 | 2026 | 2038 | 2063 | 2212 | 2226 | 2408 | 2455 | 2473 |
| Box Count | 50 | 50 | 50 | 50 | 50 | 50 | 50 | 50 | 50 | 50 | 50 | 50 | 50 | 50 | 50 |

**NEW for 1997–8:** 6.5 mm GS Soft Point. **Diameter:** .264". **Weight:** 140 grams. **Ballistic coefficient:** 0.385. **Part no.:** 1444.

# SPEER HANDGUN BULLETS

## Speer Handgun Bullets

| Caliber & Type | 25 Gold Dot Hollow Pt. | 32 Gold Dot Hollow Pt. | 9mm Gold Dot Hollow Point | 9mm Gold Dot Hollow Point | 9mm Gold Dot Hollow Point | 9mm Gold Dot Hollow Point | 357 Sig Gold Dot Hollow Point | 38 Gold Dot Hollow Point | 38 Gold Dot Hollow Point | 9mm Makarov Gold Dot Hollow Point | 40/10mm Gold Dot Hollow Point | 40/10mm Gold Dot Hollow Point | 40/10mm Gold Dot Hollow Point | 44 Gold Dot Soft Point | 45 Gold Dot Hollow Point | 45 Gold Dot Hollow Point |
|---|---|---|---|---|---|---|---|---|---|---|---|---|---|---|---|---|
| Diameter | .251" | .311" | .355" | .355" | .355" | .355" | .355" | .357" | .357" | .364" | .400" | .400" | .400" | .429" | .451" | .451" |
| Weight (grs.) | 35 | 60 | 90 | 115 | 124 | 147 | 125 | 125 | 158 | 90 | 155 | 165 | 180 | 270 | 185 | 230 |
| Ballist. Coef. | .091 | .118 | 0.101 | 0.125 | 0.134 | 0.164 | 0.141 | 0.140 | 0.168 | 0.107 | 0.123 | 0.138 | 0.143 | 0.193 | 0.109 | 0.143 |
| Part Number | 3985 | 3986 | 3992 | 3994 | 3998 | 4002 | 4360 | 4012 | 4215 | 3999 | 4400 | 4397 | 4406 | 4461 | 4470 | 4483 |
| Box Count | 100 | 100 | 100 | 100 | 100 | 100 | 100 | 100 | 100 | 100 | 100 | 100 | 100 | 50 | 100 | 100 |

**NEW for 1997–8:** 45 Gold Dot Hollow Point. **Diameter** .451". **Weight:** 185. **Ballistic coefficient** 0.138. **Part no.:** 4478.

## Speer Handgun Bullets

| Caliber & Type | 25 TMJ | 32 JHP | 9mm TMJ | 9mm JHP | 9mm TMJ | 9mm JHP | 9mm SP | 9mm TMJ | 9mm TMJ | 357 Sig TMJ | 38 JHP | 38 JSP | 38 JHP | 38 TMJ | 38 JHP | 38 JHP-SWC |
|---|---|---|---|---|---|---|---|---|---|---|---|---|---|---|---|---|
| Diameter | .251" | .312" | .355" | .355" | .355" | .355" | .355" | .355" | .355" | .355" | .357" | .357" | .357" | .357" | .357" | .357" |
| Weight (grs.) | 50 | 100 | 95 | 100 | 115 | 115 | 124 | 124 | 147 | 125 | 110 | 125 | 125 | 125 | 140 | 146 |
| Ballist. Coef. | 0.110 | 0.167 | 0.131 | 0.111 | 0.177 | 0.118 | 0.115 | 0.114 | 0.208 | 0.147 | 0.122 | 0.140 | 0.135 | 0.146 | 0.152 | 0.159 |
| Part Number | 3982 | 3981 | 4001 | 3983 | 3995 | 3996 | 3997 | 4004 | 4006 | 4362 | 4007 | 4011 | 4013 | 4015 | 4203 | 4205 |
| Box Count | 100 | 100 | 100 | 100 | 100 | 100 | 100 | 100 | 100 | 100 | 100 | 100 | 100 | 100 | 100 | 100 |

## Speer Handgun Bullets

| Caliber & Type | 38 TMJ | 38 JHP | 38 JSP | 38 JSP-SWC | 38 TMJ-Sil. | 38 TMJ-Sil. | 9mm Makarov TMJ | 40/10mm TMJ | 40/10mm TMJ | 40/10mm TMJ | 40/10mm TMJ | 41 AE HP | 41 JHP-SWC | 41 JSP-SWC | 41 TMJ-Sil. |
|---|---|---|---|---|---|---|---|---|---|---|---|---|---|---|---|
| Diameter | .357" | .357" | .357" | .357" | .357" | .357" | .364" | .400" | .400" | .400" | .400" | .410" | .410" | .410" | .410" |
| Weight (grs.) | 158 | 158 | 158 | 160 | 180 | 200 | 95 | 155 | 165 | 180 | 200 | 180 | 200 | 220 | 210 |
| Ballist. Coef. | 0.173 | 0.158 | 0.158 | 0.236 | 0.230 | 0.236 | 0.127 | 0.125 | 0.135 | 0.143 | 0.208 | 0.138 | 0.113 | 0.137 | 0.216 |
| Part Number | 4207 | 4211 | 4217 | 4223 | 4229 | 4231 | 4375 | 4399 | 4410 | 4402 | 4403 | 4404 | 4405 | 4417 | 4420 |
| Box Count | 100 | 100 | 100 | 100 | 100 | 100 | 100 | 100 | 100 | 100 | 100 | 100 | 100 | 100 | 100 |

## Speer Handgun Bullets

| Caliber & Type | 44 MAG. JHP | 44 JHP-SWC | 44 JSP-SWC | 44 MAG.JHP | 44 MAG JSP | 44 TMJ-Sil. | 44 MAG. SP | 45 TMJ-Match | 45 TMJ-Match | 45 JHP | 45 MAG. JHP | 45 TMJ | 45 MAG. JHP | 45 SP | 50 AE HP |
|---|---|---|---|---|---|---|---|---|---|---|---|---|---|---|---|
| Diameter | .429" | .429" | .429" | .429" | .429" | .429" | .429" | .451" | .451" | .451" | .451" | .451" | .451" | .451" | .500" |
| Weight (grs.) | 200 | 225 | 240 | 240 | 240 | 240 | 300 | 185 | 200 | 200 | 225 | 230 | 260 | 300 | 325 |
| Ballist. Coef. | 0.122 | 0.146 | 0.157 | 0.165 | 0.164 | 0.206 | 0.213 | 0.090 | 0.129 | 0.138 | 0.169 | 0.153 | 0.183 | 0.199 | 0.149 |
| Part Number | 4425 | 4435 | 4447 | 4453 | 4457 | 4459 | 4463 | 4473 | 4475 | 4477 | 4479 | 4480 | 4481 | 4485 | 4495 |
| Box Count | 100 | 100 | 100 | 100 | 100 | 100 | 50 | 100 | 100 | 100 | 100 | 100 | 100 | 50 | 50 |

## Speer Handgun Bullets Lead

| Caliber & Type | 32 HB-WC | 9mm RN | 38 BB-WC | 38 DE-WC | 38 HB-WC | 38 SWC | 38 HP-SWC | 38 RN | 44 SWC | 45 SWC | 45 RN | 45 SWC |
|---|---|---|---|---|---|---|---|---|---|---|---|---|
| Diameter | .314" | .356" | .358" | .358" | .358" | .358" | .358" | .358" | .430" | .452" | .452" | .452" |
| Weight (grs.) | 98 | 125 | 148 | 148 | 148 | 158 | 158 | 158 | 240 | 200 | 230 | 250 |
| Part Number | -- | 4601 | 4605 | -- | 4617 | 4623 | 4627 | 4647 | 4660 | 4677 | 4690 | 4683 |
| Bulk Pkg | 4600 | 4602 | 4606 | 4611 | 4618 | 4624 | 4628 | 4648 | 4661 | 4678 | 4691 | 4684 |

**Abbreviation Guide:** JHP-Jacketed Hollow Point, TMJ-Totally Metal Jacketed, SP-Soft Point, JSP-Jacketed Soft Point, Sil-Silhouette, WC-Wadcutter, SWC-Semi-Wadcutter, HB-Hollow Base, BB-Bevel Base, RN-Round Nose, HP-Hollow Point
Ⓗ -HOT-COR   Ⓤ -UNI-COR

# SWIFT BULLETS

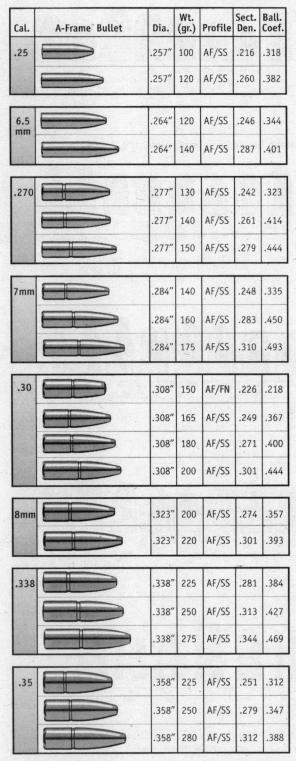

| Cal. | A-Frame Bullet | Dia. | Wt. (gr.) | Profile | Sect. Den. | Ball. Coef. |
|---|---|---|---|---|---|---|
| .25 | | .257" | 100 | AF/SS | .216 | .318 |
| | | .257" | 120 | AF/SS | .260 | .382 |
| 6.5 mm | | .264" | 120 | AF/SS | .246 | .344 |
| | | .264" | 140 | AF/SS | .287 | .401 |
| .270 | | .277" | 130 | AF/SS | .242 | .323 |
| | | .277" | 140 | AF/SS | .261 | .414 |
| | | .277" | 150 | AF/SS | .279 | .444 |
| 7mm | | .284" | 140 | AF/SS | .248 | .335 |
| | | .284" | 160 | AF/SS | .283 | .450 |
| | | .284" | 175 | AF/SS | .310 | .493 |
| .30 | | .308" | 150 | AF/FN | .226 | .218 |
| | | .308" | 165 | AF/SS | .249 | .367 |
| | | .308" | 180 | AF/SS | .271 | .400 |
| | | .308" | 200 | AF/SS | .301 | .444 |
| 8mm | | .323" | 200 | AF/SS | .274 | .357 |
| | | .323" | 220 | AF/SS | .301 | .393 |
| .338 | | .338" | 225 | AF/SS | .281 | .384 |
| | | .338" | 250 | AF/SS | .313 | .427 |
| | | .338" | 275 | AF/SS | .344 | .469 |
| .35 | | .358" | 225 | AF/SS | .251 | .312 |
| | | .358" | 250 | AF/SS | .279 | .347 |
| | | .358" | 280 | AF/SS | .312 | .388 |

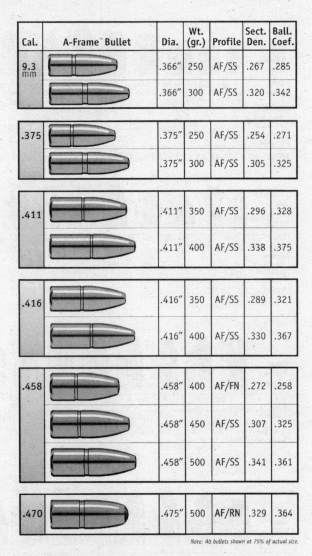

| Cal. | A-Frame Bullet | Dia. | Wt. (gr.) | Profile | Sect. Den. | Ball. Coef. |
|---|---|---|---|---|---|---|
| 9.3 mm | | .366" | 250 | AF/SS | .267 | .285 |
| | | .366" | 300 | AF/SS | .320 | .342 |
| .375 | | .375" | 250 | AF/SS | .254 | .271 |
| | | .375" | 300 | AF/SS | .305 | .325 |
| .411 | | .411" | 350 | AF/SS | .296 | .328 |
| | | .411" | 400 | AF/SS | .338 | .375 |
| .416 | | .416" | 350 | AF/SS | .289 | .321 |
| | | .416" | 400 | AF/SS | .330 | .367 |
| .458 | | .458" | 400 | AF/FN | .272 | .258 |
| | | .458" | 450 | AF/SS | .307 | .325 |
| | | .458" | 500 | AF/SS | .341 | .361 |
| .470 | | .475" | 500 | AF/RN | .329 | .364 |

*Note: All bullets shown at 75% of actual size.*

## HANDGUN BULLET SPECIFICATIONS

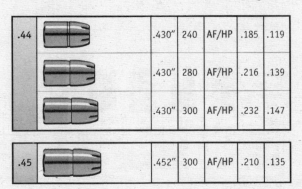

| Cal. | A-Frame Bullet | Dia. | Wt. (gr.) | Profile | Sect. Den. | Ball. Coef. |
|---|---|---|---|---|---|---|
| .44 | | .430" | 240 | AF/HP | .185 | .119 |
| | | .430" | 280 | AF/HP | .216 | .139 |
| | | .430" | 300 | AF/HP | .232 | .147 |
| .45 | | .452" | 300 | AF/HP | .210 | .135 |

*AF/SS = A-Frame Semi-Spitzer*   *AF/FN = A-Frame Flat Nose*   *AF/RN = A-Frame Round Nose*   *AF/HP = A-Frame Hollow Point*

# ALLIANT SMOKELESS POWDERS

Reloder 12

Reloder 15

Reloder 19

Reloder 22

2400

Reloder 7

Bullseye

Herco

Red Dot

Blue Dot

Green Dot

Unique

Power Pistol

American Select

# HODGDON SMOKELESS POWDER

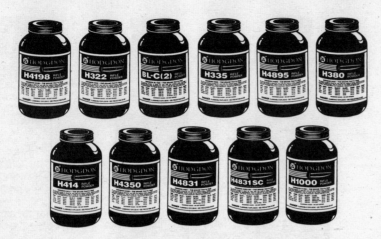

## VARGET RIFLE POWDER

## RIFLE POWDER

### H4198

H4198 was developed especially for small and medium capacity cartridges.

### H322

Any extruded bench rest powder which has proved to be capable of producing fine accuracy in the 22 and 308 bench rest guns. This powder fills the gap between H4198 and BL-C(2). Performs best in small to medium capacity cases.

### SPHERICAL BL-C®, Lot No. 2

A highly popular favorite of the bench rest shooters. Best performance is in the 222, and in other cases smaller than 30/06.

### SPHERICAL H335®

Similar to BL-C(2), H335 is popular for its performance in medium capacity cases, especially in 222 and 308 Winchester.

### H4895®

4895 may well be considered the most versatile of all propellants. It gives desirable performance in almost all cases from 222 Rem. to 458 Win. Reduced loads, to as low as 3/5 of maximum, still give target accuracy.

### SPHERICAL H380®

This number fills a gap between 4320 and 4350. It is excellent in 22/250, 220 Swift, the 6mm's, 257 and 30/06.

### SPHERICAL H414®

In many popular medium to medium-large calibers, pressure velocity relationship is better.

### H414®

A spherical powder developed especially for 30-06, 220 Swift and 375 H&H.

### H4350

This powder gives superb accuracy at optimum velocity for many large capacity metallic rifle cartridges.

### H50 BMG

Designed for the 50 Browning Machine Gun cartridge. Highly insensitive to extreme temperature changes.

### H4831®

The most popular of all powders. Outstanding performance with medium and heavy bullets in the 6mm's, 25/06, 270 and Magnum calibers. Also available with shortened grains **(H4831SC)** for easy metering.

### H1000 EXTRUDED POWDER

Fills the gap between H4831 and H870. Works especially well in overbore capacity cartridges (1,000-yard shooters take note).

### HP38

A fast pistol powder for most pistol loading. Especially recommended for mid-range 38 specials.

### CLAYS

A powder developed for 12-gauge clay target shooters. Also performs well in many handgun applications, including .38 Special, .40 S&W and 45 ACP. Perfect for 1 1/8 and 1 oz. loads.
Now available:
**Universal Clays.** Loads nearly all of the straight-wall pistol cartridges as well as 12 ga. 1 1/4 oz. thru 28 ga. 3/4 oz. target loads.
**International Clays.** Perfect for 12 and 20 ga. autoloaders who want reduced recoil.

### HS-6 and HS-7

HS-6 and HS-7 for Magnum field loads are unsurpassed, since they do not pack in the measure. They deliver uniform charges and are dense to allow sufficient wad column for best patterns.

### H110

A spherical powder made especially for the 30 M1 carbine. H110 also does very well in 357, 44 Spec., 44 Mag. or .410 ga. shotshell. Magnum primers are recommended for consistent ignition.

### H4227

An extruded powder similar to H110, it is the fastest burning in Hodgdon's line. Recommended for the 22 Hornet and some specialized loading in the 45-70 caliber. Also excellent in magnum pistol and .410 shotgun.

# IMR SMOKELESS POWDERS

## SHOTSHELL POWDER

**Hi-Skor 700-X Double-Base Shotshell Powder.** Specifically designed for today's 12-gauge components. Developed to give optimum ballistics at minimum charge weight (which means more reloads per pounds of powder). 700-X is dense, easy to load, clean to handle and loads uniformly.

**PB Shotshell Powder.** Produces exceptional 20 and 28-gauge skeet reloads; preferred by many in 12-gauge target loads, it gives 3-dram equivalent velocity at relatively low chamber pressures.

**Hi-Skor 800-X Shotshell Powder.** An excellent powder for 12-gauge field loads and 20 and 28-gauge loads.

**SR-4756 Powder.** Great all-around powder for target and field loads.

**SR-7625.** A fast-growing favorite for reloading target as well as light and heavy field loads in 4 gauges. Excellent velocity-chamber pressure.

**IMR-4227 Powder.** Can be used effectively for reloading .410-gauge shotshell ammunition.

## RIFLE POWDER

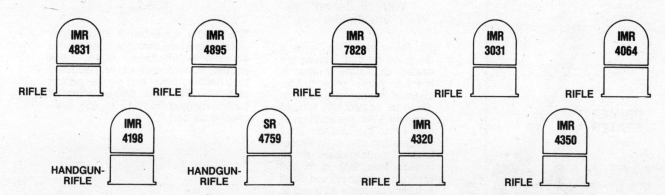

**IMR-3031 Rifle Powder.** Specifically recommended for medium-capacity cartridges.

**IMR-4064 Rifle Powder.** Has exceptionally uniform burning qualities when used in medium and large-capacity cartridges.

**IMR-4198.** Made the Remington 222 cartridge famous. Developed for small and medium-capacity cartridges.

**IMR-4227 Rifle Powder.** Fastest burning of the IMR Series. Specifically designed for the 22 Hornet class of cartridges.

**SR-4759.** Brought back by shooter demand. Available for cast bullet loads.

**IMR-4320.** Recommended for high-velocity cartridges.

**IMR-4350 Rifle Powder.** Gives unusually uniform results when loaded in Magnum cartridges.

**IMR-4831.** Produced as a canister-grade handloading powder. Packaged in 1 lb. canister, 8 lb. caddy and 20 lb. kegs.

**IMR-4895 Rifle Powder.** The time-tested standard for caliber 30 military ammunition; slightly faster than IMR-4320. Loads uniformly in all powder measures. One of the country's favorite powder.

**IMR-7828 Rifle Powder.** The slowest burning DuPont IMR canister powder, intended for large-capacity and magnum-type cases with heavy bullets.

## PISTOL POWDER

**PB Powder.** Another powder for reloading a wide variety of centerfire handgun ammunition.

**IMR-4227 Powder.** Can be used effectively for reloading Magnum handgun ammunition.

**Hi-Skor 700-X Powder.** The same qualities that make it a superior powder contribute to its excellent performance in all the popular handguns.

**Hi-Skor 800-X Powder.** Good powder for heavier bullet handgun calibers.

**SR-7625 Powder.** For reloading a wide variety of centerfire handgun ammunition.

**SR-4756.** Clean burning with uniform performance. Can be used in a variety of handgun calibers.

# FORSTER RELOADING

### CO-AX® BENCH REST® RIFLE DIES

**Bench Rest Rifle Dies** are glass hard and polished mirror smooth with special attention given to headspace, tapers and diameters. Sizing die has an elevated expander button to ensure better alignment of case and neck.

| | |
|---|---|
| Bench Rest® Die Set | $68.00 |
| Weatherby Bench Rest Die Set | 75.00 |
| Ultra Bench Rest Die Set | 84.00 |
| Full Length Sizer | 31.50 |
| Bench Rest Seating Die | 38.00 |

### PRIMER SEATER
**With "E-Z-Just" Shellholder**

**PRIMER SEATER**

The Bonanza Primer Seater is designed so that primers are seated Co-Axially (primer in line with primer pocket). Mechanical leverage allows primers to be seated fully without crushing. With the addition of one extra set of Disc Shell Holders and one extra Primer Unit, all modern cases, rim or rimless, from 222 up to 458 Magnum, can be primed. Shell holders are easily adjusted to any case by rotating to contact rim or cannelure of the case.

| | |
|---|---|
| Primer Seater | $64.50 |
| Primer Pocket Cleaner | 7.00 |

### HAND CASE TRIMMER
**$55.25**

Shell holder is a Brown & Sharpe-type collet. Case and cartridge conditioning accessories include inside neck reamer, outside neck turner, deburring tool, hollow pointer and primter pocket cleaners. The case timmer trims all cases, ranging from 17 to 458 Winchester caliber.

### CO-AX® INDICATOR

Bullets will not leave a rifle barrel at a uniform angle unless they are started uniformly. The Co-Ax Indicator provides a reading of how closely the axis of the bullet corresponds to the axis of the cartridge case. The Indicator features a spring-loaded plunger to hold cartridges against a recessed, adjustable rod while the cartridge is supported in a "V" block. To operate, simply rotate the cartridge with the fingers; the degree of misalignment is transferred to an indicator which measures in one-thousandths.

| | |
|---|---|
| **Price:** Without dial | $53.20 |
| Indicator Dial | 60.40 |

# FORSTER RELOADING

## ULTRA BULLET SEATER DIE

Forster's new Ultra Die is available in 56 calibers, more than any other brand of micrometer-style seater. Adjustment is identical to that of a precision micrometer—the head is graduated to .001″ increments with .025″ bullet movement per revolution. The cartridge case, bullet and seating stem are completely supported and perfectly aligned in a close-fitting chamber before and during the bullet seating operation.
**Price:** . . . . . . . . . . . . . . . . . . . . . . . . . . . . . . . . . . . . . . . . **$57.30**

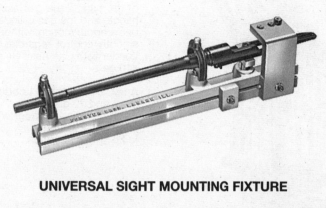

## UNIVERSAL SIGHT MOUNTING FIXTURE

This product fills the exacting requirements needed for drilling and tapping holes for the mounting of scopes, receiver sights, shotgun beads, etc. The fixture handles any single-barrel gun—bolt-action, lever-action or pump-action—as long as the barrel can be laid into the "V" blocks of the fixture. Tubular guns are drilled in the same manner by removing the magazine tube. The fixture's main body is made of aluminum casting. The two "V" blocks are adjustable for height and are made of hardened steel ground accurately on the "V" as well as the shaft.
**Price:** . . . . . . . . . . . . . . . . . . . . . . . . . . . . . . . . . . . . . . . . **$364.00**

**CO-AX LOADING PRESS B-2**

## CO-AX® LOADING PRESS MODEL B-2

Designed to make reloading easier and more accurate, this press offers the following features: Snap-in and snap-out die change • Positive spent primer catcher • Automatic self-acting shell holder • Floating guide rods • Working room for right- or left-hand operators • Top priming device seats primers to factory specifications • Uses any standard $7/8$″×14 dies • No torque on the head • Perfect alignment of die and case • Three times the mechanical advantage of a "C" press
**Price:** . . . . . . . . . . . . . . . . . . . . . . . . . . . . . . . . . . . . . . . . **$294.00**

**BENCH REST POWDER MEASURE**

## BENCH REST POWDER MEASURE

When operated uniformly, this measure will throw uniform charges from $2^{1}/_{2}$ grains Bullseye to 95 grains #4320. No extra drums are needed. Powder is metered from the charge arm, allowing a flow of powder without extremes in variation while minimizing powder shearing. Powder flows through its own built-in baffle so that powder enters the charge arm uniformly.
**Price:** . . . . . . . . . . . . . . . . . . . . . . . . . . . . . . . . . . . . . . . . **$107.00**

# HORNADY

**APEX 3.1 SHOTSHELL LOADER w/GAS ASSIST**

## APEX 3.1 AUTO SHOTSHELL RELOADER

This versatile shotshell reloader features a new hold-fast shell plate. Other features include: extra-large shot hopper, short linkage arm, automatic dual-action crimp die, swing-out wad guide, and extra-long shot and powder feed tubes. The reloader is now available with Gas-Assist Indexing. With each downstroke of the handle the gas assist cylinder compresses, storing energy. Raise the handle and the gas cylinder transfers its energy to the shellplate, rotating it in one smooth motion, without jerking, and advancing the shells and primers with smooth control regardless of handle speed. The Apex 3.1 Auto Shotshell Loader with Gas Assist is available in four models: 12 ga., 20 ga., 28 ga., and 410 ga.

**Apex 3.1 Shotshell Loader (Automatic)**
In 12 and 20 gauge . . . . . . . . . . . . . . . . . . . . . . . . . . . . . . . . . . . . . . . . . . . $299.95
**Apex Shotshell Loader with Gas Assist**
In 12 and 20 gauge . . . . . . . . . . . . . . . . . . . . . . . . . . . . . . . . . . . . . . . . . . . 349.95
In 28 and .410 gauge . . . . . . . . . . . . . . . . . . . . . . . . . . . . . . . . . . . . . . . . . 369.95

## LOCK-N-LOAD CLASSIC PRESS

Hornady introduces two new presses that lets the operator change dies with a flick of the wrist. This new feature, called Lock-N- Load, is available on Hornady's single stage and progressive reloader models. This bushing system locks the die into the press like a rifle bolt, simply by threading a die into the Lock-N-Load bushing. The die is then inserted into a matching press bushing on the loader and locked in place with a clockwise turn. Instead of threading dies in and out, the operator simply locks and unlocks them with a slight twist. Dies are held firmly in place like a rifle bolt, but release instantly for changing. The die bushing stays with the die and retains the die setting. Single stage reloading has never been simpler with Hornady's new Lock-N-Load Classic press. Instead of screwing dies in, the Lock-N-Load system lets the operator change dies with a simple twist. Die settings remain firm and the die is held perfectly solid in the loader. The Lock-N-Load Classic Press features an easy grip handle, an O-style frame made of high-strength alloy, and a positive priming system that feeds, aligns and seats the primer smoothly and automatically.

**Lock-N-Load Classic Press** (includes three die bushings,
primer catcher, positive priming system, Automatic Primer Feed
and accessories) . . . . . . . . . . . . . . . . . . . . . . . . . . . . . . . . . . . . . . . . . . $239.95

**LOCK-N-LOAD CLASSIC RELOADING PRESS**

# HORNADY

## NEW DIMENSION CUSTOM GRADE RELOADING DIES

Features an Elliptical Expander that minimizes friction and reduces case neck stretch, plus the need for a tapered expander for "necking up" to the next larger caliber. Other recent design changes include a hardened steel decap pin that will not break, bend or crack even when depriming stubborn military cases. A bullet seater alignment sleeve guides the bullet and case neck into the die for in-line benchhrest alignment. All New Dimension Reloading Dies include: collar and collar lock to center expander precisely; one-piece expander spindle with tapered bottom for easy cartridge insertion; wrench flats on die body, Sure-Loc™ lock rings and collar lock for easy tightening; and built-in crimper.

**New Dimension Custom Grade Reloading Dies:**
| | |
|---|---|
| Series I Two-die Rifle Set | $26.95 |
| Series I Three-die Rifle Set | 28.50 |
| Series II Three-die Pistol Set (w/Titanium Nitride) | 37.75 |
| Series III Two-die Rifle Set | 32.25 |
| Series IV Specialty Die Set | 53.75 |

Also available:
| | |
|---|---|
| **50 Caliber BMG Dies (Two-Die Set)** | $260.00 |

## LOCK-N-LOAD AUTO PROGRESSIVE PRESS

The Lock-N-Load Automatic Progressive reloading press, featuring the Lock-N-Load bushing system, delivers consistently accurate loaded rounds, changing forever the way handloaders switch from one caliber to another. This task can now be done with a flick of the wrist and allows the operator to stop loading, change dies and start loading another caliber in seconds. Five Lock-N-Load die stations offer the flexibility to add a roll or taper crimp die. Dies and powder measure are inserted onto Lock-N-Load die bushings, which lock securely into the press. The bushings remain with the die and powder measure, retaining their settings. Hornady's Case Activated Powder Drop releases powder only when a case is ready and removes in seconds. It also fits on other presses and mounts like dies using the Lock-N-Load bushing system. Other features include: Deluxe Powder Measure, Automatic Indexing, Off-Set Handle, Power-Pac Linkage, Case ejector.

**Lock-N-Load Auto Progressive Press** (includes five die bushings, shellplate, primer catcher, Positive Priming System, powder drop, Deluxe Powder Measure, automatic primer feed) .............. **$349.95**

## MODEL 366 AUTO SHOTSHELL RELOADER

The 366 Auto features full-length resizing with each stroke, automatic primer feed, swing-out wad guide, three-stage crimping featuring Taper-Loc for factory tapered crimp, automatic advance to the next station and automatic ejection. The turntable holds 8 shells for 8 operations with each stroke. The primer tube filler is fast. The automatic charge bar loads shot and powder. Right- or left-hand operation; interchangeable charge bushings, die sets and Magnum dies and crimp starters for 6 point, 8 point and paper crimps.

**Model 366 Auto Shotshell Reloader:**
| | |
|---|---|
| 12, 20, 28 gauge or .410 bore | $340.00 |
| Primer Tube Filler | 12.25 |
| Powder and Shot Baffles (per set) | 5.50 |
| Riser Legs (per set) | 6.45 |
| Shot and Powder Hoppers (each) | 11.30 |

# LYMAN BULLET-SIZING EQUIPMENT

## MAG 20 ELECTRIC FURNACE

The MAG 20 is a new furnace offering several advantages to cast bullet enthusiasts. It features a steel crucible of 20-pound capacity and incorporates a proven bottom-pour valve system and a fully adjustable mould guide. The improved design of the MAG 20 makes it equally convenient to use the bottom-pour valve, or a ladle. A new heating coil design reduces the likelihood of pour spout "freeze." Heat is controlled from "Off" to nominally 825° F by a calibrated thermostat which automatically increases temperature output when alloy is added to the crucible. A pre-heat shelf for moulds is attached to the back of the crucible. Available for 100 V and 200 V systems.

**Price:** 110 V . . . . . . . . . . . . . . . . . . . . . . . . . . . . . **$250.00**
220 V . . . . . . . . . . . . . . . . . . . . . . . . . . . . . **250.00**

## BULLET-MAKING EQUIPMENT

**Deburring Tool**
Lyman's deburring tool can be used for chamfering or deburring of cases up to 45 caliber. For precise bullet seating, use the pointed end of the tool to bevel the inside of new or trimmed cases. To remove burrs left by trimming, place the other end of the deburring tool over the mouth of the case and twist. The tool's centering pin will keep the case aligned . . . . . . . . . . . . . . . . . . . . . . . . . . . . . . . . . . . **$10.75**

**Mould Handles**
These large hardwood handles are available in three sizes single-, double- and four-cavity.
**Single-cavity handles** (for small block, black powder and specialty moulds; 12 oz.) . . . . . . . . . . . . . . . . . **$24.00**
**Double-cavity handles** (for two-cavity and large-block single-cavity moulds; 12 oz.) . . . . . . . . . . . . . **24.00**
**Four-cavity handles** (1 lb.) . . . . . . . . . . . . . . . . . . **28.00**

**Rifle Moulds**
All Lyman rifle moulds are available in double cavity only, except those moulds where the size of the bullet necessitates a single cavity (12 oz.) . . . . . . . . . . . . . . . . . . . . . . **$49.95**

**Hollow-Point Bullet Moulds**
Hollow-point moulds are cut in single-cavity blocks only and require single-cavity handles (9 oz.) . . . . . . . . . . . . . **$49.95**

**Shotgun Slug Moulds**
Available in 12 or 20 gauge; do not require rifling. Moulds are single cavity only, cut on the larger double-cavity block and require double-cavity handles (14 oz.) . . . . . . . . . . . . **$45.00**

**Pistols Moulds**
Cover all popular calibers and bullet designs in double-cavity blocks and, on a limited basis, four-cavity blocks.
**Double-cavity mould block** . . . . . . . . . . . . . . . . . . . **$49.95**
**Four-cavity mould block** . . . . . . . . . . . . . . . . . . . . . **76.50**

**Lead Casting Dipper**
Dipper with cast-iron head. The spout is shaped for easy, accurate pouring that prevents air pockets in the finished bullet . . . . . . . . . . . . . . . . . . . . . . . . . . . . . . . . . . . . . **$12.95**

**Gas Checks**
Gas checks are gilding metal caps which fit to the base of cast bullets. These caps protect the bullet base from the burning effect of hot powder gases and permit higher velocities. Easily seated during the bullet-sizing operation. Only Lyman gas checks should be used with Lyman cast bullets.
**22 through 35 caliber** (per 1000) . . . . . . . . . . . . . . . **$24.75**
**375 through 45 caliber** (per 1000) . . . . . . . . . . . . . **29.75**
**Gas check seater** . . . . . . . . . . . . . . . . . . . . . . . . . . **8.00**

**Lead Pot**
The cast-iron pot allows the bullet caster to use any source of heat. Pot capacity is about 8 pounds of alloy and the flat bottom prevents tipping . . . . . . . . . . . . . . . . . . . . . . **$12.95**

**Universal Decapping Die**
Covers all calibers .22 through .45 (except .378 and .460 Weatherby). Can be used before cases are cleaned or lubricated. Requires no adjustment when changing calibers; fits all popular makes of $7/8 \times 14$ presses, single station or progressive, and is packaged with 10 replacement pins **$10.75**

## UNIVERSAL CARBIDE FOUR-DIE SET

Lyman's new 4-die carbide sets allow simultaneous neck expanding and powder charging. They feature specially designed hollow expanding plugs that utilize Lyman's 2-step neck-expansion system, while allowing powder to flow thru the die into the cartridge case after expanding. Includes taper crimp die. All popular pistol calibers. . . . . . . . . . . . **$49.95**

# LYMAN RELOADING TOOLS

**MODEL 1200 CLASSIC TURBO TUMBLER**

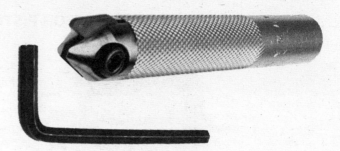

## "INSIDE/OUTSIDE" DEBURRING TOOL

This unique new tool features an adjustable cutting blade that adapts easily to any rifle or pistol case from 22 caliber to 45 caliber with a simple hex wrench adjustment. Inside deburring is completed by a conical internal section with slotted cutting edges, thus providing uniform inside and outside deburring in one simple operation. The deburring tool is mounted on an anodized aluminum handle that is machine-knurled for a sure grip.

**Deburring Tool** . . . . . . . . . . . . . . . . . . . . . . . . . . . . . **$13.50**

Features a redesigned base and drive system, plus a stronger suspension system and built-in exciters for better tumbling action and faster cleaning

| | |
|---|---|
| **Model 1200 Classic** . . . . . . . . . . . . . . . . . . . . . . | $ 82.95 |
| **Model 1200 Auto-Flo** . . . . . . . . . . . . . . . . . . . . . | 109.95 |
| Also available: | |
| **Model 600** . . . . . . . . . . . . . . . . . . . . . . . . . . . . . | 74.95 |
| **Model 2220** . . . . . . . . . . . . . . . . . . . . . . . . . . . . . | 116.95 |
| **Model 2200 Auto-Flo** . . . . . . . . . . . . . . . . . . . . . | 125.00 |
| **Model 3200** . . . . . . . . . . . . . . . . . . . . . . . . . . . . . | 164.95 |
| **Model 3200 Auto-Flo** . . . . . . . . . . . . . . . . . . . . . | 184.95 |
| **Mag-Flo** . . . . . . . . . . . . . . . . . . . . . . . . . . . . . . . | 229.95 |

## TUBBY TUMBLER

This popular tumbler now features a clear plastic "see thru" lid that fits on the outside of the vibrating tub. The Tubby has a polishing action that cleans more than 100 pistol cases in less than two hours. The built-in handle allows easy dumping of cases and media. An adjustable tab also allows the user to change the tumbling speed for standard or fast action.

**Tubby Tumbler** . . . . . . . . . . . . . . . . . . . . . . . . . . . **$58.50**

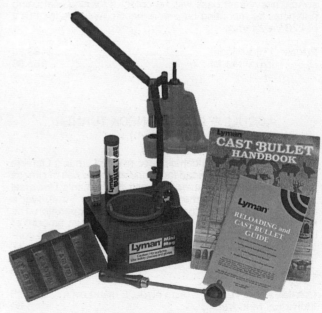

## MASTER CASTING KIT

Designed especially to meet the needs of blackpowder shooters, this new kit features Lyman's combination round ball and maxi ball mould blocks. It also contains a combination double cavity mould, mould handle, mini-mag furnace, lead dipper, bullet lube, a user's manual and a cast bullet guide. Kits are available in 45, 50 and 54 caliber.

**Master Casting Kit** . . . . . . . . . . . . . . . . . . . . . . . . **$152.00**

# LYMAN RELOADING TOOLS

## FOR RIFLE OR PISTOL CARTRIDGES

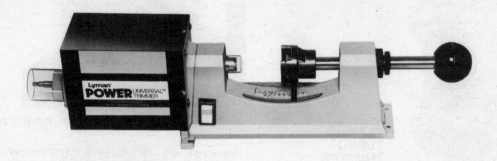

### POWER CASE TRIMMER

The new Lyman Power Trimmer is powered by a fan-cooled electric motor designed to withstand the severe demands of case trimming. The unit, which features the Universal™ Chuckhead, allows cases to be positioned for trimming or removed with fingertip ease. The Power Trimmer package includes Nine Pilot Multi-Pack. In addition to two cutter heads, a pair of wire end brushes for cleaning primer pockets are included. Other features include safety guards, on-off rocker switch, heavy cast base with receptacles for nine pilots, and bolt holes for mounting on a work bench. Available for 110 V or 220 V systems.

**Prices:** 110 V Model . . . . . . . . . . . . . . . . . . . . . . . . **$183.25**
220 V Model . . . . . . . . . . . . . . . . . . . . . . . . **185.00**

### ACCULINE OUTSIDE NECK TURNER
### (not shown)

To obtain perfectly concentric case necks, Lyman's Outside Neck Turner assures reloaders of uniform neck wall thickness and outside neck diameter. The unit fits Lyman's Universal Trimmer and AccuTrimmer. In use, each case is run over a mandrel, which centers the case for the turning operation. The cutter is carefully adjusted to remove a minimum amount of brass. Rate of feed is adjustable and a mechanical stop controls length of cut. Mandrels are available for calibers from .17 to .375; cutter blade can be adjusted for any diameter from .195″ to .405″.

**Outside Neck Turner** w/extra blade, 6 mandrels. . . . **$27.95**
**Individual Mandrels**. . . . . . . . . . . . . . . . . . . . . . . . . **4.00**

### CRUSHER II PRO KIT

Includes press, loading block, case lube kit, primer tray, Model 500 Pro scale, powder funnel and *Lyman Reloading Handbook*.

**Starter Kit** . . . . . . . . . . . . . . . . . . . . . . . . . . . . . . **$149.95**

### LYMAN CRUSHER II
### RELOADING PRESS (see photo below)

The only press for rifle or pistol cartridges that offers the advantage of powerful compound leverage combined with a true Magnum press opening. A unique handle design transfers power easily where you want it to the center of the ram. A 4½-inch press opening accommodates even the largest cartridges.

**Crusher II Press**
With Priming Arm and Catcher . . . . . . . . . . . . . . . . . **$108.00**

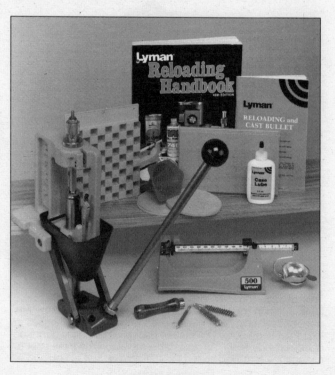

**STARTER KIT**

# LYMAN RELOADING TOOLS

### T-MAG II TURRET RELOADING PRESS

With the T-Mag II you can mount up to six different reloading dies on our turret. This means you can have all your dies set up, precisely mounted, locked in and ready to reload at all times. The T-Mag works with all $7/8 \times 14$ dies. The T-Mag II turret with its quick-disconnect release system is held in rock-solid alignment by a $3/4$-inch steel stud.

Also featured is Lyman's Crusher II compound leverage system. It has a longer handle with a ball-type knob that mounts easily for right- or left-handed operation.

**T-Mag II Press** w/Priming Arm & Catcher . . . . . . . . **$149.95**
    Extra Turret Head. . . . . . . . . . . . . . . . . . . . . . . .   **34.95**

Also available:
**EXPERT KIT** that includes T-MAG II Press, Universal Case Trimmer and pilot Multi-Pak, Model 500 powder scale and Model 50 powder measure, plus accessories and Reloading Manual. Available in calibers 9mm Luger, 38/357, 44 Mag., 45 ACP and 30-06 . . . . . . . . . . . . . . . . . . . . . . . . . . . . **$339.95**

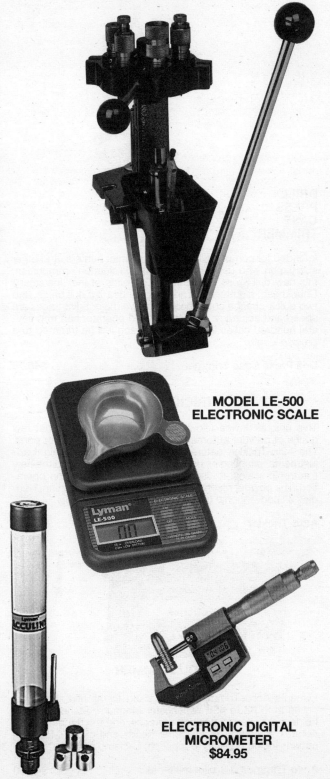

### ELECTRONIC SCALE MODEL LE: 1000

Accurate to $1/10$ grain, Lyman's new LE: 1000 measures up to 1000 grains of powder and easily converts to the gram mode for metric measurements. The push-botton automatic calibration feature eliminates the need for calibrating with a screwdriver. The scale works off a single 9V battery or AC power adaptor (included with each scale). Its compact design allows the LE: 1000 to be carried to the field easily. A sculpted carrying case is optional. 110 Volt or 220 Volt.

**Model LE: 1000 Electronic Scale** . . . . . . . . . . . . . . **$259.95**
**Model LE: 300 Electronic Scale** . . . . . . . . . . . . . . . . **166.50**
**Model LE: 500 Electric Scale** . . . . . . . . . . . . . . . . . **183.25**

**MODEL LE-500
ELECTRONIC SCALE**

### PISTOL ACCUMEASURE

Lyman's Pistol AccuMeasure uses changeable brass rotors pre-drilled to drop precise charges of ball and flake pistol propellants (the tool is not intended for use with long grain IMR-type powders). Most of the rotors are drilled with two cavities for maximum accuracy and consistency. The brass operating handle, which can be shifted for left or right hand operation, can be removed. The Pistol AccuMeasure can be mounted on all turret and single station presses; it can also be hand held with no loss of accuracy.

**Pistol AccuMeasure** w/3-rotor starter kit. . . . . . . . . **$35.00**

Also available:
**ROTOR SELECTION SET** including 12 dual-cavity rotors and 4 single-cavity units. Enables reloaders to throw a variety of charges for all pistol calibers through 45 . . . . . . . . . **$46.00**

**ELECTRONIC DIGITAL
MICROMETER
$84.95**

# LYMAN RELOADING TOOLS

## DRILL PRESS CASE TRIMMER

Intended for competitive shooters, varmint hunters, and other sportsmen who use large amounts of reloaded ammunition, this new drill press case trimmer consists of the Universal™ Chuckhead, a cutter shaft adapted for use in a drill press, and two quick-change cutter heads. Its two major advantages are speed and accuracy. An experienced operator can trim several hundred cases in a hour, and each will be trimmed to a precise length.

**Drill Press Case Trimmer** . . . . . . . . . . . . . . . . . . . . . . $45.75

## AUTO TRICKLER (not shown)

This unique device allows reloaders to trickle the last few grains of powder automatically into their scale powder pans. The Auto-Trickler features vertical and horizontal height adjustments, enabling its use with both mechanical and the new electronic scales. It also offers a simple push-button operation. The powder reservoir is easily removed for cleaning. Handles all conventional ball, stick or flare powder types.

**Auto-Trickler** . . . . . . . . . . . . . . . . . . . . . . . . . . . . . $37.50

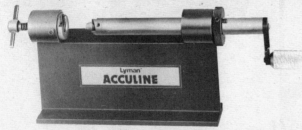

## ACCU TRIMMER

Lyman's Accu Trimmer can be used for all rifle and pistol cases from 22 to 458 Winchester Magnum. Standard shellholders are used to position the case, and the trimmer incorporates standard Lyman cutter heads and pilots. Mounting options include bolting to a bench, C-clamp or vise.

**Accu Trimmer** w/9-pilot multi-pak . . . . . . . . . . . . . . $40.50

## UNIVERSAL TRIMMER WITH NINE PILOT MULTI-PACK

This trimmer with patented chuckhead accepts all metallic rifle or pistol cases, regardless of rim thickness. To change calibers, simply change the case head pilot. Other features include coarse and fine cutter adjustments, an oil-impregnated bronze bearing, and a rugged cast base to assure precision alignment and years of service. Optional carbide cutter available. Trimmer Stop Ring includes 20 indicators as reference marks.

| | |
|---|---|
| **Replacement carbide cutter** . . . . . . . . . . . . . . . . . . | $39.95 |
| **Trimmer Multi-Pack** (incl. 9 pilots: 22, 24, 27, 28/7mm, 30, 9mm, 35, 44 and 45A) . . . . . . . . . . . | 64.95 |
| **Nine Pilot Multi-Pack** . . . . . . . . . . . . . . . . . . . . . . | 10.50 |
| **Power Pack Trimmer** . . . . . . . . . . . . . . . . . . . . . . . | 74.95 |
| **Universal Trimmer Power Adapter** . . . . . . . . . . . . . | 16.50 |

## UNIVERSAL TRIMMER POWER ADAPTER

## ELECTRONIC DIGITAL CALIPER (not shown)

Lyman's 6″ electronic caliper gives a direct digital readout for both inches and millimeters and can perform both inside and outside depth measurements. Its zeroing function allows the user to select zeroing dimensions and sort parts or cases by their plus or minus variation. The caliper works on a single, standard 1.5 volt silver oxide battery and comes with a fitted wooden storage case.

**Electronic Caliper** . . . . . . . . . . . . . . . . . . . . . . . . . . $79.95

# LYMAN RELOADING TOOLS

## PRO 1000 & 505 RELOADING SCALES

Features include improved platform system; hi-tech base design of high-impact styrene; extra-large, smooth leveling wheel; dual agate bearings; larger damper for fast zeroing; built-in counter weight compartment; easy-to-read beam.

Pro 1000 Scale ............................... $56.95
Pro 505 Scale ............................... 39.95

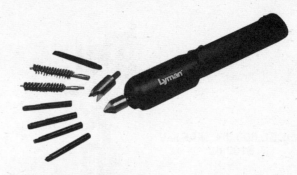

## POWER DEBURRING KIT

Features a high torque, rechargeable power driver plus a complete set of accessories, including inside and outside deburr tools, large and small reamers and cleaners and case neck brushes. No threading or chucking required. Set also includes battery recharger and standard flat and phillips driver bits.

Power Deburring Kit ......................... $54.95

## AUTOSCALE

After setting this new autoscale to the desired powder charge, it dispenses the exact amount of powder with the push of a button, over and over again. Features solid-state electronics and is controlled by a photo transistor to ensure accurate powder charges.

Autoscale ................................. $296.00

## DELUXE RELOADERS' PRO KIT

Includes Accupress with compound leverage; Pro 505 Scale; Accutrimmer with 9 popular pilots; ram prime die; deburr tool; powder funnel; Quick Spray case lube; shellholders (4); Lyman's 47th *Reloading Handbook*.

Deluxe Reloaders' Pro Kit ................... $132.50

# MEC SHOTSHELL RELOADERS

## MODEL 600 JR. MARK V
### $162.62

This single-stage reloader features a cam-action crimp die to ensure that each shell returns to its original condition. MEC's 600 Jr. Mark 5 can load 6 to 8 boxes per hour and can be updated with the 285 CA primer feed. Press is adjustable for 3″ shells. Die sets are available in 10, 12, 16, 20, 28 and .410 gauges at: . . . . . . . . . . . . . . . . . . . . . . . . . . . . . . . . . **$59.50**

## MODEL 8567 GRABBER
### $458.78

This reloader features 12 different operations at all 6 stations, producing finished shells with each stroke of the handle. It includes a fully automatic primer feed and Auto-Cycle charging, plus MEC's exclusive 3-stage crimp. The "Power Ring" resizer ensures consistent, accurately sized shells without interrupting the reloading sequence. Simply put in the wads and shell casings, then remove the loaded shells with each pull of the handle. Optional kits to load 3″ shells and steel shot make this reloader tops in its field. Resizes high and low base shells. Available in 12, 16, 20, 28 gauge and .410 bore. No die sets are available.

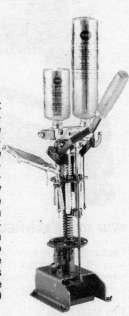

## MODEL 650
### $319.80

This reloader works on 6 shells at once. A reloaded shell is completed with every stroke. The MEC 650 does not resize except as a separate operation. Automatic Primer feed is standard. Simply fill it with a full box of primers and it will do the rest. Reloader has 3 crimping stations: the first one starts the crimp, the second closes the crimp, and the third places a taper on the shell. Available in 12, 16, 20 and 28 gauge and .410 bore. No die sets are available.

## MODEL 8120 SIZEMASTER
### $245.00

Sizemaster's "Power Ring" collet resizer returns each base to factory specifications. This generation resizing station handles brass or steel heads, both high and low base. An 8-fingered collet squeezes the base back to original dimensions, then opens up to release the shell easily. The E-Z Prime auto primer feed is standard equipment (not offered in .410 bore). Press is adjustable for 3″ shells and is available in 12, 16, 20, 28 gauge and .410 bore. Die sets are available at: **$88.65 ($104.00** in 10 ga.).

# MEC RELOADING

## STEELMASTER SINGLE STAGE

The only shotshell reloader equipped to load steel shotshells as well as lead ones. Every base is resized to factory specs by a precision "power ring" collet. Handles brass or steel heads in high or low base. The E-Z prime auto primer feed dispenses primers automatically and is standard equipment. Separate presses are available for 12 gauge 2³/₄", 3", 12 gauge 3¹/₂" and 10 gauge.

Steelmaster . . . . . . . . . . . . . . . . . . . . . . . . . . . . . . $255.00
In 12 ga. 3¹/₂" only . . . . . . . . . . . . . . . . . . . . . . . . . 280.66

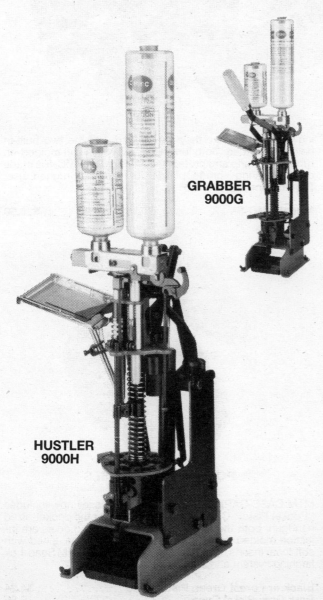

**GRABBER 9000G**

**HUSTLER 9000H**

## E-Z PRIME "S" AND "V" AUTOMATIC PRIMER FEEDS

From carton to shell with security, these primer feeds provide safe, convenient primer positioning and increase rate of production. Reduce bench clutter, allowing more free area for wads and shells.
- Primers transfer directly from carton to reloader, tubes and tube fillers
- Positive mechanical feed (not dependent upon agitation of press)
- Visible supply
- Automatic. Eliminate hand motion
- Less susceptible to damage
- Adapt to all domestic and most foreign primers with adjustment of the cover
- May be purchased separately to replace tube-type primer feed or to update your present reloader

E-Z Prime "S" (for Super 600, 650) or
E-Z Prime "V" (for 600 Jr. Mark V & VersaMEC) . . . $39.70

## MEC 9000 SERIES SHOTSHELL RELOADER

MEC's 9000 Series features automatic indexing and finished shell ejection for quicker and easier reloading. The factory set speed provides uniform movement through every reloading stage. Dropping the primer into the reprime station no longer requires operator "feel." The reloader requires only a minimal adjustment from low to high brass domestic shells, any one of which can be removed for inspection from any station. Can be set up for automatic or manual indexing. Available in 12, 16, 20 and 28 gauge and .410 bore. No die sets are available.

MEC 9000H . . . . . . . . . . . . . . . . . . . . . . . . . . . . . $1386.00
MEC 9000G Series . . . . . . . . . . . . . . . . . . . . . . . . 557.00

# MTM RELOADING

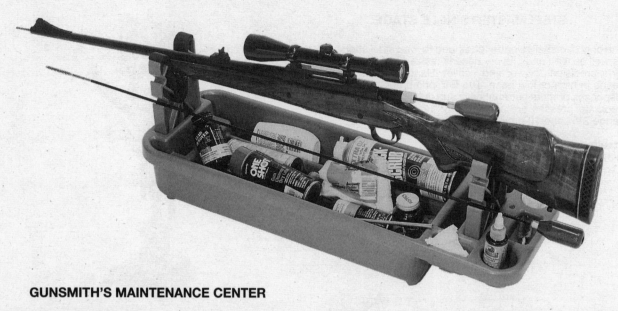

## GUNSMITH'S MAINTENANCE CENTER

MTM's Gunsmiths Maintenance Center (RMC-5) is designed for mounting scopes and swivels, bedding of actions or for cleaning rifles and shotguns. Multi-positional forks allow for eight holding combinations, making it possible to service firearm level, upright or upside down. The large middle section keeps tools and cleaning supplies in one area. Individual solvent compartments help to eliminate accidental spills. Cleaning rods stay where they are needed with the two built-in holders provided. Both forks (covered with a soft molded-on rubber pad) grip and protect the firearm. The RMC-5 is made of engineering- grade plastic for years of rugged use. **Dimensions:** 29.5″ × 9.5″

**Model RMC-5** . . . . . . . . . . . . . . . . . . . . . . . . . . . . . . . . **$26.50**

## PISTOL REST MODEL PR-30

MTM's new PR-30 Pistol Rest will accommodate any size handgun, from a Derringer to a 14″ Contender. A locking front support leg adjusts up or down, allowing 20 different positions. Rubber padding molded to the tough polypropylene fork protects firearms from scratches. Fork clips into the base when not in use for compact storage. **Dimensions:** 6″ × 11″ × 2.5″

**Pistol Rest Model PR-30** . . . . . . . . . . . . . . . . . . . . . $15.25

## POCKET PISTOL CASES

MTM CASE-GARD's℠ line of hard gun cases now includes "Pocket Pistol" Cases. Designed solely for the pocket-sized handgun, both the 802C and deluxe 802CD models are injection molded from high-impact polypropylene. Lined with soft foam inserts, they feature the CASE-GARDTM Snap-Lok latching system and are tabbed for a padlock.

**Black or Forest Green Pistol Case** . . . . . . . . . . . . . **$4.24**
**Dark Gray Pistol Case** . . . . . . . . . . . . . . . . . . . . . . . . 5.85

# RCBS RELOADING TOOLS

### ROCK CHUCKER
### PRESS
### $128.63

With its easy operation, out-standing strength and versa-tility, a Rock Chucker press is ideal for beginner and pro alike. It can also be upgraded to a progressive press with an optional Piggyback II conversion unit.
- Heavy-duty cast iron for easy case-resizing
- 1" ram held in place by 12.5 sq. in. of rambearing surface
- Toggle blocks of ductile iron
- Compound leverage system
- Pins ground from hardened steel
- 1¼"-12 thread for shotshell die kits and Piggyback II
- ⁷⁄₈"-14 thread for all standard reloading dies and accessories
- Milled slot and set screws accept optional RCBS automatic primer feed

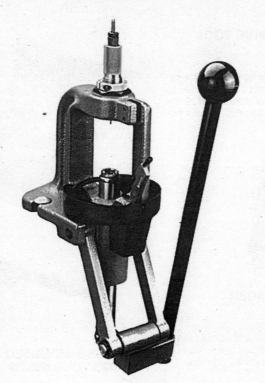

### RELOADER SPECIAL-5
### $100.13

### ROCK CHUCKER
### MASTER RELOADING KIT
### $335.25

For reloaders who want the best equipment, the Rock Chucker Master Reloading Kit includes all the tools and accessories needed. Included are the following: • Rock Chucker Press • RCBS 505 Reloading Scale • Speer TrimPro Manual #12 • Uniflow Powder Measure • RCBS Rotary Case Trimmer-2 • deburring tool • case loading block • Primer Tray-2 • Automatic Primer Feed Combo • powder funnel • case lube pad • case neck brushes • fold-up hex ket set.

### AMMOMASTER
### SINGLE STAGE

The Reloader Special press features a comfortable ball handle and a primer arm so that cases can be primed and resized at the same time.
- Compound leverage system
- Solid aluminum black "O" frame offset for unobstructed access
- Corrosion-resistant baked-powder finish
- Can be upgraded to progressive reloading with an optional Piggyback II conversion unit
- 1¼"-12 thread for shotshell die kits and Piggyback II
- ⁷⁄₈"-14 thread for all standard reloading dies and accessories

### AMMOMASTER
### RELOADING SYSTEM
### Single Stage $178.38
### Auto $394.63

The AmmoMaster offers the handloader the freedom to configure a press to his particular needs and preferences. It covers the complete spectrum of reloading, from single stage through fully automatic progressive reloading, from .32 Auto to .50 caliber. The **AmmoMaster Auto** has all the features of a five-station press.

# RCBS RELOADING TOOLS

## APS BENCH-MOUNTED PRIMING TOOL
### $83.38

The APS Bench-Mounted Priming Tool was created for re-loaders who prefer a separate, specialized tool dedicated to priming only. The handle of the bench-mounted tool is designed to provide hours of comfortable loading. Handle position can be adjusted for bench height.

## APS PRIMER STRIP LOADER
### $21.50

For those who keep a supply of CCI primers in conventional packaging, the APS primer strip loader allows quick filling of empty strips. Each push of the handle seats 25 primers.

## POW'R PULL BULLET PULLER (not shown)
### $24.25

The RCBS Pow'r Pull bullet puller features a three-jaw chuck that grips the case rim—just rap it on any solid surface like a hammer, and powder and bullet drop into the main chamber for re-use. A soft cushion protects bullets from damage. Works with most centerfire cartridges from .22 to .45 (not for use with rimfire cartridges).

## RELOADING SCALE MODEL 5-0-5
### $72.50

This 511-grain capacity scale has a three-poise system with widely spaced, deep beam notches to keep them in place. Two smaller poises on right side adjust from 0.1 to 10 grains, larger one on left side adjusts in full 10-grain steps. The first scale to use magnetic dampening to eliminate beam oscillation, the 5-0-5 also has a sturdy die-cast base with large leveling legs for stability. Self-aligning agate bearings support the hardened steel beam pivots for a guaranteed sensitivity to 0.1 grains.

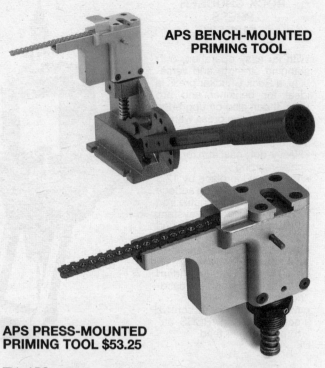

APS BENCH-MOUNTED PRIMING TOOL

## APS PRESS-MOUNTED PRIMING TOOL $53.25

This APS press-mounted priming tool provides the same features as the bench-mounted tool except it attaches to any single-stage press that accepts standard 7/8"×14 dies.

TRIM PRO™ POWER CASE TRIMMER

## TRIM PRO CASE TRIMMER
### $202.38 (Power)   $67.45 (Manual)

Cartridge cases are trimmed quickly and easily with a few turns of the RCBS Trim Pro case trimmer. The lever-type handle is more accurate to use than draw collet systems. A flat plate shell holder keeps cases locked in place and aligned. A micrometer fine adjustment bushing offers trimming accuracy to within .001". Made of die-cast metal with hardened cutting blades. The power model is like having a personal lathe, delivering plenty of torque. Positive locking handle and in-line power switch make it simple and safe. Also available:

**Trim Pro Case Trimmer Stand** . . . . . . . . . . . . . . . . $14.25
**Case Holder Accessory** . . . . . . . . . . . . . . . . . . . . . . 30.35

# RCBS RELOADING TOOLS

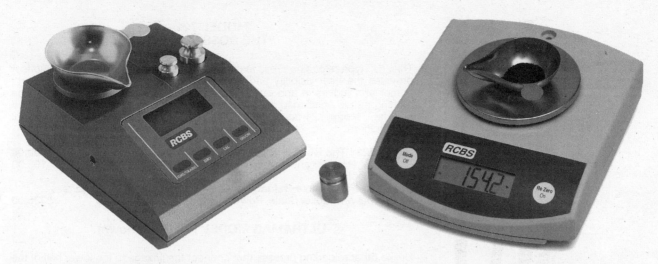

### POWDER PRO™ DIGITAL SCALE
### $203.38

The RCBS Powder Pro Digital Scale has a 1500-grain capacity. Powder, bullets, even cases with accuracy up to 0.1 grain can be weighed. Includes infra-red data port for transferring information to the Powdermaster Electronic Powder Dispenser.

### POWDERMASTER ELECTRONIC
### POWDER DISPENSER
### $214.13

Works in combination with the RCBS Powder Pro Digital Scale and with all types of smokeless powder. Can be used as a power trickler as well as a powder dispenser. Accurate to one-tenth of a grain.

### RELOADING SCALE MODEL 10-10
### $115.15

**Up to 1010 Grain Capacity**
Normal capacity is 510 grains, which can be increased, without loss in sensitivity, by attaching the included extra weight.

Features include micrometer poise for quick, precise weighing, special approach-to-weight indicator, easy-to-read graduations, magnetic dampener, agate bearings, anti-tip pan, and dustproof lid snaps on to cover scale for storage. Sensitivity is guaranteed to 0.1 grains.

### RANGERMASTER ELECTRONIC POWDER SCALE
### $220.38

Includes programmable battery shut-off to save battery life. Operates on AC power or single 9V battery. Ensures one-tenth of a grain sensitivity and accuracy from zero to 1500 grains. Will accommodate powder trickler. Non-spill aluminum pan provided.

### POWDER CHECKER (not shown)
### $22.59

Operates on a free-moving rod for simple, mechanical operation with nothing to break. Standard $7/8 \times 14$ die body can be used in any progressive loader that takes standard dies. Black oxide finish provides corrosion resistance with good color contrast for visibility.

### PARTNER
### ELECTRONIC POWDER
### SCALE $146.25

Accurate from +/− one-tenth of a grain up to 300 grains and +/− two-tenths up to 750 grains. Large LCD display is angled for easy reading over a wide range of positions. Powered by 9-volt battery.

# REDDING RELOADING TOOLS

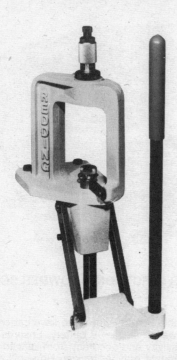

## MODEL 721
## "THE BOSS" PRESS

This "O" type reloading press features a rigid cast iron frame whose 36° offset provides the best visibility and access of comparable presses. Its "Smart" primer arm moves in and out of position automatically with ram travel. The priming arm is positioned at the bottom of ram travel for lowest leverage and best feel. Model 721 accepts all standard 7/8-14 threaded dies and universal shell holders.

**Model 721 "The Boss"** ....................................... $129.00
    With Shellholder and 10A Dies............................. 165.00
Also available:
**Boss Pro-Pak Deluxe Reloading Kit.** Includes Boss Reloading Press, #2 Powder and Bullet Scale, Powder Trickler, Reloading Dies ...... **$336.00**

## ULTRAMAG MODEL 700 (Not Shown)

Unlike other reloading presses that connect the linkage to the lower half of the press, the Ultramag's compound leverage system is connected at the top of the press frame. This allows the reloader to develop tons of pressure without the usual concern about press frame deflection. Huge frame opening will handle 50 × 3 1/4-inch Sharps with ease.

**No. 700 Press,** complete ..................................... $289.50
**No. 700K Kit,** includes shell holder and one set of dies ........... 324.00

**COMPETITION BUSHING NECK DIE**

**TYPE S BUSHING NECK DIE**

## BUSHING-STYLE NECK-SIZING DIES

Redding introduces two new Bushing Style Neck Sizing Dies—a simplified version (dubbed "Type S") and a Competition model—with interchangeable sizing bushings available in .001 increments. The Type S comes in 42 calibers and has an adjustable decapping rod to allow positioning of the bushing to resize only a portion of the neck length, if desired. The Competition Model features a cartridge case that is supported and aligned with the interchangeable sizing bushings before the sizing process begins.

**Competition Bullet Seating Die**.................. $96.00
**Type S Bushing Neck Die** ..................... 52.50
**Competition Bushing Neck Die**................ 96.00

## METALLIC TURRET RELOADING PRESS
## MODEL 25

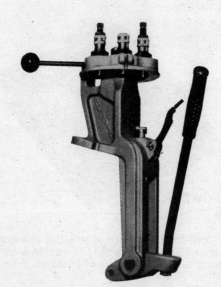

Extremely rugged, ideal for production reloading. No need to move shell, just rotate turret head to positive alignment. Ram accepts any standard snap-in shell holder. Includes primer arm for seating both small and large primers.

**No. 25 Press,** complete ..................................... $289.50
**No. 25K Kit,** includes press, shell holder, and one set of dies ...... 324.00

# REDDING RELOADING TOOLS

## MASTER POWDER MEASURE MODEL 3

Universal- or pistol-metering chambers interchange in seconds. Measures charges from $1/2$ to 100 grains. Unit is fitted with lock ring for fast dump with large "clear" plastic reservoir. "See-thru" drop tube accepts all calibers from 22 to 600. Precision-fitted rotating drum is critically honed to prevent powder escape. Knife-edged powder chamber shears coarse-grained powders with ease, ensuring accurate charges.

**No. 3 Master Powder Measure**
(specify Universal- or Pistol-Metering chamber) . . . . . . **$120.00**
**No. 3K Kit Form,** includes both
Universal and Pistol
chambers . . . . . . . . . . . . . 144.00
**Bench Stand** . . . . . . . . . . . . 27.50

## MASTER CASE TRIMMER MODEL 1400

This unit features a universal collet that accepts all rifle and pistol cases. The frame is solid cast iron with storage holes in the base for extra pilots. Both coarse and fine adjustments are provided for case length.

The case-neck cleaning brush and primer pocket cleaners attached to the frame of this tool make it a very handy addition to the reloading bench. Trimmer comes complete with:
• New speed cutter shaft
• Six pilots (22, 6mm, 25, 270, 7mm and 30 cal.)
• Universal collet
• Two neck cleaning brushes (22 thru 30 cal.)
• Two primer pocket cleaners (large and small)

**No. 1400 Master Case Trimmer** complete . . . . . . . **$93.00**
**No. 1500 Pilots** . . . . . . . . . . . . . . . . . . . . . . . . . . . 3.90

## COMPETITION MODEL BR-30 POWDER MEASURE (not shown)

This powder measure features a new drum and micrometer that limit the overall charging range from a low of 10 grains (depending on powder density) to a maximum of approx. 50 grains. For serious competitive shooters whose loading requirements are between 10 and 50 grains, this is the measure to choose. The diameter of Model 3BR's metering cavity has been reduced, and the metering plunger on the new model has a unique hemispherical or cup shape, creating a powder cavity that resembles the bottom of a test tube. The result: irregular powder setting is alleviated and charge-to-charge uniformity is enhanced.

**Competition Model BR-30 Powder Measure** . . . . **$180.00**

## MATCH GRADE POWDER MEASURE MODEL 3BR

Designed for the most demanding reloaders—bench rest, silhouette and varmint shooters. The Model 3BR is unmatched for its precision and repeatability. Its special features include a powder baffle and zero backlash micrometer.

**No. 3BR** with Universal or Pistol
Metering Chamber . . . . . . . **$150.00**
**No. 3 BRK** includes both
metering chambers . . . . . . 189.00

## MASTER CASE TRIMMER MODEL 1400

## STANDARD POWDER AND BULLET SCALE MODEL RS-1

For the beginner or veteran reloader. Only two counterpoises need to be moved to obtain the full capacity range of $1/10$ grain to 380 grains. Clearly graduated with white numerals and lines on a black background. Total capacity of this scale is 380 grains. An over-and-under plate graduate in 10th grains allows checking of variations in powder charges or bullets without further adjustments.

**Model No. RS-1** . . . . . . . . . . . . . . . . . . . . . . . . . . . . . **$49.50**

Also available: **Master Powder & Bullet Scale.** Same as standard model, but includes a magnetic dampened beam swing for extra fast readings. 505-grain capacity . . . **$75.00**

# THOMPSON/CENTER

## BLACKPOWDER TOOLS

### U-VIEW POWDER MEASURE
### $16.90

This measure shows the exact level of powder in the tube. Eliminates the guesswork of loading consistent charges. Includes loading spout that swivels out of the way to fill measure. Locking shaft is easy to adjust.

### U-VIEW POWDER FLASK
### $21.90

### HOT SHOT NIPPLE
### $4.75

This see-through powder flask makes it easy to monitor powder supply. It's small enough to fit in the pocket yet holds enough powder for a dozen reloads or more. A spring-loaded plunger helps to control dispensing operation.

Allows more even and controlled flow of pressurized gases from cap into ignition channel. Also releases gases through the side ports to prevent gas blowback. Made of hardened stainless steel to tight tolerances. Use with ¼-28 threads for T/C caplocks (except T/C Scout).
Also available:
**DELUXE NIPPLE WRENCH:** . . . . . . . . . . . . . . . . . **$12.90**

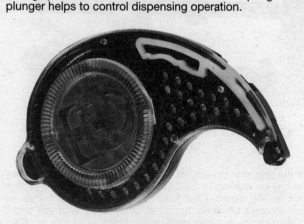

### U-VIEW CAPPER
### $22.90

### DELUXE NIPPLE WRENCH

### MAXI-SHOK BULLET PERFORMANCE TOOLS
### $27.95 (not shown)

Holds an entire box of 100 caps. Traditional shape makes it easy to use with both inline ignition muzzleloaders and sidelock actions. Simple thumb-actuated mechanism. Rugged construction.

Seat bullet or round ball with one of 4 tips on the end of the ramrod to improve terminal ballistics. By changing front of the soft lead bullet, maximum energy transfer is assured through increase in projectile expansion. Includes 3 bore guides: .45, .50 & .54 cal., plus ⁵/₁₆ adapter.

Reference

# DIRECTORY OF MANUFACTURERS AND SUPPLIERS

The following manufacturers, suppliers and distributors of firearms, reloading equipment, sights, scopes, ammo and accessories all appear with their products in the catalog and/or "Manufacturers' Showcase" sections of this SHOOTER'S BIBLE.

**ACCURATE ARMS CO., INC.**
5891 Hwy, 230W
McEwen, Tennessee 37101
Tel: 615-729-4207   Fax: 615-729-4211

**AIMPOINT** (sights, scopes, mounts)
420 West Main St.
Geneseo, Illinois 61254
Tel: 309-944-5631   Fax: 309-944-3676

**ALLIANT TECH SYSTEMS** (gunpowder)
Route 114, P.O. Box 6
Radford, Virginia 24141
Tel: 800-276-9337   Fax: 540-639-7189

**AMERICAN ARMS** (handguns; Franchi shotguns; Uberti handguns, rifles, blackpowder)
715 E. Armour Road
N. Kansas City, Missouri 64116
Tel: 816-474-3161   Fax: 816-474-1225

**AMERICAN DERRINGER CORP.** (handguns)
127 North Lacy Drive
Waco, Texas 76705
Tel: 817-799-9111   Fax: 817-799-7935

**AMERICAN FRONTIER FIREARMS** (blackpowder arms)
P.O. Box 744
Aguanga, California 92536
Tel: 909-763-2209   Fax: 909-763-0014

**ARCADIA MACHINE & TOOL INC.** (AMT handguns, rifles)
6226 Santos Diaz Street
Irwindale, California 91702
Tel: 818-334-6629   Fax: 818-969-5247

**ARMES DE CHASSE** (AyA shotguns; Francotte rifles, shotguns)
P.O. Box 86
Hertford, North Carolina 27944
Tel: 919-426-2245   Fax: 919-426-1557

**ARMSCOR** (handguns, rifles, shotguns)
Available through K.B.I., Inc.

**ARMSPORT, INC.** (Bernardelli handguns, shotguns)
3590 NW 49th Street, P.O. Box 523066
Miami, Florida 33142
Tel: 305-635-7850   Fax: 305-633-2877

**ARNOLD ARMS CO. INC.** (rifles)
P.O. Box 1011
Arlington, Washington 98223
Tel: 360-435-1011   Fax: 360-435-7304

**A-SQUARE COMPANY INC.** (rifles)
One Industrial Park
Bedford, Kentucky 40006
Tel: 502-255-7456   Fax: 502-255-7657

**ASTRA** (handguns)
Available through European American Armory

**AUSTIN & HALLECK** (blackpowder rifles)
1099 Welt
Weston, Missouri 64098
Tel: 816-386-2176   Fax: 816-386-2177

**AUTO-ORDNANCE CORP.** (handguns, rifles)
Williams Lane
West Hurley, New York 12491
Tel: 914-679-7225   Fax: 914-679-2698

**AyA** (shotguns)
Available through Armes de Chasse

**BAUSCH & LOMB/BUSHNELL** (scopes)
Sports Optics Division
9200 Cody
Overland Park, Kansas 66214
Tel: 913-752-3433   Fax: 913-752-3489

**BENELLI**
Handguns avail. through European American Armory
Shotguns avail. through Heckler & Koch

**BERETTA U.S.A. CORP.** (handguns, rifles, shotguns)
17601 Beretta Drive
Accokeek, Maryland 20607
Tel: 301-283-2191   Fax: 301-283-0435

**BERNARDELLI** (handguns, shotguns)
Available through Armsport

**BERSA** (handguns)
Available through Eagle Imports Inc.

**BLASER USA, INC.** (rifles)
c/o Autumn Sales, Inc.
1320 Lake Street
Fort Worth, Texas 76102
Tel: 817-335-1634   Fax: 817-338-0119

**BLUE BOOK PUBLICATIONS** (books)
8009 34th Ave. South, Suite 175
Minneapolis, Minnesota 55425
Tel: 612-854-5229   Fax: 612-853-1486

**BLOUNT, INC.** (RCBS reloading equipment; Speer bullets; Weaver scopes)
P.O. Box 856
Lewiston, Idaho 83501
Tel: 208-746-2351   Fax: 208-799-3904

**BONANZA** (reloading tools)
*See* Forster Products

**BRNO** (rifles)
Available through Magnum Research

**BROLIN ARMS** (handguns, shotguns)
P.O. Box 698
Laverne, California 91750-0698
Tel: 909-392-2352   Fax. 909-392-2354

**BROWN PRECISION, INC.** (custom rifles)
7786 Molinos Avenue; P.O. Box 270 W.
Los Molinos, California 96055
Tel: 916-384-2506   Fax: 916-384-1638

**BROWNING** (handguns, rifles, shotguns)
One Browning Place
Morgan, Utah 84050
Tel: 801-876-2711   Fax: 801-876-3331

**BURRIS COMPANY, INC.** (scopes)
331 East Eighth Street, P.O. Box 1747
Greeley, Colorado 80631
Tel: 970-356-1670   Fax: 970-356-8702

**CABELA'S INC.** (blackpowder arms)
812 13th Avenue
Sidney, Nebraska 69160
Tel: 308-254-5505   Fax: 308-254-6669

**CHRISTENSEN ARMS** (rifles)
385 North 3050 East
St. George, Utah 84790
Tel: 801-674-9535   Fax: 801-674-9293

**CLIFTON ARMS** (custom rifles)
P.O. Box 1471
Medina, Texas 78055
Tel: 210-589-2666

**COLT BLACKPOWDER ARMS CO.** (blackpowder arms)
110 8th Street
Brooklyn, New York 11215
Tel: 718-499-4678   Fax: 718-768-8056

**COLT'S MANUFACTURING CO., INC.** (handguns, rifles)
P.O. Box 1868
Hartford, Connecticut 06144-1868
Tel: 800-962-COLT   Fax: 860-244-1449

**CONNECTICUT SHOTGUN MFG. CO.** (A. H. Fox shotguns)
35 Woodland Street, P.O. Box 1692
New Britain, Connecticut 06051-1692
Tel: 860-225-6581   Fax: 860-832-8707

**COONAN ARMS** (handguns)
1745 Highway 36E
Maplewood, Minnesota 55109
Tel: 612-777-3156   Fax: 612-777-3683

**COOPER FIREARMS** (rifles)
P.O. Box 114
Stevensville, Montana 59870
Tel: 406-777-5534   Fax: 406-777-5228

**COR-BON BULLET CO.** (ammunition)
1311 Industry Road
Sturgis, South Dakota 57785
Tel: 800-626-7266   Fax: 800-923-2666

**COUNTY** (shotguns)
10020 Whitman Lane
Tamarac, Florida 33321
Tel: 954-720-5090   Fax: 954-722-6353

**CUMBERLAND MOUNTAIN ARMS** (black-powder rifles)
1045 Dinah Shore Blvd., P.O. Box 710
Winchester, Tennessee 37398
Tel: 615-967-8414   Fax: 615-967-9199

**CVA** (blackpowder arms)
5988 Peachtree Corners East
Norcross, Georgia 30071
Tel: 800-251-9412   Fax: 770-242-8546

**DAEWOO PRECISION INDUSTRIES, LTD.** (handguns)
Available through Kimber of America

**DAKOTA** (handguns)
Available through E.M.F. Co., Inc.

**DAKOTA ARMS, INC.** (rifles, shotguns)
HC 55, Box 326
Sturgis, South Dakota 57785
Tel: 605-347-4686   Fax: 605-347-4459

**CHARLES DALY** (shotguns)
Available through K.B.I., Inc.

**DAVIS INDUSTRIES** (handguns)
11186 Venture Drive
Mira Loma, California 91752
Tel: 909-360-5598   Fax: 909-360-1749

**DESERT EAGLE** (handguns)
Available through Magnum Research Inc.

**DESERT MOUNTAIN MFG.** (rifle rests)
P.O. Box 130184
Coram, Montana 59913
Tel: 800-477-0762 .

**J. DEWEY MFG. CO.** (cleaning rods)
P.O. Box 2014
Southbury, Connecticut 06488
Tel: 203-264-3064   Fax: 203-262-6907

**DIXIE GUN WORKS** (blackpowder guns)
P.O. Box 130, Highway 51 S.
Union City, Tennessee 38261
Tel: 901-885-0561   Fax: 901-885-0440

**DOCTER OPTIC TECHNOLOGIES** (binoculars, scopes)
4685 Boulder Highway, Suite A
Las Vegas, Nevada 89121
Tel: 800-290-3634   Fax: 702-898-3737

**DOWNSIZER CORPORATION** (handguns)
P.O. Box 710316
Santee, California 92072-0316
Tel: 619-448-5510   Fax: 619-448-5780

**DYNAMIT NOBEL/RWS** (Rottweil shotguns)
81 Ruckman Road
Closter, New Jersey 07624
Tel: 201-767-1995   Fax: 201-767-1589


**EAGLE IMPORTS, INC.** (Bersa handguns)
1750 Brielle Avenue, Unit B1
Wanamassa, New Jersey 07712
Tel: 908-493-0333   Fax: 908-493-0301

**E.M.F. COMPANY, INC.** (Dakota handguns; Uberti handguns, blackpowder arms)
1900 East Warner Avenue 1-D
Santa Ana, California 92705
Tel: 714-261-6611   Fax: 714-756-0133

**ERMA** (handguns)
Available through Precision Sales Int'l.

**EUROARMS OF AMERICA INC.** (blackpowder guns)
1501 Lenoir Drive, P.O. Box 3277
Winchester, Virginia 22601
Tel: 540-662-1863

**EUROPEAN AMERICAN ARMORY CORP.** (Astra handguns; Benelli handguns; E.A.A. handguns, rifles)
P.O. Box 122
Sharpes, Florida 32959
Tel: 800-536-4442   Tel: 407-639-4842
Fax: 407-639-7006




**FEDERAL CARTRIDGE CO.** (ammunition)
900 Ehlen Drive
Anoka, Minnesota 55303-7503
Tel: 612-323-2300   Fax: 612-323-2506

**FEG** (handguns)
Available through Interarms and K.B.I., Inc.

**FLINTLOCKS, ETC.** (Pedersoli replica rifles)
160 Rossiter Road
Richmond, Massachusetts 01254
Tel: 413-698-3822   Fax: 413-698-3866

**FORREST, INC.** (ammo magazines)
P.O. Box 326
Lakeside, California 92040
Tel: 619-561-5800   Fax: 619-561-0227

**FORSTER PRODUCTS** (reloading)
82 East Lanark Avenue
Lanark, Illinois 61046
Tel: 815-493-6360   Fax: 815-493-2371

**A. H. FOX** (shotguns)
Available thru Connecticut Shotgun Mfg. Co.

**FRANCHI** (shotguns)
Available through American Arms

**FRANCOTTE** (rifles, shotguns)
Available through Armes de Chasse

**FREEDOM ARMS** (handguns)
One Freedom Lane, P.O. Box 1776
Freedom, Wyoming 83120
Tel: 307-883-2468   Fax: 307-883-2005




**GARBI** (shotguns)
Available through W. L. Moore & Co.

**GLASER SAFETY SLUG, INC.** (ammunition, gun accessories)
P.O. Box 8223
Foster City, California 94404
Tel: 415-345-7677   Fax: 415-345-8217

**GLOCK, INC.** (handguns)
6000 Highlands Parkway
Smyrna, Georgia 30082
Tel: 770-432-1202   Fax: 770-433-8719

**GONIC ARMS** (blackpowder rifles)
134 Flagg Road
Gonic, New Hampshire 03839
603-332-8456   Fax: 603-332-8457

**GSI (GUN SOUTH INC.)** (Mauser rifles; Merkel shotguns; Steyr-Mannlicher rifles)
108 Morrow Ave., P.O. Box 129
Trussville, Alabama 35173
Tel: 205-655-8299   Fax: 205-655-7078

**GUNLINE TOOLS** (gun checkering tools)
P.O. Box 478
Placentia, California 92670
Tel: 714-993-5100   Fax: 714-572-4128

**HÄMMERLI U.S.A.** (handguns)
19296 Oak Grove Circle
Groveland, California 95321
Tel: 209-962-5311   Fax: 209-962-5931

**HARRINGTON & RICHARDSON** (handguns, rifles, shotguns)
60 Industrial Rowe
Gardner, Massachusetts 01440
Tel: 508-632-9393   Fax: 508-632-2300

**HARRIS GUNWORKS** (rifles)
3840 N. 28th Ave.
Phoenix, Arizona 85017-4733
Tel: 602-230-1414   Fax: 602-230-1422

**HECKLER & KOCH** (handguns, rifles; Benelli shotguns)
21480 Pacific Boulevard
Sterling, Virginia 20166
Tel: 703-450-1900   Fax: 703-450-8160

**HENRY REPEATING ARMS CO.** (rifles)
110 8th Street
Brooklyn, New York 11215
Tel: 718-499-5600   Fax: 718-768-8056

**HERITAGE MANUFACTURING** (handguns)
4600 NW 135 St.
Opa Locka, Florida 33054
Tel: 305-685-5966   Fax: 305-687-6721

**HI-POINT FIREARMS** (handguns)
MKS Supply, Inc.
5990 Philadelphia Drive
Dayton, Ohio 45415
Tel/Fax: 513-275-4991

**HIGH STANDARD MFG CO.** (handguns)
4601 S. Pinemont, #148B
Houston, Texas 77041
Tel: 713-462-4200   Fax: 713-462-6437

**HODGDON POWDER CO., INC.** (gunpowder)
6231 Robinson, P.O. Box 2932
Shawnee Mission, Kansas 66201
Tel: 913- 362-9455   Fax: 913-362-1307

**HORNADY MANUFACTURING COMPANY** ( ammunition, reloading)
P.O. Box 1848
Grand Island, Nebraska 68802-1848
Tel: 308-382-1390   Fax: 308-382-5761

**HOWA** (rifles)
Available through Interarms

**HUNTER CO. INC.** (slings, accessories)
3300 West 71st Avenue
Westminster, Colorado 80030
Tel: 303-427-4626   Fax: 303-428-3980

**IGA SHOTGUNS**
Available through Stoeger Industries

**IMR POWDER COMPANY** (gunpowder)
1080 Military Turnpike
Plattsburgh, New York 12901
Tel: 518-563-2253

**INTERARMS** (FEG handguns; Howa rifles;
Rossi handguns, rifles; Star handguns;
Walther handguns)
10 Prince Street, Alexandria, Virginia 22314
Tel: 703-548-1400   Fax: 703-549-7826

**ISRAEL ARMS INT'L. INC.** (handguns)
5709 Hartsdale
Houston, Texas 77036
Tel: 713-789-0745   Fax: 713-789-7513

**ITHACA GUN CO.** (shotguns)
891 Route 34-B
Kings Ferry, New York 13081
Tel: 315-364-7171   Fax: 315-364-5134

**JARRETT RIFLES INC.** (custom rifles)
383 Brown Road
Jackson, South Carolina 29831
Tel: 803-471-3616

**JENNINGS, INC.** (handguns)
P.O. Box 20135
Carson City, Nevada 89721
Tel: 800-518-1666   Fax: 702-882-3129

**KAHR ARMS** (handguns)
P.O. Box 220
Blauvelt, New York 10913
Tel: 914-353-5996   Fax: 914-353-7833

**K.B.I., INC.** ( Armscor rifles, handguns, shot-
guns; Charles Daly shotguns; FEG hand-
guns)
P.O. Box 6346
Harrisburg, Pennsylvania 17112
Tel: 717-540-8518   Fax: 717-540-8567

**KIMBER OF AMERICA, INC.** ( handguns,
rifles; Daewoo handguns)
9039 Southeast Jannsen Road
Clackamas, Oregon 97015
Tel: 503-656-1704   Fax: 503-656-5357

**KNOUFF & KNOUFF, INC.** (gun cases)
P.O. Box 9912
Spokane, Washington 99209
Tel: 800-262-3322   Fax: 509-326-5436

**KONGSBERG AMERICA** (rifles)
Merwin's Associates
2 Merwin's Lane
Fairfield, Connecticut 06430
Tel: 203-259-0938   Fax: 203-259-2566

**KOWA OPTIMED, INC.** (scopes)
20001 South Vermont Avenue
Torrance, California 90502
Tel: 310-327-1913   Fax: 310-327-4177

**KRIEGHOFF INTERNATIONAL INC.** (rifles,
shotguns)
337A Route 611, P.O. Box 549
Ottsville, Pennsylvania 18942
Tel: 610-847-5173   Fax: 610-847-8691

**L.A.R. MANUFACTURING, INC.** (Grizzly
handguns, rifles)
4133 West Farm Road
West Jordan, Utah 84084
Tel: 801-280-3505   Fax: 801-280-1972

**LASERAIM TECHNOLOGIES INC.** (hand-
guns, sights)
P.O. Box 3548
Little Rock, Arkansas 72203-3548
Tel: 501-375-2227   Fax: 501-372-1445

**LAZZERONI ARMS CO.** (rifles)
P.O. Box 26696
Tucson, Arizona 85726
Tel: 520-577-7500   Fax: 520-624-4250

**LEUPOLD & STEVENS, INC.** (scopes, mounts)
1440 N.W. Greenbriar Parkway, P.O. Box 688
Beaverton, Oregon 97075
Tel: 503-646-9171   Fax: 503-526-1455

**LLAMA** (handguns)
Available through SGS Importers Int'l

**LUGER,** American Eagle (pistols)
Available through Stoeger Industries

**LYMAN PRODUCTS CORP.** (rifles, blackpowder guns, reloading tools)
475 Smith Street
Middletown, Connecticut 06457
Tel: 860-632-2020   Fax: 860-632-1699

**MAGNUM RESEARCH INC.** (Desert Eagle
handguns; CZ handguns; Brno rifles)
7110 University Avenue N.E.
Minneapolis, Minnesota 55432
Tel: 612-574-1868   Fax: 612-574-0109

**MAGTECH RECREATIONAL PRODUCTS**
(shotguns)
5030 Paradise Rd., Ste A104
Las Vegas, Nevada 89119
Tel: 702-736-2043   Fax: 702-736-2140

**MARLIN FIREARMS COMPANY** (rifles,
shotguns, blackpowder)
100 Kenna Drive
North Haven, Connecticut 06473
Tel: 203-239-5621   Fax: 203-234-7991

**MAROCCHI** (Conquista shotguns)
Available through Precision Sales Int'l.

**MAUSER** (rifles)
Available through GSI (Gun South Inc.)

**MAVERICK OF MOSSBERG** (shotguns)
Available through O. F. Mossberg

**MEC INC.** (reloading tools)
c/o Mayville Engineering Co.
715 South Street
Mayville, Wisconsin 53050
Tel: 414-387-4500   Fax: 414-387-2682

**MERIT CORP.** (sights)
P.O. Box 9044
Schenectady, New York 12309
Tel: 518-346-1420

**MERKEL** (shotguns)
Available through GSI (Gun South Inc.)

**M.O.A. CORP.** (handguns)
2451 Old Camden Pike
Eaton, Ohio 45302
Tel: 513-456-3669   Fax: 513-456-9331

**MODERN MUZZLELOADING INC.** (black-
powder guns)
P.O. Box 130, 234 Airport Rd.,
Centerville, Iowa 52544
Tel: 515-856-2626   Fax: 515-856-2628

**WILLIAM L. MOORE & CO.** (Garbi, Piotti
and Rizzini shotguns)
31360 Via Colinas, No. 109
Westlake Village, California 91361
Tel: 818-889-4160

**O. F. MOSSBERG & SONS, INC.** (shotguns)
7 Grasso Avenue; P.O. Box 497
North Haven, Connecticut 06473
Tel: 203-230-5300   Fax: 203-230-5420

**MTM MOLDED PRODUCTS** (reloading tools)
P.O. Box 14117, Dayton, Ohio 45413
Tel: 513-890-7461   Fax: 513-890-1747

**NAVY ARMS COMPANY, INC.** (handguns,
rifles, blackpowder guns)
689 Bergen Boulevard
Ridgefield, New Jersey 07657
Tel: 201-945-2500   Fax: 201-945-6859

**NEW ENGLAND FIREARMS CO., Inc.** (hand-
guns, rifles, shotguns)
Industrial Rowe
Gardner, Massachusetts 01440
Tel: 508-632-9393   Fax: 508-632-2300

**NIKON INC.** (scopes)
1300 Walt Whitman Road
Melville, New York 11747
Tel: 516-547-4200   Fax: 516-547-0309

**NORTH AMERICAN ARMS** (handguns)
2150 South 950 East
Provo, Utah 84606
Tel; 801-374-9990   Fax: 801-374-9998

**NOSLER BULLETS, INC.** (bullets)
P.O. Box 671
Bend, Oregon 97709
Tel: 503-382-3921   Fax: 503-388-4667

**NYGORD PRECISION PRODUCTS**
(Unique handguns, rifles)
P.O. Box 12578
Prescott, Arizona 86304
Tel: 520-717-2315   Fax: 520-717-2198

**OLIN/WINCHESTER** (ammunition, primers,
cases)
427 No. Shamrock, East Alton, Illinois 62024
Tel: 618-258-2000

**PARA-ORDNANCE** (handguns)
980 Tapscott Road
Scarborough, Ontario, Canada M1X 1E7
Tel: 416-297-7855   Fax: 416-297-1289

**PARKER REPRODUCTIONS** (shotguns)
124 River Road
Middlesex, New Jersey 08846
Tel: 908-469-0100   Fax: 908-469-9692

**PEDERSOLI, DAVIDE** (replica rifles)
Available through Flintlocks Etc.

**PEIFER RIFLE CO., INC.** (blackpowder
  rifles)
153 North 5th St., P.O. Box 192
Nokomis, Illinois 62075
Tel: 217-563-7050   Fax: 217-563-7060

**PENTAX** (scopes)
35 Inverness Drive East
Englewood, Colorado 80112
Tel: 303-799-8000   Fax: 303-790-1131

**PERAZZI U.S.A.** (shotguns)
1207 S. Shamrock Ave.
Monrovia, California 91016
Tel: 818-303-0068   Fax: 818-303-2081

**PIOTTI** (shotguns)
Available through W. L. Moore & Co.

**PRAIRIE GUN WORKS** (rifles)
1-761 Marion St.
Winnipeg, Manitoba, Canada R2J 0K6
Tel: 204-231-2976

**PRAIRIE RIVER ARMS LTD.** (blackpowder
  arms)
1220 North 6th St.
Princeton, Illinois 61356
Tel: 815-875-1616   Fax: 815-875-1402

**PRECISION SALES INTERNATIONAL**
  (Erma handguns; Marocchi shotguns)
P.O. Box 1776
Westfield, Massachusetts 01086
Tel: 413-562-5055   Fax: 413-562-5056

**PRECISION SMALL ARMS** (handguns)
155 Carleton Rd.
Charlottesville, Virginia 22902
Tel: 804-293-6124   Fax: 804-295-0780


**QUARTON USA** (laser sights)
7042 Alamo Downs Parkway, Suite 250
San Antonio, Texas 78238-4518
Tel: 800-520-8435   Fax: 210-520-8433


**RCBS, INC.** (reloading tools)
Available through Blount, Inc.

**REDDING RELOADING EQUIPMENT**
  (reloading tools)
1089 Starr Road
Cortland, New York 13045
Tel: 607-753-3331   Fax: 607-756-8445

**REDFIELD** (scopes)
5800 East Jewell Avenue
Denver, Colorado 80227
Tel: 303-757-6411   Fax: 303-756-2338

**REMINGTON ARMS COMPANY, INC.**
  (rifles, shotguns, blackpowder, ammunition)
870 Remington Drive, P.O. Box 700
Madison, North Carolina 27025-0700
Tel: 800-243-9700

**RIFLES, INC.** (rifles)
873 West 5400 North
Cedar City, Utah 84720
Tel: 801-586-5995   Fax: 801-586-5996

**RIZZINI** (shotguns)
Available through W.L. Moore

**ROSSI** (handguns, rifles)
Available through Interarms

**ROTTWEIL** (shotguns)
Available through Dynamit Nobel/RWS

**RUGER** (handguns, rifles, shotguns, blackpowder guns). *See* Sturm, Ruger & Company, Inc.


**SAFARI ARMS** (handguns)
c/o Olympic Arms, Inc.
624 Old Pacific Highway Southeast
Olympia, Washington 98513
Tel: 360-459-7940   Fax: 360-491-3447

**SAKO** (rifles, actions, scope mounts, ammo)
Available through Stoeger Industries

**SAUER** (rifles)
c/o Paul Company, Inc.
27385 Pressonville Road
Wellsville, Kansas 66092
Tel: 913-883-4444   Fax: 913-883-2525

**SAVAGE ARMS** (rifles, shotguns)
100 Springdale Road
Westfield, Massachusetts 01085
Tel: 413-568-7001   Fax: 413-562-7764

**SCHMIDT AND BENDER** (scopes)
Schmidt & Bender U.S.A.
P.O. Box 134
Meriden, New Hampshire 03770
Tel: 800-468-3450   Fax: 603-469-3471

**SGS IMPORTERS INTERNATIONAL INC.**
  (Llama handguns)
1750 Brielle Avenue
Wanamassa, New Jersey 07712
Tel: 908-493-0302   Fax: 908-493-0301

**SHILOH RIFLE MFG. CO., INC.** (Shiloh
  Sharps blackpowder rifles)
P.O. Box 279, Industrial Park
Big Timber, Montana 59011
Tel: 406-932-4454   Fax: 406-932-5627

**SIERRA BULLETS** (bullets)
P.O. Box 818
1400 West Henry St.
Sedalia, Missouri 65301
Tel: 816-827-6300   Fax: 816-827-6300

**SIGARMS INC.** (Sig-Sauer handguns, shot-
  guns)
Corporate Park
Exeter, New Hampshire 03833
Tel: 603-772-2302   Fax: 603-772-9082

**SIMMONS OUTDOOR CORP.** (scopes)
2120 Killarney Way
Tallahassee, Florida 32308-3402
Tel: 904-878-5100   Fax: 904-893-5472

**SKB SHOTGUNS** (shotguns)
4325 South 120th Street
P.O. Box 37669
Omaha, Nebraska 68137
Tel: 800-752-2767   Fax: 402-330-8029

**SMITH & WESSON** (handguns)
2100 Roosevelt Avenue
Springfield, Massachusetts 01102-2208
Tel: 800-331-0852   Tel: 413-781-8300
Fax: 413-731-8980

**SPEER** (bullets)
Available through Blount, Inc.

**SPRINGFIELD INC.** (handguns, rifles)
420 West Main Street
Geneseo, Illinois 61254
Tel: 309-944-5631   Fax: 309-944-3676

**STAR** (handguns)
Available through Interarms

**STEYR-MANNLICHER** (rifles)
Available through GSI (Gun South Inc.)

**STOEGER INDUSTRIES** (American Eagle
  Luger®; IGA shotguns; Pro Series hand-
  guns; Sako ammo, bullets, actions,
  mounts, rifles; Tikka rifles, shotguns)
5 Mansard Court
Wayne, New Jersey 07470
Tel: 800-631-0722   Tel: 201-872-9500
Fax: 201-872-2230

**STURM, RUGER AND COMPANY, INC.**
  (Ruger handguns, rifles, shotguns, black-
  powder revolver)
Lacey Place
Southport, Connecticut 06490
Tel: 203-259-4537   Fax: 203-259-2167

**SWAROVSKI OPTIK NORTH AMERICA**
  (scopes)
One Wholesale Way
Cranston, Rhode Island 02920
Tel: 800-426-3089   Fax: 401-946-2587

**SWIFT BULLET CO.** (bullets)
210 Main st., P.O. Box 27
Quinter, Kansas 67752
Tel: 913-754-3959   Fax: 913-754-2359

**SWIFT INSTRUMENTS, INC** (scopes,
  mounts)
952 Dorchester Avenue
Boston, Massachusetts 02125
Tel: 800-446-1116   Fax: 617-436-3232


**TASCO** (scopes, mounts)
7600 N.W. 26th Street
Miami, Florida 33122
Tel: 305-591-3670   Fax: 305-592-5895

**TAURUS INT'L, INC.** (handguns)
16175 N.W. 49th Avenue
Miami, Florida 33014-6314
Tel: 305-624-1115   Fax: 305-623-7506

**THOMPSON/CENTER ARMS** (handguns,
  rifles, reloading, blackpowder arms)
Farmington Road, P.O. Box 5002
Rochester, New Hampshire 03867
Tel: 603-332-2394   Fax: 603-332-5133

**TIKKA** (rifles, shotguns)
Available through Stoeger Industries

**TRADITIONS, INC.** (blackpowder arms)
1375 Boston Post Rd., P.O. Box 235
Deep River, Connecticut 06417
Tel: 203-526-9555   Fax: 203-526-4564

**TRIUS PRODUCTS, INC.** (traps, targets)
221 South Miami Avenue, P.O. Box 25
Cleves, Ohio 45002
Tel: 513-941-5682    Fax: 513-941-7970


**UBERTI USA, INC.** (handguns, rifles, black-
powder guns). *See also* American Arms,
EMF, Navy Arms
362 Limerock Rd., P.O. Box 469
Lakeville, Connecticut 06039
Tel: 860-435-8068

**ULTRA LIGHT ARMS COMPANY** (rifles)
214 Price Street, P.O. Box 1270
Granville, West Virginia 26534
Tel: 304-599-5687    Fax: 304-599-5687

**UNIQUE** (handguns, rifles)
Available thru Nygord Precision Products

**U.S. REPEATING ARMS CO.** (Winchester
rifles, shotguns)
275 Winchester Avenue
Morgan, Utah 84050
Tel: 801-876-3440    Fax: 801-876-3331

**VIVATAR** (sports optics)
1280 Rancho Conejo Blvd.
Newbury Park, California 91320
Tel: 805-498-7008


**WALTHER** (handguns)
Available through Interarms

**WEATHERBY, INC.** (rifles, shotguns, ammunition)
3100 El Camino Real
Atascadero, California 93422
Tel: 805-466-1767    Fax: 805-466-2527

**WEAVER** (scopes, mount rings)
Available through Blount, Inc.

**WHITE SHOOTING SYSTEMS** (blackpowder rifles)
25 East Highway 40, Box 330-12
Roosevelt, Utah 84066
Tel: 801-722-5996    Fax: 801-722-5909

**WICHITA ARMS** (handguns)
P.O. Box 11371
Wichita, Kansas 67211
Tel: 316-265-0661

**WILDEY INC.** (handguns)
458 Danbury Road
New Milford, Connecticut 06776
Tel: 860-355-9000    Fax 860-354-7759

**WILLIAMS GUN SIGHT CO.** (sights, scopes,
mounts)
7389 Lapeer Road, P.O. Box 329
Davison, Michigan 48423
Tel: 800-530-9028    Tel: 810-653-2131
Fax: 810-658-2140

**WINCHESTER** (ammunition, primers, cases)
Available through Olin/Winchester

**WINCHESTER** (rifles, shotguns)
Available through U.S. Repeating Arms Co.


**ZEISS OPTICAL, INC.** (scopes)
1015 Commerce Street
Petersburg, Virginia 23803
Tel: 804-861-0033    Fax: 804-733-4024

# CALIBERFINDER

How to use this guide: To find a 22 LR handgun, look under that heading in the **HANDGUNS** section below. You'll find several models of that description, including the Beretta Model 21 Bobcat Pistol. Next, turn to the **GUNFINDER** section, locate the heading for Pistols—Semiautomatic, and find **Beretta**. The Model 21 appears on p. 105.

## HANDGUNS

**17 REM.**
**Thompson/Center** Contender Super "14"

**22 HORNET**
**Magnum Research** Lone Eagle SS Action
**MOA** Maximum
**Thompson/Center** Contender Bull Barrel and Super "14"
**Uberti** 1871 Rolling Block Target

**22 LONG RIFLE**
**American Derringer Models** 1, 7, 11, 38 DA Derringer
**Beretta** Models 21 Bobcat and 89 Gold Standard Pistols
**Bernardelli** Model PO10 Target Pistol
**Bersa** Model Thunder 22
**Browning** Buck Mark 22 and 5.5 Target Series
**Colt** .22 Semiauto DA and Target
**Daewoo** Model DP52
**Davis** D-Series Derringers
**EMF/Dakota** Hartford Scroll Engraved Revolver
**Erma** ESP 85A Competition Pistols
**European American Armory** Small Bore Bounty Hunter
**FEG** Mark II AP22 (Interarms), SMC-22 Auto Pistol and SMC-380 (KBI)
**Freedom Arms** Model 252 Silhouette & Varmint Class
**Hämmerli** Models 160 Free Pistol, 162 Electronic, 208S Standard Pistol, 280 Target Pistol
**Harrington & Richardson** Sportsman 999, Models 929 Sidekick, Forty-Niner Classic Western and 939 Premier
**Heritage** Rough Rider SA
**High Standard** Supermatic Citation, Trophy and Tournament Models; Victor
**Jennings** Model J-22 Target
**New England Firearms** Standard Revolver, Ultra/Ultra Mag Revolver
**North American Arms** Mini-Revolvers and Mini-Master Series; Companion Cap & Ball Mini-Revolver
**Rossi** Model 518
**Ruger** Bisley SA Target, New Bearcat, Mark II Pistols, New Model Single-Six, Model SP101 Revolver
**Smith & Wesson** Models 17, 22A Sport, 41, 63, 317 Airlite, 617, 2213/2214 Rimfire Sportsman
**Stoeger** Pro Series 95
**Taurus** Models 94, 96, PT-22
**Thompson/Center** Contender Bull Barrel, Octagon Barrel and "Super 14"
**Uberti** 1871 Rolling Block Target Pistol
**Unique** Models DES 69U, International Silhouette and Sport
**Walther** Model TPH DA
**Wichita Arms** International Pistol

**22 RIMFIRE MAGNUM**
**American Derringer** Models 7, 11
**AMT** 22 Automag II
**D-Series Derringer**, Long-Bore D-Series
**Freedom Arms** Model 252
**Heritage** Rough Rider Revolver
**North American** Mini-Revolver and Mini-Master Series; Companion Cap & Ball Mini-Revolver
**Rossi** Model 515 Revolver
**Smith & Wesson** Model 651 Kit Gun
**Taurus** Model 941 Revolver
**Uberti** 1871 Rolling Block Target
**Unique** International Silhouette
**Wichita Arms** International Pistol

**22 SHORT**
**Harrington & Richardson** Model 929 Sidekick, Model 949 Classic Western, 939 Premier Target, Sportsman 999
**High Standard** Olympic Rapid Fire Pistol, Olympic Military
**New England Firearms** Standard, Ultra/Ultra Mag.
**Unique** Model DES 2000U Pistol

**22 WIN. MAG.**
**American Derringer** Model 6
**Davis** Big Bore D-Series
**Heritage** Rough Rider Revolver
**New England Firearms** Ultra Revolver
**North American** Mini-Revolvers and Mini-Master Series
**Uberti** 1871 Rolling Block Target Pistol
**Unique** Int'l Silhouette and Sport Pistols

**22-250**
**Magnum Research** Lone Eagle SS Action

**223 REMINGTON**
**American Derringer** Model 1
**Magnum Research** Lone Eagle SS Action
**Thompson/Center** Contender Bull Barrel, Hunter, "Super 14" and "16", Encore

**243**
**Magnum Research** Lone Eagle SS Action
**Thompson/Center** Encore

**25 AUTO**
**Beretta** Model 21 Bobcat, Model 950 Jetfire
**Davis** D-Series Derringers
**Heritage** Model H25S Semiauto
**Precision Small Arms** Model PSA-25 Pistols (Traditional, Nouveau, Featherweight, Renaissance, Imperiale)
**Taurus** Model PT-25
**Walther** Model TPH Pistol

**270 WIN**
**Thompson/Center** Encore

**7mm BR**
**Thompson/Center** Encore
**Wichita** Silhouette Pistol

**7mm T.C.U.**
**Thompson/Center** Contender Bull Barrel
**Unique** International Silhouette

**7mm SUPER MAG.**
**Wichita Arms** International Pistols

**7mm-08**
**Magnum Research** Lone Eagle SS Barreled Action
**Thompson/Center** Encore

**7X30 WATERS**
**Thompson/Center** Contender Series, (Hunter, Super "14" and "16")
**Wichita Arms** International Pistol

**30 CARBINE**
**AMT** Automag III Pistol

**30-06**
**Magnum Research** Lone Eagle SS Barreled Action
**Thompson/Center** Encore

**30-30 WIN.**
**American Derringer** Model 1
**Magnum Research** Lone Eagle SS Action
**Thompson/Center** Contender Bull Barrel and Hunter, Super "14"
**Wichita Arms** International Pistol

**300 WHISPER**
**Thompson/Center** Contender Super "14" & "l6", Bull Barrel

**308 WINCHESTER**
**Magnum Research** Lone Eagle SS Barreled Action
**Thompson/Center** Encore
**Wichita Arms** Silhouette Pistol

**32 AUTO**
**Beretta** Model 3032 Tomcat
**Davis** D-Series Derringers, Model P-32
**Sig-Sauer** Model P32
**Walther** Model PP DA Pistol

**32 H&H MAGNUM**
**Davis** Long-Bore D-Series, Big Bore D-Series
**Wichita** International Pistol

**32 MAGNUM**
**American Derringer** Models 1, 7, 11, Lady Derringer
**New England** Lady Ultra, Standard Revolver
**Ruger** Model SP101

**32 S&W LONG**
**American Derringer** Model 1, 7
**Hämmerli** Model 280 Target Pistol
**New England** Standard Revolver

**32 S&W WADCUTTER**
**Erma** ESP 85A Competition Pistols
**Unique** Model DES 32U Pistol

## 32-20
**American Derringer** Model 1

## 35 REMINGTON
**Magnum Research** Lone Eagle SS Action
**Thompson/Center** Contender Hunter and Super "14"

## 357 MAGNUM
**American Arms** Regulator Revolver, Mateba Auto Revolver
**American Derringer** Models 1, 4, 6, 38 DA, Lady Derringer
**Colt** King Cobra, Python Elite
**Coonan Arms** 357 Mag. Pistol Cadet
**Compact**
**Downsizer** Pistols
**EMF/Dakota** Model 1873 Dakota SA, 1875 Outlaw, 1890 Remington Police, Hartford Scroll Engraved Revolvers, Pinkerton Detective
**European American** Armory Big Bore Bounty Hunter, Windicator DA
**Freedom Arms** Model 353, Silhouette/Competition Models
**L.A.R.** Mark I Grizzly Pistol
**Magnum Research** Desert Eagle Mark XIX Component System Pistol, Lone Eagle SS Action
**Rossi** Model 971, 971 VCR, Cyclops, Models 877 and 677 Revolvers
**Ruger** New Model Blackhawk, Vaquero, Model GP-100, Model SP101, Bisley SA Target Revolvers
**Sig-Sauer** Model P229 Pistol
**Smith & Wesson** Models 13 Military & Police, 19, 60 Chiefs Special Revolvers, 65, 65 LadySmith (36-LS and 60-LS), 66, 586, 640 Centennial, 686, 686 Plus, 686 Powerport
**Taurus** Models 605, 606, 608, 669, 689 Revolvers
**Thompson/Center** Contender Bull Barrel Pistol
**Uberti** 1871 Rolling Block Target Pistol; 1873 Cattleman & 1875 Outlaw Revolver
**Unique** Model Int'l Silhouette Pistol
**Wichita Arms** International Pistol

## 357 MAXIMUM
**American Derringer** Models 1, 4
**Magnum Research** Lone Eagle SS Action

## 357 SIG
**AMT** Backup Pistol
**Laseraim** Velocity 357/400 High Speed Series
**Sig-Sauer** Models P226, P239 Pistols

## 358 WINCHESTER
**Magnum Research** Lone Eagle SS Action
**MOA** Maximum SS

## 375 WINCHESTER
**Thompson/Center** Contender Hunter and Super "14" Pistols

## 38 S&W
**Smith and Wesson** Models 10, 13, 14, 15, 36, 38 Bodyguard, 60, 64, 649 Bodyguard, LadySmith Models 36-LS and 60-LS Revolvers

## 38 SPECIAL
**American Derringer** 1, 7, 10, 11, Lady Derringer, DA 38, Texas Double Derringer Comm.
**Colt** King Cobra DA, Python Elite DA, Model 38 SF-VI Revolvers
**Davis** Big Bore D-Series, Long Bore D-Series
**European American Armory** Windicator DA
**Heritage** Sentry DA Revolver
**KBI** Armscor Models M200DC/TC Revolvers
**Rossi** Models 68, 851, Lady Rossi Revolvers
**Smith & Wesson** Models 10 & 13 Military & Police, Model 14 K-38 Masterpiece, Models 15 and 67 Combat Masterpiece, Model 19 & 66 Combat Magnum, Models 36-LS & 60-LS LadySmith, Models 37 & 637 Chiefs Special Airweight, Models 38 and 638 Bodyguard Airweight, Model 649 Bodyguard, Models 442 & 642 Centenial Airweight, Model 586 Distinguished Combat Magnum, Model 640 Centennial, Models 686, 686 Plus, 686 Powerport Revolvers
**Taurus** Models 82, 83, 85, 605, 606 Compact

## 38 SUPER
**American Derringer** Model 1
**AMT** Backup
**Auto-Ordnance** Model 1911A1 Thompson
**European American Armory** Witness, Gold & Silver Teams
**Sig-Sauer** Model 220 "American" Pistol
**Springfield** Model 1911-A1 Mil-Spec, Standard and Lightweight Factory Comp, High-Capacity Factory Comp Pistols

## 380 AUTO
**American Arms** Escort Pistol
**American Derringer** Models 1, 7 and 11
**AMT** Model Backup Pistol, Backup II
**Beretta** Cheetah Models 84, 85 and 86 Pistols
**Bernardelli** PO18 Compact Target Pistol
**Bersa** Model Thunder 380, Series 95 Pistols
**Browning** Model BDA-380 Pistol
**Colt** Government Model, Government 380 MKIV Pony Series Pocketlite, Mustang, Mustang Plus II, Mustang PocketLite 380 Pistols
**Daewoo** Model DH380 Pistol
**Davis** P-380 Pistol
**European American Armory** European SA Compact
**FEG** Mark II APK, Mark II AP (Interarms); Model SMC 22 Auto Pistol and Model SMC-380 (KBI)
**Hi-Point** 380 Polymer Pistol
**Llama** Small Frame Automatic
**Sig-Sauer** Model 232 Pistol
**Smith & Wesson** Sigma Compact Series
**Walther** Model PP DA, Model PPK and PPK/S

## 9mm MAKAROV
**FEG** Model SMC-380 Pistol (KBI)

## 9mm PARABELLUM (LUGER)
**American Derringer** Model 1, Model DA 38 Double Derringer
**Astra** Models A-75 and A-100
**Beretta** Cougar Series, Models 92 FS, 92D, Centurion
**Bernardelli** Model PO18 Target and Compact Target Pistols

**Bersa** Thunder 9 DA Pistol
**Browning** 9mm Hi-Power, Model BDM DA
**Daewoo** Model DP51, DP516 (Compact)
**Davis** Long Bore D-Series, Big Bore D-Series
**Downsizer** Pistols
**European American Armory** Witness, Witness Fab, Witness Gold Team, Witness Silver Team, Witness Subcompact
**Glock** Models 17, 17L Competition; Model 19 Compact, Model 26 FEG Model PJK-9HP Pistol
**Heckler and Koch** Models P7M8, HK USP, USP45 Universal, HK USP Compact Universal
**Heritage** Stealth Compact
**Hi-Point** Firearms Model 9mm
**Israel Arms** Kareen MKII Compact, Golan DA
**Jennings** Lazer Nine
**Kahr Arms** Model K9 Pistol
**Llama** Max-1 Pistol
**Ruger** P-Series Pistols, SP101 Spurless DA
**Sig-Sauer** Models 210, 225, 226, 228, P229, P239
**Smith & Wesson** Model 900 Series, 910, Model 940 Centennial, Model 3900 Compact Series, 5900 and 6900 Compact Series, Sigma Series Pistols
**Springfield** Model 1911-A1 Standard & Lightweight, Trophy Match, High Capacity Standard and Ultra Compact Pistols
**Star** Models Firestar M43, Ultrastar, Firestar Plus
**Stoeger** American Eagle Luger
**Taurus** Models PT92, PT92AF, PT-92AFC, PT99, PT-908, PT911 Compact, PT Pistols
**Walther** Model P 9, P 88 Compact

## 10mm
**American Derringer** Model 1
**Auto-Ordnance** Model 1911A1 Thompson
**Glock** Model 20 Pistol, Model 29
**L.A.R.** Mark I Grizzly Pistol
**Laseraim** Technologies Laseraim Series I, III Pistols

## 40 AUTO
**Beretta** Cougar Series
**Ruger** P-Series Pistols

## 40 S&W
**American Derringer** Model 1, 38 DA Derringer
**AMT** Backup
**Astra** Models A-75, A-100
**Beretta** Models 92, 96, 96D, Centurion
**Bernardelli** Model P.018 Compact Target
**Browning** Hi-Power SA
**Daewoo** Model DH40
**Downsizer** Pistols
**European American Armory** Witness, Witness Fab, Gold & Silver Teams, Subcompact
**Glock** Models 22, 23, 24, 27 Pistols
**Heckler and Koch** HK USP, USP Compact Universal and Universal
**Israel Arms** Kareen MKII Compact, Golan DA
**Kahr** Model K9
**Llama** Classics/Max-1 Auto Pistols
**Para-Ordnance** Model P10 and P16 Pistols
**Smith & Wesson** Model 410, Model 4000 Compact Series and Full Size, Sigma Series, Model 4013 Tactical
**Star** Model Firestar M40, M43, M45, UltraStar

## .410
**American Derringer** Models 4 and 6

## 44 MAGNUM
**American Derringer** Models 1, 4
**Colt** Anaconda Revolver
**European American Armory** Big Boar Bounty Hunter
**Freedom Arms** 454 Casull and Model 555 Premier and Field Grades, Silhouette/Competition Models
**Magnum Research** Desert Eagle Mark XIX Component System, Lone Eagle SS Action
**Ruger** Redhawk, Super Redhawk, New Model Super Blackhawk SA, Bisley SA Target, Vaquero SA Revolvers
**Smith & Wesson** Model 29, Models 629, 629 Classic & Powerport
**Taurus** Model 44 Revolver
**Thompson/Center** Contender Bull Barrel & **Hunter**, "Super 14", Encore Pistol
**Unique** Int'l Silhouette Pistol
**Wildey** Pistols

## 44 SPECIAL
**American Derringer** Models 1, 7
**Colt** Anaconda
**EMF/Dakota** Hartford Model Revolvers
**Rossi** Model 720
**Smith & Wesson** Model 629, 629 Classic, Model 696
**Taurus** Models 431, 441, 445

## 44-40
**American Arms** Regulator SA
**American Derringer** Model 1, Texas Double Derringer Comm.
**Colt** Single Action Army
**EMF/Dakota** Hartford Scroll Engraved SA, **Hartford** Models, New Hartford Percussion Revolvers, Models 1873 Dakota SA, 1875 Outlaw, 1890 Remington Police, Pinkerton Detective
**Navy Arms** 1873 SA Revolver, 1875 Schofield, "Deputy" SA Revolver, Bisley Model SA
**Ruger** Vaquero SA Revolver
**Uberti** 1873 Cattleman, 1875 Outlaw/1890 Police Revolvers

## 444 MARLIN
**Magnum Research** Lone Eagle SS Action
**Thompson/Center** Encore

## 45 ACP (AUTO)
**American Derringer** Models 1, 4, 6, 10
**AMT** Backup, Longslide, 1911 Government, 1911 Hardballer
**Astra** Models A-75, A-100
**Auto-Ordnance** Model 1911A1 Thompson, Deluxe, "The General," Pit Bull, WWII Parkerized
**Brolin Arms** Legend, Patriot and Pro Series Pistols
**Colt** Combat Commander, Gold Cup Trophy, Government Model, Model 1991A1 (Compact and Commander), Officer's ACP
**Downsizer** Pistols
**European American Armory** Witness, Witness Fab, Gold and Silver Teams, Subcompact
**Glock** Model 30 Pistol

**Heckler and Koch** Model HK USP, USP 45 Universal, Mark 23 Special Operations, HK USP45 Match
**Israel Arms** GAL 45 ACP
**KBI** Armscor Model M1911-A1P
**Kimber** Model Classic Series .45
**L.A.R.** Mark I Grizzly Pistol
**Laseraim Technologies** Series I, III
**Llama** Automatic (Compact Frame), Government Model, Classics/Max-I Auto Pistols
**Para-Ordnance** Models P12 and P14
**Ruger** P-Series Pistols
**Safari Arms** Cohort, Enforcer, Matchmaster
**Sig-Sauer** Model 220 American
**Smith & Wesson** Model 457, Model 625, Model 4500 Series Compact/Full Size
**Springfield** Model 1911-A1 Champion Series, Model 1911-A1 Ultra Compact Series, PDP Series (Champion Comp, Lightweight Compact Comp, High Capacity Factory Comp) Defender, Factory Comp, Model 1911-A1 Standard, Mil-Spec, Lightweight Compact, High Capacity Series, Trophy Match, Ultra Compact Series, Super Tuned Series
**Star** Firestar M40, M43, M45
**Uberti** 1873 Cattleman

## 45 COLT
**American Arms** Regulator SA
**American Derringer** Lady Derringer, Models 1, 4, 6, 10, Texas Double Derringer Commemorative, M-4 Alaskan Survival
**Colt** Single Action Army Revolver, Anaconda DA
**EMF/Dakota** Hartford Models (Artillery, Single Action, Cavalry Colt), Models 1873 (Sixshooter, Buntline), 1873 Dakota SA, 1875 "Outlaw," Model 1890 Remington Police, Pinkerton Detective SA, Hartford Scroll Engraved SA, 1893 Express
**European American Armory** Big Bore Bounty Hunter SA Navy Arms 1873 SA Rev., 1873 U.S. Cavalry, "Flat Top" Target, 1873 "Pinched Frame" SA, 1875 Schofield Rev., "Deputy" SA Rev., Bisley Model SA, 1895 U.S. Artillery
**Ruger** Model Bisley SA Target, New Model Blackhawk, Vaquero
**Uberti** 1873 Cattleman, 1875 Outlaw/1890 Police

## 45 WIN. MAG.
**AMT** Automag IV
**American Derringer** Model 1
**L.A.R.** Mark I Grizzly
**Wildey** Hunter and Survivor Pistols

## 45-70 GOV'T.
**American Derringer** Models 1 and 4, M-4 Alaskan Survival
**Thompson/Center** Contender Super "16", Hunter

## 454 CASULL
**American Arms** Uberti SA
**Freedom Arms** 454 Casull, Model 555 Field and Premier Grades

## 475 WILDEY MAG.
**Wildey** Survivor Pistols

## 50 MAG. AE
**L.A.R.** Grizzly 50 Mark 5
**Freedom Arms** Model 555
**Magnum Research** Desert Eagle Mark XIX Component System

## RIFLES

### CENTERFIRE
### BOLT ACTION
### STANDARD CALIBERS

## 17 BEE
**Francotte** Bolt Action

## 17 REMINGTON
**Cooper Arms** Model 21 Varmint Extreme
**Kimber** Model 84C SuperAmerica
**Remington** Model 700, BDL
**Sako** Deluxe, Super Deluxe; Hunter Lightweight, Varmint
**Ultra** Light Model 20 Series

## 22 HORNET
**Browning** A-Bolt II Micro Medallion
**Dakota Arms** Model 76 Varmint Grade
**KBI** Standard 22 Models M-1400S, M-1500S, M-1800S
**Ruger** Model 77/22RH Hornet, K77/22VH Varmint
**Ultra** Light Model 20 Series

## 22 PPC
**Cooper Arms** Model 21 Varmint Extreme
**Dakota Arms** Model 76 Varmint Grade

## 22-250
**AMT** Standard & Deluxe Repeaters
**A-Square** Genghis Khan
**Blaser** Model R93
**Browning** A-Bolt II Series (except Gold Medallion)
**Dakota** 76 Classic, Varmint Grades
**Harris** Gunworks Classic Sporter, Stainless Sporter, Standard Sporters; Talon Sporter, Varminter
**Howa** Lightning
**Kimber** Swedish Mauser 96 HB SS Varmint
**Remington** Models 700 BDL, Varmint LS, Synthetic & HB
**Ruger** Models M-77VT MKII HB Target, M-77RP MKII All-Weather
**Sako** Deluxe, Super Deluxe; Hunter Lightweight, Left-Handed Models, Varmint, 75 Hunter
**Savage** Models 111G, 111F Classic Hunter; Models 112 BVSS & 112FV Varmint, 112FVSS
**Tikka** Continental Varmint, Whitetail Hunter, Synthetic
**Ultra** Light Model 20 Series
**Weatherby** Mark V Lightweight Series
**Winchester** Models 70 Classic Stainless, Heavy Barrel Varmint, Walnut Classic Featherweight

## 220 SWIFT
**Dakota Arms** Model 76 Varmint Grade
**Harris** Varminter
**Remington** Model 700VS Varmint Synthetic
**Ruger** Model M-77VT MKII HB Target
**Winchester** Model 70 Heavy Barrel Varmint

## 221 FIREBALL
**Cooper Arms** Model 21 Varmint Extreme

## 222 REMINGTON
**Cooper Arms** Model 21 Varmint Extreme
**Francotte** Bolt Action
**Kimber** Model 84C Classic, SuperAmerica
**Remington** Models 700, BDL
**Sako** Deluxe, Super Deluxe, Hunter Lightweight, Varmint Ultra Light Model 20 Series
**Winchester** Model 70 HB Varmint

## 223 REMINGTON
**AMT** Standard & Deluxe Repeaters
**Brown Precision** High Country Youth and Tactical Elite
**Browning** A-Bolt II Series (except Medallion)
**Cooper Arms** Models 21, Varmint Extreme
**Dakota Arms** Model 76 Varmint Grade
**Harris** Gunworks Varminter
**Howa** Lightning
**Kimber** Model 84C Classic, SuperAmerica, Varmint Stainless
**Remington** Models Seven Carbine; 700, BDL; Varmint LS, Synthetic & HB
**Ruger** Models Mark II, M-77RL Ultra Light, M-77RP All-Weather, M-77VT HB Target, 77R
**Sako** Deluxe, Super Deluxe, Hunter Lightweight, Varmint
**Savage** Models 110FP Tactical, 110CY; 111G, 111F Classic Hunter; 112 BT Competition, 112FV/FVSS, 112BVSS Varmint; 116FCS/116FSS "Weather Warrior"
**Tikka** Continental Varmint, Whitetail Hunter, Synthetic Ultra Light Model 20 Series
**Winchester** Models 70 Ranger, Ranger Ladies/Youth, HB Varmint

## 243 WINCHESTER
**AMT** Standard, Deluxe Repeaters
**Arnold Arms** African Safari, African Synthetic, African Trophy, Serengeti Synthetic
**A-Square** Genghis Khan
**Blaser** Model R93
**Brown Precision** High Country Youth
**Browning** A-Bolt II Series (except Varmint, Gold Medallion)
**Francotte** Bolt Action
**Harris** Gunworks Benchrest; Classic Sporter, Stainless Sporter, Talon Sporter, Varminter
**Howa** Lightning
**Kimber** Swedish Mauser 96 Sporter
**Kongsberg** Hunter 393 Series
**Mauser** Model M94
**Remington** Models Seven Carbine, Youth, Stainless Synthetic; Models 700 ADL, ADL Synthetic, BDL, BDL DM-B, Mountain (DM), Varmint HB (Laminated & Synthetic)
**Ruger** Models Mark II M-77R, M-77RS, M-77VT HB & All-Weather (KM-77RP & RSP), Ultra Light; M-77RSI International Mannlicher
**Sako** Classic, Deluxe, Super Deluxe, Hunter Lightweight, Left-Handed Models, Mannlicher-Style Carbine, Varmint
**Sauer** Models 90 & 202
**Savage** Models 111G/111F Classic Hunter; 116FSS "Weather Warrior"
**Steyr-Mannlicher** SSG PI & PII, SBS
**Mannlicher** European, Prohunter, Forester
**Tikka** Whitetail Hunter, Synthetic Ultra Light Model 20 Series
**Unique** Model TGC

**Weatherby** Mark V Lightweight Series
**Winchester** Models 70 Classic Stainless; Heavy Barrel Varmint; Ranger, Ranger Ladies/Youth; Walnut Classic Featherweight/Stainless

## 6mm BR
**Harris** Gunworks Benchrest; Classic and Stainless Sporters

## 6mm PPC
**AMT** Standard & Deluxe Repeaters
**Dakota Arms** Model 76 Varmint Grade
**Harris** Gunworks Benchrest

## 6mm REMINGTON
**A-Square** Genghis Khan
**Brown Precision** High Country Youth
**Harris Gunworks** Benchrest, Varminter, Classic & Stainless Sporter, Talon Sporter
**Ruger** Model M-77R MK II Ultra Light Model 20 Series

## 25-06
**AMT** Standard, Deluxe Repeater
**A-Square** Hamilcar, Genghis Khan
**Browning** A-Bolt II Composite & Stainless Stalker, Hunter, Medallion, Eclipse
**Harris Gunworks** Classic and Stainless Sporter; Talon Sporter, Varminter
**Marlin** Model MR-7
**Mauser** Model 96
**Remington** Models 700 BDL, BDL (DM), Mountain (DM), Sendero
**Ruger** Models 77RS MKII, M-77VT MKII HB Target
**Sako** Deluxe, Super Deluxe; Fiberclass, Hunter Lightweight, Left-Handed Models, Long-Range
**Hunter**, TRG-S
**Sauer** Model 90
**Savage** Models 110FP Tactical, 111G/111F Classic Hunter, 112 FVSS Varmint, 112BVSS Varmint
**Steyr-Mannlicher** SBS Mannlicher European Model, Prohunter, Forester
**Tikka** Whitetail Hunter, Synthetic, Continental Long-Range Hunting, Ultra Light Model 24 Series
**Weatherby** Mark V Lightweight Series

## 257 ACKLEY
**Ultra Light** Model 20 Series

## 257 ROBERTS
**Arnold Arms** Alaskan Guide, Alaskan Synthetic
**Dakota Arms** Model 76 Classic
**Lazzeroni** Models 2000 SP-F, ST-F, ST-W
**Ruger** Model M-77R MKII, M-77RL MKII Ultra Light
**Ultra Light** Model 20 Series

## 260 Rem.
**Remington** Model Seven Carbine, SS

## 264 Win.
**A-Square** Hamilcar

## 6.5X06
**A-Square** Hamilcar

## 6.5X55mm/SWEDISH
**Kimber** Swedish Mauser 96 Sporter
**Winchester** Model 70 Classic Featherweight

## 270 WINCHESTER
**AMT** Standard, Deluxe Repeaters
**A-Square** Hamilcar
**Beretta** Mato
**Browning** A-Bolt II Series (except Micro-Medalliion, Varmint
**Dakota Arms** Model 76 Classic
**Francotte** Bolt Action
**Harris Gunworks** Alaskan; Classic and Stainless Sporters; Talon Sporter, Titanium Mtn.
**Howa** Lightning
**Kimber** Mauser 98 Sporter, Model K770 Classic
**Kongsberg** Hunter 393 Series
**Magnum Research** Mountain Eagle
**Marlin** Model MR-7
**Mauser** Models 96, M94
**Remington** Models 700 ADL, BDL, BDL (DM), BDL SS (DM), Mountain (DM), Sendero
**Ruger** Models Mark II M-77RP/RSP All-Weather, M-77R/LR, M-77RL Ultra Light, M-77RS; M-77RSI International Mannlicher
**Sako** Classic, Deluxe, Super Deluxe; Fiberclass, Hunter Lightweight, L. H. Models, Mannlicher-Style Carbine, Long-Range Hunter, TRG-S
**Sauer** Models 90, 202
**Savage** Models 111G, 111GC, 111F, 111FC Classic Hunter; 114CE "Classic European," 116FCS, 116FSK, 116FSS "Weather Warrior"
**Steyr-Mannlicher** Sporter, SBS Mannlicher European Model, Prohunter
**Tikka** Continental Long-Range Hunting, Whitetail Hunter, Synthetic
**Ultra Light** Model 24 Series
**Unique** Model TGC
**Weatherby** Models Mark V Lightweight Series
**Winchester** Models 70 Classic Series; Sporter Classic SM, Classic Sporter Super Grade, Classic Walnut/Stainless Featherweight, Classic Stainless

## 280 REMINGTON
**A-Square** Hamilcar
**Beretta** Mato
**Browning** A-Bolt II Composite/Stainless Stalker, Hunter, Medallion
**Dakota Arms** Model 76 Classic
**Harris Gunworks** Classic and Stainless Sporters; Alaskan, Talon Sporter, Titanium Mountain
**Magnum Research** Mountain Eagle
**Remington** Models 700 BDL, DM-B, BDL (DM)
**Ruger** Model M-77R MKII, M-77RP MKII All-Weather
**Sako** Deluxe, Fiberclass, Hunter Lightweight, Left-Handed Models
**Weatherby** Mark V Lightweight Series
**Winchester** Model 70 Walnut Classic Featherweight

## 284 WINCHESTER
**Harris Gunworks** Classic and Stainless, Sporters; Talon Sporter
**Lazzeroni** Models L2000 SP-F, ST-F, ST-W
**Ultra Light** Model 20 Series

## 7mm BR
**Harris Gunworks** Classic and Stainless Sporters; Talon Sporter

## 7mm EXPRESS
**Ultra Light** Model 24 Series

**7mm STW**
**A-Square** Hamilcar

**7X57mm (ACKLEY/MAUSER)**
**Ultra Light** Model 20 Series

**7mm-08**
**Brown Precision** High Country Youth
**Browning** A-Bolt II Series (except Gold Medallion, Varmint, Eclipse)
**Harris Gunworks** Classic and Stainless Sporters; National Match, Talon Sporter, Varminter
**Kimber** Swedish Mauser 96 Sporter
**Remington** Models Seven Carbine, Stainless Synthetic, Youth; 700 BDL DM-B, BDL SS, BDL (DM), VLS HB
**Sako** Deluxe, Super Deluxe; Hunter Lightweight, Left-Handed Models, Varmint
**Savage** Models 111G/111F Classic Hunters
**Steyr-Mannlicher** SBS Mannlicher European Model, Prohunter, Forester
**Ultra Light** Model 20 Series
**Unique** Model TGC
**Weatherby** Mark V Lightweight Series
**Winchester** Model 70 Walnut Classic Featherweight, Ranger Ladies/Youth

**30-06**
**AMT** Standard, Deluxe Repeaters
**A-Square** Hamilcar
**Beretta** Mato
**Blaser** Model R 93
**Browning** A-Bolt II Long Action Std.
**Clifton Arms** Scout
**Dakota Arms** Model 76 Classic
**Francotte** Bolt Action
**Harris Gunworks** Alaskan; Classic and Stainless Sporters; Talon Sporter, Titanium Mountain
**Howa** Lightning
**Kimber** Mauser 98 Sporter, Model K770 Classic
**Kongsberg** Hunter 393 Series
**Magnum Research** Mountain Eagle
**Marlin** Model MR-7
**Mauser** Models 96, M94
**Remington** Models 700 ADL, BDL, BDL (DM), BDL SS DM-B
**Ruger** Models Mark II M-77R/LR, M-77RL Ultra Light, M-77RP/RSP All-Weather, M-77RS; M-77RSI International Mannlicher
**Sako** Classic, Deluxe/Super Deluxe, Fiberclass, Hunter Lightweight, Left-Handed Models, Long Range Hunter, Mannlicher-Style Carbine, Model TRG-S
**Sauer** Models 90, 202
**Savage** Models 111F, 111FC, 111G, 111GC Classic Hunters; 110FP Tactical; 112FVSS, 112BVSS Varmint; 116FCS, 116FSK "Weather Warrior," 116FSS
**Steyr-Mannlicher** Sporter, SBS Mannlicher European Model, Forester
**Tikka** Whitetail Hunter, Synthetic
**Ultra Light** Model 24 Series
**Unique** Model TGC
**Weatherby** Mark V Lightweight Series
**Winchester** Models 70 Classic Featherweight Series; Classic Stainless Sporter, Ranger, Super Grade

**300 SAVAGE**
**Ultra Light** Model 20 Series

**300 WINCHESTER**
**A-Square** Hamilcar

**308 WINCHESTER**
**AMT** Standard, Deluxe Repeaters
**Blaser** Model R 93
**Browning** A-Bolt II Short Action
**Brown Precision** High Country Youth, Tactical Elite
**Clifton Arms** Scout
**Francotte** Bolt Action
**Harris Gunworks** Benchrest; Classic and Stainless Sporters; National Match, Talon Sporter, Varminter
**Howa** Lightning
**Kimber** Swedish Mauser 96 Sporter, HBSS Varmint
**Kongsberg** Hunter Sporter 393 Series
**Lazzeroni** Models L2000 SP-F, ST-F, ST-W
**Mauser** Model 96, Models SR 86, M94
**Remington** Models 700 ADL, BDL DM-B, BDL SS, Varmint HB, Varmint Synthetic; Models Seven Carbine, Stainless Synthetic
**Ruger** Models Mark II M-77 All Weather, M-77R, M-77RL Ultra Light, M-77RS, M-77VT HB Target; M-77RSI International Mannlicher
**Sako** Deluxe/Super Deluxe, Hunter Lightweight, Left-Handed Models, Mannlicher-Style Carbine, TRG-21, Varmint
**Sauer** Models 90, 202
**Savage** Models 110FP Tactical, 111G, 111F Classic Hunters; Models 112FVSS & 112BVSS Varmint, 116 FSS "Weather Warrior"
**Steyr-Mannlicher** Models SSG-PI/SSG-PII/SSG P-IV Urban, SBS Mannlicher European Model, Prohunter, Forester
**Tikka** Continental Varmint, Whitetail Hunter, Synthetic
**Ultra Light** Model 20
**Unique** Model TGC
**Weatherby** Mark V Lightweight Series
**Winchester** Models 70 Classic/Boss Stainless; Heavy Barrel Varmint; Ranger Ladies/Youth; Walnut Classic Featherweight/Stainless

**338-06**
**A-Square** Hamilcar

**358 WINCHESTER**
**Ultra Light** Model 20 Series

# CENTERFIRE BOLT ACTION MAGNUM CALIBERS

**222 REM. MAG.**
**Cooper Arms** Model 21 Varmint Extreme
**Dakota Arms** Model 76 Varmint Grade
**Ultra Light** Model 20 Series

**240 WBY. MAG.**
**Weatherby** Mark V Accumark, Lightweight Series

**257 WBY. MAG**
**Arnold Arms** Alaskan Synthetic Rifle, Alaskan Guide
**A-Square** Genghis Khan, Hamilcar
**Blaser** Model R93
**Weatherby** Models Mark V Accumark, Deluxe, Euromark, Eurosport, Lazermark, Stainless, Sporter, Synthetic

**264 WIN. MAG.**
**Blaser** Model R93
**Ultra Light** Arms Model 28 Series
**Winchester** Models 70 Classic Sporter

**270 WBY./WIN. MAG.**
**Weatherby** Models Mark V Deluxe, Euromark, Eurosport, Lazermark, Sporter, Stainless, Synthetic
**Winchester** Models 70 Classic Sporter, Classic Stainless

**7mm REM. MAG./7mm WBY. MAG.**
**AMT** Standard, Deluxe Repeaters
**A-Square** Caesar, Hamilcar
**Beretta** Mato
**Blaser** Model R93
**Browning** A-Bolt II Series (except Eclipse, Varmint, Micro-Medallion)
**Dakota Arms** Model 76 Classic Grade
**Harris Gunworks** Alaskan; Classic and Stainless, Sporters; Long Range, Talon Sporter, Titanium Mountain
**Howa** Lightning
**Kimber** Mauser 98 Sporter, K770 Classic
**Kongsberg** Hunter 393 Series
**Magnum Research** Mountain Eagle
**Mauser** Models 96, M94
**Remington** Models 700 ADL, BDL, BDL (DM), BDL SS (DM), BDL Synthetic; African Plains, Alaskan Wilderness, Sendero
**Ruger** Models Mark II M-77R/LR, M-77RS, M-77RS/RSP All-Weather
**Sako** Classic, Deluxe/Super Deluxe, Fiberclass, Hunter Lightweight, Left-Handed Models, Long-Range Hunter, TRG-S Magnum
**Sauer** Models 90, 202
**Savage** Models 110 FP Tactical; 111GC, 111G, 111F, 111FC Classic Hunters; 112 FVSS, 112BVSS Varmint; 114CE "Classic European," 116FSK/116FSS "Weather Warrior"
**Steyr-Mannlicher** Luxus, Sporter, SBS Mannlicher European Model
**Tikka** Continental Long-Range Hunting, Whitetail Hunter, Synthetic
**Ultra Light** Arms Model 28 Series
**Unique** Model TGC
**Weatherby** Mark V Accumark, Deluxe, Euromark, Eurosport, Lazermark, Sporter, Stainless, Synthetic
**Winchester** Models 70 Classic/Boss SM, Classic/Boss Stainless, Classic Sporter Stainless, Classic Featherweight/Boss All-Terrain, Classic Super Grade, Ranger

**7mm STW**
**A-Square** Caesar and Hamilcar
**Harris Gunworks** Classic and Stainless Sporters; Talon Sporter
**Remington** Model 700 Mountain, Sendero, BDL DM-B

**8mm REM. MAG.**
**A-Square** Caesar and Hannibal
**Remington** Model 700 Safari, Safari KS 300 H&H
**Harris Gunworks** Alaskan; Classic and Stainless Sporters; Safari, Talon Sporter

**300 PEGASUS**
**A-Square** Hannibal

**300 PHOENIX**
**Harris Gunworks** Long Range, Safari, .300 Phoenix

## 300 WBY. MAG.
**A-Square** Caesar, Hamilcar
**Blaser** Model 93
**Harris Gunworks** Classic and Stainless
Sporters; Alaskan, Safari, Talon Sporter
Magnum Research Mountain Eagle
**Remington** Models 700 BDL SS, BDL SS DM-
B, African Plains, Alaskan Wilderness,
Sendero SF
**Sako** Deluxe/Super Deluxe, Hunter Lightweight,
Left-Handed Models, Model TRG-S Magnum
**Sauer** Model 90
**Ultra Light** Arms Model 40 Series
**Weatherby** Models Mark V Accumark, Deluxe,
Euromark, Eurosport, Lazermark, Sporter,
Stainless, Synthetic
**Winchester** Models 70 Classic/Boss Stainless,
Classic Sporter

## 300 WIN. MAG.
**AMT** Deluxe, Standard Repeaters
**Arnold Arms** Alaskan Rifle, Alaskan Trophy,
Grand Alaskan, Serengeti, Synthetic,
Alaskan Guide
**A-Square** Caesar, Hamilcar
**Beretta** Mato
**Blaser** Model R93
**Brown Precision** Tactical Elite
**Browning** A-Bolt II Long Action Series (except
Micro-Medallion, Varmint), including Model
M- 1000 Eclipse
**Dakota Arms** Model 76 Safari & Classic
Grades
**Harris Gunworks** Alaskan; Classic and
Stainless Sporters; Safari, Talon Sporter,
Titanium Mountain, Long Range
**Howa** Lightning
**Kimber** Mauser 98 Sporter, K770 Classic
**Kongsberg** Hunter 393 Series
**Magnum Research** Mountain Eagle
**Mauser** Models 96, M94
**Remington** Models 700, BDL, BDL (DM), BDL
SS (DM-B), BDL SS, African Plains, Alaskan
Wilderness, Sendero
**Ruger** Models Mark II  M-77R/LR, M-77RS, M-
77RS/RSP All-Weather
**Sako** Deluxe/Super Deluxe, Fiberclass, Hunter
Lightweight, Long-Range Hunter, TRG-S
Magnum, Left-Handed Models
**Sauer** Models 90, 202
**Savage** Models 110 FP Tactical; 111G, 111GC,
111F, 111FC Classic Hunters; 112 FVSS,
112BVSS Varmint; 112 BT Competition
Grade; 114CE "Classic European, 116FCS,
116 FSS, 116FSK/FSAK "Weather Warrior";
116SE Safari Express
**Steyr-Mannlicher** Luxus, Sporter, SBS
**Manlicher** European Model, Magnum Model
**Tikka** Continental Long-Range Hunting,
Whitetail Hunter, Synthetic
**Ultra Light** Arms Model 28 Series
**Unique** Model TGC
**Weatherby** Models Mark V Accumark,
Euromark, Eurosport, Sporter, Lazermark,
Stainless, Synthetic, Lightweight Synthetic
**Winchester** Models 70 Classic/Boss SM,
Classic/Boss Stainless, Classic
Featherweight/Boss All-Terrain, Classic
Sporter, Super Grade

## 338 A-SQUARE MAG.
**A-Square** Caesar, Hannibal

## 338 LAPUA MAG.
**Harris Gunworks** Long Range, Safari
**Sako** Deluxe, TRG-S Magnum, TRG-21

## 338 WIN. MAG.
**AMT** Deluxe, Standard Repeaters
**Arnold Arms** Alaskan Guide, Alaskan
Synthetic, Grand Alaskan, Alaskan Rifle
**A-Square** Caesar, Hannibal
**Beretta** Mato
**Blaser** Model R93
**Browning** A-Bolt II Long Action Series (except
Gold & Micro Medallions, Varmint, Eclipse)
**Dakota Arms** Model 76 Safari & Classic
Grades
**Harris Gunworks** Classic and Stainless
Sporters; Safari, Talon Sporter
**Howa** Lightning
**Kimber** Mauser 98 Sporter, K770 Classic
**Kongsberg** Hunter 393 Series
**Lazzeroni** Models L2000 SP-F, ST-F, ST-W
**Magnum Research** Mountain Eagle
**Remington** Models 700 African Plains, Alaskan
Wilderness, BDL (DM), BDL SS, BDL
**Ruger** Models Mark II  M-77R, M-77RP All-
Weather, M-77RS
**Sako** Deluxe/Super Deluxe, Fiberclass, Hunter
Lightweight, Left-Handed Models,
Mannlicher-Style Carbine, Safari Grade,
Model TRG-S Magnum
**Savage** Models 116FSK, 116FSS "Weather
Warrior"; 116SE Safari Express
**Tikka** Whitetail Hunter, Synthetic
**Ultra Light** Arms Model 28 Series
**Weatherby** Models Mark V Euromark,
Eurosport, Sporter, Stainless, Synthetic
**Winchester** Models 70 Classic/BOSS SM,
Stainless, Sporter, Super Grade

## 340 WBY. MAG.
**A-Square** Caesar and Hannibal
**Harris Gunworks** Alaskan; Classic and
Stainless Sporters; Safari, Talon Sporter
**Magnum Research** Mountain Eagle
**Weatherby** Models Mark V Deluxe, Lazermark,
Euromark, Sporter, Accumark, Eurosport,
Stainless, Synthetic

## 35 WHELEN
**Clifton Arms** Scout

## 350 REM. MAG.
**Harris Gunworks** Classic and Stainless
Sporters; Talon Sporter, Varminter

## 358 WIN./NORMA
**A-Square** Caesar, Hannibal
**Harris Gunworks** Alaskan

## 375 H&H
**AMT** Deluxe, Standard Repeaters
**A-Square** Caesar, Hannibal
**Beretta** Mato
**Blaser** Model R93, Safari
**Browning** A-Bolt II Medallion, Stainless Stalker
**Dakota Arms** Model 76 Safari, Classic Grades
**Francotte** Bolt Action
**Harris Gunworks** Alaskan; Classic and
Stainless Sporters; Safari, Talon Sporter
**Magnum Research** Mountain Eagle
**Remington** Models 700 African Plains, Alaskan
Wilderness, Classic, Safari, Safari KS, BDL
SS (DM)
**Rifles, Inc.** - Classic, Lightweight Strata
Stainless
**Ruger** 77RSM MKII Magnum
**Sako** Deluxe/Super Deluxe, Fiberclass, Hunter
Lightweight, Left-Handed Models,
Mannlicher-Style Carbine, Safari Grade,

Model TRG-S Magnum
**Sauer** Models 90, 202
**Weatherby** Models Mark V Euromark,
Eurosport, Sporter, Stainless, Synthetic
**Winchester** Models 70 Classic Stainless,
Classic Super Express

## 375 J.R.S.
**A-Square** Caesar, Hannibal

## 375 WEATHERBY
**A-Square** Caesar, Hannibal

## 378 WIN./WBY. MAG.
**A-Square** Hannibal
**Harris Gunworks** Talon Safari
**Weatherby** Models Mark V Deluxe, Euromark,
Lazermark

## 404 JEFFERY
**A-Square** Caesar, Hannibal
**Dakota Arms** 76 African Grade
**Harris Gun Works** Safari

## 416 REM./WBY. MAG.
**AMT** Deluxe, Standard Repeaters
**A-Square** Caesar and Hannibal
**Blaser** Model R93, Safari
**Clifton Arms** Scout
**Harris Gunworks**  Alaskan; Classic and
Stainless Sporters; Safari, Talon Safari
**Lazzeroni** Model L2000ST-F
**Magnum Research** Mountain Eagle
**Remington** Model 700 Safari, Safari KS
**Sako** Deluxe/Super Deluxe, Fiberclass, Hunter
Lightweight, Left-Handed Models, Safari
Grade, Model TRG-S Magnum
**Weatherby** Models Mark V Deluxe, Euromark,
Lazermark,
**Winchester** Model 70 Classic Super Express

## 416 RIGBY/DAKOTA
**AMT** Deluxe, Standard Repeaters
**A-Square** Hannibal
**Dakota Arms** 76 African Grade
**Francotte** Bolt Action
**Harris Gunworks** Talon Safari
**Ruger** 77RSM MKII Magnum
**Ultra Light** Arms Model 40 Series

## 416 TAYLOR and HOFFMAN
**A-Square** Caesar, Hannibal

## 425 EXPRESS
**A-Square** Caesar, Hannibal

## 450 ACKLEY/DAKOTA
**A-Square** Caesar, Hannibal
**Dakota Arms** 76 African Grade

## 458 WIN. MAG./LOTT
**AMT** Deluxe, Standard Repeaters
**Arnold Arms** African Safari, Synthetic &
Trophy; Alaskan Rifle, Trophy; Grand African
& Alaskan
**A-Square** Caesar, Hannibal
**Dakota Arms** Model 76 Classic, Safari Grades
**Francotte** Bolt Action
**Harris Gunworks** Safari
**Remington** Models 700 Safari, Safari KS
**Sauer** Safari
**Savage** Model 116SE Safari Express
**Winchester** Models 70 Classic Super Express
460 SHORT
**A-Square** Caesar, Hannibal

## 460 SHORT
**A-Square** Caesar, Hannibal

## 460 WIN./WBY. MAG.
**A-Square** Hannibal
**Francotte** Bolt Action
**Harris Gunworks** Talon Safari
**Weatherby** Models Mark V Deluxe, Lazermark

## 470 CAPSTICK
**A-Square** Caesar, Hannibal

## 495 A-SQUARE MAG. 500 A-SQUARE
**A-Square** Hannibal

## 577 TYRANNOSAUR
**A-Square** Hannibal

## 505 GIBBS
**Francotte** Bolt Action

# CENTERFIRE LEVER ACTION

## 22-250 REM.
**Browning** Model Lightning BLR

## 243 WINCHESTER
**Browning** Model Lightning BLR
**Savage** Model 99C

## 270 WINCHESTER
**Browning** Model Lightning BLR

## 7mm REM. MAG.
Browning Model Lightning BLR

## 7mm-08 REM.
**Browning** Model Lightning BLR

## 30-06 SPRGFLD.
**Browning** Model Lightning BLR

## 30-30 WINCHESTER
**Marlin** Models 30AS, 336CS
**Winchester** Models 94 Standard Walnut, Legacy, Ranger, Trapper Carbine, Wrangler

## 307 WINCHESTER
**Winchester** Model 94 Big Bore Walnut

## 308 WINCHESTER
**Browning** Model Lightning BLR
**Savage** Model 99C

## 35 REMINGTON
**Marlin** Model 336CS

## 356 WINCHESTER
**Winchester** Model 94 Big Bore Walnut

## 357 MAGNUM
**Marlin** Model 1894CS, 1894 Cowboy II
**Rossi** Models M92 SRS and SRC, Carbine, Stainless
**Uberti** 1873 Sporting, Carbine
**Winchester** Model 94 Trapper Carbine, Trails End, Legacy

## 38 SPECIAL
**EMF** Model 1866 Yellow Boy Rifle/Carbine
**Marlin** Model 1894CS, 1894 Cowboy II
**Rossi** Model M92 SRC, SRS, Carbine, Stainless
**Uberti** Models 1866 Sporting, 1866 Yellowboy Carbine

## 44 REM. MAG.
**Marlin** Model 1894S, 1894 Cowboy II
**Rossi** Model 92 Large Loop
**Winchester** Model 94 Trapper Carbine, Wrangler, Trails End, Legacy

## 44 SPECIAL
**Marlin** Model 1894S, 1894 Cowboy II
**Winchester** Model 94 Trapper Carbine, Wrangler

## 44-40
**American Arms** 1860 Henry, 1866 Winchester, 1873 Winchester
**EMF** Model 1860 Henry, 1866 Yellow Boy Rifle/Carbine, Model 1873 Sporting
**Marlin** Model 1894 Cowboy II
**Navy Arms** 1866 Yellowboy Rifle/Carbine; Henry Military, Carbine, Iron Frame Henry and Trapper Henry Models, 1873 Winchester-Style and Winchester Sporting
**Uberti** Model 1866 Sporting, Yellowboy Carbine, 1873 Sporting & Carbine; Henry Rifle, Carbine, Trapper

## 444 MARLIN
**Marlin** Model 444SS

## 45 COLT
**American Arms** 1860 Henry, 1866 Winchester, 1873 Winchester
**EMF** Model 1860 Henry, 1866 Yellow Boy Rifle/Carbine, 1873 Sporting/Short Rifle, Carbine
**Marlin** Model 1894S, 1894 Cowboy II
**Navy Arms** 1873 Winchester Sporting, Winchester-Style
**Rossi** Model 92 Large Loop
**Uberti** Model 1873 Sporting, Carbine; Henry Rifle, 1866 Sporting, 1866 Yellowboy CarbineWinchester Model 94 Trapper Carbine, Trails End, Legacy

## 45-70 GOV'T.
**Marlin** Model 1895SS

# CENTERFIRE SEMIAUTOMATIC

## 5.56mm
**Springfield** Model SAR-4800 Sporter

## 22-250
Browning BAR Mark II Safari

## 223 REMINGTON
**Colt** Competition H-Bar II; Match Target, Match Target H-Bar, Match Target Lightweight, Colt Accurized Rifle
**Ruger** K-Mini-14/5R, Mini-14/5, Mini-14/5R Ranch

## 243 WINCHESTER
**Browning** BAR Mark II Safari & Lightweight
**Remington** Model 7400

## 25-06
**Browning** BAR Mark II Safari

## 270 WIN.
**Browning** BAR Mark II Safari & Lightweight
**Remington** Model 7400

## 280 REM
**Remington** Model 7400

## 30-06
**Browning** BAR Mark II Lightweight
**Remington** Model 7400

## 300 WIN. MAG.
**Browning** BAR Mark II Safari & Lightweight

## 308 WINCHESTER
**Browning** BAR Mark II Safari & Lightweight
**Heckler and Koch** PSG-1 High Precision Marksman's
**Remington** Model 7400
**Springfield** Basic M1A, M1A National Match, M1A Standard, M1A-A1 Bush, Super Match 7.62X39
**Colt** Match Target Lightweight
**Ruger** Mini-30
**Springfield** Models SAR-8 and SAR-4800 Sporters, M1A Standard

## 338 WIN. MAG.
**Browning** BAR Mark II Safari

## 40 AUTO
**Ruger** Model PC9 Carbine

## 45 ACP (AUTO)
Auto-Ordnance Thompson Models M1 Carbine, 1927A1, 1927A1C Lightweight & Commando
**Marlin** Model 45

## 7mm REM. MAG.
**Browning** BAR Mark II Safari

## 7mm-08
**Springfield** M1A Standard

## 9mm
**Colt** Match Target Lightweight
**Marlin** Model 9 Camp Carbine

# CENTERFIRE DOUBLE RIFLES

## 308
**Krieghoff** Model Classic S/S Standard
**Tikka** Model 512S

## 30-06
**Krieghoff** Models Classic S/S Standard
**Tikka** Model 512S

## 7X65R
**Francotte** Sidelock S/S, Boxlock S/S
**Krieghoff** Classic S/S Standard

## 8X57JRS
**Francotte** Sidelock S/S, Boxlock S/S
**Krieghoff** Classic S/S Standard
**Pedersoli** Kodiak Mark IV

## 8X75RS
**Krieghoff** Classic S/S Standard

## 9.3X74R
**Francotte** Sidelock S/S and Boxlock S/S
**Krieghoff** Classic S/S Standard
**Pedersoli** Kodiak Mark IV
**Tikka** Model 512S

## 375 H&H
**Krieghoff** Classic Side-by-Side

## 45-70
**Navy Arms** Deluxe/Kodiak Mark IV
**Pedersoli** Kodiak Mark IV

**470 N.E., 500/416 N.E., 500 N.E.**
Krieghoff Classic Side-by-Side

## CENTERFIRE/RIMFIRE PUMP ACTION

**22 S, L, LR**
Remington Model 572 BDL Deluxe Fieldmaster
Rossi Models M62 SAC and SA

**243 WIN./270 WIN.**
Browning Model BPR
Remington Model 7600 (also calibers 280 Rem., 30-06, 308 Win., 35 Whelen) 308 Win./30-06/7mm Rem. Mag./300 Win. Mag.
Browning Model BPR

## CENTERFIRE/RIMFIRE SINGLE SHOT

**17 REMINGTON**
Kimber Model 84C Varmint
Thompson/Center Contender Carbine

**218 BEE**
Ruger No. 1B Standard, No. 1S Medium Sporter

**22 HORNET**
AMT Single Shot Standard & Deluxe
Browning Model 1885 Low Wall
New England Handi-Rifle, Super Light
Ruger No. 1B Standard
Thompson/Center Contender Series (Kit, Carbine Stainless)
Uberti Model 1871 Rolling Block Baby Carbine

**22 MAG.**
Uberti Model 1871 Rolling Block Baby Carbine

**22 PPC**
AMT Single Shot Standard & Deluxe

**22 S, L, LR**
Dakota Arms Model 10
European American Armory HW 660 Weihrauch Rimfire Target
KBI Model M-12Y Youth
Marlin 15YN "Little Buckaroo," Model 2000L Target
Remington Models 40-XR BR, 40-XR KS Sporter
Savage Mark I-G
Thompson/Center Contender Series (Youth Model Carbine, Kit, Carbine Stainless)
Uberti Model 1871 Rolling Block Baby Carbine
Ultra Light Arms Model 20RF

**22-250 REM.**
AMT Single Shot Standard & Deluxe
Browning Model 1885 High Wall
Cooper Arms BR-50 Bench Rest, Model 22 Varmint Extreme

**220 SWIFT**
Cooper Arms Model 22 Pro Varmint Extreme, BR-50 Bench Rest
Ruger No. 1B Standard, No. 1V Special Varminter
Savage Models 112BVSS Varmint, 112FVSS
Thompson/Center Encore

**222 REMINGTON**
AMT Single Shot Deluxe, Standard

**223 REMINGTON**
AMT Single Shot Deluxe, Standard
Browning Model 1885 Low Wall

Harrington & Richardson Ultra Varmint
New England Handi-Rifle, Survivor
Ruger No. 1B Standard, No. IV Special Varminter
Savage Models 112 FVSS/112 BVSS
Thompson/Center Contender Series, Youth Model Carbine, Encore

**243 WINCHESTER**
AMT Single Shot Deluxe, Standard
Cooper Arms Model 22 Varmint Extreme, BR-50 Bench Rest
New England Handi-Rifle
Ruger No. 1A Light Sporter, No. 1B Standard, No. 1 RSI International
Thompson/Center Encore

**25-06**
Cooper Arms Model 22 Varmint Extreme, BR-50 Bench Rest
Harrington & Richardson Ultra Single-Shot
Ruger No. 1B Standard, No. 1V Special Varminter

**6mm PPC**
AMT Single Shot Deluxe, Standard
Cooper Arms Model 22 Varmint Extreme, BR-50 Bench Rest
Ruger No. 1V Special Varminter

**6mm REMINGTON**
Ruger No. 1B Standard, No. 1V Special Varminter

**257 ROBERTS**
Ruger No. 1B Standard

**270 WBY. MAG./270 WINCHESTER**
Browning Model 1885 High Wall
Harrington & Richardson Ultra Comp
New England Handi-Rifle
Ruger No. 1A Light Sporter, No. 1B Standard, No. 1 RSI International
Thompson/Center Encore

**280 REMINGTON**
New England Handi-Rifle
Ruger No. 1B Standard

**30-06**
Browning Model 1885 High Wall
Harrington & Richardson Ultra Comp
New England Handi-Rifle
Ruger No. 1A Light Sporter, No. 1B Standard, No. 1 RSI International

**30-30 WIN.**
Browning Model 1885 Traditional Hunter
New England Handi-Rifle
Thompson/Center Contender Series

**300 WBY. MAG.**
Ruger No. 1B Standard

**300 WIN. MAG.**
Ruger No. 1B Standard, No. 1S Medium Sporter
Savage Models 112 BT Competition, 112 FVSS/112BVSS
Thompson/Center Encore

**308 WIN.**
AMT Single Shot Standard & Deluxe
Cooper Arms Model 22 Varmint Extreme, BR-50 Bench Rest
Harrington & Richardson Ultra Single-Shot

**7mm REM. MAG.**
Browning Model 1885 High Wall
Ruger No. 1S Medium Sporter, No. 1B Standard

**7mm-08**
AMT Standard, Deluxe
Thompson/Center Encore

**7X57mm**
Ruger No. 1A Light Sporter, No. 1 RSI International

**7-30 WATERS**
Thompson/Center Contender Series

**338 WIN. MAG.**
Ruger No. 1S Medium Sporter, No. 1B Standard

**357 MAG.**
New England Survivor
Pedersoli Calvary, Infantry, Long Range Creedmoor, Rolling Block Target
Uberti Model 1871 Rolling Block Baby Carbine

**357 REM. MAX.**
Harrington & Richardson Ultra Single Shot

**375 H&H/WIN.**
Ruger No. 1H Tropical
Thompson/Center Contender Series

**40-65**
Browning Model 1885 BPCR

**416 REM./RIGBY**
Ruger No. 1H Tropical

**44 REM. MAG.**
New England Handi-Rifle

**45-70 GOV'T.**
Browning Model 1885 High Wall, Model 1885 Traditional Hunter, Model 1885 BPCR
Harrington & Richardson Whitetails Unlimited 1997 Commemorative
Navy Arms Remington Style Rolling Block Buffalo, Sharps Plains, 1873 Springfield Cavalry Carbine, 1874 Sharps Cavalry Carbine, 1874 Sharps Sniper, Sharps Buffalo, No. 2 Creedmoor Target
New England Handi-Rifle
Pedersoli Calvary, Infantry, Long Range Creemoor, Rolling Block Target
Ruger No. 1S Medium Sporter

**458 WIN. MAG.**
Ruger No. 1H Tropical

**50 BMG**
L.A.R. Grizzly

**54**
Pedersoli Sharps Carbine Model 766

## CENTERFIRE/RIMFIRE RIFLE/SHOTGUN COMBOS

**22 LR, 22 HORNET, 223 REM./12 or 20 Ga.**
Savage Model 24F

**22 LR/.410 Ga.**
Springfield Model M-6 Scout

## 22 Hornet/.410 Ga.
**Springfield** Model M-6 Scout

## 45-70 GOVT./20 Ga.
**Pedersoli** Kodiak Mark IV

## RIMFIRE—BOLT ACTION ▪

### 22 S, L, LR
**Dakota Arms** Model 22 LR Sporter
**KBI** M-12 Y Youth, M-1400S, M-1500S, M1800-S
**Kimber** Model 82C Series (Classic, Stainless, SVT, SuperAmerica, Custom Match)
**Magtech** Models MT 122.2.S/R/T
**Marlin** Models 25N, 880, 880SS, 880SQ, 881, 2000L Target
**Remington** Models 541-T and 581-S
**Ruger** Model 77/22 Series
**Savage** Model 900B Biathlon, 900S Silhouette, 900TR Target Repeater
**Ultra Light** Arms Model 20
**Unique** Model T Dioptra Sporter, T UIT Standard, T/SM Silhouette

### 22 MAGNUM RIMFIRE
**KBI** M-1400S, M-1500S, M-1800S
**Ruger** Model 77/22 Series
**Unique** Model T Dioptera Sporter, Model T/SM Silhouette

### 22 WMR
**Marlin** Models 25MN, 882, 882L, 882SS, 883, 883SS
**Savage** Model 93G Magnum, Model 93 FSS "All Weather"

## RIMFIRE—LEVER ACTION ▪

### 22 S, L, LR
**Browning** Model BL-22 (Grades I and II)
**Henry** Rifle
**Marlin** Model Golden 39AS, Model 1897 Century Limited
**Uberti** Model 1866 Yellowboy Carbine
**Winchester** Model 9422 Series

### 22 MAG. (WMR)
**Uberti** Model 1866 Yellowboy Carbine
**Winchester** Models 9422 Walnut, WinCam, WinTuff

## RIMFIRE—SEMIAUTOMATIC

### 22 S, L, LR
**AMT** Target Model
**Browning** Model 22 SemiAuto Grades I and VI
**Cooper Arms** Models 36 Classic, 36RF BR-50, 36RF/CF Featherweight, Custom Classic
**KBI** M-2000 S Classic, M-2000SC Super Classic, Standard M-20P
**Marlin** Models 25N, 60/60SS, 70PSS "Papoose," Models 7000, 880, 880SS, 880SQ, 881, 995SS
**Remington** Model 522 Viper, Model 552 BDL Deluxe Speedmaster, Model 597 Series
**Ruger** Model 10/22 Carbine Series
**Savage** Models Mark II-FSS/G/GY/GXP, Mark II-LV, 64GF/64G

### 22 WMR
**AMT** Rimfire Magnum
**Brno** Model ZKM 611
**Marlin** Models 25MN, 882, 882L, 882SS, 883, 883 SS, 922 Mag.
**Remington** Model 597 Magnum

## BLACKPOWDER

## HANDGUNS ▬

### 22
**American Frontier** Firearms Pocket Remington, Pocket Richards & Mason Navy Conversion

### 31
**Colt** Blackpowder Colt 1849 Pocket
**EMF** 1849 Baby Dragoon

### 32
**American Frontier** Firearms Pocket Remington, Pocket Richards & Mason Navy Conversion

### 36
**American Arms** 1851 Colt Navy
**Colt** Blackpowder Colt 1851 & 1861 Navy, Trapper Model 1862 Pocket Police Dixie 1851 Navy Brass-Frame Revolver, Spiller and Burr Brass-Frame Revolver
**EMF** Model 1862 Police, 1851 Navy
**Euroarms** Model 1120 Colt 1851 Navy
**Navy Arms** 1851 Navy "Yank" Revolver, Reb Sheriff's Model 1860, 1862 New Model Police Revolver
**Uberti** 1851 and 1861 Navy, Paterson

### 38
**American Frontier Firearms** Richards 1851 Model Navy Conversion, Richards & Mason Conversion 1851 Navy Model, Remington New Army Cavalry, Pocket Remington, 1871-2 Open-Top Frontier & Tiffany, Pocket 1860 Army Model Conversion & 1861 Model Navy Conversion
**Dixie Pedersoli** Mang Target Pistol

### 44
**American Arms** 1858 Remington Army and Army SS Target, 1860 Colt Army
**American Frontier Firearms** Richards 1851 Model Navy Conversion, Richards & Mason Conversion 1851 Navy Model, Remington New Army Cavalry, Pocket Remington, 1871-2 Open-Top Frontier & Tiffany, Pocket 1860 Army Model Conversion & 1861 Model Navy Conversion
**Colt** Blackpowder Colt Third Model Dragoon, Colt 1860 Army, Cavalry Model 1860 Army, Colt 1847 Walker, Colt Walker 150th Anniversary Model CVA 1851 Navy Brass-Framed Revolver, 1858 & 1860 Army Revolvers
**Dixie** Pennsylvania Pistol, Remington 44 Army Revolver, Walker Revolver, Wyatt Earp Revolver
**EMF** Model 1860 Army, 1848 Dragoon, 1847 Walker, 1851 Sheriff's Models, 1851 Navy, 1858 Remington Army, 1863 Texas Dragoon
**Euroarms** Rogers and Spencer Models 1005, 1006 and 1007, Remington 1858 New Model Army, Model 1210 Colt 1860 Army
**Navy Arms** Colt Walker 1847, 1851 Navy "Yank", 1858 Target Model, Reb Model 1860 Revolver, 1860 Army Revolver, Reb 60 Sheriff's Model, Rogers and Spencer Revolver, 1858 Target Remington and Deluxe New Model Revolvers, Stainless Steel 1858

Remington New Army, LeMat Revolvers, Le Page Flintlock/Percussion Pistols and Cased Sets, First Model Dragoon
**Uberti** 1st Model Dragoon, Walker, 1858
**Remington** New Army, 1860 Army

### .445
**Dixie** Screw Barrel (folding trigger) Pistol

### 45
**American Frontier Firearms** Remington New Army Cavalry Model
**Dixie** LePage Dueling Pistol, Pedersoli English Dueling Pistol
**Gonic** Arms Model GA-90
**Ruger** Old Army Cap and Ball
**Traditions** Pioneer Pistol

### .451
**Dixie** 1860 Army Revolver

### 50
**CVA** Kentucky Pistol, Hawken Pistol
**Traditions** Buckskinner, Buckhunter Pro In-Line, Kentucky, William Parker & Trapper Pistols

### 54
**Traditions** Buckhunter Pro In-Line Pistol

### 58
**Navy Arms** 1806 Harpers Ferry Pistol

## RIFLES AND CARBINES ▬

### 32
**Dixie** Tennessee Squirrel
**Navy Arms** Pennsylvania Long
**Thompson/Center** Fire Hawk Blued
**Traditions** Deerhunter

### 40-65
**Cumberland Mountain Arms** Plateau Rifle, 1874 Sharps Silhouette
**Dixie** 1874 Sharps Silhouette

### 41
**White Systems** Model Super 91, Whitetail and Bison (G Series)

### 45
**Cabela's** Hwken Rifle
**Dixie** Hawken, Kentuckian, Pedersoli Waadtlander, Tryon Creedmoor, Pennsylvania
**Gonic** Arms Model 87 Mag.
**Navy Arms** Pennsylvania Long
**Peifer** Models TS-93/93BA
**Thompson/Center** Hawken
**White Systems** Model Super 91, African Series, "G" Series (Whitetail & Bison models)

### 45-70
**Cumberland Mountain Arms** Plateau Rifle
**Dixie** 1874 Sharps Lightweight Target/Silhouette
**Remington** No. 1 Rolling Block (Creedmoor-style) Mid-Range, Shiloh Sharps Model 1874 Business, Sporting Rifle No. 1 & 3

### 45-90
**Shiloh Sharps** Model 1874 Business, Sporting Rifle 1 & 3

### 45-120
**Shiloh Sharps** Model 1874 Business, Sporting Rifle No. 1 & 3

## 451
**Navy Arms** Tryon Creedmoor

## 50
**Austin & Halleck** Models 320 & 420, Mountain Rifle

**Cabela's** Rolling Block Rifle & Carbine, Hawken Rifle

**Colt** Blackpowder Arms Colt Gamemaster .50

**CVA** Accubolt Pro, In-Line Apollo Brown Bear; In-line Buckmaster Stag Horn & Stag Horn; Firebolt Series, St. Louis Hawken

**Dixie** Hawken, Tennessee Mountain, In-Line Carbine

**Gonic Arms** Models 87 Mag. Rifle, 93 Mag., Safari

**Lyman** Deerstalker Rifle and Carbine, Great Plains, Cougar In-Line, Trade Rifle

**Marlin** Model MLS-50

**Modern** Muzzleloading Knight MK-85 Series, LK-93 Wolverine & Thumbhole Wolverine, Magnum Elite, Disc Rifles

**Navy Arms** "Countryboy" In-Line, Ithaca-Navy Hawken, Kodiak Double, Smith Carbine

**Peifer** Models IS-93/93BA

**Prairie River Arms** Bullpup & PRA Classic

**Thompson/Center** Fire Hawk Blued, Grey Hawk, Hawken, New Englander, Pennsylvania Hunter (rifle and carbine), Renegade, Scout Rifle and Carbine, Thunder Hawk, Thunder Hawk Shadow, Traditions Buckhunter & Buckhunter Pro In-Line Rifle Series, Buckskinner Carbine, Deerhunter, Deerhunter Scout, Hawken Woodsman, Pennsylvania, Shenandoah, Kentucky, Tennessee, Lightning Bolt-Action Rifles

**White Systems** Model Super 91 and "G" Series (Whitetail & Bison models)

## 50-70
**Shiloh Sharps** 1874 Business, Sporting Rifle No. 1 & 3

## 50-90
**Shiloh Sharps** 1874 Business, Sporting Rifle No. 1 & 3

## 54
**Cabela's** Hawken Rifle, Rolling Block Muzzleloader

**CVA** In-line Apollo Brown Bear, Eclipse, Buckmaster Stag Horn & Stag Horn, St. Louis Hawken, Elk Master, Firebolt Series

**Dixie** Hawken, In-Line Carbine, Sharps New Model 1859 Carbine and 1859 Military Rifle

**Euroarms** 1803 Harpers Ferry, 1841 Mississippi

**Lyman** Deerstalker Rifle, Great Plains, Cougar In-Line, Trade Rifle

**Marlin** Model MLS-54 Modern Muzzleloading

**Knight** MK-85 Series, LK-93 Wolverine & Thumbhole Wolverine, Magnum Elite

**Navy Arms** 1803 Harpers Ferry, 1841 Mississippi, 1859 Berdan Sharps, 1859 Sharps

**Cavalry** Carbine, Ithaca/Navy Hawken, Mortimer Flintlock and Match Flintlock

**Prairie Rover Arms** Bullpup & Classic

**Thompson/Center** Fire Hawk Blued, Grey Hawk, Hawken, New Englander, Renegade, Scout Carbine and Rifle, Thunder Hawk, Thunder Hawk Shadow

**Traditions** Buckhunter In-Line Rifle Series, Hawken Woodsman

**Uberti** Sante Fe Hawken, Deerhunter; Lightning Bolt-Action Rifles

**White Systems** "G" Series (Bison)

## 58
**Colt** Blackpowder Colt Model 1861 Musket

**Dixie** 1858 Two-Band Enfield Rifle, U.S. Model 1861 Springfield (Rifle-Musket), Mississippi,

1862 Three-Band Enfield Rifle Musket, 1863 Springfield Civil War Musket

**Euroarms** Model 2260 & 2361 London Armory Co. Enfield 3-Band Rifled Musket, Models 2270 and 2280 London Armory Co. Enfield Rifled Muskets, Cook and Brother Confederate Carbine, J. P. Murray Carbine, Model 2301 Cook & Brother Field, 1861 Springfield, 1863 Remington Zouave, C. S. Richmond Musket, 1841 Mississippi

**Navy Arms** Mississippi Model 1841, 1853 Enfield Rifle Musket, 1858 Enfield, 1861 Musketoon, 1861 Springfield, 1863 Springfield, J.P. Murray Carbine, 1862 C. S. Richmond Thompson/Center Big Boar Caplock, Fire Hawk Blued

**Traditions** Model 1853 3-Band Enfield Rifled Musket, Model 1861 U. S. Springfield Rifled Musket

## 69
**Dixie** U.S. Model 1816 Flintlock Musket

**Navy Arms** Brown 1816 M.T. Wickham Musket

## 75
**Navy Arms** Brown Bess Musket

## DOUBLE RIFLES ▬▬

### 50 52 54 58
**Cabela's** Kodiak Express (50, 52, 54 cal)

**Navy Arms** Kodiak Double Rifle (50, 54, 58 cal.)

## SHOTGUNS ▬▬

### 10 Gauge
**Dixie** Double-Barrel Magnum

**Navy Arms** Steel Shot Magnum

### 12 Gauge
**CVA** Classic Turkey Double-Barrel & Trapper Single-Barrel Shotguns

**Dixie** Double-Barrel Magnum

**Navy Arms** Mortimer Flintlock, Fowler, T&T

**Thompson/Center** New Englander

**Traditions** Buckhunter Pro In-Line

### 20 Gauge
**Dixie** Double-Barrel Magnum

---

## DISCONTINUED FIREARMS

The following models have been discontinued or are no longer imported, or are now listed under a different manufacturer/distributor.

### HANDGUNS ▬▬

**ASTRA** Model A-70 Pistol

**AUTO ORDNANCE** 1911A1 Competition, Duo-Tone

**BENELLI** Model MP95E

**COLT** MKIV Series '80 Pistol models Combat Elite, Delta Elite, Delta Gold Cup, Pocketlite; MKII Series '90 Double Eagle, Combat Commander, Officer's ACP; Revolver models Realtree Anaconda, Special Lady

**CZ** Models 75, 75 Compact, 83, 85 Standard, 85 Combat, 100

**DAEWOO** Model DP51S Pistol

**ERMA** Model 777 Standard, Match

**FEG** GKK-45 Auto Pistol

**HARRINGTON & RICHARDSON** Amtec 2000 DA Revolver, Competitor Single Shot Pistol

**HIGH STANDARD** Citatopm MS Pistol

**KBI** FEG-GKK-45 Pistol

**MAGNUM RESEARCH** Baby Eagle, Mountain Eagle, Mtn. Eagle Compact and Target Editions

**MITCHELL ARMS** Baron, Jeff Cooper Signature, 44 Magnum Pistol, Gold Series, Guardian Angel, IPSC Ltd., Medalist, Medallion, Monarch, Sovereign, Sportster

**ROSSI** Revolver Models 720 Covert Special and 971 Compact Gun

**RUGER** New Model Super Single-Six Revolver

**SMITH & WESSON** Pistol Models 422 Rimfire, 909, 2206, 2206 Target, 3914, 4053; Revolver Models 49 Bodyguard, 622VR, 625 Mountain Gun

**TAURUS** Pistol Models PT-58, PT-92 AFC, PT-100, PT-101, PT-101D, PT-908, PT-908D, PT-910, PT-940D Deluxe; Revolver Models 65, 66, 80, 431, 441, 607

**UBERTI** Buckhorn 1873 SA Target Replica Revolver

**WALTHER** Models P5 and P5 Compact

### RIFLES ▬▬

**BROWNING** A-Bolt II Euro-Bolt

**COOPER** Model 40 Custom Classic

**CZ** Models CZ527, CZ550, ZKK 602, ZKM452

**EUROPEAN AMERICAN ARMORY** Sabatti Model SP1822

**HARRINGTON & RICHARDSON** Erma SR-100 Precision, Rocky Mtn. Elk Foundation, Wesson & Harrington 125th Ann. Rifles

**KIMBER** Model 82C Varmint Synthetic, Custom Shop SuperAmerica; Model 84C Custom Match

**MITCHELL ARMS** Models LW22 and LW9 Carbines

**RUGER** M-77EXP Mark II Express

**SAVAGE** Model 114CU Classic Ultra

**STEYR-MANNLICHER** AUG SA Semiauto, Luxus and Sporter Series, SPG Match UIT

**WINSLOW** Plainsmaster and Bushmaster stock models

### SHOTGUNS ▬▬

**AMERICAN ARMS** Grulla #2

**BENELLI** Model M1 Super 90 Defense and Super 90 Slug

**CONNECTICUT VALLEY CLASSICS** 12 gauge Classic Series

**KBI/SABATTI** Over/Under Shotgun

**MAVERICK** by Mossberg Model 88 Series, Model 95 Bolt Action

**MERKEL** Models 200E, 200ET Trap, 200SC Sporting Clays

**PERAZZI** Combo Model MX9

**REMINGTON** Model 11-87 SPS-Camo

**STOEGER IGA** Reuna Single Barrel and Youth

### BLACKPOWDER ▬▬

**ARMSPORT** Revolver Models 5120, 5121, 5133, 5136, 5138, 5139 and 5140, 5149 Stainless Target, 5150 Stainless

**CVA** Vest Pocket Derringer; Revolver Models 1861 Navy, New Model Pocket, Pocket Police, Remington Bison, Sheriff's Model, Walker; Frontier Hunter LS Carbine; In-line Apollo Series Comet, Classic, Dominator; Bobcat Hunter, Kentucky, Lynx and Varmint Rifles

**DIXIE** Winchester '73 Carbine and Engraved Rifle

**MODERN MUZZLELOADING** Model BK-92 Black Knight

**MOUNTAIN STATE** Golden and Silver Classic Rifles

**STONE MOUNTAIN** 1853 Enfield, Harpers Ferry, Mississippi and Silver Eagle Hunting Rifles

**TRADITIONS** Buckhunter In-Line Rifle Series

**UBERTI** Santa Fe Hawken Rifle

# GUNFINDER

To help you find the model of your choice, the following index includes every firearm found in this SHOOTER'S BIBLE 1998, listed by type of gun.

# PRODUCT INDEX

The Product Index below is intended to give the reader a general overview of the contents of this edition of SHOOTER'S BIBLE. For detailed listings of firearms, see the Gunfinder and Caliberfinder indexes that precede this. For complete addresses and phone/fax numbers of the companies listed below, please turn to the Directory of Manufacturers and Suppliers on page 554.